D0148402

WITHDRAWN FROM
TCC LIBRARY

TALLAHASSEE
COMMUNITY COLLEGE

The
Eugene O'Neill
Companion

For Ralph and Caroline

The Eugene O'Neill Companion

MARGARET LOFTUS RANALD

Greenwood Press
Westport, Connecticut • London, England

Library of Congress Cataloging in Publication Data

Ranald, Margaret Loftus.
  The Eugene O'Neill companion.

  Bibliography: p.
  Includes index.
  1. O'Neill, Eugene, 1888-1953—Handbooks, manuals,
etc. 2. O'Neill, Eugene, 1888-1953—Dictionaries,
indexes, etc. I. O'Neill, Eugene, 1888-1953.
II. Title.
PS3529.N5Z792 1985   812′.52   83-22671
ISBN 0-313-22551-6 (lib. bdg.)

Copyright © 1984 by Margaret Loftus Ranald

All rights reserved. No portion of this book may be
reproduced, by any process or technique, without the
express written consent of the publisher.

Library of Congress Catalog Card Number: 83-22671
ISBN: 0-313-22551-6

First published in 1984

Greenwood Press
A division of Congressional Information Service, Inc.
88 Post Road West
Westport, Connecticut 06881

Printed in the United States of America

10 9 8 7 6 5 4 3 2 1

Contents

081533

091933

Preface

This *Eugene O'Neill Companion* has been planned for both a general and a scholarly audience. Consequently, the synopses of plays and scenarios are very full, for the general audience, and the critical, bibliographical, and production information has been developed largely for the scholarly audience. An attempt has been made to analyze every completed play (including unpublished versions) and most of the unpublished scenarios. In order to avoid redundancy, I have omitted detailed analyses of the unpublished material recently edited by Virginia Floyd (*Eugene O'Neill at Work*, 1981) except for a few major projects which O'Neill left uncompleted. Character analyses are offered for all but a very few minor figures in the plays, and cast lists of original productions and a selected number of revivals are included, Jordan Y. Miller (*Eugene O'Neill and the American Critic*, 2d ed., 1973) having already compiled a comprehensive list with more attention to revivals than space would here allow.

Essays on specific theatrical companies closely affiliated with O'Neill and his works are included, as are biographies of some of the more important persons involved in the production and design of first performances of O'Neill plays. Biographical sketches of O'Neill himself, his family, friends, and other persons very closely associated with him are given, together with selected biographies of actors and actresses who created important O'Neill roles, who have performed in numerous O'Neill plays, or who have become intimately linked with O'Neill roles. Of necessity, these biographical pieces are not exhaustive, and since O'Neill seems to have known almost everyone worth (or not worth) knowing, many people had to be omitted. In most cases, their names will be found in the index.

A chronology of the plays, according to O'Neill and the most recent scholars in the field, is included as Appendix A. Film, musical, operatic, and balletic adaptations (with analyses) appear in Appendix B, while biographies of composers appear in the main part of the book, in alphabetical order. Cross-references indicate the existence of film and musical adaptations. The arrangement of the book is alphabetical, with the first reference to another entry being provided with an asterisk to alert the user to further material. Where necessary, sources are noted both in the text and at the end of a given entry.

Full publication data are given in the "References." (In view of the excellent bibliographical work of Jordan Y. Miller (1972) and Jennifer McCabe Atkinson (1974), the bibliography does not aim at exhaustive completeness, but rather selection, mainly from material written since 1960. The section on dissertations does, however, contain some new material, and most of those works listed are available from University Microfilms.

I hope that the *Eugene O'Neill Companion* will prove a useful guide to both American and foreign readers. Perhaps it may stimulate its users to look more closely at the works of America's premier playwright and reassess his use of political as well as autobiographical elements. After all, O'Neill concerned himself with race relations at a time when such a topic was considered either appalling or irrelevant. In addition, he concerned himself with attempting to forge a new philosophical-religious synthesis in a world which was rapidly changing. He took the American theatre he found and turned it upside down, making it a vehicle for ideas as well as emotions. It is a trifle regrettable that his last, great, naturalistic autobiographical plays have become so popular that some of his earlier, fascinating, and more experimental plays have been ignored. They are now ripe for revival.

NOTES TO THE USER

Production Data On a number of occasions this is of necessity incomplete, because of an absence of reliable data. In their early years the Provincetown Players did not list designers or directors for all their productions. Indeed, in accordance with their "amateur" status, the company expected playwrights to direct their own plays — a policy not strictly followed. I have indicated the absence of documentary evidence by the word "Unknown." Similarly, when I have been unable to establish the performer of a given role, I have made the notation "Unknown." Finally, the number of performances is exceptionally difficult to ascertain. When I am reasonably certain of my figures I have included them. However, with the early productions of the Provincetown Players, records are not reliable. Deutsch and Hanau (1931) give opening dates, and Sarlós (1982) also gives closing dates of a run. However, one cannot be certain whether runs were of three or six days, and information concerning matinees or Sunday performances is lacking. Additionally, one cannot be sure whether a given play was withdrawn in the course of its announced run. Accordingly, I have chosen not to estimate, but rather to list such performance statistics as "Unknown."

References All references cited in the text are given in a short form: author's surname and date of publication, sometimes with page numbers. Full bibliographical citations will be found in the section entitled "References," which immediately follows the text.

Acknowledgments

The most pleasant task of any book is acknowledging those who have helped: editors, librarians, scholars, authors, colleagues, friends, relations, and even pets. First I wish to thank Marilyn Brownstein, Margaret Brezicki, Cynthia Harris, and Lynn Sedlak Flint of Greenwood Press for their patience. Particular thanks go to my copy editor, Sharon Skowronski, whose eagle eye for detail was invaluable. I thank also my colleague Myron Matlaw, for his confidence in recommending me for this project. It enabled me to take a sabbatical from Shakespeare to work on America's greatest playwright. I thank also those librarians whose assistance has been exemplary and beyond the call of duty: Dorothy Swerdlove, Richard Buck, Daniel Patri, and Betty Corwin of the New York Public Library at Lincoln Center; Jeanne Newlin and Martha Mahard of the Harvard Theatre Collection; the helpful staff of the Copyright Division and Rare Book Room of the Library of Congress; the staff of the manuscript division of the Huntington Library; the staff of the rare book division of Princeton University. The library of Amherst College also allowed me to peruse some uncatalogued O'Neill material, remembering my interest from an earlier visit. And, of course, I must not omit the help of the Paul Klapper Library, Queens College of the City University of New York, particularly Richard Wall and the reference staff, and also the circulation desk for their immense patience in allowing me to hold so many books for so long.

As always, colleagues and friends have been highly supportive: William Green (Queens College) contributed enthusiasm and useful suggestions; Myron Matlaw (Queens College) contributed the entry on James O'Neill from his own research; and Gary Jay Williams (Catholic University of America) contributed the articles on The Experimental Theatre, Inc., and the Provincetown Players. Dr. Gerald J. Griffin (New York City) a former associate of Dorothy Day, contributed reminiscences, while Arnold and Sharon Levin (Santa Monica, California) recalled original productions and provided me with an introduction to Dr. Irma Gruenberg, widow of the composer of the opera *The Emperor Jones*. She gave me some important information concerning her late husband and his work. I also thank Robert K. Sarlós for his offer of help, but his book was sufficient indeed. Travis Bogard (University of California, Berkeley) helped arrange an enlightening tour of Tao House, with Miss Turner as an admirable guide. Gerald Stram (Sausalito, California) read the entry on his grandmother, Carlotta Monterey, and permitted the use of some of her letters. Mrs. Dorothy Commins read the entry on her late husband, Saxe Commins, answered my questions, and offered gracious hospitality. Paul Avrich (Queens College) supplied some information on Terry Carlin and Hippolyte Havel. Special thanks to Eleanor Linn, who compiled the index, and to her consultant, John G. Linn.

In terms of published material, my debt to those who have done major research in the field will be obvious from the citations within the text and the "References" afterward. Without their work, this book would have been impossible. I have tried to be scrupulous in citing all works; and if at times I seem to echo them without citation, this is the result of inadvertence and too great familiarity with their excellence of phrase. Unless otherwise specified, quotations from the works of Eugene O'Neill are taken from texts published by Random House.

I must also thank the dedicated staff of the Queens College word processing unit (Jefferson Hall Division). Dean John Reilly (Queens College) gave me permission to use this division; Pearl Sigberman and Wendy De Fortuna scheduled the work (and held my hand in moments of stress), and the following ladies typed the lengthy (and sometimes difficult) manuscript with great efficiency, good cheer, and genuine interest. Rebecca Amann typed the major portion (becoming adept at mindreading in the process), followed by Ida Pizzo and Thelma Silver. Without their help I could not have managed. I also thank Copymasters (79th St. and Amsterdam Avenue, New York City) for their efficiency and understanding, in the face of my anxiety over leaving portions of my single manuscript.

Lastly, because this is the most conspicuous place, I thank my husband Ralph, and my daughter, Caroline, for their immense patience and interest during this long project. In addition, Demelza and Roxelana (cats) provided warm companionship and volunteer service as paperweights, as well as reminders that it was time to break for dinner.

Copyright Acknowledgments   Random House, New York, and Jonathan Cape, London, for permission to quote from all the plays of Eugene O'Neill not mentioned elsewhere in this listing.

Yale University Press, for permission to quote from *Hughie*, © 1959, *Long Day's Journey into Night*, © 1955, *More Stately Mansions*, © 1964, *A Touch of the Poet*, © 1957.

The Collection of American Literature, the Beinecke Rare Book and Manuscript Library, Yale University, which holds copyright to all hitherto unpublished writing by Eugene O'Neill © 1984 for permission to quote from "The Ancient Mariner," "The Ole Davil," "S.O.S.," "The Personal Equation," "The Reckoning," and "The Revelation of Saint John the Divine." The last four titles were seen at Harvard University.

The Huntington Library, San Marino, for permission to quote from the following letters:

MS 85 Carlotta M. O'Neill to Frances McComas, April 30, 1927

MS 87 Carlotta M. O'Neill to Frances McComas, January 8, 1930

MS 90 Carlotta M. O'Neill to Frances McComas, February 2, 1948

MS 91 Carlotta M. O'Neill to Frances McComas, February 24, 1948

MS 92 Carlotta M. O'Neill to Frances McComas, April 3, 1948

MS 93 Carlotta M. O'Neill to Frances McComas, January 1, 1949

The BC Research Company, Columbia, South Carolina, for permission to quote from *"Children of the Sea" and Other Unpublished Plays by Eugene O'Neill*, edited by Jennifer McCabe Atkinson with foreword by Frank Durham. Washington, D.C.: NCR Microcard Editions, © 1972. A Bruccoli Clark Book. [Also includes "Bread and Butter," "Now I Ask You," and "Shell Shock."]

Ticknor & Fields/Houghton Mifflin for permission to quote from *The Calms of Capricorn*, a play developed from O'Neill's scenario by Donald Gallup, 1982, copyright © 1981 by Yale University.

Harper and Row, New York, and Curtis Brown, New York, for permission to quote from *O'Neill* by Arthur and Barbara Gelb, © 1960, 1962, 1973 by Arthur and Barbara Gelb.

The University of Chicago Press for permission to quote from Dorothy Commins, *What is an Editor? Saxe Commins at Work*, © 1978.

Oxford University Press for permission to quote from Travis Bogard, *Contour in Time*, © 1972.

Frederick Ungar, New York, for permission to quote from Virginia Floyd, ed., *Eugene O'Neill at Work: Newly Released Ideas for Plays*, © 1981; and *Eugene O'Neill: A World View*, © 1979.

Little, Brown and Company for permission to quote from Louis Sheaffer, *O'Neill: Son and Playwright*, © 1968; and *O'Neill: Son and Artist* © 1972.

The
Eugene O'Neill
Companion

Eugene O'Neill at the time of his marriage to Carlotta Monterey. Photograph by Albert de Mayer, Paris, 1929. Courtesy of the Performing Arts Research Center, The New York Public Library at Lincoln Center, New York, N.Y.

A

ABEL. In *Gold*,* the ship's boy of the *Triton*. He is fifteen years old, emaciated, and dressed in ragged clothing. He complains about needing water, and Butler,* the ship's cook, shares his private store with him because the boy had not treated him with contempt. Abel, along with Butler, is murdered by Jimmy Kanaka* with the connivance of other members of the crew who wish to keep their "buried treasure" for themselves. Abel's name indicates kinship with the biblical character: a virtuous and innocent young man destroyed by the corruption of others.

ABORTION, a one-act play. The scene is a room on the ground floor of a dormitory at a large Eastern university in the United States during the annual class reunion and commencement week festivities. The room is of college gothic with a large bow window, a fireplace, and furnishings of the Morris chair and leather divan style. The walls "are hung with flags, class banners, framed photographs of baseball and football teams." All in all, it is a "rah! rah!" type of room, indicative of its inhabitants: Donald (Bull) Herron,* an All-American tackle type in white flannels, and Jack Townsend,* the epitome of the blonde, blue-eyed, tanned, eminently successful college athlete, captain of the victorious baseball team. Jack's family, consisting of his parents, Mrs. Townsend* and Mr. Townsend,* and his sister, Lucy Townsend,* have come to the celebration, along with Jack's fiancée, Evelyn Sands.* This day has been the crowning one of Jack's college career: he has captained the baseball team to the championship; and as the hero of the hour, he has been delayed by an adulatory crowd. Joe Murray,* a frail, tubercular-looking eighteen-year-old, enters to ask for Jack. Herron, with the arrogance of an upper-class student toward an uncultured "townie," tells him not to wait. This menacing intrusion of the outside world on Jack's moment of triumph underscores the joy of Evelyn and Jack as they bask in the glory of his success and their dreams of marriage in three months. Mr. Townsend gets his son alone for a serious conversation which reveals that Jack has seduced a poor girl, a "townie" stenographer; and with the help of a "loan" of two hundred dollars from his father, he has managed to procure an abortion for her (at that time an illegal operation). The operation was performed the previous week, and Jack assumes that all has gone well since he has not heard from the girl, though he does admit that he has not answered her letter or telephoned her. Mr. Townsend, himself "no St. Anthony" during his four years at the same college, remonstrates with his son and also expresses surprise at his choice of company, which Jack justifies as the act of "the male beast who ran gibbering through the forest after its female." Mr. Townsend shows some concern on hearing that the girl and her brother are the sole support of the family and elicits a penitential statement from Jack that he has "played the scoundrel all the way through." Still, Jack persists in believing that the ethics of society and its views of right and wrong are also to blame and with a curious logic says, "In bitter self-abasement I have paid, and I am sure the result of it all will be to make me a better man, a man more worthy to be Evelyn's husband." Mr. Townsend, touched by his son's confidence in him, leaves on this note of reconciliation to participate in the "parade." "All's well that ends well. You've learned your lesson."

At that moment, Joe Murray enters to tell Jack that his sister, Nellie Murray,* has died as the result of the bungled abortion. Joe, speaking with a working-class accent, tells how he threatened the doctor with his revolver and was given Jack's two hundred dollars to keep him quiet. Joe accuses Jack of being a "dirty murderer" and attacks the irresponsible behavior of upper-class students like Jack: "lazy, no-good dudes, sponging on your old men; and the goils, our goils, think yuh're grand!" Jack claims that "the thought of it will torture me all my life," and then, in response to Joe's apparent threat of blackmail, offers to pay him anything he wants: "My father is rich. We'll get you a good position, do anything you wish, only do not punish the innocent." Joe, enraged that "you want—to pay me—for Nellie," draws his revolver, which Jack wrests from him, but then offers it back: "Here, take it! I was a fool to stop you. Let the thing end with me and leave the innocent." Joe malevolently tells him that he's going to the police. As he leaves, the parade passes by with a flare of torches, band music, and singing. The revellers rush into the dormitory. Jack takes refuge in the bedroom, and when they leave he comes out to hear the cry, "A long cheer for Townsend, fellows! Hip! Hip!" As the cheering swells, Jack shoots himself in the temple. He dies as the crowd sings "for he's a jolly good fellow." Evelyn enters, discovers the fatal wound, and faints as the curtain falls, with the students still singing in the background in ironic contrast to the tragedy that has just been enacted: "For he's a jolly good fellow, which nobody can deny."

Comments: This play, though clumsy and melodramatic, has considerable biographical interest in demonstrating O'Neill's preoccupation with his responsibility for the pregnancy of Kathleen Jenkins* who became his first wife and the mother of his son, Eugene Gladstone O'Neill, Jr.* Its evocation of the Eastern college-town atmosphere also shows the influence of O'Neill's unsuccessful year at Princeton University (1906–1907). The conflict between town (the blue-collar Trentonians) and the privileged upper-class students of Princeton is O'Neill's earliest treatment of class conflict and indicates his sympathy for the underdog. At the same time, it shows O'Neill's somewhat superior attitude toward women.

In this play, Mrs. Townsend seems rather vague and overprotective, Lucy an enthusiastic little nitwit, and Evelyn a beautiful creature prepared to abase herself before her idol, while Nellie, the victim of the abortion, "died game," refusing to utter a word against the man who had wronged her. This early play was considered as a possible vaudeville skit, and James O'Neill* offered to appear in it. On the whole, the importance of this play is historical rather than literary or dramatic because it started O'Neill on his career. The play, along with several others, was forgotten until it was republished in 1950 in *"Lost" Plays of Eugene O'Neill* without his consent when its copyright ran out. It does, however, show some skill in melodramatic construction and has a fine, old-fashioned, ironic curtain.

Production Data: Written 1913–1914. Produced with *The Movie Man** and *The Sniper** at the Key Theatre, St. Mark's Place, New York City, October 27, 1959. No further information located.

A Note on the Text: The text used is that appearing in *Ten "Lost" Plays of Eugene O'Neill* (New York: Random House, 1964).

ADAMS, Gabriel. In *Now I Ask You*,* romantic poet, later revealed as the husband of Leonora Barnes.* He plays Marchbanks to the Candida of Lucy Ashleigh,* a role which does not endear him to Lucy's husband, Tom Drayton.* Tom sees through him as a poet who makes love to everyone. In reality, Gabriel is secretly married to Leonora Barnes, the painter, but they pretend to be living in free comradeship in order not to seem provincial among members of the Greenwich Village art world. Like Lucy, Gabriel plays a role but does not wish to be fully committed to an affair; he needs Leonora's care. Physically, this poet, with his dark eyes and dark hair, bears a resemblance to O'Neill himself.

AH, WILDERNESS! a play in four acts and seven scenes, O'Neill's only performed comedy, set in "a large small-town in Connecticut," July 4–5, 1906.

Act I: "Sitting-room of the Miller home...about 7:30 in the morning of July 4th, 1906." It is a sunny, cheerful room "furnished with scrupulous medium-priced tastelessness of the period." There is a sofa on the left wall and at center "a big, round table with a green-shaded reading lamp," connected to an overhead chandelier. Five chairs, three rockers, and two armchairs are around the table. There are two bookcases, one with sets for show, and the other a messy one— for reading. A door leads into the back parlor and a dining room beyond from which voices are heard. Essie Miller* is trying to get her eleven-year-old son, Tommy Miller,* to finish his milk, while he wants to go outside and set off his fireworks. The Miller family is introduced: Mildred Miller* is a slender, vivacious, attractive fifteen-year-old; Arthur Miller* is a nineteen-year-old Yale football player type, "solemnly collegiate"; Essie Miller is fifty, short, stout, with graying hair and "a bustling, mother-of-a-family manner"; Lily Miller,* her sister-in-law, is forty-two, a spinster schoolteacher type, even to her spectacles, but her voice is "soft and full of sweetness"; Nat Miller,* owner of the *Evening*

Globe, is in his late fifties, thin, a trifle stooped, with "fine, shrewd, humorous gray eyes"; Sid Davis,* his brother-in-law, is a forty-five-year-old permanent juvenile. Their conversation is punctuated by the sound of Tommy's firecrackers.

The family is discussing its plans for the day. Mr. Miller wants to go to the Sachem Club picnic, but Sid is not sure until Lily says he is a reformed character. It is obvious that Sid is rather too fond of the bottle, but now that he is working on the Waterbury paper, things have changed. He says he will take Lily to the fireworks in the evening and she agrees, as long as he comes home sober. Mildred and Arthur tease them about "spooning" in the evening. The last member of the Miller household to appear in the play is then introduced, seventeen-year-old Richard Miller,* a blend of both of his parents with "something of extreme sensitiveness added—a restless, apprehensive, defiant, shy, dreamy self-conscious intelligence." He is addicted to reading, but his mother is concerned about the suspect quality of the books he is choosing and keeping hidden in his room. When he is asked his plans for the day, he scornfully says he won't go to "that silly skirt party" on the beach with Mildred and then launches into a cliché-ridden socialist speech against capitalism on the Fourth of July. He considers himself intellectually superior to the rest of the family, including Arthur, the Yale student, and throughout the play his speech is larded with quotations from his reading: Oscar Wilde, Shaw, Ibsen, Swinburne, and Fitzgerald's translation of the *Rubáiyát of Omar Khayyám*. To Richard's surprise, his newspaper-editor father reveals a knowledge of Carlyle's *French Revolution* which the young man is currently reading. Mrs. Miller shows herself a mine of misinformation about books, while Sid and Lily both know parts of the *Rubáiyát*.

Suddenly, David McComber,* a "dried-up little man" in his fifties with a rather nasty primness about him, comes up the garden path. The family scatters, leaving Mr. Miller to meet "about the most valuable advertiser I've got." McComber comes quickly to the point: Richard has been writing obscene poems to his daughter, Muriel McComber,* and he pulls out the evidence, which consists of scraps of paper on which are written quotations from Swinburne's *Anactoria*. Appalled by what he sees as an attempt to contaminate the mind of his daughter, he has confined her to the house for a month, given her an 8 P.M. curfew, and has insisted that she write Richard a letter of renunciation, which he now delivers. He tells Nat that it is his duty to punish Richard "to protect other people's children." McComber threatens Richard with possible arrest if he tries to see Muriel and then says he will withdraw his advertisement from Nat Miller's paper if he does not get a written apology from Nat. In reply, Miller furiously refuses to publish the ad starting the next day and threatens to encourage the opening of a competitive store in the town to ruin McComber's business. After McComber leaves, Sid enters to congratulate Nat on his stand and the two of them read with amusement the overripe verse that Richard has sent to Muriel. But then Nat wonders whether his son might be "hanging around her to see what he can get...I've got to draw the line somewhere!"

With that Richard enters, rather "nervous about McComber's call." His father asks him about his relations with Muriel and is pleased to be told that he loves and respects her and certainly has no intention of exploiting her sexually. "We're engaged!" They then discuss the pieces of poetry, and Richard says he had hoped they would make Muriel less afraid of life and of her father. Nat then hands him Muriel's letter of renunciation, which at first wounds him bitterly, but then he turns to "humiliation and wronged anger." Mr. Miller has left him in embarrassment, but now Mrs. Miller enters, eager to find out what McComber had wanted. Richard desperately claims that he is ill, arousing his mother's sympathy and also that of Lily, but finally, to the accompaniment of more of Tommy's firecrackers, the family leaves Richard at home and departs for the picnic.

Act II: The Miller dining-room, a little after 6 P.M. the same day. The dining table has been expanded with all its leaves, overfilling the small room which also contains a china cabinet with the good glass and china and the three pieces of old silver on top of the ugly sideboard. As before, the furniture is medium-priced and impressively tasteless. Mrs. Miller and Norah,* the clumsy, "green-horn" Irish second girl, are setting the table. The girl seems totally unable to do anything right, whether it be turning on the chandelier, setting the table, shutting the door, or serving from the correct side. As Mrs. Miller is bemoaning the thickness of Norah, Lily tries to help with the table: "It makes me feel I'm some use in this house instead of just sponging," a notion Mrs. Miller refutes. Lily is sensitive to her own image as "a cranky old maid." The discussion shifts to Sid's proclivity for liquor. Lily broke off their engagement some sixteen years ago because of an episode "with bad women," which she sees as symptomatic of what he would do when married, even though Sid has always protested his innocence. Mrs. Miller calls Sid "a stupid dumb fool," but Lily, who obviously has affection for him, sees him as a permanent juvenile and a bad marriage risk. She is not embittered, however, because she has been able to enjoy the Miller children as if they were her own.

Suddenly Mrs. Miller realizes that she must tell Tommy not to say that the evening's meal is bluefish, a dish to which Nat believes himself allergic. Actually, he has been eating it for years under another name, but this is the first time that Tommy is aware of the deception and must be told to keep a straight face. This leaves Lily alone when Richard enters in a state of utter tragedy. Asking what has happened between him and Muriel, Lily tries to console him. But Richard refuses all consolation, rejecting Lily's optimism with dramatically pessimistic and cynical remarks. When Mrs. Miller hears that Richard is through with Muriel, she expresses her displeasure at the "indecent" quotations he has sent her, to which Richard replies with a cryptic quotation from Shaw's *Candida*—the romantic renunciation of Marchbanks—and leaves, somewhat to his mother's amusement.

As they depart, Richard re-enters to sneak some olives from the table, much to Norah's annoyance. True love does not transcend food. As he stands there, Wint Selby,* Arthur's Yale classmate, enters. He is a "hell-raising sport type" and is looking for Arthur to accompany him with "a couple of swift babies from New Haven." Richard tells him that Arthur plans to spend the evening at the house of his girlfriend, Elsie Rand, and then Wint suggests that Richard might like to accompany him. Richard, anxious to prove himself socially and filled with rage against Muriel, agrees, lying boldly about his experience with both liquor and women. A meeting at the Pleasant Beach House is set up, and Wint leaves just as Tommy enters to announce the arrival of "Pa and Uncle Sid." The youngster is ravenous, Mrs. Miller warns him about the fish deception, and in the background Sid is heard singing. Obviously, as Mildred points out with mirth, he is merrily drunk, while Lily is mortified.

They sit down to dinner and the soup arrives as Miller enters "mellow and benignly ripened," to the amusement of Mildred and Tommy and aloof unconcern of Richard. Norah finds the situation uproarious, much to Mrs. Miller's annoyance, and the girl's innate clumsiness is thereby accentuated. After a mild drunk scene by Nat, Sid enters "in a condition that can best be described as blurry." He wishes everyone good evening, attempts to apologize to Lily as he bumps into her chair, and then tries to eat his soup, finding hand-eye-mouth coordination impossible. Much to the hilarity of everyone—except Lily—he drinks his soup, declaiming loudly all the time.

The fish course then arrives, and Miller, because of Tommy's mirth, discovers that he has been eating bluefish for years. The lobster course follows, and Miller tries to manage cheerful conversation with "reminiscent obsession" while Sid interrupts and finally takes him down a peg. Sid continues his performance and descends to parody of Nat and then ritually asks Lily to marry him. With a hysterical giggle she refuses, and Sid proceeds as if she is the "slave to rum." He exits with a parody of a Salvation Army meeting as the family explodes with laughter. At this, Lily stands up to berate them for their collective encouragement of Sid and then leaves. Nat is ashamed and suggests that he take her to the fireworks that evening, but Mrs. Miller vetoes the idea. She understands that Lily will never outgrow her affection for Sid, who, Nat tells her, has just lost his job on the Waterbury paper. Nat will take him on, but only if he stops his foolishness. Richard, however, takes Sid's side, blaming Lily's hardheartedness for his continued drinking, again quoting poetry. Both Nat and Mrs. Miller turn against Richard, so that after their exit, he leaves with a scornful smile: "Aw, what the hell do I care? I'll show them!"

Act III, Scene i: The seedy "back room of a bar in a small hotel...dimly lit" with player piano, three stained tables, each with four chairs, and the door to the "Family Entrance" and stairs to the bedrooms. It is about 10 P.M. the same night, and Richard and Belle* are sitting at the center. She is a peroxide blond, tawdrily and flashily dressed, but "is a fairly recent recruit to the ranks [of college tart] and is still a bit remorseful behind her make-up and defiantly careless manner." Richard has a half-empty glass of beer and Belle is drinking a gin rickey. The piano is playing "Bedelia." The bartender, a cunning-looking young Irishman, is watching. Richard, clearly unused to drinking, is toying with his beer, which he treats with some distaste. Belle attempts to liven him up, but he makes no motion toward her. She taunts him into ordering "a man's drink" and he orders a sloe-gin fizz, while she and the bartender conspire to make it a powerful mix. In his attempt to appear the man of the world, Richard tells the bartender to take a drink for himself, receiving a cigar in exchange, and then grossly overtips. But when Belle attempts to smoke, Richard is naively shocked. As the gin warms him up he gets as far as kissing her shyly but is shocked at the seductive kiss he is given. She tries to talk him into going upstairs with her—Wint Selby has long left the bar for the bedroom—but Richard demurs, offering to pay for her room rent if she doesn't have enough money. At this Belle orders another round of drinks, this time on her. As Richard gets a trifle muzzy he becomes more affectionate. But then he tries to reform Belle, and when that fails, he sinks into gloom.

A salesman enters. Belle is quick to see a better customer as Richard starts reciting a combination of poetic snatches, so she leaves him and moves over to the salesman, who encourages Richard's performance. Finally, Richard rises, this time quoting from Ibsen's *Hedda Gabler*, "Eilert Lovborg will come—with vine leaves in his hair," and constitutes himself the protector of Belle's virtue against the onslaughts of the salesman. The result is that Richard gets himself thrown out of the bar, but Belle tells the salesman who Richard is. This shocks him and he tells the bartender, who then throws Belle out.

Act III, Scene ii: The Miller sitting room at about 11 P.M. the same night. Mr. and Mrs. Miller are reading and crocheting, respectively, but both seem worried. Lily is pretending to read and looks "submissive and resigned again." Mildred is writing two words over and over with intense concentration. Tommy is desperately sleepy but won't admit it and is valiantly trying to stay awake. Mildred asks for approval of her new signature, complete with numerous cur-licues, while Mr. and Mrs. Miller express concern about Richard's whereabouts. Mildred says that he just wants to arouse their sympathy. Tommy is sent to bed after one false start, and finally Art appears, looking pleased with himself. He suggests that despite all his socialist rant, Richard has gone to the fireworks. He then "very importantly" speaks of his meal at the Rands and starts to bicker with Mildred. To calm and distract his wife, Nat suggests that Art sing and Mildred play the piano accompaniment. To the sound of extremely sentimental songs sung in the same exaggerated style, a slightly recovered Sid enters to apologize to Lily, who finally forgives him. He even joins in the chorus of "Waiting at the Church," but this recalls memories of his trip to New York which are less than pleasant for Lily. The sound of popular songs continues as the Millers become progressively more apprehensive until Richard appears, dirty, disheveled, and maudlin, quoting again from Ibsen with a soused defiance. But suddenly he says, "Ma! I feel—rotten!" With this, Sid takes him upstairs, while Mrs. Miller worries that he has been "talking about some Hedda," whom she is sure must be "one of those bad women." She hides her face on her husband's shoulder and weeps as Lily, Mildred, and Arthur stand about, embarrassed.

Act IV, Scene i: The Miller sitting room at about 1 P.M. the next day. The family, except for Richard, enters after dinner. Sid is a trifle bloodshot and sleepy; Lily is sad and depressed; Arthur, self-consciously virtuous; Mildred and Tommy subdued. Mr. Miller has come home to punish Richard, who is still in bed but has eaten the dinner that his mother had sent him. Mrs. Miller is now attempting to intercede for Richard, especially now that she has discovered Hedda Gabler's identity. Meanwhile, however, Mr. Miller has received an anonymous note, obviously about spiking Richard's drink. Sid and Nat discuss the situation, agreeing with amusing indirection that Nat should give him the same sex education lecture he had given to his other three sons. Mrs. Miller still has not woken Richard, and finally Nat leaves, angry at having made a trip home for nothing.

Shortly after Mr. Miller's departure, Richard appears, having deliberately avoided any meeting with his father. Richard is sulky, depressed, and still somewhat sick; his self-dramatization again comes from Oscar Wilde and Ibsen: "It's lucky there aren't any of General Gabler's pistols around—or you'd see if I'd stand it much longer!" Mrs. Miller takes him literally and, with her usual practicality, offers a Bromo Seltzer. Sid enters to tease him about his drinking, and when Richard speaks of his wounded heart Sid is initially flippant but then turns sad: "Love is hell on a poor sucker. Don't I know it?" Richard then falls asleep. Mildred returns to ask about Richard's punishment. She has brought him a letter which Muriel had handed through her parlor window, in defiance of parental edicts, disclaiming the earlier letter of renunciation her father had made her write. She says she loves Richard and will sneak out to meet him tonight. At first Richard is joyful, but then (strictly for Mildred's benefit) he adopts the pose of "cynical pessimist," claiming that he knew she couldn't stay away from him and saying he is not sure whether he will meet her this evening. Mildred reminds him that he is forbidden to go out, but then Richard says that he'll go, no matter what punishment he will receive, and begs Mildred to keep quiet about it. She is admiring of his courage but nonetheless bargains with him for a suitable recompense—in kind. He will sneak out now and wait until evening, for he would "wait a million years." His exit line to Mildred is delivered with superior scorn: "The trouble with you is, you don't know what love means!"

Act IV, Scene ii: A strip of beach, a bank overhung with willow trees, a path, and "at center front a white, flat-bottomed rowboat." A new moon is rising, and "in the distance, the orchestra of a summer hotel can be heard very faintly at intervals." Richard is sitting on the gunwale of the rowboat near the stern, in wait for Muriel and meditating on the punishment he is likely to receive for sneaking out. He then thinks about the previous night's escapade with considerable disgust; now he is full of romance, but at the same time he doesn't want to seem too eager when Muriel appears. Muriel McComber is a pretty, plump girl of fifteen or sixteen with "fluffy, light-brown hair, big naive wondering dark eyes, a round dimpled face, a melting, drawly voice." Richard knows she is there but continues whistling "Waiting at the Church" until she calls to him. He acts as if "disturbed in the midst of profound meditation." His apparent indifference hurts her, as does his suggestion that she is afraid of life because she does not want to be seen in the moonlight. However, they eventually sit together on the boat, Muriel telling him about how she sneaked out. Not to be outdone, Richard starts to describe the previous night. Romantically, he claims he had been thinking of suicide because of her rejection of him, so he took the eleven dollars he had saved up for a birthday present ("I've still got almost five left") and went to a low dive. He somewhat upgrades the tale of the Pleasant Beach House, making Wint Selby a Yale senior and the tarts New York chorus girls with whom he drank champagne. However, he warms too much to his subject and Muriel bites his hand when he tells of one girl who sat on his lap and kissed him. She threatens to go home and the two have a lovers' quarrel. But then they make up, Richard suggesting that maybe he needn't go to Yale and instead will work for his father so he and Muriel can be married sooner. Muriel, very practically, opposes that plan. As always, when in doubt, he falls back on quotations as they speak of their honeymoon, Muriel suggesting Niagara Falls, but Richard quoting Kipling: "on the road to Mandalay! We'll watch the dawn come up like thunder out of China."

Act IV, Scene iii: The Miller sitting room at about 10 P.M. the same night. Mrs. Miller is working happily on a doily while Mr. Miller is reading some of the books confiscated from Richard's room. He is amused by Shaw and thinks Swinburne has "a fine swing to his poetry" despite his choice of "loose women" as subject. He has also re-read *The Rubáiyát of Omar Khayyám* and enjoyed it—except for the parts about drinking. Mildred has told her parents of Richard's tryst, and while they are pleased, they are also concerned about disciplining him for disobedience and drunkenness. Mr. Miller says he won't let Richard go to Yale, but his wife thinks that would not be proper, since the other boys have gone. This, of course, is bluff, as Mr. Miller hastens to explain, and Mrs. Miller thinks about the great career Richard is going to have as a lawyer, doctor, or writer. They discuss Muriel and decide that he could do a lot worse, though Nat suggests that the infatuation won't last after he leaves home. Mrs. Miller, a true romantic, is glad that he will always have this moment to remember. Lily is out walking with Sid, Arthur is with Elsie Rand, and Mildred is with her latest beau. Everyone seems to be in love, and even Mr. McComber has been reconciled, apologizing to Nat, who has also gained some new business. "It's been a good day."

The sound of the front door is heard and Richard enters "like one in a trance, his eyes shining with a dreamy happiness." He sits down on the sofa, unconscious of anyone; it is not liquor this time, but love. Nat sends his wife away and talks to his son about his behavior the previous night. Richard insists that he had not gone to bed with Belle. Then, "with a shamefaced, self-conscious solemnity," Nat delivers the necessary lecture on sexuality, prostitution, and finally exclaims, "I never had anything to do with such women, and it'll be a hell of a lot better for you if you never do!" Richard is shocked that his father might have thought

him capable of such infidelity since he plans to marry Muriel. Then Richard
asks about his punishment. Nat replies that he had thought of refusing Richard
the chance to go to Yale, a suggestion that the young man greets with joy.
However, on hearing that Muriel believes that Nat will not wish his son to forgo
college, he insists that his son go to Yale: "Muriel's got good sense and you
haven't."

Richard is then sent to call his mother, and they all talk about the beauty of
the evening. Mr. Miller says he remembers very few nights of similar beauty,
"they were so long ago, when your mother and I were young and planning to
get married." Richard is momentarily astonished at this comment and then
realizes that they, too, were once young like him: "You sort of forget the moon
was the same way back then—and everything." He kisses both his parents with
shy reconciliation and goes out to sit on the piazza. The Millers gaze out at the
moonlight. Nat is feeling happy that Richard can take care of himself now. They
prepare to go up to bed, Mr. Miller saying he is too tired to say his prayers.
They look at Richard "like a statue of Love's Young Dream," and Nat quotes
from the *Rubáiyát*, going on to say that "there's a lot to be said for Autumn.
That's got beauty, too. And Winter—if you're together." Mrs. Miller kisses
him as they move out of the moonlight.

Comments: This comedy is completely out of character for O'Neill, for he
has taken autobiographical elements and manipulated them with romantic nostalgia, unabashed sentiment, and humor instead of the bitterness he displayed
in later autobiographical plays. Aspects of O'Neill himself can be perceived in
Richard, but the structure of this Connecticut family is somewhat different from
that of the O'Neills, with the Millers having four boys and one girl. The basic
situation, a young man's discovery of love, is a stock situation, as are the
characters. We have the clumsy servant, the family drunk, the old maid aunt,
the college athlete and the college sport, and the parents who don't quite understand their children but who eventually overcome the generation gap. Similarly, there are stock scenes, particularly those in which Mrs. Miller takes Richard's
posturings literally, and when Mr. McComber is appalled by Richard's obscene
poetry. The repetition of drunk scenes is also a series of variations on a stock
theme, while the lovers' meeting and the series of reconciliations are the stuff
of romantic sentimentality rather than reality. Nonetheless, the play works and
has remained deservedly popular, despite the fact that there is little character
drawing and the situations tend to telegraph their outcome in advance. The tone
of amused tolerance and the nostalgia for lost innocence that pervade the play
recall a simpler age, and as a result, the playwright's deliberate manipulation
of stock characters and situations becomes a legitimate dramatic device rather
than a subject for hostile criticism. To a considerable extent, the play owed its
acceptance and long run to the casting of George M. Cohan, the original Yankee
Doodle Dandy (whose ad-libbing became legendary), in the role of Nat Miller
and later, in a Los Angeles production, to the performance of Will Rogers in
the same role.

For O'Neill himself, the play was easy to write and represented a pleasant vacation from the seriousness of *Mourning Becomes Electra** and *Days Without End,** that ultimately unsuccessful play which had occupied him for five years. After these plays O'Neill did not produce a new stage work until 1946, with *The Iceman Cometh.**

Production Data: Written 1932 and revised in production, 1933. Produced by the Theatre Guild* at the Nixon Theatre, Pittsburgh, September 25, 1933; moved to the Guild Theatre, New York City, October 2, 1933 (Total of 285 performances).

Director: Philip Moeller
Designer: Robert Edmond Jones*
Cast: Nat Miller: George M. Cohan
      Richard Miller: Elisha Cook, Jr.
      Sid Davis: Gene Lockhart
      Essie Miller: Marjorie Marquis
      Arthur Miller: William Post, Jr.
      Mildred Miller: Adelaide Bean
      Tommy Miller: Walter Vonnegut, Jr.
      David McComber: Richard Sterling
      Muriel McComber: Ruth Gilbert
      Wint Selby: John Wynne
      Belle: Ruth Holden
      Norah: Ruth Chopenning
      Bartender: Donald McClelland
      Salesman: John Butler

Revived at the Guild Theatre, New York City, October 2, 1941 (29 performances). [*See also* Appendix B for two film adaptations (one entitled *Summer Holiday*), and the musical *Take Me Along*.]

ALLEN, Mrs. in "The Personal Equation,"* a plump, middle-aged woman, housekeeper to Thomas Perkins.* She objects to the way Tom Perkins,* the son, treats his father, never even coming to visit. She is little more than an expository device and almost reveals the unconventional nature of the relationship between Olga Tarnoff,* a young revolutionary, and Tom.

ALL GOD'S CHILLUN GOT WINGS, a drama in two acts and seven scenes set in lower New York at an unspecified time; "years ago." The title comes from a Negro spiritual.

Act I, Scene i: "A corner in lower New York, at the edge of the colored district," at a point where three streets merge, at the end of a spring afternoon. The tenement fire escapes are crowded with people, all white faces on the street to the left and all black on the right. Street noises are heard: the clatter of the Elevated, the clip-clop of the horse cars, and music differentiating the two groups. From the white side is heard the sentimental chorus of "Only a Bird in a Gilded Cage," while from the blacks is heard the snappier, jazzy rhythm of "I Guess

I'll Have to Telegraph My Baby.'' Even the laughter of the two faces is different, the whites seem constrained while the blacks are more uninhibited, more instinctive. Eight children, four boys and four girls, two of each sex white and two black, are playing marbles together. A white girl is trying to get her brother, Mickey,* to hurry home before he gets into trouble, while a black girl is doing the same for her brother, Joe.* As they leave, Mickey announces to Jim Harris,* a black, "You's de winner, Jim Crow," the first of a series of racist remarks that will be heard throughout the play. Jim Harris and Ella Downey,* a pretty, blonde, white girl of eight, are being teased about their friendship. When she starts to cry, Jim chases them away and protectively calls her by her hated nickname, "Painty Face"; he thinks her high color is "purty" while she wishes she was black, even if she were called "chocolate," "Crow," or "nigger." Jim confides that he has been drinking chalk in the belief that it might eventually make him white, and Ella allows that it might be working, "maybe—a little bit." The two decide to be "feller" and "girl" to each other as the organ grinder plays "Little Annie Rooney."

Act I, Scene ii: Nine years later, the same corner, at a slightly later time of year than in the preceding scene. Nothing much has changed, except the street noises are now more rhythmically mechanical, electricity having taken the place of horse and steam. The songs, though different, indicate the same racial differences, the white song being "Gee, I Wish That I Had a Girl" and the black one being "All I Got Was Sympathy." There is an exchange of laughter, and as it grows darker the street lamps sputter on. Two young toughs slouch to the corner, one the white Shorty,* and the other the black Joe of Scene i. The two are discussing Mickey's latest boxing victory when Mickey himself drops by. He has become a loud-mouthed, loud dresser with a battered boxer's face. He announces his proprietary interest in Ella Downey, who is to graduate from high school that night. Jim Harris is also to graduate, and he appears dressed in a stiff white collar and dark suit. He has developed into a quiet young man "with a queerly baffled, sensitive face" (a stage direction which will recur throughout the play). Mickey treats Jim with a superior air and becomes threatening when Jim tells him not to fool around with Ella, flaunting the fact that he, Mickey, has a date with her and claiming that "she hates de sight of a coon." Jim is in agony over Ella, and Mickey tells him that he doesn't have a chance: "yuh're trying to buy white and it won't get yuh no place, see!" Jim tells him he had better "act square" with Ella, when the young woman herself comes in. She is pretty but has developed a somewhat bold air, and she starts to leave with Mickey. Jim, desperately hurt, and remembering their past friendship, asks if it is true that she hates "colored people," a charge Ella unconvincingly denies with "Why some of my oldest—," the usual reply of a bigot. She treats Jim's warning concern with contempt and flounces off as Joe tries to explain to Jim that he shouldn't try to make it in the white world. The only difference between him and his friend is that Jim's father has made some money in his trucking business. He asks if Jim is trying to "buy white wid yo' ol' man's dough" and forces him to answer the question, "Is you a nigger, Nigger?" to which Jim replies, "We're both niggers." With that, the two are reconciled and Jim goes off to his graduation.

Act I, Scene iii: Five years later, the same corner. The scene looks much the same, but the people seem listless and tired. The contrast in songs this time is "When I Lost You" from the white side and "Waitin' for the Robert E. Lee" from the black. Both singers are slightly drunk. Shorty enters, looking tougher than before, "the typical gangster," singing a section of the ballad "Frankie and Johnny" as Ella enters. Shorty has been waiting for her in order to give her news about Mickey. Ella looks much older; she seems ill and is poorly dressed. Shorty says that Mickey is almost through in the ring—he has worn himself out with too many women—and he has sent her money either for her or "the kid." Ella says that the child has died of diphtheria and she has not bothered to tell Mickey. He'd be glad, and now they are both free. Shorty suggests that Ella join his "stable," but Ella says she's through with that. When she allows that she has been seeing Jim Harris, "The only white man in the world! Kind and white. You're all black—black to the heart," he throws money at her, shouting "nigger-lover!" Ella drops the cash into the hat of a Salvation Army captain, with a mocking "Here. Go save yourself. Leave me alone."

Ella is alone when Jim Harris enters, "a quietly dressed, studious-looking Negro with an intelligent yet queerly baffled face." He has failed his law examinations once more—after five years, he is where he should have been at the end of two. No matter how hard he studies and how much he knows, he finds himself the victim of the psychic warfare waged by the whites against the blacks: "They're kind. They're good people. They're considerate, damn them! But I feel branded!" Ella treats him with sympathy, telling him that he is the only person who has been "white" to her. She doesn't really understand why Jim wants to be a lawyer because she thinks him better than "they [whites] are in every way." Jim then proposes marriage to Ella and is surprised by the speed with which she accepts: "I'm alone. I've got to be helped. I've got to help someone—or it's the end—one end or another." Jim goes into "a frenzy of self-abnegation," saying they will go abroad where the color of one's skin does not matter. He will adore Ella, love and protect her, and he'll "become your slave!—yes, be your slave—your black slave that adores you as sacred!"

Act I, Scene iv: A few weeks later, "a street in the same ward in front of an old brick church." The church is set back from the sidewalk behind an iron fence with a gate. The buildings look stern and forbidding, and all the window shades are drawn. The neighborhood seems to be waiting, breathless, and the silence is broken by a Negro tenor singing "Sometimes I feel like a mourning dove," then "Sometimes I feel like an eagle in the air," and finally the stanza beginning "Sometimes I wish that I'd never been born." Again there is silence which "is broken by one startling, metallic clang of the church-bell." As if called by a signal, people pour out of the tenements and "form two racial lines" as the church door swings open and Ella and Jim seem almost be be spewed out of it. They must run this gauntlet, and as they stand there, an organ grinder enters to play the chorus of "Old Black Joe." The newly married pair walk slowly through the segregated lines, and in near hysteria, Jim tries to keep up their courage. As they reach the curb, Ella's face has "an expression of trance-like calm and peace" while Jim is close to collapse as he looks for a taxi to take them to the steamer.

Act II, Scene i: Two years later, the parlor of an apartment in the Negro district, one of "the better sort." The furniture is a curiously clashing mixture of the garishly ornate and the soberly severe. Two objects on the wall act almost as icons of this confusion of vision. The first is a gold-framed colored photograph of an elderly black man "with an able, shrewd face but dressed in outlandish lodge regalia," and the second is a primitive mask from the Congo, "a grotesque face, inspiring obscure, dim connotations...but...conceived in a true religious spirit." It dominates the room "by a diabolical quality that contrast imposes upon it." Everything in the room is clean and gleaming with polish; the wallpaper is new, as is the brilliant carpet. In a rocking chair by the table at the center sits Mrs. Harris,* Jim's mother, a woman of about sixty-five dressed in old-fashioned Sunday best. Walking nervously around the room is Jim's sister, Hattie Harris,* age about thirty. She looks high-strung and defiant, with an intelligent face "showing both power and courage." She is dressed severely, almost asexually.

They are awaiting the return of Jim and Ella, and the two women show differing responses to their own negritude. Mrs. Harris appreciates the difficulty Ella faces in an interracial marriage because its "harder for de white dan for de black." Hattie cannot understand this, and it is clear that she disapproves of the marriage. Mrs. Harris is also opposed: "De white and de black shouldn't mix dat close." She accepts her place in the world, while Hattie struggles against it. Hattie thinks Jim and Ella were cowards to run off to Europe—they should have stayed and conquered prejudice: "We don't deserve happiness till we've fought the fight of our race and won it!" Jim enters alone, saying that Ella has an attack of "nerves" and must rest. She has been dreadfully lonely in France, and apparently the marriage was not consummated for over a year. Hattie asks whether Ella does indeed love him, and Jim replies that he'd drown himself if he didn't know that she does. However, as the time went on in France, Ella became more and more closed in; she spoke of wishing for there to be always just the two of them, and slowly Jim began to feel that he was a "quitter" for running away after their marriage. He had even given up his ambition to become a lawyer and felt that he wasn't "a real man." Now they have come back to confront the situation bravely, and Jim will return to study.

Ella then enters, looking pale and haunted. She runs to Jim as if to a protector and gazes at Mrs. Harris and Hattie "with a frightened defiance." She acts toward Hattie with an air of condescending superiority, infuriating Hattie into boasting of her educational accomplishments. Ella recalls how easy it was for her to pass her own examinations and how very difficult for Jim, giving him "a tolerant, superior smile but one full of genuine love." She recalls "the law school examinations Jim hardly ever could pass,'' and Hattie angrily says Jim will pass them now "if you'll give him a chance." Suddenly Ella sees the Congo mask and is frightened by it. Hattie forces her to touch it and tells her that it is as good a work of art as something by Michelangelo. To Ella it is "ugly" and "stupid." She leaves it in its dominant position, "where I can give it the laugh," and announces that she won't allow Jim to take any more examinations, a statement that brings Hattie to complain about "white justice!—their fear for their superiority." Ella begs Jim to send Hattie away, and the two black women leave with dignity as Jim collapses. Penitently, Ella tells Jim that she didn't mean what she said about the examinations: "I want you to be the best lawyer in the country!...I want the whole world to know you're the whitest of the white! I want you to climb and climb—....I love you, Jim!''

Hattie and Mrs. Harris reappear to announce that they are moving to the Bronx, "the heart of the Black Belt—the Congo—among our own people," giving the house to Jim and Ella as a gift. As Jim leaves to escort them out, Ella examines the room, looking sneeringly at Mr. Harris's photograph "all dolled up like a circus horse! Well, they can't help it. It's in the blood, I suppose. They're ignorant, that's all there is to it." After this racist remark, she tries a mocking tone to the Congo mask and looks out the window at all the black faces. Suddenly she sees Shorty and calls out to him, but he does not reply. She realizes that even a pimp and dope-peddler thinks her a pariah, as she runs out "whimpering like a child" calling for Jim.

Act II, Scene ii: The same scene but six months later. The walls and ceiling of the parlor seem to have shrunk so that they oppress the occupants, and the portrait and the mask both appear abnormally large. Jim is seated at the table, law books piled everywhere, and is trying to study, but he cannot concentrate. He groans, slams the book shut, and goes to the window as Hattie enters. Ella has declined into insanity, and Jim has convinced himself that once he passes his examinations things will be better. He won't take Hattie's advice and send Ella away because he is all she has in the world and she loves him. Jim is feeling depressed but claims he really knows his material this time. Hattie, however, is afraid that Jim, too, may be headed for a breakdown, and she is also afraid for herself in that she may kill Ella in order to set Jim free. Jim swears he must prove himself worthy: "I've got to prove I'm the whitest of the white." This statement stings Hattie to fury, and she tells Jim that Ella, in her ravings, has said she cannot have a child by Jim "because it'll be born black." She begs Jim to commit Ella to a mental institution, but Jim refuses, even when Hattie tells him of the anger and hatred Ella spews out in her madness. Hattie fears for her brother's safety; but Jim realizes that he is all Ella has in life, and from now on he is going to lock the door against the rest of the world, except for the doctor.

Left alone, Jim attempts to memorize his law books as Ella enters in a dressing gown, carrying a carving knife. She advances murderously on Jim, but he turns and sees her, catching her wrist. She speaks of her nightmares with "terrified pleading...like a little girl.'' She wants him to be her "Uncle Jim, who's been with us for years and years,'' addressing him almost as if he is a slave. When Jim sends her to bed, she looks at him with an expression of vicious hatred and calls, "You dirty nigger.'' Momentarily she recovers, but as she leaves she calls out "Nigger" once more as Jim bows his head on his arms. The curtain falls.

Act II, Scene iii: Six months later, just after sunset; the same scene. The walls and the ceiling of the room appear even more shrunken; and by contrast, the furniture, the books, the picture, and particularly the Congo mask are magnified. Ella enters and addresses the mask. Jim has gone out, and now she can tell the mask what she thinks. It is to blame for "all this.'' She sees it as a diabolical presence that has destroyed their relationship. It has made her "black as dirt! You've poisoned me! I can't wash myself clean.''

Ella sinks down in a chair as Jim comes back from looking for his examination results. He holds an opened letter and looks utterly devastated. Once again he has failed in "God's country!'' It would "be against all natural laws, all human rights and justice'' for "Jim Crow Harris'' to be allowed to succeed, to become a member of the bar. Ella is overwhelmed with joy to hear that Jim has not passed: "You're still my old Jim—and I'm so glad.'' With this, she grabs the mask and plunges a knife through it, exorcising it. Jim is appalled: "You devil! You white devil woman! You devil!'' Ella, however, believes she is killing the devil that has tormented them both; and as Jim sits down, tired to death, Ella admits that she has deliberately kept him awake so that he would fail because if he had passed his examinations, the devil would win. That was why she carried the knife around—to prevent his studying. Jim tells her that he has been continually frightened of what "they'' would do to her "after.''

Ella now regresses to the happy days of childhood, when racial differences did not matter. Jim blames God for what has happened as she hints that she will not live much longer. But Jim then reacts in an almost mystically ecstatic way, thanking God and asking His forgiveness: "Let this fire of burning purify me of selfishness and make me worthy of the child You send me for the woman You take away.'' Ella still joyously regresses: "Be my little boy, Jim. Pretend you're Painty Face and I'm Jim Crow. Come and play!'' Jim, still in a state of exaltation, replies, "Honey, Honey, I'll play right up to the gates of Heaven with you,'' and the curtain falls.

Comments: *All God's Chillun Got Wings* opened under circumstances of extraordinary bigotry, and attempts were made to prevent its performance. When it was bruited abroad that a white actress, Mary Blair,* would kiss the hand of a black actor, Paul Robeson,* and that the play was about an interracial marriage, there was a furor. Finally, local government was approached in an attempt to close the play. On the day of the first performance New York City refused to grant work permits for the children who were to play in the opening scene, with the result that James Light, the play's director, was forced to make an announcement and read the opening lines (Gelb and Gelb, 1973, p. 554; Sheaffer, 1973, p. 143). Helen Deutsch and Stella Hanau (1931, p. 112) maintain that it was the stage manager who read the first lines and they also include a picture of Harold McGee reading. The play was not closed, and the scene continued to be read. Attempts to have the ban lifted were continued, but "except for a few performances late in the summer" (Deutsch and Hanau, 1931, p. 112), the children were not permitted to appear. Obviously, the play was far ahead of its time in choosing to deal with the theme of an interracial marriage, and to some extent the social situation still militates against the play's revival. Prejudiced language, simplistic racial sentiments, and inherent stereotypes have dated the play more than might have been initially anticipated. But the passage of time and the cooling of passions about this *succès de scandale* have meant that one can now look more critically at the play itself and place it more specifically in the mainstream of O'Neill's development.

As O'Neill himself said, the racial issue is not the most important thing in the play, which, of course, is really about the problems of a mismated couple. In this way, one can place *All God's Chillun* in the same line of development as O'Neill's other exercises on this theme. From *Bread and Butter,** *Servitude,** and *The First Man,** to *Beyond the Horizon** and *Welded,** O'Neill had dealt with woman as the destroyer of the ambition of man as artist, researcher, and adventurer, and this play clearly belongs with them. Also, because of the curious choice of names for the central characters—James and Ella, the names of O'Neill's own parents—the play can be seen as disguised autobiography and a forerunner of *Long Day's Journey into Night** with James Tyrone* and Mary Tyrone.* However, J. H. Raleigh (1964, p. 113) suggests that the name of Jim should be seen as an echo of the character of the same name in Mark Twain's *Huckleberry Finn* and hence the type of noble and generous black who is superior to the whites around him. But that parallel does not apply to the marriage of James O'Neill* and Ella Quinlan O'Neill.* Perhaps in the destructiveness of Ella Downey there is an echo of the devastation caused to James O'Neill's own career by his wife's drug dependence.

The play also contains nuances of *The Emperor Jones** in its use of the Congo mask and its suggestion of atavism. Also, of course, *All God's Chillun* attempts expressionism in the use of the two "icons," represented by the lodge picture and the mask, but even more important is its attempt to show the crushing nature of environment on Jim and Ella. The room shrinks in size and begins to oppress its inhabitants, who cannot escape from it. These two individuals have overturned an established order of things, and the clashing culture of their surroundings helps to destroy them. O'Neill said that in this play he was dealing with the essential unity of all humankind, and this theme is a logical sequel to the treatment of unity in *The Fountain.** Basically, though, *All God's Chillun Got Wings* is really about two human beings who try to solve their racial and cultural differences through love. In this situation, Ella is the weaker of the two because she cannot overcome her innate (and learned) behavioral prejudices. Jim, on the other hand, becomes what in many of O'Neill's "marriage" plays would seem to be the perfect helpmate in serving his beloved. This action follows with O'Neill's definition of love in his early play, *Servitude**: "Love means servitude, and *my* love is *my* happiness."

But though it is possible to treat this play entirely in terms of the marital situation, O'Neill has also broadened his scope so that to some extent it even prefigures some of Lorraine Hansberry's characters in *A Raisin in the Sun*. Hattie, for instance, prefigures the young woman Beneatha who has just discovered both Africa and her own negritude. Hattie will make her own way in the world while asserting her blackness, even though it costs her her femininity. Mrs. Harris, on the other hand, accepts her status and prefers to segregate herself, while Jim attempts to succeed in the white world on white terms. Curiously, this is something that Jim's father had been able to do in his trucking business, but Jim, in trying to succeed on intellectual terms, is continually defeated because of his vulnerability to psychic murder. Ella herself is also a practitioner of this skill. She continually sends mixed signals to Jim, knowing that she will lose him should he succeed. She slips into neurosis and finally insanity, and in that insanity she indicates her true, suppressed feelings: she is afraid to have a child because it will be black; she despises black people; she is afraid of sex. She regresses to the only stage in American society in which racial differences are unimportant—childhood—and the only two relationships she really wants with Jim are those of playfellow or white child in the care of "Uncle Jim," as if he is the family's old black retainer. Success for Jim would leave Ella without a real place in his new existence, and therefore she must intervene to prevent his achievement.

In general, the play contains some rather stereotypical qualities. The blacks are supposed to be more instinctual, more musical, more in tune with the seasons, while the whites sing sentimentally, without the "Negro richness" of which O'Neill speaks. Also, the old black-white dichotomy, together with all the pejorative connotations of blackness, is now somewhat dated. As a result, Jim's wish to be Ella's "black slave" and her wish for him to be "the whitest of the white" grates on today's sensibilities, as does Jim's curious remark that "all love is white." Despite all these problems, some of which are not of O'Neill's making, the play remains the first important and thoroughly serious treatment of white-black relations of this century, though the conclusion is rather too romantically contrived and fails to resolve the conflicts of the play. This attempt to convey the essential oneness of humanity is less successful, less precisely stated, than *The Fountain*.

Production Data: Written 1923. Produced by Kenneth Macgowan,* Robert Edmond Jones,* and Eugene O'Neill at the Provincetown Playhouse, New York City, May 15, 1924 (43 performances). Reopened, Greenwich Village Theatre, New York City, August 18, 1924 (62 performances).

Director: James Light
Designer: Cleon Throckmorton

   Cast: *Child Characters:*
             Jim Harris: William Davis
             Ella Downey: Virginia Wilson
             Shorty: George Finley
             Joe: Malvin Myrck
             Mickey: James Ward
             Little Girls: Grace Burns, Alice Nelson, Evelyn Wynn
             Adult Characters:
             Jim Harris: Paul Robeson*
             Mrs. Harris: Lillian Greene
             Hattie: Dora Cole
             Ella Downey: Mary Blair*
             Mickey: James Martin
             Shorty: John Taylor
             Joe: Frank Wilson
             Organ Grinder: James Meighan
             Salvationists: Barbara Benedict, Clement O'Loghlen, William Stahl
             Men and Women: Kirk Ames, Eloise Anderson, Harold Bryant, Polly Craig,
             Hume Derr, Oscar Flanner, Lila Hawkins, Paul Jones, Spurgon Lampert, Sadie
             Reynolds, Kathleen Roarke.

[*See also* Appendix B for operatic adaptation.]

ALVARADO, Luis de, in *The Fountain,** a friend of Juan Ponce de Leon.*
He first appears in 1492 when he brings a Moorish minstrel to a Spanish Conqueror's entertainment and the Moor sings of the sacred fountain. Alvarado is
initially a swashbuckling young rake, but he is discontented with the life of
action. Twenty years later, in Porto Rico, he is seen again, this time as a man
who has spent the previous five years as a Dominican monk. He has now found
peace and is a good counselor to Juan Ponce de Leon, remaining his friend until
the end. Alvarado is a symbolic figure, that of a man who has found his peace
in religion. He is one of the four religious apparitions who appear to Juan in the
fountain and personifies the ability to reconcile the warring factions of man's
soul. In his priestly garb he also represents Christianity, one of the four main
world religions, which are shown in the fountain to indicate their essential unity.

AMES, Amos. In *Mourning Becomes Electra,** a carpenter, a fat man in his
fifties. He and his wife, Louisa Ames,* come with Seth Beckwith* to look at
the Mannon house. Ames comes dressed in his best Sunday clothes to gaze at
the gentry. His function in both *Homecoming* and *The Haunted* is that of a
member of the Chorus of Townsfolk who comments on the Mannon clan. In
The Haunted, he is one of those who encourages Abner Small* to accept a wager

that he will stay all night in the shuttered Mannon home, which is believed to be ghost-ridden. "In character he is the townsfolk type of garrulous gossip-monger. . .devoid of evil intent."

AMES, Louisa. In *Mourning Becomes Electra*,* the wife of Amos Ames.* She appears in the first play, *Homecoming*, as a member of the Chorus of Townsfolk used for purposes of exposition and comment on the activities of the Mannon family. She is taller and heavier than her husband, Amos Ames,* and is in her fifties. She has a delight in scandal, and "her tongue is sharpened by malice."

AMINDRA, the hell ship in *The Long Voyage Home*.* Olson* has once shipped on her, and in this play he is shanghaied aboard her.

ANCIENT MARINER, THE, an experiment in "plastic theatre" and an adaptation of Samuel Taylor Coleridge's poem. O'Neill used a copy of the poem published by G. P. Putnam's Sons in an undated edition; he omitted a few stanzas and added stage directions and about a dozen lines. The play opens at night outside a lighted house, with dancers whirling by a shaded window to the tune of Tchaikowsky's "Doll's Funeral March." Three Wedding Guests appear, two looking like smug marionettes, while the third has attributes of real life. This third guest is the one the Mariner forces to hear his tale. The Chorus, composed of "six old sailors wearing the masks of drowned men," brings on portions of a ship, which they put together on stage. The Bride and Bridegroom appear briefly, looking like dolls. The Ancient Mariner has a long white beard and looks like a Biblical prophet dressed in sailor clothes.

The plot of the poem does not need rehearsal here, but the use of costumes and masks is heavily symbolic. At its first appearance, the Albatross looks like a "Dove of the Holy Ghost," and then it is offered bread, symbolizing communion wafers. After it is shot, the bird's spirit appears as "a figure all in white planes like a snow crystal"; and when the body of the bird is hung on the guilty Mariner, it looks like a white cross. The Mariner is pushed to the bow of the vessel by the Chorus, who then recoils from him as if he is a leper. The figure of Death is portrayed as "a *black* skeleton—the mask of a black skull on a robe of verdigris and rust." Life-in-Death is a woman with "a face like a white skull—(make up not mask)—vampirish and terrible in a robe of pale red like blood [?] diluted with water." As the voyage proceeds, the sails of the vessel look "like the wings of the Albatross—faintly luminous," and the Chorus of dead sailors awakens to reveal new masks, "those of holy spirits with haloes about their heads." A white spirit appears bearing the body of the Albatross and asks other spirits for vengeance, which is refused. In anger he curses the Mariner, who, along with the Third Wedding Guest, is unconscious during this colloquy. The Chorus now wears the masks of old men. A hill with lighthouse appears after the curse is finally removed, and the Chorus puts on Angel masks to represent angelic spirits; their spirits fly to heaven like shooting stars. The Pilot, his Boy, and the Hermit appear to the strains of a hymn, and the ship sinks with a roar; the stage is darkened, and momentarily the Mariner appears as if floating like a drowned corpse to reappear in the dory. The Pilot has a fit, the Boy goes crazy, and the Hermit shrives the Mariner who has knelt before him and told his story. The scene then shifts back to the wedding, and the music of the "Doll's Funeral March" is heard again. The Mariner turns to the audience and addresses the last lines directly to it:

He prayeth best who loveth best
All things both great and small;
For the dear God who loveth us,
He made and loveth all.

He crosses himself, turns, and leaves. O'Neill omits the last two stanzas of the poem, and the action concludes with the Third Wedding Guest staring after the departed Mariner. Then he rushes into the house to the sounds of welcome; he shuts and locks the door, and his shadow is seen on the lighted window shade as he dances with the Bride.

Comments: The play had the usual three-week run at the Provincetown Playhouse, New York City, on a double bill with Molière's *George Dandin*, translated by Stark Young, but it was not a success. Robert Edmond Jones* believed that *The Ancient Mariner* was an advance in the concept of "plastic theatre," and O'Neill enjoyed the experiment in the use of masks "to show the eye of tragedy and the face of exaltation." Despite its lack of critical success, O'Neill thought highly enough of the dramatization to consider allowing it to be revived by the Federal Theatre Project in 1937; however, this was not done. One scene was given in a program of rehearsals from Provincetown productions at the Garrick Theatre, New York City, November 17, 1929, but it has not been revived. This adaptation is similar to what O'Neill also attempted in the unperformed and unfinished "The Revelation of John the Divine."*

The Ancient Mariner was part of a deliberate experiment in the development of a theatrical experience resulting from the joint skills of designer, director, and playwright to create spectacle and a total involvement of the senses of the audience without dependence on the actor or on the text. In effect, then, the playwright would provide a scenario on which the director would exercise his skills, together with those of his costume and set designers. Masks, music, and movement were important in this aesthetic approach, which owed much to the theories of Edward Gordon Craig.

Production Data: Written 1923. Produced by Kenneth Macgowan,* Robert Edmond Jones* and Eugene O'Neill* at the Provincetown Playhouse, New York City, April 6, 1924, as part of a double bill with Molière's *George Dandin*, translated by Stark Young (29 performances).

Directors: Robert Edmond Jones and James Light
Design: Robert Edmond Jones
Masks: James Light
Cast: Ancient Mariner: E. J. Ballantine
        First Wedding Guest: James Shute
        Second Wedding Guest: H. L. Rothschild
        Third Wedding Guest: Charles Ellis
        Chorus: Robert Forsyth, Benjamin Keiley, Harold McGee, William Stahl, John
        Taylor, Clement Wilenchik
        Helmsman: James Meighan
        Bride: Rosalind Fuller
        Bridegroom: Gerald Stopp
        Life-in-Death: Rita Matthias
        First Spirit: Henry O'Neill
        Second Spirit: Gerald Stopp
        Pilot: Rupert Caplan
        Pilot's Boy: John Brewster
        Hermit: Henry O'Neill
Text published in *Yale University Library Gazette*, 35 (1960):61–86.

ANDERSEN, Paul. In *Chris Christophersen** (the first draft of what later becomes *"Anna Christie,"**), the second mate aboard the steamer *Londonderry.**
He is a tall, broadshouldered blond young fellow of about twenty-five but with
a weak expression, especially his "self-indulgent mouth." He is a curiously
misconceived character, chiefly because he had to be developed to complement
an equally misconceived Anna. He comes from a farming family; but since he
is not the eldest son, he does not inherit the farm. He therefore goes to the
university for two years; but then he drops out to drift around, taking office jobs
and generally feeling discontented until he signs on as an able seaman and
discovers that the sea is his spiritual home. With his clearly superior intellectual
equipment, he advances quickly to the berth of second mate. But then his native
weakness takes over and he decides that he does not wish any further advancement. He is happy with what he considers the easiest job on the boat, since the
position of second mate carries the privileges of an officer without too much
responsibility. After deciding to marry Anna, whom he finds to be a kindred
spirit, he says he will study for his Master's Ticket so that she will be able to
travel with him. He is a romantic, somewhat impractical fellow.

ANDERSON, Jimmy. In O'Neill's only published short story, "Tomorrow,"*
a failed journalist. Jimmy Andersen had been a student at Edinburgh, was from
a good family, and went to South Africa as a journalist. There he had married
an English girl named Alice, who was unfaithful to him with a British officer.
As a result, Jimmy had turned to drink.
    At the beginning of the story, Jimmy has finally managed to translate his
dream of "tomorrow" into reality by getting a job. Art,* his roommate (a

surrogate for Eugene O'Neill), is pleased; but after a five-day binge, he realizes that Jimmy's bed has not been slept in and that Jimmy has not even taken care of his beloved geranium which has never bloomed. Late that night, Jimmy returns with the news that he has been fired announcing that "I couldn't do the work." He realizes all at once that he is a total failure. He goes upstairs with Art and tells him the story of Alice. Left alone in his room, he accidentally knocks the geranium off the fire escape and it smashes. He rushes down to tell Art and then goes back upstairs and jumps to his own death.

"Tomorrow" represents an early version of several characters who appear in *The Iceman Cometh.** James Cameron* is the Jimmy Tomorrow* journalist of the play, Captain Cecil Lewis* finds his wife in bed with a staff officer, and Don Parritt* commits suicide. [*See also* Byth, James Findlater.]

"AND GIVE ME DEATH," the proposed third play in the abandoned cycle "A Tale of Possessors, Self-Dispossessed."* This play, covering the period 1793-1805, was designed to tell the story of Deborah (formerly Abigail) Harford* and her marriage to Henry Harford. Gradually O'Neill came to realize that this play ought to be divided into two. He finally destroyed the completed longhand draft in February 1943. This play was originally entitled "Greed of the Meek"* and was the first play of the eight-play version of the cycle. It then received part of its title from the first play of the nine-play version, "Give Me Death," and became the second play of the nine-play series, dropping to third when O'Neill decided to subdivide the first two plays, bringing the number of proposed cycle plays to eleven.

"ANNA CHRISTIE," a play in four acts; awarded the Pulitzer Prize, 1922.
Act I. The saloon of "Johnny-the–Priest"* near South Street, New York City. The stage is divided into two sections, a bar room and a back room, in a realistic representation of a typical drinking establishment of the area. "It is late afternoon of a day in fall." Johnny-the–Priest, a white-haired, clerical-looking man wearing an apron, is tending bar. He is deceptively mild in appearance and manner, but one senses the hardness and callousness beneath this exterior. As the play opens he is lounging in a chair, reading the evening paper, with his spectacles on his nose. Two Longshoremen enter and are served drinks. Larry,* a young fellow of twenty or so, arrives to take Johnny's place at the bar when a Postman appears with a letter addressed to Christopher Christopherson,* in care of Johnny, with the postmark of St. Paul, Minnesota. As Johnny leaves, Chris, "a short squat, broad-shouldered man of about fifty," enters. His face is "round, weather-beaten," with short-sighted, kindly blue eyes. His neck is thick, and "he walks with a clumsy rolling gait" on unusually short legs. He is the captain of a coal barge. At this moment, he is happily inebriated, ready and willing to oblige with a song. He downs another drink and says that he has just returned from a dirty voyage to Norfolk. Suddenly he remembers that Marthy Owen* has come with

him. She is a "Tugboat Annie" type of about forty or fifty, fat, flabby, with
greasy gray hair in an untidy topknot over a "jowly, mottled face" and red
nose. She is dressed in grimy men's clothing, oversize brogans, and a calico
skirt. Her voice is loud and mannish, but she has retained a certain lusty, gusty
quality despite the obvious ill usage she has suffered. She is living with Chris.
Chris is given his letter, which is from Anna, his daughter, who is coming "right
away" because she has been sick. The old sailor recalls that he has not seen
her in fifteen years because she has been living with his wife's relatives in
Minnesota. By now she is twenty years old and expects to stay with her father
on her arrival. Chris is most embarrassed over how to explain Marthy, who
instantly understands and says she'll be off the boat before Anna arrives. She
will always be able to find another bargeman to live with. The two decide to
celebrate Anna's imminent arrival, but Marthy suggests that Chris get something
to eat so that he will be sober when she comes.

Anna Christopherson* then enters the bar through the "family entrance."
"She is a tall, blond, fully developed girl of twenty, handsome after a large,
Viking-daughter fashion." Clearly she is not in good health and, equally ob-
viously, is a prostitute. She is cheaply and tawdrily dressed. She orders, "gimme
a whiskey—ginger ale on the side. And don't be stingy, baby," as she sinks
into a chair by the table opposite Marthy. Each woman has another drink after
Anna speaks of her journey from Minnesota and Marthy realizes her identity.
Each assesses the other, but Marthy refuses to be taken for a prostitute. As Anna
Christopherson continues her life story, she reveals that she now calls herself
"Anna Christie." She is shocked to hear from Marthy that Chris is not a janitor
but a coal barge captain, but Marthy rushes to his defense: "That's what comes
of his bringing yuh up inland—away from the old devil sea—where yu'd be
safe." With bitter irony, Anna tells of her life as a poor-relation-slavey, of the
way her cousin "started" her sexually when she was only sixteen. In an outburst
of rage, she says that she hates all men. Marthy, however, says that Chris is
one of the good ones and warns Anna that the old man thinks the world of her.

Chris returns and asks after Marthy. Larry tells him that she is in the back
room with "another tramp"; and when Chris enters, Marthy leaves for the barge
to pack her things, first informing him that her companion is Anna. Chris enters
the back room with embarrassed emotion, looking shyly at Anna, whose brilliant
clothes impress him with their "class." The two kiss clumsily and then start
talking. Anna is at first resentful that her father had never visited her, but Chris
tries to explain about "dat ole davil sea" which makes sailors act irrationally.
Anna is scornful of his working on a coal barge since she has thought he held
a respectable job as a janitor. In reply Chris lies, claiming he needed a job in
the open air because he has been sick. To this Anna says that she just got out
of the hospital two weeks earlier. This calls forth Chris's protective instincts,
and it is ironic to remember that Anna has told Marthy that her stay in the hospital
came after the "house" in which she had worked was raided by the police.
Chris suggests that life on the barge will improve her health and gently suggests

that she drink some port wine to increase her strength. With the eyes of love, he sees her as a defenseless, innocent girl, embarrassing Larry by this revelation. Anna, in Chris's absence, doesn't know what to do and collapses into sobs. The act ends as Chris and Anna drink a toast with "Skoal," Anna "downing her port at a gulp like a drink of whiskey."

Act II. It is ten days later, and Anna is with her father on board the "barge, *'Simeon Winthrop,'* at anchor in the outer harbor of Provincetown, Mass." It is 10 P.M., and the vessel is enshrouded in dense fog. The curtain rises to show Anna wearing an oilskin and no hat, looking "healthy, transformed, the natural color has come back to her face." "She is staring into the fog astern with an expression of awed wonder," reveling in this new experience: "I feel as if I was—out of things altogether." The more Chris complains about the sea, the more Anna is coming to love it, and she refuses to go inside, asking about the other members of her family who followed the sea. Chris tells the tale—all but one never returned: "He's the only one dat ole davil don't kill." Shyly he tells her that he was once a boatswain and continues with his attack on sea life and "dat ole davil, sea," which swallows up those who follow her. He tells Anna that a woman is a fool to marry a seafarer, but no matter what Chris says, Anna claims that "I feel clean, somehow—like you feel yust after you've took a bath. And I feel happy for once—yes, honest!—happier than I been anywhere before!" Chris has a premonition that this voyage was a bad idea. But Anna claims that what happens will be "Gawd's will, like the preacher said," to which Chris protests, "No! Dat ole davil, sea, she ain't God!"

Suddenly there is a hail and four Sailors from a wrecked vessel come aboard; all but one, Mat Burke,* are unable to stand from sheer exhaustion. Mat is a powerful man of six feet, aged about thirty; and when Anna comes out to give him a drink of whiskey, he is overwhelmed to find someone like her on the barge: "I thought you was some mermaid out of the sea come to torment me." Anna, though at first repelled by him, is amused by his ability to joke with her after his experience, and Mat boastfully tells of his feat of strength in rowing for two days while his companions were too weak. Thinking she is Chris's mistress, he makes a clumsy pass at her, asking for a kiss. She pushes him away and catches him off balance so that he falls. She then explains her relationship to Chris, and he apologizes to "a fine, dacent girl the like of yourself," with a grudging admiration for one who has managed to fell him. They shake hands, and Anna is hurt by the strength of his grip. Mat then tells the tale of the wreck and of the misery of a sailor's life in which the only women he meets are out to roll him for the money he brought ashore. Continually, he refers to Anna as "a dacent girl" and has clearly decided that he wants to marry her. Chris comes upon them and orders Anna to bed and Mat to the forecastle. Both refuse, Anna because she won't be ordered like a slave and Mat because he wants to show his strength. But then he remembers that Chris is Anna's father. Anna defends Mat and helps him inside as Mat announces, "You're the girl of the world and we'll be marrying soon and I don't care who knows it!" As Chris hears this, he shakes his fist and bitterly berates the sea: "Dat's your dirty trick, damn ole davil, you! But py God, you don't do dat! Not while Ay'm living! No, py God you don't!"

Act III. The interior of the barge, the *Simeon Winthrop*, in Boston Harbor about a week later on a sunny afternoon. The cabin is spruce and clean with fresh white curtains on the windows. Anna is sitting in a rocking chair with a newspaper, "not reading but staring in front of her," unhappily. Chris is also uneasy and moves restlessly about the cabin looking at her and moving things around. Finally he starts to sing, which calls forth a sarcastic remark from Anna that she wishes they were back in New York. Chris says that she has been having a good time going to movies, "All with that damn Irish fallar!" Anna bridles and asks if he thinks they have been doing anything wrong. Chris apologizes, but then he objects to her swearing, claiming that she learned it from Mat. He tells her that a stoker is not a real sailor and makes it clear that he wants Anna to marry a man who will live on land with a "little home in country all your own," a suggestion that Anna rejects brusquely. She has just told Chris that she isn't good enough for a man like Mat, when Mat himself appears dressed in his best cheap suit and newly shined shoes to tell Chris that he intends to marry Anna that very day. The two men engage in an altercation, Chris suggesting that Anna was making a fool of Mat; but when Mat won't accept that, Chris speaks of the loneliness he will feel without his daughter, saying that Mat would be better off with a wife in every port. Mat counters those arguments by saying that Anna is the only woman in the world for him and that after their marriage Chris would see her more often than he did when she lived in the West. Chris guiltily says he thought it "better Anna stay away, grow up inland where she don't ever know ole davil sea." Mat considers this argument that of a weakling and berates Chris for his gutlessness. One charge leads to another until Chris draws a knife on Mat, who disarms him with the utmost ease.

Anna enters, noting the signs of violent argument, and asks for an explanation. Mat declares his love for her, and finally Anna tells hers for him. They embrace passionately, and Anna says "goodby" as she fights back sobs. Chris and Mat, still angry with each other, are not sure what to make of this until Anna repeats herself more clearly: "I can't marry you, Mat." As the two men continue to bicker over her, Anna tells them both to "go to hell" because they are just like all men, treating her as "a piece of furniture." She berates Mat for saying that nothing mattered to him as long as she was not married to someone else and continues her tirade: "But nobody owns me, see?—'cepting myself. I'll do what I please and no man, I don't give a hoot who he is, can tell me what to do! I ain't asking either of you for a living. I can make it myself—one way or another. I'm my own boss. So put that in your pipe and smoke it! You and your orders!"

After this declaration of independence, Anna tells the whole story of her past, which Chris tries to deny as a lie. But Mat, at first shocked, then explodes into rage and violence, swinging a chair at her. He moves into "a lamentation that is like a keen," saying that his heart is broken and crying to God for an explanation of His allowing him to live and fall in love with such a whore. Enraged and desperately hurt, Anna orders him out, and Mat swears that he will go on an almighty drunk. Chris then "stupidly" suggests that it is better for Anna to marry Mat now, but the stoker refuses, cursing Anna as he leaves. Chris seems devastated by this new knowledge, but as Anna mockingly suggests that she too should leave, he softens: "Ain't you fault, Anna, Ay know dat. It's dat ole davil sea, do this to me." Even the arrival of Mat out of the fog is perceived as a plot of the sea against him. With that, Anna suggests he go ashore and get drunk; Chris asks if she will stay on the barge, and Anna, in a voice devoid of hope, is noncommittal.

Act IV. The cabin of the *Simeon Winthrop*, the same as Act III, about nine o'clock of a foggy night two days later. Anna is found sitting in a rocking chair, dressed in the tawdry finery of Act I. She looks tired and worn out from sleeplessness. Chris enters, suffering from a bad hangover but carrying a pail of beer. They exchange sympathy, and Chris looks at Anna's suitcase and realizes that she has planned to go back to her life as a prostitute. He also discovers that Anna does indeed love Mat, and she wishes he would return—even if it were to beat her up. Chris says that he will agree to the marriage, if she wants it, and asks her forgiveness, something Anna is quick to do. "There ain't nothing to forgive, anyway. It ain't your fault, and it ain't mine, and it ain't his neither. We're all poor nuts, and things happen, and we yust get mixed in wrong, that's all." Chris seizes on this with his refrain, "It's dat ole davil, sea!" But Anna refuses to accept that. She then returns to Chris's earlier comment that he had "fixed something up" for Anna, and he says that he has decided to give himself back to "dat ole davil" as a kind of ransom for Anna. He has decided to ship as boatswain on the *Londonderry* bound for Cape Town, South Africa, and in the course of this revelation Anna discovers that Chris has bought a gun. Shocked, Anna takes charge of it, even though Chris says he has not even bought bullets.

Chris goes off to bed, nursing his head. Anna waits dejectedly until she hears Mat's footsteps. At first "her face lights up with joy," but then terror seizes her. She grabs the revolver from the drawer in which she had hidden it and shrinks down into a corner out of sight. Mat then flings open the door. Obviously he has been on a monumental binge, and he has been fighting. He looks around, and not seeing Anna, he thinks she has gone. But then he sees her suitcase and thinks that she probably has gone ashore. He instantly suspects that she has gone out as a streetwalker, and again he curses her. At this Anna reveals herself, revolver in hand. She threatens him with it, but Mat is too far gone in despair to care as he advances on her: "Let you end me with a shot and I'll be thanking you, for it's a rotten dog's life I've lived the past two days since I've known what you are, 'til I'm after wishing I was never born at all!" Anna drops the revolver and Mat continues his lament. He is a coward because he cannot bring himself to kill her or forget her. He cannot even stay away from her. He begs her to put him out of his misery and tell him that what she had told him the other day was a lie. "Imploringly," Anna says she cannot do that, but she assures him that she has changed. She had planned to return to New York but has come back to the barge to wait for Mat, and now she begs desperately for his forgiveness. Again Mat rages at her and her past, so Anna orders him out. Mat asks what she plans to do, and Anna says she will return to prostitution: "Don't you see I'm licked? Why do you want to keep kicking me?"

She then asks why he hasn't followed his original plan to find "that ship was going to take you to the other side of the earth where you'd never see me again." To Anna's secret and ironical amusement, he has also signed up on the *Londonderry*. Anna taunts him with references to a "dame" in every port, and Mat swears he is through with women; but Anna asks whether she has been any worse than he in the past. Mat then asks whether she had ever been in love with any of her customers, and Anna stoutly denies it. She begs him to believe her, and Mat clearly wants to believe. As Anna swears that she has changed, Mat wishes that he could bring her to forget her past, which was not really her fault anyway. He brings her to swear an oath on the crucifix given him by his mother that "I'm the only man in the world ivir you felt love for. . . . And that you'll be forgetting from this day all the badness you've done and never do the like of it again." Solemnly, Anna swears, and Mat is joyfully about to kiss her when it occurs to him to ask if she is a Catholic, wondering whether the oath is sound since she is not. Anna disclaims all religious belief, and Mat decides that he must take Anna's "naked word" because he loves her so much. As they embrace and Mat promises they will be married in the morning, Chris appears, looking on the two, first with hatred then with "resignation and relief." He brings out his can of beer and offers a toast of "Skoal!" Revealing that the two of them are to be shipmates, Anna says she will get a little house and make a home for them both. Mat promises Chris a grandchild as soon as possible. Struck with a sudden thought, Mat inquires after the Christophersons' religion. "Ve vas Lutheran in ole country," a comment Mat first greets with horror and then with resignation: "Yerra, what's the difference? Tis the will of God anyway." Chris still persists that "it's dat funny vay old davil sea do her worst dirty tricks, yet. It's so." Mat acquiesces, gloomily; but Anna, "with a determined gaiety," offers another toast for the three of them: "Here's to the sea, no matter what. Be a game sport and drink to that!" Mat "banishes his superstitious premonitions" and drinks, but Chris looks moodily out: "Fog, fog, all bloody time. You can't see vhere you vas going, no. Only dat ole davil, sea—she knows!" The curtain falls as the sound of steamers' whistles is heard from the harbor.

Comments: "*Anna Christie*" was well received by the critics, and it established O'Neill as a major playwright, even more than did *Beyond the Horizon** of the previous year. Both plays were awarded the Pulitzer Prize in drama. Nonetheless, there were some critical complaints about the verbosity of the second act and the rather obvious dramatic contrivance of the fourth. O'Neill, however, was unhappy with the entire play, despite its success, because some critical comment insinuated that he had sold out his talent for a quick success and that the happy ending was tacked on as a commercial afterthought. He was particularly stung by that kind of comment and wrote at considerable length in the *New York Times* specifically denying the allegation. Later, when his plays were being collected, he wished to have *"Anna Christie"* suppressed, considering it one of his worst failures because he thought he had failed to communicate to his audience the serious meaning he had intended. In response to the "happy ending" allegations, he pointed out that at the end of the play Mat agrees with the superstitious forebodings of Chris, and it is this rather negative note that precipitates Anna's "Gee, Mat, you ain't agreeing with him, are you?" and the "determined gaiety" with which she raises her defiant toast to the sea. With similar foreboding, the curtain falls on Chris's melancholy musing.

Part of the reason that O'Neill was so dissatisfied with *"Anna Christie"* is that it was really a third draft of a play he had intended to be otherwise. The original draft, entitled *Chris Christophersen** (note change in spelling of the surname among drafts after O'Neill learned about Swedish surnames), had tried out in Atlantic City under the title *Chris* and closed in Philadelphia. A second draft, entitled *"The Ole Davil,"** moves closer to *"Anna Christie,"* but in that text Chris's gloomy premonitions are not taken seriously. The titles of the first and third drafts indicate quite clearly the change of emphasis the material underwent in the shift from Chris to Anna as the central figure. And certainly, one cannot really complain about the best feminine role that O'Neill had written up to this time. In Anna, O'Neill has portrayed a woman with courage and independence, to some extent a victim but at the same time a woman who has the courage to confront and even defy life.

This statement brings one to the sea, "dat ole davil sea," with which O'Neill had been preoccupied from his earliest plays and toward which he had a distinctly ambivalent attitude. The sea is for its followers a most jealous mistress, and she destroys those who refuse to follow their destiny in her company. In *Bound East for Cardiff** this aspect is particularly well shown, as Yank* is destroyed (it is implicitly suggested) because of his disloyalty to the sea. Yet, in *In the Zone** (a play of the S.S. *Glencairn** group and another play that O'Neill subsequently considered a pot-boiler), the sea is for Smitty* a means of escape and renewal to some extent. Even in O'Neill's first Broadway success, *Beyond the Horizon,** the sea plays a major part. In that play, Robert Mayo* refuses to follow his destiny, represented by the sea, and as a result his life is destroyed. For Anna Christie, the sea plays the opposite role. She has been brought up away from the sea, and as a result she is rootless, unwanted, exploited, and unloved. It is only when she discovers her true milieu, the destiny of her family from time beyond memory, that she is cleansed. For Anna, the sea is affirmative, life renewing, even welcoming, curative, and loving. She willingly gives herself up to its dictates and accepts its premises. Therefore, for her the sea is ennobling.

For Chris, on the other hand, the sea is fickle, demanding, and hostile. He continually fights against its will and excoriates it for its acts. As a result, one can believe that his premonitions will indeed be fulfilled. Even Mat Burke, who glories in his strength as a stoker, is ambivalent about the sea at the end of the play, and Chris may very well have understood why, when he maintains that a stoker isn't really a sailor at all. Thus, in a moment of happiness, Mat's glimmer of understanding that the sea can both give and take away is important, particularly when one realizes that he and Anna were brought together as the result of the sea's will. Mat had lived through a shipwreck in order to meet Anna, but who knows what else may happen. In a sense, Anna Christie reminds one of Shakespeare's Miranda in *The Tempest*, itself a sea play. As Miranda gazes upon the denizens of civilization she says, "O brave, new world, that has such creatures in it," to which her father, Prospero, replies with a caution: " 'Tis new to thee." Similarly, Anna, having discovered what she takes to be her true place, can drink defiantly to the sea "no matter what," because she sees herself a part of it, while Chris, like Prospero, cautions, "You can't see vhere you vas going, no. Only dat ole davil, sea—knows." The ambivalence between the sea as ever renewing, ever cleansing, and malevolently destructive thus quite clearly underlines the conclusion of the play, so much so that it is hard to understand exactly why it was taken as a "happy ending." O'Neill, in a letter to the *New York Times* (December 18, 1921), maintained that the moment one mentions marriage, all listeners forget what occurs later; but Travis Bogard (1972, p. 162) makes the interesting comment that there is perhaps some doubt about which ending was actually used for the original production, the one customarily printed or that of "The Ole Davil" which does indeed end in laughter.

Overall, the play succeeds by its portrayal of the character of Anna, whose first line, "Gimme a whiskey—ginger ale on the side," is an actress's dream. To be sure, there are stereotypical characters—Marthy Owen, for instance, is a development of the "prostitute" with a heart of gold. To some extent, Anna is a younger edition of the same character, but her independence and refusal to admit of a double standard for her and Mat distinguish her from the rest of the sisterhood. And of course, she has also a symbolic significance within the O'Neill canon as a character who is not afraid to embrace the truth of her destiny, "no matter what," when she perceives it. Furthermore, Anna is reformed less by Mat than by her experience with the sea, and then by one of its denizens, the stoker himself. O'Neill does become rather melodramatic and contrived in his fourth act when he brings on a revolver and in so doing breaks one of the so-called rules for the "well-made play"—if a revolver is brought onstage it must be fired. Similarly, there is rather clumsy use of coincidence in both Chris and Mat shipping on the same boat for Cape Town, though that is not beyond the realm of possibility. Last, the curious interlude of Anna's religion seems a concession to humor rather than dramatic necessity, even though it does force Mat to trust Anna's word, without an oath.

Production Data: Written 1919–1920. First produced by Arthur Hopkins at the Vanderbilt Theatre, New York City, November 2, 1921 (177 performances).

Director: Arthur Hopkins

Designer: Robert Edmond Jones*

Cast: Johnny-the-Priest: James C. Mack
First Longshoreman: G. O. Taylor
Second Longshoreman: John Hanley
Postman: William Augustin
Chris Christopherson: George Marion
Marthy Owen: Eugenie Blair
Anna Christopherson: Pauline Lord*
Mat Burke: Frank Shannon
Johnson (a deckhand): Ole Anderson
Larry: Unknown
Three Sailors: Messrs. Reilly, Hansen, and Kennedy

[*See also* Appendix B for film versions and a musical, *New Girl in Town*.]

ANTHONY, Dion. In *The Great God Brown*, son of Mr. Anthony* and Mrs. Anthony* and husband of Margaret Anthony.* He appears first as a lean, wiry young man, very restless and nervous. Even when he walks with his parents he walks alone, as if totally apart from them. At this early age of about eighteen, Dion Anthony already wears a mask: "a fixed forcing of his own face—dark, spiritual, poetic, passionately supersensitive, helplessly unprotected in its child-like, religious faith in life—into the expression of a mocking, reckless, defiantly, gayly scoffing and sensual young Pan." His parents send him to the university so that he can be an architect (and do better than William A. [Billy] Brown,* later the Great God Brown). But Dion marries Margaret, drops out of the university, has three sons, and turns to drink; and while employed by Brown, he dies.

Yet this is only the surface tale of Dion Anthony, for O'Neill has planned him as a symbolic figure, embodying in his names the dichotomy of his existence: Dion for Dionysus, and Anthony for the tormented ascetic, Saint Anthony. The two sides of Dion Anthony are in conflict, and the Anthony side of him is so afraid of being hurt that it must wear the mask of Dionysus/Pan. Dion pretends that he mocks life, but he also projects the image of one who surrenders to life and *is* both Life and Love themselves. However, Dion does not really appear to love life or surrender to it as much as he says. Even at the moment in which he possesses Margaret for the first time, he is mocking in his comments, putting on an "ironic mastery" which detracts from his declaration of love and seems to indicate a withholding of total commitment. As he grows older, the Pan mask becomes Mephistophelean, demonic and dissipated because no one can bear to see his vulnerable countenance without the mask, except the earth-mother prostitute, Cybel.* Whenever Dion tries to gain understanding from his wife while not wearing his mask, she does not know him—she cannot perceive the reality beneath the appearance—and therefore Dion is forced to love "by proxy" and even die by proxy. But as his mask becomes more and more frightening, his real face becomes purified, almost ascetic, like that of a Christian martyr, so that finally he is able to leave life without regret. He has cared so greatly about life that he has had to go masked in order to endure; but at the end of his days, he realizes that life was not worth very much and that he has cared too much for it. For example, he asks forgiveness of Margaret without wearing his mask, but she is terrified of the Christian martyr's face she sees there. When Dion dies, he wills his mask to William A. Brown, who puts it on and becomes Dion for Margaret, with the ironic conclusion that when Brown himself dies, Margaret then embraces the Dion mask, remembering Dion Brown rather than Dion Anthony. It is through the help of Cybel that Dion achieves the strength to die while understanding the transitory nature of life and being able to renounce it. Cybel has achieved the oneness with nature that Dion/Dionysus had sought because she is the personification of nature's rhythms and understands its circularity. When Dion reaches that point, he is then under the control of the Saint Anthony side of his personality—his soul—and is ready to ask forgiveness and die. But curiously, even though O'Neill does give the audience the idea of renunciation, he allows Dion a mode of revenge on the materialism of those such as Billy Brown who have injured him. Pan will take vengeance on materialism, which is the Apollonian life-denying principle; but ironically, out of this vengeance also comes a kind of purification for Brown.

In the characters of Dion Anthony and Billy Brown, O'Neill has conveyed very well the torment implicit in such dual souls, but the motivations for each are rather flimsy. Dion remembers Billy's destruction of a sand picture at an early age, and from that time on he questioned God and wore the mask of Pan. He says that he is Love, but yet he does not fully give himself up to love. Similarly, Brown's envy of Dion's supposed ability to control life does not seem sufficient, even when combined with love for Margaret, to motivate him into taking over the identity of his dead friend and rival. Also, the playwright seems to have drawn back in his conception of Dion and to some extent of Brown also. If Dion was designed to be Dionysus-Antichrist, then he could logically be expected to embody the anti-Apollonian, antireligious principles of existence in contrast to Billy Brown, who follows another kind of antichrist, the god of material success. But O'Neill draws back from both of these logical extensions, and as a result the emphasis of the play shifts and the theological focus becomes a trifle confused.

Nevertheless, *The Great God Brown* remains an important play in the development of O'Neill's lyrical gift, despite some curious lapses into banality. It is a valiant attempt to convey through the use of visual means the pathos of a human soul, something that is, in fact, ultimately uncommunicable, for each human being must live in the private hell of his own innermost being.

ANTHONY, Margaret. In *The Great God Brown*,* wife of Dion Anthony.* She first appears as a lithe, healthy-looking, seventeen-year-old blonde, vivacious yet also dreamy and romantic. She is in love with Dion Anthony and marries him, putting up with all of his problems and mothering him throughout their married life. During the course of the play, which covers about twenty years, Margaret becomes the "three mothers in one person" about whom Dion Anthony speaks. She is the woman who marries Dion and takes the place of his own mother; she is the mother of his three sons; and she is the feminine principle of Nietzsche and of Goethe in *Faust*. It is no accident that she is named Margaret after Goethe's Gretchen-Margaret.

She is given several masks to wear throughout the play: first the transparent mask of "The Girl," then the mask of brave hopefulness, and last the mask of "proud, indulgent mother." She is a symbolic figure rather than one to be read literally, but she does bear a resemblance to earlier O'Neill women characters. First, she recalls Maud Steele* in O'Neill's first play, *Bread and Butter*,* the young woman of extreme practicality who ignorantly destroys the life of her husband, John Brown,* who wants to be an artist. Similarly, Margaret reminds one of Ruth Atkins* Mayo in *Beyond the Horizon** because Ruth, too, thwarts the dream of Robert Mayo* and also of his brother, Andrew Mayo.* Margaret also recalls Eleanor Cape* of *Welded** in her ecstatic attitude toward marriage and Alice Roylston* of *Servitude** in her acceptance of service to her husband. Margaret thinks she loves Dion Anthony, but she really loves the Pan mask of her husband; and whenever he shows her his true countenance, she is appalled. She later loves the Pan mask when it is worn by William A. Brown,* with whom, perhaps, she might have made a more conventionally successful match than with Dion Anthony. Basically, Margaret is a straightforward, conventional, practical, maternal, and loving woman, but essentially is a person lacking in psychological or emotional depth.

ANTHONY, Mr. In *The Great God Brown*,* father of Dion Anthony.* "Mr. Anthony is a tall lean man of fifty-five or sixty with a grim, defensive face, obstinate to the point of stupid weakness." He is dressed in a cheap, black, funereal-looking suit for the high school's commencement dance. He is in partnership with Mr. Brown* (father of Dion's friend, William A. Brown*), and Mr. Anthony is the practical, limiting member who refuses to allow Brown any adventurous approaches to business. He upholds the school of hard knocks as the best university training. However, when he realizes that young Billy Brown is being sent to college to study architecture, he orders his son to go and turn out well—or else be thrown out into the gutter. Mr. Anthony is a totally rigid character, and Dion Anthony later says that he knew his father "only at the second of my conception." They were never able to communicate because Mr. Anthony is a repressive character who deeply wounds the psyche of his son so that the young man must perpetually wear the mask of a mocking Pan in order to avoid further hurt.

ANTHONY, Mrs. In *The Great God Brown*,* mother of Dion Anthony.* Mrs. Anthony "is a thin, frail, faded woman, her manner perpetually nervous and distraught," but with a face that shows signs of past beauty. She "wears a cheap, plain, black dress." She wants Dion to go to the university and is convinced, like any upwardly mobile proud mother, that he has artistic talent beyond what he actually possesses. She loves her son to excess, and he reciprocates; but he has to hurt her with his Pan mask in order to avoid being hurt by his father.

ARGHUN. In *Marco Millions*,* King of Persia, betrothed of Kukachin,* and father of Ghazan.*

ARNOLD, Jack. In *Shell Shock*,* major of infantry, U.S.A. "He is a tall, broad-shouldered and sinewy-built man of about thirty with black hair and mustache." He joined the Canadian Army even before the United States entered World War I and has become a hero as the result of holding an advanced trench for three days and nights without relief. He also saved Herbert Roylston,* wounded in No Mans Land. Amnesiac after a nervous breakdown, Arnold now believes that he performed this gallant action merely to get the cigarettes Roylston had in his possession. He is certain Roylston was dead when he brought him in. Later, after discussing the incident with an old college friend, Robert Wayne,* Arnold recalls that he had actually heard Roylston's screaming and it was that sound that had motivated his action. With relief, he finds Roylston alive and vows that he will never smoke a cigarette again. Certainly, there is some legitimate doubt about the precise motivation of Arnold's act, but he now adopts the more acceptable one and his nervous affliction is cured.

Jack Arnold is the principal character of this slight sketch and has several graphic speeches on the horrors of trench warfare.

ARNOLD, Madeline. In *Strange Interlude*,* the fiancée of Gordon Evans.* She is nineteen years old, dark-haired and dark-eyed, athletic, tall and healthy, reminiscent of a young Nina Leeds* (Gordon's mother). Madeline is a determined young woman who is accustomed to getting what she wants, but she is a good sport when she does not and as a result is popular among both men and women. Nina is opposed to the impending marriage because she does not want to lose her son, but Sam Evans,* Gordon's father, is in favor. During Gordon's final regatta crew race, Nina tries to break up their engagement by telling of the family's hereditary insanity, but she is prevented by Edmund (Ned) Darrell.* Madeline is at first exasperated by Nina's behavior but admires her later for the way in which she has nursed Sam Evans until his death. Madeline does not believe that Nina could ever have been unfaithful to her husband because then she would not have remained with him. A young woman of good sense and practicality, but not much introspection—Madeline is a fit wife for Gordon Evans, who is sure to be a material success.

ART. In "Tomorrow,"* the first-person narrator of O'Neill's only published short story. He is the equivalent of Eugene O'Neill during the playwright's residence at the saloon of James J. Condon* (a.k.a. Jimmy-the-Priest*) at 252 Fulton Street. Art has just returned from a voyage to Buenos Aires as an able-bodied seaman on a British tramp steamer and is currently living on a small allowance from his family and staying drunk most of the time. His roommate, Jimmy Anderson,* commits suicide after he is fired from his job and thereby loses his dream that "tomorrow" he will be successful.

ASHLEIGH, Lucy. In *Now I Ask You*,* wife to Tom Drayton.* She is slender, dark, and beautiful, with large eyes, an enthusiast who adopts all the latest fads. She has run through futuristic painting, five-act tragedy in free verse, the ukulele, captive poets, sculptors, psychoanalysis, and Yoga before she embarks on a siege of role playing. She begins with a Russian heroine, then moves to a disciple of free love, to Hedda Gabler, Candida, and then to attempted suicide as Hedda Gabler once again. Throughout all this confusion, both Mrs. Mary Ashleigh,* her mother, and Tom Drayton humor her until finally she comes to her senses. O'Neill suggests in the stage directions that she is "suffering from an overdose of undigested reading."

ASHLEIGH, Mr. In *Now I Ask You*,* father of Lucy Ashleigh* and husband of Mrs. Mary Ashleigh.* He is a portly retired banker of "sixty and rather bald." "Inefficiently pompous, he becomes easily aroused to nervous irascibility when his own respectable dogmas are questioned." He is completely incapable of understanding the wild enthusiasms and role playing of Lucy.

ASHLEIGH, Mrs. Mary. In *Now I Ask You*,* mother of Lucy Ashleigh.* Mrs. Ashleigh "is a handsome, white-haired woman of fifty, calm, unruffled, with a charmingly-girlish smile and dark eyes dancing with a keen sense of humor." She is surprisingly modern in her outlook and understands the folly of her daughter, treating her with an amused tolerance. She is the puppet-mistress of the play as she manipulates Tom Drayton* and to a certain extent Lucy in order to bring Lucy to her senses.

ASWAD, Ibnu. In *The Fountain*,* an elderly Moor of Granada. His house is requisitioned by Juan Ponce de Leon* as the site of his evening party. Aswad is the symbol of resignation.

ATKINS, Mrs. In *Beyond the Horizon*,* mother of Ruth Atkins.* Mrs. Atkins appears three years into the play's action as "a thin, pale-faced, unintelligent woman of about forty-eight, with hard bright eyes." She has long been confined to a wheel chair, the victim of partial paralysis, and "has developed the selfish, irritable nature of the chronic invalid." She is critical of everything and everyone, particularly of Robert Mayo,* Ruth's husband, always complaining about his inefficiency as a farmer and moaning about the way the two family farms are being ruined by his inability to make the land productive. She upbraids Ruth for not marrying Andrew Mayo,* Robert's older brother; then she also complains that Kate Mayo,* Robert's mother, is altogether too acquiescent in letting her son do whatever he pleases. Mrs. Atkins helps her daughter financially but always complains about having to do so.

ATKINS, Ruth. In *Beyond the Horizon,** wife of Robert Mayo.* She turns Robert aside from his obvious destiny as a romantic, poetic wanderer, and she brings about their mutual destruction. As the play opens, Ruth is a pretty, slender, blonde woman of twenty with great blue eyes. She is an outdoorsy figure, but ''her small regular features are marked by a certain strength—an underlying, stubborn fixity of purpose hidden in the frankly-appealing charm of her fresh youthfulness.'' She is the daughter of a crippled widow, the owner of the farm adjoining that of the Mayos. Obviously, both Robert and his brother, Andrew Mayo,* have affection for her, and their father hopes that she will marry Andrew and join the two holdings together. Clearly, this would be a good practical idea, and Robert and Andrew seem to assume that this will occur; yet each has affection for Ruth.

On the eve of Robert's departure for a three-year sailing voyage Robert tries to explain to the uncomprehending Ruth his reasons for wishing to go ''beyond the horizon.'' His romantic eloquence casts a spell over her, and then he declares that he must leave for another reason: he loves Ruth and believes her in love with his brother. To his surprise Ruth declares that she has never loved Andy, ''You stupid thing! I've loved you right along.'' She now begs him to stay. At first Robert thinks of taking Ruth with him, but she, with great practicality, reminds him that she cannot leave her invalid mother. Robert tries to resolve the conflict between his two sets of wishes, and finally he gives into Ruth's tears and her appeal to his love for her. He then chooses love as ''sweeter than any distant dream'' and decides to forego the voyage. Even at this moment, there is a premonition of disaster when Robert wishes to announce their happiness instantly but Ruth counsels delay. ''Little Miss Common Sense'' wins the day.

That this marriage is a dreadful mistake is clear from the moment of its announcement, when Andrew and his father, James Mayo* fight bitterly and unforgivingly. Andrew, desperate at losing Ruth, takes Robert's place on the sea voyage, leaving his manifestly impractical younger brother to take care of the farm that had been the older son's birthright and desire to have.

As the play progresses, Ruth becomes progressively more hopeless. The farm is clearly falling apart, and there is now something ''hard and spiteful'' in Ruth's face as she complains bitterly about Robert's inefficiency, his lateness for meals, and his continual escape into books. Ruth seems quite unable to cope with the reproaches of her peevish mother and the whining of her own daughter as well. The only thing she depends on is the return of Andrew, a man who has made something of himself. She now realizes her ghastly mistake in choosing the romantic, impractical Robert whom she has come to hate. Now, with a complete change of heart she tells her husband that it is Andy she has always loved and that Andy loves her. Robert is shocked to discover the "creature" he has been living with—"mean and small."

With the return of a changed Andy, Ruth starts to take a little trouble with her appearance. Andy, however, claims to have completely recovered from his broken heart, and tells Robert this. Robert says he should not mention this fact to Ruth, but Andy does so anyway. Ruth is now stunned into the realization that she is trapped forever, as Andy leaves almost immediately for Buenos Aires to make his fortune.

In the final act of the play, Ruth "has aged horribly. Her pale, deeply lined face has the stony lack of expression of one to whom nothing more can ever happen, whose capacity for emotion has been exhausted." She is slovenly, hardly even clean, the embodiment "of the apathy in which she lives." She looks on her husband with a look of "dull annoyance" as he comes out from his sickroom. Sorrow and hatred have destroyed all that was buoyant in Ruth. For the past five years they have merely lived in the same house, but to judge from what she says to Andrew, they have been barely communicating. Andrew is enraged at the shocking physical condition of his brother and blames Ruth for it, but she scarcely has the strength or the will to respond to anything. As far as she knows, Robert may still believe that she loves Andrew, but "I wouldn't know how to feel love, even if I tried, any more." Furious at the discovery of the misery in which his beloved brother has been living, Andrew orders Ruth to lie to Robert, to tell him she has always loved him—"anything that'll bring him peace." Ruth seems beyond even this kind of gesture, but she goes to do so, only to discover that Robert has left his room.

The three of them meet on the side of the road as Robert lies there, dying. He speaks of learning through suffering and again asks Andy to take care of Ruth. She has not told Robert the saving lie. At that, Andrew turns on her and denounces her as the cause of everything. Ruth can do nothing but weep and remind Andy that Robert recognized that she, too, has suffered. At that, Andrew asks Ruth's forgiveness and says "we must try to help each other." He obviously intends to carry out his brother's wishes. "But Ruth, if she is aware of his words, gives no sign. She remains silent, gazing at him dully with the sad humility of exhaustion, her mind already sinking back into that spent calm beyond the further troubling of any hope."

Ruth Atkins is another female character, like those in *Bread and Butter** and *Before Breakfast,** who has married an artistic, romantic man and destroyed him. These women have tried to make their men accept a mode of life limited by their own lack of intelligence and their almost appalling practicality. They are shown as ineffably selfish creatures, destroyers of dreams, hostile to what they are incapable of understanding. However, in *Beyond the Horizon*, unlike the other plays mentioned earlier, O'Neill does show that the husband retains some sympathy for his wife, if not love, and understands with an astonishing generosity of spirit that she has also suffered. And although Ruth is seen by

Andrew as the bringer of destruction, after Robert's death Andy will try to carry out Robert's wishes to care for Ruth. Ruth, however, seems incapable of any emotion. She, too, is destroyed.

ATLANTIC QUEEN, steam whaling ship, locus of *Ile.**

"ATROCITY," a pantomime, written 1915–1916, shortly after O'Neill left Harvard and while he was still under the influence of George Pierce Baker.* The text has not survived.

AUNT, of Mildred Douglas* in *The Hairy Ape.** The Aunt appears in one scene only and is used partially for expository purposes, but she is also a symbol of the female representative of capitalist society. She is the epitome of the dowager: pretentiously dressed, double-chinned, wearing a lorgnette. She is Mildred's reluctant chaperone on the transatlantic voyage.

B

BAIRD, Father Matthew. In *Days Without End*,* uncle of John Loving* and for a while his guardian after the death of John's parents when he was fifteen years old. Father Baird is seventy, "erect, robust, with thick white hair, ruddy complexion." He is a healthy and kindly man, alert, observant, confident, radiating the inner certainty of a man who knows his goal and is sustained by his religious commitment. Because he has had a mystical premonitory warning, Father Baird fears that John is in spiritual danger, and therefore he has come to New York to see if he can help. He is most concerned for John's eternal salvation and has not been discouraged by his nephew's years of blasphemous argument or social and religious experimentation. In fact, he believes that John will return to the Catholic religion of his boyhood. Father Baird is continually insulted by Loving,* John's Mephistophelian alter ego, who brings John to the brink of suicide and almost causes the death of Elsa Loving,* John's wife. To Father Baird's joy, John returns to the Church and Elsa lives. As with most of the characters in this play, Father Baird is not deeply drawn and indeed is rather stereotypical.

BAKER, George Pierce (1866–1935), university professor, teacher of playwriting. Born in Providence, Rhode Island, April 4, 1866, to Dr. George Pierce and Elizabeth (Cady) Baker. Married 1893 to Christina Hopkins of Cambridge, Massachusetts; four sons. Graduated from Harvard 1887; instructor to full professor of English, 1888–1905. Professor of dramatic literature, 1910.

In 1905, Baker offered an experimental course in playwriting at Radcliffe College and in 1906 began teaching it at Harvard. After *Salvation Nell* (by one of Baker's most famous pupils, Edward Sheldon) became a Broadway hit in 1908 as a vehicle for Minnie Maddern Fiske, the English 47 Workshop at Harvard became very popular, as did its highly selective following course, 47A, which was limited to twelve students admitted only by invitation. English 47 continued throughout the 1913–1924 period, despite opposition from Harvard alumni and trustees who considered the course to be too narrowly vocational and who seriously curtailed the activities of the program. Baker was not permitted to solicit funds to support the courses and was not given adequate theatre facilities, a serious disadvantage since much of his teaching was done in rehearsal of student plays. In 1919 he lectured at the Lowell Institute, distilling his lecture notes, dating from 1913, into a theory of drama which resulted in his book, *Dramatic Technique* (1919). In 1925 he was enticed to Yale to become head of the Department of Drama in the School of Fine Arts, which possessed a fine theatre thanks to the generosity of Edward Harkness, a Yale alumnus. Baker regretted leaving Harvard after his long career there but was consoled by obtaining better facilities and also by the fact that New Haven was a Broadway tryout city and was closer to New York than was Cambridge. His presence at Yale was instrumental in the founding of the Yale Drama School. He died of pneumonia in New York City, January 6, 1935.

Eugene O'Neill was a member of the English 47 Workshop in 1914-1915, during which time he wrote "Dear Doctor"* (destroyed); "Belshazzar,"* with classmate Colin Ford (destroyed); *The Sniper**; and "The Personal Equation."* Of these four, only *The Sniper* has been published. On the whole, O'Neill does not seem to have learned much from Baker, chiefly (as Louis Sheaffer, 1968, pp. 295–296, suggests), the method of drafting a scenario first and then refining it into drama by dint of careful revision. The two surviving plays are notable for strong confrontation scenes, which Baker favored. After his initial year, O'Neill was invited to return in the fall, but he chose not to do so. On the whole, he was already farther advanced in his own dramatic interests than Baker, who favored the work of mid- and late-nineteenth-century playwrights and slighted the work of such experimenters as Strindberg and Ibsen.

Baker's students included: Edward Sheldon, Philip Barry, Sidney Howard, Robert Edmond Jones,* Kenneth Macgowan,* Van Wyck Brooks, Herman Hagedorn, Theresa Helburn,* Maurice Wertheim, Maurine Watkins, Edward Knoblock, and Robert Benchley. The members of this interesting, and somewhat heterogeneous, group all continued their interests in the theatre, ranging from play reviewer through humorist to producer, technical personnel, and Broadway angel.

BALDWIN, Arthur. In *Recklessness,** husband of Mildred Baldwin.* He is "a stocky, undersized man of about fifty," a puffy-faced dissipated-looking person with a thick-lipped mouth that "seems perpetually curled in a smile of cynical scorn....He is rather foppishly dressed in a perfectly fitting dark gray suit of extreme cut." He is a moderately wealthy man, much older than his wife, whose parents have forced her into marriage with him because of his wealth. He is a distinctly unpleasant person; and when he hears of Mildred's affair with Fred Burgess,* the chauffeur, he contributes to Burgess's death by sending him off to the village on the fictitious errand to fetch a doctor, alleging that Mildred has been taken seriously ill. He tells Fred to "drive like hell," knowing that the steering wheel of the car is defective and that Fred will be unable to negotiate the difficult road at high speed. Baldwin seems also to have been flirting with Gene,* the lady's maid, who reveals the affair between Mildred and Fred out of her own jealousy. Baldwin plays cat and mouse with Mildred until she finally admits her love for Fred, and cynically Baldwin says he will give her a divorce. This entire conversation is playing for time until Fred's body is brought in and Mildred goes upstairs and shoots herself, something for which Baldwin does not seem to have bargained. He is a stock character, the wealthy man who looks upon his beautiful young wife as nothing more than a piece of property.

BALDWIN, Mildred. In *Recklessness*,* wife of Arthur Baldwin.* She is a tall, strikingly voluptuous young woman of about twenty-eight, with reddish-gold hair, violet eyes, pale skin and full lips. She wears a low-cut gray evening gown that matches her eyes. Her husband is about fifty, and she was married to him (through the machinations of her parents) in a match that was strictly monetary. The two have little in common, and Mildred has been left alone much of the time and has fallen in love with Fred Burgess,* the chauffeur. She begs him to take her away, claiming that she will sell her jewels and that she has no fear of poverty. Fred says that they must wait until he passes his engineering examinations, at which time he will be able to support her. When Baldwin discovers the affair, he leads Mildred along until she reveals the truth. He mocks her by saying that he will "let" her get a divorce, all the time knowing that Fred has been killed in a motor accident which he has arranged. When Mildred sees Fred's body, she faints. Immediately upon recovery, she goes upstairs and shoots herself. Mildred is a character with little individuality, even though she has a superficial resemblance to Nora Helmer in Ibsen's *A Doll's House* when she discusses herself as Baldwin's "plaything," his piece of property. The relationship between her and Fred is not very well developed, and one does not become very involved emotionally with their fate. Consequently, the suicide at the end of the play seems obligatory and melodramatic rather than the only possible response to a life that has become unbearable for Mildred, the victim of malign circumstances beyond her control.

BARNES, Leonora. In *Now I Ask You*,* "synchromist" painter, later revealed as wife to Gabriel Adams.* She is tiny, pale, anemic-looking, "dressed in a pink painter's smock, dark skirt," sandals, and wearing a blond Dutch-boy bob. She is a merry, iconoclastic character who talks a great deal about free love and tells Tom Drayton* that she finds him sexually attractive because she sees him as the Nietzschean "Great Blond Beast." She engages in a flirtation with Tom. Her "liberated" statements, however, are really a pose. She is, in fact, a nurturing person who looks after Gabriel, the totally impractical poet. Like Lucy Ashleigh,* she enjoys playing a part. In Leonora's case, it is the role of the liberated artist; hence, she changes her name from Pearl to Leonora, or Leo, and engages in such iconoclastic behavior as rolling her own cigarettes and preaching against both marriage and sex. She and Gabriel hide their marriage and pretend that they are living in a free comradeship so that they will not be considered provincial by members of the Greenwich Village art world.

BARTLETT, Captain Isaiah. In *Where the Cross is Made*,* the initial version of the later melodrama, *Gold*,* father of Nat Bartlett* and Sue Bartlett.* He is tall, stern, formidable, with white hair, bristly mustache, weatherbeaten face, and bushy gray eyebrows overhanging ''the obsessed glare of his fierce dark eyes.'' He is a retired sea captain who has lost his mind as the result of his obsession with the imminent return of an expedition he had sent out three years earlier to recover a chest of treasure. Some years before, Bartlett and his ship-wrecked crew had discovered this chest, but chose to rebury it on the desert island (intending to return for it) rather than share it with their rescuers. The search vessel, the *Mary Allen*, has been lost, but Bartlett, believing that it will return, has spent that last three years waiting in his ''cabin'' on the top of his house. Nat is planning to have his father committed to a mental institution so that the family home can be sold. Sue is opposed to this decision. Captain Bartlett, in a hallucination shared by Nat and the audience, believes that his ghostly companions have returned with the treasure. He dies at that moment; his companions have come to fetch him just as the doctor from the mental institution arrives to take him from the house.

In *Gold*, the later and less successful recension of *Where the Cross is Made*, the captain of the shipwrecked *Triton* is shown on the desert island at the moment the ''treasure'' is first discovered. He and four other members of the crew take a chest full of junk jewelry for the real thing. The fact that Captain Bartlett announces that he has only wanted to find a cache of ambergris in his whaling expeditions, together with his dreams of what he will do with his share of the treasure, indicates a man who is obsessed by greed. This leads him to order indirectly the murder of Abel* and Butler,* the only two members of the crew who seem to possess some charity. Bartlett suffers from the guilt of his complicity in the murders, though he continues to assert, ''I gave no word.'' His guilt causes the death of his wife, Sarah Allen Bartlett,* as the result of a complete nervous breakdown. At the end of the play, he realizes that the schooner he has sent in pursuit of the treasure, which was christened with the name of his wife, *Sarah Allen*, will not return and also that with his obsession he is driving his son to madness. He then confesses his sin publicly: ''I gave the order—in my mind—to kill them two, I murdered them in cold blood.'' At this point, he brings out an anklet as a sample of the treasure, which Nat instantly identifies as junk. The captain is now capable of recognizing the truth about himself and his crime and in effect dies of this knowledge. By his confession, which is an act of love for his son, he has exorcized the devils that have tormented him, but he cannot live with the knowledge and consequences of the original deed. This becomes clear from his appearance at the end of the play, where in a single year he has aged astonishingly. Altogether, he is not a deeply conceived character, and the underlying symbolism of the play seems a trifle heavy for such a slight melodrama.

BARTLETT, Nat. In *Where the Cross is Made*,* a one-act version of *Gold*,* son of Captain Isaiah Bartlett* and brother of Sue Bartlett.* Nat "is very tall, gaunt, and loose-framed. His right arm has been amputated at the shoulder." He is thirty years old but seems older, as if worn down by some experience. "His face is long, bony, and sallow, with deep-set black eyes, a large aquiline nose, a wide thin-lipped mouth shadowed by an unkempt bristle of mustache. His voice is low and deep with a penetrating, hollow, metallic quality." He is planning to put his father in a mental institution. Nat hates his father, who had forced him to go to sea, where Nat lost his arm in an unspecified accident. He also blames his father for the death of his mother. Nat is a frustrated writer and his chief desire is to finish his book. As the play progresses, the audience begins to realize that Nat's own sanity is as suspect as that of his father. Nat tells the tale of buried treasure to [Dr.] Higgins* of the mental hospital with a mixture of skepticism and belief. He draws attention to the romantic melodrama of the tale yet later seems to be so committed to belief in the treasure that he must destroy the map indicating the site of the cache, "where the cross is made." The fact that he shares in his father's hallucination when the ghosts of the captain's companions appear from under the sea indicates that the obsession is mutual. Upon his father's death, just before he is to be taken to the mental hospital, Nat inherits not the treasure but the obsession. The horrified Sue tries to drag him away, but Nat seems to have lost his mind.

In *Gold*, a four-act recension of *Where the Cross is Made*, Nat also appears. This time he is a young man of eighteen who is in the process of being seduced by his father's obsession. He has hung around the boat house where his father has been equipping an expedition to seek the buried "treasure." He is desperately anxious to accompany his father, but his mother, Sarah Allen Bartlett,* refuses to permit this, being afraid that he will become a sinner like her husband. Nat is furious when Daniel ("Danny") Drew* takes the vessel out, as the result of a subterfuge arranged by Nat's sister. By the end of the play, he is partaking of his father's obsession with the "treasure" and even briefly believes, contrary to evidence, that the expedition's vessel, the *Sarah Allen*, has returned. However, after his father confesses his guilt in the murder of two crewmates and shows him an anklet as sample of the treasure, Nat's eyes are opened and he perceives that the "treasure" is junk. There is an implication that this ability to distinguish the false from the true may assure Nat's salvation.

BARTLETT, Sarah Allen. In *Gold*,* a recension of the earlier one-act play, *Where the Cross is Made*,* wife of Captain Isaiah Bartlett,* and mother of Nat Bartlett* and Sue Bartlett.* Mrs. Bartlett "is a slight slender woman of fifty" who is in extreme ill health. She is prematurely white-haired and walks with a cane. Though she appears physically weak, her eyes still have a resolution about them and her face bears "a look of fixed determination." She has pieced together, from her husband's nightmares, an account of the murders in which he was involved while trying to protect what he believes to be a buried treasure. As a result, she is totally opposed to her husband's wish to outfit a schooner to search for this treasure, even refusing to "christen" the vessel with her name since it will be sailing in an unholy cause. She finally consents only to save her son, Nat, whom the captain threatens to take with him if she does not agree. This action contributes to her nervous breakdown, which leads to her death. Throughout the play, she attempts to force the captain to confess his sin and give up his obsession with the buried treasure. Clearly, she sees him as leading the life of a damned soul. After her death, Captain Bartlett declares that she hounded him to confess until her dying day, but finally he does so. As a character, O'Neill undoubtedly planned to make her a kind of nemesis; but in this rather ineffective play, he succeeds only in making her appear to be a religious fanatic.

BARTLETT, Sue. In *Where the Cross is Made*,* daughter of Captain Isaiah Bartlett* and sister of Nat Bartlett.* She is a tall, slender woman of twenty-five, with red hair, pale complexion, blue eyes, full lips, and a sad expression. She loves and cares for her father and is opposed to Nat's decision to put him in a mental institution. She is told that she can have a share in the proceeds of the sale of the family house for her marriage portion, but she refuses it as "blood money." At the end of the play, she tries in horror to pull Nat away from his obsession with the buried treasure, for she is the only sane member of the family, something that is communicated by the fact that she does not see the ghosts of the departed shipmates as her father and Nat (and the audience) do. Her grasp of reality is strong.

In *Gold*,* a four-act recension of *Where the Cross is Made*, Sue is a healthy, outdoorsy girl of twenty, engaged to Daniel ("Danny") Drew,* who has just achieved his captain's papers. The two of them hatch a plan to prevent Captain Isaiah Bartlett from leaving his dying wife, Sarah Allen Bartlett,* in order to go on a mysterious expedition. They do not know that he is seeking a supposed buried "treasure." They only know that his departure on this voyage will kill Mrs. Bartlett. Danny takes out the ship and survives; but Mrs. Bartlett dies, and Sue is left to look after her obsessed father, who is also driving Nat insane. She tries to make her father see reality. Finally, when he confesses his complicity in the death of two of his crew, he allows Nat to see the sample of treasure that he has carried with him. Nat, his eyes opened, recognizes it as junk and says so. This brings about his father's death. Sue is a sensible young woman with a firm grasp of reality. She nurses her mother in her final illness and also cares for her brother. One curious action in the play does seem out of character: Sue's sending off her fiancé on what turns out to be a singularly dangerous voyage in order to ease her mother's pain.

BARTON, James (1890–1962), actor. Born in Gloucester, New Jersey, November 1, 1890; died in Mineola, Long Island, February 19, 1962. Son of James Barton (of West and Primrose Minstrels) and Clara (Anderson) Barton. Married (1) Marilyn Miller, (2) Kathryn Penman.

James Barton began his career in vaudeville when he was carried onstage by his parents in 1892 in *The Silver King*. He appeared again in 1894 in a sketch performed in Louisville, Kentucky. After touring as Topsy in *Uncle Tom's Cabin*, he spent a number of years in Middle Western and Southern repertory and stock companies, also showing skill as a tap dancer. He first appeared on Broadway in *The Passing Show of 1919*, following that by roles in *The Last Waltz* (1921); *The Rose of Stamboul* (1922); *Dew Drop Inn* (1923); *The Passing Show of 1924*; *Artists and Models* (1925); *Palm Beach Nights* (1926); *Ziegfeld Follies of 1926*; and *Moonshine, Forty-Sixth Street*, and *Sweet and Low* (all in 1930). Well established in musicals, his greatest success came in 1934 when he took over the part of Jeeter Lester in *Tobacco Road* from Henry Hull and continued in it for the next five years, in effect typecasting himself as the hard-drinking, grizzled character with a heart of gold, a role he later transmitted in films.

His film roles, which had begun in the silent era with *Why Women Remarry* and *Captain Hurricane*, as well as the 1935 talkie, *The Family Tree*, were entirely character parts, on the order of *Tobacco Road*. He appeared in *The Shepherd of the Hills* (1944); *The Time of Your Life* (1948, as Kit Carson); *Yellow Sky* (1948); *The Daughter of Rosie O'Grady* and *Wabash Avenue* (1950); *Here Comes the Groom*, *The Scarf*, and *Golden Girl* (1951); *The Naked Hills* (1956); *Quantez* (1957); and *The Misfits* (1961).

In 1946 he played Theodore Hickman* ("Hickey") in the rather disastrous premiere of *The Iceman Cometh*.* Originally, Eddie Dowling had been scheduled for this role as well as directing the production. When it was decided that this double duty would constitute too heavy a load, Barton, who had been cast as Harry Hope,* succeeded Dowling in the part, while Dudley Digges* took Barton's place as Hope. Unfortunately, Barton, whose strength lay in his portrayal of broad, drunken characters, proved unequal to the role, even having difficulty in remembering his lines. In addition, on the opening night he used the dinner intermission to socialize with his friends instead of husbanding his vocal and emotional resources for his long monologue in Act II. As a result, he lacked sufficient strength to carry it off; and in the course of the performance, the prompter's voice was heard all too frequently. The reviews were originally reserved but not hostile, despite Barton's inadequacy, and the play did achieve a respectable run of 146 performances. However, it did not contribute greatly to O'Neill's box office reputation (even though some intellectual reviewers considered that it contained some of his best work), and when *A Moon for the Misbegotten** closed out of town in the same year, O'Neill was considered finished. It is tempting to blame the relative failure of *Iceman* on Barton (and certainly he was a contributing factor), but perhaps in 1946 the American theatre was not yet ready for Hickey, *The Iceman Cometh*, or for O'Neill's darkening vision of humanity.

BARTON, Ralph (1891–1931), caricaturist, bon vivant. Born in Kansas City, Missouri, to Abraham Pool and Catherine Josephine Barton. Educated in public schools and in 1909 began his career on the *Kansas City Post*. Studied art in Paris and worked for almost all the "smart" magazines like the *New Yorker*, *Harper's Bazaar*, and *Vanity Fair*. Also did the illustrations for the original publication of Anita Loos' *Gentlemen Prefer Blondes*.

Ralph Barton was married four times, his third wife being Carlotta Monterey,* the third wife of Eugene O'Neill.* That marriage lasted from 1923 to 1926, when he married the composer Germaine Tailleferre, a marriage that was dissolved in April 1931, shortly before his suicide on May 20, 1931. He left a curious suicide note, regretting the unhappiness he had caused "my beautiful lost angel, Carlotta," asking her to forgive him, and asserting that she was "the only woman I ever loved." Since Eugene and Carlotta O'Neill had just returned from Europe, there was speculation that this was the motivation for Barton's shooting himself in the head, and Barton's brother said that there had been "a friendly visit" with the O'Neills, a statement that they denied. Barton, in his suicide note, said that from his childhood he had been afflicted with melancholia, and despite his "glamorous" life, this had become worse and "in the last five years [it] has begun to show definite symptoms of manic-depressive insanity." He was survived by an actor-brother in New York and by two daughters, his mother, and sister, who were surprised because his recent letters had not shown any such depression. Indeed, he had been discussing with them his recent friendship with Charles Spencer [Charlie] Chaplin.* This situation may also partly explain O'Neill's later opposition to the marriage of his daughter, Oona (see Chaplin, Oona O'Neill) to Chaplin. There seems to have been a curious mixture of impulse and planning in Barton's suicide, because he had carefully opened a copy of *Gray's Anatomy* to illustrations of the heart, before apparently changing his mind and shooting himself in the head. He also possessed tremendous self-hatred, which expressed itself in the somewhat cynical tone of his suicide note in which he also said that people could attribute any motives they wanted to his act, including the fact that he was currently short of cash, and went on to say, "I present my remains, with my compliments, to any medical school that fancies them, or soap can be made of them" (Sheaffer, 1973, p. 374, quoting *New York Times*, May 21, 1931, pp. 1, 16).

BAYAN, General. In *Marco Millions*,* the Commander-in-Chief of the army of Kublai Kaan.* Bayan wishes to make war on the West while the Kaan has the advantage of possessing the ultimate weapon of destruction invented by Marco Polo*—the cannon. He wants to wage a "just war" to establish by force the reign of Buddha, "the Prince of Peace," in the Western World. Basically, he is a parody of those army officers who, having untried and untested weapons, are desperate for an occasion on which to use them. Also he is a parody of those patriotic windbags who attempt to justify with religious arguments the destruction that runs counter to the tenets of that same religion. He is easily turned aside from attacking the West and toward making war on Japan because Japanese silkworms are threatening the silk industry of the Kaan's dominions. In other words, the real cause of this and other wars is economic, not religious.

BECKWITH, Seth. In *Mourning Becomes Electra*,* gardener and man of all work to the Mannon family. He is seventy-five years old, stooped by rheumatism; his face seems hardened into a grim mask, but his eyes are alert "and his loose mouth has a strong suggestion of ribald humor." He possesses "the wraith of what must once have been a good baritone" voice, and he is several times heard singing the chantey "Shenandoah," the song which embodies "the brooding rhythm of the sea" for the entire play. He has long been a retainer of the Mannons and understands their past history as well as if not better than they do themselves. In the final play of the cycle, *The Haunted*,* he knows what will happen to Lavinia Mannon* once she re-enters her house of ghosts. He is the Leader of the Chorus of Townsfolk and also an expository device for the play because he knows all the family scandals and where the skeletons are hidden. It is he who first notices Adam Brant's* resemblance to the Mannon family and recalls the old scandal of David Mannon* and the French Canadian nurse, Marie Brantôme.*

BEFORE BREAKFAST, a monologue. The scene is "a small room serving both as kitchen and dining room in a flat on Christopher Street, New York City." The room is dingily furnished with stove, sink, neglected potted plants, oilcloth-covered table, two cane-bottomed chairs, a wooden dish-closet, and pegs with assorted men's and women's clothing. "It is about eight-thirty in the morning of a fine sunshiny day in the early fall." Mrs. Rowland,* a bedraggled woman in her early twenties who looks much older, enters and looks around the room drowsily. She seems as exhausted as if she had not slept. Clumsily, she puts on an apron, starts the coffee, and calls "Alfred! Alfred!" On getting no answer, she goes to the dish-closet and takes out a bottle of gin and a glass, trying unsuccessfully to avoid making a noise. After gulping down a large glass of gin, she seems more animated, and also more vindictive. Again she calls "Alfred," and when there is again no reply she searches through her husband's pockets until she finds a letter in his inside vest pocket, which she reads. "At first her expression is one of hatred and rage, but as she goes on to the end it changes to one of triumphant malignity." She replaces the letter, hangs up the clothes, and then proceeds to the bedroom door and looks inside. She berates her husband for sleeping late and for pawning his watch, "the last valuable thing we had." She complains shrilly about having to go out sewing while he refuses to get a job and simply plays "the gentleman," loafing "around barrooms with that good-for-nothing lot of artists from the Square." She repeatedly tells him that there would be nothing on the table if it wasn't for her slaving. The rent is due and she doesn't have the money: "You've got to come to your senses. You've got to beg, borrow, or steal it somewheres.... You're too proud to beg, and you've borrowed the limit, and you haven't the nerve to steal." She then says she knows about his drunkenness and his "goings-on" and berates him for his slovenliness. As she sweeps around the house, she recalls the circumstances of their marriage: he, "the millionaire Rowland's only son, the Harvard graduate, the poet, the catch of the town" had got her, the grocer's daughter, "into trouble" and insisted on marrying her, despite his father's offer to buy her off. But the child was stillborn, and the reputed millionaire died owing everyone money.

As she nags on, she reveals that she has read Helen's letter to her husband, asserting her right to do so and triumphantly saying that she'll never divorce him so that he can remarry. Alfred, who has now gotten out of bed and commenced shaving, cuts himself, as his wife again complains that he has been drinking so much that his hands are unsteady—and indeed, when he had put out his sensitive, long-fingered poetic hand to take the bowl of shaving water, the tremor had been appallingly evident. His wife tells him to wipe the blood off his face because she cannot stand the sight of blood. She rages on, inveighing against Helen, asking whether she knows that Alfred is married, asserting that he is to blame for the unhappiness of their marriage and even her own ill health. Clearly, she has become an alcoholic. Finally, she reaches a height of insult: "I think your Helen is no better than a common streetwalker, that's what I think." There is a groan of pain from the next room, and then Mrs. Rowland complains that she can hear the water dripping on the floor. Suddenly she becomes afraid, and the noise of something crashing to the floor is heard. She rushes to the bedroom door and stands there "transfixed with horror," then runs out the other door screaming madly.

Comments: This melodramatic little monologue is a development of several themes that O'Neill had treated earlier: the nagging wife who leads her husband to suicide is found in *Warnings** and *Bread and Butter*,* also containing the theme of the incompatible couple which prefigures its later treatment in *Beyond the Horizon** and *The Great God Brown*.* The shrew with her continual insistence on economic security is perceived, as in the last two of these plays, to be a hindrance to the artistic development of the husband. *Servitude*,* which takes up the theme of the young woman got "in trouble" by the artistic young man, gives what would seem to be O'Neill's version of the perfect marriage: one in which the woman gives up everything to the service of her husband's art and glories in her slavery. The general attitude toward Mrs. Rowland seems to be like that of Strindberg in his portraits of wives who bring about the ruin of their husbands by their limited understanding of their men.

Production Data: Written 1916. Produced by the Provincetown Players* at the Playwrights' Theatre, New York City, December 1, 1916 (Performances unknown).

Director: Advice given by James O'Neill,* redirected by Eugene O'Neill
Designer: Unknown

Cast: Mrs. Rowland: Mary Pyne
      Alfred: Eugene O'Neill

O'Neill appeared for the last time on the dramatic stage in this play, contributing the momentary vision of his elegant, tremulous hand, and an offstage groan.
Revived at the Provincetown Playhouse, New York City, March 5, 1929 (30 performances).

Director: James Light
Designer: Unknown
Cast: Mrs. Rowland: Mary Blair*
      Alfred: Unknown

[*See also* Appendix B for operatic adaptation by Thomas Pasatieri.*]

BELLA. In *The Moon of the Caribbees*,* a West Indian Negress, "oldest, stoutest, and homeliest" of the women.

BELLE. In *Ah, Wilderness!** the peroxide-blonde "tart." She is one of the "swift babies from New Haven" whom Wint Selby* has met. He is responsible for bringing Richard Miller* to the Pleasant Beach Inn for an evening of drinking and sex. Belle is tawdrily dressed, but she seems to be "a fairly recent recruit to the ranks, and is still a bit remorseful behind her make-up and defiantly careless manner." She tries to get Richard to take her to bed and conspires with the bartender to mix him a singularly powerful sloe-gin fizz. When nothing seems to wake Richard up, she turns to a salesman who seems a better customer. She is responsible for getting Richard and later herself thrown out of the bar and then writes a letter to Nat Miller,* Richard's father, informing him of the night's events. She does not know what to make of the innocent Richard, particularly when he offers to pay her room rent without going to bed with her.

"BELSHAZZAR" (or "Balshazzar"), a Biblical drama in six scenes, written in collaboration with Colin Ford, a fellow student in the English 47 Workshop of George Pierce Baker* at Harvard, 1914–1915. The text of this play has not survived.

BEN. In *Beyond the Horizon**, "a hulking, awkward young fellow with a heavy, stupid face and shifty, cunning eyes. He is dressed in overalls, boots, . . . and a broad-brimmed hat of coarse straw pushed back on his head." Ben is the hired man on Robert Mayo's* farm. He gives notice at the height of the haying season, partly because Robert has failed to pay him, but more particularly because he resents being made fun of by the other laborers of the area. They all despise Robert as a hopeless farmer, and even this rather cloddish young man is afraid that Robert's reputation will rub off on him.

BEN. In *Ile*,* the cabin boy of the whaling ship `Atlantic Queen*, "an over-grown, gawky boy with a long, pinched face." He is used as an expository figure in the play, and through his remarks the tragic figure of Annie Keeney* is introduced.

BENTLEY, Abraham. In *The Rope*,* father of Luke Bentley* and Annie Swee-ney.* He is "A tall, lean, stoop-shouldered old man of sixty-five." Abraham is crippled by rheumatism and hatred, and walks with a cane. His face is gaunt, chalky-white, furrowed with wrinkles," and he seems to be senile. He is the miserly patriarch who hates his daughter Annie because she has married Pat Sweeney,* a Roman Catholic, despite the fact she is looking after him. He believes that all they want is his money. His pennypinching is said by Annie to have driven her mother into her grave. His second wife, a "harlot," according to Annie, left him; Luke, their son (on whose paternity Annie casts aspersions) ran away from home five years ago, stealing a hundred dollars from his father. Old Bentley then rigged up a noose in this house of hatred for the young man to hang himself on his return. When Luke does come home, Bentley quotes from Scripture the section on the welcome given by the father to the returned prodigal son. He then gleefully encourages the young man to hang himself, and earns a beating from the son as a result. The old man seems curiously upset at Luke's failure to try the noose, and the reason becomes clear only when Mary Sweeney,* his granddaughter, tries to swing on it. A bag containing Bentley's hoard of fifty twenty-dollar gold pieces falls to the floor. It had been used as a counterweight and Bentley's perverse wish to have Luke try out the noose was his way of "giving him" the money that everyone in this house covets. Despite his crustiness, Old Bentley loves Luke.

BENTLEY, Luke, in *The Rope*,* son of Abraham Bentley* and half-brother of Annie Sweeney.* Luke is tall, about twenty-five (though the text of the play would indicate twenty-one), rather coarse-featured, sunbronzed, fairly hand-some, unintelligent-looking, but with a certain foolish, raffish charm. He ran away from home when he was sixteen, stealing a hundred dollars from his father. Now, five years later (the play's chronology is confused), he has returned, apparently to renew old hatreds. His father greets him with the scriptural greeting given by the father to the prodigal son, and then leads the young man to the noose that he has prepared so that he can hang himself. When Luke realizes that the old man really wants him to hang himself, he beats him. Over whiskey with Pat Sweeney,* Annie's husband, he plots to torture the old man into revealing the whereabouts of his money. What Luke does not know is that his father had rigged up the noose with his moneybag as counterweight. In encouraging Luke to try out the noose the old man was really attempting to have him find the money that everyone in the house wants. This is his way of killing the fatted calf for the returning prodigal. Old Bentley has loved his son after all.

BENTON. In *Servitude*,* man-servant to David Roylston* and also to his late father. Benton is a clean-shaven, fifty-five-year-old man in livery with one badly crossed eye which gives him "a look of sly villainy." He is used primarily as an expository device, and he hints at the premarital misconduct of David and Alice Roylston.* He seems to believe that David married beneath him.

BERGMAN, Ingrid (1915–1982), actress. Born in Stockholm, Sweden, August 29, 1915, to Justus and Friedel (Adler) Bergman. Her father was a painter and photographer. Educated at the Lyceum School for Girls, 1922–32; studied at the Royal Dramatic Theatre School, Stockholm, 1933–34. Married to Dr. Peter Lindstrom (1937–50) one daughter; Roberto Rossellini (1950–57) two daughters, one son; Lars Schmidt (1958–82). Died of cancer in London on her sixty-seventh birthday.

Miss Bergman is best known for her screen roles in such films as *Intermezzo* (1937, Sweden, and 1941, U.S.A.), *Casablanca* (1942), *For Whom the Bell Tolls* (1943), *Gaslight* (1944), *Stromboli* (1950), *The Visit* (1963), *Murder on the Orient Express* (1974), and many others. However, she also played Anna in *Anna Christie** (Lobero, Santa Barbara, and San Francisco, California, 1941) and Deborah Harford* in *More Stately Mansions** in its first American production (Los Angeles and New York, 1967).

Miss Bergman's performance as Anna was seen by Carlotta Monterey,* and as a result she was invited to visit O'Neill at Tao House. She recalled (at a meeting of the Modern Language Association, New York City, December 1978) that she lunched with them both and was taken into O'Neill's office where he was working on nine plays of his projected cycle, "A Tale of Possessors, Self-Dispossessed."* O'Neill explained his project, telling her that he wished to form a repertory company to perform it and would like her to be a part of it. However, she would have to commit herself to the project for four years, a term which she felt would be too long in view of the fact that she wished to have a film career. Accordingly she refused, with regret, and remembers that O'Neill said, "You're abandoning me," and Miss Bergman replied that perhaps she might do the plays "later." When approached by José Quintero* to create the part of Deborah Harford in *More Stately Mansions* for American audiences, she recalled that meeting with O'Neill and accepted Quintero's offer. Both O'Neill and Carlotta had considerable praise for Miss Bergman as a person and an actress, as material in the O'Neill Collection at Yale attests. *See* Floyd (1979).

BERRY, Doctor. In *Gold*,* a four-act recension of *Where the Cross is Made*,* a kindly-looking man of about sixty with white hair. He is an old family friend. Sue Bartlett* shares her letter from her fiancé, Daniel ("Danny") Drew,* with him, and in this way O'Neill conveys news of the loss of the schooner *Sarah Allen*, outfitted to go on a curious voyage which obsesses Captain Isaiah Bartlett.*

Bartlett is now quite mad, and the doctor advises Sue to commit him to a mental institution as a means of salvaging the sanity of her brother, Nat Bartlett.* In the earlier play, the doctor's name is Higgins* and his role is different.

BEYOND THE HORIZON, a play in three acts and six scenes; awarded the Pulitzer Prize, 1920. The action takes place in the farmhouse and on the farm owned by the Mayo family. The locale is unspecified, but it is not far from the sea and is probably like the area near Truro familiar to O'Neill.

Act I, Scene i: "A section of country highway" with a road that winds off toward the horizon between "low, rolling hills with their freshly plowed fields clearly divided from each other...by the lines of stone walls and rough snake fences." It is twilight of a May evening, with the glow of the sunset still visible in the sky as the play opens. It fades as the act progresses. This scene constitutes a visual image for the action of this play of broken dreams.

Robert Mayo,* age twenty-three, is sitting on the fence, reading, as Andrew Mayo,* his twenty-seven-year-old brother, enters. The two young men are in marked contrast, Robert being delicately and refinedly built, with "a touch of the poet about him expressed in his high forehead and wide, dark eyes." Andrew, on the other hand is "husky, sun-bronzed, handsome in a large-featured, manly fashion—a son of the soil." It is the night before Robert is to start a three-year sea voyage under the tutelage of his uncle, Captain Dick Scott* on his sailing ship, the *Sunda*. Andrew laughingly chides Robert for daydreaming and then starts to read from his brother's book of poetry, disclaiming all interest in poetry or learning. He is happy he didn't go to college for a year, like his brother, because his destiny is to work the Mayo family farm. Robert confides that he had not returned to college because he knew that James Mayo,* their father, was not very happy about the idea and also needed the money for the farm. Anyway, he had not been "keen on being a student." What he really wants to do is wander, keep moving, and not put down "root in any one place." Clearly the two young men have always been close, even as they discuss their differences: Andy is really committed to the farm, like his father, while Robert wishes to follow the quest of "beauty that's calling me, the beauty of the far off and unknown,...the need of the freedom of great wide spaces, the joy of wandering on and on—in quest of the secret which is hidden over there, beyond the horizon." Andrew, more down to earth, laughs, and leaves to go home since Ruth Atkins* and her mother, Mrs. Atkins,* are expected for dinner. At the mention of Ruth, there is a tension between the two men. Robert starts to say something but cannot finish, and Andrew notes, "We can't help those things, Rob."

Ruth Atkins then enters. "She is a healthy, blonde, out-of-doors girl of twenty." Like Andrew, she tells Robert that she regrets his going away and tells of the difficult life she leads with her querulous, bedridden mother. She wishes that she could go away too, and like Andy, she asks why Robert feels he must go. Again, Robert attempts to explain, recalling that when he was very ill as a child he used to look out of his window and wonder what the sea was like beyond the hills, and he promised himself that someday he would "follow that road, and it and I would find the sea together.... Those were the only happy moments of my life then." Ruth says that she begins to understand his feelings, but then Robert announces another reason for leaving: he loves Ruth, while she loves Andy who reciprocates. To his astonishment, Ruth announces "I don't love Andy!" and begs him not to leave. "You stupid thing! I've loved you right along." The only reason she and Andy were always together was Robert's preoccupation with books, and her own feeling that Robert's year away at college might have made him "stuck-up." At this moment the basic elements of their destructive relationship are shown: Ruth may love the romantic man, but as the scene progresses she shows her great practicality, and the two will obviously prove to be incompatible. Again Ruth begs him not to leave, and momentarily Robert thinks of taking her with him, but she reminds him of her commitment to her invalid mother. She appeals to his sympathies, his love of family, concluding with "We'll be so happy here together where it's natural and we know things." Robert agrees, saying "love must be the secret...that called to me from over the world's rim." Robert wants to tell the assembled family immediately, but Ruth, "little Miss Common Sense" persuades him to wait until after she and her mother have gone home. As they leave Robert and Ruth look up to the evening star "and the dying sunset flash." Ruth breaks the spell and starts to lead him away as Robert shakes his head, "as though he were throwing off some disturbing thought."

Act I, Scene ii: "The small sitting room of the Mayo farmhouse about nine o'clock the same night." The room is neat, clean, well ordered, with an "atmosphere...of the orderly comfort of a simple hard-earned prosperity, enjoyed and maintained by the family as a unit." James Mayo, who is the picture of what Andrew will be at the age of sixty-five, is sitting with his wife, Kate Mayo,* "a slight, round-faced, rather prim-looking woman of fifty-five who had once been a school teacher." Her air of refinement remains, despite her hard life as a farmer's wife, and one can easily see that Robert takes after her. Her brother, Captain Dick Scott, is fifty-eight, "short and stocky, with a weatherbeaten, jovial face and a white mustache—a typical old salt." As the scene opens, the Captain is telling a long tale which has bored his listeners, who are more concerned with Robert's imminent departure. Mrs. Mayo regrets the loss of her youngest child, while the Captain says the journey will make a man of him. Andrew counters with a reminder that Robert himself wants to go, but then Andrew seems just a trifle uneasy, implying that there is a chance that Rob may change his mind.

After Andrew leaves, the Captain says that he wishes he were taking him, because "there's the boy that would make a good, strong sea-faring' man—if he'd a mind to." This comment calls forth a protest from James Mayo that Andrew is a born farmer and that he will take over the property and make it "one of the slickest, best-payin' farms in the state." The farm should be expanded, but the family currently lacks the capital to do so. Further discussion among the older adults reveals that something has seemed to be going on between Robert and Ruth, while Mr. Mayo says that he had hoped that Ruth and Andy would marry some day, particularly because her mother's farm adjoins the Mayo property and the widow could use "a first-class farmer, to take hold of things." Abruptly, Mrs. Mayo says that she believes that Ruth does not love Andy.

At that moment, Robert enters to announce that he plans to give up the idea of the voyage, in order to stay home and marry Ruth. Unnoticed by Robert, who is carried away by his passion and the poetry of his words, Andy has overheard and tensely offers his congratulations, hiding his emotions with difficulty. Captain Scott is extremely disconcerted by this sudden change of plans and complains that he will be the laughing stock of his crew if the newly decorated cabin destined for Robert remains unoccupied. The crew will think he was jilted by a woman. Andrew then announces that he will sail with Captain Scott in Robert's place. At first Robert remonstrates with him, and then his father angrily berates Andrew for walking out just when he is needed for the busy time on the farm. Andrew suggests he should get a man to help and that comment sends Mayo into an angry frenzy. He accuses Andrew of lying when he claims that he had always wanted to leave, saying that the young man is "runnin' against your own nature, . . . You're runnin' away 'cause you're put out and riled 'cause your own brother's got Ruth 'stead o' you. . . . '' Finally, Andrew loses his temper and claims he's "sick and tired" of the farm, welcoming the "chance to move on." At this, James Mayo orders Andrew out of the house by morning and tells him never to return while he [James Mayo] is alive. Captain Scott tries to smooth things over, Mrs. Mayo begs her husband to retract his statements, and finally the two brothers are left alone. Both know that Andy's alleged desire to leave is a lie, and Rob agrees that in a similar situation he, too, would have to leave, telling his brother that he would never have spoken to Ruth had he known the depth of his brother's affection. However, the die is now cast, and Andy and Rob both know it.

Act II, Scene i: The sitting room of the Mayo farmhouse, "about half past twelve in the afternoon of a hot, sun-baked day in midsummer, three years later." The room has the same furnishings, but their sparkle has gone, giving "evidence of carelessness, of inefficiency, of an industry gone to seed." The sound of dishwashing is heard, interrupted by the whining of a child and the irritated voice of a woman. Kate Mayo, whose face has "disintegrated, become a weak mask," seems constantly on the verge of tears and devoid of all willpower. Mrs. Atkins, "a thin, pale-faced, unintelligent-looking woman of forty-eight, with hard, bright eyes," is sitting in a wheel chair and her manner has the peevish irritability of the chronic invalid. The two women are talking, Mrs. Atkins complaining over Robert's tardy appearance at meals, while Mrs. Mayo weepily tries to justify her son's general inefficiency as a farmer. "You can't expect him to learn in a day." Obviously everything has been going downhill at the farm, and Mrs. Atkins is angry that her own property is being dragged down as well. Robert is even about to raise a loan on the Mayo farm, to carry them until harvest. Everyone is waiting for the imminent return of Andy but for different reasons. Mrs. Mayo wishes that her husband had lived long enough so that he could have forgiven Andy. Mrs. Atkins comments that that would never have happened, and she proceeds to inveigh against Robert, saying that his marriage to Ruth was "a crazy mistake" and that Andy would have been a better match; Mrs. Mayo agrees.

Ruth then enters with her sickly little girl, Mary Mayo.* Ruth has aged noticeably, and her youthful, fresh appearance has taken on an expression that is faintly "hard and spiteful." She seems exhausted, and Mrs. Atkins starts instantly to complain about Robert's tardiness and the everlasting whining of the child. The two women go outside to get some fresh air, Mrs. Mayo pushing the wheel chair, as Ruth mechanically starts to put the child to bed for a nap. As the child ignores her, Ruth goes to the desk and takes out a letter which she reads with great interest, though her furtive behavior indicates some fear of discovery. As a flush of excitement brightens her cheeks, Robert enters. He has also aged, and his expression is one of hopeless resignation—the incipient weakness of his face being now fully in evidence. He cares little for his personal appearance and has not shaved for days. Ruth greets him irritably, and Robert turns to Mary, whom he treats with gentle affection. This annoys Ruth, who complains that he will excite the child, just before she sleeps. In the course of this conflict, Robert is able to get the child to sleep; his gentleness succeeds where Ruth's complaints cannot. Robert notes that Ruth has been reading Andy's letter and must know it by heart by now. Jealous of Robert's affection for the child, Ruth ill-naturedly brings Robert his food, but he continues to read, oblivious to everything.

The bickering resumes, beginning with Robert's tardiness at mealtimes and proceeding to his inefficiency as a farmer. They are interrupted by Ben,* the hired man, who announces that the mowing machine is broken and that he is quitting because he is a good man and doesn't want to be the laughing stock of the area because he works for such a poor farmer as Robert. Coldly, Robert agrees to pay him off, and Ruth notes that Ben would not have acted that way with anyone else, spitefully saying, "It's lucky Andy's coming back," a sentiment with which Robert unresentfully agrees. As he expresses his envy at the experiences his brother has had, Ruth bitterly asks, "I 'spose you're sorry now you didn't go?" Unhearing, Robert proceeds vindictively to curse his lot, saying that Mary is the only person who keeps him in this "prison" of a farm. He wants to breathe freely and to have experiences. Indeed he should have left, because Andy seems to be incapable of understanding the romance of foreign ports, the East—his attitude is too practical. This speech arouses Ruth's anger and she attacks Robert for his inefficiency, berating him for "findin' fault— with your own brother who's ten times the man you ever was or ever will be." In the escalation of her rage, she tells Robert she hates the sight of him and has known since the first month of her marriage that she had made a mistake. Robert counters with anger at "finding out...what a—creature I've been living with," but Ruth in fierce exultation tells him she doesn't need Robert now that Andy's coming home. She loves him and he reciprocates. As Robert throws her away from him, Andy's voice is heard and Ruth rushes to the door—but Robert's commanding voice stops her from opening it. Robert opens the door as the curtain falls.

Act II, Scene ii: A hilltop on the farm with the sea in the distance at about 11 A.M. the next day, which is hot and cloudless. Robert is sitting on a rock gazing despondently at the sea, while Mary frolics nearby. He asks the child whether she would mind if he went away and asks if she loves Uncle Andy. The child insists, "Mary loves Dada," and Robert says he was only joking. Andy then comes up to the top of the hill, joshing with Robert about the way he used to "mope and dream" in the old days. He starts to discuss the state of the farm, but Robert interrupts him, asking for details of Andy's travels, discovering to his amazement that his brother had "forgotten" to mention such an extraordinary adventure as a typhoon. Andy declares that he hates the sea and wants nothing more than a berth to Buenos Aires to go into the grain business. He consoles Robert over the run-down state of the farm, declaring that it is just bad luck, and offering to invest his savings in helping Robert to get on his feet. They discuss their dead father, and then Andy tells Robert that he now comes to the conclusion that he had never really loved Ruth. However, when he says he is going to tell Ruth as well, Robert suggests that he should not.

At that moment Ruth appears, having taken some care with her appearance, and sends Robert and Mary away on a business errand. Ruth talks to Andy as if she is expecting him to stay and save the farm and is shocked when he announces his intention to go to Buenos Aires. She begs him to stay, but Andy says he feels "ripe for bigger things than settling down here." She then asks whether Robert has discussed her with Andy, and on being told no she wonders if Andy is lying. Finally, Andy says that he isn't going away for the same reason he had had before: "I want you to believe I put all that silly nonsense back of me a long time ago." Ruth, deeply hurt, then finds out that the two brothers have been discussing her and that Robert knows what Andy has just said. At this moment, Captain Scott enters, accompanied by Robert and Mary, to tell Andy that a sudden chance at a berth on a steamer bound for Buenos Aires has just come up and Andy must leave tomorrow. This time it is Robert who insists that Andy not lose "a piece of good luck," and Ruth resentfully says, "Yes, go, Andy." As Andy and the Captain walk back to the house, Ruth breaks down. Robert looks grimly at her as he comforts their concerned child.

Act III, Scene i: The sitting room of the Mayo farmhouse about 6 A.M. toward the end of October, five years later. "The room...presents an appearance of decay, of dissolution.... The whole atmosphere...contrasted with that of former years, is one of habitual poverty too hopelessly resigned to be any longer ashamed or even conscious of itself." Ruth is sitting by the stove, wrapped in a heavy shawl covering a dress of deep mourning. She has aged appallingly, and her face has the hopeless "expression of one to whom nothing more can ever happen, whose capacity for emotion has been exhausted.'' Her voice is tonelessly monotonous and her appearance "slovenly.'' Her mother is wrapped in a blanket, asleep in her wheel chair beside the stove. As a noise is heard from the bedroom, Ruth turns with annoyance and Robert enters, barely able to stand. He is emaciated, his hair is long, "his eyes are burning with fever,'' and there are hectic crimson patches on his cheeks. Ruth irritably tells him to go back to bed, because the doctor has told him not to move around. Robert, however, claims he is feeling better and that the doctor doesn't know anything. Andy is coming, bringing a specialist with him, and Robert asks bitterly if that is why Ruth has been waiting up all night. To Ruth's comment of "Someone had to. It's only right for someone to meet him after he's been gone five years,'' Robert notes, "Five years! It's a long time. . .to wait!'' He rereads Andy's telegrams, saying bitterly, "Business first was always Andy's motto.'' Robert is irritable and feverishly sensitive, yet he continually insists that all he has is a bad cold.

However, there is a moment of tender sympathy when he tells Ruth that he knows how dreadful the past years have been for her, and "especially the last eight months since Mary—died.'' They agree that the child is better off dead, but Robert exasperatedly tells Ruth that she must stop her mother from blaming the child's death on the weak constitution she inherited from her father. He blames his wife's resentment on his refusal to beg help from Andy. He recognizes that he has been an utter failure and has dragged Ruth down with him, but then he pathetically attempts to look forward to a new future after Andy's return. He will borrow money from his brother and leave the farm which has ruined their lives and will start anew in the city: "I'll prove to you the reading I've done can be put to some use.'' But with dull practicality, Ruth reminds him of their obligation to her mother. She would never consent to move. This enrages Robert, who sees this as another excuse to thwart him, so in some fear Ruth agrees to his proposal. Robert then starts optimistically looking ahead to this future and announces that he wants to go out to see the sun rise. But as he peers out of the window, reality takes hold and he sees only "the black rim of the damned hills outlined against a creeping grayness.'' She gets him back to bed, and her mother wakens, grumbling as usual, working herself up to a fit of rage and reminding Ruth that she has been supporting them for some time on the savings she had put aside for her old age. She regrets that Ruth ever married the man. Disasters have proliferated: the hired man has quit since he had not been paid for three months, and there is but one piece of firewood left in the house. The noise of an automobile is heard, and Mrs. Atkins asks to be wheeled out. She still has a little pride and doesn't wish Andy to see her in her disheveled state.

Andy then enters with Doctor Fawcett.* Andy's face seems tense, highstrung, and "his eyes are keener and more alert'' than before. "There is even a suggestion of ruthless cunning about them.'' While the doctor examines Robert, Ruth gives Andy a recital of the disasters that have befallen them. They are now penniless, and Robert was too proud to ask for money. She has even had to telegraph Andy collect. After the death of Mrs. Mayo, Robert had begun to lose interest in life, and his hired men had cheated him; but the death of Mary turned him inward on himself so that he simply took to his books as an escape. Now Ruth supposes he is used to Mary's death. She herself has reached a point where nothing can touch her emotionally. Andy then apologizes for his anger at Robert's condition and tells the story of his own failure. He had made money, but not quickly enough for his wishes, so he began speculating and has lost all but ten thousand dollars, which will be enough to start again. He has become like a gambler whose last throw will be profitable. At this point, the doctor tells them that Robert has only a few days, perhaps just a few hours, to live. Six months ago things might have been different, but now the case is hopeless.

Andy refuses to accept this verdict and talks wildly about taking Robert to Arizona, as Robert enters on the words, "There *must* be a chance!" Robert, however, says gently, "Why must there, Andy?" Quite clearly he has renounced the idea of living and sees death as a welcome release. He has no belief in the miracle the doctor said *might* occur, and he talks with Andy about his achievements. Ruth sits with her face in her hands as the two brothers speak as if she were not there. Robert is surprised to learn that Andy is, like him, also a failure; in fact, he suggests Andy is "the deepest-dyed failure of the three" because he has spent eight years running away from himself and from the "harmonious partnership" between himself and the farm. For that he will be punished. He begs Andy to marry Ruth after his death and then faints from weakness. Andy helps him back to bed, and Ruth reveals to Andy that she had very soon found that she had not loved Robert; not even Mary had helped her love him. In fact, she had come to hate him and finally realized that Andy was the one she had really loved. But then she recalls the day on the hilltop when Andy had laughed and said that all such foolishness was over and tells him that she had told Rob of her love for Andy and they had had a bitter fight. Andy then turns on her. His love for his brother is stronger than any affection for Ruth, and he berates her for causing her husband such torture. Now Robert has asked him to marry Ruth whom he has come to hate. Ruth suggests that he lie, but Andy insists that *she* will have to do the lying in order to undo some of the suffering she has caused: "Go in to him! Tell him you never loved me—it was all a mistake. . . . Tell him something, anything, that'll bring him peace!" Ruth acquiesces without emotion and goes to the bedroom to find the room empty. Robert has crawled out the window into the yard.

Act III, Scene ii: A section of country highway, as the sun is rising behind the dark hills. Robert staggers in, "stumbles into the ditch," crawls to the top of the bank from which he can see the sun rise, and then collapses. Ruth and Andrew hurry on after him. Andy tries to take him back home, but Robert refuses, wishing to die in this spot: "You mustn't feel sorry for me. Don't you see I'm happy at last—free—free!—freed from the farm—free to wander on and on—eternally!" He sees the rising sun as a "free beginning—the start of my voyage! I've won my right to my trip—the right of release—beyond the horizon!" Once again he asks Andy, "Remember Ruth—," and as Andy promises to take care of her, Robert speaks of his wife's sufferings. As the sun rises over the rim of the hills, he calls out, "The sun!" and dies. Enraged, Andy turns on Ruth, "God damn you, you never told him!" but Ruth counters by saying that he was so happy at that moment that it does not matter. Andy turns violently toward his brother: "This is your doing, you damn woman, you coward, you murderess!" Weeping, Ruth reminds him of Robert's insistence that she too had suffered. With this, Andy begs Ruth's forgiveness and promises that they must try to help each other, and in time they will "come to know what's right." But Ruth seems incapable of anything except despairing inertia, "her mind already sinking back into that spent calm beyond the further troubling of hope."

As the play had opened with the sun setting beyond the horizon, it closes with a sunrise beyond the horizon. The sunset indicated the decision of Robert to give up his dream, to deny his true nature, and the remainder of the play constitutes his "dark night of the soul," his time of suffering. But with the end of that suffering, he has earned the right in death to go beyond the horizon of human existence. Only then can he escape the imprisonment that results from his failure to fulfill his true destiny.

Comments: *Beyond the Horizon* was O'Neill's first Broadway success, and it concerns itself with a theme which the playwright continually treated: the necessity of being true to one's own nature. Robert Mayo, the dreamer, attempts to be a farmer and in so doing destroys everything he possesses and everyone he loves. His brother, Andrew, a true son of the soil, is piqued at Ruth's decision to marry Robert. As a result, he turns away from his own agricultural destiny, goes first to sea, and then to Buenos Aires, where, rather than cultivating grain, he tries to speculate in it. He has removed himself from his own roots, the kind of life to which he was eminently suited. Both brothers are destroyed by their attempt to follow other paths: Robert ruins both the farm and his own health by foregoing his dream of traveling "beyond the horizon," while uncomplicated Andy, in leaving the farm, causes a lasting breach between himself and his disappointed, unforgiving father. His attempts at speculation fail, and his essential decency is transmuted into bitter disappointment and a kind of "ruthless cunning." But what is worse is that their decision to work against their respective destinies brings about the destruction of lives other than their own. Ruth, Robert's wife, suffers the total loss of love and hope; Mrs. Mayo and Ruth's mother, Mrs. Atkins, witness the ruin of the farms of which they had been so proud; Mr. Mayo dies bitter and unforgiving; and the innocent Mary, the child of Ruth and Robert, also dies. At the end of the play, there is nothing but a very bleak hope that Andy and Ruth may perhaps work out something once they know "what's right."

In a sense, this play may also be seen as the paradigm of the plight of the artist and hence applicable to O'Neill himself. A human being must use his "one talent," and to ignore it causes destruction. Whatever the cost, one must surrender to one's role and play it properly, for failure to do so brings both destruction and despair. At the same time, O'Neill shows the destructive power of Woman, in the person of Ruth, who selfishly lures Robert away from his natural path and hence is the reason for the disaster that befalls the Mayo brothers and their family. Both Robert and Andrew castigate her for her part in events; yet each does have some lingering sympathy for Ruth as a fellow victim, despite their hatred for her as the cause of their disasters. Each human being must follow his destiny or suffer the ultimate consequence—failure and despair.

Beyond the Horizon is conventional in structure, with its three acts of two scenes apiece, though there is considerable use of visual reflections of the inner disaster which has struck the characters. The Mayo living room declines from neatness into squalor as the characters move from security to despair. The characters are also conventional, with contrasting brothers, one a born farmer and the other a delicate, poetic young man who is all intellect and sensitivity. No one except his mother has any real understanding of Robert Mayo. The practical people like Ruth, Mrs. Atkins, and even Andy cannot quite understand the nature of his dreams. However, through suffering Robert realizes his own error, and Andy and Ruth now have a glimmering vision of something better. Maybe they can work something out. The play shows a considerable advance in the use of dialogue, though at times the high-flown poetic language given to Robert Mayo does not quite ring true, and the unfriendly portrait of Ruth, the creature of instinct who destroys both the dreamer and the dream, sometimes seems a trifle too vindictive.

Production Data: Written in early 1918 and revised (to an unknown extent) by Richard Bennett. First produced at the Morosco Theatre, New York City, February 2, 1920. Moved to the Criterion Theatre, New York City, February 23, 1920; Little Theatre, New York City, March 9, 1920 (111 Performances).

Producer: John D. Williams

Director and Designer: Homer Saint-Gaudens

Cast: Robert Mayo: Richard Bennett
       Andrew Mayo: Edward Arnold
       Ruth Atkins: Helen MacKellar
       Captain Dick Scott: Max Mitzel
       Mrs. Kate Mayo: Mary Jeffery
       James Mayo: Erville Alderson
       Mrs. Atkins: Louise Closser Hale
       Mary Mayo: Elfin Finn
       Ben: George Hadden
       Dr. Fawcett: George Riddell

Revived November 20, 1926, at the Mansfield Theatre, New York City (79 performances).

BIGELOW, Edward. In *The First Man*,* friend of Curtis Jayson* and Martha Jayson.* He is "a large handsome man of thirty-nine. His face shows culture and tolerance, a sense of humor, a lazy unambitious contentment." He has recently been widowed after a singularly unhappy marriage to a strait-laced woman, during which he scandalized the town of Bridgetown, Connecticut, by flaunting his affairs before them. However, with the acquisition of freedom, Bigelow has become a changed man, even taking care of his three children, whom he hardly noticed while his wife was alive. He becomes the friend of Martha, arousing the malicious gossip of the entire Jayson clan, who convince themselves that Martha's child is Bigelow's rather than Curt Jayson's. Bigelow is a pleasant, humane character, a good friend and confidant to Curt, and he is used mainly as an expository figure and plot device.

BIG FRANK. In *The Moon of the Caribbees*,* a fireman on the S.S. *Glencairn*, a huge man with a Swedish accent.

BLAIR, Mary (1895–1947), actress. Born in Pittsburgh, Pennsylvania, 1895; daughter of James G. Blair, a newspaperman. Died in Pittsburgh, September 18, 1947. After being divorced from Charles Meredith and Edmund Wilson, she married Constant M. Eakin, a businessman, in 1930, who survived her.

One of the earliest graduates in the theatre from Carnegie Institute of Technology, Miss Blair created more major O'Neill women characters than anyone else, both for the Provincetown Players and the Theatre Guild (of which she was one of the original three actresses). She began her career in a stock company and played the woman in *Before Breakfast** in the 1929 revival. In 1920 she created the role of Emma Crosby* in *Diff'rent*.* She received excellent reviews for this part, particularly for her ability to convince as both a young woman and a desiccated spinster of fifty. In 1922 she created the role of Mildred Douglas* in *The Hairy Ape** but was replaced in the uptown production by Carlotta Monterey* on the insistence of the sponsor of the play, Arthur Hopkins, who believed that Carlotta would be a better box office draw. To be sure, Carlotta was one of the reigning beauties of New York at the time, and while O'Neill was impressed by her appearance, he was not overwhelmed by her acting. Apparently, Miss Blair did not bear O'Neill any grudge over her replacement and created the part of Ella Downey* in *All God's Chillun Got Wings** (1924), when she played opposite Paul Robeson* and kissed his hand to the tumultuous outrage of newspapers, politicians, and other thoughtless New Yorkers. The voluminous hate mail was so filthily vituperative that much of it was kept from her. When the production was finally staged (it had been delayed for several weeks by Miss Blair's pleurisy), it did so under difficulties because the city invoked child labor laws against it and refused to permit the appearance of child actors in the initial scenes. In 1925 she replaced Mary Morris on Broadway as Abbie Putnam* in *Desire Under the Elms*,* while Miss Morris was on the road with the play. Miss Blair also had the part of the prostitute in *Marco Millions*,* partly at O'Neill's insistence, because he felt gratitude to her for accepting the part of Ella and some embarrassment at her replacement in *The Hairy Ape*. She played in a number of the Theatre Guild Productions, particularly *The Rise of Silas Lapham* (1919). Other notable roles were in *The Faithful* (1920), *The*

World We Live In (1921), *The Crime in the Whistler Room* (1924, written by
her then husband, Edmund Wilson), *Fashion* (1924), *The Spook Sonata* (1924),
The Homicide (1929), a Philadelphia lampoon of *Lysistrata* (1930), and *The
American Dream* (1933)—after she had made the mistake of turning down *Tobacco Road*. In 1935 her career was interrupted by the illness of her husband,
and then her own tuberculosis, which sent her into retirement.

BLAKE, Doctor. In *The Hunted*, the second play of the trilogy, *Mourning
Becomes Electra*,* an "old, kindly best-family physician." He is "a stout, self-
important old man with a stubborn opinionated expression." He has earlier been
contacted by Christine Mannon,* who has told him symptoms of her husband's
illness which lead him to diagnose a severe, rather than minor, heart problem.
Therefore, he has no difficulty in accepting the story that Ezra Mannon* died
of heart failure; possibly "it was love killed Ezra," he suggests. He forms part
of the Chorus of Townsfolk who appear just after the death of Ezra Mannon to
comment on the Mannon family (particularly Christine Mannon) and the events
with which they have been involved.

"BLEMIE." *See* Silverdene Emblem.

"BLIND ALLEY GUY," notes for a proposed gangster play, originally entitled "Gag's End," worked on from December 16, 1940 to June 1, 1943.
"Blind Alley Guy" was originally conceived as an autobiographical play. But
as O'Neill became more and concerned with European politics and his own "war
jitters," he changed the central character of Walter White into that of quasi-
Hitler totalitarian, married to an "amoral, selfish, aggressive" and bigoted wife.
The scene is the United States, and the theme concerns a man who thought
himself "greater than Hitler." It expresses O'Neill's hatred of "bigotry and
fanaticism." A very full analysis of all the notes for this play appears in Virginia
Floyd (1981, pp. 352–360). The manuscript materials are at Yale University.

BORDEN, Emma. In *The Hunted*, the second play of the trilogy, *Mourning
Becomes Electra*,* wife of Josiah Borden.* She is about fifty, "a typical New
England woman of pure English ancestry, with a horse face, buck teeth and big
feet, her manner defensively sharp and assertive." She, along with her husband,
forms part of the Chorus of Townsfolk which appears just after the funeral of
Ezra Mannon* to comment on the Mannon family (particularly Christine Mannon*) and the events in which they have been involved.

BORDEN, Josiah. In *The Hunted*, the second play of the trilogy, *Mourning
Becomes Electra*,* manager of the Mannon shipping company. "He is around
sixty, small and wizened,...[with a] rasping nasal voice and little sharp eyes."
He along with his wife, Emma Borden,* forms part of the Chorus of Townsfolk

which appears just after the funeral of Ezra Mannon* to comment on the Mannon family (particularly Christine Mannon*) and the events in which they have been involved.

BOULTON, Agnes (1893–1968), writer, second wife of Eugene O'Neill. Born in London, September 19, 1893; died, Point Pleasant, New Jersey, November 25, 1968; daughter of a painter, Edward W. Boulton. Educated privately and at the Convent of the Holy Child, Sharon Hill, Pennsylvania, and the Philadelphia School of Industrial Arts. Her first husband died, leaving her with a daughter, Barbara Burton. She married O'Neill on April 12, 1918, in a ceremony at the home of the Reverend William J. Johnson in Provincetown, Massachusetts. Divorced in Reno, Nevada, July 1, 1929, on the grounds of desertion.

Before meeting O'Neill, Agnes had tried to support herself, her daughter, and her parents on a dairy farm she owned near Cornwall Bridge, Connecticut, but it did not pay its way. She then decided to come to New York to work at magazine writing, at which she had had some experience, having written short stories for pulp magazines for the past seven years or so. She later wrote a novel entitled *The Road Before Us* (1944) which was well received. In *Part of a Long Story* (1958), she recounts dramatically her meeting with O'Neill, then an extraordinarily intense, dark, young man. At first he may have been attracted to her by her superficial resemblance to Louise Bryant.* They first met in the Golden Swan bar, nicknamed the Hell Hole, making a foursome with Christine Ell and James "Jamie" O'Neill, Jr.* At their very first meeting, Eugene O'Neill escorted her home, and his parting words to her were, "I want to spend every night of my life from now on with *you*,...I mean this. *Every night of my life*." A few nights later they met again, and in her book Agnes recounts the theatrical gesture with which O'Neill turned back a clock on the mantel with the words, "Turn back the universe,/ And give me yesterday." At this time O'Neill was trying to forget Agnes, but without success, and one night he ordered her to bed with him, planning to kill his feelings for her by sexual intercourse based on hatred rather than love; however, the weather was cold and they merely slept together, but the next day he berated her with the filthy language he had learned as a seaman. Agnes fled to her room at the Brevoort Hotel, and later O'Neill sent her the manuscript of *The Moon of the Caribbees*,* which she greatly admired. From that time on, it was decided that she and O'Neill would go to Provincetown together, though Agnes was warned that his passion for Louise Bryant was not yet finished. After the death of his friend Louis Holladay* from an overdose of heroin, O'Neill tried to drink himself senseless, moved in with Jamie, and then returned to Agnes. Shortly afterward, the two of them went to Provincetown. As expected, Louise Bryant tried to regain O'Neill in 1918, but was unsuccessful, and he and Agnes lived in Provincetown along with Jamie, while O'Neill continued to write.

They stayed in Provincetown until November 1918, returning to New York for rehearsals of *Where the Cross Is Made** and then going in December to Old

House, West Point Pleasant, New Jersey, which Agnes owned in the seaside village where she had been brought up. With some embarrassment she was forced to turn out her parents, her daughter, and her sisters, who had recently moved into the house without her knowing it. O'Neill did not want to have any communication with her family, and Agnes honored his wish. While there, Agnes became pregnant with Shane Rudraighe O'Neill,* and at the end of May 1919, O'Neill and Agnes moved to Provincetown to the old Coast Guard station at Peaked Hill Bars, remodeled by Mabel Dodge, which James O'Neill* [Sr.] had bought for his son. During their time in New Jersey, O'Neill had written several plays and had worked in rehearsal with *Moon of the Caribbees*. On October 30, 1919, in Provincetown, Shane Rudraighe O'Neill was born, named after "Shane the proud" or, as O'Neill sometimes said, according to Agnes, "Shane the loud." After the child's birth, Agnes remained in Provincetown while O'Neill stayed mainly in New York overseeing rehearsals of *Chris Christophersen** (to be produced under the title *Chris*), and *Beyond the Horizon*,* coming up to Provincetown for the summer. When James O'Neill died in New London, Connecticut, on August 10, 1920, they were together again for the funeral. The pattern of their lives now was to live at Peaked Hill during the summer and move to winter quarters in Provincetown, with O'Neill periodically traveling to New York to oversee rehearsals, and Agnes sometimes coming down for productions. Throughout this time, his ambivalent attitude toward his role as a parent became more and more obvious, as did his relationship with Agnes. Apparently, it always possessed an undercurrent of hostility which would surface when he became drunk; but curiously, Agnes does not seem to have tried to stop his drinking, though his anger sometimes frightened her. Her personality is the counterpart of the character of Eleanor Cape* in *Welded*,* O'Neill's account of a love-hate matrimonial relationship.

In 1922 the O'Neills bought Brook Farm, Ridgefield, Connecticut, an estate of thirty acres with a fifteen-room colonial house. Now they alternated between this one and Peaked Hill, with excursions into New York, particularly for O'Neill to look at new productions and work with Kenneth Macgowan* and Robert Edmond Jones.* By 1924, however, O'Neill had come to dislike Brook Farm, a hostility that may have contributed to the farm depicted in *Desire Under the Elms*.* Meanwhile, tensions in the household were mounting as Agnes also tried to continue with her writing. That O'Neill felt some guilt in this regard can be seen in his inscription in the published play *Welded* which he gave to her; he quotes a speech of Michael Cape* imploring his wife's forgiveness for "all I've ever done, all I'll ever do." In 1922 Agnes reworked an old scenario of her husband's, "The Reckoning,"* into a full-length play, "The Guilty One,"* which was optioned by William Brady but was later withdrawn at O'Neill's request. (See Floyd, 1981, pp. 84–91.)

By September 1924, O'Neill decided to winter in Bermuda because he found the Ridgefield winters oppressive. In November 1924, the family sailed there, where Oona (*see* Chaplin, Oona O'Neill) was born, May 14, 1925. The couple returned separately to the United States, spending the summer of 1925 together in Nantucket and Provincetown, returning to Ridgefield in the fall, with O'Neill drinking again but swearing off liquor on December 31. In late February 1926, they returned to Bermuda, first to their leased house at Bellevue but then to "Spithead," a two-hundred-year-old house which they bought. In June 1926, they returned to the United States and after a short time in New York went to Loon Lodge, Belgrade Lakes, Maine, for the summer with Eugene, Jr. (*see* O'Neill, Eugene Gladstone, Jr.) and Barbara Burton, Agnes's daughter, and assorted visitors, including Carlotta Monterey.*

O'Neill, however, was beginning to feel dissatisfied with himself, his career, and particularly with his relationship with Agnes. It was at this time that his relationship with Carlotta became a threat to the marriage. O'Neill began to visit Carlotta in New York while Agnes remained in Ridgefield, leaving for Bermuda with the children on November 20, 1926, and O'Neill following a week later. On his return he informed Agnes about Carlotta, claiming that he had not slept with her, and Agnes apparently believed him. Throughout the early part of 1927, the Bermuda house was renovated. In March they moved in, but their relations were volatile, O'Neill believing that Agnes was sorry that he had stopped drinking because she could no longer control their situation, and Agnes herself perhaps regretting that her unconventional lover had turned out to be a conformist after all. During this year, O'Neill undertook a brief visit to New York, returned to Bermuda, and then in August went back to New York alone, Agnes wishing to stay on because they were short of money. Initially, he wrote of his loneliness for her, once even wondering whether she had a lover in Bermuda, a suggestion for which he later apologized. She, however, seems to have been equally lonely and deeply hurt by his suspicion, writing him an angry letter and proposing to return to Brook Farm, Ridgefield. O'Neill cabled her to remain, which she did. During the fall, he and Carlotta resumed their affair, but he still claimed love for Agnes. In October, he went to Bermuda for a rest, staying for several weeks, during which nothing appeared different; but on November 15, 1927, he left for New York and never returned.

By early December, he asked Agnes to forward manuscripts he had left with her at Spithead and suggested that from now on each should be allowed complete freedom in personal relationships. By Christmas, O'Neill offered her complete freedom, making clear that he thought the marriage was finished. Agnes tried to hold him by stating that she could understand the situation, but O'Neill replied that he had fallen in love with someone else (Carlotta) who returned his affection. Agnes quickly returned to New York; and during her brief stay, they resumed sexual relations for the last time and also decided on a divorce settlement, with Agnes to receive one-third of his annual income plus twenty-four hundred dollars per year support and a life interest in Spithead, either as her own residence or rental property.

Agnes returned to Bermuda on Janury 14, 1928, accompanied by her daughter Barbara. On February 10, O'Neill and Carlotta left for Europe, expecting that Agnes would proceed to Nevada for a Reno divorce as soon as possible. At this point the stories diverge, Agnes claiming that she was not sure what agreement she was to sign, Carlotta seeing her action as meanly obstructive, and O'Neill wishing for an early divorce, yet claiming to be conscience-stricken and still deeply fond of the children. In April 1928, Agnes was back in New York and was quoted in the press as saying that she did not plan to sue for divorce. But by late June she had told the press that she would sue and, as the New York *News* headline said, "Grant O'Neill his 'Illusion of Freedom'." After this, O'Neill never wrote to her again. By February 1929, Agnes agreed to go to Reno, accepting the original financial agreement, which also made financial provision for the children's education at good boarding and preparatory schools. O'Neill claimed that the real reason for her delay was his insistence that she agree not to write about him or their marriage in any way, including the giving of interviews and the writing of memoirs or fiction; a clause in the agreement enjoined her in this regard, invoking a financial penalty for violation. After establishing residence in Nevada, Agnes was divorced on the grounds of desertion on July 1, 1929, with the final decree issued two days later and the records sealed permanently.

After the divorce, the two communicated only through intermediaries, O'Neill remembering his marriage with a resentment that mounted yearly with the payment of the agreed alimony. He did maintain some contact with the children, both in letters and occasional visits. Agnes dropped out of his life, except financially, living in Connecticut, New York, and Point Pleasant, New Jersey, bringing up her children and having some difficulty with Shane. In 1947 she agreed to settle accounts with O'Neill for a lump sum payment of seventeen thousand dollars and shortly afterwards married an old acquaintance, Morris "Mack" Kaufman, a writer and movie producer, many years her junior from whom she later separated. In 1958, after O'Neill's death had negated her earlier agreement, she published her own, slightly untrustworthy and romantic account of her life with O'Neill, *Part of a Long Story* (1958), and also wrote a well-received novel, *The Road is Before Us* (1944). She helped support Shane and his family, both in Bermuda and New Jersey, but does not seem to have remained close to her daughter Oona after her marriage to Charles Spencer (Charlie) Chaplin* in 1943. Oona's visit in 1967 after her mother was hospitalized for treatment of malnutrition, was her first in about fifteen years. Agnes Boulton died in Point Pleasant Hospital, New Jersey, on November 25, 1968 after surgery for an intestinal ailment.

Accounts of O'Neill's acquaintances and friends are frequently unkind to Agnes Boulton, suggesting that the two were temperamentally unsuited and that Agnes's haphazard housekeeping interfered with the playwright's work. Her insistence on continuing her own career of writing "pulp" novels and short stories was also a distraction to a man who wished total commitment and even "servitude" from his wife.

See in "References": Alexander (1962); Boulton (1958); Gelb and Gelb (1973); Sheaffer (1968 and 1973). Ninety-nine letters from Agnes Boulton to Eugene O'Neill are in the Harvard Theatre Collection.

BOUND EAST FOR CARDIFF, a one-act play, part of the S.S. *Glencairn**
group, revision of *Children of the Sea.**

The play is set in the forecastle of the S.S. *Glencairn* on a foggy night midway
on a voyage from New York to Cardiff. Five seamen are sitting on their bunks,
and Yank* is lying seriously injured after a fall into the hold. Cocky,* Olson,*
Davis,* Paul,* and later Ivan* try to keep their minds off the imminent possibility
of Yank's death by telling tales of female conquests and complaining about the
captain, conditions aboard the ship, and the sea in general. Obviously all the
men fear burial at sea, because in that way the sea will have defeated them.
Driscoll,* who has been Yank's shipmate for five years, remains with Yank to
see him through his last voyage. They swap yarns about old fights, old loves,
old crimes, Yank becoming concerned that God will judge him harshly for killing
in self-defense. Yank and Driscoll find that each, independently, has nourished a
hope to leave the sea and buy a farm together, but such escape is impossible—the
sea is their implacable fate. Just before his death, Yank recalls the kindness of a
barmaid, Fanny, who had wanted to lend him money, and he asks Driscoll to buy
her a big box of candy. He also thinks of Driscoll's sorrow. As the fog of death
covers Yank's eyes, the physical fog lifts. Cocky enters with a mocking remark
but is awed into silence as he sees Driscoll make the sign of the cross over his dead
friend. Yank's wish to be buried on land is not fulfilled.

Comments: The play is really a duologue between Yank and Driscoll as they
look back on their lives spent in battle with the sea which they fear. Yet as the
sea is O'Neill's symbol of fate, all humankind clearly belongs to it. The lifting
of the fog is a sign of reconciliation because the sea has now claimed as its
victim the rebellious Yank, who had tried to break free by thinking of buying
a farm. The unspoken implication that the sea punishes such disloyalty pervades
the death scene. The chief characters have tried to find some meaning in their
lives, and even if they cannot escape their fate, both Yank and Driscoll illustrate
the ultimate decency of human friendship.

Production Data: Written in Spring 1914. First produced by the Provincetown
Players* at the Wharf Theatre, Provincetown, Massachusetts, July 28, 1916.
(Performances, unknown).

Director: Eugene O'Neill
Set Designer: unknown
Cast: Partial List
        Yank: George Cram Cook*
        Driscoll: Frederick Burt
        Cocky: E. J. Ballantine
        Davis: Harry Kemp
        Second Mate: Eugene O'Neill
        With: John Reed,* Wilbur Daniel Steele

This was the first production of an O'Neill play. The actors whose names are
italicized recreated their roles in the New York production of November 3, 1916,
at the Playwrights' Theatre.

Revived frequently as part of the *S.S. Glencairn* series. *See* that entry for performance statistics.

[*See also* Appendix B for film adaptation of the entire series under the title *The Long Voyage Home*.]

BRADY, Alice (1892–1939), actress. Born in New York City, November 2, 1892, to William A. Brady, theatrical producer, and Rose René Brady, French musical theatre actress. Died of cancer in New York City, October 28, 1939. Educated at a convent school in Elizabeth, New Jersey, and at the Boston Conservatory where she sang in Gilbert and Sullivan. Married James Lyon Crane in 1920, later divorced.

Alice Brady made her Broadway debut in 1911 in a musical, *The Balkan Princess*, following that in 1912 with roles in Gilbert and Sullivan and *Little Women*. A charming and elegant personality, she made her name chiefly in romantic comedy, though she did have considerable ability in serious roles. Her long list of credits includes: *The Family Cupboard* (1913), *Sinners* and *You Never Can Tell* (1915); *Forever After* (1918, a two-year run and tour); *Anna Ascends* (1920); *Drifting* (1922, a commitment which forced her to turn down *Rain*); *Zander the Great* (1923); *Oh Mama* (1925); *The Bride of the Lamb* (1926); *A Most Immoral Lady* (1928); *The Game of Love and Death* (1929); *The Brass Ankle* (1931); and *Mademoiselle* (1932).

Miss Brady had a curious history of declining roles in O'Neill plays. In 1921 she turned down the role of Eileen Carmody* in *The Straw** and in 1928 passed over the part of Nina Leeds* in *Strange Interlude*,* a mistake, she later admitted. Then in 1931, she had a major triumph in creating the role of Lavinia Mannon* in *Mourning Becomes Electra*,* with Alla Nazimova* as Christine Mannon,* thereby gaining new status as a serious actress. However, she declined another O'Neill role later, that of Elsa Loving* in *Days Without End** (1932).

That year she abandoned Broadway for Hollywood. Already an experienced film actress, she had made thirty-two films between 1914 and 1923, and a sampling of titles indicates their content: *As Ye Sow*, *Bought and Paid For*, and *The Gilded Cage*. Altogether, she made over fifty films, her most notable ones being: *The Vinegar Tree*, *When Ladies Meet*, *Broadway to Hollywood*, *Stage Mother*, *Beauty for Sale*, *Should Ladies Behave* (all in 1933); *Gay Divorcee* (1934, with Fred Astaire and Ginger Rogers); *Gold Diggers of 1935*; *Three Smart Girls* and *A Hundred Men and a Girl* (both with Deanna Durbin), *Mama Steps Out*, *Joy of Living* (all in 1937), *Good-Bye Broadway*, and *In Old Chicago* (1938, for which she received an Academy Award). Her last film, completed a few months before her death in 1939, was the Henry Fonda vehicle, *Young Mr. Lincoln*.

BRANT, Adam. In *Mourning Becomes Electra*,* he appears in both *Homecoming* and *The Hunted*, clipper ship captain of the *Flying Trades*, son of David Mannon* and a French Canadian nurse, Marie Brantôme,* and lover of

Christine Mannon.* He is murdered in *The Hunted* by Orin Mannon* with the connivance and prodding of Lavinia Mannon.* For Christine, he represents romantic love and escape from her loveless marriage, while to Lavinia he represents a threat to her beloved father. At the same time, there is some truth to Christine's suggestion that Lavinia is jealous that Adam Brant pays no attention to her. Brant's motivations are also mixed. He hated his father, who was disinherited by his family and then became a drunkard, abusing Adam's mother, whom Adam loved. He also hates the Mannon family for their refusal to aid his mother when she was in great need, a time, incidentally, during which Adam himself had almost forgotten her. As a result, he wants revenge on all the Mannons for what they did to his mother; and for the same reason he has not adopted the name of Mannon, though he is legally entitled to it since his parents were indeed married. He enjoys humiliating the Mannons, yet his love for the sensual Christine seems genuine. He aids in the murder of Ezra Mannon,* her husband, by obtaining the poison she administers to him in place of his cardiac medicine, and Adam is happy to learn that his dying enemy knew the truth about him and Christine. But when she comes to his vessel, begging him to take her away, there is some sadness in Brant's heart because he must then give up his ship, which seems to mean almost as much to him as Christine. However, he promises her that they will leave as passengers bound for the South Sea Islands he has told her of, where love is not sinful. Left alone, he regrets the loss of the *Flying Trades*: "I wasn't man enough for you!" At this confessional moment, Lavinia and Orin break in, Orin killing Brant with a pistol fired at point-blank range. When Christine hears about Brant's death, she shoots herself.

In terms of the mythical interpretation of the trilogy, Brant represents Aegisthos, the lover of Clytemnestra (Christine) who is murdered by Orestes (Orin) with the connivance and suggestion of Electra (Lavinia), while Ezra Mannon is the Agamemnon of the piece. Brant also represents the Freudian Id, the passions that canot be denied, only controlled or repressed, and hence his begetting in illicit passion runs counter to the Puritan tradition represented by the Mannons. Brant's resemblance to Ezra Mannon is also important because by killing Brant, Orin discovers within himself his own Orestes complex in killing his "father" and also his Oedipus complex in wishing to sleep with his mother.

BRANTÔME, Marie, the name of the "French Canuck nurse" with whom David Mannon* ran away and later married, abusing her. Their son is Adam Brant,* who hates his father's family and eventually takes a self-destructive revenge on the clan. Marie does not appear in the trilogy, *Mourning Becomes Electra,*￼ but she is frequently discussed. In particular, her liveliness and vivacity are remembered, as well as her "low" origin.

BREAD AND BUTTER, a four-act play.
   Act I: The scene is the sitting room of the home of Edward Brown, Sr.,* a prosperous hardware merchant of Bridgetown, Connecticut. "The room is suf-

ficiently commonplace and ordinary to suit the most fastidious Philistine,'' with ''pretentiously stupid paintings of the 'Cattle-at-the-Stream,' 'Sunrise-on-the-Lake' variety''; easy chairs; dull crimson walls; embroidered, fringed center-piece; and Mission clock on the mantel. Mr. and Mrs. Brown* are sitting with their eldest son, Edward Brown, Jr.* The elder Brown is a lean, fifty-eight-year-old man, ''dressed as becomes a leading citizen,'' while Mrs. Brown is a ''tired-looking woman about fifty years old,'' with ''a meek expression and an apologetic demeanor.'' Edward, Jr., is a pudgy, thirty-year-old alderman. Brown is criticizing an advertisement for the family hardware business that Edward has written in order to attract the ''better class of people in town,'' pointing out that the trade of the working people is preferable because ''they pay cash.'' Quite clearly, Brown has never forgotten his humble origins as a ''working man and a farm hand, and all the education he's got beyond grammar school he picked up along the way.''

Edward then turns to a discussion of the future of John Brown,* his youngest brother, and there is clearly some jealousy because John has been allowed four years at Princeton while Edward has gone into the family business. Brown announces that he and his wife have decided that John should go into a profession, preferably to become a lawyer. Edward is obviously jealous of John, as is the second son, Harry Brown,* a pleasant-looking, twenty-five-year-old, young-man-about-town type. Both older boys had been expected to work during vacations, but not John; and further, they have not heard John express any desire for a profession—in fact Harry says that John wants to be a painter. Edward, with his stolid practicality, completely misunderstands and thinks this means tradesman rather than artist. Meanwhile, John, the subject of this conversation, is visiting his fiancée, Maud Steele,* the daughter of a wealthy Bridgetown citizen. Edward himself earlier asked Maud to marry him, but she preferred John.

The two girls, Mary Brown* and Bessie Brown,* now enter and join the conversation. They are a remarkable contrast, Mary twenty-eight, angular, and bespectacled, Bessie ''small, plump, with a mass of wavy black hair and great hazel eyes,...laughing mouth, and...quite adorable.'' Mary holds the opinions of her businessmen brothers, while Bessie sticks up for John: ''He is an altogether different type from the other members of the family; a finer, more sensitive organization.'' He has large, black ''dreamer's eyes'' and wears his hair long and brushed back. ''His mouth is full lipped and small,...his nose straight and thin with the nostrils of the enthusiast.'' The two older boys instantly put him on mock trial and discover that Maud Steele has just accepted John's offer of marriage, with the understanding that the engagement must be a long one because John has to make his way. But before John can finish, Harry breaks the news that John is ''condemned to be a lawyer.''

Shocked, Bessie, John's confidante, breaks out, ''but John doesn't want to be a lawyer,'' and John corroborates her statement, announcing that he wants to go to art school in New York with his friend, ''Babe'' Carter.* Shocked,

Brown asks if Mr. Steele* has agreed to this plan, and John claims that his future father-in-law "said it was a good idea and told me he didn't think much of your law school plan." Steele then arrives to discuss the future of the young people. He says that there are too many lawyers but obviously understands that Brown wants John to pursue such a career for social reasons. He believes that John ought to test his talent as an illustrator: "Give him a year in New York and don't allow him any more money than is absolutely necessary, and I'll guarantee at the end of that time he'll have lost his high-fangled notions.... He'll come gradually to see the commercial aspects of the case."

As they leave, John enters, followed by Maud Steele, "a remarkably pretty girl of twenty," with a kittenish manner and the pouting air of a spoiled child. They kiss, and John talks of going to art school, while Maud says her father "thinks you'll just make oodles and oodles of money in New York when you get started." She produces a magazine with the kind of commercial art that she and her father favor, and John looks contemptuously at it: "I want to do much finer things than that, don't you understand?"

Act II: "A studio in New York on a cold evening in March, a year and a half later." The room is seedily furnished, full of paintings and furnishings of the thrift-shop or street-scavenged variety. John and his two roommates are trying to impose order on the chaos. "Babe" Carter, John's Princeton roommate, "is a broad-shouldered giant with a mop of blond hair and feeble attempt at a blond mustache." He is very handsome. Steve Harrington* "is a tall slender fellow of about twenty-eight, with large irregular features, light brown hair and brown eyes." John "has aged considerably," and his face is lined. He is unhealthily pale and nervous. Babe is on his way to Bridgetown to see Bessie in secret, and Mr. Brown is coming to visit the studio. The young men engage in banter as Eugene Grammont,* the art teacher, enters. Babe and Steve speak with him about the hostility Mr. Brown shows to John's ambitions to be a serious painter. Bessie alone is sympathetic; Maud is so philistine that she is shocked by nude paintings, but she does try to understand. Grammont speaks of John's talent as one of the finest he has ever encountered, but he also notes that the young man is too sensitive to "fight against discouragement and lack of appreciation through long years of struggle." His work has suffered, probably, as the roommates suggest, the result of Maud's letters begging him to return home and paint there.

Mr. Brown then appears, more dour and disapproving than ever, angry that Babe has been "meeting Bessie on the sly." Brown has taxed his daughter with this, and the self-willed young woman has left home, saying that she intends to marry Babe Carter. John makes his pleasure obvious: "She must be true to herself. Her duty to herself stands before her duty to you." In reply to Brown's anger, John tells him, "You consider your children your possessions, your property, to belong to you. You don't think of them as individuals with ideas and desires of their own. It's for you to find out the highest hope of each of them and give it your help and sympathy." Clearly he is speaking for himself as much as for Bessie, but Brown is furious that Bessie has turned down a wealthy older man for "that scamp Carter" and intends to refuse to see her if she marries Babe. Turning to the subject of John's future, Brown tries to persuade him to come home—for Maud's sake, and if nothing else, Mr. Steele has promised John a house and a position in his own business. Obviously, Brown is incapable of understanding what John is trying to do and wants his son to start making some money soon instead of wasting his time on paintings like an impressionistic nude that no "decent family would ever hang...up in their house."

Into this family argument lurch Ted Nelson,* another roommate, and his friend Helene,* a cloak and suit model. Both have been drinking to celebrate Ted's sale of a story to a magazine. Ted obviously considers it prostitution of his art, but it did bring in money. He introduces Helene to Brown as his "wife," to the joint consternation of John and Helene. Steve gets them out of the way as Grammont enters and attempts to change Brown's mind, but the outraged father takes a highly moral view of the situation and suggests to John that Grammont is simply out to make money by keeping John as a student. He sees all the relationships of this studio in their worst light. Enraged, he delivers an ultimatum to John: "You either come home with me in the morning or you needn't look to me for help in the future. I'll bring you to your senses. Starve awhile, and see how much bread and butter this high art will bring you! No more coming to me for money, do you understand?" John refuses, and as a parting shot, Brown says that Steele won't keep his promised position open for John forever. John calls out, "Oh, to hell with Steele!" as the curtain falls.

Act III: "The studio about three o'clock on a hot Sunday afternoon in July of the same year." John, Steve, and Ted are there. John, looking "haggard and dissipated," is trying to work on an unfinished portrait. Steve, wearing his dark suit, is sprawled on a chair, while Ted, looking shabby and down at heel, stares out the window. All seem to be exceedingly depressed, with little money and nothing to do. John has been working as checker on the docks, and Sunday is his only day for painting. He is rebellious because he knows that his routine job has destroyed his creativity. He knows "only a great sickness and lassitude of soul, a desire to drink, to do anything to get out of myself and forget." But there is more than just that. Maud has been writing to him, and "it's hell to love and be loved by a girl who can't understand; who, you know, tries to and cannot; who loves you, and whose life you are making miserable and unhappy by trying to be true to yourself." Steve and Ted suggest two possible alternatives—either go home, get married, and work for a while in order to finance his painting, or "a year at the salary you'll get from father-in-law you ought to save enough to stay down here for an age." Maud will surely understand him better after the marriage. John, however, foresees that he will be destroyed by the pettifogging philistinism of Bridgetown.

Babe and Bessie enter, happily married now, to try to invite the inhabitants of the studio to the museum with them. When she hears what they have been talking about, she advises John against marriage, saying that she knows both

Maud and John better than they know themselves. John has had a commercial nibble at some of his work, he tells her, but nothing more. Bessie is both encouraging and worried about John, particularly about his drinking; John denies that he is drinking but nonetheless sits down with Ted and a pint of whiskey, which they share as Maud Steele and Mrs. Brown appear.

Mrs. Brown is appalled by John's state of painterly undress, while Maud laughs at her, though she remains shocked at the picture of the nude dancer. The two women have come to New York because they have not been receiving letters from John. They have come to "rescue" him. As Maud puts it, "you've simply got to stop breaking people's hearts and homes. We're going to take you back to Bridgetown, a prisoner." Everything has been arranged: Mr. Steele has a job waiting for him in the store, Maud has picked out a house and her father will give it to them as a wedding present, and Mr. Brown "has the dandiest surprise in store for you." At first John refuses, but then Edward, dressed with "sober immaculateness," enters, looking scornfully at John's scruffiness. When he hears that John will not return, he starts to lecture him: "It's my duty to show him the wreck he is making of his own life." At first John is politely curt, but when Edward speaks of the unhappiness he is causing Maud, he erupts: "Yes, I *can* refuse, for Maud's sake most of all. Would you have me give up like a craven; be untrue to my highest hope; slink home a self-confessed failure? Would you have Maud married to such a moral coward? You, with your bread and butter viewpoint of life, probably can't appreciate such feelings." Then he suddenly realizes that Edward may be harboring a hope that he will refuse and leave the way open for Edward to marry Maud. With cold fury Edward suggests, "You are mixed up with some woman down here and—" With that John punches him in the face and Edward forgives, but he refuses to retract his statement. Edward and Mrs. Brown leave, but Maud remains behind, weeping. She makes one last appeal to him to return "for my sake," and John's will is broken. They kiss as the curtain falls.

Act IV: The sitting room of Maud and John Brown's home in Bridgetown, two years later. It is furnished in a manner reminiscent of the sitting room of the senior Browns, with lace-curtained windows and a generally "commonplace aspect." Two paintings in the impressionist style are rather out of key with the rest of the room. Maud and Edward enter. She has aged fretfully, and her face, though still pretty, has hardened. She "wears the air of one who has been cheated in the game of life and knows it; but will even up the score by making those around her as wretched as possible." Edward, too, has aged but is still as "faultlessly staid" in dress and appearance as ever. He was elected mayor last fall and is now a congressional candidate; Maud congratulates him. There is still bad blood between him and John, and, in fact, John practically put him out of the house some six months earlier. Maud speaks enviously of the way "it must be fine to keep going upward step by step and getting somewhere, instead of sticking in one place without hope of advancement." She asks Edward to promise not to forget "us poor, unhappy small-town people." John is staying out late at the club on Saturday nights and drinking too much with Harry Brown's low women friends. Edward says he has heard about this and is grieved to see Maud in such a state. He recommends that she sue for divorce because John has failed "in his duties as a husband. He has no stability." Reports of an extramarital affair are circulating, so that Maud would have the sympathy of everyone. And, as Maud admits after Edward's questioning, they are no longer living together as man and wife. However, Maud vindictively says she won't divorce him because she is sure he could find another wealthy wife very speedily. At this, Edward begs her to reconsider and tells of his love for her, expressing the hope that she might "come to love me ever so little." As Edward kisses Maud's hand, John enters.

He watches the pair cynically. He has grown stout, flabby, and pasty faced, with "dull and lusterless eyes." Bitterly and cruelly he interrupts: "Thou shalt not covet thy neighbor's wife.... Never try to make love, Edward. You look a fearful ass; and remember Maud is expressly forbidden to covet such animals in that same commandment. Sorry to disturb you. I'll cough next time." He leaves as Edward begs Maud not to forget her promise at least to consider his suggestion. She throws herself on the sofa, weeping bitterly as John returns. Instantly they start bickering about John's appearance, his late nights, his drinking, his failure to return for dinner, his trip to New York to see Bessie, and the rumor of his being seen with another woman. Exasperatedly, John pours himself a drink while Maud goes to answer the door. At first he is a trifle ashamed, but he soon turns on her: "your tongue is calculated to drive anyone to drink." Then come the usual recriminations. Both were foolish, Maud for giving up "the righteous citizen Edward" and John for giving up his career. Maud then berates John for his lack of interest in the family business and calls him a failure. As she continues, John suggests that she should get a divorce: "When nothing is left of the old love but wrangling and distrust, it's high time for us to give up this farce of life together." Then she would be free to marry Edward. Once again Maud refuses, admitting that Edward has made the same suggestion. She takes a lofty moral tone: "I was brought up to regard marriage as a sacred thing; ...If I were to get a divorce, think of the scandal, think of what people would say." Once again Maud accuses John of infidelity as he reads the paper. Suddenly he discovers a highly favorable criticism of Babe Carter's work and is overjoyed: "Won't Bessie be tickled to death when she reads that?" With singular nastiness, Maud reveals that "they say he was forced to marry her on account of their previous intimacy." Enraged, John almost strikes her, but the doorbell rings and Bessie enters. Maud, having announced that she refuses to see Bessie, has left the room, and John must lie to cover up.

Bessie asks about Maud, and then John reveals the hell his marriage has become: "We're two corpses chained together." Bessie says she isn't surprised: "The pity of it is, you're neither of you really to blame. It's simply the conflict of character. You'll grind together until both are worn out." Bitterly, John agrees: "You're right; Death is the only cure for this marriage." Bessie also suggests divorce, but John says that Maud does not agree. She doesn't want to leave him free to marry again, and if he deserted her, she would glory in her martyrdom. Further, John has no money of his own. He no longer paints, and as Bessie reminds him of the drawings he has sold, he wishes that he had turned back to his career when he received a check the night before his marriage. Instead, he had put even his drawing behind him when he married Maud. Bessie is astonished at the depth of John's misery because he has always written so enthusiastically to them. She suggests that his drinking may be the cause of his "degeneration," but John no longer cares.

To change the subject, Bessie tells of the success of Steve Harrington in Paris and says that she and Babe are going over there for a year, since Babe has sold three paintings. She suggests that John come to Paris with them, but he refuses, partly from fear of further failure and partly because Bessie and Babe "are just becoming reconciled with the family." He then shows Bessie Babe's favorable notice, and she suggests that he visit the Brown household with her. But again he refuses, suggesting that she visit him tomorrow night. After she leaves, Maud, who has overheard everything, loses all self-control, and enraged that Bessie should suggest his going to Paris, finally attacks her reputation: "She lived with Carter before." That is the last straw for John, who starts to throttle her. Then he "realizes what he is doing and pushes her from him. She falls to the floor,... sobbing convulsively," and John cries out, "By God, there's an end to everything!" He rushes out of the room and up the stairs. "Then for an instance a great silence broods over the house. It is broken by the muffled report of a revolver sounding from the floor above," followed by the sound of a heavy fall. "Maud springs to her feet,... listening." Suddenly she comprehends and rushes out, screaming with terror.

Comments: This early play, probably written in the spring of 1914, is O'Neill's first full-length play. It is also noteworthy for its unusual length of four acts rather than the customary three. In terms of content, *Bread and Butter* has both characters and themes which O'Neill used very frequently throughout his dramatic career. The theme of the artist who is turned away from his true *métier* by a philistine wife appears here for the first time and is repeated in *Beyond the Horizon** and *The Great God Brown.** The theme of the hostile wife who drives her artistic husband to suicide is repeated in *Before Breakfast,** while the unhappy economic practicalities of a wife were anticipated in *Warnings.** O'Neill's attitude toward the philistine rectitude of the business community appears also in the characters of the Businessman in *Fog** and the husband in *Recklessness.** The portrait of the artist character, John, in this play is also strikingly like that of the poet in *Fog*, and the similarity to O'Neill's own appearance is surely more than coincidence. The artist's plea for self-realization is also repeated in a slightly different context in *Servitude,** where both Ethel Frazer* and David Roylston* speak of this theme. While the theme of philistinism and the world of art is the main one here, it is important to note that O'Neill had begun his career with a curiously ambivalent attitude toward marriage. It seems that even at this early stage, O'Neill regarded the matrimonial relationship as destructive to men unless the wife is prepared, like Alice Roylston* in *Servitude*, to devote herself fully to her husband. Otherwise, marriages degenerate into Strindbergian hostility and bickering, cause the destruction of masculine idealism, or, in the case of *Warnings*, result in the destruction of a ship. It is interesting in this context to note the torment that most of O'Neill's married couples seem to endure and how little they understand each other.

This is a well-made problem play in which one incident is carefully articulated into the next, giving an appearance of inevitability. Central conflicts are reiterated, and the play ends with a melodramatic curtain—a shot and a suicide. One is reminded of the number of times Ibsen concluded in this manner and also of Chekhov's glee when he noted that *The Cherry Orchard* did *not* end with a shot.

The characterization in *Bread and Butter* is very broad, and individuals seem rather to be representatives of their particular point of view. They are not deeply drawn, and even the internal conflict of John, the frustrated artist, is not probed. Actions are eminently predictable, and some of the dialogue, especially the exchanges among the young men at the studio, is rather jejune. In general, these are stock characters playing their stock roles, and as a result, there is little sense of human beings being caught up and victimized by a hostile universe. John's suicide is purely a private matter, the result of his own weakness. This point of view is narrower than that attempted in the one-act plays written at about the same time. In *Thirst*,* for instance, the sun is like the eye of an angry God, while in both *Warnings* and *The Web** there are some socioeconomic factors which are not fully exploited here.

Production Data: Written Spring 1914. Unproduced.

A Note on the Text: The text used is that appearing in *"Children of the Sea" and Three Other Unpublished Plays by Eugene O'Neill*. Edited by Jennifer McCabe Atkinson with Foreword by Frank Durham. Washington, D.C.: NCR Microcard Editions, 1972. A Bruccoli Clark Book.

BRENNAN, Mrs. In *The Straw*,* she "is a tall, stout woman of fifty, lusty and loud-voiced, with a broad, snub-nosed face, a large mouth, the upper lip darkened by a suggestion of a mustache, and little round blue eyes." She has a perpetually irritated expression. A widow who had reared a family of her own, she is hired as housekeeper to the Carmody family when Eileen Carmody* was sent to the hospital. She marries Bill Carmody,* and in her he seems to have met his match because she will not put up with any nonsense from him. A domineering woman, she has effectively ruined the sweetness of Mary Carmody,* the youngest of the children, whom Eileen has loved most.

BROWN, Bessie. In *Bread and Butter*,* daughter of Edward Brown, Sr.* She is "small, plump, with a mass of wavy black hair and great hazel eyes, a red, pouting, laughing mouth, glowing complexion and small restless hands and feet." She is an adorable twenty-three. Bessie is the confidante of her brother,

John Brown,* and is the only one who understands him. She follows her own desires and marries "Babe" Carter* for love. The result of this is that she is exceedingly happy and is eventually reconciled to her family, who originally opposed the match. She advises John to get a divorce from Maud Steele,* his wife, once the marriage has turned sour, as she had fully expected it would. She understands the psychodynamics of each party better than they do themselves, and she tries to give John a chance by inviting him to Paris. In response, Maud claims that Bessie and Babe Carter have lived together before their marriage, an accusation which so enrages John that he nearly throttles her. When he realizes what violence Maud has induced in him, he shoots himself.

BROWN, Edward, Jr. In *Bread and Butter*,* son to Edward Brown, Sr.* He is a true son of his father, though with more social pretensions. He "is tall and stout, pudgy-faced, dark-haired, small of eye, thick of lip and neck." He is an alderman of Bridgetown at the beginning of the play, later rising to mayor and congressional candidate. He dresses always with sartorial immaculateness, and the tidiness of his exterior is indicative of the philistinism of his mind. He is highly moral, ultraconservative, dedicated to success, and exceedingly dull as a personality. He was a candidate for Maud Steele's* hand, but she chose to marry the artistic John Brown,* Edward's youngest brother, of whom Edward remains jealous. Edward helps coerce John to return to Bridgetown and then later, when the marriage of John and Maud turns sour, suggests that she get a divorce because he still loves he (after his fashion) and hopes to marry her. In fact, he is really the right sort of husband for her. Edward takes over his father's business and cannot understand why John should be treated with partiality. He and his brother, Harry Brown,* were always expected to work. Edward is a foil for John.

BROWN, Edward, Sr., in *Bread and Butter*,* is a successful hardware merchant in Bridgetown, Connecticut. He "was a working man and a farm hand, and all the education he's got beyond grammar school he picked up along the way." He is ambitious for his youngest son to become a lawyer, but John Brown* wants to be a serious painter. Brown cannot understand this attitude, but he does allow John a year in New York to prove himself. At the end of this time, Brown cuts off his support in order to force John to return home to philistine respectability and marriage to Maud Steele.* He does not understand Bessie Brown,* John's favorite sister, either, and forces her to choose between "Babe" Carter* and himself. Bessie chooses to marry Carter, and her father refuses to see her again, until they are reconciled at the end of the play. John accuses him of considering "your children to be your possessions, your property, to belong to you. You don't think of them as individuals with ideas and desires of their own. It's for you to find out the highest hope of each of them and give it your help and sympathy." Instead, Brown thinks of nothing except economic security.

In appearance, he is "a tall, lean old man with a self-satisfied smile forever on his thin lips. He is smooth-shaven, a trifle bald, fifty-eight years old, and dressed as becomes a leading citizen."

BROWN, Harry. In *Bread and Butter*,* son of Edward Brown, Sr.,* and brother of John Brown,* whom he later leads into dissipation. Harry is the younger brother of Edward Brown, Jr.,* who takes over the family business. Harry is "a tall, dark, pleasant-looking young fellow of twenty-five with a good-natured air and breezy manners of a young-man-about-small-town." He is "a bit of a sport," and he dresses rather foppishly in light checks. Like Edward, he is jealous that John is treated better than they; but after John's return to Bridgetown, the two frequent the same clubs, bars, and women.

BROWN, John. In *Bread and Butter*,* son to Edward Brown, Sr.* He is the artistic youngest son of the family. He has been favored above his brothers Edward Brown, Jr.,* and Harry Brown* by being sent to Princeton. His father wishes him to become a lawyer, but John, with the help of his future father-in-law, Mr. Steele,* persuades the elder Brown to give him a year in New York at art school to study painting. During this time, John starts to develop his very considerable talent, but his father refuses to continue financing him. After a few months working at a routine job as a checker on the docks, John is profoundly discouraged. He feels that his creative spark is gone, and he starts to drink too much. Finally, when Maud Steele,* his spoiled, kittenish fiancée, and John's mother and brother Edward come to New York, he agrees to return to Bridgetown with them.

After two years of marriage, John has discovered that by selling himself for "bread and butter" to the philistine world of business and marriage, he has lost everything that matters to him. No longer able to paint, and having turned his back on the art world completely, he is left with recriminations. The very night before his wedding, he received a check for some drawing that had been accepted, but he decided that for Maud's sake he should put art behind him. Two years later, their marriage has degenerated into a hellish existence of drink, women, and everlasting quarreling which turns into open hatred and abuse. John suggests divorce to Maud, as does Edward; and later Bessie Brown,* John's sister, also makes the same suggestion to her brother. Maud, however, loftily refuses, having reached such a stage of bitterness that she wants to make John suffer as much as she has. Finally, when she overhears Bessie suggesting that John accompany her and her husband to Paris she becomes totally enraged, raving out of control about her hatred for John as an utter failure. John manages to put up with this, but when she attacks the morals of his favorite sister, Bessie, he nearly throttles her. Realizing what he has done, he rushes upstairs and shoots himself, believing that, as he had said before, "Death is the only cure for this marriage."

John Brown is a character who physically resembles Eugene O'Neill himself, being slender, dark, bronzed, graceful, with long black hair brushed back over his head, large dark eyes, a small, full-lipped mouth, and a straight thin nose "with the nostrils of an enthusiast." He is "a finer more sensitive organization" than any other member of the family. He is shown as torn between his love for Maud and his artistic desires. He turns away from his proper course and is destroyed by an unhappy marriage to an eminently unsuitable woman. On the whole, John is basically a weak character, and his degeneration is so predictable that we do not feel the full measure of sympathy for him that O'Neill apparently wished to evoke. The character does not gain the symbolic stature of the artist destroyed by a philistine society.

BROWN, Mary. In *Bread and Butter*,* daughter of Edward Brown, Sr.* She is twenty-eight years old, plain, angular and bespectacled, dressed in an unfashionable black gown. She clearly belongs to the philistine side of the family represented by Edward Brown, Jr.*

BROWN, Mr., father of William A. Brown.* In *The Great God Brown*,* he is a "bustling, genial, successful, provincial business man, stout and hearty in his evening dress." He is about fifty and is a partner of Mr. Anthony,* whom he sees as preventing him from expanding his contracting business. He sends his son to college so that he may become an architect and make more of the family business. Mr. Brown is essentially a limited mentality, a man of materialistic practicality.

BROWN, Mrs., mother of William A. Brown.* In *The Great God Brown*,* she is the proud mother and the dutiful wife. She "is a dumpy woman of forty-five, overdressed in black lace and spangles." She wishes Billy to go to college for a profession and is convinced that he possesses talent in excess of what he actually has.

BROWN, Mrs. In *Bread and Butter*,* wife to Edward Brown, Sr.* She "is a small grey-haired, tired-looking woman about fifty years old, neatly dressed in black. She has a meek expression" and a self-deprecating manner. She seems genuinely puzzled by the behavior of her son, John Brown,* when he decides to become a painter.

BROWN, William A., the character after whom *The Great God Brown** is named. He first appears as a tall, athletic, blond, all-American boy of eighteen. He ages through the play (which lasts twenty years or so) into a successful, well-preserved businessman-architect, without much imagination or emotional depth until he wears the mask of his friend, Dion Anthony.*

Billy Brown is desperately in love with Margaret (Anthony)* but loses her to Dion, who better fits her romantic turn of mind. Billy remains a bachelor, and when Margaret and the family are in need of help, he employs Dion Anthony in his business. Secretly, Billy has always envied Dion because his friend has seemed to master life and to enjoy himself, while Billy has always been conventional and practical. He disapproves of the way Dion acts towards Margaret, and indeed he never ceases to love her. He tries to understand what it is that makes Dion so attractive and tries to buy the same joy that he thinks Dion experiences by helping Margaret and also keeping the prostitute Cybel,* who loves Dion. Through the first part of the play to the end of the second act, Brown is a thematic descendant of Edward Brown, Sr.,* the businessman of *Bread and Butter*,* and of the crassly material Marco Polo* in *Marco Millions*.* Success and prosperity form The Great God Brown, and he lives accordingly. However, when Dion dies, Brown takes on the mask of his friend in order to love Margaret, and from that time on he knows no rest. He comes to learn the pain of loving "by proxy," as Dion has done, and finally he learns to love so that when he finally dies, he has gone beyond materialism and has become a character for whom the audience must feel sympathy.

The character of William A. Brown is not fully successful because of this total psychological and emotional opposition. To be sure, O'Neill is trying to convey the conflict within the soul of an individual, but the shift of emphasis from Dion Anthony to Brown in the middle of the play results in too great a shift of focus. Brown, whom the audience has been expected to dislike and discount, is now almost heroic in his own struggle. He gradually comes to learn about the nature of life and happiness, achieving an understanding of both only upon his deathbed. Part of the problem with Brown is that O'Neill makes him a composite of symbol and reality, with the result that when he wears the symbolic mask of Dion, reality continually intrudes, and Brown is forced into a series of quick changes, almost reminiscent of the later Superman when he is trying to keep secret his real identity. Nor can O'Neill quite make up his mind whether he is castigating the business mentality or showing a tortured human being in the character of William A. Brown who can act unselfishly. Brown has envied Dion in the past, and by getting "inside" his friend's skin, or identity, he manages to learn how to love and how to treat life; thus he shows an admirable capacity for growth and departs from his original stereotype.

BRYANT, Louise (1887–1936), American revolutionary and journalist. Born in San Francisco, 1887 (exact date uncertain). Died in Paris, January 6, 1936, after a cerebral hemorrhage. Daughter of Hugh J. and Louisa (maiden name unknown) Mohan. Her father was a former Pennsylvania coal miner and later journalist who abandoned the family. Her mother was said to have been of Spanish extraction. She later married Sheridan Bryant, a railway conductor in Wadsworth, Nevada. Louise used his name, but never legally took it. Educated at Nevada public schools, University of Nevada, Reno, and the University of Oregon, B.A. 1909. Married Paul Trullinger (1909–1916); John Silas Reed* (1916, died 1920); William C. Bullitt (1923–1930), one daughter. After graduation she moved to Portland, Oregon, where she used her sorority connections to become society reporter on the weekly *Spectator*.

In 1909, Louise Bryant married Paul Trullinger, a Portland dentist, who encouraged her artistic endeavors by allowing her a studio in the city where she tried to write poetry and sketch, as well as having several love affairs. She met John Silas Reed* in late 1915 during his speaking tour and within a few weeks followed him to Greenwich Village. Divorced by Trullinger for desertion in 1916, she married John Reed on November 9 of the same year. During the previous summer, she and Reed had summered in Provincetown, Massachusetts, in the company of those Greenwich Village friends who founded the Province-town Players.* There she met Eugene O'Neill and they became lovers, Louise having falsely informed O'Neill that she and Reed were living as brother and sister because Reed's kidney ailment prevented their having sexual intercourse. She told O'Neill that Reed understood the situation and that she was seeking consolation from the playwright. Apparently O'Neill believed her, and the result was a curious romantic triangle of which Reed seems to have been unaware, helping O'Neill to further his career through the use of his own contacts. Louise played the Dancer* in O'Neill's *Thirst** at its first performance, while O'Neill played the West Indian Mulatto Sailor.* This triangular relationship seems to have contributed to O'Neill's *Strange Interlude** and also, to some extent, to *Beyond the Horizon.** Curiously, John Reed later wrote a one-act play, *The Eternal Quadrangle*, satirizing the vogue for plays containing *ménages à trois*. During this summer, Louise also wrote a one-act morality play, *The Game*, which was produced by the Provincetown Players with Reed in the role of Death. Along with Reed, she is said to have been present at the historic first reading of O'Neill's *Bound East for Cardiff** in the Provincetown house of George Cram Cook* and Susan Glaspell.*

Her relationship with O'Neill continued through 1916, and she followed him to Provincetown in the spring of 1917, where he had returned to write in peace. There the affair was resumed, and Louise used influence to have "Tomorrow,"* O'Neill's only published short story, accepted by *The Seven Arts*. She also visited New London with him.

In June 1917, after a bitter quarrel with Reed over his extramarital affair, she went to France as a war correspondent, where she was unsuccessful in getting even one story published. She returned in July 1917, and in August she and Reed went to Russia to look at the Bolshevik Revolution. From this came Louise Bryant's *Six Red Months in Russia* (1918) though in fact she spent only four months there, and *Mirrors of Moscow* (1923), as well as other articles, written after her return in February 1918. Having left Reed in Russia at the end of January, she attempted to renew her relationship with O'Neill, who was by then living with Agnes Boulton.* Louise, believing that O'Neill's new love was merely a rebound romance as a result of her own departure, importuned him in impassioned letters to return to her in New York, even after his marriage to Agnes on April 12, 1918. In *Part of a Long Story* (1958, pp. 113–122), Agnes Boulton gives her account of the relationship and of Louise's unsuccessful attempt to resume it. She believed that Louise was actually "a very artful woman" given to twisting the truth, particularly when she circulated the false story that she had broken O'Neill's heart and had turned him out of her apartment after her return from Russia, with the result that O'Neill had become drunk and followed her around. The truth was that O'Neill had refused to see her, apparently breaking off the relationship in a letter which has not survived.

John Reed returned to New York in April 1918, and during the rest of that year, he and Louise were involved in speaking engagements and then in a Senate hearing before a committee investigating Bolshevism in 1919. In late February 1919, Louise Bryant undertook a national speaking tour on the subject of the Bolshevik Revolution, while Reed finished writing *Ten Days that Shook the World*. In September 1919, he left for Russia, arriving there in November. In an attempt to return to the United States, he was imprisoned in Finland for five months, finally returning to Moscow in June 1920. Louise Bryant left New York clandestinely in August 1920, and the two met in Moscow on September 15, 1920, after Reed's return from the great Bolshevik meeting at Baku. On September 28, he became ill with typhus and died October 17, 1920. On October 24, 1920, he was buried in the Kremlin.

In 1923, Louise Bryant married William C. Bullitt, later Franklin D. Roosevelt's ambassador to the Soviet Union, after his divorce from Ernesta Drinker. A daughter, Anne Moen, was born in 1924. This was an excellent society marriage, for Bullitt was a wealthy man with homes in both Paris and New York. But ultimately it was unsuccessful, and Louise began to drink heavily. In 1930 he divorced her and arranged for the divorce records to be closed permanently. She went downhill after that, becoming involved in increasingly odd situations, even bringing suit against a lover, Julius Mack, in 1932. She seems to have had very little money, and finally in 1935 she left Greenwich Village, where she was drinking heavily, and went to Paris, where she is said to have taken to drugs as well, finally dying of a cerebral hemorrhage after climbing the stairs to her hotel room on January 6, 1936. As late as the last months of her life, she was still talking about John Reed and her love for him.

On the whole, Louise Bryant is a peripheral figure in journalism, having had a gushing, exclamatory style which has frequent non sequiturs. Her importance resides in her relationship with the men in her life, particularly Eugene O'Neill, rather than in her own artistic talents and achievements. She was given to romanticizing herself, and as a result her comments on her origins and actions are often suspect. She liked dressing in Russian style and projected the image of a thoroughly emancipated and fearless woman. *See*: Barbara Gelb, (1973), and Rosenstone (1975) as well as brief mentions in biographies of O'Neill. Note also the romantic, and erroneous, film *Reds* (1981) in which Louise Bryant does meet O'Neill after her return from Russia, something that never happened.

BURGESS, Fred. In *Recklessness*,* chauffeur to Arthur Baldwin* and lover of Mildred Baldwin.* Fred is about twenty-five, tall, clean-shaven, dark complexioned, ''with clear-cut regular features, big brown eyes and black curly hair." He wears the gray uniform of a chauffeur with black puttees. He is shown as the lover of Mildred, wishing to leave Baldwin's employ, but is waiting until he has passed his engineering examinations and can support her. He understands what it is to be poor and with considerable practicality knows that she will not be able to put up with economic hardship. Apparently Gene,* Mildred's maid, is also in love with him and according to Baldwin is Burgess's lover. However, Baldwin's motives for this statement are suspect. Gene reveals Mildred's affair to Baldwin, who arranges for Fred to rush off at high speed to the village in an automobile whose steering mechanism Baldwin knows to be defective. Fred drives into a boulder and is killed.

Fred Burgess has very little to say in the play, in which the major emphasis is on the conflict between Mildred and her husband. At first sight, one might consider him the equivalent of Jean in Strindberg's *Miss Julie*, but the resemblance is quite superficial. Burgess is really a stock character, very lightly drawn, but with a curiously practical streak which leads him to investigate Mr. Baldwin's past, discovering a shady business deal.

BURKE, Mat. In *"Anna Christie"*,* he is a powerfully-built young stoker of about thirty. He is about six feet tall, "his face handsome in a hard, rough, bold, defiant way." On his first appearance, he has just survived a shipwreck and has been rowing alone for the past two days because his three companions were too exhausted to help him. He takes pride in the fact that with his own strength he was able to defeat the sea which had wanted to claim them. When he meets Anna Christopherson* on board her father's coal barge which has rescued them, he is overwhelmed with admiration. This affection speedily ripens into love, and at their very first meeting he proposes marriage, because he has had such little chance to meet "a fine dacent girl—the like of yourself, now." The two obviously have something in common in their love of the sea. Though he hates some of its aspects, Mat knows that otherwise he would be "digging spuds in the muck from dawn to dark." He is confident that with his strength he can meet all adversity.

What he is unable to meet is the shock to his idealism when he discovers Anna's past. He had said that as long as she had not been married to anyone else nothing mattered, but the knowledge that she had been earning a living from prostitution appalls him. Finally Anna convinces him that she has indeed changed, but he makes her swear on his mother's crucifix that she has not *loved* any other man but him. Anna does as she is asked, but Mat is concerned that the oath may not be valid since she professes no religion. However, he realizes that his love of and need for her are such that he must and will take her "naked word."

In the final reconciliation scene, Christopher Christopherson,* Anna's father, gives his consent, and Mat accepts the fact that even if Anna is a "Luthers", " 'Tis the will of God, anyway." However, even this moment of joy is tempered by Chris's gloomy premonitions of disaster. Who knows what the sea will have in store for them—all their plans of children and living all together in a little home may yet be frustrated. This is the subliminal message that makes Mat momentarily fearful along with Chris. However, he "banishes his superstitious premonitions with a defiant jerk of his head, grins up at Anna and drinks the toast she offers: Here's to the sea, no matter what?''

Mat Burke is a true child of the sea, reminiscent of Yank* in the S.S. *Glencairn** plays and the later Yank* in *The Hairy Ape.** He glories in his strength, and in his powerful physical build he considers himself almost impregnable against the assaults of the sea. He has found his place! Nonetheless he has a softer, romantic side, as he falls so quickly in love with Anna, and a superstitious, almost reflective aspect when he momentarily agrees with Chris's fears. After all, their meeting was the result of a shipwreck, and the sea can also take away what it gives.

Mat Burke appears also in *"The Ole Davil"*,* the second draft of the play that ultimately became *"Anna Christie."* His role is essentially the same, but O'Neill developed his lines with more careful recreation of dialect/brogue. One curious little difference is Mat's reference to the alleged cowardice of the captain of the wrecked steamer as he prayed for help. He speaks of the ineffectual quality of the "prayers of a Protestant pup," a comment which foreshadows of the scene in which Mat asks Anna to what religion she adheres. But though the whole matter of religion is treated more fully in *"Anna Christie,"* this foreshadowing comment does not occur, and hence the situation is contrived. At the end of "The Ole Davil," when Mat and Anna are to be married, the young people do not take Chris's anger at the sea seriously, and the play ends in laughter. In *"Anna Christie,"* however, Mat briefly shares Chris's qualms.

BUTLER, the ship's cook of the *Triton* in *Gold.** He is "past middle age," emaciated and dressed in ragged clothing. He shares his private store of water with the ship's boy, Abel,* because Abel has not, like other members of the crew, treated Butler with contempt. He along with Abel is murdered by Jimmy Kanaka,* with the connivance of the rest of the crew, who wish to keep their "buried treasure" for themselves. It is significant that Butler is the first to recognize the treasure as "junk," possibly because unlike those who discovered the chest of "jewels," he is not blinded by greed. He shows compassion to Abel and is thereby shown to be clear-eyed and not corrupt.

BYTH, James Findlater. Press agent and advance man for James O'Neill,* the father of Eugene O'Neill. Byth was allegedly a war correspondent in South Africa during the Boer War, but by the time O'Neill met him again, after his own return from South America in 1911, Byth had become a hopeless alcoholic denizen of James J. Condon's* (Jimmy-the-Priest's*) bar. He is the original of James ("Jimmy Tomorrow") Cameron* in *The Iceman Cometh.** He is also the original of Jimmy Anderson* in "Tomorrow,"* O'Neill's only published short story. Byth attempted suicide by jumping out of a window and died without regaining consciousness.

"BY WAY OF OBIT," an uncompleted series of eight monologue-plays designed more for a book than for the stage. Each would consist of one scene, with "one character, one marionette (life-size) The Good Listener." (Floyd, 1981, p. 346). The Work Diary lists the proposed eight plays as follows:

11/29/40 Pig H[ell]. H[ole]. play
11/29/40 R.R. man play
11/29/40 J[immy]. the P[riest]. idea of guy who recited Homer
11/29/40 Hughie*
11/29/40 Minstrel man idea
12/1/40 Miser one
12/2/40 Rudie (the chambermaid play
12/2/40 Blemie one (Information from Floyd, 1981, p. 346).

Of these proposed works, only *Hughie* was completed.

C

CABOT, Abbie Putnam. In *Desire under the Elms*,* wife of Ephraim Cabot* and lover of Ephraim's son, Eben Cabot.* Abbie is the thirty-five-year-old third wife of the seventy-six-year-old Ephraim. She is a buxom, good-looking woman whose face is marred by an obstinate chin and a "gross sensuality." She has married Ephraim solely to gain possession of a home and the farm. She had a hard life until Ephraim came along. Yet she has no love for him, only a desire to find a place where she can belong, and in fact she has a physical aversion to her husband.

When Abbie arrives at the farm, she is attracted by Eben's youthful good looks and uses her most seductive tone to gain his acceptance of her as his mother. Eben, however, sees her as a conniving interloper, a harlot who sold herself for the farm. Two months later, on a hot afternoon, Abbie accosts Eben. Clearly their physical attraction is almost unbearable, and she takes advantage of the situation. She herself is a ripe woman who responds to the stirrings of nature, and indeed finds herself one with it.

Eben fights against her, arousing her jealousy. However, as Abbie had predicted, nature proves too strong for Eben. Even though he repulses her once more, she finally persuades him to court her in the best parlor, the room in which his mother's funeral wake had taken place. When the two of them consummate their love in that room, it becomes theirs, and the restless spirit of Eben's mother vanishes. Here the myth of Phaedra and Hyppolytus is relived in the union of the two, together with the inclusion of the Oedipus situation by which Eben supplants his father.

By the following year, a son is born to Abbie and Eben, as all the world well knows, except Ephraim. But the balance of the lovers' existence has been disturbed by the arrival of their child; Eben detests pretending that what is rightfully his belongs to his father—just like the farm. The farm, fertility, and ownership all become one to him, but when Ephraim taunts him by saying that the farm will go to Abbie or "his" son, Eben wishes the child dead, turning against Abbie in hatred. She, by now the slave of her destiny and physical desire, smothers the baby, in an attempt to regain Eben's love. Here again, O'Neill uses myth, this time that of Medea, who killed her own children because she had lost the love of Jason. But, as Abbie herself later realizes, she should have killed the old man, because Eben is devastated by the discovery that Abbie has murdered his own flesh and blood. All she can do is attempt to make him understand her motivation—that she loves him, Eben, better than anything else in the world. She could bear anything, if only Eben would again say he loved her.

But Eben rushes off to inform the Sheriff, and Abbie is left to face the Old Testament wrath of Ephraim. When Eben returns, Abbie discovers with strange joy that he has come to claim participation in the crime and plans to share her punishment because of his love for her. As they depart from the farm in the custody of the Sheriff, they go toward a rising sun and into a new existence which will be made easier by love, a love that, like that expressed by Saint Paul, surpasses all other virtues.

The character of Abbie, then, must be taken on a symbolic, nonliteral level as well as a literal one. She is the modern embodiment of a series of mythic resonances, coming from Ancient Greece, through Old and New Testaments, American history, Sigmund Freud, and even Nietzsche, even though he saw women as little more than recreation for mankind. She is Phaedra attempting to seduce Hippolytus, Jocasta who loves her son as child and husband, Medea who murders her children, and the victim of a malevolent deity and hence unable to escape her destiny. This deity is both the wrathful God of Puritanism and the Old Testament and the Apollonian God of Nietzsche. Yet even in her tragedy she finds some consolation in the other side of the Nietzschean dichotomy, that is, in the Dionysian ecstasy of her love for Eben. It is this deeper level of meaning that makes this play an important contribution to the American theatre and makes the character of Abbie Putnam tragic, rather than merely weak or pathetic.

CABOT, Eben, third son of Ephraim Cabot* and half-brother of Simeon Cabot* and Peter Cabot.* In *Desire under the Elms,** Eben is twenty-five years old, "tall and sinewy," dark and rather good-looking, but with an expression that "is resentful and defensive. His defiant, dark eyes remind one of a wild animal's in captivity." There seem to be smouldering fires within him and "a fierce repressed vitality." He hates his father, as do his older half-brothers. Eben, the son of Ephraim's gentle second wife, hates his father for having worked her to death, but even more for having held the farm as his. Ephraim had married Eben's mother because she had a legitimate claim to ownership of the farm. Now the son believes that his father has stolen his rightful inheritance. Of all three sons Eben is most like his father in his attachment to this hard-scrabble farm. He buys up the shares of his half-brothers, using Ephraim's own secret hoard of gold, and wishes for the death of his father (who has been away for two months), for then the farm would be his, and with the death of family hatred his mother's unquiet ghost would be exorcized.

But Ephraim continues his pattern of filching from his son and outdoing him in everything. Even when visiting the town prostitute Eben knows that his father has preceded him. Now, when Ephraim returns with a new wife, Abbie Putnam Cabot,* the cycle continues and Eben realizes that Abbie will get the farm. But despite his initial hatred of her, he is eventually seduced by her. In mythic terms, Phaedra has seduced Hippolytus, and Oedipus has slept with his mother. In Freudian terms the son has supplanted the father. But love has also entered this house, and with the consummation of Abbie and Eben's relationship, the ghost of Eben's mother leaves; her hostile spirit has turned kind.

As a result of this affair a son is born to Abbie. Ephraim rejoices in it as his, though all the world knows differently. Once again Ephraim has stolen something belonging to Eben, and the son commences to hate the child, especially when Ephraim taunts him with the announcement that the farm will go to the child or Abbie. He now wishes for the death of the child and turns against Abbie. Several myths now come together here: the Oedipus myth, the myth of Phaedra and Hippolytus, and now the myth of Jason and Medea. Like Medea, Abbie kills her child, but her motivation is to regain the love of Eben.

His first reaction is to impose the same Old Testament justice that his father espouses. Abbie has sinned in killing her own flesh and blood and therefore she must pay; while on another level, the son would have preferred the death of his father, a Freudian view. Therefore his initial reaction is to follow the path of the angry God of retributive justice and he informs on Abbie. But then Eben wavers as his instinctual side comes into the ascendant. He is a child of nature and the land, subject to their rhythms and laws, the laws which brought them together in love. For that reason he returns to the farm to share Abbie's blame and punishment. Both have sinned in the name of love, and both must share their doom together. They depart from the farm for prison as the sun is rising and go forth in a shared devotion, almost a transfiguration.

Both Eben and Abbie are characters who seem to be doomed by some malevolent deity, partly because they are both too close to the natural order of human existence. They are the two who seem to be most attuned to the rhythms of nature and therefore cannot escape their destiny. It is important to note the significance of the farm for both of the lovers. For Abbie it means home and a place to belong and set down roots; for Eben it is a place of kinship with the earth, a small world insulated against what is outside. For him the stone walls that imprisoned his brothers are protection, where he lives with the spirit of his mother but also with classic Oedipal hatred of his father. Yet he is the only son who can have any comprehension of what the farm means both to him and his father, and therefore he must wrest ownership from his father. Eben and the farm are one.

Though he does have some of his father's characteristics, Eben is not quite so punitive in his conception of God. He also follows the Dionysian God of instinct, even more than his father, and in surrender to that God he achieves a different kind of fertility. Nonetheless, when he hears of his child's murder, the Apollonian, judgmental, wrathful God makes him inform on Abbie, in unexpected contrast to Ephraim, who says he would never have told. This episode of Puritanism, of Old Testament rage, is short-lived, and in love he returns to Abbie. He then offers her a love which renounces everything, including life, to share in her punishment by accepting part of the guilt. This is the love, the charity of which Paul spoke in the New Testament; "Now there remaineth Faith, Hope, and Love, these three; and the greatest of these is Love."

Obviously, Eben and his love for Abbie are not to be taken literally, otherwise one would have merely a melodrama of incest. In bringing his material together on a strong basis of myths reinterpreted in an American setting, O'Neill has obtained resonances from the Greeks, the Old and New Testaments, Nietzsche, Freud, and American history. As a result he has communicated the sense of doom, the feelings of pity and terror of which Aristotle spoke. Oedipus, Hippolytus, Judas Iscariot, and finally Jesus as interpreted by Saint Paul, all provide qualities of Eben Cabot, and it is through the sensitive use of all these myths that O'Neill has managed to give extraordinary power to the characters of a play which remains one of the finest in the American theatre.

CABOT, Ephraim. In *Desire under the Elms*,* father of Simeon Cabot,* Peter Cabot,* and Eben Cabot,* and husband of Abbie Putnam Cabot.* He is seventy-five years old, "gaunt, with great wiry power, but stoop-shouldered from toil." His face is as hard as the rocks on his farm, yet at the same time "there is a weakness in it, a petty pride in its own narrow strength." His eyes are close-set and myopic.

Ephraim is the archetypal New England Puritan, the believer in hard work as a means to glorification, the man who thinks himself to have a pipeline to the deity and actually hears God speaking to him. His God is an angry god, one of toil and punishment, not one of consolation, and as a result, Ephraim's life has become one of great loneliness. However, the "weakness" in his face indicates his occasional "lapses" from this harsh creed. Once he went away from his rock-riddled farm, following others from the locality to the Middle West where he found the land so rich that one merely had to plant the crops and sit back until they grew. But this ease distressed him, and finally he heard God speaking to him to say that this is not what He wanted. "God's hard, not easy," as Ephraim constantly says. Cabot believes that God, in fact, ordered him back to the farm, where he built his stone walls and forced the earth into fertility. Ephraim has also married three times. First to a woman like himself, a hard worker, who bore Simeon and Peter. Second, to Eben's mother, a softer person, but whose parents had some claim to the farm; she died, like her predecessor, worked to death by Eben's driving destiny. The third marriage, that to Abbie Putnam, a much younger women, is a curious response to the stirrings of nature within Ephraim in a spring some twenty-five years after his second wife's death.

This indicates not so much a "lapse" from service to the severe God of Puritanism, but rather an instinctive unity with the very farm itself. As he himself recognizes, Ephraim has become in effect the rock-strewn, hardscrabble farm, both in its difficulty and its fertility. For this reason, he identifies with both the land and its livestock. In fact, the only place where he really finds comfort is sleeping in the barn with the cows. This identity with nature sends him forth to seek a wife, to gratify his loneliness, but also, as he reads it, in response to the will of an Old Testament God. He wants to have a suitable son to whom he can leave the farm, but none of his boys seems right. Each is a rebel against the hardness of the father, though their responses are different. After years of slavery to the old man, the older boys decide to follow the demands of the "easy" God and go to California for gold. Nonetheless, they are so identified with the farm by their very "bovine" appearance that they regret leaving it. Significantly, they relate to the "fust-rate, number one prize stock" they have bred, not to the imprisoning stone walls they have built to make the land fertile. Eben, despite his alleged "softness," is the closest to the old man in his desire to own the farm, in his vengefulness, and finally in his acceptance of punishment from the "hard" God.

But Ephraim is more than merely a God-fearing, God-obsessed patriarch of the New England persuasion. He is the Oedipal father whom, in Freudian psychological theory, the son seeks to destroy and supplant in his mother's bed. He is also briefly a participant in an almost Dionysian revel when he capers like a satyr at the celebration of the birth of Abbie's child by Eben. He then becomes the personification of the punishing God when he hears of the murder of the child, but in momentary despair thinks of renouncing his harsh God, following his "easy" one to California, and destroying the results of his service to the harsh God of Puritanism or, in the Nietzschean terms, the Apollonian God. For this reason, he will turn the livestock loose and burn everything, but by the end of the play, the hardness has won and Ephraim's life on the farm will continue. He is hounded by his own destiny and must pay for even his minor attempts to escape. In this manner, Ephraim becomes a mythic figure, a combination of the forces of New England Puritanism, Greek myth, Freudian psychology, and Nietzschean theory; in addition, he is emblematic of Nature herself, which cannot be denied. He should not be taken literally, though such a reading is possible, but symbolically, against the background of these varied sources. The key to his character is the long monologue in Part II, Scene ii, in which his dialect reaches a level of poetic eloquence that O'Neill does not always manage. Here, too, the excellent use of Biblical quotation when lyricism is beyond Ephraim's personal vocabulary is both totally in character and indeed inspired.

But one must not forget the ineffable loneliness of the man, which must also arouse pity, as well as terror for the fate which engulfs him. In his own way, he has sought love and wants to love. He is sensitive to the loneliness and the coldness he finds within his house and among other people. His farewell words to Abbie indicate these qualities: "Ye'd ought t'loved me. I'm a man. If ye'd loved me, I'd never told no Sheriff on ye no matter what ye did, if they was t'brile me alive." This loss of Abbie makes him "lonesomer than ever"; but then the wrathful God controls him again as he returns to find Eben and Abbie in each other's arms, awaiting the Sheriff: "Ye'd ought t'be both hung on the same limb an' left thar t'swing in the breeze an' rot—a warnin't t'old fools like me t'b'ar their lonesomeness alone—an' fur young fools like ye t'hobble their lust." His theology is bleak and seems to offer no true happiness: his vision of heaven is to have a farm "up thar," and one wonders whether the cultivation will be as difficult "thar" as on earth. The Sheriff's concluding remark contains tremendous irony: "It's a jim-dandy farm, no denyin'. Wished I owned it!" Ephraim Cabot is a titanic figure who must both fight and serve an angry God, and in a sense he is a symbol of a singularly bleak view of the human condition.

CABOT, Peter. In *Desire under the Elms*,* second son of Ephraim Cabot,* brother of Simeon Cabot,* and half-brother of Eben Cabot.* Peter is thirty-seven years old, heavily built, fleshy, and "bovine" in countenance. He has worked resentfully on his father's farm all his life and cannot wait to leave. Although he has some sensitivity to the beauty of the sunset, it reminds him of "gold in the sky—in the West—Golden Gate—Californi-a! Goldest West!— fields o'gold." For him, as for Simeon, the stone walls they have helped to build on the farm imprison them, and he is happy to take from Eben his thirty pieces of gold (a significant number, reminiscent of the price paid Judas Iscariot) to try his fortune and find freedom in California. He is a trifle more practical and less sensitive than Simeon but he too has some regrets about leaving the farm—for the "number one prize stock" that he and his brother have raised. He hates his father and, like his brother, possesses some symbolic significance as a character. An unwilling follower of the Protestant ethic, Peter is a son who must revolt against patriarchal tyranny, the Puritan wrathful God of the Old Testament, or the Nietzschean Apollonian God. As he leaves he becomes the ecstatic, intoxicated follower of the "easy" God his father forsook; and in his departing song and dance he, with his brother, foreshadows the boasting, drunken, Dionysiac satyr-dance performed by Ephraim Cabot at the celebration for the birth of Abbie Putnam Cabot's* son. As a departing act, Peter and Simeon heave rocks through the parlor window.

CABOT, Simeon. In *Desire under the Elms*,* oldest son of Ephraim Cabot,* brother of Peter Cabot,* and half-brother of Eben Cabot.* Simeon is thirty-nine years old, heavily built, fleshy, and "bovine" in countenance. Like Peter, Simeon has worked resentfully on his father's farm all his life and cannot wait to leave it. His character, however, is not as hard as Peter's. When Simeon sees a golden sunset he recalls his wife Jenn, dead for the past eighteen years: "She'd hair long's a hoss's tail—and yaller like gold." His occasional recollection of her "makes it lonesome." For him, as for Peter, the farm's stone walls imprison them and he is happy to take from Eben his thirty pieces of gold (a significant number, reminiscent of the price paid Judas Iscariot) to free himself from slavery to his father and to seek his fortune in California. Nonetheless, he identifies with the "number one prize stock" that he and his brother have helped raise. Significantly, it is Simeon who announces the theme of escape from prison when he speaks of the walls "crumblin' and tumblin!" and takes the gate off the hinges: "We harby 'bolishes shet gates, an' open gates, an' all gates, by thunder!" He hates his father and as a character possesses the same symbolic significance as Peter: he is the son who must revolt against patriarchal dominance and exploitation and against the Puritan, Old Testament, wrathful God, or the Nietzschean Apollonian God. Also like Peter, he foreshadows the Dionysiac satyr-performance of Ephraim at the celebration for the birth of Abbie Putnam Cabot's* son. As a last act of defiance, Simeon joins Peter in heaving rocks through the parlor window.

CADE, Leda. In the scenario of *The Calms of Capricorn*,* a prostitute and passenger on the clipper *Dream of the West* on its voyage from New York to San Francisco. She is the companion of Ben Graber,* a failed banker who seems to have ruined himself for her. She is a beautiful woman of twenty-five, with a "frankly sensual face. She represents femininity, emotion and instinct. Her appearance strikes everyone into stunned silence." She later tells her story. On the advice of her dying mother, she married an old family friend, thirty years older than the seventeen-year-old girl. Leda obeyed but began to feel that she was in effect prostituting herself to him and so decided to undertake the profession on a paying basis. She sees beneath the social "masks" with which each character hides his or her true self, forcing them to strip them away. Her purpose is to make individuals trust their instincts, change their luck, attempt to fulfill their dreams, and admit the existence of sensuality. She goes to bed with almost every man on the ship and teaches Elizabeth Warren* how to use her body to get what she wants, namely, Jonathan Harford.* Almost every character in the action is defined in relationship to Leda, and she exercises a kind of superiority over them because of her amoral concept of life. However, she meets her match in Wolfe Harford,* the deliberately detached gambler, who refuses to commit himself to anyone or anything. Consequently, she sets out to ensnare him because he is a challenge, the only person who remains impervious to her, and finds herself almost enslaved to him. When her companion, Ben Graber, the failed banker, finally loses everything through playing cards with Wolfe, she forces Graber to wager herself, his last possession, as a means of freeing himself from his conscience. When Wolfe wins her and tries to return her to Graber, who refuses her, Leda turns to Wolfe: "You think you can get rid of me,...Never! I love you, you fool—can't you see I love you?"

Leda Cade is a curious character, a kind of inverted Cybel* in *The Great God Brown*,* who acts as a catalyst in the play, forcing most characters to re-evaluate themselves. She represents instinct and emotion, a gambler's daring, and yet, as Sara Melody* Harford says, she is not quite as hard a woman as she pretends to be. In the process of drafting the *Calms of Capricorn* scenario, O'Neill does not seem to have developed her character fully, as his three choices of names may indicate: Goldie, Lisa, and lastly Leda.

CALIGULA. In *Lazarus Laughed*,* a twenty-one-year-old Roman noble, later Caesar. He wears a mask of sensuality and calculating ambition, but beneath his half-mask he has a mouth which is delicate, "weak but domineering." He has an air of "boyish cruelty...naively insensitive to any human suffering but its own." He believes himself to be utterly ruthless and celebrates death rather than life. In this way he acts as a total opposition to Lazarus,* who affirms life. However, his ambition and cruelty do not satisfy him, and he longs to be able to laugh joyously like Lazarus, whom, unwillingly, he realizes that he loves. Eventually he succeeds in his ambition to become Caesar through strangling Tiberius Caesar,* as Lazarus dies at the stake. Then, Caligula runs the gamut of emotions through laughter and acceptance of the life-affirming principle of Lazarus, then grief and remorse, and finally, the knowledge that the world is not yet ready for Lazarus: "Men forget!" But Lazarus's life has not been in vain, for he has managed, momentarily, to touch the heart of Caligula; and this time Caligula Caesar, who has in the past found himself dancing unwillingly to Lazarus's tune, comes to know himself.

CALMS OF CAPRICORN, THE, the proposed seventh part of the abandoned eleven-play cycle devoted to the fortunes of the Harford family entitled "A Tale of Possessors, Self-Dispossessed."* The central theme of the cycle, and also of this proposed play, was to be the corrupting influence of possessions upon their owners, and the Harford family was designed as a microcosm of the development of American society from its foundation in 1775 to 1932. The scenario for this play survives and it has been developed into play form by Donald Gallup. (*See A note on text*, below.) The action covers the years 1857–1858 in four acts and ten scenes. O'Neill began work on this proposed drama in 1931. When the cycle consisted of four plays, this one stood first and gave its name to the entire corpus.

Act I, Scene i: "Potato field on Sara's farm, late afternoon, Spring 1857." This scene is supposed to be the same as the Epilogue of *More Stately Mansions*ation of the script which does not appear in the published American version and which was not staged in the American production). Cato,* an elderly former slave, is hoeing and grumbling about the problems of being a free man in Massachusetts, recalling the companionship of his fellow slaves and wishing that he had never allowed himself to be talked into running away and that Simon Harford* had never purchased his freedom. Sara Melody* Harford enters. She is age forty-seven and presents a mixture of aristocratic and peasant characteristics. While her nose is small and straight and her ears small, her hands and feet are large, her ankles thick, and her mouth has an air of sensuality about it, with a jaw that shows masculine determination. She remains a "fine figure" of a woman, but "there is a look of resigned sadness in her eyes" and some streaks of white in her hair. She offers to help Cato, who is appalled at what visiting white quality might think, telling her that "Massa Harford" has specifically told him to prevent Sara's working on the farm.

Captain Enoch Payne,* captain of the clipper ship *Dream of the West*, enters with his wife, Nancy Drummond Payne.* He is in his sixties, a man of average height, "solid and imposing," with white hair, giving "an impression of conservatism." His wife is thirty-eight, pretty, with "brown hair,... [and] big brown eyes,...shy, bashful, reserved, gentle." She shows great respect for her husband and he shows love for her. They have just returned from a voyage and discuss Ethan Harford,* Sara's eldest son, who is the second mate on the ship. Captain Payne perceives Ethan as a fool who would sacrifice his ship to break a speed record. The captain leaves Nancy with Sara, who asks the younger woman whether she is tired of life on the ship. Nancy replies that the clipper is now like home to her and that this new life has healed the wound caused by the death of her baby five years ago.

They then turn to a discussion of Ethan, and Nancy recommends that Ethan be encouraged to change ships because there is no opportunity for advancement for him in his present post. She draws attention to Ethan's "fierce pride in preserving his independence" and also notes that he is "so sensitive under his hard reserve, and so isolated and lonely in his freedom." Sara says that this is "the touch of the poet" he has inherited from his father and says that she will indeed try to persuade the stubborn Ethan to make a move. At this, Nancy seems a trifle frightened and begs Sara not to reveal what she has said. They then turn to a discussion of Simon Harford,* Sara's husband, who has just recovered from an illness. He has ceased work on his book because the task was becoming impossibly large, and he has been accompanying his second son, Honey Harford,* a tin peddler.

At this, Ethan Harford enters, a young man of twenty-eight, who gives the impression of being taller than medium height. He has "a visionary's intense blue eyes set in a square, handsome, hawk-nosed face." Nancy is embarrassed by his arrival and hurriedly leaves. Sara tests him by observing how pretty Nancy is, but Ethan says he hasn't noticed because he has "no interest in women." He has not returned home after his last few voyages because he is ashamed of still being a second mate, but he is back now because he is disturbed over Sara's reports of his father's illness. They discuss Simon Harford and his project to write on "The Meaning of Life." Sara tells Ethan that her husband has completely given up on the project, realizing that it is all a fake; and though he now seems happy working with Honey, he appears to be driving himself. Ethan speaks of the inability of the Harfords to belong. Simon should have chosen to live solitarily because he has always "remained a child first tied to his mother's apron strings, then to yours." Sara suggests that Ethan consider changing ship, since he seems unhappy with his present post, but Ethan launches into an exposition of his love-hate relationship with the sea and his desire to master that element. He had once perceived the sea as freedom, but he finds himself still obeying orders. He wishes to tear gold from the mountains and to conquer. Sara asks why he has not gone after the gold in California, and Ethan reproaches her with her desire for material possessions; he wants something intangible, "Victory

over the sea—and so, freedom and rebirth.'' For this triumph he will pay any
price, be it the wreck of his ship or his own death. They briefly discuss his
assessment of his brothers; he likes Honey, dislikes Jonathan Harford,* and
respects Wolfe Harford* ''because he respects nothing.'' Sara tells him, ''it's
a hard fate for a woman to have been the daughter and wife and mother of men
touched with the curse of the poet'' because they always seek the moon.

At this Simon enters, accompanied by Honey Harford. Simon is fifty but is
so emaciated that he looks older. His eyes ''have a groping and bewildered
stare.'' He is tall, with ''a long Yankee face, with Indian resemblances.'' Honey
is twenty-four, ''all peasant Irish,'' with a tall, heavy figure ''beginning to run
a little to fat.'' He seems an amiable soul with eyes which ''sparkle...[with]
sly, droll humor.'' Sara and Honey leave, and Ethan and Simon discuss their
relationship and their basic identity of soul, so alike that they have always been
strangers. Simon has ''a dream of unity'' while Ethan has ''a lust for power and
possession—but in the spirit, not the flesh.'' Simon is sure that Ethan will
probably lose his battle to ''possess'' the sea, but in losing he will find a ''final
victory and release.'' He believes that his son is doing the only thing possible
for him: ''to choose a dream and then to follow that dream to the end.'' [O'Neill
did not fully think through the father-son relationship here.] Sara returns and
suggests that Simon go inside. Ethan leaves, and Simon speaks to Sara of his
love for life and for her. He wishes to give himself ''to life and love and beauty''
rather than material possessions, and at this moment he feels that he and Sara
are truly one. He embraces her, and Sara realizes that he is shivering. She tries
to hustle him indoors, but as she hugs him to her he says he ''is warmed in the
warmth of your heart...warmed forevermore.''

Act I, Scene ii: The farmhouse sitting room, about ten (or fourteen) days
later, two days after Simon's death from pneumonia. The four Harford sons are
waiting for the undertaker. Jonathan Harford, the third son, looks like his father;
he is twenty-five, ''with a long New England bony face.'' He appears older than
he is, with ''a tense nervous vitality'' tempered with self-discipline and self-
confidence. Wolfe Harford, the second son, is twenty-seven ''tall and thin,
handsome, distinguished, fastidious,'' who presents a facade ''of smiling indifference.'' Jonathan suggests that they sell the farm and go to California to help
Sara forget and make up to her for the life she has had while ministering to
Simon's craziness. Honey observes that Simon was not crazy but was really a
poet. When asked his opinion of Jonathan's project, Ethan contemptuously disclaims all interest in ''money-grubbing values,'' while Wolfe agrees to go through,
without any particular enthusiasm. Honey, however, will go anywhere where
money is to be made, but then, ''conscience-stricken,'' he thinks of Sara, who
is grieving bitterly. He brings her into the room, and they perform their parts
in the service Simon has dictated for them: ''each has part of a poem to read,
then Honey a verse of a song to sing,'' and Sara reads a letter Simon has left
for her, telling her that she must forget him and embark on a new life of freedom.
Sara ''reacts to this with reproachful, despairing tenderness,'' regretting that she

had ever forced her husband into business, recalling his poetic soul, speaking of the glory of the love he had given to her, and recounting his relationship to her as her lover, husband, and child. As the undertaker arrives, she returns once more to look on his body, begging him who had always been withdrawn from her; "only this once—give me all of you for the all of me!" Then she realizes that now Simon has found freedom, even from her, and that he has also set her free to do what she has always wanted with the assistance of her sons. But then she berates herself for her greed and hopes Simon has not heard. All this time her comments are punctuated by the sound of hammering as the coffin is closed.

Act II, Scene i: "After-cabin of the clipper ship *Dream of the West* at dock in New York six weeks later." In this scene, all the voyagers on this ship of fools are introduced. First Honey and Jonathan enter, exclaiming about the luxury of their stateroom. Then the Reverend Samuel Dickey,* a Protestant minister, arrives. He is thirty-four, "rather shabbily dressed,...slightly unctuous.... He wears glasses that give him a faintly myopic look." He is the cabin-mate of Wolfe Harford, who spends part of this scene and much of the remainder of the play occupied with solitaire, a game which suits him because of its pointlessness and total lack of commitment to anyone or anything. Sara and Nancy enter, Sara exclaiming over the quality of the accommodations and Honey teasing her about arriving too early. They discuss Wolfe's preoccupation with solitaire, and he articulates his philosophy of uninvolvement, of total detachment, which allows him to laugh at both himself and other people. Ethan has just been appointed first mate, despite Captain Payne's misgivings, because Thomas Hull,* the former one, has been told to stay ashore to recuperate from a heart attack. Wolfe, when asked if he is not "enthusiastic" over Ethan's promotion, replies that he would first have to be certain "that it is fortunate to get what one wants."

The next passengers to appear are the owner of the ship, Theodore Warren,* and his daughter, Elizabeth Warren.* Mr. Warren is forty-eight, tall, successful-looking, and is dressed with expensive conservatism. Elizabeth is eighteen, "tall, dark, slender, with a boyish figure [and] a coldly beautiful, calm, disciplined exterior" which hides "intense nervous energy." The last two passengers then board; Ben Graber,* a banker, and his companion, Leda Cade.* Graber is fifty-three, somewhat gross, and slightly drunk. He has an aura of failure about him; he is "unkempt" with a furtive air. It is later revealed that Graber's bank "went bust" (III.i). Leda is an opulent, beautiful woman of twenty-five, with a "frankly sensual face. She is all emotion, intuitive, female instinct. ... Her appearance strikes everyone into stunned silence." Leda is introduced to the women by the captain, and she assesses them openly. She tells Sara she is sure they will understand each other and announces to Nancy, "I think I know you." She says the same thing to Elizabeth, adding cryptically that she knows "what you want from me." As for the men, Leda says she needs no introduction because she has "met them all before." She leaves as Warren and Elizabeth are angered by what has occurred.

Suddenly Thomas Hull, the ex-first mate, enters, saying that he is well enough to make the trip. Payne is relieved, and Hull "caustically" tells Ethan to move his things from the first mate's cabin. Angered, Ethan leaves. Nancy is furious, and Leda comforts her with the possibility that Hull may fall overboard, "or we can give him a push." As Graber leaves the two women alone, Leda warns Nancy not to show her feelings so openly because others may notice. Ethan then returns, and Leda asks for an introduction. Nancy introduces her as Mrs. Graber, and Leda commiserates with Ethan, suggesting that bad luck can change. Hull then enters, treating Ethan insultingly. The young man at first says nothing, but goaded by a remark from Leda, he punches Hull on the jaw. The first mate falls down, hits his head on the stairs, and dies. Instantly Leda takes charge, sending Ethan out on deck, after asking if that was what he had "really meant." She tells Nancy to say that Hull fell while coming down the stairs and also suggests that Nancy is glad he is dead and would be pleased if "another old man" were also. Nancy denies it and shrieks at the thought. Leda joins her to give the impression of a scream of horror.

Act II, Scene ii: "The same, a few minutes later." Captain Payne has just verified that Hull is dead, and Warren notes it as an inauspicious omen. Nancy is barely in control and nearly gives everything away with her hysterical outburst that Ethan had nothing to do with Hull's death when Captain Payne calls him merely to tell him of his promotion. Warren attempts to shield his daughter from the knowledge of the death, while Leda suggests that it might wake her up to start living. Payne regrets the death of his old friend and turns with anger on Wolfe, who continues to play solitaire with a supreme indifference that Leda enjoys.

At that moment, Ethan arrives and, to Captain Payne's rage, expresses no sorrow for the death of the man with whom he had always been at enmity. Nonetheless, in reply to Ethan's query, Payne says that he will appoint Ethan first mate for this voyage only, "no promises beyond that," warning him not to increase sail when the captain is asleep and insisting on strict obedience to orders. With considerable prescience, he notes that Ethan has been promoted to both second mate and the first mate as the result of accidents and perhaps he hopes that a similar disaster will befall his captain. Nancy rushes to Payne, denying that Ethan wants him dead and saying that it is the same thing as saying that *she* wants her husband dead. As both men leave, Leda congratulates Nancy on her performance, and Sara comments that Leda is "a strange, hard woman, but not half as hard as you'd like to make out." She leads Nancy into her cabin. Left alone with Leda, Wolfe, who has started playing cards again, asks her whether Ethan really did murder Hull, saying that he's "interested in seeing Ethan get what he thinks he wants in order to watch him throw it away." As for himself, he doesn't want anything, not even Leda. But finally he agrees that he will bet *himself* against Leda that she will make him want her before the voyage is over. At this moment Graber and Honey enter, very drunk, from the forward part of the ship where they have been carousing with the gold-seekers. Discovering that Hull is dead, Graber runs to Leda as if for protection, and

Honey crosses himself. Mr. Dickey enters to say a service over the dead man, and Leda offers to sing a hymn, claiming that she owes her success to her religious upbringing. She sings "Fields of Eden" as Graber and Honey applaud and Dickey kneels beside the corpse to pray.

Act III, Scene i: The vessel, "becalmed in the South Atlantic in late November, evening, looking astern." The interior of Ethan's cabin is at right-center, front, and he is restlessly asleep. Above on the poop deck, grouped on either side of the mast, are Nancy, Sara, and Jonathan (on the right) and Warren, Elizabeth, and Dickey (on the left). They are seated on deck chairs, discussing the fact that they will probably not break the record of the *Flying Cloud*. Warren says that when the captain reprimanded Ethan for adding more sail during his watch, he, as owner, had approved; but now he is not so sure, remarking that when the possibility of achieving a record "is thrust on one," then one should "follow one's luck." Jonathan suggests that "one makes one's luck with one's will." Nancy replies, "that makes life so terrible," and Dickey says that "this's not a very Christian sentiment;" one should follow God's will and strive "to save one's soul." Jonathan claims he knows nothing of the soul, and he speaks of the importance of striving after a goal, and in that attempt one will find happiness or unhappiness as "by-products." Sara believes that "a woman often finds happiness by accepting unhappiness," while Elizabeth talks of the unimportance of love. The conversation turns to Ethan, whom Jonathan considers incapable of love, but Nancy defends him. Sara sensibly suggests that Nancy go to her cabin, and Elizabeth begins to discuss Leda, "Mrs. Graber." Elizabeth insists that Leda is evil, because she can feel her prying, and complains when Leda asks her, "What do you want?" But perhaps, her father suggests, Elizabeth has provoked such a response because she does not ignore Leda. The sound of singing is heard. Honey is with the gold-seekers, trying to learn everything they know so he can make use of it. Impatiently, Jonathan wishes for a wind, and Elizabeth suggests that their situation is the result of Leda's influence.

Left alone, Sara speculates on the desirability of a marriage between Elizabeth and Jonathan, while down below Nancy approaches Ethan's door, wanting to knock, but hesitating as Leda advises against chasing him. Leda draws an admission of love from Nancy and promises not to "squeal" on her. Leda then tells the story of her life. She was born of a good family, but her father died when she was young; and following the advice of her dying mother, she married an old friend of her father, a man thirty years older than she, who was a mere seventeen. She began to realize that all he wanted was money and her body, and she felt like a prostitute. Finally she decided that she might as well enjoy her role, and so she became a professional. Yet she took up with Graber because she felt sorry for him. She praises the healthiness of human copulation and promises that she will work to make Ethan discover that he loves Nancy, suggesting that Nancy should not be too much around him. Leda then enters Ethan's room, as Nancy leaves her own door slightly open to hear what happens. She speaks of Nancy's desire for him, and then kisses him.

On the poop deck Captain Payne joins Sara, telling her that he had a foreboding that their good sailing luck would not last and asks what is bothering Ethan. Is he in love, and if so, is it with Leda or Elizabeth? Sara suggests Leda, and Payne is relieved. Nonetheless, he is concerned about Nancy's strange behavior on this trip, because she seems to dislike him. Down below, Ethan comes out of his room and confronts Nancy, who stammers something about the calm. With this, he kisses her passionately, but then they break apart guiltily and Ethan rushes on deck to meet Payne's apology for their earlier quarrel. The Captain's action increases Ethan's feelings of guilt and rage, while Nancy, below, wishes that Payne would fall and die so that she can possess Ethan.

Act III, Scene ii: The same, the tenth day of the calm. Sails are set, but there is no wind. On the poop deck in the wheelhouse, the helmsman, Captain Payne, Graber, and Warren are playing cards. Elizabeth and Dickey are on deck, nearby. Sara and Jonathan are on deck forward of the mizzen sail. Nancy is in her cabin, while Leda and Honey are in Leda's. In a recess, Wolfe sits playing solitaire. The action on all these parts of the stage should be perceived as simultaneous, beginning as Leda finishes dressing after giving herself to Honey, who shows no trace of guilt. The song of the gold-seekers is heard, followed by a sea chantey, which interrupts Leda's jocular comments. She curses the song, and in the wheelhouse Warren tells Payne to stop the singing, which Payne sees as an emotional safety valve. The scene now moves to Jonathan and Leda. She tells the young man he should seduce Elizabeth so that she will marry him. The action then moves to Elizabeth and Dickey; she, too, damns the song and says she has lost faith in God. Jonathan, talking to Sara, suddenly realizes that the ship is losing way, going backward, and he swears that he will wipe sailing vessels off the face of the earth, because he hates the sea.

Sara and Jonathan discuss the various interrelations on the boat, Sara suggesting Elizabeth as a good match for Jonathan, who agrees that it would be a good business proposition. Jonathan is concerned that Nancy will make a fool of Ethan and wishes that Payne would die to solve their problems. Meanwhile, Dickey is stroking Elizabeth's arm as she upbraids him with too much interest in Leda, claiming that Leda will "end up committing fornication with every man on board." Elizabeth has even heard her father go to Leda. At this, the scene shifts to Warren, who sounds very angry as he plays cards with Graber, who is out-cheating him. The two discuss Leda, and Graber admits that they are not married. Dickey and Elizabeth are then heard continuing their conversation. He speaks of his love for her, but Elizabeth says that she plans to "marry a man with brains and ability who will be rich, whom I can help with my brains to become rich." She has come to realize that Nancy and Ethan are having an affair, and the scene shifts to the Captain, who is reaching the same conclusion. Then Nancy is seen in her room, longing for Ethan and speaking of her hate for Payne. The scene then moves to Leda and Honey, Leda saying that Wolfe would be the perfect match for herself.

This continual shifting of scene echoes the shifting relationships of the characters: Ethan, Honey, and Wolfe discuss Leda, then Sara and Elizabeth do the same, followed by Payne and Dickey. The clergyman says she is corrupting the whole ship, but he is too afraid to speak to her. Payne, stung by Dickey's remark that he is an old man, tries to remonstrate with Leda, but she manages to make him want her, even though he loves his wife. Leda seems to have cast a spell on all the characters, except Wolfe, who declares that he cannot love. Ethan maintains that possessions are all that count, and the only reason he has not possessed Nancy is honor. Meanwhile, Payne wishes for death, and Nancy in her room also hopes he will die. Contrapuntally, Ethan and Wolfe discuss the viability of dreams, Wolfe finally saying, ''I accept fate,'' while Ethan replies, ''I'll make fate.'' As Ethan leaves, he runs into Leda, who refuses to sleep with him because she knows he wants Nancy. Wolfe is the only man *she* wants, yet he scorns her. As eight bells sounds, the captain goes down the companionway, filled with a death wish, and slips as Nancy calls out to him to be careful (in a denial of her own secret wish). Captain Payne falls; both Nancy and Ethan think he is dead and embrace, but Payne is only injured. Momentarily, they both think of helping him into death but then deny it. Nancy, guilt-ridden, promises to nurse her husband.

Act III, Scene iii: The same on the twentieth day of the calm, with Warren and Graber playing cards in the wheelhouse while Wolfe looks on. Elizabeth and Dickey are on the left in the wheelhouse, Sara and Jonathan are below in Sara's stateroom, while Nancy sits by her husband's bunk. The same intercutting of scenes takes place, the action moving from place to place, unified by a single word. Nerves are strained. The card-players are quarrelling about cheating, while Warren upbraids Ethan, suggesting that Payne is a Jonah. Down below, Captain Payne opens his eyes and reads the hatred in Nancy's look, while above in the wheelhouse Warren praises her as a paragon because of the way she has nursed her husband.

Meanwhile, Dickey is not pawing Elizabeth, sure evidence that he, too, has been with Leda. She has made him feel innocent: ''There was no sin, no God! Life was innocent and beautiful, without guilt.'' Elizabeth wishes for a similar experience, for her nerves are made ragged with the everlasting song of the materialistic gold-seekers. She loathes Leda yet feels alive when she comes around. Slowly she is coming to Leda's conclusion ''that nothing matters except to want and to be wanted.'' But Elizabeth has no desires. She looks at her father cheating at cards, while Graber is trying desperately and unsuccessfully to lose. Warren speaks of wishing to marry her off but says that, ''like her mother, she's as cold as a dead fish.'' Stung, Elizabeth insists that Jonathan loves her, but Dickey says that even he had found her too cold. With this, she slaps his face, just as Leda appears and again asks, ''what do you want from me.'' Leda tells her she must make men want her physically, not for her money. Confidentially, Elizabeth says that she thinks Jonathan is interested, and Leda suggests that she give herself to him; ''You are only hiding from yourself your fear that men do not want you because they feel you cannot give yourself." Elizabeth says she will do so, and Leda challenges her to perform.

Leda moves to the wheelhouse to observe the card game, taunting Wolfe for his refusal to commit himself to the game as Elizabeth decides to seek out Jonathan. Dickey enters the wheelhouse to be snubbed by Wolfe as Leda approaches Ethan, who leans over the rail just above the captain's stateroom. He realizes that he wishes that they had murdered the captain when they had the chance, a sentiment that is echoed below by Nancy. The scene returns to the rail, and Leda tells Ethan not to feel guilty, because his murderous thoughts are only natural under the circumstances. Ethan says he finds the sea terrible now, because it seems about to beat him. Leda then confides her desire for Wolfe, whom she does not love. She despises him for having pierced her armor; through his indifference he has brought her to despise herself. She claims there is no distinction between lust and love and that she will win in the end, though she is currently becoming Wolfe's slave. She would not hesitate to murder for love, and she laughs at Ethan's sense of honor, which has so far prevented him from possessing Nancy. She hopes that the murder will come soon.

Down below, Captain Payne tells Nancy that he wishes to die: "and you know the reason. I'm dead already. You have murdered me." The scene shifts to Sara and Jonathan, who are discussing the economics of his proposed match with Elizabeth. Leda and Elizabeth are then seen coming out of Jonathan's cabin. Elizabeth tells Leda that she would have given herself to Jonathan had he returned, a sentiment on which Leda congratulates her. The two then go to see Nancy, both of them agreeing that in Nancy's position, each would murder "that old fool." Again Leda congratulates Elizabeth on the progress of her education, and Elizabeth says that she believes Leda to be "the only one on board who knows what life is about." But when she asks Leda to teach her, the older woman replies that Elizabeth is now able to teach herself. They then go into the captain's room to persuade Nancy to walk with them. She refuses, but Payne, with some understanding of the situation, tells her to go. As they leave they meet Honey, who is drunk, and then Sara and Jonathan. Elizabeth offers to kiss Honey, somewhat brazenly, allowing that she would prefer to kiss Jonathan, and telling him that she had waited for him in his room.

Honey has been appointed by the gold-seekers and the crew to "demand" that Payne resign as captain in favor of Ethan. Honey and Jonathan plan to deliver the message, which Nancy says would kill Payne; but in answer to Honey's suggestion that Payne's death would be a blessing, she agrees. Down below, the captain furiously refuses to resign, while in the wheelhouse above, Ethan thinks of murdering him. As Ethan comes down the stairs, Honey announces the proposition of the gold-seekers and the crew, but Ethan refuses to consent. Honey announces a double-cross, in that he will tell his supporters that the plan has been fulfilled, and leaves, while those in the wheelhouse prepare to go below for a party.

In the captain's room, Payne thanks Ethan for his loyalty in this matter and asks whether he has made love with Nancy; on hearing Ethan's denial, he announces that he can now sleep peacefully. The scene now switches to the after-cabin where the women are having their own party. Leda announces her credo of "ruthless lust for giving ourselves to power. The spirit is of no importance, it's the body that counts." Back in the captain's cabin, Payne drifts off to sleep, telling Ethan he can wait for both Nancy and command of the ship. However, Nancy, in the after-cabin, gets up and with ruthless cruelty says she is sick of waiting; she goes to the stateroom in time to see Ethan advancing on Payne with a pillow ready to smother him. She cries, "No! Give me what is mine!" She snatches the pillow and smothers Payne herself, as Leda announces that men are afraid to face love and that is why they write poetry about the emotion. The song of Honey in the wheelhouse is echoed by everyone on the vessel; as if the murder has set them free, all join in the song of the gold-seekers, and the third mate enters to announce that there is a squall coming that may mean wind.

Act IV, Scene i: The same, late January 1858, with the vessel just off Golden Gate. Only the exteriors of the wheelhouse and cabins are revealed, and the clanking of the pump is heard. All passengers, except Graber and Wolfe, are on deck, excited and jubilant. All discuss the speed of their voyage from the calms. Never has anyone seen the risks Ethan has taken; he has overdriven the ship, and now she is leaking from the strains put upon her hull, but it appears that she may well beat the record of the *Flying Cloud*. Warren says that even if the ship is ruined, he will be able to sell her in England (patched up) for a good price. Ethan and Nancy were married "right after" Payne's burial.

The sound of victory is everywhere, and each person celebrates the devious means by which this end has been achieved. Elizabeth speaks of her father's sly business deals, Nancy of her relief when Payne died, and Warren of the way Payne's end was hastened. Jonathan announces, "the end justifies the means," but yet he is sure that "Ethan's victory is a dead thing" because sail is finished. Sara, who has regretted Simon Harford's lack of business acumen, now celebrates Ethan's coming success by comparing his duel with the sea to the dueling abilities of her own father [in *A Touch of the Poet**]. Nonetheless, she hopes that Ethan will now give up the sea and devote his determination to a "dream of wealth and power on land." Elizabeth announces that that is Jonathan's dream, and perhaps the two brothers can work together with Nancy, Elizabeth, and also Sara; "we will help our men take possession of the world—and we will possess the world by possessing them." Elizabeth's match with Jonathan is not quite sure, but Elizabeth maintains that her father will wish to avoid a scandal and will therefore consent. As for Leda, she is not forgotten. She wants Wolfe and she will get what she wants; she, too, is one of this cabal of power-lustful women and at this moment is watching Graber and Wolfe play cards, the younger man winning in a strangely joyless manner. Elizabeth and Jonathan approach Warren and receive his reluctant consent to their marriage, which Dickey will perform. At this moment, Ethan comes out to announce that the sailing record is within their grasp, but as the cheers of everyone die away, so too does the wind. Nancy falls into Ethan's arms, terrified, and he says, "No, after what we did, she [the sea] can't do that to us," and commands the wind to return—which it does. There are varied reactions to this phenomenon: Nancy feels momentarily frightened, Dickey doubts God, and Sara suddenly feels horror at seeing Ethan and Nancy embracing. Nancy then confesses to a feeling of guilt, which Sara dismisses: "You are lovers and love is worth all it costs."

Act IV, Scene ii: The same at sunset, some hours later, in a dead calm. "The clanking of the pump is louder and quicker now, the chantey is a more powerful groundswell, while the gold-seekers' song is beaten and exhausted, with only occasional bursts of desperate assertion." The same group is on deck, but "their mood is even more strained than in the previous scene." They are beginning to doubt, though Nancy clings desperately to hope. Warren wonders if the calm might not be a judgment for "Ethan's crime and Nancy's and Leda's lust." Dickey perceives the hand of God here and confesses his sin openly, at which all except Jonathan sing a hymn and bow their heads. Jonathan speaks with businesslike practicality about the death of sail, while Sara, Elizabeth, Warren, and Dickey blame both themselves and each other for their sins. Jonathan alone refuses to accept guilt, telling Elizabeth he is interested in her brain rather than her body. Nancy, "in a daze of love," pities Ethan for losing his dream and is in turn berated by both Elizabeth and Sara for her crime. Sara, however, does have a sense of justice, absolving Nancy of the guilt, which Nancy willingly accepts as wholly her own. Jonathan now thinks of Ethan's coming disgrace, and Dickey suggests that the sinners be sacrificed to the sea.

As Nancy and Ethan come out of the wheelhouse, they are greeted with "a howl of execration." Ethan draws a pistol, but Honey restrains both Ethan and the rest of the passengers and crew in a speech which points out that all on this vessel are sinners "and proud of it." He will drink with them tonight, and the next day he promises they will achieve their heart's desire. Dickey looks on the situation as a successful revival meeting, while Warren begins to assess the situation of his vessel and fires Ethan for negligence in risking his vessel and passengers (the old charge of "suffering a vessel to be hazarded"), as well as failure to beat the speed record. Ethan accepts the situation but notes that the breeze has risen once more and that they should reach Golden Gate by midnight.

Act IV, Scene iii: The same, midnight, with moonlight shining through the fog. The interiors of the wheelhouse, Sara's stateroom, the captain's stateroom, and the after-cabin are shown. Leda is sitting beside Graber as if she is playing against Wolfe, while Honey and Jonathan observe. Ethan stands in the starboard doorway, looking at the fog. Sara is in her stateroom, and Elizabeth is by the rail to the left of the wheelhouse. Graber has lost the game, but Leda offers triple stakes to Wolfe, who, despite Jonathan's advice, cynically accepts, saying, "Your values are nothing to me." Jonathan, somewhat disgusted, turns away to speak with Honey about the folly of gambling, when Elizabeth calls him. He goes to her, and the two hammer out a very materialistic matrimonial relationship based on brains and acquisitiveness rather than love or sex; they agree to be married that night, and Elizabeth informs her father of her decision and of the economic expediency that underlies it. Warren leaves to fetch Dickey to perform the ceremony, while in the wheelhouse Graber loses once more and Leda doubles the stakes.

Eight bells sounds, and though the watch is about to be relieved by Jackson,* the new first mate, Ethan does not move. Jonathan suggests that he go below and not take this defeat by the sea so seriously; he should try something else. But for Ethan the sea is the symbol of life, and he has twice murdered for it, a confession that shocks both Honey and Jonathan. In reply, Ethan says that Jonathan will succeed "in the world" but fail in life, while Jonathan suggests that Ethan is covering up for Nancy. However, Ethan insists on his guilt, and Jonathan becomes afraid that he will confess and jeopardize the success of the Harford family in the West. Ethan promises silence. Warren calls Elizabeth, who calls Jonathan, and he leaves. Ethan and Honey then talk together, Ethan telling his brother that he is trying to come to a decision of which Sara will approve. Then he will go to Nancy with his decision. However, he is glad he has staked all, committed crimes, and tried to win, even though he has failed; in fact, he has reached the decision for himself—suicide—in order to find peace. But he still must decide "what to do with love." Honey leaves to go to Sara, and below, Nancy goes into Ethan's room in a state of guilt; seeming to see Enoch Payne lying on the bed, she flees from the room. Ethan is wavering between going down to face Nancy and committing immediate suicide, but he decides against this final step as an unconditional surrender. In order "to avoid temptation," he enters the wheelhouse, to discover that Wolfe, much to Leda's horror, fully expects him to jump. In Sara's stateroom, she and Honey discuss Ethan and Wolfe. She looks on Wolfe as "a great gambler" like her own father and asks why Ethan has not come down. When Honey tells her he is making a decision, she senses instantly what it is, but Honey reassures her it is "whether he'll leave the sea or not." Sara speaks of the Harford honor and her fear that Payne didn't die naturally, but Honey tells her that is nonsense. Nancy, in a state of nerves, calls up for Ethan, as Leda, Graber, and Wolfe continue raising stakes.

In her stateroom, Nancy and Ethan speak of their mutual sins. They embrace, but Ethan seems curiously self-contained. She says that she has decided to accept all the guilt so that Ethan may go free; he tests her resolve but then breaks down, saying that he, too, has his pride: "No, we'll go together." Nancy rejoices in this discovery of his love, and Ethan goes to tell Sara of his decision, since Nancy has just taught him how "to face everything alone, without fear." In her cabin Nancy echoes this resolve: "I can face all my crimes proudly, without fear. Hell together with Ethan *will* be heaven!" Sara cannot agree to Ethan's proposal but tells him to do what he wishes. He is right in believing that she would not have forgiven him if he had not told her, but now she begs him to leave, "and God damn the honor of the Harfords"; as she had said earlier, they always bring their honor to her and expect her support. Ethan leaves, and Honey returns to find Sara wishing to get drunk and fulminating in vulgar style against the Harford honor. But when Honey offers her a drink, she refuses to be "a sodden coward like my father, drunk, afraid of life." She will face life with honor.

Ethan and Nancy go up on deck; Ethan bids farewell to Wolfe, who understands, though Leda momentarily tries to dissuade them. They disappear into the fog, as Ethan says they will "swim out together—until the fog lifts. And then the sea will be alight with beauty forevermore—because you are you." As they disappear, Graber announces that he has lost everything and now is free of every cent he has stolen for Leda. She points out that he is not yet free of his conscience and forces him to play Wolfe for one last stake—herself. He refuses, and Leda cuts cards with Wolfe, who does not wish to play; she insists, and he wins her with the queen of hearts. Still anxious to avoid commitment, Wolfe offers her to Graber, who refuses; but Leda turns to Wolfe: "You think you can get rid of me.... Never! I love you, you fool—can't you see I love you?" Below, Sara senses the moment her eldest son and Nancy leap into the sea: "Ethan! My first-born!"

Comments: An assessment of this melodramatic scenario-*cum*-play is difficult because it lacks the benefit of the many revisions that O'Neill certainly would have given it. For instance, continual repetition of the phrase, "a touch of the poet," and the references to the poetlike qualities of assorted Harford men undoubtedly would have been cut or muted. In some cases, too, O'Neill was in the process of changing his mind concerning the exact relationships he was planning to portray. This is particularly true in the first "act" in which he is undecided between having Ethan look with some contempt upon his father, Simon Harford, or sincerely making communication. The name Leda is also a third choice, earlier ones being Goldie and Lisa.

As it stands, there are many unresolved and suggestive aspects in this play, as well as echoes of many earlier works. The use of the song of the gold-seekers as a groundswell reminds one of *The Moon of the Caribbees**; the character of Leda is an inversion of Cybel* in *The Great God Brown**; while the theme of acquisitiveness recalls *Marco Millions** as well; and the suicide of Ethan and Nancy in expiation of their shared guilt echoes the departure of Abbie Putnam Cabot* and Eben Cabot* for prison and death in *Desire Under the Elms.** The use of the ship as a microcosm of society is, of course, as old as the fifteenth century, and O'Neill had already used it in the S.S. *Glencairn** plays as well as in *The Hairy Ape.** Also, the ship's name, *Dream of the West*, has mythic implications in its central theme of acquisitiveness throughout the entire cycle of plays of which this is a part. However, other aspects of both the ship and the sea echo other plays. In *Mourning Becomes Electra*,* Adam Brant's* clipper is a symbol of escape and of happiness; and in *"Anna Christie"** the sea is both "that ole davil" and a cleansing, purifying element, unlike the fickle woman that she is made out to be in *The Calms of Capricorn*. O'Neill also makes curious use of the Renaissance belief in correspondences by which the elements reflect and sometimes even influence the behavior of individuals. The calm continues while the love of Ethan Harford and Nancy Payne remains unfulfilled; but because they have committed a crime, the elements eventually betray them, and they realize that they must pay. Their dream of the West cannot be fulfilled because of their blood-guiltiness. O'Neill also repeats his almost endemic tripartite concept of the matrimonial relationship by having Sara Melody Harford speak of Simon as her lover, husband, and child, a child whom her love has brought to birth and nurtured, and marriage once again is *Servitude.**

However, woman also represents nature and passion, as in the character of Leda, who in many ways is the central figure of the play. O'Neill specifically portrays her as the embodiment of feminine emotion and intuition, and characterization is achieved in this scenario in terms of individual relations with her. She believes in a life of self-expression, but it is also an exploitive view in which woman in effect sells her body in order to possess men and drive them on. Leda perceives the essential similarity of all the characters, both men and women, evaluating them all with a certain cynicism, yet still shows a kind heart in taking up with Graber, the failed banker. Wolfe Harford fascinates her as a challenge. His detachment and deliberate uninvolvement with anything are something she has not before experienced, and therefore she is close to being defeated and enslaved by him and his indifference. Consequently, she must strive to possess him because he has also made her capable of love as a desperate venture, a desire to gain the impossible.

In *The Calms of Capricorn*, the central theme of possession and self-destruction, symbolized by the ship and the sea, is also developed through the Harford family, each member of which represents a different aspect of that theme. Ethan wants to possess something intangible, to fulfill his dream of mastering the sea. In this way, like his poetic father, he is attempting to discover "The Meaning of Life." However, his self-destructive streak leads him to crimes of desperation in order to attempt his dream, and in losing that dream, he finds death. Jonathan Harford is the cool businessman who marries for money and plans to use his wife as a partner rather than a lover. He, too, is said to have "a touch of the poet"; but unlike Ethan, he lives by the balance sheet rather than the emotions. Honey Harford is another aspect of acquisitiveness, a throwback to a simpler generation and even to his Irish past in his profession of tin-peddler combined with his exploitation of the gold-seekers. Wolfe Harford, however, refuses to play the acquisitive game, opting out in his symbolic game of solitaire. It may be that O'Neill intended to make him the detached commentator on the antics of the fools on the vessel, but he does not do so in a very positive way in this scenario. Theodore Warren is the typical sharp-practicing businessman, while Samuel Dickey is the somewhat insincere representative of organized religion, and Graber is the victim and failed practitioner of the doctrine of acquisition. Of the women, Nancy Payne lives for the emotions, and Sara Harford (still acquisitive) shows herself lusting after possessions but also understanding the poetry of love. Elizabeth Warren remains the sexual operator throughout, and love for her is little more than lust.

Structurally, O'Neill is attempting to press on the limits of the theatre once more, this time with simultaneity of scene. He develops the web of interrelationships in a nonlinear manner, shifting from one part of the set to another and unifying the actions by word echoes and repetition of thought and movement, which indicate a sometimes unspoken parapsychological empathy between characters. On paper, this can sometimes be confusing, but such a simultaneous development of conflict and unity can be portrayed effectively on the stage. Even in this rough draft, one can also sense the strain and ragged nerve ends of the assembly of characters 'during the calm; and after the deliberately slow pace of these scenes, the action builds to a momentary climax of expected victory but then declines into the necessity of submission to inexorable fate.

Production Data: A staged reading was given by members of the O'Neill Seminar (Theatre and Drama 911) at the University of Wisconsin-Madison on December 13, 1981. The seminar was taught by Esther M. Jackson and John D. Ezell, and the reading was directed by Edward Amor. The presentation was given by special arrangement with Yale University.

A note on text: The text used for this section is that edited and adapted by Donald Gallup, *The Calms of Capricorn: A Play Developed from O'Neill's Scenario...With a Transcription of the Scenario* (New Haven: Ticknor and Fields, 1982). As Gallup notes in his introduction, some critics will doubtless consider publication of this 1935 scenario and its adaptation into a play as running counter to the playwright's own wishes, but it does provide an extraordinary insight into the creative processes of a remarkable playwright and an astonishing (though abortive) concept. One does wonder, however, whether it should be produced as a play.

CAMERON, James ("Jimmy Tomorrow"). In *The Iceman Cometh*,* a former Boer War correspondent. He is a small man in his late fifties, dressed in black, with "a face like an old well-bred, gentle bloodhound's." He looks intelligent and speaks in an educated manner with a slight Scottish rhythm; his manner is prim. He is said to be based on the personality of James Findlater Byth,* former publicity man for James O'Neill,* Eugene O'Neill's father. Cameron rents a room above the saloon operated by Harry Hope.* His pipe dream is that someday he will lay off the booze and will go back to his job in publicity. Under the influence of Theodore Hickman,* the salesman who comes to the bar annually to celebrate Hope's birthday, he toys with the idea of translating the dream into reality but then recognizes its impossibility. After Hickey's arrest for the murder of his wife, Cameron and other denizens of the bar seize on his plea of insanity, a pipe dream explanation which discredits what he has taught them. They then gladly get drunk to forget the outside world and to regain illusions. Cameron's nickname is important because he is always saying that he will spruce up and get a job "tomorrow." Larry Slade* calls him "the leader of our Tomorrow Movement."

CAPE, Eleanor. In *Welded*,* the actress wife of playwright Michael Cape.*
She is tall, thirtyish, with "high, prominent cheekbones. . . passionate, blue-gray
eyes," and a mass of dark brown hair combed straight back from a high forehead.
She possesses a charm that is both "innate" and also the product of intense
self-discipline. She is really a portrait of Agnes Boulton,* O'Neill's second wife,
and the action of this Strindbergian play is believed to recreate some of the
battles of the O'Neills' stormy marriage. Eleanor has been the prime interpreter
of her husband's works, yet he considers her merely an actress, while his contribution is the truly creative one—a situation that mirrors the split between
O'Neill the playwright and Agnes Boulton, the short-story writer. As a character,
Eleanor has little psychological depth, and she moves between total submission
to her husband and complete defiance and rage against the imprisonment that
she finds in marriage.

As before in plays such as *Bread and Butter** and *Servitude*,* O'Neill discusses
the problems of human beings in the matrimonial situation, but he has moved
somewhat ahead. In *Welded*, Eleanor is given some credit for interpretive abilities, and clearly she is not expected to show complete submission to her master.
Nonetheless, the attitude toward marriage is not very affirmative, as the very
title of the play implies. Eleanor as a character is really rather stereotypical and
little psychological motivation is given, while her emotionalism and posturing
are tiresome rather than affecting. Altogether, the chief importance of this play
would seem to lie in its autobiographical elements and its development of another
aspect of matrimonial conflict: the battles between two egotistical characters,
both asserting the claims of their work, as well as attempting to continue in a
marriage. The self-absorption of both Eleanor and Michael is shown visually in
their external illumination by individual follow-spots and by the way in which
they sometimes talk past each other rather than communicating.

CAPE, Michael. In *Welded*,* the playwright-husband of the actress, Eleanor
Cape.* He is thirty-five, dark, tall, with a face that "is a harrowed battleground
of supersensitiveness." His contradictory personality is shown by his thinker's
forehead and dreamer's eyes contrasted with "the nose and mouth of a sensualist." He is both "sympathetic and cruel at the same time." He is also an
idealist who believes that love is necessary to his very existence, but his is an
overpoweringly possessive love which allows no room for the outside world. At
the same time, he is dedicated to his work, as can be seen from his stern reaction
to Eleanor, his wife, when she hopes his loneliness for her did not bring him to
hurry completion of the final act of his play. He believes that his own work is
superior in creativity to that of his actress-wife, and therefore, he is intolerant
of her artistry. "You actress!" is for him an ultimate insult. He is an egotistical
artist, a quality that O'Neill signifies visually by having him surrounded by the
halo of a follow-spot.

Clearly, Michael Cape is the autobiographical character of O'Neill himself,
and this rather overwritten play indicates some of the playwright's own attitude

towards marriage, and it is not a very affirmative one when characters are "welded" to each other. Altogether, this Strindbergian battle of the sexes lacks deep psychological insight, and Michael's use of language is inflated, as befits his posturing behavior.

CAPTAIN (unnamed), of the S.S. *Glencairn*, "an old man with gray mustache and whiskers" wearing a simple blue uniform in *Bound East for Cardiff.**

CARLIN, Terry (1855–1934), sometime anarchist, dedicated alcoholic, the original of Larry Slade* in *The Iceman Cometh.** Born Terence O'Carolan somewhere in Ireland (exact place unknown), died in Boston, 1934, of pneumonia. Carlin was brought to the United States as a child in the 1860s. He began working in a sweatshop at an early age and between the ages of ten and twenty he became a tanner and currier. He lived for a time in Chicago with a mistress named Marie, a former prostitute. An Irish charmer, he also read widely, becoming interested in the work of Ibsen and writing about him in anarchist journals. He became an anarchist after an unsuccessful foray into business during which he was cheated by the employer of his brother, Jim. Carlin became secretary of the Liberty Group in Chicago, and later became part of the group surrounding the bookshop of Benjamin Tucker in Greenwich Village. O'Neill met Carlin in Greenwich Village in 1915–1916, when Carlin was well advanced on his course of drinking himself to death in the Golden Swan Bar (the Hell Hole) and elsewhere. In the summer of 1916 they inhabited a cottage near Provincetown, and O'Neill was introduced to the Provincetown Players* group through Carlin, who knew some of them from his time in New York. During the winter of 1916, he and O'Neill lived a handout-to-mouth existence in Greenwich Village, and in the summer of 1917 they rented an apartment in Provincetown with Arthur McGinley, an old friend of O'Neill from his New London, Connecticut, days. Again O'Neill worked with the Provincetown Players. During this time, he and Carlin were drinking heavily, often in company with James ("Jamie") O'Neill, Jr.,* the playwright's brother. Carlin may have supplied Louis Holladay* with the heroin he used for his suicide.

After O'Neill's marriage to Agnes Boulton,* he and Carlin were less close, particularly after the birth of Shane Rudraighe O'Neill* because both Agnes and her housekeeper, Mrs. Fifine Clark, disapproved of the alcoholic Carlin and eventually forbade him the use of the house. Carlin adored Shane, and O'Neill allowed him the use of a shack in the dunes near Peaked Hill Bars during summers. Prohibition failed to still Carlin's craving for alcohol or his very imaginative ways of obtaining the forbidden substance. O'Neill continued to look after his old drinking partner, contributing to his support, even during the Great Depression, until Carlin's death in Boston in 1934 at the age of seventy-nine. O'Neill and Carlin were almost reunited just before the latter's death because the playwright was working on *Days Without End,** which was trying out in Boston. However, a storm prevented their meeting. O'Neill paid Carlin's medical and funeral expenses, and his ashes were scattered over the water at Provincetown. O'Neill celebrated the deep sensitivity his friend kept hidden from most people behind a veil of alcohol when he developed Carlin into the character of Larry Slade, "The old Foolosopher," in *The Iceman Cometh*. It is possible that O'Neill gained insight into Ibsen from Carlin, and Arthur and Barbara Gelb (1973, pp. 289–290) credit Carlin with helping O'Neill develop sympathy for the poor, the underprivileged, and life-damaged. See in "References": Avrich (1980); Gelb and Gelb (1973); Sheaffer (1973).

CARMODY, Bill. In *The Straw*,* the widowed father of five children. He later marries his housekeeper, Mrs. Brennan.* Fifty years old, he is "heavy-set and round shouldered, with long muscular arms and swollen-veined hairy hands. His face is bony and ponderous; his nose, short and squat; his mouth large, thick-lipped and harsh." His complexion shows the mottled appearance of the habitual drinker, and his head has a bald spot on the crown. His small, blue eyes have an expression of "selfish cunning." "His voice is loud and hoarse." His manner is bullying with his family and whining to his superiors. He seems to feel that life has dealt badly with him, and in such moments he resorts to the bottle. He is miserly and lacking in sympathy for his daughter, Eileen Carmody,* seeing her illness, tuberculosis, as another problem with which he must deal and doing so most grudgingly. Even the seven-dollars-per-week fee for the sanitorium is something he agrees to pay only after the doctor threatens him with reporting to the Society for the Prevention of Tuberculosis. When he learns that her case is hopeless, he prefers to send her to the state farm to die rather than spend more of his own money on her. At the end of the play, when he has met his match in Mrs. Brennan, he shows some tenderness toward his dying daughter but then once again descends into self-pity.

CARMODY, Billy, In *The Straw** the son of Bill Carmody.* Billy is a fourteen-year-old replica of his father and a troublemaker at school who therefore has been allowed to leave and get a job. He seems preoccupied with himself. At the end of the play, he has been given a raise; but because he has to be with his girlfriend, he is not able to visit the dying Eileen Carmody,* his sister.

CARMODY, Eileen. In *The Straw*,* she is the central character. She is just over eighteen when the play opens, with a "wavy mass of dark hair parted in the middle" and gathered in a knot at the back of her head. Her almost perfect oval face has a "long heavy Irish jaw," and her eyes are large, blue, and candidly sweet. Her full lips have "an expression of wistful sadness." Her figure is slight and undeveloped, and her complexion has that startling and hectic color often seen in tubercular patients. As the mainstay of the family since her mother's death just over a year ago, she has been working herself to exhaustion taking care of her selfish, drunken father, Bill Carmody,* and her four younger siblings.

She is unofficially engaged to Fred Nicholls,* an old school friend and the son of a local manufacturer. His parents approve of her, but not of Bill Carmody.

When Eileen is diagnosed as having tuberculosis, her father complains bitterly about the expense he is being put to, and only when Dr. Gaynor* threatens to report him to the Society for the Prevention of Tuberculosis does he agree to send her to Hill Farm Sanitorium at a cost of seven dollars per week. Reactions to Eileen's illness are interesting. She herself is devastated that she must leave her "babies," particularly her youngest sister, Mary Carmody,* age eight, and fears that the family might have become infected through contact with her. Fred Nicholls, far from being the strong support that the doctor had hoped, is more frightened of infection than concerned for Eileen and speedily shows that his affection for her is not deep. Whatever he does for her seems to be performed as a necessity rather than as an act of love.

At the sanitorium Eileen meets Stephen Murray,* and once again displays her self-sacrificing, nurturing qualities by helping him with his writing. These same virtues also prevent her recovery, because she remains concerned about her family, who are more preoccupied with themselves than with her. Gradually she falls in love with Murray and tells him so the night before he is discharged as cured. Murray is surprised by her admission; he agrees to her request that he write to her, but soon forgets. Eileen's illness progresses until she is incurable and is about to be transferred to the state farm, because her father wishes to save money on his dying daughter. She has totally lost her will to live because of her loneliness and lack of affection. Her engagement has been broken, her father has married again, her favorite sibling, Mary Carmody,* seems afraid of her, and Stephen Murray has not kept up his correspondence. She is in despair; she has given herself to others and they have not cared.

After a four-month absence Stephen returns and is shocked at Eileen's deterioration. She realizes that he is not going to talk of love, and turns aside his reference to his last night in the sanitorium with a jocular remark. As Stephen leaves, Miss Gilpin,* the nurse in charge of the infirmary, suggests that Stephen make Eileen's last months happy by becoming engaged to her, moving her to another sanitorium and working nearby. Stephen, overcome with guilt and sorrow, romantically insists that he will marry Eileen, and in order to gain her acceptance, he appeals once more to her unselfish qualities by alleging (untruthfully) that he has had a recurrence of tuberculosis. Eileen, desperately happy, looks forward to working together toward a cure for both of them. Stephen does not destroy this hope.

The character of Eileen Carmody was founded on the real-life personality of Catherine (Kitty) Mackay, a fellow-patient of O'Neill's at the Gaylord Farm* in 1912–1913. She was the eldest of ten children and on one occasion was released because she was concerned about the problems faced by her widowed father and her siblings. Photographs indicate that O'Neill used her physical characteristics for those of Eileen. There seems to have been a mild flirtation between them but no commitment on O'Neill's side. She did not see O'Neill after his release from Gaylord, and she died in 1915.

Eileen Carmody represents another development of the O'Neill feminine ideal: the woman who gives generously and unstintingly of herself to assist the talent of the man she loves without counting the cost to herself.

CARMODY, Mary. In *The Straw*,* the daughter of Bill Carmody* and sister of Eileen Carmody* and three other siblings. At the beginning of the play, Mary is a quiet, dark-haired child of about eight who loves to read. Eight months later, when she comes to visit the dying Eileen, she has turned into a skinny girl, dressed in an outgrown dress, whose initial sweetness has disappeared during the time she has spent with Mrs. Brennan,* the housekeeper who is now her stepmother, and Mary's expression is that of "hangdog sullenness, a stubborn silence, with sulky, furtive glances of rebellion directed at her stepmother." When Eileen, who has always thought of Mary as her "baby," attempts to embrace her, Mary is unwilling and apprehensive. Clearly, Mrs. Brennan has been trying to wean Mary away from memories of her sister, and she has succeeded. The finer side of Mary's character seems to have disappeared, and her remark, "Eileen—you look so—so funny," is devastating to the sick girl.

CARMODY, Nora. In *The Straw*,* the eleven-year-old daughter of Bill Carmody* and sister of Eileen Carmody* and three other siblings. She "is a bright, vivacious red-haired girl." Later, Bill Carmody speaks of her as "the smartest girl in her school." The sorrows of her family do not seem to greatly affect her. At the end of the play, she has an obligation at school and cannot visit the dying Eileen.

CARMODY, Tom. In *The Straw*,* the son of Bill Carmody* and brother of Eileen Carmody* and three other siblings. He is "a healthy, good-humored youngster with a shock of sandy hair." He is ten years old, a year younger than Nora, whose merry disposition he shares. At the end of the play, he has an obligation at school and cannot visit the dying Eileen.

CARTER, "Babe." In *Bread and Butter*,* husband to Bessie Brown* and former roommate of John Brown.* Babe "is a broad-shouldered giant with a mop of blond hair and a feeble attempt at a blond mustache." He is handsome, blue-eyed, and successful. He follows his artistic bent and marries for love. At the end of the play, he is receiving excellent critical reviews, and he and Bessie are off for Paris.

CASTILLO, Manuel de. In *The Fountain*,* a swashbuckling young man. As the action progresses, he remains exactly the same in his ambitious aims. He is the type of bold adventurer who went forth to conquer the world for Spain and line his own purse. His only advance is in cruelty.

CATES. In *Where the Cross Is Made*,* bosun of the wrecked *Mary Allen*, "squat and stout,...dressed in dungaree pants and a shredded white sailor's blouse." He was drowned when the ship was lost. He appears (along with his companions, Silas Horne,* the mate, and Jimmy Kanaka,* the harpooner) in an hallucinatory scene in which only the obsessed Captain Isaiah Bartlett* and the half-insane Nat Bartlett* see them. The three men bring in two inlaid chests, presumably containing the treasure; but it is only an illusion.

In *Gold*,* a four-act recension of *Where the Cross is Made*, Cates has the same physical characteristics as in the earlier play, but his piglike eyes show his greed. He survives the wreck of the *Triton* and is shown in Act I as actively wishing for the death of Abel* and Butler,* two other crew members, in order to deny them their share of the buried "treasure." He goes out to seek this "treasure" on the vessel *Sarah Allen*. The crew attempts to murder Danny Drew,* the acting captain and fiancé of Sue Bartlett,* in order to prevent him from knowing the true reason for the journey. He, along with Horne and Jimmy Kanaka, is lost when the *Sarah Allen* is wrecked.

CATHLEEN. In *Long Day's Journey into Night*,* the second girl in the Tyrone household. She is a clumsy "thick" Irish peasant girl in her twenties. She gets tipsy during the course of the play when she is talking to Mary Tyrone,* and she is used as an expository device to indicate the shame that attaches to Mary's addiction to morphine. She is innocently outraged when she recounts the suspicion with which the druggist treated her request for the "prescription" for rheumatism.

CATO. In *The Calms of Capricorn*,* an elderly black slave. He is hoeing the potato patch of Sara Melody* Harford's farm, lamenting that he had ever allowed himself to be talked into running away from Georgia. He remembers his time as a slave as one of happy companionship. After his capture in Massachusetts, Simon Harford* purchased his freedom, something he now regrets. Cato is also mentioned, in slightly different circumstances, as the coachman of Deborah Harford* in *A Touch of the Poet*.*

CEELY ANN. In *The Dreamy Kid*,* "a stout [black] woman of fifty or so with gray hair and a round fat face. She wears a loose-fitting gingham dress and a shawl thrown over her head." She has been taking care of Mammy Saunders.* She knows very well that Dreamy* has turned out to be a young tough, and she is enraged when Irene,* the black prostitute, appears looking for Dreamy. Ceely Ann is basically an expository figure and is very lightly drawn.

CHANTEYMAN. In *The Hunted*, the second play of the trilogy, *Mourning Becomes Electra*,* "a thin wiry man of sixty-five or so." He is dissipated-looking, but curiously romantic, a "troubadour-of-the-sea." In Act IV of *The Hunted*, he sings the chantey, "Shenandoah," which pervades the trilogy, and here it represents Adam Brant's* love for the sea and what he must give up for Christine Mannon.* In a mythic sense, the Chanteyman also represents Charon, the boatman of the Styx, and his song reinforces the theme of the sea which runs through the plays. His conversation with Brant and his warning against "gals" also foreshadows the fatal consequences of Adam's choice, while his song of "Hanging Johnny" reinforces the guilt Brant feels for his part in the death of his old enemy, Ezra Mannon,* Christine's husband.

CHAPLIN, Charles Spencer (Charlie Chaplin; 1889–1977), actor, comedian, film director. Born in London to theatrical parents; died in Vévey, Switzerland, December 25, 1977.

Chaplin is noted for his creation of the film character of the little tramp with baggy pants, which he portrayed in silent and sound films such as *The Kid*, *The Gold Rush*, *The Champion*, *City Lights*, and *Modern Times*. He also made more conventional films, like *Limelight*, *Monsieur Verdoux*, and the satirical *The Great Dictator*, which attempted to lampoon Hitler (1940). In 1919 he offered to play one of the ghosts in O'Neill's *Gold*,* under an assumed name, but withdrew when he realized that his appearance would unbalance the play. On June 16, 1943, at the age of fifty-four, he married as his fourth wife eighteen-year-old Oona O'Neill (*see* Chaplin, Oona O'Neill) daughter of Eugene O'Neill and Agnes Boulton.* O'Neill was highly incensed, partly because Chaplin was involved in a paternity suit. O'Neill's anger may also have been compounded by the fact that Chaplin had been a close friend of Ralph Barton,* the *New Yorker* caricaturist who had been the third husband of Carlotta Monterey* prior to her marriage to O'Neill. Chaplin was one of the last people to see Barton before he shot himself, allegedly over the loss of Carlotta, though he also claimed to be a depressive personality. In any case, O'Neill never again communicated with his daughter, cutting her out of his will. In 1952, Chaplin came under fire from conservative politicians and moralists, as well as the House Un-American Activities Committee. While he and his family were in the course of a European trip, Chaplin received word that he might be refused readmission to the United States as an undesirable alien on grounds of alleged subversive activities. Accordingly, they took up residence in Switzerland, with visits to England where Chaplin was knighted in the New Year Honours List of 1975 and where Oona became a naturalized British citizen. In 1972 he revisited the United States to celebrate his contributions to film, including a showing of *The King in New York* at Lincoln Center, New York, and the award of a special Academy Award "Oscar" for services to the motion picture industry.

He and Oona O'Neill had eight children, some of whom have gone into the theatre: Geraldine, Michael, Josephine, Victoria, Eugene, Jane, Annette, and Christopher. From all accounts, the union proved a happy one. His earlier marriages were to Mildred Harris, Lita Grey, and Paulette Goddard.

CHAPLIN, Oona O'Neill (1925–   ), daughter of Eugene O'Neill and his second wife, Agnes Boulton*; sister of Shane Rudraighe O'Neill*; wife of

Charles Spencer ("Charlie") Chaplin.* Born in Bermuda, May 14, 1925. Her name, the Irish translation of Agnes, was suggested by Padraic Colum, the Irish poet, and his wife, the critic Mary Colum, at the request of O'Neill and his wife.

Oona was educated for two years in a Virginia private school, briefly at a Manhattan Catholic school, and then the Brearley School, New York City. She was admitted to Vassar College but chose instead to attempt a career in the theatre, playing a small part in a summer stock production of *Pal Joey* at the Maplewood Theatre, Maplewood, New Jersey. She was also offered screen tests and modeling assignments but chose to go to Hollywood in the company of a friend, who became Mrs. William Saroyan. At this time, she was also corresponding with J. D. Salinger, later to become famous for writing *The Catcher in the Rye*. She had been the Number One debutante of the 1942–1943 season, a distinction which did not please O'Neill because he felt that she was deliberately trying to garner publicity, though when asked to define herself as either Lace-curtain Irish or Shanty Irish, she quickly chose the latter.

In Hollywood she made the acquaintance of some important people, including Charlie Chaplin, who considered casting her in a film production of Paul Vincent Carroll's *Shadow and Substance*. On June 16, 1943, she became Chaplin's fourth wife. O'Neill was furious, partly because of the difference in age, Oona being eighteen and Chaplin fifty-four, and also because Chaplin was currently embroiled in a particularly nasty paternity suit. O'Neill never communicated with his daughter again, despite her several attempts to heal the wound, and cut her out of his will. Nevertheless, from all accounts, the union proved to be a happy one, Oona once saying that her husband gave her maturity and that she kept him young. The Chaplins had eight children, some of whom have gone into the theatre: Geraldine, Michael, Josephine, Victoria, Eugene, Jane, Annette, and Christopher.

Oona's marriage, however, was merely the final blow to an already shaky relationship with her father. She had been only two years old at the time of O'Neill's separation from Agnes Boulton, and she saw very little of him after that. At the age of six she was taken to visit him and Carlotta Monterey,* his next wife, in New York City, unfortunately becoming carsick during the visit. He did not see her again for eight years, until she visited her father and Carlotta at Tao House and this time made an excellent impression on both of them during her ten-day visit. In the summer of 1941, Oona again visited at Tao House but made a slightly less favorable impression by saying that she planned to marry "a really rich man" so that she would not have to work as hard as the monumentally efficient Carlotta. O'Neill was extremely displeased with Oona's expedition to Hollywood in 1942, and their break in correspondence dates from that decision, Oona's marriage merely confirming what had already occurred. He believed that she was exploiting his name and also that Agnes Boulton, her mother, was trying to push her into society. Except for the first four years of her life—which included O'Neill's time in Bermuda and at Belgrade Lakes,

Maine, and Nantucket during two summers—Oona had little contact with her father, except in letters. Any closeness with him was the result of two short vacations in California. However, it is clear that she regretted the estrangement, and in a letter to José Quintero* after his successful production of *Long Day's Journey into Night** in 1956–1958, she stated that through it she had come to know her own father.

Along with her older brother, Shane Rudraighe O'Neill, Oona was brought up by their mother in West Point Pleasant, New Jersey, in Connecticut, and in New York City, and in later years Oona helped Shane with monetary support. After her marriage, she does not seem to have remained very close to her mother, not visiting for almost fifteen years and seeing her in West Point Pleasant only once, in 1967, a year before Agnes Boulton's death when she, Agnes, was in the hospital suffering from malnutrition. However, when Spithead, the O'Neill-Boulton home in Bermuda, was sold, Oona gave her share of the proceeds (about nine thousand dollars) to her mother.

Since Chaplin's death in 1977, Oona has lived quietly in Vévey, London, and Paris, only visiting New York. She is rumored to be writing. Altogether, she seems to possess the greatest psychological strength of all O'Neill's children and remains today an extremely beautiful woman. After the death of Carlotta O'Neill in 1970, she and Shane shared equally in the lucrative royalties from *A Moon for the Misbegotten** and in equal thirds with Yale University of the royalties from sundry other O'Neill plays whose copyrights were renewed. Oona gave her share to Shane, who was at that time in financial straits.

CHILDREN OF THE SEA, a one-act play, the original version of *Bound East for Cardiff*.* As in the later version, "the action takes place in the forecastle of a British tramp steamer on a foggy night, midway in the voyage from New York to Cardiff. [The ship is unnamed in this version; only later it is called the S.S. *Glencairn*.] Five men are sitting on benches and talking, while a blond Norwegian sitting on a top bunk is playing his "battered" accordion. Yank* is lying on a lower bunk, clearly suffering considerable pain. Cocky* is telling a long and preposterous yarn as the play opens, and then the conversation turns to Yank's accident, a fall to the bottom of Number 2 hold, the circumstances of which are recounted in some detail. The sailors are convinced that "it's over the side for 'im," but Driscoll* tries not to admit this. He complains bitterly of the captain's lack of medical knowledge and his inability to give any proper treatment and then tells how he and Yank have been shipmates for the past five years: "Many's the time I'd 'a been on the beach, or worse, but for him." Certainly they have fought, but only when drunk, and they always made up. As Yank sleeps uneasily, the talk turns to the miserable food on the vessel—a classic sailor's complaint. With the mention of the fog outside, Driscoll recounts the way he and Yank survived the wreck of the *Dover* [an account shortened considerably in the later version]. Similarly, in a conversation with Yank, Driscoll gives another long anecdote, this time based on a mutiny on a starvation ship some fifteen years earlier, after which Driscoll pushed the mate over the side. [This was cut out in the later version. Yank's fear of death is less graphically portrayed than in the revision, and his fear of being buried at sea is less emphasized.] Both Yank and Driscoll speak of the misery of sea life and mutually confess their desire to have a farm someplace, Yank saying that he has tried to put some money aside for this purpose, and to his surprise finds Driscoll has had the same idea. But as Yank says, "Such things are not for the like av us." As Driscoll remains with his dying shipmate, Yank reminisces about their times in Buenos Aires [possibly based on O'Neill's own memories, a section shortened in the revision]. Yank also expresses fear of God's judgment for a killing he has committed, but Driscoll reassures him by saying that it was in self defense. [There is also a more detailed treatment of Yank's memory of the Cardiff barmaid, Fanny, who tried to lend him some money, and his charitable wish to have Driscoll buy her "the biggest box of candy yuh c'n find in Cardiff," but Driscoll suggests that she would prefer some gin. In this version, O'Neill makes her the "common property of the whole British merchant marine."] As Yank dies, death comes to him as "a pretty lady dressed in black." At that moment, Cocky enters to find Driscoll praying.

Comments: This play is a remarkable document as indicating O'Neill's ability at revision, because the second version is infinitely better than the first. The notion of the inevitable fate of the "children of the sea" is more clearly developed in *Bound East for Cardiff*, the lengthy anecdotes of Driscoll are cut down or omitted, and the character of Fanny is softened. But above all, the sailor's fear of being buried at sea is stressed in the later version, and the treatment of the sea as a malevolent mistress who will eventually claim her own is better developed. The use of dialect is also more skillful in the later text.

The source of this drama is Joseph Conrad's *The Nigger of the Narcissus*, first published in the United States under the title *Children of the Sea*, the title O'Neill used when he copyrighted this first version of *Bound East for Cardiff*.

Production Data: Written 1913–1914. Unproduced in this form. *See Bound East for Cardiff.*

A Note on the Text: The text used is that appearing in *"Children of the Sea" and Three Other Unpublished Plays by Eugene O'Neill*, edited by Jennifer McCabe Atkinson with foreword by Frank Durham (Washington, D.C.: NCR Microcard Editions, 1972). [A Bruccoli Clark Book.]

CHIPS. In *The Moon of the Caribbees*.* the carpenter of the S.S. *Glencairn*, "a lanky Scotsman."

CHRIS, the title of the unsuccessful 1920 production of *Chris Christophersen*.*

CHRIS CHRISTOPHERSEN, a play in three acts and six scenes; the first draft of "The Ole Davil"* (unpublished) and *"Anna Christie."*

Act I, Scene i: " 'Johnny-the-Priest's' " bar near South Street, New York

City, . . . late afternoon of a day in the fall of the year 1910.'' Johnny-the-Priest,*
Adams, and Jack Burns are discovered. "Johnny is a deceptively mild-looking
man, but cynical, callous, hard as nails.'' Adams is a fiftyish, unshaven, grizzled,
bleary drunk in a gray suit. Burns, a bull-necked man with a battered-looking
face, "is middle-aged, dressed in a patched working suit.'' Burns wakens Adams
and they engage in rough banter. Two Longshoremen enter and order drinks,
and then Larry,* the relief bartender, arrives, "a boyish, red-cheeked, rather
good-looking young fellow of twenty or so.'' The Postman leaves a letter from
Leeds, England, addressed to Christopher Christophersen [*see* Christopherson,
Christopher], in care of Johnny. Larry and Johnny surmise that it is from Chris's
daughter, and they discuss Chris's past. He used to be a deep-sea sailor, a
boatswain on sailing ships, but is now captain of a coal barge. Adams makes
some drunken comments, and Johnny sends him out.

As Johnny leaves for the day, Chris enters, "a short, squat, broad-shouldered
man of about fifty with a round, weather-beaten, red face'' with short-sighted,
good-humored eyes. He walks clumsily, "with a rolling gait,'' and speaks in
either "a hollow boom'' or "a sly, confidential half-whisper.'' He is dressed in
clumsy blue shore clothes and is happily intoxicated. He laughs, sings his signature song, "My Yosephine'' and asks for a drink. Larry gives him his daughter's letter, which tells him she is coming from England to live with him, the
father she has not seen for fifteen years, since she was five years old. She has
been brought up by cousins since her mother's death. In answer to Larry's
question, Chris recalls that he had also had two sons older than Anna (*see*
Christopherson, Anna) but that both were drowned. Above all else, Chris hopes
that Anna will not marry a sailor and that is why he has left her in England.
For the first time he expresses his hatred of the sea, which becomes a *leitmotif*
of the play: "Dat damn, dirty sea, she spoil all tangs. She's dirty ole davil.''
Chris realizes that Anna's arrival is imminent and hence he must get Marthy
Owen,* his companion, off the barge. He plans to have Anna live with him and
not work. Larry scoffs at the idea of Anna on a coal barge, but Chris says he
won't worry "so long's dat ole davil, sea don't gat her.'' Burns and Chris drink
to Anna's coming.

Mickey* and Devlin* enter. Mickey is a forty-five-year-old monkey like man,
and Devlin is "a lanky, loose-jointed man of about thirty-five.'' Both are dressed
in dungarees. There is an interval of Chris's drunken singing, and then Mickey
recognizes his old shipmate. He and Devlin talk of Chris's rotten job on the coal
barge after having been boatswain on the *Neptune*, but Chris objects strenuously.
They try to talk him into shipping with them, but Chris says he won't allow
"dat ole davil sea'' to get him back. The curtain falls as Chris sings "My
Yosephine.''

Act I, Scene ii: "The interior of the cabin of the barge *Simeon Winthrop* at
dock in New York.'' Chris and Marthy Owen are there. She is about forty or
fifty, fat, jowly, ugly, with teeth missing, but she still has in her eyes "a youthful
lust for life.'' She wears a man's cap and coat, a grimy skirt, and oversized

men's shoes. Chris tells Marthy to get a drink, and Marthy replies that she understands he wants to be rid of her and has her bag already packed. Chris explains that Anna is coming to live with him, and as Marthy leaves, she passes Anna.

Anna is "a tall, blond, fully-developed girl of twenty,...statuesque,...with an English accent...dressed simply in a blue tailormade suit." She and Chris greet each other and he makes her a cup of tea, which she pronounces to be bad. Anna is astonished at the cramped quarters and believes Chris's lie that he has had to return to the sea because of his health. The two talk of Anna's mother, an educated woman, a clergyman's daughter, whose relatives disapproved of her marriage to Chris—a love match on both sides. Continually Chris emphasizes that the barge isn't a real sea job, and much to his joy, Anna declares that she doesn't much like what she sees. She has trained to be a typist and her nurse-governess position was only temporary. She hated the way she was treated and was forced to leave when her employer engaged in sexual harassment. She sees typing as a means of achieving independence and possibly a college degree. Marriage, she says, is not for her. In answer to her inquiry after Chris's reason for not coming to see her, Chris says, "Dat ole davil sea...[makes men] crazy fools with her dirty tricks." After some comments on Chris's poor English, Anna gets dinner. She is appalled at the way in which her father lives and says that she will take him away from the sea as soon as she is able to find work and rent a little house somewhere. Chris suggests that things will be better once they leave port, and Anna agrees to make one trip with him. After another English lesson, the curtain falls as Chris sings "My Yosephine,...Long time Ay vait for you."

Act II, Scene i: Ten days later, on the stern of the *Simeon Winthrop* in impenetrable fog. Anna, dressed in dripping black oilskins, is standing on the deck with an expression of "awed wonderment." Chris, wearing yellow oilskins, is operating a box foghorn. The barge has lost its tow-line and is drifting help-lessly. Anna is overwhelmed with the beauty of the moment, but Chris, highly concerned for their safety, complains that that "damn ole davil, sea" is playing another trick on him. The foghorn suddenly fails, and Chris talks about this trip as a Jonah voyage, but Anna disagrees, saying that she has had a wonderful experience. Chris rages against the drunken tugboat captain who has used a rotten line, and they drift further into the shipping lanes. Anna, however, seems to surrender herself to the sea and its whims. The two start to talk about Anna's cousins and their farming, but Anna wants to hear about the seafarers and their women who make up Chris's and her family. Chris says that all the men were able seamen, except for him—"Ay vas bo'sun"—and that all the women married sailors, except for Anna's grandmother, the "only one gat sense." Anna waxes lyrical about the sea, feeling "as if this were the place for me to be," and far happier than at any other time. Chris's fears increase, the sound whistle is heard, Chris shows Anna how to launch the dinghy, the two don life preservers, and

Chris waves the lantern frantically, hailing the steamer. As the steamer hits the barge on the port bow, the two jump overboard and the curtain falls.

Act II, Scene ii: "The main cabin on board the British tramp steamer, *Londonderry*," within minutes of running down the barge. Captain Jessup,* a dapper, kindly-looking sixty-year-old, and Mr. Hall,* a tall, gaunt, middle-aged, determinedly grim-faced officer, are discussing the accident. They plan to continue with their voyage and not put back to Boston with the persons they have rescued. On questioning the steward, the captain is surprised to learn that one of the survivors is a woman. Paul Andersen,* the second mate, then enters. He is "a tall, broad-shouldered, blond young fellow of about twenty-five" whose handsome features are "marred by a self-indulgent mouth." He reports that there is little damage to the *Londonderry* and says of Anna, "as far as looks go— she's a corker." In a few moments Chris and Anna enter, he with the uneasy deference due to an officer, and Anna "with eager curiosity." Captain Jessup is at first astonished and then berates Chris for poor seamanship, but Anna stands up for him. The captain, learning of Chris's windjammer experience, says that he must work his passage while Anna will be a passenger, taking Paul Andersen's quarters, which the second mate relinquishes with alacrity. After this night Chris must remain in the forecastle—"bad for discipline" otherwise. With joy Anna discovers that the *Londonderry* is bound for Buenos Aires, six thousand miles without a stop.

Anna and Andersen are left alone, and he realizes to his surprise that she has no fear of the sea but instead has a fatalistic acceptance of what has happened. She tells him that for her the sea represents freedom: "As if you'd come home after being away a long, long time." Andersen agrees, and when Anna tells him of her seafaring relatives, he says that his family were farmers but other relatives were sailors. He himself had tried two years at university but then dropped out to drift into office work, until he suddenly resigned to sign on as a seaman on a tramp steamer. Then he began to experience something similar to Anna—he felt he had come home. Anna is amazed that in three years Andersen has advanced to the rank of second mate and declares that he will soon be a captain. Andersen, however, disclaims all ambition, saying that he has the easiest berth on the ship and intends to stay in it because it offers both freedom and limited responsibility as a "citizen of the sea which belongs to no one," without a single love, but a chance to sample the love of "women of all kinds and races." Apart from that comment, Anna agrees. The two have enjoyed exchanging ideas and finding common interests, but when Andersen presumes so far as to kiss Anna, she repulses him and berates him so that he apologizes. As they shake hands prior to Andersen's exit, Chris enters to say goodnight. He warns Anna against Andersen, saying "Ay know this kind fallar. . . . Ay svear, Anna, Ay vould like better you vas never born dan you marry man dat go to sea." Again he curses the sea, and Anna, laughingly, kisses him goodnight, but after her exit, Chris shakes his fist at that "damn ole davil."

Act III, Scene i: A month later in the forecastle of the *Londonderry* at anchor in Buenos Aires at 9 P.M. Chris, Jonesy,* and Edwards* are discovered. Jonesy "is a stout, heavy-faced, good-looking young fellow" who is trying hard to write a letter to his wife. Edwards, a "lanky, dark-complected boy of eighteen," watches with amusement. They discuss the illness of the boatswain and jokingly suggest that Chris might be offered the job. They also suggest that Anna won't be his "gel" long if the second mate has anything to do with it. Chris angrily replies that he wants Anna to remain with him. Glass,* the messroom steward, then enters. He is a sharp, thin young man of twenty-five who has come to play a practical joke on Chris by alleging that Paul is "a good sport and a real seaman of the old school—like you, Old Chris." He suggests that Chris keep an eye on Anna and Paul since they plan to elope. Chris is enraged and launches himself at Glass, who has suggested that he go after Andersen with a pistol. After Chris's departure the three sailors laugh at him, and Glass admits that Anna had refused Paul's offer of marriage. The three now await Chris's next move, and Glass is warned that Chris will be after him when he finds out the truth. When Chris returns, he takes out his sheath knife and starts mumbling about Paul as one of the dirty tricks of "ole davil sea," swearing that he will defeat her yet. As Chris goes out with his knife to find Paul, the curtain falls.

Act III, Scene ii: "A section of the amidships of the *Londonderry*." Everything is painted white, and the stage is lit with "bright intense moonlight." Chris can be seen dimly, squatting in the shadows as Andersen comes out to stare over the water, apparently waiting for someone. As Paul presents his back to Chris, the older man moves forward, clutching his knife; but the ship's bell tolls six as he is about to spring, so Chris withdraws. Anna enters and the two start to talk. Anna and Chris must leave the ship tomorrow for "the old dull life all over again." Chris cannot attack Paul while Anna stands between them, and therefore he is forced into the role of listener as Paul tries to reopen an earlier conversation; "You don't have to go back to the old life, Anna," but she refuses, despite the fact that she now wants to remain "forever sailing here and there, watching the sun rise and sink into the sea again day after day—and never do anything but love the sea." Paul persists and then sarcastically suggests she act as her father's housekeeper on another barge. This leads Anna to speak concernedly about Chris and his fear that the sea will swallow her up: perhaps his mind is affected. Paul suggests that Chris is afraid: "It's life he's really afraid of, if he only knew it—his own life." Andersen goes on bitterly to say that he too has "swallowed the anchor" of fear by becoming second mate to avoid responsibilities, but he will have to pay in the end. He is now stuck in his current position, and Anna will go back. Paul asks her to marry him, and then Chris realizes that Glass had played a joke on him by saying that their marriage was already agreed on. As Anna struggles with Paul, Chris seems ready to spring. The two young people struggle, cajole, plead, until Paul realizes triumphantly that Anna is fighting against herself. Finally she admits her love but says she can never marry him because she is afraid of his past. And no matter what his protestations, he will never leave the sea; if he were to do so, he would regret his decision and come to hate her. She cannot live the way her mother did, waiting out the long intervals between voyages and looking for men who never return, having found other women elsewhere. But Paul has another suggestion whereby they can both keep the sea and remain together. He will get his master's certificate as soon as possible, because "a captain can have his wife to live on board with him if he gets the right ship and insists upon it." In the meantime he will get a passenger-steamer berth and Anna can sometimes accompany him as a passenger.

Paul, changed by love, now welcomes responsibilities, but Anna reminds him that she has still not accepted his marriage proposal; Paul teasingly says that she has promised to marry him tomorrow in Buenos Aires. Anna laughingly assents, and they embrace. As Chris sees this tableau, he drops his knife and stumbles toward them, crying "Anna," revealing that he has overheard everything. Gradually he becomes resigned to their plan: "It's all right—yes—Ay tank it must be so—it's all right." Anna kisses him and Paul shakes his hand. Chris remains alone, but as he moves he kicks his knife, picks it up, looks at it, and flings it over the side. "You take him. He's your dirty trick, ole davil." At that moment, Captain Jessup enters and is at first angered to see Chris away from his proper place, the forecastle, but then offers him the berth of boatswain for the return voyage. Chris accepts. "Dat's your best dirty trick, ole davil," he says, and departs singing his old ditty, "My Yosephine," as the curtain falls.

Comments: This first draft of the later *"Anna Christie"* achieved a total of nineteen performances at its opening in Atlantic City, under the title *Chris*, and its closing in Philadelphia. In general, it is fair to say that the play in this draft lacks focus, largely because of O'Neill's wish to concentrate on Chris and the male figures. As a result, there is a considerable amount of somewhat undramatic discussion and banter in Johnny-the-Priest's bar, with all the denizens given specific names and detailed descriptions, which are not really necessary. A similar situation is found in the last act where Glass, the steward, plays a practical joke on Chris by asserting that Anna is planning to marry Andersen, the second mate. Thus, a considerable amount of dramatic time is consumed in the characterization of other forecastle inhabitants. The character of Chris is well realized even here, and he changes little throughout the next drafts. However, he displays more incipient violence against Paul Andersen than he shows in the later drafts against Mat Burke.*

In terms of plotting, the basic difference between this draft and those that follow is that here the barge is run down by the steamer *Londonderry* with the result that Anna and Chris must remain on board until the boat reaches Buenos Aires. The conclusion, with the marriage of Anna and Paul, is paralleled by the offer of a boatswain's job to Chris. Therefore, the tricks of "that ole davil, sea" continue, but ironically, they have brought happiness.

The most noteworthy weakness is to be found in the characterization of Anna. She is a totally incongruous figure for the purposes of the play, with her English accent, her training as a typist, and her simple, blue, tailored suit. Clearly, she belongs to a social class (or has been educated into it) which is superior to that of Chris or Paul Andersen. As a result, O'Neill has to upgrade the character of Paul to say that he has had two years of university education and has dropped out to discover finally that the sea is his proper home. Paul's lack of ambition and his wish to avoid responsibility also seem to be a trifle unmotivated. In other words, O'Neill has found himself forced to develop a character worthy of Anna in terms of expectations and social class. This weakens the central situation of the play, which O'Neill wanted to be that of Chris and the "dirty tricks" of "that ole davil, sea." Similarly, the banter between Chris and Anna over his bad tea and his poor English seems contrived, while Anna's sudden discovery of the magnificence of the sea lacks motivation and immediacy. All told, it is the failure in the conception of Anna as a character that weakens this draft.

Production Data: Written 1919. Produced under the title *Chris* by George C. Tyler at Nixon's Apollo Theatre, Atlantic City, New Jersey, March 8, 1920. Moved to Philadelphia, March 15, 1920—closed March 26, 1920 (total of 19 performances).

Director: Frederick Stanhope
Designer: Unknown
Cast: Jack Burns: Claude Gourand
      Adams: Max L. Schrade
      Longshoremen: Frank Devlin, and another, name unknown
      Johnny-the-Priest: James C. Mack
      Larry, the Bartender: William E. Hallman
      Postman: Harry MacFayden
      Chris Christophersen: Emmett Corrigan
      Mickey: Dan Moyles
      Devlin: George A. Lawrence
      Marthy: Mary Hampton
      Anna Christophersen: Lynn Fontanne*
      Captain Jessup: Roy Cochrane
      Steward: George Spelvin
      Paul Andersen: Arthur Ashley
      Edwards: William Smith
      Jonesy: John Rogers
      Glass: Gerald Rogers

Note: The published version reproduces O'Neill's original spellings of Christophersen and Andersen.

A Note on the Text: The text used is Eugene O'Neill, *Chris Christophersen*. Foreword by Leslie Eric Comens (New York: Random House, 1982).

CHRISTIE, Anna. *See "Anna Christie,"* the play. *See also* Christopherson, Anna, for character analysis.

CHRISTOPHERSEN, Anna. *See* Christopherson, Anna.

CHRISTOPHERSEN, Chris. *See* Christopherson, Chris.

CHRISTOPHERSON, Anna. In *"Anna Christie,"** she is the title figure, for she has adopted this name instead of her given one. She is the daughter of Christopher Christopherson,* the captain of a coal barge. When she first appears, "she is a tall, blond, fully-developed girl of twenty, handsome after a large Viking-daughter fashion but now run down in health, and plainly showing all the outward evidences of belonging to the world's oldest profession. Her youthful face is already hard and cynical beneath its layer of make-up. Her clothes are the tawdry finery of peasant stock turned prostitute."

Anna had been taken by her mother to live with relatives on a farm in Minnesota, where she remained after her mother's death. Her father, Chris, wished her to remain there so that she would avoid contact with "that ole davil, sea" which he considers a malevolent, destructive force. However, his planning went seriously awry because after her mother's death, Anna was treated like a slavey poor relation and was seduced by a cousin when she was sixteen. After that, she took a job as a children's nurse and was further exploited, so that she eventually began to work in a house of prostitution, was arrested, and later hospitalized. After these experiences she writes to her father and comes to New York to live with him under the impression that he is a janitor.

She is rather disappointed to discover that he is the captain of a coal barge but is reassured by Marthy Owen* that her father is a good man. Chris is overjoyed when he sees her at Johnny-the-Priest's* saloon and is so blinded by his affection that he does not realize her true occupation, something that the other denizens of the bar instantly note. She moves onto the barge with Chris, and by the second act of the play she has undergone a transformation because of her association with the sea. Her health appears to have returned and she feels cleansed, free from the evils that she had found in her life on land. For her, "dat ole davil, sea" is curative because it is clearly her spiritual home. Like all her male ancestors, she must follow the sea, and like all her female ancestors, she will marry a seafaring man. This is her destiny, and Anna discovers this in the course of the play.

First, she and her future husband, the stoker, Mat Burke,* need to develop a tolerance of their respective past lives. He resents her having been forced into prostitution, and she asks whether he has been any better in the way he has acted when on shore. She attacks the double standard of morality and objects when both Chris and Mat treat her as "a piece of furniture." She needs another chance: "Don't you see I'm licked? Why d'you keep kicking me?" In her final reconciliation with Chris and proposed marriage to Mat she is returning to the primordial rhythm of her seafaring ancestry. She willingly accepts this destiny, because for her the sea possesses a curative, ennobling power. By living inland she had been fighting against her fate, and therefore she has sinned. Anna has discovered hope partly through love, but more through the healing power of the sea which has given her Mat, and has also prepared her to love him by showing her the futility of her former life. It is this emphasis on the power of the sea over Anna that makes her different from the conventional prostitute figure with the proverbial heart of gold. She is a symbolic character, one who seizes on her destiny, "no matter what!" once it has been revealed to her.

The character of Anna is the development of her role in two earlier drafts, *Chris Christophersen** and "The Ole Davil"* (the latter an unproduced and unpublished version). In the first of these (note altered spelling), the emphasis is clearly on Chris, and the character of Anna is totally misconceived. Her mother was a clergyman's daughter, and since her death Anna was brought up by her cousins in Leeds, England. As a result, when she arrives by steamer (steerage), she has an English accent, has trained as a typist so as to ensure her independence (possibly by gaining a college degree), and knows nothing at all about the sea. Her transatlantic crossing has not shown her anything out of the ordinary. However, she has been unhappy with her cousins, who everlastingly spoke of farming. Obviously, she is distinctly out of place on the coal barge, and therefore her sudden discovery of the glory and magnificence of the sea seems a trifle unmotivated and romantic. It is also hard to imagine such an Anna wishing to take care of Chris as he is portrayed in this play. Even her marriage to Paul Andersen* seems contrived and exceedingly romantic, despite its air of practicality. Paul says that he will get his master's ticket so that Anna can travel with him, but in Buenos Aires she wishes to remain "forever sailing here and there, watching the sun rise and sink into the sea day after day—and never do anything but love the sea." This sounds more like a permanent Caribbean cruise than the life of a seafarer as perceived by Chris elsewhere in the play. In effect, Anna is a most unlikely daughter for Chris because she seems to belong to a totally different social class, and O'Neill clearly recognized the problem because of the way in which he includes some banter about Chris's bad tea and his Swedish accent, which Anna tries at first to correct. One really wonders how and why Anna's mother had married Chris. O'Neill also has to devise Paul Andersen as an unusual character to preserve credibility in his marriage to Anna.

In "The Ole Davil," the emphasis changes, and though O'Neill tries to keep it on Chris, it has shifted to Anna. The major change in Anna is that she is now the prostitute down on her luck who is familiar from "*Anna Christie.*" The circumstances of her early life have changed, and so has her social class; hatred of men because of her mistreatment appears here, as does her memorable opening line. Anna is also given a much longer conversation with Marthy Owen, whose character is further developed. In general, the character in "The Ole Davil" is that of the Anna Christie of the final draft. There are, however, some notable differences. At the end of the play, Anna does not take Chris's anger against "the ole davil" seriously, and neither does Mat Burke, the man she is going to marry. They treat the entire restatement of the theme as a joke, and the play ends in laughter and the mutual discovery that Chris and Mat are to be shipmates. Anna in this draft is also more practical than in *Chris Christophersen*, something that arises from her changed social status. She will get a little house somewhere and live on the money that Chris and Mat send her. Despite her background, this Anna is infinitely more independent than the Anna of *Chris Christophersen*. Her hatred of men is adequately motivated because of their exploitation of her, and so is her refusal to be ordered about by Chris or treated as an object by Mat. She has a sense of her own integrity which is reinforced by her cleansing experience with the sea. To be sure, this also has elements of the romantic, but it is better motivated because of the sordid nature of her earlier experiences. It is easier to imagine this Anna as the daughter of Chris than her prototype, and similarly, her marriage with Mat Burke seems better motivated and more suitable than the match with Paul Andersen. This second draft of the character is immeasurably superior to the portrayal in *Chris Christophersen*, even though O'Neill has not quite solved the problem of central emphasis. Quite clearly, the character of Anna is stealing the play, but in one way O'Neill makes no alteration: he always allows her a happy ending, though he always claimed that it carried tragic potential.

CHRISTOPHERSON, Christopher ("Chris"). In *"Anna Christie,"** the seaman father of Anna Christopherson.* He is short and squat, about fifty years old, "with a round, weather-beaten red face from which his light blue eyes peer short-sightedly, twinkling with a simple good humor." His mouth is large, partially hidden by "a thick, drooping, yellow mustache," and its expression is "childishly self-willed and weak, of an obstinate kindliness." His neck is thick, his arms heavy, hands freckled and hairy, his legs are short and stumpy and his feet large and flat. His voice varies between "a hollow boom" and "a shy, confidential half-whisper with something vaguely plaintive in its quality."

Chris comes from a family of seafarers in Sweden, yet he hates the sea because he perceives only its malevolence. He long ago left his wife in Sweden, and some fifteen years ago she came to the United States and left their daughter, Anna, with her relatives in Minnesota, where she died. Chris is glad that Anna has been brought up inland, away from "dat ole davil, sea." These words run like a refrain through Chris's character, and he blames all his misfortunes on the hostility of the sea. However, despite his detestation and fear of the sea, he cannot drag himself away and is currently the captain of a coal barge—a great decline for one who had formerly been a boatswain. As the play opens, he is living with Marthy Owen* aboard the barge when he receives a letter from Anna saying that she is coming to see him "right away." Chris wants her to stay with him on the barge, and Marthy cheerfully says she will move on.

When Anna arrives, it is clear to everyone except Chris that she has been earning her living as a prostitute. Her father treats her as if she is quite innocent, offering to buy her sarsparilla and then port wine, when the audience has already seen her order "whisky—ginger ale on the side." She goes with him on the barge, and Chris is concerned because she seems to be falling in love with the sea—a fate he doesn't wish for her. As they are talking on the fogbound barge in the outer harbor of Provincetown, Massachusetts, four survivors from a wrecked steamer hail them. Three of the men are seriously ill, but Mat Burke,* the stoker, has managed to survive in surprisingly good condition.

As Mat Burke falls in love with Anna, Chris becomes both angry and frightened. He does not want his daughter to have anything to do with a seaman, especially a stoker, whom he regards as less than a true sailor. He wants Anna to have a small home on land divorced from any connection with "dat ole davil, sea." He is firmly convinced that Mat is not good enough for his daughter, and he does his best to prevent their marriage. Once he attempts to fight Mat, but the powerful younger man easily disarms him of his knife. Finally, Anna reveals to both Chris and Mat that she has been a prostitute, information that devastates Chris and enrages Mat. After Mat leaves, Chris goes on a drunken binge and signs on as boatswain on a vessel bound for Cape Town, South Africa. He is at first so eager to kill Mat that he gets a revolver, but then he doesn't even buy bullets. Eventually, as he sees Anna's sorrow at Mat's departure, he forgives her for her past and begs her to forgive him. He blames the sea for what has occurred in the past and says that if she wants to marry Mat, he will not mind.

At the conclusion of the play, Mat and Anna are indeed going to be married, and Chris and Mat discover that they are to be shipmates on the voyage to Cape Town. Yet even in this moment of joy, Chris is troubled by his distrust of the sea. He believes that the meeting of Mat and Anna was a trick of "dat ole davil" and that she has more mischief in store for them. His gloomy premonitions even infect Mat momentarily, and the play ends with Chris still concerned with whatever the inimical element will bring. Even Anna's defiant toast, "Here's to the sea, no matter what!" fails to arouse him.

Chris is a character who was based on real life, an acquaintance of O'Neill who was drowned in New York Harbor, under circumstances which have been retailed differently. However, Chris is also a character who has affinities with some of the characters to be found in the S.S. *Glencairn** plays. He is one of those persons in thrall to the sea but always fearful of it and always rebellious against the total commitment that it exacts. His character remains constant throughout the three versions of *"Anna Christie."* In *Chris Christophersen* (produced under the title of *Chris*) he is given the signature tag of the song "My Yosephine, long time ay vait for you," and in the second revision "The Ole Davil," his continual repetition of the title and variants like "Dat ole Davil Sea," becomes tedious.

CHU-YIN. In *Marco Millions,** the philosopher-advisor of the Great Kaan, Kublai Kaan.* He is old, stooped, with a white beard, and is dressed in "a simple black robe." He is a believer in resignation, humanity, and the emotions. He thinks that Marco Polo* may indeed learn to develop feelings, but he is mistaken. He tries to aid Kukachin,* the daughter of the Kaan, in the hope that Marco may come to understand her love for him. He gives Marco what he says are "secret orders" from the Kaan to look daily into the princess' eyes during their voyage to Persia and remark what he sees there. But Marco is imperviously practical and sees only medical symptoms. At the end of the play, Chu-Yin asserts that Kukachin "loved love. She died for beauty." As he leaves the grieving Kaan with the body of his daughter, he who has preached resignation looks with compassion on his master: "Then weep, old man. Be humble and weep for your child. The old should cherish sorrow." In this play, Chu-Yin is an example of disinterested service, an honest advisor who seeks the way of virtue without desire for power, an Oriental stoic who endures.

CNEIUS CRASSUS. In *Lazarus Laughed*,* a Roman general of about sixty. He commands the troops in Athens. He is a short, squat figure who wears a mask of "coarse humor." Despite his hardboiled exterior, he finds himself touched by the laughter of Lazarus.* He is astonished by the fact that his legionaries do not have the chance to kill Lazarus's followers, who seize the soldiers' weapons and joyously kill themselves. He offers to make Lazarus a god, but the new prophet-redeemer refuses.

COCKRAN, Jack, also known as Jack Gardner. In "The Reckoning"* (unpublished scenario), the young helper of Stephen Donohue,* the blacksmith. He gets Bessie Small,* his employer's daughter, pregnant and initially refuses to marry her because he is in love with Alice (who never appears). When Donohue hears of Bessie's pregnancy he wants to force the marriage, and he picks a fight with Jack Gardner, who hits him over the head with a hammer. Believing that he has killed Donohue, Jack follows Bessie's advice and flees to Chicago where he lives under the assumed name of Cockran. Bessie follows him and blackmails him into marrying her by threatening to reveal his crime; in fact, she is lying because Donohue was merely stunned. Cockran explains that he is marrying her without love and has no intention of continuing any real relationship with her because he considers their union as tainted with guilt. Ten years later Bessie again blackmails him, this time into running for senator, using the same threat. Cockran has now become a successful businessman, a partner in a northeastern mill, rising from mill hand and gaining the respect of labor and management alike. This time, Cockran drives a hard bargain with Bessie; he will run for senator on condition that their ten-year-old son be removed from her influence and sent to boarding school. By 1917 the United States is about to enter the war and Senator Cockran is preparing a speech in favor of this policy, but Bessie tries to blackmail him into speaking against it so that Jack Cockran, Jr.,* can avoid the draft. Cockran, knowing that he will be destroyed politically, capitulates when Bessie threatens to tell Jack, Jr., the truth. But their son has already enlisted, and Bessie realizes that she has ruined her husband. However, the senator has followed his conscience and spoken in favor of the war, as he had originally planned. Bessie now reveals the story of Cockran's past to Jack, who is appalled at her deception, but when Cockran is confronted with Bessie's version of the facts, he realizes that she has omitted the detail of her premarital pregnancy. He then also realizes that she has tried to protect their son from the knowledge of his sin and also that it is through Bessie's "blackmail" that he has become successful. The three of them are then reconciled, Jack forgiving his parents and Cockran discovering love for his wife as Jack goes off to war.

It is unfair to attempt a full analysis of the motivations of this character because the source material is merely a draft. Suffice it to say that the character of Cockran is barely developed and the events of the scenario are not fully worked out, while the theme of crime and punishment (with an ironic twist) is rather trite.

COCKRAN, Jack, Jr. In "The Reckoning"* (unpublished scenario), son of Jack (Gardner) Cockran* and Bessie Small.* He is first seen as a child of ten who is very attached to his mother. Later, age about seventeen, he is a super-patriotic young man who rushes off to enlist in the aviation corps in 1917, with the enthusiastic approval of his girlfriend, Harriet Lathrop.* In some respects he is an earlier development of the character of Gordon Evans* in *Strange Interlude*.* In the last scene, he is asked to forgive his parents for their earlier sin of begetting him out of wedlock and also for the way in which he was deliberately separated from his mother through his father's vindictiveness. He delivers a somewhat inflated speech of reconciliation in which he equates his familial relationships with his patriotism: "right or wrong, my country." He is an undeveloped figure in a draft scenario.

COCKY. A Cockney seaman on the S.S. *Glencairn*, "a wizened runt of a man with a straggling gray mustache," who appears in all the plays of the S.S. *Glencairn** group. See also *Children of the Sea*.

COCKY. In "The Personal Equation,"* a squat, broad-shouldered, pasty-faced stoker. He is simply a representative of one ethnic group in O'Neill's portrait of the stokehole, which prefigures his later treatment of the same scene in *The Hairy Ape*.* Cocky takes part in the attempt to sabotage the engines of the S.S. *San Francisco*.

COLUMBUS, Christopher. In *The Fountain*,* he is the great "Admiral of the Ocean Sea" who appears the night before landfall on his second voyage. He tells Diego Menendez* that his real motivation in wishing to gain wealth is to finance "The Last Crusade" against the Infidel and free the Holy Sepulchre. He has sworn to the pope that he will do so. Juan Ponce de Leon* mocks him for this wish and tells him that to establish the old religious law of Spain on the Infidel and indeed the New World is really a fanatic's dream. In turn, Columbus uses Juan for all the routine and dangerous work, but he himself gets the credit. O'Neill does manage in this short scene to give some indication of the strength of the man who is able to get others to follow him beyond the ends of the known world.

COMMINS, Saxe (1892–1958), editor, sometime dentist. Born Saxe Comminsky in Rochester, New York, in 1892. Died in Princeton, New Jersey, July 17, 1958. One of the six children of emigrants from Kovno, Lithuania, now Russia. His father was a tinsmith and his mother a sister of Emma Goldman, the noted anarchist and friend of John Silas Reed.* Educated in the public schools of Rochester and at the University of Pennsylvania. Had originally planned to follow a medical career, but when the family incurred heavy expenses because his older brother contracted tuberculosis, he had to choose a less expensive and less time-consuming degree and chose dentistry, graduating in 1918. Married Dorothy Berliner, a concert pianist, December 24, 1927, and had two children, Frances Ellen and Eugene David.

During his time at the University of Pennsylvania, where he helped support himself by ''ghosting'' term papers for classmates, Commins frequently visited Greenwich Village, where his sister, Stella, was living with her husband, the artist Edward (Teddy) Ballantine. They were original members of the Provincetown Players,* and Commins wrote one unsuccessful play for them in the 1916–1917 season, *The Obituary*. Commins first met Eugene O'Neill in the Village, and their acquaintance continued during the summer of 1916 in Provincetown. After completing his dental training, Commins built up a good practice in Rochester, and Eugene O'Neill became one of his patients. At the same time, Commins kept up his literary contacts in New York and continued to vacation with O'Neill and his second wife, Agnes Boulton,* at Peaked Hill Bars and later in Bermuda. He helped O'Neill in his arrangements for purchasing Spithead there, and the two were so close that Commins escorted Agnes to the opening night of *The Hairy Ape** while O'Neill was dealing with his drunken brother, James [Jamie] O'Neill, Jr.,* and trying to arrange the funeral of their mother, Ella Quinlan O'Neill.* Commins was also O'Neill's confidant in his divorce from Agnes and his subsequent marriage to Carlotta Monterey.* By the time of his own marriage, Commins had also collaborated with Lloyd Coleman on a book entitled *Psychology: A Simplification* (New York; Liveright, 1927). He was given a contract for six similar books, but they were not published, owing to the firm's financial problems.

On December 24, 1927, he married concert pianist Dorothy Berliner in a quiet ceremony and then returned to Rochester to wind up his practice by the following May. He had decided to leave dentistry and try a career in the literary world. Dorothy continued with her teaching and playing, both of them saving money so that they could spend a year abroad. In June 1928, they sailed for Europe, and after a brief stay in England they moved to Paris, where O'Neill, who had left the United States with Carlotta the previous February, wrote Saxe from Guéthary, asking him to perform some literary business for him. Saxe then visited O'Neill and apparently helped with the typescript of *Dynamo** and is said also to have read a rough draft of *Mourning Becomes Electra** (Commins, 1978 p. 7). Sheaffer suggests that Commins heard of it in a letter of August 4, 1929. Back in Paris, where the Comminses had the loan of an apartment, Saxe worked on *Dynamo* and also became part of the Parisian literary scene which at that time included James Joyce, T. S. Eliot, Ezra Pound, Gertrude Stein, Sherwood Anderson, Ernest Hemingway, Hart Crane, and others. By this time, Saxe was beginning to function as O'Neill's communications link with both his literary agent, Richard Madden, and his personal and business friends. The Comminses also visited with the O'Neills after their return from the Orient, and Carlotta's letters to them at that time reflect ecstatic happiness and deep friendship.

The Comminses returned to the United States in June 1929, laden with commissions from O'Neill, who had also written to his publisher, Horace Liveright, recommending Saxe Commins for a position as editor. Unfortunately, the Liveright firm was in financial difficulties, so Saxe Commins joined the firm of Covici-Friede, where he was soon working on some of their most prestigious publications, like the Chaucer edition with illustrations by Rockwell Kent. Financially, things were difficult for the Commins family, which now included a daughter, but Dorothy managed to supplement Saxe's small salary by obtaining a thirty-nine-week radio series, "Movements from Celebrated Sonatas for the Piano," which she was asked to repeat at the time that David Sarnoff, a family friend, was developing network broadcasting. In addition, she played with the American Pro Arte Quartet. After a year at Covici-Friede, where he was not very happy, Commins was able to transfer to Liveright because Manuel Komroff, O'Neill's editor there, wished to leave to devote himself to his own work. He recommended Saxe as his replacement, and O'Neill sent his congratulations, accepting Saxe's "offer to handle his affairs at Liveright's" (Commins, 1978, p. 15). [Note that the Gelbs' account of this transfer differs slightly in details, Gelb and Gelb, 1973, p. 711.] During his time there, Saxe Commins saw through the press all the plays that O'Neill wished to publish, gaining particular success with *Strange Interlude*.* Whether the idea was O'Neill's or some one else's is not quite clear, but what is certain is that O'Neill's plays managed to make a considerable amount of money for their author because of their almost simultaneous publication and production. This approach to marketing was new at the time. (One suspects that James O'Neill, Sr.,* would have enjoyed the situation.) However, during the summer of 1931 Commins worked with O'Neill on *Mourning Becomes Electra*, a title he had some difficulty getting past the management because of its obscurity. It was published in November 1931; and while it was modestly successful (110,000 copies), it did not solve the increasing financial problems of Liveright's, and Saxe Commins and others were forced to take pay cuts.

Things were then particularly bad for the Commins family, which now also included a son, and in May 1932, O'Neill, in a letter redolent of breezy masculine camaraderie, wrote to Saxe and told him to forget a loan made earlier to his old friend: "I really owe that money to you for your services as Doctor Commins in Rochester long ago. . . . I'm your friend, ain't I? That used to mean that what's mine is yours—and I'm old-fashioned" (Commins, 1978, p. 17). In the same year, Saxe Commins had worked out a means of safeguarding the finances of

O'Neill in case Liveright's folded. O'Neill forced Arthur Pell, treasurer of the company, to sign an agreement to the effect that in the event of Liveright's bankruptcy, the publication rights of O'Neill's plays would revert to the author. He and Commins went farther, drawing up terms to be presented to O'Neill's next putative publisher to include a royalty of 20.0 percent instead of the 17.5 percent he was currently receiving from Liveright's, plus a ten-thousand-dollar advance on the signing of the contract (Sheaffer, 1973, p. 415). Thanks to Commins, O'Neill was well prepared for Liveright's collapse in May 1933, particularly because Saxe had also noticed (with some comments from O'Neill) that royalty payments were past due. Commins called "a meeting of the principal stockholders...to place an ultimatum before them. Either a certified check covering all of O'Neill's royalties would be...[issued] within twenty-four hours, or I [Commins] would announce on the book page of the *New York Times* that O'Neill had decided to transfer his publishing program to any one of the five leading publishers of the country" (Commins, 1978, p. 19). Commins was able to take this stand because he "had a virtual power of attorney in O'Neill's behalf and had been authorized specifically to exercise...judgement, as his editor and in the protection of his royalties" (Commins, 1978, p. 19). Later that day the check was prepared, and Commins took the train to Georgia to deliver it personally to O'Neill, without discussing the circumstances that had led to its issuance.

In May 1933, the firm of Liveright finally went bankrupt. The reorganization of 1930 had only prolonged the agony. Thanks to Saxe Commins's prescience, O'Neill suffered no loss, and many other publishers were bidding for him because his works were desirable properties. At this time, O'Neill repaid some of Saxe's many acts of friendship: "Out of generosity and loyalty he made it plain that he would sign no contract without my counsel and consent. Furthermore, he wanted it stipulated in writing that no arrangement to publish his plays could be made unless the agreement included a clause which guaranteed...[Commins] a job as his editor and a general editor of the company of his choice for the duration of his contract" (Commins, 1978, p. 26). To this last clause Saxe raised a typically unselfish objection, noting the inadvisability of irrevocably binding the two of them together since Saxe "might conceivably embarrass him." O'Neill agreed to Saxe's reservation but insisted that he remain as his editor. The bidding for the O'Neill properties continued, and Commins recommended that O'Neill move his publishing program to Random House, whose president, Bennett Cerf, and his partner, Donald Klopfer, never regretted the decision. Commins moved to Random House on July 9, 1933, where he remained until his death just over twenty-five years later. Many years later, Cerf said "that Commins was 'almost more important to us than O'Neill,' while...Klopfer, going further, called Saxe 'our prize acquisition of the two' " (Sheaffer, 1973, p. 417).

At Random House, Saxe Commins was editor for such outstanding and varied authors as S. N. Behrman, Sinclair Lewis, Robinson Jeffers, John O'Hara, Theodor Giesel ("Dr. Seuss"), James Michener, Budd Schulberg, Adlai Stevenson, W. H. Auden, Henry Steele Commager, Stephen Spender, Isak Dinesen, Etienne Gilson, and, perhaps most important, William Faulkner, with whom the Commins family developed a very warm relationship. In addition, Saxe was also director of the Modern Library for many years and frequently wrote the introductions to individual volumes. He also "edited and provided a foreword to each of the two volumes in Scribner's Wilderness Edition of *The Plays of Eugene O'Neill* (New York, 1935), though the forewords were signed by O'Neill" (Commins, 1978, p. 100). He also "wrote a statement about *Bound East for Cardiff,** likewise signed by O'Neill and edited and supplied with a foreword the Armed Services Edition of *Selected Plays of Eugene O'Neill* (1945).

The friendship of Saxe and Eugene continued on both a personal and business basis, O'Neill customarily giving his first-night tickets to the Comminses because he preferred to stay away. He also enlisted his friend to send him the books he needed for his work. After O'Neill left Georgia for California in Fall 1936, Commins visited him at Tao House on more than one occasion. In 1939–1940, he typed the revised manuscript of *The Iceman Cometh** there and took it back to New York for safekeeping, for production was not planned until after the war. He also retyped *Long Day's Journey into Night** from Carlotta's typescripts during another visit in 1942, one of a very select group who read it prior to O'Neill's death (others were Eugene Jr., Carlotta, Russel Crouse, Dudley Nichols, and Sophus and Eline Winther).

After the O'Neills' return to New York, the two families renewed their friendship with frequent visits. Dorothy Commins assisted O'Neill in 1946 in reconstructing the music he wanted to use in *The Iceman Cometh*. However, as the personal relations between O'Neill and Carlotta deteriorated, Saxe was the embarrassed observer of some very unfortunate incidents in which he saw Carlotta as the aggressor and O'Neill as long-suffering victim. One of these confontations was shockingly vindictive. Apparently, O'Neill was unable to find the manuscripts he had brought from California, and Carlotta taunted him with senility and loss of memory while he and Saxe Commins ransacked their Hotel Barclay suite. Carlotta kept suggesting places to search, even insisting that they look through her underwear drawer, but they found nothing. Finally Saxe went home, very upset, leaving O'Neill almost frantic. A couple of days later, O'Neill told Saxe that Carlotta had deliberately removed them as a punishment for some offense of which O'Neill claimed ignorance, though it has been suggested by his biographers that it may have been his relationship with a younger woman (of which Saxe was uninformed—see Commins, 1978, pp. 65–67, and Sheaffer, 1973, p. 560). Carlotta always distrusted her husband's roving eye.

The other appalling incident, which led to the O'Neills' temporary separation in 1948 and subsequent departure for Boston, also led to an irrevocable break between Commins and Carlotta. Saxe again was present when O'Neill agreed to lend a small sum of money to M. Eleanor Fitzgerald, his old friend from Provincetown days, who needed to make an advance payment to a hospital she was entering for exploratory surgery. Carlotta took the telephone call and passed the instrument to O'Neill "icily." Naturally O'Neill agreed, but during the conversation Carlotta paced the floor, growing more and more enraged: "She was close to hysteria, her eyes blazing and her voice hoarsely incoherent with words of imprecation" (Commins, 1978, p. 69). As soon as O'Neill left the phone, she started cursing all of his friends, "Fitzi" in particular. O'Neill tried to explain, but Carlotta would not be placated, while Saxe "cowered" in his chair, waiting for a moment at which he could decently leave. When the servant came to clear away the coffee cups, he made his excuses and left, so he was not a witness to the scene of violence that followed, though O'Neill later told him of it. Carlotta smashed the glass top to his dresser, tore up the only picture he had of his mother and himself as a baby, and screamed, "Your mother was a whore!" (Commins, 1978, p. 70). At this O'Neill slapped her, so she went to her room, packed a bag, and moved out.

Once again, Saxe came to the rescue. When O'Neill telephoned him with the tale of the night's events, he enlisted the aid of Walter Casey, an old friend from New London, who came to stay with O'Neill. The playwright was pitiably remorseful, blaming himself for the altercation. His tremor became more acute, so a doctor was called; he prescribed sedatives, frequent cups of black coffee, and suggested that someone remain with him at all times. Consequently, Casey and Saxe alternated on "sentry duty" for ten days, while Carlotta had pairs of detectives keeping the apartment under constant surveillance. On the night of January 28, 1948, when Saxe had gone home, exhausted, O'Neill fell on his way to the bathroom and broke his right arm, Casey being deeply asleep with the aid of some drink and unable to hear his cries. Saxe promptly arranged for O'Neill to go to Doctors Hospital for treatment and saw to it that Casey supervised the removal of O'Neill's manuscripts to the vaults of Random House in accordance with his request. Carlotta then telephoned Commins at his office and abused him as a thief for removing the manuscripts and reviled him with such gross obscenities that Saxe forbore to write them down. Particularly hurtful seem to have been "her last three whiplash words" which concluded that telephone call and appear to have been "crooked Jew Bastard." This incident made a deep impression on this sensitive and caring human being; that night when he went home, he broke into tears (Sheaffer, 1973, p. 609; Commins, 1978, pp. 68–74).

After this, Saxe knew that his friendship with O'Neill must end if Eugene returned to Carlotta because she would intercept all mail and telephone calls. After O'Neill's departure for Boston with Carlotta, Saxe no longer communicated with O'Neill, and when Dorothy sent him a congratulatory telegram on his sixtieth birthday, she received a reply from Carlotta filled with domestic inanities and without any reference to Saxe. Carlotta was vindictive enough to sacrifice an extraordinary friendship to her own possessiveness. Even after this kind of treatment, Saxe Commins remained a good friend. He had assisted Eugene Gladstone O'Neill, Jr.,* in co-editing with Whitney J. Oates of Princeton a two-volume translation of *The Complete Greek Drama* for Random House which was published in 1948. Now he helped the young man in an unsuccessful attempt to raise money to fund a radio series (Sheaffer, 1973, p. 629). Commins was also the first person informed in 1950 when Eugene, Jr., committed suicide. Instantly he contacted O'Neill's lawyer, who volunteered to inform O'Neill. According to Commins's account, Carlotta, on hearing the news answered, " 'How dare you invade our privacy?' and slammed the receiver down'' (Commins, 1978, pp. 79–80). Commins never heard O'Neill's reaction.

During 1951, when the O'Neills briefly separated again after a cataclysmic series of incidents, Commins had another battle with Carlotta. Once again, he and other friends such as Lawrence Langner* (of the Theatre Guild*) rallied around O'Neill when he was hospitalized in Boston with a broken leg. They persuaded him to come to New York in what "Carlotta chose to call a conspiracy to kidnap and transport her husband from Salem, Massachusetts, to New York City" (Commins, 1978, p. 80). His full account of the situation is given by his wife (pp. 80–85) and Carlotta comes out of it very badly. (*See also* Monterey, Carlotta.) The whole chapter entitled ''The Sequestration and Death of Eugene O'Neill'' is one of great pathos, showing the way in which Carlotta, with what seems to be singular malice, forced a complete break in a friendship of almost forty years, attempting to gain total control of her husband and to make him totally dependent on her. The ties of this torturing relationship were too strong for O'Neill to break, and therefore he decided that he should return to Boston on her terms to spend what was left of his life with her. Saxe and Dorothy Commins were devastated. They even offered O'Neill a permanent home with them in Princeton where Dorothy could nurse him, but O'Neill refused. After his departure for Boston in 1951, Commins never saw his friend again.

Saxe was not yet finished with Carlotta, however, and had another brush with her in 1954, the year after Eugene's death, this time over the publication of *Long Day's Journey into Night*. Commins wished to honor the signed instrument of November 29, 1945, by which O'Neill stipulated that the text of this work was to remain sealed until twenty-five years after his death. Carlotta requested Bennett Cerf, president of Random House, to break the seals and publish the text. He initially refused, and he consulted with Commins, who suggested that they get a legal opinion and in addition stipulated, if they did publish the work, that Carlotta sign a statement to be printed with the text indicating that she had authorized the publication. When she heard of this, Carlotta's old animosity was rekindled. She accused Commins of plotting against her and, most hurtful of all, "of having ruined all the O'Neill plays on which I had worked" (Commins, 1978, p. 58). Bennett Cerf stood behind Commins in a letter to Carlotta, but the two men were shocked when lawyers for both Random House and Carlotta agreed that she had the right to publish the work on the grounds that ''the instructions of the deceased may be superseded by those of the *sole* beneficiary and executrix of a will.'' Commins believed that this was ''why Eugene O'Neill had been *induced* to disown his two surviving children'' (Commins, 1978, p. 58), in order that Carlotta would have control of this property before the expiration of the twenty-five-year period—which would have been 1978. Bennett Cerf relinquished the rights of publication rather than go against the wishes of O'Neill, and in 1956 the play was published by Yale University Press.

Commins was by now having health problems. After an initial heart attack in 1953, he had continued to work with his other authors; but in 1955 he stepped down as editor-in-chief at Random House, continuing his work at home, with a reduced schedule in New York. One author with whom he worked with particular closeness was William Faulkner, whom he had looked after since the mid-1930s. Faulkner frequently visited the Commins family and was also assigned a desk and typewriter at Random House where he could work undisturbed—and also where he could find Saxe Commins on the days he came into New York. Where O'Neill had developed an almost cruelly self-centered discipline in regard to his work, Faulkner had not, and Commins worked very closely with him, helping him to hone his ideas for *A Fable* and the last two volumes of his Snopes series, *The Town* and *The Mansion*, as well as a volume of short stories. Saxe Commins and his wife continued with Faulkner the same generous psychic and professional support they had given O'Neill, one of their five Nobel prize-winning authors (Pär Lagerqvist, Isak Dinesen, and Sinclair Lewis were the others). Commins was instrumental in having Faulkner come to Princeton as writer-in-residence in 1954, and he himself was always readily available to students.

In Fall 1957, Commins underwent surgery and was unable to attend the Eugene O'Neill Pipe Night at the Players Club, New York City. He recuperated well, and by mid-year, he and Dorothy were planning a sea voyage to Sweden for their son's marriage. A few weeks before they were due to sail, he was hospitalized with a mild heart attack, but by July 4, he was working on the galley proofs of Isak Dinesen's *Last Tales* and Edgar Snow's *Journey to the Beginning*. He finished the galleys on July 16, 1958, and gave them to Dorothy to mail to Random House. She returned to the hospital and stayed as late as she was allowed. The next morning, she was told that he had died during the night.

Saxe Commins, along with Maxwell Perkins, was one of the legendary editors of American book publishing. The services he rendered were incalculable to his authors, whether they involved the meticulous checking of facts or the acquisition of a tuxedo. Commins was not a creative artist, but he was capable of perceiving and nurturing the creativity of others, self-effacingly managing to bring order out of seeming chaos, yet never violating the author's purpose. He was a man of the utmost tact, sensitivity, and consideration, capable of the most unselfish friendship; and fortunately for him, he married in Dorothy Berliner, a woman of equal sensitivity. Her 1978 volume, *What Is an Editor? Saxe Commins at Work*, is a monument not only to her husband but also to her and a remarkable matrimonial union. *See* in "References: Commins (1978); Gelb and Gelb (1973); Sheaffer (1973). Random House has some material which includes correspondence concerning the publication of *Long Day's Journey into Night*. *See also* Andrew B. Myers, "Hysteria Night in the Sophomore Dormitory: Eugene

O'Neill's *Days Without End,*'' *Columbia University Library Columns*, vol. 28, no. 2 (1979), pp. 3–13, for an example of this material. Saxe Commins's own papers are in the Princeton University Library.

CONDON, James J., proprietor of a saloon at 252 Fulton Street, near the old Washington Market, New York City. He was nicknamed Jimmy-the-Priest.*

COOK, George Cram (''Jig''), (1873–1924), friend of Eugene O'Neill and a founder of the Provincetown Players.* Born in Davenport, Iowa, October 7, 1873, to Edward and Ellen Katherine Cook. Died in Delphi, Greece, January 14, 1924. Father, a corporation lawyer. Educated in the public schools of Davenport, preparatory school of Griswold College, Iowa State University, and Harvard University, graduating B.A. in 1894 with a major in classics and M.A. the following year. Spent the next year in Heidelberg, preparing for a teaching career in an American university and traveling through Europe. Returned to become an instructor in English at Iowa State University where he seems to have tried to give his rather provincial students an education in European culture. His passionate involvement with classical literature, particularly Greek language and culture, continued, and in later years he spoke to Floyd Dell, an old friend, about trying to found a new Athens in Iowa, the place that, according to his third wife, Susan Glaspell,* he both loved and hated. He left teaching in 1898–1899 to write *Roderick Taliaferro* (published 1901), a romantic novel set in the Mexico of the Emperor Maximilian, and also *The Faggot and the Flame* (1900).

In 1901 he married a young woman from Chicago and went to teach at Leland Stanford Junior University (now Stanford University). However, he speedily became discontented with teaching and the restrictions of academic life and returned to his family's log cabin in Iowa to write. Finding difficulty in proceeding with his new novel, *The Balm of Life*, he turned seriously to farming, keeping a ''Farm Journal'' that detailed his agricultural experiences. As a result of his complete change in life style and his shortage of money, his marriage broke up in 1905. Cook was at that time beginning to feel the loneliness of rural life, expressing concern about finding time to write, and thinking about the advantages of beginning an entirely new course of study. Left alone, he had an unsuccessful love affair (one of many during his life), but this time he seriously thought of suicide. Slowly he put himself back together, partly through reading the work of Nietzsche, some of which he translated himself. In 1906 he met and later married Mollie Price, the mother of his two children, Nilla and Harl. He also became interested in politics and was introduced to socialism through seventeen-year-old Floyd Dell, who became a lifelong friend. Together they founded the Monist Society of Davenport. At this time Cook wrote *The Needle and the North*, a triangle tale of two men and one woman, and *The Chasm*, a political novel.

In 1912, Cook moved to Chicago to become an associate to Francis Hackett and Floyd Dell on the Friday literary review of the *Chicago Evening Post*. By this time, his second marriage had been dissolved, and on April 14, 1913, he married Susan Glaspell, whom he had first met in 1907, in a civil ceremony in Weehawken, New Jersey, conducted by the mayor of that town. They moved to Provincetown, Massachusetts, for this and many succeeding summers, spending winters in New York.

In Provincetown, Cook devoted himself to remodeling his house, later installing an elevator to spare his wife's heart from strain. Many of their friends from Greenwich Village also summered in Provincetown and it was there that the Provincetown Players* began in 1914 as an outgrowth of amateur theatricals and private performances of plays written among the group. Cook and Glaspell collaborated on *Suppressed Desires* (1914), a comedy-satire on Freudian psychology, and *Tickless Time* (1918), a play about idealism in a mechanistic world. On his own he wrote *Change Your Style* (1915), a satire on art schools; *The Athenian Women* (1918), an antiwar play based upon *Lysistrata*; and *The Spring* (1912), a symbolic play. From 1914 to 1922, with a "sabbatical" break for writing in 1919–1920, Cook and Glaspell were guiding forces of the new group, which now offered performances during the summer at the Wharf Theater, Provincetown, and at the Playwrights' Theater, Macdougal Street, Greenwich Village, New York City, during the winter. Cook had long been disappointed in the quality of the contemporary American theatre, and he looked back to the theatre of ancient Greece as an ideal of serious, communal theatre. He envisaged "a whole community working together, developing unsuspected talents" (Susan Glaspell, *The Road to the Temple*, 1927; reprinted 1941, p. 251), believing that "true drama is born only of one feeling animating all the members of a clan— a spirit shared by all and expressed by the few for the all. If there is nothing to take the place of the common religious purpose and passion of the primitive group, out of which the Dionysian dance was born, no new vital drama can arise in any people." (Quoted by Glaspell, 1927, reprinted 1941, pp. 252–253.)

This was the faith on which the Provincetown Players was founded, and this was the belief to which Cook devoted the next eight years of his life, contributing his idealism, his encouragement, his literary ability, and his eminently useful skill in carpentry. He was solely responsible for constructing the dome for the stage of the Playwrights' Theater for the first performance of O'Neill's *The Emperor Jones** (1920), the play whose success was ironically the eventual cause of the destruction of Cook's own dream because it turned the group toward commercial and economic considerations as a barometer of success. But in 1916, when the Provincetown Players first discovered Eugene O'Neill and his alleged "trunkful of plays," this was far in the future. Speaking of the first reading of O'Neill's *The Moon of the Caribbees,** Glaspell wrote, with romantic enthusiasm "Then we knew what we were for." This partnership between playwright and company continued until the group disbanded in 1922, and it remained fruitful for both. O'Neill found a group of intelligent, sympathetic performers, producers, designers, and an audience devoted to change in the theatre, while the company found a playwright destined to shake the American theatrical establishment to its roots, a playwright whose ideals matched its own. The Cooks and the O'Neills became very close during the years that O'Neill summered at the converted Coast Guard station at Peaked Hill Bars, O'Neill once performing an ultimate act of friendship by putting the Cooks' beloved dog out of its misery.

As the Provincetown Players began to adopt the "uptown point of view of money and notoriety" (Glaspell, 1927; reprinted 1941, p. 305), Cook began to withdraw from the group and in 1922 wrote its obituary: "Our individual gifts and talents have sought their private perfection. We have not, as we hoped, created the beloved community of life givers. . . . We have valued creative energy less than its rewards—our sin against our Holy Ghost. . . .

Since we have failed spiritually in the elemental things—failed to pull together. . .and since the result of this is mediocrity, we keep our promise. We give this theater we love a good death. The Provincetown Players end their story here." (Glaspell, 1927, reprinted 1941, pp. 309–310.)

With the demise of this experiment Cook had decided to go to Greece. In romantic reminiscence, Glaspell recounts finding him sitting alone in the Playwrights' Theater with the blue light playing on the dome he had built for *The Emperor Jones*. He sat in silence for some time and finally announced, "It is time to go to Greece" (Glaspell, 1927, reprinted 1941, pp. 310–311). And so in March 1922 they did, eventually settling in Delphi among the shepherds where "Kyrios Kouk," as he came to be called, tried to awaken in the memory of Greece's modern inhabitants a sense of their historic past. Cook spoke ancient Greek, but he began to learn the modern language as well. From Susan Glaspell's account, Cook was happy in the last eighteen months of his life there, but she herself was less so, possibly because the practicalities of daily living devolved upon her, and also because she did not learn the language. She went back briefly to the United States when her father died and then returned to Greece with Cook's daughter, Nilla, who was to be educated in Athens. Cook adopted the clothes of the Greek shepherds, listened to their tales, translated his play, *The Athenian Women*, into modern Greek, developed a village play on the Cain-Abel theme (dreaming of another Oberammergau), and even rebuilt a Cyclopian wall with his own hands. While Glaspell saw, with some justified fear, the violence that underlay existence on Parnassos, Cook, though somewhat disillusioned, took refuge in the historic past and in his multifarious activities. Once again, as in Provincetown, they adopted a dog, and were distressed over its death, because they had saved it from ill-treatment. Cook died painfully on January 14, 1924, of glanders, a horse disease which had been transmitted to him by this dog. He was buried in Delphi after a Greek Orthodox funeral in which ceremonies were organized by the inhabitants of Delphi according to their folk customs. The Greek government, in an unprecedented move, ordered that a stone from the ruins of the Temple of Apollo be used to mark the gravesite.

Cook's life was a curious one, full of enthusiasms both spiritual and physical. He seems to have been too busy encouraging the gifts of others to care for his own, and as a result he left a small quantity of written work. Above all, he was able to kindle fire in others and maintain their affection for his ideals, even if they later departed from them. Susan Glaspell gives a moving account of his funeral (1927, reprinted 1941, pp. 442–444), noting that "in the stadium of Delphi, in memory of George Cram Cook, Greeks have revived the Pythian games," but today guides make no mention of him. See in "References": Cook (1925); Deutsch and Hanau (1931); Gelb and Gelb (1973); Glaspell (1927; reprinted 1941); Hapgood (1939); Sarlós (1982); Sheaffer (1968); Vorse (1942).

CORA. In *The Iceman Cometh*,* a thin, peroxide-blonde prostitute in her mid-twenties, whose pimp is Chuck Morello.* She is a roomer at Harry Hope's* saloon, and her pipe dream is that she will someday marry Chuck, who will lay off the drink, and they will move to a farm in New Jersey or Long Island, despite the fact that they know nothing of farming. Under the influence of Theodore Hickman,* the salesman who comes to the bar annually to celebrate Harry's birthday, she attempts to translate the dream into reality. But she gets drunk and Chuck leaves her, realizing the impossibility of the dream. After Hickey's arrest on the charge of murdering his wife, Cora and other denizens of the bar seize on his plea of insanity, a pipe dream explanation which discredits what he has taught them. Then she is happy to get drunk in order to forget the outside world and to regain illusions.

CORDOVA, Beatriz de. In *The Fountain*,* the eighteen-year-old daughter of Maria de Cordova* and Vicente de Cordova.* Her mother had been in love with Juan Ponce de Leon,* but he was too dedicated to Spain to trouble himself with love. Beatriz's father fought a duel with Juan, who had to leave Spain. On the death of both parents, Beatriz is sent to Porto Rico as Juan's ward. Her mother had given her instructions to bring him "tenderness," that same tenderness Maria had told him she would pray would come to him. Juan is overwhelmed with love for the young woman but realizes that she is too young for him. He departs on his obsessional quest for the fountain of youth and begs her not to marry before his return.

   In Florida, Juan is wounded as a result of a plot against him by Nano,* an Indian, and there he undergoes a revelation in which Beatriz becomes for him the spirit of the fountain, the spirit of youth, the instrument of redemption. Her face and voice singing the song of the fountain lead Juan to an understanding of the essential mystery of life—the oneness of creation and of religions, the principle of flux, and the participation of the individual soul in the vastness of eternity. On his return, purged of all ambition, Juan discovers that Beatriz has fallen in love with his own nephew, also named Juan. He gives his consent and they depart happily.

   Beatriz is more of a symbolic than a human character, and she appears to have the same function as Dante's Beatrice, who leads the poet to an understanding of the sempiternal rose that signifies eternity.

CORDOVA, Maria de. In *The Fountain*,* a beautiful woman of thirty-eight, wife of Vicente de Cordova.* She is unhappily married and for a long time has been in love with Juan Ponce de Leon.* He, however, is dedicated to the service of Spain and considers their relationship to be "a rare friendship," and he refuses to reduce it to the common status of love. She retires from court, and after Juan has fought a fairly harmless duel with Vicente, (which necessitates his departure from Spain) she and her husband have a daughter, Beatriz de Cordova,* who later becomes Juan's ward. Maria sends Beatriz to Juan to bring him the "tenderness" she had told him she would pray for as his consolation "when his hard youth dies."

CORDOVA, Vicente de. In *The Fountain*,* husband of Maria de Cordova* and father of Beatriz de Cordova.* He is about forty-five, and his marriage is unhappy. He believes that Juan Ponce de Leon* has impugned his honor (and possibly that of his wife), so he challenges Juan to a duel in which the older man is pinked by Juan, who could easily have killed him. The ensuing scandal forces Juan to leave Spain with Christopher Columbus.*

CORSARO, Frank (1924–   ), director, actor, teacher, librettist, playwright. Born Francesco Andrea Corsaro in New York to Joseph and Marie (Quirino) Corsaro. His father was a tailor. Graduate of DeWitt Clinton High School, 1944; attended Yale University School of Drama, 1945–47; studied at Actors Studio (1954–67). Married Mary Cross Lueders, 1971.

Corsaro has directed many plays, both on and off-Broadway, as well as in summer stock, also playing small roles. Since 1966, he has been most notable for his productions of opera, particularly at the New York City Opera and the Opera House, Kennedy Center, Washington, D.C. He wrote the libretto for *Before Breakfast*,* a one-act monologue opera with music by Thomas Pasatieri,* loosely based on O'Neill's one-act play of the same name. The Woman (here unnamed) is portrayed as a former successful marathon dancer for whom everything afterward has been disastrous. The opera, in effect a forty-minute mad scene, includes a three-minute jazz-dance sequence. The opera, first performed by the New York City Opera at the New York State Theatre, Lincoln Center, New York City, with Marilyn Zschau, October 9, 1980, was not well received, being evaluated as a "weak piece." The music was considered derivative, resembling the work of Gian Carlo Menotti.

"COUGH, THE." Original title of *The Web*.*

CREGAN, Jamie. In *A Touch of the Poet*,* former corporal in the Seventh Dragoons at the Battle of Talavera, July 27, 1809. He is a middle-aged, tall, gaunt Irishman with an old saber scar over one cheekbone. He is neatly dressed, but his clothes are old and worn. Clearly down on his luck, he happens to visit Cornelius Melody's* tavern and discovers that its owner is the major under whom he had served at Talavera. Cregan had also been brought up on the Melody estate in County Galway, Ireland, and he is used as an expository device early in the play to communicate the details of Con's past, particularly his womanizing and the true facts of his marriage to Nora Melody.* He gets drunk with Melody and also comes to his aid in his attempt to do battle with the Harford clan. Melody "pulls rank" on *Corporal* Cregan, but Jamie has a reluctant admiration for the way in which Con manages to keep the past alive as a means of refusing to face the present. When Melody shoots his horse, Cregan considers that he is mad.

CROSBY, Captain. In *Diff'rent*,* husband of Mrs. Crosby* and father of Emma Crosby* and Jack Crosby.* He is a sixty-year-old weatherbeaten sea captain, almost as wide as he is tall, with a large jovial bellow for a laugh. He is full of health and strength and also of the joy of living. He cannot believe that Emma is serious about not marrying Caleb Williams* because of his sexual escapade in the South Seas when in fact he was not really to blame. Crosby has not been a "plaster saint" himself, as his wife well knows. She obviously rules him at home.

CROSBY, Emma. In *Diff'rent*,* daughter of Captain Crosby* and Mrs. Crosby* and engaged to Caleb Williams.* She is slender, somewhat plain, but with thick light-brown hair and "large soft blue eyes which have an incongruous quality of absent-minded dreaminess about them." The conflict in her personality, signified by her plain features and romantic eyes, is further underlined by the furnishings of the room, which are of a stern, scrupulous cleanliness contrasted with a small piano. The juxtaposition of the family Bible and romantic novels shows a similar contradiction. She refuses to marry Caleb Williams because of one sexual peccadillo, in which he was not totally to blame. She has an exaggerated and imperfectly articulated ideal of marriage, wishing to place a husband on a pedestal of purity. But whether this means that she would desire an asexual marriage is not made clear. Certainly, her family seems more tolerant of masculine faults than is Emma. Exactly how Emma acquired these high moral standards is never stated; but if it is from romantic novels, then one wonders whether O'Neill intended her to be a Madame Bovary in reverse, and certainly the name is evocative.

Thirty years pass and Emma is a "scrawny" dried-up woman of fifty who flings herself at the cruel, oafish, fortune-hunting Benny Rogers,* again in a manner which seems unmotivated. Once more, the furnishings of the room signify Emma's internal attitudes and contraditions. She has renovated it in the perfect (though studied) style of the jazz age, yet she has retained the marble clock (symbol of the passage of time) and the family Bible (symbol of continuity and righteousness). She agrees to marry Benny Rogers, and her contradictory attitude toward sex is now compounded by prurience and the remnants of prudishness. She breaks Caleb Williams's heart by telling him that she loves the worthless Benny more than she had ever loved Caleb, but she is repaid by Benny's callous rejection of her when he thinks he may be able to get Caleb to buy him off. Caleb, in despair, commits suicide after her rejection of him, and in turn, Emma goes out to hang herself in imitation of Caleb. Her final gesture of dismantling all the furniture of the renovated parlor is dramatically good, but overall the characterization of both principal figures is shallow, though O'Neill seems to be attempting some kind of psychological insight.

CROSBY, Jack. In *Diff'rent*,* "a hulking, stocky-built young fellow of twenty-five," brother to Emma Crosby* and son of Captain Crosby* and Mrs. Crosby.* He is later drowned in company with Alf Rogers.* Jack is a born practical joker and tells the tale of Caleb Williams's* loss of virginity during a whaling voyage. He has little care that he might hurt either Caleb or his sister Emma. As a result of his coarse tattling, Emma refuses to marry Caleb.

CROSBY, Mrs. In *Diff'rent*,* the wife of Captain Crosby* and mother of Emma Crosby* and Jack Crosby.* "She is a large, fat, florid woman of fifty," weighing over two hundred pounds. "She exudes an atmosphere of motherly good nature." She cannot believe that Emma will not marry Caleb Williams because of a single sexual error, when he was not really to blame. She tells her daughter that if she had kept her eyes open around town, she would know the way men act. She accepts a double standard and tries to convince Emma to do the same.

CYBEL. In *The Great God Brown*,* a prostitute, friend of Dion Anthony* and protected by William A. ["Billy"] Brown.* Cybel first appears as "a strong, calm, sensual blonde of about twenty." She has a healthy, fresh complexion, a full-breasted and full-hipped figure, with "movements slow and solidly langorous like an animal's." She appears throughout the play, and at the end, when Billy Brown dies, she looks like an earth-mother idol. Her name is significant as being that of the earth-goddess of Asia Minor, and such is the role she plays throughout the play. She takes Dion Anthony* into her room when she finds him lying drunk on her doorstep, and she mothers him. She understands the emotional turmoil of Dion, and she alone can bring him peace because she, unlike Margaret Anthony,* Dion's wife, is not afraid of his real face. As the symbolic figure of fertility, or nature, she is beyond the trammels of conventional morality, and therefore she must wear the mask of the hardened prostitute so that the rest of the world can accept her. Otherwise they would not understand. She can see beneath the surface of appearances to the spirit beneath. Her symbol is a battered old player piano which can play sentimental ditties. Billy Brown, who perceives only outward appearances, dislikes the piano, but Dion and Cybel understand it. She removes Dion's mask from Brown as he dies, telling him he cannot take it to bed with him. He must die in his own person, not that of Dion. Cybel helps both Dion and Billy to die well, achieving a renunciation of life through a realization that life is merely a phase of existence, and one should not care too much about it. She speaks of the rhythm of the seasons, of birth, growth, decay, and even death—but always there is spring, always renewing—and humanity is part of that great cycle. At first, Cybel may seem the conventional prostitute with the heart of gold, but O'Neill uses her as a symbolic figure. As the play progresses, she becomes more and more like an idol. Actually, her character is not completely successful in the play, because she seems too removed from the action, and she is not sufficiently drawn to fulfill her purpose in the play with any real authority.

D

DANCER, A. In *Thirst*,* a young woman "dressed in a complete, short-skirted dancer's costume of black velvet covered with spangles." Her hair is long and blonde. "Her silk stockings are baggy and wrinkled and her dancing shoes swollen and misshapen;" but she wears a fine diamond necklace. She is emaciated from hunger and thirst, which have turned a once beautiful creature "into a mocking specter of a dancer." She is desperate for water and food and is terrified of the sharks which swim about the raft that contains three shipwreck survivors. She has been an extremely successful dancer, and her necklace is the gift of an elderly British duke who once proposed marriage to her. A Gentlemen,* one of her two companions, recalls her beauty, and she recalls that the second officer of the ship had loved her and had managed to save her by placing her on this raft. But beauty and success mean little when survival is the only reality, and so she tries to bribe the West Indian Mulatto Sailor,* the third person on the raft, first with the gift of her diamond necklace and then with the offer of her body. She wants the water she believes he has secreted away from the other two. When he refuses, she goes mad, rises up, and performs a dance of death before falling lifeless. The Sailor suggests that he and the Gentleman consume her body. That leads to the final struggle in which her body is thrown overboard, the Gentleman is stabbed, and he drags the Sailor with him to the sharks. Irony pervades this play, and the Gentleman and the Dancer constantly rail against a hostile God and universe. The Sailor, more attuned to survival, says nothing. All are equal here, caught up by circumstance.

DARRELL, Edmund (Ned). In *Strange Interlude*,* the lover of Nina Leeds* and the father of her son, Gordon Evans.* He is twenty-seven at the beginning of the twenty-five-year span of the play and is a promising neurologist working at a hospital for wounded veterans of World War I. He had been a friend of Gordon Shaw,* Nina's dead fiancé, and the dorm-mate of Sam Evans.* When Nina asks for employment at the hospital, he agrees, for Gordon's sake, but is appalled to discover that she is hopelessly promiscuous, having decided that only by giving herself to any of these men can she purge herself of her guilt for not having consummated her relationship with Gordon. As a means of saving her from herself, Darrell recommends marriage with Sam Evans, who worships the memory of Gordon. Darrell considers this his experiment in working with human lives or, as Nina suggests, playing "God the Father." Unfortunately, Sam comes of a family with hereditary insanity, and Nina has an abortion on the advice of Sam's mother. She does not, however, tell Sam.

Nina is devastated by the situation but feels she must remain with Sam. She tells Darrell of her predicament and, following Sam's mother's suggestion, asks Darrell to father her child so that Sam can be happy in thinking the child is his. In a very scientific way Darrell agrees, but then the two of them fall passionately in love. Finally, Nina becomes so desperate that she thinks of divorcing Sam, but Darrell dissuades her. He tries repeatedly to stay away from Nina, to try to forget her, but always he returns at her bidding, allowing everything, including his career, to flounder. The two do not resume physical intercourse, though there are opportunities. Darrell looks at Gordon Evans, his son who is not aware of his true parentage, and the two of them become disenchanted with each other. Gordon hates Darrell because he once saw him kissing Nina, and Darrell dislikes the fact that his son is being made into the image of the dead Gordon Shaw.

As he grows older, Darrell comes into a little money, which Sam manages to parlay into a comfortable fortune so that Darrell can play at biology, having long ago given up on neurology. He becomes enthusiastic about the work of his young assistant, Preston, who becomes for him a surrogate son, and finally he manages to break the tie with Nina, though he will always remember their afternoons. At times, Darrell seems desperate for happiness, and as a result he can even detest the inoffensive Sam. For Darrell, Nina is a destructive possessor, and he himself is too weak to break from her. He finally realizes that he was nothing more than a body to Nina, and that even during their lovemaking Gordon Shaw was figuratively present. He has been the ghost haunting their relationship throughout the play. This is the reason that he roots for Gordon Evans to lose his final regatta crew race, much to Sam's rage.

When Sam has his stroke, which leads to his death a few months later, Darrell sees his innermost wish fulfilled; but when it occurs, he knows that he no longer cares. Once Sam is dead, Ned Darrell discovers from Gordon that Sam has left a half-million dollars to Darrell's Caribbean research station. Then Gordon confesses that he had once seen Ned kissing Nina and reveals his awareness that Nina has loved Darrell more than Sam, and therefore, he expects them to marry. Darrell makes a pro forma proposal of marriage to Nina, because Gordon expects it, but asks her to refuse him. This she does, because their "ghosts" would haunt them otherwise. When Nina asks Charles Marsden* if he will marry her, Darrell gives them his blessing and leaves with his memories of Nina who has in effect destroyed his life.

Ned Darrell is the image of man as lover throughout the play.

DARROW, Susannah. In the unpublished scenario, "S.O.S."* Susannah is the forty-year-old daughter of a retired whaling captain and has nursed her father until his death. She marries John Lathrop,* the local telegraphist, and turns him away from drink. When he loses his job, she moves with him to New Jersey and later to Brooklyn. She accompanies him on his voyages as a wireless operator on the *Rio Grande* for two years but is forced to remain behind to look after her business interests on one occasion. That is the time that John accidentally contributes to the loss of the vessel because his deafness has made it impossible for him to hear a warning signal. However, his hearing is suddenly restored, and John becomes a hero by warning the American cruiser, *New Orleans*, of a raider's position. He is executed by the Germans and Susannah is lionized as a hero's widow. She returns to Acropolis, her home town, and moves into Mrs. Perkins's boarding house, where John had lived before he was married. She has no other home now, having had to sell her house because of financial reverses. However, by living where John had lived, she now feels close to him. She never finds out the story of John's contribution to the loss of his vessel. She is a sketchily drawn character, devoted to her husband, and in that she is quite different from Mary Knapp* in the earlier *Warnings*.* A typescript is in the Harvard Theatre Collection.

DAVIDSON, Mrs. Elizabeth. In *The First Man,* the only decent member of the Jayson clan. She is seventy-six years old, a "sinewy old lady, old-fashioned, unbending and rigorous in manner . . . dressed aggressively in the fashion of a bygone age." She is the family matriarch who remains untouched by the scandal surrounding the paternity of Martha Jayson's* child. She is contented finally to have a Jayson carry on the family name and is the only one of the family to rejoice in his birth. Curtis Jayson* gives her custody of the child as he rushes off to his five-year anthropological expedition in Asia. He tells Aunt Elizabeth that she is the only member of the family with "unmuddled integrity." Obviously, this is a rather impractical move on Curt's part, but quite clearly O'Neill was simply trying to bring the play to a close.

DAVIDSON, Sidney. *See* Smitty.

DAVIS, a seaman on the S.S. *Glencairn*, "a short dark man," who appears in all the shipboard plays of the S.S. *Glencairn* group.

DAVIS, Sid. In *Ah, Wilderness!* brother of Essie Miller* and permanent wooer of Lily Miller,* Nat Miller's* sister. He is forty-five, short, with the look of a permanent adolescent. He dresses in clothes that were once natty and loud but are now shabby and shapeless. His problem is the bottle, and he becomes intoxicated at the July 4 picnic, once again. He is such an amusing drunk that everyone encourages him, much to Lily Miller's anger. Nonetheless, he is a sympathetic, understanding person where members of the family are concerned. He and Nat Miller get along well, and Nat tries to help when Sid loses his job as a reporter. Lily Miller loves Sid, and he loves her (after his fashion), making a ritual proposal of marriage almost every day. She had once been engaged to him but broke it off as the result of his drunken escapade with prostitutes. He has some self-knowledge but seems powerless to change his ways. He is the stock figure of the weak family member with some brains, and even talent as a reporter, but unable to translate potential into achievement. He is mildly romantic and, like Lily, he quotes from the *Rubáiyát* but particularly the parts about liquor.

DAY, Dorothy (1897–1980), social activist. Born in Brooklyn, New York, on November 8, 1897, the third of four children to John and Grace (Satterlee) Day. Died in New York City, November 29, 1980. She had one child, Tamar, born of a relationship with Forster Batterham. Her father was a journalist and racetrack entrepreneur. Educated in the public schools of Oakland, California, and Chicago, graduated from Waller High School in 1914, winning a three-hundred-dollar cash college scholarship in the Chicago *Examiner* competition. Attended the University of Illinois 1914–16, leaving before graduation. She was an adequate but undistinguished scholar there as she worked her way through college. She became interested in writing, joining ''The Scribblers'' and also writing for *The Daily Illini*, where she was introduced to socialism. In June 1916, she moved to New York City with her family to seek a journalistic career. She was first employed as a feature writer for the *Call* and moved to the Lower East Side where she attended various socialist lectures and also met Michael Gold, later a well-known communist writer, who became a lifelong friend. In April 1917, she joined the staff of the *Masses*, under Max Eastman and Floyd Dell, at times taking on a great deal of the editorial responsibilities. In November 1917, she was arrested and briefly imprisoned as the result of a women's suffrage rally in Washington, D.C.; she went on a brief hunger strike in Occoquan prison before being released.

During 1917–1918, she was the close companion of Eugene O'Neill during his Greenwich Village period. Details of this relationship (which she later said covered a mere four months) are hard to establish. William Miller, her biographer, maintains that it was totally Platonic, even though they did go to bed together, with Dorothy clasping the drunken and shivering O'Neill in her arms (Miller, 1982, p. 110). He also suggests that the virginal and comforting Josie Hogan* in *A Moon for the Misbegotten*ary recalls something of this relationship (Miller, 1982, pp. 111–112). Another informant, Gerald Griffin, one of Dorothy Day's earliest associates in the Catholic Worker movement who worked with her for eleven years in the days before she had developed an image which needed to be protected, tells a different story. He asserts categorically that she and O'Neill were lovers, that Dorothy Day had a notable capacity for drink (though she was no alcoholic), and that she was certainly sufficiently in love with O'Neill to make an attempt to beat the competition she saw coming from Agnes Boulton.*

In later years, Dorothy Day also resented the comments made by Malcolm Cowley about her drinking propensities. Cowley clarified his comments by saying that ''she was rather admired for her ability to put down several belts of whiskey and remain sober'' (quoted by Miller, 1982, p. 105). It is generally accepted that she was one of the habitués of the Golden Swan (the Hell Hole) and that she and O'Neill would often bar-hop after it closed, somewhat to the resentment of her friend, Michael Gold, and then they would repair to her room on the Lower East Side. One frequently recorded incident tells of her, Max Bodenheim, and O'Neill composing a poem in alternate stanzas while they were all sitting in the Hell Hole (The Golden Swan bar). She was also noted for her knowledge of the text of *Frankie and Johnny*, including the most ribald verses. At this time, she is often said to have dropped into Roman Catholic services at Saint Joseph's Church, Sixth Avenue, in Greenwich Village. This is sometimes cited, to Gerald Griffin's skepticism, as early evidence of a desire to convert to Catholicism. It seems more likely that this was really a way of keeping warm during a bitter winter.

Agnes Boulton, O'Neill's second wife, gives an account of her first meeting with Dorothy Day, which was also her third meeting with O'Neill, considering Day ''extremely attractive in a strange way . . . [giving] the impression of being a sort of genius herself'' (Boulton, 1958, p. 41). As soon as she had ordered drinks, she broke into *Frankie and Johnny* while members of the local gang, the Hudson Dusters, looked on with some admiration. Some days after that meeting, Agnes, Dorothy and O'Neill went to a restaurant together; Agnes left early on this occasion but at a later meeting realized that O'Neill had eyes only for her.

By this time, Agnes had moved from the Brevoort Hotel into Waverly Place. One day, to her surprise, Dorothy Day appeared at about 10 A.M. saying that she had been up all night and needed sleep. Curious about how Dorothy had found her, Agnes interrupted her writing to ask and was told that O'Neill had given her the information and planned to meet her there that afternoon. Agnes, to her chagrin, realized that Dorothy must have spent the night with O'Neill when she herself had pleaded her work as an excuse. Dorothy then announced that she wished to move in with Agnes, paying half the expenses. Agnes refused, citing her need for quiet in order to work. Dorothy insisted, Agnes eventually agreed, and so they and O'Neill made a threesome. This incident seems to confirm that Dorothy wanted to keep O'Neill, but in later years when the battle was long lost, she claimed that she had been in love with O'Neill's work while Agnes had been in love with the man (Miller, 1982, p. 113; Sheaffer, 1968, p. 407). Agnes also recalls O'Neill's reciting Francis Thompson's ''The Hound of Heaven'' to Dorothy when they were in the Golden Swan. Later, after her religious conversion (and at a time when she was trying to tone down her early raffish image), Dorothy said that O'Neill gave her ''an intensification of the religious sense that was in me,'' going on to say that ''since he brought me such a consciousness of God—since he recited to me 'The Hound of Heaven,' I owe him my prayers (Miller, 1982, p. 118).

Dorothy, Agnes, and O'Neill were also involved in events surrounding the suicide on January 22, 1918, of Louis Holladay,* the brother of Polly Holladay who owned the Golden Swan. Holladay had stopped drinking at the request of his girlfriend, Louise Norton, whom he planned to marry; but on his return to New York, she informed him she now intended to marry someone else. That night at the Hell Hole (the Golden Swan), Holladay started drinking again. Agnes left early, and after her departure the group went to Romany Marie's restaurant, where somehow Louis obtained some heroin (the details differ with the teller). O'Neill allegedly told Louis not to be a fool and left after his acquaintance had taken some heroin. Shortly afterward, Holladay collapsed on Dorothy Day's shoulder and died. Everyone else seems to have fled in fear, but Dorothy took possession of what was left of the drug and concealed it from the police, disposing of it either by passing it to Max Bodenheim or flushing it down a toilet (again accounts differ). Polly Holladay was called, and when she told the police that her brother had a history of heart trouble, which was true, a verdict of heart attack was given and the matter of the heroin was never raised. After this, Dorothy went to Agnes's apartment, where O'Neill had earlier taken refuge, shaking so badly that Agnes thought him drunk. Dorothy insisted that the two of them accompany her to Romany Marie's, but O'Neill went to the Hell Hole where he tried to drink himself into insensibility. The two women went briefly to the restaurant and then to a cafeteria where Agnes says they were accompanied by "a certain shifty, rather elusive friend of Gene's" (Boulton, 1958, p. 88), who tried to tell them how Holladay had obtained the heroin. After this, they went to pick up O'Neill but realized they could do nothing for him and started off home. Dorothy separated herself from Agnes on the way but apparently did not return to O'Neill as her companion had supposed. Their paths diverged greatly after that. In April 1918, Dorothy started nursing training in Brooklyn and in July of the same year Agnes and Eugene O'Neill were married. Apparently, Dorothy did not see either of them until Agnes met with her in early 1958, à propos of her writing about the three of them in *Part of a Long Story*, the manuscript of which Mrs. Sue [Light] Jenkins (one of the early Provincetown Players)* had brought her to read before publication.

Dorothy Day's later years seem to have continued her initial quest for some kind of purpose in life. While she was in nursing training she fell passionately in love with Lionel Moise, an eminently unstable, tough, hard-drinking, former newspaperman. She threw herself at him, moved in with him, and became completely subservient to his wishes. Even after being locked out of his apartment she returned to him. By May 1919 she was pregnant, and William Miller maintains that she had an abortion, while Gerald Griffin insists that it was a miscarriage. Whatever the truth, the affair was over, and a few months later she married Berkeley Tobey in Spring 1920, on the rebound, and traveled to Europe with him. The two were divorced about a year later. Tobey was a man of some means but also of matrimonial instability, finally going through eight marriages. She then reactivated her affair with Moise and returned to him in Chicago, even though she knew that two other women were in love with him. She was briefly arrested in Chicago and jailed with one of them, Mae Cramer, because of her connection with the Industrial Workers of the World. By 1923 Lionel Moise was out of her life and Dorothy was working on the *Liberator*, now a Communist monthly in Chicago. Tiring of that city, she and her sister went to New Orleans where Dorothy worked for a short time as a reporter on the New Orleans *Item*.

By April 1924, she was back in New York and engaged in an affair with Forster Batterham which became a common-law relationship a year later. He was "a philosophical anarchist" from North Carolina who did not agree with marriage. Through him she met a number of interesting literary people in New York during 1925. She had also bought a small cottage on Staten Island and spent a considerable amount of time there. In 1927 her daughter Tamar was born, and Dorothy decided that the child should be baptized a Catholic. This took place in July, but it was not until December 28 of the same year that Dorothy herself was baptized, chiefly because of complications arising from her chequered matrimonial career. Once she severed her connection with Batterham, there were no obstacles. Nonetheless, she seems to have continued to care for him, and many years later at his request she nursed his then common-law wife, Nanette, until her death from cancer. He was also present at Dorothy Day's funeral in 1980. He played Olson in *The Moon of the Caribbees* (1918).

She returned to her writing and in 1928 took up a three-month dialogue-writing contract with Pathé in Culver City. She and Tamar went to Mexico for about six months while she wrote some commissions for *Commonweal*; but the child having become ill, she cut her stay short and spent the fall and winter of 1930–1931 in Florida where her father was involved with the Hialeah racetrack. She seems to have returned to New York in 1932 and then have gone to Washington with the unemployed workers' march in November–December of that year as a reporter for the Jesuit monthly, *America*.

At this time, she came under the influence of Peter Maurin and in 1933 founded *The Catholic Worker* newspaper, the organ of the movement that made her famous. At one point her influence spread across the United States with her philosophy of personal charity and individual commitment to the needy. Maurin preached agricultural communes, but Dorothy Day's attempts to implement them were unsuccessful. She found her real calling in ministering to the derelicts and the unwanted in such cities as New York, Boston, Chicago, and Los Angeles. Though many members of the Roman Catholic establishment considered her dangerously radical, her work appealed to many idealists, and during the depression years of the thirties the movement flourished. It faltered during World War II, largely because of her commitment to the pacifist stance she had always held, even in World War I; and during the early fifties, particularly the years of the "Red Scare," she became somewhat unpopular. However, by the early sixties, with anti-Vietnam war feeling growing and with renewed popular interest in civil rights and the plight of the underprivileged, Dorothy Day was again in the mainstream of social activism, almost part of the establishment. She participated in civil rights marches and supported voter-registration movements and the United

Farm Workers movement of Cesar Chavez, all the time continuing her work within the cities, though it was now less extensive than in the earlier years. She raised money for her houses of hospitality by her speeches and writing and continued to live in one, on the Lower East Side, until her death there in Maryhouse, West Third Street, on November 29, 1980. Nowadays she is being spoken of as a saint, and for many years she was indeed part of the charitable conscience of America. *See* in "References": Boulton (1958); Gelb and Gelb (1973); William Miller (1982); Sheaffer (1968). This entry was prepared with the help of Gerald J. Griffin.

DAYS WITHOUT END, an expressionistic play in four acts and six scenes, the second in the abandoned trilogy "Myth-Plays for the God-Forsaken,"* of which *Dynamo** is the first; originally titled "Without Ending of Days."

Act I: "Plot for a Novel": The scene is "John Loving's private office in the offices of Eliot and Company, New York City." It is a spring afternoon in 1932. At first the light is "chill and grey," but it gradually rises to illuminate two people seated at a table. John Loving* is forty, conventionally good-looking in a slightly heavy American way, but with a wide, sensitive mouth. He is conservatively dressed in a dark suit. Loving* sits at the rear of the table, dressed exactly the same, of the same age and figure, but masked. His mask is an exact reproduction of the features of John's face, "the death mask of a John who has died with a sneer of scornful mockery on his lips. And this mocking scorn is repeated in the expression of the eyes which stare bleakly from behind the mask." Throughout the play he is visible only to John and, of course, to the audience. Other members of the cast can hear him but not see him. He presents the rational, hostile, atheistic, cynical aspect of John Loving's disintegrated personality.

John is writing an autobiographical novel and discussing the plot with Loving. Cynically, Loving mocks John's proposed conclusion in which the hero confesses his sin and "she forgives." Loving sees this as "ridiculous conscience" and suggests that the conclusion will have to be "so obviously fictitious" that "she" (John's wife) will not suspect any autobiographical elements in the novel. He then suggests that John "have the wife die," a notion that gives John a start, and comments that "it would be interesting to work out your hero's answer to his problem, if his wife died." John, appalled by this idea, is confronted with Loving's rationalism: "Afraid to face your ghosts—even by proxy?" John maintains that he is writing this novel as a means of explanation "to get at the real truth and understand what was behind—what evil spirit of hate possessed me." Sneeringly, Loving calls John a "poor damned superstitious fool," claiming "there is nothing—nothing to hope for, nothing to fear—neither devils nor gods—nothing at all!"

A knock is heard, and William Eliot,* John's partner, enters. He, too, is about forty, a round, humorous-natured man with horn-rimmed spectacles. He is surprised to discover that John has again been bitten by "the literary bug" because he had thought that John was finished "when you got engaged to Elsa

[Loving*] and decided to come in with me and make some money.'' Eliot recalls when John was given to writing denunciations of capitalism and religion: "I remember one article where you actually tried to prove that no such figure as Christ had ever existed." Loving's answer indicates in a "cold and hostile" tone that he still feels the same way, and in a way of mitigating Eliot's surprise, John tries to change the subject. Eliot then says that Lucy Hillman* has just telephoned and will call back. The two men then discuss the marriage of Lucy and Walter Hillman; he is a philanderer and a drunkard, while Lucy seems to be "going to pieces, too," not with affairs, as John suggests, but with liquor. After wondering why Lucy doesn't divorce her husband and receiving little reaction from John, Eliot leaves while John reacts with Loving in a very guilty manner, Loving leaning toward suicide as a logical conclusion for his hero and John defiantly saying, "He must find a faith somewhere." At this, Loving speaks of John's "old secret weakness—the cowardly yearning to go back" which he plans to force John to face. At this moment Eliot re-enters to announce the arrival of Father Matthew Baird,* the uncle who had briefly acted as John's guardian. Throughout this scene, Loving attempts to shock the priest with his bitterly hostile and atheistic remarks, while John tries to be a trifle kinder. The priest doesn't take the atheistic pose too seriously because he has faith that John will find his own way back to faith. Father Baird and Eliot discuss John's missionary past when he harangued his friends and family with lectures on atheism, socialism, Nietzschean theory, Karl Marx, and then the Eastern religions and Greek philosophy. The priest sees this quest as an attempt to hide something that Loving angrily denies; but now that John is married, his uncle believes that he seems to have found a religion of love, and he wishes to meet Elsa, John's wife. He sees John as "running away from the truth in order to find it" until finally "the road turns back toward home" to belief.

Uncle and nephew discuss John's "continued estrangement" from religion, and the priest wonders whether he himself might in some measure have been responsible, a comment which calls forth diametrically opposed reactions from John and Loving. But then the priest tells of a religious experience he recently had which made him certain that John was in some spiritual danger. The image of the crucified Christ seemed to command him to take action, and for that reason the priest decided to take a vacation in the East to see for himself. John and Loving again have opposed reactions, as Father Baird quotes from Francis Thompson's poem, "The Hound of Heaven": "I am He Whom thou seekest!/ Thou dravest love from thee, who dravest Me." Defensively, John asserts that he has love, but the priest insists that someday he will need God: "Beyond the love for each other should be the love of God, in Whose Love yours may find the triumph over death." Again, Loving sneers, and John speaks with fear about imagining the death of Elsa.

To change the subject, Loving speaks of the novel that John is writing, and the priest asks for a synopsis. In telling the tale, John overinsists that it is not autobiographical, but it transparently is. He tries to tell the plot straight, but

Loving continually interjects bitter cynical remarks. The novel concerns a young boy brought up by devout Catholic parents knowing nothing but their love and the love of God. Not until school did he learn about the God of punishment. But when he was fifteen, both his parents died during an epidemic of influenza, first his father and then, despite his prayers, his mother. According to Loving, the boy "cursed his God . . . and, in revenge, promised his soul to the Devil" in a kind of Faustian bargain "when everyone thought he was praying." The priest is shocked, and the Mephisteles-Faust equation of Loving and John is now made clear to the audience. John, however, laughs off the autobiographical coincidences and invites his uncle home to dinner. But the priest is still troubled about John. After his departure, John and Loving quarrel about him until there is a telephone call from Lucy Hillman suggesting that she visit Elsa, who has been ill. Loving sneeringly remarks, "your terrible sin begins to close in on you," and then suggests that he should continue his novel by having the hero's wife die "of influenza that turns into pneumonia." John reacts furiously as the curtain falls.

Act II: "Plot for a Novel (Continued)": The living room of the Lovings' duplex apartment "later the same afternoon." Elsa enters. "She is thirty-five but looks much younger," appearing to be a woman who has finally found love, and is loved in return, but who has reached that state "comparatively late in life and after much trouble." Obviously she is recovering from an illness. She calls for her maid, Margaret,* and as they speak about the forthcoming visit of Father Baird, the hall telephone rings to announce Lucy Hillman. Elsa, wishing that she looked better, is nonetheless pleased to see Lucy, who is about the same age as Elsa but shows it. "She is well dressed, but in a manner that is a shade too youthful and too fashionable, indicating a basic insecurity." Elsa chides Lucy for not having visited, and the two women indicate totally different outlooks. Lucy is discontented and unhappy, envious of "the old perfect marriage" of John and Elsa. As conversation continues, Lucy seems on the verge of telling a secret, but then she moves on to discuss her unhappy marriage, while Elsa expresses her concern about Lucy, recalling the misery of her own first marriage and the faith that sustained her—that somewhere there was a man she could really love. As a result, she could never do anything cheap or "deliberately disfigure myself out of wounded pride and spite." This comment starts Lucy on a tale in which she recounts the way she deliberately seduced a friend at her husband's party as a means of getting even with her philandering husband. When she finally got him into her bedroom, she discovered him to possess depths of hate and evil she had never suspected. Then, without any preparation, she asks Elsa, "suppose John were unfaithful to you—," a remark that frightens her friend, who claims that John is an idealist about love and marriage; "I know he never had a single affair in his life before he met me." Lucy is not totally impressed as Elsa launches into a paean of praise to John and his ideal of love and marriage: "He said no matter if every other marriage on earth were rotten and a lie, our love could make ours into a true sacrament...of faith in which each of us would find the completest self-expression in making our union a beautiful thing.'' And this is the marriage that Elsa believes she has found. Lucy, deeply moved, kisses her ''God bless you—and preserve your happiness!'' Lucy jumps up, ready to leave as John, with Loving behind him, arrives home, looking sneeringly and sinisterly at her as she stands, stiff and strained.

Left alone with Lucy as Elsa departs on a domestic errand, John guiltily asks Lucy if she has been careful not to reveal their fleeting affair. She replies that she has not told Elsa but has informed Walter, her husband, without revealing John's identity, in order to give herself the satisfaction of revenge. She asks John the nature of his vengeance. Loving answers, ''perhaps on love. Perhaps in my soul, I hate love,'' a remark that frightens Lucy. Now both John and Lucy feel guilty, and John thinks he will have to tell Elsa, an action Lucy advises against: ''I'm thinking of what it would do to her.'' But John wonders, ''You think she couldn't forgive?'' After Lucy's departure, Loving suggests a discussion of John's new novel, as Elsa enters to look lovingly at him and nestle close to him, asking what has been troubling him. She has known something was wrong ever since she returned from Boston. Innocently, she guesses that it concerns business and says that money means nothing to her as long as she has him. She asks to hear the novel—later when she is entertaining Father Baird— and John says he hasn't decided on the conclusion. Left alone, John castigates himself as ''You God-damned rotten swine!'' while Loving recalls that there is always one way out: ''There is always death to wash one's sins away.''

Act III, Scene i: ''Plot for a Novel (Continued)'': The living room of the Loving apartment, as in Act II, immediately after dinner the same evening. Elsa is on the sofa, with John beside her. Loving is behind him, dressed in identical evening clothes. Elsa is in a simple white gown; Father Baird, in clerical suit, sits left-front. John is proudly displaying Elsa to his uncle, who is gallantly admiring, but then John taxes her with not eating enough to help her recovery from influenza. Elsa, however, senses that he does not wish to tell them his plot for the novel, but they both ask him to continue. John insists once more that the events of the novel happened to a former acquaintance, except for the conclusion, ''which is wholly imaginary.'' Elsa asks if she ever knew the man and is answered with a hostile negative by Loving, the tone of which surprises her. John proceeds with his plot and tells of the young man's inner conflict when his parents died. At times he really believed that he had given his soul to an evil power, and then he would long to pray for forgiveness. At other times he believed ''that he had forsworn all love forever,'' and then he wished for death. ''Once he even took his father's revolver,'' and then Loving mocks his refusal to accept ''the warm dark peace of annihilation.'' As John recounts the events of the ''novel,'' Loving continually interjects blasphemously rationalistic comments whenever John talks of love, forgiveness, or religion. John speaks of his hero's search for the truth until he finally found his truth in love for a woman and, as Loving scornfully puts it, ''immediately began building a new superstition of love around her.'' But he became afraid of this happiness, fearing that his wife might die, and then he was unfaithful to her.

As Elsa and Father Baird listen, John recounts his adventure with Lucy Hillman. When Elsa realizes what she is hearing, Loving twists the knife in the wound, interpreting John's actions as hatred of love: "He really wanted to deliver himself from its power and be free again. He wanted to kill it!'' John stammers out "it wasn't he,'' and Loving ridicules as a mere excuse the notion that the "hero'' believed himself "possessed by a demon,'' but Father Baird understands: "One may not give one's soul to a devil of hate—and remain forever scatheless.'' Loving continues his sneering, but John speaks of the forgiveness his "hero'' craved, and he asks Elsa if she would forgive if she were the "hero's'' wife. Elsa replies "No. She could never forgive him.'' At this, John attempts an explanation, but Loving insists that the wife must die: "Yes. I need her death for my end. That is, to make my romantic hero come finally to a rational conclusion about his life!'' Elsa is devastated by these words and makes an excuse to go to bed. John is solicitous, and Loving meaningfully notes that it is cold and raining outside. As she leaves the room, she can be seen turning toward the entrance door of the apartment, not her bedroom. Loving remains watching her while Father Baird and John go into the study, and then he follows them.

Act III, Scene ii: "John Loving's study on the upper floor of the apartment,'' with bookcases, a long table, chairs, and a chaise longue. Father Baird is sitting on the chaise longue, looking at the floor. John is in the chair in front of the table, and Loving sits in a chair at the left of the table staring coldly at John, who continues to talk rather aimlessly, probably as a way to avoid thought. He is giving what Loving calls his "soap box'' speech about ideals, and then the alter ego suggests that "we know we are all the slaves of meaningless chance— electricity or something which whirls us—on to Hercules!'' John takes up that cry and speaks of "a new ideal to measure the value of our lives by!'' A new savior is needed, but Father Baird expresses his content with the old one, and Loving speaks of his "pseudo-Nietzschean savior'' who he admits is "an equally futile ghost.'' Finally, Father Baird insists on a return to the matter of the novel, wishing to discover what happens to the "hero'' after his wife's death. Again there is a conflict between John and Loving, a psychomachia, a struggle between good and evil for the soul of John. John speaks of his hero's return to the church of his youth, while Loving insists that the man curses God and defies Him. John then says that the "hero'' walks out of the church "daring to face his eternal loss and hopelessness, to accept it as his fate and go on with life.'' The priest, John, and Loving then discuss the meaning of life, in which Father Baird believes and suggests that John kneel for forgiveness. Loving calls out "Rot!'' and the priest is momentarily angered. John again insists that his novel is "only a story,'' but the priest understands the truth. With that, he turns away to look at John's books as John goes to hunt for Elsa.

At this moment Elsa enters. Her skirt, stockings, and shoes are soaking wet, and clearly she is running a new fever. She treats the attentive John with coolness and tells him that she understands that his novel is a lie and that she has understood that he has been talking about himself and Lucy. She turns on him for wanting to destroy that ideal marriage "which had become all the beauty and truth of life to me!" She has decided to follow out the scenario that John has prescribed for her in his novel: "it all seemed to fit so perfectly—like the will of God." She is not blasphemous, because "I've never had any God, you see—until I met John." As she goes to her room, both he and Father Baird begin to pray, but Loving interrupts: "I tell you there is nothing—nothing!" And the curtain falls as John repeats, "There's nothing—nothing to fear!"

Act IV, Scene i: "The End of the End": The study, as in the last scene, but the interior of Elsa's bedroom is revealed at the left. Elsa is in bed, "eyes closed, her face pallid and wasted." John looks to be on the verge of total collapse as he sits in a chair at the foot of the bed, with Loving standing behind him, looking like evil personified. "Father Baird is standing by the middle of the bed, at rear" talking with Dr. Herbert Stillwell* as they watch Elsa anxiously. A nurse is at the rear. It is about a week later, and obviously the crisis of Elsa's illness is approaching. She moans, "How could you? Our dream!" and John begs, "Elsa! Forgive!" but Loving mockingly says, "She will never forgive!" John is barely coherent as the doctor removes him from the room. Panic-stricken, John is beginning to believe that his novel was prophetic and is coming true. Father Baird and Doctor Stillwell discuss Elsa's case, with the doctor saying that "the pneumonia has been more a means than a cause. . . . A little casting out of devils would have been of benefit."

As the priest watches John, he prays to God, "grant me the grace to bring Jack back to Thee." Loving, fighting the good, insists that "nothing can save her" and reinforces the thought that the novel is coming true: "It was a cunning method of murder!" Now the priest and Loving fight for the soul of John, as he vacillates between the desire to kneel for forgiveness and the wish to bargain with God: "Let Him prove to me His Love exists! Then I will believe in Him again!" John rushes back into the room as Loving and he fight their battle further. Loving plays a trump card: "But if you love her, how can you desire to go on—with all that was Elsa rotting in her grave behind you!" With this, John swears that he will commit suicide, but Elsa suddenly calls out, "No, John! No!" Loving thinks himself triumphant at this moment—that John has accepted the meaninglessness of life and the comforting annihilation of death, as Elsa again in her delirium pleads, "No!" But suddenly, John feels the need to go to the church, to gaze once more upon the cross. As Loving tries to bar his way, John walks out of the room as Elsa comes out of her semicoma, calling him to come back with "I'll forgive!" She then falls back—not dead, but with renewed will to live.

Act IV, Scene ii: "A section of the interior of an old church." In the middle of one wall is a large, finely-carved, wooden crucifix set about five feet from the floor. The dawn light filters through the stained glass window on the wall and around the cross. The church doors suddenly crash open to admit John and Loving. Loving is retreating before John, trying to bar his way, "but John is the stronger now and, with a look of obsessed resolution in his eyes, he forces Loving back." The battle for John's soul continues as he kneels before the cross and Loving mocks him. Finally, John realizes, "Thou hast heard me at last! Thou hast not forsaken me! Thou hast always loved me! I am forgiven! I can forgive myself—through Thee! I can believe." Loving attempts once more to override John, but John continues: "At last I see! I have always loved! O Lord of Love, forgive Thy poor blind fool!" As Loving cries "No!" his legs crumple, and John prays, "Thou art the Way—the Truth—the Resurrection and the Life, and he that believeth in Thy Love, his love can never die." At this, Loving falls on the floor dead with his arms flung out to form another cross, saying as his last words those of Julian, the apostate: "Thou has conquered, Lord. Thou art—the End. Forgive—the damned soul—of John Loving." At this surrender, the personality of John Loving is reintegrated in an epiphany in which he stretches up to the cross, "an expression of mystic exaltation on his face" illuminated by the light of the stained glass window and the refulgent light of the crucifix.

Father Baird enters to tell John Loving that "Elsa will live," and exultantly John calls that "Death is dead!" He asks if his uncle hears that "life laughs with God's love again! Life laughs with Love!" Thus the play concludes with an echo of O'Neill's earlier *Lazarus Laughed,** for life and love have defeated death.

Comments: And here, too, ends O'Neill's literary quest for belief, but it would be total folly to suggest that this play signifies a return to the beliefs of Catholicism for the playwright himself, though during its writing he had been discussing religion with Roman Catholic clerical acquaintances. Insofar as can be ascertained from the playwright's papers, *Days Without End* owes its title to the conclusion of the evening prayer in the Episcopalian *Book of Common Prayer*: "World without end, Amen." At the same time, it is also an intensely auto-biographical play, less in the matter of religious commitment than a kind of exorcism of O'Neill's past conflicts with his own parents, his relationship with his father, and also his discovery of his mother's drug addiction which took place when he was fifteen and for which he felt that he was to blame since it began as the result of a prescription for postpartum pain when he was born. At the same time, it was a tribute to O'Neill's third wife, Carlotta Monterey.* The dedication to the published version reads, "To Carlotta," while his inscription in her personal copy takes the lines in which Elsa speaks of marriage as a sacrament in Act II and adds the words, "And ours has, hasn't it, Darling One?"

The play, however, had a long and difficult gestation, going through eight drafts. It was begun in 1927 in Bermuda, just when O'Neill was beginning to break away from his second wife, Agnes Boulton,* and for that reason perhaps questions about marriage which had been in a sense "solved" in *Welded** surfaced again, and some of the same conclusions about sacramentality are found in both. Similarly, the crucifixion-image that completes the earlier play is re-peated in a more romantic and flamboyant manner here. It is also important to note that it was not completed until 1933, after O'Neill and Carlotta were married and living at Casa Genotta, in Georgia. For him, then, this was Carlotta's play, as *Welded* belonged to Agnes, and hence O'Neill was extraordinarily attached to it as an act of love. He agonized over its writing even more than over most of his plays, and like John Loving, the novelist, he vacillated over the ending, finally deciding upon the Catholic conclusion. This was, however, not greeted with critical acclaim, leading O'Neill to complain that critics dislike religious endings, especially if that religion happens to be Roman Catholicism. Perhaps this opposition led him personally away from the return to the religion of his childhood, for there is some evidence that he had again become interested in that religion, and Carlotta told a friend that she was willing to follow him into the church, should he return.

With regard to technique, *Days Without End* is a return to the use of masks with which O'Neill had experimented in *The Hairy Ape,** *Lazarus Laughed,* and *The Great God Brown.** O'Neill wrote an important defense of his use of masks both in this play and elsewhere, "One's outer life passes in a solitude haunted by the masks of others; one's inner life passes in a solitude hounded by the masks of oneself." ("Memoranda on Masks," 1932; reprinted in Cargill, 1961.) However, as he later complained, critics tended to see the play as "a drama of spiritual faith and love in general" (Letter to Kenneth Macgowan,* February 14, 1934, quoted by Floyd, 1981, p. 167). In addition, the critics did not in general perceive the play as the psychological study O'Neill had intended it to be, while the Faustian equivalence seemed to escape their understanding entirely. He wished it to be considered "A Modern Miracle Play" (Ibid.), presumably recreating the medieval psychomachia, but this too eluded the critics, as well as the audience.

Dramatically, the play is clumsy, with entrances and exits very obviously contrived, the exposition heavy-handed, and the epiphanic reintegration of John Loving ill-prepared and even trite. Even the use of the mask for Loving, the ironically named "damned soul of John Loving," seems gratuitous, almost an act of desperation rather than organic to the nature of the play, as in *The Great God Brown*. Nonetheless, O'Neill persisted in his high opinion of *Days Without End*, even its language, which to others has often seemed curiously self-conscious and a great falling off from *Ah, Wilderness!** which he stopped off to write before finishing this work. The fact of this failure led O'Neill to drop plans for completion of the trilogy, "Myth-Plays for the God-Forsaken," which he had begun with *Dynamo*. Though the play failed in New York, it later achieved some success in Ireland, the Netherlands, and Sweden. After this play, O'Neill was not represented by a newly produced play until *The Iceman Cometh** (1946).

Production Data: Written 1931–1933. Produced by the Theatre Guild.* First

performed at the Plymouth Theatre, Boston, December 27, 1933, and then at
Henry Miller's Theatre, New York City, January 8, 1934 (57 performances).
   Director: Philip Moeller
   Designer: Lee Simonson
   Cast: John: Earle Larimore*
         Loving: Stanley Ridges
         William Eliot: Richard Barbee
         Father Matthew Baird: Robert Loraine
         Elsa: Selena Royle
         Margaret: Caroline Newcombe
         Lucy Hillman: Ilka Chase
         Dr. Herbert Stillwell: Frederick Forrester
         Nurse: Margaret Swope

"DEAR DOCTOR," or "The Dear Doctor," title uncertain. A one-act comedy written at Harvard during O'Neill's participation in the English 47 Workshop
of George Pierce Baker* (1914–1915). Baker thought that this one-act might
have some possibilities as a vaudeville skit. O'Neill later discovered that the
short story he had used for his source was itself pirated from an earlier vaudeville
skit. The text of this play has not survived.

DESIRE UNDER THE ELMS, a tragedy in three parts and twelve scenes laid
"in, and immediately outside of, the Cabot farmhouse in New England, in the
year 1850." The house faces south "to a stone wall with a wooden gate at center
opening onto a country road. The house is in good condition but in need of
paint." The wood siding has weathered to gray, and the shutters are faded. On
either side of the house are two huge elms which bend down over the roof,
appearing to protect and at the same time to subdue: "They brood oppressively
over the house. They are like exhausted women resting their sagging breasts and
hands and hair on its roof, and when it rains their tears trickle down monotonously
and rot on the shingles." A path runs "around the right hand corner of the house
to the front door." The side of the house facing the audience has four windows,
the upstairs ones being of the bedrooms of the father and the brothers, and the
larger, downstairs ones being of the parlor on the right and the kitchen on the
left.
   Part I, Scene i: Sunset on an early summer day. The air is still and the sky
above the farmhouse is filled with color, but the house itself is in shadow. Eben
Cabot* comes out on to the porch, looks down the road, mechanically swings
a dinner bell, and then looks up appreciatively at the sky. He is a tall, sinewy,
twenty-five-year-old, with a handsome face marred by a "resentful and defensive
expression." He has dark hair and eyes which have the look of a trapped animal
about them. "He is dressed in rough farm clothes." As he gazes at the sky he
says, "God! Purty!" then spits on the ground and goes in. Simeon Cabot* and
Peter Cabot,* Eben's half-brothers, come in from their work. Simeon is thirty-

nine and Peter is thirty-seven. They are rather "bovine" men, bent somewhat from years of hard farm work, and as they move they jostle each other slightly "like two friendly oxen." They are dressed in farm work clothes and heavy muddy boots. They stop for a moment in front of the house and look at the sky. Their faces soften and they begin a laconic conversation which repeats Eben's "purty!" Simeon recalls that it was eighteeen years ago that his wife died. Now and then he recalls, "Makes it lonesome. She'd hair long's a hoss's tail—an' yaller like gold!" Peter gives a brief recognition to the dead woman but then says, "They's gold in the West, Sim," and excitedly speaks of the fortunes that can be made for the asking in California, "Golden Gate—Californi-a!—Goldest West!—fields o' gold." The excitement communicates itself to Simeon as Peter recalls the everlasting misery of their lives on the farm, raising one stone on top of another to build "stone walls fur him to fence us in!" The two begin to speculate on the whereabouts of their father, Ephraim Cabot,* who has been gone for the past two months. He last left the farm thirty years ago to marry "Eben's maw." Eben, who has been listening out the window, says, "I pray he's died," much to the surprise of his brothers. Again the three of them gaze at the sun, Eben remarking, "Sun's downin' purty," while Simeon and Peter together speak of "gold in the West." Initially Eben misunderstands "Yonder atop o' the pasture, ye mean?" But the two brothers answer as one: "In California!" With that, they go inside for dinner.

Part I, Scene ii: The color is fading, and with the coming of twilight the inside of the kitchen becomes visible. The kitchen is clean and neat but thoroughly masculine in appearance. There is a ship's poster saying "California" on the rear wall center. Places have been laid for three, and Eben serves boiled potatoes and bacon together with "a loaf of bread and a crock of water." The two older men sit down and start eating while Eben picks at his food, "glancing at them with a tolerant dislike." Finally the silence is broken when Simeon and Peter both upbraid Eben for wishing their father dead. Eben considers himself his mother's son and has never forgotten the way Ephraim worked her to death. Simeon and Peter also remember her kindness, but they don't react quite like Eben. Peter, in fact, notes that Ephraim is slaving himself and his sons to death, On'y none o' us hain't died—yit." Simeon perceives that there is "something' " driving the old man to act as he does, but he does not understand what it might be. Eben then asks what is driving his brothers to California, suggesting that they'll never get there because they are waiting for their share of the farm, their two-thirds. But he maintains that the farm really belonged to his mother: "Didn't he steal it from her? She's dead. It's my farm." Gradually it comes out that Eben cannot forgive his brothers for not trying to save his mother from overwork, and the two older men recite a laconic litany of the farm chores that came first, until Eben finally speaks again of the stone walls: "makin' walls till yer heart's a stone ye heft up out o' the way o' growth onto a stone wall t'wall in yer heart." Peter asks him why he did nothing, and Eben takes refuge in the same excuse—"chores." However, he believes that she still haunts the place, and "sooner'r later, . . . I'll see t' it my Maw gits some rest an' sleep in her grave."

Again the brothers wonder what has become of Ephraim, who had driven off looking unusually spic and span. He had felt the stirrings of spring, "an' now I'm ridin' out t' learn God's message t' me in the spring, like the prophets done."And, after an admonition to the two older men not to run away, he had gone—singing a hymn. Eben asks why they had not prevented his departure and asserts that he is stronger than they. They are mildly amused by this and even more so when Eben announces that he is going up the road, and the brothers realize that it is to see the town prostitute, Min, whom each one of them had known, including Ephraim; "He was fust! . . . We air his heirs in everything." At first Eben thinks of bashing Min, but then when he is left alone, he softens: "By God A'mighty she's purty, an' I don't give a damn how many sins she's sinned afore mine or who she's sinned with, my sin's as purty as any one on 'em!"

Part I, Scene iii: It is pitch dark and just before dawn as Eben goes in the front door, "chuckling bitterly and cursing half-aloud." He goes upstairs. He enters their bedroom with a lighted candle, and the interior of the bedroom becomes visible, with its low sloping roof, the double bed in which Simeon and Peter are sleeping, and Eben's cot at the rear. With a combination of "silly grin and malicious scowl" Eben tells his news: Ephraim has married a woman of thirty-five. This news makes Simeon and Peter decide to depart for California, and Eben pulls out a paper in which he offers to buy their shares in the farm for three hundred dollars apiece, which he can get from Ephraim's secret hoard: "I know whar it's hid. . . . Maw told me." The older men don't quite commit themselves and tell Eben to fix some "vittles" for them. He tells them that he has indeed been with Min and suggests that "this cow the Old Man's hitched t'! She'll beat Min, I got a notion!" Simeon's curious suggestion, "Mebbe ye'll try t' make her your'n, too?" calls forth a disgusted denial from Eben. Left alone, the brothers discuss Eben's offer, noting shrewdly that "if Paw's hitched we'd be sellin' Eben somethin' we'd never git nohow!" In the meantime, while waiting for Eben to return, they will laze around and drink. Both men wish Ephraim damned, and Simeon ironically recalls his departure to seek God's will when "I'll bet right then an' thar he knew plumb well he was goin' whorin', the stinkin' old hypocrite!"

Part I, Scene iv: The interior of the kitchen as in Scene i, with a candle on the table. Simeon and Peter have just finished breakfast, and almost as a reflex action they are about to leave for work when Simeon remembers that they have decided not to work at all if Eben wants to be sole owner. As soon as he hears this, Eben races off to milk the cows: "I'll work my durn fingers off fur cows o' mine." Again, Simeon and Peter note his likeness to Ephraim. The two of them sit down and start drinking. They look at the farm, the sky, and their future with very mixed emotions. They resent how much of themselves they have put into the farm, yet they are also proud of what they have done and regret leaving it. Their defiant assertion of freedom from "stone walls" masks a certain apprehension, and so they go "help Eben a spell," for the habits of a lifetime are hard to break.

Just as they start to move, Eben enters with the news that Ephraim and his woman are on the way, and the two older men hasten to get their bundles before he returns. Eben asks whether they'll sign the paper before they go, and Peter counters by asking to see the money. As the brothers go upstairs, Eben pulls up a floorboard under the stone and extracts a canvas bag containing thirty twenty-dollar gold pieces (a significant number, recalling Judas Iscariot). After testing and counting the coins, Simeon and Peter sign and go out to the gate. Eben seems in a delighted trance, while the two brothers mock Ephraim, who is unhitching. Simeon and Peter are in a state of euphoria as they celebrate their freedom from "this stinkin' old rock-pile of a farm." Simeon takes the gate off the hinges and declares that he "bolishes . . . all gates, by thunder!" With this, Peter suggests that they take it with them and let it "sail free down some river."

As Ephraim and his wife enter, the brothers freeze. Ephraim is seventy-five, gaunt, toilworn; his face is hard, yet still "with a weakness in it, a petty pride in its own narrow strength." His eyes are myopic, small and close-set, and "he is dressed in his dismal black Sunday suit." Abbie Putnam Cabot* "is thirty-five, buxom, full of vitality." She has a pretty round face "marred by its rather gross sensuality." She has an obstinate jaw and determined eyes "and about her whole personality the same unsettled, untamed, desperate quality which is so apparent in Eben."

Abbie looks at the farm with a curious echo of the three brothers: "It's purty—purty! I can't b'lieve it's r'ally mine." This last comment galvanizes Ephraim into an assertion of ownership and then a relenting "Our'n—mebbe!" recalling his loneliness in the past. Simeon and Peter greet him with assorted insults which culminate in their heaving two stones through the parlor window as they dance drunkenly away, intoxicated both by liquor and freedom, singing the gold-seekers' words to the tune of "Oh Susannah!" Abbie, meanwhile, has gone into the house to meet Eben, after Ephraim has warned her not to assert her ownership of the farm to him. As the older brothers leave, Abbie looks after them from the bedroom window. "Is it my room, Ephraim?" When her husband replies "Our'n!" she makes an uncontrollable grimace of aversion and shuts the window. Suddenly the thought strikes Ephraim that his sons might have injured the stock or caused some other damage, and he rushes off to the barn.

After a moment, Abbie pushes open the kitchen door and enters to look at Eben, who does not see her at first. She looks at him calculatingly, and is "dimly awakened by his youth and good looks." Throughout the rest of this scene, Abbie uses "her most seductive tones" to Eben, as he, "obscurely moved, physically attracted to her," listens to the tale of her life. She understands his rage in seeing her take his mother's place, she says, and recalls that she herself was orphaned early and had to go into service "in other folks' hums." Then she married, but her husband was a drunk, her baby died, and she was once more working for others. After her husband's death, her lot did not change until Ephraim came along—"An' bought yew—like a harlot," says Eben, enraged that the price for Abbie is his mother's farm. The two of them level with each other, Abbie saying quite frankly that that was the only reason she married Ephraim and Eben threatening to tell his father. In turn, Abbie threatens to get Ephraim to drive Eben off the place, and she carefully and specifically asserts her ownership of the farm, home, kitchen, and bedroom, yet finally asks that they be friends. Eben, hypnotized, at first agrees, but then he flings out of the room, finding his father offering a Bible curse on Simeon and Peter. Eben mocks the old man, who replies by telling his son, "Ye'll never be more'n half a man!" As they walk off to the barn, the faint song of Simeon and Peter can still be heard, and Abbie, in the kitchen, washes *her* dishes as the curtain falls.

Part II, Scene i: Two months later, outside the Cabot farmhouse, on a hot, Sunday afternoon. Abbie is sitting, rocking listlessly on the porch, as Eben pokes his head out the window to see if the porch is empty. Abbie senses his presence and stops rocking, while Eben, realizing that she is there, scowls and spits "with exaggerated disdain." Abbie waits breathlessly until Eben comes out dressed in his best suit. As he passes her, she chuckles tauntingly and rouses his ire. She asks where he is going "all slicked up like a prize bull," and he replies in kind. But as they look at each other, "their physical attraction becomes a palpable force quivering in the hot air." Abbie very softly tells Eben that no matter what he says, he is attracted to her, and he has been fighting against his nature ever since she entered the house. She speaks of nature, the heat of the day, the burning inside, humanity's kinship with nature: "Nature'll beat you Eben. Ye might's well own up t'it fust 's last." Eben tries to break away from her, claiming that he is fighting both her and his father for his mother's rights to the land. Abbie then gets him to admit that he is going out to visit Min, the prostitute, who he insists is better than Abbie because she acts honestly and isn't working to steal what is his—the farm. This gives Abbie a chance to throw a tantrum and order him out as Ephraim enters.

The old man seems to have softened somewhat since his marriage, and his eyes have become dreamy. However, he is as physically strong as ever. He inquires as to the reason for all the shouting, and she claims that Eben had declared his father was getting soft. As Ephraim looks up at the sky—"Purty, hain't it?"—and compares it to a warm field, Abbie laughs at him. He allows, "I'd like t'own my place up thar," because he is beginning to feel "ripe on the bough." But above all else, he is lonely, because the house is always cold—even when the outside temperature is boiling. In the barn, however, with the cows, it is always warm and comforting. He begins to talk almost kindly of Eben, but Abbie finesses this approach with "Hain't I yer lawful wife?" At this, Ephraim covers her hand with kisses and showers her with praises from The Song of Solomon.

Satisfied that she has him under control, Abbie taxes him with planning to leave the farm to Eben, but Ephraim swears that he has no intention of leaving it to anyone—he would rather burn and destroy it all, except for the cows—and except for Abbie, whom he would turn free. At this, Abbie tells Ephraim that Eben has gone to visit Min and alleges that his trying to make love to her had caused the uproar Ephraim had heard. Enraged, Ephraim suggests that he horsewhip his son off the farm, but Abbie refuses, because Ephraim needs another hand. Sadly, Cabot says that none of his sons will bother to stay with the farm: "Simeon an' Peter air gone t' hell—an' Eben's follerin' 'em." She then suggests that "mebbe the Lord'll give *us* a son" and claims that she has long been praying for this. Ephraim swears that if that were to happen, he would do anything for her. He kneels down and pulls her down too so that they can pray for a son: "An' God hearkened unto Rachel!"

Part II, Scene ii: It is about 8 P.M. the same day, and "the interior of the two bedrooms on the top floor is shown." Eben is sitting on the side of his bed in his undershirt and underpants in the room on the left. Cabot and Abbie are seated side by side on the edge of their large, old-fashioned feather bed, he in his nightshirt and she in a nightdress. By the flickering light of the tallow candles, Ephraim speaks of the way Abbie and the farm have become one to him: "Me an' the farm has got t' beget a son."

Then in a long monologue, Ephraim tells of the way he came to the farm, made "fields o' stones" fertile land: "When ye kin make corn sprout out o' stones, God's livin' in yew!" Ephraim's God is a hard deity, as he has learned. Once, after two years on this hardscrabble farm, Cabot had given into weakness like the rest of the folk in the area. He had trekked West with them and found easy, rich land: "Ye'd on'y to plow an' sow an' then set an' smoke yer pipe an' watch thin's grow." But the voice of his God came to him saying, "This hain't with nothin' t' Me. Git ye back t' hum!" With that, Ephraim walked away from his land and returned because "God's hard, not easy! God's in the stones!" And as God founded His church on a rock, so Ephraim built his farm out of stones, in efforts that made him hard, too. In his loneliness he took his first wife, the mother of Simeon and Peter, but even then his loneliness was unassuaged. When she died after twenty years, he was less lonely, and his boys helped him with the farm, his own land: "When I thought o' that I didn't feel lonesome." But then he married Eben's mother, partly because of his loneliness and also to bring her family to drop an ownership claim against the farm. But he remained lonely, even though she bore Eben; she never understood him, and after sixteen years she, too, died. Then he lived with the boys, all of whom hated him because of his hardness, while he reciprocated by hating their softness: "They coveted the farm without knowin' what it meant." Then in the past spring he heard again the voice of God telling him "t' go out an' seek an' find!" He turns to Abbie again with the words of Solomon, "Yew air my Rose o' Sharon!" but he is greeted with a blank stare of resentment. At this he pushes her away angrily, almost threateningly, saying, "If ye don't hev a son t' redeem ye . . ." In reply, Abbie promises him a son, "I kin foretell." Lonely and cold in his own house, Ephraim returns to the barn: "I kin talk t' the cows. They know the farm an' me. They'll give me peace."

As Ephraim clumps down the stairs, Eben, on the other side of the wall, sits up, listening. Abbie, "conscious of his movements" stares at the wall. Meanwhile, Ephraim goes out of the house and raises his arms: "God A'mighty, call from the dark!" Then, receiving no answer, he goes to the barn. "Eben and Abbie stare at each other through the wall." Eben sighs, "and Abbie echoes it." Abbbie listens at the wall, and Eben reacts as if he can see what is going on. Then, as she enters his room, he turns away. She stands looking at him and then rushes to embrace and kiss him. At first he submits, then hurls her away. Abbie asks why, and Eben says he hates her, but Abbie recalls that his lips were burning with desire. Eben suggests that he might have been thinking of someone else, and Abbie responds that she wouldn't love a weak thing like him: "I on'y wanted yew fur a purpose o' my own—an' I'll have ye fur it yet 'cause I'm stronger'n yew be!" At this, he orders her out of his room, and she taunts him as nothing more than hired help. She says there is still one room in the house which she does not own, and she will now go down there, light the candles, and make it hers. "Won't ye come courtin' me in the best parlor, Mister Cabot?" In confused horror, Eben recalls that the room hasn't been opened since his mother's funeral. Abbie leaves with "I'll expect ye afore long, Eben," and the young man, almost mechanically, puts on his white shirt, tie, coat, and hat, but no shoes. He looks around in bewilderment—"Maw! Whar air yew?"—and slowly walks out.

Part II, Scene iii: A few minutes later in the parlor, "a grim, repressed room like a tomb in which the family has been interred alive." The candles are all lit, and Abbie is seated on the edge of the horsehair sofa looking unexpectedly "awed and frightened, ready to run away." Eben opens the door, dressed as before, with "an expression of obsessed confusion." The spirit of Eben's mother, which seems to haunt the room, has frightened Abbie, but now that Eben has entered, it seems "soft an' kind." Eben recalls his mother and says that the farm was really hers. Gradually, Abbie answers his recollections of his mother with comparisons to her own lot and asks him to kiss her, "Same's if I was a Maw t' ye." But lust overcomes her and frightens him while she pleads, saying that *she* (his mother) wants him to love Abbie. Revelation comes to Eben: "It's her vengeance on him—so's she kin rest quiet in her grave." With this, Abbie stretches her arms out to him as Eben throws himself on his knees and admits that he has been "dyin' fur want o' ye!" They embrace and kiss violently.

Part II, Scene iv: The "exterior of the farmhouse. It is just dawn." Eben, dressed in work clothes, comes out and goes to the gate. He seems changed and more confident, "grinning to himself with evident satisfaction." The parlor window is flung open just as he reaches the gate, and Abbie looks out, her hair over her shoulders and eyes filled with longing. She calls him back and they kiss several times. Abbie declares that Ephraim won't suspect anything, and now that the parlor is her room, or "our room," as she corrects herself to Eben, she will let in the sun. Eben says, "Maw's gone back t' her grave. She kin sleep now." Abbie says she isn't going to bother to get Ephraim's food, and just then Ephraim appears in the distance, looking vaguely up at the sky he is barely able to see. Eben treats his father with a curious blend of humor and mild insolence, something Ephraim cannot understand, and accuses Eben of being drunk, but Eben says, " 'Tain't likker, jest life. Yew'n me is quits. Let's shake hands." Mystified, Ephraim looks at him as Eben asks whether he had felt his mother going back to her grave: "She's quits with ye." Ephraim, not knowing what to say, says he has slept with the cows: "They know how t' sleep. They're teachin' me." Eben acts so jovially that the balance of authority seems to have shifted and Ephraim senses it, particularly when Eben begins to treat him like a fool: "I'm the prize rooster o' this roost." But Ephraim looks scornfully after his son. "A born fool," he says as he goes to look for breakfast. The curtain falls.

Part III, Scene i: The following year, a night in late spring. Each of the two upstairs bedrooms is lighted by a candle. Eben lies on his bed, scowling at the floor through which he can hear the noise of a dance from the kitchen. In the master bedroom there is a cradle by the bed. Downstairs, the floor has been cleared for dancing, with benches placed against the wall. Ephraim Cabot is in "a state of extreme hilarious excitement" as a result of all the whiskey he has drunk, and he is serving drinks to all the men. Married couples and young people from the neighborhood are crowded in, and a musician busily tunes his fiddle. Abbie sits in a rocking chair with a shawl around her shoulders. She is pale, thin, and drawn, and her eyes stray continually to the open door as if she is expecting someone. The entire company is chattering, laughing, and exchanging broad winks. Abbie asks where Eben is, and a young girl replies scornfully that he has spent most of his time at home since *she* came. A man suggests himself for consideration as a successor to Eben if Abbie gets tired. All in all, the company is having a bawdy time at the expense of Abbie and Ephraim, the latter of whom is quite oblivious to what is being said as he calls on his guests to dance for him. There is a short square dance sequence in which everyone participates in one way or another, dancing or clapping, except Abbie. Suddenly, Cabot is unable to restrain himself and "prances into the midst of the dancers, scattering them, waving his arms wildly." Everyone stops and watches as the fiddler works harder and harder on "Pop Goes the Weasel" and Cabot capers higher and higher, kicking with both legs, looking "like a monkey on a string," and punctuating his dancing with comments on his physical stamina. Finally, the fiddler stops, and Cabot then stops.

Upstairs, Eben enters the master bedroom and looks at the child in the cradle, confusedly yet with "a trace of tenderness, of interested discovery." At that moment, Abbie seems to sense something, almost by telepathy, and goes up to the baby. Cabot orders the music to resume and goes outside for some air as the company start whispering among themselves, making "a noise as of dead leaves in the wind." As Cabot leans on the gate and stares at the sky, Abbie and

Eben kiss and bend over the baby. Eben says he doesn't want to continue with "lettin' on what's mine's his'n." He has been doing that all his life and is getting to the end of his rope. Abbie comforts him with a kiss, saying that something will happen, and they remain in an embrace. Ephraim, at the gate, feels somehow lonesome, finding himself uncomfortable in the house. "Somethin's always livin' with ye." And in search of peace he goes down to the barn. The fiddler strikes up "Turkey in the Straw" and the real merriment begins.

Part III, Scene ii: The outside of the farmhouse a half-hour later. Eben is "looking up at the sky, an expression of dumb bewilderment on his face," as his father appears. When he sees Eben, he becomes cruelly triumphant, comes up, and slaps him on the back, while in the background the sound of the dance can be heard. He asks Eben why he isn't inside looking for a girl: "Ye might 'arn a share o' a farm that way." This angers Eben, who taxes Ephraim with the way he got title to his farm, through marriage. Ephraim denies the charge, but when Eben says, "An' I got a farm anyways," Ephraim treats him with scornful confidence, telling him that he will never get any of the farm. It will belong to the new child and to Abbie, who has told him about the way Eben had tried to make love to her. When he sees the impression this information has made on Eben, he embroiders further, claiming that Abbie had wanted Eben cut off so that she could have the farm. At this, Eben threatens to murder Abbie, and the two men grapple. But Ephraim is too strong for Eben, who is rescued by Abbie.

Eben engages in bitter recriminations with Abbie, who frantically protests her love. Eben tells her she has made a fool of him by getting his father to disinherit him if Abbie has a son. Pleadingly, Abbie explains that she was after vengeance then because of Eben's going to Min, but she "didn't mean t' do bad t' ye!" and begs for forgiveness. Eben, however, wants revenge on both of them and threatens to leave for the California gold fields. Then, when he is rich, he will return and kick out Abbie and his father, and the child too. As far as the infant is concerned, Eben wishes it would die: "I wish he never was born! I wish he'd die this minit! I wish I'd never sot eyes on him! It's him—yew havin' him—a-purpose to steal—that's changed everythin!." In answer to Abbie's pleading, Eben admits that he had indeed loved her "like a dumb ox!" and his hatred arises from the belief that she had tricked him. So, he will leave the next morning. Abbie says that if Eben hates the child, so too will she: "He won't steal [the farm]! I'd kill him fust! I do love ye! I'll prove t' ye!" Desperately, Abbie asks for a kiss, and when Eben refuses, she asks whether he would love her once more if she could make it so that things were as they were before the baby came, and Eben replies laconically, "I calc'late not. But ye hain't God, be ye?" As Eben leaves to get drunk and dance, Abbie calls after him: "I'll prove I love ye better'n . . . Better'n anything else in the world!"

Part III, Scene iii: It is just before dawn, and the kitchen and the Cabots' bedroom are visible. Eben is in the candlelit kitchen, sitting at the table, his carpetbag on the floor in front of him. Upstairs, the bedroom is lighted by an oil lamp; Cabot is asleep, and Abbie is leaning over the cradle with a look of "terror yet with an undercurrent of triumph." She seems about to break down and fling herself on her knees by the cradle, but Ephraim moves and groans. She pulls herself together, goes out, and in a moment reappears in the kitchen. She runs to Eben, "flings her arms around his neck and kisses him wildly." He remains stiff and unmoved, looking straight ahead. Hysterically, Abbie announces, "I done it, Eben!" but Eben doesn't understand. He reiterates his plan to leave, leaving "Maw t' take vengeance on ye." He won't tell his father the truth because "the old skunk'd jest be mean enuf to take it out on that baby." And then he expresses his own love for the child, because it is his, it looks like him, and some day he will come back. Abbie, not hearing Eben, then announces, "I—killed him, Eben." However, Eben thinks she means Ephraim and manufactures an alibi—that the old man killed himself while he was drunk. Instantly Abbie realizes, "But that's what I ought t' done, hain't it? I oughter killed him instead! Why didn't ye tell me?" Eben, horrified at the discovery that his son has been smothered, cries out, "Oh, God A'mighty! A'mighty God! Maw, whar was ye, why didn't ye stop her?"

Eben's grief then turns to rage as Abbie tells of her desperation and her reason for doing an act she regrets—she loves Eben more even than her own child. But Eben is blinded by his anger and maintains that she plans to blame him for the murder. "But I'll take vengeance now! I'll git the Sheriff! I'll tell him everythin! Then I'll sing 'I'm off to California!' an' go—gold—Golden Gate—gold sun— fields o' gold in the West!" Abbie calls after him, "Eben, I love ye! I don't care what ye do—if ye'll on'y love me agen," as she faints to the floor.

Part III, Scene iv: One hour later, just after dawn with a brilliant sunrise. Abbie is sitting at the kitchen table with her head on her arms. Upstairs, Cabot has just woken and starts to talk to Abbie. Then he gets up, blaming himself for oversleeping. With pride, he looks at the cradle and his "purty" son and then goes downstairs, asking for his breakfast. Abbie, at first almost like stone, then tells him she has smothered the child. Ephraim reacts with stunned fury, shaking her and asking why she did it. Abbie then pushes him away furiously and springs to her feet, spewing out the hatred and rage she feels towards her husband, wishing she had murdered him instead, and finally admitting the child's paternity. Cabot's face hardens: "I got t' be—like a stone—a rock o' jedgment!" If Abbie's statement is true, then Ephraim is glad the child is dead, and "I'll deliver ye up t' the jedgment o' God an' the law!" But to his surprise, he learns that Eben has already gone to do so. "In a voice full of strange emotion," he tells Abbie, "Ye'd ought t' loved me. . . . I'd never told no Sheriff on ye no matter what ye did."

At that moment Eben comes running back, and when Cabot learns that he has indeed told the Sheriff, he pushes his son away, warning Eben to get off the farm before he murders him. Ephraim then leaves. Eben, unhearing, enters the kitchen, falls on his knees beside Abbie, and begs her forgiveness, telling her that as he waited for the Sheriff to appear, he realized that he had loved Abbie and always would. That is why he has run back, to talk to her before she can be taken away so they can run off together. Abbie refuses, because she must pay for her sin. Eben says he will share it with her by alleging that he planned the murder and must pay, too: "I want t' share with ye, Abbie—prison 'r death 'r hell 'r anythin'!" Finally Abbie realizes that she can't talk him out of his plan.

Footsteps are heard; it is Cabot, back from the barn. He enters to find Eben kneeling beside Abbie with his arms around her, both staring straight ahead. Almost maniacally, he wishes them both hanged and then announces that he has turned his stock loose and by so doing has freed himself. He will set fire to house, barn, everything and go to California. He breaks into a caper. But then he looks for his hoard and discovers that Eben had given it to Simeon and Peter for their passage money. After a moment of shock Ephraim resigns himself: "I calc'late God give it to 'em—not yew! God's hard, not easy! . . . God's hard an' lonesome." The ease of the West is not for him, and Eben is His instrument to save Ephraim from his weakness.

At this moment, the Sheriff enters with two other men, and Eben tells his story of participation in the murder. Cabot looks at Eben "with a trace of grudging admiration" and goes out to round up his stock and recommence life. The two prisoners bid him good bye and then embrace each other, to the embarrassment of the Sheriff and his men. They go out the door hand in hand, and Eben says, "Sun's a-rizin'. Purty, hain't it?" Abbie agrees, and they stand momentarily looking upwards, with a curiously detached air mingled with devotion. The Sherifff delivers the final ironic line: "It's a jim-dandy farm, no denyin'. Wished I owned it!"

Comments: With this play Eugene O'Neill established himself as a playwright of genius. Here everything seems to have fallen into place to create a major work of tragic art. It is sometimes said that tragedy is impossible of achievement by modern playwrights, but with *Desire Under the Elms*, I believe that O'Neill has given that statement the lie. He has developed a play with an American setting and a recognizable locale with its historial and emotional connotations of Puritanism, Protestant ethic, and hardness, but he has superimposed that mythic structure on the ancient myths of Greek drama. One can easily recognize the three basic myths included in this tragedy, Oedipus, Phaedra, and Medea. But the important thing about this play is the freedom with which O'Neill melds these elements into something different by the addition of other psychological-philosophical sources—Friedrich Nietzsche and Sigmund Freud. And out of this collection of materials he managed to create a modern approximation of the Aristotelian pity and fear. His characters seem indeed to be the prisoners of their own destiny, and a hostile first principle broods over their acts, forever forbidding happiness in this life. Only at the end, in a spiritual union, a renunciation of life through love that is unselfish, do the central characters gain a glimmer of something better as they look up at the sunrise.

The Oedipal struggle between father and son is clear from the beginning in the way that Eben's close relationship with his mother is conveyed and also his rage that he has been cheated of Ephraim's farm. It is, then, but a short step to Freud and Eben's acting out of the Oedipal aspect of man's existence by having sexual intercourse first with Min and then with Abbie. Abbie is, of course, a combination of Phaedra and Medea, a statement which also gives Eben some of the qualities of Hippolytus, and certainly he is at first reluctant to recognize his physical longing for Abbie. But the intrusion of the Medea myth is unexpected in the play, and Abbie realizes that she should have murdered Ephraim, but it nonetheless strengthens her characterization as a woman who gives up everything for love. In her case, she has married in hope of possessing the farm, and she feels herself to be part of nature and even of the farm. As a result, in killing the baby she is cutting herself off from her place, her dreams, her love, and her true identity. She is a creature of Nature and physicality, yet she murders the product of that part of her in order to regain the love of Eben. Here, certainly, the myth gives added resonance.

From Nietzsche, O'Neill has taken the concept of the Apollonian and Dionysian duality which he later used more specifically in *The Great God Brown*.* Here he transposes the situation to Ephraim and his vision of God, who is "hard an' lonesome." The whole metaphor of the stones and the hardness of life imposed by the Apollonian-Puritan God upon Cabot is contrasted with his occasional longing for the "easy" God which he had found in the Middle West where one had merely to plant a field and watch the crops grow. Even at the end of the play, Ephraim has a sneaking desire to follow that "easy" God when he speaks of leaving for the West and the goldfields. The stern God does not always remain in total control of Ephraim, as is evidenced by his two momentary lapses in the spring but even more particularly in the Dionysian revel celebrating the birth of Abbie's son. There he turns into a satyr-figure—laughing, capering, drinking, celebrating—reaching a momentary intoxication of joy that blinds and deafens him to what is being said and done around him. His Dionysian side is also in tune with nature because he is in tune with the seasons when he leaves his farm to seek God's will. Here, he also follows the voice of his commanding Apollonian-Puritan God, but in marrying Abbie, he follows the instincts of Dionysus. The great key to the theology of the play (and I do not think this word is too strong) is Ephraim's long monologue to Abbie in Part II, Scene ii, where he tells of his attempt to quit the farm, of his time in the Middle West, and then his return to the rock-strewn farm which had made him as hard as the stone walls he has built. He sees them as a testament to God, but his sons Simeon and Peter perceive them as prison walls. Eben, on the other hand, considers them more as a protective device for his own world—the farm, from which he fears displacement. Both Eben and his father feel themselves part of the farm, and their kinship with nature and the seasons makes their basic conflict credible. The two men are more alike than they realize, but Eben has the ability to love, while Ephraim has not. For this reason Ephraim is always lonesome, always private, revealing himself only to his wrathful, judgmental God, and also to the cows, the only living things with whom he really feels comfortable because, as animals, they do not threaten him into giving too much rein to his physical, Dionysian nature.

In two other aspects O'Neill succeeded brilliantly in this play—in the use of language and sets. The language is spare, laconic, and dialectal, yet through it O'Neill is able to convey an extraordinary emotional power and also communicate theological and philosophical concepts without resort to the lyricism which sounds so strained in plays such as *The Fountain*.* For instance, the almost monosyllabic speeches of the brothers in the first two scenes indicate, through their differing reactions to the sunset, quite separate people. Eben thinks of the farm as his own, Simeon remembers his dead wife, and Peter thinks of the gold in California. Even Ephraim's long monologue is pure dialect, yet at the same time it achieves a kind of poetry which O'Neill in his more self-conscious moments was unable to manage.

In terms of the set, O'Neill was himself largely responsible for its design, and he specified his requirements in drawings. It is a permanent set, with the scenes shifting among the various rooms which are emphasized by means of light. One possible defect in this set would seem to be the elms themselves. The stage directions speak of their "sinister maternity" and the way their branches rest on the roof like "hands and hair"; but the trees are never exploited, and certainly it never rains in the course of the play so that "their tears trickle down monotonously and rot the shingles." Perhaps they are meant to give some sense of the fatal destiny of the house of Cabot, but the stone walls of the farm are a better symbol. Nevertheless, throughout the play O'Neill shows himself completely cognizant of the action as it develops on this particular set, and his contrapuntal use of words and images is excellent. The celebration scene in Part III, Scene i, for instance, is brilliant in its contrasts, while the bedroom scene in Part II, Scene i, with Eben on one side and Abbie and Ephraim on the other, is superb in showing the almost telepathic communication between the lovers. The farmhouse and the farm are really central characters in the play, and hence the Sheriff's ironic closing lines seem most à propos. Those lines are an epitaph for Ephraim and for the farm itself, and an act of devout respect to the God who made it possible—but at a cost the Sheriff can neither know nor understand. Only the three Cabots understand as they go off into their sunrise. In their imprisonment, they all find freedom under the aegis of a mighty and cruel God.

The subject matter of the play caused it to be banned in Boston, and it was refused a public performance in England until 1940. With other audiences, however, *Desire Under the Elms* was well received and has since become one of the most frequently revived of O'Neill's plays. O'Neill himself claimed that he had dreamed the play and that he wrote it at great speed; perhaps that accounts for the tightness of the writing and the spare dialogue. But his growing experience with the stage is undoubtedly the reason for the skillful construction, the use of association (notably the quotations from The Song of Solomon), and the excellent curtain lines. But above all else, O'Neill's skillful fusion of classical and American myth gave to this play a power not before seen in the American theatre.

Production Data: Written 1924. Produced by Kenneth Macgowan,* Robert Edmond Jones,* and Eugene O'Neill at the Greenwich Village Theatre, New York City, November 11, 1924 (208 performances).

Director: Robert Edmond Jones

Designer: Robert Edmond Jones

Cast: Simeon Cabot: Allen Nagle
  Peter Cabot: Perry Ivins
  Eben Cabot: Charles Ellis
  Ephraim Cabot: Walter Huston
  Abbie Putnam: Mary Morris, later replaced by Mary Blair*
  Young Girl: Eloise Pendleton
  Farmers: Romeyn Benjamin, Arthur Mack, William Stahl, Jim Taylor
  Fiddler: Macklin Marrow
  Sheriff: Walter Abel
  Deputies: Arthur Mack, William Stahl
  People from Surrounding Farms: Albert Brush, Hume Derr, Donald Oenslager, Alma O'Neill, Lucy Shreve, Mary Ture, Ruza Wenclawska

Revived January 16, 1952, at the ANTA Playhouse, New York City (45 performances). *Revived* January 8, 1963, at the Circle in the Square, New York City, (384 performances).

[*See also* Appendix B for operatic adaptation by Edward Thomas.]

DEVLIN. In *Chris Christophersen*,* "a lanky, loose-jointed man of about thirty-five," dressed in dungarees. He is one of the denizens of Johnny-the-Priest's* bar. He is an expository figure who tells of Chris's past.

DEVLIN, Al. In *The Movie Man*,* cameraman with the Earth Motion Picture Company. He is "short, dark, with a goodnatured irregular face, middle-aged." Like Henry Rogers,* Devlin is dressed in the colonialist's "uniform" of Stetson hat, khaki shirt, riding breeches, and puttees. His most notable characteristic is his interest in chasing women. He tries to make a pass at Anita Fernandez,* who contemptuously looks through him. He is totally prejudiced against the Mexican people and has no good words to say for them. His language is full of colloquialism and slang, much of which is now dated. He is a one-dimensional, stock character.

DEWHURST, Colleen (19??–   ), actress. Born in Montreal, Canada. Educated at Downer College for Young Ladies, Milwaukee, Wisconsin; studied at the American Academy of Dramatic Art, 1947. Married to James Vickery (1947–59); George C. Scott (1960–65, 1967–72).

Miss Dewhurst made her acting debut in 1947 and first appeared on Broadway as one of the Neighbors in *Desire Under the Elms** (ANTA Theatre, New York City, 1952). She has become very closely associated with the role of Josie Hogan* in *A Moon for the Misbegotten*,* which she first played under the direction of José Quintero* at Spoleto (Summer 1958), repeating it in Buffalo, New York (1965). She again played it in 1973–1974, touring opposite Jason Robards, Jr.* as James Tyrone, Jr.* (Academy Theatre, Lake Forest, Illinois; Eisenhower Theatre, Washington, D.C.; Morosco Theatre, New York City; Ahmanson Theatre, Los Angeles). This performance won her the Antoinette Perry Award, a Drama Desk Award, and the Los Angeles Drama Critics Circle Award. She repeated the role with Jason Robards, Jr., on ABC-T.V. (May 27, 1975).

Miss Dewhurst, an actress of great range, versatility, and talent has shown extraordinary ability in the playing of O'Neill characters and has had some of her greatest successes with them. In 1963 she received the *Village Voice* Off-Broadway Award for her role as Abbie Putnam* in *Desire Under the Elms** (Circle in the Square). In 1967 she played Sara Melody* Harford, opposite Ingrid Bergman* as Deborah Harford,* in *More Stately Mansions*,* directed by José Quintero (Ahmanson Theatre, Los Angeles; Broadhurst Theatre, New York). She also played Christine Mannon* in *Mourning Becomes Electra** (Circle in the Square/Joseph E. Levine Theatre, 1972), also directed by Quintero.

DICK. In *The Moon of the Caribbees*,* a fireman on the S.S. *Glencairn.*

DICKEY, Reverend Samuel. In the scenario of *The Calms of Capricorn*,* a Protestant minister. He is one of the passengers on the clipper *Dream of the West* on a voyage to San Francisco. He is thirty-four, "rather shabbily dressed,...slightly unctuous....He wears glasses which give him a faintly myopic look." He seems to represent organized religion with its limitations as he speaks of the necessity of following God's will and saving one's soul. As a result of meeting with Leda Cade,* a prostitute and fellow passenger with whom he goes to bed, he entertains doubts about his calling. He also lusts after Elizabeth Warren.* He buries the murdered Captain Enoch Payne* and almost immediately performs the marriage ceremony for the murderers, Ethan Harford* and Nancy Drummond Payne,* the captain's widow. He also officiates at the *mariage de convenance* of Jonathan Harford* and Elizabeth Warren.* When the vessel is again becalmed just outside of San Francisco, he suggests throwing the "sinners," Ethan and Nancy, into the sea.

DIFF'RENT, a naturalistic domestic drama in two acts.

Act I: "Parlor of the Crosby home on a side street of a seaport village in New England—mid-afternoon of a day in late spring in the year 1890." The room "has an aspect of scrupulous neatness" and is furnished in the typical overstuffed and horsehair style of the period. Notable articles of furniture are a black horsehair sofa, two plush-covered armchairs, a tiny old-fashioned piano, a Rogers group, marble clock, and clumsy marble-topped table with a large family Bible. The bookcase "is half filled with old volumes," but on the table near the Bible are "several books that look suspiciously like cheap novels."

Enlarged photos of "stern-looking people" are on the walls. Altogether, the room conveys a sense of formality belonging to an earlier age. Emma Crosby* and Caleb Williams* are discovered sitting side by side on the sofa, both dressed in their black Sunday best. She is twenty, slender, giving an impression of prettiness whose "soft, blue eyes . . . have an incongruous quality of absent-minded dreaminess about them." Nonetheless, she also gives an impression of vitality and good health. Caleb, age thirty, is a ruggedly healthy, bronzed man with black hair and dark eyes. He is sitting awkwardly with his arm about her waist, while she holds one of his hands and leans dreamily on his shoulder. But despite his rigid pose, Caleb looks tenderly down at her. He has just returned from a whaling expedition which has taken him to the South Seas, and their marriage is to take place in two days. As Emma contentedly wishes they could sit like this forever, Caleb replies, "Hell, yes!" and Emma reproves him for swearing, saying that that may be all right for her father and her brother, "But you're diff'rent. You just got to be diff'rent from all the rest." This comment dismays Caleb, who with good-natured amusement says he is like all other men; "Sailors ain't plaster saints." But Emma pleads that he will promise to "stay diff'rent . . . even after we're married years and years." In short, Emma has extraordinarily high ideals concerning marriage, believing that prenuptial virginity is an essential element. The more she tries to impress upon Caleb the necessity of his being "diff'rent" the more he insists that he is "a plain, ordinary cuss," and he will not try to pretend otherwise. He speaks of the problems that other whalers have found when they returned home to find "out some funny things that's been done when they was away." Emma says that she is "diff'rent" in that regard and further that she has "never doubted" him in the years he was away, "and I won't when you sail away again, neither." Caleb laughingly says it would be difficult to be jealous of a whale, and anyway, in the course of his two-year voyage, he was so concerned with making enough money for their marriage that he had no time for anything. The vessel had not even touched a port, except for one occasion when they were blown south and had to put in at an island for water. Emma is startled by this revelation, because she had not heard this, and Caleb suddenly remembers that he has an errand to run.

Just before he leaves, Jack Crosby* enters, "a hulking, stocky-built young fellow of twenty-five, . . . handsome in a coarse, animal, good-natured fashion." He is carrying a string of cod heads and laughs uproariously as he catches Emma and Caleb in the process of a kiss. Jack banters with Emma and Caleb about their forthcoming marriage and starts teasing Emma: "Caleb's a Sunday go-to-meetin' Saint, . . . one o' them goody-goody heroes out o' them story books you're always readin'." Then with a meaningful look he suggests, "You ought to have a talk with Jim Benson, Emmer." This angers Caleb, who in response to Emma's enquiry suggests that Jim ought to "keep his tongue from waggin'." After Caleb leaves, Jack tells the story of the way in which Caleb was seduced by a native girl, largely as the result of practical joke played on him by some drunken crew members. He had stayed away from the women until one of them was told to swim out to the vessel because the captain (Caleb) had allegedly asked for her. Uproariously, he tells of the way in which the young woman pursued the boat after their night together until finally the crew had to shoot at her in the water before she ceased her screaming after Caleb. The entire incident is treated by everyone on the boat as a hilarious joke, and it has become the talk of the town bars.

Emma is stunned—"He ought to have acted diff'rent"—and announces, "I ain't going to marry him." This reaction astounds Jack and also Harriet Williams,* Caleb's sister. She counsels a bit of tolerance, saying that she is well aware of the peccadilloes of her fiancé, Alf Rogers,* but realizes that men will be men. Mrs. Crosby,* Emma's mother, says the same thing, and comments that when Captain Crosby* had told her about the incident, "I thought it was a good joke on Caleb." Both women try to convince Emma that "if you've been wide awake to all that's happened in this town since you was old enough to know, you'd ought to realize what men be." As Harriet says, "A girl'd never git married hereabouts if she expected too much." But Emma refuses to budge. She no longer can marry Caleb because she loved what she thought he was, not what he is. Captain Crosby, a sixty-year-old, squat, broadly built, weatherbeaten sailor, also tries to talk Emma out of her idealism. Caleb returns, to find Emma with the marks of her inner conflict upon her face, and he confesses the whole incident, saying that though he did indeed lose his virginity to the importunate native girl, "I was sorry for it, after. I locked myself in the cabin and left her to sleep on deck." Emma says she can forgive what has happened—"I know that most any man would do the same"—but she still will not marry him.

She has loved Caleb because he was "diff'rent," and now that he has proved himself to be like other men, she cannot marry him: "You've busted something way down inside me—and I can't love you no more." Gloomily, Caleb says that she shouldn't have put him on such a pedestal, but perhaps after another two-year voyage she will reconsider and realize that Caleb is not as bad as he currently seems: "And I'll wait for ye to change your mind, I don't give a durn how long it'll take—till I'm sixty years old—thirty years if it's needful!" Mournfully, Emma tells him that it will be no use. She has decided that there are worse things in the world than being an old maid. As Emma goes upstairs to lie down, Caleb slowly goes out the door, his face set "in its concealment mask of emotionlessness."

Act II: Thirty years later, "late afternoon of a day in the early spring of the year 1920," the same room as in Act I. However, the room has had its aspect altered alarmingly and "has a grotesque aspect of old age turned flighty and masquerading as the most empty-headed youth." It is now as typical of the "jazz age" as the earlier room was of Victoriana: the curtains are orange rather than stiff white, the cream wallpaper has pink flowers, the carpet is gone, to be replaced by hardwood varnished to a high gloss with three precisely placed garish rugs. "The plush-covered chairs are gone, replaced by a set of varnished oak. The horsehair sofa has been relegated to the attic. A cane-bottomed affair with fancy cushions serves in its stead.'' The mahogany chest has been replaced by a Victrola, and instead of the tiny antique piano there is a new, modern one. The bookcase is modern and so are the ''installment-plan sets of uncut volumes'' that fill it. The varnished oak center table is piled with fashion magazines. Only the marble-topped table with the family Bible and the marble clock on the mantle have survived from the old room, and they emphasize the incongruity of the renovation.

As the curtain rises, Emma and Benny Rogers* are discovered. She is sitting in a rocker by the table and clearly shows the effects of the passage of thirty years. She seems dried out but has dyed her hair black, has attempted the use of modern make-up, and is dressed in a style that is grotesquely, even obscenely, youthful, ''a mockery of undignified age snatching greedily at the empty simulacra of youth . . . a passé stock actress of fifty made up for a heroine of twenty.'' Benny ''is a young fellow of twenty-three, a replica of his father in Act One, but coarser, more hardened and cocksure. He is dressed in the khaki uniform of a private in the United States Army.'' He is listening to a record on the Victrola and is dancing to the music. Emma has picked out this particular jazz record from the list that Benny had given her. She bridles at Benny's congratulations and compliments, saying that she prefers jazz which puts ''life and ginger in an old lady like me—not like them slow, old-timey tunes.'' She wants to learn the latest dances and tells Benny not to call her ''Aunt Emmer.''

Gradually, Benny unburdens himself of his resentment against ''Uncle Caleb,'' whom he describes as ''a darn, stingy, ugly old cuss,'' whom he has hated ever since his own ''Pa died and Ma and me had to go live next door to him.'' He cannot understand what Emma ever saw in him, but she defends him as being ''kind at bottom, spite of his rough ways.'' Obviously Benny's real hatred arises from the fact that Caleb has been the family disciplinarian and also because he is tight with money: ''He's got piles of money hoarded in the bank but he's too mean even to retire from whalin'.'' Caleb is about to return and he will undoubtedly come straight over to see Emma. Benny recalls his own father and also Jack Crosby (both drowned), ''they were good sports,'' a comment that Emma takes rather primly. Calculatingly, Benny starts to worm his way into Emma's confidence until he asks her for a hundred dollars with which to have a good time in Boston. Emma's amazement gives way to pity as Benny complains that everyone treats him ''like a wet dog,'' even though he's ''sweatin' blood in the army after riskin' my life in France.'' He tells Emma she is the only one to understand him, and she rises ''kittenishly'' and ''coquettishly'' to the bait. She allows that she has had the place fixed up specially for him ''so's you'd have a nice, up-to-date place to come to when you was on vacation from the horrid old army.'' Emma then tries to give some advice concerning the town prostitute, suggesting that he should promise not to visit her any more. Gradually, Benny wheedles her, telling her about the French girls, and Emma with strange eagerness wants to know more. She goes upstairs ''to tidy up'' as Harriet arrives dressed in old-fashioned black and her face wears a permanently careworn, fretful expression. She tells Benny that his uncle has come home and he knows now that Benny has stolen money from her and has heard about his "drunken carryin's-on with that harlot, Tilly Small." She is enraged also at "the sneakin' way you're makin' a silly fool out of poor Emmer Crosby." Benny thinks this is funny and with a lascivious wink says, "You oughter see her perform sometimes. You'd get wise to something then." Harriet is furious and contemptuously tells him that neither she nor Caleb will give him one penny more, and she will tell Emma how rotten he is. She tries to appeal to some decent part of him, reminding him that Caleb still hopes that Emma will marry him: "And she will, I believe, if she comes out of this fit in a sane mind—which she won't if you keep fussin' with her."

After Harriet leaves, threatening Benny with Caleb's violence, Benny debates whether to go or stay, and then with a cruel grin he has an idea: "By God, that's it! I'll bet I kin work it, too! By God, that'll fix 'em!" He calls Emma down and with pretended grief says good-bye and thanks for everything she has done. Caleb and Harriet have thrown him out and have told him never to return. Emma believes this edited version of the facts and offers to talk to Caleb, but Benny refuses, saying that Caleb will not believe anything except his mother's lies. He repeats Harriet's comment that Emma may yet accept Caleb, a remark that Emma rejects, suggesting that Benny may be a trifle jealous of his uncle. Benny picks up this suggestion, saying that Caleb may well believe the lies about her relationship with his nephew. Emma is "shocked but pleased," and then Benny suggests that the two of them get married tomorrow. Emma, "dazed with joy," accepts, "if I'm not too old for you."

As they embrace and Emma kisses Benny full on the lips, Caleb knocks on the door and is amazed at the transformation he sees in the room. Plainly uncomfortable with it, he asks after his favorite chair, and Emma with a pitying smile, "not without a trace of malice," looks at Caleb, still hale though white-haired and looking much the same as in Act I. Seeing him as "a sot, old-fashioned critter," she lightly remarks, "It didn't fit in with them new things." Caleb is appalled at the grotesque changes he sees in Emma's appearance—her dyed hair, her rouge and powder, her absurdly youthful costume. She says that Benny is going to teach her to dance, and Caleb barely keeps his rage under control. He then reminds her that he has waited thirty years for her to change her mind, and "we both got to realize now and then that we're gettin' old . . . Seems to me, Emmer, thirty o' the best years of a man's life ought to be proof enough to you to make you forget—that one slip o' mine." Emma treats the situation in a careless, yet forced tone: "Land sakes, I forgot all about that long ago. And here you go remindin' me of it!" With dogged persistence, Caleb says that he thinks Emma may well need him more than she realizes, and the conversation turns to Harriet and Benny.

Caleb tries to make Emma see that Benny is no good, but she defends him and finally accuses Caleb of jealousy, revealing their plan to be married tomorrow. With rage, Caleb says he will prevent the marriage, but in answer to Emma's pleas he says he won't do Benny any violence; if he wanted to get even with Emma he'd let the marriage go through, "or else I'd offer him money not to marry ye—more money than the little mite you kin bring him—and let ye see how quick he'd turn his back on ye." Emma, who has hurt Caleb to the heart by her proclamation of love for Benny, refuses to believe Caleb's allegation, and with rage he leaves: "Thirty o' the best years of my life flung for a yeller dog like him to feed on." . . . I kin only see one course out for me and I'm goin' to take it. 'A dead whale or a stove boat!' we says in whalin'—and my boat is stove." As he leaves, Emma collapses into a chair, "sobbing hysterically." Benny then returns and treats Emma with swaggering braggadochio, eventually coming to the point: he will accept Caleb's bribe not to mary Emma "if he'll put up enough money. I won't stand for no pikin'." With utter viciousness he makes it quite clear that he will marry Emma only if Caleb's bribe is insufficient. As Emma hysterically sends him away, he turns on her: "This is what I get for foolin' around with an old hen like you that oughta been planted in the cemetery long ago! Paintin' your old mush and dressin' like a kid! Christ A'mighty."

At this moment, Harriet knocks at the door to ask Benny to investigate a "big thumpin' noise" in her barn. He goes with her, and Emma remains sitting in her chair. Then, "with quick mechanical movements," she removes the curtains, cushions, and pictures and puts them in a pile on the floor. She then adds the rugs, and without any change in her expression, "sweeps everything off the table on to the floor." Benny rushes in and in answer to his inquiry she says, "The junk man's coming for them in the morning." Benny then tells her that Caleb has hanged himself and gives her specific details. He asks Emma to comfort Harriet. Emma says she will be over "in a minute," but first she has to do something. Benny is nonplussed, but Emma enlightens him: she has to go down to the barn. As Benny leaves in exasperation—"Everyone's lost their heads but me"—Emma whispers, "Wait, Caleb, I'm going down to the barn," and exits like a sleepwalker as the curtain falls.

Comments: This play is another in O'Neill's continuing treatment of domestic relations; and even though it was not successful with audience or critics, it has elements of interest. O'Neill himself thought it one of the best things he had done to date, and it achieved performance at matinees during the run of *The Emperor Jones*.* Travis Bogard (1972, p. 145) suggests that it shows O'Neill's first essay into Freudianism, and to some extent he may be correct; but the psychology is very clumsy. Motivation for Emma's actions is extraordinarily scanty, though the stern-looking photographs may be expected to provide a clue. However, the actions of the other members of the Crosby family deny that possibility, for they seem to be tolerant of sexual peccadilloes. Perhaps the differing furnishings of the room in Acts I and II are meant to indicate Emma's psychological state, and certainly her action at the end, in tearing apart all the misconceived redecorations in the parlor, is both dramatically effective and psychologically viable.

Yet, the major problem of the play lies in the nature of Emma's ideals for matrimony. Does she wish for a totally chaste marriage, or does she instead merely wish for prenuptial virginity for both of them? This is not clearly explained. As for the origin of Emma's "romantic idealism," O'Neill seems to look for it in the romantic novels she enjoys reading—a situation which would make her character that of Emma Bovary in the reverse, and the choice of name is thus significant. Visually, the conflict between the family Bible and the romantic novels is stated but not developed. Similarly, O'Neill restates this opposition in the second act with the marble clock, the Bible, and the uncut installment-plan books. However, again, this is not developed. In short, O'Neill fails to communicate the exact nature of Emma's ideal in marriage, and as a result, the central conflict is not properly defined. One must also quarrel somewhat with the reversal of Emma's character in Act II. She has turned almost completely around, and once again, motivation is lacking. Her primness has become a prurience that undermines her characterization, particularly since she claims that Caleb's sin is now forgotten. As for Caleb, his dogged pursuit of Emma is likewise unmotivated and remains unexplained. Certainly he has an implicit ideal of marriage that is much more realistic than Emma's. The double suicide is also a trifle too melodramatic. Nonetheless, this play does start O'Neill on an examination of the wellsprings of human motivation, even if he does not succeed here, and it is another step forward in his long attempt to portray the matrimonial relationship in his dramas. The performance of Mary Blair* in the role of Emma Crosby was highly praised.

Production Data: Written 1920. Produced by the Provincetown Players at the Playwrights' Theatre, New York City, December 27, 1920. Moved to matinee schedule, Selwyn Theatre, New York City, January 21, 1921; transferred to the Times Square Theatre, New York City, February 4, 1921, and the Princess Theatre, New York City, February 7, 1921 (Total performances 100).

Director: Charles O'Brien Kennedy

Designer: Cleon Throckmorton

Cast: Emma Crosby: Mary Blair*
   Captain John Crosby: H. B. Tisdale
   Mrs. Crosby: Alice Rostetter
   Jack Crosby: Eugene Lincoln
   Caleb Williams: James Light
   Harriet Williams: Elizabeth Brown
   Alf Rogers: Iden Thompson
   Benny Rogers: Charles Ellis

Revived January 25, 1938, at Maxine Elliott's Theatre, New York City (4 performances).

Revived October 17, 1961, at the Mermaid Theatre, New York City (88 performances).

DIGGES, Dudley (1879–1947), actor. Born in Dublin, Ireland, 1879; died in New York City, October 24, 1947. Married Maire Quinn. Educated at Saint

Mary's College (high school), Rathmines, where he played his first stage role as the Earl of Pembroke in Shakespeare's *King John* (1890).

Digges began his stage career as an amateur playing melodrama in the company of W. G. Fay, from which he was co-opted into the fledgling Irish National Theatre, playing Naisi in the *Deirdre* of Æ (George Russell) at the celebrated opening performance of the group at the hall of Saint Theresa's Total Abstinence Society (1902). Participants in the other presentation of the evening included W. B. Yeats's beloved Maud Gonne, and Maire Quinn, whom Digges later married. He came to the United States in 1904 to perform with the Irish National Theatre at the Irish Pavilion of the St. Louis World's Fair (1904), where another headline performer was an unknown Irish tenor named John McCormack. The company was fired in a dispute with its management over its material, and Digges came to New York where he worked very briefly as a sales clerk for Rogers Peet men's clothiers and joined Arnold Daly's company as a super. The next year he moved to Ben Greet's Shakespearean Players and then toured with Minnie Maddern Fiske's company in *The New York Idea*. In 1908 he became stage manager for Charles Frohman, and from 1912 to 1919, he acted as stage manager for George Arliss. In 1919 he played in *Someone in the House*, a flop in which Lynn Fontanne* also appeared. In that same year, he became a charter member of the Theatre Guild, participating in its first production, *Bonds of Interest* (a flop), and in its first success, *Mr. Ferguson*. From this time on, his success as a character actor was assured, and he was perpetually busy on stage and screen for the rest of his life. He appeared in a variety of films and plays, ranging from classics to modern plays of all genres.

Digges was closely associated with the O'Neill plays produced by the Theatre Guild, playing Chu-Yin* in *Marco Millions** (1938, with Alfred Lunt*), Mr. Fife* in *Dynamo*,* and the original Harry Hope* in *The Iceman Cometh** (1946). He also played Henry Smithers* in the 1946 film of *The Emperor Jones*,* with Paul Robeson.*

Throughout his long career Digges remained profoundly interested in Ireland and in the fortunes of the Irish National Theatre. In 1931 he returned to the Abbey Theatre to play in *The Hour Glass* in which he had appeared in 1903. A gifted and versatile character actor, he understood all aspects of the theater.

DILLMAN, Bradford (1930–   ), actor. Born in San Francisco, California, April 14, 1930, to Dean and Josephine Dillman. Father an investment banker. Educated at Hotchkiss Preparatory School, Yale University (B.A., 1951), Actors' Studio (1955–   ) with Lee Strasberg, and with John Lehne (1962–   ). Married to Frieda Harding (1956–62, one son, one daughter); Suzy Parker (1963–   , 2 sons, 1 daughter). Served in the U.S. Marine Corps, 1951–53.

Dillman made his professional debut in *The Scarecrow* (Theatre de Lys, New York, 1953) and played off-Broadway and in summer stock. He created the role of Edmund Tyrone* in *Long Day's Journey into Night** in the first American production (1956) directed by José Quintero,* winning the *Theatre World* award for his portrayal. (For an account of the progress of this production, *see* the memoir by Quintero, *If You Don't Dance They Beat You*, 1974). Dillman repeated this role at the Theatre of Nations Festival, Paris, France (1957). He also played the role of Willie Oban* in the 1973 American Film Theater production of *The Iceman Cometh*.* He has had a successful career in film and television in both specials and series.

DONATA. In *Marco Millions*,* the betrothed of Marco Polo* and daughter of Paulo Loredano.* At the beginning of the play, she appears as a young girl of twelve seen only through a barred Venetian window, being serenaded by Marco Polo and exchanging vows of love with him. In the last scene of the play, which takes place some twenty years later, she is seen as fat and rather "bovine" in face. She has waited twenty years for Marco to return to marry her. The match is an economic one, a union of two business houses, and love does not enter into it. Donata, like a good Venetian woman, has remained faithful to Marco, though he has had some amorous adventures. She gives him a locket which he later returns to her, damaged, claiming falsely that it was the result of an encounter with pirates rather than the rage of the woman who loved him, Kukachin.* As Marco knows, she is not very bright, but she is a good bourgeois type who will run a smooth household for him. Significantly, she nearly swoons, not at Marco's return and proposal but at the sight of the piles of worldly wealth of which she will be mistress. She is a fit wife for a crassly materialistic businessman, unthinking and devoted to display.

DONKEYMAN. In "The Ole Davil," the Donkeyman of Chris Christopherson's* barge. He comes to Anna Christopherson,* his daughter, to offer his help and express his concern that Chris might lose his job if he stays away much longer getting drunk. Anna addresses him as "Mr. Donk."

DONKEYMAN. *See* Old Tom.

DONOHUE, Stephen, "Big Steve." In "The Reckoning"* a blacksmith and stepfather of Bessie Small.* When he hears that Bessie is pregnant by his helper, Jack Gardner, he tries to force their marriage. In the fight which ensues, Gardner hits him over the head with a hammer, knocking him senseless. Both young people believe him to be dead, and Jack (on Bessie's advice) flees to Chicago, changing his name to Jack Cockran.* Donohue recovers and later traces Jack and Bessie (who has married him) to their new home in a northeastern mill town. He confronts Bessie and tells her that Cockran's blow has permanently damaged him so that he has lost his business and has been forced to lead a nomadic existence. He swears he will kill Jack if he can find him. Bessie refuses to admit that she is Donohue's stepdaughter and buys him a ticket to Ireland to get him out of the way. Apart from gaining vengeance, Donohue's dearest wish is to die in his home country. As a character, he is merely a dramatic instrument in a scenario which is by no means fully developed.

DONOVAN, Fred (and also Tom), alias of Tom Perkins* in "The Personal Equation."*

DOUGLAS, Mildred. In *The Hairy Ape,** a jaded, bored, fretful, pretty girl of twenty dressed in white. She is seeking additional experiences on her transatlantic crossing. She looks with a certain *frisson* of sexual interest on the second engineer, who is to escort her to the stokehole to see how the other half lives. She has also been playing at social work on New York's Lower East Side and is en route to look at conditions in London's Whitechapel. With these credentials, and her father's influence as head of the Steel Trust and owner of the shipping line, she manages to get permission to visit the stokehole, despite the opposition of both captain and chief engineer. When she enters that inferno, she is almost overwhelmed by the horror of the scene but manages to hold herself together momentarily until Yank* whirls around, after shouting obscenities at the commanding steam whistle in the compartment. She looks at him as if he is an animal, and he thinks her a ghost. Her personality totally collapses, she covers her face with her hands, cries out, "Oh, the filthy beast!" and faints. She disappears from the play after that, but she has made such an impression on Yank that she has destroyed the very wellsprings of his being, hence he tries to gain revenge on her and her class for his loss of certainty. Originally played by Mary Blair,* the role of Mildred Douglas was given in the uptown performance of the play to Carlotta Monterey,* later to become O'Neill's third wife.

DOVER. In *Children of the Sea** and *Bound East for Cardiff** this is the vessel from whose wreck Driscoll* and Yank* escape.

DOWNEY, Ella. In *All God's Chillun Got Wings,** Ella, a white girl, grows up and marries Jim Harris,* a black man, after she has a child by Mickey,* a young, neighborhood hoodlum-boxer, and lives for a brief time as a prostitute. She marries Jim so that they can help each other, but she discovers that she cannot exist in her limbo-world of interracial marriage. She is basically a very prejudiced character, as her behavior when she is insane indicates, and she does not wish Jim to succeed in his law school examinations because she is afraid that she will lose him. She may also be interpreted as a destructive aspect of white society or as the frequent O'Neill character of the wife who is a stumbling block in the path of her husband's achievement of his potential. She gradually regresses to childhood, when racial differences meant nothing. She fears negritude, and as a result she is afraid of the Congo mask on the wall of the parlor, finally stabbing it with a knife as a kind of exorcism. She will not have a child by Jim because she is afraid that it will be black. She threatens Jim with a knife, and in her insanity she calls him a dirty nigger. Her attitude toward Jim is tripartite. First she sees him as a protector, then as "Uncle Jim," the type of household retainer, then as child-playmate once more, but she never seems to perceive him fully as a husband.

DRAYTON, Tom. In *Now I Ask You*,* husband of Lucy Ashleigh.* He is a tall, extremely handsome, blond businessman who is extraordinarily patient in dealing with the amusingly foolish role-playing of Lucy. He follows his mother-in-law's tolerant advice in suggesting that he give Lucy her head and wait for her to calm down into common sense. He engages in a flirtation with Leonora ("Leo") Barnes,* a "synchromist" painter, in an attempt to show Lucy the folly of her alleged commitment to "Free Love." Leonora sees him as the "Great Blond Beast" of Nietzsche and admits that she finds him sexually attractive. Tom, however, is impervious to all but Lucy.

DREAM OF THE WEST, the name of the clipper ship in the scenario, *The Calms of Capricorn*,* which is part of the uncompleted cycle, "A Tale of Possessors, Self-Dispossessed."*

DREAMY. In *The Dreamy Kid*,* "a well-built, good-looking young Negro, light in color. His eyes are shifty and hard, their expression one of tough, scornful defiance. His mouth is cruel and perpetually drawn back at the corners into a snarl. He is dressed in well-fitting clothes of a flashy pattern." He is the beloved grandson of Mammy Saunders,* who has raised him from a baby after the death of his mother, her daughter, Sal. He has joined a gang of young blacks and has killed a white man, for which crime he is being hunted by the police. In answer to a plea by Ceely Ann,* he has come to visit his grandmother, who is dying in her Greenwich Village apartment. His "woman," Irene,* a black prostitute, comes to warn him that the police are looking for him there, but Dreamy says he cannot go because his grandmother has promised to curse him with bad luck if he leaves her. Irene offers to stay with him, but Dreamy threatens her and even punches her as he pushes her out, telling her to get help from his gang. At the end of the play, he is crouched on the floor with his revolver in one hand and the other clasped in his grandmother's as he awaits the police, determined not to be taken alive. His expletive, "Lawd Jesus," is taken by his grandmother to be a prayer as the curtain falls.

Dreamy is a stock figure, the gangster who is caught when he returns home for a sentimental reason. No motivation is given for his turning to crime, and Mammy Saunders believes in his goodness and innocence. His exterior is tough and hard, but underneath he is still somewhat vulnerable and even superstitious. His character is notable as being an early O'Neill attempt at a serious black character.

DREAMY KID, THE, a one-act play. The action takes place in "Mammy Saunders's bedroom in a house just off Carmine Street, New York City." The furnishings are meager, consisting of a "heavy, old-fashioned wooden bedstead with a feather mattress" covered with "a gaudy red-and-yellow quilt," a chest, lamp, rocking chair, and a washstand with pitcher, bowl, medicine bottles, spoon and glass. The window is covered with "ragged white curtains. It is soon after nightfall in early winter." By the light of the streetlamp outside the window, Mammy Saunders,* a black woman of about ninety years of age, can be seen lying in bed as she calls weakly but querulously for Ceely Ann,* a black woman of about fifty, who enters sobbing quietly as she rearranges Mammy's covers. As Ceely Ann fumbles to light the lamp, Mammy complains that her strength has left her, and she is convinced that she can last the night only "wid de blessin' er God." Ceely Ann reassures her, but with obvious unbelief, that she will be up and around within a week or so. Mammy continually calls for Dreamy,* her grandson, asking when he will come to see her. A knock is heard at the door, and Irene,* a black prostitute, enters, also asking for Dreamy. Ceely Ann treats Irene with scorn as a bad woman as Irene tries to tell her of Dreamy's trouble, "Worser'n bad." She has come to find Dreamy, believing that as "they" have said, he will come to his grandmother's deathbed. Ceely Ann, hearing this, says that she had always expected that something like this would happen since Dreamy started hanging out with "dat passel er tough young niggers—him so uppity 'cause he's de boss er de gang. . . . De low-flung young trash." Mammy, however, thinks him "de mos' innercent young lamb in de worl'." Clearly, Dreamy has become a gangster, "fightin' wid white folks, an' totin' a pistol in his pocket." Irene says that she wants to warn Dreamy to stay away before he gets "pinched." She leaves as Mammy Saunders wakens and calls again for Dreamy. Her mind is wandering as she mistakes Ceely Ann for her grandson and then asks whether Ceely Ann remembers her own "dead Mammy."

At this moment Dreamy slinks in, the picture of a scornful, defiant young tough, with a weapon in his pocket. His first words reveal that he is in flight from the police because he has "croaked a guy, . . . a white man." He is enraged at Ceely Ann for having sent for him since that will alert the police, but nevertheless he has come to see Mammy, even though he had not at first thought that she was quite as ill as she is. He, too, tries to reassure her, but the old woman talks on, recalling that the best thing she has done in her life is to raise Dreamy from a baby, after his mother died. As she speaks, there is a noise from the hall, and Dreamy draws his revolver, unlocking the door in response to a "sharp rap." It is Irene who has followed Dreamy to be with him, even if he will be captured. The young man now shows the violent side of his nature as he threatens to beat Irene for revealing his whereabouts, but the woman tells what she has found out in the neighborhood liquor store—that the police are after him and that the house is already surrounded. Dreamy looks outside to find a plain-clothes man already watching the house. He orders Irene to leave, but she refuses. He finally raises his fist to her and pushes her into the hall, giving her orders to tell the gang to come and get him out, though he knows quite well they will not take any action. He really wishes to save Irene but he is also afraid to leave Mammy, because she has threatened to curse him if he does so and he will never have good luck again. Dreamy is by now quite fatalistic about the outcome of the situation.

Ceely Ann having already left, Dreamy and Mammy are left alone, as the old woman recalls him as a child with "yo' big eyes jest a-dreamin' an' a'dreadin'," while the grown-up gangster is saying, "Dey don't get de Dreamy alive—not for de chair!" He puts his left hand into his grandmother's hand, holding the revolver in his right hand as he faces the door, listening to a noise in the hall and repeating, "Dey don't git de Dreamy! Not while he's 'live! Lawd Jesus, no suh!" The dying old woman joins in what she thinks to be a prayer as the noise of stealthy footsteps in the hallway is heard again as the curtain falls.

Comments: This play is really a melodramatic and sentimental little sketch, but it is notable for being one of the first plays in which a "white" company engaged a group of black players to play black roles. (Gelb and Gelb, 1973, pp. 399–400.) Prior to this, the custom had been to use white players in blackface. Also in this piece, O'Neill has written serious roles for black actors, in this way prefiguring his later work in *The Emperor Jones** and *All God's Chillun Got Wings.** The use of black English is carefully maintained throughout, and the inherent predictability of the situation, together with the stereotypical characters, is masked by the ethnicity of the participants. O'Neill does, however, show restraint in the conclusion of the play in that he does not have an exchange of gunfire, opting instead for the curtain fall in that moment of quiet that precedes the violence. Nonetheless, the importance of this piece rests in its use of black characters in serious roles, showing O'Neill's early recognition of their theatrical possibilities in integrated companies. Originally, he had considered making Irene a white prostitute, but audiences would not then have accepted such a possibility. Later, of course, he did use interracial marriage as a theme in *All God's Chillun Got Wings.*

Production Data: Written 1918. Produced by the Provincetown Players* at the Playwrights' Theater, New York City, October 31, 1919, after having been considered for performance the previous year. (Performances, unknown).

Director: Ida Rauh
Designer: Glenn Coleman
Cast: Mammy Saunders: Ruth Anderson
       Ceely Ann: Leathe Colvert
       Irene: Margaret Rhodes
       Dreamy: Harold Simmelkjaer
Revived as part of a double bill with *The Emperor Jones*, February 11, 1925, at the Fifty-Second Street Theatre, New York City (24 performances).

DREW, Daniel ("Danny"). In *Gold,** a tall, tanned young man of thirty, a typical ship's officer, engaged to Sue Bartlett.* He supports Sue in her attempt to prevent her father, Captain Isaiah Bartlett,* from taking out his ship, the *Sarah Allen*, because he is "not in any way fit to take a ship to sea." Sue also wants him and her brother, Nat Bartlett,* to remain because her mother, Sara Allen Bartlett,* is dying. She persuades Danny to take the vessel out secretly, leaving the captain and Nat behind. She is sure that the crew needs only an officer, and Danny has just received his master's papers. The crew, all of whom had sailed with Bartlett in the shipwrecked *Triton*, are qualified, and Silas Horne,* the boatswain, surely knows the nature of the voyage. The vessel is reported lost, and a year after its departure a letter from Danny arrives telling of the disasters that had occurred and of his survival. Members of the crew had stabbed him and left him for dead, and he had never learned the nature of the expedition, a hunt for buried treasure. He is recovering his health in a Rangoon hospital. Danny Drew is a lightly drawn character, little more than a dramatic device. He agrees to take Bartlett's vessel out for love of Sue, but one wonders about her motivation in subjecting Danny to possible danger.

DRISCOLL, an acquaintance of O'Neill from Jimmy-the-Priest's* bar in New York City. He was a fireman on the S.S. *New York*, the same boat on which Eugene O'Neill shipped for a transatlantic round-trip contract. He was the model for such characters as Yank* in *The Hairy Ape*,* Driscoll* and Paddy* in the S.S. *Glencairn* plays, and also Paddy* in *The Hairy Ape*. He is also Lyons* in "Tomorrow,"* the only short story published by O'Neill. Driscoll attempted suicide by jumping off a passenger liner. He was rescued but later was successful in killing himself in the same manner a couple of voyages later. O'Neill was unable to understand how such a man, who gloried in his strength and sense of place in the world, could give up in this way.

DRISCOLL, a seaman on the S.S. *Glencairn*, "a brawny Irishman with the battered features of a prizefighter", who appears in all plays of the S.S. *Glencairn* group. In general he is portrayed as a sympathetic character, a hard drinker, but a man with understanding and humanity. This is particularly true in *Bound East for Cardiff** where he keeps a death-watch for Yank* and discovers that they have both had the same dream of leaving the sea and farming together. He consoles the dying Yank, assuring him that God will not judge him for having killed in self-defense. Driscoll yearns to leave the sea, but that wish is shown always to be impossible. He is the victim of his fate. His sensitivity to the problems of others is also demonstrated by his reaction to the reading of Smitty's* love-letters in *In the Zone*.* See also *Children of the Sea*, and Driscoll (1).

DYNAMO, a play in three acts and ten scenes, originally projected as part of a trilogy (later abandoned) of "Myth-Plays for the God-Forsaken,"* which was to include other plays to bear the titles of "Without Ending of Days" [*Days Without End**] and "It Cannot Be Mad," "On to Betelgeuse," or "On to Hercules." *See also* "The Life of Bessie Bowen" and "Hair of the Dog."

Act I: The general scene for this act and the first two scenes of Act II shows "the exterior of the homes of the Lights and the Fifes in a small town in Connecticut." They face front, side by side, with strips of lawn between and a lilac hedge showing the property line. The two houses are in marked contrast: the Light home is a little, white, New England cottage with green shutters, while the Fife house is "a small, brownish-tinted modern stucco bungalow type, recently built." As with a doll's house, the wall, in this case the front wall, is removed so that the interiors of the houses are visible. Both have small rooms, particularly the Light home. It is May, "the lilacs are in bloom, the grass a fresh green." The time is "the present day (1929)."

Act I, Scene i: "The Light sitting room and Reuben's bedroom above it." Reuben Light's* room has a four-poster bed, table, chair, books, "washstand with bowl and pitcher," and kerosene lamp on the table. The sitting room has a table at the center with an oil lamp, the Bible, and some magazines. The minister's chair is at left, and his wife's rocking chair is at the right. The ceilings are low, the wallpaper is faded, but the impression is one of extreme cleanliness and excellent order. Rev. Hutchins Light,* a "ponderously built" man in his early sixties, is trying to compose his weekly sermon. Amelia Light,* his wife, is fifteen years younger, stout, with big breasts and hips. "She must have been pretty as a girl" and still retains vestiges of dark-haired, dark-eyed, dark-complexioned attractiveness. Her expression is resigned, but her mouth looks "rebellious." She is pretending to read. Reuben Light, age seventeen, is in his room. He is tall and thin with "shy and sensitive" gray-blue eyes. "His jaw is stubborn, his thick hair curly and reddish-blond." He speaks diffidently, and his manner is timid unless he feels threatened; then he adopts a "booming, overassertive" tone, like that of his father. He is looking eagerly toward the window of his bedroom.

Mr. Light is thinking about something his neighbor, Ramsay Fife,* superintendent of the hydroelectric plant, has said earlier to him about keeping his son at home evenings. He is determined that Reuben will follow the family tradition and become a minister—"It is God's manifest will"—while Amelia Light is equally determined that he go to college and "marry a nice girl with money" so that he will never have to experience "the poverty and humiliation I've had to face." Voices are raised as Hutchins Light again asserts that it is God's will. Fearfully, Reuben hears his father's voice and thinks that he must have heard about him and Ada Fife,* whose signal he is waiting. As soon as she puts on the victrola, he will go down to see her. Downstairs, Mr. and Mrs. Light discuss Reuben, Mr. Light still trying to fathom the meaning of Fife's remark and wondering whether Reuben has been "having anything to do with that cursed pack next door." Mrs. Light, who has also been complaining about the primitive conditions of their cottage, which doesn't even have electric light, says that Reuben doesn't care about girls, and he wouldn't lie to her. But Mr. Light immediately suspects Reuben with Ada and is appalled by the thought. Mrs. Light, likewise worried, decides to go upstairs to talk to Reuben, but when she gets there she finds the bedroom empty. As she looks out the window, a lightning flash reveals Reuben crouched in the shadow of the hedge, waiting for Ada.

Act I, Scene ii: The outer walls of the Light home have been replaced, and the interior of the Fife home is visible, the sitting room downstairs and the parents' bedroom above. They are brilliant with electric light. Ramsay Fife is sitting at the sitting room table, center-front, reading a book on hydroelectric engineering. He is a wiry little Scotch-Irish man of about fifty, with the "malicious" expression of the practical joker. "He has a biting tongue but at bottom is a good-natured man except where the religious bigotry of his atheism is concerned." May Fife,* his wife, is a tall, very stout woman who must once have been pretty, and even though she weighs over two hundred pounds, she gives an impression of "inert strength" rather than shapelessness. Her hair is copper-colored, her expression "blank and dreamy. Her voice is sentimental and wondering. She is about forty years old." She is lying on a chaise longue, looking out the window. Upstairs, Ada Fife, their daughter, age sixteen, is busy putting on heavy make-up. She looks more like her father than her mother, with "his alert quality," but underneath her assertiveness "one senses a strong trace of her mother's sentimentality."

Mrs. Fife is listening to Ada upstairs and dreaming of her own past springtimes, recalling her first meeting with Ramsay when he was a linesman; she had allowed him to seduce her, despite her mother's warning, but then he marrried her, and Ada was born, and she would not wish anything otherwise. Fife reads the electrical textbook impatiently and then throws it down, saying he doesn't care to go for his engineer's papers; everyone knows that he knows more about the practical working of the plant than anyone else. Upstairs, Ada looks at herself, assessing Reuben as a decent, honest boy, but "I'd never love him . . . he's too big a Mama's boy for me." She wants to see if he'll have the courage to kiss her. As Ada enters the sitting room, Mr. Fife is exploding with rage over a news item telling the tale of a man named Clark who had murdered a man many years ago in Ohio, in a fight over a girl. Then, with the help of the girl, he managed to escape, marry her, and settle down to a respectable life on the West Coast. His daughter became engaged to the minister's son, and just before the wedding, her father told his future son-in-law about his past, with the result that the young man "breaks off with the girl and goes to the police with the story, saying he's bound by his conscience to squeal on him!" Fife warns Ada that that is the kind of thing she can expect from Reuben, too, as a minister's son, and suggests that they have a wager: Fife will prove Reuben yellow or Ada will have a new dress. She agrees and goes outside to bring Reuben into the house. Much to the horror of the watching Mrs. Light, Ada kisses Reuben in fun, and he kisses her back, hungrily, and then agrees, with a certain amount of fear, to visit her house and her father. Mr. Fife has had an inspiration for a trick and has sent Mrs. Fife away.

Act I, Scene iii: The interiors of the Light and Fife sitting rooms are both shown. Mrs. Light is now hiding behind the little hedge, watching. Mr. Light is castigating himself for his anger that Reuben desires a woman, thinking with puritanical rage that his relationship with his own wife has been "one long desire of the senses." Mrs. Fife leans dreamily out her window, thinking first of Ada and then of the dynamos at the electric plant: "I could sit forever and listen to them sing." Mrs. Light looks up, sees Mrs. Fife, and is ashamed and frightened.

Downstairs in the Fife house, Ada and Reuben enter to confront Ramsay, who asks the young man whether his father is going to accept his challenge to a religious debate. Reuben says he doesn't think so, and in reply to Fife's assumption that he too will become a minister, he denies it: "I've never felt the call. You have to feel God calling you to His service." This leads Fife to blasphemous literality, suggesting that God wouldn't use "telegraph, or telephone, or radio for they're contraptions that belong to his archenemy Lucifer, the God of Electricity!" As he finishes, there is a flash of lightning that unnerves Reuben, much to Fife's glee. Ada is a bit disturbed by her father's irreligious comments, and Reuben is filled with guilt. Fife then turns on him and asks what his intentions are concerning Ada, forcing Reuben to say, "I'm going to marry her!" Outside and upstairs, Mrs. Light and Mrs. Fife react differently to the conversation they are partly overhearing. Mrs. Light is appalled, while Mrs. Fife thinks she hears a skunk in the garden and meditates on her desire for a skunk coat and then on Fife's jokes, but ruminates that "he's the kindest man in the world." Downstairs, Fife tells the story of the news item he has just read, alleging that *he* was Clark, the murderer, and swearing Reuben to silence. Reuben is overwhelmed by the magnitude of this secret and is forced into a battle with his conscience, telling Fife that he should give himself up. "You know you're guilty in the sight of God!" At this, Fife jeers at him. Reuben leaves, while Ada turns on her father: "It wasn't fair! He never had a chance!" But then she turns aside from her father, and another lightning flash causes Light in his house to jump with fear. He goes upstairs to see what his wife and Reuben have been doing.

Act I, Scene iv: The walls of the Light and Fife sitting rooms have been replaced, and the interior of Reuben's bedroom is visible. Mrs. Fife still looks out of her bedroom window, and Mrs. Light remains behind the hedge, waiting for her to go in. Mrs. Fife says how much she loves to watch the lightning and then goes in as Mrs. Light slinks home. Reuben enters, torn with guilt and indecision, wondering why Fife has not been punished for his sin—and at this moment there is another lightning flash. Upstairs, Mr. Light has just found Reuben's room empty, and Mrs. Light tells him that Reuben has said he will marry Ada. She pushes him into the closet so that he can overhear as Reuben rushes in and flings his arms around his mother, sobbing. As the lightning flashes, striking terror into Reuben, he repeats the story of the murder that Fife has told him, after first extracting a pledge of secrecy from her because he loves Ada "with all my heart." But Light erupts from the closet to confront his son, and Reuben discovers that even his mother has turned against him, wanting his father to beat and hurt him—but Reuben is stoic, especially when he realizes that his father is afraid of lightning. As Light leaves to inform the police, Reuben jeers at his father's fear and turns against his mother, who has called Ada a harlot. Meanwhile, Fife has been awaiting the expected outcome of his practical joke and calls out to Light as he comes into view, "You wouldn't give me up to the police"; but Ada, angry that the game has gone too far, tells the truth, which she then repeats to Reuben, calling him "a yellow rat" and saying that it was her father's test of him.

Angrily, Reuben turns his back on Ada and his family; as the lightning flashes, he enrages his father by defying God: "If there is a God let Him strike me dead this second! I dare him!" Fearfully, Mr. Light twists his lapel from his son's grip and drags his wife away as Reuben turns his back on them, blasphemously crying out, "There is no God! No God but Electricity!" As he exits, the sound of wind and rain is heard.

Act II, Scene i: Fifteen months later; the Light sitting room is visible. Mrs. Fife is leaning out of her sitting room window, "basking contentedly in the sun." She meditates on the warmth of the day and the death of Mrs. Light. Ada enters, looking untidy and acting in an irritable manner. They talk about Reuben, Mrs. Fife wishing he would return and Ada claiming falsely that she doesn't care. However, she has held a grudge against her father since that night. She says about herself, "You poor boob! . . . it must be love!" In his sitting room, Mr. Light looks at the wreck of his life, for Amelia's death has aged him dreadfully; he wonders if his dream of his dead wife means Reuben's death also, but he seems to care very little about him, recalling the blasphemous postcards Reuben had sent monthly: "We have electrocuted your God. Don't be a fool!" And Amelia's last words to her husband were "Don't be a fool!"

Meantime, Mrs. Fife and Ada are talking amicably, Mrs. Fife trying to smooth things over between father and daughter, and Ada kisses her impulsively, with real affection. As Mrs. Fife basks in this moment of demonstrativeness, Reuben enters. He is now nineteen, tanned, weatherbeaten, filled out, hardboiled. His gentle eyes have developed "a queer devouring intensity." He is roughly dressed in faded dungarees, open-necked shirt, old suit coat, and he carries a half-dozen books held together by a strap. He looks around in a jeering manner and laughs aloud as Mrs. Fife tells him Ada will be pleased to see him. At first Reuben sounds careless, but then he says that he understands now that he really was a "dope" and now he is more experienced sexually. He also believes in Fife's God, Electricity, suddenly asking Mrs. Fife is she has ever watched dynamos. Her reply indicates that he has met a kindred spirit: "I love dynamos. I love to hear them sing. They're singing all the time about everything in the world." She imitates their sound, and he takes her hand. At her suggestion, Reuben goes to his old hiding place to surprise Ada, who is happy to see him; but he puts on a callous swagger, knowing that "she's easy now!" Ada is a trifle afraid of this new Reuben, who tells her that he has changed and has learned a lot. He starts to compliment her, finally inviting her to walk with him later in the evening.

He wants to go back to Long Hill where he had forced himself to confront the lightning fifteen months ago. Now he works with electricity. "Did you ever think that all life comes down to electricity in the end, Ada?" He wants to get a job in Fife's plant, and he asks her to get her father to help. Obviously, he does not know of his mother's death, and Ada does not tell him.

When Reuben enters his father's sitting room, Mr. Light is sitting with his head on his arms on the table. Reuben awakens him "with mocking geniality" and is appalled when his father speaks: "Murderer! You killed her!" Mr. Light then bursts into tears as Reuben tries to comprehend the situation. Reuben tries to blame his mother's death on the dampness in the house, but Light blames his son's flight and the everlasting blasphemies which broke her heart. She had written letters continually but had no address to which to send them, and when Light had discovered the letters, he destroyed them because he felt betrayed and full of hatred. He confesses himself further: "She never mentioned your name! . . . I—I had forbidden her to." Then when Reuben hears that her last words were "Don't be a fool!" he believes that she has accepted his new god and tells his father that he is going to work in the hydroelectric plant: "Did you ever watch dynamos? Come down to the plant and I'll convert you! I converted Mother, didn't I?" At this, Ada comes to tell him that he can indeed work at the plant. He moves to kiss her, but recalling that his mother had hated her, he leaves to visit her grave: "Wait till later, Ada."

Act II, Scene ii: Reuben's bedroom at about 11:30 P.M. the same night. Reuben and Ada enter; she is hanging on his arm as if afraid that he will leave her, while he has an expression of "gratified vanity" and an air of "nervous uneasiness." Ada looks upon the sexual consummation of their relationship as a momentous act of love, but Reuben says it "was just plain sex," something that makes one forget everything for an instant, but then one must wake up to reality and attempt to think things through. Curiously, it is Ada, the daughter of an atheist, who feels guilt about their act, while Reuben acts hardboiled, insisting that at his mother's grave he realized that there is nothing to pray to: "You can't pray to electricity unless you're foolish in the head." Ada offers sympathy, but Reuben coldly dismisses it and sends Ada home, crying softly to herself. Left alone, Reuben recalls his mother, wishing he could have seen her after she had come over to his side; then he notes how easy it was for him to seduce Ada.

He doesn't intend to marry her, but she will be useful to have around. He wonders about the relationship between his parents and whether his mother had loved his father. Then he begins to feel the lack of something in the house with his mother dead, and he wonders whether the urge to pray to electricity had come from her, perhaps through some kind of extrasensory perception. Unable to sleep, he decides to go out to look at the dynamos.

Act II, Scene iii: "A half hour later. Exterior of the Light and Power Company's hydro-electric plant." Through a window in the red-brick building "there is a clear view of a dynamo, huge and black, with something of a massive female idol about it, the exciter set on the main structure like a head with blank, oblong eyes above a gross, rounded torso.'' There is the sound of water running over the dam and over all other sounds is ''the harsh, throaty, metallic purr of the dynamo.'' Reuben comes in, stands in front of the dynamo, and listens to it. He meditates on its meaning: ''what electricity is . . . what life is . . . what God is . . . it's all the same thing.'' He sees the dynamo as ''a great dark idol . . . a great dark mother.'' Listening to the hum of the dynamo is more satisfying to him than ''all organs in church.'' Electricity sings ''about everything in the world,'' he says, quoting Mrs. Fife. If one could only learn what it means ''then you'd know the real God!'' Somehow there must be a way for him to achieve this knowledge, and so he kneels and prays to the dynamo: ''Mother of life, my mother is dead, she has passed back into you, tell her to forgive me, and to help me find your truth!'' After this, he feels himself forgiven, purged, and knows that he can now sleep.

Act III, Scene i: The exterior of the power house some four months later, a little after sunset. Reuben enters, followed by Mrs. Fife. He has grown extremely thin, while she looks the same, but her expression is even more dreamy as she listens to Reuben, who is talking excitedly. He is talking about the origin of life in the sea and equating it with the sound of water over the dam and the song of the dynamo like purifying water over his body, like a mother singing him to sleep. Mrs. Fife, spellbound, offers, ''I'll be your mother—yours and Ada's. I've always wanted a boy.'' At this Reuben leans against her, his head almost on her shoulder: ''Yes. You're like her—Dynamo—the Great Mother—big and warm.'' In an intensity of excitement he tries to explain his new belief that ''all things end up in her,'' the dynamo. The sea, the water that drives the dynamo, and the entire cosmos are driven by a central power, ''the Great Mother of Eternal Life, Electricity, and Dynamo is her Divine Image on earth! Her power houses are the new churches,'' and she wants one man to love her totally and purely—to him she will show the secret of life. Reuben sees himself as that new savior of mankind, and he wants Mrs. Fife to be a witness to the forthcoming miracle which he is sure will happen because he has had a vision of his mother this night and he knows ''she came from the spirit of the Great Mother into which she passed when she died to tell me she had at last found me worthy of her love.''

Mr. Fife is concerned about Reuben's renunciation of Ada, but the young man explains that he must purify himself from all taint of the flesh until he knows the secret of life that the dynamo has to tell him; but, in his mind, he recalls that Ada continually appears to him in his dreams, despite his self-flagellation. He then goes into the dynamo room to pray to her, the dynamo, as Fife enters the plant, exasperated with Reuben's oddness and knowing that he would fire Reuben if Ada would not object. He sees his wife and wonders why she has come to the plant; she tries to explain what Reuben has been telling her, but he cannot understand and instead asks when Reuben is going to marry Ada, also enquiring whether they have gone to bed together. On receiving an affirmative answer, he goes home as Mrs. Fife enters the dynamo room to find Reuben kneeling on the floor with his hands stretched out in supplication to the dynamo, begging for a sign, "the miracle of your love!"' When nothing is forthcoming, he blames himself, saying that he has frustrated the miracle because he has not yet killed all physical desire for Ada, who is looking for him at that moment, but he has not seen her. Then, when Mrs. Fife suggests he should "do the right thing by Ada," he decides he must face her "right now." As he leaves, he finds Ada and tells her that "she," the dynamo, had forced her to come and that someday he will make both his father and Ada adore the Dynamo. Ada tries to calm him by putting her arms around him and telling him of her love, but Reuben pushes her away, telling her that "you've got to believe in Dynamo, and bow down to her will!" Ada agrees, in order to calm him, and follows Reuben as he goes to the dam and up to the roof of the dynamo room. He holds her hand as he explains the song of the dynamo as "the hymn of eternal generation, the song of eternal life!" But as he looks at Ada he realizes that he still wants her physically, and he wishes that the miracle were over. Ada, somewhat concerned, tells him that she is afraid of the height and suggests that they go down. And Reuben says, "Yes, down to her! . . . She's waiting for me!" as he pulls Ada into the interior galleries of the power plant.

Act III, Scene ii: The interior of the power plant with an upper and a lower gallery. Reuben and Ada are "just inside the door to the dynamo-room roof at the top of the stairway." Ada looks around in fear, saying, "It looks as if it was alive!" This remark makes Reuben think Ada is beginning to understand, but he will not let her press close to him because "we're in her temple now!" Puzzled and piteous, Ada tells Reuben of her love for him. But Reuben is listening to the sound of the dynamo, believing that "she" is not angry that Ada is with him. He asks Ada to go upstairs to the platform by the dynamo and pray to "her" in the same position as before "her arms, stretching out for me," with the intent that the dynamo will find him worthy. Ada does as she is asked, and Reuben comes up too. When Ada again tells of her love, Reuben decides he must kiss her once as evidence to the dynamo that he has been purified. He kisses her, but the test turns into a kiss of frantic passion, and he bends her to the ground. As she cries out in fear, darkness falls.

Act III, Scene iii: The same scene, a short time later. Reuben can be heard sobbing from the upper gallery. Jennings,* the engineer, is the operator on duty. Mrs. Fife is just under the observation balcony, listening to the dynamo and reacting to its sound by humming in tune with it. Ada is revealed bending tenderly over Reuben as he thinks himself forever shut out from the apprehension of the miracle because of his betrayal of his mother whose spirit has passed into the dynamo. In recompense he offers to kill Ada to show his commitment to the dynamo-mother. But he cannot do this with his hands; so he seizes Jennings, takes his revolver, and locks him up. He recalls his mother's hostile remarks about Ada in the beginning of their relationship, and as Ada, who is coming down from the platform, approaches him, he fires twice, hitting her, so that she "pitches sideways on the stairs."

He then runs down to the dynamo-room floor, climbs up the rungs on the outside of the dynamo, and pleads childishly to the machine, "I don't want to know the truth! I only want you to hide me, Mother! Never let me go from you again! Please, Mother!" With this "he throws his arms out over the exciter" and causes a blinding flash of short circuit; the noise of the dynamo is almost silenced, while Reuben cries out "in a moan that is a mingling of pain and loving consummation" that dies into a baby's sound as he crumples to the platform. As the lights go up again and the dynamo resumes its purring sound, Mrs. Fife rushes to him, asking whether he is badly hurt. Then, "with childish bewildered resentment and hurt" she turns to the dynamo, "What are you singing for? I should think you'd be ashamed! And I thought you was nice and loved us." As the lights come up full, Mrs. Fife starts pummeling the dynamo's side, but when she hurts her hand, she ceases and begins to weep.

Comments: This play represents another of O'Neill's attempts to forge for himself a new theology, which had begun with *The Fountain** and proceeded through *Marco Millions*, *The Great God Brown,** *Lazarus Laughed,** and even *Strange Interlude**. Here, as in these earlier plays, O'Neill set himself the task of revealing the sickness of American society as he perceived it, and he attacks repressive organized religion with its fear of human sexuality and physicality, together with its unthinking approach to natural phenomena which makes a lightning flash a tool of God's justice. But in *Dynamo*, his solution is not Nietzschean, and there is no opposition between the Apollonian and Dionysian views of existence. Here he is closer to the characters of Cybel* in *The Great God Brown* and Josie Hogan* in *A Moon for the Misbegotten* in creating Mrs. Fife as the figure of the earth-mother, the fecund woman who is in tune with the seasons and also in tune with the dynamo.

A most important influence on this play was *The Education of Henry Adams*, particularly Chapter 25, "The Dynamo and the Virgin (1900).* (*See* Bogard, 1972, pp. 319–320, and other critics.) This essay celebrates creative force, or energy. As Adams says, "Symbol or energy, the virgin had acted as the greatest force the Western World ever felt, and had drawn man's activities to herself more strongly than any other power, natural or supernatural, had ever done." He believed that the historian's task was "to follow the track of the energy; . . . its complex source and shifting channels." Woman, symbolized by the Virgin, had once been supreme in the West: "She was goddess because of her force; she was the animated dynamo; she was reproduction—the greatest and most mysterious of all energies; all she needed was to be fecund." But in America, the woman was no longer so important because to the Puritan mind "sex was sin." Also, to Adams, as he gazed upon the dynamo at the 1900 Paris Exposition "the dynamo became a symbol of infinity . . . [and] he began to feel the forty-foot dynamos as a moral force, much as the early Christians felt the Cross . . .

Before the end, one began to pray to it; inherited instinct taught the natural expression of man before silent and infinite force.''

These selected quotations (from Henry Adams) form almost a summation of O'Neill's attempt here to reforge a modern belief independent of existing religions. Hutchins Light, a name significant to the play (as well as an "in" joke among O'Neill's contemporaries) is a strict Puritan who finds difficulty in even thinking of sex and who ruthlessly represses natural instincts. His spiritual backwardness is symbolized in the architecture of his New England-style cottage, which is without the light of the new symbol of energy, electricity, which is produced by the dynamo. By contrast, the Fife household, headed by an avowed atheist, is brilliantly lighted, while Mrs. Fife, in her Cybel-like, earth-mother appearance, is also the human embodiment of the energy of the dynamo. O'Neill repeatedly notes that she has "inert energy" and that she responds frankly and openly to the passage of the seasons and to her own physical impulses. And of course her response to the dynamo, which O'Neill describes as being like a giant female idol, is one which recognizes the kinship of energy. Reuben Light also comes to perceive the importance of this energy of the dynamo in his long monologue of III.i, in which he speaks of life beginning in the sea, suggesting the participation of the dynamo in this energizing of existence given that it produces its power from that water in which life began. The dynamo, then, becomes the symbol of the fecund mother; and hence, when his own mother dies, Reuben believes that her spirit has in effect passed into the realm of electricity, into "the Great Mother of Eternal Life, Electricity and Dynamo . . . her Divine image on earth,'' while Mrs. Fife is the human embodiment of that fecund mother. But Reuben's Puritan conscience will not be denied, and so he, in a manner that O'Neill sees as symbolic of American society, does not follow the natural path of Mrs. Fife but instead attempts to tear at the secret, to seek after it by self-denial and masochistic punishment, rather than surrendering to it like Mrs. Fife. Instead of accepting his physical desires, he kills Ada, and then in effect crucifies himself upon the dynamo who rejects him because he has misunderstood her message and attempted to master her.

Reuben Light, like Yank* in *The Hairy Ape** and Nina Leeds* in *Strange Interlude*,* is also seeking to belong, trying to find a place of rest, of happiness; but where Nina does find a place of rest, Yank and Reuben Light are left searching until they find a pessimistic answer in their own destruction. Yank as the human personification of a machine, does have a place, but he is destroyed when he is forced to look beyond it. Reuben Light comes to a religious conversion to the Goddess of Energy, the Dynamo, and finally wants a union with her as the Great Mother; he no longer needs a miracle or the knowledge of the secret, but he, perhaps like American society, is destroyed because he is not worthy of the machine.

This play was not well received, and after completing *Days Without End*,* O'Neill abandoned work on this trilogy, "Myth-Plays for the God-Forsaken."* One would like to say that *Dynamo* is a noble failure, and indeed the theme is fascinating, but it does represent a regression from the immediately preceding *Strange Interlude*. The interior monologue is used extensively here as well, but the dramaturgy is a trifle clumsy. It was chiefly remembered for its remarkable stage set and the appearance of Claudette Colbert as Ada in a tight red dress, displaying her wonderful legs (Helburn, 1960, p. 261.) The characters are also stereotypical, possessing mainly symbolic importance. It should be noted that O'Neill revised the text after production to emphasize the psychological aspects of the play, and hence the cast list indicates one character not in the printed text (*See* Bogard, 1972, p. 320).

Production Data: Written 1924–1928. Produced by the Theatre Guild* at the Martin Beck Theatre, New York City, February 11, 1929 (50 performances).

Director: Philip Moeller

Designer: Lee Simonson

Cast: Rev. Hutchins Light: George Gaul
Mrs. Amelia Light: Helen Westley
Reuben Light: Glenn Anders
Ramsay Fife: Dudley Digges*
Mrs. May Fife: Catherine Calhoun Doucet
Ada Fife: Claudette Colbert
Jennings: Hugh Forrester
Rocco: Edgar Kent

E

"EARTH IS THE LIMIT, THE," the proposed eighth part in the abandoned cycle, "A Tale of Possessors, Self-Dispossessed."* This play, set the 1860s, was designed to tell the story of Wolfe Harford,* the gambler. The outline of this play was destroyed either in 1943 or 1953.

EDWARDS. In *Chris Christophersen,** he is a "lanky, dark-complected boy of eighteen," a shipmate of Chris (*see* Christopherson, Christopher) in the forecastle of the steamer *Londonderry* which ran down Chris's coal barge. He and Jonesy* teasingly suggest that Chris might be offered the job of boatswain and also annoy him by suggesting that Anna Christopherson,* Chris's daughter, might be romantically involved with Paul Andersen,* the second mate.

ELDRIDGE, Florence (1901–   ), actress. Born in Brooklyn, New York, to James and Clara Eugenie McKechnie. Educated at Girls' High School, Brooklyn. Married to Fredric March in 1927.

Miss Eldridge began her Broadway career as a member of the chorus of *Rock-a-Bye Baby* (1917) and since then appeared in numerous plays, including Pirandello's *Six Characters in Search of an Author* (1922), *The Skin of Our Teeth* (1942), *An Enemy of the People* (1950). She also toured with her husband (1927–28) and played in a number of films, including *Les Misérables* (1935), *Mary of Scotland* (1936), *Another Part of the Forest* (1948), and *Inherit the Wind* (1960). She played the role of Mary Cavan Tyrone* in *Long Day's Journey into Night** in its first American production (Helen Hayes Theatre, New York City, November 7, 1956; later, Sarah Bernhardt Theatre, Paris, France, July 1957). She won the *Variety* drama critics' poll as best actress for this performance, which set a standard for the role of Mary Cavan Tyrone as the fey, detached victim-heroine, completely different from the later interpretation by Geraldine Fitzgerald.* José Quintero* gives a fascinating account of the history of this production in his memoir, *If You Don't Dance They Beat You* (1974). *See* also Eldridge's account in Floyd (1979).

ELIOT, William, in *Days Without End*,* a rubicund man of about forty, bald, with horn-rimmed spectacles. He is John Loving's* partner. He appears only in the first act where he is used as an expository device to reveal John's past and also to introduce the characters of Father Matthew Baird* and Lucy Hillman.*

EMPEROR JONES, THE, an expressionist play in eight scenes; a monodrama. The action "takes place on an Island in the West Indies as yet not self-determined by White Marines. The form of native government is, for the time being, an Empire."

Scene i: The audience chamber of the palace of the Emperor Jones, late in the afternoon of an oppressive tropical day. Brutus Jones* is a black former Pullman porter (then a high-status, unionized, black monopoly). He has murdered two people, one black and one white, and is a gaolbird, but he has risen "from stowaway to Emperor in two years" by means of his cunning. He treats the "low-flung bush niggers" with contempt and has convinced them that he can be killed only with a silver bullet. He has actually had one made, telling his "subjects" that when the time comes, he will kill himself with it. He enjoys exploiting his people, and in lining his pockets he has quite cynically put aside his Baptist religion and laid his "Jesus on de shelf for de time bein'." His manner exudes self-confidence, but it is attacked when Henry Smithers,* a seedy white cockney trader, tells him of a rebellion brewing against him in the hills under the leadership of Lem.* At first taken aback, Jones recovers himself, but then he hears the sound of a tom-tom at exactly seventy-two beats per minute, the rate of the normal pulse beat. This drumming continues throughout the play, and its speed and volume increase. With a certain bravado, Jones decides he had better carry out his escape plan, certain that he can defeat the forest. To Smithers's amazement, Jones insists on walking out through the front door— departing as the Emperor Jones, not sneaking out the back way like a fugitive. He takes his revolver with him.

Scene ii: At "the end of the plain where the Great Forest begins." It is night, and the wind moans in the trees. Jones, dog-tired, has lost his way and cannot find the cache of food he had prepared for himself. No longer confident of his ability to defeat the jungle, he once again becomes conscious of the tom-tom, and the "Little Formless Fears" with their glittering eyes creep around him. As fear starts to overcome Jones, they utter "low mocking laughter like a rustling of leaves." In panic Jones shoots once at them, but as the Fears hurry back into the forest, the tom-tom quickens. Jones forces himself into the forest, trying to convince himself "ain't nothin' dere but de trees!"

Scenes iii–vii: Different parts of the forest at night. By the light of the just risen moon, Jones meets the ghost of Jeff, the Pullman porter he had killed with a razor after a gaming dispute. At first Jones thinks he is seeing a living human being, but then he realizes the truth as the ghost of Jeff continues to play dice in an automatic way. In panic, he fires at the ghost, who disappears, but in response the beat of the "tom-tom is perceptibly louder and more rapid." Jones, realizing that he has revealed his whereabouts with the shots, "lunges wildly into the underbrush."

Scene iv: In another part of the now fully moonlit forest. Jones's uniform is ragged and torn. He is trying to escape the sound of the tom-tom, which seems to be getting closer. He tears off his uniform coat and spurs in order to travel lighter, and suddenly he asks himself, "How'd dis road evah gid heah?" He is afraid of meeting more ghosts but then recalls that "de Baptist parson" had told him there are no such things; after all, Jones knows himself to be civilized, not "like dese ign'rent black niggers heah." However, he still hopes that he won't meet any more of them. Suddenly a black prison road gang enters, and Jones chokes with fear, "Lawd Jesus!" as the prison guard cracks his whip and Jones almost hypnotically obeys the guard's motion to join the others. He goes through the motions of shoveling dirt until the Prison Guard approaches him angrily and cuts at him with his whip. As the guard turns contemptuously away, Jones rushes at him as if he is indeed carrying a shovel but realizes his hands are empty. Struggling with his rage, he frees his revolver and shoots the guard, thus reenacting his second murder. The walls of the forest close in, darkness falls, and Jones flees in terror as the sound of the distant tom-tom increases in volume and beat.

Scene v: Jones is in a clearing in the woods where another chapter in the history of American blacks is replayed. This time it is a slave auction, and Jones, "his pants...in tatters, his shoes cut and misshapen," is placed on a tree stump that serves as an auction block and is bid for. In rage, Jones asserts his rights as "a free nigger" and fires two shots at the Auctioneer and the Planter. Darkness descends as Jones exits, crying with fear, followed "by the quickened, even louder beat of the tom-tom."

Scene vi: Jones's clothing has been so torn away that he is wearing little more than a breech-cloth made out of the remnants of his pants. The clearing in the forest is surrounded by treetrunks and creepers so that it looks like the hold of an ancient ship. Two rows of seated figures, apparently shackled to the trees, are rocking back and forth with despairing moans. Yet another scene in black history is being dramatized—this time the slave ship, with Jones as one of the participants. The low melancholy murmur which rises to a cry of pain seems almost to be directed by the insistent tom-tom in the distance. As Jones joins with the others, "his voice reaches the highest pitch of sorrow, of desolation." The light fades slowly, and Jones moves away as "the tom-tom beats louder, quicker, with a more insistent, triumphant pulsation."

Scene vii: Jones is "at the foot of a gigantic tree by the edge of a great river," the Congo. Jones's voice is heard in the wail of the despairing slaves, delivered to the beat of the tom-tom. He enters bewildered, almost like a somnambulist, and falls on his knees before a moonlit, rough stone altar. Fearfully, he discovers some latent memory of this frightening place as he invokes the Christian God, "Oh Lawd, pertect dis sinner!" As he cowers to the ground in hysterical fear, the Congo Witch-Doctor appears, dancing to the "fierce, exultant boom" that his stamping seems to have evoked from the tom-tom. He sways, swings his rattle, dances, and croons to the ever-insistent beat in a dance that is clearly meant to pacify an "implacable deity demanding sacrifice." Jones, by now completely hynotized, joins with the Witch-Doctor, crooning, beating time with his hands, swaying from the waist. The Witch-Doctor indicates that Jones must be that sacrifice, but the fallen emperor is terrified and continues to ask "Mercy, Oh, Lawd! Mercy! Mercy on dis po' sinner." At this moment, a huge crocodile appears from the river and fixes its eyes on Jones, who stares, fascinated. The Witch-Doctor touches Jones with his wand, and Jones squirms on his belly toward the crocodile, still pleading, "Mercy, Lawd! Mercy!" The monster heaves itself on land, Jones moves toward him, the Witch-Doctor "shrills out in furious exultation, the tom-tom beats madly," and Jones calls, "Lawd, save me! Lawd Jesus, heah my prayer!" With that cry, Jones has come full circle from the first scene in which he boasted of having laid his Jesus on the shelf, and he remembers the silver bullet, the only one left him, and with it he shoots the crocodile. The symbolism of the silver bullet used to exorcise a god is quite clear. The Witch-Doctor disappears, and Jones lies on the ground "whimpering with fear as the throb of the tom-tom fills the silence about him with a somber pulsation, a baffled but revengeful power."

Scene viii: The final scene is the same as Scene ii, "the dividing line of forest and plain." Lem, "a heavy-set, ape-faced old savage of the extreme African type," appears dressed in a loin cloth, followed by a small squad of nearly naked soldiers carrying rifles. Smithers is there also, contemptuously telling the primitive Lem that they will never catch the resourceful Brutus Jones. A shot is heard in the forest, and Lem announces "We cotch him," revealing that they have made silver bullets by melting down coins. The play ends as Jones's dead body is carried in and Smithers delivers an awe-struck epitaph; "Silver bullets! Gawd blimey, but yer died in the 'eighth o' style any'ow!" Jones's psychic journey has ended in a return to the real world which brings him death.

Comments: This play gave the Provincetown Players* their first big hit, and it ironically led to their demise. It attempts to probe the collective unconscious of the black race, following the principles of C. G. Jung, in whose theories O'Neill was then much interested. Gradually the veneer of civilization is stripped from Jones as he falls from his high imperial estate, through reenactment of his crimes, of injustices perpetrated against blacks, to the primitive, instinctive, superstition of the Congo Witch-Doctor. But there is more to this play than a simplistic racist statement showing the black man regressing to the jungle, for in some ways it looks ahead to *The Hairy Ape,** to Yank* who crawls in with the ape, seeking in its fatal embrace a chance to belong. Brutus Jones is forced to relive his own history and the history of his people and in so doing is ultimately forced to make a choice between accepting the old, dark gods or the new. As he squirms toward the crocodile, he is about to accept his sacrificial fate, to accept himself as being at one with the old gods before whom he had instinctively knelt. But instead of submitting to that sacrifice, Jones rejects the old god, calling upon that Christian Savior he had so flippantly dismissed in Scene i, and he uses his silver bullet to destroy the crocodile god, the god who had called him and whom he had refused. As it is with vampires, to too with this crocodile god. Two divergent interpretations are possible here: (1) that Jones, by refusing to accept the crocodile god, condemns himself to a spiritual as well as a physical death, for he has denied his own inner being; (2) Jones in this action has asserted his own will, and thus he is a symbol for modern man attempting to break the chains of history, though in reality he is forging new fetters. In either case, the crocodile god gets his revenge, and Jones dies by a silver bullet.

Technically, this expressionist play is a development of O'Neill's earlier attempt to involve his audience instinctually, as well as intellectually, to make them participants in a shared experience rather than be mere spectators. In *Where the Cross Is Made*,* the audience shared the hallucination of Captain Isaiah Bartlett* and his son, Nat.* In *The Emperor Jones*, O'Neill experiments with the power of music, the hypnotic sound of the tom-tom, first keyed to the normal pulse beat but then played with increased volume and rapidity so that one's entire physical and emotional being responds. This music, devised by Austin Strong, is of paramount importance to this play.

The Emperor Jones is essentially a monodrama, for only the first and last scenes, as the realistic frame of the play, contain dialogue. Throughout, it is the psyche of Jones that is revealed, and his thoughts, visions, hallucinations, fears, his conscious and unconscious memories are played out for the audience. O'Neill makes skillful use of black English, but he is less successful with his cockney Smithers. The character of the Emperor Jones is modeled after Toussaint L'Ouverture (1746–1803), the Haitian revolutionary leader and former slave, treacherously mistreated by the French and also Vilbrun Guillaume Sam, of Haiti. O'Neill's character is a man of "cunning intelligence," one who has attributes of shrewdness but has learned evasions and suspicion in order to survive. He seems also to have understood the desire of his "subjects" for grandeur, and that (in a slightly garish way) he provides, but he also possesses intelligence and manipulative ability, qualities that emphasize his declension into atavistic fears and superstitions.

Clearly, this play requires an extraordinary actor for its main role, and O'Neill was most fortunate in its creator, Charles Gilpin,* the first black actor to star with a white company on Broadway. The role was played by Paul Robeson* in the 1924 revival prior to *All God's Chillun Got Wings*.* Robeson also played the role in the London production of 1925 and the New York revival of 1933. Robeson's performance was also filmed in a bastardized adaptation, but it is a record of this great artist. However, those who saw both actors claim that although Robeson did a fine job, he lacked the passionate intensity of Gilpin.

As a play for today's audience, *The Emperor Jones* presents serious difficulties because of its racist overtones. It is all too easy to see Brutus Jones and Lem as little removed from the jungle life of instinct rather than as intelligent human beings. The play also projects an air of condescension, and today the continued repetition of the word "nigger" grates. Nonetheless, it should be taken as a serious attempt at the use of the new theme, the black psyche. There is also the implicit suggestion that modern civilization has not helped the black man at all, first enslaving him and then showing him little more than a life of crime and manipulation, so that when Jones is in control he is no better than his original oppressors. Overall, the play's greatest strength lies in its successful blending of disparate influences, from Joseph Conrad's *Heart of Darkness* through the Vachel Lindsay poem, "The Congo," and the well-known power of music to engender frenzy—as modern devotees of rock-and-roll can testify. O'Neill's original title for this play was "The Silver Bullet", but it was never performed under that name.

Production Data: Written 1920. First produced by the Provincetown Players* at the Playwrights' Theatre, New York City, November 1, 1920; moved to the Selwyn Theatre, New York City, December 27, 1920 (total of 204 performances).

Director: George Cram Cook*

Designer: Cleon Throckmorton

Music: Austin Strong

Cast: Brutus Jones: Charles S. Gilpin
      Harry Smithers: Jasper Deeter
      Old Native Woman: Christine Ell
      Lem: Charles Ellis
      Soldiers: S. I. Thompson, Lawrence Vail, Leo Richman, James Martin, Owen
        White
      The Little Formless Fears: unknown
      Jeff: S. I. Thompson
      The Negro Convicts: Leo Richman, Lawrence Vail, S. I. Thompson, Owen
        White
      The Prison Guard: James Martin
      The Planters: Frank Schwartz, C. I. Martin, W. D. Slager
      The Spectators: Jeannie Begg, Charlotte Grauert
      The Auctioneer: Frederick Ward Roege
      The Slaves: James Martin, S. I. Thompson, Leo Richman, Owen White,
        Lawrence Vail
      The Congo Witch-Doctor: S. I. Thompson

Revived May 5, 1924, at the Provincetown Playhouse, New York City (21? performances).

Director: James Light

Designer: Cleon Throckmorton

Cast: Partial list
      Brutus Jones: Paul Robeson
      Henry Smithers: Charles Ellis
      Old Native Woman: Kirah Markham
      Lem: William Stahl
      Soldiers: John Brewster, Robert Forsyth, James Meighan, William Stahl,
        Clement Wilenchick

The Little Formless Fears: Unknown

Jeff: Clement O'Loghlen

The Negro Convicts: John Brewster, James Meighan, William Stahl, John Taylor, Clement Wilenchick

The Prison Guard: James Martin

The Planters: Robert Forsyth, James Meighan, William Stahl, Clement Wilenchik

The Spectators: Jeannie Begg, Kirah Markham

The Auctioneer: Clement O'Loghlen

The Slaves: John Brewster, Robert Forsyth, James Meighan, William Stahl, Clement Wilenchick

The Congo Witch Doctor: John Taylor

Revived December 15, 1924, at the Provincetown Playhouse, New York City (14 performances).

Revived November 2, 1925, as part of double bill with *The Dreamy Kid** at the 52nd Street Theatre, New York City (24 performances).

Revived December 1, 1925, at the Punch and Judy Theatre, New York City (20 performances).

Revived February 16, 1926, at the Provincetown Playhouse, New York City (35 performances).

Revived November 10, 1926, at the Mayfair Theatre, New York City, with Charles Gilpin (61 performances).

[*See also* Appendix B for operatic adaptation by Louis Gruenberg,* and ballet by José Limón.]

EMPRESS, S.S., steamer, see *Warnings*.

ENWRIGHT. In ''The Personal Equation,''* (unpublished scenario), a middle-aged, thin, round-shouldered revolutionary. He is a stereotypical revolutionary who appears only in the first act as an expository device.

EVANS, Gordon. In *Strange Interlude*,* the child of Nina Leeds* and Edmund Darrell,* though he bears the name of his putative father, Sam Evans.* Nina deliberately conceives this child by Darrell so that Sam can think he is the father of a healthy baby. Nina, Sam's wife, chooses to have an abortion so that the child she is carrying will not inherit the insanity of the Evans family. Gordon is brought up to surpass the exploits of Gordon Shaw,* Nina's dead fiancé, for whom he is named. Sam brings him up to follow the cult of the college athlete, and as a result, the boy draws closer to Sam and away from Nina, something that she finds difficult to endure. Gordon hates his real father, Darrell, because he has seen him kissing Nina and fears Nina's love for this other man. He breaks every gift Darrell brings him when he is a child, and the hostility persists when he becomes an adult. At one point in the final act, he strikes his own father, but such is his repentance for his dishonorable act that he doesn't understand the revelation of his parentage which Nina cries out in anger.

Gordon is a golden boy, the ultimately successful athlete, the best of his class, rather materialistic and lacking in introspection, but not totally insensitive. He even wishes Nina and Darrell happiness when he thinks they will marry after Sam's death. He is engaged to Madeline Arnold,* age nineteen, a young woman who resembles Nina but without the neuroses. As Darrell and Nina renounce each other, he and Madeline circle overhead in their private airplane in departure. He is breaking the bond with his overpossessive mother, and at the same time he is closing the circle with Gordon Shaw. As Shaw fell out of the heavens in flames in World War I, Gordon flies up; and like the other Gordons of the world, he is going to be successful.

EVANS, Mrs. Amos. In *Strange Interlude*,* mother of Sam Evans.* She is forty-five but looks sixty. She is a tiny woman who has once been lonely, but now there is a tension and a grimness about her. Her eyes are dark with sorrow, though there is still a trace of "sweet loving-kindness" about the mouth. She informs Nina Leeds* about the hereditary insanity in Sam's family and tells her to have an abortion so that the taint will cease. Mrs. Evans had married in ignorance of this illness, and Sammy was an accident which eventually was the cause of her own husband's insanity. She has also been looking after poor, idiot Aunt Bessie for most of her married life. She sympathizes with Nina, "the daughter of my sorrow," and suggests that Nina should perhaps consider having someone else father a healthy child for Sam in order to preserve his happiness, since he wants a child so badly. She begs Nina to stay with Sam, whether she loves him or not, and make him happy: "Being happy, that's the nearest we can ever come to knowing what's good." After this revelation, the two never meet again.

EVANS, Sam. In *Strange Interlude*,* at the beginning of the twenty-five-year span of the play he is twenty-five years old, coltishly collegiate, an amiable duffer, looking younger than his years. He is in love with Nina Leeds,* whom he had met at a college prom when she was with Gordon Shaw,* the great college hero. After Gordon's death, Sam wishes to marry Nina, and the two meet through their mutual acquaintance, Edmund Darrell,* Sam's college dorm-mate. Ned advises Nina, who has had a breakdown following the death of Gordon, to marry Sam, have a child, and forget the past. Nina does so, and the two of them seem to worship at the shrine of Gordon. However, Sam's mother, Mrs. Amos Evans,* reveals to Nina that there is hereditary insanity in Sam's family; his father had died of it and Sam should never have been born. Mrs. Evans suggests that the pregnant Nina obtain an abortion and then arrange for someone else to father a child to keep Sammy happy and sane. Sam is desperate for a child, and as a result he is not performing well at his job, while Nina treats him with indifference bordering on hostility. She becomes pregnant deliberately by Darrell, and Sam is led to believe that the child is his. But the baby gives Sam the necessary impetus to make a complete material success of his life. He brings up his son, Gordon Evans,* to re-create the image of Gordon Shaw and be everything that he himself could not be at college. He dies sometime after a stroke induced by overexcitement when his son wins his last regatta crew race after a strenuous battle. He adores Nina and is unaware of either his own weakness or Nina's adultery; he is a decent, honest, simple-minded man with uncomplicated emotions and desires, a Babbitt, perhaps, but a good-hearted person, despite his materialism. He typifies man as husband for this play.

EXORCISM ("A Play of Anti-Climax"), a one-act play written in 1919. Destroyed. Apparently O'Neill felt that this play, based on his suicide attempt during his residence at Jimmy-the Priest's,* was too autobiographical. It was produced once and received mixed reviews. From what can be pieced together of the plot, it appears that Ned Malloy, the protagonist, is in the process of getting a divorce and, because of the archaic laws in New York State, must go through the humiliation of supplying evidence of adultery (then the only allowable ground for divorce) by being "discovered" in bed with a prostitute. The young man, originally of a good family, has reached rock bottom and is so totally depressed that he refuses the offer of a new life on a Western farm and takes an overdose of morphine. Twenty-four hours pass: he has been revived by two drunken friends and realizes that he has been forced to return to the life he has been trying to escape. However, he has also discovered the existential truth that though he did not succeed in the act of suicide, the nature and quality of his act is the equivalent of a successful suicide. He is now ready for a new life in a new world.

Production Data: Written 1919. Produced by the Provincetown Players at the Playwrights' Theatre, New York City, March 26, 1920 (performances, unknown).

Director: Edward Goodman

Cast: Ned Malloy: Jasper Deeter
Jimmy: Alan MacAteer
Major Andrews: William Dunbar
Mr. Malloy: Remo Bufano
Nordstrom: Lawrence Vail

EXPERIMENTAL THEATRE, INC., THE. The Experimental Theatre, Incorporated, was the legal name of the organization which succeeded the Provincetown Players* at the Macdougal Street Playhouse beginning in the fall of 1923. Distinctions have not always been made between the offspring and the original Players, but the policies and practices of the new organization were much different. The new group was organized under the management of "the triumvirate" of O'Neill, critic Kenneth Macgowan* who would be the producer, and designer Robert Edmond Jones.* The new operation was still known popularly as "the Provincetown" and even the Provincetown Players, although it had been the intent of some of the original founders, including O'Neill, to retire that name with the official dissolving of the original group.

The new Experimental Theatre was no longer to be an amateur workshop for new American playwrights. Clearly defined artistic goals and efficient organization were to replace George Cram Cook's* blend of communalism, paternalism, inspiration, and sometimes conflicting goals. The intent now was to marry the production methods of the new theatre aesthetic, with its directors and new stagecraft, with selected American, modern European, or classical plays. The emphasis was upon collaborative experimentation in production, professionally finished results, and efficient management. Sizable private subsidies were sought to make this possible (the Provincetown Playhouse seated only two hundred), but not even the generous gifts of Otto Kahn nor the promotional efforts of the indefatigable M. Eleanor Fitzgerald were enough to offset the eventual deficits.

The first season's plays included Strindberg's *The Spook Sonata,* Molière's *George Dandin,* an arrangement of *The Ancient Mariner** by O'Neill, and O'Neill's *All God's Chillun Got Wings.** (In the latter O'Neill play, the portrait of racial intermarriage brought playwright and playhouse notoriety and ugly letters.) *The Emperor Jones** was revived successfully with Paul Robeson* in the lead. In the second season, the operation was enlarged to encompass productions at the larger Greenwich Village Theatre, in part to help offset the rising production costs. Eight shows in the overly ambitious season at the old Provincetown Playhouse included Edmund Wilson's *The Crime in the Whistler Room,* the grouping of four of O'Neill's sea plays known as the S.S. *Glencairn* Series,* Walter Hasenclever's *Beyond,* Sherwood Anderson's *The Triumph of the Egg,* and Gilbert and Sullivan's *Patience.* At the Greenwich Village Theatre, the group produced Stark Young's *The Saint,* O'Neill's *Desire Under the Elms,** and William Congreve's *Love for Love.* The latter two were probably the best new productions of the 1923–1925 seasons.

In 1925 a reorganization resulted from dissatisfaction with the complexities of managing and financing the two professional theatres and, on the part of several in the group, the desire for more leisurely experiment and the nurturing once again of the works of new, unknown writers. The artistic directorship of the Provincetown Playhouse was given over to James Light and M. Eleanor Fitzgerald, both of whom had been key figures in the original Players. O'Neill, Macgowan, and Jones continued management of the Greenwich Village Theatre, where in the next season they mounted, among other things, *The Great God Brown** and *The Fountain.** With the end of the season the partners went their separate ways—O'Neill to the Theatre Guild. Meanwhile, the Experimental Theatre, Inc., began a struggle of four and one-half seasons during which it was unable to engender an exciting new vision of its own or to rally sufficient, sustained support. There were productions of interest, the most notable among them being Paul Green's *In Abraham's Bosom* and E. E. Cummings's *Him,* both of which stirred much controversy. Even chamber opera was tried with Gluck's *Orpheus* and Mozart's *La Finta Giardiniera.* But with its vision and its finances faltering and with the stock market crash, "the Provincetown" closed its doors on December 14, 1929. Among the actors, directors, and designers who worked at the Provincetown and Greenwich Village theatres in these years were (in addition to those already mentioned): Walter Abel, Bette Davis, Walter Huston, Sam Jaffe, Clare Eames, Marie Ouspenskaya, Leo Carrillo, Donald Oenslager, Harold Clurman, Samuel Selden, Richard Boleslavski, Reginald Marsh, and Mordecai Gorelik.

For further reading, *The Provincetown: A Story of the Theatre* (1931) by Helen Deutsch and Stella Hanau briefly surveys all phases from 1915 to 1929, with emphasis on the later phases in which the authors joined the theatre. A full-length study of the original Players to 1922, with different emphases, is Robert K. Sarlós's *Jig Cook and the Provincetown Players: Theatre in Ferment* (1982). On the Experimental Theatre, Inc., see *"The Theatre We Worked For": The Letters of Eugene O'Neill to Kenneth Macgowan*, edited by Jackson R. Bryer and Ruth M. Alvarez, with introductory essays by Travis Bogard (1982). © Gary Jay Williams.

F

FATHER OF LAZARUS. In *Lazarus Laughed*,* a "thin feeble old man of over eighty, meek and pious." He is among the Orthodox who cannot accept Lazarus's doctrine. He dies in the course of the first conflict of the play, this one between the followers of Lazarus and a combination of Nazarene and Orthodox Jews, which escalates into an attack on both by the Roman soldiers. He is thus among the first martyrs to Lazarus's cause.

FAT JOE. In *The Long Voyage Home*,* proprietor of a London waterfront dive, "a gross bulk of a man with an enormous stomach," red bloated face, and little piggish eyes.

FAWCETT, Doctor. In *Beyond the Horizon*,* the specialist whom Andrew Mayo* has brought to examine his brother, Robert Mayo,* who is dying of tuberculosis.

FERNANDEZ, Anita. In *The Movie Man*,* the daughter of the prisoner, Ernesto Fernandez, who is to be shot the next morning. She is beautiful with dark eyes and masses of black hair. She comes to plead with General Gomez* for the life of her father but meets Henry Rogers,* who manages to negotiate with Gomez: the General may fight a night battle in violation of his movie contract, but in exchange he must spare Fernandez. Gomez agrees. Anita is clearly a young woman of a high social class, and she looks with contempt on Al Devlin,* who attempts to make a pass at her. She is the stock figure of the maiden in distress who is able to enlist the help of men through her tears. O'Neill uses her to some extent as a comic figure in her fractured English dialogue with Rogers.

FIFE, Ada. In *Dynamo*,* daughter of Ramsay Fife* and Mrs. May Fife.* She goes from sixteen to eighteen in the course of the play. At the beginning, she is pretty, alert, most like her father but with her mother's large, blue eyes. She has short, brown, bobbed hair, speaks slangily, and has some of her father's malicious humor. As the play opens, she is talking as if she plans to play around with Reuben Light* but not fall in love with him because he is too much of a mother's boy. She agrees to go along with her father in a bet to prove Reuben "yellow," but when Mr. Fife plays a cruel joke on the young man by pretending to let him in on a family secret since he is going to marry Ada, she becomes annoyed. The joke goes too far when Fife alleges that he has committed a murder, and Reuben is devastated by the discovery because his conscience is seriously divided. When Reuben leaves home as the indirect result of this jape, Ada is angry with her father and is happy to give herself to Reuben when he returns. She loves him and wants to marry him, but he perceives her as a temptation of the flesh who prevents him from achieving the deepest knowledge that the dynamo has to offer him. When he discovers that his passion for her still exists, he grabs a revolver and shoots her before flinging himself on the dynamo. As a character, Ada is not deeply drawn; she loves Reuben and she does not fully understand his obsession with the dynamo, though her mother is very sympathetic to it.

FIFE, Mrs. May. In *Dynamo*,* wife of Ramsay Fife* and mother of Ada Fife.* She is the human equivalent of the dynamo and its earth-mother image. She is about forty, stout, but not ungainly; even though she is over two hundred pounds, she gives the impression of "inert strength." Her hair is copper-colored, her mouth small yet sensuous, her eyes dark blue, her voice "sentimental and wondering." Her husband sees her as rather bovine, but she has an interesting inner life of her own, which is concerned almost entirely with the physical. She recalls how Fife seduced her and married her; she understands the way Ada also feels. She is like Cybel* in *The Great God Brown*,* a fecund earth-mother, but Mrs. Fife is quite literally attuned to the hum of the dynamo, which she can imitate precisely, and she seems to have attributed anthropomorphic qualities to the machine. At the end of the play, when Ada has been killed by Reuben Light* and Reuben is destroyed in an act of self-immolation by the dynamo, she upbraids the machine and hits it: "And I thought you was nice and loved us!"

FIFE, Ramsay. In *Dynamo*,* husband of Mrs. May Fife* and father of Ada Fife.* He is a man of about fifty, small, wiry, a practical joker, but not really an evil man. He is the local atheist who enjoys infuriating his next-door-neighbor, the Reverend Hutchins Light,* trying to get Light to debate with him on topics of religion. When Ada starts seeing Reuben Light,* Mr. Fife decides to play a practical joke on him to prove to Ada that the minister's son is "yellow." After Reuben, who has been dragged into the house by Ada, says he plans to marry her, Fife tells a false tale of his having committed a murder and having fled to avoid arrest. As Fife had expected, Reuben wrestles with his conscience, and the tale is revealed to the Lights. Fife is very amused that Hutchins Light falls for the tall tale. When Reuben returns, Fife gets him a job in the power plant. All he really wants is for Reuben "to do the right thing by Ada."

FIRST MAN, THE, a naturalistic domestic drama in four acts, originally entitled "The Oldest Man."

Act I: The living room of Curtis Jayson's* house in Bridgetown, Connecticut, The room is large and comfortable, with bookcases, grand piano, magazines, and a large rug. It is an early fall afternoon. Martha Jayson,* Curtis Jayson, and Edward Bigelow* are discovered. Martha is a healthy-looking, outdoorsy woman of thirty-eight with a direct gaze, "outspoken and generous." Curtis "is a tall, rangy, broad-shouldered man of thirty-seven." He gives an impression of good health and nervous energy, while his expression, though one of "thoughtful, preoccupied aloofness," still shows "an eager boyish enthusiasm." Edward Bigelow, "a large, handsome man of thirty-nine," is a cultured-looking person, but he has a quality of "lazy, unambitious contentment." Curtis reads from a scientific journal while Martha and Bigelow chat and laugh together. Bigelow is discussing his children, and then the conversation turns to Martha's upbringing in Nevada, and finally to Curt's career to date. Bigelow maintains that Curt is a "romanticist." First he took up mining engineering at Cornell, because he believed the tales of Bret Harte. Next he got a job in a Nevada mining town, where he met Martha, and then became interested in geology. Finally he turned his hand to anthropology. Curtis is about to set out on "a five-year excavating contest to discover the remains of our gibbering ancestor, the First Man." He is extremely pleased that he has been picked for this expedition and has just decided that he must go. Martha, however, seems rather hurt that he has made up his mind without consulting her. He says that he knows that there will be hardships, but after the past ten years when he and Martha have shared them together all over the world, he will be able to deal with them. She has accompanied him to many remote places, and indeed she has given up her life to his work. As Curt exits to his study, Martha and Bigelow continue talking, and Martha recalls the death of their two children, ages three and two, both girls. Martha tells how "the nurse girl fell asleep—or something—and the children sneaked out in their underclothes and played in the snow. Pneumonia set in— and a week later they were dead." According to Martha, she and Curt "were real lunatics for a time," but when they calmed down, they swore they would never have children again "to steal away their memory." Curt threw himself into his work, and Martha followed him: "he needed me—then—so dreadfully!" Work has taken the place of children for Curt, but Martha seems a trifle doubtful.

Lily Jayson* enters to break up the conversation. She raises her eyebrows to see Martha and Bigelow alone and obviously disapproves of him. After he leaves, Lily begins to have a confidential conversation with Martha. Lily is twenty-five, intellectually pretentious, rather pretty, and has a great deal of "nervous, thwarted energy." She tells Martha the story of Bigelow's life: he hated his wife and "flaunted his love affairs in everyone's face," but after the death of that "terrible strait-laced creature," he suddenly became guilt-ridden and started to pay attention to his children. Lily, for one, doesn't believe in the depth of his repentance, and she has been deputed by Jayson's family to warn Matha that the townspeople's tongues are beginning to wag about their relationship. Martha is appalled. She has not been used to this kind of backbiting, and her first reaction is to tell the whole town where to go. In conversation with Lily, Martha speaks of marriage and children. Lily asks whether Martha might not have a child now; she is not getting any younger, and she surely won't want to tag along after Curt to the ends of the universe all her life. Martha admits that indeed the nomadic life has begun to pall in the last few years, but Curt loves the romance of expeditions and hates children because "he's never become reconciled" to the loss of their two babies. Lily recommends that Martha deliberately get pregnant and then see how Curt reacts, only to be told that Martha is already two months pregnant.

At this point, the first contingent of the Jayson clan appears for afternoon tea. They are a dreadfully Philistine group. Mrs. Elizabeth Davidson,* the best of them, is an old-fashioned and unbending lady of seventy-five. Esther (Jayson) Sheffield,* Curt's sister, is stout, contented and unenquiring, sheltered and enjoying "an assured position in her little world." Mark Sheffield,* her husband, "is a lean, tall, stooping man of about forty-five," his face marked with "the superficial craftiness of the lawyer mind." As Lily had warned, they speedily start to discuss the childless state of Curt and Martha. Curt then calls for Martha to come to his aid, and further criticism of Martha takes place. She is too much of "a slave to Curt's hobbies than any of my generation were to anything but their children." In answer to Mrs. Davidson's enquiry as to the whereabouts of Martha and Curt's children, Lily says in a curious way, "They died, Aunt, as children have a bad habit of doing." She hints that Martha might be pregnant, but before a full-dress conversation can begin, the rest of the "Grand Fleet" of Jaysons appears: John Jayson* "is a short, stout bald-headed man of sixty," a typical small-town family banker, querulous and fussy. His son, John Jayson, Jr.,* age about forty, a younger edition of his father, is pompous, complacent, authoritarian, "emptily assertive and loud." Richard Jayson* is a good-looking, college-bred young man, a country-club type who "has been an officer in the war and has not forgotten it." Emily Jayson* is a mousy-looking woman whose sweetly innocent manner cloaks "a very active envy, a silly pride, and a mean malice."

As soon as they all arrive, Lily starts to serve tea, and the criticism of Martha begins again. Lily tells them that Martha had consigned her critics to perdition, and Esther notes that Martha had even forgotten about the arrival of her husband's family for tea and had planned to take a drive with Mr. Bigelow—and his three children. After some more malicious criticism, Lily changes the subject by announcing that Martha is going to have a son. Instantly the tongues start wagging and suspicions are voiced that the child might be Bigelow's rather than Curt's. Martha then returns, and the sparring recommences. She sees right through the petty malice of her in-laws and obviously dislikes the narrowness of Bridgetown. As Bigelow's car horn is heard, Martha calls Curt to entertain the family and leaves. Curt tells his relatives that he has made arrangements to take Martha on the five-year Asian scientific expedition. He will tell her the next day as a birthday surprise. There is a short conversation at cross purposes, during which Curt says that it is "impossible" for them to have children. After his departure, the backbiting resumes, and the curtain falls as Jayson, Sr. hopes that there will not be scandal; obviously, the family suspect that Bigelow is the father of Martha's child.

Act II: Curtis Jayson's study, mid-morning of the following day. The room looks like a combination of professorial office and hunter's trophy room, with books and papers lying around and animal skins and heads on walls and chairs. Curtis and Bigelow are talking as Martha is outside playing with Bigelow's children. Bigelow tells Curtis that the entire Jayson clan is treating Martha rather badly and that he should tear himself away from his book to help her fight them. Much to Bigelow's surprise, Jayson tells him that he is planning to take Martha with him on the expedition and that he will tell her later today, her birthday. As Martha returns, the two men tease her about getting old, and when they are left alone, Martha and Curt speak lovingly to each other. Curt tells her she has been the best wife possible, and "I owe everything to you—your sympathy and encouragement." Martha then asks Curt not to go on the expedition because she is afraid of loneliness. He says that he has to go, and then Martha reveals her pregnancy to him. Curt is stunned and sees the coming child as merely a hindrance, something that will interrupt his plans after all the trouble he has taken to have Martha included. She admits that she would have "accepted" the trip if she had not been pregnant, and Curt is indignant when he discovers that the coming son (as she insists it will be) is not a mistake. She tells him that she has felt incomplete without a child and that she wishes he could understand her feminine longing for a child, but he has too much masculinity to comprehend. However, it was that very masculinity that made her love him. "I love the things you love—your work—because it's a part of you. And that's what I want you to do—to reciprocate—to love the creator in me—to desire that I, too, should complete myself with the thing nearest to my heart!" In an attempt to make him understand, she recalls one night when they were sleeping on the Tibetan frontier and she suddenly felt herself "out of harmony . . . like an outcast who suddenly realizes the whole world is alien." All her desire for a child came back to her, and when they came back to Bridgetown "to have a home at last, I was so happy because I saw my chance of fulfillment—before it was too late." But Curt cannot understand: "It seems like treachery to me . . . I feel you're deliberately ruining my highest hope." He cannot imagine living with a child, "a stranger who will steal away your love, your interest—who will separate and deprive me of you!"

He will not and cannot share her with anyone. He even goes so far as to hint at abortion. His work is everything to him, and Martha asks where work leaves off and Curt begins. He insists she is selfish, and Martha sadly says that she has spoiled him "by giving up my life so completely to yours," suggesting that love is a changing process: "We must, both of us, relearn to love and respect— what we have become." Curt then gives his definition of their relationship: "You are me and I am you! What use is this vivisecting?" But Martha, in a whisper, asks, ''Yes, you love me. But whom am I? You don't know.'' As they gaze questioningly at each other, the curtain falls.

Act III: The same scene as in Act II, 3 A.M. on an early spring morning of the next year. Mr. Jayson is looking into the fire as Richard enters. Through the open door, muffled cries of pain are heard. Martha is having an exceptionally difficult childbirth, and her groans and screams punctuate the dialogue throughout this act. Curt is walking in the garden, with something other than Martha's pain obviously torturing him. He has asked for Bigelow, but Mr. Jayson has given orders that he is not to be sent for. The entire family is quite convinced that the child is Bigelow's, and they are afraid of scandal, even to the extent of wishing that the child be stillborn. Emily and Esther look on Martha's ordeal as punishment for sin, but the one person who does not know of their suspicions is Aunt Elizabeth Davidson. By now most of the Jayson clan have assembled, and Curt telephones Bigelow and discovers that his family has not passed along the messages left for him by his oldest friend, Bigelow. Alone and totally confused, he paces up and down, hearing Martha's moans, until Bigelow arrives. They patch up their friendship, Curt having thought that Big's children put the idea of a baby into Martha's head, and Bigelow having heard rumblings of scandal.

Savagely, Curt tells Bigelow that he has arranged to join the expedition in a month or so and will take Martha with him. He quite frankly hopes that the child will die because he actively hates it. He is certain that Martha knows: ''I couldn't keep it out of my eyes . . . she read only my hatred there, not my love for her.'' He feels that Martha can never forgive him, and indeed he cannot forgive himself, yet he remains angry with her: ''She had made the life, our life—the work, our work. Had she the right to repudiate what she'd built because she suddenly has a fancy for a home, children, a miserable ease?'' He hates the coming child as the cause of her suffering. Finally, the screaming stops, and Mrs. Davidson enters to announce the birth of a son.

Curt races upstairs while Emily and Esther chatter maliciously after Bigelow leaves, Emily saying, ''I never want to lay eyes on it.'' Jayson remarks, ''We must keep up appearances,'' and at that moment the nurse appears, supporting Curtis, who is petrified with grief. She announces the death of Martha. The baby, however, is fine—''eleven pounds—that's what made it so difficult.'' The malicious family tries to apologize as Curt recalls Martha's last moment: ''But she loved me again— only me—I saw it in her eyes! She had forgotten—*it*. It has murdered her! I hate it—I will never see it—never—never—I take my oath! Let me Go! I am going back to her!'' And the curtain falls.

Act IV: The same scene as in Act I, on the afternoon of a fine day, three days later. The Jayson clan enters—Mr. Jayson, Esther, Mrs. Davidson, Lily, Dick, Sheffield, then John and his wife Emily. All are in mourning, but the only one who seems to show sincere grief is Mrs. Davidson. They discuss the funeral in a forcedly flippant manner (on Lily's part) and speak of the hypocrisy of those who wept. Curt is in the garden talking to Bigelow, and the tongues start wagging again. Sheffield, however, notes that Bigelow is the only person who can make

Curt see reason: "Then again, I feel that it is to Bigelow's own interest to convince Curt that he mustn't provoke an open scandal by running away without acknowledging this child." Obviously, Curt has kept his word and has not even seen the baby. He plans to leave this very evening for his five-year expedition.

As the Jayson clan retires, Bigelow and Curt enter, Bigelow trying to convince Curt that he should postpone his departure and be reconciled to his child; but Curt says that he might be tempted to violence if he saw it. After Bigelow leaves, having failed to convince Curt to stay, the family returns to the living room, and Sheffield tries to make Curt realize that he has to make arrangements for his son. He tells Curt he must remain for at least a month to acknowledge the child so that the family honor will be preserved "in the eyes of the public." Gradually, as Mr. Jayson and Emily add their comments, Curt realizes that they suspect Bigelow of being the father of the child. As Curt rushes off to the child, Mrs. Davidson speaks lovingly of the baby, apologizes for her dislike of Martha, and attacks them all: "Now I love her and beg her forgiveness. She died like a true woman in the performance of her duty. She died gloriously—and I will always respect her memory. I feel that you are all hostile to her baby—poor, little defenseless creature! Yes, you'd hate the idea of Curtis having a son—you and your girls."

After this outburst, Curt returns: "Well—my answer to you—your rotten world—I kissed him—he's mine! He looked at me—it was as if Martha looked at me—through his eyes." Then he turns to Aunt Elizabeth and announces that he will leave the baby in her care because she is the only member of the family "with unmuddled integrity." He begs her to "teach him his mother was the most beautiful soul that ever lived." He then prepares to leave, kissing only Lily: "You loved her, didn't you? You're not like—Take my advice and get away before you become—But I see by your face it's too late." As he leaves, Jayson asks for forgiveness, and Curt finally says, "you are forgiven," but only because he knows that Martha would have done so. As the family stands awkwardly around, Lily breaks down: "Oh, I hate you—and myself." But nothing can convince Richard: "He did acknowledge the kid—before witnesses too." Jayson testily tells him to keep quiet, but the curtain falls on a family that is "already beginning to look relieved." In the long run, Curt has not learned from suffering. He has retained his freedom and his romanticism. He will teach his son "to know and love a big free life . . . Martha shall live again for me in him."

Comments: This play is one of O'Neill's weakest efforts. It reverts to the scene of one of his earliest plays, *Bread and Butter*,* which also is set in the confining atmosphere of Bridgetown, Connecticut. It takes up the question of matrimonial relationship that is treated both there and in *Servitude** as well as in *Beyond the Horizon.** Similar to the husband in *Servitude*, Curt Jayson wants a wife who will give her entire life to him and to his work, and as in *Beyond the Horizon* and *Bread and Butter*, family life means the destruction of dreams and limitation of the freedom of the romantic—whether he be artist or scholar.

Finally, as in *Bread and Butter*, the multiple meannesses of a small town destroy, or attempt to destroy, human relationships. O'Neill seems here to be restating a sacrificial view of marriage which he quite consciously held and which he expected to achieve in his own marriages. In fact, it is likely that the attitude of Curt Jayson toward his son may be a parallel to O'Neill's own reaction to Agnes Boulton's* pregnancy and the birth of his second son, Shane Rudraighe O'Neill.* In *Part of a Long Story* (1958) Agnes Boulton recalls that O'Neill's "first reaction to her announcement was that the doctor had made a mistake; his second reaction was silence. . . . He was withdrawn, deep in himself, not hostile, not even perturbed, so far as I could see. But there was no contact between us and I was miserable because I could not follow him, could not understand." (p. 275).

The First Man is clumsy, both in its shuffling of characters on and off the stage without any real motivation, and also in its stereotypical character drawing. The entire Jayson family shows no development from their counterparts in *Bread and Butter*, while the interpolated screams of Martha are exceedingly difficult to play without causing either offense or laughter. It is interesting to note that at this time O'Neill had something of an obsession with repetition of words, patterns, themes, and sounds throughout a play: "That ole davil, sea," for instance, is exclaimed repeatedly in *"Anna Christie"**; the drumbeats in *The Emperor Jones**; "Diff'rent"* in the play of that name; and "I spoke no word" in *Gold*.* O'Neill wanted these repetitions to be signaled through dull tone, or a kind of hypnotic approach, but on more than one occasion his directors overruled him. Psychological motivation is rudimentary, and indeed it seems to be little more than the unthinking acceptance of Strindberg's view of the battle between the sexes. In *The First Man*, both dialogue and situations are contrived, and the major interest of the play is autobiographical. The piece also lacks focus because O'Neill seems unable to decide between putting the emphasis of the action on satirizing the small-mindedness of the Bridgetown inhabitants with their malice toward and jealousy of Martha, whose life has been different from theirs, and his own attitude toward marriage, as enunciated by the character of Curtis Jayson.

Production Data: Written 1920–1921. Produced by Augustin Duncan at the Neighborhood Playhouse, New York City, March 4, 1922 (27 performances).

Producer and Director: Augustin Duncan

Designer: Unknown

Cast: Curtis Jayson: Augustin Duncan
    Martha: Margaret Mower
    John Jayson: Harry Andrews
    John, Jr.: Gordon Burby
    Richard: Ian Bunce
    Esther: Margherita Sargent
    Lily: Marjorie Vonnegut
    Mrs. Davidson: Marie L. Day

Mark Sheffield: Eugene Powers
Emily: Eva Carder
Maid: I. Hill
Trained Nurse: Isabel Stuart

FIRST MATE (unnamed), an officer on the S.S. *Glencairn*, ''a tall strongly built man dressed in a plain blue uniform,'' in *The Moon of the Caribbees*.*

FITZGERALD, Geraldine (1914–   ), actress, director, singer, writer. Born in Dublin, Ireland, to Edward and Edith Fitzgerald. Father an attorney. Attended the Dublin Art School and before beginning her theatre career in 1932 at the Gate Theatre, Dublin, she was a painter. Married to Edward Lindsay Hogg (1936–46); Stuart Scheftel (1946–   ).

Miss Fitzgerald continues to have a most distinguished career in the theatre, beginning with her first Broadway appearance in 1938 in *Heartbreak House*. While playing in both classical and contemporary theatre, at the same time she has appeared in numerous films, including *Wuthering Heights* (1939), *Watch on the Rhine* (1943), *The Pawnbroker* (1964), and *Arthur* (1981). In addition, she has been seen in television performances since 1950, both in series and special productions, notably her Long Wharf Theatre Performance in *The Widowing of Mrs. Holroyd* (1974) and her virtuoso performance in *The Jilting of Granny Weatherall* (1979). She has also given concerts of readings, of street songs and clown songs, and has collaborated with Brother Jonathan in *Everyman and the Roach* (1971) and *Everyman at La Mama* (1972). She directed *Mass Appeal* in 1981–82.

Miss Fitzgerald has also become closely associated with the work of Eugene O'Neill, particularly *Ah, Wilderness!** in which she first appeared as Essie Miller* in 1969 (Fords Theatre, Washington, D.C.) and again, in the same role in the Long Wharf Theatre Production, New Haven, Connecticut, December 20, 1974. She also played Mary Tyrone* in *Long Day's Journey into Night** (Promenade Theatre, New York City, April 21, 1971) for which she was named in the *Variety* drama critics poll as best actress in a leading role off Broadway, while the director and cast received the Vernon Rice award. In 1978 she played Deborah Harford* in *A Touch of the Poet** with Milo O'Shea as Cornelius Melody.*

Miss Fitzgerald's interpretation of Mary Tyrone differed markedly from those of Florence Eldridge* in the original production and Katharine Hepburn in the film. Fitzgerald chose to play the character with considerable vigor, even a sense of bitter humor, noting that the detached quality of which O'Neill spoke does not have to mean ''semicomatose.'' In comments made at a meeting of the Modern Language Association in New York in 1978 printed in Floyd, 1979, pp. 290–292, she remarked that she had researched the effects of morphine in discussions with doctors who told her that there is such a thing as a ''cat'' reaction to morphine which makes both women and cats ''overactive and excitable rather than drowsy.'' This behavior is indeed mentioned in the play itself, indicating that Mary has a level of suppressed aggression as well as guilt. Miss Fitzgerald thus played her as "satirical, . . . witty, . . . needling" and to some extent the aggressor, with James Tyrone* as the victim who is attempting to keep things together. In Fitzgerald's interpretation, Mary Tyrone is also guilty, fearful that her son's illness is a kind of judgment on her, and hence she is trying to escape into a kind of dream world where her son will not be in danger. She cuts off Edmund Tyrone* when he wishes to speak about his illness because she wants to prevent *him* from even thinking about it. Thus her dream-return to the simplicity of the convent is an attempt to "un-bear" Edmund (as Miss Fitzgerald pointed out in a filmed interview), trying to remove herself from motherhood and even from the family. And what is noteworthy is that this is a very close-knit family, for all its "cathartic bloodletting," which cares very greatly about its individual members. For that reason, they continually criticize each other and the masks they present. Mary Tyrone's ladylike façade masks turmoil within, as James Tyrone's loquacity and posturing hide the disappointment of chances lost. The drinking and whoring of James Tyrone, Jr.,* are defense mechanisms against despair, and Edmund's sensitivity finds expression in writing, which also hides his fear of illness. Above all, as Miss Fitzgerald has said, this family has a "mutuality of needs." O'Neill commented that the family in *Ah, Wilderness!* represents the family he would like to have had, but the family in *Long Day's Journey into Night* perhaps conveys a more universal account of the deep truths of family life, so that all can relate to it on a personal level, despite what Miss Fitzgerald notes as the distinctly unusual problems of each of its members, three alcoholics and a drug addict. Miss Fitzgerald has brought a keen intelligence, intense understanding, and brilliant acting to her O'Neill roles, and the veiled rage of her final words in *Long Day's Journey into Night* is frighteningly effective.

FLAVIUS. In *Lazarus Laughed,** the commander of the troops of Tiberius Caesar.* Flavius is placed on the throne of Caesar by Tiberius, as Lazarus and his followers come into the throne room at Capri. Calling out, "I will save you, Lazarus," Caligula* attacks Flavius, mistaking him for Tiberius, and kills him.

FLYING TRADES, the name of Adam Brant's* clipper ship in *The Hunted*, the second play in the trilogy, *Mourning Becomes Electra.**

FOG, a one-act play. The scene is the lifeboat of a passenger steamer which is drifting without oars in dense fog off the Grand Banks of Newfoundland. Four persons are aboard: a Poet,* a Man of Business,* a Polish Peasant Woman,* and a dead child. It is daybreak and two male voices are heard, but no human figures can be seen because of the intense fog. The first voice, "appallingly brisk and breezy under the circumstances," clearly belongs to the practical, materialistic Man of Business, while the second, "more refined than the first, clear and unobtrusively melancholy," is that of the Poet. They discuss their chances of being rescued and then turn to the sleeping Polish Peasant Woman and the dead child. The Poet propounds a thesis, astounding to the Man of Business, that the child is better off dead rather than having to endure "poverty— the most deadly and prevalent of all diseases." The Man of Business, with the insulation of money, is rather amused by such a statement concerning this "pretty necessary sickness and you'll hardly find a cure of it. I see you're a bit of a reformer." After all, he finds life "pretty good." The Poet, on the other hand, continually feels the injustice of the human condition, for he is a "humanist," so discouraged by life that has "become so sick of disappointment and weary of life in general that death appeared...the only way out." So deep was this desire that he had hidden in the steerage after the ship had struck the derelict obstacle which sank her, so as not to be saved. There, however, he had discovered the Polish Peasant Woman and her child and had rescued them and himself by lowering one of the remaining lifeboats. He now believes that this experience is a supernatural omen "to convince me my past unhappiness is past and my fortune will change for the better." Nonetheless, had he known the suffering that the Polish Peasant Woman would have to undergo in her grief for her child, dead just twenty-four hours, he would have preferred immediate drowning for them all. The Man of Business is unable to comprehend the Poet's depth of feeling, and suddenly they hear a steamer's whistle in the distance. As it comes closer, the lifeboat grazes an enormous iceberg, and the Poet physically prevents the Man of Business from hailing the steamer because to do so would endanger another vessel: "We can die but we cannot risk the lives of others to save our own." The fog then lifts, revealing the iceberg "like the facade of some huge Viking temple" and a boat rowing toward them. The Man of Business regains his former importance and optimism, while the Poet, with "drawn and melancholy" countenance, contemplates "the unexpected return to life." The two make peace, at the initiative of the Man of Business, and the Third Officer of the approaching lifeboat tells the pair that his vessel had been guided to them by the cries of a child which "stopped just as the fog rose." The Man of Business greets this account "with an expression of annoyed stupefaction on his face," while the Poet goes to the Polish Peasant Woman to waken her, only to discover that she is dead, "Poor happy woman." The Man of Business steps into the rescue boat, but the Poet prefers to remain with the dead, "with eyes full of a great longing as the lifeboat is towed back to the vessel—to life." The Man of Business, unable to accept a nonrational explanation, has the last word: "—the exact truth. So you see that, if you will pardon my saying so, Officer, what you have just finished telling us is almost unbelievable."

Comments: This play uses setting and atmosphere as a means of intensifying the action, while the situation parallels *Thirst** without the violence. The notion of a hostile cosmos, expressed in *Thirst* by heat, is here conveyed by the fog and the cold, while the iceberg may have been suggested by a combination of the loss of the *Titanic* (1912) and a reading of Coleridge's *The Rime of the Ancient Mariner*. One wonders, as with *Thirst*, about the staging problems of such an intricate setting. The interaction of action and setting is well developed here, but the characters are nonetheless stereotypical. The Poet, with his face "oval with big dark eyes and a black mustache and black hair pushed back from his high forehead," is clearly a portrait of O'Neill, whose melancholy had led him to make one suicide attempt in 1912. The Man of Business is the person-ification of a successful man, whose parochial instincts do not extend beyond money, his home in Connecticut, and his trips to New York. He is totally lacking in imagination and is insulated from the problems of humanity by his position and personal choice. The Poet has visited the steerage to talk to the people, while the Man of Business finds no interest in such a strange pursuit.

Part of the problem with this undeniably moving play is that its two characters are such stock figures that their predictable comments at times are more suitable to comedy than to tragedy, and neither is given sufficient motivation. This comment is particularly true of the Poet, whose world-weariness is completely unexplained. In form, the play is a dialogue concerning humanity, but because of the integration of setting, atmosphere, and the supernatural, it is moving toward expressionism. The use of the child's cry as a means of guiding the rescue ship is an extremely successful use of symbolism which transcends rational explanation (one wonders, intellectually, how a child's cry could be stronger than the sound of a steamship's engines), but the nature of the symbolism is not exploited.

Production Data: Written 1914. First produced by the Provincetown Players* at the Playwrights' Theatre, New York City, January 5, 1917 (performances, unknown).

Set Designers: Margaret Swain and B.J.O. Nordfeldt.

Cast: Poet: John Held
      Man of Business: Hutchinson Collins
      Polish Peasant Woman: Margaret Swain
      Third Officer: Karl Karstens

A note on text: The text used is that appearing in *Ten "Lost" Plays of Eugene O'Neill* (New York: Random House, 1964).

FONTANNE, Lynn (1887?–1983), actress. Born Lillie Louise Fontanne in Essex County, England, December 6, 1887(?), to Jules Pierre Antoine and Frances Ellen (Thornley) Fontanne. Father a brass-type founder. There is con-fusion concerning Miss Fontanne's exact date of birth because after her husband's death in 1977 she confessed to a benign long-term deception, having lowered her age by some five years or so when she married Alfred Lunt,* May 26, 1922. (It is also suggested that the birthdate of 1882 was really that of an older sister.) One wonders whether the motivation was less one of vanity than the result of Lunt's own close relationship with his mother.

Miss Fontanne studied acting with Ellen Terry (1903), making her stage debut in a touring production of *Alice-Sit-By-The-Fire* (1905) and her first London appearance in the pantomime, *Cinderella* (1905). After a distinguished London career, she came to the United States in 1916, playing both out of town and on

Broadway. She met her future husband in a Washington, D.C. production of *A Young Man's Fancy* (1919), marrying him three years later. From the time of their marriage, they became almost inseparable, co-starring almost continuously and gaining an enviable reputation for their perfectionism, skill in ensemble playing, and matrimonial happiness. Their names were a tremendous box-office attraction from *Sweet Nell of Old Drury* (1923) and *The Guardsman* (1924) to *The Visit* (1957–60), and their performances rescued many a mediocre play, and the Theatre Guild,* from disaster. Throughout her career, Miss Fontanne managed to project an aura of superb personal beauty, well counterbalanced by her husband's suavity. Between them, they seemed capable of defeating time, remaining permanently fixed in early middle age in the eyes of theatregoers.

Miss Fontanne created the role of Anna Christophersen (*see* Christopherson, Anna) in *Chris [Christophersen],* the first staged version of "*Anna Christie*"* (Nixon's Apollo, Atlantic City, New Jersey, March 8, 1920, and which closed later in the month at the Broad Street Theatre, Philadelphia). She also created the role of Nina Leeds* in *Strange Interlude*, her first major attempt at serious drama, (John Golden Theatre, New York, June 30, 1928).

Lunt and Fontanne (always billed in that order) became almost inseparable theatrical names, jointly receiving the United States Medal of Freedom (1964) and having a New York theatre named for them the same year. Miss Fontanne also made four films and appeared on television several times, both as an actress and a guest. Died of pneumonia at Ten Chimneys, the Lunt-Fontanne farm in Genesee Depot, Wisconsin, July 31, 1983.

FOUNTAIN, THE, a play in three parts and eleven scenes concerned with the search for the fountain of youth undertaken by Juan Ponce de Leon.* The period covered is 1492–ca. 1514, and O'Neill takes conscious liberties with historical fact throughout. It is another exercise in expressionism.

Part I, Scene i: "Courtyard of the house of Ibnu Aswad,* Granada, Spain—the night of the Moorish capitulation, 1492." The scene is roughly the equivalent of the Court of the Lions in the Alhambra of Granada, seen diagonally, with the apex of the triangle seen to the right. "In the centre of the courtyard [is] a large splendid fountain of green marble with human and animal figures in gilt bronze." "It is early night," and the curtain rises on the empty courtyard with the only noise being the splashing of the fountain. Suddenly an imperious and violent knocking is heard, as if the hilt of a sword is being used. Ibnu Aswad, an elderly Moor with a long white beard, enters with an expression of broken pride and humiliation. He goes out through the *porte cochère* and returns with Juan Ponce de Leon and his servant Pedro. Juan is age thirty-one, a tall, handsome, Spanish noble dressed in full uniform. His expression is a combination of arrogance and romanticism, signifying the two parts of his personality, the ambitious noble and the dreamer. Aswad greets the Spaniards with hauteur since they are to be quartered in his house, the Moorish rule of Granada being no more. Juan graciously denies his role as conqueror, offering himself as a "stranger grateful for hospitality," a courtesy which causes the Moor to unbend: "The waters of the fountain fall—but ever rise again, Sir Spaniard." He accepts the defeat of the people as the will of Allah, but "whosoever the victor, there is no conqueror but Allah!" Juan has invited friends to the house and receives Ibnu Aswad's cold compliance. The Spaniard looks around him, wondering what he might do to assuage the sorrows of the Moor, and then his eyes fall on Pedro, who is gazing at the fountain: "Lazy lout! Does the fountain cause you, too, to dream?"

Maria de Cordova,* "a striking-looking woman of thirty-eight or forty" with a face marked by discontent or sorrow, enters. Juan greets her with astonishment mingled with alarm, for her husband is to be his guest this night and her presence would degrade his own honor. Maria tells Juan that she is about to leave the court and admits her love for Juan, who brushes her declaration away as a cheapening of their "rare friendship." "Life is nobler than the weak ties of poets—or it is nothing." Maria indignantly tells him that if he had fought as hard for love as he has for glory he might know differently, and Juan apologizes. Maria has received permission to go into retirement and look for her peace in God, now that there is no longer war in Spain. Juan, however, sees peace as a time of stagnation and vows to depart with Christopher Columbus,* the Genoese, because "he dreams of glory . . . he plans to conquer for Spain that immense realm of the Great Khan which Marco Polo saw." Maria asks if he is fleeing from love, and Juan denies it, saying that Spain alone is his mistress and that he will serve only her and his own ambitions, for the two are one. Maria says that she cannot understand, but as her last penance, she has told him of her love and now promises to pray for his success: "but I shall add, Dear Savior, let him know tenderness to recompense him when his hard youth dies."

Juan remains melancholy for a moment, and then Luis de Alvarado,* "a dissipated-looking noble, a few years older than Juan," enters. He is a merry character and slightly drunk. He suggests that Juan has been indiscreet in seeing Maria, but they are interrupted by the noise of an argument. Luis says that he has brought with him Yusef,* a Moorish minstrel whom he has saved from instant execution by Diego Menendez,* a churchman. Luis has invited the minstrel for sport. He has a lute and knows only Arabic and therefore he can sing whatever he wishes: "If he is wily, he will chant such curses on our heads as will blight that fountain dry—and no one of us but me will understand." Luis again warns Juan about Maria and leaves to save his Moor from the clutches of Diego. Luis returns with the minstrel, a wizened old man wearing the turban that signifies his having made the Hajj to Mecca. He is exhausted yet resigned. Diego Menendez, a Franciscan monk, follows. He is about the same age as Juan but with the thin cruel lips and cold gaze of the religious fanatic. Vicente de Cordova, a gray-haired, scholarly looking soldier-noble of about forty-five, accompanies him. After them come three nobles, Alonzo de Oviedo,* Manuel de Castillo,* and Cristoval de Mendoza,* typically courageous, reckless, picturesque young cavaliers of that uneducated type of new hidalgo which set forth to conquer the New World with cross and sword.

Menendez is furious that the infidel minstrel is to remain with them, and Castillo and Mendoza suggest torturing him to find where the townsfolk have hidden their valuables. Juan suggests that he be removed and manages to annoy Vicente, but Luis, as a means of quieting the situation, sings the song of the fountain which will recur, often with variations, throughout the play:

> Love is a flower
> Forever blooming.
> Life is a fountain
> Forever leaping
> Upward to catch the golden sunlight,
> Striving to reach the azure heaven;
> Falling, falling,
> Ever returning
> To kiss the earth that the flower may live.

Juan greets this poem as a lie, and Luis insists that his dream is that "life is love." Vicente and Juan here come very close to a duel, but Luis prevents it momentarily, and Juan and the three young adventurers talk of Columbus, his crack-brained theories of the earth, and his plans to find the wealth of the East. Juan announces his intention to go, and Luis suggests that the Moor who has been to the East should sing to them of treasure.

The minstrel sings a curious song in words they do not understand but which captures them with its hypnotic rhythms. Luis de Alvarado translates the words almost in a trance as he gazes at the fountain, telling of "a spot that Nature has set apart from men and blessed with peace." Here everything is in an Edenic state, and in the center of this sacred grove is "the Fountain of Youth." Young maidens dance around it and bathe in it, and the old come to drink of it and become young again. Those who drink are purified and revered as holy ever after, but this fountain is revealed only to the "chosen." Juan scoffs at this tale, but in a *sotto voce* comment to Alvarado manages to offend the honor of Vicente, who thinks himself taunted because of his age. They draw their swords but are interrupted by a shriek as Diego Menendez appears with dagger in hand. He has slain the minstrel. Luis rushes on him, but Juan prevents violence. The duel with Vicente is postponed until the next day, and Juan will treat him gently— a minor wound—so that Maria will love her husband. Something is troubling Juan, but he and Luis drink mutual healths to "Sir Lying Poet" and "Sir Glory-Glutton" as the curtain falls.

Part I, Scene ii: "About a year later [1493]—Columbus's flagship on the last day of his second voyage." It is just before dawn, and the ship is crowded with people. A large number of richly-dressed nobles are huddled in sleep, but one small group, including Oviedo, Castillo, Mendoza, and Luis, are playing at dice;

apparently it has been an all-night game. They speak of Juan's disgrace and of Columbus's enmity toward him, because of the scandal resulting from the duel with Vicente. Vicente finally apologized and then retired from court with his wife, who was rumored to be pregnant. At the request of Luis, Juan (a frequent winner) joins the game, but he loses the throw to Oviedo after having said, "Let the cast be an augury for me." Again the group discusses politics and Columbus's theories, but Juan expresses loyalty to him as a commander. As the others sleep, Juan asks Luis to explain what he has heard about Vicente and a child. Discussing the rumor, they speak of reconciliation. Perhaps Juan may again be welcome at Court—but now he is far away.

Christopher Columbus* then appears, a tall, white-haired man in full uniform. He is waiting for a landfall, and his gaze shows "the fixed enthusiasm of the religious devotee." He calls for Menendez and they speak of Juan, whom Columbus dismisses as an egotist, one of those "who seeks only selfish ends." There is no place for such men on this voyage. In reply to Menendez's suggestion that he may wish to confess, Columbus speaks of the lies that have been told against him. He does not desire wealth for himself. With his share of the wealth of the East he intends to outfit an army against the infidel. He has promised the pope that he will finance the last crusade to rescue the Holy Land and "reconquer the Blessed Tomb of Christ for the True Faith!" Juan calls mockingly from the dimness, "The Crusades are dead—and the wealth of East is still unwon," and to Columbus's rage, he suggests that "a new era of world empire dawns for Spain. By living in the past you will consecrate her future to fanaticism!" Juan's vision is to see Spain mistress of the world, but the means to both their ends will be those of cruelty and looting, with the result that "stronger looters" will destroy Spain. Enraged at this distinction between ends and means, Columbus asks to see his tormentor, and Juan reveals himself. At this moment there is a cry of "Land Ho," and all leap to look at it. Juan looks at "Greater Spain," but Columbus raises the cross: 'The earth is God's! Give thanks to Him! Kneel, I command you! Raise the cross!" But Juan defiantly raises his own cross, "a soldier's cross—the cross of Spain," as he sticks his sword point into the deck and falls down before it. All the other nobles do likewise as the monks begin to chant the *"Te Deum"* and all join in, but their excitement gives it "a hectic, nervous quality." The curtain falls on this contrast of cross and sword.

Part II, Scene iii: "Courtyard of the Government House, Porto Rico, an afternoon twenty years or so later" [1513]. It is filled with tropical greenery, cocoanut palms, orange trees, and so forth, and in the center is a large, handsome fountain resembling that in Scene i. Juan is discovered sitting on a stone bench in front of the fountain basin, eager to get some respite from what is still a blisteringly hot day. The years have not been kind to him: his face is lined, "His hair and beard are gray. His expression and attitude are full of great weariness." His gaze is "disillusioned," and the lips are bitter. Luis enters dressed as a Dominican monk. He has aged, but his is a face that shows a man at peace with himself. Luis chides Juan for not forgiving his entering the church, "My friend deserting to my enemy," as Juan puts it. But Luis says that Juan had always had his dream of reaching Cathay while he, Luis, had been nothing but "an aimless posing rake," living a life without meaning until he answered God's call, learning that "you must renounce in order to possess."

Juan speaks of the opposition his governmental policies are meeting from the church. Diego Menendez and his company convert the Indians by force, while he seeks to construct. Luis reminds him that his armies had crushed the Indians before their conversion, and again their argument ends in a stalemate as they await the arrival of a fleet from Spain. Friar Quesada,* a thin fanatical monk, enters, accompanied by Oviedo and Nano,* a fifty-year-old Indian dressed in breech-clout, moccasins, and a head-dress of feathers. He is loaded with chains. Quesada *demands* justice, and Juan puts him in his place. Since Nano and his tribe have refused to pay their tithes and Nano has rejected baptism, Oviedo suggests enslaving them until their taxes are paid, but Juan disagrees and Oviedo warns him there will be a day of reckoning when Diego Menendez returns from Spain. Left alone with Luis and Nano, Juan asks whether the Indian knows of the great countries of the East and then tells Luis that there is a fountain legend among the Indians of Nano's tribe. Nano, in answer to a question, says it is called "The Spring of Life," which can be found only by those whom the gods love. Juan recalls the Moorish minstrel's "only to the chosen" as a curious echo.

At this moment the fleet from Spain arrives, and Luis offers to take charge of Nano to convert him, but Juan orders the Indian to prison. He is disturbed by the arrival of this fleet, fearing that Diego Menendez will undermine his policies. He wishes for a patent to discover new lands; even though he is governing Porto Rico, the shadow of Columbus, who discovered it, still stifles him. The great discoverer took all the credit, ignoring Juan's contribution: he held the outposts and "suffered wounds and fevers," while Columbus prospered. But the dream of Cathay endures, though Juan is beginning to fear that he is too old to pursue it. Menendez enters in time to hear these sentiments. He has become "the crafty schemer made complacent by a successful career, the oily intriguer of Church politics." He claims to have brought great news for Juan, but its delivery "is reserved for a worthier hand." Luis and Juan debate whether it might be the exploration patent, when a crowd appears led by Beatriz de Cordova,* a beautiful young girl of eighteen, accompanied by her Duenna. She greets Don Juan, introduces herself as the daughter of Maria de Cordova who has appointed him her guardian, and then hands him the patent to find Cathay. She speaks of her mother's memory of Juan as the "ideal of Spanish chivalry, of a true knight of the Cross." She had prophesied that Juan "would be the first to find Cathay." The governor greets these words with sadness and wonders whether in sending Beatriz, who is the embodiment of his own lost youth, Maria is mocking him. In reply, Beatriz says that her mother's charge to her was to "bring him tenderness, . . . That will repay the debt I owe him for saving me for you." Juan instead wishes for the past to return, and as Beatriz comments

that he is older than she had expected, he recalls the past with some bitterness—
"that night in Granada." But then he returns to his old gallantry: "Welcome,
dear ward, to Porto Rico!"

Part II, Scene iv: "Cabinet of Bishop Menendez in the Government House—
an evening three months later." The room is dark, gloomy, like a monk's cell
with an altar with candles burning before it, and an enormous crucifix. "The
atmosphere [is] that of a rigid, narrow ecclesiasticism." Menendez waits anxiously, and Quesada enters wearing a sword and pistols over his robe, which is
tucked up over riding boots with spurs. He is the personification of the church
militant. He has been riding hard and brings news that a meeting hostile to Don
Juan is being held. He will be forced to resign his patent for Cathay if he does
not leave soon.

Menendez's plan is working; with the departure of Juan's expedition he will
be rid of his enemy and all dissident elements, becoming free to implement his
own plans for governing the island. The crowd also calls for the burning of
Nano as an infidel, for Quesada has told the mob that Juan was bewitched by
him. This was not part of Menendez's plan, and so he orders Quesada to go
with the Cathay expedition. But now the city is aflame and the mob is about to
march on the palace. The bishop knows that only Juan can control such a mob,
but there is some truth in the statement that Juan is bewitched "between Luis'
influence and the girl's meddling." At this, Juan enters to accuse Menendez of
plotting to get rid of him by insisting on this expedition. Menendez counters by
telling him he has become a weakling, misgoverning the island, and says he
must surrender his patent for Cathay if he is not prepared to take it up. Juan,
somewhat shaken, says he will sail, "but first I must—know for a certainty,
beyond all doubt—exactly where—" For his voyage he needs specific information that Nano alone can give him. Menendez replies that he had thought
affection for Beatriz had detained him, a statement that calls forth a vehement
negative from Juan. After Juan leaves, Menendez calls for Beatriz and blames
her for the rebellion because she has made Juan soft and lax in enforcing discipline
because she has "pitied the suffering of the Indians." She has made him forget
his dreams of Cathay, and now she must "urge him to sail at once! Rouse the
hero in him! Give him back his sanity!" Beatriz believes Menendez, but she is
confused and wishes to pray for guidance. Oviedo enters, also booted and spurred
after a hard ride, saying that the time has come for them to lead this rebellion
and abandon Don Juan. Beatriz leaps to her feet with a contemptuous "Coward"
and departs. Menendez hopes she will perhaps be able to push Juan to undertake
the voyage: "we may still win, my friend!"

Part II, Scene v: "A prisoner's cell in the Government house—same time"
as Scene iv. Nano is suspended by his wrists, semiconscious, his body wasted,
his feet barely touching the floor, a charcoal brazier and bellows are in the center
of the room, and several irons are heating in the fire. A brutal-looking soldier
is operating the bellows as Juan enters to dismiss him. Juan has kept Nano alive
in order to learn the location of the fountain of youth; he has even tortured the

Indian to gain information, but a subtle displacement has occurred. Nano has become superior to his captor, who must plead with him for information. Nano is the strong one, while Juan has lost all sense of purpose and direction. Juan offers Nano the position of pilot of his fleet, and finally Nano agrees to lead them. As Juan feels a sense of triumph, the voice of Beatriz is heard—"A happy omen!"—and he hurries up the stairs, his will to live restored. The curtain falls as Nano begs forgiveness: "Great Spirit, forgive my lie. His blood shall atone!"

Part III, Scene vi: "Same as Scene iii—immediately following Scene v." It is a stifling twilight. Beatriz's voice calls as in Scene v and Juan enters, as if from the prison cell. He is in a state of almost hysterical excitement, with his sword drawn. He greets her in words which make no sense to her: "Was it the fountain called—or you, Beatriz? You, for you are the fountain!" At this, he seizes her hand and kisses it as she tells him she has come to warn him. He realizes that she has spoken with Diego Menendez and tells her that his will has returned. He then proceeds to woo her, but they are speaking at cross purposes, for the girl has never perceived him as a possible lover. However, many of her comments are misconstrued by the infatuated Juan, "The search will make you young," for instance, and also her description of the ideal lover, "Your double— You as my mother described you in the wars before Granada." But Juan frightens her with the suggestion that he might indeed become that double. Finally she tells him to "sail and find Cathay." This he agrees joyously to do; she has given him a knightly task and in turn agrees not to marry before Juan returns, sealing the bargain with a kiss. At this moment Luis enters, telling Juan that the mob demands that Nano burn at the stake.

Juan refuses, and Luis accuses him of preferring the Indian's myths, suggesting that he has wrung from Nano by torture the secret of the fountain. Enraged, Juan declares that "I do not believe Nano, I believe in Nature. Nature is part of God. She can perform miracles." He instances their own extraordinary discoveries in the tropics and announces that he will seek the fountain in Cathay, which is the "flowery land" of which Nano has spoken. Then, when Luis dismisses this as fable, Juan asks what evidence he has of the birth of Christ. Shocked, Luis accuses him of heresy, and Juan makes his choice: "Let me be damned forever if Nature will only grant me youth on this earth again!" In answer to Luis's horrified cry, he says, "There is no God but Love—no heaven but youth!" Luis now understands Juan's love for Beatriz, and Juan confesses it openly to his old friend.

Beatriz returns and also tells him that the mob is calling for Nano's blood. At this Juan calls for Nano to be brought. He defies the mob, cutting down some of them and then informs them that Nano will be the pilot for their voyage to Cathay because he was born on the mainland. He defies Quesada: "Can this monk lead you to conquest? You must decide between us." The mob decides to follow Juan, who may lead them to the cities of gold. Beatriz is filled with admiration at the courage of Juan, but he rejects her praise. He is not what he was, but he cares only for "the golden city of Youth" where Beatriz is queen.

Part III, Scene vii: "A strip of beach on the Florida coast—a night four months later." It is a bright moonlit night, and an old Indian is standing like a statue, dressed only in a piece of deerskin at his waist, a knot of feathers, and paint. He peers out to sea and, puzzled, calls to the Medicine Man,* a being of incredible age and paint, with many shell and bone ornaments. Other Indians also peer out to sea, unsling their bows and arrows as if to use them, as Nano walks up from the beach, glistening with sea water drops. He speaks to the assembled Indians and warns them against the Spanish vessels, insisting that those who sail in them are "thieves and rapers of women." They want nothing but gold, which is their god. He tells of the way in which the Spaniards killed their "God who came to them in the form of a man. . . . He taught them to look for the spirit behind things." And so they killed him, torturing him, crucifying him "as a sacrifice to their Gold Devil." He tells the incredulous Indians that he has lied to the Spaniards in saying that he knows the location of the "Spring of Life" and suggests that they hide by a spring in a clearing in order to ambush those who come. Nano has made war on the Spaniards and has refused to submit to the image of their dead God. After Nano departs to swim back to the Spanish ships, the Indians decide that they should try to "propitiate their devils."

Part III, Scene viii: "The same—noon the following day." The Indians are discovered erecting a small altar as they watch the Spaniards putting off from their ships. They devise a cross in the manner Nano had described to them, but in their ignorance they raise it upside down. They then add gold to the altar. As the boats draw near, they circle the altar in an apparent worship of gold and the Spanish "totem pole," but in fact they are praying to the sky. Juan enters first, worn and wild, accompanied by Luis and followed by soldiers guarding Nano, in chains, and four Franciscan monks led by Quesada who is wearing a sword and pistol over his robe. Again he is the figure of the church most militant. After them come richly dressed nobles and more soldiers. Juan asks Luis to stop the Indian ceremony and get Nano to talk to them; but as he does, Quesada sees the inverted cross, symbol of the Black Mass, and enraged, he shoots the Medicine Man, only to be knifed in the back by him.

Juan is disturbed by this bloody meeting with Cathay, but he sees no flowers. Nano tells him of the secret spring, and then Juan claims the land for Spain, naming it Florida. Suddenly, as the nobles whisper about Juan's obsession with the fountain, they spy the gold on the altar and clutch for it. Juan calls them to order and asks that the "*Te Deum*" be sung. But the sound is exhausted and dispirited, as if the Spaniards sense themselves defeated by something they do not understand.

Part III, Scene ix: "A clearing in the forest—that night." It is about midnight. Gigantic trees surround the clearing, entwined with flowering vines and festooned with Spanish moss. The clearing is flooded with moonlight, and in the center a spring bubbles from the ground with a soft murmur. The scene is perceived through a network of trees. The Indians are visible in ambush as Nano and Juan

enter. Juan looks at the spring and finds it no different from any of the others
to which Nano has led him, but he nonetheless feels himself subject to a strange
enchantment there. He looks into the pool made by the spring, hoping to see
himself made young, but all he sees is his face like that of a corpse. He prays,
but without faith in anything he prays to Beatriz, whose "spirit inspires all things
wherever there is beauty." He drinks as Nano darts off to tell the Indians to
shoot when Juan rises. As he drinks from the spring he feels a kind of joy, but
again he sees himself as old. Leaping up and calling Nano a traitor, he is felled
by the arrows of the Indians. Nano then leads the Indians back to the Spanish
camp, where the sounds of massacre are heard.

Part III, Scene x: "The same, some hours later." But this time there is no
network of trees between the clearing and the audience. At first, the curtain rises
on a pitch-black scene, and nothing is heard except the spring and then a groan
of pain. Juan's voice is heard asking if this, his fate, is indeed justice, and he
begs for a miracle. At first nothing happens, but then there is an unearthly light
and he sees the figure of a woman. In answer to his call he hears the voice of
Beatriz as she sings the same song of the fountain that Luis had sung in the first
scene. As the song is sung, a mystical light envelops the spring, becoming like
"a shimmering veil" hiding the background. Beatriz appears in the spring,
dancing as if she is its spirit. He tries to move toward it in order to drink, but
he cannot and he sinks down. The vision vanishes and in its place he sees a
venerable Chinese poet who writes with a brush upon a block. This form is
followed by the Moorish minstrel of Scene i, then the form of Nano, and finally
Luis as he was at Granada. The Chinese poet seems to be reading what he has
written to the other three as the four apparitions join hands and Beatriz's voice
is heard singing a new song of the fountain, on the cyclic flow of life and nature.
With this song, the apparitions disappear.

Juan seeks the answer to their riddle, and other figures materialize one by
one: the Chinese poet in the garb of a Buddhist priest, the Moorish minstrel
dressed as a priest of Islam, the Medicine Man in full regalia, and last Luis as
a Dominican monk, each carrying the symbol of his religion. They can be seen
clearly for a moment and then dissolve from sight in the fountain. Juan looks
and tries to understand: "All faiths—they vanish—are one and equal—within."
He tries to define the fountain: "What are you, Fountain? That form which all
life springs and to which it must return—God! Are all dreams of you but the
one dream?" He calls for youth to return to tell this secret, and again the voice
of Beatriz, the spirit of youth, is heard singing another song of the fountain:

> Death is a mist
> Veiling sunrise.

And as she sings, an old Indian woman enters. Juan at first curses her and then
reaches out to help her. As he touches her she turns into Beatriz, and Juan
realizes: "Beatriz! Age—Youth—They are the same rhythm of eternal life!"

Beatriz disappears into the fountain and the figure of the woman is now discovered to be Beatriz, as the light "envelops her until her figure seems like the heart of the flame." Juan looks again: "Soaring flame of the spirit transfiguring Death! All is within! All things dissolve, flow on eternally! O aspiring fire of life, sweep the dark soul of man! Let us burn in thy unity!" Beatriz's voice is heard once more in the last song of the fountain:

> God is a flower
> Forever blooming
> God is a fountain
> Forever flowing.

Juan sobs in happiness and prays to God: "Fountain of Eternity, Thou are the All in One, the One in all—the Eternal Becoming which is Beauty!" He falls unconscious. Luis appears with a brother Dominican, and together they raise Juan, who is praying. As they carry him out, the dawn breaks.

Part III, Scene xi: "Courtyard of a Dominican Monastery in Cuba—several months later." There is a crude, home-made fountain in the center, two crude statues of the Holy Family and Saint Dominic in niches, and vines climbing over the top of the wall and palms visible over it. Nature seems to push into the courtyard as the sunset flames in the sky. Juan is discovered, pale and emaciated, but with a face of "deep spiritual serenity." Luis and the Father Superior wonder how he has lived so long, but he has been waiting for his desire to see Beatriz to be fulfilled. Luis says that it will be for him "the cup of gall and wormwood."

Juan awakens. Luis tells him that Beatriz has come and that Diego Menendez has been killed in an Indian uprising. Juan admits that he has lived only to see Beatriz again. She represents the only time beauty has touched his life and he wishes to lay before her the only "Golden City" he has ever conquered—his heart. Luis tells him to be silent and then informs him that his nephew, Juan,* has come from Spain and has accompanied Beatriz.

When the two young people enter, it is obvious that they are deeply in love. She speaks of the young man's valor in defense of the palace, while the youth says, "I do not care for riches; and as for Golden Cities, I only wish to plant Spain's banner on their citadels." He is a reincarnation of Juan Ponce de Leon, and the old man realizes that Beatriz has indeed found his double. He keeps silent about the tale he had intended and instead gives his blessing to the young couple. They kiss, and the nephew picks up his lute; but Beatriz looks at the sleeping Juan. They go out beyond the walls into the realm of nature, and Juan looks after them: "Yes! Go where Beauty is! Sing!" And from outside, their two youthful voices are heard singing the original song of the fountain. Luis hears this and is shocked, but Juan restrains him with his suddenly strong voice speaking of renunciation, of oneness with nature: "Oh, Luis, I begin to know eternal youth! I have found my Fountain! O Fountain of Eternity, take back this drop, my soul!" With that he dies, and the voices of Beatriz and young Juan swell contrapuntally with the deep, strong chant of the monks as the curtain falls.

Comments: O'Neill took tremendous care with *The Fountain* with its theme of the central mystery of life, but it also reveals his greatest difficulty as a dramatist. He was not a poet and could never become one. The play was, in fact, originally written in a kind of blank verse, but it was then cut into prose, except for the songs, in order to make it more palatable to the audience. It has been said by critics that O'Neill did not have a good ear for language, but this statement should be amended to state that he had an excellent ear for dramatic dialogue and dialect. He understood the speech of everyday people and frequently managed to reproduce it with uncanny accuracy. Where he fails is in his attempts at formal language and the language of poetry. Then he becomes inflated, sometimes bombastic, and even inadvertently amusing because his sense of speech rhythm can desert him in his search for the formal, the Latin-rooted word, where simplicity might be preferable.

In *The Fountain*, he is trying to communicate a philosophy of life, the essential oneness of man and nature, the Heraclitean flux, the Neoplatonic notion of the world soul with each human soul a part of it, and also the oneness of all religions, together with the shabbiness of Christianity as embodied in the Spanish conqueror-churchmen. Altogether, this is a tall order and perhaps incommunicable, and indeed O'Neill does not seem to have thought the whole corpus of ideas into a workable form. Perhaps this is the reason that his symbolism is sometimes flaccid and undeveloped and his language convoluted. The fountain of youth becomes the fountain of eternity and change, yet Juan's revelation is not fully clarified. What, too, is the significance of the name of Beatriz? Is she to be taken as the Dantesque Beatrice who leads the poet finally to a vision of the sempiternal rose? Certainly in this play, Beatriz is the instrument which brings Juan to his discovery, but then she is also the spirit of youth. And finally, though Juan has discovered what for him is the central mystery of life, he seems unable to pass on the message to others. Is it renunciation, tenderness, or return to the purity of a religion of nature? But then all the religions shown in the fountain have themselves been guilty of cruelty as human institutions, and therefore they cannot be an answer. James A. Robinson (1982, pp. 100–108) sees the influence of Tao philosophy here.

It has been suggested (Gelb and Gelb, 1973, pp. 468–469) that O'Neill was trying in some measure to exorcize his Catholic conscience in this play, but this is not necessarily so. He does show the dichotomy between the purity of what might be termed "natural religion" and its institutional human counterpart, which is corrupted by the cruelty of conquest and ambition, but his solution remains vague.

Juan embodies this split vision of the universe in his search for the extension of Spain's boundaries and his romantic dream of finding the fountain of youth. The notion of Cathay, then, is in effect the unification of these two dreams. While Juan is unsuccessful in finding that mythical land (though he does annex

Florida) he is (in his own mind) successful in achieving his spiritual quest for the secret of the fountain. That particular scene of revelation (Scene x) is the most dramatically successful of the entire play; and though it is philosophically flawed, it does project a considerable emotional impact. Like the entire play, it is a good attempt, but essentially a failure, and is difficult for scenic designers.

Nonetheless, there is something to admire in O'Neill's careful dramatic structure. The first scene introduces almost every theme that is later taken up in the play, from the dream of conquest, to the dream of the revelatory fountain, and including the essential unity of all religions. He also uses repetition of song and motif, as he had earlier done in *The Emperor Jones** and *The Hairy Ape,** and here he attempts to extend the expressionistic technique he had tried in the earlier plays, including some use of masks for the apparitions, this time working toward a poetic expressionism. Characters are also shown as changing, but the circumstances of those changes are not fully developed. For O'Neill, the theme of life's secret is important, and ultimately it may well be undiscoverable, incommunicable, or intensely private. The playwright seems to have set himself a task here that was impossible for him to achieve and perhaps impossible for anyone save Shakespeare or Dante. Nonetheless, the attempt remains highly interesting; and though it was originally unsuccessful, there are some very stageworthy moments in it. And structurally, O'Neill shows great discipline and force, though perhaps the ending is a trifle simplistic. All in all, a valiant effort.

Production Data: Written 1921–1922. Produced by Kenneth Macgowan,* Robert Edmond Jones,* and Eugene O'Neill with A. L. Loves and Morris Green at the Greenwich Village Theatre, New York City, December 10, 1925 (25 performances). Musical setting by Macklin Morrow.

   Director: Robert Edmond Jones
   Designer: Robert Edmond Jones
   Cast: Ibnu Aswad: Stanley Berry
         Juan Ponce de Leon: Walter Huston
         Pedro: William Stahl
         Maria de Cordova: Pauline Moore
         Luis de Alvarado: Egon Brecher
         Yusef: John Taylor
         Diego Menendez: Crane Wilbur
         Vicente de Cordova: Edgar Stehli
         Manuel de Castillo: Morris Ankrum
         Alonzo de Oviedo: Perry Ivins
         Cristoval de Mendoza: Ralph Benzies
         Christopher Columbus: Henry O'Neill
         Helmsman: Philip Jones
         Friar Quesada: Edgar Stehli
         Nano: Curtis Cooksey
         Beatriz de Cordova: Rosalind Fuller
         Duenna: Liza Dallet
         Soldier: William Stahl
         Indian Chief: Ray Corning

Medicine Man: John Taylor
Father Superior: Henry O'Neill
Juan: John Taylor
His Servant: Philip Jones
Revived at the Jolson Theatre, New York City (28 performances).

FRAZER, Ethel. In *Servitude*,* wife of George Frazer* and admirer of David Roylston.* "She is a tall, strikingly beautiful woman about twenty-eight years old. Her complexion is pale; her eyes large, expressive, dark; her hair black and wavy; her figure inclining a little toward voluptuousness." She has a troubled expression and dark shadows under her eyes. She is dressed in a "black dress such as is worn by the poorer class of working women." She has attempted to put David Roylston's theory of individual self-realization into practice but has found herself unable to bear the loneliness and opprobrium she has found. She has been married for seven years to George Frazer, a stockbroker, whom she has left after reading all of Roylston's works and seeing all his plays. Now, frightened, discouraged, and dispirited, she visits Roylston, seeking "advice" and words of encouragement. These Roylston gives, as is his custom, but for the first time he has temporarily lost control of such a situation. His wife is out of town and Mrs. Frazer has missed her last train, so she must stay the night. In her innocence, Ethel Frazer thinks that Roylston indeed follows his own defiance of conventions. With the unexpected return of Alice Roylston,* Mrs. Frazer tells her the truth, that they are both innocent, and is astonished to discover the depth of Alice's love for her husband. Humbly, Mrs. Frazer realizes that Alice, in her willingness to give up her husband if that would make him happy, is a truly heroic personality. She learns that her own ideal, Roylston, is nothing more than a selfish egotist, and she brings him to a realization of his faults. At the same time, she comes to understand the depth of her husband's love for her and discovers a truth that "happiness is servitude." Having rethought her matrimonial relationship and realized that she is unable to live alone, she is reconciled to her husband.

Ethel Frazer is O'Neill's version of the "new woman," and she seems to be drawn as a serious, rather than a satiric, character. She is also a combination of Ibsen's Nora and Shaw's Candida, perhaps meant as an exemplum for the modern woman that liberation does not bring happiness. She is a mouthpiece for O'Neill's ideas rather than a fully developed character.

FRAZER, George. In *Servitude*,* the stockbroker husband of Ethel Frazer. He is about "thirty-five, thick-set, of medium height, black hair grey at the temples, square jaw, irregular features, broad clean-shaven face, and shrewd blue eyes." His expression is haggard and troubled, and he is dressed in a dark business suit. He is deeply in love with Ethel and has tried to make her happy. When she leaves him to pursue her own destiny, he cares for her sufficiently to have her followed in case something should happen to her. When she discovers that

David Roylston,* her idol, has feet of clay, she returns to George. There is a melodramatic moment, which seems a trifle out of key with the rest of the play, in which Frazer appears with a revolver ready to shoot Roylston when he sees the two of them standing together. Ethel Frazer has thought her husband to be rather crass, but she has remained in love with him, while he has demonstrated an unexpectedly romantic and faithful streak.

FREDA. In *The Long Voyage Home*,* a prostitute in Fat Joe's London waterfront dive, "a little sallow-faced blonde."

G

GADSBY, Nicholas. In *A Touch of the Poet*,* the Harford family lawyer a man "in his forties [with] bald head, round, florid face, and small, blue eyes." He is dressed in the "rigidly conservative" manner of a "best-family attorney" and projects all the pomposity and self-satisfaction of his professional position. He is sent by the Harford family to Cornelius Melody's* tavern on the night of his annual Talavera Day Dinner to buy him off with a payment of three thousand dollars to prevent a marriage between Sara Melody* and Simon Harford.* Gadsby is astonished to find the major in his full uniform, and he engages in a dialogue at cross purposes with the drunken Melody, who believes the lawyer has come to offer a marriage settlement. When the tavernkeeper realizes the truth, he calls out his shanty Irish spongers, Dan Roche,* Paddy O'Dowd,* and Patch Riley,* who beat up the attorney.

Gadsby reappears briefly in *More Stately Mansions** when, with Joel Harford,* he comes to Deborah Harford* to convince her to allow her son Simon to take control of the failing family company and share living arrangements with Simon, Sara, and their children. He treats Deborah with affectionate gallantry and for one moment shows a romantic streak when he compares himself with Napoleon and speaks of having dreamed of finding love, perhaps with Deborah (this is implicit). Otherwise, he is a sternly practical figure.

"GAG'S END." *See* "Blind Alley Guy."

"G.A.M.," a one-act comedy on the Industrial Workers of the World (the IWW, or "the Wobblies"). Written 1915–1916 after leaving Harvard and still under the influence of George Pierce Baker.* The text has not survived. Title may be "G.A.N." The significance of the initials is unknown.

GARBO, Greta (1905–   ), actress. Born Greta Louisa Gustafsson, September 18, 1905, in Stockholm, Sweden, to an unskilled laborer who was frequently jobless. He died when she was thirteen and the following year she went to work in a menial position in a barber's shop, later becoming a salesgirl in a Stockholm department store.

Miss Garbo's first film appearance came in a publicity film entitled *How Not to Dress* (1921) sponsored by the store for which she worked. This led to another film, this time for a bakery, *Our Daily Bread* (1922), and in the same year she gained the lead in a slapstick comedy, *Peter the Tramp*. Bolstered by these successes, she applied to the Royal Dramatic Theatre training school in Stockholm and was accepted with a scholarship. While there, she was discovered by Mauritz Stiller, then Sweden's foremost director, and given the lead in *The Story of Gösta Berling* (1924). From this time on, she and Stiller became very close, he coaching her, introducing her into society, and even controlling her personal life. When Stiller was offered a Hollywood contract with Metro Goldwyn Mayer, he insisted to Louis B. Mayer that Garbo be made part of the package. At first Mayer was reluctant because this tall, uncommunicative woman did not fit the usual screen-star image.

Her American success was immediate in *The Torrent* (1926), and she was launched on her career as the quintessential screen legend, a star whose films are still shown and whose mysterious personality still interests fans, even though she retired from films in 1941 after the release of the unsuccessful *Two-Faced Woman*. She survived the transition from silent films to "talkies" better than most other stars (including her beloved co-star, John Gilbert). Her first talking role was that of Anna in the second film version of "*Anna Christie*"* (1930), which was also issued in German and in a silent version. Her husky, accented English made her a natural for the role and further enhanced her standing as an actress. The film, scripted by Frances Marion, was also notable for the return of Marie Dressler, of *Tugboat Annie* fame, in the role of Marthy Owen,* a role which was enhanced by the scriptwriter. Dressler even managed to out-act Garbo in this production, which was one film from which O'Neill made some money.

Garbo's most famous films were: *Mata Hari* (1931), *Grand Hotel* (1932), *As You Desire Me* (1932), *Queen Christina* (1933), *The Painted Veil* (1934), *Anna Karenina* (1935, with Fredric March,*) *Camille* (1937, also scripted by Frances Marion), *Conquest* (1937), *Ninotchka* (1939, which contains the famous scene in which "Garbo laughs!"). Curiously, Garbo did not receive a regular academy award, despite being nominated for both *Anna Karenina* and *Camille*. This oversight was remedied in 1954 with a belated special Oscar "for her unforgettable screen performances." She did not attend the ceremony.

Since her unexplained and sudden retirement in 1941, Garbo has lived a reclusive life, dodging reporters and photographers, and dividing her time among her residences in Switzerland, the French Riviera, and the Upper East Side of New York. Garbo has never married, though she has been linked romantically with a number of interesting men, including Mauritz Stiller, Rouben Mamoulian, John Gilbert, Leopold Stokowski, Gaylord Hauser, and Cecil Beaton.

GARDNER, Jack. *See* Cockran, Jack.

GAYLORD FARM, Wallingford, Connecticut, was a tuberculosis sanitorium noted for its innovative treatment. O'Neill was a patient there during 1912–1913. Several persons from among the staff and patients appear in *The Straw*,* notably the superintendent, Mr. David Russell Lyman (Dr. Stanton*), Mrs. Florence R. Burgess, senior nurse (Mrs. Turner*), Miss Mary Clark (Miss Gilpin*), Misses Wilhelmina Stamberger and Catherine Murray (Miss Howard*), Catherine (Kitty) Mackay (Eileen Carmody*), and O'Neill himself (Stephen Murray*).

GAYNOR, Doctor. In *The Straw*,* "a stout, bald, middle-aged man," an authoritarian figure who dictates to rather than advises members of the lower classes. He diagnoses Eileen Carmody's* illness as tuberculosis and both threatens and hectors Bill Carmody* into sending her to the Hill Farm Sanitorium.

GENE. In *Recklessness*,* maid to Mildred Baldwin.* She is vindictive and dark-eyed. She observes Fred Burgess,* the chauffeur, and her mistress embracing. In her jealousy, she reveals their affair to Arthur Baldwin,* who procures Fred's death in an accident with an automobile whose steering mechanism Baldwin knows to be defective. Baldwin treats her with a mocking salacity and later alleges that she had also been Fred's lover. This is not established as fact, but certainly Gene's vindictive jealousy arises from love for Fred. She is a lightly drawn character.

GENTLEMAN, A. In *Thirst*,* "a middle-aged white man" dressed in the tattered and soaked remnants of an evening suit. He is one of three survivors of a shipwreck and is drifting with a Dancer* and a West Indian Mulatto Sailor* on a raft surrounded by sharks. All are slowly being driven mad by hunger and thirst. The Gentleman continually complains about the circumstances that have brought them to this situation and rails against the hostile universe and the hostile God who rules it. He sees humankind as pitiable. He suspects the Sailor of having stolen and hidden the remainder of the store of water and manages to enlist the help of the Dancer in trying to coerce the Sailor to share the nonexistent water. The Gentleman operates to some extent as a symbolic figure, showing that in the matter of survival, the ship's first class passengers are equal to the denizens of the forecastle. He cannot accept the Sailor's suggestion that the pair consume the body of the Dancer, and he flings it overboard. Enraged, the Sailor stabs the Gentleman, but held in the dying grasp of the "civilized" man, he, too, falls into the sea to be eaten by sharks. All perish.

GHAZAN, King of Persia, son of Arghun,* betrothed of Kukachin,* in *Marco Millions*.*

GIEROW, Karl Ragnar (1904–1982), theatre director, playwright, and poet. Managing director of the Royal Dramatic Theater, Stockholm, 1951–1963, when he resigned and was succeeded by Ingmar Bergman. During his tenure at the state-supported theatre, he was responsible for the world premieres of *Long Day's Journey into Night** (1957), *Hughie** (1958), and *More Stately Mansions** (1962), all in translations by Sven Barthel. Gierow also reworked the manuscript of the last of these, reducing it from a playing time of about ten hours to four. Both Eugene O'Neill and Carlotta Monterey* had very friendly relations with the Royal Dramatic Theater because the company had continued to perform O'Neill's plays when they were considered "box office poison" in America. It was partly as a result of her rage at this neglect that Carlotta violated her husband's express wish that *Long Day's Journey* not be published or performed until twenty-five years after his death and gave it to Gierow for its premiere, following it with the other posthumously produced plays. Gierow, along with other Swedish producers and scholars, also felt a kinship with O'Neill both because of his Nobel Prize for Literature (1936) and his often expressed debt to the Swedish playwright, August Strindberg. In fact, the traditional companion piece to *Hughie** has become Strindberg's monologue, *The Stronger*.

Gierow was appointed to the Swedish Academy in 1961, later becoming its permanent secretary, charged with presenting the Nobel Prize for Literature. Two controversial Nobel awards during his tenure were to Jean-Paul Sartre (1964), who refused it, and Alexander I. Solzhenitzyn (1970). The propriety of accepting this award was disputed by the author and the Soviet government for two years. The medal was finally presented in 1974, two years after Solzhenitzyn left Russia for the West.

GILPIN, Charles (1878–1930), actor. Born in Richmond, Virginia, November 20, 1878; died in Eldridge Park, New Jersey, May 6, 1930. Father worked in a steel mill; mother was a trained nurse. Youngest of fourteen children, Gilpin worked at a variety of odd jobs, including elevator operator, Pullman porter, compositor, as well as acting in vaudeville and in black stock companies.

In 1919, Charles Gilpin played the small role of William Curtis, an elderly slave, in John Drinkwater's play, *Abraham Lincoln*, for which he received favorable notices. Accounts differ over what he was actually doing at the time that Jasper Deeter suggested he be auditioned for the role of Brutus Jones* in *The Emperor Jones*.* But whether it was elevator man at Macy's or ticket clipper on the Sixth Avenue elevated railway, the fact remains that as a black actor he had not been able to support himself in the legitimate theater. *The Emperor Jones* began its run at the Playwrights' Theater, New York City, and was then transferred uptown to the Selwyn Theatre for a total of 204 performances. Gilpin's performance was universally praised, and late in his life O'Neill praised him as the one actor who fully created the character the playwright had in mind. But at the time, O'Neill was not always happy with Gilpin, and for the London production he introduced Paul Robeson* in the title role.

Gilpin was in many ways the victim of racial prejudice, not only in the South but also in New York City. An invitation to be guest of honor at a New York

Drama League dinner in 1921 was issued only after protests from theatre people. In addition, very few parts in the legitimate theatre were available to him, for it was not until O'Neill that "integrated" casts were used. His performance in the role of Brutus Jones was a remarkable achievement, and theatre historians who saw the performances of both Gilpin and Robeson suggest that Gilpin was actually superior, possessing greater energy and conveying emotion more physically. As the run of the play continued, Gilpin began to object to some of the subliminal racism that does indeed exist in the play, rewriting lines, refusing to use the word "nigger," for instance, and sometimes drinking too much before a performance. He never played another major role; and years later when he saw Robeson re-create the part, he knew his own superiority in it, saying, "That role belongs to me. That Irishman, he just wrote the play" (Gelb and Gelb, 1973, p. 450). He retired to his farm in New Jersey and died there.

GILPIN, Miss. In *The Straw*,* the superintendent of the infirmary. She is "a slight, middle-aged woman with black hair, and a strong, intelligent face, its expression of resolute efficiency softened and made kindly by her warm, sympathetic grey eyes." She is very fond of Eileen Carmody* and remembers the way she herself had felt as a young woman when she, too, had loved someone who did not love her. She wishes to protect Eileen and so begs Stephen Murray* to propose marriage and take Eileen to a private sanitorium so that she will have some happiness in her last days. When Stephen takes her plan even farther and asks Gilpin's corroboration in the lie that he has suffered a recurrence of his tuberculosis, she very unprofessionally assents. She cannot hope for Eileen's recovery, but she thinks she has acted for the best. "God bless you both," she says as she leaves.

Miss Gilpin's character was modelled after that of Mary Clark, who had come to Gaylord Farm* as a patient and stayed on to work there. O'Neill met her while he was a patient and kept in touch with her for many years, even sending her a volume of his plays including *The Straw*.

"GIVE ME DEATH." The original title of "And Give Me Death."*

GLASPELL, Susan (1882–1948), playwright and novelist. Married to George Cram ("Jig") Cook* (1913–24) and Norman Matson (1925–31, divorced). Born in Davenport, Iowa, July 1, 1882 (though university records suggest an earlier date of 1876) to Elmer S. and Alice Keating Glaspell. Died of virus pneumonia in Provincetown, Massachusetts, July 27, 1948. Educated in the public schools of Davenport, and at Drake University, Des Moines, Iowa, graduating Ph.B. in 1899.

Immediately after graduation, Susan Glaspell joined the reportorial staff of the Des Moines *Daily News*, first as a political and legislative reporter and later achieving her own column, which was aimed at the feminine leadership, with the by-line, "The News Girl." These essays, based on personal observation, proved good training for her later regional short stories and novels. She returned to Davenport in 1901 to become a full-time writer and in 1903 enrolled at the University of Chicago for graduate work in English. Between 1903 and 1922, she published two or three short stories a year, twenty-six of them about "Freeport," a rather transparent pseudonym for Davenport. One of her most successful short stories is "Jury of Her Peers," an adaptation of her 1916 play *Trifles*, written for the Provincetown Players,* of which she was a founding member. In 1909, her first novel, *The Glory of the Conquered*, was published, royalties from which enabled her to spend a year abroad and then some time in Colorado. A second novel, *The Visioning* (1911), and a collection of short stories, *Lifted Masks* (1912), followed.

On April 14, 1913, she became the third wife of George Cram ("Jig") Cook, whom she had met in Iowa in 1907. They were married in a civil ceremony in Weehawken, New Jersey, by the mayor of the town, and moved to Provincetown, Massachusetts, buying a summer house there and returning to New York for the winters. She and Cook became intimately bound up with the early history of the Provincetown Players. Her plays, all but two of which were first produced by the company, are: *Suppressed Desires* (1914), written with Cook; *Trifles* (1916); *The People* (1917); *Close the Book* (1917); *The Outside* (1917); *Tickless Time* (1917), with Cook; *Woman's Honor* (1918); *Bernice* (1919), her first full-length play; *Inheritors* (1921); *The Verge* (1921); *Chains of Dew* (1922), a comedy in three acts; *The Comic Artist* (1971), with Norman Matson (1893–1965); and *Alison's House* (1930), based on the life of Emily Dickinson, the poet, for which she won the 1931 Pulitzer Prize for Drama.

Her most popular one-act play remains *Trifles*, later reworked into the short story "Jury of Her Peers." It concerns a midwestern woman who has murdered her husband. While she is awaiting trial, three men (the sheriff, the county attorney, and a neighbor) and two women come to the house seeking evidence to prove her guilt. From small things, which the men find inconsequential, the women discover the action which triggered the crime. And in their understanding sisterhood, they suppress the evidence, having acquitted her in their hearts, whatever the law may say.

Later, in *The Verge* (1921), Glaspell undertook the study of a woman who pays the price of her ambition and rebellion against convention. She kills her lover and crosses the borderline into insanity. This work was perhaps too advanced for its time, and Hutchins Hapgood (1939) disliked its sentimentality and "expression of half-mad feminism." [*A Victorian in the Modern World* (1939)]. Her two collaborations with George Cram Cook were both very successful, comedy-satires: *Suppressed Desires* (1914) dealing with the contemporary faddish commitment to Freudian psychology, and *Tickless Time* (1917), examining the tension between idealism and realism in a mechanistic world revealed in the image of a sundial.

Glaspell becomes important in the history of the American theatre both in the context of the Provincetown Players and in the history of women in the American theatre. The Provincetown Players helped the career of Eugene O'Neill by providing an experimental place for his early work because his first produced play, *Bound East for Cardiff*,* epitomized the ideals of the group. As Glaspell herself wrote of the initial reading of this play, "Then we knew what we were for. We began in faith, and perhaps it is true when you do that 'all these things shall be added unto you.' '' (Glaspell, 1927, reprinted 1941, p. 254). Others, however, including another founding member of the Provincetown Players, Hutchins Hapgood, maintain that O'Neill's talent was such that it would have triumphed even without the support of the group. In her own right, Glaspell made a specific contribution to the American theatre in her insistence on writing plays of intellectual substance, plays of ideas. Only in recent years has the full impact of her very advanced feminism been properly appreciated, and her work is now being reevaluated in the context of the women's movement.

The influence of Susan Glaspell and George Cram Cook on the Provincetown Players began to decline after their "sabbatical" absence from New York during the theatre season of 1919–1920. On their return from their writing leave, they began once more to work with the Playwrights' Theatre, the New York branch of the group where Susan Glaspell was considered one of the group's finest actresses. However, the extraordinary success of O'Neill's *The Emperor Jones** (1920) began the decline of the Provincetown Players. Because of the expensive uptown Broadway production, the company was seriously depleted, and the original high ideals of the group began to turn to an evaluation of success in "uptown" economic terms. As a result, George Cram Cook decided in 1922 to fulfill a lifelong ambition and go to Greece. Susan Glaspell accompanied him, less committed to the revivification of the ideals of ancient Greece in the modern world than her husband (perhaps because the practicalities of daily existence devolved upon her). After his death in 1924, she married Norman Matson (1893–1965) in 1925, with whom she collaborated in *The Comic Artist* (1927). They were divorced in 1931, the year of her Pulitzer Prize for *Alison's House*.

Apart from her plays, Glaspell wrote *The Road to the Temple* (1927), an impressionistic account of the life of George Cram Cook, drawn largely from his notes and writings. It includes useful material on the early days of the Provincetown Players and a moving account of Cook's funeral at Delphi, Greece. Her novels are mainly regional pieces placed in the geographical and moral setting of the American Middle West. They are less distinguished than her plays and indeed have become somewhat dated, though they were well received in their day. They are: *The Glory of the Conquered* (1909); *The Vision* (1911); *Fidelity* (1915); *Brook Evans* (1928); *Ambrose Holt* (1931); *The Morning is Near Us* (1939, the Literary Guild Selection for 1940); *Cherished and Shared of Old* (1940); *Norma Ashe* (1942); and *Judd Rankin's Daughter* (1945). She died of virus pneumonia in Provincetown, July 27, 1948.

See in "References": Deutsch and Hanau (1931); Gelb and Gelb (1973); Glaspell (1927; reprinted 1941); Hapgood (1939); Sarlós (1982); Sheaffer (1968); Waterman (1966).

GLASS. In *Chris Christophersen*,* he is a sharp, thin young man of twenty-five, the messroom steward of the steamer *Londonderry* which ran down Chris's coal barge. He plays a practical joke on Chris, enraging him to near violence by saying that his daughter Anna [*see* Christopherson, Anna] is planning to elope with Paul Andersen,* the second mate. Glass later admits that Anna had refused Paul's offer of marriage.

GLENCAIRN, S.S., a British tramp steamer, locus of *The Moon of the Caribbees*,* *Bound East for Cardiff*,* and *In the Zone.** Some seamen from the S.S. *Glencairn* also appear in *The Long Voyage Home*,* the land-based play of the S.S. *Glencairn* cycle.

GOLD, a four-act melodrama, a development of *Where the Cross Is Made*,* which is a one-act play, based on "The Captain's Walk," a short story idea by Agnes Boulton,* O'Neill's second wife.

Act I: "A small, barren coral island on the fringe of the Malay Archipelago." It is noon, and the island is baking and shimmering in the heat. Abel,* the ship's boy, age fifteen, is lying on the ground, emaciated and prostrate with thirst. Butler,* the ship's cook, a man "over middle age," shares a few drops of water from his own private flask with the boy. He will not share with the other members of the crew because of the contemptuous way in which they have treated him. The boy asks the meaning of the screaming and shouting he has just heard and Butler tells him that the other shipwrecked sailors of the whaler *Triton** have found a chest full of jewelry. The skipper, Captain Isaiah Bartlett,* had ordered Butler away, but the cook had looked at the treasure and says he is sure that it is junk. The four other crew members, Captain Bartlett, Silas Horne,* Cates,* and Jimmy Kanaka,* then enter, with Cates and Jimmy carrying the disputed chest.

Cates is desperate for water, but Captain Bartlett tells them they will soon be picked up and that the contents of the chest will make them rich forever. The Captain dreams of what he will do with the money and reveals that he has always hated whaling. His sole aim has been to find a cache of ambergris and make his fortune. Once before he passed up a chance to search for buried treasure, but this time he has found it himself. Bartlett forces Abel and Butler to agree that the treasure is gold and precious stones, though Butler clearly knows better. Bartlett then knocks the cook down, refusing to allow a share to either him or Abel. After this incident, Butler looks again at the sample piece, an anklet, and Bartlett says he can keep it. Horne, however, objects, and Butler throws it back as junk. Abel and Butler withdraw, while the others discuss their treasure, their shares, and their need for water. Jimmy Kanaka shins up a coconut palm and sees a schooner approaching. Fearful of having the treasure discovered, Horne, Cates, and Jimmy bury it, while Bartlett draws a map with a cross indicating the spot. Then they think of Abel and Butler and discuss killing them. Jimmy volunteers to do it, "Horne makes violent motions to Jimmy to go," and Jimmy seems "to read a direct command in Bartlett's face." After Jimmy knifes the two, Bartlett declares (as he will continue to do throughout the play), "I spoke no word." The treasure is buried, Bartlett keeps the anklet sample, and the schooner picks them up.

Act II: The "interior of an old boat-shed on the wharf of the Bartlett place on the California coast. . . . late afternoon of a day six months later." Bartlett and Silas Horne are there. Horne looks unchanged, but Bartlett's hair has turned white. He has aged shockingly and seems to be fighting continually against some weakness. A schooner has just been readied for the search voyage, but Sarah Allen Bartlett,* the captain's wife, has refused to christen the boat with her own name. She has pieced together the tale of the treasure and the murders from Bartlett's nightmares. The knowledge has wrecked her health, and she begs her husband not to sail, asking him to confess his crime. He forces her to christen the boat by saying that otherwise he will take their son, eighteen-year-old Nat Bartlett,* with him. She reluctantly agrees.

Act III: Dawn, the next day, outside the Bartlett house. Cates, Horne and Jimmy are eager to sail. Though Mrs. Bartlett has totally collapsed, Bartlett plans to leave immediately. Nat begs to go too, but his father refuses, afraid that he knows about the treasure. Sue Bartlett* does not wish her mother to die alone and tricks her father into comforting his dying wife while Sue's fiancé, Daniel ("Danny") Drew*, newly qualified as ship's master, takes the vessel out. Sarah rejoices fanatically as Bartlett rages.

Act IV: "About nine o'clock of a moonlight night one year later," in Captain Bartlett's "cabin" at the top of the house, "fitted up like the cabin of a sailing vessel." Sue and Doctor Berry* are sitting by the table. Mrs. Bartlett has died; Sue is in mourning and looks older. She has just received a letter from Danny and is sharing its contents with the doctor, who is obviously a family friend. The *Sarah Allen* has been lost, and Danny is the sole survivor, because the crew tried to murder him and left him for dead. Fortunately he recovered but then became ill with fever and is currently in a hospital in Rangoon. He has never learned the purpose of the voyage. Captain Bartlett refuses to believe the loss of his beloved schooner, and his obsession with the buried treasure has made him quite mad so that the doctor advises Sue to commit him to an asylum.

Nat, looking much older, gaunt, moody, and preoccupied, now enters to say that he has certain evidence of the loss of the *Sarah Allen*. After reading Danny's letter, Nat wishes that he had gone because he would not have let Cates, Horne, and Jimmy get away with things the way they did with Danny. After Doctor Berry leaves, Nat says that he dislikes his "sneaking around all the time." Captain Bartlett, now clearly insane from his obsession, enters, moving like an automaton. He takes out his treasure map and says he is sure the seekers will return tonight, exactly one year after their departure. In his ravings he recreates the occurrences of Act I. Nat attempts to tell him of the conclusive evidence that the vessel is lost, but Captain Bartlett disbelieves. He shows the map and then tells him of the murders, "but I spoke no word." He goes up the companionway and hails the *Sarah Allen*, certain that he can see her lights. He convinces Nat that the footsteps he hears are those of the crew returning, but when Nat flings open the door in welcome he discovers Sue. Nat runs to the beach to check, while Sue tries to convince her father to tell the truth and save Nat's sanity. Eventually he admits that there were no lights, but still goes upstairs to check once more. Nat returns in a confused state, first saying that he saw nothing, and then announcing that he has seen the *Sara Allen*. Bartlett now returns claiming that he too has seen her, as Sue begs him again to tell Nat the truth. Finally, he confesses that the vessel is indeed lost and admits that "I gave the word—in my mind—to kill them two. I murdered them in cold blood." He then takes the anklet sample from his pocket and asks Nat to say whether it is real or not. With scorn, Nat identifies it as junk. With this news Bartlett shrinks into feebleness, his dream destroyed; he tears up the map and totally collapses. Sue calls to Nat to run for the doctor: "Oh Nat—he's dead, I think—he's dead."

Comments: The play is one case in which a first version is superior to the second, and O'Neill himself realized this. Even technically, the earlier one-act, *Where the Cross Is Made*, is more innovative in its attempt to induce a collective hallucination in the audience, but the later expansion errs in the direction of overstatement, improbability, and unconvincing moral symbolism. Most curious is the collective assessment of the treasure as genuine by all except Butler, and later by Nat, and also Captain Bartlett's refusal to have the sample anklet checked for fear that the treasure might be discovered.

The answer appears to lie in the symbolic meaning of the play. To begin with, the ship's boy is named after Abel, the biblical character destroyed by his brother, Cain; and equally significant, both Abel and Butler are drawn as characters who demonstrate the virtue of charity, Abel by not ridiculing Butler, and the cook by sharing his water flask with the boy. Significantly, Butler, the man of virtue, can perceive the difference between appearance and reality, and hence he readily dismisses the "treasure" as the "junk" it is. Captain Bartlett, however, is the prisoner of his own greed; Horne's face is marked by "crass lusts and mean cruelty"; while Cates's figure indicates a disposition to gluttony. Jimmy Kanaka, the harpooner, may well be considered one of their kind, both as an infidel and also as a murderer. In other words, those who are blinded by their sin cannot distinguish the false from the true. But above all, their besetting sin is greed, one of the seven deadly or capital sins, from which other sins flow. For them "the love of money is the root of all evil," and there are no actions that they will not take to gain their end, be it the double murder of Abel and Butler or the attempted murder of Danny Drew. ·

In this reading, the play becomes a treatment of crime and punishment. Captain Bartlett must pay for his crime, and the gnawing of his conscience drives him to nightmares and madness, while his wife's knowledge of the crime, gleaned from his ravings, eventually kills her. Nat, too, is affected because he has learned the reason for the voyage of the *Sarah Allen*, named after his religious mother who did not wish to lend her name to "christen" the ship in an unholy cause. Nat, then, like his father, falls victim to the sin of greed; but though his corruption does not proceed as far as his father's, he begins to participate in the captain's hallucinations and obsession. He believes, despite his earlier "certain knowledge" of her loss, that the *Sarah Allen* has returned. It is this discovery, that Nat is sliding into madness, that brings Sue to appeal to her father's love for his son, begging him to release Nat from "this crazy dream." Bartlett picks up this pleading: "Confess, ye mean? Sue, ye be houndin me like your Ma did to her dying hour." She begs him once again to save his son, and finally he does indeed confess his sin of murder. After that, Nat tries to hold to the dream of riches; but his father, who now sees things clearly, reconfesses his guilt and his greed, and hands the anklet to Nat, who, with his eyes now opened, instantly identifies it as false. Bartlett, likewise, can now perceive the truth and collapses: "What a damned fool I've been." With this, he slumps over and dies. There is clearly a suggestion now that Nat will be saved from his obsession, his incipient madness, as a result of his confession. Here, too, one must not overlook Sarah Allen Bartlett, whose continual fear for her husband's spiritual well-being leads her to death, yet paves the way for his eventual confession. She may be read as religiously obsessed, but at the same time she sacrifices herself for the good of her son when she finally agrees to "christen" the schooner so that Nat will not go with his father to partake of the same corruption. This kind of sacrifice also explains Sue's otherwise strangely motivated part in the subterfuge that sends her fiancé, Danny Drew as acting captain in place of Bartlett. She is making a sacrifice of her love for the good of another, her mother, and finally of both Nat and her father.

But when all is said and done, the play is a failure, and O'Neill was quite right in his later assessment of this effort. The moral symbolism is far too weighty for the curiously improbable material. The characters are not deeply drawn, existing mainly as stereotypes; Sarah Allen Bartlett, who should be the voice of conscience, seems to be a religious fanatic, and Bartlett himself is a slight figure compared with other guilt-ridden persons in literature. Even Sue seems curiously confused in her priorities when she sacrifices her fiancé and not a character whose strength and love eventually help bring about repentance.

Production Data: Written 1920. First produced by John D. Williams at the Frazee Theatre, New York City, June 1, 1921 (13 performances).

Director: Homer Saint-Gaudens

Designer: Unknown

    Cast: Abel: Ashley Buck
           Butler: George Marion
           Captain Isaiah Bartlett: Willard Mack
           Silas Horne: J. Fred Holloway
           Ben Cates: Charles D. Brown
           Jimmy Kanaka: T. Tamamoto
           Mrs. Bartlett: Katherine Grey

Sue Bartlett: Geraldine O'Brien
Danny Drew: Charles Francis
Nat Bartlett: E. J. Ballantine
Dr. Berry: Scott Cooper

GOMEZ. In *The Movie Man,** general of the insurgents. He is tall and heavily built, with a bloated, dissipated-looking face and a bristly black mustache. He has signed a contract with Henry Rogers* of the Earth Motion Picture Company giving Rogers exclusive rights to film his battles in exchange for arms. He agrees to release a condemned prisoner, Ernesto Fernandez, in exchange for permission to fight a night battle, in violation of his film contract. He is drawn as a caricature of a Mexican general, drunken and irresponsible.

GRABER, Ben. In the scenario, *The Calms of Capricorn,** companion of Leda Cade* on the voyage of the clipper *Dream of the West*. He is fifty-three, a failed banker, with an aura of defeat about him. He is slightly unkempt and is usually drunk. He plays cards and usually loses, but at the end of the play he loses everything and then declares himself free of Leda, refusing Wolfe Harford's* offer of her when Wolfe wins her in the final stakes. Leda encourages Graber in his continual betting, pointing out that he is not yet free of his conscience. He may have lost every cent he stole for Leda, but he still has one possession—Leda herself—which he must also lose in order to be completely free.

GRAMMONT, Eugene. In *Bread and Butter.** Master of the art school attended by John Brown.* "He is a slight stoop-shouldered old man of sixty or more with a mass of wavy white hair and white mustache and imperial. His keen, black eyes peer kindly out of his lean ascetic face. He is dressed entirely in black with a white shirt and collar and a black Windsor tie." He looks foreign "but speaks English without an accent." So reads the stage direction, yet Grammont is given to exclaiming "Mon Dieu." He is extremely impressed with John Brown's talent and attempts to persuade Edward Brown, Sr.* to allow John to continue his studies. Mr. Brown, however, sees this genuine appeal as a crude attempt to bring him to keep paying his son's tuition so that Grammont will make more money. Grammont is also perceptive enough to see John's essential weakness—that he is too sensitive to fight against discouragement and opposition.

GREAT GOD BROWN, THE, a play in four acts, eleven scenes, with prologue and epilogue.
   Prologue: "The Pier of the Casino. Moonlight in Middle June." The set bears a curious resemblance to a courtroom, with benches on three sides and a rail at the back enclosing the wharf. It is the night of the high school commencement dance, and sentimental music is heard in the background as William A. Brown* enters with his mother and father. Billy Brown is an athletic-looking, wiry youth of eighteen, blonde, blue-eyed, with an open, pleasant face, the very

normal all-American boy. He is in evening dress. "The MOTHER is a dumpy woman of forty-five, overdressed in black lace and spangles. The FATHER is fifty or more, the type of bustling, genial, successful, provincial businessman, stout and hearty in his evening dress." Mrs. Brown* begins by criticizing the arrangements for the dance and then notes that Dion Anthony* was wearing "dirty flannel pants," which, it later appears, was to win a bet with Billy, a very disciplined, restrained young man who clearly admires Dion for being "a real sport." Mr. Brown,* Billy's father, and Mr. Anthony,* Dion's father, are the somewhat incompatible partners in a contracting firm, incompatible because Brown believes himself squelched by the other's conservatism. Mrs. Brown wants Billy to go to college and take up a profession, and Mr. Brown suggests architecture in order to extend the work of the firm. Billy, who has been listening at the rail, looking "like a prisoner at the bar," dutifully agrees and promises to work hard. The parents then leave to watch the dancing, and Billy follows meekly.

After a moment or two of silence, broken only by the sound of the music and the waves lapping against the pier, the Anthony family enters. Mr. Anthony "is a tall, lean man of fifty-five or sixty with a grim, defensive face, obstinate to the point of stupid weakness. The mother is a thin frail faded woman, her manner perpetually nervous and distraught, . . . [whose] sweet and gentle face" shows signs of past beauty. He is wearing a cheap, funereal, black suit; she is dressed in a cheap black dress. Following them, but "as if he were a stranger, walking alone, is their son, Dion," wearing an open-necked gray flannel sports shirt, dirty white flannel trousers, with his bare feet thrust into sneakers. He is wiry, like Billy, but seems nervous, and "his face is masked. The mask is a fixed forcing of his own face—dark, spiritual, poetic, passionately supersensitive, helplessly unprotected in its childlike, religious faith in life—into the expression of a mocking, defiant, gayly scoffing and sensual young Pan." The two halves of his personality, his soul, are expressed in his name: Dion for Dionysus and Anthony in the life-denying Saint Anthony, who was continually assailed by devils. He stands at the rail, where Billy had also stood, looking like a prisoner at the bar, but his air is one of "studied carelessness," which puzzles his parents.

Mrs. Anthony pleads with her husband to send Dion to college, but his father extolls the virtues of the school of hard knocks which helped him become a success. Dion interjects a blasphemously mocking remark: "This Mr. Anthony is my father, but he only imagines that he is God the Father." Like his partner, Mr. Anthony complains about the way the business is being run, that Brown is impractical; but when his wife informs him that Billy is going to college, Mr. Anthony changes his tune. He furiously orders Dion to go to college and become "a better architect than Brown's boy or I'll turn you out in the gutter without a penny!" Dion agrees, ironically pretending that the choice is difficult but stating that "architecture sounds less laborious." Mrs. Anthony, like Mrs. Brown, overrates her son's abilities; but where Billy says nothing, Dion becomes resentful, ironically thanking his father for the "opportunity to create myself—in my mother's image'' of upward mobility. He sits where his father had just sat, and his mask stares at them. To break the discomfort of the situation, Mrs. Anthony notes the chill in the June air, not as it was when she was carrying Dion. At that time she felt as if she were wrapped in the night "like a grey velvet gown." Mr. Anthony, practically, refers to his mother's superstition concerning the full moon and then complains of his rheumatism. As they exit, Dion bitterly says, "Hide! Be ashamed!" The father is bitterly hopeless, but the mother is proud, as Dion mocks them, cuts a grotesque caper, and exits. The Anthonys' reaction to the moonlight is quite different from that of the Browns, who remember their past Junes with a sense of affection. Curiously, Mrs. Brown recalls bathing in the moonlight, while Mrs. Anthony maternally recalls her pregnancy.

Again there is a silence except for the sound of the waves, and Margaret [Anthony*] enters, "followed by the humble worshiping Billy Brown." "She is a "pretty vivacious" blonde seventeen-year-old, "with big romantic eyes, her figure lithe and strong, her facial expression intelligent but youthfully dreamy." She is wearing a mask, a transparent one, almost the same as her own features, "giving her the abstract quality of a Girl" rather than her own self. She looks up at the moon and starts singing a song which Billy instantly identifies. He tries desperately to make conversation, but the topic moves from himself to Dion, and even when he manages to propose to Margaret, all she can think about is Dion. She loves Dion and considers Billy's love for her simply that of a big brother. Heartbroken, Billy starts to leave, promising always to be her "best friend" as Margaret confesses to annoyance that Billy is there when all she wants is Dion. Billy promises to send Dion, and Margaret speaks again to the moon: "I'll be Mrs. Dion—Dion's wife—and he'll be my Dion—my own Dion—my little boy—my baby." Her maternal, wifely attitude is here specifically shown as the character she will project throughout the rest of the action. She leaves, "her upturned unmasked face like that of a rapturous visionary."

Once again there is silence, except for the dance music and the waves, and Dion enters, walks quickly to the bench, sits down, hides his masked face in his hands, and asks why he must remain masked. Slowly he bares his face, asking why he cannot show his true self to the world, why is he afraid of love; why must he show scorn instead of pity? "Why was I born without a skin, O God, that I must wear armor in order to touch or be touched?" Then, after a short silence, he resumes his mask, covering his "shrinking, shy and gentle [countenance], full of a deep sadness," bitterly asking, "why the devil was I ever born at all?" At this moment Billy enters, telling him that Margaret has refused him and is in love with Dion. Sportingly, Billy says he is glad she loves his chum, but Dion is very flippant until Billy tells him that he knows his friend is in love with Margaret. Billy makes the suggestion that they room together at college and Dion says, "Billy wants to remain by her side." With a forced grin, full of hurt, Billy leaves.

Dion then goes to Margaret, who is waiting for him. In a rapture of joy he sees her as his protectress: "Her arms are softly around me! She is warmly around me! She is my skin! She is my armor! Now I am born—I—the I!—one and indivisible—I who love Margaret!" With this he looks at his mask, telling it he has outgrown it; he no longer needs it, for in this love he will need no mask. But just then Margaret enters, her mask in her hands, and fails to recognize Dion's own countenance. Only when he replaces his Pan-mask does she recognize or relate to him and say that she loves him. They embrace, and "with ironic mastery" Dion tells his love, draws her to him, kisses her, and then speaks of their dissolving "into dew—into silence—into night—into earth—into space— into peace—into meaning—into joy—into God—into the Great God Pan." At this moment of sexual union they will become one with nature in a Dionysiac ecstasy. A cloud has passed over the moon, and darkness ensues until Dion suddenly awakens to the world of reality: "Time to exist! . . . Learn to pretend! Cover your nakedness! Learn to lie! Learn to keep step! Join the Procession! Great Pan is dead! Be ashamed!" And that is exactly what Margaret says: "Oh, Dion, I am ashamed!" Afraid that Dion will hate her for giving herself to him, she weeps on his shoulder, and he passionately tears off his mask, attempting to embrace and comfort her in his own person. However, he only succeeds in frightening her and bitterly resumes his mask, proposing to her: "By proxy, I love you." And with a tender joking quality, he speaks the beginning of the marriage vows, asking "Mrs. Dion Anthony" for the next dance. With joy, Margaret repeats it, "You crazy child!" as they go out together.

Act I, Scene i: "Seven years later. The sitting room" of the Anthony home in one-half of a two-family house in a monotonously designed development. Four pieces of mass-produced furniture are in keeping with the house: armchair at left, table and chair at back-center, and a sofa at right, repeating the "courtroom effect" of the Prologue. The backdrop is painted with relentless realism. "It is afternoon of a gray day in winter." Dion is sitting at the table with his mask hanging around his neck. "His real face has aged greatly, grown more strained and tortured, but at the same time, . . . more selfless and ascetic, more fixed in its resolute withdrawal from life." The mask has also changed, becoming "older, more defiant and mocking, . . . its Pan quality becoming Mephistophelean. It has already begun to show the ravages of dissipation." Dion picks up the New Testament, puts his finger in at random, and reads, "Come unto Me all ye who are heavy laden and I will give you rest." At this moment, the Saint Anthony side of him speaks as he invokes the Savior. But as soon as he hears the sound of the outer door he claps on his mask of Pan, and the Dionysian, antichrist side of him takes control, mocking his faith.

Margaret enters, stylishly dressed, expensively and with a fur coat, but clearly the clothes have been remodeled and are well used. She is still pretty, fresh, and healthy and has grown maternal looking, but her face shows "the beginning of a permanently worried, apprehensive expression about the nose and mouth— an uncomprehending hurt in her eyes." She kisses him, reminding him that he was asleep when she had left. She has left the children with someone else rather than disturb Dion; she wishes he would take more interest in them, but then she treats him as if he is the oldest of her brood. As he says, he is in too ''delicate a condition'' to be a father before breakfast. After this initial sparring, Margaret starts to become practical, taxing Dion with continuing the hard drinking and gambling he had begun while they were abroad. Dion dropped out of college to marry Margaret when his father died and left him his share of the business. He sold out to Billy and his father, who has since died, so now Billy owns the entire establishment. Dion took the money with which he and Margaret have been living merrily abroad for the past five years, ''living and loving and having children.'' Now, however, they are very short of money, and Margaret mentions that she has seen Billy Brown in the street and he had commented that Dion had had the makings of a good architect—if only he had stuck to it. She suggests that he speak to Billy for the sake of the children, but Dion at first stands on his pride. Protectively, Margaret then says she will get a job in the library so that Dion can start his painting again, and reaches out to tell him again that she loves him. At this, Dion slumps into his chair, pulls off his mask, and with his saintly face he seems as if he is ''exorcizing a demon.'' ''Pride is dead! Blessed are the meek! Blessed are the poor in spirit!'' he quotes from the Sermon on the Mount. Margaret calls him a ''poor boy,'' and resuming his mask, Dion ''with wild mockery'' says he will go and ''implore'' Billy Brown ''to be a generous hero and save the woman and her children!'' With a laugh he leaves. Margaret asks him to do a couple of errands, and Dion says he will not return for dinner. She ''sighs with a tired incomprehension,'' goes over to the window and stares out, hoping, with practical maternal consideration, that the children will watch out when they cross the street.

   Act I, Scene ii: The office of Billy Brown at 5 P.M. The courtroom furniture arrangement continues, this time with a good mahogany desk in the center flanked by an armchair to the left and an office sofa to the right. The backdrop is a meticulously detailed rear wall. Billy Brown is seated at his desk, looking over some blueprints. He looks like a good, solid, clean-cut, college-trained business-man ''with the same engaging personality.'' The telephone rings, Billy registers surprise, and Margaret enters, wearing ''the mask of the pretty young matron, . . . [with] a bravely hopeful view of the world.'' She is dressed as in Scene i, but has taken a little extra care with her appearance. They exchange greetings, and Margaret remarks on how well Billy is doing. He says that it has been mostly luck, but then shows her his design for the new municipal building, which the committee wants touched up with ''an original touch of modern novelty,'' asking for her suggestions. She recalls how well Dion used to paint, and Billy, a trifle piqued, repeats that Dion would have made an excellent architect. Margaret, ever the proud wife, says he could be anything he wants to be, putting the best face on her family situation, lying loyally where necessary to obscure the truth. Brown embarrassedly inquires about their financial affairs, and Margaret acknowledges that she has applied for a library position. ''Won't it be fun! Maybe it'll improve my mind! And one of us has got to be practical, so why not me?'' Brown, touched, first offers help, but then, being rebuffed, he says that he has a proposition for Dion: "I need a crack draftsman darn badly." Margaret agrees that Dion might well consider it, but when Brown suggests that he "nail" down Dion right away, she becomes defensive about his whereabouts. As she leaves, Brown speaks admiringly of her and says he will "give Dion a good talking-to one of these days!"

Act I, Scene iii: Cybel's* parlor, "an automatic, nickel-in-the-slot player piano is at center, rear, on the right is a dirty gilt second-hand sofa. At the left is a bald-spotted crimson plush chair." The rear-wall backdrop "is cheap wall-paper of a dull yellow-brown, resembling a blurred impression of a fallow field in early spring. There is a cheap alarm clock on top of the piano," with Cybel's mask beside it. The semi-courtroom configuration remains but with the player piano at the center to indicate an emotional rather than a judicial, rational center for the scene, while the "fallow field" color also indicates a oneness with nature and the emotional life. The piano is playing sentimental "Mother-Mammy tunes" as Cybel is revealed seated at the stool. "She is a strong, calm, sensual blonde girl of twenty or so, her complexion fresh and healthy, her figure full-breasted and wide-hipped, her movements slow and stolidly langorous like an animal, her large eyes dreamy with the reflected stirring of profound instincts." She is the "earth-mother" type, whose name well befits her. She looks at Dion, sleeping on the sofa with his mask fallen onto his chest revealing his real face, which is "singularly pure, spiritual, and sad." Cybel looks at the clock as the piano runs down and then moves to awaken Dion.

He wakens with a start of surprise, first quotes from a healing New Testament passage, then, momentarily disoriented, reaches for his mask. Cybel tells him she had found him sleeping on her steps, and since she didn't want any more trouble from the police because of her profession as prostitute, she had taken him in to sleep it off. Dion mockingly thanks her for her pity, and she tells him to "beat it home to bed"; at this he again mocks her maternal instincts, "Miss Earth," and becomes superficially lyrical about the coolness of her hand. She looks at his mask and then calmly resumes hers, that of a "hardened prostitute." The masks look at each other, she starts the piano again, and then offers a truce: "Shoot! I'm all set! It's your play, Kid Lucifer," a significant epithet. Humbly, Dion removes his mask and she stops the music. He apologizes, "It has always been such agony for me to be touched." Cybel removes her mask and speaks with understanding and sympathy to him. Dion suddenly looks closely at her, perceiving a strength that he needs, and asks that they be friends; "And never nothing more?" says Cybel; "Let's say, never anything less," he replies.

At this, Brown rings the doorbell, having come to seek Dion. As Cybel goes out, with her mask in place, she smiles invitingly to Brown and tells him to come back sometime. Left alone, Billy and Dion start awkwardly, and then Billy offers Dion the proposition he had mentioned to Margaret. Dion is mocking, as usual: "Then my poor wife did a-begging go?" Billy angrily defends her, castigating Dion for his feckless behavior and telling him of Margaret's loyalty.

Dion then makes a fine distinction: "She was lying about her husband, not me, you fool!" Finally Dion, "wearily bitter," agrees to take the job: "One must do something to pass away the time, while one is waiting—for one's next incarnation." He then asks if his father's chair can be located; "I'd like to sit where he spun what I have spent," and Brown agrees to look for it.

Taking off his mask, Dion muses on his relations with other human beings. He and his father were "aliens," and only in death did Mr. Anthony's face seem familiar—as it must have been at the moment of Dion's conception. He remembers his mother "as a sweet, strange girl, with affectionate bewildered eyes as if God had locked her in a dark closet without any explanation." Dion was her doll, and she played the role of mother and child in the household until she died "with the shy pride of one who has lengthened her dress and put up her hair." As a result of his alienation, Dion "shrank away back into life," supersensitive to it, until he met another girl, Margaret, who married him "and became three mothers in one person, while I got paint on my paws in an endeavor to see God." Dion here seems to mean that Margaret is a composite of his own mother, the mother of his children, and the Virgin-Mother, perhaps also with overtones of Faust's Marguérite, or Gretchen, since they share the same name. Now, Dion says, he must follow another god, that of material success embodied by "the Omnipresent Successful One, the Great God, Mr. Brown." As they leave, Dion blasphemously parodies, "I am thy shorn, bald, nude sheep! Lead on, Almighty Brown, thou Kindly Light!" He will now serve the God of Material Success.

Act II, Scene i: Seven years later, spring, about sunset. Cybel's parlor has changed. The furniture arrangement is the same as in Act I, but the pieces are new and expensive, except for the player piano with the alarm clock and the masks of Dion and Cybel on either side. The backdrop is now brilliant wallpaper with flowers and fruits in profusion. Dion is sitting in the chair on the left and Cybel on the sofa with a card table between them. They are each playing solitaire, a symbolic indication of their separateness.

Dion has aged noticeably; his hair is gray and his face has become "that of an ascetic, a martyr, furrowed by pain and self-torture, yet lighted from within by a spiritual calm and human kindliness." The Saint Anthony side of him now dominates his real countenance, his real self. Cybel has grown heavier, "more voluptuous," and has the aspect of "an unmoved idol of Mother Earth." Cybel remarks that hearing the old "sob tunes" makes her understand people because they reveal what is inside: "crying jags set to music." Dion replies that "every song is a hymn. They keep trying to find the Word in the Beginning." Cybel speaks of the necessity of keeping one's real self hidden in order "to keep our real virtue." People try to know too much, but she has given them an image, that of a tart, and that they can handle and understand. With this she wins her solitaire game, telling Dion that the game knows he still wants to win and therefore thwarts him, whereas since she merely plays for the sake of the game, she wins. In other words, she accepts life as a game and cares little for it, while

Dion is still desperately trying to play his solitary game to win. He has not learned renunciation fully, but Cybel can take life as it is, insulated against its shocks by a unity with its rhythms. The sensitivity which still bedevils Dion is clearly shown when Cybel mentions Mr. Brown's dislike of the player piano. He despises its shabby appearance and cares nothing for what is inside it. He has been keeping Cybel for the past seven years, and she evaluates him as handsome but "too guilty. What makes you pretend you think love is so important, anyway? It's just one of the things you do to keep life living." She is happy with the relationship she and Dion have had; and as he goes to her she removes his mask, and he lays his head in her lap as she comforts him like a mother: "You were brave enough to look into your own dark—and you got afraid." Cybel, the earth-mother, knows the secret of life; what is important is "the you inside." Everything else is worthless. Dion sadly says that she has given him the strength to die.

He kneels to pray "with an ascetic fervor": "Into thy hands, O Lord." But then fear overcomes him and he claps on his mask, laughing and quoting Shelley's invocation to death; "Swift be thine approaching flight! Come soon—soon!" Cybel consoles him by saying that "when the time comes, you'll find it's easy." Dion then confesses that he is very ill; the doctor has warned him never to drink again, or he will risk death. At this, he suggests they should drink together. Cybel tells him to do so, to please himself, but she then asks about the cathedral plans about which he had been raving. Dion replies in a wildly mocking manner that they have been accepted: Brown does the mathematically correct "barns" for his clients while Dion "doctor[s] them up with cute allurements." This he does with "devilish cleverness." Once he had dreams, "but pride is a sin"; and as he quotes the Sermon on the Mount, "blessed are the poor in spirit," he "subsides weakly on his chair, his hand pressed to his heart." Cybel sends him home to sleep, and he speaks mockingly of Margaret's loyalty and also of the way Brown seems to need him: in keeping Cybel, "he wanted what he thought was my love of the flesh!" Brown steals Dion's ideal, but Cybel replies, "You're brothers, I guess, somehow," suggesting that Brown will pay one way or another. Momentarily, Dion permits himself some sympathy for Brown and asks forgiveness for the wrong he has done him. Then "with forced harshness" he leaves: "Well, homeward Christian Soldier! I'm off! Bye-bye, Mother Earth!" Suddenly Cybel calls him back, asking him to kiss her without his mask. Gently removing it, she says in a maternal manner, "Haven't I told you to take off your mask in the house?" Obviously realizing that she will never see him again, she tells him to "remember it's all a game, and after you're asleep I'll tuck you in." With a heartbroken cry, Dion calls her "Mother"; but then returning his mask "with a terrible effort," he leaves on a mocking note: "Go to the devil, you sentimental old pig! See you tomorrow." He exits whistling. Cybel, as the earth-mother idol, asks, "What's the good of bearing children? What's the use of giving birth to death?"

As she sits wearily before the piano, listening to the sentimental tunes she has started, Billy Brown, now a prosperous, well-groomed forty, enters too quickly for her to replace her mask. He starts to castigate her for having broken her word and having seen Dion, but then he looks at her real face as if she is a stranger and does not recognize her. Cybel instantly begins a charade, claiming that she is Cybel's sister and that she was entertaining Dion. Brown is relieved and soon finds himself confiding in this unknown woman. When Cybel teases him with loving Margaret and helping Dion for that reason, Brown at first denies Cybel's allegations and then wonders what it is that makes Dion so attractive to women: his looks, his sensuality, his wildness? Cybel replies cryptically, ''He's alive!'' Brown, unable to understand that Cybel is referring to the agony of living, then suggests that he keep her also, as he has Cybel. Perhaps he can buy what Dion is able to obtain for himself. Perhaps he can supplant Dion. But Cybel refuses, telling him that ''Cybel'' will be back soon; and in reply to Brown, the unmasked lady swears she will never see Dion again—for she knows that he left her as a dead man. With that assurance, Brown leaves jubilantly.

Act II, Scene ii: ''The drafting room in Brown's office.'' The same pattern of furniture arrangement persists. Dion's drafting table with a high stool before it is at the center, a stool to the left and a sofa to the right. The backdrop has windows and a view of houses across a dimly lighted street. Dion is seated at his table, reading aloud to his mask from *The Imitation of Christ* of Thomas à Kempis, the meditation on death, while ''his own face is gentler, more spiritual, more saintlike and ascetic than ever before.'' He looks tenderly at his mask: ''Peace, poor tortured one, brave pitiful pride of man, the hour of our deliverance comes. Tomorrow we may be with Him in Paradise.'' He kisses his mask and sets it down, but then as he hears footsteps coming up the stairs, he claps it to his face ''in a sudden panic.'' A knock is heard at the door, and Dion calls out mockingly, ''Come in, Mrs. Anthony, come in!'' Margaret enters, carrying behind her back her ''mask of the brave face she puts on before the world to hide her suffering and disillusionment. . . . Her own face is still sweet and pretty, but lined, drawn and careworn . . . sad, resigned, but a bit querulous.''

She is relieved to find him, but wearily reproves him for staying out and drinking for the past two days. She has sent the boys out to look for him and asks him to come home. She will make him some food. With wonderment, Dion asks, ''Can Margaret still love Dion Anthony?'' and Margaret replies ''I suppose I do, Dion. I certainly oughtn't to, had I?'' Dion, in that same tone of wonder, says, ''And I love Margaret!'' He looks back to their ghostly past, and they kiss, Margaret gently upbraiding him for ''all you've made me go through in the years since we settled down here.'' Only the existence of the boys has made things possible for her, but then I've always been such a big fool about you.'' Dion speaks mockingly of Margaret's ability to be magnanimous—with ''three strong sons!'' Margaret says that they are coming to meet her at the office if they have not found their father first, and at this news, Dion sinks to his knees: ''Margaret! Margaret! I'm lonely! I'm frightened! I'm going away! I've got to say good-by.'' Margaret pats him on the head and treats him as her ''poor boy!''

telling him to come home to sleep. She does not understand, so Dion springs up again. He is not her boy but a man; he begs her to look at him: "It's the last chance! Tomorrow I'll have moved on to the next hell! Behold your man—the sniveling, cringing, life-denying Christian slave you have so nobly ignored in the father of your sons!" He tears the mask from his face, which is radiant with a great pure love for her and begs her forgiveness for the wrongs he has done her. But Margaret, unable to understand the reality beneath the appearance, is terrified by the face that is revealed to her. As before, in the Prologue at the casino, she does not recognize the real Dion: "You're like a ghost! You're dead!" She falls back, onto the bench, and Dion takes her hand with the mask, looks at it, kissing first the mask and then her face: "Thrice blessed are the meek!" Heavy footsteps are heard on the stair, and Dion replaces his mask. The three boys enter; they are aged about fourteen, thirteen, and twelve, healthily normal in the all-American, Billy Brown mold. They stop, startled, not recognizing their mother without her mask, but they had heard her cry out. When Dion replaces her mask, they run to her. Dion then tells them he must visit Mr. Brown's house to "pay him a farewell call" and asks the boys to look after Margaret: "You must inherit the earth for her. Don't forget now, boys. Good-by." And the boys self-consciously reply, in order, "Good-by."

Act II, Scene iii: "The library of William Brown's home—night of the same day." The backdrop is one of bourgeois prosperity and culture—bookcases with expensive bindings in sets, for example. The furniture follows the same pattern: expensive table in the middle, leather armchair at left, and sofa on the right—all "opulently comfortable." Brown is sitting in the chair, reading from an architectural journal, and looking as monumental as a "Roman consul on an old coin." A loud knocking is heard on the front door, and Dion is heard to say, "Tell him it's the devil come to conclude a bargain." When Dion enters, he is disheveled and his mask looks "deathlike . . . its mocking irony becomes so cruelly malignant as to give him the appearance of a real demon, tortured into torturing others." Brown asks him to sit down and tells him to be quiet for the sake of the neighbors. Dion then speaks with "deadly calm," recalling the day that Billy Brown had ruined the picture he had been drawing in the sand when he was a mere four years old. When Dion had wept, he had been called a "cry baby," but what he was crying for was the loss of his faith in a friend, another human being, and in the God who permitted such injustice. From that day on, Dion fashioned for himself the "mask of the Bad Boy Pan in which to live and rebel against that other boy's God and protect himself from his cruelty." As a result, Billy Brown, secretly ashamed, went on to become "the good boy, the good friend, the good man, William Brown!"

Billy shamefacedly remembers the incident and then offers Dion a drink. As he downs it, to Brown's disapproval ("It's your funeral!"), Dion announces that for the past week he had been celebrating the success of *his* design for the cathedral. Brown teasingly remarks that he had indeed helped a lot on it, but Dion turns on him: "Brown will still need me—to reassure me that he's alive!"

He believes himself to have been life's lover, one who gave himself fully to the living of life, "and the only reason she's [life] through with me now is because I was too weak to dominate her in turn." Brown, says Dion, has merely lived a neutral, duty-ridden life, following a conventional mode of existence, and will "never live until his liberated dust quickens into earth." Brown has stolen Dion's creative life, because he has a "question mark of insecurity in his blood," and now Dion wants to see what will happen as that consumes him. In reply to Brown's comment that Dion is sometimes evil when he is drunk, Dion replies, "When Pan was forbidden the light and warmth of the sun he grew self-conscious and proud and revengeful—and became Prince of Darkness." This, apparently, is the motivation for Dion's mode of existence, and now at the hour of his death, Dion reveals it to Billy Brown. In this moment he reveals the obscene trick he has played in his design for the cathedral. "It's one vivid blasphemy from sidewalk to the tips of its spires!—but so concealed that the fools will never know. They'll kneel and worship the ironic Silenus who tells them the best good is never to be born." However, blasphemy itself is a faith, and faith is something that Brown has never had. "He only believes in the immortality of the moral belly!" Then Dion utters his curse that from this time on, Brown will not be able to design anything, "He will devote his life to renovating the house of my Cybel into a home for my Margaret!" Dion twists the knife in the wound, asking why no woman has ever loved Brown, "why has he tried to steal Cybel, as he once tried to steal Margaret? Isn't it out of revenge and envy?" Why has Brown had no children? Slowly he dissects Brown's life with its success and its inner emptiness. Money could not buy Cybel, who loved Dion better than Brown could understand. Brown cannot love; he does not really love Margaret. "Brown loves me! He loves me because I have always possessed the power he needed for love, because I am love!" With this, Brown leaps on Dion and tells him he is looking into a mirror to see himself. Dion then speaks his "last will and testament," bequeathing Dion Anthony to Brown, who will then become Dion in order that Margaret and her sons may love Brown in Dion's image. With this, Dion's mask falls off, and his "Christian Martyr's face at the point of death" is revealed. His words are again from the Sermon on the Mount, "Blessed are the meek and the poor in spirit," an interesting conflation because the first "shall possess the earth" and the second "shall see God." Brown begins the Pater Noster, and the dying Dion begins, "Our Father," and dies.

Brown looks with contempt on the real face of his dead friend and rival: "So that's the poor weakling you really were! No wonder you hid! And I've always been afraid of you— . . . in awe of you." He looks at "this man who willed himself to me," and "struck by an idea," he starts to don Dion's mask but, when he hears a knocking at the door, puts it back on the table. But he picks it up again, takes Dion's body and carries it off to bury it in his garden. He reappears almost instantly to ask who is at the door, only to find that it is Margaret, who has come looking for Dion. She enters wearing her mask, accompanied by the three boys, and Brown tells her that Dion is sleeping, just tired, for he has said he has sworn off drinking. Margaret is thrilled but then defends Dion as a light drinker. Brown leaves, and the boys and Margaret discuss Mr. Brown, whom the boys obviously admire. Margaret sends them home as Brown enters, dressed in Dion's clothes and wearing his mask. Margaret greets "Dion" joyfully and congratulates him on his vow to give up liquor. "Give Mother a kiss," she says, but Brown kisses her with real sexuality which arouses her, much to her surprise: "You haven't kissed me like that in ages." Brown's reply, "I've always wanted to, Margaret," brings her to think of a miracle. Perhaps he was afraid she would spurn him, she says, but now, with "Dion" restored, she no longer needs her mask, which she throws away to embrace him as they walk to the door.

Act III, Scene i: "The drafting room and private office of Brown are shown," on left and right respectively, with a dividing wall down the center. The furniture is arranged as in the previous scenes. It is 10 A.M. about one month later. "The backdrop for both rooms is of plain wall with a few tacked-up designs and blueprints painted on it." Two Draftsmen are discussing the eccentric behavior of William Brown "ever since he fired Dion." He has also fired all his servants and uses his home just as a place in which to sleep. Curiously, Dion has been seen in his own home, looking sober and fine.

Unexpectedly, Margaret enters. She no longer needs to wear a mask because her face has regained the prettiness and confidence of her youth. She asks to see Dion, even though she knows that Brown has given orders that Dion must not be disturbed. The Draftsmen are nonplussed when Margaret announces that "Dion" goes to the office daily. At this moment Brown enters, wearing a mask that is the exact copy of his own features. He greets Margaret, confuses the Draftsmen even more by speaking of how busy Dion is, and then invites her into his office. Margaret asks for an explanation, while Brown says that "Dion" is working very hard on his designs for the new state capitol and that he, Brown, will give him full credit and take him into partnership once the designs are accepted. After that, Brown plans to go to Europe for a couple of years and leave "Dion" in charge. Margaret says that "Dion" has indeed told her of these plans, and she is now exceedingly happy. But momentarily Brown slips and starts to sound like "Dion," and when Margaret notices, "he tears off his mask to reveal a suffering face that is ravaged and haggard, his own face tortured and distorted by the demon of Dion's mask." He tells Margaret he loves her and begs her to go away with him, but Margaret is appalled by what she both sees and hears. Brown replaces his mask with the explanation that he is on the verge of a nervous breakdown. As she leaves, asking him not to work Dion too hard, Brown takes off the mask, looks at it, and realizes that he is "dead beyond hope of resurrection." Dion has usurped his innermost self and has killed his identity. Now he enjoys "Paradise by Proxy! Love by mistaken identity!" But, and this is most important, he does indeed love. His musings are interrupted by a Client who wants to have Brown's design for his house revised to make it more livable, less "like a tomb." The Client recalls that he has heard that Anthony, who used to do such things, has been fired, but Brown suavely denies this, saying that Mr. Anthony is still with him but doesn't want that known. Certainly he will revise the design.

Act III, Scene ii: "The library of Brown's home about eight the same night." Brown fumbles his way across the room, turning on the reading lamp, to reveal Dion's mask on a stand directly under it. Brown removes his own mask and puts it on the table in front of Dion's, "flings himself down in the chair and stares . . . into the eyes of Dion's mask." Then he begins to speak of the narrow escape "they" had had earlier in the day. He has already made his will and now must run off to Europe and murder Mr. William Brown there so that Billy Brown, in the mask of Dion, can live "happily ever after" with Margaret. She will bear his children. Already, Brown claims, Margaret and her sons love him more than ever they did Dion. Someday, Brown will reveal all, when Dion is forgotten and when Margaret will have come to know and understand what is beneath the mask. But then a moment of fear strikes him as the mask seems to tell him otherwise. In despair he calls on God, quoting from the Sermon on the Mount: "Blessed are the merciful! Let me obtain mercy!" He reaches out to the mask of Dion, and as he holds it he seems to gain strength to love from it. "Then, with bravado," he invites the mask to come with him: "I need the devil when I'm in the dark!" After his departure he can be heard saying that Dion's clothes now fit him better than his own. When he reappears, having changed clothes, he again invites the mask to come with him to see his triumph—but then he kisses it: "I love you because she loves you." And in his Dion mask he leaves by the back way, for secrecy is essential.

Act III, Scene iii: The sitting room of Margaret's house. She is sitting on the sofa waiting the arrival of Dion. She seems young once more and deeply in love. She hears the door, rushes to it, and embraces Brown/Dion. She recalls the commencement dance, and Brown winces with pain while Margaret expounds on her recent happiness. Everything is just as it was when they were first married. All those years she had felt that Dion was lost and that she could do nothing to help him, but now "you're my long-lost lover, and my husband, and my big boy too!" The Anthony boys are all out at a dance, and Margaret tells how much they have enjoyed their father in his new manifestation, a comment that makes Brown weep. When Margaret remarks on that, Brown asks her whether she had ever known "Dion to cry about anyone?" And Margaret replies, "You couldn't—then. You were too lonely. You had no one to cry to." Brown then says he must work, and he mentions Margaret's unannounced visit, at which she says that "the Great God Brown" is becoming rather eccentric and should take a vacation. His face had scared her because it looked like that of a corpse, and he had declared his love. She found it "too disgusting for words to hear him." The masked Brown, in "a show of tortured derision," then promises to kill Brown for her; but finally, he controls himself, pats her on the head, and says, "Mr. Brown is now safely in hell. Forget him!" As the curtain falls,

Brown is preparing to dress up the state capitol: "We'll adroitly hide old Silenus on the cupola." He is becoming more and more like Dion.

Act IV, Scene i: Same as Act III, Scene i. Brown, wearing his Dion mask, with his own on the table beside him, has just finished the plans of the state capitol. He has incorporated his own blasphemy into them: "Only to me will that pompous façade reveal itself as the wearily ironic grin of Pan." With that he starts dancing goatishly around his office, putting himself in all the state offices: "Oh, how many persons in one God make up the good God Brown?" The Draftsmen outside wonder together, while Brown replaces the Dion-mask with his own, momentarily revealing his real countenance which is "sick, ghastly, tortured, hollow-cheeked and feverish-eyed." In anguish he wonders, "Why am I not strong enough to perish—or blind enough to be content?" and asks for the strength to destroy both Dion and himself.

At this moment, Margaret enters to castigate Brown for working Dion too hard. To her surprise, Brown seems irrational, perhaps drunk, and even makes difficulty about her seeing Dion. Then, recovering himself, he exits and returns as Dion, saying that he will get Brown off to Europe as soon as he can. He is "soused to the ears all the time! Soused on life! He can't stand it! It's burning his insides out!" Suddenly, Margaret notices that the clothes "Dion" is wearing are those of Brown, but she is calmed by Brown's excuse: "It's his! We're getting to be like twins. I'm inheriting his clothes already!" The committee of the state government, three important-looking gentlemen, then enter, and "Dion," telling Margaret to receive them, leaves to return as Brown. In his absence, Margaret tells the delegation that the design was entirely the work of Dion Anthony. Discovering that Brown has not given "Dion" any credit, Margaret speaks of her hatred of Brown, who, however, corroborates Margaret's statement, saying that he had planned to surprise the Committeemen with the announcement of Dion's part. Then he openly attacks the design, pointing out the blasphemous insult that it embodies: "An insult to you, to Margaret—and to Almighty God." He tears the plans to pieces, and Margaret picks them up and hugs them to her, calling for Dion. Brown skips out to return as Dion, who consoles Margaret: "A little paste, Margaret! . . . And all will be well! Life is imperfect, Brothers! Men have their faults, Sister! But with a few drops of glue much may be done! . . . Man is born broken. He lives by mending. The grace of God is glue!" Then he prances out to the Draftsmen telling them to look in the little room for Mr. William Brown who is dead. The terrified employees run out and then return, carrying the mask of William Brown as if it were a body. The Committeemen watch in horror and then go for the police as Margaret proclaims Dion's innocence.

Act IV, Scene ii: Brown's library. The mask of Dion is on the table, and kneeling beside the table, facing front, is Brown, who has stripped himself almost naked in a symbolic renunciation of life's materialism, while he tries to pray. "Finally a voice seems torn out of him," and he cries out to the "Compassionate Savior" for mercy. Hearing no answer, he turns to mocking despair,

wishing the whole world to suffer as he is suffering. The door is pushed open
and Cybel enters, looking stouter and even more like an idol. She takes off her
own mask and then looks from Brown to the Dion mask and understands: "You
are Dion Brown!" Brown explains himself as "the remains of William Brown!
I am his murderer and his murdered." Cybel has come to warn him to flee:
"They've got to quiet their fears, to cast out their devils, . . . They've got to
absolve themselves by finding a guilty one!" Billy, naked, "must be Satan."
But Billy, tired of running, opens the windows as the sound of pursuit draws
near, puts on the Dion-mask, and invites the shots of the police. Cybel picks
him up, puts him on the couch, and removes the Dion-mask: "You've got to
sleep alone." When Margaret enters, she takes the mask from the table where
Cybel has left it and kisses it heartbrokenly. The puzzled Police Captain then
asks Cybel how she came to be here and asks the name of the dying man. Cybel
answers "Billy," and removing her mask, she sits down at his head, helping
him into death like a mother comforting a child. Billy starts the Pater Noster
and then in his death-vision sees joy after pain: "Only he that has wept can
laugh!" Out of the pains of earth comes the laughter of man, and those pains
have sprung from the laughter of heaven, words which repeat those of Nietzsche's
conclusion to *The Birth of Tragedy*. At this he dies. Cybel kisses him gently,
arranges his body, and speaks of the coming of spring, bearing life and its
seasonal cycle: "always, love and conception and birth and pain again—spring
bearing the intolerable chalice of life again." "She stands like an idol of Earth,
her eyes staring out over the world." Margaret kisses the Dion-mask: "You're
not dead, sweetheart! You can never die till my heart dies! You will live forever!
You will sleep under my heart. I will feel you stirring in your sleep, forever
under my heart." The Police Captain crudely interrupts this scene by asking the
name of the victim, and to Cybel's reply, "Man," he asks, "How d'yuh spell
it?" Even in death Billy Brown has no identity.

Epilogue: It is four years later, in the same spot on the same dock as in the
Prologue. Once again there is a dance, and this time Margaret, wearing the
"mask of proud, indulgent Mother," enters with her three boys. She is beautiful,
but older, and somehow a trifle lonely having accomplished her maternal purpose
in life. She echoes Dion's mother's words about "the Junes when I was carrying
you boys" and then sends them off to their girls, admonishing them always to
remember their father. She looks at the moon and the waves, again expressing
her yearning and love for Dion. Then she takes out the Dion-mask and addresses
it in the very words she used at Billy Brown's death, wishing Dion to sleep
"forever under my heart." She, the mother-figure, wishes to carry him with her
as if in her womb, forever as her child.

Comments: This play represents one of O'Neill's most interesting experiments
in expressionism, and it is also one of his most poetic plays though, in justice,
one must admit that at times poetry declines into bombast or prosiness (one
wonders about "the grace of God is glue"). The playwright had experimented
with the use of masks in *The Fountain*,* where some of the apparitions are

masked, and also in *The Hairy Ape*,* where, however, their use was suggested by the costumer of the Provincetown Players. Later, O'Neill wished he had made more use of masks in the latter play, and in *The Great God Brown*, he made full-dress use of the device. He later explained his purpose in using masks in a famous article written in defense of *Days Without End**: "One's outer life passes in a solitude haunted by the masks of others; one's inner life passes in a solitude hounded by the masks of oneself." ("Memoranda on Masks," 1932, reprinted in Cargill, 1961). To some extent, it is the masks which have attracted critics so much to this play, but there are also times when their use becomes virtuosic or clumsy, rather than communicative, and they even hinder the development of the action. Part of the problem may be that O'Neill does not fully seem to trust his audience. He uses the expressionistic technique of masks but at the same time takes care to ground the action in very specific realism. For instance, the backdrop of each scene is usually very realistic, with the exception of the "fallow field" color in the initial view of Cybel's room; the interior furnishings are also very realistic, but with a touch of expressionism signified by the court-room arrangement in each scene. The characters are in effect on trial throughout the play. But then, after Brown assumes the mask of Dion, O'Neill seems to want things both ways simultaneously. When Margaret appears to see "Dion," she is given a plausible, though rather irrelevant, excuse to visit Brown's office. And again, when Brown suddenly reappears as Dion, Margaret notes the similarity of their clothing, which Brown/Dion explains as their becoming like twins. In true expressionism, such realistic details are superfluous. Similarly, the repeated exits and entrances of Brown in the last two acts in order to recostume and remask himself become almost farcical because of the mixed-mode approach O'Neill has chosen.

But why does O'Neill use masks, and what is their purpose? By their use, he wants to show the individual human's conflict among the soul, the spirit, and the adaptations each person must make in order to exist. One must wear a mask: in order to avoid hurt, as in the case of Dion; to hide secret sorrow, as with Margaret; to preserve integrity and respond to an imposed image, as with Cybel; and additionally, as with both Dion and Brown, to signify the conflict within the individual human being. But in this last situation, the use of masks is a trifle inconsistent and even a little muddling, particularly in the case of Dion Anthony. His very name indicates a dichotomous existence: Dion, which stands for Dionysian ecstasy and subversion of established order—almost an antichrist—and Anthony, which stands for the ascetic, almost masochistic Saint Anthony, whose temptations have a lurid life of their own and seem almost Dionysian but must be rejected. But at the same time, Dion's mask and attitude are made to signify something not quite clear. As he grows older, his mask becomes demonic, almost Mephistophelean, but his true face becomes ascetic, purified into a renunciation of life. The psychological and spiritual conflict is then to be shown by the change of both mask and man, but the gulf between the two finally seems almost unbridgeable. As Travis Bogard (1972, p. 265) suggests, the wearing of masks is a kind of enforcement, for they cannot be removed, and man is in the position of Marcel Marceau's famous mask maker who finds himself panic stricken, unable to escape the mask he has fashioned. O'Neill said that his aim in the use of these masks was to convey the psychological depths of individual characters, to objectify the invisible and even the incommunicable.

Obviously, all the characters have symbolic force: Dion, as O'Neill said in a letter to the New York *Evening Post* (February 26, 1926), is "creative pagan acceptance of life, fighting eternal war with the masochistic, life-denying spirit of christianity." But Dion's own acceptance of life is at best questionable. He also echoes the character of the failed artist, John Brown,* in *Bread and Butter*,* O'Neill's first full-length work, while Billy Brown recalls John's father, Edward Brown, Sr.,* and also Marco Polo* in *Marco Millions*.* He is the crass materialist who cares nothing for art, lacks imagination, and is a total pragmatist. However, William Brown does have some capacity for love in a self-sacrificing manner and in this way reminds one of the romanticism of Juan Ponce de Leon* in *The Fountain*.* Even in Brown there are elements of Dionysus, and therefore he is so envious of Dion that he adopts his friend's mask, almost becoming his "twin," something neither of the earlier plays' characters would ever have done. However, in each case, O'Neill does not take his anti-christ-Dionysus theme to its logical conclusion, in Brown's case becoming too bogged down in the practicalities of costume-changes, wills, and economics.

O'Neill has returned to the Nietzschean opposition of Dionysus and Apollo which he had used in *Desire Under the Elms*,* and embodied them in the opposition of Dion and Brown. But he has somewhat muddled the issue, first by putting the same dichotomy into a Christian framework with Apollo/Saint Anthony, within Dion, and making a different opposition of Dionysus/materialistic Brown, who then takes on some aspects of Christian self-sacrifice. To some extent, O'Neill's symbolism gets away from him, but it always remains suggestive, even if a trifle inconsistent because the opposition of Dion and Brown is so blurred that one can feel sympathy for both characters and total commitment to neither. To be sure, one ought not to look for absolute and complete answers to living in this play, but O'Neill invites, even raises, questions and then draws back from offering answers. Moreover, the play does lose both intensity and focus after the death of Dion, for the audience must now feel sympathy for the materialistic "Great God Brown."

In addition to his debt to Nietzsche, O'Neill demonstrates other influences: in his use of Goethe's *Faust* for the character of Margaret, the Gretchen of Goethe, and the Marguérite of Barbier and Carré in Gounod's opera. She is "three mothers in one person," a female trinity, representing the replacement mother of Dion, the physical mother of his three children, and the everlasting maternal principle, symbolized by both the Virgin Mother and Margaret/Gretchen, with aspects of the Nietzschean woman whose sole purpose it is to continue the race. Yet Margaret also includes elements of several other earlier O'Neill characters: she is Maud Steele* in *Bread and Butter*, the extremely practical, materialistic, unimaginative girl who destroys the artist in John Brown; she is also Ruth Atkins* Mayo in *Beyond the Horizon** who turns Robert Mayo* aside from the fulfillment of his dream and destroys both him and his brother, Andrew Mayo.* However, in her loyalty and service, Margaret reminds one of Alice Roylston* in *Servitude*,* and in her ecstatic view of marriage, she recalls Eleanor Cape* at the end of *Welded*.* But above all else she is a mother-figure, as is shown in her final words which repeat her eulogy over her dead hero, "Dion," at the end of Act IV. Here she very specifically refers to a pregnancy image, to a desire to keep her Dion, her boy, forever living under her heart. Once again, the attitude of the playwright is ambivalent, and one must ask whether she is to be an affirmative creature or a destructively blind figure; and yet one must have sympathy for her, whatever the verdict.

The truly important figure for this play is that of Cybel, and curiously, she is probably the least well developed. Her name is significant as that of the mother-goddess of Asia, and she is clearly designed as a pagan opposition to the Margaret-trinity of Christian mothers. Therefore, she is a prostitute, outside the realm of society's approval, but she is the symbol of a oneness with nature, of that Dionysian unity with the pulse of creation which Dion Anthony seeks through one side of his personality. The "fallow field" color of the backdrop of her room initially reveals that oneness with nature, and as the play progresses, she becomes more and more like an idol of Mother Earth, attuned to the rhythm of the seasons, of birth, growth, and even death. Always, in the spring there is rebirth, and in this way she is the symbol of hope for the play, and it is through her that both Dion and Brown are reconciled to their fate, even seeing that final vision, summed up in the beatitudes of the Sermon on the Mount: "Blessed are they that weep, for they shall laugh." Thus O'Neill looks ahead to his next effort, *Lazarus Laughed*.* Cybel, then, is the expansive female principle, that of creative unity with nature and immersion in the rhythms of existence, as opposed to Margaret, who is the more limited creature, embodying the principle of racial continuance, of strangulating maternity, and of sorrowing virgin-mother victim.

The play itself is, like Cybel, a structural celebration of circularity, of repetition, of continuity. It ends as it began, with a high school commencement dance, in the same place, with echoes of the words of the Prologue, and simply a different cast of characters, ready to set off and make the same mistakes. As in the Prologue, and throughout the play, the sets have a curious relationship to a courtroom, for mankind is on trial throughout his pilgrimage of life, that pilgrimage mentioned by Thomas à Kempis in the "Meditation on Death" from *The Imitation of Christ*. Comfort for mankind only comes, so O'Neill seems to say, from the renunciation of life spoken of in the New Testament and by à Kempis; yet always there is Cybel to celebrate earth and its continuity as individual man passes through it on his spiritual journey.

Overall, this play has immense importance in the O'Neill canon because it shows him as attempting a great deal more than mere entertainment or experimental art theatre approaches. Now he is trying to forge a theology to communicate a philosophy and to force his audience into the rigors and terrors of thought to reassess the human condition.

Production Data: Written 1925. Produced by Kenneth Macgowan,* Robert Edmond Jones,* and Eugene O'Neill at the Greenwich Village Theatre, New York City, January 23, 1926. Moved to the Garrick Theatre, New York City, March 1, 1926, and the Klaw Theatre, New York City, May 10, 1926 (total performances, 283).

Director: Robert Edmond Jones
Designer: Robert Edmond Jones
Cast: William A. Brown: William Harrigan
      His Father: Milano Tilden
      His Mother: Clifford Sellers
      Dion Anthony: Robert Keith
      His Father: Hugh Kidder
      His Mother: Eleanor Wesselhoeft
      Margaret: Leona Hogarth
      Cybel: Anne Shoemaker
      Margaret's Sons: Starr Jones, Paul Jones, Teddy Jones
      Draftsmen: Frederick C. Packard, Jr., John Mahin
      Client: Seth Kendall
      Committeemen: Stanley Barry, Adrian Marsh, William Stahl
      Police Captain: Ellsworth Jones
      Margaret's Sons (four years later): Tupper Jones, Starr Jones, Paul Jones

Revived October 6, 1959, at the Coronet Theatre, New York City, (32 performances).

Revived December 10, 1972, at the Lyceum Theatre, New York City, New Phoenix Repertory Co. (19 performances).

[*See also* Appendix B for song with words from this play; also a ballet scenario by Beatrice Laufer.]

"GREED OF THE MEEK," the proposed first play in the abandoned cycle "A Tale of Possessors, Self-Dispossessed."* This play, apparently covering the period 1755–1775 introduces the Harford family and carries them from the farm to the eve of the American Revolution. O'Neill slowly began to realize that this play ought to be divided in two. He finally destroyed the completed longhand draft in February 1943. This play (often cited as "The Greed of the Meek") was originally entitled "Give Me Death" and was then the first play of the nine-play version of the cycle. It received its new title from the first play of the eight-play version of the cycle.

GRUENBERG, Louis (1884–1964), composer. Born August 3, 1884, in Brest-Litovsk, Russia; died in Beverly Hills, California, June 9, 1964. Composer-librettist of the operatic adaptation of *The Emperor Jones* (1933; *see* Appendix B). Brought to the United States in 1885. Studied piano with Adele Margulies in New York (1892–1903), then went to Germany where he studied composition with F. E. Koch and piano with Ferruccio Busoni (1904–08). Taught at the Vienna Conservatory (1912–19) and made his professional debut as a pianist in Berlin (1912).

Gruenberg completed two successful operas, *The Witch of the Brocken* (1912), a children's opera, and *The Bride of the Gods* (1913), libretto by Busoni, while continuing with orchestral composition. In 1919 he won the Flagler Prize for his piece, *The Hill of Dreams*, abandoned his performing career, and decided to concentrate on composition, returning to the United States in that year. During the 1920s, he helped found the League of Composers and devoted himself to an attempt to forge a distinctly American musical style. To this end he experimented with jazz rhythms, writing *The Daniel Jazz* (1924), a vocal and orchestral piece based on a poem by Vachel Lindsay. He followed this with *Jazzberries* (1925), *Jazzettes* (1926) for violin, *Jazz Masks* (1929–31), *Jazz Epigrams* (1931), and *Jazz Dances* (1931). His interest in Afro-American music was further shown in *Creation* (1925), based on a spiritual, and *Twenty Negro Spirituals* (1926). From 1934 to 1937, he taught composition at the Chicago Musical College and then moved to California.

Gruenberg was also the composer of some distinguished film scores. He was most proud of the one he wrote for Per Lorenz's *The Fight for Life* (for which he received an academy award), which was based on the maternal welfare sections of Paul de Kruif's book of the same title. Convinced of the seriousness of his musical craft, Gruenberg arranged a special screening for music critics, only to discover that they were not interested. His exploitation of the heartbeat throughout indicates some similarity to his technique in *The Emperor Jones*. Other award-winning scores were *So Ends Our Night* and *Commandos Strike at Dawn*. He also wrote scores for *Arch of Triumph, American Romance, Gangster, Smart Woman, Counterattack,* and *All the King's Men.* Essentially a composer of serious music, Gruenberg endeavored to keep his Hollywood work separate, but he was often evaluated unfairly, with his serious work being dismissed as theatrical or commercial while his film scores were sometimes considered too serious. Nonetheless, he persevered with serious composing.

His most important opera was *The Emperor Jones* (performed 1933), for which he himself wrote the libretto (contrary to some published reports), consulting with O'Neill as he did so. The sometimes criticized changes at the end of the opera were actually seen by O'Neill himself. Gruenberg submitted the text to the playwright and discussed it with him at a late-night meeting at the Hotel du Rhin, Paris, January 22, 1931. The piece was given eleven times (with Lawrence Tibbett) in the 1933 and 1934 seasons of the Metropolitan Opera. It was also given an all-black production in New York (1934) with Jules Bledsoe and was performed in Chicago (1946) and Rome (1950). Paul Robeson* also sang in a concert version. Attempts by NBC-T.V. to present it as a television opera began in 1950, and William Warfield was signed for the role. Unfortunately, the project foundered as a result of the civil rights movement which perceived racism in the work, a charge which deeply hurt the composer in view of his own continuing interest in Afro-American music.

Gruenberg's instinctive understanding of O'Neill's questing mind has not been fully appreciated. Originally, Gruenberg had hoped to write an opera based on *The Fountain*,* and in 1927 he wrote to the playwright asking him to do the libretto. When O'Neill refused, Gruenberg then turned to the idea of adapting *Marco Millions*,* while O'Neill showed himself receptive to the idea of one based on *Lazarus Laughed*.* This series of events is illuminating because it indicates an empathy between the two men in their quest for an understanding of the commonalty of all religions of the world and solutions to the problem of existence. Where O'Neill conducted his search throughout these three plays, Louis Gruenberg made his statement in *Song of Faith* (1959–62), recently revived in Los Angeles, a choral and orchestral work which was the outcome of much philosophical and religious thinking but which critics dismissed as simplistic.

His chief operatic works (apart from those already mentioned) are: *The Sleeping Beauty* (1922), children's opera; *Jack and the Beanstalk* (1929), libretto by J. Erskine; *The Dumb Wife*, libretto after Anatole France (this work remains unperformed because of a copyright dispute); *Helena of Troy; Antony and Cleopatra* (unperformed because of the competing work by Samuel Barber); and *The Miracle of Flanders* (1945). He also wrote several symphonies, one of which (Symphony No. 1) won the RCA-Victor Prize in 1930, and in 1944 Jascha Heifetz played the premiere of the Violin Concerto Op. 47, which he had commissioned. In the twenty years prior to his death in 1964, Gruenberg had become an unjustly neglected composer, though recently some reevaluation of his serious work has begun. A considerable amount of his work remains unpublished and unperformed. His papers are in the process of being deposited in the Music Division, New York Public Library at Lincoln Center. (This entry was prepared with the assistance of Dr. Irma Gruenberg.)

"GUILTY ONE, THE", a four-act play completed in 1924 by, or with the help of, Agnes Boulton* O'Neill. It was based on the scenario of "The Reckoning"* and was placed under option by Matthew Brady, who asked for some revisions. It was withdrawn in 1925 after Brady's favorable stance on theatrical censorship. Virginia Floyd, who has seen "the extant fragment" of this play, sees it as "a veiled version of *Long Day's Journey into Night*,* particularly in the hostile treatment of the wife. *See* in "References": Floyd (1981), pp. xxiv–xxv, 84–91; Sheaffer (1973), pp. 147–148, 166.

H

"HAIR OF THE DOG," the proposed last play in the abandoned cycle, "A Tale of Possessors, Self-Dispossessed."* The history of this play begins in 1927 as "It Cannot Be Mad," part of the uncompleted cycle "Myth-Plays for the God-Forsaken,"* when it was planned to show man's search for a new faith in a world of machinery. It passed through other titles, "On to Betelgeuse," and "On to Hercules," before becoming "The Life of Bessie Bowen,"* (or Bolan or Bowlan) and "Twilight of Possessors, Self-Dispossessed." In its revision "Hair of the Dog," the play covered the years 1900–1932 and dealt with the automobile industry. In February 1943 O'Neill finally became convinced of the intractability of the material and destroyed the longhand draft. This title was also the original one for the play that became *A Touch of the Poet.** See in "References": Floyd, 1981, pp. 219–220.

"HAIRY APE, THE," a short story written in 1917. Destroyed. It is concerned with a stoker who joins the Industrial Workers of the World. It was rejected for publication, but later made into a play.

HAIRY APE, THE. "A Comedy of Ancient and Modern Life in Eight Scenes" is what O'Neill called this play, also noting that "it seems to run the whole gamut from extreme naturalism to extreme expressionism—with more of the latter than the former" (letter to Kenneth Macgowan,* December 24, 1921).

Scene i: "The firemen's forecastle of an ocean liner—an hour after sailing from New York" on a transatlantic crossing. The room is crowded with shouting, drunken men dressed in singlets and dungarees or stripped to the waist. Voices mingle into a general confused uproar. "The treatment of this scene, or of any other scene in the play, should by no means be naturalistic. The effect sought after is a cramped space in the bowels of a ship, imprisoned by white steel." There are tiers of bunks, uprights supporting them, and a low ceiling which forces all the men to stoop into a position reminiscent of Neanderthal Man. The men look like his popularly portrayed image, hairy chested, simian foreheads, and so forth, while the criss-cross pattern of the steel irresistibly recalls a cage. The denizens of this zoo show a representation of "all the civilized white races," which is indicated by their dialect conversation out of which individual remarks suddenly surface. The central figure, the character to whom all the men show a grudging respect, is Yank.* "He seems broader, fiercer, more truculent, more powerful, more sure of himself than the rest." He seems most in command of the situation, ordering Paddy,* the romantic Irishman, to shut up so that he (Yank) can think. At this the entire forecastle repeats the word "think!" The stage direction says, "The chorus has a brazen metallic quality as if their throats were phonograph horns. It is followed by a general uproar of hard, barking laughter." As in *"Anna Christie,"* where "the ole davil sea" is a leitmotif, and *The Emperor Jones,* where drumbeats hypnotize the audience, this stage direction is repeated throughout Scenes i and iv in order to give an impression of the stokers as machines. Yank glories in his role; he is the strongest and the best, and the ship is his home. He stands alone, without any need for women or anyone else. Long,* the labor radical, takes up from Yank's commitment to ʌie ship and dismissal of customary ideas of home and family, twisting his words "To 'ell with home" slightly: "And 'e says 'ome is hell. And 'e's right! This is 'ell. We lives in 'ell—and right enough we'll die in it." With this he proceeds with the usual arguments about the Biblical equality of man and the violation of individual rights by the capitalist class.

This outburst arouses Yank's contempt, and he turns on Long, calling him "yellow," asserting the superiority of those in the stokehole to the inhabitants of the first-class cabins. The stokers make the ship run and are therefore necessary. They belong; but none of the passengers could possibly endure the conditions and therefore are superfluous. After another round of drinks, Paddy begins a long lament for the past of the tall ships, where men were *Children of the Sea,* when the moon was high, the sails were full, and Trade Winds were blowing. After this paean of praise to an editorialized version of the days of sail, Paddy recalls, " 'Twas them days men belonged to ships, not now. 'Twas them days a ship was part of the sea, and a man was part of a ship, and the sea joined all together and made it one." Now, the dirty smoke from the funnels and the hellish conditions in the stokehole offer a violation of that ancient order of things. Paddy wishes to return to that lost harmony of existence, and he asks, "Is it a flesh and blood wheel of the engines you'd be?"

Yank seizes on this comment and praises the wonder of machinery and those who serve it. He glorifies speed, not "all dat crazy tripe about suns and winds, fresh air and de rest of it." That is a dream of the past, and Paddy as its representative is too old to belong to the present. Yank makes the ship move, as something makes everything else in the world move: "Den yuh get down to me. I'm at de bottom, get me! Dere ain't nothin' foither. I'm de end! I'm de start! I start somep'n and de woild moves!" Yank sees himself as the spirit of steel, the first mover of the mechanized universe—the one indispensable creature of modern times who glories in his strength and his ability to absorb hardship. As the next watch is called into the stokehole, Paddy remains to drink and dream while Yank strides out to the stokehole delivering his crowning insult, "Yuh don't belong!"

Scene ii: "Two days out. A section of the promenade deck." Mildred Douglas* and her Aunt* are discovered reclining in deck chairs. Mildred is a pale, delicate, twenty-year-old dressed in white, whose pretty face has a "self-conscious superiority." She looks "fretful, nervous and discontented." Her Aunt is the stereotypical dowager, with "double chin and lorgnettes. She is dressed pretentiously." The day is bright, the air is clear and fresh, but "these two incongruous, artificial figures, inert and disharmonious" mar the picture. Their conversation is effete, with bitchy literate snobbishness. Mildred recalls the great-grandmother who smoked a clay pipe and the grandfather who "puddled steel." But now her father is the head of Nazareth Steel and obviously a millionaire. All energy seems to have disappeared from Mildred, and her air of affectation and boredom is very self-conscious. Her Aunt is acting as chaperone on this ocean voyage, and from her the audience discovers that Mildred has been playing at social work on the Lower East Side of New York: "how they must have hated you, by the way, the poor that you made so much poorer in their eyes." She has now transferred her attention to London's Whitechapel district and intends to investigate conditions there. There is a possibility that Mildred may wish to be sincere, but feeling has been bred out of her: "I'm afraid I have neither the vitality nor integrity." She has made arrangements to visit the stokehole to see how the other half lives and to experience "a new thrill" as well as to garner further social service credentials. Both the captain and the chief engineer have been opposed, but Mildred has exerted influence and has won permission. The Second Engineer comes to escort her. "He is a husky fine-looking man of thirty-five or so," whom Mildred later characterizes as "an oaf—but a handsome virile oaf," in order to enrage her Aunt. The Second Engineer tries to talk Mildred out of this whim by accentuating the problems of heat, access, and dirt, particularly dirt on her white dress, but she brushes all objections aside. With some subliminal and titillating wish for sexual assault, she sets off as her aunt calls her "Poser." With that, Mildred slaps her across the face; "Old hag," she says, as her Aunt again screams the insult after her.

Scene iii: The Stokehole. There is one large electric light, barely sufficient to illuminate the murky atmosphere, the outlines of furnaces and boilers, and the shadows of coal piles and working men. The men work like automata, moving "with a strange, awkward, swinging rhythm," their shovels almost appearing to be part of them. "There is a tumult of noise . . . with [a] rending dissonance." Yet at the same time "there is order in it, a mechanical regulated recurrence, a tempo" and a "quiver of liberated energy." As the curtain rises, the furnace doors are shut and the men are either resting or rearranging the coal into heaps. Paddy is complaining about his back, and Yank upbraids him scornfully. Then a whistle is heard, and the men swing into action, opening the furnace doors so that a red glow lights the stage from the back. Yank rallies the men in words that have obvious sexual overtones: "Sling it into her! Let her ride! Shoot de piece now! Call de toin on her! Drive her into it! Feel her move!'' Then the tempo quickens and the words sound like those of "the gallery gods at the six-day bike race.'' "Let's see yuh sprint! Dig in and gain a lap! Dere she go-o-es!'' With that he slams his furnace door shut and the others do likewise. But the pause is only momentary, and the whistle sounds again. This time Yank is contemptuous: "Take it easy dere, you! Who d'yuh tink's runnin' dis game, me or you? When I get ready, we move. Not before! When I get ready, get me!'' The other stokers growl approvingly at Yank, and then he again starts to work—but for himself and "de baby,'' not for those above: "Him and his whistle, dey don't belong. But we belong, see!''

He starts on his own furnace, and at this moment Mildred, accompanied by both the Second and Fourth engineers, enters. At first she is frightened, and her pose is about to crumble, but she forces herself to move further in, and out from between the two men. The other men see her and they stop, dumbfounded, while Yank, hearing the whistle again, starts to rage at it, waving his shovel in the air, beating on his chest like a gorilla, and shouting obscenities (mild by today's standards) at it. Suddenly he becomes conscious of the other men staring at something behind him, and he turns around to see "Mildred, like a white apparition in the full light from the open furnace doors." He utters "a snarling, murderous growl, crouching to spring, . . . He glares into her eyes, turned to stone." The effect on Mildred is appalling. As his eyes bore into her, her personality collapses; she puts her hands before her eyes. Yank's mouth falls open and he looks bewildered as she says, "Take me away! Oh, the filthy beast!'' and faints. The Engineers remove Mildred, and the sound of an iron door clanging shut is heard. Yank, somehow assaulted in the depth of his being, furiously shouts, "God damn yuh!'' and "hurls his shovel after them." It hits the bulkhead and clashes to the ground, while the whistle begins again.

Scene iv: The firemen's forecastle, just after Yank and his watch have come off duty. All except Yank have washed, though coal dust still clings around their eyes. Yank remains apart from them. "He is seated forward on a bench in the exact attitude of Rodin's 'The Thinker'.'' The others are smoking, sitting around, and looking fearfully at Yank as if they are expecting another outburst. They tell him to wash, and Yank tells them he's trying to think. They pick up on his words in the same mechanical manner detailed in Scene i, and then they respond similarly to Paddy's suggestion that he has fallen in love. Yank snorts, "Love, Hell! Hate, dat's what. I've fallen in hate, get me?'' Paddy starts assessing Mildred's behavior with ironical scorn, and Long calls it insult, falling into the rhetoric of the union leader and the politician. As before, words are picked up and repeated: "Governments!'' "God!'' Paddy continues to tease Yank, claiming that he has fallen in love with Mildred, but Yank insists that he had thought he was seeing a ghost. He asks Paddy if she had called him "a hairy ape,'' and Paddy says, "She looked it at you if she didn't say the word itself." This starts Yank off into a rage-filled monologue, punctuated with comments from the forecastle. He says that her ghostly appearance at first scared him, and then when he realized the way she was looking at him, anger took over. Now he wants some kind of vengeance. "She don't belong, get me!" But at the same time he realizes that "she grinds the organ and I'm on de string." He threatens to throw her into the furnace: "Speed, dat'll be her! She'll belong den!" He then threatens to take off to look for her but is held down by the other men. The curtain falls as Yank cries out, "She done me doit! . . . Lemme up! I'll show her who's a ape!"

Scene v: Three weeks later on a corner of Fifth Avenue on a fine sunny Sunday morning. The whole atmosphere is one of cleanliness, tidiness, and opulence. There are shop windows in the background, a jewelry establishment, and a furrier's. There "the adornments of extreme wealth are tantalizingly displayed," each with enormous price tags whose numbers wink on and off. This scene is an expressionistic one and is, in effect, seen through the eyes of Yank. Yank enters with Long; he has not washed and is wearing his fireman's cap on the side of his head and dirty dungarees. Long is dressed in shore clothes and with an expansive gesture announces, "Fif' Avenoo. This 'ere's their bleedin' private lane, as you might say. We're trespassers 'ere. Proletarians keep orf the grass." Yank then tells Long about his childhood and upbringing on the Brooklyn waterfront. He says that nothing "belongs" as far as his life is concerned except his time in the stokehole. He is impressed with the cleanliness and elegance of the neighborhood as Long tries to explain to him that "we pays for it wiv our bloody sweat." When they look into the jeweler's window, he tries to raise Yank's class consciousness. One single piece is "more'n our 'ole bloody stokehole makes in ten voyages sweatin' in 'ell. . . . One of these 'ere would buy scoff for a starvin' family for a year." If Yank wants to get his back at Mildred, he will have to fight " 'er class," the whole capitalist class. From the jeweler's they move to the furrier's, and Yank notes a price of two thousand dollars for monkey fur with a sense of "queer excitement."

At that moment a church lets out, and a company of capitalists emerges. They are all overdressed, especially the women, with the men in Prince Alberts, complete with accoutrements of elegance of a bygone age: "hats, spats, canes, etc." They all speak in "toneless simpering voices." Obviously, they are not realistic; rather they are stereotypes of capitalists, as seen through Yank's eyes. As they approach, Yank's hostility increases, and he bumps into one man who merely replies, "I beg your pardon." He then lasciviously approaches a lady who passes on without seeming to see him. Gradually he moves into another monologue expressing his feeling of "belonging" in this modern industrial society. He perceives himself as the moving force not only of the ship but also of high steel construction: "I'm steel and steam and smoke and de rest of it." As his rage increases, he bumps viciously into one after another of the men, "not jarring them the least bit." He is the one who is pushed off balance. Finally he hears a lady announce ecstatically, "monkey fur," and the tone of her voice recalls Mildred. He tries to uproot a lamp post to use as a weapon and then attempts to punch in the face a man who has knocked him down while trying to get a bus. The punch has no effect on the man, who first complains about missing his bus and then calls for the police, who club Yank to the ground. None of the crowd seems to notice anything amiss: they are totally oblivious to Yank. Long, in the meantime, has fled the scene as Yank becomes violent.

Scene vi: "Night of the following day. A row of cells in the prison of Blackwell's Island." The cells stretch diagonally back endlessly. There is one electric bulb which illuminates a portion of the cell in which Yank, who has been given a thirty-day sentence, sits on the edge of his cot "in the attitude of Rodin's 'The Thinker'." He is bruised, and a bloodstained bandage is wrapped around his head. Looking around him at the bars of the cell, Yank announces, "Steel. Dis is de Zoo, huh?" a comment which brings forth the same "hard, barking laughter" familiar from Scenes i and iv. Yank attempts to communicate what had happened to him, explaining that a woman is to blame, and then he identifies her as the daughter of Douglas of the Steel Trust. At this, one of the prisoners suggests that he ought to join the Industrial Workers of the World (IWW) if he wants to get even with the likes of Douglas. He reads from an article hostile to the IWW which concludes by saying that they plan to "make of our sweet and lovely civilization a shambles, a desolation where man, God's masterpiece, would soon degenerate back to the ape." This comment reaches Yank; he asks for the newspaper to find out more about the IWW because "dey blow up tings, . . . Dey turn tings around." He sits down again in the attitude of "The Thinker" and then has a revelation: Douglas is the president of the Steel Trust, and by making half the steel in the world, he oppresses and imprisons Yank. At this, he starts to pull on the cell bars: "Steel! *It* don't belong, dat's what! Cages, cells, locks, bolts, bars—dat's what it means—holdin' me down wit him at de top!" He resolves to be the fire that drives through and melts steel, "fire dat never goes out—hot as hell—breakin' out in de night." He seizes one bar with his hands and braces against it with his feet—like an ape. The bar bends, and the guards enter with a hose to subdue him, astonished to see the damage Yank has done with his brute strength.

Scene vii: "Nearly a month later. An I.W.W. Local near the waterfront." There is moonlight and the room is minimally lit, but it is dingy, cheap, commonplace, and certainly not mysterious. A secretary is making entries in a ledger, and eight or ten men, "longshoremen, iron workers, and the like, are grouped about the table. Two are playing checkers. One is writing a letter." This scene is announced by a signboard as "Industrial Workers of the World—Local No. 57." Yank appears, knocks carefully, and enters. He asks to join the organization, and for the first time the audience learns his real name, Robert Smith. To his surprise, all he has to do to become a member is sign his name and pay fifty cents. The Secretary welcomes Yank as a representative of an as yet barely organized group of workers and tells him to take some literature for his friends. Yank cannot understand this bureaucratic approach from what he thinks to be a revolutionary enterprise and explains that he is interested in blowing things up, particularly the factory belonging to Douglas of the Steel Trust. "Dat's what

I'm after—to blow up de steel, knock all de steel in de woild up to de moon.''
He doesn't care if he gets caught: ''I'll soive life for it—and give 'em de laugh!
and I'll write her a letter and tell her de hairy ape done it. Dat'll square tings.''
With this, the Secretary moves away, signaling to his goons who pinion Yank
and search him. The Secretary then accuses him of being an ''agent provocator''
and tells him that whoever has sent him is wasting his time. Yank wouldn't be
able to do anything anyway: ''You're a brainless ape.'' Even as a revolutionary,
Yank does not belong, and he is thrown out of the office. He starts to attack the
closed door of the office but then stops, confused and powerless, sitting down
in the attitude of ''The Thinker'' once again, trying to understand. The IWW
is as impotent as the Salvation Army. He tries to figure out what runs the world.
He has thought himself to be the motive principle, but ''I don't tick, see?—I'm
a busted Ingersoll [watch], dat's what. Steel was me, and I owned de woild.
Now I ain't steel, and de woild owns me.'' Everything is ''dark'' to him, and
so he asks the man in the moon for ''the inside dope from de stable—where do
I get off at, huh!'' With this a Policeman arrives and tells Yank to move along
or else he'll be arrested. ''Lock me up! Put me in a cage,'' says Yank. His only
offense was that he was born. The Policeman tells him he's drunk and to move
along.

Scene viii: The monkey house at the zoo, the next day. One cage is visible
and it is labeled ''Gorilla.'' Inside, the huge animal is squatting rather in the
manner of ''The Thinker'' as Yank enters. The gorilla eyes him but remains
soundless and motionless. Yank looks at him and starts a long monologue,
beginning with admiration of the gorilla's strength, and the animal seems to
respond as Yank claims kinship: ''Ain't we both members of de same club—
de Hairy Apes?'' Now he realizes what Mildred saw as she looked at him. He
has been sitting on a bench in Battery Park all night; he has seen the sun rise,
and it was as beautiful as Paddy had said, but he didn't belong, so he came up
to visit the gorilla to see how he feels: ''On'y yuh're lucky, see? Yuh don't
belong wit 'em and yuh know it. But me, I belong wit 'em—but I don't, see?
Dey don't belong wit me, dat's what.'' At least the gorilla has memories of the
past, the jungle, but Yank has nothing: ''I ai't on oith and I ain't in heaven, get
me? I'm in de middle trying to separate 'em, takin' all de woist punches from
bot' of 'em.'' That is his definition of hell. But the gorilla is fortunate because
he really does belong at the bottom, and he is the only one who does. That's
why ''they'' have had to put him in a cage. The gorilla has become for Yank
the symbol of his own oppression, and therefore Yank decides to release him
so that the two of them may get even: ''Wanter wind up like a sport 'stead of
croakin' slow in dere?'' Between them they will take on the world. Yank then
jimmies the lock on the cage door and throws it open: ''Pardon from de governor!
. . . I'll take yuh for a walk down Fif' Avenoo.'' In answer to Yank's invitation
to shake hands, the gorilla embraces him, crushing his ribs, and then, after
looking around uncertainly, shuffles off. Yank drags himself to his feet, realizing
that he is finished: ''Christ, where do I get off at? Where do I fit in?'' Then he

painfully crawls into the gorilla's cage and stands holding the bars: "Croak wit your boots on," and "in the strident tones of a circus barker," he announces, "Ladies and gents, step forward and take a slant at de one and only—one and original—Hairy Ape from de wilds of—" and slips to the ground dead. "And," says the stage direction, "perhaps the Hairy Ape at last belongs."

Comments: This play, though at first not well received by the critics, was a success with the audience, and it represents O'Neill's most interesting play, technically, since *The Emperor Jones*.* It contains elements of experimentation which range from naturalism through symbolism to expressionism. The first part of the play, on board the ship, is realistic and bears a resemblance to the earlier plays of the S.S. *Glencairn** group. The name of Yank reappears, and the character of Paddy seems to be a repetition of Driscoll* in the earlier plays. Paddy may also be a study of O'Neill's own acquaintance from Jimmy-the-Priest's (James J. Condon's*) bar in New York, the fireman named Driscoll who committed suicide, and O'Neill here may have been seeking an explanation for his action. Overall, the scenes in the stokehole and the forecastle are realistic in their execution but expressionistic in their use of scenery. The cage motif of the forecastle and the inferno motif of the stokehole are well defined. So, too, is the frequently misunderstood attitude of Rodin's "The Thinker." This statue is often considered an optimistic, even uplifting sculpture, but one must not forget that it was designed for the central piece of the monumental work, "The Gates of Hell." Perhaps that motif is a trifle overdone in *The Hairy Ape*, but nonetheless it does underline both Yank's psychological and intellectual difficulties. Significantly, the pose appears only after Yank's confrontation with Mildred when he starts to discover the hell of his own existence.

Actually, the only truly expressionistic scene in the play is the Fifth Avenue scene, for there O'Neill refracts all the happenings through the distorted mental processes of Yank. The manifest impossibility of Yank's banging without result into the representatives of wealth and power is indicative of the approach employed. This scene is also notable as being the first occasion in an O'Neill play that masks were used. Here they are a means of signifying the stereotypical anonymity of the capitalist characters; O'Neill was later to use this technique more fully and more originally in *Lazarus Laughed,** *The Great God Brown,** and *Days Without End*.* Finally, the last scene of *The Hairy Ape* operates on a symbolic rather than an expressionistic level, but again the treatment is realistic. O'Neill is endeavoring to break new ground by his fusion of techniques, but this is not a truly expressionistic play—and there is no reason to regret the fact. One does, however, wonder whether the conclusion actually communicates the final words of the stage direction, with their singular pessimism. Of all the plays O'Neill had written so far, *The Emperor Jones* comes closest to *The Hairy Ape*, with its repetitions of motifs—the cages, the "loud barking laughter" like the sound of a phonograph, the reduction of human beings to automata, the praise of steel, and Yank's final attempt to get to the very bottom of the question of human existence. Both Brutus Jones* and Yank try to find out where they belong, but Jones's conclusion, in which he rejects his old gods, is less pessimistic than that of Yank, who is shown as accepting kinship with the primates.

The Hairy Ape was considered by some critics to be propagandistic and polemical, but this does not necessarily have to be the case. The characters should be taken as symbolic rather than realistic. Yank is symbolic of any victim of modern industrial civilization. At first he believes that he is an essential part of it; he accepts its premises and, like Arthur Miller's Willy Loman in *Death of a Salesman*, he lives by them. It is only when his dream is destroyed, when his "saving lie" is revealed to him as a falsehood, that Yank starts to question.

Mildred's intrusion into the world in which Yank is king brings about his own psychological destruction, and similarly, Yank's intrusion into the world in which the gorilla is king also brings about his physical destruction. Yank, then, is not simply representative of the oppressed working classes, the victim of the capitalistic system, but is a symbol of the displacement of modern man in general. This is a theme which O'Neill often treats: the place of a human being with reference to his function and his dreams. In the S.S. *Glencairn** plays, Driscoll speaks of the old oneness of man and sea, a theme that Paddy echoes here. Industrialization has destroyed the old certainties, but it has not yet provided new ones; and as in *The Emperor Jones*, one is forced to question the so-called benefits of modern civilization.

The play was written quickly, in just a few weeks, and O'Neill rightly saw it as a great advance. Indeed, it remained, for a long time, one of the most popular of all his plays, up to the arrival of the autobiographical dramas which were produced at the end of his life and posthumously. It is extraordinary how O'Neill manages to make the inarticulate Yank communicate important concepts, and this is where his symbolic and expressionistic techniques are important. But they exist on the groundwork of a solid realism born of the playwright's own observation of life in the stokehole. One curious footnote to the original production of *The Hairy Ape* is that when it was moved uptown, the part of Mildred was played by Carlotta Monterey,* who met O'Neill then for the first time. There was some talk of making this play into an opera, and Eric Coates, the British composer, was interested, but nothing came of the proposal. Judging by Coates's "London" suite, he would have been a good choice, for his music makes interesting use of the dissonances and noises of a great city. *Note*: The use of masks in the Fifth Avenue scene came from a suggestion by the costumer, Blanche Hays, not the playwright.

Production Data: Written December 1921, in a mere three weeks. Produced by the Provincetown Players* at the Playwrights' Theatre, New York City, March 9, 1922. Moved to the Plymouth Theatre, New York City, April 17, 1922 (total performances, 127).

Director: James Light, assisted by Arthur Hopkins
Designer: Cleon Throckmorton, assisted by Robert Edmond Jones*

Cast: Robert Smith ("Yank"): Louis Wolheim*
    Paddy: Henry O'Neill
    Long: Harold West
    Mildred Douglas: Mary Blair* (replaced by Carlotta Monterey* when the play
       moved uptown)
    Aunt: Eleanor Hutchison
    Guard: Harry Gottlieb
    IWW Secretary: Harold McGee
    Second Engineer: Jack Gude
    Policeman: Unknown
    Fourth Engineer: Unknown
    Ladies, Gentlemen, Stokers: Greta Hoving, Josephine Hutchinson, Esther Pinch,
       Lucy Shreve, Jack Gude, Clement O'Loghlen, Anterio Argondona, Em Jo,
       Allen Delano, Patrick Barnum, Harold McGee, Harry Gottlieb, Alexander
       Boije, George Tobias.
[*See also* Appendix B for film adaptation.]

HALL, Mr. In *Chris Christophersen** a tall, gaunt, determined-looking, grim-faced officer aboard the steamer *Londonderry* which ran down Chris's coal barge.

HARDER, T. Stedman. In *A Moon for the Misbegotten,** heir to Standard Oil money, and neighbor of Phil Hogan* and his daughter, Josie Hogan.* Harder is in his late thirties, living the life of a country gentleman, and endeavoring to look the part. He is offended by the existence of the raffish Hogans and unsuccessfully tries to buy their farm for ten thousand dollars from the legal owner, James Tyrone, Jr.* He comes to the Hogan farm to complain about their breaking down his boundary fences to allow their pigs into his pond. He is no match for the Irish wit and comic malice of the Hogans, who trip him up both literally and figuratively. A short account of this incident also appears in *Long Day's Journey into Night.** In *A Moon for the Misbegotten* it becomes the central comic piece.

HARDWICK, Captain. In *Warnings,** master of the S.S. *Empress.* "He is a stocky man about fifty, dressed in a simple blue uniform. His face is reddened by sun and wind." He has a "gray beard and mustache." Hardwick is the same age as his deaf radio operator, James Knapp.* He is understandably short with him at first, but then shows unexpected sympathy: "If you're sick, why don't you say so?" He can even find it in his heart to tender rough comfort: "Brace up! Poor beggar!" However, when he discovers that Knapp's deafness has caused him to miss a radio warning about the derelict which he has just hit, he is enraged: "I won't touch him; but that miserable, cowardly shrimp has lost my ship for me." Hardwick then takes care that Knapp is informed in writing of his responsibility in missing the warning transmission. He and Knapp seem to be designed as foils for each other, but the contrasts are not developed.

HARFORD, Deborah, mother of Simon Harford* and Joel Harford.* In *A Touch of the Poet** (which is part of the abandoned cycle, "A Tale of Possessors, Self-Dispossessed"*), she is forty-one, a tiny, youthful figure who appears about thirty. Her face "is small with high cheekbones, . . . broad forehead, . . . square chin framed by thick wavy, red-brown hair." She has a "slightly aquiline" nose, a mouth that is a trifle too large for her face, even teeth, enormous "long-lashed green-flecked brown eyes, under heavy, angular brows." She comes to Cornelius Melody's* tavern in search of her son Simon, who is being nursed there by Sara Melody* because he had become ill while trying to live a life close to nature in a nearby log cabin. Deborah meets Cornelius Melody, who tries his practised seducer approach on her, almost kissing her until she pushes him away complaining that he smells of liquor. However, he is later proved right in his suggestion that she was responsive, for in *More Stately Mansions** (also part of the proposed eleven-play cycle) she has dreams about herself as a courtesan in the court of King Louis (a revelation which arouses Simon's mirth). She is adamantly opposed to the possibility of marriage between Sara and Simon and warns the young woman of the dangers of marrying into the acquisitive Harford clan with their admiration of Napoleonic despotism and their desire to possess everything and everyone. Deborah has managed to escape their claws because there was not enough of her for them to catch, and, as one finds out, she flees into dreams, thinking of herself also as the Empress Josephine. Her shrewdest warning is "that the Harfords never part with their dreams even when they deny them." She is used in *A Touch of the Poet* as an expository device to tell the past history of the Harford family.

In *More Stately Mansions*, which picks up the action four years later, O'Neill has Deborah and Sara in conflict over the possession of Simon. Deborah seems to have had a love-hate relationship with her son, loving him as the dreamer and hating him for the acquisitive instincts of the Harfords. She has encouraged him in his idealism, inviting him into her symbolic enclosed garden in which nature is artificially manipulated into strange topiary shapes. Yet at the same time, she admits that she had hated him as a child, even hated her pregnancy because it meant possession by someone or something. She wanted freedom to dream her own curiously erotic dreams. Deborah is also greedy, almost devouring her son as his mother-wife and confusing him in the priorities of his affections. She agrees to Simon's becoming head of the failing family business after her husband's death and even humbles herself to ask Sara to share her house with her. However, she despises Sara as an "Irish biddy" and loathes her acquisitiveness, which she sees as destroying the dreamer in Simon and drawing him away from her.

While they all live together, Deborah adopts the role of happy grandmother until Simon begins to realize that the two women have shut him out of their lives. Sara as wife-mother with her four sons no longer needs him as a husband. Consequently, Simon attempts a reordering of their relationships, perceiving that Deborah and Sara have united against him as Woman to destroy him. He puts the two women at enmity with each other by defining their roles: Deborah will stay in her garden of dreams, while Sara will become his wife-mistress at the office. Finally, Deborah realizes that she must give up her son to the arms of his wife to show the superiority of love to lust, and she deliberately opens the red door in her summer house, "the Temple of Love" she calls it, to walk into the world of insanity. She has known that with this symbolic act she also opens a door in the mind and will leave life, the world outside the wall of her garden, and forever after be "the great Princess on her grand estate," as Sara puts it. Deborah chooses renunciation to show Sara which of them "is the one who loves him most!"

Deborah Harford is another of the portraits of predatory women whom O'Neill frequently draws. She is uncannily reminiscent of Nina Leeds* in *Strange Interlude** who embodies more than one aspect of devouring womanhood. Deborah is Simon's mother and wife, and in her own dreams she is a mistress, of King Louis, in *More Stately Mansions*, and the Empress Josephine, wife of Napoleon, in *A Touch of the Poet*. This confusion of roles inflicts a deep psychic wound upon her son, who is forced to choose between Deborah and Sara as symbols of his divided self. Deborah is a symbolic rather than a realistic character, as is shown by her always dressing in white and in the way her physical characteristics change. During the final act of *More Stately Mansions*, she changes from an emaciated death's head to a woman who "looks beautiful and serene, and many years younger." She has found peace in insanity and also in that renunciation of self for the good of a man (in this case Simon) which O'Neill seems to see as the proper mission of a woman.

HARFORD, Ethan, eldest son of Sara Melody* Harford and Simon Harford*; brother of Wolfe Harford,* Jonathan Harford,* and Honey Harford.* He is the principal male character in the scenario of *The Calms of Capricorn** (part of the abandoned cycle, "A Tale of Possessors, Self-Dispossessed"*). He is the second mate on the clipper ship *Dream of the West* captained by Enoch Payne,* who distrusts the twenty-eight-year-old Ethan, perceiving him as a fool who would sacrifice his ship to break a speed record. Certainly Ethan seems almost fanatical, with his "visionary's eyes set in a square, handsome, hawk-nosed face," so dedicated to his dream of conquering the sea that he has "no interest in women," telling his mother that he hasn't noticed how pretty Nancy Drummond Payne,* the captain's wife is, a foreshadowing of their future relationship. Ethan and his father have a basic identity of soul, which Simon recognizes. He understands Ethan's desire to subdue or "possess" the sea and prophesies that his son will lose this battle, but in losing he will find a "final victory and release," because he must follow his dream no matter what the consequences.

On the aptly named clipper ship, *Dream of the West*, Ethan displays the innate ruthlessness of the Harford clan (and also his mother, Sara), the romanticism of his father, Simon, and the expiatory renunciation of his grandmother, Deborah Harford.* Goaded to rage by Leda Cade,* he accidentally kills Thomas Hull,* the first mate of the *Dream of the West*, and succeeds to his position, against the wishes of Captain Enoch Payne, who perceives Ethan's fanaticism. As the ship remains becalmed in the Tropic of Capricorn the passengers' nerves become ragged and true feelings are revealed on this ship of fools. Ethan and Nancy find their passion for each other unbearable; they even wish Captain Payne dead so that they can marry. An accidental fall presents them with an opportunity. As Payne is lying injured, Ethan attempts to smother him with a pillow, but is prevented by Nancy, who commits the murder herself—but both share in the guilt. They are now free to consummate their love; until now Ethan's honor has prevented them from doing so. They marry immediately and the calm is broken, a good omen, but their guilt begins to torment them. The twin themes of the dream and ruthlessness in achieving it come together in Ethan's singleminded attempt to beat the record of the *Flying Cloud* for the New York-San Francisco run, even at the cost of straining and ruining the ship of which he is now captain. Like those Harford men of whom Deborah Harford spoke in *A Touch of the Poet*,* Ethan will not give up on his dream. By the time the vessel is off San Francisco she is leaking badly and is once again becalmed. Denied a chance at the record, Ethan is also dismissed by the owner of the vessel, Theodore Warren,* for negligence. Ethan and Nancy take these happenings as judgment on them. Realizing the impossibility of achieving their dreams or of finding peace in life, they decide to choose death together; and in expiation of their sin, they jump overboard and are lost in the fog just before the ship enters San Francisco harbor.

Ethan, like other Harford men, has pursued his romantic dream and failed, but at the end he has preserved his honor by bowing to fate and punishing himself for the murders he has committed in his attempt to "possess" or subdue the sea. Sara sees her eldest son as a great duelist like her father, Cornelius Melody* in *A Touch of the Poet*.

HARFORD, Honey. In the scenario of *The Calms of Capricorn*,* fourth son of Simon Harford* and Sara Melody* Harford, brother of Ethan Harford,* Wolfe Harford,* and Jonathan Harford.* He is twenty-four, "all peasant Irish," with a tall, heavy figure "beginning to run a little to fat." He seems to be an amiable soul whose eyes "sparkle . . . [with] sly, droll humor." Honey is a tin peddler; and after Simon Harford abandons his writing project, he accompanies his son on his route. At his father's funeral service, Honey is given a song to sing, an action that sets him apart from his brothers who are given parts of a poem to read. He seems to remain fairly close to his mother throughout the action, but his most important characteristics are those of the classic Irish politician, hail-fellow-well-met, an operator, one who will manage to be the leader of a group. He spends a great deal of his time on the voyage to San Francisco cultivating the group of gold-seekers who are traveling on the clipper *Dream of the West*, trying to find out everything they know about the possibilities of striking it rich. He is deputized by the gold-seekers and the crew to demand on their behalf that the "Jonah," Captain Enoch Payne,* resign in favor of Ethan Harford. He goes to bed with Leda Cade,* a prostitute and passenger on the *Dream of the West*.

Honey Harford was destined to be the central character of "Nothing Is Lost But Honor," one of the plays in the abandoned cycle, "A Tale of Possessors, Self-Dispossessed,"* which was to follow his career as a politician. At the end of the eleven-play cycle O'Neill had planned for him to be the only surviving son of Simon Harford and Sara Melody Harford.

HARFORD, Joel. In *More Stately Mansions** (part of the abandoned cycle, "A Tale of Possessors, Self-Dispossessed"*), son of Deborah Harford* and older brother of Simon Harford.* He "is twenty-nine, tall and thin, with a slight stoop. . . . His face is pale and handsome. . . . He has brown hair, cold light-blue eyes, a pointed chin, an obstinate mouth." He seems "prematurely old." He is the head bookkeeper of the Harford family business with all the qualities of "methodical mediocrity" that the position would seem to require, including "determination and rigid integrity." He lacks both the ambition and imagination to run the company, something his father understood when he left orders that Simon should take over the failing family business. Joel's "prim and puritanical" conservatism annoys the more flamboyant and unscrupulous Simon who once says, "He isn't a man. He's a stuffed moral attitude." He remains concerned with the future of the company and is distinctly disapproving of the wife-mistress relationship between Sara Melody* Harford and Simon at the office. However, it seems subtly to have corrupted him too, because he looks with smirking desire at Sara and she responds subliminally.

HARFORD, Jonathan. In the scenario of *The Calms of Capricorn*,* third son of Simon Harford* and Sara Melody* Harford; brother of Ethan Harford,* Wolfe Harford,* and Honey Harford.* He is twenty-five, with a close resemblance to his father, having inherited his "long New England bony face." He appears older than his years, given "a tense nervous vitality" tempered with self-discipline and self-confidence. He is a railroad clerk. Throughout the action of the scenario, Jonathan is the calculating businessman, thinking always of the main chance to be taken and the possibilities of making money. He is the one who suggests that the family leave New England and go to San Francisco to make a new start where money is to be made. He is concerned lest the crimes of his brother Ethan and his wife, Nancy Drummond Payne,* should become common knowledge because that might hinder his chances of economic success since he would start out with a tarnished reputation. Jonathan's commitment is to practicality and material success; business for him is a kind of poetry. He marries Elizabeth Warren,* daughter of the businessman Theodore Warren* who also is owner of the clipper *Dream of the West*. She has offered her body to him and he has accepted, but with lust, not love. He tells her that their marriage will be one of economic convenience, a business proposition; he proposes a kind of economic partnership because he can use her intelligence to help him get ahead.

In return he says he will be faithful to her, but again for reasons of appearance rather than affection.

Jonathan Harford was destined to be the central figure of "The Man on Iron Horseback,"* one of the plays of the abandoned cycle, "A Tale of Possessors, Self-Dispossessed,"* which was to follow his life "as railroad and shipping magnate." [*See* Donald Gallup, introduction to "The Calms . . ."]

HARFORD, Sara. *See* Melody, Sara.

HARFORD, Simon. In *A Touch of the Poet,** *More Stately Mansions,** and *The Calms of Capricorn,** son of Deborah Harford,* husband of Sara Melody* Harford, father of Ethan Harford,* Wolfe Harford,* Jonathan Harford,* and Honey Harford,* brother of Joel Harford.* He is a prominent figure in the abandoned cycle, "A Tale of Possessors, Self-Dispossessed." He plays an important part in *A Touch of the Poet** (though he never actually appears onstage), is the central figure in *More Stately Mansions,** and dies at the beginning of *The Calms of Capricorn** (uncompleted scenario). He is apparently twenty-two in the first play (which takes place in 1828), twenty-six at the beginning of the second (which covers the years 1832–1841). He dies in 1857, aged fifty (O'Neill's chronology is not fully worked out). He represents in himself the two opposed personalities of the Harford men: the romantic, poetic spirit, and the hard-driving, acquisitive businessman. Both types have dreams and follow them relentlessly to the end.

In *A Touch of the Poet* Simon has romantically retired to a lakeside log cabin, planning to write a book about an ideal society in which men and women will live in harmony, without moneygrubbing acquisitiveness. When he marries Sara Melody,* partly because he feels bound in honor to do so, he must forgo his dream and make money, for he has been disowned by his father. Four years later, at the beginning of *More Stately Mansions*, Simon has been following his acquisitive side and has become a successful businessman, with three sons and another who is born in the course of the play. Nevertheless, his poetic dream is not dead, and despite his success in business, he hates both it and the counting-house mentality of people like his brother Joel. These sentiments are shown in his opening meeting with his mother, Deborah Harford, a secret one at that same log cabin in which he had attempted to bring his poetic dream into reality. She ministers to Simon's dreams by telling of her own. Hidden in the cabin, Sara overhears, and after Simon's departure the symbolic meaning of the two hostile women becomes discernible: they represent the different selves of Simon which are at war within him, and they dramatize his internal conflict between romantic dream and materialism as they battle for possession of him.

With the death of Simon's father, Henry Harford, Simon is asked by his brother, Joel, and Nicholas Gadsby,* the family lawyer, to take over the failing family business. Symbolically, Harford had been gambling in western lands. Simon agrees, on the arrogant condition that his firm absorb that of his father.

There may be a psychological significance here; the son supplants the father. He is, however, disturbed by the arrangement worked out by Deborah and Sara, that they should all live in Deborah's house, but with Sara in charge. Quite rightly he suspects trouble and tries to prevent it by warning both women that he wants a tranquil domestic life; by psychological extension this can mean that he wants to be an integrated personality. Simon's torture begins as Deborah and Sara seem to become one woman, a predatory and destructive female principle trying to destroy him. With Simon's four sons as their personal possessions, Deborah, the mother-wife, and Sara, the wife-mother, now need him only for economic support. Simon, who has turned aside from his dream, working to make Sara proud of him, no longer takes pride in his business achievements.

In an attempt to fight back, Simon tries to separate the literal and psychological functions of the two women so that they will both minister to his divided spirit. He asks Sara to work for him in his office as wife-mistress and secret partner. She must "buy" her influence and shares in the family business with her physical favors. In short she must prostitute herself to him in order to gain the economic security and power she wants. Deborah, on the other hand is relegated to her walled garden of dreams where her "Temple of Love" waits for her to pass through its red door. In her company Simon will be able to retreat into his dream world, his old romantic relationship with her. But this precarious balance cannot be maintained. His romantic side begins to strengthen and his business deals become risky. He is even late for his amorous "assignations" with Sara, who now realizes that he has made her a prostitute and that her power over him is waning as he spends more time with Deborah, neglecting the world of daily business.

The real problem with Simon is that he is being torn apart by the conflicting attitudes toward woman and toward life which are symbolized by Deborah and Sara. The almost surreal Deborah with her erotic fantasies evokes the dreamy side of him, while Sara embodies the Harford acquisitiveness. Curiously, like Cornelius Melody* in his desire to live in a world removed from reality, Simon even quotes the same stanza from Byron's *Childe Harold*, "I have not loved the world, nor the world me," when he is with his mother. For Sara he quotes from Oliver Wendell Holmes's *The Chambered Nautilus*, the line which gives the title to the play, "Build thee more stately mansions, O my soul," but here he is ironic because Sara, like other Harfords, is concerned with the building of material rather than spiritual mansions. He is anguished by the battle between the women to control him completely (when they work together as Woman) or possess him singly (when they work apart). He cannot function as either a divided or integrated personality.

Finally, in the last act of the play, Simon forces the now reluctant Sara to continue her pursuit of money and power, suggesting also that she "rid our life of that damned greedy evil witch," Deborah, hinting that he might even mean driving her into insanity. In other words, Simon has now pitted the women against each other, wishing them to fight until only one survives, a battle that is symbolic of his own divided mind. In fact, both of them think that one solution might be to "throw him in the pit—to fight it out with himself" as they watch "with gratified womanly pride." Then they would finally be rid of him. When Simon hears this, he shocks them with his new morality which turns idealism topsy-turvy. Man is not naturally good, but "a hog. It is that idealistic fallacy which is responsible for all the confusion in our minds, the conflicts within the self, and for all the confusion in our relationships with one another, within the family particularly, for the blundering of our desires which are disciplined to covet what they don't want and be afraid to crave what they wish for in truth. . . . All one needs to remember is that good is evil, and evil good." Within himself he realizes that the forces of the conflicting self are so "evenly matched" that they cannot battle it out, so one alone will survive and he will have to choose between their two feminine embodiments.

He first attempts to choose Deborah and her shadow world, begging her to take him with her beyond the red summerhouse door, to open the door in the mind which will lead him to "peace and happiness" in the magic kingdom of which she has told him. Insanity, then, will be his release. Sara, however, who has previously prevented Deborah from taking this step, now offers to renounce Simon to his mother, to go away, just as long as that door remains closed. But Deborah romantically proves the superiority of her love to Sara's "lust" (both for sex and power), by walking alone through her red door, into insanity. Each of the two women has attempted to remake Simon into her image of him, while Simon is not permitted his own choice. By the end of the play, Simon is free because Deborah is insane and Sara knows herself beaten. She renounces her own image of Simon and is now prepared to allow him to fulfill his own desires and dreams with her loving and unquestioned support. She is mother, wife, and mistress, all at the service of Simon in the marital relationship which O'Neill purveys throughout his plays as the ideal in which the artist, the dreamer, the masculine creative force, is nurtured, supported, and gratified by woman—by his wife, who has renounced everything except service to him.

But Simon has been broken in the struggle. In *The Calms of Capricorn* sixteen years have passed and the family have returned to Sara's old farm, but the curative power of nature does not seem to have worked. Simon looks much older than his fifty years and he has abandoned his dream, his projected book on the meaning of life, recognizing it as a fake. He is still trying to find himself, perhaps through his sons. He accompanies his practical son Honey, the tin peddler on his rounds, but business still makes him unhappy. He finds more kinship with his estranged seafaring son, Ethan, who has "a touch of the poet." Finally he reaches a stage of resignation and dies of pneumonia, tenderly thanking Sara for all she has done for him. His carefully orchestrated funeral service shows how well he understood all members of the family. In his last letter he tells Sara to go and be free; presumably freeing her to follow her dream, whatever that may be. As Sara and her sons realize, Simon has remained the eternal romantic, the eternal child.

Simon Harford's divided psyche is really the central battleground of these dramas, but Simon also seems to have been designed to represent the conflict between the Babbittry of someone like Marco Polo* in *Marco Millions** and the seeker after truth like Juan Ponce de Leon* in *The Fountain** and the Kublai Kaan* in the former play. In this way, Simon constitutes a criticism of American society, but almost more important is the manner in which he represents the victim, the man, who is almost destroyed by female possessiveness.

HARFORD, Wolfe. In *The Calms of Capricorn** (part of the abandoned cycle, "A Tale of Possessors, Self-Dispossessed"*), second son of Simon Harford* and Sara Melody* Harford; brother of Ethan Harford,* Jonathan Harford,* and Honey Harford.* He is twenty-seven, "tall and thin, handsome, distinguished, fastidious," who adopts an air "of smiling indifference." He is a bank clerk. Throughout the action he resolutely tries to avoid all emotional involvement and commitment to any person or thing. His deliberate opting out is shown by his choosing to play solitaire, a game which he considers utterly pointless, subject to chance, and independent of the operation of any other human being; in this way he shows his refusal to join in the "game" of life. Leda Cade,* the prostitute who represents feminine emotion and intuition, tries to force him into emotional involvement because she first perceives him as a challenge and then, as the action progresses, finds herself becoming almost enslaved to him. She finally forces him to cut the cards for possession of herself. He wins but instantly tries to return her to Ben Graber,* the man with whom she is traveling, but he refuses her and Leda announces her love for Wolfe.

Wolfe, the gambler, was destined to be the central figure of "The Earth Is the Limit,"* another of the plays in the proposed cycle. His mother, Sara, sees him as a great gambler like her father, Cornelius Melody,* in *A Touch of the Poet.**

HARRINGTON, Steve. In *Bread and Butter,** one of John Brown's* studio-mates in New York. Steve is "about twenty-eight, with large irregular features, light brown hair, and wide-set brown eyes." He is quiet and reserved with a pleasing voice. He tries to help John when he is depressed. At the end of the play, Steve is a successful artist in Paris.

HARRIS. In "The Personal Equation,"* a wiry, grey-haired stoker. He is simply the representative of one ethnic group in O'Neill's portrait of the stoke-hole, which prefigures his later treatment of the same scene in *The Hairy Ape.** Harris takes part in the attempt to sabotage the engines of the S.S. *San Francisco.*

HARRIS, Hattie. In *All God's Chillun Got Wings,** sister of Jim Harris. She is a proud young woman of thirty who is not ashamed of being black. She has worked her way through college and has become a schoolteacher, but she, too, has paid a price because she seems to lack sympathy and to have become extremely severe. She has denied her femininity. She is angry with Jim for marrying Ella Downey* and tries to get Jim to institutionalize Ella when she becomes insane. Hattie believes in his commitment to a legal career and cannot understand the way in which he will remain bound to the destructive Ella.

HARRIS, Jim. In *All God's Chillun Got Wings*,* a studious-looking black man "with a queerly baffled, sensitive face." He marries Ella Downey,* a white woman who eventually becomes insane. He wants desperately to become a lawyer, but no matter how hard he studies and how well he knows the answers, he is always intimidated into failing by the psychic murder inflicted on him by whites. Ella contributes to his failure because she prevents his development, wanting him to remain her playmate rather than become her husband. He is the son of a successful black businessman, but he wants to make it intellectually and professionally in the white world. When he finally accepts the impossibility of this dream, he follows his wife into her childhood world.

HARRIS, Mrs. In *All God's Chillun Got Wings*,* mother of Jim Harris* and Hattie Harris.* She is about sixty-five and appears in one scene in her parlor dressed in her old-fashioned Sunday-best dress. She accepts her place in society and prefers to remain in the black world. She is proud of the business success her husband achieved. She does not approve of Jim's marriage to Ella Downey* but does not openly object. She does not believe that the two races should mix, but she has some sympathy for Ella, believing that it is harder for her to marry black than the other way around. She gives her house in Lower New York to Jim and Ella and moves to the Bronx, then a black neighborhood.

HARTMANN. In "The Personal Equation,"* a revolutionary. He is a short man in his early forties with black hair brushed straight back in artistic style. He wears a black suit, white shirt, and a "flowing black Windsor tie." His head, with its thick-rimmed spectacles to correct myopia, seems too big for his short body. He is a totally committed revolutionary, believing in the cause of the International Workers of the Earth. He plans a means of sabotaging the engines of the S.S. *San Francisco*, a vessel belonging to the Ocean Steamship Company, the leader of the shipping cartel. He is convinced that the executive of the union representing firemen and dockworkers has arranged to sell out the members and therefore deputes Tom Perkins* to ship as a stoker and pick up dynamite in Liverpool to damage the engines. The scheme fails, and Tom is so seriously wounded that he becomes a brain-damaged vegetable. Hartmann is scarcely drawn as an individual and is the stereotype of the committed revolutionary. His name recalls the well-known anarchist Sadakichi Hartmann.

HAUNTED, THE. The third play in the trilogy, *Mourning Becomes Electra*.*

HAVEL, Hippolyte (1869–1950), anarchist, lover of Emma Goldman and Paula ("Polly") Holladay, sister of Louis Holladay.* Havel is the original of Hugo Kalmar* in *The Iceman Cometh*.* Born August 21, 1869 in the village of Burowski, Bohemia, then part of Austria-Hungary, to a Czech father and a gypsy mother. Havel was educated in Vienna, where he became a journalist for the anarchist press. His first imprisonment for revolutionary activities came in Vienna in 1893, when he was sentenced to eighteen months in jail as the consequence of delivering an inflammatory May Day speech. On his release he was deported to Burowski, his home village, but soon after was arrested in Prague after a demonstration. He then traveled through Germany lecturing and writing on anarchism. On his return to Vienna he was jailed for violating his banishment and incarcerated in an insane asylum on the grounds that his actions against the government constituted certifiable lunacy. Fortunately he was examined by the famous Dr. Krafft-Ebing, who attested to Havel's sanity so that he was released and deported. He went first to Zurich, then Paris and London, where he supported himself by shining shoes and sweeping floors.

In 1899 he became the lover of Emma Goldman, the celebrated revolutionary (and aunt of Saxe Commins,* O'Neill's editor at Random House), traveling with her to Paris for an anarchist conference. Goldman brought him with her to the United States, where he finessed an immigration check by claiming to have been born in Chicago in 1871, the year of the Great Fire in which city records were destroyed. In 1901 he was briefly detained as a result of anti-anarchist feeling following the assassination of President McKinley. Moving to New York, he helped Goldman with her periodical, *Mother Earth*, until her deportation in 1919. He also wrote a pamphlet, *What Is Anarchism?* and was founder of and writer for the following revolutionary journals: *The Social War, The Revolutionary Almanac*, and *Revolt*.

O'Neill met him in Greenwich Village when Havel was the lover of Polly Holladay and acted as cook at her restaurant at 137 Macdougal Street. Havel's relationship with Polly was extremely volatile because of his jealousy and her frequent infidelities. She often complained that Havel had broken his word to her by failing to commit suicide as he had promised. Havel also traveled to Provincetown where he acted as cook in Polly's restaurant there. In the summer of 1916 he lived with John Silas Reed* and Louise Bryant* as cook, and their house consequently became a gathering place for the Provincetown Players.*

Havel was also an important figure in the Ferrer School, an anarchist educational enterprise, along with Sadakichi Hartmann. O'Neill appropriated the latter's name for his revolutionary character Hartmann* in the unpublished play, "The Personal Equation."* However, Havel's chief claim to fame arises from his bohemian life, for he was an unsuccessful revolutionary, being impatient and unable to withstand protracted argument. His customary practice was to resort to personal invective and foul-mouthed insult. Like Hugo Kalmar in *Iceman* he was given to calling opponents "bourgeois pigs," and "Little monkey-face." Havel was the stereotypical anarchist in appearance, short, plump, with wild black hair, black eyes, spectacles, small beard and silver cane. He was never able to concentrate long enough to write a full-length work and declined into alcoholism. In 1924 he moved to an experimental anarchist colony in Stelton, New Jersey, remaining there for the rest of his life, irascible, garrulous, drunken, and tiresome, living on handouts. He still continued to visit Greenwich Village, and in 1934 undertook one last lecture tour of the United States. He died insane in the Marlboro Psychiatric Hospital, Marlboro, New Jersey, probably as the result of chronic alcoholism. O'Neill, a romantic rather than a doctrinaire anarchist, took Havel seriously, feeling sympathy for him because he had suffered for his political beliefs. *See* in "References": Avrich (1980); Gelb and Gelb (1973); Sheaffer (1973).

HELBURN, Theresa (1887–1959). Playwright, producer, long-term executive director of the Theatre Guild* which produced many of O'Neill's plays. Born in New York City, January 12, 1887. Second child and only daughter of Julius and Hannah (Peyser) Helburn. Died in Norwalk, Connecticut, August 18, 1959. Married 1920 to John Baker Opdycke, but continued to use her maiden name professionally. No children. Educated in private schools in New York and Boston. A.B., Bryn Mawr, 1908. Graduate study, Harvard University. Honorary degrees from Tufts University, Franklin and Marshall College, Columbia University. Her father was a leather merchant in Boston, where he spent the work week, returning to New York on weekends to be with his family who were living with his wife's parents. Hannah Helburn, a teacher before her marriage, remained interested in education and founded an experimental elementary school for her daughter and other children. She was also "a driving force in the Browning club" (Helburn, 1960, p. 6) and tried to encourage the work of young painters. She did not, however, think of the theatre as more than entertainment and Theresa Helburn did not see her first play until she was nine years old. At that time the child decided "the theater [*sic*] was not a dream or a goal—it was home" (Helburn, 1960, p. 7). After attending private schools in New York and Boston she went to Bryn Mawr College, Pennsylvania, where she produced the class play every year she was there, and also directed and acted in student productions. She retained her interest in her college and in 1936 appeared as Queen Elizabeth at the Bryn Mawr College May Day Festival.

Shortly after her graduation she suffered a nervous breakdown and the pattern of the rest of her life was indicated. She would have a period of intense activity which would be followed by exhaustion. However, she seems to have kept this potentially dangerous situation under control. Her parents bought her a farm in the Berkshires, Massachusetts, where she recuperated and began to write. She enrolled at Radcliffe College as a graduate student and took classes at Harvard, taking George Pierce Baker's* "English 47" workshop in 1909–1910.

Returning to New York in 1910 she supported herself with a variety of odd jobs, writing poetry (published in the *Century*, *Harper's* and the *New Republic*, as well as in poetry publications). She also taught drama at Miss Merrill's

Finishing School, Mamaroneck, New York, where one of her students was Katherine Cornell. She became a governess in the household of the Christian Herter family, where she developed an appreciation of chamber music. She travelled with their youngest daughter to Paris, where she met Gertrude Stein, discovered avant-garde art, studied ballet with Isadora Duncan, and explored the French theatre. Caught in Europe with her parents at the outbreak of World War I, they made their way to England where Helburn hoped to remain to help in the war effort, but because of her father's precarious health they returned to New York.

She continued writing, amassing a drawer full of rejected short stories and having no better luck with her plays. *Crops and Croppers* (later retitled *Alison Makes Hay* and bought by the producer, B. Iden Payne) managed twenty performances in 1918. Another play, *Enter the Hero*, was withdrawn in rehearsal, but later achieved some success among amateur groups. She became drama critic of the *Nation* and in 1919 was a play reader for the Theatre Guild, a development of the Washington Square Players,* with which O'Neill had been associated. The Guild's directors included Lawrence Langner,* Philip Moeller, Lee Simonson, Helen Westley, and Maurice Wertheim, all of whom were associated with O'Neill in the production and acting of his plays.

In 1920, the year of her marriage to John Opdycke, she became temporary executive secretary of the Theatre Guild. Her original plan was to stay two weeks until a permanent replacement was found (Helburn, 1960, p. 81), but she stayed nearly forty years, retiring as Executive Director in 1958. Together with Lawrence Langner she was responsible for overseeing a large number of O'Neill premieres (*see* Theatre Guild, The*). Helburn is credited with the original professional pairing of Alfred Lunt* and Lynn Fontanne,* and with guiding revision of the musical *Oklahoma* into its current form. This production quite literally rescued the Guild from bankruptcy. Prior to that time, they had achieved solvency largely as a result of their numerous productions of Bernard Shaw.

Theresa Helburn had a long professional relationship with Eugene O'Neill and their illuminating correspondence is in the Beinecke Library of Yale University. At times their relations were strained, partly as a result of Guild politics and policies, but overall, the Guild did very well by O'Neill, staging some of his most difficult plays like *Marco Millions** and *Strange Interlude*,* though they balked at *Lazarus Laughed** and to their lasting regret, turned down *"Anna Christie."** Helburn was also supportive of O'Neill's abandoned cycle "A Tale of Possessors, Self-Dispossessed,"* visiting the O'Neills at Casa Genotta, Sea Island, Georgia, in 1936 to investigate the then eight-play plan. The thought of producing this *comédie humaine*, as she called it, fascinated her and she talked of setting up a special repertory company to produce it. However, she asked for a draft, and O'Neill backed off, saying that he wanted first to complete the work. Later, in 1940, she visited Tao House, asking O'Neill to release *The Iceman Cometh** for production, but he decided to hold it until after the end of World War II. The Guild remained interested in the cycle, and Lawrence Langner even thought of forming a company in San Francisco so that the playwright could oversee production from his Tao House location, but even that possibility failed to budge O'Neill from his insistence on waiting for completion. In 1946 the Guild produced *The Iceman Cometh* to mixed reviews, and in 1947 it produced *A Moon for the Misbegotten*,* which closed in tryouts, ostensibly for "recasting," but it was not revived by the Guild. This failure signified the end of O'Neill's professional relationship with the Guild, though he remained friends with Lawrence Langner and his wife Armina Marshall, until the 1948 split between O'Neill and his wife, Carlotta Monterey.* O'Neill never seems to have been personally as close to Helburn as he was to the Langners. (*See* Helburn, 1960, pp. 256–280 for her account of the Guild's work with O'Neill.)

Theresa Helburn had a great influence on the development of American theatre from 1920 to 1958, when she retired. Often criticized as autocratic, she admitted to a blind spot in refusing to recognize that the French theatre, with its irony, did not appeal to American tastes. Early criticism of her regime suggested that she staged too many European and not enough American plays, and later comments claim that she was too devoted to commercial success in the 1930s. But in view of the Great Depression, who can blame her? She also founded the short-lived Theatre Guild School for Young Playwrights in conjunction with the New School for Social Research, New York City. She briefly essayed acting in *Suzanna and the Elders* (1939), but was not well received. Her directing credits included *Chrysalis* (1932, with 23 performances) and *Mary of Scotland* (1933, with 236 performances). In 1957 she set up the Theresa Helburn Human Freedom Award to encourage playwrights to deal with this theme. She died in Norwalk Hospital, Connecticut, after a heart attack suffered at "Terrytop," her residence in Westport, Connecticut. *See* in "References": Helburn, 1960; Langner, 1951; Mannes, 1930.

HELENE. In *Bread and Butter*,* a cloak and suit model, friend of Ted Nelson.* She is twenty, blond, blue-eyed, wearing a great deal of make-up. Her figure is beautiful and voluptuous, and she wears the latest styles from a French magazine. She appears, slightly drunk, on the arm of Ted Nelson and scandalizes Edward Brown, Sr.,* who does not believe the introduction of her as Ted's "wife." Mr. Brown sees her as evidence of immorality in artistic circles.

HENDERSON. In "The Personal Equation,"* a tall, thin Scot, friend of Thomas Perkins.* He is the engineer of the S.S. *San Francisco* and has worked with Perkins for thirty years. He is about to leave the vessel for a job in the marine works in Liverpool, and Perkins is distressed at the imminent departure of his old friend. In the second act of the play, he is used as an expository device. The two men play cards, squabble, and discuss their past and also Perkins's son, Tom Perkins.* Henderson prevents Mrs. Allen,* the housekeeper, from revealing the unconventional relationship of Tom and Olga Tarnoff,* a young revolutionary.

HERRON, Donald (Bull). In *Abortion*,* roommate of Jack Townsend.* A huge, swarthy six-footer with a bull neck and an omnipresent grin, slow to anger and to understanding but—an All-American tackle. His immense frame is decked out in white flannels which make him look gigantic." He is the butt of numerous nicknames; Lucy Townsend,* Jack's sister, calls him Jumbo and Pluto. He has the unthinking arrogance of the upper classes in his attitude toward Joe Murray,* the "townie" whose sister has died as the result of a bungled abortion. He represents one type of college athlete, the rather clumsy hulk.

HICKEY. *See* Hickman, Theodore.

HICKMAN, Theodore ("Hickey"). In *The Iceman Cometh*,* a stout salesman of about fifty. He visits Harry Hope's* bar annually to go on a monumental binge himself and to treat the denizens of the saloon to a celebration in honor of Hope's birthday. "He exudes a friendly, generous personality that makes everyone like him on sight" and is obviously very good in his line. "His clothes are those of a successful drummer whose territory consists of minor cities and small towns." He has a good sense of humor and can play jokes on others and laugh at those played on himself. His continual jokes about finding his wife, Evelyn, "in the hay with the iceman" give one meaning to the title of the play.

This year, however, the Hickey who appears at the bar is different. He is sober and does not mention his wife. Also, he has given up drinking, though he still treats his friends and tells them, "The only reason I've quit is—Well I finally had the guts to face myself and throw overboard the damned lying pipe dream that'd been making me miserable, and do what I had to do for the happiness of all concerned—and then all at once I found I was at peace with myself and I didn't need booze any more."

The rest of the play shows his attempt to teach this new philosophy of existence to the inhabitants of the bar, and Hickey is a persuasive salesman. He manages to get some of them to test out their pipedreams so they can shape up, spruce up, give up the drink, and translate their illusions into reality. He also tries to make others look at themselves without euphemisms. Of course, Hickey is well aware that the dreams are impossible of fulfillment, but he believes that through this facing of the truth his friends will find a peace which is the result of going beyond all hope. Three people do not follow this new doctrine of salvation: Hugo Kalmar,* the old anarchist, who remains drunk most of the time but who fears the questions Hickey is making him ask himself; Larry Slade,* a disenchanted anarchist whom Hickey calls "the old foolosopher"; and Don Parritt,* the eighteen-year-old informer son of an imprisoned anarchist mother. Hickey particularly wants to convince Larry of this discovery of truth because in the "foolosopher's" pipedream of detachment and announced detestation of life, Hickey sees the greatest challenge.

As the play progresses, the other bar-friends fail to convert their dreams into reality, but they do not find the peace that Hickey expects, and the same is true for those who are forced to see other truths about themselves. The result of Hickey's campaign is to sow dissension and bring misery, something he cannot understand. The group gathers to murmur against him, wondering why he has not mentioned his wife. At his birthday party, Hickey delivers another speech, attempting to convince them of the joys of truth. Then he tells them, "my dearly beloved wife is dead," but then continues that he must feel glad for her sake because she was "married to a no-good cheater and drunk" but now is at peace. This devastates the group, and the next day Larry, Rocky, and Parritt speculate on what happened. Larry perceives the truth and tries to stop the conversation, but that evening Hickey makes a full confession, after having called the police— he had killed Evelyn with a bullet in the head. In a long monologue Hickey tells the story of his life: the ne'er-do-well son of a minister; he loved Evelyn from childhood, and she loved him. He went away and told her to forget him, but she did not. Finally, she married him, still believing in his ultimate goodness, no matter what he might do. She never wavered in this belief and forgave Hickey for every act of drunkenness and infidelity, even when he infected her with venereal disease. "Love always won," and Hickey began to feel more and more guilty. This year he kept swearing to her that he would not come to Hope's bar, but as the day came closer he knew he would have to come, even though this time he would not be able to bear her forgiveness. That would mean he could not return to her, and that would break her heart because to her it would mean he no longer loved her. Therefore he killed her—to give her peace.

Hickey talks on, trying to convince himself of the truth of this statement, but inadvertently reveals everything when he repeats what he had said over the body of his dead wife: "Well, you know what you can do with your pipe dream now, you damned bitch!" This is his true motivation. Now his assertion of the necessity of truth, of facing oneself, is shown as the true pipedream for him. This is underscored by his immediate adoption of an excuse: "I couldn't have said that! If I did, I'd gone insane!" He pleads with Harry Hope for confirmation, and the barroom denizens quickly seize on this as an acceptable, if illusory, explanation. Even as the policemen he had telephoned move to arrest him, he pleads insanity, but Larry alone sees that he may find his peace only with expiation in the electric chair. The iceman of death has indeed come for him.

Theodore Hickman, whose name has resonances of God "Theo" and "Hick" man, represents the bankruptcy of his preaching of salvation. He comes to the bar-microcosm with the aim of selling the ideal of life without the saving lie, but Larry Slade well knows that "the lie of the pipe dream is what gives life to the whole misbegotten mad lot of us." When Hickey comes, he brings death with him, as Hugo understands and therefore retreats into drunkenness. It has been suggested by Cyrus Day (1958) that Hickey is an antichrist and Parritt a Judas Iscariot; hence they recognize each other, but in another sense they are both betrayers, and thus their recognition is perhaps even more explicable. But the irony of Hickey is that his dream of peace is a pipe dream which he himself is unable to recognize for what it is. Further, he is a salesman, a drummer, and, as Arthur Miller later pointed out in commenting on his own *Death of a Salesman*, all his character sold was himself. In a sense, this is also true of Hickey, but what he has to sell is a philosophy of pessimism—of suicidal annihilation which only Parritt puts into practice (out of despair rather than understanding) and only Larry can comprehend. Everyone else at the bar gladly gets drunk in an attempt to forget the world and regain illusion.

HIGGINS. In *Where the Cross Is Made*,* doctor on the staff of the local mental hospital, a medium-sized man, very professional-looking, about thirty-five. He is asked by Nat Bartlett* to take his father away. The character of Higgins is not very carefully drawn, and his chief function is to act as expository device as Nat tells his father's story.

HILLMAN, Lucy. In *Days Without End*,* a sadly discontented, unhappily married woman of about thirty-five who shows her age and who wears clothes that are a trifle too youthful and too "extreme." She is the wife of the philanderer Walter Hillman; and in an attempt to avenge herself on him, she seduces John Loving,* the husband of Elsa Loving,* partly because she envies the perfection of their marriage. She goes to see Elsa while she is recuperating from influenza and tells the story of her affair, but she suppresses John's name because she finds herself ashamed of her actions. She feels the necessity of confessing her fault, but she does not wish to hurt Elsa, realizing that Elsa would never forgive her husband. Lucy's character is, like many in this play, a stereotype, and she is not deeply drawn.

HILLS, Everett, D.D. In *The Hunted*, the second play of the trilogy, *Mourning Becomes Electra*,* a Congregationalist minister. He is in his fifties, "stout and unctuous, snobbish and ingratiating, conscious of godliness, but timid." He, along with his unnamed "flabby, self-effacing" wife, forms part of the Chorus of Townsfolk who appear just after the funeral of Ezra Mannon* to comment on the Mannon family (particularly Christine Mannon*) and the events with which they have been involved.

HOGAN. In "The Personal Equation,"* a drunken stoker. He is simply one of the ethnic characters in O'Neill's treatment of the stokehole of the S.S. *San Francisco*, which prefigures his portrayal of the same scene in *The Hairy Ape*.* Hogan is used as a dramatic device to move characters on and off stage.

HOGAN, Josie. In *A Moon for the Misbegotten*,* daughter of Phil Hogan* and sister of Mike Hogan.* She is an almost freakish woman of five feet eleven inches weighing about 180 pounds, with a rough tongue, a bad reputation, and a heart of gold. When her mother died giving birth to her brother Mike, now twenty, Josie acted as mother to him and her other two brothers, all of whom she assists to leave the rockstrewn tenant farm which Phil Hogan rented first from James Tyrone, Sr.,* and now from his son. She manages to keep Phil in order with rage and blows, but inwardly she pities his weakness. She loves James Tyrone, Jr.,* the ne'er-do-well son of the old actor; and her brother, Mike, seems to be correct when he alleges that she is scheming to get Jim in bed with her and have her father catch them and force a marriage. Josie vigorously denies the suggestion, but later on, when Phil leads her to believe that Jim has welshed on their understanding that Phil would have first refusal of the farm, she determines to go through with the plot. However, despite all her blather, Josie is really a virgin who covers up her essential undesirability to men by pretending promiscuity, while all the young men who claim they have known her sexually are really covering up the fact that she has actually punched them away. But with Jim Tyrone, things are different on this moonlit September night. Josie discovers that Phil has lied to her and that Jim will indeed sell him the farm. First she is furious with her father, and then she looks at Jim, who wants nothing from her except her maternal love. To be sure, he does make one serious pass at her but then decides not to go through with it because he, alone among the young men, has seen through Josie's defense mechanism and sees her brazen exterior as a means of covering a deeply wounded woman who knows herself undesirable but who has much love to give.

Josie understands the sadness of Jim Tyrone, his weakness, and his sorrow for the death of his mother. Throughout that long night, she cradles his head on her breast, like the Virgin and the dead Christ in the "Pietà," as he confesses himself to her, obtaining forgiveness from her and assurance that his own mother forgives him. Josie is a combination of feminine characters earlier portrayed by O'Neill. She is Cybel,* the earth-mother prostitute of *The Great God Brown*￼* who comforts both Dion Anthony* and William A. Brown,* and like her, she understands how to bring peace to Jim. She also knows how to help her weaker brothers to escape their fate on the farm, giving them the chance to fulfill their ambition at the expense of her own. She is the only prop on whom Phil Hogan is able to lean, for she manages to maintain his self-respect, even if it is only by chasing him with a broom handle when he gets drunk. She supports him in his chicanery, laughing at his tricks, and at the same time saving him from himself. With Jim Tyrone she is also the unattainable Virgin, the mediatrix in mankind's salvation, and also his mother and in these roles speaks words of absolution to Jim so that he need no longer feel guilt. At the same time she echoes the spirit of Nora Melody* in *A Touch of the Poet*,* who takes pride in her love, in her tending the dreams of others, regardless of her own wishes. She is content to have had the chance to bring peace to the tortured soul of the man she loves dearly yet without hope.

HOGAN, Mike. In *A Moon for the Misbegotten*,* youngest son of Phil Hogan* and brother of Josie Hogan.* He is twenty years old, a "primly self-righteous" young man of about five feet seven with a "common Irish face, . . . a New England Irish Catholic Puritan, Grade B, and an extremely irritating youth to have around." His sister, Josie, has brought him up since his mother had died at his birth. Josie helps him escape from the rockstrewn farm of their father, as she had also done for his two older brothers. Mike is shrewd enough to see Josie's affection for James Tyrone, Jr.,* and also smart enough to understand that his sister would like to trick Tyrone into marrying her. Nonetheless, Mike is an unlikable young man who fortunately disappears early from the play.

HOGAN, Phil. In *A Moon for the Misbegotten*,* father of Josie Hogan* and Mike Hogan.* Phil is a tenant of James Tyrone, Jr.,* on a rockstrewn farm in Connecticut. He is a feisty, stocky little Irishman of around fifty-five, about five feet six in height, with a wicked sense of verbal humor and an enormous capacity for liquor. He dislikes his youngest son, Mike, partly because Phil's wife had died giving birth to him but mainly because he is a "priest's pet," an extremely upright, rather mean-minded young man. He frequently berates his Amazonian daughter, Josie, who keeps him in line and who also helps Mike (and her older brothers, Thomas and John) to escape from the farm. In truth, Phil respects Josie because she keeps alive his image of himself as a sharp practiser (helping him to do so in a very practical way) and also shares his sense of humor. He understands her love for James Tyrone and as a result attempts to trick them into bed together as a means of forcing their marriage—or so he says. He tells Josie that James is about to sell the farm to an heir of Standard Oil, T. Stedman Harder,* on whom both he and Josie have played a practical joke (also recounted in *Long Day's Journey into Night*). Josie believes her father and as a result attempts to seduce Jim Tyrone, only to discover that Phil has lied to her and that Jim is even more wounded than she. Out of love and pity, she spends her last evening with him cradling his head on her breast in maternal comfort. When Phil returns, he claims that he had misinformed Josie so that the two of them might find solace in each other. Josie is really heartbroken, but she realizes that she must stay with Phil, who knows that he cannot exist without her support.

HOLLADAY, Louis (?   –1918), longtime friend of Eugene O'Neill, dating from his Princeton days in Spring 1906. In that term, Holladay supplied O'Neill with absinthe which the two consumed in O'Neill's Princeton dormitory until, to the horror of Holladay and some of the undergraduates, O'Neill became berserk. He and O'Neill, together with Edward Keefe and George Bellows, Princeton acquaintances, also frequented the notorious Tenderloin district of New York on occasion. After dropping out of Princeton, O'Neill retained his acquaintanceship with Holladay and his sister Polly, the lover of Hippolyte Havel,* among many others. Louis Sheaffer (1968, pp. 161–162) suggests that Holladay *may* have shipped on board the *Charles Racine* with O'Neill in 1910 as quasi-passenger-crew-members for a voyage to Buenos Aires.

Holladay, along with Polly, became part of the Liberal Club life of Greenwich Village, and O'Neill began to move back into their circle in 1915, particularly through his patronage of Polly's restaurant, which was in the same building as the Liberal Club. In 1915–1916, Holladay attempted to run a bar, but the operation was closed and Holladay given a jail sentence for violation of the liquor laws since he did not have a liquor license. By then he wished to marry Louise Norton, whose money had started him in the bar business; and in order to gain her approval, he stopped drinking and followed her suggestion that he go to Oregon "to manage an apple orchard owned by her family" (Sheaffer, 1968, p. 410). On his return after a year, she told him that she had decided to marry someone else. On January 22, 1918, Holladay became exceedingly drunk and took a deliberate overdose of heroin. O'Neill, who was present at the time, told him not to be foolish and left, along with others. Shortly afterwards, Holladay expired on Dorothy Day's* shoulder. She summoned O'Neill and Agnes Boulton,* but O'Neill chose to go to a bar rather than return to the restaurant where Louis lay dead. Uncertainty surrounds the details of Holladay's procuring the heroin, and accounts differ with the teller; Terry Carlin* is suggested as the source, but narcotics charges were not filed, apparently because Dorothy Day managed to hide the evidence and Polly Holladay told the police that her brother was known to have heart trouble (which was indeed true). The death certificate read "chronic endocarditis."

Holladay's importance in O'Neill's life arises from his Princeton acquaintanceship, his companionship in exploring the red-light district of New York, and his possible trip to Buenos Aires with the playwright, as well as his presence in Greenwich Village. O'Neill's reaction to Holladay's death also prefigures his later response to the deaths of friends and relations. Unlike most Irishmen, O'Neill avoided funerals, even when he himself was in good health, preferring to have his wife, whether Agnes Boulton or Carlotta Monterey,* perform the suitable obligatory acts of funeral arrangements or sending flowers whenever possible.

HOMECOMING. The first play in the trilogy entitled *Mourning Becomes Electra.**

"HONOR AMONG THE BRADLEYS," a play written in 1919. Destroyed. It seems to have been based on a curious family who lived near O'Neill and Agnes Boulton* in West Point Pleasant, New Jersey. There were a father, mother, and seven beautiful blond girls, each of whom in turn became pregnant and had to drop out of school. Whatever happened to either the girls or their babies is unknown. They were, according to Agnes Boulton O'Neill, the town outcasts. *See* in "References": Boulton (1958, pp. 236–238) and Floyd (1981, pp. 2–3).

HOPE, Harry. In *The Iceman Cometh,** proprietor of a saloon and rooming house. He is sixty, white-haired, extraordinarily thin, horse-faced, a very likable fellow, "a soft-hearted slob, without malice, . . . a sinner among sinners, a born easy mark." He tries to hide his vulnerability "behind a testy truculent manner" that fools no one. He is a little deaf, sometimes pretending to be more so, wears dime-store spectacles which are badly out of alignment, and his ill-fitting false teeth click when he is angry.

Harry's name is an ironic comment on the situation of the denizens of his bar, for they have lost all hope. Harry rents upstairs rooms to them and often allows them drinks on the house, though he claims that he is going to stop this privilege "tomorrow." Harry's wife, Bessie Mosher, died twenty years ago, and Harry has almost sanctified her, forgetting her shrewish disposition. Since her death he has become a recluse, staying inside his bar all the time but continually saying that one of these days he will "take a walk around the ward" and look up his old acquaintances in politics, for he had once been a small-time Tammany Hall politician.

When Theodore Hickman* ("Hickey") arrives to help Harry celebrate his birthday, he persuades Harry to take this much-promised walk, but Harry finds himself totally scared. He gets to the middle of the street and bolts back to the security of his tiny world with its pipe dreams, manufacturing another for himself as a support—that he had nearly been run down by an automobile. He is a character for whom the saving lie is essential for existence, and he does not wish to face the truth about himself. After the disaster of the birthday party, when Hickey tells of murdering his wife, Evelyn, and is arrested, Hope and his friends seize on his plea of insanity, a pipe dream explanation which discredits what Hickey has taught them. However, they speedily get drunk once more in a wish to forget the outside world and to try to regain their old illusions.

Harry Hope's bar is a combination of places Eugene O'Neill frequented in his early New York years: James J. Condon's* Saloon, The Golden Swan (The Hell Hole), and the bar of the Garden Hotel (near the old Madison Square Garden). Harry Hope himself is based on both Tom Wallace, a recluse who lived above The Hell Hole after his wife's death, and Condon, who was also known as Jimmy-the-Priest. [For this and other identifications, *see* in "References": Sheaffer (1973).]

HORNE, Silas. In *Where the Cross is Made*,* first mate of the wrecked *Mary Allen*, "a parrot-nosed, angular old man dressed in grey cotton trousers and a torn singlet." He was drowned when the ship was lost. He appears (along with his companions, Cates* the bosun, and Jimmy Kanaka,* the harpooner) in an hallucinatory scene in which only the obsessed Captain Isaiah Bartlett* and the half-insane Nat Bartlett* see them. The three men bring in two inlaid chests presumably containing the treasure, but it is only an illusion.

In *Gold*,* a four-act recension of *Where the Cross is Made*, Horne has the same physical characteristics but with the notable addition of a face marked by "crass lusts and mean cruelty." He "makes violent motions to Jimmy Kanaka" to murder Abel* and Butler,* the only two persons of the crew who seem uncorrupted, in order to deny them their share of the buried "treasure." Later he goes out to seek this "treasure" on the vessel *Sarah Allen*. The crew attempts to murder Danny Drew,* the acting captain and fiancé of Sue Bartlett,* in order to prevent him from knowing the true reason for the journey. Horne, along with Cates and Jimmy Kanaka, is lost when the *Sarah Allen* is wrecked.

HOWARD, Miss. In *The Straw*,* she is a pretty, blonde nurse in training. She knows that she is attractive but nonetheless has an underlying air of seriousness. She is twenty years old and frequently jokes with Stephen Murray.* She has probably been drawn from real life and is a composite of two nurses that O'Neill knew at the Gaylord Farm,* Wallingford, Connecticut. Their names were Wilhelmina Stamberger and Catherine Murray. Miss Stamberger had the physical appearance of Miss Howard and had once had tuberculosis. Miss Murray, however, was the nurse at Gaylord whom O'Neill knew best.

HUGHES, Charlie. In *Hughie*,* night clerk in a seedy westside New York hotel. He is in his early forties, is married to a nagging wife named Jess, and has three children. He was born in Saginaw, Michigan, and has come to New York in order to seek success and has failed. He is tall, thin, long-faced, with a pimply complexion, bad teeth, a prominent Adam's apple, horn-rimmed glasses, and a blank expression. He is dressed "in an ill-fitting blue serge suit, white shirt and collar, a blue tie." His suit is well worn and shiny at the elbows. He has just recently replaced Hughie, the former night clerk who has recently died. "Erie" Smith,* a long-time resident of the hotel, tries to engage Charlie in conversation because he is desperately lonely now that Hughie, his former confidant, is dead. However, Erie cannot establish communication with Charlie Hughes, who is too busy spinning his own pipedreams of adventure which are triggered by the night sounds of city life impinging on the lobby of the hotel. Eventually, Charlie realizes that he ought to listen to the guest, if not for courtesy, then for the reason that he, too, needs companionship. He asks a few questions about Arnold Rothstein, the gambler, "the Big Shot," and this manages to buoy up the lonely Erie. At the end of the play, Erie and Charlie are rolling dice with Erie's loaded "bones," as Hughie and Erie had done. Charlie is titillated and made to feel important by Erie's supposed connection with Rothstein, while Erie's grief is assuaged and his confidence restored by the discovery of another "sucker," another uncritical listener who will bolster his confidence and keep up his spirits. In short, both men need each other in order to face life. In return for his listening, Charlie enjoys vicariously the apparently exciting life of a Broadway gambler. He plays the role of the good listener in this monologue.

HUGHIE, a one-act play with two characters, set in the "lobby of a small hotel on a West Side Street in midtown New York . . . between 3 and 4 A.M. of a day in the summer of 1928." It is the only completed play of a projected cycle of eight one-acts with the overall title, "By Way of Obit."* Essentially, the play is composed of two monologues, one spoken by "Erie" Smith* and the other acted, with the help of the extensive stage directions, by Charlie Hughes.*

The spoken monologue is played against a background of city noises, the elevated railway, garbage cans, an ambulance, and a fire truck, all of which trigger thoughts in the mind of the night clerk which run parallel to the words of Erie Smith, and only occasionally is there a spoken bridge of communication until the end of the play, which runs barely an hour.

The night clerk is tall and skinny with a pimply face, large characterless nose and mouth, bad teeth, a pronounced Adam's apple, thinning hair, horn-rimmed spectacles, and a blank expression. His "ill-fitting blue serge suit" is shiny at the elbows. "He is in his early forties." Erie Smith is about the same age but quite different in appearance. He is stout with unusually short, fat legs, so that he appears less than his actual medium height. His head is large and set on a thick neck that disappears into "beefy shoulders." He has a round face, snub nose, shifty blue eyes with pouches under them, and thinning sandy hair. He is dressed in a tight-cut "Broadway" gray suit, bright blue shirt, red-and-blue tie, tan-and-white shoes, white silk socks, "a braided leather belt with a brass buckle," and he carries a Panama hat. He perspires profusely and mops his face with a red-and-blue silk handkerchief. "In manner, he is consciously a Broadway sport and a Wise Guy—the type of small fry gambler and horse player." However, beneath his slightly conspiratorial manner there is "some sentimental softness . . . which doesn't belong in the hard-boiled picture."

Erie enters and asks laconically, "Key." The night clerk has obviously not seen Erie before, and therefore he has to introduce himself as "492," his room number. To his surprise, Erie discovers that the night clerk is named Charlie Hughes, the same surname as that of the recently deceased night clerk whose funeral has sent Erie off on a drunk. The two men, however, are not related, though they have some similarities. Both are married, "Hughie" having two children and the current night clerk three, and both share the same age, forty-three or forty-four. Charlie Hughes is from Saginaw, Michigan, and that leads Erie to recount the fact that he was born in Erie, Pennsylvania, hence his nickname, but he ran away when a girl in the town accused him of getting her pregnant. He fled to Saratoga to follow the horses, and he claims to have been following "the bangtails" ever since, with varying degrees of success.

All through this speech, the night clerk has been busy with his own thoughts as Erie continues, this time with reminiscences of Hughie, who had always greeted him with cheery inquiries and tried to follow Erie's career vicariously, though Hughie was too frightened of his wife to act out his fantasies with women or with gambling. What distresses Erie is that he has been unable to win a bet "since Hughie was took to the hospital," but then he takes refuge in the fatalistic philosophy, "Hell, we all gotta croak. . . . When a guy's dead he's dead. He don't give a damn, so why should anybody else?" But despite this, Erie still misses Hughie, who obviously provided a sounding board for him and also a reinforcement for his dream of being a big-shot Broadway gambler and horse-race handicapper. Hughie also gave Erie a chance to be superior to him as "a sucker," and now Erie misses him: "He sure was one grand little guy." But he gets no response from Charlie Hughes, whose mind is away with the night sounds of the city which tell him the time even better than a clock and signify also the passage of life. But then Charlie recalls his duty to a guest and offers a cliché, for which Erie is grateful, because it starts him off again on reminiscences of Hughie, this time concerning the way he used to play with Erie's loaded dice—so innocent that the trickery never occurred to him, and full of wonder at Erie's never-failing luck. One day Erie took Hughie out to Belmont race track where he fell in love with the horses and even won. But then, when Hughie gave Erie two dollars he had stolen from his wife's purse in order to bet, Erie refused and made him return it: " 'Nix,' I told him, 'if you're going to start playin' sucker and bettin' on horse races, you don't get no assist from me'." This, he recalls, is the one good deed he has done in his life.

Erie then looks back on his first meeting with Hughie, whom he had "sized up for a sap the first time I see him," and tells the dead man's life story. Hughie had come from upstate New York to find success in the city but had ended up as a night clerk and then met a girl on a subway train, fell in love, and married her. Once Hughie took Erie to his cheap Brooklyn flat to meet Irma and the children, but Irma had disapproved of Erie: "She had me tagged for a bum, and seein' me made her sure she was right." The invitation was never renewed, and when Hughie tried to apologize, Erie "switched the subject." The night clerk has been letting his mind wander after a policeman on the beat, a passing ambulance, and then a fire engine, continually dreaming of participation in some excitement. As a result, he barely replies to Erie's direct questions.

Despite the night clerk's lack of interest, Erie cannot break off the conversation and go to bed. He needs companionship desperately as he stands at the desk "twirling his key frantically as if it were a fetish which might set him free," again wishing that Hughie were there to respond to his tall tales of gambling and sexual conquests. He hastens to assure the new night clerk that the tales were not all lies but were things that happened to other people in most cases. "I sure took him with me in tales and showed him one hell of a time." Erie is also well aware that Hughie's appreciation made him feel better, especially when he was broke and "feeling lower than a snake's belly." On those occasions he would exaggerate his successes to impress Hughie. Suddenly the word "truth" percolates into the night clerk's consciousness and he asks, "What's the truth?" feeling guilty that he has been ignoring Erie, who at least offers something approaching company in his current mood, when he finds himself thinking vaguely of death.

Almost as if in response to the night clerk's unspoken thoughts, Erie starts to talk to himself about Hughie's death and funeral, which would have been very meager indeed without Erie's one-hundred-dollar floral piece in the shape of a horseshoe with the legend, "Good-by, Old Pal" in forget-me-nots. As Erie stands there forlornly, the night clerk starts to feel guilty for his inattention and decides he must say something. Dimly recollecting that Erie had said something about gambling, he takes a plunge by asking, "Do you, by any chance, know the Big Shot, Arnold Rothstein?'' But this time Erie does not hear him, talking of the tales he could tell Hughie—while in his own thoughts the night clerk is dreaming about playing a high-rolling game with Rothstein, until he reaches a state of exaltation like ''a holy saint, recently elected to Paradise.'' But then Erie breaks the silence by saying that Hughie is ''out of the racket. I mean, the whole goddamned racket. I mean life.'' The night clerk makes an inconsequential remark of acquiescence, which triggers communication, and he again asks if Erie knows Arnold Rothstein. The gambler claims that he does and that he occasionally runs errands for him, but then he confesses to considerable fear because he has borrowed the money for Hughie's funeral flower piece and now must pay it back, something that he cannot do at the moment. His creditors are likely to beat him up, and now that his usual run of luck has deserted him since Hughie's illness and death, he believes he has lost both luck and confidence permanently: ''He used to give me confidence.'' Again the night clerk returns to the topic of Arnold Rothstein, and Erie responds, seeing another Hughie in Charlie Hughes as he speaks of his successes in crap games and at the race track, looking ahead to a success ''tomorrow'' at Saratoga. By now the night clerk is ''ingratiatingly pally,'' and Erie suggests a crap game to be played with Erie's money. He asks if the night clerk wishes to inspect the dice, and he refuses: ''I know I can trust you.'' With this, Erie says he will stop ''carryin' the torch for Hughie.'' He is dead, and death is man's common fate. Erie's grief is now over and his confidence has returned as he starts rolling the dice, winning the first throw over the night clerk and looking at him with ''the slyly amused, contemptuous, affectionate wink with which a Wise Guy regales a Sucker.''

Comments: This play operates almost as a sequel to *The Iceman Cometh** with its depiction of pipe dreams which give hope to the wounded and the unsuccessful. Both Erie and Hughie needed each other, as the night clerk also needs Erie, while the gambler can now transfer Hughie's role to his replacement. In this play, however, O'Neill has moved into a singularly spare kind of drama which leaves almost everything to the actors. Gone are the spoken interior monologues of *Strange Interlude*,* and instead one is expected to read the mind of the night clerk as he ruminates about the street noises, dreaming of participation in exciting incidents in the same way that Erie speaks his tales aloud. Each depends on an imaginative existence in order to live in a world where they are both close to total failure; the two of them also need each other as they stand in the lobby, temporarily apart from the daily and nightly existence which is conveyed through the noises of the city. In this way, their temporary abdication from life is exemplified, and through their mildly grandiose dreams, they manage to survive. In some respects, O'Neill has, however, refined his technique so much that he has become undramatic, while his reliance on extensive, almost poetic, stage directions seems to be leading him in the direction of the novel.

Note: In the 1964 New York production Charlie's thoughts were spoken.

Production Data: Written 1941. First produced at the Royal Dramatic Theatre (Kungl. Dramatiska Teatern), Stockholm, Sweden, September 18, 1958, by Karl

Ragnar Gierow in a translation by Sven Barthel (64 performances). Originally, it played along with *The Emperor Jones*,* an unsuccessful production which was later withdrawn and replaced by August Strindberg's *The Stronger*. This latter pairing has become traditional.

 Producer: Dramaten
 Director: Bengt Ekerot
 Set Design: Marik Vos
 Costumes: Gunnar Gelbort
 Cast: "Erie" Smith: Bengt Eklund
   Charlie Hughes: Alan Edwall

First American Production: Produced by Theodore Mann and Joseph Levine in association with Katzka-Berne at the Royale Theatre, New York City, December 22, 1964 (51 performances).

 Director: José Quintero*
 Set Design and Lighting: David Hays
 Costumes: Noel Taylor
 Cast: "Erie" Smith: Jason Robards, Jr.*
   Charlie Hughes: Jack Dodson

A Note on Text: The text used is that published by Yale University Press, 1959.

HULL, Thomas. In *The Calms of Capricorn*,* the predecessor of Ethan Harford* as first mate of the clipper, *Dream of the West*. Hull is an old friend of Captain Enoch Payne* and is the enemy of Ethan Harford, knowing that Ethan will sacrifice everything, including the safety of ship and crew, to break the sailing record of the *Flying Cloud*. Hull has had a heart attack at the beginning of the action of the scenario of *The Calms of Capricorn*,* and since he has been told to remain ashore to recuperate and miss this current voyage, Ethan is temporarily given his job. However, Hull returns to the vessel to resume his position (much to Payne's relief), and Hull treats Ethan with cynical rudeness and even enmity. When he caustically berates Ethan for being below with the women, the younger man at first absorbs the insult, but, goaded by Leda Cade,* he suddenly punches Hull in the jaw. Hull falls, striking his head, and dies.

HUNTED, THE. The second play in the trilogy entitled *Mourning Becomes Electra*.*

I

ICEMAN COMETH, THE, a play in four acts set in "a cheap ginmill . . .
situated on the downtown West Side of New York." The action covers two days
and nights in early summer, 1912.

Act I: "The back room and a section of the bar of Harry Hope's saloon,"
early morning. A dirty black curtain at the right separates the bar from the back
room, which is crowded with round tables and chairs arranged in three rows,
"front to back." In the left corner is a toilet, built out like a telephone booth;
a nickel in the slot-phonograph is on the middle left wall, along with two grimy
windows onto an interior courtyard. The walls and ceiling, once white, are now
filthy. The floor, with iron spittoons here and there, is sawdust-covered. Four
single wall brackets offer what illumination there is. Through the drawn back
curtain at the right, the bar is visible by the light which filters in through windows
onto the narrow street. It is obviously the morning after a habitually drunken
evening for the denizens of the hotel who are sleeping it off.

At the left-front table is Hugo Kalmar,* "a small man in his late fifties" with
a large head, "crinkly long black hair streaked with gray,...square face with
a pug nose, a walrus mustache, black eyes . . . thick-lensed spectacles," the
stereotypical anarchist. He is asleep in his chair, his head resting on his arms
folded on the table. Seated at the same table is Larry Slade,* the only man in
the room who is not asleep. He is a tall, raw-boned sixty-year-old with a gaunt,
unshaven, Irish face and "a mystic's pale-blue eyes with a gleam of sharp
sardonic humor." He is filthy and lice-ridden. Four men are asleep at the front-
middle table: Piet Wetjoen,* a huge Boer farmer type in his fifties who has run
to fat but still owning "a suggestion of old authority"; Joe Mott,* a light-skinned
black, about fifty, in a derelict sporty suit, yet with an air of nattiness; James
Cameron* ("Jimmy Tomorrow"), about the same size and age as Hugo, in
clean but threadbare black with "a face like an old, well-bred, gentle bloodhound's," educated voice and prim manners; Cecil Lewis* ("The Captain"), a
typical former English army officer of about sixty, lean figured, with white
military mustache and bright blue eyes and "the big ragged scar of an old wound"
visible on his shirtless left shoulder. Three men sit at the right-front table: Pat
McGloin,* a slovenly, sandy-haired, jowly man who looks like the ex-policeman

he is; Ed Mosher,* sixtyish, the habitual drunkard who shows "the influence of his old circus career in his [flashy] get-up"; and Harry Hope,* the proprietor of the hotel. Hope is sixty, white-haired, and extraordinarily thin, instantly likable, "a softhearted slob, . . . a born easy mark" with a bark worse than his bite; he is a trifle deaf and wears badly aligned dime-store spectacles and cheap false teeth which click audibly. Alone at a table in the second line is Willie Oban,* a Harvard law school alumnus in his late thirties, thin, haggard, dissipated, dressed in the remains of cheap clothes and shoes. "He keeps muttering and twitching in his sleep."

Rocky Pioggi,* the night bartender, a swarthy, squat "Neapolitan-American in his late twenties," enters and slips Larry a quiet drink, laughing at the way Harry Hope has decided not to allow any more drinks on the house—"beginnin' tomorrow." In this way, the "touching credulity concerning tomorrow" is introduced as the theme which gives form to the play and identity to the characters, for this is a world of total failures, of people who live by what Ibsen in *The Wild Duck* called the saving lie. Larry, "de old Foolosopher" of the group, sums it up well: "The lie of a pipe dream is what gives life to the whole misbegotten mad lot of us, drunk or sober." Each one of these characters has an illusion which makes existence, if not really living, possible. For Larry, it is the belief that he has achieved a sense of philosophical detachment about existence; he thinks he no longer cares about life because all his dreams are behind him: "What's before me is the comforting fact that death is a fine long sleep, and I'm damned tired, and it can't come too soon for me." However, he takes no steps to seek out the death he claims he so much desires. Once upon a time he, like Hugo, had been involved with "the Movement," but when he saw "that men didn't want to be saved from themselves, for that would mean they'd have to give up greed," he decided to adopt the role of "philosophical detachment." He shakes Hugo awake for confirmation, but the old anarchist mouths a few revolutionary slogans and then tries to wheedle a drink from Rocky before falling asleep again. No one takes Hugo seriously any more, even in the Movement, but he doesn't realize it. However, he does hit Rocky on a tender spot when he asks after the part-time pimp's "leedle slave girls."

Everyone is waiting for "Hickey" (Theodore Hickman*), the salesman who always comes to the hotel on Harry's birthday to treat the denizens to a party. He always arrives on "his periodicals" two days before the date, joking about his wife "in de hay with de iceman." He has only until tonight to be in time for the birthday, and the drunks are beginning to give up hope of his arrival. Rocky and Larry then turn to consider Willie, who has pawned and repawned clothes until he is down to the last rags available. Usually Willie's mother has helped out, but this time her lawyer has told Harry that she is through with her son, and since he has no money to pay for drinks, he is in the middle of the d.t.'s. Rocky has been enforcing Harry's rule on Willie but then is told to use his own judgment, and Willie takes a long swig from the bottle.

Joe wakes up and asks whether Hickey has arrived yet because he is desperately thirsty and is waiting for Hickey to treat them all. But on hearing that Hickey has not come, Joe asks Larry whether Don Parritt,* a young man who has just arrived to look for Larry, might not give them money. Parritt has claimed to be a friend of the "old Foolosopher," but Larry denies it, saying only that he and Don's mother were friends in the Movement on the West Coast. He tells Joe that Rosa Parritt, the young man's mother, has been arrested for her part in a bombing and will probably be sentenced to life in prison. Larry and Joe engage in some political banter as Don Parritt enters, a tall, good-looking eighteen-year-old with something shifty and ingratiating about him "and an irritating aggressiveness in his manner." He looks out of place in this dive, and with a certain nastiness, he stands Joe a drink and starts to tell the story of his life to Larry. First he complains about the dive which Larry calls "the No Chance Saloon. It's Bedrock Bar, The End of the Line Café, the Bottom of the Sea Rathskeller," populated by those "with a few harmless pipe dreams about their yesterdays." Parritt says he has been devastated "by that business on the Coast," and since his mother's arrest he has been on the run from the police while looking for Larry: "He's the one guy in the world who can understand" because in the old days of the Movement, Larry had been like a father to him. Indeed, he has contacted Larry through some old letters that his mother had kept. Larry is distressed about the West Coast incident because it seems an informer within the Movement went to the police; he also wonders how Parritt has managed to avoid capture. The two discuss Larry's leaving the Movement; Larry claims that his reason was disillusionment, but Rosa had believed that she was the reason, according to Parritt. The young man professes himself worried about his mother in gaol, "She's always been so free," but he also tells of his bitter argument with her about his political commitment. He tries to enlist Larry's sympathy with his disillusion, but something does not quite ring true, an impression that is confirmed when Hugo wakes up enough to call him "Got-tamned stool pigeon" and is nearly punched for it. Larry has respect for Hugo because he served ten years in gaol in his own country, much of it in solitary confinement; but now the Movement considers him a drunken has-been.

Larry then recounts the lives of the other bar occupants. Captain Lewis and General Wetjoen fought on opposite sides in the Boer War (1899–1902), met at the St. Louis Fair, became friends, and have been fighting the old war ever since. James Cameron ("Jimmy Tomorrow") had been a war correspondent in South Africa. Harry Hope has become a recluse since his wife died twenty years ago, but he still stays in business and helps his friends. These include his brother-in-law Ed Mosher, a former circus worker, and Pat McGloin, a former police lieutenant dismissed from the force for graft. Joe, the black man, once ran a black gambling house, and Willie tells his own story. He is the son of a well-known criminal who died in gaol; Willie went to Harvard law school, but then came the booze. Now he touches Parritt for a drink, which the young man rather testily refuses. Oban is also waiting for Hickey to bring "the blessed bourgeois long green" and launches into a drunken song which nearly gets him thrown upstairs. But his fear of "the Brooklyn boys," the d.t.'s, is so abject that Harry Hope relents.

By this time everyone is more or less awake and more or less communicating with one another: Lewis and Wetjoen reminisce about the Boer War and refer to Joe as "Kaffir," while Jimmy joins with them in a sentimental reference to "brothers within the Empire united beneath the flag on which the sun never sets." He will straighten out—tomorrow. Meanwhile, Joe has been brooding about his past when he had a fine gambling house, partly as a result of Harry Hope's connections with Tammany Hall and the chief of police. After more nostalgic comments, Harry Hope speaks fondly of his wife, prompted by the calculated praise of McGloin: "A sweeter woman never drew breath." In fact, the late Bessie Mosher Hope had made his life miserable, but Harry claims that with her death, he gave up politics. However, one of these days, he plans to go out, "walk around the ward," and try to get back into political life. His dream is followed by Jimmy's that he will smarten up and go back to work in the publicity department of a newspaper. Similarly, Lewis speaks of the settlement of a family estate and invites Wetjoen to travel to London with him to see England in the spring, while the Boer recalls the beauty and vastness of the South African veldt to which he plans to return. McGloin and Mosher start to discuss Bessie Hope, and then the ex-policeman asserts his innocence while Willie offers to defend him and have him reinstated. Mosher also speaks wistfully of getting back his old circus job. This collection of pipe dreams is repeated with some variations many times throughout the play to indicate their life-giving importance to the dreamers.

It is now time to open the bar, and Margie* and Pearl,* two prostitutes, enter. "Margie has brown hair and hazel eyes," and Pearl is typically Italian. They are plump, vestigially pretty, "dollar streetwalkers," whose pipe dream is that they are "tarts," not prostitutes, while Rocky, the bartender who runs them, purveys his own illusion that he is not a pimp but takes care of their money—for a consideration. They treat him affectionately like "a bullying brother," and he looks on them like "the owner of two performing pets he has trained to do a profitable act under his management." The girls are "sentimental, feather-brained, giggly, lazy, good-natured and reasonably contented with life." They discuss their evening's business, hand over their money, and agree with Rocky, "Yuh don't live offa us. You're a bartender." Cora,* a thin, peroxide-blonde prostitute, a few years older than they, then enters with Chuck Morello,* her pimp, "a tough, thicknecked, barrel-chested Italian-American" in a loud suit. Their pipe dream is that someday they will marry and settle down on a farm, once Chuck gives up drinking. Their discussion usually focuses on the location of this farm—Long Island or New Jersey. Like the other girls, Cora also talks about her previous night's clients, but then she suddenly mentions having seen Hickey, an announcement that wakes up everyone except Hugo and Parritt. Hickey has sent a message to the "gang" that he will be around, but Chuck and Cora feel that he is different—sober, something none of the group has ever seen before, and he has said, "I'm just figurin' the best way to save dem and bring dem peace."

At this moment Theodore Hickman ("Hickey") enters. "He is about fifty, a little under medium height, with a stout, roly-poly figure." His smooth face is boyish with bright blue eyes, and his head is bald except for a fringe all around. His manner shows the affability of a professional salesman, a well-developed sense of humor, together with "an efficient, businesslike approach . . . an easy flow of glib convincingness." He looks like "a successful drummer whose territory consists of minor cities and small towns." He enters theatrically, greets the gang, and then, hand on heart, sings two drinking songs, one falsetto, the other bass; and while everyone laughs, he orders drinks for all "in a lordly manner" and proceeds to greet all the denizens of the bar. To everyone's surprise, Hickey announces that he has given up drink: "I don't need it any more." However, he feels "exactly the same as I always did. If anyone wants to get drunk, if that's the only way they can be happy, and feel at peace with themselves, why the hell shouldn't they? . . . The only reason I've quit is—Well, I finally had the guts to face myself and throw overboard the damned lying pipe dream that'd been making me miserable." The more he protests, the more atypical his behavior becomes; he has walked from Astoria, Queens, to Lower Manhattan, a six-hour trip, and he is offering a new sales pitch: "Honesty is the best policy— honesty with yourself, . . . Just stop lying about yourself and kidding yourself about tomorrows." He has decided that his mission now is to help all the "gang" to translate their individual pipe dreams into action, even Larry, "The Old Grandstand Foolosopher." Parritt applauds this move, and Hickey notices him for the first time, recognizing some kind of kinship between them, even though they have never met before: "I can tell you're having trouble with yourself." Still talking, Hickey starts to fall asleep, but before he does, he speaks about "real peace. . . . [When] you can let go of yourself at last. Let yourself sink down to the bottom of the sea. . . . Not a single damned hope or dream to nag you." Again he orders drinks for all, and collapses.

No one can quite figure out this new Hickey. Larry is sure that he is not kidding, and Parritt is highly suspicious of him; "He's too damned nosey." Hope and Cameron allow that he is speaking some sense, but Hope thinks him a wet blanket for a birthday party. Mosher is unimpressed and says that he will recover from "almost fatal teetotalism." Hugo momentarily awakens with his anarchist slogans, concluding with his favorite quotation, "The days grow hot, O'Babylon! 'Tis cool beneath thy willow trees!" He receives the usual "chorus of amused jeering," while Mosher goes on to talk of an old medicine pitchman he knew with a cure for everything. The roar of laughter called forth by this talk awakens Hickey briefly, who sleepily exhorts them to have a good time.

Act II: The back room, near midnight the same day. The room has been prepared for a party. Four circular tables have been pushed together to make one long one and are covered with borrowed table cloths. An "uneven line of chairs" follows the contours of the tables, bottles of bar whiskey have been placed within easy reach of all diners, and the table is laid with glasses and cutlery. The rest of the room has been cleared for dancing, and "an old upright piano and stool have been moved in and stand against the wall at the left, front." Right-front is a table without chairs. The floor has been scrubbed and the walls washed, and the light sconces are decorated with red ribbon. In the middle of the separate table is a birthday cake with six candles and some packages containing gifts. Cora, Chuck, Hugo, Larry, Margie, Pearl, and Rocky are discovered, all except Larry and Hugo dressed for the occasion. Larry is "in frowning, disturbed meditation," while Hugo is, as usual, passed out. Their manner indicates an undercurrent of artificiality, "nervous irritation and preoccupation." They are discussing Hickey and his new "line of bull about yuh got to be honest wid yourself and not kid yourself, and have de guts to be what yuh are," as Rocky puts it. But he sees himself as different: "I don't kid myself wid no pipe dream." Hickey has made an impression on Jimmy Tomorrow and Harry Hope, while the rest are hiding out in their rooms to escape from this bearer of a new gospel. Hickey has even tried to get after Cora and Chuck, who claim they will be married tomorrow, but their conversation deteriorates into argument when Margie and Pearl tell Rocky that they have admitted to Hickey that they are whores, and therefore that makes Rocky "a dirty little Ginny pimp." Real violence is about to occur, but the tension is broken by Larry's sardonic laughter and his comments on Hickey as "the great Nihilist." With this Hugo wakes up; clearly Hickey has been after him, too, questioning his commitment to a new social order, but he returns to sleep. No one knows what to make of the situation; Hickey has not yet mentioned his wife, nor has he played the old gag about finding her with the iceman. All the old camaraderie seems to have vanished, and the group members act scratchily toward one another. Larry is particularly puzzled, noting Hickey's recognition of Parritt, and wonders whether he is really dying to tell something to his old drinking companions but at the same time is afraid to do so. Perhaps this is the reason for his new sobriety.

Hickey reappears, laden with packages; he ribs Larry as "Old Cemetery, the Barker for the Big Sleep" and then speaks of his mission to help Larry "and the rest of the gang" to find their own personal peace. But then he offends the girls by calling them whores; they forgive him. And as the drinking continues, he tries to make Larry admit that he's "just an old man who is scared of life, but even more scared of dying." The philosophical detachment he has cultivated is just a defense mechanism. Hickey attempts to explain himself further and suggests that for Parritt "there is only one possible way out you can help him to take." He tries to find out more about this stranger, but Larry becomes angry, particularly when Hickey suggests that he is still committed to the Movement and that a woman is behind Parritt's troubles. But Hickey remains tolerant, having expected Larry to be "the toughest to convince of the gang," claiming that Larry, Harry, and Jimmy are the three he most wishes to help.

With this, he starts to plan the party, and Cora, with Joe's assistance, tries to play the piano. Under cover of the noise, Willie Oban announces his plan to get his clothes out of pawn tomorrow and go to the district attorney to ask for a job. Larry tells him to have another drink, and Willie moves away in anger. Parritt then comes in to talk to Larry. Obviously, he is somewhat afraid of Hickey and wants Larry's support. He returns once more to the subject of his mother and Larry's relationship with her, recalling their fight when Larry walked out, calling her a whore, an allegation Larry denies; but Parritt continues to speak of his mother's lovers and recalls that Larry alone had treated him "like a father." He expresses his anger with Hickey and then suggests that Larry has guessed his secret. Angrily, Larry denies it, and Parritt goes on to speak about his disillusion with the Movement and his duty to his country (a hint of his identity as informer), but Larry sees through "such hypocrite's cant," insisting that he has forgotten Rosa Parritt and no longer cares about life. Parritt counters with the insult, "You'll never die as long as there's a free drink of whiskey left," and Larry controls himself with difficulty. A noise of fighting and cursing is heard, and Wetjoen and Lewis enter. They have been fighting; after some words with Hickey, their good-natured ribbing has turned to nastiness. Then McGloin and Mosher come in, concerned over Harry Hope's behavior and the consequences it may have for them, particularly if he visits Bessie's family. However, they, too, are affected by Hickey, for Mosher plans to leave tomorrow to look for his old job, and McGloin is going out to seek reinstatement.

It is now just about midnight, and Hickey pulls the whole gang together to greet Harry, who comes downstairs with Jimmy Tomorrow to the sound of a dispirited shout of "Happy Birthday, Harry!" Harry is distinctly "pugnacious" while Jimmy seems afraid. Cora is trying to sing and play the piano, but Harry screams angrily at everybody, telling them to keep quiet, reducing Cora to tears and bringing a rebuke from Hickey. As Harry and others try to resuscitate the party spirit, Hickey continually exhorts individual members of the group to face themselves and life; but then when the champagne comes, he, too, drinks a toast, even seeing that Hugo, who complains that the wine is not iced, is wakened for the occasion. However, Hickey's speech is curious: "I meant it when I say I hope today will be the biggest day in your life, and in the lives of everyone here, the beginning of a new life of peace and contentment where no pipe dreams can ever nag at you again." In reply, Harry Hope speaks belligerently of not being an easy mark for all the spongers he sees around him and asserts that he really will show them all that he has the courage to go out and take "a walk around the ward." But then his belligerence collapses and he apologizes. With this, Hickey rises and delivers a long, hortatory monologue in which he tries to explain his tactics and extolls the glories of self-recognition, concluding with the comment, "I don't give a damn about anything now. And I promise you, by the time this day is over, I'll have every one of you feeling the same way!" Larry sneeringly asks for an explanation of what has led Hickey to this discovery: "Did this great revelation of the evil habit of dreaming about tomorrow come to you after you found your wife was sick of you?" The mood of the party shifts to open hostility against Hickey, and they taunt him as a cuckold, Willie leading his "Sailor Lad" tune. Hickey replies good-naturedly and then reveals that "I'm sorry to tell you my dearly beloved wife is dead." The mood instantly shifts to shame and sympathy, as Hickey apologizes for being a wet blanket, saying that at least Evelyn has found peace in being rid of him, "a no-good cheater and drunk." She had loved him, but now in death she is better off. But "she wouldn't want me to feel sad. Why, all that Evelyn ever wanted out of life was to make me happy." And as everyone stares "in bewildered, incredulous confusion," the curtain falls.

Act III: The barroom, including part of the back room showing the tables arranged as in Act I. It is around mid-morning of Harry Hope's birthday, a hot summer day, but the sunlight does not filter into the room. Joe Mott is strewing sawdust on the floor; Rocky is irritably tending bar; Larry is sitting without a drink, staring straight ahead; Hugo has passed out; Parritt sits at a front table staring tensely in front of him. Rocky and Larry discuss the "Reform Wave" that Hickey has begun. He has dragged Jimmy out to get his clothes ready to look for a job and has given Willie the money to redeem his stuff from the pawnbroker, while the others are all busy shaving and getting presentable. Larry remarks that Hickey hadn't called on him, perhaps because he was scared. Parritt sneeringly notes that Larry had locked his door, and Rocky recalls what Hickey had said about Larry's illusion that he really wants to die. Defiantly Larry says that suicide is a coward's way out, but Parritt suggests that "he's all quitter," a comment that rouses Larry's anger.

When Rocky falls asleep, Parritt starts to confide in Larry, first noting his discomfort and even fear of Hickey, especially since Hickey gave the news of his wife's death. This has started Parritt thinking about his mother as if she were dead, and finally he tells Larry, "I once had a sneaking suspicion that maybe, if the truth was known, you were my father," a suggestion Larry vehemently denies. His mother will never forgive him (Parritt) for giving up the Movement, Parritt says, and then confesses that he was the one who sold information to the police, in order to get money for a whore. Larry, angered, shakes him into silence. Rocky wakes up, and he and Larry discuss the death of Hickey's wife, concluding that it probably wasn't suicide. Larry says he feels the "cold touch" of death on Hickey, and then Rocky tells what has happened to him as a result of Hickey's work of salvation: Margie and Pearl have taunted him with being a pimp and so he slapped them; in turn they claim they want to work for a proper pimp, not a part-timer like Rocky, and so they have gone on strike to visit Coney Island for the day. Chuck then comes in all dressed for his wedding to Cora, asking for a sherry flip for her. She has kept him awake with her doubts all night, and he would dearly love a drink, but, as he says to Rocky, "Yuh'd like me to stay paralyzed all de time, so's I'd be like you, a lousy pimp!" At this, Rocky's violent side is shown and he reaches for his gun; Joe attempts to patch things up, but Rocky calls him a "doity nigger," so Joe pulls a knife. This time Larry stops them, and Hugo wakes up briefly. Joe, however, is not so easily placated; he asks for the drink he has earned, turns in his room key, and after draining his glass, he breaks it to save Rocky trouble; "so's no white man kick about drinkin' from de same glass." He's off to open up his "old gamblin' house for colored men."

Willie then comes in, very shaky, but dressed in his good clothes, washed and spruced up. He really needs a drink, but that won't help him get a job. Captain Lewis and Piet Wetjoen then enter separately, also dressed up but with last night's enmity smouldering, trading allegations of cowardice and peculation. Both claim they will get temporary jobs and then go home, but they independently decide to wait to say good-bye to Harry. Chuck then realizes that he has forgotten about Cora, who is waiting, and goes back to her with a drink. Meanwhile, Willie starts to talk to Parritt, offering his legal expertise in the young man's defense, because a position with the D.A. may not materialize for some time, and a few independent successes would look good. Parritt says that the cops are not after him, but Larry comments, 'I wish to God they were! And so should you, if you'd the honor of a louse!" In retaliation, Parritt suggests that Larry is still in love with the Movement, but even more, still in love with Rosa Parritt. Again he claims he sold out the Movement to get money for a whore, and when Larry becomes enraged, Parritt begs his help. Mosher and McGloin now enter separately, also spruced up and ready to go out. Again Willie offers legal assistance, this time to McGloin, who refuses it. As both men turn in their room keys, Cora enters, very drunk, with Chuck behind her, to announce that they are off to get married but want to avoid Hickey who is shepherding Harry and Jimmy down the stairs, both looking as if they are on their way to the electric chair.

Hickey looks around him and tries to encourage one and all to go out and "lead the forlorn hope." Lewis goes first, followed by Wetjoen, Mosher, McGloin, and Willie. Jimmy attempts to break for a drink, but Hickey heads him off, and he too goes out. Harry Hope is left, and he confesses fear of the automobiles outside, asking Hickey to accompany him. But Hickey tells him he must go alone, and after considerable lingering and discussion Hope leaves, and his progress across the street is monitored by Rocky. Larry then turns to Hickey and asks whether Hickey wants him to admit that he is eager to hang onto life, and when Hickey points out that he has indeed just made such an admission, Parritt jeers. Meanwhile, Harry Hope has gotten to the middle of the street and has stopped there, frozen with fear; then he turns and rushes back into the bar, calling for a drink and telling of nearly being knocked down by a nonexistent automobile. Rocky pours him a drink, threatening to give up his job, and also says, "Dey wasn't no automobile! Yuh just quit cold." Rocky has lost a bet. Hope appeals to Larry for corroboration, and Larry agrees that he had a narrow escape; but Hickey insists on absolute truth, claiming that Larry has offered "the wrong kind of pity." When forced by Hickey to rethink the situation, Harry Hope collapses, tries to pour himself a drink, and in so doing wakes Hugo, who doesn't say his usual things but starts to attack Hickey: "Peddler pimp for nouveau-riche capitalism." But then he looks at Harry more closely: "You look

funny. You look dead. Vat's happened?'' He feels some sympathy with him
because he feels he is dying from drink, but "I can't sleep here vith you. You
look dead.'' Larry, "with bitter condemnation,'' points out to Hickey ironically
that Harry is "another one who's beginning to enjoy your peace!'' Hickey insists
that he will come through, but Hope tells him he sounds "a worse gabbler than
that nagging bitch, Bessie, was'' and then says, "I want to pass out like Hugo.''
Larry angrily says that all that Hickey has brought Harry is "the peace of death,''
but Hickey will not be persuaded, though he is a trifle shaken, recalling "it hit
me hard, too. But only for a minute. Then I felt as if a ton of guilt had been
lifted off my mind.''

Larry now asks very specifically what happened, and Hickey tells him, "It
was a bullet through the head that killed Evelyn.'' Larry believes that Hickey
means that Evelyn committed suicide, but Hickey disabuses him, saying, "My
poor wife was killed.'' The reactions of Larry and Parritt differ: Larry thinks
she was murdered, and Parritt that she is still alive. Rocky, with total practicality,
asks, "Moidered? Who done it?'' But Larry, looking "with fascinated horror
on Hickey,'' tells Rocky not to ask. Hickey sees this as "the old grandstand
bluff,...Or...some more bum pity? The police will soon know, anyway.''
Hope suggests, "my bets are on the iceman,'' but now for him the booze doesn't
matter. However, there are other reactions: Parritt calls on Larry, "You've got
to believe what I told you! It had nothing to do with her! It was just to get a
few lousy dollars!'' At this, Hugo awakens in rage, pummels the table, suddenly
afraid, and collapses in tears: "Please, I am crazy drunk!...do not listen to
me!'' The scene turns into a curious tableau: Larry shrunk against the bar with
Rocky leaning over it, both staring at Hickey, while Parritt looks pleadingly at
Larry. Hickey, however, looks "with worried kindliness at Hope,'' wondering
why he has not yet begun to feel happy now that he has killed his "nagging
pipe dreams.''

Act IV: The same setting as Act I, 1:30 A.M. the next day, with a new
arrangement of tables. Larry, Hugo, and Parritt are at one table; Hugo is passed
out; Larry looks at the floor; and Parritt "keeps staring at him with a sneering,
pleading challenge.'' Cora, Captain Lewis, McGloin, and Wetjoen are at another
table, while Willie, Hope, Mosher, and Jimmy Tomorrow form a third group.
"There is an atmosphere of oppressive stagnation in the room,'' and the last
two groups seem to be getting drunk mechanically. In the bar section, Joe is
sprawled out, asleep, while Rocky stands behind his chair, hostile, looking like
a minor gangster. He rouses Joe, "Yuh damned nigger,'' and orders him into
the back room because it is after hours. Chuck enters, drunk, and has obviously
been fighting. He says he is through with Cora and admits that marriage to her
was one of the pipe dreams about which Hickey had spoken. He goes up to her
and she hands over her money with "Jees, imagine me kiddin' myself I wanted
to marry a drunken pimp.'' Parritt then takes out after Larry, telling how the
older man had locked himself up with a bottle of booze because he was afraid.
But Parritt seems confused about himself and his motives. One minute he taunts

Larry with inability to commit suicide, but then Larry counters, "Are you trying to make me your executioner," and Parritt starts to attack the sincerity of The Movement, finally suggesting that Larry "ought to take a hop off the fire escape!" Rocky's "Who cares?" calls forth an echo of total despair from the rest of the room, but only for an instant, and silence descends until Rocky tries to enlist both Larry and Parritt as pimps. When they refuse, he suggests that they keep away from Hickey, who is bound for the Chair. Larry has momentary sympathy for him; but now at least three suspect what has happened, and Larry is sure Hickey will return because "he's lost his confidence that the peace he's sold us is the real McCoy, and it's made him uneasy about his own."

At this, Hickey enters, denying the statement. He looks around and castigates all the drunks because they are complaining, "We can't pass out! You promised us peace!" He is fed up with them "That's why I phoned—" but he does not say whom. "By rights you should be contented now, without a single damned hope or lying dream left to torment you!" He claims he has only a little time left because he has made a date for 2 A.M., and he tries to make them understand the advantages of their new condition. Tomorrow is dead, so they no longer need to care about anything; but their silence makes him believe they hate him. Again he speaks about facing the truth and seeing "the one possible way to free poor Evelyn and give her the peace she'd always dreamed about." They don't want to hear, but Hickey continues with his confession: "I had to kill her." This revelation shocks them all, and Larry tells him to keep quiet. They don't want to know anything that would send Hickey to the chair; but Parritt suggests that Larry is still refusing to face facts, saying, "It's worse if you kill someone and they have to go on living." Hickey wants no more to do with Parritt, because their crimes have nothing in common. "There was love in my heart, not hate," says Hickey. Parritt claims he did not hate his mother and calls on Larry for support, which he does not get. Hickey then turns to his friends to tell them what "a pipe dream did to me and Evelyn." His long monologue is interrupted once by Jimmy; and just before Hickey begins the full account of his motivations in murdering his wife, two detectives, Moran and Lieb, arrive to arrest him, and they hear everything.

Hickey speaks of his early life as a minister's son, his love for Evelyn, and hers for him. She had always stuck up for him and later married him against her parents' wishes, even though he had tried to break with her when he left town to try his luck as a salesman. She told him, "I'll wait, and when you're ready you send for me and we'll be married. I know I can make you happy, Teddy, and once you're happy you won't want to do any of the bad things you've done any more." This was her pipe dream. So Hickey went off to "the Big Town," enjoying the salesman's life, getting drunk, and then hearing from Evelyn. Finally they were married, and then Hickey would get bored, get drunk, and be unfaithful—and Evelyn would always forgive him. Once he contracted venereal disease and accidentally infected her; but even then she forgave him, and his sense of guilt commenced to pile up. This year he had sworn to her that he wouldn't come to Harry Hope's birthday party for his annual drunk. But soon he realized he would have to go, yet at the same time knew that ''I'd never have the guts to go back and be forgiven again, and that would break Evelyn's heart because to her it would mean that I didn't love her any more.'' That is why he shot Evelyn—to give her peace—and as he looked at her, feeling a weight of guilt lifted, he found himself saying, ''Well, you know what you can do with your pipe dream now, you damned bitch.'' Suddenly, however, Hickey is shocked into denial and appeals to Harry Hope: ''You know I must have been insane, don't you, Governor.'' He has found another pipe dream; but at this he is arrested and leaves protesting that he must have been insane when he spoke to his dead wife as he did. Hope tries to support this contention and offers to testify to his insanity, as do some of the others.

Left alone, they start to drink: ''maybe it'll have the old kick.'' Larry delivers an epitaph for Hickey: ''May the Chair bring him peace at last, the poor tortured bastard.'' The emphasis now shifts to Parritt, who speaks of his guilt in his mother's arrest and imprisonment. He remembers saying in words which prove an ironic echo of Hickey's, ''You know what you can do with your freedom pipe dream now, don't you, you damned old bitch!'' In fury, Larry turns on him: ''Get the hell out of life, God damn you, before I choke it out of you! Go up—!'' Parritt is almost transformed at this: ''Thanks, Thanks, Larry. I just wanted to be sure. I can see now it's the only possible way I can ever get free of her.'' Then, after a brief farewell from Larry, ''Go, for the love of Christ, you mad tortured bastard, for your own sake!'' Parritt leaves, telling Hugo he will buy him a drink ''tomorrow—beneath the willow trees!'' In this cryptic exchange, Larry, ''the old foolosopher,'' has finally been goaded into giving Parritt the advice the young man has been seeking. Parritt does not deserve to live and he really has no choice but to commit suicide, ''take that hop from the fire escape.'' Death is for him the only answer, because he has committed the ultimate crime for a revolutionary—he has been an *informer*.

Hugo now expresses relief that Hickey has been taken away because he caused him bad dreams; ''He makes me tell lies about myself. . . . He was selling death to me, that crazy salesman.'' Hope attempts to salvage something of himself by claiming that he had gone out into the street to humor ''a lunatic's pipe dream'' and was nearly run down by an automobile. Rocky supports him ''On de woid of an honest bartender,'' a remark that causes laughter at both him and Chuck, the other pimp. Then Harry Hope offers a sentimental toast to Hickey, 'the kindest, biggest-hearted guy ever wore shoe leather.'' All drink to that, but Larry sits by the table, waiting tensely, as the others talk about the folly of trying to translate their dreams into reality. They continue to get drunker, but Hugo becomes concerned about Larry: ''You look dead. What you listen for in back-yard?'' Hugo moves away in fear, drinking with Harry: ''Gottamned stupid bourgeois! Soon comes the day of Judgment!'' They laugh at him, and at the height of the merriment in come Margie and Pearl: ''Gangway for two good whores!'' They are very drunk and proceed to become more so, while Larry is still "torturedly arguing with himself" over the advice he has given Parritt. He is waiting for the sound that will show that Parritt has committed suicide by jumping off the fire escape, in that way making reparation for the crime of informing on a revolutionary associate (in this case also his mother). Larry's tension increases until he says, "I'll go up and throw him off!—like a dog...you'd put out of misery!" With that the sound of something falling is heard and then "a muffled, crunching thud." Hope also hears the noise, but no one thinks to investigate, while Larry quietly mumbles, "God rest his soul in peace." He knows now that for him life means that he is a "weak fool looking with pity at the two sides of everything." And then he realizes that "I'm the only real convert to death Hickey made here." Meanwhile the party is getting merrier and everyone sings, "but not the same song." Out of the cacophony Hugo's rendering of the French Revolutionary song, "La Carmagnole," takes over; but he is shouted down, and the curtain falls on his favorite line, " 'The days grow hot, O Babylon' " which is taken up by the rest of the company (in enthusiastic jeering chorus) " 'Tis cool beneath thy willow trees!' " Larry remains by the window, "oblivious to their racket."

Comments: This play marked O'Neill's return to the Broadway theatre in 1946 after a twelve-year absence during which he was awarded the Nobel Prize for Literature (1936). The portrayal of Hickey by James Barton* was weak in this production, and while most critics praised the play, they also complained about its length and repetitiousness. A well-known anecdote of Lawrence Langner* concerning this original production has him remonstrating quietly with O'Neill during rehearsal that the playwright had repeated the same point eighteen times. To this O'Neill replied quietly, "I *intended* it to be repeated eighteen times" (*see* Bogard, 1972, pp. 408–409). Also, Langner suggested that the true greatness of the play would be discovered only when it would be possible to make cuts in the text—after the expiration of copyright (Gelb and Gelb, 1973, pp. 874–875). To some extent this comment represents the truth, because when the play was revived in 1956 at the Circle in the Square, with Jason Robards, Jr.,* as Hickey and under the direction of José Quintero,* it was extremely successful, making Robards a star and beginning his career as an O'Neill actor. It also began Quintero's preoccupation with O'Neill and his as yet unfinished task of producing the entire canon. But even more important, it reestablished O'Neill's reputation as a playwright of the classic American theatre—no longer dated, not box-office poison—and began the currently continuing O'Neill revival.

Agreed, this play is long, at times tedious, but an audience attuned to the deliberate experiential *longueurs* of writers of the theatre of the absurd is more able to deal with the situation than the audience of 1946. Superficially, *The Iceman Cometh* has almost no action, and indeed what happens can be summarized very baldly and very briefly. However, its use of contrapuntal characterization and dialogue, and the interplay of the literal and symbolic, make this play extraordinarily interesting and challenging. In addition, its known autobiographical elements and renditions of actual characters lend added fascination.

O'Neill's only published short story, "Tomorrow,"* also offers a preliminary study for *Iceman*.

But what does it mean? That is a question which, as with all great works of dramatic art, is almost impossible to answer. The title is allied to the parable of the wise and foolish virgins who await the arrival of the Bridegroom in Matthew 25. There, of course, the Bridegroom represents Christ and the virgins those who have prepared for salvation. In such a reading, Theodore Hickman, whose name has a curious combination of God's gift, and "hick" human character, is the savior for whom this particular microcosm of human existence is waiting. Certainly O'Neill does seem to have made some attempt to convey a sense of human variety, though not as much as in *The Hairy Ape*.* All the characters of the ironically named Harry Hope's saloon are the failures, the misfits, the petty criminals of society; and in this setting, Gorki's *The Lower Depths* is automatically recalled. So, too, is Ibsen's *The Wild Duck* with its insistence on the necessity of the saving lie which alone provides identity and, in this case, hope to the hopeless. But Hickey is the savior who cannot save, and the only salvation he can offer is that of annihilation, of death, of the iceman in the title. The Iceman is death; but at the same time, O'Neill combines a series of meanings in his use of this character, which gives added resonance. Hickey is a travelling salesman, with the usual tales of drunkenness and infidelity which that occupation has drawn to itself. In addition, he tells tales of Evelyn, his wife, in bed with the iceman, which recall the old bawdy vaudeville joke concerning the husband who calls up the stairs to his wife, "Has the iceman come yet?" and the answer, "No, but he's breathing hard." Similarly, "The Sailor Lad" song of Willie Oban is one familiar to barrooms and undergraduate drinking parties. So there is no salvation except death for these characters and by extension no salvation for mankind—certainly not the religious solution for John Loving* in *Days Without End*.*

There are other interpretations, too, and Cyrus Day in a well-known article (1958), lists correspondences between Harry Hope's birthday party and Christ at the Last Supper, seeing Hickey as an antichrist and Parritt as a Judas Iscariot. Day notes the number of the "disciples" at the party, among other similarities; and while they may not be identical, the referential resonances remain important. Here also, the play is perceived pessimistically, and as Travis Bogard has suggested (1972, p. 415), O'Neill has come, after a long poetic search, to accept the view of Nietzsche, that man lives in a world without God.

The autobiographical elements are in themselves fascinating, and they have been investigated very thoroughly. Harry Hope's saloon is a combination of several that O'Neill frequented: Jimmy-the-Priest's (James J. Condon's* saloon), the Hell Hole (the Golden Swan), and the taproom of the Garden Hotel (near the old Madison Square Garden). The year is important, for it was in 1912 that O'Neill himself attempted to commit suicide by mixing alcohol and drugs. Harry Hope is closely modeled on one Tom Wallace who lived above the Hell Hole; Hugo Kalmar represents Hippolyte Havel,* an old radical; "Jimmy Tomorrow" Cameron is James Findlater Byth,* a former press agent of O'Neill's father; while Larry Slade is Terry Carlin,* a former anarchist acquaintance of O'Neill.

The anarchist incident on the West Coast also has its basis in fact in the McNamara case, which involved the bombing of the *Los Angeles Times*. The perpetrators were arrested when Donald Vose, the son of a woman anarchist, informed on them. Further ramifications of the case are noteworthy, for Emma Goldman, on whom the character of Rosa Parritt is based, was a friend of Vose's mother and was also aunt to O'Neill's editor at Random House, Saxe Commins.* The Boer General Wetjoen's name is also a consolidation of the names of the two famous guerrillas, De Wet and Viljoen. Ed Mosher was based on Bill Clarke, a former circus man. Altogether, this play offers dense structure, symbolic meaning, careful orchestration of characters and dialogue, skillful shifting of relationships, subliminal understandings, and calculated ambiguities. One never knows, for instance, whether Parritt is, as he suggests, the son of Larry, but certainly both have betrayed Rosa Parritt and the Movement, and both suffer for it. Hickey, too, is a betrayer, for he has betrayed Evelyn, and for that reason he perceives a kinship with Parritt and must also try hard to make Larry understand his new philosophy of death, in the purveying of which he is indeed a most persuasive salesman. O'Neill clearly understood the pessimistic nature of this play and consequently withheld it from production during World War II, thinking that the postwar years might be more receptive. In this he was right, as production history corroborates.

Production Data: Written 1939. Produced by the Theatre Guild* at the Martin Beck Theatre, New York City, October 9, 1946 (136 performances).

Director: Eddie Dowling

Design and Lighting: Robert Edmond Jones*

Cast: Harry Hope: Dudley Digges*
  Ed Mosher: Morton L. Stevens
  Pat McGloin: Al McGranery
  Willie Oban: E. G. Marshall
  Joe Mott: John Marriott
  Piet Wetjoen: Frank Tweddell
  Cecil Lewis: Nicholas Joy
  James Cameron: Russell Collins
  Hugo Kalmar: Leo Chalzel
  Larry Slade: Carl Benton Reid
  Rocky Pioggi: Tom Pedi
  Don Parritt: Paul Crabtree
  Pearl: Ruth Gilbert
  Margie: Jeanne Cagney
  Cora: Marcella Markham
  Chuck Morello: Joe Marr
  Theodore Hickman: James E. Barton
  Moran: Michael Wyler
  Lieb: Charles Hart

Revived at The Circle in the Square, New York City, May 8, 1956 (565 performances); produced by Leigh Connell, Theodore Mann, José Quintero.

Director: José Quintero

Set Design and Lighting: David Hays

Costumes: Deirdre Cartier

   Cast: Harry Hope: Farrell Pelly
          Ed Mosher: Phil Pheffer
          Pat McGloin: Albert Lewis
          Willie Oban: Addison Powell
          Joe Mott: William Edmonson
          Cecil Lewis: Richard Bowler
          James Cameron: James Greene
          Hugo Kalmar: Paul Andor
          Larry Slade: Conrad Bain
          Rocky Pioggi: Peter Falk
          Don Parritt: Larry Robinson
          Pearl: Patricia Brooks
          Margie: Gloria Scott Backe
          Cora: Dolly Jonah
          Chuck Morello: Joe Marr
          Theodore Hickman: Jason Robards, Jr.*
          Moran: Mal Throne
          Lieb: Charles Hamilton

Revived in cut version with James Earl Jones at The Circle in the Square, Joseph E. Levine Theatre, New York City, December 13, 1973 (85 performances). [*See also* Appendix B for film adaptation.]

ILE, a one-act play. The scene is the captain's cabin of the whaling vessel *Atlantic Queen*, icebound somewhere in North Atlantic waters at 1 P.M. in 1895. The Steward* and Ben,* the cabin boy, two expository characters, explain what has happened in the past. For almost the entire two years of the voyage, the vessel has been imprisoned in the ice and as a result has obtained only four hundred barrels of whale oil, approximately half its capacity. Captain David Keeney* has developed an obsession about returning to Homeport in this situation and adamantly refuses to return home even though the water to the south is now open and the men's contracts are up. With Joe,* the harpooner, as spokesman, they tell Captain Keeney that they will proceed no further north. Enraged by such defiance of his authority, Keeney knocks Joe down, with the result that the men draw their knives and rush Keeney and Slocum,* the second mate, who draw their revolvers, breaking up any attempt at mutiny. Mrs. Annie Keeney,* the wife of the captain, is an inadvertent witness to this incident. She has fallen into profound depression because of the length of this voyage, and has constantly begged him to return. Now she seizes the opportunity, begging her husband to turn back, recalling their love. She confesses that she had envied Keeney the glorious freedom of his seafaring life and for that reason had begged to accompany him. But now the brutality, the feeling of imprisonment, and the everlasting sameness have brought her to hate the sea, and she fears she is going mad. In anguish, Captain Keeney agrees to return, but at that moment the ice opens up to the north and Keeney returns instantly to his quest, deriding himself for thinking of turning for home "like a yaller dog." As Annie implores him, Keeney turns on her, saying that she cannot possibly understand his feelings and should not meddle in his business. He has to prove himself as a man in order to be a good husband for her. As he departs to hunt after a school of whales that has just been sighted, she falls into insanity. At first Keeney cannot believe what has happened, but then as she plays an old hymn tune on her organ, swaying in time to the music, his face hardens into determination and after an anguished backward look, he turns away to continue the quest which has cost him everything.

Comments: The play has a late point of attack, and the action is psychological rather than physical, though there is a confrontation scene of some violence among Keeney, Slocum, and the mutineers. The real conflict, however, is between Captain David Keeney and his wife, Annie. He has devoted himself to his quest for whales with such an Ahab-like obsession that he is almost incapable of thinking rationally. Annie manages to break through this fanaticism by reminding him of their love when the violence of the mutineers had made no impression. Clearly, Keeney loves his wife, but when he must choose between love and dedication to his calling, he will sacrifice everything in order to succeed in his profession. His motivation, then, is not merely vanity but rather the pursuit of perfection, no matter what the cost; and in the case of Annie, it is indeed high. Women, however, should not interfere in man's pursuit of his art—and if they do, they pay for it. Captain Keeney should not be read as a man of wounded vanity but rather as a paradigm of the artist, to whom dedication to his calling is all-important. The play depends rather heavily on coincidence and disappointed expectation, especially in its final section.

Production Data: Written 1916–1917. First produced by the Provincetown Players* at the Playwrights' Theater, New York City, November 30, 1917 (performances unknown).

Director: Nina Moise
Designer: Louis B. Ell
Cast: Ben: Harold Conley
The Steward: Robert Edwards
Captain Keeney: Hutchinson Collins
Mr. Slocum: Ira Remsen
Mrs. Keeney: Clara Savage
Joe: Louis B. Ell

Revived as part of a triple bill, April 18, 1918, at the Greenwich Village Theatre (52 performances).

[*See also* Appendix B for operatic version by Beatrice Laufer.]

IN THE ZONE, a one-act play, part of the S.S. *Glencairn** group. The scene is the forecastle of the S.S. *Glencairn*, which is carrying ammunition from the United States to England. The steamer has just entered the war zone, and despite their extra 25 percent danger pay, the men are understandably edgy. The play opens with Smitty* stealthily removing a black iron box from his suitcase and hiding it under his mattress. He is observed by Davis,* who then awakens the crew, including Smitty who has been feigning sleep. Davis finds that a porthole has been left open—perhaps as a deliberate invitation to a submarine attack. He is suspicious that Smitty might be a German spy, and he tells the crew what he has seen; his statement is corroborated by Scotty,* and gradually all the jumpy seamen become convinced. When Smitty is on deck, they purloin the box and submerge it in a pail of water (in case it is explosive). After a considerable struggle they wrest the keys from Smitty and open the box. It contains a rubber-covered package of love letters addressed to a Sidney Davidson from a woman named Edith, who has been studying voice in Berlin (a circumstance that makes the semiliterate seamen suspect a spy code). In the final letter Edith says an angry farewell to Sidney, because he has let the ''dark shadow'' of drunkenness overcome him: his drinking means more than her love. She also berates him for running away to sea like a coward. A dried flower falls out of the rubber package. Driscoll* replaces both the letters and the flower and releases Smitty, who had been bound. Smitty leans against the wall, sobbing silently, and the play concludes with Driscoll exploding, ''God stiffen us, are we never going to turn in fur a wink av sleep.'' The seamen, as if awakening from a bad dream, turn in, and Driscoll turns out the light.

Comments: Throughout the S.S. *Glencairn** plays, O'Neill has created the idea of Smitty as too well-educated and of too high a social class for the rest of the crew. *In the Zone* reveals Smitty's past. The themes of revelation and man's cruelty to others constitute the real center of the play; its rather melodramatic skeleton of wartime fear and suspicion is atmospheric and incidental. O'Neill manages to maintain suspense very well, although the device of disappointed expectation lends a certain predictability to the play.

Production Data: Written in 1916–1917. First produced by the Washington Square Players* at the Comedy Theatre, New York City, October 31, 1917 (performances unknown). This piece, which capitalized on the war situation, became quite popular on the vaudeville circuit and generated considerable royalties for O'Neill.

Director: Unknown.

Designer: Unknown.

Cast: Smitty: Frederick Roland
      Davis: Robert Strange
      Yank: Jay Strong
      Olson: Abram Gillette
      Scotty: Eugene Lincoln
      Ivan: Edward Balzerit
      Driscoll: Arthur Hohl
      Cocky: Rienzi de Cordova

Revived frequently as part of the S.S. *Glencairn** group.

[*See also* Appendix B for film adaptation of the entire series under the title, *The Long Voyage Home*.]

IRENE, a black prostitute, heavily made up and flashily dressed. In *The Dreamy Kid*,* she comes to Mammy Saunders' Greenwich Village apartment to warn her grandson, Dreamy,* that he is being hunted by the police. Irene wants to stay with him, even at the risk of her own life, but Dreamy sends her away on the pretext of getting some aid from his gang. She is a variation on the character of the prostitute with a heart of gold and is portrayed as fiercely loyal to her man. As a character, she is lightly drawn, and her motivations are unspecified.

"IT CANNOT BE MAD," the third and uncompleted play in the abandoned trilogy, "Myth-Plays for the God-Forsaken."* The completed plays were *Dynamo** and *Days Without End.** It was later given the tentative titles "On to Betelgeuse" and "On to Hercules." Its scenario survives in the Yale Collections and reveals the planned play to consist of two parts, each with two acts, covering the years 1894–1915 and later. The topic is the automobile industry and the heroine is Bessie Wilks [*sic*] (for a detailed analysis, *see* Floyd, 1981, pp. 169–193). The material was later considered for inclusion in the last play of the abandoned cycle, "A Tale of Possessors, Self-Dispossessed,"* under other titles: "The Life of Bessie Bowen"* (or Bolan or Bowlan), "Twilight of Possessors, Self-Dispossessed," and finally "Hair of the Dog."* At this point it was to be the last play of the cycle and covered the years 1900-1932. O'Neill seems to have had a real desire to make use of this topic, but in February 1943 he destroyed his last revision.

IVAN, a Russian seaman in the S.S. *Glencairn** plays. He has very few lines altogether, none at all in *The Moon of the Caribbees.**

J

JACK, or John Sloan, in *A Wife for a Life*,* partner of the Older Man.* He is a miner about thirty years old. He has saved his partner from drowning in the Transvaal, and they have been through many disappointments together. Now they have struck it rich, and Jack suggests that he return to the East to form a company to work the mine. The Older Man, who has opened a telegram from New York reading, "I am waiting. Come," suggests that Jack's desire to go East is the result of a woman. Jack then tells the heroic story of Yvette,* after whom he has named the mine, a young woman married to a drunken brute of a mining engineer. She has refused to consummate their mutual love because of her loyalty to her marriage vows. However, since her husband has disappeared she will be free to marry at this moment if her husband does not reappear. Throughout this recital, the Older Man has become progressively more agitated, and it is clear that he is that mining engineer. Jack does not realize this and departs for the East rejoicing in his good fortune. The characterization in this play is almost nonexistent, and Jack is really an expository device who reacts to the questions put to him by the Older Man.

JACK. In *In the Zone*,* a seaman on the S.S. *Glencairn*, "a young American with a tough, good-natured face," wearing dungarees and a heavy jersey.

JACKSON. In the scenario of *The Calms of Capricorn*,* the successor of Ethan Harford* as first mate of the clipper *Dream of the West*. He enters merely to announce that there is a squall approaching which may signify the end of the calm. This occurs just after the killing of Captain Enoch Payne.*

JAYSON, Curtis. In *The First Man*,* husband of Martha Jayson* and friend of Edward Bigelow.* He is a tall, rangy, graying man of thirty-seven, one year younger than his wife. He is, as Bigelow says, a romantic who has found his way into anthropology from mining engineering and geology. He is highly successful and has returned to his provincial-minded hometown of Bridgetown, Connecticut, to write a book. He and Martha had two baby daughters who died of pneumonia about ten years earlier at the ages of three and two. Devastated by the experience, he and Martha swear never to have more children in order to keep alive the memory of their dead babies. Curt flings himself into his work, and Martha becomes his total helpmate, looking after all the practicalities of existence and following him all over the globe, sharing hardships in order to advance the progress of science. On his return to Bridgetown he expects to continue this existence for a short time in the bosom of his extended family while he writes up his findings, and then he will go out on a five-year expedition in search of the Missing Link. He makes arrangements for Martha to go with him, after great difficulty, because she will be the only woman, only to discover that she has deliberately become pregnant. He is appalled by this betrayal of their vows, their ideal existence. He cannot understand that Martha does not feel herself fulfilled; indeed she thinks herself alien to the general scheme of things because she is childless. Angrily, Curt upbraids Martha for her violation of their marital scheme, and when she suggests that love is an evolutionary thing, he responds, "You are me and I am you," a statement that mirrors O'Neill's own attitude toward parenthood at this time. Similarly, this play restates attitudes toward marriage which O'Neill had dramatized earlier in *Bread and Butter** (which also takes place in Bridgetown), *Servitude,** and *Beyond the Horizon.** In these plays, the desired helpmate is totally dedicated to the service of her husband and his work; family life, together with its practicalities, seems to be an interruption in the creative work of the artist, scientist, or poet. This was apparently O'Neill's own attitude at this time.

Curt is so enraged that he even suggests that Martha consider an abortion, but she refuses. However, he remains unreconciled throughout her entire pregnancy and continues with his plans to depart on the expedition. Even as Martha is screaming in the agony of a difficult childbirth, he speaks of her as being able to travel with him in a month or so, hating the coming child so much that he would prefer it to die. When Martha dies, forgiving him on her deathbed, Curt transfers all his hatred to the child because "it" has murdered Martha. Finally, when he realizes that his malicious family believes that his friend Bigelow might be the father, he goes to see the child and acknowledges it as his own. The play ends with Curt asking his seventy-six-year-old aunt, Mrs. Elizabeth Davidson,* to look after his son because she alone of the family has "unmuddled integrity." He is as impractical as ever, and although his grief is suitably intense, one might consider that the death of Martha is another chance for Curt to pursue his dream without encumbrances. He plans to leave for the five-year trip to Asia, despite what has happened. When he returns (and when the child is bigger) he intends to inculcate in it the same kind of dream that he has had.

Altogether, the character of Curt Jayson is single-minded and indeed rather selfish, while his ideal of marriage indicates O'Neill's retrogression to attitudes of the early plays.

JAYSON, Emily, wife of John Jayson, Jr.* In *The First Man,** she is a small, mousey woman concealing "beneath an outward aspect of gentle unprotected innocence a very active envy, a silly pride, and a mean malice." She is the worst of the entire clan of Jayson women because she not only believes that Martha Jayson's* child is really Edward Bigelow's,* but she self-righteously looks upon Martha's suffering as a judgment upon her.

JAYSON, Esther. *See* Sheffield, Esther.

JAYSON, John, father of Curtis Jayson* and others. In *The First Man,** he is sixty, stout, bald, the epitome of the conservative small-town banker, with all the prejudices thereunto appertaining. He is dignified, but under the mask he is querulous and fussy. He is obsessively concerned with the family honor and is willing to believe the worst of Martha Jayson*—that her child is that of Edward Bigelow* rather than of his son, Curt.

JAYSON, John, Jr. In *The First Man,** son of John Jayson* and brother of Curtis Jayson.* He is a younger edition of his father, the conservative small-town banker, but with the addition of a pompous and authoritarian manner, "emptily assertive and loud." He is "purse-proud and family proud," exceedingly concerned with the family honor. He readily believes that Martha Jayson's* coming child is Edward Bigelow's.* John, Jr., is one of the members of the Jayson clan who wants Curt to recognize the child, simply for appearance's sake. John is married to Emily Jayson.*

JAYSON, Lily. In *The First Man,** sister of Curtis Jayson.* She is "a slender, rather pretty girl of twenty-five." She has been at college and has an air of intellectual superiority about her. She is clearly finding herself stifled by the life of Bridgetown. "Now that I'm through with college, my occupation's gone. All I do is read book after book. The only live people are the ones in books, and the only live life." She is fond of Martha and tries to warn her against scandal because of her friendship with Edward Bigelow,* the reformed town rake. She loves Martha, but discovers that she herself has been corrupted by the mean-spiritedness of her family, though she took no part in the accusations against her sister-in-law.

JAYSON, Martha. In *The First Man,** wife of anthropologist Curtis Jayson.* She is a healthy, direct woman of thirty-eight, "outspoken and generous," qualities which O'Neill indicates may be the result of her upbringing in the West, in Goldfield, Nevada. She and Curtis are childless, their two daughters (ages three and two) having died of pneumonia. As a result, Martha and Curt enter into a pact never to have any more children in order to keep the memory of the lost babies intact. During the next ten years, Martha gives her life entirely to Curt and his work, accompanying him on expeditions to many out-of-the-way places and acting as his secretary, research assistant, organizer, everything. As the play opens, Martha and Curtis have returned to Curt's home town of Bridgetown, Connecticut, the same mean-spirited place populated by malicious and small-minded people that O'Neill had drawn in *Bread and Butter*.* All the Jayson clan are jealous of Martha because of her interesting life and also highly critical because of her childless state. Furthermore, they suspect that she may be sexually involved with Edward Bigelow,* Curt's oldest friend. Bigelow is recently widowed after a singularly unhappy marriage during which he became the town rake, but with the acquisition of freedom he has reformed and become an excellent father to his three children.

Martha, with angry directness born of innocence, is furious when she is warned against Bigelow, and she continues to see him. However, when it becomes known that she is pregnant, the gossip begins all over again. In actual fact, Martha has deliberately worked at becoming pregnant (by her husband, of course) because she has realized that she has little time left for motherhood and feels that she has not fulfilled her true function in life. Curt cannot understand this, believing that he and his work—their work—should be sufficient for her. Martha begs him to "love the creator in me," but Curt hates the coming child because it will bring a stranger into their lives, which should be complete as a two-person partnership. Curt is all the more angry with Martha because he has arranged to have her accompany him on a five-year expedition to Asia to search for the Missing Link. Martha asks him not to go, but Curt refuses. Martha has the baby, after an extremely difficult childbirth, and dies. Curt is enraged against his son because "it" has murdered Martha, and he refuses to see it. The family, now firmly convinced that Bigelow is the father, tries to convince Curt to acknowledge the child. This he finally does and then leaves for Asia, after castigating his suspicious family.

The character of Martha lacks careful psychological motivation and is rather inconsistent. For instance, she seems curiously vague about the circumstances of her babies' death: "The nurse girl fell asleep—or something—and the children sneaked out in their underclothes and played in the snow. Pneumonia set in— and a week later they were dead." This seems to indicate a lack of feeling rather than the intensity of frustrated motherhood that she later professes to feel. Certainly we are meant to take this seriously, but O'Neill is not able to convey it very well. The children in this play seem expendable, and even Lily Jayson,* who is supposed to love Martha, is curiously matter of fact when she is asked, "Where are her children?" Lily replies only that "they died, Aunt, as children have a bad habit of doing." And right through the play, Martha's child is the object of active hatred and suspicion.

Martha is a stereotypical character: the generous, direct Westerner who cannot understand the manners and mores of a world seen by azimuthal projection from Bridgetown. She conforms at first to the early O'Neill image of a wife, as in *Servitude*,* the kind of helpmate and complete sacrificer of self that he endeavored to find in his own marriages. Her pregnancy is therefore seen as a betrayal of the ideal relationship which an artist needs in order to flower. Martha thus also becomes for O'Neill similar to Ruth Atkins* Mayo in *Beyond the Horizon*,* a woman who prevents the full flowering of the artist. Martha's death is therefore rather fortuitous because Curt manages to keep his romantic dream and will continue it by passing it on to his son—after he returns from the expedition. One can only feel sorry for Martha, because it is clear that Curt would never have accepted parenthood if it interfered with his self-expression. She is said to forgive him on her deathbed, but in view of Curt's attitude toward parenthood, one can only consider Martha's death a preferable fate to life in suspicious Bridgetown with a husband who does not want a child and a family who dislike her. The facts of Martha's pregnancy and Curt's attitude toward it mirror the reaction of O'Neill himself when he discovered that Agnes Boulton* O'Neill was pregnant.

JAYSON, Richard (Dick). In *The First Man*,* son of John Jayson.* He is "a typical young Casino and country club member." He has been to college and is a pleasant enough young man. A former officer in World War I, he "has not forgotten it. His manner is mocking, sardonic." He represents another aspect of the philistinism of Bridgetown, Connecticut, and the Jayson clan in particular. He dislikes anything that disturbs his own comfortable bachelor life-style. He also believes that Martha Jayson's* son is really that of Edward Bigelow.*

JEAN. In *The Sniper*,* a fifteen-year-old peasant boy. He appears, mudstained and with a cut on his head, to tell Rougon* that his wife Margot, and his dead son's fiancée, Louise, have both been killed by the Germans.

JEFF. See *The Emperor Jones*.

JENKINS, Kathleen (1889–1982), first wife of Eugene O'Neill. Born in New York State to Charles and Kate (Camblas) Jenkins. Her parents separated when Kathleen was ten because of her father's drinking, and she and her mother returned to New York City from Chicago where they had been living. James O'Neill* was opposed to their marriage, thinking Kathleen a gold digger, and arranged for his son to go as a mining engineer to Honduras. But Eugene and Kathleen eloped to Hoboken, New Jersey, and were married there on October 2, 1909, in Hoboken Trinity Church, with the Reverend William C. Gilpin as officiating minister. Though Kathleen was pregnant at the time, they agreed to keep their marriage secret while O'Neill went to Honduras. Their son, Eugene O'Neill, Jr.,* was born on May 6, 1910, and the news item concerning his birth stated that the marriage had taken place the previous July. It also said that the child would be baptized a Catholic.

She and O'Neill were divorced in 1912, after an uncontested suit which began June 10, 1912, on the only grounds for divorce then admitted in New York State—adultery, committed during the months of June through August 1911 and specifically on December 29, 1911. At the trial, the date of their marriage was given as July 6, 1909. The interlocutory decree was awarded on July 5, 1912, and the final judgment was signed on October 11, giving Kathleen custody of the child; she did not request alimony. In 1915 she married George Pitt-Smith (died 1947), a divorced office manager with a son a little younger than Eugene, Jr. O'Neill did not see his son until the boy was twelve years old, when Kathleen asked for some help in his education. The child had been given the name of Richard Pitt-Smith but reverted to his original name after meeting with his father. Mrs. Pitt-Smith seems to have borne no animosity toward Eugene O'Neill, and he found this fact rather admirable, noting that of all the women with whom he had been involved, she had given him the least trouble. Louis Sheaffer corroborates this account by thanking her for assistance in the writing of his book, *O'Neill: Son and Playwright* (1968), and more particularly in *O'Neill: Son and Artist* (1973, p. 721), noting that "her forbearance was impressive."

Widowed in 1947, she was active in her community of Little Neck, Long Island, serving for many years as editor of the *Little Neck-Glen Oaks Ledger*. She died at the Grace Plaza Nursing Home, Great Neck, New York, August 30, 1982.

JENNINGS. In *Dynamo*,* the shift operator at the power plant. He is aged about thirty. Reuben Light* takes Jennings's revolver in order to shoot Ada Fife.*

JESSUP, Captain. In *Chris Christophersen*,* he is the dapper, kindly looking sixty-year-old captain of the steamer *Londonderry* bound for Buenos Aires which ran down Chris's coal barge. Jessup allows Chris to work his passage in the forecastle and eventually offers him a job as boatswain. He allows Chris's daughter to travel as a passenger.

"JIMMY-THE-PRIEST," a nickname for James J. Condon, who ran a saloon 252 Fulton Street, near the old Washington market, New York City, where O'Neill lived for a time after his return from Honduras. *See also* Johnny-the-Priest.

"JIMMY TOMORROW." *See* Cameron, James.

JOE. In *All God's Chillun Got Wings*,* a young black friend of Jim Harris.* Joe tries to make Jim come to terms with his negritude, asking if he is trying to "buy white" with his father's money. Joe is essentially a pragmatist, who is certain that a black will not be permitted to succeed in the white world. He forces Jim to admit that he is a "nigger."

JOE. In *Ile*,* a harpooner on the whaling ship *Atlantic Queen*, "an enormous six-footer with a battered, ugly face." He is the leader of the mutineers who is felled by Captain David Keeney* with a punch to the head.

JOHN. In *Welded*,* a tall, loose-limbed man of about fifty with gray hair, the director-friend of Michael Cape,* a playwright, and his actress-wife, Eleanor Cape.* John has long been *in* love with Eleanor, but they have never been lovers. He enters suddenly upon Eleanor and Michael just after Michael has returned from the country where he has just finished a play. Michael is piqued at this interruption of the couple's first night back together, and an argument ensues. Eleanor visits John and throws herself at him, but John soon realizes that she is merely using him as an instrument of vengeance on Michael, and he takes her home to meet Michael when he returns, penitent. John will continue to hope, and the three of them will share in the success of Michael's play.

"JOHNNY-THE-PRIEST." In *"Anna Christie,"** he keeps a saloon near Street, New York City. His voice and manner "are soft and bland. But beneath all his mildness one senses the man behind the mask—cynical, callous, hard as nails." He is loosely based on the real-life character of James J. Condon,* Jimmy-the-Priest,* the keeper of a Fulton Street rooming house in New York City where O'Neill stayed after his voyage to Buenos Aires. Johnny-the-Priest also appears in the two preliminary versions of *"Anna Christie," Chris Christophersen,** and "The Ole Davil."**

JOHNSON. In *Anna Christie*, and "The Ole Davil." Deckhand on the *Simeon Winthrop*.

JONES, Brutus. In *The Emperor Jones*,* he is the main character. "A tall, powerfully built negro of middle age. His features are typically negroid, yet there is . . . an underlying strength of will, a hardy, self-reliant confidence in himself that inspires respect." He has an air of intelligence, yet at the same time he is "shrewd, suspicious, evasive." He wears a somewhat garish uniform of a pale blue coat, "sprayed with buttons" and covered with gold braid, and red trousers, with a light blue stripe at the side; he sports patent leather boots with spurs, and carries a pearl-handled revolver in his belt. Nonetheless, he still projects an air of dignity rather than the merely ridiculous.

Brutus Jones had arrived on this unnamed island two years ago as a stowaway, fleeing from the consequences of having killed a prison guard with a shovel during road work while serving time for killing a fellow Pullman porter, Jeff, in a gambling dispute. Helped along by Henry Smithers,* Jones moves "from stowaway to Emperor in two years." At the beginning of the play he is supremely self-confident, making sure that Smithers realizes who is in charge and suggesting that the white man has himself been in prison, an allegation the cockney trader denies. Smithers offers a shock to this confidence by revealing that Lem,* a native chief who had previously tried to have Jones killed, is plotting a revolution in the hills. Jones, however, has nothing but contempt for his subjects, whom he calls "low-flung bush niggers," and he has played on their superstition by claiming that he can be killed only by a silver bullet. He has even had one made and tells his simple subjects that he will kill himself when the time comes, " 'cause I'm de on'y man in de world big enuff to git me. No use deir tryin.' " Jones, however, underestimates the cunning of Lem, who melts down coins and makes some silver bullets, one of which finally kills Jones. This is only the skeleton of Jones's character which is gradually revealed throughout the course of this expressionistic monodrama.

After hearing Smithers's warning, Jones hears a tom-tom in the distant hills beating at seventy-two per minute, the "normal pulse beat," a drumming that will continue with accelerating beat and increasing volume without interruption throughout the play. He then decides it is time to put his plan of escape into effect, and to Smithers's rather "puzzled admiration," he leaves by the front door as the Emperor Jones, conscious of his own intellectual superiority and sure of his ability to outwit the forest. However, he is wrong, and the next six scenes of the eight-scene play demonstrate the decline of Brutus Jones from self-sufficient ruler who had easily put away his Baptist religion and laid "Jesus on de shelf" into a panic-stricken, almost naked creature calling, "Lawd Jesus, heah my prayer!" In the course of those scenes, Jones is driven almost mad by the obsessive and incessant drumming which has pursued him through reenactment of his own crimes and the history of the black race in the United States. First, Jones confronts the ghost of Jeff, the Pullman porter he had murdered with a razor, and fires his first bullet at him. Next, in another part of the forest, he reenacts the killing of the prison guard and disperses this image with another shot. His own personal history then goes back into the collective unconscious of the black race following the theories of C. G. Jung, in which O'Neill was then interested, and Jones is placed on the auction block and bid for by a planter. In terror and rage, Jones asserts his rights as "a free nigger" and shoots both the auctioneer and the planter. His clothing reduced now to little more than a breech cloth, and maddened by the drumming, Jones, with only a single silver bullet left, reenacts the horrifying experience of the slave ship.

Finally, he finds himself on the banks of the Congo, almost naked, before a low stone altar. Feeling that he has been in this sacred place before, he kneels fearfully before it, and the Congo Witch-Doctor comes to dance out a supplication to a malevolent deity who requires sacrifice. Jones, now hypnotized by the drumming and the dancing, sways with the Witch-Doctor, who indicates that Jones is to be the sacrifice to the dark god who comes up from the water in the form of a huge crocodile. Jones writhes toward the crocodile, which slowly advances toward him, as Jones calls not upon the gods of the Witch-Doctor, but upon that Baptist God, whom he had put aside in Scene i, yet repeatedly invoked against the forces of the supernatural. Finally, as he calls on Jesus, he remembers his revolver and the silver bullet. With that last shot the crocodile disappears, a deity of darkness vanquished by a silver bullet. In the next scene Jones himself is killed, also by a silver bullet, this one cast by Lem and his allies.

It is exceedingly easy to see this play as one which shows that Jones's thin veneer of civilized intelligence is quickly stripped away to reveal the true nature of the man, a creature of superstition and instinct rather than reason. Yet it is also a parable of a different nature, because Jones as a character has shown also the falseness of modern civilization. From the "white quality" he met on the Pullmans, then a high-status unionized job for blacks, he has learned how to survive in modern society, by crime and by exploiting others lower than himself. He has adopted the "new" God of Christianity, whom he will quickly put aside when He becomes inconvenient. However, Jones is not a complete member of modern society, as the garish furnishings of his throne room and the faintly ridiculous nature of his uniform indicate. In the play he is taken back to his very roots, and the Witch-Doctor leads him toward a submission to the dark gods of his racial unconscious. But unlike Yank* in *The Hairy Ape*,* Jones does not choose to "belong" in this environment and calls upon his new God for aid. But the crocodile god will nonetheless be revenged; the forces of darkness will not be denied. Hence it is fitting that Jones also dies by a silver bullet.

Notable performances of this exceedingly difficult role were by Charles Gilpin,* the creator of the role, and later by Paul Robeson* in the 1924 New York revival and in London in 1925. Robeson also performed the role in a film adaptation.

[*See also* Appendix B for 1933 opera by Louis Gruenberg* which served as a starring vehicle for Lawrence Tibbett, the 1933 film, and a 1956 ballet by José Limon.]

JONES, Robert Edmond (1887–1954), theatrical designer, director, and writer. Born in Milton, New Hampshire, December 12, 1887, son of Fred and Emma Jane (Cowell) Jones. Father was a farmer and mother a piano teacher. Died in Milton, New Hampshire, November 26, 1954. In 1933 married Margaret (Houston) Carrington, sister of Walter Huston, the actor. She was the expert who trained John Barrymore for his famous *Hamlet* performance. She predeceased him in 1942.

Jones showed very early interest in both art and music, displaying promise in violin. In 1906 he went to Harvard University, where he played that instrument in the school orchestra. Graduating *cum laude* in 1910, he remained for two years as a graduate assistant and later instructor in the Department of Fine Arts. He then went to New York to work as a costume designer for Comstock and Gest. In 1913 he went to Europe, intending to study with Edward Gordon Craig, who refused to accept him. One product of this period was a highly original stage design for *The Cenci*, later exhibited in New York to critical acclaim. Jones then moved to Berlin to work for a year in the Deutsches Theater of Max Reinhardt where he became acquainted with the theory and practice of what was termed the "new stagecraft," which aimed at the artistic unity of all aspects of production and directing.

After the outbreak of World War I in 1914, Jones returned to New York and in 1915 designed the set and costumes of *The Man Who Married a Dumb Wife*, offering a simple set, aimed at projecting the playwright's intentions through imaginative use of color and lighting. In the summer of 1915 he began to design for the Provincetown Players* and also designed *The Glittering Gate*, the first production of the Washington Square Players,* using wrapping paper and scrap materials. Attracting the attention of Arthur Hopkins, the theatrical producer, Jones was hired to design *The Devil's Garden* in the fall of 1915, beginning a nineteen-year collaboration with Hopkins. During this time he designed sets, and usually costumes as well, for thirty-nine plays, including O'Neill's *"Anna Christie"* and *The Hairy Ape.* He also collaborated with Joseph Urban on *Caliban by the Yellow Sands* for the New York Shakespeare Tercentenary celebration (1916), a masque performed in the Lewisohn Stadium of the City College of New York. In ballet, he designed sets for the Metropolitan Opera production of Nijinsky's ballet, *Til Eulenspiegel.* He also tried directing, with *Simon the Cyrenian*, for the Colored Players, an early black company. In 1920 he held the first one-man art show of theatrical designs, an indication of the seriousness with which he regarded his craft.

In 1923 he joined with the critic Kenneth Macgowan* and Eugene O'Neill to form "the triumvirate" which would manage the Experimental Theatre, Inc.,* the successor group to the Provincetown Players,* at the old playhouse at 133 Macdougal Street, Greenwich Village, New York. Macgowan was to be the head, with Jones and O'Neill as associate directors. Their opening effort was a production of Strindberg's *The Spook Sonata.* From that time, Jones was a frequent designer, and sometimes director as well, of O'Neill plays, including *Welded,* *The Ancient Mariner,* *All God's Chillun Got Wings,* *Desire Under the Elms,* which he also directed (all in 1924), *The Fountain* (also directed, 1925), and *The Great God Brown* (also directed, 1926). Even after "the triumvirate" was dissolved in 1925–26, Jones continued to design for O'Neill plays, doing *Mourning Becomes Electra* (1931), *Ah, Wilderness!* (1933), *The Iceman Cometh* (1946), and *A Moon for the Misbegotten* (1947), all for the Theatre Guild.* For this group he also designed *The Seagull, The Philadelphia Story, Othello, Mary of Scotland, The Joyous Season,* and *Everywhere I Roam.* His last important work, *The Lute Song* (1946), was also done for the Guild. This was an adaptation by Sidney Howard of a Chinese play in three acts and seventeen scenes. For it, Jones designed impressionistic sets, a project which took him fourteen months to complete. He also designed for the Group Theatre and produced and designed the Laurence Olivier/Vivien Leigh offering of *Romeo and Juliet.* He also designed the sets for Noël Coward's *Tonight at 8:30.* Jones worked in other areas of production and design, serving briefly as art director of Radio City Music Hall, New York, for which he designed the inaugural program in 1932. He designed the Metropolitan Opera production of *Green Pastures*, an adaptation of Marc Connelly's play of the same name. He also designed the inaugural season (1932) of the Annual Play Festival in Central City, Colorado, working with the festival for the next ten years. In 1934 he did the "color designs" for *Becky Sharp*, the first technicolor movie, coincidentally produced by Kenneth Macgowan.

Jones was a revolutionary theatre designer, believing in the self-abnegation of the designer, who "should be translucent, like a medium," in placing himself at the service of the play. He liked to think of himself as a poet of the theatre who aimed to present not the real world but "an abstract evocation and release of desire, a dream that is living with 'life beyond life'." To some extent, O'Neill's overly literal and specific stage directions limited Jones's imagination, particularly in *Desire Under the Elms* and *Mourning Becomes Electra*, but he remained faithful to his doctrine of self-effacement and put his talents to the service of the plays. He and O'Neill believed that in *The Ancient Mariner* they were breaking new ground in the development of a poetic theatre, but the critics did not agree and the production folded.

As a prolific and lyrical writer on the theater, Jones preached his imaginative gospel in books and frequent articles in theatre journals. His writing career really began to assume importance in 1922 when he and Macgowan toured Europe together to gather material for their joint work *Continental Stagecraft* (1922). He continued to publish voluminously on aspects of stage production, including *Drawings for the Theater* (1925), *The Dramatic Imagination* (1941), and *Towards a New Theater* (four recorded lectures, 1955–65). Long recognized as the dean of American theatrical designers, Jones was awarded Yale's Howland Memorial Prize, as well as the Fine Arts Medal of the American Institute of Architects for conspicuous attainment as a theatrical designer. *See* in "References": Larson (1969); Pendleton (1958); and Simonson (1932).

JONESY. In *Chris Christophersen*,* "a stout, heavy-faced, good-looking young fellow," a shipmate of Chris in the forecastle of the steamer *Londonderry* which runs down Chris's coal barge. He seems barely literate as he strives very hard to write a letter to his wife. He and Edwards* teasingly suggest that Chris might be offered the job of boatswain and also annoy him by suggesting that Chris's daughter Anna [*see* Christopherson, Anna] might be romantically involved with Paul Andersen,* the second mate.

JUAN. In *The Fountain*,* the nephew of Juan Ponce de Leon.* He "is a slender, graceful young cavalier," almost the double of his uncle at twenty. He is in love with Beatriz de Cordova,* daughter of Ponce de Leon's old love, Maria de Cordova.* The forthcoming marriage of the young people epitomizes the cyclic flow of the universe, the essential unity of man and nature. Ponce de Leon gives his blessing to this match, realizing that his own time is past, but that he, too, is partaking of that eternity of existence in which youth and age are one.

K

KAAN, Kublai. In *Marco Millions*,* the Great Kaan, "father of Kukachin.* The Kaan has sent the older Polo brothers to ask the pope for one hundred wise men to dispute the superiority of the Eastern religions of Taoism, Confucianism, Buddhism, and Islam over the Christianity of the West. He is a philosopher-king and is a trifle surprised when the pope sends Marco Polo,* the ultimate Western salesman, with the comment that he will be worth more to the Kaan than a million wise men "in the cause of wisdom." The Kaan rightly perceives the cynicism involved in the situation and keeps Marco and his relatives around for the purposes of experimentation and observation. He wishes to discover whether Marco in particular possesses an immortal soul since his god seems to be profit motivated. If Marco had been able to listen, the Kaan would have been his instrument of conversion rather than, as Marco thought, the other way around. After intense observation of Marco's behavior, the Kaan concludes that "the Word became their flesh, they say. Now all is flesh! And can their flesh become the Word again?"

Unfortunately for Kaan's experiment, Kukachin, his beloved daughter, has fallen in love with this swashbuckling, ruthless man of action. She defends Polo against the charge of having no soul and asks that he captain her ship that is to take her to Hormuz, where she is to marry the king of Persia. With heavy heart the Kaan agrees, and as she leaves he knows that her heart will be broken. On her death she requests that her body be returned to her father. When the Great Kaan hears the news of her death, he is both heartbroken and enraged against Marco Polo. Earlier he had forbidden general war against the West in order to enforce Buddhism on that part of the world. Now he wishes destruction but he is saved by his philosopher-adviser, Chu-Yin,* who preaches resignation.

Throughout his reign, Kublai Kaan has tried to learn about the nature of religion and of man. He is at first amused by the brash confidence and materialistic ambitions of Marco Polo, seeing him as a young man who will learn. But as Polo becomes merely more and more grasping, even tyrannical, in his quest for power, the Kaan finds his "spiritual hump" a real deformity. Polo seems to possess no emotions, and when he breaks the heart of Kukachin, the Kaan cannot forgive. He tries to discover the justice of his daughter's fate and the truth of human existence. All he can see is the truth of his own power and the fact that "she died for love like a fool!" However, the philosopher-adviser suggests, "No. She loved love. She died for Beauty." But the ultimate truth for the Great Kaan seems to remain in human relationships, in his love for his daughter, not the acquisition of wealth which is the creed of the Polos.

KALMAR, Hugo, "one time editor of Anarchist periodicals." In *The Iceman Cometh,** he rents a room over the saloon operated by Harry Hope.* "Hugo is a small man in his late fifties," with a big head, black hair, walrus mustache, thick spectacles, dressed in clean, threadbare black. He looks like the stereotypical bomb-throwing anarchist. He is said to have been based on the real life character of Hippolyte Havel.* Hugo has done ten years in prison for his beliefs, much of it in solitary confinement in his own country, but "the Movement" now sees him as a drunken has-been. He spends most of the play passed out at one of the tables of the back room, waking occasionally to declaim a few anarchist speeches and once to complain that the champagne is not iced. His pipe dream is that capitalism will someday be destroyed, though he does nothing about it nowadays. He is frightened by Theodore Hickman,* the salesman who comes to the bar annually to celebrate Hope's birthday, because Hickey makes him have bad dreams and questions his commitment to the Movement. Hugo perceives that Hickey has brought death with him this year. After Hickey's arrest for murdering his wife, and the assertion by other bar denizens that they will support his plea of insanity, which is a new pipe dream, Hugo starts to sing his revolutionary songs as the merriment gets more drunken. The curtain falls on his favorite quotation: "The days grow hot, O Babylon! 'Tis cool beneath thy willow trees." He is treated with good-natured jeering by the rest of the bar, and because he is continually sleeping off a drunk, he is not really affected by Hickey's pleas for an end to illusions.

KANAKA, Jimmy, the Hawaiian harpooner of the wrecked *Mary Allen,* "a tall, sinewy, bronzed young Kanaka," wearing only a breech cloth. He was drowned when the ship was lost. In *Where the Cross is Made,** he appears (along with his companions, Silas Horne,* the first mate, and Cates,* the bosun) in an hallucinatory scene in which only obsessed Captain Isaiah Bartlett* and the half-insane Nat Bartlett* see them. The three men bring in two inlaid chests, presumably containing the treasure; but it is only an illusion.

In *Gold,** a four-act recension of *Where the Cross Is Made,* Jimmy volunteers to murder Abel* and Butler,* the only two members of the crew who appear uncorrupt. He also spots the rescue schooner. Later, he ships out on the *Sarah Allen* to seek this "treasure." The crew attempts to murder Danny Drew,* the acting captain and fiancé of Sue Bartlett,* in order to prevent him from knowing the true reason for the journey. He, along with Horne and Cates, is lost when the *Sarah Allen* is wrecked.

KATE. In *The Long Voyage Home*,* a short and dark prostitute in Fat Joe's* London waterfront dive.

KEENEY, Captain David. In *Ile*,* the captain of the whaling ship *Atlantic Queen*, "a man of about forty, around five feet ten in height but looking much shorter on account of the enormous proportions of his shoulders and chest." He is the fanatical captain devoted entirely to the pursuit of whale oil. He has been icebound for almost two years and has obtained only half of his self-set quota of oil. He fears ridicule on his return to Homeport, since he has always brought home a full ship before. The dark lines of his face and the bleakness of his expression reveal the psychic price he is paying for this devotion to an impossible search. He has also brought his beloved wife, Mrs. Annie Keeney,* on this voyage, and the brutality and stasis of the journey have driven her nearly mad. Keeney's men attempt a mutiny, but the captain and the officers quell it with fists and threats of gunfire. In a tender moment with Annie, he is convinced that he should turn for home since there is clear water to the south, a request that his officers and men had earlier made. However, just as he gives his consent, there is a cry that the ice has opened to the north and a large school of whales has been spotted. Keeney instantly turns away from Annie, and at that moment she loses the last shreds of her reason. Keeney tries to convince himself that she is fooling him, but when he realizes that she is indeed mad, he looks back on her with anguish. Then with a face that has hardened into determination, he turns away to pursue this quest which has cost him everything. Keeney is one of those O'Neill characters who devotes himself utterly to a quest and as a result loses all that is dear to him.

KEENEY, Mrs. Annie, wife of Captain David Keeney* of the whaling ship, *Atlantic Queen*, "a slight, sweet-faced little woman primly dressed in black." In *Ile*,* she has accompanied her husband on his ill-fated whaling expedition, during which he has been icebound for most of two years and has managed to gain only four hundred barrels of oil, about half the capacity of his vessel. The Keeneys have been married six years and are childless. In the course of the play, Annie reveals the depth of her loneliness in the absence of her husband and her envy of the fine, free life she believed him to lead on the ocean while she wandered along the seashore filled with envy. The reality of this voyage, with its brutality and its virtual imprisonment, has caused such a profound mental depression in her that she is almost insane, weeping, sewing, and occasionally playing her organ. Ben,* the cabin boy, recalls how nicely she used to treat him before this occurrence. She is an inadvertent witness to the mutineers' confrontation with her husband and his officers, and she is profoundly disturbed. She tries in vain to get her husband to turn back, telling him that there is clear water to the south and that she wants nothing more than to return to Homeport. She recalls the flower-covered trellis of her home and swears that she now hates the sea and wishes that she had never come on this voyage. She wishes that they had had children and thinks that might have helped her misery. Captain Keeney reminds her that he had tried to dissuade her from the voyage and had worried so much about her well-being that he had brought along an organ to keep her amused. Finally Keeney agrees to return as she begs, "For the love of God, take me home." But just at that moment of tenderness, word comes that the ice has opened to the north where the whales will be.

Captain Keeney berates himself for thinking of "going home like a yaller dog." He then turns on Annie, telling her that she shouldn't meddle in his business. As he leaves to go after the whales, Annie's last shreds of sanity leave her and she turns to the organ to play an old hymn tune. Keeney first cannot believe the truth of her condition, but then he watches with anguish and realizes the price he has paid for his quest. As Annie plays and sways to the music, Keeney's face hardens into bleak determination as he goes on deck. She is the epitome of the O'Neill victimized woman who is sacrificed to the necessity of a "driven" man.

KNAPP CHILDREN. Charles, Dolly, Lizzie, and Sue—children of James Knapp* and Mary Knapp.* In *Warnings*,* these children are fifteen, fourteen, eleven, and eight, respectively. There is also a squalling baby aged one year. Charles seems to be a responsible young man, able to understand the economic problems of his father, even though he feels forced to ask for a new suit. He readily accepts his father's refusal, even though he is justifiably self-conscious about his slightly grotesque appearance in outgrown clothes. He has just discovered girls. Dolly, likewise, has just discovered boys, and the two bicker at considerable volume. Lizzie and Sue quarrel most of the time they are on the stage.

O'Neill has treated these children with considerable dislike. They seem very little more than pests. Curiously, O'Neill never has success with juvenile characterizations, and one wonders whether part of the reason was his unfamiliarity with children in general.

KNAPP, James. In *Warnings*,* the wireless operator of the S.S. *Empress.* He is a slight, stoop-shouldered, thin-faced man of about fifty," almost completely bald. "His face has been tanned by the tropic sun. . . . His eyes are small, dark, and set close together; his nose stubby and of no particular shape; his mouth large and weak." He has a "drooping gray mustache." His outward appearance is that of a depressed weakling. He has been warned by an ear specialist that his hearing is defective and that he will go stone deaf as the result of any sudden shock. The doctor cannot say when this will occur, but it may be some long time away. Knapp, understanding the responsibility of his position, tells his wife, Mary Knapp,* that he will tell his superiors; but she replies that if he is dismissed from his current position, he will not be able to get another. She begs him to remember what happened the last time he looked for another job and reminds him of the way they and their four (now five) children had almost starved. When she attacks him with scorn as a complete loser, he agrees to make one last voyage: "I got to do the right thing."

The scene shifts from the Knapps' cramped Bronx apartment to the listing boat deck of the S.S. *Empress*, where James is working his wireless, methodically sending out distress calls but receiving no replies. What the doctor predicted has happened, and Knapp has become completely deaf. He has not heard the transmissions from a nearby vessel warning of the derelict which the *Empress* has just struck. Captain Hardwick,* enraged at Knapp's reiterated "Yes, sir, No, sir" asks, "Are you deaf?" Knapp breaks down and piteously tells the story of how he has made this last voyage because "we're so poor and I couldn't get another job." The Captain's initial sympathy turns to rage when he discovers that Knapp's deafness was a direct cause of his losing the ship. When Knapp is told (in writing) of the earlier warnings which he had not heard, he is appalled, and when he sees that the life boats are being lowered, he goes to his cabin and shoots himself because he cannot live with the consequences of his error.

James Knapp is a character whom O'Neill has cast in a tragic role but has drawn as the pathetic victim of a nagging wife. Knapp is responsible for the disaster, and he must pay for it, but the motivation, largely because of the character drawing, seems pathetic rather than tragic. Knapp is a small man, though nonetheless a decent person. Clearly, O'Neill has sympathy for him, but it is questionable whether this arises from his dislike of the nagging Mary Knapp or from the economic determinism which has victimized this representative of the common man. As is frequent among these early O'Neill characters, the character drawing is mainly external, and the internal conflicts are only hinted at.

KNAPP, Mary. In *Warnings*,* wife of James Knapp,* who is the wireless operator of the S.S. *Empress*. "She is a pale, thin, peevish-looking woman of about forty, made prematurely old by the thousand worries of a penny-pinching existence. She wears her greying brown hair drawn back into a knot, her mouth has a sorrowful droop," and her faded blue eyes have an expression of fretful weariness. "She wears a solid gray wrapper and black carpet slippers." She is the mother of five children. [*See* Knapp Children]. The depressing and cramped Bronx apartment in which they live is filled with tension and quarreling. Mary Knapp seems to think of nothing but money, and with good reason. She even has to take in washing to make ends meet. When her husband James tells her that he is losing his hearing and will suddenly go deaf at some unspecified time in the future, she tries to suggest the doctor doesn't know what he is talking about. When James says that he must give up his responsible job because of his handicap, she is at first afraid that they will starve; then she berates him scornfully for thinking that he is capable of finding another job. She reproaches him, "And this is all the thanks I get for slavin' and workin' my fingers off! What a father for my poor children!" Her attitude toward her children shows a querulous hopelessness as well.

O'Neill has drawn Mary Knapp without any sympathy. She is made to seem nothing more than a shrewish nag, devoid of moral sense and concerned only with economic subsistence. This is unfortunate, because such a portrait also affects the character of James, who is made to seem a mere weakling under the thumb of a shrew when in fact he does indicate real affection for his son. This rather harsh treatment of Mary thus tends to diminish the death of James. Certainly both of them are the victims of an unforgiving economic system, but O'Neill has not indicated the existence of any past or present affection between them, and therefore the play seems rather one-dimensional. The inner feelings of Mary are not delineated. She is the first of the numerous nagging wives to be found in O'Neill, and like them she demonstrates a practicality which indicates a poverty of spirit.

"KNOCK AT THE DOOR, A,"   a one-act comedy. Written 1915–16 after leaving Harvard and still under the influence of George Pierce Baker.* The text has not survived.

KUKACHIN. In *Marco Millions*,* the exquisitely beautiful daughter of Kublai Kaan.* She first appears as a beautiful embalmed corpse, the twenty-three-year-old wife of the king of Persia. Her body at her own request is being returned to her father. As four travelers—representative of the Christian, Magian, Buddhist, and Mahometan religions—gaze upon her, she seems to generate light, and then she speaks with infinite musicality: "Say this, I loved and died. Now I am love, and live. And living, have forgotten. And loving, can forgive. Say this for me in Venice." The Christian merchant rightly assumes that this is a message for the Polos, but he does not understand its import or that it is meant specifically for Marco Polo.*

In Act II, Scene i, in a flashback, she is in the throne room at Xanadu. She is twenty years old and in love with the dashing Marco Polo, whom she has known since her childhood. She does not believe that he is as grossly materialistic as her father and his counselor, Chu-Yin,* think. She defends him when the Kaan suggests that he does not have a soul, recalling occasions when he has been touched by emotion and performed disinterested acts. She requests that he captain her ship on its voyage to Hormuz where she must meet with her betrothed, the king of Persia. Princesses must follow duty, not the dictates of love.

During the course of the voyage, Kukachin barely escapes death on three separate occasions but is saved by Marco Polo, not for love but as a means of protecting his investment—a future bonus. She, however, wishes for death. On their last night together, he importunes her for an additional bonus because of these extra services, and she tries desperately to make him feel love for her. She asks him to look into her eyes and say what he sees there—in accordance with the instructions of Chu-Yin. Marco looks and at that moment is almost overwhelmed with emotion. They nearly kiss, but then Marco hears the counting-house voice of his uncle, "one million," and is recalled to materialistic reality.

He says that the princess is perhaps delirious and suggests that she go to sleep. At this, she draws a dagger to kill herself, but Marco disarms her. When he tries to explain his behavior, he reveals that he is engaged to Donata* and shows her picture. He also notes the economic significance of the marriage as a union of two business houses and says that what he wants is a well-run household with a bourgeois wife who is not too bright. Enraged, Kukachin grinds Donata's locket underfoot, and later when she sees the magnificent Order of the Lion on the chest of Ghazan, the new king of Persia whom she is to marry, she places it on his chest, "the bosom of a sheep." She has offered herself to an "ox" and can no longer bear the shame of living. She therefore decides to die.

At the end of the play, her coffin, which had been in procession from Persia to Tartary in the prologue, reaches the palace of the Great Kaan at Cambaluc where Kublai, Chu-Yin, and four priests—Taoist, Confucian, Buddhist, and Moslem—try to find the secret of death and life. Kublai says, "She died for love like a fool," but Chu-Yin says, "No. She loved love. She died for beauty." Kukachin, however, in the prologue says she has forgiven, and in that way the play comes full circle, affirming the superiority of love over materialism.

L

"LAMENT FOR POSSESSORS, SELF-DISPOSSESSED,"* the title of the nine-play version of the abandoned cycle, "A Tale of Possessors, Self-Dispossessed."*

LAMPS, the lamptrimmer of the S.S. *Glencairn*, "a fat Swede," in *The Moon of the Caribbees.**

LANGNER, Lawrence (1890–1962), producer, playwright, patent lawyer, friend of Eugene O'Neill and a founding member of the Theatre Guild.* Born May 30, 1890, in Swansea, Wales; died in New York, December 26, 1962. Married Armina Marshall (1899–   ), an Oklahoma-born actress, in 1925; one son, Philip.

After a somewhat unconventional childhood, Langner was brought to London in 1903 where he worked as a junior clerk for Bannister Howard, manager of the Ben Greet Players, leaving that firm to study patent law. In 1910 he was sent to New York as representative of his British firm and remained there, eventually becoming senior partner in the firm of Langner, Percy, Card, and Langner. He divided his time between patent law and the arts, managing a remarkable balance between both. As a patent attorney, he was a government consultant on European patents in World War I and helped write the patent clause of the Treaty of Versailles in 1919. During World War II, he spent much time in Washington working for the war effort with the National Inventors' Council, an organization he helped found.

In 1914–1915, he helped organize the Washington Square Players* and also wrote plays (under the pseudonym of Basil Lawrence). The opening bill of the Players, February 19, 1915, included his one-act play *Licensed*. Susan Glaspell,* John Silas Reed,* and other members of the Provincetown Players* also supplied plays. In 1917, Eugene O'Neill's *In the Zone** was presented and *The Rope** in 1918. In that year he founded the Theatre Guild,* later joined by Theresa Helburn,* a production unit that was to become influential because of its performances of Shaw, assorted modern European drama, classical works, and some of the greater works of Eugene O'Neill. The Theatre Guild produced premiere performances of *Marco Millions*** (1928), *Strange Interlude*** (1928), *Dynamo*** (1929), *Mourning Becomes Electra*** (1931), *Ah, Wilderness!*** (1933), *Days Without End*** (1934), *The Iceman Cometh*** (1946), and *A Moon for the Misbegotten*** (1947), which closed out of town. However, since the Guild made decisions by committee, and perhaps for other reasons, it turned down other plays that O'Neill offered to it: *The Straw,*** *Gold,*** *The First Man,*** *Welded,*** *The Fountain,*** and (to its later regret) *"Anna Christie."**

Langner also became a close and considerate friend of Eugene O'Neill, even trying to arrange financial help for him to devote himself to full-time writing as early as 1922. He visited O'Neill in Bermuda and was one of the first outsiders to read *Strange Interlude*, being so impressed that he campaigned vigorously for its production. O'Neill also stayed with Langner and his wife, Armina Marshall, during rehearsals for this play. After O'Neill's marriage to Carlotta Monterey,* the Langners remained friends with the playwright, visiting the couple at Chateau du Plessis; Casa Genotta, Sea Island, Georgia; and Tao House, California. At Casa Genotta, O'Neill confided to Langner his plan for the cycle, "A Tale of Possessors, Self-Dispossessed,"* later suggesting that the Guild organize a special repertory company for its performance. In his autobiography, Langner also gives a first-hand account of O'Neill's less than idyllic residence in Georgia, telling of the unconquerable humidity and the permanent presence of snakes, which necessitated the clipping of all undergrowth to destroy their hiding places.

After O'Neill's move to Tao House in Danville, California, rumors persisted that O'Neill planned to break with the Guild. However, in 1940 he permitted Lawrence Langner and Theresa Helburn to read *The Iceman Cometh* with a view to postwar production by the Theatre Guild. In 1941 the Langners visited at Tao House, finding O'Neill in poor health but ready to discuss the lamentable state of the Broadway theatre. After the sale of Tao House, the Langners visited the O'Neills at the Huntington Hotel, San Francisco, when O'Neill discussed plans for the Guild production of *The Iceman Cometh*. He also allowed them to read three more plays: *A Moon for the Misbegotten, A Touch of the Poet,* and *Hughie,** despite Carlotta's disapproval. The first two of these were eventually produced by the Guild, with Armina Marshall as associate producer.

Earlier, in 1937, the Langners had founded the Westport Country Playhouse, with an acting company called the New York Repertory Company. Langner's idea was to produce each summer plays that he himself liked, without having to consider the preferences of other members of the Theatre Guild. Later, in 1951, he was instrumental in founding the American Shakespeare Festival and Dramatic Academy in Stratford, Connecticut.

With O'Neill's return to New York and concomitant sociability (much to Carlotta's annoyance), the Langners remained friends with the O'Neills. However, their attitude toward Carlotta differed somewhat from that of Saxe Commins,* O'Neill's editor, particularly during the couple's rather violent and brief separation in 1948. Langner and his wife believed that O'Neill and Carlotta were necessary to each other and consequently were later among the few remaining friends that Carlotta welcomed to their Marblehead residence on Point O'Rocks Lane. However, even the Langners were eventually cut off, largely because of their activities during the O'Neills' last rupture in 1951. Langner called in a psychiatrist, Dr. Merrill Moore, who curiously was a cousin of Carlotta's third husband, Ralph Barton.* He examined both O'Neill and Carlotta and concluded that O'Neill ought to separate from his wife and that a guardian should be appointed for her since he considered her incompetent to handle her affairs. Both the Langners and the Comminses supported O'Neill's move to New York from Boston, and both now hoped that he would remain either in New York or in Princeton, where Saxe and Dorothy Commins had offered him a permanent home. However, O'Neill decided otherwise. As he was about to leave for Boston by train, O'Neill asked Armina Marshall if the Theatre Guild would lend him five thousand dollars in case he might need some ready cash. Miss Marshall obliged, asking for a *pro forma* IOU which O'Neill gladly signed, just to keep the Guild books in order. Shortly after his return to Boston, Carlotta sent Miss Marshall a check for the amount and requested the return of the IOU. From that time on, the Langners were also shut out.

Lawrence Langner, as well as being a dedicated theatrical producer, was also a playwright, collaborating with his wife on numerous occasions, most notably in *The Pursuit of Happiness* (1934), *On to Fortune* (1936), and *Suzanna and the Elders* (1939). He also wrote a number of plays alone, notably *Moses* (1924), *These Modern Women* (1926), and *Henry Behave* (1927). His one-act play *Matinata* shared the opening bill for the first performance of *The Emperor Jones** at the Provincetown Playhouse (1920). Langner, like Saxe Commins, another of O'Neill's oldest, closest, and most considerate friends, was a man whose interests (and profession) included both the idealistic and the practical, a combination which seems to have attracted O'Neill. On the death of Lawrence Langner, his work with the Theatre Guild was carried on by his wife, Armina Marshall, and his son, Philip. He also wrote two books of memoirs: *The Magic Curtain* (1951), which recounts his experiences in both chosen professions, and *G.B.S. and the Lunatic* (1963), an account of his acquaintance with George Bernard Shaw.

See in "References": Gelb and Gelb (1973); Sheaffer (1968 and 1973); Helburn (1960); Langner (1951).

LARIMORE, Earle (?–1947), actor. Born in Portland, Oregon, son of Eugene Elton and Margaret Grace (Hughes) Larimore. Died after a long illness in New York City, October 23, 1947. Educated at Lincoln High School, Portland, and Oregon Agricultural College where he was a member of a little-theatre group. Served in France during World War I and after his return founded his own advertising agency, selling bonds on the side. Then became a technical engineer and helped design ships.

Larimore was encouraged in acting by an aunt whose sister was the actress,

Laura Hope Crews. He joined a stock company in Astoria, Oregon, and when it broke up he tried vaudeville in New York, without success. Crews then sent him to Jessie Bonstelle, who engaged him for bit parts and second leads. He stayed with this company for a year, touring in *Steve, May the Third,* and *So This Is London.* In 1925 he had his New York debut in *Made in America,* following this in 1926 with *Love City, Nirvana,* and *Stranger in the House* (Baltimore), *Juarez and Maximilian* and *Ned McCobb's Daughter.* Joining the Theatre Guild in the same year, he played in *The Silver Cord* and opposite Lynne Fontanne* in *At Mrs. Beam's.* He soon established himself at the Guild as a romantic actor, appearing in *The Second Man* and *The Doctor's Dilemma* (with Lynn Fontanne and Dudley Digges*) in 1927.

In 1928 he created the roles of Sam Evans* in *Strange Interlude** and Marco Polo* in *Marco Millions,** repeating the latter role in a one-week revival in 1930. O'Neill had liked Larimore's performance as Sam Evans and was therefore happy when he was cast as Orin Mannon* in *Mourning Becomes Electra** (1932) with Alla Nazimova* as Christine Mannon* and Alice Brady* as Lavinia Mannon.* He received enthusiastic reviews. On June 1, 1932, he married Selena Royle, the actress, after a first marriage had ended in divorce in 1925. In 1934 he created the part of John Loving* in the unsuccessful *Days Without End,** with Selena Royle as Elsa Loving* and Ilka Chase as Lucy Hillman.* In 1946 he understudied E. G. Marshall as Willie Oban* in *The Iceman Cometh,** a role he subsequently played on tour. In 1947 he understudied the role of James Tyrone, Jr.,* in *A Moon for the Misbegotten,** which closed out of New York. Larimore was a singularly gifted interpreter of O'Neill roles, making a dramatic impact even in those plays which were not critical successes. Larimore's career included roles in many other plays. He also performed on radio and television.

LARRY. In *"Anna Christie,"** the relief bartender, about twenty years old, "boyish, red-cheeked, rather good looking." He speedily realizes that Anna Christopherson* is a prostitute and suspects that Chris Christopherson* may be trying to pick her up. He is embarrassed to discover that Anna is Chris's daughter. Larry plays the same role (relief bartender) in the two earlier drafts of this play, *Chris Christophersen** and *"The Ole Davil."**

"LAST CONQUEST, THE," notes for a proposed play, originally entitled "The Thirteenth Apostle," worked on August 30, 1940–December 13, 1942. Apparently O'Neill remained committed to this work as late as 1948, when he was no longer capable of doing further work on it. Ten sets of notes exist for this play at Yale University. A very full analysis of all this material appears in Floyd, 1981, pp. 317–345.

The play apparently was to be based on the themes of the duality of man, the conflict between good and evil and between Christ and the Devil. The action ranges from the temptation of Christ to His crucifixion and concerns "the attempted last campaign of Evil to stamp out even the unconscious memory of

God in Man's spirit'' (O'Neill, quoted by Floyd, 1981, p. 319). Satan fails. O'Neill was forced to abandon the play, not because of an inability to write a final confession of faith in good but because of his ill-health. Floyd believes that this might have proved to be O'Neill's greatest work.

LATHROP, Harriet. In "The Reckoning"* (unpublished scenario), girlfriend of Jack Cockran, Jr.* She is the super-patriotic young woman who goes with young Jack when he enlists in the aviation corps in 1917. She has a few qualities of the later Madeline Arnold* in *Strange Interlude*,* largely because of her relationship to Jack's basically possessive mother, Bessie Small.* Harriet is an undeveloped character in this draft scenario.

LATHROP, John. In the unpublished scenario "S.O.S."* he is the sixtyish telegraphist of Acropolis. He also goes on weekly drinking bouts. He reforms after marrying Susannah Darrow,* but he is shortly afterwards discharged from his position for being too old. They then move to New Jersey, and John gets a position as a wireless operator on board a steamer, the *Rio Grande*. Susannah accompanies him as a passenger. After two years of this, Susannah must remain at home for one voyage, just at the time that John discovers that he is becoming hopelessly deaf. He decides he must make one last voyage because they need the money. During the voyage John loses his hearing completely and as a result fails to monitor a signal warning of a German raider in the vicinity. The *Rio Grande* is captured and sunk, and John's responsibility for the incident is revealed. His crew-mates treat him like a pariah, but the raider's captain makes a mild "hero" out of him, giving him the run of the ship. John's hearing is suddenly restored by the concussion of the ship's guns. He then kills the German wireless operator and sends out a signal giving the raider's position. As an American cruiser heaves into sight, John is shot by a firing squad and is buried at sea. He then becomes a real hero, and his responsibility in the loss of the ship is forgotten. His character is sketchily drawn but bears some resemblance to that of James Knapp* in *Warnings*.* However, the matrimonial relationship between Susannah and John is one of great happiness, not the bickering found between the Knapps.

LAZARUS, the husband of Miriam* and brother of Martha* and Mary.* In *Lazarus Laughed*,* he has been raised from the dead by Christ before the play opens, and as a result of this voyage beyond the grave, he has emerged as the personification of life's affirmation and its Dionysian spirit. He is given the role of Nietzschean redeemer, and in his laughter he reveals to those who will listen that "life is" and that death is merely the fear between life on earth and an after-life. His message of affirmation leads him into confrontations with both Nazarenes and Orthodox Judaism in which his family, with the exception of Miriam, is killed. Later, in a confrontation with Greco-Roman civilization, his followers are killed, then Miriam, and finally he himself is burned at the stake.

But through his life he manages to touch his followers, if only for a brief period, and leads them to a joyous acceptance of death. By the end of the play even Tiberius Caesar* and Pompeia* have learned from Lazarus, and at the last there is even some hope for Caligula,* who speaks the most pessimistic lines of Lazarus as the curtain falls: "Men forget!" Lazarus is so committed to life that he becomes progressively younger as the play proceeds. Being able to overcome the fear of death, he thus defeats the ravages of time and partakes of eternity in the course of mortal life. Lazarus's dedication to the superiority of man as god in himself is the Dionysian incarnation of which Nietzsche speaks in *Thus Spake Zarathustra*, and it is the culmination of O'Neill's attempts to preach this gospel.

LAZARUS LAUGHED, a "play for an imaginative theatre" in four acts and eight scenes, with over 420 roles.

Act I, Scene i: Lazarus's* home in Bethany, exterior and interior, shortly after the miracle of his being raised from the dead. The main room has long tables and seats for guests; the exterior shows the roadway with many men, and through a doorway one sees the yard where a crowd of women has gathered. Inside the house are Seven Male Guests and a Chorus of Seven Old Men, all of whom are watching Lazarus. All the characters—crowds, guests, chorus— are masked in the seven ages of man (Boyhood or Girlhood, Youth, Young Manhood or Young Womanhood, Manhood or Womanhood, Middle Age, Maturity, Old Age). Each of these age divisions has seven representatives, each masked with the following aspects of general character traits probably drawn from Carl G. Jung's *Psychological Types*: "the Simple, Ignorant; the Happy, Eager; the Self-Tortured, Introspective; the Proud, Self-Reliant; the Servile, Hypocritical; the Revengeful, Cruel; the Sorrowful, Resigned." The Seven Male Guests are composed of one representative of each period and trait. Each crowd consists of "forty-nine different combinations of period and type," each distinguished by a different color for each character type. The Seven Old Men of the Chorus are given masks twice the size of the others, and their type is the "Sorrowful, Resigned type of Old Age." All the masks in this scene and the succeeding one are noticeably Semitic. Lazarus alone is unmasked because he is "freed now from the fear of death." He has the face of a "statue of a divinity of Ancient Greece" with a dark complexion, a face calm but wrinkled with suffering, displaying fortitude rather than resignation, high forehead, dark eyes, and an expression which seems to see beyond the mundanities of everyday existence. Kneeling beside him are Miriam,* his wife; his sisters, Martha* and Mary*; his Father*; and Mother.* Miriam wears a mask on the upper part of her face which is that of "Woman" while her mouth is sensitive and sad. Her ruddy complexion contrasts with the marble pallor of the mask. Martha, Mary, and the parents wear full stylized masks: Martha, the "buxom middle-aged housewife"; Mary, "young and pretty, nervous and high-strung"; the Father, "a thin, feeble old man of over eighty, meek and pious"; the Mother, "tall and stout, over sixty-five, a gentle, simple woman.'' It is twilight, some time after the miracle, and Jesus has departed.

The Chorus of Old Men begins with a chant, the last lines of which are taken up by the crowd: "He that believeth/ Shall never die!" Then they call, in an echo of Jesus's command, "Lazarus, come forth!" As they wait, the Seven Guests, covering the age types, recount the tale of Lazarus's unsuccessful life: he had lost his money through his innocence, and all his children had died, even his one son. Now, since the miracle, he seems to have changed: his accustomed pallor has been replaced by ruddiness, and his face seems to "have forgotten sorrow in the grave." They then recount the events of the miracle: as Lazarus came forth he looked at Jesus and said, " 'Yes' as if he were answering a question in Jesus' eyes." Then he knelt before Jesus and kissed his feet, "and both of them smiled and Jesus blessed him and called him 'My Brother' and went away." And then Lazarus "began to laugh softly like a man in love with God." Such was the power of this laugh that the watcher found that he himself was laughing, too.

Again the crowd calls for Lazarus, and he rises from his seat in the main room, embracing his Mother and Miriam as his Father and sisters kiss his hands. The crowd presses in and the Father calls for a toast. But Lazarus stands there oddly majestic and silent. As the toast is raised Lazarus speaks, "No! There is no death!" and in answer to the question of what is beyond the grave, he gives his listeners the secret of his existence for the rest of his life: "There is only life! I heard the heart of Jesus laughing in my heart; 'There is Eternal Life in No!' it said, 'and there is Eternal Life in Yes! Death is the fear between'." And with this affirmation of life, Lazarus laughs in such a manner that all laugh with him, and the scene concludes with the entire crowd chanting, "Laugh! Laugh!/ Death is dead!/There is only laughter!"

Act I, Scene ii: The exterior of Lazarus's house in Bethany, some months later, on a clear, bright, starry night. The house is now known as the House of Laughter. The low, one-story house is lighted with flickering candles, and "the sound of flutes and dance music can be heard" as dancers pass by the windows. "There is continually an overtone of singing laughter, emphasizing the pulsing rhythm of the dance." Outside are two approximately equal groups of Jews, divided this time not by sex but by religious orientation. Martha and Mary are among the Nazarenes, adherents of Jesus, while Lazarus's Father and Mother are among the Orthodox. The two groups are separated by the Chorus of Old Men. From inside the house comes the song: "Laugh! Laugh/There is only Life!/ There is only Laughter!" Mary, outside the house, asks how the Nazarenes can laugh because laughter is a betrayal of Jesus. The Orthodox Priest is enraged at the blasphemy that the followers of Lazarus are committing. Both the Nazarenes and the Orthodox are opposed to Lazarus, who seems to have become a devil. As the two groups taunt and sneer at each other, Lazarus's Mother faints, and both sides revile Lazarus. But then when the Orthodox Priest begins to insult Jesus, Mary asserts His identity as the Messiah and begs her Mother to go with them, to give up everything, even her husband's love. At this the Father curses, "the devil in you," in Martha and in Lazarus. But as he reaches the lament, "My children are dead," the voice of Lazarus is heard: "Death is dead! There is only laughter."

The followers then stream out of the house, and the warring factions outside forget their differences and unite against this common enemy. As before, the followers are forty-nine in number, masked by age and character type, with a Chorus of seven wearing double-sized masks. Dressed in bright, diaphanous robes, they sway in the rhythm of the dance, laughing to the music as the outsiders hoot at them and then speak of their fecklessness. Slowly the crowd starts to join in "a queer excitement." They begin to fall into the movements of a "grotesque sort of marionettes' country dance" which becomes more and more "hectic" and turns into a hostile, animalistic chant: "Beware, Lazarus!/We burn! We kill!/We crucify!/Death! Death!"

As they move toward the gateway, Lazarus appears and silence falls. He is dressed in a white robe and looks ten years younger, about forty, while Miriam has aged about five years. His face looks more Greek, his complexion is that of "the red-brown of rich earth." He signs, the music ceases, and silence and immobility fall, but as he begins to speak his own dancers start to move and the music begins again, softly. He speaks of the affirmation of life: "You forget the God in you! You wish to forget! Remembrance would imply the high duty to live as a son of God—generously—with love!—with pride—with laughter!" Living with sadness and resignation is a paltry thing, and Lazarus speaks of abandonment to life itself: "The greatness of Man is that no god can save him— until he becomes a god."

At this instant, a Messenger arrives to tell the crowd that Jesus is dead. With that, violence erupts between the groups of Jews, and a squad of eight Roman soldiers enters, all masked with the Roman face, "heavy, domineering self-complacent," and all of the period of manhood of the "Simple, Ignorant Type." They charge the warring mobs, and Lazarus remarks that "sometimes it is hard to laugh—even at men." They separate and identify their dead: Mary, Martha, and Lazarus's parents are all dead; and Miriam, grief-stricken, recalls that Jesus, too, is dead. However, Lazarus still insists that "even a Son of Man must die to show men that Man may live! But there is no death!" With this the Centurion orders Lazarus to come with him to Rome, and Lazarus obeys, kissing each of his dead relatives. Then looking upward he says, "Yes! . . . and begins to laugh from the depths of his exalted spirit." Gradually his followers and even the Romans start to join in. Even the mourning Chorus of Old Men begins to adopt the rhythm of the laughter and the movement of the dancers, finally reaching a point at which they too cry out, "Death is no more!/Death is Dead!/Laugh!" But there is a test at hand for Lazarus's followers as the Old Men announce in remorse, "Oh, shame and guilt!/We forget our dead!" The crowd echoes this grief; the followers of Lazarus slow their dancing, and their chanting certainty remains unfinished: "Fear is no—/Death is—/Laugh—" The music and dancing cease and the lights go out. Then all break into a "chorus of forlorn bewilderment." The followers call for the return of laughter; but all fall into hopelessness, and finally they join in a chorus of despair and denial of life: "Life is a fearing,/ A long dying,/From birth to death!/God is a slayer!/Life is death!" And the curtain falls on this lament.

Act II, Scene i: "Some months later. A square in Athens about ten o'clock at night." The facade of a temple is at the rear, and a crowd of Greeks, masked in accordance with the pattern in Act I, is waiting as if for a festival. The masks are Grecian, and the Chorus of Seven is masked as "the Proud, Self-Reliant type, in the period of Young Manhood." They are clothed in a manner reminiscent of the devotees of Dionysus: in goat skins, daubed with wine. They seem to think Lazarus may be a reincarnation of that god. Roman legionaries, masked as in Act I, serve as police and keep back the crowd. Caligula,* a twenty-one-year-old Roman noble, paces up and down in the front. He wears a half-mask of crimson-purple, emphasizing "his prematurely-wrinkled forehead, his hollow temples and his bulbous, sensual nose." His eyes are feverish and suspicious, but his mouth is delicate and "weak but domineering." He projects an aura of "boyish cruelty . . . naively insensitive to any human suffering but its own." Cneius Crassus,* a Roman general of sixty, walks beside him, a short, squat figure wearing a mask of coarse humor.

Following the pattern of Act I, the Chorus is first heard, this time invoking Dionysus, while seven Greeks speculate about Lazarus and discuss his deeds. But one troubling thing is noted, that when he has gone people cannot remember his laughter, that the dead are dead again and the sick die, and the sad grow more sorrowful." Another hopes that Lazarus will lead them against the Romans and drive them out. As the crowd presses closer, Caligula calls upon Crassus to be ruthless: "Corpses are so educational." He looks with scorn upon the people who stretch their arms toward the direction from which Lazarus is expected, "A Jew becomes a god!" But Crassus wonders whether Lazarus really is a Jew: "he teaches people to laugh at death. That smacks of Roman blood!" The emperor, Tiberius Caesar,* has heard of Lazarus and his claim that "there is no death at all," and therefore he fears Lazarus's influence among the multitudes. Clearly Tiberius wishes to kill Lazarus and has sent Caligula to escort him to Rome. But Caligula also has ambition, and he is determined someday (the sooner the better) to be Caesar. Therefore, he is concerned lest Lazarus has discovered the secret of defeating old age and will divulge it to Tiberius. However, he does not consider the possibility of killing this new prophet. Perhaps, as Cneius Crassus suggests, Caligula is afraid of Lazarus.

Gradually the rhythmic chant of the Chorus excites the crowd: "Fire-born! Redeemer! Savior!/Raise from the dead our freedom!/Give us back our lost laughter!/Free us from Rome!" They press closer and closer upon the Romans, who are ordered to draw swords. But then the sound of music is heard, and Caligula "begins to dance grotesquely and chant." But the crowd, now savage, calls, "Death to Caligula," as he raises his own sword and calls, "Death!" The entire group, Romans and Greeks alike, echo "Death!" And at that moment the voice of Lazarus rings out, "There is no death!" Then the sound of gay and mocking laughter is heard, and his crowd of followers come "dancing into the square, preceded by a band of musicians and by their chorus." Here, each member of the Chorus wears a mask with a different ethnic characteristic. They sift into the crowd singing their chant, "There is no death!/There is only life!/ There is only laughter!" "Caligula and Crassus are swept to one side," and the entire company calls, "Lazarus!" The Roman soldiers now march in pulling Lazarus, their prisoner, in a chariot. He is dressed in white and gold and now seems no more than thirty-five years of age. He seems to radiate light, and he looks like Dionysus, the Greek god "closest to the soil . . . the soul of the recurring seasons, of living and dying as processes in eternal growth." Miriam, dressed in black, is with him, seeming to be over forty-five. The Greeks rush upon him, dress him in the bull's hide, put the rod of Dionysus in his hands, and then prostrate themselves before him as their "Savior!/Redeemer!/Conqueror of death!" Lazarus laughs, and Caligula panics, drawing his sword; but as he looks at Lazarus, who tells him, "Death is dead," he stops and finally collapses like a child: "Death would have been my slave when I am Caesar. He would have been my jester and made me laugh at fear!"

Lazarus tries to teach Caligula, telling him that he loves to kill because he himself is afraid to die. He lives in fear of death and like so many men, "their fear becomes their living. They worship life as death!" This is what Lazarus learned in the grave, that men have invented death in their fear and that "they must be taught to laugh again!" This is Lazarus's mission. And the Chorus first, followed by the multitude, takes up the cry, "There is only God!/We are his laughter!/Laugh! Laugh!" They then pick up the chariot traces and draw Lazarus off, while Caligula and Crassus are left alone, the young man brooding and the older man trying to control himself, but struggling with laughter until he collapses. Caligula, surprised by this, leaps up and lops off the heads of a handful of flowers, saying, "Laugh! Laugh! Laugh!" Lazarus has begun to influence even him.

Act II, Scene ii: Rome, at midnight, some months later. It is a threatening night with thunder and lightning but no rain. The members of the Senate are seated on a series of steps ranged on either side of a temple portico. They are dressed in white robes and masked in the Roman manner, with the arrogance attenuated into "exhausted cynicism." The periods of "Middle Age, Maturity and Old Age are represented in the types of the Self-Tortured, Introspective; Proud, Self-Reliant; the Servile, Hypocritical; the Cruel, Revengeful; and the Resigned, Sorrowful." The Chorus of Seven Senators, wearing double-sized masks, shows "the Servile, Hypocritical type of Old Age." Lazarus stands in the rear-center, dressed in white, "his body seeming to glow more brightly than ever." Miriam, dressed in black and grown much older, kneels near and behind him. On the opposite side Caligula squats on an ivory and gold throne. He is dressed in bright colors, "a victory wreath on his head," looking at Lazarus and the praying Miriam. As the scene opens, the sound of "departing troops" is heard, and their uniforms and helmets are momentarily visible as they go out to the gate which is heard to clang shut.

After a short silence, the Chorus of the Senate "intones wearily, as if under a boring compulsion," a chant in praise of the senate. Caligula sings an old camp song hoarsely and drunkenly. He stares at Lazarus and tells him that the legions have left, but Lazarus does not seem to have heard. Then, following the pattern of earlier scenes, the Seven Senators discuss Lazarus and the state of Rome. They are concerned with an encampment of Lazarus's followers outside the walls of the city: "Probably the legions are to butcher them in their sleep." Everyone is waiting for Caligula to give a signal, for Tiberius has fled to Capri. Miriam pleads for mercy, but Lazarus seems to glow more magnificently than before: "I will awaken my beloved ones that their passing may be a symbol to the world that there is no death!" And with this he laughs, and his mirth spreads awkwardly to the Senators themselves; their discordant laughter is echoed by the thunder and lightning of the heavens, and the sound of flutes, cymbals, and marching feet is heard as Miriam kneels with arms outstretched, looking like a figure of crucified grief. In counterpoint, the followers of Lazarus reiterate, "Fear is no more! Death is dead!" All, except Miriam, Caligula and the Legionaries, are by now caught up in the chant, and Caligula attempts to assert his belief in death. But laughter overcomes him, too, until finally he collapses into a be-seeching cry, "Forgive me! I love you, Lazarus! Forgive me!" All, including the Senators and even the Legionaries, now sing of the triumph of life over death: "Death is dead!"

As the returning soldiers become visible, Crassus tells the tale of the massacre of Lazarus's followers. They did not wait for the Legionaries, but "they charged upon us, laughing! . . . They stabbed themselves, dancing as though it were a festival! They died, laughing, in one another's arms! We laughed, too, with joy, because it seemed it was not they who died but death itself they killed!" And with this, Crassus hails Lazarus as a leader, and he is echoed by his troops: "Hail, Lazarus Caesar! Hail!" Caligula, seeing his ambition about to be de-stroyed, begs Lazarus to refuse. Lazarus's reply is a mockery, "What is—Caesar?" and with this Crassus offers to make him a god; but again, Lazarus laughs and tells the departing soldiers and Senators, "Wait! When you awake tomorrow, try to remember! Remember that death is dead! Remember to laugh!" Left alone with Miriam and Lazarus, Caligula threatens, "I swear you shall not laugh at death when I am Death!" but then he breaks into a harsh laugh and leaves, terrified. Miriam, broken with grief, speaks of the death of those followers of Lazarus who have believed in him, but Lazarus exults, tenderly explaining to his aging wife, as he kisses her, "But God, their Father, laughs!"

Act III, Scene i: Capri, some days later, the exterior of the villa of Tiberius, about 2 A.M. on "a clear black night." A marble terrace with massive columns and a triumphal arch are visible. A cross has been erected in the center of the arch, and "a full grown male lion has been crucified" on it. The windows of the palace are lighted by lamps, and the noise of a drunken revel is heard as the Guard, in the uniform of the Chorus and masked as Roman soldiers, enters, followed by their commander, Flavius,* and by Lazarus, Miriam, and Caligula, with his sword drawn. He seems ''in a state of queer conflicting emotion,. . . with a nervous dread and terror of everything about him, while. . . perversely excited and elated by his tension.'' Lazarus is younger than ever, now seeming about twenty-five, while Miriam seems ever more aged, ''a figure of a sad, resigned mother of the dead.'' Flavius bows to Caligula and then, awkwardly, to Lazarus and goes to announce them.

As they watch over him, Miriam and Caligula see the crucified lion. Miriam utters a cry of horror, but Caligula speaks callously, saying that such trees ''usually bear human fruit.'' He takes the lion as a lesson for Lazarus and ''other lions—not to roar–or laugh—at Caesar!'' He tells Lazarus he should not have come, because last night Caligula's legions were his and he could have been Caesar. But Lazarus sadly recalls the short memories of mankind, for the very next morning ''the legions had forgotten. They only remembered—to go out and pick up their swords! They also pillaged the bodies a little, as their right, believing now that they had slain them.'' Lazarus laughs softly, remembering that men are men. Caligula taunts Lazarus with the possibility of his soon taking the place of the crucified lion and brutally pokes at the dying beast which Lazarus addresses with such pity that it licks his hand. In reply to Caligula's astonishment, Lazarus repeats, ''There is no death,'' what Caligula sees is ''Your fear of life!'' With fear, Miriam sees nothing but evil in Roman civilization and dreads the coming death of Lazarus, ''the going away from me of your laughter which is to me as my son, my little boy!'' She recalls the peace of the hills of Bethany, and Lazarus promises that she must wait ''only a little longer'' and then she will find ''God's laughter on the hills of space.'' Confusedly, Caligula speaks to Miriam, finally confessing that he loves Lazarus: ''Yet why can I not laugh, Jewess?'' Miriam replies that laughter is impossible for her, too: ''The miracle could not revive all his old husband's life in my wife's heart.''

At this point Marcellus,* a thirty-five-year-old Roman patrician, enters. He is richly dressed, and his eyes are cold and hypocritical in a face marked with dissipation. Nonetheless, Lazarus's luminescent form astonishes him. He announces his wish to speak alone with Lazarus, who orders Caligula away, and then Marcellus raises his dagger against Lazarus who commences to laugh softly; Marcellus's dagger is stopped in mid-air and Miriam cries out in fright. As the dagger drops from the Roman's hand, he smiles ''the curious, sheepish, bashful smile of one who has fallen in love and been discovered.'' Lazarus speaks to him as one ''who believes in death! But soon you will laugh with life!'' And as he departs, Marcellus begins to laugh and the files of the Guard join with Lazarus in his laughter. Caligula mocks Marcellus for his weakness and his confession of love for Lazarus until Marcellus stabs himself, dying on the line, ''There is no death!'' The Guard join in the Chorus, ''Death is dead!'' and Caligula calls after the departing Lazarus and Miriam: ''I will defend you! There is death inside there—death! Beware Lazarus.'' But Lazarus's laughter is heard from inside the palace as the Chorus and the entire Guard join in the chant, "Death is dead!''

Act III, Scene ii: "The banquet hall in the palace of Tiberius.'' It is a huge chamber with long couches and low tables lining the walls, except for the rear, which is broken by an arch. A dais with the chair of Caesar is in the center, with a table in front and couches on either side. On the right are reclining young women and girls, and on the left, an equal number of youths. They are masked in the Roman manner "of the periods of Boyhood (or Girlhood), Youth, and Young Manhood (or Womanhood), and there are seven individuals of each period and sex in each of the three types of the Introspective, Self-Tortured; the Servile, Hypocritical; and the Cruel, Revengeful—a crowd of forty-two in all.'' The male masks appear effeminate and corrupt, and "the female have a bold, masculine expression.'' The men are dressed as women and vice versa. "The whole effect of these two groups is of sex corrupted and warped, of invented lusts and artificial vices.'' The Chorus "is composed of three males and four females— the males in the period of Youth, one in each of the types represented'' and the females correspondingly. "The fourth female is masked in the period of Womanhood in the Proud, Self-Reliant type.'' Their masks are double-sized, and they sit four and three on either side of the dais. Pompeia,* Caesar's favorite mistress, sits front-right, wearing an olive-colored half-mask "with the red of blood smouldering through, with great, dark, cruel eyes—a dissipated mask of intense evil beauty.'' But the lower part of her face is unmasked and "is set in an expression of agonized self-loathing.'' Tiberius Caesar, "dressed in deep purple, fringed and ornamented with crimson and gold,'' is standing on the dais. He is seventy-six, "tall, broad and corpulent but of great muscular strength still.'' He is bald, and his "mask is a pallid purple, as if the imperial blood in his veins had been sickened by age and debauchery. The eyes are protuberant, leering, cynical slits, the long nose, . . . now gross and thickened, the forehead lowering and grim.'' Beneath the mask is the face of a statesman with a stern expression, strong chin, and a healthy complexion. "As the curtain rises, slaves are hurriedly putting out the many lamps'' as from outside Lazarus's laughter is heard over that of the Guards. Everyone in the hall is listening with fascination and with varied reactions. Flavius and a squad of the Guard surround the dais.

Tiberius, in a combination of fear and awe, orders "Strike him down! Stab him!'' But the chant of the soldiers is heard: "Laugh! Laugh! Laugh!/Death is dead!'' Then "the shining figure of Lazarus'' appears to strike fear into Tiberius, who orders Flavius to stand in his place while he seeks the protection of the Guards. Caligula "is heard screaming above the chorus of Laughter! "Beware of death! I will defend you, Lazarus!'' as he rushes in with drawn sword and kills Flavius. With that he commences to laugh because now that he has saved Lazarus, he is able to laugh "a clear laughter of selfless joy.'' But as soon as Lazarus, followed by Miriam, appears, his joyous mirth ceases and once again "becomes full of his old fear and blood-lust.''

Confronting Lazarus, he claims the title of Caesar. But Lazarus goes over to where Tiberius is hidden and draws him forth, removing the toga from his face and forcing the emperor to look into his eyes. Tiberius realizes that Lazarus is not evil and has not come to seek his office but then puzzles at Lazarus's laughter against Caesar. "Yet I like thy laughter. It is young. Once I laughed somewhat like that—so I pardon thee." He orders Caligula down from the dais, pardoning him, "for where could I find another heir so perfect for serving my spite upon mankind?" But he also warns Caligula by pointing out the corpse of Flavius. Seated again upon the dais, Tiberius questions Lazarus about his "magic," to which Lazarus replies, "There is no death, Caesar," a comment which brings Tiberius to ask him to prophesy whether he himself will die soon. On hearing the affirmative reply, Tiberius turns against the prophet, but overcome with awe he asks Lazarus, "What cured thee of death?" to which Lazarus replies, "There is only life, Caesar."

As he laughs softly, Pompeia is impelled to rise and walk to the dais, trying to gain Caesar's attention. When she fails, she goes over to interrogate Caligula: "His laughter is like a god's. He is strong. I love him." Caligula coarsely takes this as an expression of lust and tells her that Lazarus is faithful to his old wife and has remained so though many women have flung themselves at him. He wagers that Lazarus will laugh at Pompeia rather than sleep with her, and the woman plots Miriam's death by poison: "I want to see him suffer, to hear his laughter choke in his throat with pain!" At first opposed, Caligula comes to approve of the plan, so she approaches Tiberius to awaken him from his trance and challenge the power of Lazarus. As she mocks him, Lazarus asks, "Do you fear peace?" and Pompeia rebukes him. Tiberius then tells once again the tale of the miracle of Lazarus and the death of Christ, but Pompeia remains impervious, suggesting that Lazarus "prove there is no death." The assemblage takes up the suggestion, wishing to relieve its boredom by beholding a miracle: "Raise the dead!" Pompeia then shows Tiberius a piece of poisoned fruit she has taken from his bowl: she will give it to Miriam to eat, "and he must laugh!" Cruelly, Tiberius agrees, and Pompeia offers it to Miriam, while Caligula says that the test is a good one: "I know he loves her!"

With meekness and longing, Miriam asks Lazarus's permission to accept death in the poisoned fruit because she is tired of life, overcome with the accumulated griefs of existence, and wishes to rest in the tomb of Bethany. Tenderly, Lazarus tells her to "go in peace—to peace!" though he will be lonely. She has never participated in his laughter, and for her, life after the miracle has been hard. As Miriam gratefully takes the peach with a courtesy, Lazarus involuntarily motions her away as Pompeia and the crowd jeer at Lazarus's fear of death. But Miriam eats quickly and starts to talk of the past "like a garrulous old woman," of her return home, and of her love for Lazarus, a man unlike any other. Then, as she falls into his arms, he lays her down, saying he will be lonely. Tiberius mocks him, and Lazarus begs Miriam, "Call back to me! Laugh!" as he had asked her to do before she ate the fruit. But there is silence, broken only by the jeering of the assemblage: "There is death!" Caligula hops up and down in cheated rage while Tiberius threatens the scourge, but just as the soldiers are about to attack Lazarus, Miriam's voice is heard: "Yes! There is only life! Lazarus be not lonely!" and she laughs and sinks back. Lazarus now realizes his total commitment to "this new faith and joy," for with Miriam the last remnants of his old self-pity and loneliness have gone. "But there is no death, no fear, nor loneliness! There is only God's eternal laughter! His laughter flows into the lonely heart!" He begins to laugh again, "the laughter of a conqueror arrogant with happiness and the pride of a new triumph." He picks up the body of Miriam and lays it on the dais of Caesar as "an abject, submissive panic spreads" through the room, affecting everyone, and "an agonized moan of supplicating laughter comes from them all." "Let us die, Lazarus!/Mercy, Laughing one!/ Mercy of Death!"

Act IV, Scene i: The same, a short time later. All lamps have been extinguished "except the one on the table on the dais," which illuminates the face of Miriam. "Lazarus sits on the couch on the right of the dais" looking like a young son keeping vigil by the body of his mother. Tiberius sits on the other side of the table, talking to, but not looking at either Lazarus or the corpse. Pompeia sits to the right at Lazarus's feet at the top step of the dais, gazing up into Lazarus's face. On the step below, "Caligula squats on his haunches, his arms on his knees, his fist pressed to his temples."

Each of the four is attempting to evaluate what has just occurred. Tiberius asks specifically whether Miriam was dead when she spoke, or whether these were merely her last words of comfort; Pompeia rejoices in Lazarus's laughter, saying to Caligula that this has increased her love for Lazarus—her desire for a master; Caligula bitterly says that Lazarus loves no one. Pompeia returns to the wager with Caligula, saying she is glad that she has lost but that now she cannot pay: "Now that I know love, I may not give myself to any man save him!" The three Romans try to redefine their relationship with Lazarus, and Tiberius asks Lazarus what he had found "beyond death," to which Lazarus replies, "Life! God's Eternal Laughter!" In answer to Tiberius's request for hope, Lazarus advises the Emperor to "dare to love Eternity without your fear desiring to possess her! Be brave enough to be possessed!" He tries to make Tiberius understand that man should interpret his "first cry . . . fresh from the womb as the laughter of one who even then says to his heart, 'It is my pride as God to become a Man. Then let it be my pride as Man to recreate the God in me!' " The reaction of each of his listeners is conditioned by their own personalities: Pompeia thinks of bearing his child; Caligula is tortured by his inability to laugh with joy; while Tiberius is afraid that there is no sleep beyond death. Lazarus momentarily solves all these difficulties by saying, "There is peace!"

But this answer is only a temporary satisfaction and Tiberius insists on rational answers, in particular demanding an explanation for Lazarus's reversal of the aging process. Lazarus's answer is another affirmation of life: "I know that age and time are but timidities of thought." Tiberius does not really hear, but instead he speaks as one touched by the presence of Lazarus and brought to see "the swinish and contemptible" life he has led. He asks rhetorically, "who would believe Tiberius if he said, "I want youth again because I loathe lust and long for purity!" In answer Lazarus says he believes, and Tiberius speaks with sorrow of his life, his family, and the assorted crimes they have committed, finally bowing his head, half-sobbing. At this Caligula speaks to Pompeia of his ambition. He will soon be Caesar now that the "old lecher" is becoming senile. Then he says, "I shall laugh!" Against this counterpoint of ambition, Tiberius continues to speak of his crimes. But then he turns against Lazarus, threatening him with death. Lazarus says, "I have heard your loneliness," and in reply Tiberius promises, "So much more the reason why my pride should kill you." Looking after the departing Tiberius, Caligula starts his legionary's song and dance, looking ahead to his accession to the title of Caesar. But suddenly he collapses in front of Lazarus, fearfully wondering why he should love this man and speaking of the pain he will endure at his death, a sentiment that is echoed by Pompeia, who confesses that she too loves Lazarus. In reply Lazarus says that "if you can answer yes to pain, there is no pain," a sentiment that causes Caligula to claim that "it is our one truth." But then he goes on to wish that he could be as Lazarus, that he could laugh, that he could love instead of despising mankind. But in reply to Lazarus's expression of love, Caligula rages against him, hating the pity shown him. But Lazarus asks an ultimate question of the young man, "What if there is no evil?" For in that case Caligula has lost the god by which he has lived: he exhorts Caligula to "believe in the healthy god called Man in you" and to laugh at the self who worships evil. "Believe in the laughing god within you." Momentarily, Caligula does believe and bursts out in joyous laughter which continues as he exits. But again Lazarus recalls with sadness, "They forget! It is too soon for laughter!"

With this, Pompeia kisses his hand and tells him of her love, as he replies in kind. She asks him to kiss her. When he does, she speaks of her hateful past and of the way in which she poisoned Miriam in the hope of gaining Lazarus's love, a love which she now says she will spurn; she will wish instead to have Lazarus tortured. Distractedly she departs, calling upon "my Caesar" to kill the man who laughs at Caesar, but her own laughter is picked up by the girls and youth of the palace who appear with the Chorus, taunting Lazarus: "Let us see you laugh!" Lazarus moves, silence falls, and he picks up the body of Miriam, looking tenderly upon her: "But what am I? Now your love has become Eternal Love! Now, since your life passed, I feel Eternal Life made nobler by your selflessness! Love has grown purer! The laughter of God is more profoundly tender." As he comes down from the dais and leaves through the assembled youths and Chorus, they take up his refrain: "Love is pure!/Laughter is tender!"

Act IV, Scene ii: It is later the same night in the amphitheatre, just before dawn. Tiberius Caesar sits on his throne, watching as Lazarus is being burned alive. Pompeia, "half-kneeling before Tiberius, . . . also stares at Lazarus." The Chorus, consisting of seven men masked in the period of "Middle Age, in the Servile, Hypocritical type,'' are grouped on either side of Caesar on a lower tier. The Chorus chants with mockery, "Burn and laugh!/Laugh now, Lazarus!" Pompeia says she cannot bear Lazarus's eyes as they gaze at her, asking Tiberius to put them out, but Caesar wishes to look upon them as they see death. He now regrets having acceded to Pompeia's request for Lazarus's execution, and he rises up to call to the doomed man, who has been gagged lest he should laugh. But then the ruler asks, "Is there hope of love somewhere for men on earth?"The Chorus takes up this as a refrain, and Tiberius asks, "Wherein lies happiness?" which the Chorus also takes up. But then Tiberius gives the command to allow Lazarus to speak, and the dying man joyously calls out, "O men, fear not life! You die—but there is no death for Man!" These words silence the mocking crowd, and then Lazarus commences to laugh. The hearers join in as Pompeia, almost hypnotized, leaves her place to go to Lazarus, following him, laughing, right into the flames as the assemblage laughs with him. In panic, Tiberius asks, "what is beyond there, Lazarus?" Lazarus's reply is exultant: "Life! Eternity! Stars and dust! God's Eternal Laughter!" And with this the assemblage joins in. Tiberius now wishes for death, and Caligula rushes on him, strangling him in a fury, and then goes toward the funeral stake ready to stab Lazarus. But the crowd is still hypnotized into oblivion by Lazarus, who speaks again: "Hail, Caligula Caesar! Men forget!" "Laugh! Laugh!" replies the crowd, but then Caligula announces, "I have killed God! I am Death! Death is Caesar!" With this, the crowd offers homage to Caesar and then slinks away as Caligula attempts to assert himself in the face of the dying Lazarus, but Caligula falls into "a paroxysm of terror": "Lazarus! Forgive me! Help me! Fear kills me! Save me from death!" And Lazarus's voice is heard in comfort: "Fear not, Caligula! There is no death!" And with that, Caligula finds himself able to laugh like Lazarus, with love; but then he goes through the emotions of grief, "I will remember, I will!" then cruelly, "All the same, I killed him and I proved there is death!" and finally remorsefully "Fool! Madman! Forgive me, Lazarus! Men forget!"

Comments: This play, which for obvious reasons of expense has yet to achieve a full professional performance, remained O'Neill's favorite, and he always believed that some of his finest writing and thinking went into this creation. It is also the culmination of a series of plays, from *The Fountain** through *Marco Millions** and *The Great God Brown*,* in which he attempted to forge a new theology of life, largely under the influence of the work of Friedrich Nietzsche. In *The Fountain*, Juan Ponce de Leon* is the philosopher-hero who finally discovers that the mystery of life lies in love. In *Marco Millions*, it is the Great Kaan* who speaks of the essential mystery of existence over the body of his dead daughter, Kukachin,* "Death is." By the time of *The Great God Brown*, O'Neill is more firmly under the influence of Nietzsche, particularly *The Birth of Tragedy* and its opposition of Dionysian and Apollonian aspects of life. But in *The Great God Brown*, the Dionysian is defeated, even though at the conclusion, Cybel* speaks of man's oneness with the rhythms of nature.

Here, in *Lazarus Laughed*, O'Neill is working under the influence of *Also Sprach Zarathustra* (Thus Spake Zarathustra), in particular the affirmation of the supremacy of man himself as god. Man should, as O'Neill echoes, recreate the god in man. Rather than man's being created in the image of God, man is his own godlike self and therefore should be committed to the affirmation of life. As O'Neill has his Lazarus say, "There is no death." Death is simply the fear between one life and the next. In such a theology there is no room for a punitive or judgmental god, and as a result, one can easily see that this play is really a distinctly subversive piece of work, despite the aspects of Christianity that surround it. In both *The Fountain* and *Marco Millions*, the playwright had searched for his answer in the great religions of East and West. Here he pits his new theology of man against the great civilizations and religions of the West and finds them all wanting.

The structure of the play is repetitive. Each act begins with Lazarus touching and influencing the representatives of one of the great civilizations, temporarily bringing them to an acceptance of his affirmation of life which leads them joyously into an acceptance of death; but "men forget," and Lazarus must begin again in a new venue. First, Lazarus influences his Jewish neighbors, but then his philosophy causes division within Judaism, followed by a massacre and the death of many of his followers, and even Christ dies. In his translation to Greece, Lazarus is seen specifically as a new Dionysian redeemer, but again his followers are massacred by a master race, this time by the Romans. In Rome itself, Lazarus's followers joyfully kill themselves and momentarily influence the Roman legionaries sent to destroy them—but the next day the Legionaries come to pillage the bodies, and again "Men forget." In Capri, Miriam finally dies joyfully—she has been the Mother of Grief, committed to life but not to Lazarus's vision, and therefore she has feared death and has aged. With her death, Lazarus has seen another of his followers die, and for a time even he thinks grimly of his passage from one life into the next. Finally he even influences Pompeia, Tiberius's mistress, into an act of self-immolation and manages to work some change in both Tiberius and Caligula. But the conclusion is less than affirmative: "Men forget!" and more and more Lazaruses must die. Finally, even Lazarus himself dies as an example to all his followers, but one wonders whether his example has changed the world any more than the death of any other god in any other religion. In a sense, then, O'Neill's relentless affirmation of life in the rational manner of laughter is not really as successful as he might have hoped. Laughter is important in this play, not as hysteria but rather as a means by which the problems and difficulties of existence are treated rationally. For, curious as it may sound, laughter is both a release of tension and also a rational perception of the irrationality of human existence, which attempts to seize the transitory and overlook the changeless and important.

The difficulty of staging this play has always militated against its performance, and its first production in 1928 at the Pasadena Community Playhouse was achieved only at the cost of much doubling, so that the 420 parts were reduced to 159—itself a very large number. A university performance was given at Berkeley, California, in 1950 without cuts in the dialogue, but laughter was confined to the unbelievers. Instead of Lazarus's laughter, the director had complete silence fall upon the entire Chorus, while Lazarus's mood of exultation was reinforced by music (Bogard, 1972, p. 289). This was said to be most effective, even though the Chorus was reduced to twenty men and women. Bogard suggests that this production emphasized the essential humanity of the play. Though it was received quite favorably in Pasadena, a 1948 production at Fordham University was not. According to Louis Sheaffer (1973, p. 203), Brooks Atkinson called it "practically unbearable theater" and Richard Watts, Jr., referred to the production as "verbose and strangely tedious." This play, then, is one of O'Neill's beloved failures insofar as stage performance is concerned, but it remains important as indicating his philosophic groping toward a new, personal theology. In it he also carried his use of masks to an ultimate and logical conclusion, but in so doing, he made the play almost impossible of production on the professional stage. He also showed understanding of the musical possibilities of a chorus, and it is important to note the extraordinary economy of lines given to both chorus and crowds; obviously, O'Neill realized that complex choric utterances would not be comprehensible and therefore confined himself to repetition of refrains in few words which can almost be vocalized. It is pointless to discuss character drawing in this play because all the characters exist for their symbolic rather than psychological validity.

Production Data: Written 1925–1926. First produced by the Pasadena Community Players at the Pasadena Playhouse, Pasadena, California, April 9, 1928 (28 performances).

Director: Gilmor Brown
Designer: James Hyde
Music: Arthur Alexander
Movement: Katharine Edson
Cast: (Partial List)
    Lazarus: Irving Pichel
    Father of Lazarus: Maurice Wells
    Mother of Lazarus: Esther M. Cogswell
    Martha and Mary (his sisters): Margaret Morrow, Dorothy Warren
    Miriam (Lazarus's wife): Lenore Shanewise
    Orthodox Priest: William Earle
    Messengers: Ralph Urmy, Charles Bruins
    Orthodox Jew: Jerome Coray
    Centurion: Richard Menefee
    Caligula: Victor Jory
    Crassus: Max Turner
    Flavius: Richard Menefee

Marcellus: Maurice Wells
Tiberius: Gilmor Brown
Pompeia: Dore Wilson
Soldier: Jerome Coray

Plus a cast of 159 players doubling in approximately 420 roles. *Revived* at Collins Auditorium, Fordham University, New York, April 8, 1948 (8 performances). *Revived*, 1950, in the outdoor Greco-Roman Theatre of the University of California, Berkeley, directed by Fred Orin Harris. (For details *see* Bogard, 1972, p. 289n.)

LEEDS, Nina. In *Strange Interlude*,* daughter of Professor Leeds,* fiancée of Gordon Shaw,* wife of Sam Evans,* lover of Edmund (Ned) Darrell,* mother of Gordon Evans,* and finally wife-to-be of Charles Marsden.* She is twenty when the play opens and has had a nervous breakdown as the result of the death of her fiancé, Gordon Shaw, who was shot down in flames just before the 1918 armistice. She blames herself for not insisting that they consummate their relationship physically before he left for war, even if they were not married. Gordon had taken the professor's advice to heart and decided that it would not be the honorable thing to marry Nina until he returned from the war and had managed to get started in life. Nina feels herself bereft, and so she arranges to work at a hospital for war veterans. There she becomes quite promiscuous, believing that only by giving herself to all these men can she expiate her sin against Gordon. Her father is devastated by her decision, though he knows nothing of her behavior at the hospital, and dies several months after she goes to work there. Nina returns to her home to find Charles Marsden waiting to help her with her grief; but she has brought Dr. Edmund Darrell, a neurologist, with her, and also Sam Evans, a young man who hopes to marry her and who worships the ideal of Gordon Shaw.

As Darrell suggests, she marries Sam, only to discover from Sam's mother that there is hereditary insanity in the family and that she should not bear the child she is carrying. Nina is appalled by this discovery because she has married Sam solely for the purpose of having a child, not for love of him. Mrs. Evans begs her to make Sam happy, even suggesting that she find some healthy male to father a child for Sam, to keep him happy and to save him from his father's madness. Nina has an abortion secretly and feels little more than misery and contempt for Sam, who thinks himself incompetent because he has not impregnated her and who is in the process of losing his job.

When Darrell returns, Nina suggests that he be the father of her child, purely as a means of helping Sam, his old dorm-mate from college. With the utmost objectivity and scientific detachment, the two agree to this course of action, but they have reckoned without their passions. They fall hopelessly in love, and Nina thinks seriously of divorcing Sam, but Darrell will not allow this. Instead he tells Sam that he is to be a father. Later, the situation is reversed and Darrell wants Nina to go away with him, but this time she refuses, for Sam's sake.

Desperately, Darrell tries to drown his sorrows in dissipation, but that does not work, and always he finds himself drawn back to Nina, either by her wish or his own weakness.

Throughout the play, Nina represents the history of woman, to some extent the Strindbergian destructive woman but also all aspects of woman in her relationships with men. There are six men with whom Nina is entwined and four basic relationships: her father, Gordon Shaw, Sam Evans, Ned Darrell, Charles Marsden, and Gordon Evans, her son. The relationships are those of father, lover, husband, son; Charles Marsden finally adopts the triple role of father-husband-friend as the play concludes. In a most important scene (Act VI), the pregnant Nina mentally evaluates the importance of the adult men in her life, realizing that she has need of them all: "My three men!...I feel their desires converge in me!...to form one complete beautiful male desire which I absorb...and I am whole...they dissolve in me, their life is my life...I am pregnant with the three!...husband!...lover!...father...and the fourth man!...little man...little Gordon!...he is mine too!...that makes it perfect."

In this way, Nina becomes a composite woman, dedicated to procreation and to wifeliness, as well as to passion. Her predatory sexuality requires her to be wife, mistress, and mother. Later, as Gordon grows, she is too possessive of her son, but ironically, because both she and Sam, her husband, share a devotion to the memory of Gordon Shaw, she is fated to lose her son to the masculine world of athletic achievement and material success, as well as to the arms of another woman. It is as a wife that Nina probably achieves the greatest success, in terms of the O'Neill view of matrimony. Like the wife in *Servitude*,* Nina finds some happiness in submission to her husband and to the fulfillment of his wishes, but inwardly she still rebels. She is continually looking for a totally comfortable and perfect relationship, but it cannot exist for her except in this quadripartite form. As she grows older, her hold on three of the men lessens: her lover, Ned, has declined into a friend; her husband is wrapped up in the achievements of his putative son; and Gordon has likewise left Nina's ambience. Alone of all, Charles Marsden remains, and she is finally happy to marry this latent homosexual novelist in a completely asexual marriage more like the relationship of father and daughter at the beginning of the play. Now that all the turmoil of passion is over, she wishes merely "to rot in peace" because she is weary of life which is but a "strange interlude in the pyrotechnical display of God the Father."

Throughout the play, Nina has been seeking a belief, an explanation of the pain that life has inflicted upon her, and she believes that part of her problem of belief is that God has been perceived as a male, not a female. Had God been personified as God the Mother, then humanity would have been perceived as coming from the birth pangs of the Mother, and hence pain would have some creative value. But all she can see is that she is to some extent the plaything of something stronger than herself—her own procreative urge, which must be fulfilled, and after that, she can decline into the asexual peace of old age. Yet curiously, one must recall that, though she may appear older, the Nina of Act IX is still only forty-five. For her, life has been a constant conflict, and it is with relief that she finally turns away from everyone except the one man who expects nothing of her physically, "dear old Charlie," who will occupy her father's house and study and will put her to bed at night. Finally, she has found a place and a relationship in which she belongs.

LEEDS, Professor, father of Nina Leeds.* In *Strange Interlude*,* he is a timid, intelligent, small, slender, gray-haired man of fifty-five. His meticulously ordered room, full of the ancient classics, and nothing more modern than Thackeray, indicates that to some extent he is in retreat from the real world of daily events. Widowed for some time, he is bossed by his daughter Nina. Professor Leeds interfered with the course of his daughter's love affair with Gordon Shaw,* suggesting that they delay marriage until after the war (1914–1918). Despite Gordon's desire to marry Nina, he agreed that waiting would be the honorable thing to do, and the professor really rather hoped that he would never come back because he thought Nina could do better for herself. When Gordon is killed, Nina goes to pieces, and the professor is devastated. He dies after the first act when Nina has gone away to nurse wounded soldiers. She does not see him at all during that last year or so, though she does write. Charles Marsden* was one of the professor's students and remains close to him. When her father dies, Nina realizes that in fact he had died for her when Gordon Shaw did. He typifies man as father at the beginning of the play, a role that is adopted by Marsden at the end.

"LEGEND OF POSSESSORS, SELF-DISPOSSESSED,"* the title of the eight-play version of the abandoned cycle "A Tale of Possessors, Self-Dispossessed."*

LEM, a native chief in *The Emperor Jones*,* a heavy-set, ape-faced old savage of the extreme African type, dressed only in a loin cloth." He leads the opposition to Brutus Jones,* even deputing someone to kill the emperor. As a result of a misfire, Jones kills his would-be assassin and proclaims that he could only he harmed by a silver bullet. Lem, whom O'Neill does not consider intelligent, believes this piece of superstition and manages to manufacture silver bullets of his own by melting down coins. It is with one of these that Jones is killed. As emperor, Jones had contempt for the "low flung bush niggers," yet they manage to kill him.

LEVY, Marvin David (1932–   ), composer. Born August 2, 1932, in Passaic, New Jersey. Educated in the public schools of Passaic and Newark, New Jersey. Graduated B.A. from New York University (1954) where he studied musicology with Gustave Reese and composition with Philip James. Took his M.A. at Columbia University, New York (1956), studying musicology with Paul

Henry Lang and composition with Otto Luenberg. He also studied piano, first with an aunt and then with Jane Carlson and Carl Friedberg at the Juilliard School, New York. During 1952–58, he was archivist for the American Opera Society and music critic for various newspapers and magazines. He was awarded two Guggenheim fellowships (1960 and 1964) and two Prix de Rome Awards (1962 and 1965).

A prolific composer of orchestral and chamber music as well as songs, he has also written several operas, his most important being *Mourning Becomes Electra* (*see* Appendix B), with libretto by Henry Willis Butler, a work commissioned by the Metropolitan Opera Association, New York City, in 1961 and first performed by it in 1967. His other, shorter operas include: *Sotoba Komachi*, after a Nōh play (1957), translation by Sam Houston Brock; *The Tower* (1957), libretto by Townsend Brewster; *Escorial* (1958), after Michel de Ghelderode, translation by Lionel Abel. He has also written a Christmas oratorio, *For the Time Being* (1959), text by W. H. Auden; a Sabbath Eve Service, *Shir Shel Mushe* (1964); and another oratorio, *Masada* (1973).

Initial reactions to *Mourning Becomes Electra* were mixed, particularly because of its length (over 3.5 hours). It was repeated after the first season in a version that showed revision, an orchestral interlude being cut out. The libretto was particularly praised as a skillful truncation of O'Neill's three plays. Levy's lyric gift was commended in this opera, though at least one critic objected to the amount of "heightened recitative." In general, Levy's music has been praised for his classic lyrical and coloristic qualities, while his work for vocal artists has been noted for its genuine consideration for the artist. *Mourning Becomes Electra* has recently been revived outside of New York.

LEWIS, Cecil, a sixty-year-old former British army captain in the Boer War (1899–1902). In *The Iceman Cometh*,* he rents a room above the saloon operated by Harry Hope.* He is still trim, with white hair, military mustache, blue eyes, mottled complexion, and an old wound scar on his left side. He has struck up a curious friendship with Piet Wetjoen,* a former Boer general whom he met at the St. Louis World's Fair. Lewis has been forced out of the army for peculation and misappropriation of funds, but he tells a tale about finding his wife Marjorie in bed with a fellow officer, thus denying the truth about himself. His pipe dream is that one day the family estate will be settled in England and he will return; and on one occasion he offers to take Wetjoen with him. Under the influence of Theodore Hickman,* the salesman who comes to the bar annually to celebrate Hope's birthday, Lewis attempts to translate the dream of returning home into reality, by getting a job, but he cannot go through with it and temporarily breaks off his friendship with Wetjoen. However, he realizes the impossibility of his dream, and after Hickey's arrest for the murder of his wife, Lewis seizes on Hickey's plea of insanity, a pipe-dream explanation which discredits what he has been shown about himself. Then, along with the others, Lewis gladly gets drunk in order to forget the outside world and to regain illusion.

LIEB, in *The Iceman Cometh,** a plain clothes policeman in his twenties who comes with his companion, Moran,* to arrest Theodore Hickman.*

"LIFE OF BESSIE BOWEN, THE" (or Bolan or Bowlan). This play was begun in 1927 as "It Cannot Be Mad," with the heroine's name being Bessie Wilks. It was designed as part of the uncompleted trilogy "Myth-Plays for the God-Forsaken,"* the other two being *Dynamo** and *Days Without End.** It was also given the titles "On to Betelgeuse" and "On to Hercules." The material was considered for inclusion in the last play of the abandoned cycle, "A Tale of Possessors, Self-Dispossessed,* and it was then entitled "Twilight of Possessors, Self-Dispossessed," and finally "Hair of the Dog."* In February 1943 O'Neill decided that it was unusable and destroyed it. It concerned the automobile industry.

LIGHT, Amelia. In *Dynamo,** wife of Rev. Hutchins Light* and mother of Reuben Light.* She is about forty-five and looks younger. Mrs. Light is stout but still active, "with large breasts and broad, round hips," the image of a very sensual woman. Once she must have been pretty, in a dark-complexioned way with dark wavy hair. "Her expression is one of virtuous resignation," but her mouth is "rebellious...determined and stubborn." She wants her son Reuben to go to college and marry a young woman with money so that he won't have to live in the genteel poverty they currently endure, without electricity in the house and with a roof that leaks. Her husband, however, insists that "it is God's manifest will" that Reuben become a minister. She is appalled to discover that Reuben has said he will marry Ada Fife,* the daughter of their neighbor, the local atheist, who enjoys humiliating Light. She hides behind the hedge to hear all that goes on in the Fife residence and tells her husband, who hides in the bedroom closet to overhear Reuben's confidences. He hears more than he bargains for because Reuben tells his mother the false tale of Fife's having committed a murder. This whole tale brings Light out to beat his son, and later he is humiliated when Fife tells him that it was all a joke. Reuben, enraged at what he sees as his mother's betrayal of a confidence, leaves home and continually sends her postcards saying, "We have electrocuted your God! Don't be a fool!" She gets pneumonia and dies, her last words being, "Don't be a fool!" words which Reuben takes to mean that he had converted her to his new God, electricity. He then believes that she has gone to the realm of the "Great Mother," the energy of life who is embodied on earth in the Dynamo.

LIGHT, Rev. Hutchins. In *Dynamo,** husband of Amelia Light* and father of Reuben Light.* He is a "ponderously built" man of about medium height in his early sixties. Light has a square face with a low forehead, heavy nose, stubborn jaw, yet a "weak, indecisive mouth," small pale eyes, and reddish, grizzled hair. His voice has a tendency to boom, especially when he "is the victim of an inner uncertainty." He is determined that his son Reuben will follow the family tradition and become a minister, continually asserting that ''it is God's will.'' He is a stern man, living in a kind of puritan past in a house where there is no electric light and in which the roof leaks. He bullies his family and is particularly hostile to Reuben, especially after he finds out that the young man has said he will marry Ada Fife,* the daughter of the local atheist next door. Ramsay Fife,* her father, plays a practical joke on both Reuben and, by extension, Mr. Light. After being beaten by his father and humiliated by Fife, Reuben leaves home and Mrs. Light dies. Mr. Light finds less comfort in religion than one might expect, because he follows a God of fear and of punishment. For Light, every flash of lightning strikes terror into him, perhaps as a symbol of judgment. He is so unsure of himself that he will not consider a debate with Fife on the topic of religious faith. When Reuben returns, Mr. Light is a man broken by grief.

Hutchins Light is a symbol of the bankruptcy of organized religion in this play, a believer who thinks only of doom, who is humiliated by any suggestion of human physical desire, who tries always to subdue the flesh, and who finds no room for love in his heart.

LIGHT, Reuben. In *Dynamo*,* son of Rev. Hutchins Light* and Amelia Light.* He ages from seventeen to nineteen. At the beginning of the play, he is tall and thin, with large, sensitive eyes, the same gray-blue as his father's. He is a reddish blond, with a sensitive mouth and a stubborn chin. He speaks timidly but, like his father, sometimes booms out as a protective mechanism. He is fascinated by Ada Fife,* the daughter of the next-door neighbor, the local atheist. Ada is interested in him, but considers him too much of a mother's boy. She goes along with a trick dreamed up by her father to prove Reuben is ''yellow.'' When Ramsay Fife* entrusts Reuben with a mock ''secret'' concerning his alleged killing of a man, Reuben's conscience gives him so much trouble that he tells his mother and is also overheard by his father, who is enraged to hear from Mrs. Light that Reuben has said he wants to marry Ada. When his father beats him and then discovers from Fife the joke that was played on him, Reuben's hostility comes into the open. He realizes that his father is afraid of lightning and forces the frightened man to remain looking at the flashes as he blasphemously announces that ''there is no God but electricity.'' He then goes away for fifteen months to learn about electricity and sends his mother monthly postcards which say, ''We have electrocuted your God. Don't be a fool!'' When he returns, he is thinner, more tense, and curiously excited. He goes to see Ada and then his father, discovering that his mother is dead from pneumonia. He blames Light because of the dampness of the house. He does not intend to stay with his father because he has asked Ada to get her father to find him a job at the power plant.

This she does, and Reuben, who now thinks himself experienced, seduces Ada without any intention of marrying her, thinking she will be useful to have around. He speaks continually of the dynamos and believes that his mother's spirit, on her death, has gone into the realm of the ''Great Mother,'' the divine source of energy which is embodied on earth in the dynamo. He discovers a kindred spirit in Mrs. May Fife,* Ada's mother, who also feels the relationship between herself and the dynamo. He tries to explain his new theology to her. All life began in the sea, water comes from the sea to form rivers, and these rivers drive the dynamo which is the source of energy. The power plants of the world are the temples of this new god, a female god, the god of electricity. He wishes to become worthy of being initiated into the deepest secrets of the dynamo by means of a miracle, and for that reason he has forsworn sex and has flagellated himself in a curious parody of puritan sexual disgust. He prays to the dynamo, but there is no miracle. He tries one ultimate act of renunciation by kissing Ada to prove that he is strong, but he finds himself again prey to physical longing for her. Finally, thinking himself unworthy, he grabs a revolver from the operator on duty, kills Ada, and then immolates himself on the exciter of the dynamo, begging it as a mother to hide him.

Reuben Light is a character who is not deeply drawn, but he represents the seeker after truth, a young man who has moved away from the old ways and is seeking a new religion, that of energy. He cannot accept the beliefs of the past and is destroyed, like Yank* in *The Hairy Ape*,* in an attempt to "belong."

LONDONDERRY, S.S., a steamship in *Chris Christophersen*,* "The Ole Davil,"* and *"Anna Christie."* In *Chris Christophersen*,* (the first version of *"Anna Christie"*) it is the vessel which runs down Christopher Christopherson's* barge, and on which Anna Christopherson* finds love in the person of Paul Andersen,* the second mate. In "The Ole Davil" (the second version of the same play) and *"Anna Christie"* (the final version) it is the ship on which Chris and Mat Burke* independently sign.

LONG. In *The Hairy Ape*,* a fellow-fireman with Yank.* He is the stereotypical radical who is given to polemical and revolutionary statements about the equality of man and the tyranny of the capitalist class. He attempts to raise Yank's social consciousness.

LONG DAY'S JOURNEY INTO NIGHT, a play in four acts and five scenes, "a play of old sorrow, written in tears and blood," awarded the Pulitzer Prize in 1957. This autobiographical play takes place from 8:30 A.M. to around midnight on an August day, 1912. The single set is the living room of James Tyrone's* summer home. A round table with a green-shaded reading lamp attached by a cord to an overhead chandelier is at center on an "inoffensive" rug which covers almost the entire floor. Three wicker armchairs and an oak rocker surround the table. There are two bookcases, the smaller one with philosophical and political tracts, modern poetry, novels, and assorted plays; the larger, a glass-enclosed one, is filled with complete sets of great writers, world literature, Shakespeare, histories of Ireland, and others—all of which seem to have been well read. There are windows on each side of the stage, with the backyard to the left and the front lawn and harbor to the right, with a screen door opening onto the porch. Doors at the rear lead to the seldom-used front parlor and to the windowless back parlor, really a passageway to the dining room.

Act I: A sunny morning, about 8:30 A.M. Mary Cavan Tyrone* and her husband, James, enter from the back parlor, having come from breakfast. She is fifty-four, plump but still graceful, with a curiously thin face, devoid of makeup, framed by white hair which accentuates the size of her beautiful dark brown eyes. "Her extreme nervousness" is manifested by the ceaseless movements of her hands, whose slender beauty is now warped and gnarled with rheumatism. Her voice has a soft Irish lilt, and her manner retains the "innate unworldly innocence" of the convent girl she once was. James Tyrone, age sixty-five, "looks ten years younger" with a military bearing that makes him seem taller than his five feet eight inches. Though his face is starting to go, he is still remarkably handsome, and his voice is "fine, resonant and flexible." In movement and manner he shows a conscious technique, reminiscent of his past as a romantic actor, but his simplicity and humble beginnings show in his current dress which is "commonplace shabby. He believes in wearing his clothes to the limit of usefulness," and since he is to do some gardening, he is unconcerned with appearance. He is a curious combination of "stolid, earthy peasant...sentimental melancholy and rare flashes of intuitive sensibility."

The two enter, with "Tyrone's arm around his wife's waist." As he twits her about gaining twenty pounds, she counters by saying she must reduce, and Tyrone asks if that is why she has eaten so little at breakfast; he himself is accustomed to a large meal, and he rejoices in the youthful quality of his digestion. They both sit down as Mary wonders what is keeping the two boys at the table; James jokingly, yet a trifle resentfully, suggests that "they're cooking up a scheme to touch the Old Man." As he puffs contentedly on his cigar, Mary teases him about his real estate deals—all but one unsuccessful—and then speaks worriedly about Edmund Tyrone,* the younger son, who has "a bad summer cold." James then shows concern about Mary's own health because she seems upset; after being her "dear old self again," Mary remarks that she did not sleep well the previous night because of the noise of the foghorn, and then she teases James about his snoring. They are interrupted by the sound of laughter from the dining room, and it becomes clear that James is angry with his older son, James ("Jamie") Tyrone, Jr.,* who is nearly thirty-four and has not yet made anything of himself—but Mary defends him. With this, Mary calls on them to finish breakfast, and the two young men enter.

Jamie resembles his father rather than his mother but has never been as handsome as he. Similarly, he looks shorter and stouter than James "because he lacks Tyrone's bearing and graceful carriage." His face is beginning to show signs of dissipation, and with its aquiline nose and expression of perpetual cynicism, it has "a Mephistophelian cast." His personality is that of the charming irresponsible Irishman, though the charm is beginning to wear thin. He is dressed in a shabby suit with collar and tie, and his fair skin is sunburnt. Edmund, the younger, is twenty-three, taller than Jamie and wiry. He looks more like his mother, having her large dark eyes set in a long thin Irish face, a high forehead and a sensitive mouth, though his profile is his father's. His dark brown hair is slightly sun-bleached, but he does not appear to be in good health and is "much thinner than he should be." His eyes look feverish and his cheeks are sunken. He is dressed in old flannel trousers, a tieless shirt, and sneakers.

Mary becomes even more nervous, putting her hands to her hair and saying that it is hard for her to do it properly. She also complains that her eyes are bad and she cannot find her glasses. This search continues throughout the play and she never does find them. Jamie and his mother discuss Tyrone's snoring with an air of easy companionship, and Tyrone starts to needle Jamie. In an attempt to smooth over differences, Tyrone asks what had been amusing the boys, and Edmund tells the tale of Shaughnessy, a tenant of Tyrone, and his outsmarting of Harker [sic], the Standard Oil millionaire (an incident that is fully dramatized in *A Moon for the Misbegotten**). With the completion of the tale, Tyrone denies his enjoyment of it and once more turns on Jamie, a situation that annoys Edmund, who leaves to get a book. In his absence they discuss Edmund's health, Jamie and Tyrone showing themselves concerned that it might be more than the "summer cold" that Mary Tyrone maintains to be the cause. When her husband suggests that Doctor Hardy thinks it might be malaria contracted during Edmund's sojourn in the tropics, Mary flares up, saying that Hardy, like all doctors, doesn't know anything. But her outburst causes both Jamie and his father to look so long at her that she becomes discomfited, being reassured only when Tyrone flatters her about the beauty of her hair; she recalls that she didn't have a single gray hair "until after Edmund was born." Still rather pleased by Tyrone's flattery, she goes out to look after the day's menu, telling him not to allow Edmund to work in the garden.

Left alone, Tyrone and Jamie continue to discuss Edmund's health, and Tyrone says that Hardy thinks he might have consumption and will telephone him today with the result; Jamie angrily suggests that this wouldn't have happened if Tyrone had been less miserly and had gone to a decent doctor first. With this, Tyrone rounds on Jamie, claiming that he is a ne'er-do-well who would never even have had an acting job had it not been for his father's position. Finally, Jamie agrees, "I'm a bum," just to stop the argument. Tyrone speaks again of Edmund's illness in such final terms that Jamie is shocked, but his father blames him for Edmund's malady because of his evil influence. Jamie denies it and says that he really loves "the Kid," pointing out that Edmund is exceedingly stubborn and further that he has played fast and loose with his constitution during his travels as a sailor through his drinking and living in low dives. Jamie notes that his brother has always come home broke, and even though Edmund is currently working, it is only on a small-town paper.

But then they speak of Mary and forget their enmity, expressing their joy in having her at home again. She has been back for the past two months and seems "strong and sure of herself." Nonetheless, Jamie is still suspicious that she might be regressing because she had wandered around all night and even moved into the spare room as she had done before. Tyrone tries to reassure himself and as a result argues once more with Jamie, recalling that Mary's "curse" began with Edmund's birth, a comment that Jamie counters by claiming that it was the fault of the "cheap quack like Hardy" whom Tyrone had summoned to treat her. Again Tyrone loses his temper with Jamie, but when Mary returns, they both compliment her, Jamie telling her not to worry about Edmund and warning her to be careful, a comment that Mary takes with resentment. As the two men go out to the garden, leaving Mary alone, she looks nervous, frightened, and even a trifle desperate; but as she hears Edmund come downstairs, momentarily seized by a fit of coughing, she composes herself with a book. The two discuss Edmund's health and then Tyrone's meanness in buying a second-hand car. Mary feels that she is alone, cut off from friends, partly because of the cheapness of the house and Tyrone's preference for the bar room. Edmund tries to comfort her and warns her to be on her guard: "You know what's happened before." Again, Mary seems defensive, complaining about the constant suspicion with which everyone is treating her and asking why it has surfaced today. Edmund confides that he had noticed her night-time wandering and move to the spare room. She then says she is worried about Edmund's health. He reassures her, and again they speak of her promise on her word of honor, as before. But then she makes a remark that serves as a theme for the play: "That's what makes it so hard—for all of us. We can't forget." With this she decides to go upstairs for a nap since she has not slept all night, "Or are you afraid to trust me alone?" Edmund, torn between trust and fear, tells her to take her nap while he goes out to watch the others work. Mary sits back down but grows very tense, clearly fighting "a desperate battle with herself." In this act, Mary Tyrone's addiction to morphine is discussed only in euphemisms.

Act II, Scene i: About 12:45 p.m., Edmund is trying to concentrate on a book. Cathleen* the second girl, enters with a bottle of bonded bourbon and glasses on a tray. She is a somewhat dense, well-meaning, Irish servant. As she goes to call Jamie and Tyrone, Edmund manages to grab an extra drink, but he is concerned over Cathleen's revelation that his mother has not been sleeping but is lying down with "a terrible headache." As he hears Jamie, Edmund puts back his empty glass, and the two manage another surreptitious drink, watering the bottle to keep the liquid level constant. Jamie suggests to Edmund that he cut out the liquor and also warns him that he may be really ill, something Edmund himself suspects. But then Jamie asks where his mother is and berates Edmund for leaving her alone so long, telling him that he really doesn't understand the situation; he, Jamie, has known and lived with the secret of his mother's addiction ten years longer than his brother. At that, Mary comes downstairs, looking less nervous than earlier in the day, but her eyes are brighter and her manner shows a somewhat withdrawn quality; Jamie realizes that his suspicions were correct, and his face and manner collapse into "embittered, defensive cynicism." They exchange a few remarks, but when Jamie makes a cynical comment about Tyrone's dilatoriness, Mary turns on him resentfully, realizing that he knows what she has been doing. But then she withdraws, saying that "none of us can help the things life has done to us." With an automatic sense of grievance which lacks inner conviction, she complains about her husband, her difficulty in getting decent servants because he won't pay high enough wages, and his refusal to spend money on a home because he has lived too much of his life in second-rate hotels. Nonetheless, he is even proud of "this shabby place" because deep down he does want a home. Edmund goes out to call Tyrone, and Jamie taxes his mother with having started on drugs once more. On his return, Edmund is at first angry with Jamie, but then he realizes that Jamie is right, but he won't admit it. Tyrone appears, and the three men bicker over the size of their drinks, while Mary is in the kitchen organizing the help. When she comes back, she begins to speak of the old grievance of "second-rate hotels" and so forth, and Tyrone realizes that she has slipped again. "He suddenly looks a tired, bitterly sad old man." Edmund tries to stop his mother, who turns on Tyrone for allowing Edmund a drink against doctor's orders. They wait for Mary to go in, all of them looking at her as she flutters about her hair, her lost glasses, and complains about their accusations, reacting to Tyrone's "I've been a God-damned fool to believe in you" with the excuse of worry about Edmund. Then she tells him that she really has tried to break her habit, but when he turns against her, griefstricken, she takes an attitude of "stubborn denial." They go into lunch as Tyrone says, "Never mind. It's no use now."

Act II, Scene ii: About a half-hour later. The family enters from lunch, Tyrone no longer with his arm about Mary; he seems to avoid touching her, while Jamie has put on his mask of "defensive cynicism." Edmund tries to do likewise but without success; he is both physically and spiritually sick. Mary is talking nonstop about the servant problem, the end of summer, their imminent return to the road, to "second-rate hotels," her inevitable loneliness, and Tyrone's return to the bar room. She claims that "in a real home one is never lonely," recalling that she gave up a home, her father's, to marry Tyrone, who thinks only of "buying property but never to give me a home." In the course of concern over Edmund's health, there is a telephone call from the doctor wishing to see Edmund that afternoon. Again Mary starts talking, this time about cheap doctors, like Hardy, who spoke to her about will power when she was desperate, and then she returns to the past: "it was exactly the same type of cheap quack who first gave you the medicine—and you never knew what it was until it was too late." Edmund and Tyrone try to stop her talking, and she decides to go upstairs to fix her hair, "if I can find my glasses," suggesting that her husband come upstairs "If you're so suspicious"; but he knows it is of no use. As she leaves, Jamie cynically says, "Another shot in the arm," a remark which makes the others turn on him; but then he says he does indeed have pity but realizes that "the truth is there is no cure." Edmund mimics his cynicism, but then they quarrel about Nietzsche, which brings from Tyrone a denunciation of both young men for falling away from Catholicism. Edmund then quotes from Zarathustra: "God is dead; of His pity for man hath God died." Tyrone and Jamie seem to consider Mary's case as hopeless, but Edmund says he will go up to speak with her.

Left alone with Jamie, Tyrone confides that Edmund does indeed have consumption and will have to go to a sanitorium. Jamie tells his father to be sure that he sends his brother to a good one, not "a cheap dump" because of his "Irish bogtrotter idea that consumption is fatal." Jamie suggests that he go uptown with Edmund for company when his brother hears the bad news, and Tyrone warns against getting him drunk. At this Mary enters, her eyes brighter and her manner becoming progressively more detached. First she complains about Tyrone's treatment of Jamie, blaming his shortcomings on his never having had a real home, then talking of the fog (which won't worry her tonight, she says), and going on about Tyrone's drinking, for which, he says, "No man has ever had a better reason." She tries to get him to stay, but he suggests that she take a spin in the car which he has bought for her, even hiring a chauffeur to drive it. Again Mary complains of his miserliness in buying a second-hand car and getting a cheap driver, but says she realizes that he had made the investment out of love for her. This touches Tyrone and he embraces her, begging her to stop the drug, but she returns to her defensive manner, making it quite clear that she will not make the attempt, again returning to a recital of past wrongs. When she married an actor, a lot of her convent friends dropped her; especially when Tyrone's former mistress sued him; when Edmund was born, "a cheap hotel doctor" gave her medicine for pain; when Jamie had measles, he went into the room where his baby brother Eugene was, and the child contracted measles and died. She still blames her son for that but also blames herself for ever having another child. Yet she assures Tyrone that she did want Edmund, though she knows he is doomed because "he was born too nervous and sensitive, and that's my fault."

Edmund then enters, dressed up to visit the doctor; he touches Tyrone for the carfare and to his surprise receives ten dollars. Mary, by now excessively nervous, has decided to go uptown to the drugstore–to "lay in a good stock ahead," Tyrone says bitterly, recalling the night she had screamed for "it" and threatened suicide. Edmund is a trifle suspicious about this sudden generosity of his father, asking whether the doctor has said he was going to die, a remark that angers Tyrone and evokes an apology from Edmund.

Tyrone goes upstairs to change, suggesting that Edmund talk to his mother. She tries to persuade him to stay with her and not go to visit Hardy, who preaches "will power." Edmund seizes the opening and begs her to stop—they will all help her. But Mary openly denies everything and speaks in her "remote and objective" manner of lying to herself and not being able to call her soul her own. One day, when Edmund is "healthy and happy and successful," things will be all right, and the Blessed Virgin Mary will forgive her and give her back the simple faith of her convent days so that she will be able to bear things. She then announces that she is going to the drugstore: "You would hardly want to

go there with me. You'd be so ashamed.'' She asks if Edmund is going to divide
the money with Jamie to help his dissipations and begs Edmund not to drink.
With this, all three men leave the house. Mary at first complains of her loneliness
but then realizes that she had wanted them to leave: "Their contempt and disgust
aren't pleasant company. You're glad they're gone. Then Mother of God, why
do I feel so lonely?'' she asks as the curtain falls.

Act III: It is 6:30 P.M. on a dusky, foggy evening with the sounds of the
foghorn and ships' bells in the background. Mary and Cathleen are standing at
the table on which is a tray of whiskey and glasses, the girl having obviously
been drinking. Mary is paler than before, and her eyes are unnaturally bright.
She seems to have "found refuge and release in a dream where present unreality
is but an appearance to be accepted and dismissed." She is well-dressed, but
she wears her clothes in a slovenly way and her hair is disarranged. She talks
to Cathleen as if she were an old friend, and her manner seems curiously girlish.
Mary complains about the foghorn, while the girl complains about the chauffeur,
who makes passes at her. Cathleen continues to drink and waters the bottle to
deceive Tyrone. In answer to the girl's query why she had not gone into the
theatre, Mary reveals her distaste for the life and her early desire to be a nun.
Cathleen then tells of the difficulty she had had in getting the druggist to fill the
prescription for rheumatism medicine for her mistress, and Mary, unhearing,
goes back to her happy time at the convent where she had been a promising
pianist. That had been her second dream, to be a concert pianist. She is now
far back in the past, the time of happiness, which alone seems real now that she
is drugged, as she recalls her meeting with Tyrone backstage when he was a
matinee idol. All she wanted then was to marry him, and they have been husband
and wife for thirty-six years. As she speaks she seems to revert to those early
years, but Cathleen recalls her to reality by asking permission to take a drink to
Bridget, the cook, and suggesting that Mary eat: "It's a queer medicine if it
takes away your appetite." Left alone, Mary sits dreamily and then suddenly
looks cynical as she denigrates her sentimentality about Tyrone but longingly
wishes she could call back her simple faith. She commences to say a Hail Mary
but then berates herself as "a lying dope fiend reciting words."

She is about to go upstairs—"When you start again you never know exactly
how much you need—but Tyrone and Edmund return, finding "their worst
expectations" confirmed. Mary offers them drinks, asking Jamie's whereabouts
and suggesting that he wishes to destroy Edmund out of jealousy, recalling his
dislike of the dead baby, Eugene. Tyrone agrees that Edmund should beware of
Jamie's cynicism, but Mary babbles on obliviously, about Jamie as a child, about
the dead Eugene, about Jamie's failures at school, and now about his drinking,
which is the result of Tyrone's giving him whiskey to quiet him as a baby. This
stings him into response, and Edmund recalls that his father had done the same
thing to him. Then Mary continues, telling Edmund, "You were born afraid."
They start to drink, and Tyrone realizes how much the liquor has been watered.

Mary becomes momentarily normal, telling Tyrone of her love for him, while he reciprocates, but then she taxes him with too much drinking, recalling one honeymoon evening when he was brought home literally dead drunk. This brings Edmund to look accusingly at his father, but Mary rambles on, recalling the beauty of her wedding and the glory of her wedding gown, wondering where it is, probably the attic. Tyrone leaves to get another bottle of whiskey, and she slips in and out of reality, one moment talking of the past and then of her love for Tyrone, asking Edmund to understand his father despite his miserliness about such things as light bulbs. She recalls the often-told story of Tyrone's youth, his desertion by his father, and his going to work in a machine shop at the age of ten. Edmund tries to tell her of his illness and that he must go to a sanitorium, but she is incapable of real understanding, seeing the situation as an attempt to separate Edmund from her. But when he mentions the word consumption, the disease which killed her father, Mary forbids him to remind her of it. With this Edmund condemns her bitterly: "It's pretty hard to take at times, having a dope fiend for a mother!" But almost instantly he repents and goes out as Mary thinks of taking more dope, hoping one day that she will accidentally give herself an overdose, something she could never do deliberately. Tyrone returns with a new bottle (having outwitted Jamie's attempt to get to his store because of a new padlock) and is surprised to find Edmund gone, but then Mary breaks down, afraid that Edmund is going to die. Tyrone denies it, saying that the doctor has said he will be cured in six months; but Mary is inconsolable, saying she should never have borne him; then he would never have known of her addiction and have come to hate her. Tyrone attempts to calm her as Cathleen enters "woozily" to announce dinner. Mary says she must go to bed and rest because of the pain in her hands, but Tyrone knows the truth: "You'll be like a mad ghost before the night's over!" Once again Mary resorts to outright denial as she leaves, and Tyrone, brokenly, goes to dinner.

Act IV: Around midnight. The hall light has been extinguished, and in the dining room only the reading light is on. The fog has grown denser, and the noise of the foghorn and ships' bells can be heard. Tyrone, wearing his old dressing gown and pince nez, is drunkenly playing solitaire. He has the air of "a sad, defeated old man, possessed by hopeless resignation." Edmund's voice is heard in answer to Tyrone's call, which is then followed by a thump as Edmund bangs into the hatstand in the darkness. This precipitates an instant argument about Tyrone's stinginess over light bulbs, which culminates in Tyrone's ordering his son to turn out the hall light or risk a thrashing. But then he recalls Edmund's illness and turns on all three bulbs in the chandelier, dramatically speaking of the poorhouse at the end of the road. The two discuss Jamie, who has not yet returned, and they drink together. Edmund has just walked home in the fog, and he quotes Ernest Dowson on the evanescence of life, saying that in the fog he had felt the peace of being "nothing more than a ghost within a ghost," explaining that one doesn't want to see life as it is. In reply, Tyrone suggests that Edmund has something of a poet in him, "but it's a damned morbid one!" He suggests a return to Shakespeare and quotes Prospero's speech from

The Tempest: "We are such stuff as dreams are made of." The two then discuss their situation, "trying to forget" or "try[ing] to be resigned—again," or as Edmund suggests, to "be so drunk you can forget." With this he quotes from Baudelaire, on drink, and from his "Epilogue," then from Dowson's "Cynara." Tyrone finds these poems "morbid filth" as Edmund continues to apply the last two poems to Jamie's plight, and Tyrone inveighs against the kind of literature that Edmund reads, from Baudelaire to Zola, "whoremongers and degenerates!" suggesting once more that he read Shakespeare. Edmund whimsically recalls once winning a bet from the old man that he would learn *Macbeth*, "letter perfect," and his father remembers "approvingly"; but then they hear Mary moving around upstairs, and they drink together.

Tyrone speaks of Mary's recollections of the past, suggesting that they need considerable modification to conform to the reality. Her father became an alcoholic (drinking only champagne) when he was forty, and that and tuberculosis soon killed him. Even "her wonderful home was ordinary enough," and as for her pianistic talent, that was the flattery of the nuns who loved her because she was so devout. Her religious vocation was not really strong: "She was bursting with high spirits and the love of loving." They start a game of Casino, afraid that Mary might come downstairs, Edmund detesting "the bank of fog in which she hides and loses herself," almost as if she hates the three men in her life. Tyrone suggests that she is concerned about Edmund's health, and with that Edmund turns on his father, accusing him of guilt in his mother's addiction to morphine because he "put her in the hands of a cheap hotel quack" because of his own "stinginess." He berates Tyrone for not sending her for a cure earlier, "while she still had a chance," and again blames his miserliness. Tyrone claims that for years he didn't know, and he has spent thousands on cures, none of which has worked; but Edmund continues to attack his father for never giving Mary a home "except this summer dump in a place she hates and you've refused even to spend money to make this look decent." It is no "wonder she didn't want to be cured. Jesus, when I think of it I hate your guts." Tyrone counters by recalling that Mary had followed him on the road because she had wanted to and always had a nurse for the children. Finally, Tyrone taxes Edmund with being the cause of her addiction, something that the young man knows, but then Tyrone repents of having said so. The two make up "with real, if alcoholic, affection."

The subject changes to the sanitorium to which Edmund is to go, and Edmund tells Tyrone that he has found out that his father has chosen the state institution merely to save money, even though the old man owns plenty of property. Edmund has tried to understand and tried to be fair, remembering Tyrone's past. He also recalls the rotten things he himself has done, but he appeals to his father's "pride and shame" in this instance, before collapsing in a fit of coughing. This gives Tyrone a momentary pause in which he recites once more the litany of his boyhood troubles, the source of his fear of poverty, claiming that Edmund's "fling of hard work" was merely "a game of romance and adventure"; but the son tells him that he attempted suicide at Jimmy-the-Priest's* once, when he was completely sober. Again Tyrone returns to past hardships, his father's death, their poverty, his working in the machine shop, and his resultant miserliness. Then he offers Edmund the choice of any sanitorium he likes, "within reason," suggesting another one that the doctor had recommended: "It's only seven dollars a week but you get ten times that value" because it is heavily endowed. Edmund agrees to it as "a good bargain." The two return to their game, but then Tyrone wanders off again, speaking of the way a dollar perhaps meant too much for him, "and the time came when that mistake ruined my career as a fine actor." Like O'Neill's own father with his perpetual role as Edmond Dantès in *The Count of Monte Cristo*, James Tyrone bought a play cheaply and made such a great success in the role that "it ruined me with its promise of easy fortune," and finally he woke up to the fact that he was a slave to the property, so "identified with that one part" that no one wanted him in anything else. He talks of the way he had educated himself, read Shakespeare, studied elocution, and developed into an actor worthy of praise from Edwin Booth as a leading man. His ambitions were fulfilled, he married Mary, but then he fell into the trap of this single part which gave him a net profit of thirty-five to forty thousand dollars per season. Edmund is touched by this account, but Tyrone is not sure whether it will make him even more contemptuous of his father, and it certainly doesn't teach the value of money. At this, Tyrone looks up and asks if he can turn off the extra lights: "There's no use making the Electric Company rich." As he extinguishes them, he says he wouldn't care now if he had only the poorhouse to look forward to in old age if he could look back on his past as a fine artist. Edmund starts to laugh at the irony of life as his father wonders where the piece of paper with Edwin Booth's words of praise is now. Edmund suggests that it could be in the attic in an old trunk along with his mother's wedding dress.

This precipitates Edmund's own reminiscences, delivered "as if he were deliberately giving way to drunkenness and seeking to hide behind a maudlin manner." He tells of his memories of the sea, the occasions on which he has felt at one with nature, in "ecstatic freedom, . . . Like a saint's vision of beatitude," in which "for a second there is meaning!" but then the fog draws in again and one stumbles on. He believes he would have been more successful as a seagull or a fish than as a man because now he is a permanent stranger "who can never belong, who must always be a little in love with death." Tyrone is very impressed and declares that Edmund has "the makings of a poet," but Edmund turns aside the praise, saying that he will never be a real poet: "I couldn't touch what I tried to tell you just now. I just stammered." His strength will be in "faithful realism, at least. Stammering is the native eloquence of us fog people."

At that moment Jamie appears, monumentally drunk. Tyrone, in order to avoid a fight, leaves Edmund to deal with his brother. He downs a large drink and then tells Edmund that he really does love him, refusing him a drink until Edmund convinces him that he will go on the wagon tomorrow. Jamie asks whether Tyrone is going to send Edmund to the state farm to avoid expense, but the younger man says that they have decided on another place and shows sympathy and understanding toward his father. Jamie then tells the story of his evening on the town, starting with a quotation from Oscar Wilde's "The Harlot's House." He visited the local brothel and took up with Fat Violet because he felt sorry for her. He has reached a somewhat maudlin stage, but then he seems to remember his mother and asks, "Where's the hophead? Gone to sleep?" This cruel remark calls forth a punch in the face from Edmund. But Jamie is not really malicious. He has simply lost hope: "I'd begun to hope, if she'd beaten the game, I could, too," a remark that plunges him into tears and starts him on his own confidences. He has known about his mother's addiction much longer than Edmund, once having "caught her in the act with a hypo." Edmund's illness has really hit him hard because he would do anything for his brother, but then Jamie suggests that perhaps Edmund thinks Jamie is hoping his brother will die so that he and his mother can inherit all of Tyrone's cash. Edmund tells him to shut up, but Jamie starts to cut his brother down to size, saying that his success is only with a hick newspaper. But then he changes, asserting that he has really taught Edmund everything he knows, from literature through drinking to whores, confessing that he has consciously been a bad influence—out of jealousy toward "Mama's baby, Papa's pet," the cause of his mother's addiction. In fact, he loves Edmund more than he hates him but nonetheless wishes with one part of himself to make his brother fail, hoping he will die. The part of him that's dead also hopes that Mary will not break her habit: "He wants company, he doesn't want to be the only corpse around the house!" Then, having "gone to confession," he expresses his love for Edmund and falls into a drunken sleep. Tyrone returns, looks with bitterness at his failure of an older son, who wakes up enough to insult him with two quotations, one from Shakespeare's *Richard III* and the other from Rossetti on "Might-Have-Been." He then suggests a revival of *The Bells*, with Tyrone playing Gaspard the miser, and insults him before falling asleep. Tyrone then dozes off as well, waiting for Mary to go to bed.

Suddenly Edmund hears something. All the lights go on in the front parlor and someone starts playing the piano rather like "an awkward schoolgirl." Then the playing stops and Mary enters, wearing a blue dressing gown, nightdress, and dainty slippers. "Her eyes look enormous. They glisten like polished black jewels," while her face looks astonishingly youthful, shy, inexperienced. Over one arm she carries her white satin wedding dress "trimmed with Duchesse lace." She looks at the three men without recognition as Jamie remarks, "The Mad Scene. Enter Ophelia!" Both Tyrone and Edmund round on him, and Edmund slaps him across the mouth. Jamie admits he "had it coming" and then starts to weep as Mary speaks. She has regressed to her life at the convent and talks of her stiff fingers, which she will ask the infirmarian to check. Tyrone finally realizes that she is carrying her wedding gown and takes it from her as she looks at it without seeming to comprehend what it is, and without recognizing Tyrone. She identifies it as a wedding gown which she has found in a trunk in the attic but says that she is planning to be a nun. She knows she has lost something, but cannot remember what it is, ''Something I miss terribly'' presumably her religious faith. Jamie is the first to realize that she has gone beyond their comprehension and recites two stanzas of Swinburne's ''A Leave-Taking,'' and after the second, Mary continues with her search for ''something I need terribly. I remember when I had it I was never lonely nor afraid.'' She moves around like a somnambulist, unaware of everyone. For a brief moment, Edmund seems to get through to her as he pulls at her like a little boy, telling her, ''I've got consumption.'' Her initial reaction is to cry out ''NO!'' but then she tells him not to touch her because she is going to be a nun. Again Jamie says there is no hope, and again he quotes from Swinburne, with Tyrone telling him to stop. They steady themselves with drinks. None of them has ever seen her quite so far gone as she is now, as she tells of her visit to Mother Elizabeth concerning her vocation and her vision of the Blessed Virgin giving her consent. But Mother Elizabeth had told her to test her vocation for a year by living like other girls. Mary was shocked and prayed again to the Virgin, who told her she would always love her ''and see no harm ever came to me so long as I never lost my faith in her.'' Then Mary becomes uneasy, recalling that the following ''spring something happened to me. Yes, I remember. I fell in love with James Tyrone and was so happy for a time.'' As she stares before her in a dream, Tyrone moves slightly while the two sons remain still, and the curtain falls.

Comments: This remarkable autobiographical play is generally considered to be O'Neill's finest work, and he himself believed that the last scene was the best he had ever written. It is a play of little outward action but a great deal of interaction of past and present, in terms of the lives of four members of this intertwined family which cannot forget. It observes the Aristotelian unities scrupulously and has refined dramatic action to a minimum, being an orchestration of confessional and self-exculpatory monologues interspersed with familial interactions. The autobiographical elements are clear, and for that reason O'Neill restricted its release, refusing to allow it to be printed or played until twenty-five years after his death when all the participants would be dead. But he reckoned without Carlotta Monterey,* his third wife who insisted on its release. Later, Karl Ragnar Gierow,* director of the Royal Dramatic Theatre of Stockholm, with the assistance of the then secretary of the United Nations, Dag Hammarskjold, managed to obtain permission for its presentation in Stockholm, where it was a resounding success. A New York production followed shortly after, and the play has since been ranked as possibly the greatest naturalistic American drama to date, winning O'Neill, posthumously, a fourth Pulitzer Prize.

In this drama, O'Neill resurrects and exorcises old ghosts, coming to terms with his father but not with his mother, for whom he shows some sympathy but never forgiveness or understanding. Jamie [James O'Neill, Jr.*] is celebrated in *A Moon for the Misbegotten** while *Long Day's Journey* belongs primarily to the playwright's father James O'Neill,* with O'Neill's own exculpation of himself in the character of Edmund. The tale of his tuberculosis in 1912 is true, as was his father's original intent to send him to the state farm. In fact, O'Neill actually did spend a little time there before transferring to Gaylord Farm,* the locus of *The Straw*.* The accounts of O'Neill's sea travels and attempted suicide are also true, but O'Neill is easy on himself as Edmund, for he edits out the fact of his first marriage and first son, as well as the help his father gave him to leave the country. The circumstances of Mary Tyrone's addiction are also identical to those of Ella Quinlan O'Neill,* including the death of a child from measles, though O'Neill omits her breaking of the habit. But the play is more than mere autobiography because it shows the struggle of human beings in torment, and at times O'Neill assesses things with the greatest clarity, especially his own poetic talent. In general, he did just "stammer," though he had the feelings and intellect of a poet; but in this play, he reaches greater heights than elsewhere, partly because of his intense emotional involvement. The setting, in Monte Cristo Cottage, New London, goes beyond either realism or naturalism because this little world encapsulated in fog becomes symbolic of the human condition and the traps in which human beings find themselves caught, without possibility of release, because they are so disoriented by fog that they have lost their bearings, both psychological and spiritual—a metaphor for loss of faith, for unfulfilled ambitions, for wasted lives which end in death without ever having celebrated life but continually avoided it whether through liquor or morphine. Only Edmund seems to have the possibility of escape, though in this play it is tenuous. *Long Day's Journey* also has affinities with the earlier *Ah, Wilderness!** which might be termed the comic view of O'Neill's family life in New London and which has also gained considerable popularity. The later play, however, is by far the greater achievement both emotionally and dramatically. Here O'Neill has come to trust his actors, giving each one of them a chance to shine, for every part requires a professional of great ability, even star quality, for the success of a production.

A Note on Names: That O'Neill named his dramatic family Tyrone is very important because it underlines his interest in his own Irish heritage. Hugh O'Neill, Earl of Tyrone, who took upon himself the clan title of "The O'Neill" in 1593, kept the forces of Elizabeth I occupied in Northern Ireland from 1598 to 1603, submitting six days after her death and being permitted by James I to retain his earldom. An earlier O'Neill, "Shane the Proud," an uncle of Hugh O'Neill, also led a rebellion against Elizabeth. O'Neill's son, Shane Rudraighe O'Neill,* was consciously named after this great Gaelic chieftain. The name Edmund is also significant because it corresponds to that of the heroic Edmond Dantès, the Count of Monte Cristo, the role with which O'Neill's father was irredeemably associated, and also to Edmund Burke O'Neill, the middle child of James and Ella O'Neill who died at the age of eighteen months.

Production Data: Written 1939–1941. First produced at the Royal Dramatic Theatre (Kungl. Dramatiska Teatern), Stockholm, Sweden, February 2, 1956, by Karl Ragnar Gierow in a translation by Sven Barthel (130 performances).

Producer: Dramaten
Director: Bengt Ekerot
Design: Georg Magnusson
Cast: James Tyrone: Lars Hanson
      Mary Tyrone: Inga Tidblad
      James Tyrone, Jr.: Ulf Palme
      Edmund Tyrone: Jarl Kulle
      Cathleen: Caterine Westerlund

First New York Production: Produced by José Quintero* at the Helen Hayes Theatre, New York City, November 7, 1956 (390 performances).

Director: José Quintero
Setting: David Hays
Costumes: Motley
Cast: James Tyrone: Fredric March*
      Mary Tyrone: Florence Eldridge*
      James Tyrone, Jr.: Jason Robards, Jr.*
      Edmund Tyrone: Bradford Dillman*
      Cathleen: Katherine Ross

Note: An excellent account of the progress of this production is given by José Quintero, *If You Don't Dance They Beat You*, pp. 203–264.

Other New York City Productions:

Royal Dramatic Theatre Company, Stockholm, Sweden, the Cort Theatre, New York City, May 16, 1962 (2 performances).

The Promenade Theatre, New York City, April 21, 1971 (121 performances), originally produced at the Long Wharf Theatre, New Haven, Connecticut, May 1971.

Producers: Edgar Lansbury, Jay H. Fuchs, Stuart Duncan, Joseph Beruh
Director: Arvin Brown
Set Design: Elmon Webb and Virginia Dancy
Costume Design: Whitney Balusen
Lighting: Ronald Wallace
Cast: James Tyrone: Robert Ryan
      Mary Cavan Tyrone: Geraldine Fitzgerald*
      James Tyrone, Jr.: Tom Atkins
      Edmund Tyrone: James Naughton
      Cathleen: Paddy Croft

The Actors Studio, December 10, 1973 (9 performances).

A Note on Text: The text used is that published by Yale University Press.

A Note on Publication: At the very specific request of O'Neill, the manuscript, in four copies (including two for future copyright application), was sealed and placed in the vaults of Random House Publishers. In a legal document dated November 29, 1945, drawn up by the publisher, in terms stipulated by O'Neill, signed by him and countersigned by Bennett A. Cerf, president of the company, publication was not to take place until twenty-five years after the death of the playwright. Only five people had read it at this time: O'Neill himself; Eugene

Gladstone O'Neill, Jr.*; Carlotta Monterey O'Neill; Russel Crouse; and Saxe Commins,* O'Neill's editor at Random House. Commins maintained that O'Neill wished to withhold publication "until everyone involved, particularly the members of his family, was dead or old enough not to be hurt or even disturbed by it" (Commins, 1978, p. 55). Saxe Commins, who spoke with Eugene O'Neill, Jr.,* about the play, believed that he remained unaware of his father's publication restriction and that it is "hardly likely" (p. 54) that he in any way influenced his father's decision in this matter. Certainly, when Commins visited O'Neill at Tao House in early 1942 and worked with him on the play, O'Neill made no mention of his son's alleged wish that publication be delayed because the work might cause some academic embarrassment to him. By mid-1954, only one year after the playwright's death, Carlotta O'Neill telephoned Bennett Cerf to ask whether he had read the manuscript of the play. Cerf replied that he had not and that since he was not legally entitled to do so, he had neither seen nor opened the package. Further, he intended to respect O'Neill's wishes. Mrs. O'Neill then requested him to break the seals and read the work, which she wished to have published as soon as possible. Cerf consulted with his lawyers, who suggested that the work could be published by Random House only if Mrs. O'Neill allowed the printing of a statement that she fully authorized the publication even though it was contrary to the wishes of her dead husband. After some outrage from Carlotta O'Neill and some litigation, Random House relinquished the rights to publication, and the work was brought out by Yale University Press. Commins believed that Carlotta's wish to gain control of this property was the reason that O'Neill had been "*induced* to disown his two surviving children" (Commins, 1978, p. 58). In a 1956 interview in the *New York Times*, Carlotta O'Neill maintained that her husband had chosen to withhold it because of the specific urging of Eugene, Jr., who was now dead. All in all, it seems that the publication initiative came from Mrs. O'Neill, who also maintained that her husband did not really intend to uphold the twenty-five-year restriction because (she said) he frequently referred to it as a nest egg in case they might run out of money. Carlotta O'Neill's actions and explanations seem to be more expedient than accurate in this matter, and as a result of Bennett Cerf's actions in following her husband's instructions she vilified the devoted Saxe Commins and severed connections with Random House as far as possible.

[*See also* Appendix B for film version.]

LONG VOYAGE HOME, THE, a one-act play, part of the S.S. *Glencairn** group. The scene is Fat Joe's* London waterfront dive. Mag,* the drunken barmaid, and Joe are talking to Nick,* the crimp, who is trying to procure a seaman to make up the complement of the *Amindra*, a ship with a most unsavory reputation. The S.S. *Glencairn* has just paid off "three Britishers and a square'-ead." Driscoll,* Cocky,* Ivan,* and Olson* (known as Ollie) enter in their uncomfortable and ill-fitting shore clothes. All except Ollie are drunk and proceed to get drunker. Driscoll recognizes the dive as the place where he was stripped of his money on a previous visit and continually admonishes Joe to "play fair." All react differently to liquor: Cocky becomes weepy; Driscoll sings, "We are the boys of Wexford"; and Ivan eventually passes out. Freda* and Kate,* two prostitutes, are brought in to entertain the men, and Freda latches on to Ollie. He relates his life story to her and confides that he is not drinking because he knows that once he starts he cannot stop. He has now saved enough money to return to Stockholm and take up farming there. Freda claims that she, too, is from Stockholm, and that elicits more confidences from Ollie. Driscoll and Cocky leave to take the unconscious Ivan to their lodgings. Meantime, Ollie, who has heard from some bar room roughs that the *Amindra* is in port, recalls her as a hell-ship on which he once sailed. Joe and Nick mix something into Ollie's ginger beer. He passes out and is rushed aboard the *Amindra* by the two roughs. Freda grabs Ollie's money and tries to keep some for herself, but Joe hits her and gets it all. Driscoll and Cocky return for Ollie but are told that he has gone away with Freda. They believe this story, laugh at it, and order more drinks.

Comments: This play, like the others in the series, indicates that the land is an alien environment for those who are children of the sea. Unlike the other plays, it takes place on land, and the ill-fitting shore clothes are a good symbol of alienation. The theme of rebellion against the sea is shown in Ollie's desire for a farm, but, as is always the case, such disloyalty to the sea is punished. In this play, the idea of the sea as exacting a penalty from its unfaithful minions is less clear than elsewhere. Ollie is an innocent who is fleeced. What is clear is that there is a supportive camaraderie among the men of the S.S. *Glencairn.*

Production Data: Written in 1916–1917. First produced by the Provincetown Players* at the Playwrights' Theatre, New York City, November 2, 1917 (performances, unknown).

   Director: Unknown
   Set Designer: Unknown
   Cast: Bartender: George Cram Cook*
            Olson: Ira Remsen
            Driscoll: Hutchinson Collins
            Cocky: O.K. Liveright
            First Girl: Ida Rauh
            Second Girl: Alice MacDougal

Revived with *The Moon of the Caribbees,* * *In the Zone,* * *Bound East for Cardiff,* * October 29, 1937, at the Lafayette Theatre, New York City (68 performances).
Revived with *The Moon of the Caribbees, In the Zone, Bound East for Cardiff,* May 29, 1948, at the New York City Center (14 performances).
Revived December 4, 1961, at the Mermaid Theatre, New York City (32 performances). *Revived* frequently as part of the S.S. *Glencairn* * group. See that entry for performance statistics.
[*See also* Appendix B for film adaptation of the entire S.S. *Glencairn* series under the title *The Long Voyage Home.*]

LORD, Pauline (1890–1950), actress. Born in Hanford, California, August 18, 1890; died of a heart attack in Alamagordo, New Mexico, October 10, 1950. Married O. B. Winters, 1929; divorced 1931.

Miss Lord made her debut at the age of thirteen in San Francisco as a maid in *Are You a Mason*? She gained her professional training as an understudy with Nat Goodwin's repertory company. Beginning in 1912 with *The Talker*, she appeared in a very large number of Broadway productions, most importantly playing opposite Jacob Ben-Ami of the Yiddish Theatre in *Samson and Delilah* (1920). Other important roles were in *They Knew What They Wanted* (1924); *Sandlewood* (1927), for which she received the New York Drama Critics' Award; *The Late Christopher Bean* (1932); *Ethan Frome* (1936); *Suspect* (1941); *The Walrus and the Carpenter* (1941); and *Sleep, My Pretty One* (1944). Her best-remembered film appearance was in *Mrs. Wiggs of the Cabbage Patch*.

In 1921 Miss Lord created the role of Anna Christopherson* in *"Anna Christie"** for which she received superb reviews in what was considered to be the best part she had ever been given. She managed to convey the two sides of Anna, the somewhat sympathetic vulnerability and the smouldering outraged femininity, with extraordinary credibility. Her tempestuous quality combined with subtlety of interpretation were praised in what was considered to be the finest performance of an already distinguished career. When the Theatre Guild* mounted a road company of *Strange Interlude** in 1928, Pauline Lord recreated the role of Nina Leeds,* originally played by Lynn Fontanne.* Critics who saw both actresses were almost unanimous in preferring the more emotional, subjective, intuitive approach of Lord to the intelligent, technically polished performance of Fontanne, which did not communicate quite the same passion. Pauline Lord seems to have been unjustly neglected by theatre historians, perhaps because she appeared in so many plays, including a large number of flops. Those who saw her in performance speak of the delicacy of her art, the way in which she could portray the hidden depths of passion by giving the impression that she was attempting to conceal rather than communicate it; in this way she conveyed feminine vulnerability without mawkish sentimentality in a style that depended on emotional intensity yet avoided flamboyance. As an actress, she is said to have lacked self-confidence, and she seems to have worked her way into a role in a Stanislavsky-like manner (without ever having learned the method). Her four greatest roles all indicate her brilliant intuition and skill, as well as the kind of part which suited her best: Anna in *"Anna Christie,"* Amy in *They Knew What They Wanted*, Zenobia in *Ethan Frome*, and Nina Leeds* in *Strange Interlude.** In many ways, she seems to have been the quintessential O'Neill heroine, and it is unfortunate that she did not portray more of these characters.

LOREDANO, Paulo. In *Marco Millions*,* father of Donata,* the betrothed of Marco Polo.* He is pleased that his daughter is to marry Marco Polo because he needs a business alliance with the house of Polo Brothers and Son.

LOVING. In *Days Without End*,* the Mephistophelian alter ego of John Loving.* John Loving, in despair over the death of both his parents, "promised his soul to the Devil—on his knees, when every one thought he was praying!" Now, when John is forty and happily married, Loving represents the rationalistic, blasphemous side of his personality. Throughout the play, Loving, an ironically named character, is masked with "the death mask of a John [Loving] who has died with a sneer of scornful mockery on his lips." He operates like Mephistopheles in *Faust*, continually trying to obtain John's soul by forcing him into the final act of despair—suicide. He manages temporarily to destroy Elsa Loving's* affection for her husband and works toward her demise by suggesting that the conclusion of her husband's autobiographical novel is the death of the wife. Almost hypnotized by this notion, Elsa goes out in the rain and brings on an attack of pneumonia which is nearly fatal because she has lost the will to live since her husband's infidelity has destroyed her "sacramental" ideal of matrimony. Throughout the play, Father Matthew Baird* and Loving engage in a struggle for John's soul. Finally the priest is successful, through a combination of spiritual and quasi-parental love, reinforced by the sacrificial love of Elsa, which finally brings her to forgive her husband rather than have him damn himself forever in suicide. As a result, John and Loving go to John's old church where John undergoes an epiphanic reintegration of his personality, and Loving surrenders to the love of Christ, dying on the ground in a cruciform attitude, and saying the words of Julian the Apostate, "Thou has conquered, Lord!"

LOVING, Elsa. In *Days Without End*,* wife of John Loving.* She is thirty-five years old but appears younger with an "Indian summer" kind of beauty that has come to her with the discovery of an ideal love rather late in life. She has had an unhappy first marriage, but she has not let that "disfigure" her by doing anything she might regret because she has always held onto the possibility that somewhere there would be someone who would be able to fulfill her ideal. She believes that she has found that relationship in her marriage with John Loving. At first she had not wanted to marry him, thinking herself through with marriage for good, but John had converted her to his ideal of the "true sacrament" of marriage, "a sacrament of faith in which each of us would find the completest self-expression in making our union a beautiful thing." This ideal bears comparison with that expressed by Michael and Eleanor Cape* in the earlier play, *Welded*,* which celebrates the O'Neill ideal of marrage while he was married to Agnes Boulton.* *Days Without End*, however, is specifically dedicated to Carlotta Monterey,* his third wife, and the character of Elsa (who recalls the Wagnerian chaste woman falsely accused in *Lohengrin*) is based upon Carlotta. Elsa, however, also shows some differences from the earlier Eleanor Cape, in her resemblance to Nina Leeds* in *Strange Interlude*,* for she tells her unhappy friend (and unbeknown to her, John's lover) Lucy Hillman* that John has "become my child and father now, as well as being my husband—[lover]."

Elsa is devastated by the discovery of John's momentary infidelity to her and as a result is vulnerable to the suggestion of Loving,* John's evil alter ego, that she court pneumonia by going out into the rain to get wet while she is recovering from influenza, the illness that killed John's parents when he was fifteen. She is unable to forgive her husband's violation of their ideal and loses the will to live. However, just as John is seriously contemplating suicide at the prodding of Loving, she springs out of her half-coma calling "No!" She then forgives him in an act of love that prefigures the crucifixional epiphany in John's boyhood church, the reintegration of his fragmented personality, damaged by his loss of faith in God. The title of the play and to some extent the philosophy of marriage both come from *The Book of Common Prayer* (and also the Roman Catholic marriage service) which sees the relationship of man and wife as reflexive of the relationship between Christ and His church. Thus John is saved through love, the Mephistophelian Loving surrenders, and the play ends with John standing before the cross, in much the same way as Michael and Eleanor Cape are finally seen at the end of *Welded*. As a character, Elsa is a loving tribute to Carlotta rather than a fully developed dramatic creation, while the play itself suffers badly from weak dramaturgy and characterization.

LOVING, John. In *Days Without End*,* husband of Elsa Loving,* opposed personality to Loving,* and nephew of Father Matthew Baird*. He is forty years old, handsome in a conventionally American manner, with "a straight nose and square jaw, a wide mouth that has an incongruous feminine sensitiveness." He is a writer who, since his marriage, has gone into a business partnership with William Eliot,* and as the play opens he is once more dabbling with the plot of a novel. This new work is obviously autobiographical, though John continually insists that it is not, and the project is mainly a means of covering up his momentary affair with Lucy Hillman.* Throughout the entire action of the play he is mocked, criticized, and incited to suicide by Loving, his Mephistophelian alter ego, who represents the rebellious, rationalistic, blasphemous, searching, and hostile qualities of John Loving's disintegrated personality. With his "John" side he loves Elsa with an idealistic, sacramental matrimonial affection, while the "Loving" side wishes to destroy love. Father Baird is the influence which leads John back to the Roman Catholic faith of his childhood, while Loving, the embodiment of the potentially damned soul of John Loving, represents the forces of darkness striving for possession of that vacillating soul. Loving is masked with the death-mask of a John Loving who died with a cynical sneer of mockery upon his lips—and he is invisible to all characters in the play, except to John himself.

While Elsa was away, John allowed himself to be momentarily seduced by the unhappy Lucy Hillman, and when the play opens, he is attempting to exorcise the affair by writing it into a confessional novel, which Loving continually mocks while taunting John with the folly of his guilt feelings. With the arrival of his uncle, Father Baird, John is even more defensive, particularly when the priest tells of a mystical experience warning him of some spiritual danger to his former ward. John had lost both his parents to influenza when he was fifteen years old, and enraged against a hostile God, he had sworn himself to the devil in a kind of Faustian bargain. Now, after having tried atheism, socialism, Marxism, and Eastern religions, he believes himself to have reached a quiet harbor in Elsa's love. He starts to tell his uncle the plot of the novel, while Loving interjects insulting and blasphemous comments and also suggests that the death of the wife is required by the plot.

That evening, John again tells the plot of his novel, this time with Elsa present; she recognizes the specifically autobiographical content of it and his infidelity with Lucy Hillman. Seeing John as having violated the sacramentality of their marriage, she is receptive to Loving's suggestion that she deliberately court pneumonia and die. Without faith in John's love she is unable to muster the will to live because she cannot forgive him his sin. Eventually John, who has flirted with suicide, decides to choose the path of love, and he goes to the old church of his boyhood where he achieves an epiphanic reintegration of his personality by vanquishing Loving, the personality of blasphemy and hate, through the power of Christ's love and the love of Elsa.

The character of John is to a great extent autobiographical, for it recounts O'Neill's own disillusionment with his father and also his mother, whose addiction to morphine he discovered at the age of about fifteen, believing himself somewhat responsible for it. Ella Quinlan O'Neill* had begun her long slavery to drugs as the result of prescriptions given her to ease postpartum pains after the birth of Eugene. At the same time, the play is also a paean to O'Neill's third marriage, to Carlotta Monterey.* As *Welded** had celebrated the ideal relationship during his marriage to Agnes Boulton,* so *Days Without End* is a celebration of his love for Carlotta. The action of the play is what O'Neill himself called "A Modern Miracle Play," and in effect it is a recreation of the medieval psychomachia, the struggle of good and evil for the soul of man and the triumph of Christian love—here in a marital setting. Through love, John Loving's fragmented personality is reintegrated and his purpose in life rediscovered. Unfortunately, the play itself is less competent than the passion that went into it, and the expressionistic use of masking seems an act of dramatic contrivance rather than the organic device it was in *Lazarus Laughed** or *The Great God Brown.** The psychological and nonsectarian spiritual content of the play was also not clear to most of the reviewers and audience of the play because it was seen instead as showing O'Neill's return to Catholicism—an event which never occurred. Further, the character drawing and dramaturgy are both rather clumsy; for instance, the first two acts are subtitled "Plot for a Novel," and to some extent the material might have been better served in that genre. Exposition is obvious, and the great crucifixional epiphany unfortunately degenerates into triteness, despite the recollection of the earlier *Lazarus Laughed* in John Loving's final lines. O'Neill's emphasis on the crucifix is not good Roman Catholic theology, which sees the resurrection as all important.

LUALDI, Adriano (1885–1971), composer. Born March 22, 1885, at Larino, Campobasso; died in Milan, January 8, 1971. He was the composer-librettist of the one-act opera, *La luna dei Caraibi* (1944, performed 1953), derived from O'Neill's *The Moon of the Caribbees* (*see* Appendix B). Studied music in Rome and under Wolf-Ferrari in Venice, gaining his diploma in 1907 and starting his career as a conductor. He became an interesting and influential music critic during the 1920s and in 1929 was "elected" (or appointed) to the Italian Fascist parliament as representative of the Sindicato Nazionale de Musicisti. He was one of the first organizers of the International Festivals in Venice (1930–34) and was principal of the Conservatory of San Pietro a Maiella, Naples (1936–43). An enthusiastic Fascist, he was forced into retirement after the fall of Mussolini, but was restored to political respectability in 1949 when he was appointed director of the Conservatory of Florence, a post he held until 1956. As a musician, his reputation has risen and fallen along with Fascism. In the 1930s he was overrated, and since then he has been dismissed (probably unfairly) by musicologists. His work is considered as lacking unity of style, but he is praised for his coloristic sense and skill in evoking emotions and atmosphere, qualities which would well serve his O'Neill opera. He seems to have enjoyed working with the bizarre, as his opera *Il diavolo nel campanile* (1919–23), based on a tale by Edgar Allan Poe, indicates. There the music deliberately dissolves into stylistic chaos. His other major operas are: *Le nozze di Haura*, libretto by Orsini (1908, revised 1913); *Le furie di Arlecchino*, libretto by Orsini (1915); *Lumawige e la saetta*, libretto by M. Lualdi (1936, revised 1956). Operas for which Lualdi was his own librettist are: *La figlia del re* (1914–17); *Il diavolo nel campanile* (1919–23); *La Granceola* (1932); *La luna dei Caraibi* (1944, performed 1953); and *Euridikes diatheke–Il testamento di Euridice–*(1962).

LUNT, Alfred (1892–1977), actor. Born August 19, 1892, in Milwaukee, Wisconsin, to Alfred Davis and Henrietta Washborn (Briggs) Lunt. Died in Detroit, August 3, 1977, after an operation for stomach cancer. Married to Lynn Fontanne,* May 26, 1922. Educated at Carroll College, Waukesha, Wisconsin, and the Emerson College School of Oratory, Cambridge, Massachusetts.

Lunt's interest in the stage was sparked by his stepfather, Dr. Carl Sederholm, who took him to opera performances in Chicago. His father had died when Alfred was two, and his mother remarried in 1900. He made his stage debut on October 7, 1912, in a repertory production of *The Aviator* with the Castle Square Theatre, Boston, Massachusetts, serving his apprenticeship there in small roles (1912–14). He toured with Margaret Anglin's repertory company (1914–16) where he began a lifelong friendship with Howard Lindsay. In 1916 he toured in vaudeville with Lily Langtry and made his Broadway debut in *Romance and Arabella* (1917). He first appeared with Lynn Fontanne in *A Young Man's Fancy* (Washington, D.C., 1919). After a long courtship and after solving problems allied to his close attachment to his mother, he and Fontanne were married in 1922. Lunt and Fontanne (always billed in that order) co-starred almost exclusively with each other for the remainder of their theatrical lives, retiring together to their farm in Genesee Depot, Wisconsin, in 1970s. Throughout their joint career, from *Sweet Nell of Old Drury* (1923) to *The Visit* (1957–60), they gained an enviable reputation for perfectionism, superb ensemble playing, and matrimonial harmony.

Alfred Lunt created the role of Marco Polo* in O'Neill's *Marco Millions*,* in a performance that was generally considered to be below his usual high standard (perhaps the result of health problems). O'Neill was less than pleased with the entire production, but did not attack Lunt, whose wife, Lynn Fontanne, was about to appear in *Strange Interlude** which Lunt had irreverently called "a six-day bisexual race" (Gelb and Gelb, 1973, p. 649). The Lunts, whose true métier was comedy of manners, were not great successes in serious O'Neill roles.

Lunt and Fontanne became almost inseparable as theatrical names, receiving the United States Medal of Freedom (1964) in a joint award and having a theatre named for them in New York in the same year. Alfred Lunt also had a good career in films, on television, as producer, director, and even operatic director for the Metropolitan Opera House, New York City. Somehow Lunt and Fontanne managed to defeat time in the course of their theatrical careers, remaining fixed somewhere in early middle age in the public mind, even in their last active years together.

LYONS, the stoker, in O'Neill's only published short story, "Tomorrow."* He is based on Driscoll,* a companion of O'Neill when the playwright was living at the saloon of James J. Condon* at 252 Fulton Street, near the old Washington Market. Driscoll is the same character who appears under his own name in the S.S. *Glencairn** plays. He committed suicide by jumping out a window. In the short story, he, Paddy,* and Art* (the character representing O'Neill) frequently get drunk. They all are roomers at "Tommy-The-Priest's",* which is really the saloon of James J. Condon. This story contains elements of the later play, *The Iceman Cometh.**

M

MACGOWAN, Kenneth (1888–1963), dramatic critic, author, producer, university professor. Born in Winthrop, Massachusetts, November 30, 1888, son of Peter Stainforth and Susan Arletta (Hall) Macgowan. Married Edna Behre. Died in West Los Angeles, California, April 27, 1963. Educated at Harvard University.

Macgowan began his career as a drama critic on the *Boston Transcript* (1910–13), later serving in that capacity on the *Philadelphia Evening Ledger* (1914–17), the *New York Tribune* (1918), the *New York Globe* (1919–23), *Vogue* (1920–24), and *Theatre Arts Magazine* (associate editor and drama critic, 1919–25). His producing career began when he worked with Joseph Verner Reed, importing English plays for the American theatre. Altogether he produced some thirty-five plays on Broadway, including several by Eugene O'Neill whom he had met as a result of praising *Beyond the Horizon** in an article in the *New York Globe*.

Macgowan and O'Neill soon became close friends in a relationship that lasted almost until the end of the playwright's life. Macgowan was one of the few earlier acquaintances of O'Neill who was welcomed by Carlotta Monterey* after her marriage to the playwright, probably because he approved of the match. During O'Neill's marriage to Agnes Boulton,* Macgowan, either with or without his wife, visited the O'Neills at their various residences at Peaked Hill Bars, Brook Farm, Loon Lodge, and Bermuda. Macgowan, however, came to the conclusion that Agnes was not the ideal wife for O'Neill because of her commitment to her own writing and her sociability, as well as her impractical housekeeping and apparent inability to control his drinking—in fact Macgowan believed that she encouraged it. Macgowan also became O'Neill's professional and personal confidant, and in numerous letters to him O'Neill confided his ideas for new plays and his hopes for the American theatre. (*See* Bogard [1972] and Bryer and Alvarez [1982]). O'Neill's trust of Macgowan was such that he consented to undergo a short course of psychological therapy with Dr. Gilbert V. Hamilton, whose book, *Research on Marriage*, Macgowan had reorganized and popularized into *What Is Wrong With Marriage* (1929). The playwright also took Macgowan into his confidence concerning his divorce from Agnes Boulton and departure for Europe with Carlotta. He even made use of Macgowan as "go-between" in asking him to send flowers to Carlotta while he was courting her at long distance from Bermuda. The voluminous O'Neill-Macgowan correspondence was punctuated by visits to the playwright at Chateau du Plessis; Sea Island, Georgia; Tao House, California; and Marblehead, Massachusetts. Only after the last separation of Carlotta and O'Neill in 1951 did Macgowan consider the possibility of its permanence, though he, more than anyone else, seems to have understood the nature of their mutual dependence on each other.

Professionally, Macgowan was most important to O'Neill's career not only as a friendly critic but also as one member of "the triumvirate" which included the theatrical designer Robert Edmond Jones* and O'Neill. The three banded together in 1923 to manage the Experimental Theatre, Inc.,* the successor organization to the Provincetown Players* at the old playhouse at 133 Macdougal Street, Greenwich Village, New York. Macgowan was the head of the group with Jones and O'Neill as associate directors. This organization gave all three a chance to put into practice the production theories they shared and of which Macgowan had written in *The Theatre of Tomorrow* (1921). In 1922 he undertook a tour of European theatres with Jones, and *Continental Stagecraft* was the result. During this association, Macgowan, Jones, and O'Neill produced and designed their first production, Strindberg's *The Spook Sonata*, following this with O'Neill's plays, *Welded,* The Ancient Mariner,* All God's Chillun Got Wings** and *Desire Under the Elms** (all 1924), *The Fountain** (1925), and *The Great God Brown** (1926). It is interesting, in view of O'Neill's use of masks in *All God's Chillun* and in *Brown,* to note that Macgowan had earlier collaborated with Herman Rosse on an anthropological study entitled *Masks and Demons* (1923). Later he was also to write a study of the state of the American theatre entitled *Footlights across America* (1929). After the triumvirate broke up in 1926, largely owing to O'Neill's residence in Bermuda, Macgowan remained in close touch with O'Neill but not with Jones, though they subsequently did work together again. During the period of the triumvirate, the three friends attempted to bring a new approach to drama, with nonrealistic, unobtrusive sets, careful attention to lighting, and a holistic approach to production. They were often highly successful, though sometimes O'Neill's specific demands interfered with Jones's imaginative creativity, and their attempt at poetic drama, *The Ancient Mariner* was not well received. From 1925 to 1927, Macgowan was producer for the Actors' Theatre. Other Macgowan productions included *Fashion, Outside Looking In, Bride of the Lamb, Young Love, These Modern Women, Children of Darkness, Twelfth Night, Art and Mrs. Bottle, The Lady with the Lamp,* and *Springtime for Henry.*

After having learned the film business through work as publicity director for Metro-Goldwyn-Mayer, Macgowan finally cast in his lot with the movies, producing forty-five films for RKO, Paramount, and Twentieth-Century Fox. Notable among them were: *Alexander Graham Bell, In Old Chicago,* and *Becky Sharp,* the first feature-length color film, for which Robert Edmond Jones did the color designs. He was also the founder of the theatre arts department at the University of California, Los Angeles, where he was professor (1947–58), receiving an Honorary Litt.D. in 1959. The theatre arts building at UCLA is named for him.

Kenneth Macgowan was both an active participant in and a philosopher of the theatre. He believed in the Off-Broadway Theater Movement as the "conscience of American Theater," and in his work with O'Neill and Jones he put his theories into practice. He was a champion of the influences of the new European theatre as exemplified by Edward Gordon Craig and Max Reinhardt, and was not afraid to experiment. As a reviewer and editor he was most influential, and as a theatre scholar he wrote important studies like those already mentioned as well as *The Living Stage* (with William Melnitz). Though working in films, he did not prostitute his talents but continued to maintain contacts with Broadway, though distance had attenuated them. Finally, he remained a most loyal friend and confidant of Eugene O'Neill.

MACKEL, Ira. In *The Haunted*, the last play of the trilogy, *Mourning Becomes Electra,** a farmer who "hobbles along with the aid of a cane." He is bald with a white "chin whisker" and sly brown eyes. "He talks in a drawling wheezy cackle." He forms part of the Chorus of Townsfolk who comment on the Mannon family and the events in which they have been involved. He is one of those who successfully bets Abner Small* that the latter cannot stay overnight in the haunted Mannon mansion.

MAG. In *The Long Voyage Home,** the slovenly, drunken barmaid in Fat Joe's London waterfront dive.

"MALATESTA SEEKS SURCEASE." The original title of a proposed gangster comedy, "The Visit of Malatesta."*

MALOY, Mickey. In *A Touch of the Poet,** the barkeep. He "is twenty-six, with a sturdy physique and an amiable, cunning face, his mouth usually set in a half-leering grin." He is used as an expository device early in the play, questioning Jamie Cregan* about Cornelius Melody's* past. In a moment of rage, Melody insists that Maloy would make a better match for his daughter, Sara Melody,* than Simon Harford.* Maloy has some sympathy for Nora Melody,* Con's wife, and admires her as a long-suffering wife.

MAMMY SAUNDERS. In *The Dreamy Kid,** an old black woman of ninety or so. She is the grandmother of Dreamy,* the gangster, whom she still believes to be the most innocent young man in the world. She has raised him from babyhood when his mother, Sal, her daughter, died, and she gave him the sobriquet of "Dreamy" because his eyes were "jest a-dreamin' an' a-dreamin'." She is dying in her Greenwich Village bedroom as the play opens and wants nothing more than to see Dreamy again. He comes to see her at the risk of being captured, and she begs him to stay with her, threatening him with her curse if he leaves. At the conclusion, Dreamy is determined to shoot his way out and not be taken alive, but his defiant "Lawd Jesus" is taken by his grandmother as a prayer in which she joins as the curtain falls. As a character, Mammy Saunders is a stock figure, that of the earth-mother black mammy. However, she is important as being portrayed as a serious, not a comic, character.

MANNON, Christine. In *Mourning Becomes Electra*,* she appears in the first two plays of the trilogy, *Homecoming,* and *The Hunted*, wife of Ezra Mannon,* mother of Lavinia Mannon* and Orin Mannon,* paramour of Adam Brant.* She is a tall, handsome woman of forty with spectacularly lovely copper-bronze hair. She has "a fine voluptuous figure and she moves with a flowing animal grace." Her face in repose looks almost like "a wonderfully lifelike pale mask, in which only the deep-set eyes, of a dark violet-blue are alive.' In *Homecoming*, she no longer has any love for her husband, Ezra, who is away at the Civil War, and dreads his return because it will put an end to her liaison with Adam Brant, the illegitimate son of Ezra's brother, David Mannon,* and a French Canadian nurse, Marie Brantôme.* Christine detests her daughter, Lavinia, because her existence recalls the horror of her honeymoon and her early marriage. However, she loves her son, Orin, in an abnormal way because when he was born his father was fighting in the Mexican War. As a result she has lavished affection on the boy because he seemed to belong entirely to her. Her anger against Lavinia is increased by the fact that she has informed both her father and Orin there has been "gossip" about her mother and Brant. In addition, Christine cannot forgive Lavinia for pushing Orin into the war in which he has been wounded.

When her husband returns, Christine treats him coldly, even though Ezra begs her to tear down the emotional wall that separates them and speaks of the love he feels for her. Christine, however, sees this as mere lust, and later that night she gives herself to him, but with disgust. Later, as they talk she reveals to Ezra the truth about Adam Brant's identity and her liaison with him, knowing that this news might cause Ezra to have a heart attack. This is indeed what happens, and instead of medicine, Christine administers to him a poison which she had Adam Brant procure for her. As he dies (in the presence of Lavinia), Ezra accuses his wife of killing him. Christine faints and accidentally drops the box which had contained the poison. Lavinia finds it and later places it on top of Ezra Mannon's body as a means of convincing Orin of their mother's guilt. In *The Hunted* Orin and Lavinia hunt down Adam Brant, and Orin kills him. When Christine is told of this, she goes into Ezra's study and shoots herself with his pistol as she stands in front of his judicial portrait. This concludes the action of the second play of the trilogy.

Christine Mannon is really a romantic, sensual woman who is married to a man of overdeveloped Puritan conscience, one who comes from a long line of repressed ancestors whose portraits darken the walls of the Mannon house. Through her liaison with Adam, she becomes awakened to her own sexuality and dreams of the "Blessed Islands," the romantic South Seas, where love is not a sin. Yet at the same time, her relationship with Orin is abnormal in its possessiveness and almost incestuous ardor. In some respects it is Orin's turning away from her that is even more contributory to her suicide than the death of her lover.

In terms of the mythic structure of *Mourning Becomes Electra*, Christine Mannon is Clytemnestra and Jocasta, Ezra Mannon is Agamemnon and Laius, and Adam Brant is Aegisthos, while Lavinia is Electra, and Orin the avenging Orestes and also Oedipus. The trilogy shows the workings of destiny in the house of Mannon/Atreus, but the overall myth is reworked through the influences of Aeschylus, Euripides, Sophocles, Jung, Freud, and the combined traditions of puritanism and American history. The relations between parents and children, and also those of Orin and Lavinia, are heavily indebted to twentieth-century Freudianism.

MANNON, David. In *Mourning Becomes Electra*,* brother of Ezra Mannon,* lover and later husband of Marie Brantôme,* a "French Canuck nurse" in the employ of the Mannon family. He is frequently discussed, though he does not appear at all. His son, Adam Brant,* hates his father because of the way Mannon abused Marie. Adam also detests the Mannon clan for disinheriting his father and for refusing aid to his mother when she was in need. David Mannon is the first of the Mannon family skeletons to be revealed. He represents an unsuccessful attempt to break out of the puritan mold; he later turns to drink and dies, leaving his wife destitute.

MANNON, Ezra. In *Homecoming*, the first play of the trilogy, *Mourning Becomes Electra*,* a brigadier general in the Union Army, "a tall, spare, big-boned man of fifty." He returns from the Civil War to his wife, Christine Mannon,* and his daughter, Lavinia Mannon.* His son, Orin Mannon,* has been wounded. Ezra is a grim-faced man, a graduate of West Point who fought in the Mexican War, but on the death of his father he resigned to go into the family shipping business. Finding that his wife had apparently lost her affection for him, he flung himself into seeking after business success, and once he achieved that, he studied law and became a judge in the town, then mayor, resigning from that position to go to the Civil War. His portrait, made some ten years earlier, showing him in his judge's robes, hangs in his study where it seems to preside over the happenings of much of the trilogy. He is a strict, repressed-looking man with a masklike countenance, whose military bearing is stiff and almost mechanical, while his voice is hollow and lacking in emotion.

On his return from the war, he begs Christine to tear down the wall that seems to have grown between them. He asks for her love, but she withholds it because she has now fallen in love with Adam Brant,* the illegitimate son of Ezra's brother, David Mannon,* and a French Canadian nurse, Marie Brantôme.* Lavinia, abnormally attached to her father, has informed him that there is some gossip about Christine and Brant. Later that night, after Ezra has taken Christine to bed with him, she reveals her liaison, which leads Ezra to have a heart attack; but instead of medicine, Christine administers to him the poison she had Brant obtain for her. With his dying words Ezra accuses her of murder, in the hearing of Lavinia, who vows vengeance on her mother.

In the terms of the mythic structure of *Mourning Becomes Electra*, Ezra Mannon represents Agamemnon who has just returned from the wars to discover that his wife, Clytemnestra, has a lover, Aegisthos. In the *Oresteia* of Aeschylus and in related plays by Euripides and Sophocles, the fate of the House of Atreus is shown. Clytemnestra kills Agamemnon, Orestes kills Aegisthos and Clytemnestra and is hunted by the Furies, who eventually become for him ''the Kindly Ones,'' and finally he is pardoned. However, the character of Electra in O'Neill's rendition of the myth is taken largely from the interpretation of Sophocles and Euripides.

MANNON, Lavinia. In the trilogy *Mourning Becomes Electra*,* daughter of Christine Mannon* and Ezra Mannon,* sister of Orin Mannon.* In *Homecoming* she is engaged in conflict with her mother because she has discovered her involved in a liaison with Adam Brant,* captain of a Mannon company clipper ship and a romantic figure. To her horror she discovers that Adam is the son of David Mannon,* her father's brother, and a ''French Canuck nurse,'' Marie Brantôme,* formerly in the employ of the Mannon family. She taxes her mother with this crime, seeing it as an act of disloyalty to the father with whom she has an extraordinarily close, even abnormal, relationship. She is a stern personality, dressed in black and moving with an almost military precision which proves to be almost a copy of her father's manner. When her father returns from the Civil War, after being informed by Lavinia of the ''gossip'' about Christine and Brant, the two women compete for Ezra Mannon's attention. Christine hates Lavinia because she reminds her of her honeymoon and early marriage, but she loves her son, Orin, because he was born while her husband was away at the Mexican War. As a result he seems totally her own. Ezra has realized this, and seeing that he had lost Christine, he had turned to his daughter, ''but a daughter's not a wife.''

After Ezra's death through Christine's poisoning, Orin returns from the war, and the two women again compete—this time for Orin in *The Hunted*. Christine wants him almost as a lover, while Lavinia wants to use him as an instrument of vengeance on her mother both for her liaison with Adam and her murder of Ezra, which she had tricked Christine into revealing by her reaction to the poison box Lavinia placed on her father's body in *Homecoming*. In this first play their competition included a contest for the affections of Adam Brant, who had also flirted with Lavinia, and Christine had taunted the girl with her lack of success with this romantic figure. To some extent, this is additional motivation for Lavinia's wishing to do away with Adam Brant. Orin, however, acts as his mother's rejected lover when he discovers the truth of Lavinia's allegations. Together they go to Brant's ship and overhear the lovers planning to run away together. After this, the murder of Adam Brant is easy for both of them, and Orin shoots him at point-blank range.

Returning to the Mannon home, Lavinia is pleased with the justice of the deed, but Orin's reaction is Oedipal as he begs his mother's forgiveness. Lavinia, a puritanical Mannon with strict rules of vengeance and punishment, tells her mother that the death of Brant was justice but is frightened when she realizes that her mother might be contemplating suicide, saying, "You can live!" But Christine commits suicide, and again Lavinia implacably repeats, "It is justice."

In *The Haunted*, the third play of the trilogy, a curious change has come over Lavinia. She has become beautiful and has even taken on the physical voluptuousness and sensual beauty of her mother. Obviously, she has been sexually awakened during the voyage, and she and Orin have taken to the South Seas. Earlier, she seems to have had no physical desire or sexual experience. She had refused Peter Niles's* proposal of marriage in *Homecoming* because "I can't marry anyone, Peter. I've got to stay home. Father needs me." And her expression of hatred toward Adam Brant is a curious mixture of rejection of a lover and rage against a man who is supplanting her father. After the South Sea voyage she is eager to marry Peter as a means of returning to a normal life, but she realizes that she cannot do so as long as Orin is alive because she is afraid that he will tell the tale of the family crimes. But as Lavinia has taken on the physical and even the nurturing qualities of her mother toward Orin, so too her brother has taken on the role of her father. In this way Lavinia still cannot marry: "Father [Orin] needs me!" But this time the existence of the impediment chafes her because she has now become a passionate woman who wishes for sexual fulfillment, while Orin has taken on the brooding, puritanical, judgmental, and repressive qualities of all his ancestors, including his own father who had refused to help Marie Brantôme in her time of need. He sees that since he is paying for his participation in the Mannon crimes, so too must Lavinia.

He therefore tries, like a possessive father, to frustrate Lavinia's marriage plans to Peter by writing down the family history for Peter to read before his marriage to Lavinia, but withholds it on receiving Lavinia's promise to do anything for him. Now Lavinia is asked to give up Peter and engage in an incestuous relationship with Orin, who is standing almost in Ezra's position to her. Whereas she had wanted to compete with her mother for possession of her father, now her brother, rejected lover of their mother, is offering to become her lover, having already become her punitive father. This proposition appalls her, and she taunts Orin with cowardice for being afraid to commit suicide.

After Orin kills himself, she throws herself at Peter, despite Hazel Niles's* earnest request that Lavinia leave him to pursue his happiness without her. Hazel knows that there is something that Orin had wanted to tell Peter and begs her to renounce her brother because Lavinia's influence has already caused a rift in the family. She appeals to Lavinia's conscience and then to her love for Peter. At first Lavinia is adamant in her refusal, and in desperation she flings herself at Peter, begging him to consummate their relationship without waiting for marriage. He is shocked, though somewhat aroused, by what he now sees as almost indecent sexuality, and his suspicions are aroused concerning Orin's message. Obviously, the dead are influencing the living here, and Lavinia slowly comes to realize that she can never find happiness and can never leave the Mannon house. She cannot kill herself because she is a Mannon, with all the masochistic puritanism that implies, and Orin's curse will be fulfilled—her ghosts will haunt her the rest of her life. She realizes too that Peter is already beginning to sound bitter and resentful and that she is destroying him. Then, when he asks what had happened on the South Sea island, she sees a way out of her dilemma. She tells him, in as coarse a way as she can, that she was the "fancy woman" of the native of whom Orin had spoken. This information shocks Peter into leaving her, and Lavinia orders the Mannon house shuttered against the daylight. She turns, takes a last look at the sun, and then walks inside. Curiously, as she does this, she moves in her square-shouldered, almost military manner of *Homecoming*, and after Orin's death her black dress has made her look once more like the spinsterish asexual creature of that play. The Mannon blood has again come to control her, and the Mannon destiny cannot be avoided.

In the mythic interpretation of this trilogy, Lavinia is obviously the Electra figure who wishes to destroy Aegisthos (Brant) the lover of Clytemnestra (Christine) and avenge her mother's murder of Agamemnon (Ezra). Orin quite clearly is Orestes but also is Oedipus in killing Brant, who looks like his father, to supplant him with Christine/Jocasta. Lavinia's abnormal relationship with her father is quite obviously what in psychological parlance is referred to as an Electra complex, as her competition with her mother indicates. But once she is sexually awakened, Lavinia/Electra takes on the physical characteristics of her dead mother, with the result that Orin/Ezra now conceives an incestuous passion for her as they replay the roles of their parents almost against their wills. A malevolent destiny seems to be pursuing them—the Eumenides of the Oresteia cannot be denied—and these Furies destroy everyone but Lavinia, whom they will hound.

However, it is important to notice that the character of Lavinia/Electra is not modeled after Aeschylus, but rather Sophocles and Euripides, who treat her character more fully and sympathetically. At the end of his trilogy, then, O'Neill has managed to make Lavinia a character who evokes pity and fear, rather than the condemnation of narrow justice. This he does by means of the complex mingling and interweaving of a series of mythic themes and happenings ranging from the Oresteia to modern psychology, particularly Freud, through the chivalric gallantry mingled with horror that was the American Civil War, the masochistic judicial puritanism of witch-hunting forebears, and the dreams of primal innocence that are attached to the South Seas. As a result, the character of Lavinia Mannon achieves an inevitability, a deep significance arising from the myths of the Jungian racial unconscious which raises her actions beyond the strictures of realism or even conventional morality.

MANNON, Orin. In *Mourning Becomes Electra*,* son of Christine Mannon* and Ezra Mannon,* brother of Lavinia Mannon,* and fiancé of Hazel Niles.* He appears in two plays of this trilogy, *The Hunted* and *The Haunted*, and he is frequently mentioned in *Homecoming*. In the first play, he is the subject of dispute between Christine and Lavinia because the latter encouraged him to go to war with the Union Army and follow his father, a brigadier general. Christine has always loved Orin more than her daughter, who reminds her of her honeymoon and the early days of her now loveless marriage. Orin, however, was born during his father's absence at the Mexican War, and as a result his mother considers him a child almost of her own begetting, and indeed she has coddled him so much that the relationship between the two is almost one of lovers rather than mother and son. As a result, Ezra found himself neglected, and the relationship between father and son is unsatisfactory.

While he has been away as a first lieutenant of infantry, Orin is wounded in a curious action in which he suddenly perceived the folly of war and "began to laugh and walked toward their lines" with hand held out in a gesture of greeting. He is wounded, but then "went mad, wanted to kill and ran on, yelling. Then a lot of our fools went crazy, too, and followed" with the result that an unexpected advance was made, and his father treated him as a hero. But above all else, Orin has returned with a horror of war, because as he continued in that business, he discovered "a queer feeling that war meant murdering the same man over and over, and that in the end I would discover the man was myself! Their faces keep coming back in dreams—and they change to Father's face—or to mine." He is further disturbed by Lavinia's allegations of Christine's liaison with Adam Brant,* son of their uncle, David Mannon,* and a "French Canuck nurse," Marie Brantôme,* formerly in the employ of the Mannon family. Brant is the captain of a Mannon shipping company clipper ship, a man of great romantic charm. At Christine's request, he obtained the poison which she later used to murder her husband, Ezra Mannon. Lavinia had hinted at Christine's affair in letters to both Ezra and Orin and now wishes to convince her brother of Christine's involvement with Brant and also of her guilt in the murder of Ezra.

On Orin's return in *The Hunted*, Christine and Lavinia vie for his affections, Christine enlisting the help of Hazel Niles in her attempt to cosset Orin and woo him away from his sister. Orin enjoys the attention but has the curious feeling that everything in the house has changed—"everything but Father," a shocking remark to everyone since Ezra has just died. Christine tries to make light of the Adam Brant affair, suggesting that Lavinia's allegations are the result of disappointment that Brant did not pay enough attention to her, and begs her son to protect her against his sister. As she pleads, he soothes her, telling her, "I love you better than anything in the world." Then he talks with her about his dream of life on the South Sea islands, when he was wounded and delirious: "There was no one there but you and me. And yet I never saw you, . . . I only felt you all around me. The sky was the same color as your eyes. The warm sand was like your skin. The whole island was you." This scene develops the intense and abnormal feeling that exists between mother and son as Orin declares, ''I'll never leave you again now. I don't want Hazel or anyone. You're my only girl!'' He recalls his joy in brushing her hair, and now with his father dead they can ''get Vinnie to marry Peter and there will be just you and I.'' Clearly their relationship is somewhat Oedipal, and unconsciously Orin welcomes the loss of his father, whom Lavinia worships in an equally abnormal way. He looks with a curious detachment on his father's body, thinking that they might be friends now that he is dead. Orin is appalled at Christine's guilty reaction when she sees the poison box that Lavinia has placed on Ezra's body as a test.

He turns against her as his ''lost island'' of peace and goes with Lavinia to Brant's ship in Boston where they overhear Christine and Brant planning their departure together for the South Seas. Their suspicions confirmed, Orin has no compunction in killing Brant with his pistol at point-blank range and ransacking the cabin to make the murder look like a robbery. But then he looks at the face of Adam Brant with its extraordinary likeness to Ezra Mannon and recalls how the faces of other men he had killed ''came back and changed to Father's face and finally became my own . . . Maybe I've committed suicide.'' But then he looks longer and his submerged motivation becomes clear: ''If I had been he I would have done what he did! I would have loved her as he loved her—and killed Father too—for her sake!''

On their return from Boston, Orin and Lavinia confront Christine with their account of Adam Brant's death and claim responsibility for it. Orin, however, tries to exculpate his mother, but when he perceives that she had indeed loved Brant, he acts like a rejected lover, angry that she had told him about ''our island'' and begging her to go away with him: ''I'll make you forget him! I'll make you happy! We'll leave Vinnie here and go away on a long voyage—to the South Seas—'' But then he realizes that she still loves Brant and asks, ''Will you always love him? Do you hate me now? Mother! Answer me! Say you forgive me!'' Lavinia forces him away with her. When she is left alone, Christine shoots herself, leaving Orin in a state of hysterical grief because he must remain unforgiven.

In *The Haunted*, Orin and Lavinia have returned from a voyage to the South Seas, but while Lavinia has been sexually awakened there, Orin has become more and more guilt-ridden; haunted by the horror of his crimes, he is Orestes pursued by the avenging Furies. He looks on Lavinia with disgust, while she lives in constant fear that he will someday tell the truth. The result is, as Orin himself realizes, that they have become the embodiment of their parents: Orin has become the judgmental Ezra, and Lavinia the voluptuous, sensual Christine. She suggests that the two must return to a normal life through the friendship and love of Hazel and Peter Niles, but Orin denies their right to love. Now that they have returned, the Mannon dead will exert their influence on them again. He is jealous of Lavinia's new beauty, and now that she resembles their mother, he begins to act like his father and to subvert her attempts at romance, continually talking maliciously about her relationship with a native in the islands, where he discovered that *HIS* islands had become "Vinnie's islands." Again he finds himself the rejected lover. He attempts to break off Lavinia's engagement with Peter by writing an account of the family crimes which he plans to give to Hazel so that Peter can read it if Vinnie attempts to marry him.

In terror, Lavinia promises to do anything for Orin if he will retain the manuscript, and he agrees, after making her promise to give up Peter. But then Orin proposes an incestuous relationship: "I love you now with all the guilt in me—the guilt we share! Perhaps I love you too much, Vinnie!" In this way alone can Orin be sure that she will never leave him. But then he turns to pleading that they "confess and pay the penalty for Mother's murder, and find peace together!" With this he loses his advantage, as Vinnie calls him a coward, repeating that Christine's death was justice, and finally telling him, "You'd kill yourself if you weren't a coward!" Rejected once again by the woman he loves, his sister and his partner in guilt this time, Orin does indeed shoot himself, leaving his ghost to haunt Lavinia through her own conscience.

In the mythic interpretation of the play, Orin Mannon is a complex figure. In the first instance, he is Orestes who kills his mother's lover, Aegisthos (Adam Brant), and yet at the same time he is the Oedipal murderer of his "father," Laius, so that he can marry his mother. In this way for Orin, Christine is both Clytemnestra and Jocasta. But for him the incest-taboo is carried farther through his guilt-ridden thoughts. His private Eumenides, combined with the puritanical influence of the Mannon family history, lead him to adopt the personality and even the office of his own father, while Lavinia adopts that of her mother. Thus their relationship moves, on Orin's part, closer to that incestuous consummation he was unable to achieve with his mother. Far from reaching peace through the intervention of any gods, Orin can find his release through suicide. The character of Orin Mannon is in effect an amalgam of myths, ranging from Orestes and Oedipus, to the puritan, Apollonian, judicial one O'Neill had used in *Desire Under the Elms*,* to the curiously romantic and chivalric Civil War and the dreams of the Blessed Islands of the South Seas where love is natural and sinless. Without doubt, his character is given depth by this dense interweaving of psychology, myth, and history, with the result that the central characters seem unable to escape from the fate that has been decreed for them by some malevolent destiny.

MAN OF BUSINESS, A. In *Fog*,* the stereotypical businessman. He has a "round, jowly, and clean-shaven countenance." He lacks imagination, is self-centered, materialistic, and unsympathetic to the ills of humanity. He and the Poet* engage in a discussion concerning the nature of life.

"MAN ON IRON HORSEBACK, THE." The proposed tenth play in the abandoned cycle, "A Tale of Possessors, Self-Dispossessed."* This play, cov-

ering the period 1876–1893 was designed to tell the story of Jonathan Harford*
and his career as railroad and shipping magnate. The outline, written in August
1935, was destroyed in February 1943.

MARCELLUS. In *Lazarus Laughed*,* a thirty-five-year-old Roman patrician.
He is a dissipated-looking man who confronts Lazarus* with his dagger raised
ready to kill him. However, Marcellus is overcome by the luminescence of this
prophet-redeemer who laughs softly at him. The dagger stops in mid-air and
then falls from his hand, and Marcellus finds himself in love with Lazarus. He,
too, begins to laugh, along with the assembled troops, and then, when Caligula*
mocks him for his weakness, he stabs himself with his own dagger. He, too,
has learned to accept death as part of life.

MARCH, Fredric (1897–1975) actor. Born Ernest Frederick McIntyre Bickel
in Racine, Wisconsin, August 31, 1897; died in Connecticut, April 14, 1975.
Educated at the University of Wisconsin, but interrupted his studies during World
War I, becoming an artillery lieutenant.

Returning to the University of Wisconsin, March began to play parts in college
dramatics. In 1920, after his graduation, he went to New York to join National
City Bank but during a period of enforced meditation in the hospital as the result
of an appendicitis operation, he decided to try his luck at acting. His first part
was a two-line bit in *Deburau*, produced by David Belasco in Baltimore (1920)
which also came to New York. March worked as actor, model, and extra in
films produced in the New York area. He played in Al Jolson's New York
production of *Lei Aloha* (1923) and moved into a stock company in Dayton,
Ohio (1924). He played the lead in the European tour of *Melody Man* (1925),
returning to stock. In 1926 he had his first Broadway lead in *The Devil in the
Cheese*. He married Florence Eldridge* in 1927, and they took a working honeymoon with the first traveling company of the Theatre Guild.* He made his
first film appearance as a featured actor in *The Dummy* (1929), and after his
parodic performance in *The Royal Family* on the West Coast, he was signed by
Paramount Pictures. He played in a great number of films, including *Anna
Karenina* (1935, with Greta Garbo*), and *Les Misérables* (1935, as Jean Val-
jean). He received Academy Awards for his performances in *Dr. Jekyll and Mr.
Hyde* (1932) and *The Best Years of Our Lives* (1946).

March was always careful in his choice of roles, avoiding possible typecasting
as a romantic light-comedy lead or actor in costume drama. His list of screen
credits is extraordinary, and he acted with an astonishingly large number of top-
ranked female stars, including Greta Garbo, Bette Davis, Janet Gaynor, Jennifer
Jones and Grace Kelly, among others. As he matured and the subtlety of his
acting deepened, he moved into increasingly serious roles, frequently being
chosen for the screen adaptations of notable plays because he combined box-
office appeal with acting skill. He was cast as *Christopher Columbus* (1949); as
Willy Loman in *Death of a Salesman* (1951); appeared in *Inherit the Wind*

(1963), *The Condemned of Altona* (1964), and played Theodore Hickman* in *The Iceman Cometh* (1973), (*See* Appendix B). He appeared as featured actor or lead in over forty films.

At the same time, he worked sporadically in the theatre, often with his wife, Florence Eldridge, appearing in *Your Obedient Husband* (1939), *Hope for a Harvest* (1941), and *The Skin of Our Teeth* (1943), among others.

In 1956 he created the role of James Tyrone,* Sr., opposite Florence Eldridge in the first American production of *Long Day's Journey into Night*,* directed by José Quintero, with Jason Robards, Jr.,* and Bradford Dillman* completing the cast. For a fascinating account of the development of this production see José Quintero (1974).

MARCO MILLIONS, satiric comedy in three acts, eleven scenes, with prologue and epilogue. The title comes from the rough translation of "Il Milione," the sobriquet attached to the name of Marco Polo by those who did not believe his accounts of the riches he saw in his travels. The original title as shown on the typescript in the Library of Congress is *Marco's Millions*.

Prologue: A sacred place in Persia near the confines of India toward the close of the thirteenth century. A white Christian "merchant, carrying in each hand a strapped box that resembles a modern sample case," goes to the welcome shade of the tree, puts down his cases, mops his brow, and complains of the heat. "A Magian, a Persian, dressed in the fashion of a trader," enters. The two bow perfunctorily; the Magian puts down his small square case, mops his brow, and they exchange commiserations about the heat. A Buddhist, a Khashmiri, a traveling merchant with a pack strapped to his back, enters, and the scene is reenacted. They discuss problems of business, and the Magian announces the death of Queen Kukachin* of Persia. The Christian expresses concern because he has been sent by his trading house, Polo Brothers and Son, of Venice, in hopes of selling a fleetload of goods. Marco Polo,* the head of the house had acted as Kukachin's escort during her journey from Cathay to Persia.

The three then begin to discuss the religious significance of the tree. The Buddhist declares it sacred to Buddha, the Christian to Jesus Christ, and the Magian to Zoroaster. They are about to do violence upon each other when a funeral wagon enters drawn by thirty men of different ages, all chained and lashed, led along by two files of soldiers under the command of a Captain and Corporal. They, too, welcome the shade and announce that the tree is sacred to Mahomet. The Captain speaks to the three merchants and tells them that this is the coffin of Princess Kukachin of Tartary, Queen of Persia. As they look upon her, her face lights up, music is heard, and she speaks! "Say this, I loved and died. Now I am love, and live. And living have forgotten. And loving, can forgive. Say this for me in Venice." The Christian realizes that this is her message for Marco Polo. The Captain of the wagon train is enraged, and discovering that three of his impressed men have died, he harnesses the three merchants along with the other men. When the Christian merchant protests that he has a letter of introduction to the queen, the dead Kukachin, the Captain tears it up and lashes his "beasts" on.

Act I, Scene i: Twenty-three years earlier, the outside of Donata's* home in Venice, in moonlight. "Marco Polo, a boy of fifteen, youthfully handsome and well made is standing in a gondola. . . a guitar over his shoulder." His love song is heard before he is seen, waiting for Donata to appear at her barred window. They speak of love but also of the financial advantages of their match. As Marco says, "It'll bring the two firms into closer contact." Marco must leave in the company of his father and uncle to gain experience in the family business. They will be gone for an indefinite time to make "millions" at the court of the Great Kaan. The young people swear to wait for each other, kiss, and depart, Donata giving Marco a locket containing her picture.

Act I, Scene ii: Six months later, "the interior of the Papal Legate's palace at Acre." A church bell is heard before the scene is revealed to find the Legate, Tedaldo,* age sixty, seated on a throne between a Knight-Crusader in full armor on his right and his adviser, a Dominican monk, on his left. Nicolo Polo* and Maffeo Polo* stand humbly before the throne. Nicolo, Marco's father, is "a small thin middle-aged man, with a dry, shrewd face." Maffeo is also middle-aged but "tall and stout with a round jovial face and small, cunning eyes." Marco is sitting on a stool trying very hard to compose a poem to Donata. The Polos are awaiting the announcement of the papal election by a conclave that has been in session for two years. They are trying to deliver a message to the new pope from the Great Kaan requesting that he send one hundred wise men to dispute religion with his Taoists, Buddhists, and Confucians to determine "which religion in the world is best." Tedaldo is bored with the Polos, who talk incessantly of the wealth of the Kaan. They then look at Marco in the throes of composition, teasing him for writing a love poem. When the Legate reads it, he notes that "your lady is a bit too mineral, your heaven of love a trifle monetary." In short, the poem, which begins, "You are as beautiful as the gold in the sun," indicates the materialism that Marco will embody throughout the play. Suddenly a sealed letter arrives to announce that Tedaldo has been elected pope. The new pope falls to his knees in prayer, but the Polos want to transact their business and be gone. They use Marco to interrupt the new pope's prayers in order to obtain a message for their client. Tedaldo, amused by the Polos' total commitment to business, says he will send a monk or two, "But if the monks fail, Master Marco can be my missionary. Let him set an example of virtuous Western manhood. . . . Mark my words, Marco will be worth a million wise men—in the cause of wisdom." As they leave, Marco picks up the poem which he had crumpled up when the Legate had told him he was no poet, stuffs it into his doublet, and leaves as church bells peal out to announce the new pope.

Act I, Scene iii: Dawn, in front of a Mahometan mosque, where a Muslim ruler sits, flanked, like the Legate, by a warrior on the right and a priest on the left. His wives crouch before him like slaves. Against the sides of the stage "forming a sort of semi-circle with the throne at its center are . . . a mother nursing a baby, two children playing a game, a young girl and a young man in a loving embrace, an aged couple, a coffin.'' These Mahometan figures do not move, except for their eyes which follow the action. The Polos are at center, and Marco is carrying what look like sample cases. Marco has been bilked in his purchase of a piece of Noah's ark, and the older men note his innocence. They read their travel notes from their last visit as the Ali brothers, Muslim businessmen (and their competition), enter. They start telling ethnic jokes as Marco speaks condescendingly to the motionless people around the edge of the action, all of whom rebuff him with their silence. He proceeds to the coffin and touches it in fascination, returning to the merchants who are laughing first at their own jokes and then at Marco's innocence in purchasing a piece of junk. The Prostitute appears and offers herself to Marco—free—but he refuses. Ali speaks of the birth of Christ and His status as prophet as a dervish whirls in, Maffeo notes that he would be a good investment as an exhibit, while Marco says he must write to Donata about this. The call to prayer is heard as the Polos remark that ''all Mahometans are crazy.''

Act I, Scene iv: Dawn reveals an Indian snake charmer with his snake coming out of the basket. The scene duplicates that of Scene iii, but the costumes and the locale are Indian. Behind the throne is an immense Buddha. The Polos are in the center, as in Scene iii, and Marco, less innocent now, is carrying the sample cases. He is astonished by the snake, but Maffeo tells him it is a fake because the snake has been defanged. This scene is a replay of the earlier one, including Marco's rebuff of the prostitute, but the religion is Buddhist and the older Buddhist Merchant tells the Buddhist tale of the incarnation of God. The older Polos announce that these people are ''all crazy, like the Mahometans.''

Act I, Scene v: The sound of a Tartar kettledrum is heard in the darkness, and a section of the Great Wall of China is revealed with a huge shut gate. It is just before sunset. A Mongol ruler sits on a throne, ''with warrior and sorcerer to right and left of him,'' and the same motionless figures, recostumed, sit around. Only a Minstrel in the center moves. The ruler and the court are richly dressed in furs, the figures in ''rough robes.'' The Polos stand in the center, looking travelworn, with ''Marco still lugging the battered sample cases.'' He is now eighteen, ''brash, self-confident . . . assertive and talky.'' This scene starts to replay the two preceding ones, but Marco now scarcely looks at the figures. Tartar merchants enter, and this time Marco tries his hand at telling ethnic traveling salesman jokes. As the older Polos tell him he's doing a poor job, the prostitute enters to ask if Marco will visit her again, but he complains that she has stolen his locket. She produces his poem to Donata, but when she asks if he had written it, he denies it. She accuses him of lying: ''Don't sell your soul for nothing. That's bad business.'' With that, she stamps the poem into the ground: ''Your soul, dead and buried!'' At Marco's threat she then returns Donata's portrait locket: ''I kissed it so you'd remember my kiss whenever you kiss her!'' Just as Marco is about to pursue her, the Tartars shout, the

Minstrel chants, and "they raise their hands and arms to the sky" and pray to their two gods of heaven and earth. Again the Polos dismiss this unfamiliar religion, and the gate of the wall opens revealing soldiers and a court messenger who is surprised not to see the hundred wise men from the pope. The monks have left the Polo party for home. The party is summoned to the court of Kublai Kaan.*

Act I, Scene vi: Music from Chinese and Tartar bands reaches a crescendo. The light rises to blinding intensity to reveal the throne room of the Great Kaan of Cathay in his city of Cambulac. He is sixty years old, his person showing both the conquering force of the Chinghiz dynasty and "the humanizing culture of the conquered Chinese who have already begun to absorb their conquerors." Below the throne are an armed Mongol Warrior on the right in full armor, and on the left "Chu-Yin,* the Cathayan sage and adviser to the Kaan, a venerable old man with white hair, dressed in a simple black robe." The Kaan's sons are close to the throne, and further away, nobles, wives of the Kaan, warriors, courtiers, poets, officers, and so forth stretch away into the distance. Marco is overwhelmed; he stands spellbound as his father and uncle advance and kneel to the Kaan, frantically signalling for him to do the same. An usher approaches and fiercely gestures to him to kneel, but Marco, misunderstanding, sits on his sample cases. As the Kaan asks where are the wise men to dispute the relative merits of the teachings of Lao Tsue, Confucius, Buddha, and Christ, he suddenly sees Marco and asks his identity. When ordered, Marco approaches the throne, with an attempted air of bold self-confidence, but finally he realizes he should kneel, and in answer to the Kaan's greeting, he delivers the pope's "message" concerning the hundred wise men: "He sent me in their place. He said I'd be worth a million wise men to you." Nicolo attempts to explain that the pope had meant that Marco "might set an example that would illustrate, better than wise words, the flesh and blood product of our Christian civilization."

The Kaan tries to solve the riddle of the immortal soul, finding it hard to believe that Marco has one, but the young man, with primary certitude unsupported by evidence, asserts that he certainly does: "I'm a man made by Almighty God in His Own Image for His greater glory." At this the Kaan orders Marco trussed as a test and threatens to cut off his head, but the young man, with shaken bravado, suggests that then he might catch cold. The Kaan seizes on his fear and suggests that he is afraid to die because he knows that when he is dead he will not be better than a dead dog. Enraged, Marco calls the Kaan "a heathen liar," while his father and uncle moan in horror. The Kaan then releases him: "You cannot imagine your death. You are a born hero. I must keep you near me. You shall tell me about your soul and I will listen as to a hundred wise men from the West." Marco chaffers with the Kaan and asks how much the Kaan will pay him.

Maffeo requests permission to speak to the young man and advises him to ask for the post of second-class commission-agent, pointing out the economic advantages that could accrue from his position for the family firm. Marco asks what is in it for him, and his uncle hastily offers him a junior partnership, but Marco holds out for "a fair commission." He has learned his trade well. Marco is granted his request, but the Kaan is puzzled about him; he "touches me, as a child might, but at the same time there is something warped, deformed." Chu-Yin, the philosopher, advises that he should be allowed to "develop according to his own inclination" and given "opportunity for true growth if he so desires." Perhaps they will indeed learn from him. In granting the post to Marco, the Kaan tells him with some mockery that he will expect a report after each of his journeys, "all the observations and comments on your soul in the East." Like a true salesman Marco announces that the family business has just taken him into partnership and "any way we can serve your majesty—" The Kublai laughs, understanding what is going on, and as they are dismissed, Marco, with a curious assertion of equality, promises, "I will always serve your best interests, so help me God." He makes a grand exit, preceded by his frightened relatives, while Kublai laughs and Chu-Yin smiles.

Act II, Scene i: Fifteen years later in "the Little Throne Room of the summer palace of the Kaan at Xanadu," the retreat of a philosopher-king. It is a sunny morning in late June. The Kaan is lying on cushions, with the detached, aloof air of a philosopher. He has aged, but his face has an expression "full of philosophic calm." Kukachin, his twenty-year-old daughter, is sitting before him with a grief-stricken air. As a flute player plays a sad melody, she sings a song of winter and parting. Her father inquires after the cause of her sadness and asks whether it is because she must become queen of Persia. Arghun* is a hero that any woman could love, but then he suggests that she is behaving like any woman who has lost her lover. By this time she is weeping but recalls her duty as a princess, refusing to tell her father whether she has fallen in love.

At this moment Chu-Yin arrives to announce the unexpected arrival of Marco Polo, mayor of Yan Chau, who is making an unauthorized visit "in state." Chu-Yin suggests ironically that Marco is coming with a new account of his exploits, which so far seem to have involved the repression of beauty and joy. The Kaan, with irritation, says that Marco is no longer amusing to him as a jester. "He has not even a mortal soul, he has only an acquisitive instinct. . . . He is only a shrewd and crafty greed. I shall send him home to his native wallow." Suddenly Kukachin defends him, claiming that he has always succeeded in his assigned tasks, but he is not understood "because he is so different from other men." She also is quite certain that he has a soul. In this defense she has revealed her secret love; the Kaan tells her she must leave for Persia in ten days.

After she retires the two old men discuss the situation. Chu-Yin says that he has long known of her love and thinks it will be a "poignant memory to recompense her when . . . she is merely a Queen." Perhaps, too, Marco may someday "see into her eyes and his soul may be born." He sees Marco as an interesting case study, and he speaks of the way Kukachin sees him as a hero because of his "exotic" origin and his habit of bringing her "a humble, touching little gift" each time he returns. But the real Marco, ruling in Yan Chau, is different, as becomes obvious when Marco returns, dressed in the garish regalia of an order of his own invention, "the Mystic Knights of Confucius," of which he is the chief. Marco's manner and appearance are those of "a successful movie star at a masquerade ball, disguised so that no one will fail to recognize him." He is a trifle taken aback by the Kaan's stern manner but confidently announces that he has come to inform the ruler of the methods he has used to sweat out an unprecedented amount of taxes. Suddenly he sees the princess Kukachin, compliments her (as one not really knowing his place), and presents her with a gift, a small chow puppy.

Then, returning to business, Marco announces that he has hit upon an extraordinary system: he has repealed the tax on excess profits and replaced it with a "democratic" one on the necessities of life so that everyone from beggar to banker must pay. It quickly becomes clear that Marco is acting like a Fascist or Nazi (though Nazism was not in power when O'Neill was writing). He has abolished the right of free speech, repressed ancient culture, and imprisoned all those who are not "happy." A half-a-million citizens have already complained to the Kaan, but Marco writes them off as a "minority of malcontents." He has also installed a bureaucracy to govern, he has invented paper money, and last, he has invented the cannon as a means of speedily reducing cities to compel them to make peace. He gives a quick cost-plus analysis of the advantages of this lethal weapon over conventional methods of warfare (in an argument that sounds chillingly like that used later to justify nuclear warfare). He quite frankly says, "you can't consider souls when you're dealing with soldiers, can you?" With this invention the Kaan can conquer the world, to "become the bringer of peace on earth and good-will to men." Marco's price for this invention, the lowest possible, concomitant with the costs involved, is a million yen, in gold "if you don't mind." But he goes on in the manner of an international arms salesman: if the Kaan is not interested, he can easily find a market elsewhere. The Kaan grimly replies, "Oh, I quite realize that in self-protection I've got to buy them—or kill you!" Marco then requests permission for himself and his family to return to Venice, and when the Kaan asks what he will tell the pope about the attempt to convert him, Marco says that the Kaan will surely be converted to Christianity on his "death-bed, if not before—a man of your common sense."

With great irony, the Kaan says that Marco still has not proved that he has an immortal soul, and when Marco sticks with his primary certitude, "It doesn't need proving," the Kaan asks for an unprejudiced witness. Kukachin steps forward to verify the existence of Marco's soul, then asks that he be captain of the fleet that will take her to Persia. Kublai agrees to let the Polos return with Kukachin's fleet. The princess is overjoyed and speaks of the entertainments there will be on the ship, while Marco speaks with great practicality of the dullness of shipboard life: "I hate idleness where there's nothing to occupy your mind but thinking"; he enjoys "overcoming obstacles, getting things done." Then when Kukachin speaks of taking poets with her, Marco tells a joke on himself—that he had once written a poem of which he can remember only the first line, which is indeed prophetic: "You are as lovely as the gold in the sun."

Act II, Scene ii: The port of Zayton, the wharves of the imperial fleet, several weeks later. Slaves are loading the junk to a four-beat drum rhythm which sounds like a machine. They move like a bucket dredge and are treated with less respect. Marco later says that only six slaves had been killed in meeting the loading deadline—an acceptable figure. As the light increases, Kublai Kaan and Kukachin are seen. The Kaan looks at his weeping daughter and offers to break the contract with Arghun, "Let it mean war!" But Kukachin tells him that she wishes to take this voyage and with Marco Polo as captain: "I desire a captain of my ship on a long voyage in dangerous, enchanted seas." The Great Kaan threatens to kill Marco, but Chu-Yin's voice is heard from below preaching resignation. Then, teasingly, the Kaan charges his daughter to tell him when she reaches Persia "particularly what his immortal soul is like." With a broken-hearted wish, "May you know happiness," he leaves her. He tells her to "live," to which Kukachin adds "and love." Chu-Yin also bids her farewell, preaching a pessimistic resignation: "Life is perhaps best regarded as a bad dream between two awakenings, and every day is a life in miniature."

At this moment Marco arrives, dressed in a gorgeous uniform, to take over the operations. He tells Chu-Yin that he takes very seriously his responsibility of looking after the princess even more than if she were worth a million yen in spices. Chu-Yin charges him with what he claims are "secret last instructions" from the Kaan: "You are at some time every day of the voyage, to look carefully into the Princess's eyes and note what you see there." With total obtuseness Marco understands this as meaning to look after the princess's health. He says he looks forward to a bonus from the king of Persia if he delivers the princess safely and praises his own trustworthiness because he is on his way home to marry "the best little girl in the world." Donata, he is confident, is waiting for him. He speaks disparagingly to Chu-Yin about the harem system, commenting that one woman "at a time is trouble enough." Then, looking at the crowd coming to bid farewell to the princess, he attributes it to his own foresight in providing a band. The crowd bids her a sad, whispered farewell, and Kukachin recites a farewell poem. Marco, moved in spite of himself, notes the emotional effect of poetry upon him; then he respectfully orders the princess inside, professing care for her health, something that pleases Kukachin who misreads the motivation for his concern. He tells Chu-Yin that he has always respected her because she is not haughty, and therefore he would do anything for her—even if she were not a princess. Chu-Yin wonders whether "there may be hope—after all," but again Marco fails to understand. When the philosopher calls him "Enigma," he counters with "Take a fool's advice and don't think so much or you'll get old before your time." Then as he orders the band to play, he calls out after the old adviser that Kaan should write to him in Venice if he wants anything [and in words that have an eerie resemblance to Arthur Miller's later

Willy Loman in *Death of a Salesman*]: "they all know me there—and if they don't, by God, they're going to."

Act II, Scene iii: "Poop deck of the royal junk of the Princess Kukachin at anchor in the harbor of Hormuz, Persia—a moonlight night some two years later." Kukachin is seated on a silver throne "dressed in a gorgeous robe of ceremony." She is even more beautiful in the manner "of a woman who has known real sorrow and suffering." The sailors are working with machinelike precision as Marco barks out orders. The two older Polos are counting the contents of two bags of money and packing them into a chest. They now have almost a million "in our money." As they count, the Boatswain chants the poetic tale of the journey, answered by a chorus of sailors and women, with Kukachin providing a counterpoint: "When love is not loved it loves Death." As she sings, she speaks of three occasions on which she wished for death, and when Marco comes, he speaks specifically of those occasions: her being swept overboard, the coming of pirates, and her fever. For him they are moments in which his valor and practicality defeated death, and as a result he hopes for a large bonus from Arghun. The more they talk of these deeds, the more hysterical Kukachin becomes, which Marco sees as symptomatic and insists on looking at her tongue, treating her like a patient.

Arghun is dead, and Ghazan Khan, his son, plans to marry the princess. In these last moments together, she clearly wishes to bring Marco to a recognition of her love for him, but he is impervious. She begs him one last time to look into her eyes and say what he sees there. As he does so "Her lips part, her whole being strains out to him. He looks for a moment critically, then he grows tense, his face moves hypnotically toward hers, their lips seem about to meet in a kiss," and they say each other's names with passion—but at that moment, Maffeo reaches the count of "one million" and Marco comes to himself with a start. Despairingly, the princess again says his name, and Marco says that he had noted something disturbing in her eyes, "It made me feel feverish too," suggesting that she should go to sleep. She draws a small dagger to kill herself, but Marco (still obtuse) disarms her. Then when she says, "I implored an ox to see my soul! I no longer can endure the shame of living," he thinks she is insulted because he had presumed to call her by name. In hasty explanation he tells her that he had forgotten who she was; he had seen her as Donata who is waiting for him and shows her the miniature. In reply to Kukachin's comment that she may have married another, Marco confidently notes the economic basis of the match: "Her family needs an alliance with our house." And as for physical attraction and brains, well, Marco really wants a well-run establishment with "sound common sense," and "who needs a great thinker around the house?" With hatred and disdain, Kukachin calls him a "Pig of a Christian" and suggests that she should ask Ghazan Khan to have him flayed—at which remark the older Polos cringe for mercy.

With a song of resignation, Kukachin awaits the arrival of Ghazan Khan, the young man who will marry her. He is "fascinated by her beauty. She looks back at him with calm indifference." He speaks lyrically to her, saying that she will be for him "Queen of Love," at which Kukachin calls out "No!" and drops Donata's locket to the floor, grinding it underfoot. As Marco tries to intervene she kicks it away for him to scramble after. While he puts the pieces in his handkerchief, she asks Ghazan Khan to arrange a suitably vulgar feast for Marco: "He is an exquisite judge of quantity. Let him be urged to eat and drink until he can hold no more, until he becomes his own ideal figure, an idol of stuffed self-satisfaction!" Then she looks on the magnificent "Order of the Lion which only great heroes and kings may wear" on Ghazan's breast and asks for it. "With bitter mockery she pins it on Marco: "How well it is set off on the bosom of a sheep." She calls for a chest of gold and flings handfuls of coins at the Polos. The older men scramble for them, but Marco is insulted. Ghazan senses that something is wrong and asks if he should kill Marco, but the princess says no, asking permission to remain on board overnight. The two older Polos leave with their pockets and chests filled with gold as Marco bids farewell to Ghazan with a medical explanation for the princess's behavior. While the women sing a song of sadness, Kukachin, "in a voice which is a final, complete renunciation," calls out a farewell. Marco, "cheery and relieved," offers Ghazan Khan a perfunctory wish for happiness as the princess sinks to her knees, hiding her face in her arms.

Act III, Scene i: One year later in "the Grand Throne Room of the Imperial palace at Cambaluc." Kublai Kaan, "aged and sad," is listening to his commander-in-chief on his right hand, while Chu-Yin on his left reads. Behind General Bayan* are "a multitude of young staff officers, all gorgeously uniformed and armored." Music and laughter come from the ballroom. The general wishes to invade the West, using the "engine to batter down walls" invented by Polo. It is better to make a preemptive strike now before the enemy has similar weapons: "And it would be a righteous war! We would tear down their Christian idols and set up the image of the Buddha!" The Kaan ironically notes that Buddha is "the Prince of Peace," and the general recalls his other names: "The Gentle One, The Good, The Kind, The Pitiful, The Merciful, The Wise, The Eternal Contemplative One!...Death to those who deny Him!" And the word "death" is echoed by those present. Kublai, ever the philosopher, waits for a thunderbolt from God, and when it does not appear he remarks that "then there is no God!" He will allow war, but not with the West. He suggests that his soldiers make war for economic reasons on "a group of islands whose silk industry is beginning to threaten the supremacy of our own" (Japan, of course), and rather than a war with high-sounding slogans, he would prefer them to wage "a practical war of few words." General Bayan leaps at the chance and in reply to the joyful cry, "Down with the West," with which the assemblage greets the announcement of war, he proclaims, "Down with Japan," the new enemy. Instantly he "harangues them with the air of a patriotic exhorter" listing the "outrages" committed against the people of the Kaan, particularly the "breeding and maintaining silkworms for the purposes of aggression." Kublai notes, "War without rhetoric, please! Polo has infected you with cant! The West already invades us!''

At this moment a Courier from Persia enters, bearing a letter from Kukachin. In it she says she wishes only for death, commends the ''unremitting attention to duty'' and valor of Marco Polo, and asks the Kaan to send him another million. ''You were right about his soul. What I had mistaken for one I discovered to be a fat woman with a patient virtue'' whom Marco will by now have married. The Courier then delivers a further message, this time a memorized one from Marco Polo recounting his services, and in particular he reports that he saw in the princess's eyes no ''unnatural change'' until the last day when he ''noticed a rather strained expression . . . fever due to her Highness's spleen being sluggish after the long confinement in shipboard.'' The Kaan, almost mad with rage, threatens to destroy the entire West, leading his armies himself, and to tear Marco limb from limb. Chu-Yin dissuades him, and Kublai Kaan calls for his crystal ball.

The light goes up on the backstage, and a garishly set banquet table is revealed. It is Venice, and the procession of guests marvels at the gold plate and discusses the return of the Polos and also the now fat and somewhat bovine Donata, who has waited twenty years. She and her crafty, wizened father now enter. Actually, no one is quite sure whether these returned travelers are really the Polos—they look ''like greasy Tartars.'' Musicians play, ranks of servants bring in costly food and wines, piling them on the table to the astonishment of all. Then the Polos enter, lavishly dressed in crimson satin. They remove their outer robes and give them to the servants, revealing even more gorgeous robes underneath. These they give to the musicians and appear in their Tartar robes whose sleeves they slit, and to the accompaniment of a blare of music they pour out a profusion of precious stones. Marco and Donata embrace, with Marco claiming that the damage to her locket was caused by an encounter with pirates. They kiss and Marco announces himself worth two millions. Donata inquires about the one or two women he had mentioned, but Marco reassures her, ''I tell you I wouldn't have married the prettiest girl in Cathay.'' With this she agrees to marry him, and her father announces the betrothal. All then sit down to eat, and as they sit down their faces disappear behind the mountains of food on the table. Marco is asked for a speech. He ''begins with dramatic feeling'' but then launches ''into a memorized speech in the grand Chamber of Commerce style'' on the nature of the silk industry and the breeding of silkworms. The guests start to eat, but Marco continues to talk. One word only can be distinguished—''millions.'' Kublai Kaan offers an ironic comment on the proceedings: ''The Word became their flesh, they say. Now all is flesh! And can their flesh become the Word again?''

Act III, Scene ii: The throne room at Cambaluc about two years later. Kublai Kaan sits on his throne looking like an idol. He wears a simple, unornamented white robe and gazes sadly upon a catafalque draped in heavy white silk before him. Chu-Yin stands to his left, and as they look, the Kaan signals and general mourning commences. A funeral procession then enters with the bier and four priests, one at each corner: Confucian, Taoist, Buddhist, and Moslem. Each bows his head and reads from his holy book. The bier is raised to the catafalque, and incense is swung. The music ceases and silence falls. Each of the four priests speaks of coming to terms with death according to his own religion, and all come to the same resigned conclusion: "Death is." Kublai delivers a tender elegy to the beautiful princess, who looks like a glorious statue, until his voice breaks and he pulls himself together contemptuously—"No more! That is for poets! I am the Great Kaan!" With that the Chorus starts a discordant paean of praise which Kublai silences, commanding all to pray. He also sinks to his knees, leading a prayer.

The Chronicler and the Chorus then sing of the shortness of life, and finally the Kaan and Chu-Yin are left alone. The monarch asks if he had prayed well, and the philosopher says that he has made a statement of his own limited wisdom, and within the limitations it was "the truth of power. It was the truth." Bitterly, Kublai says, "She died for love of a fool!" The philosopher disagrees: "No. She loved love. She died for beauty." But then personal grief overtakes the Kaan, and Chu-Yin leaves him, for philosophy has no place there. The old man approaches the bier saying, "Weep for me, Kukachin! Weep for the dead!...I bid you welcome home, Little Flower! I bid you welcome home!" At this point the play in effect comes full circle. In the Prologue, Kukachin had forgiven Marco Polo because now she has passed beyond pain into love; indeed she *is* love and therefore she can forgive. Here Kublai has gone beyond power, beyond revenge, finding the ultimate reality in human relations, in human affections, in love. But yet, ironically, the play represents the triumph of the Marco Polos of the world and the defeat of the Kublai Kaans.

Epilogue: The lights go up in the theatre. A man seated in a front-row aisle seat hides a yawn, stretches his legs, and walks out with everyone else. He is dressed as a Venetian merchant of the late thirteenth century. It is Marco Polo himself, slightly puzzled and quite irritated, who mingles with the audience as it leaves the theatre. He seems quite unaware of the stir he is causing. He stands outside, recalled to reality, impatiently awaiting the arrival of his luxurious limousine which finally pulls up and carries him away to resume his life.

Comments: This play bears a resemblance to *The Fountain** in its use of history for criticism of society, and it is noteworthy that in each case O'Neill has used explorers as his material. Both plays also try to combine practical language and lyricism to express truths of human existence; and both plays fail in terms of the poetic language, which is pretentious and imprecise. *Marco Millions* is also extraordinarily expensive to stage because of the large cast and the multitudinous scenic effects which are required. As a result, though written 1923–1925, it did not achieve production until 1928, and then only after it had been turned down by David Belasco and then by the Theatre Guild* in its original six-hour, two-play format. What was finally produced was a shortened version which O'Neill did in 1927. Reviews were generally friendly, though the structure of the play was criticized.

The play is, of course, an indictment of the materialism of American society, particularly that of the American businessman immortalized by Sinclair Lewis in *Babbitt*. Marco is the quintessential successful salesman, Rotarian, and Lion; it is most fitting that the princess awards him the Order of the Lion. Marco thinks only in terms of money, profit and loss, bonuses, and economic gain—even where marriage is concerned. He is practicality personified, without emotion and without morality, as is indicated by his sales presentation for that new invention, the cannon. His capitalism is also a kind of Fascism, or even Nazism, in its oppression of the poor, suppression of free expression, and imprisonment of those perceived as malcontents. As an arms salesman, Marco also uses arguments which have later become very familiar as the doctrine of the preemptive nuclear strike.

Curiously, the crass Babbittry of Marco, though still existing in modern American society, has become less specifically relevant today than the arguments for and against war which are presented in this play. Once the Kaan's general possesses the ultimate weapon, the cannon, he is eager to use it to wage "a just war." The Kaan, however, as a philosopher, perceives the essential fraudulence of this argument as a means of forcing others to accept a prince of peace. In this argument O'Neill returns to the cross and the sword motivations he had used in *The Fountain*. The Kaan throws his general a sop in suggesting that he attack Japan instead for economic reasons, probably the only "honest" reason for war.

Other themes also are treated again, notably the viability of Christianity, which O'Neill here sees as infinitely inferior to the philosophical cast of the Eastern Religions. The notion of the oneness of all religions shown in *The Fountain* is gone here because Christianity has been perverted to serve the ends of acquisitiveness, injustice, exploitation, and destruction. The Christians are shown as those "whose God is their Belly," according to Saint Paul, and hence O'Neill's treatment of the famous recognition scene in the Marco Polo saga becomes a vulgar, gluttonous feast in honor of "self-satisfaction" as well as a parody of the testimonial, or Chamber of Commerce, dinner which is still commonly seen.

Last, O'Neill treats the theme of love. Kukachin, the princess, is the romantic heroine who loves blindly, totally, and forever, dying when she discovers the truth about Marco. Donata, on the other hand, may once have loved with emotion; but she has waited for economic reasons, and it is significant that she nearly swoons, not when she realizes that Marco has returned but when she sees the riches of which she will be mistress. Once again, O'Neill is also striving to comment on the central mystery of life, as in *The Fountain*, but Marco is too blind to be enlightened and too selfish to love (unlike Juan Ponce de Leon*) and thus achieves no vision of any after-life. He speaks of the words of Tedaldo, "rather too mineral." Overall, the work remains topical, and it is also a good parody of much of American society; but prohibitive production costs and somewhat dated theatrical devices make its revival difficult. One interesting piece of structure is the inclusion of Marco Polo "himself" within the audience. This is an unusual attempt to transcend the proscenium arch and bring audience and action together as one. Marco Polo, in his attitude toward the play he has just seen, thus becomes one with the audience—itself a bunch of Babbitts—bored with much of the message of the play, willing to be entertained, but not at all desirous of thinking about what it has seen, impatiently eager to return to daily living and its pragmatic decisions. The play is thus a sad commentary on modern society in that the Marcos live on and the Kublai Kaans are defeated.

Production Data: Written 1923–1925. Produced by the Theatre Guild* at the Guild Theatre, New York City, January 9, 1928 (102 performances).

Note: For reasons of expense the silent figures of Scenes iii-iv-v were omitted in this production, which detracted from the force of the play.

Director: Rouben Mamoulian

Design: Lee Simonson

Cast: Partial list

    Christians

    Traveler: Philip Leigh

    Marco Polo: Alfred Lunt*

    Donata Loredano: Natalie Browning

    Nicolo Polo: Henry Travers

    Maffeo Polo: Ernest Cossart

    Tedaldo: Morris Carnovsky

    Dominican Monk: Albert Van Dekker

    Knight-Crusader: George Cotton

    Papal Courier: Sanford Meisner

    Paulo Loredano, father of Donata: Philip Leigh

    Heathens

    Magian Traveler: Mark Schweid

    Buddhist Traveler: Charles Romano

    Mahometan Corporal: Albert Van Dekker

    Mahometan: Robert Barrata

    Older Ali Brother: H. H. McCollum

    Second Ali Brother: Mark Schweid

    Prostitute: Mary Blair*

    Dervish: John Henry

    Indian Snake Charmer: John Henry

    Mongol Priest: Philip Leigh

    Emissary from Kublai: Albert Van Dekker

    Kublai Kaan: Baliol Holloway

    Kukachin: Margalo Gillmore

    Chu-Yin: Dudley Digges*

    General Bayan: Robert Barrata

    Messenger from Persia: Charles Romano

    Boatswain: H. H. McCollum

    Ghazan: Morris Carnovsky

Buddhist Priest: Charles Romano
Taoist Priest: Unknown
Confucian Priest: Mark Schweid
Moslem Priest: H. H. McCollum
Tartar Chronicler: Philip Leigh

Revived March 3, 1930, at the Liberty Theatre, New York City (8 performances).
Revived February 20, 1964, at the ANTA Washington Square Theatre, New York City (49 performances).
[*See also* Appendix B for incidental music.]

MARGARET. In *Days Without End*,* the middle-aged kindly Irish maid of Elsa Loving.*

MARGIE. In *The Iceman Cometh*,* a dollar street walker just over twenty years old. She and Pearl* are whores, roomers at Harry Hope's* saloon, and are run by Rocky Pioggi.* They both have the remains of youthful freshness. "Margie has brown hair and hazel eyes, a slum New Yorker of mixed blood," and is "sentimental, feather-brained, giggly, lazy, good-natured and reasonably contented with life." Her pipe dream is that she is a "tart," not a whore, and her attitude toward Rocky, who insists that he is a bartender, not a pimp, is that of a sister "toward a bullying brother." Under the influence of Theodore Hickman,* the salesman who comes to the bar annually to celebrate Harry's birthday, the girls finally admit that they are whores, go on strike, and take the day off to visit Coney Island. After Hickey's arrest on the charge of murdering his wife, they, along with other denizens of the bar, seize on his plea of insanity, a pipe-dream explanation which discredits what he has taught them, and gladly get drunk in order to forget the outside world and to regain illusions.

MARSDEN, Charles. In *Strange Interlude*,* friend of Professor Leeds,* confidant and later husband-to-be of Nina Leeds.* He remains important throughout the twenty-five year span of the play. At first he is thirty-five, tall, thin, meticulously tailored, somewhat dreamy, "always ready to listen, eager to sympathize, to like and be liked." He is also hopelessly tied to his mother, and is devastated by her death (between Acts IV and V). He then brings his sister, Jane, to live with him and look after him. When she dies, he waits for Nina Leeds. According to Ned Darrell,* he writes novels of manners which display very little insight into human behavior.

Charles loves Nina Leeds in an asexual way and manages to make himself an indispensable, dependable friend in all crises. He perceives Darrell as a rival for Nina's affections and suspects the truth about him and Nina: that young Gordon Evans* is Darrell's child, not that of Sam Evans,* her husband. He also understands that Nina has never outgrown her love for Gordon Shaw,* but he is able to understand that and forgive her almost anything. At the end of the play, "dear old Charlie" has managed to survive and outlast all the other char-

acters in the play, one way or another knowing everything and forgiving everything. He is about to marry Nina to offer a relationship that is really that of
father and daughter; at age sixty, he is fifteen years older than she, and like her,
he wishes for peace, "all passion spent." Only once does he lose his self-
control, in Act VIII when Gordon Evans is trailing in his last crew race: then,
momentarily, he wants Gordon to lose, feeling himself threatened by the young
man's aggressive masculinity. Charles and Nina plan to return to her childhood
home where they will live out their last years together. The action of the play
and their lives have come full circle, and their past passions are a "strange
interlude."

MARTHA. In *Lazarus Laughed*,* the sister of Lazarus* and Mary.* Martha is
a typical buxom, middle-aged housewife, among the first to accept Jesus. She
dies in the course of a conflict between a combination of Orthodox and Nazarene
Jews united against Lazarus's followers. Members of all groups are destroyed
by the Roman legionaries. Martha is among the first martyrs to Lazarus's cause.

MARY. In *Lazarus Laughed*,* the pretty, young, nervous, and high-strung sister
of Lazarus* and Martha.* Mary is among the first who accept Jesus and is
devastated by the news of his death. She herself dies in the course of a conflict
between a combination of Nazarene and Orthodox Jews, united against Lazarus's
followers as the common enemy. Members of all groups are destroyed by the
Roman legionaries. Mary is among the first martyrs to Lazarus's cause.

MARY ALLEN. The name of the schooner in *Where the Cross Is Made*,* lost
in the search for buried treasure.

MASON. In *Warnings** first officer of the S.S. *Empress*. He is "a tall, clean-
shaven, middle-aged man in uniform." He looks scornfully at James Knapp*
when he discovers Knapp's responsibility for the loss of the vessel.

MAX. In *The Moon of the Caribbees*,* a Swedish fireman on the S.S. *Glencairn*.

MAYO, Andrew. In *Beyond The Horizon*,* the older brother of Robert Mayo.*
Andrew is twenty-seven, is "husky, sun-bronzed," handsome, and manly, "a
son of the soil, intelligent in a shrewd way, but with nothing of the intellectual
about him." At first "he wears overalls, leather boots," open-necked gray flannel
shirt, and "a soft, mud-stained hat pushed back on his head." He is a born
farmer, and his father, James Mayo,* looks forward to his marrying Ruth Atkins*
and joining the Mayo farm with hers to make a better holding. Andrew is in
love with Ruth but has not asked her to marry him, when the play opens. Ruth,
however, loves the more delicate, romantic younger brother, Robert Mayo. On
the eve of Robert's departure for a three-year voyage on the *Sunda* under the
tutelage of his uncle, Captain Dick Scott,* Robert and Ruth declare their love

for each other, and Robert decides to remain at home to marry Ruth. Deeply hurt by the situation, and knowing that he will be unable to observe their happiness without pain, Andrew decides to accompany his uncle on the *Sunda*. James Mayo is enraged by what he sees as disloyalty, and Andrew lies by claiming that he never wanted to stay on the farm. This alienates further his father, who orders him out of the house and refuses to forgive him.

Andrew stays away for three years, during which James Mayo dies, still unforgiving, and Robert through his incompetence allows the farm to fall apart. On Andrew's return, Ruth has told Robert that she had early discovered that she had always loved Andrew best and hopes that he will once again run the farm. Andrew, however, has now changed. His "easy-going good nature" has been replaced by an air of authority, "a breezy briskness of voice and gesture." As he tells both Ruth and Robert, he has totally recovered from his heartbreak. Having seen the exotic East, he now wants to go to Buenos Aires and go into business. The romance of travel has left him untouched, but he has become too restless to remain on the farm, and he takes off very quickly, after offering his brother some money to help pay off his debts. Robert, however, refuses the offer.

Five years later Andrew returns in response to a collect telegram sent by Ruth, bringing a specialist to examine Robert, who is dying of tuberculosis. Andrew has not made his fortune; in fact, he has lost almost everything by speculating in grain. He, the born cultivator, the natural farmer, has deliberately turned aside from the work he was most suited for, and as a result he has failed. He discovers that Ruth had continued to love him and indeed had told Robert so just before his return to the farm five years earlier. Now the dying Robert, full of pity for Ruth, whose life he has ruined, asks Andrew to promise to marry her. Andrew, overwhelmed with the way Ruth has tortured Robert with the knowledge that she did not love him, turns on her with hatred, berating her for her cruelty and telling her that she must lie to Robert claiming that she has indeed loved him. Then when Robert dies, without her doing so, he blames her: "This is your doing, you damn woman, you coward, you murderess."

The change in Andrew is now almost total. In appearance he is expensively dressed, stouter, high-strung, decisive, yet anxious, and "his eyes are keener and more alert. There is a suggestion of ruthless cunning about them." He knows now that he is a failure; as Robert told him, "You're the deepest-dyed failure of the three, Andy. You've spent eight years running away from yourself. . . . You used to be a creator when you loved the farm. You and life were in harmonious partnership." After his first rush of anger is over, Andy remembers his promise to his dying brother, "I'll take care of her, I swear," and he asks Ruth's forgiveness, saying that the two of them "must try to help each other— and—in time—we'll come to know what's right." But Ruth seems unable to respond.

Andrew Mayo, like his beloved younger brother, is a failure because he has denied his true nature. In gambling with the things that he had once loved to create, he has been punished, and he must suffer in order to win them back. He is also the victim of Ruth, who forced him to turn aside from his dream.

MAYO, James, in *Beyond the Horizon*,* a sixty-five-year-old farmer, father of Andrew Mayo* and Robert Mayo.* James Mayo is, like Andrew, a true "son of the soil," with a short, square, white beard. He has worked all his life on the small Mayo property and has secretly hoped that Andrew will marry Ruth Atkins* and join that farm to his own. He is exceedingly happy that Andrew will take over after he is gone. Unfortunately, his plans are thwarted when Ruth and Robert—the romantic, poetic, younger son—decide to marry. Andrew, distressed at the thought of seeing their happiness, decides to take Robert's place on a scheduled three-year voyage on the sailing ship *Sunda* with his uncle, Captain Dick Scott.* James Mayo is furious and Andrew tries to lie to him, claiming that he is sick and tired of the farm. This sends James Mayo into a frenzy. He threatens Andrew and then orders him out of the house by morning, telling him never to return while he himself is living. In Andrew's absence he dies, still without forgiving his son. James sees all too clearly that Andrew is denying his own manifest destiny by leaving the farm on which he was born and which he was clearly born to nurture.

MAYO, Kate. In *Beyond the Horizon*,* the wife of James Mayo* and mother of Andrew Mayo* and Robert Mayo.* She is "a slight round-faced, rather prim-looking woman of fifty-five who had once been a school teacher." Years of hard work as "a farmer's wife have bent but not broken her." She is quite unlike her brother, Captain Dick Scott,* in her refined air, which she has passed on to her younger son, Robert, who is clearly her favorite. As the play opens, she is concerned over Robert's proposed voyage with Captain Scott on his sailing vessel, the *Sunda*. She is a peaceful woman and is most distressed when James Mayo disowns Andrew when the older son decides to take Robert's place on the voyage. She continues to live on the farm with Robert and his wife, Ruth Atkins,* and Ruth's crippled mother. After the death of her unforgiving husband, James, and the gradual decline of the farm, she collapses psychologically. She seems to lose all willpower and acquiesces in disaster as her once-neat home disintegrates into squalor and the farm itself is mortgaged. She disappears from the action after the third act and dies.

MAYO, Mary. In *Beyond the Horizon*,* the pretty, yet sickly, anemic-looking, two-year-old daughter of Ruth Atkins* Mayo and Robert Mayo.* Mary and her father have great affection for each other, though Ruth seems to regard the child as a nuisance. Mary's death between Acts II and III plunges Robert into a state of total despair.

MAYO, Robert. In *Beyond the Horizon*,* younger brother of Andrew Mayo,* son of James Mayo,* and Kate Mayo,* husband of Ruth Atkins,* and father of Mary Mayo.* Robert is twenty-three years old, a dreamer with "a touch of the poet" in his high forehead and wide, dark eyes, and the delicacy of his features.

He is first discovered reading "by the fading sunset light," looking out at the horizon. It is essential to note the importance of the horizon in the play, which opens with a sunset and ends with a sunrise. The Mayo farm is hemmed in by hills, and the horizon represents the limits of experience, while beyond it lie possibilities for fulfillment and escape for Robert. When he was a sickly child he would look through his window and imagine what was beyond the road "winding off into the distance, toward the hills, as if it, too, was searching for the sea." In these, the only happy moments of his life, he promised himself that he would someday undertake that same journey. He is about to translate that dream into reality by undertaking a three-year sea voyage on the sailing ship *Sunda*, captained by Captain Dick Scott,* a maternal uncle.

On this quiet evening, the night before Robert's departure, Robert and Andy discuss their different dreams. Andy sees contentment in the beauty of the farm, for he is a true son of the soil. The brothers do not speak of the hope of James Mayo that Andy will marry Ruth Atkins, the heiress to the adjoining property. Unbeknownst to each other, both young men are in love with her. This triangle is revealed on that same evening when Robert, after a lyrical explanation of his proposed search for beauty and adventure, suddenly reveals to Ruth that he must leave because of her and her relationship with Andy. To his amazement Ruth confesses that she had always loved Robert best, but had thought him more interested in books than in herself. They fall into each other's arms and Robert decides to forgo his dream.

This decision, and the marriage, are both disasters and bring about the ruin of both Andy and Robert. Andrew, unable to bear their happiness, undertakes the sea voyage, turning his back on his manifest destiny, the farm, which Robert, equally untrue to his destiny, must now look after. He, the romantic and poetic artist, is forced into the practical world for which he is totally unsuited. Another result is the permanent breach between Andrew and his father, who knows that the older son is throwing away everything he should live by. During the three years of Andy's absence the farm begins to fail, and Ruth and Robert decline into almost complete estrangement. He takes joy in their sickly child, Mary,* but all Ruth can live for is the return of Andy so that she can tell him of her love for him. But Andy too has changed. His heartbreak over, he now plans to go to Buenos Aires to make money and both Ruth and Robert remain trapped.

With the death of Mary Mayo, Robert falls into despair and contracts tuberculosis, while Ruth lives in a permanent state of inertia. The full ruin brought about by being untrue to one's destiny is only made clear when Andy returns, at Ruth's request, to aid his dying brother. If Robert has been a failure, so too has Andy, because he has gambled in agricultural products. The things he was born to create have become mere objects to him. Andy is enraged with Ruth and blames her for all the disasters that have befallen both brothers. Robert, however, retains sympathy and understanding; he knows that Ruth has suffered and asks Andrew to promise to marry her when he (Robert) is dead.

Robert finally does achieve his dream, but only in death. He dies by the side of the road of his dreams, watching for the sun to rise. He tells Andrew and Ruth not to grieve for him because now he is taking off for distant places. He is free of the farm, "free to wander on and on—eternally!" Through suffering he has won "the right of release."

In this character, O'Neill has shown another of the numerous artistic characters he drew in this period who allow themselves to be turned aside from their dreams by a woman. As in *Bread and Butter** and *Before Breakfast,** Robert marries a woman who is unable to sympathize with his dreams. He is forced to submit to her view of the world and her image of their life, with the result that he is destroyed. Here, however, O'Neill does not depict the victim as totally hostile to the woman who has destroyed him. Robert Mayo has some sympathy for Ruth, and he understands that she, too, is suffering the consequences of their mutual mistake. At the very end of his life, he begs Andrew to marry Ruth in the hope that together they may find some happiness. In this respect, the character of Robert is gentler than those of the earlier victims, but nonetheless, the theme recurs that an artist, or anyone else for that matter, must not turn aside from exercising what Milton called "That one talent, which is death to hide." Failure to follow the prescribed course leads to destruction. It is all too easy to claim that Ruth is totally to blame, and O'Neill in this play seems to give Robert some share of the responsibility. By the end of his life, Robert is in effect the nearest thing to a success in the play. He has learned through suffering, and he has discovered in his death the fulfillment of his dreams.

MAYO, Ruth. See Atkins, Ruth.

McCOMBER, David. In *Ah, Wilderness!** father of Muriel McComber,* the girlfriend of Richard Miller.* McComber is "a thin, dried-up little man" in his late fifties, with a "long solemn horse face . . . and a tiny slit of a mouth." He is the typical heavy father and descends censoriously on Nat Miller* on July 4 to complain about the obscene poems Richard is writing to Muriel, not realizing that they are quotations from Swinburne. Nat Miller angrily sends him away, refusing to run his advertisement in the Miller newspaper. McComber insists that Muriel write a letter of renunciation, which he delivers to Nat for Richard's perusal, and he punishes his daughter, insisting that Miller also punish his son. Finally he thinks better of his actions and apologizes to Nat.

McCOMBER, Muriel. In *Ah Wilderness!** daughter of David McComber.* She is between fifteen and sixteen, pretty in a plump way with a "graceful little figure, fluffy, light-brown hair, big naive wondering dark eyes, a round dimpled face, a melting drawly voice." She is in love with Richard Miller* and is overwhelmed with the poetry (copied from Swinburne and others) that he sends her. When she is forbidden by her father to see Richard, she manages to arrange a meeting, in which the two discuss their future. She wants him to go to Yale, even though Richard talks of getting married immediately. She is the younger equivalent of Essie Miller,* Richard's mother—loving, practical, not particularly bright, and romantic.

McGLOIN, Pat. In *The Iceman Cometh*,* a big, paunchy ex-police lieutenant dismissed from the force for graft. He is the friend of Ed Mosher,* the brother-in-law of the saloon proprietor, Harry Hope,* who allows them free drinks. McGloin rents a room from Harry, and his pipe dream is that he will get himself reinstated on the force—and look for more graft. Under the influence of Theodore Hickman,* the salesman who comes to the bar annually to celebrate Harry's birthday, McGloin attempts to translate the dream into reality, but he cannot go through with it. After Hickey's arrest on the charge of murdering his wife, McGloin and other denizens of the bar seize on his plea of insanity, a pipe-dream explanation which discredits what he has taught them, and they gladly get drunk to forget the outside world and to regain illusions.

MEDICINE MAN. In *The Fountain** an extraordinarily wizened old Indian. He attempts to outwit the Spaniards when they land in Florida by giving the impression that the Indians are worshipping the Spaniards' "totem pole," but in inadvertently allowing the cross to be reversed, he gives the impression that it is a Black Mass. He is killed by Quesada,* whom he in turn kills. Later he appears in the fountain as an image of paganism, one of the four great world religions: Buddhism, Islam, his own, and Christianity. He helps to indicate the essential unity of the religions of mankind.

MELODY, Cornelius. In *A Touch of the Poet*,* part of the abandoned cycle, "A Tale of Possessors, Self-Dispossessed," husband of Nora Melody* and father of Sara Melody.* He is forty-five years old, "tall, broad-shouldered, deep-chested, and powerful, with long, muscular arms, big feet, and large hairy hands." He still has an erect military bearing, and his peasant body shows few outward signs of his hard drinking. His face is still handsome, "the face of an embittered Byronic Hero, with a finely chiseled nose over a domineering, sensual mouth." His manner is that of a polished gentleman, but it is a role that he overplays slightly so that it seems less than genuine. He is the owner of a run-down tavern on what used to be a breakfast stop on the main stagecoach run to Boston, but when the route was changed the tavern declined.

Con Melody lives in a dream of his wrecked past and lost gentility, dressing in the slightly foppish manner of the English aristocracy at the beginning of the nineteenth century, the time of the Peninsular War (1808–1814). His father had been "a thievin' shebeen keeper" who had exploited the local tenantry and made sufficient money to buy Melody Castle in County Galway, Ireland, where he soon discovered that the possession of money did not lead to acceptance by the gentry. As a revenge he took pains to educate his son Con as a gentleman, sending him to school in Dublin with sufficient money to support his gentility. Like his father, young Melody discovered that his gentlemen friends were eager to exploit him for his money but unwilling to accept him socially. As a result of a snub, he fought his first duel, and from then on he seems to have adopted a truculent manner, which led to more such encounters. Joining the British Army, he became a major in His Majesty's Seventh Dragoons (one should remember that commissions were purchased in those days) and went to the Peninsular War where he distinguished himself for bravery at the Battle of Talavera (July 27, 1809). But his lawless ways proved his undoing. He had been accepted at the noble houses of Spain and Portugal, but he abused this hospitality and eventually fought a duel, killing a Spanish nobleman who had caught him making love to his wife. Because of his bravery, Melody was permitted to resign.

He returned to Melody Castle to his wife, Nora, and his baby daughter, Sara. Nora had been a peasant girl whom he had loved and who had loved him with reckless affection. He had made her pregnant and then married her but went off to Spain, leaving her to bear her child alone. Now Melody raised all the capital he could, sold the castle, and emigrated to the United States, where he bought the failing tavern in which the entire action of A Touch of the Poet takes place. Emigration, lack of business acumen, and hard drinking have ruined and soured the once-arrogant man, but he holds steadfastly to his past gentility by keeping a dainty, thoroughbred mare, even though his family lack the credit for food. He affects to despise all the local "Yankee" gentry and all the "shanty Irish" of the neighborhood, and he treats both his wife and daughter with contempt. He continually upbraids Nora for her slatternly ways and tells those who will listen that he was forced to marry her; she slaves for him and never sneers at his dreams, always remembering the "glory" of her love for him. Sara, however, is tougher than her mother and more ambitious, and she confronts her father with his cruelty to Nora.

The two important developments of the play concern Con and Sara. She falls in love with young Simon Harford* and eventually goes to bed with him, while Con Melody is forced to admit the emptiness of his dream. This comes about through his contact with the Harford clan. When Mrs. Deborah Harford* visits the tavern to see her son, Melody tries his old tactics of seduction on her; then when Nicholas Gadsby,* the Harford lawyer, tries to buy off the Melody family, Con and his former corporal, Jamie Cregan,* attempt to assault the Harford home, as a matter of "honor." As a result, they are beaten up in a drunken brawl, on the anniversary of the Battle of Talavera, July 27, 1828. O'Neill makes Melody's dream visually significant by having him dress in his old uniform to preside over an annual dinner commemorating this battle at which only Cregan and the local spongers are present. Melody also plays the role of Byronic hero, romantic, misunderstood, alone in a hostile world. His confrontation with the Harford servants destroys this saving lie, and Melody goes out and shoots his beloved mare with his dueling pistols, planning to kill himself as well but he realized as he held her dying head that he himself had already died, for without his dream he has become nothing. He therefore adopts a new role, resuming the Irish brogue he has formerly despised and acting like "a leering peasant lout." He claims that he will now start to run the tavern properly and not play the fine gentleman. He tells Nora that he loves her, leaving her in a state of ecstatic happiness; but Sara, who has always attacked his dream, now realizes that she, too, has partaken of it.

Cornelius Melody is the "poet" of the play, and in the Irish sense he is indeed a "faker" like the characters of Harry Hope's* saloon in *The Iceman Cometh.* Once again, O'Neill shows the importance of an illusion for the psyche of a weak and flawed character. He also shows the arrogance of matrimony in which the husband expects and gets total servitude from his wife, whom he blames for having ruined him. Here O'Neill repeats attitudes from earlier plays: *Servitude,* *Bread and Butter,* *Before Breakfast,* *Beyond the Horizon,* and *Welded,* to name a few. Melody was also meant to be a chapter in the history of the progress of the Irish in the United States. Though Con Melody has seen through his dream of gentility, he is still not a whole man because all he has done is adopt a new role, and one is left wondering what he will do when he tires of it.

MELODY, Nora. In *A Touch of the Poet,* part of the abandoned cycle, "A Tale of Possessors, Self-Dispossessed,"* wife of Cornelius Melody* and mother of Sara Melody. Nora is about forty years old but appears much older as a result of overwork. She is slovenly, looking like a sack tied in the middle, with down-at-the-heel men's shoes on her bare feet and hands crippled with rheumatism. However, she still possesses a curious sweetness, and her fine eyes indicate that in her youth she must have been quite beautiful. She speaks with a rich brogue. She was pregnant by Melody when he married her, something that he frequently throws up at her, claiming that his marriage to a peasant like her was a cause of his ruin. She is also rather guilt-ridden about this "sin," but she also re-members the glory of that time and throughout the play speaks of the "pride" of her love. She lives by love, and that love consists in total servitude to the wishes of her husband. Like Alice Roylston* in O'Neill's early play, *Servitude,* she sees herself as a willing slave to Cornelius Melody, even when he treats her with revulsion. All she wishes from him is an occasional word of love to remind her of their past passion.

She is prepared to go to any lengths to make Melody comfortable, always encouraging him in the pursuit of his dreams of the past when he was Major Melody of Melody Castle, scrimping so that he can keep his thoroughbred mare, staying away from church so as not to embarrass him, and arranging for his annual Talavera Day Dinner, even though they cannot afford it. She never sneers at Melody's dreams and is totally loyal to him. Once, in Act IV, she shows her understanding of the situation: "His pride, indade! What is it but a lie? What's in his veins, God pity him, but the blood of thievin' auld Ned Melody who kept a dirty shebeen?'' But then she instantly castigates herself for disloyalty. She realizes that Melody is selfish and uncaring but believes that ''for all his scorn, he knows my love is all he has in the world to comfort him.'' She defines love as ''It's when, if all the fires of hell was between you, you'd walk in them gladly to be with him, and sing with joy at your own burnin', if only his kiss was on your mouth.'' Without this pride in love, she knows that she is merely an old, sick woman, and therefore she keeps this flame alive. At first she is sure that Sara will find it impossible to love because she has too much pride to surrender everything, but by the end of the play the two women understand each other.

Nora Melody's character seems rather too good to be true, particularly in terms of modern feminist theory, but her attitude toward love and the duties of a wife is exactly the same as that articulated by O'Neill in *Servitude, Welded,** and *Days Without End.** In real life, too, O'Neill seems to have seen the matrimonial relationship as one in which the wife is totally subordinate to the husband, living through him, defining her existence in the same manner, dreaming his dreams, and protecting him from all anxiety. At the end of the play, when Con Melody is broken and playing his new role of peasant lout, Nora takes comfort in his expression of love for her.

MELODY, Sara. In *A Touch of the Poet,** part of the abandoned cycle, ''A Tale of Possessors, Self-Dispossessed,''* daughter of Cornelius Melody* and Nora Melody.* Sara is an ''exceedingly pretty'' twenty-year-old in the typical Irish way of black hair, blue eyes, fair skin, and rosy cheeks. Overall, her appearance represents a curious mingling of aristocratic and peasant characteristics. Her forehead is fine and her nose ''thin and straight''; her head is well shaped, her neck slender, and her ears small, but her mouth ''has a touch of coarseness and sensuality and her jaw is too heavy.'' Though her waist is slim, her figure is buxom and marred by ''large feet and broad, ugly hands with stubby fingers.'' She has a low musical voice which sounds at times too careful in its articulation, perhaps to hide her brogue. She hates her father for his feckless ways, his exploitation of both her and her mother, and his devotion to his memory of past gentility, symbolized by his keeping a thoroughbred mare and refusing to work in the tavern, even though they are desperately poor. But Sara inherits some of her father's pride, and while she thinks she hates his memories of the past, she discovers at the end of the play that she has also rather enjoyed them as giving her some kind of identity.

Sara falls in love with Simon Harford,* who has become ill while living an idealistic life close to nature in a log cabin at a nearby lake. She nurses him back to health and then meets Deborah Harford,* Simon's mother, who makes it quite clear that she disapproves of any marriage between her son and Sara. This rouses Sara's fury, as also does her father's departure for town to beat up the Harford family for their humiliation of him. That night she gives herself to Simon in an act of love, not rage. She is filled with the ''pride'' and ''glory'' of her love, as was her mother before her. She loves the dreaming poet and the idealist in Simon. Though the play ends with Cornelius Melody's defeat, it also ends with the triumph of Sara's love and her understanding of Nora's total renunciation of self in the love of her husband.

More Stately Mansions,* another play in the abandoned cycle, "A Tale of Possessors, Self-Dispossessed," picks up the tale of Simon and Sara (now husband and wife), along with Deborah, some four years later, with Sara pregnant with her fourth child. She has come to the old log cabin for the specific purpose of eavesdropping on Deborah and Simon. She overhears him laugh derisively at Deborah's curiously erotic fantasy of being a courtesan at the court of King Louis. She also discovers his unhappiness with his extraordinary economic success but his joy in her own happiness and also his insistence to Deborah that he has not abandoned his old idealistic dreams. The two say good-bye and Sara reveals herself to Deborah, warning her that she has been listening and that she will fight her for possession of Simon. The two women part as enemies. With the death of Deborah's husband, Simon takes over the failing family business, and Sara agrees to move in her family with Deborah. There Deborah becomes a doting grandmother and Sara a devoted wife, and the two women start to merge into the figure of Woman herself—predatory, yet also self-sufficient. They have both become Mother-wife and Wife-mother; with four sons they seem to consider Simon superfluous except as a means of economic support. Accordingly, Simon attempts to sort out his priorities of affection by defining the place of each; Deborah in her eccentric and symbolic garden, Sara as his wife-mistress and secret partner in his office.

As time passes, Sara's acquisitiveness and desire for upward mobility increase. She sells her body to Simon for interest in the company, but then she discovers that he has in effect made a whore out of her and that she now thinks of love as lust, rather than the glorious thing it was in *A Touch of the Poet*. Meanwhile, Simon is being torn apart psychologically because of the new conflicting forces in his mind, represented by each of the women; and having put them in an adversary situation, he wants them to fight to the death so that one alone will survive and his spirit can become whole. Otherwise, he must choose between them. The major action of the play is in the conflict between Sara and Deborah for total possession of Simon, which mirrors his psychic struggle. Deborah keeps him in her garden of dreams and childhood affection, while Sara must try to hold him with her body and her business acumen, which seems to be very similar to that of her late father-in-law—unscrupulous gambling. Deborah continually despises Sara because of her low origins, and the younger woman's limitations are symbolized by the garish couch in Simon's private office and the extravaganza of their country house based on a medieval castle that she designs and hopes to build as the fulfillment of her dream of opulence.

In the final act of the play, Sara has begun to realize that material success does not satisfy her—she thinks of retiring to the old farm rather than becoming a "Napoleon of industry." Her interview with Benjamin Tenard,* the banker, shows how low she has fallen morally. Now it is Simon who seems to be pushing her into more acquisitiveness, but she also discovers that she will have to fight her mother-in-law to the finish for possession of her own husband. Deborah has for some time been frightened of insanity, and Simon indirectly gives Sara permission to drive her even to that, in order to bring him peace. Sara, however, still possesses some pity and pulls Deborah away from opening the symbolic red door in her "Temple of Love," which is also the door in her mind which will lead her into madness. But when Simon appears and Sara realizes that he is begging his mother to take him with her into this "magic" land, Sara falls on her knees before Deborah, promising to go away and leave Simon entirely to her, as long as she stays on this side of the door. She will take her children away to leave him in peace with her. In her farewell speech she shows the ultimate renunciation of her pride: "God bless you, Simon, Darling, . . . and give you peace and happiness."

This action of total self-abnegation forces Deborah into a realization of what she must do, and proclaiming the superiority of her love over the love of "a low, lustful creature like you," she deliberately enters the summer house alone, pushing Simon down the steps. Sara is overcome with this renunciation, and in turn she sits over the unconscious Simon, who has fallen and hit his head, begging forgiveness for her "greed and my father's crazy dreams . . . in leading Simon away from himself until he lost his way and began destroying all that was best in him! To make me proud of him!" She now intends to devote her life to his service, setting him free to become the man she had once loved, "the dreamer with a touch of the poet in his soul, and the heart of a boy!" She will even smash the tottering company—but not before she arranges for the future support of Deborah and her son Joel.

Suddenly Deborah reappears, and Sara in fear asks her whether she is pretending insanity to set Simon free: "That would be too great a price—" But Deborah gives no sign that can be certainly interpreted, and Sara realizes that she will never know the truth of that renunciation as the older woman returns to the summer house and shuts the door. With Simon's recovery of his senses he calls for his mother, "Let us go. Peace and happiness," thinking that he is about to follow Deborah. But Sara helps him up, promising to bathe his hurt head, and when he again addresses her as mother, she promises, "Yes, I'll be your Mother, too, now, and your peace and happiness and all you'll ever need in life."

Sara thus becomes Woman unified in all her manifestations, more like Cybel* in *The Great God Brown*,* the earth-mother and the giver of comfort, than the fragmented, manipulative Nina Leeds* of *Strange Interlude*.* She has also learned the same lesson that Nora Melody had learned: that a man's dreams must be supported. Sara has attempted to pervert the true personality of Simon, but now, having discovered the aridity of her own greed, she will serve the artist-child-husband-lover in him. Once again, O'Neill has shown Woman as predatory, manipulative, devouring, and greedy in attempting to destroy the soul of man as artist. But he has also shown that his version of reconciliation is still that of Alice Roylston* in *Servitude*,* of Eleanor Cape* in *Welded*,* and Elsa Loving* in *Days Without End*.* Woman in her love must renounce herself and find herself through her husband. One is curiously reminded of Piccarda's statement in Dante's *Paradiso*: "la sua volontate è nostra pace"—In His will is our peace.

In the scenario, *The Calms of Capricorn*,* another section of the abandoned cycle, "A Tale of Possessors, Self-Dispossessed," Sara and her family have returned to the Melody farm. She is by now forty-seven; Simon has given up on his attempt to write his book on "The Meaning of Life"; and she still sees him as her lover, husband, and child, whom she serves. In the first act, he thanks her for all she has been to him, and after his death, Sara berates herself for having forced him to deny his "touch of the poet" and go into the family business, speaking once again of the glory of love that she had experienced. In the letter Simon leaves her, he begs her to seek freedom now that he is gone. Sara remains acquisitive, and her sons speak of her desire to hold onto land. However, she goes with them on the clipper ship *Dream of the West*,* from New York to Golden Gate in search of a new start and further profit.

She understands the differing personalities of her four sons, seeing Ethan Harford,* the eldest, as the poet, though Jonathan Harford,* her third son, has some poetry in him as well; Honey Harford,* the fourth son, seems able to comfort her, but Wolfe Harford,* the second son, deliberately denies all emotional commitment. Sara and Leda Cade*, a prostitute and fellow passenger, understand each other, because each is aware of the way in which a woman must operate in order to gain power for herself through the possession of the man whom she drives to success. However, Sara is also receptive to emotional commitment, hating the Harford concept of honor because it takes those she loves away from her. At the end of this scenario, she senses the moment that Ethan Harford and Nancy Drummond Payne* leap into the sea in expiation of their sins. Her comments in this work on the glory of love echo those of her mother, Nora Melody, in *A Touch of the Poet*, and some of the action is also reminiscent of that earlier play.

MENDOZA, Cristoval de. In *The Fountain*,* a swashbuckling young man. As the play progresses he remains exactly the same in his ambitious aims. He is the type of bold adventurer who went forth to conquer the New World for Spain and to line his own pockets as well. His only advance is in cruelty.

MENENDEZ, Diego. In *The Fountain*,* a political priest. He first appears in 1492 as a young fanatic who kills a Moorish minstrel because he has sung an infidel song. Twenty years later in Porto Rico, he is an oily, glib church politician who is now a bishop. He treats the Indians harshly because he wishes to plant the cross and obtain converts by use of the sword. He finds himself in opposition to Juan Ponce de Leon,* who treats the Indians with a little more wisdom because he has noted that enslavement makes inefficient servants for the glory of Spain.

Menendez wants to get Juan out of the way and manages to get him a patent to search for "Cathay." When Juan eventually leaves, Menendez rules but is killed in an Indian uprising. Politics and plotting are his major interest in life, and O'Neill uses him as an example of the nefariously motivated churchmen who went forth to convert the New World. He should be compared with Friar Quesada* as an example of the church militant.

MICKEY. In *All God's Chillun Got Wings*,* at first a young tough and later an even tougher prize fighter. He fathers Ella Downey's* illegitimate child. He is an exceptionally prejudiced young man who will surely come to a bad end.

MICKEY. In *Chris Christophersen*,* a forty-five-year-old monkeylike man, dressed in dungarees, a denizen of Johnny-the-Priest's* bar. He is an expository figure who tells of Chris's (*see* Christopherson, Christopher), past.

MILLER, Arthur. In *Ah, Wilderness!** son of Essie Miller* and Nat Miller*; brother of Mildred Miller,* Richard Miller,* and Tommy Miller.* Art is a nineteen-year-old Yale football player on vacation, "with a square, stolid face, small blue eyes and thick sandy hair." He is a very collegiate type and is in love with Elsie Rand, who never appears in the play. He is a stock figure of the college athlete and a young man given to singing very sentimental songs.

MILLER, Essie. In *Ah, Wilderness!** wife of Nat Miller* and mother of Arthur Miller,* Mildred Miller,* Richard Miller,* and Tommy Miller,* plus two other sons who do not appear; sister of Sid Davis* and sister-in-law of Lily Miller.* Essie is around fifty, stout, with graying light-brown hair. She "must have been decidedly pretty as a girl in a round-faced, cute, small-featured, wide-eyed fashion." Her eyes are large, soft, and brown, her manner bustling and maternal. Throughout the play she is eminently practical and not very well educated. She is appalled at the advanced and wicked reading that her son Richard is doing, and her distinctive characteristics are literality and maternal fussiness. She seems to live entirely for her family and is almost always sympathetic and understanding, though not above a little deception, as in her feeding her husband bluefish under another name because she knows that his allergy is nonexistent. She is also romantic and still in love with her husband after many years of marriage. O'Neill treats her with a tolerant humor, frequently making fun of her lack of information.

MILLER, Lily. In *Ah, Wilderness!** sister of Nat Miller,* permanently and hopelessly attracted to Sid Davis,* brother of Essie Miller.* Lily "is forty-two, tall, dark and thin" with glasses. She looks like the epitome of the dried-up, old-maid schoolteacher, but when she speaks her voice is "soft and full of sweetness." She broke off her engagement with Sid sixteen years earlier because of a drunken escapade involving prostitutes, though Sid swears his innocence.

She realizes that he is not good marriage material, and therefore she refuses his almost ritual proposals. However, she still has real affection for him and is enraged when the family seems to encourage him in his adolescent comic behavior. On one occasion, she does feel sorry for herself as an old maid sponging off her relatives, but she seems to have made a good accommodation to her situation by loving the Miller children and enjoying her work. She is quite well-read and is romantic enough to quote from the *Rubáiyát*.

MILLER, Mildred. In *Ah, Wilderness!** daughter of Essie Miller* and Nat Miller*; sister of Arthur Miller,* Richard Miller,* and Tommy Miller.* She is fifteen years old, so like her father that she is not at all pretty. She has large gray eyes, "vivacity and a fetching smile." Throughout the play she is rather giggly and juvenile, like Tommy, given to laughter in the wrong places and to teasing her lovesick brother, Richard. She does perform one useful function for Richard in bringing him a letter from Muriel McComber,* his girlfriend.

MILLER, Nat. In *Ah, Wilderness!*,* husband of Essie Miller*; father of Arthur Miller,* Mildred Miller,* Richard Miller,* and Tommy Miller,* plus two more sons who do not appear; also brother of Lily Miller.* He "is in his late fifties, a tall, dark, spare man, a little stoop-shouldered," almost bald, "dressed with an awkward attempt at respectability." He is the owner of the *Evening Globe* a newspaper in a "big small-town in Connecticut." He is decent, understanding, tolerant of his children's foibles, better read than his wife, whom he loves; he can relate to Richard's voyages of literary discovery and laugh at the spicy quotations his son sends to Muriel McComber.* He even sends David McComber* away and refuses his advertising because the man attacks Richard. However, he is a trifle concerned about Richard's relationship with Muriel, in case he does something "wrong." He delivers the stock sex-education speech of embarrassed parent to his son and is happy to hear that Richard has not begun such experimentation. He believes in education and sends his sons to Yale. He is also a romantic and can relate very well to the lovesick Richard and the moonlight. He is also tolerant of the behavior of Sid Davis,* his brother-in-law, and despite Sid's past history with the bottle, Nat plans to take him on as a reporter, if he stops "that nonsense." Nat Miller is portrayed with some sentimentality as a decent, hard-working husband and father, capable of getting mildly drunk, telling interminable personal tales, and of insisting on his foibles, such as his allergy to bluefish.

MILLER, Richard. In *Ah, Wilderness!*,* son of Essie Miller* and Nat Miller*; brother of Arthur Miller,* Mildred Miller,* and Tommy Miller*; in love with Muriel McComber.* He is widely believed to illustrate elements of Eugene O'Neill himself. He is "a perfect blend of father and mother," light-brown hair, gray eyes, of medium height. He is not really a handsome seventeen-year-old, but he projects an "extreme sensitiveness . . . a restless, apprehensive, defiant, shy, dreamy, self-conscious intelligence.'' He is at that awkward stage when he is discovering and revelling in literature of all kinds and consequently has a superior air toward the rest of his family, who do not seem to understand him. He spouts socialist clichés about the Fourth of July holiday and capitalism, and is given to quoting from the books he keeps hidden from the rest of his family. His library and his dramatic posturings include Wilde, Shaw, Ibsen, Swinburne, Kipling, Carlyle, and the *Rubáiyát* of Omar Khayyám. He is surprised when his father shows knowledge of Carlyle and when both Lily Miller* and Sid Davis* know the *Rubáiyát*.

He is the central figure of the play, and the main action evolves about some Swinburne quotations he has sent to his girl friend, Muriel. Her father considered them obscene and insisted that Muriel reject him and that Richard be punished. In an attempt to gain a kind of dramatic vengeance, Richard goes with Wint Selby,* a Yale friend of his brother, to the Pleasant Beach Inn with two ''swift babies from New Haven.'' What ensues between him and Belle* is the stock situation of the young man's first visit to a prostitute (whom he tries to reform) and first acquaintance with strong drink. The innocent Richard gets very drunk and quotes poetry to the surprised ''tart,'' Belle, and the salesman she has picked up. Richard is finally thrown out of the inn. At home he becomes very sick, and his Ibsen-like posturing collapses as a result.

Receiving a letter from Muriel suggesting a meeting, he tries not to appear too eager, but at the same time he wants to impress her. He tells her rather too much of the story of the preceding night and they quarrel; however, they make up and the young man returns home, where his father gives him the stock embarrassed-father's sex-education speech. Richard is appalled that anyone would suspect him of such behavior when he loves Muriel and intends to marry her. He is also surprised to realize that his parents were once young, too. As the play ends, he is sitting dreamily in the moonlight.

MILLER, Tommy. In *Ah, Wilderness*!* son of Essie Miller* and Nat Miller*; brother of Arthur Miller,* Mildred Miller,* and Richard Miller.* Tommy is ''a chubby, sun-burnt boy of eleven with dark eyes, blond hair. . .a shiny, good-natured face.'' He is the stock juvenile brat with charm who lets off his fire-crackers at the wrong time, reveals his mother's deception about the bluefish she feeds his father under another name, and who refuses to drink his milk or go to bed.

MINNIE. In *Homecoming*, the first play of the trilogy, *Mourning Becomes Electra*,* cousin of Louisa Ames.* Minnie is one of the Chorus of Townsfolk who act as an expository device and offer commentary on the Mannon clan. She ''is a plump little woman of forty, of the meek, eager-listener type, with a small round face, round stupid eyes, and a round mouth pursed out to drink in gossip.''

MIRIAM, in *Lazarus Laughed*,* wife of Lazarus.* She is the personification of woman, the mother of grief. She continually mourns for the death of Lazarus's followers, and as a result of her commitment to death, she ages continually throughout the play until she is an elderly woman, while Lazarus, by contrast, has grown younger and younger. Time has made her its victim, while Lazarus's affirmation has defied and defeated time. She dies joyfully from eating a poisoned fruit offered her by Pompeia* and only then is she able to laugh along with Lazarus in her defeat of death.

MONTEREY, Carlotta (1888–1970), actress, third wife of Eugene O'Neill. Born Hazel Neilson Tharsing on December 28, 1888, in Oakland, California (or San Leandro), to Christian Neilson Tharsing and Nellie Gotchett Tharsing. Died in Westwood, New Jersey, November 17, 1970, of arteriosclerotic thrombosis. Father a fruit farmer of Danish origin; mother of Dutch, French, "old world" origin. (*Note*: Carlotta's true name is also variously spelled Taasinge, Tauzig, and even Tossinger. This last is given by José Quintero* (1974) and is probably a phonetic spelling of Taasinge.) In the 1890s, Mrs. Tharsing left her husband and went into the boarding-house business in San Francisco, leaving her daughter in the care of a sister, Mrs. John Shay, in Oakland. Birthplace is given as Oakland in publicity issued by her theatrical agency, Chamberlain and Lyman Brown, New York. In 1916–17, this agency circulated an amusing piece showing Carlotta as a "farmerette" working her five-acre lot in Oakland, preferring this life to the bright lights of the theatre. Altogether, the facts about Carlotta's life are difficult to substantiate since she herself was given to romantic rewriting of them.

Carlotta's early education is unknown, but it was probably either the public or parochial schools in Oakland. From thirteen to sixteen she was at Saint Gertrude's, Rio Vista, a Catholic academy. She was early given elocution lessons and later (1906–11) went abroad, studying at the Academy of Dramatic Arts, run by Sir Herbert Beerbohm Tree in London (Sheaffer, 1973, p. 221). Her theatrical publicity release claims that this was a "three-year advanced course, . . . supplemented by a year of voice culture with Mme. Yeatman in Paris, coupled with a course of stage dancing under the personal direction of Raymonde, ballet-master of the French Opera." She also claimed to have been an honor student at the Convent of the Sisters of Mercy, Paris. In 1907, as the result of her mother's submitting a photograph, she became Miss California in a national beauty contest (Sheaffer, 1973, p. 221).

Apparently her European education was designed to give the arrestingly lovely young woman sufficient social polish to make an advantageous marriage, an objective which was achieved with her first marriage to John Moffatt (1911–14), a lawyer-businessman and relative of the Coates Thread Company; whose finances were of the roller-coaster variety. Their divorce was amicable, and they remained friends. Her second husband was Melvin C. Chapman, Jr. (1916–23), a twenty-year-old Oakland law student by whom she had a daughter, Cynthia

(1917–71). Carlotta's publicity speaks of her charms as Luana [in the touring company of *Bird of Paradise*], capturing the heart of a prominent California businessman, whom she later married. Her third husband was Ralph Barton,* the *New Yorker* caricaturist (1923–26), whom in 1924 she nominated as the best-dressed man in New York: "Need I say more?" During these marriages, and over the course of about six years, she was also the mistress of James Speyer an elderly widowed Jewish Wall Street banker who belonged to the same distinguished and cultured group as Otto Kahn, the philanthropist who supported the Metropolitan Opera and also contributed to the Provincetown Players.* As well as Carlotta, with whom he never actually lived, Speyer's philanthropies included the Museum of the City of New York, to which Carlotta was instrumental in persuading O'Neill to donate some of his own longhand drafts and the papers and memorabilia of his father, James O'Neill.* Her fourth marriage was to Eugene O'Neill (1929–53). Before going to Europe with O'Neill, Carlotta apparently met with Speyer, convincing him that she needed the income from the trust fund he had set up for her (averaging about fourteen thousand dollars a year) so that O'Neill could be free to write without fear of financial liabilities. Speyer agreed to continue this annuity for her lifetime, a provision that was, after some reluctance, continued by his heirs (Sheaffer, 1973, pp. 282, 532). Until the 1940s, O'Neill apparently believed that Carlotta's money came from an inheritance from a rich aunt.

Carlotta developed into a remarkably exotic beauty, with black hair, dark eyes, white skin (though one publicity release and the accompanying picture indicate "dark olive skin"), and an imperious carriage of her head, apparently the result of an attempt to counter eye trouble in childhood (Sheaffer, 1973, p. 220). She accentuated her "foreign" appearance by her choice of a Spanish stage name which originated in the county and town of Monterey, California. Her most striking features were those of head and neck, and a partially nude Marcia Stein photograph reveals her waist to be a trifle thick and her feet and ankles a little pudgy. But Carlotta had mastered the arts of self-presentation, camouflage, and publicity. Her agency scrapbooks are filled with photographs of "the lady who looks like a painting" modeling fashions from important designers and expensive New York stores. In later years she had her clothes custom made by designers and her shoes made to order. She was also noted for her English accent, precise diction, and arresting manner. Her acting seems to have been somewhat affected and attitudinous, and judging from reviews her career was dependent upon her personal beauty and fine costuming. In 1923 she was listed as 'the perfect profile" and as one of the world's thirteen most beautiful women in a field that included Mary Pickford and Lady Diana Duff-Cooper. Her roles were usually exotica: a Hawaiian maiden (*Bird of Paradise*), assorted Eastern European figures, adventuresses, a Russian girl, a French actress, the other woman, and similar parts in assorted melodramas and bedroom farces.

Theatrical appearances included *The Geisha* (a small role, London and provincial tour); *Taking Chances*, with Lou Tellegen (1915–16, touring company);

All Night Long (1918, New York performances–4); *Mr. Barnum* (1918, New York performances–24); *Be Calm, Camilla* (1918, New York performances– 84); *A Sleepless Night* (1919, New York performances–71); *Page Mr. Cupid* (1920, closed in Brooklyn); *The Dauntless Three* with Robert Warwick (1920, joined touring company); *The Ruined Lady* (1920, New York performances– 33); *Zizi* (1921, closed out of town); *Nemesis*, in which she was hailed as "a second Nazimova" (1921, New York performances–56); *Danger* (1921, New York performances–79); *Bavu*, by Earl Carroll, which opened his theatre (1922, New York performances–25); *Voltaire*, when Abram Poole painted her portrait in the role of Mlle. Clairon (1922, New York performances–16); *The Hairy Ape** (1922, replacing Mary Blair,* her only success of the season); *Ladies for Sale*, also called *Sold* (1923, closed in Pittsburgh "for lack of theatres" after touring Buffalo and Baltimore); *The Other Rose,* in which her handsome black dress was noted (1923, New York performances–84); *Fashions of 1924*, a revue in which no one was paid (1923, New York performances–13); *This Is A Tough Season* (1923, Equity review); *The Sable Coat* (1924, closed in Atlantic City); *The Red Falcon* (1924, New York performances–15).

These roles show not only the minor status of her theatrical career but also the state of the American theatre which O'Neill was shortly to shake to its foundations. Carlotta's own view of this theatre was curiously shallow and gives rise to wonder that she attached herself to O'Neill. While touring with *Sold* in 1923 (a play compared to the work of O'Neill in its "stark realism"), she complained that since World War I the American theatre had turned "into the strange areas of sex-problem drama, lurid melodrama and exotic comedy . . . [with] coarseness and vulgarity. The stage is my life's work only because I have been brought up to feel . . . that the American drama should be a thing of vital beauty bearing always a message of joy and hopefulness and helpfulness. If the drama in America is less than this, then it is nothing" (Theatrical Scrapbook, clipping from the *Pittsburgh Post*, March 2, 1923). Clearly by 1924 her career was waning and a film career seemed highly unlikely, though her reputation as a great beauty remained. Perhaps in an attempt to improve her image she changed her managers to the firm of Frohman. She was also reputed to have come into money (probably from Speyer, her "protector" in the old European sense) and was noted for her fastidiousness and expensive dress. She is said to have hated theatrical life and to have suffered greatly from nervousness when performing.

In the summer of 1926, Carlotta was the house guest of the play agent Elizabeth Marbury in Belgrade Lakes, Maine, where Eugene O'Neill and his wife, Agnes Boulton,* and all their children were vacationing. Here Carlotta and O'Neill met for the first time since the 1922 production of *The Hairy Ape* when she had characterized him as "the rudest man I have ever met." This time she seems very consciously to have thrown herself in his way, for she was now free, having just divorced Ralph Barton for adultery, the only New York grounds at the time. After her return to New York, according to her own (somewhat suspect) account, O'Neill came to her apartment on three occasions while Agnes and the children were still out of town. He poured out his heart to her, speaking bitterly "about his early life—that he had no real home, that he had no mother in the real sense, no father in the real sense, no one to treat him as a child should be treated. . . .He kept saying 'I need you, I need you, I need you' '' (Sheaffer, 1973, pp. 233–234). Then one day she saw the contents of his suitcase, a meager collection of clothing which convinced her that the man was neglected, so she instantly went to Abercrombie and Fitch, bought a half-dozen of everything, together with an expensive toilet case, and had them sent to his hotel. That was what got "old maternal Monterey, you know" (Quoted by Gelb and Gelb, p. 963).

O'Neill returned to his family in Bermuda before Christmas 1926 and told Agnes about Carlotta, maintaining that they had not slept together. Agnes forgave him, but O'Neill continued to write to Carlotta, sending her (through Kenneth Macgowan*) a large box of roses for Christmas. In early March the O'Neill family moved into their newly remodeled home in Bermuda, "Spithead," and O'Neill proceeded with work on *Strange Interlude*,* in which Nina Leeds* seems to embody O'Neill's multiple image of a woman as wife, mistress, and mother. Later, with Carlotta, he was to add secretary, friend, and collaborator, sentiments frequently echoed by his inscriptions in copies of his plays designed as gifts to her. He continued to play one woman against the other, assuring his wife of his enduring love when she left for New Jersey in April 1927 to visit her dying father. In May of the same year, O'Neill went to New York to discuss the production of *Strange Interlude*, and perhaps also to lay further claim to Carlotta (whom he saw there) because she had just denied a rumored engagement to James Speyer (Gelb and Gelb, 1973, p. 635; Huntington Library Manuscript 85).

He returned to Bermuda, but then in August, when Agnes believed that the episode was over, he returned to New York and Carlotta. He did not return to Bermuda again, and asked for the return of his manuscripts.

By the end of January 1928, O'Neill had decided to marry Carlotta after having discussed the matter with Agnes during her flying visit to New York earlier in the month. Carlotta apparently forced the issue when she found out that Agnes was in town. The road seemed clear for their marriage since O'Neill believed Agnes was willing to get a divorce and (unknown to O'Neill) Carlotta had secured from Speyer assurance of her continued annuity. Then, as later, reactions to their relationship were highly varied. Where one person thought Carlotta admired the dramatist rather than the man, others praised her protectiveness, her managerial skills, and her superb housewifery. Where some saw her as overpossessive, others noted that O'Neill's strong and tormented personality would have destroyed a more passive character. Kenneth Macgowan believed that she was more likely than Agnes to keep him sober. Carlotta later maintained that "there was no mad love affair between us. O'Neill was a tough mick and never loved a woman who walked. He loved only his work" (Gelb and Gelb, 1973, p. 656). She also claimed that she agreed to marry him only if she could contribute 50 percent of the household expenses; he needed a well-run home in order to work, "And that is what I did for him" (Ibid.).

Almost immediately after the late January opening of *Strange Interlude*, O'Neill and Carlotta left secretly for England (February 10, 1928). They remained two weeks in London, went to Paris for a few days, toured by automobile through the Loire and Touraine, staying briefly at Biarritz, and finally renting a villa at Guéthary, keeping their whereabouts secret from everyone. In Biarritz, O'Neill bought Carlotta the stuffed monkey, Esteban, displayed prominently in all their residences. It disappeared during Carlotta's last long hospitalization. In a letter of March 16, 1928, to a California friend, Carlotta wrote ecstatically about "a new life,. . .*a really new one*!. . .I have with me, in all this a lovely soul—a keen brain & a beautiful person" (Huntington Library Manuscript 87). She also speaks of her housekeeping difficulties in words that belie her alleged French education and training: "I know about 30 words of French—altho' I understand nearly everything. Can you imagine the effort (& fun!) getting leases signed—servants engaged & running the house—! 'Gene, the devil, won't open his mouth to them & sits back & grins at me." She outlines a regimen of morning work, afternoon walk, reading, and formal dinner, which prefigures their general routine throughout their marriage, and goes on to express her resentment about Agnes: "the 'Madam' is a *quiet & law abiding blackmailer*! As Gene & I pay 50–50 on all expenditure I do not feel that I'm doing her any injustice. . . .He has offered her everything but his eye teeth now!" (Huntington Library Manuscript 87). On the whole, life proceeded quietly at Guéthary, but even then Carlotta indicated a future pattern by almost walking out on O'Neill when his old friend, Louis Kalonyme, visited and the two went on a combined reminiscence and drinking spree. Perhaps her hostility to O'Neill's old friends began here. In mid-August 1928, O'Neill having completed work on *Dynamo*,* they spent a week in Paris with Saxe Commins,* O'Neill's friend and later editor at Random House, and his wife Dorothy Berliner, a concert pianist who was meeting Carlotta for the first time. They then took a motor tour in Spain.

With O'Neill's divorce still not obtained, he and Carlotta sailed from Marseilles for the Orient on October 5, 1928, in fulfillment of his long-held desire to go there. Things did not go altogether smoothly on this trip, both in terms of health and interpersonal relationships. In Singapore, O'Neill suffered sunstroke; in Saigon, Carlotta took exception to his gambling, and then both came down with flu. In Shanghai, O'Neill was recognized by a Greenwich Village acquaintance and the two went on a series of drinking bouts, O'Neill finally having to be hospitalized. The undercurrent of violence in their relationship also surfaced when Carlotta remonstrated with him after one drinking spree; the argument grew so heated that he slapped her, calling her "an old whore" (Sheaffer, 1973, p. 315). After his hospitalization, O'Neill became almost abjectly apologetic, a pattern that was visible throughout their marriage. After his recovery they went to the Philippines and back to Singapore, but O'Neill began drinking again, and an infuriated Carlotta left the ship in Ceylon on New Year's Day, 1929, but took the next boat after him, keeping in touch by radio. Reunited in Port Said, they continued together after a tempestuous meeting that eventually simmered into reconciliation (Sheaffer, 1973, p. 322).

Problems continued, Carlotta disliking O'Neill's earlier acquaintances, opening his correspondence, "editing out" what he was to receive, and answering his telephone, as she was to do throughout their marriage. She claimed that early in their relationship O'Neill had told her that he did not wish to answer the telephone or look after his mail himself, but as Carlotta limited outside communication more and more during the next fifteen years or so, many people were hurt and wondered about O'Neill's acquiescence. Perhaps she severed connections with some old friends to prevent alcoholic backsliding, but she earned the reputation of being "the dragon at the gate" (Sheaffer, 1973, p. 333) of the castle. In later years she even refused to pass on a communication from a schoolmaster concerned about the academic performance of Shane Rudraighe O'Neill,* Eugene's son with Agnes Boulton.

After a brief sojourn at Cap d'Ail, which was not quiet enough for O'Neill, in April 1929 they rented the Chateau du Plessis in Saint Antoine-du-Rocher, Touraine, for three years and Carlotta undertook the first of her numerous building enterprises, this time trying to bring an ancient building up to American standards of plumbing, comfort, and lighting. Her curious attitude of sophisticated superiority toward her husband is indicated by an often-quoted comment that at Le Plessis "I taught him how to live," making this "rather tough Irishman" learn that living in a chateau was not "chichi" (Seymour Peck, *New York Times*, 1956, reprinted in Cargill, 1961), putting on airs, and that hand-made shoes did not a gigolo make. On July 22, 1929, they were married in a civil ceremony in Paris, exchanging plain gold rings engraved with lines from *Lazarus Laughed**: "I am your laughter" on Carlotta's, "and You are mine" on O'Neill's (Gelb and Gelb, 1973, p. 696; Sheaffer, 1973, p. 332). After a honeymoon trip to Austria, they settled into the romantic seclusion of Le Plessis where O'Neill worked on *Mourning Becomes Electra** and Carlotta ran an elegant and efficient household that revolved around him. Guests at that time recall the gracious formality of the ménage where Carlotta dressed for dinner in elegant gowns that only O'Neill generally saw. In 1930 she seemed content to nest, writing to a friend that "starting off again in boxes terrifies me." Again she asserts her happiness: "Gene...is a grand companion—he has a brain, a soul, a body & a sense of humour! Pretty nigh perfection—*I* wish I had as much to give!" (Huntington Library Manuscript 88). During the summers of 1929 and 1930 their quiet was interrupted by many guests, much to Carlotta's displeasure. Eugene Gladstone O'Neill, Jr.,* (the playwright's son with Kathleen Jenkins,* O'Neill's first wife) also visited, as also did a number of journalists. In October 1930 they toured Spain, Italy, and Morocco, returning to Le Plessis to face a monumentally dismal, wet winter. O'Neill spent his time working, and Carlotta became lonely and depressed, a fact recognized by O'Neill in his dedication of her copy of *Mourning Becomes Electra*: "mother, and wife and mistress and friend!. . . And collaborator! Collaborator, I love you!'' (*See* O'Neill, *Inscriptions*, 1960). This kind of dedication was to typify their continuing relationship, and it fed the legend of Carlotta as unselfishly ministering to the needs of the creative artist, a woman who upheld the ideal of marriage O'Neill praised in *Servitude*,* *Welded** and *Days Without End*.*

Tiring of the French climate, and angry at the way they had been bilked repeatedly by their servants and tradespeople, the O'Neills returned to New York on May 17, 1931, hoping to avoid publicity. However, they were foiled in this wish by the suicide of Ralph Barton, Carlotta's third husband, on May 20, 1931. In his suicide note he mentioned his regret at hurting Carlotta, "my beautiful lost angel," calling her "the only woman I ever loved" (Sheaffer, 1973, p. 374). Weathering this storm, they summered in Northport, Long Island, where O'Neill continued to revise *Mourning Becomes Electra* and renewed acquaintance with Shane, but he did not attend the wedding of his first son, Eugene, Jr. in June. Toward the end of summer they leased an apartment at 1095 Park Avenue where Oona O'Neill [Chaplin]* visited them, along with Shane, in a rather disastrous reacquaintance during which she became carsick. Rehearsals for *Electra* began in September 1931, and Carlotta began her pattern of continuous attendance at them, a practice she followed throughout O'Neill's career. This created a rather tense, yet slightly amusing, situation in which the unsuccessful actress was now in the position of instructing her betters.

In mid-December 1931, the O'Neills visited Sea Island, Georgia, and found the climate congenial and the location compatible with O'Neill's love of the sea. Accordingly, they bought some land, and Carlotta designed the twenty-one-room Casa Genotta (a combination of both their names), the first of her two dramatic (and slightly monumental) residences, or temples of devotion to O'Neill. Years earlier, her theatrical publicity had referred to her as "an interior decorator of merit," and both here and in California she lived up to this billing. The house was in Spanish-Italian style with a study designed in the manner of the captain's cabin of a galleon. Before their departure from New York in June 1922, Carlotta renewed acquaintance with her daughter, Cynthia Chapman, now fourteen, and her mother, neither of whom she had seen for five years. Mrs. Tharsing was soon sent back to California, and Cynthia, who had been in boarding school since the age of five, was put in another such establishment in Connecticut. Carlotta's relations with her daughter were never close because they were always secondary to those of both herself and O'Neill.

In July 1932, Eugene, Jr., and his wife visited Casa Genotta, and later Shane came also. As before, guests found the establishment superbly run, with everything geared to allowing O'Neill maximum freedom and isolation in which to work. Whatever one may say of Carlotta, domestic efficiency and total dedication to privacy were her long suit. She enjoyed formality, running her household in the manner of imperious upper-class England. She is recorded as celebrating Christmas in the English manner, with the family formal dinner on Christmas Eve so that the servants could be dismissed to their own families for Christmas

Day while the master and the mistress of the house dined on what had been left prepared for them. During their residence in Georgia, O'Neill wrote *Ah, Wilderness!** and *Days Without End*, a work which caused him inordinate difficulty and which he saw as the dramatization of his relationship to Carlotta. His 1934 dedication of it to her included the words of John Loving: " 'If every other marriage on earth were rotten and a lie, our love could make ours into a true sacrament.' And ours has, hasn't it, Darling One" (*See* O'Neill, *Inscriptions*, 1960). He also began work on "The Life of Bessie Bowen"* toward the end of 1934 and conceived the idea of his massive cycle of American history ("A Tale of Possessors, Self-Dispossessed"*) in early 1935.

However, all was not perfectly tranquil between two such temperamental people, and a servant once recalled an altercation so bitter that "for a couple of days...she sat at the table but wouldn't eat, with tears streaming down her face" (Sheaffer, 1973, p. 448). In other ways also, Casa Genotta was not the perfect residence, particularly in summer with its snakes, heat, and humidity, necessitating an escape to the Adirondacks in 1934. Working on his cycle through 1935, O'Neill finished *A Touch of the Poet** in the spring of 1936. Then, having decided to move to a cooler climate in the West, they entertained a number of friends and relations prior to their departure, while O'Neill worked in the torturing summer heat. Cynthia Chapman, now seventeen and married to her first husband, August Barnett, came, as did Shane.

On November 3, 1936, with Casa Genotta unsold, they arrived in Seattle, debilitated after medical and dental treatments in New York. They rented a house overlooking Puget Sound, and during their residence there O'Neill was awarded the Nobel Prize for Literature for 1936. However, when the award was made in February 1937, O'Neill was in the hospital in Oakland recuperating from an appendectomy. Carlotta, who had moved into the hospital to be near him and perhaps counter his roving eye for younger women, helped nurse him during a serious relapse. Their move to the San Francisco Bay Area had been prompted by the depressing fog and rain of Seattle (one wonders if it was reminiscent of the wet winter at Le Plessis), and they took a suite in the Fairmont Hotel on Nob Hill, with a view of the Bay. Cynthia, now divorced and remarried to Roy Stram, visited them occasionally, while Carlotta and O'Neill looked for a suitable new residence, finding nothing exactly to their liking.

With the sale of Casa Genotta at a loss, for a sum estimated variously between sixty-five and eighty-three thousand dollars, they were able to purchase 160 acres in the Las Trampas Hills above Danville, California, in order to build the next of Carlotta's edifices, Tao House, now a national historic site though not open to the public because of limited access, a narrow, winding road—built with O'Neill's Nobel Prize money. The two-story house was built in a modified California Spanish ranch style with an oriental interior, many of the furnishings being reproductions purchased from Gump's, the San Francisco department store. Space was provided for O'Neill's eight thousand books and Carlotta's three hundred pairs of shoes, an amusing testimony to diverse interests. The site commands a superb view of Mount Diablo and the whole San Ramon Valley, but the rather small windows were usually shielded from the sun at Carlotta's wish (probably her dislike of sunlight was the result of her eye trouble and perhaps the result of pride in her fine skin). Most of the rooms have access to the outdoors, but in general the house seems to turn in on itself, with a high concrete wall shielding the back courtyard from prying eyes. This gives further evidence of the O'Neills' almost pathological desire for privacy. No one, not even Carlotta's mother and daughter, was permitted to come uninvited, while visits from old California acquaintances and neighbors were actively discouraged. In 1948, Carlotta, writing to an old friend, alleged that this eremitic existence had been dictated by O'Neill, but at that time Carlotta was in a distinctly hostile mood toward her husband, and her comments are therefore suspect. As before, she seems to have enjoyed building and decorating this dwelling, whose name "Tao" is Chinese for "the righteous way of life." It was begun some time after June 1937 and finished in about six months, at a cost of about $150,000, their most expensive house to date. Having built Casa Genotta at much less expense and with nonunion black labor, Carlotta was horrified at the cost and fulminated frequently against President Roosevelt, whom she saw as the author of all kinds of ills, with democracy as a contributing factor. This attitude caused Eugene, Jr., to refer to her as "the old Tory," an appellation that enraged her, as she frequently informed José Quintero years later.

Nonetheless, the O'Neills were not totally isolated during their years in Tao House. Some of O'Neill's old friends visited, and Saxe Commins came in his dual capacity of editor and friend. All three of O'Neill's children visited on more than one occasion, though Carlotta disapproved of the life-style of each one. She disliked Eugene, Jr.'s left-wing politics and his marital instability; she wished that Shane would become independent; and she found Oona a trifle "snippy," particularly when she once announced her intention to "marry a rich man." It is fair to say that Carlotta could not be bothered with any children, including her own. At Casa Genotta she had told Shane that she actively resented having to write to him and Oona (Bowen, 1959, p. 245) and apparently intercepted their letters to O'Neill, including Shane's congratulatory message concerning the Nobel award. The attitude of both O'Neills was probably summed up by Carlotta when she said that their purebred Dalmation dog, Silverdene Emblem* O'Neill "is the only one of our children who has not disillusioned us" (Sheaffer, 1973, p. 518).

O'Neill resumed work on his cycle in April 1938 after recuperating from neuritis, and he finished a second draft of *More Stately Mansions** at the beginning of 1939. As usual, Carlotta typed up his longhand notes from the minuscule script which, she later told Quintero, ruined her eyesight. In 1941 he and Carlotta invited Ingrid Bergman,* then a young actress appearing in "*Anna Christie*,"* to be part of the proposed repertory company to be formed to play the cycle plays. However, wishing for a film career, Miss Bergman did not want to tie herself down for several years and refused. Her account of the visit shows

Carlotta's extraordinary protectiveness: "She stated that he was tired and would not stay long with me. She would nod, and then I would have to go" (Floyd, 1981, p. 293).

Altogether, Carlotta and O'Neill seem to have enjoyed Tao House best of all their residences, though by 1941 Carlotta was beginning to feel isolated. She even went to a reunion of her old school, Saint Gertrude's, and renewed some old acquaintances, surprising some of them by sinking theatrically to her knees before one of her former teachers (Sheaffer, 1973, p. 524). Tao House represents the last flowering of O'Neill's creativity and the writing of some of his greatest plays: *The Iceman Cometh** (1939), *More Stately Mansions* (1935–41), *Long Day's Journey into Night** (1939–41), *Hughie** (1941), *A Moon for the Misbegotten** (1941–43), and a revision of *A Touch of the Poet** (1942), as well as the massive cycle plays which were later destroyed; however, the scenario of *The Calms of Capricorn** has survived. All the first typescripts were made by Carlotta, who was sometimes overwhelmed by the tragic nature of the material.

However, difficulties began to overwhelm them. The writing of *Long Day's Journey* and *A Moon for the Misbegotten*, both plays of exorcism for O'Neill, were emotionally and physically debilitating, and his tremor was mistakenly diagnosed as Parkinson's Disease. Only after his death was it determined that he suffered mainly from familial tremor. Wartime problems began to accumulate: servants left, and the house became more difficult to run. By 1943 relations with Shane were bad, and Oona was completely cut off when she married Charles Spencer (Charlie) Chaplin* (ironically a friend of Ralph Barton) the same year. Gasoline rationing curbed their use of the car, and then their chauffeur joined the Marines. O'Neill was unable to drive because of his tremor and Carlotta had never learned, so they were marooned, dependent upon the help of local tradespeople for transportation. A few people, like Myrtle Caldwell, an old friend, and her daughter, Jane, tried to relieve their gloom and ill health. Carlotta's arthritic spine was causing her great pain, and O'Neill was having urological problems which lessened his desire for sex. One curious incident occurred at this time which indicates the suspicion with which each regarded the other. O'Neill came upon Carlotta and her masseuse in what he chose to interpret as a compromising lesbian situation, and Myrtle Caldwell had to be called to pacify him (Sheaffer, 1973, pp. 545–546).

Carlotta was by now sick of her country isolation, and by October 1943 she was anxious to sell the house, which she finally did in February 1944. Most of the oriental furniture was sold back to Gump's; the books and the player piano O'Neill enjoyed were sent to storage; and they moved into a suite in the Fairmont Hotel where Carlotta, rundown with overwork, had a serious kidney and bladder infection. As before, Carlotta kept her family at arm's length, relenting somewhat by arranging to have her mother sent to a nursing home when Cynthia was no longer able to care for her. Dissatisfied with the Fairmont, O'Neill nagged Carlotta into obtaining larger quarters at the Huntington Hotel. They then engaged on a permanent basis the nurse who had always cared for them in their illnesses.

Her job seemed to be that of companion to Carlotta more than anything else, for Carlotta had engaged Jane Caldwell to perform the secretarial tasks she was no longer capable of.

During the rest of 1944, O'Neill (against Carlotta's wishes) renewed negotiations with the Theatre Guild* in New York, showing them *Moon, Poet*, and *Hughie*, and also suggesting *Iceman* for postwar production. By the end of the year, Carlotta was almost desperate to escape from California, but their doctors advised against suddenly plunging into an Eastern winter. Further, O'Neill, always susceptible to young women, seems to have become very attached to Miss Caldwell, who was at the time engaged to a young man of her own age. Gradually this situation began to enrage Carlotta, who was always touchily jealous, and their relationship in 1945–46 was tense, with a notable battle in September 1945 when Carlotta announced her intention to leave for the East and the next morning claimed that O'Neill had attacked her physically (Sheaffer, 1973, pp. 537–538). O'Neill, too, was querulous, speaking of his dislike of hotels and reiterating his old complaint about never having had a real home, an assertion guaranteed to inflame Carlotta. The two reached a truce and left for New York on October 17, 1945. Curiously, O'Neill rather than Carlotta said good-bye to Cynthia, even though Cynthia believed that her mother was in the suite at the time.

On their return they moved into the Barclay Hotel, East Forty-eighth Street, and O'Neill, though appearing older than his fifty-seven years, began to become quite gregarious. At this time they were forced to share a bedroom for the first occasion in their marriage. Their relationship remained tense, and Dorothy Commins reprints her husband's notes on one incident that Saxe Commins, O'Neill's devoted friend and editor, called "a painfully embarrassing display of cruelty and vindictiveness" (Commins, 1978, pp. 65–67). Naturally, Commins took O'Neill's side, noting that "it was not the first time that I had been made privy to domestic scenes of spite and violence on one side and tormented meekness on the other." It appears that O'Neill was unable to find his manuscripts, and Carlotta stood there taunting him with losing his memory, continually suggesting other places to search, even forcing the embarrassed Commins and the almost frantic O'Neill to search through her underwear drawer. Two days later, O'Neill told Commins that Carlotta had known the whereabouts of the manuscripts all the time; she had removed them as a punishment for an offense of which O'Neill claimed ignorance. Perhaps it was his relationship with Jane Caldwell, of which Commins knew nothing (Sheaffer, 1978, p. 560). This strange and vindictive episode marked an increase in her possessive jealousy and her fear that she might lose O'Neill to someone younger, for Carlotta, though expensively clad, was no longer noted as a fashionable dresser. Indeed it might be argued that her slight dowdiness was less the result of economics than a deliberate fixation of dress and coiffure in the era when she was a reigning beauty—an emphatic personal statement. In justice one should also note that the O'Neills' most bitter confrontations occurred when they were living in close quarters. Perhaps their marriage needed space.

In Spring 1946, they moved from the Barclay to 35 East Eighty-fourth Street, the penthouse apartment hallowed for Saxe Commins by the memory of Edward Sheldon who had borne a twenty-year illness of incredible pain and blindness with a singularly blithe spirit (Commins, 1978, pp. 64–65; Gelb and Gelb, 1973, p. 863). Again Carlotta redecorated, while O'Neill revised *The Iceman Cometh*, but again they were bedeviled with family troubles. Eugene, Jr., was now adrift, no longer teaching classics at Yale, and O'Neill's first grandson, the child of Shane and Cathy, died of what was probably Sudden Infant Death Syndrome. Carlotta, who had visited Cathy in the hospital and had taken a layette to their cold-water-flat in Greenwich Village, chose to make dreadful allegations of parental neglect whenever she was angry. José Quintero was once treated to such a tirade. She no longer wished to have anything to do with any of O'Neill's children, and they both later refused to make bail for Shane when he was jailed for possession of heroin. Similarly, no communication with Oona was permitted, and eventually O'Neill and Eugene, Jr., were forced to meet secretly outside the apartment.

Carlotta began to tire of city life, possibly because of its frustrations and its sociability. Also, she seems to have had a pattern of nesting; she would engage in furious and happy activity redecorating a house or apartment, and then when it was finished would wish to move on to begin the cycle again. At this time, O'Neill was preparing for the October 1946 opening of *The Iceman Cometh*, and the Theatre Guild assigned Shirlee Weingarten, a production assistant, to O'Neill as his secretary. She soon proved herself indispensable to O'Neill, also playing the role of buffer between him and Carlotta, though later incurring the older woman's jealousy. O'Neill's socializing was continuing, despite Carlotta's wish to keep him sequestered. She used to arrange small dinners where she could serve something that would minimize his tremor, but on one occasion a small dinner mushroomed into a large songfest with Irving Berlin at the piano. Another time, when Burl Ives and O'Neill began trading ribald songs, Carlotta disapprovingly left for home, though she did send Russel Crouse, the host, a letter of thanks (Gelb and Gelb, 1973, p. 878). As Louis Sheaffer puts it, "gradually their life was developing into a pattern of disagreements and amnesties" (Sheaffer, 1973, p. 589). O'Neill, however, was receiving publicity, as a 1946 article in *Life*, by Tom Prideaux, and a three-part *New Yorker* profile, by Hamilton Basso in 1948, indicate.

The Iceman Cometh (1946) had not been a great success, and *A Moon for the Misbegotten* (1947) had been a failure, and relations between the O'Neills were very strained. Carlotta became suspicious of O'Neill's interest in Patricia Neal, perhaps because the smokey, dark-velvet quality of her voice reminded Carlotta of herself when young, and years later Carlotta vetoed her candidacy for the part of Abbie Putnam* in *Desire Under the Elms** (Sheaffer, 1973, p. 599). But at this time O'Neill reciprocated Carlotta's jealousy, resurrecting the old charge of lesbianism after reading *Nightwood*, (1937) a study of a destructive psycho-pathic woman, by Djuna Barnes, an old Provincetown acquaintance. Since Shir-lee Weingarten had given O'Neill this book, Carlotta was angry and chose not to attend her wedding reception; O'Neill went alone, against her wishes. By Novem-ber 1947, Carlotta's rage at her husband brought her to retail her complaints to Eline Winther, the wife of Professor Sophus Keith Winther of Seattle, while they were both visiting New York. Shortly afterward they fired Freeman, their chauf-feur, who had been with them since Georgia and whom they had brought from California after the war to look after them (Sheaffer, 1973, pp. 601-604).

Their worst quarrel took place in January 1948 after M. Eleanor Fitzgerald, the lawyer, financial expert, and mother-confessor of the Provincetown Players, telephoned to ask O'Neill for a loan in order to make an advance payment to the hospital she was entering for exploratory surgery. Saxe Commins was again present to observe Carlotta's fury. O'Neill attempted to explain what he owed to "Fitzi," but Carlotta would not be appeased, cursing her "in language that was far worse than ladylike," culminating in her ultimate insult—"bohemian" (Commins, 1978, p.69). Commins finally left, overcome by embarrassment, but returned the next day at O'Neill's request to find things worse than before. Carlotta had renewed her attack on O'Neill's friends, particularly "Fitzi," and then had rushed into her husband's room, smashed the glass top of his dressing table to smithereens, and torn up the only picture he had of his mother holding him as a baby, screaming, "Your mother was a whore!" At this O'Neill slapped her across the face. Carlotta went to her room, packed a bag, and left the house with a melodramatic promise never to return (Commins, 1978, pp. 69–70). She checked into the Weston Hotel nearby but did not inform O'Neill, routing all communications through her lawyer. She also hired detectives to keep the apart-ment under surveillance.

Carlotta's side of the story was told in telephone calls to friends and also in letters to an old friend, a woman painter in Monterey, California, with whom she suddenly renewed connections after nearly twenty years, pouring out the grievances of all those years "full of *working for* & *with* the Master." Shortly before the California period, Carlotta had taken to calling O'Neill that, but now the appellation is full of bitterness. "That's all I did. I never went to a Concert or any other thing to give me pleasure. I typed, designed & built two houses. Moved to France & back! (Oh, . . . What fools men can make of women!) . . . I have left Gene. . . . I don't like *men* who slap women — accuse them of rotten things they *know* they didn't do. The sadistic joy of hurting some-one, making them ill—a *power* over *them*" (Huntington Library Manuscript 90). She reports O'Neill's breaking his arm and says that on January 29 she had "like a sap" gone to the hospital to cheer him up. Her real reason for writing, however, was to propose that she move to Monterey "*to go West to die*," and accordingly she asks her friend to find her a room and bath somewhere, no matter how simple, but with heat, because of her arthritis, assuring her of her ability to pay from her private income. She praises her friend's work and wishes that she, too, had worked after her marriage. At this time O'Neill was in Doctors Hospital, and by February 24, 1948, Carlotta writes that she is suffering from "an arthritis attack helped on by an attack of gout" and has engaged a nurse for herself. She is clearly resigned to returning to O'Neill! "We are both getting old. There has never been any glamour in our lives—but a great deal of hard work." She complains about all the money she has had to invest in their marriage, because O'Neill's money had all gone in alimony, educational expenses, and a final settlement with Agnes, but concludes "it is a bit ridiculous &, not too dignified to step down now" (Huntington Library Manuscript 91).

For his own part, during this time O'Neill claimed that he wanted to leave Carlotta, a move that friends, and particularly Eugene Jr., and Saxe Commins, encouraged. He also told Shirlee Weingarten about the masseuse incident and revealed his knowledge that James Speyer was the source of Carlotta's money (Sheaffer, 1973, pp. 607–608). However, he also had written to Carlotta on February 10, begging her to take him back. It was the twentieth anniversary of their departure for Europe. By April 3, 1948, (Huntington Manuscript 92) she is writing from Doctors Hospital, having had herself admitted, unbeknown to O'Neill. One doctor believed that her real reason was to spy on her husband, whose progress she had been following in a series of abusive telephone calls. The earlier meeting with O'Neill, far from cheering him up, seems to have resulted in some physical pain to him, for she is alleged to have moved his injured arm. Now she is continuing to complain: "He, of course, is on the millionaires' floor! His room is $35.00 per day. (My room is $16.00 a day). He has three nurses at $70.00 a week each. . . . I was here 5 days without a nurse & then *had* to *have* one! . . .If this room is good enough for me it's good enough for him." This time, however, she claims she is going to fight and then continues her recital of grievances: "I have to eat! And with all the thousands I've spent on him & our homes—and all the years I have spent working for him, as secretary, nurse, housekeeper, builder & God knows what—he should be ashamed. . . . He wants no one but me to wait on him! *I don't cost him anything* & he could have the pleasure of bullying & insulting me. Mama's sweet little sadist" (Huntington Library Manuscript 92). This correspondence, which suggests dates different from those usually assigned to the chronology of this incident, temporarily ceases with this letter. By the middle of April, O'Neill's shoulder had healed, and after the breakdown of several truces, the two reached a reconciliation. As some of their friends understood, they needed each other, but there were serious casualties in friendships as a result. Saxe Commins had been accused by Carlotta of stealing manuscripts from their apartment, insulted with obscenities, and reviled as "You Jew Bastard." (Commins, 1978, pp. 73–74; Sheaffer, 1973, p. 609). She also demanded that he return his key to their safe-deposit box. Her suspicions of O'Neill remained, and she believed that he had detectives watching her. Perhaps as a kind of retaliation she later spread the false rumor that from this time on, his mental condition had begun to deteriorate, and that was why he had to cease writing.

By April 19, 1948, they were ensconced in the Ritz-Carlton Hotel in Boston, living together in a state of calm, and by July 1948, Carlotta had discovered what was to be the last residence they were to own, on Point o'Rocks Lane, Marblehead, Massachusetts, a six-room frame house about fifty years old anchored to the rocks by cables and as she put it, "We have one foot in the Atlantic" (Huntington Library Manuscript 93). The house required considerable remodeling (including the installation of an elevator) and winterizing in order to make it a permanent residence, for a total cost of eighty-five thousand dollars, for which Carlotta had to sell her securities. Nonetheless, there is a less querulous tone to this letter to her friend despite her complaints of hard work, perhaps because she was decorating again. She recounts the relentless progress of O'Neill's disease, "I feed him more often," inveighs again against "Dear Mr. Roosevelt," and then notes, "There is a different mood in the house—a new gentleness, & of course, a feeling that 'mama' is there to take care of her child" (Huntington Library Manuscript 93).

Gradually O'Neill came to realize that he would be unable to work again, and loneliness set in, particularly as winter drew on. Carlotta was essential to him, for he was no longer able to cut his own food or light a cigarette (Gelb and Gelb, 1973, p. 898). However, the domestic calm of which Carlotta spoke was easily shattered, and one uninvited guest was treated to an embarrassing display of open hostility (Sheaffer, 1973, pp. 618–619). On the whole, the summer of 1949 and the rest of that year were tranquil, punctuated by visits from some few, carefully screened old friends. Carlotta maintained that O'Neill's health was seriously deteriorating (though some friends thought otherwise) and complained loudly about her own aches and pains.

Some domestic storms occurred in 1950, apparently reaching violence on at least one occasion (Sheaffer, 1973, p. 625), and in September, Eugene, Jr., committed suicide. The lawyer who telephoned the news reported that Carlotta said, "How dare you invade our privacy," and slammed down the receiver (Commins, 1978, pp. 79–80). O'Neill and Carlotta sent separate floral pieces to the funeral but did not attend.

Carlotta did not wish to spend another winter in Marblehead and obtained O'Neill's consent to sell the house, but before they did, a rather ghastly set of incidents occurred. The pair had been bickering constantly, and to offset her nervous tension Carlotta increased her dosage of a prescription drug to the point where she was beginning to suffer from bromide poisoning, becoming somewhat paranoid and disoriented. Things reached a climax on February 5, 1951, when O'Neill walked out of the house without a coat, tripped, fell, and broke his right leg. Hearing his cries, Carlotta allegedly left him to lie there after delivering "in histrionic tones these lines: 'How the mighty have fallen! The Master is lying low. Now where is your greatness" (Commins, 1978, p. 81). Later she maintained that O'Neill was warmly dressed and that she had gone to him. A doctor and an ambulance were called (probably by the houseboy), and O'Neill was taken to the hospital.

Carlotta claimed that she went out on the street to call a cab shortly afterward, but it was the next evening that she was found by the local policeman walking on the street. He tried to get her to return home; she refused but finally agreed to get into a police car that had been summoned. There she became so hysterical that a doctor was called to the house, and she was placed in the same hospital as her husband but removed the next day to one which had psychiatric services. O'Neill remained in the hospital, his leg healing, and also recuperating from bromide poisoning. Old friends like Lawrence Langner,* Saxe Commins, and Shirlee Weingarten rallied around. After several weeks Carlotta wanted to visit her husband, and after an initial refusal, O'Neill agreed. Though they were apparently friendly, O'Neill seemed very upset afterward. By March 19, 1951, a Boston psychiatrist, Dr. Merrill Moore (ironically a cousin of Ralph Barton), recommended that O'Neill be declared unfit to manage his affairs and that a guardian be appointed. This suggestion was not followed. Meanwhile, Moore had also examined the anguished Carlotta, who was addressing streams of letters to Professor Winther in Seattle, and suggested the same thing. O'Neill took this advice and on March 23 asked that a guardian be appointed for her. She was released from the hospital on March 29, and her attorney filed for separate maintenance on March 30, the same day that O'Neill, at the urging of his friends, went to New York and was admitted to Doctors Hospital where he remained for 2.5 months.

Carlotta remained in Boston in the care of the nurse they had formerly employed in California. She was convinced of Carlotta's sanity, and Cynthia Stram cared sufficiently to make sure that her mother was being treated properly. Later Carlotta was furious to learn that O'Neill had changed his will, removing her as executrix. Legal maneuvering continued, and friends tried to convince O'Neill that he should separate from his wife. Saxe and Dorothy Commins even offered him a permanent home with them, but finally he decided to return to Carlotta. As Saxe Commins put it, "He realized, as we were beginning to do, that the tie that bound him to Carlotta was too firm to undo. Yet he was acutely aware that submission meant the final severance from all his old friends and repudiation of his past" (Commins, 1973, pp. 83–84). He returned on Carlotta's terms which dictated that she decide their place of residence and be renamed his executrix. By early May 1951, she had cleaned out the Marblehead house, planning to sell it and move to Boston. She moved into the Hotel Shelton, where O'Neill returned to live until his death. Two accounts of their meeting survive: Carlotta claimed that he walked past her into his room saying, "I'm sorry, forgive me, I love you" (Gelb and Gelb, 1973, p. 933), but the nurse who had accompanied O'Neill said that Carlotta hugged and kissed him and that "he was happy to be home" (Sheaffer, 1973, p. 657). She paid his bills with a portion of the forty thousand dollars she had received from the sale of the Marblehead house and settled into twenty-four-hour nursing, with a brief respite in November 1951 when O'Neill spent a time in the hospital with a gastro-intestinal complaint.

In December 1951 he gave Carlotta a typescript of *Long Day's Journey into*

Night, concluding his inscription with "I have loved you for twenty-three years now, Darling, and now that I am old and can work no more, I love you more than ever" (*Inscriptions*). Some months later he made Carlotta "irrevocably" the custodian of all his works "published and unpublished" (Sheaffer, 1973, p. 663). In July 1952 he inscribed *A Moon for the Misbegotten* to her with a further expression of love, though, according to Carlotta, his last writing to her "was quite bitter" (Sheaffer, 1973, p. 665).

In early 1953, according to Carlotta, O'Neill called for all his uncompleted manuscripts held by Random House, tore them up, and consigned them to the fireplace: "We tore up all the manuscripts together, bit by bit. It took hours. After a pile of papers had collected, I'd set a match to them. It was like tearing up children" (Sheaffer, 1978, p.667; Gelb and Gelb, 1973, p. 938). Some years later this account was questioned since there was not and never had been a fireplace in Suite 401 of the Shelton. At this, Carlotta said they had given the torn pages to the janitor, who in turn had fed them to the furnace. Other papers, which accidentally included the manuscripts of *More Stately Mansions* and *The Calms of Capricorn*, had been sent to Yale when the Marblehead house was sold.

Even these last months were not wholly tranquil. José Quintero recalls Carlotta's account of O'Neill's continually begging her for more sedation, dragging at the chain on her neck which held the key to the medicine. At least one doctor believed, however, that O'Neill was being too heavily sedated. He threatened suicide more than once and required Carlotta to remain with him constantly, lying beside him on the bed. He died on November 27, 1953, and Carlotta took elaborate precautions to ensure total privacy at the small, nonreligious ceremony he had requested. Though a Catholic priest had tried to gain access to him near the end, Carlotta had rebuffed him. In March 1954, Carlotta put up a simple gray headstone which contained simply his name, and dates of birth and death, leaving a blank space for her own.

After O'Neill's death, Carlotta devoted herself to the resurrection and preservation of her husband's reputation. She remained initially at the Shelton, taking her duties as sole executrix very seriously. She made sure that O'Neill's diaries were preserved, though she is known to have excised some material to avoid scandal. Above all, she tried to keep O'Neill's name before the public, expressing her anger when Random House allowed the collected plays to go out of print in 1954.

In the middle of that year she asked Bennett Cerf, the president of Random House, to read *Long Day's Journey into Night* because she wanted it published. O'Neill had deposited this manuscript with Random House, sealed, and accompanied by a signed instrument dated November 29, 1945, forbidding its publication until twenty-five years after his death. Therefore, Cerf was loath to go against O'Neill's wishes. On the advice of Saxe Commins, Cerf obtained a legal opinion, only to discover that Carlotta was legally able to override the earlier proviso. Cerf then relinquished publication rights, which were given to Yale.

Carlotta was furious with Commins over the delay and accused him of ruining all the O'Neill plays on which he had worked (Commins, 1978, p. 58). Partly as justification for her action in publishing this play, Carlotta reiterated her claim that Eugene, Jr., had requested his father to delay publication, but with the younger O'Neill's death in 1950, all barriers were removed. She also maintained that O'Neill had referred to this work as their private nest egg in case they needed it (Sheaffer, 1973, p. 634).

In 1955, Carlotta moved to the Hotel Lowell in New York and continued her role as keeper of the flame. In February 1956, the month of the Yale University Press publication, *Long Day's Journey into Night* was produced in a Swedish translation (by Sven Barthel) in Stockholm by Karl Ragnar Gierow* at the Royal Dramatic Theater. Carlotta stated that she had granted permission to this company because it was her belief that Sweden, which had awarded her husband the Nobel Prize for Literature, had shown itself more sympathetic to O'Neill's work than his native country, keeping his works in production when they were totally forgotten in the United States.

This was not strictly true, and with the 1956 production of *The Iceman Cometh*, directed by José Quintero and starring Jason Robards, Jr.,* a new O'Neill boom began, and Carlotta helped to foster it. She gave the rights to produce *Long Day's Journey into Night* to Quintero, Theodore Mann, and Leigh Connell, continuing and cultivating a close relationship with Quintero. She even gave him her husband's wedding ring and often spoke to him as "Gene," begging him to cease tormenting her. She also took up Carmen Capalbo and Stanley Chase, to whom she gave the rights to produce *A Moon for the Misbegotten*. Obviously she was enjoying her newfound power and celebrity, delighting in working dramatic business deals and enjoying the attention that directors were eager to pay her. An account of her approach can be found in the last chapters of José Quintero's memoir (1974).

She then moved to the Carlton House on Madison Avenue where Theodore Mann of the Circle in the Square Company, which had produced *Iceman* in 1956, was a frequent visitor. One of her enjoyments was visiting the monkey house in the Central Park Zoo. Esteban, the stuffed monkey bought for her by O'Neill on their original visit to Europe, remained a prominent part of her ménage, and she often addressed jokes to it. The monkey could not be found after Carlotta's death. During these years she began to behave more and more erratically, impulsively giving away jewelry and even production rights she did not even possess. José Quintero tells of dining with her at a time when Catherine Givens O'Neill,* Shane's wife, had asked him to tell Carlotta that they were short of funds. In reply Carlotta, who had had a number of "Monterey Cocktails," delivered a tirade against all of O'Neill's children, and at the end of the luncheon she flung her ruby earrings across the table, telling Quintero to take them instead of money. Somewhat shaken, Quintero left the earrings at the hotel desk, claiming that she had accidentally left them behind.

Among other people, she saw her lawyers; Jane Rubin, O'Neill's literary agent; and Donald Gallup, curator of the O'Neill Collection at Yale University, who eventually edited the texts of *The Calms of Capricorn* and *More Stately Mansions*. The latter was shortened for its first performance (1964) in Sweden by Karl Ragnar Gierow, a production arranged through the intervention of Dag Hammarskjold, Secretary-General of the United Nations. José Quintero also reedited it for his Broadway production starring Ingrid Bergman and Colleen Dewhurst.* It is hard to see how Carlotta justified these productions because in a 1956 *New York Times* interview with Seymour Peck, she said of O'Neill's destruction of his manuscripts, "He didn't want to leave any unfinished plays and he said, 'It isn't that I don't trust you Carlotta, but you might drop dead or get run over or something and I don't want anybody else finishing up a play of mine." (*See also* Sheaffer, 1973, p. 666.)

Slowly Carlotta began to deteriorate, complaining of being short of money and sometimes drinking too much, trying to exorcise herself of O'Neill. She had one brief spell in the hospital, made a good recovery, but was never quite the same. In November 1968, her behavior became so erratic that she was committed to Saint Luke's Hospital, Amsterdam Avenue and 114th Street. Some mystery surrounds this choice of hospitals when she was able to afford more elegant surroundings. Her condition worsened, and when José Quintero returned in January 1969 from an extended stay in Mexico, he found it difficult to discover her whereabouts. When he did, he was appalled at her condition and did his best to alleviate it, even to the extent of cutting her hair himself (see, in his memoir (1974), the chapter entitled "My Last Meeting with Carlotta"). In March 1968 she was removed to the DeWitt Nursing Home, East Seventy-ninth Street, where she still projected an air of elegance. By now she was quite senile, and in July 1970 she was transferred to the Valley Nursing Home, Westwood, New Jersey, where she died unexpectedly on November 17, 1970, of "arteriosclerotic thrombosis," according to the autopsy.

In her will, she left all O'Neill's papers to Yale and also the royalties from his plays, though through a quirk in the copyright laws, his two disinherited children, Shane and Oona, gained royalties to some plays and shared others with Yale. She left her jewelry and effects to Cynthia Stram, her daughter, who died eight months later. Carlotta did not die penniless, as she had feared, and she was able to see O'Neill's work again become respected, sharing at times in more money than O'Neill himself had seen from some of his plays.

Reactions to Carlotta still remain mixed. Some believe that she looked for glamor from her attachment to the famous playwright, a glamor which she, in self-pitying moments, claimed she had not found, while others praise her love for him. She gave him an organized environment in which to work, and she kept him sober, though probably at the price of deliberately excluding old friends; her treatment of the extraordinarily decent and faithful Saxe Commins, for example, was both vindictive and reprehensible. She seems at that time in her life to have become totally possessive, and having made O'Neill completely dependent on her, he was unable to go elsewhere, even had he wished. However, she also put up with a very great deal from a man who demanded too much from any one woman. She absorbed much, gave much, and still managed to survive. In 1961 she told the Gelbs that she had married O'Neill because she was proud of his work and wanted to help him. She claimed that there was no "wild flame" (though letters written at that time seem to belie her protestations) and said, "I really wanted to marry that man and stick to him and help him. And I think I did. This may sound boastful, but I think I did help him" (Gelb and Gelb, p. 964). And according to her lights, she did, so that may well be her fitting epitaph. *See* in "References": Bowen (1959); Commins (1978); Floyd (1979); Gelb and Gelb (1973); O'Neill, Carlotta M., Huntington Library Manuscripts; O'Neill, *Inscriptions* (1960); Quintero (1974); Sheaffer, (1973).

A MOON FOR THE MISBEGOTTEN, a semi-autobiographical play in four acts; O'Neill's tribute to his brother, James O'Neill, Jr.* The action takes place between noon on an early September day in 1923 and dawn the following morning. The setting is the farmhouse of Phil Hogan,* a tenant farmer, in Connecticut. The house is a dilapidated clapboard, two-story structure, once painted "a repulsive yellow with brown trim" but now weathered to "blackened and weathered gray" with bits of "dim lemon" paint. There is a one-story addition at the right, which is Josie Hogan's* bedroom, with tar-paper outside walls. There are three steps up to the front door of the house, to the left of this addition. There is a path which leads to the woods on one side and the county road on the other. Under Josie's window, near the house, is a flat-topped boulder. **Act I**: Just before noon on a clear hot day. Josie enters from the bedroom, an almost freakishly oversized woman of just under six feet who weighs about 180 pounds but is nonetheless firm and feminine of body. Her face, though not pretty, is a typically Irish one, with large dark-blue eyes and a rather charming smile which reveals even white teeth. Her hair and eyebrows are black and coarse, while her complexion is fair, freckled, and sunburned. She wears a cheap, sleeveless, blue cotton dress and is barefoot. She looks around and is relieved when her brother, Mike Hogan,* appears. He is "about four inches shorter than his sister . . . [with] a common Irish face. . . . Mike is a New England Irish Catholic Puritan, Grade B, and an extremely irritating youth to have around." He is in dirty, sweaty overalls, a brown shirt, and he carries a pitchfork. Josie is angry with his tardiness, but when Mike offers the excuse of being afraid of his father, "the old hog," Josie slaps his face, knocking him off balance. He cringes and begs her not to hit him as she tells him not to insult their father: "I like him, if you don't." Josie has made arrangements so that Mike can flee the farm and go to Bridgeport to their brother Thomas, a sergeant of police there; if he can't get Mike a job, then perhaps he will pass him on to John, a barkeep in Meriden. Josie has helped them escape also, and though she never hears from them, she is not really resentful. She thinks the police force or tending bar would be suitable positions for a prig like Mike: "you was born a priest's pet, and there's no help for it. . . . You're worse than decent. You're virtuous." This angers Mike, who starts to speak of Josie who is, as she puts it, "the scandal of the neighborhood," and doesn't care for his proffered prayers.

As she has done before, she has taken some money from Phil Hogan's satchel, calling it unpaid wages, to salve Mike's sensitive conscience. Momentarily she reveals real tenderness toward Mike and his two brothers, but she speedily covers it with a coarse remark which starts Mike preaching at her once more about her language and her dishonesty in helping her father cheat people by doctoring sick animals and selling them at full price, suggesting that she should leave the farm and marry a decent man, "Though it'd be hard to find a decent man who'd have you now." Josie asserts that she wouldn't want such a man because he'd be like Mike—and she doesn't want to be tied down to one man. Mike reacts by asking whether that includes James Tyrone, Jr.,* who will "be rich once his mother's estate is settled." Sarcastically he suggests that Josie has been mooning after Tyrone.

Mike suggests that she and her father have a plan to catch Tyrone by having Phil, with a shotgun and witnesses, catch him in bed with Josie. Josie keeps her temper with difficulty, as Mike continues, telling of his dislike of James Tyrone, with "his high-toned Jesuit college education," his quoting Latin, and his assumption of superiority when in reality he is "nothing but a drunken bum who never done a tap of work in his life, except acting on the stage while his father was alive to get him jobs" remarks that make him a clear portrait of O'Neill's own brother, Jamie. Mike's vindictiveness culminates in a wish that Josie will manage to "nab him . . . and skin him out of his last nickel." These comments anger Josie, who tells her brother to be off before their father returns. At this, Mike scampers off as his father runs back from his piggery to berate his idle son. Josie looks after her brother, saying that she stole the money for "the little boy you used to be that I had to mother" and not the adult he has become. Then, in order to meet her father, she gets down a broom handle for self-defense: "Not that I need it, but it saves his pride."

In a moment, Phil Hogan, a barrel-shaped man of "fifty-five, about five feet six," enters. He has short arms, stumpy legs, a fat porcine face, and skin that is sunburned and freckled. He is dressed in brogans, a coarse straw hat, filthy overalls, and a dirty undershirt. His high-pitched voice has a notable brogue. He is ready to chastise Mike, "the lazy bastard," but Josie engages in delaying tactics before telling him that Mike has left like his brothers. Phil realizes who is responsible and taxes her with having stolen money from him as well, but Josie announces her right to some of the money since she had doctored a nag to get a good price. Hogan joyfully recalls the way he beat the Crowleys, the buyers, but then Josie reveals that she had knocked one of them over when Phil was getting the worst of the battle.

Hogan remembers with resentment that his wife had died when Mike was born, and when Josie reminds him that she alone could put him in his place when he came home roaring drunk, Phil claims that his daughter is the same, "There's no liberty in my own home," but goes on to ask about Mike's "preaching'' to her. She tells him that as usual it was about her scandalous ways, asserting her own freedom to give a man ''his walking papers.'' Phil wishes that she were not such a ''terrible wanton woman'' but confesses to a certain pleasure that as a result she has not left the farm.

Josie then retells Mike's proposition that she trick Jim Tyrone into bed and force him to marry her, a comment that arouses Phil's interest, suggesting that such a trick is a very old one, ''but sometimes an old trick is best because it's so ancient no one would suspect you'd try it.'' Josie resents this approach, but Phil continues, saying they'd make a good match because neither could be superior to the other; after all, James would only be returning to the same class as his father, the actor who had worked his way up from poverty to riches, to be ''a true Irish gentleman.'' With this, Josie recalls the way Phil used to dress her up and send her to meet the elder Tyrone when, as their landlord, he would come to demand the arrears in the rent owed him. Then she would offer him a drink of the good company whiskey, and the old actor would calm down, tell her she should be an actress, and give her a half-dollar when she would admit that Phil had put her up to it. At this, Phil, unaware that James Tyrone,* Sr., knew of the trick, would claim he would vacate the place unless the rent was lowered and the house painted. But a few drinks later, the rent was forgotten.

Suddenly, Josie becomes suspicious of her father and his tricks, because he keeps insisting that Jim Tyrone likes her and is a good match, recommending that she get her wits together and grab him. Josie scoffs at his plan that she get him alone in the moonlight, saying that she wouldn't want to be married to a drunk, even though she is sure she could straighten him out. Certainly she'd love to get her hands on his money, but Jim will go back to his Broadway tarts and spend it there, though she herself ''is decent and deserving compared to those scum.'' The more Hogan speaks of Jim, the more illogical Josie becomes, and it is clear that she is indeed fond of him.

But then Hogan turns to the source of his concern—the farm. The estate of Mary Cavan Tyrone* is almost out of probate, and he is afraid that Jim will decide to sell it as soon as he can because he already has a large offer, despite the fact that they have been tenants for twenty-five years and Jim has promised that he will not sell them out. Perhaps the executors will insist on accepting an offer much greater than Phil's, or Jim will agree to a sale one night ''when he has one of his sneering Broadway drunks on.'' Josie can't believe this of him: ''He only acts like he's hard and shameless to get back at life when it's tormenting him—and who doesn't?'' This revealing comment brings Phil to dig further and prompts Josie into saying that ''Poor Jim'' is mourning for the death of his mother. Phil then suggests that Josie ought ''to be extra nice to him, for one thing,'' and not act ''brazen,'' to which Josie scornfully replies that perhaps she ought ''to pretend I'm a pure virgin,'' thus putting an end to the conversation, telling her father to get his stew from the stove while she finishes Mike's work. But then she sees Jim approaching, ''like a dead man walking slow behind his own coffin'' when he thinks himself unobserved, but sprucing up when he sees them. As Phil insists that Josie tidy herself up, she slams into her room and James Tyrone, Jr., enters.

He is in his early forties, about five feet nine, with a "naturally fine physique" which is beginning to run down from dissipation. His puffy face with its aquiline nose and sneering expression gives him "a certain Mephistophelian quality." His dark hair is thinning and he has a bald spot. However, he still retains something of a devil-may-care Irish charm, attractive to women and men (especially fellow drinkers). He is dressed in a dark brown suit which suggests a Broadway gambler trying to look like a Wall Street broker. He has drunk enough to anaesthetize his hangover, and he and Phil spar verbally with the familiarity of old contenders. Tyrone opens with a Latin quotation from Virgil applicable to the rock-strewn infertile farm and then goes on to tell the tale of his being sent down from a Jesuit university just prior to graduation because of his unsuccessful bet with a classmate that he would be able to pass off a Broadway tart as his sister. This actually happened to Jamie O'Neill. With this, Jim sits down with Phil who promptly complains about "this rockpile, miscalled a farm," suggesting that Tyrone ought to pay *him* to stay. Tyrone asks after Josie, who has been looking gently at him, "pleased to hear him laugh." She banters with him, suggesting that he probably needs a woman in bed with him to overcome the "heebie-jeebies" of the booze, but as she continues with rough talk Jim tells her to stop, clearly disgusted with it, and tells Josie that he is through with dainty tarts; now he likes big women, a remark that makes Josie blush. Obviously he has some regard for her, his "Virgin Queen of Ireland," as she also has for him.

Jim starts angling for a drink, which Phil refuses. Tyrone then tells Phil that T. Stedman Harder,* the Standard Oil man whose farm abuts Hogan's, is about to visit because Phil's pigs continually wallow in his ice pond; "somehow Harder's fence in that vicinity has a habit of breaking down." In fact it does so immediately it is repaired, and the farm manager suspects Phil Hogan as the culprit. Hogan rejoices in having Harder come to visit, and Josie kisses Jim for the great news; but suddenly she "looks startled and confused, stirred at the same time frightened," covering her emotions with a scornful "Ooh, there's no spirit in you! It's like kissing a corpse." Jim is a trifle surprised, but Josie, at Phil's request, breaks out the whiskey in celebration of the imminent arrival of T. Stedman Harder, who is seen riding with his manager in the distance. Tyrone wants to see the fun, so Josie pushes him into her room to keep him out of sight, promising to "spoon in the moonlight" with him that night.

Harder is the epitome of the privileged, wealthy, Ivy-League-university type who wants to live the life of a country squire. He is a lethargic, slightly fat, somewhat stupid man, accustomed to receiving respect from people outside his class, immaculately dressed in English riding gear and carrying a riding crop. He is a born mark for the Hogans, who are quick on verbal attack, because he speaks slowly and thinks deliberately. They insult him merrily, picking up his words and interpreting them literally, suggesting that he is a "poor crazy creature."

Then, seeing that Harder's manager is some distance away, Hogan turns the
tables, threatens him and taxes him with breaking down his own fence to entice
the pigs into the ice pond with the intent to destroy them: "How many pigs is
it caught their death of cold in his damned ice pond and died of pneumonia?"
Josie alleges ten deaths from pneumonia and ten more as the result of contracting
cholera from the water. Phil then launches into a verbal assault on Harder as "a
pig-murdering tyrant" and orders him off the property as a trespasser, giving
him a shove. With this Harder leaves and rides off with his manager, who is
barely able to stay in the saddle for laughing. Harder is a dramatization of an
anecdote in *Long Day's Journey into Night*.* When he has gone, Tyrone, whose
bursts of laughter have punctuated this exchange, reappears, and they all share
the joke. Jim then reveals that the large offer for the farm had come from Harder,
and now he expects to receive an even higher offer from the same source. Phil
quickly reminds Jim of his promise that he could have first refusal of the property,
but Jim paraphrases Kipling's "Rhyme of the Three Sealers,": "There's never
a promise of God or man goes north of ten thousand bucks." Phil claims to be
"suspicious," and Jim allows that he "could well sell it." Josie becomes angry
with him, and Jim reminds her of their date that evening, "I expect you to be
very sweet to me," going on to compliment her on "the most beautiful breasts
in the world." Josie is momentarily pleased but then tells Jim he must eat. He
tells her to go ahead and mother him as they both go inside.

Act II: The same as Act I, but the wall of the house has been removed,
revealing a small, low-ceilinged living room with bare boards, fly-specked wallpaper, and a clutter of worn-out furniture of the "fire sale" variety. The door
to Josie's bedroom is at the right. A clock on the bureau says 11:05 P.M. Josie
is sitting on the front steps, "hunched up," wearing an expression "of sadness
and loneliness and humiliation." She gets up, goes inside, and lights a kerosene
lamp, then notes the time, recalling that Tyrone had said he would be there
around nine. She angrily pulls out the flower she had pinned to her bosom,
flinging it into a corner: "The hell with you, Jim Tyrone!" The sound of Phil
Hogan singing the melancholy Irish ditty, "The Praties They Grow Small," is
heard, and he lurches in, less drunk than he appears. He shouts out to Josie,
who yells back, and then he pounds on the door. She tells him to come in, "you
drunken old loon." At this the pair argue about his inebriation, but Josie is a
trifle suspicious that he has returned before closing time at the inn.

Phil sarcastically notes that Jim Tyrone has stood Josie up, suggesting that
no one can say anything to a woman in love, something Josie denies. Then,
after a lot of drunken blather, he says that Jim Tyrone has agreed to sell the
farm to Harder for ten thousand dollars, though papers are not yet signed. Josie
cannot believe that Jim would break a promise, but Phil insists that Harder is
going to meet with the executors of Mrs. Tyrone's estate the next day. Josie is
bitterly disappointed, but then Phil tells her that she has made a fool of Jim
Tyrone because he really does seem to have affection for her, and Mike's scheme
of her catching him is not such a bad idea because it might really work—Jim

actually believes she is a virgin and that all her sluttish boasting is merely a cover. Josie is furious, and Phil says that the reason Jim has not come to visit is that he loves her too much to seduce her. She asks whether Jim has yet signed any papers and then proposes to go down to the inn, raise a fuss about his breaking their date, bring him home, and put Mike's plan into execution. Phil's part in the scheme is to arrive at sunrise with witnesses. She will fulfill her earlier intention to do anything, no matter how crooked, if Jim were to break his promise about the farm. But marriage is not on her mind; what she wants is a paper signed and witnessed to the effect that he will sell the farm to Phil Hogan at the price he offers and that he will pay Josie ten thousand dollars when the Tyrone estate is settled. But though Josie will allow him into her bed, she won't allow him anything more, so "he'll pay for nothing." She believes he will give anything to keep the Hogans quiet, to avoid publicity and preserve his vanity about his prowess with women. Phil and Josie agree to go to the inn, Phil to pick out witnesses and Josie to collect Jim, but first she goes to smarten up: "Sure, those in my trade have to look their best." But Phil notes that she doesn't even light her lamp: "God forgive me, it's bitter medicine. But it's the only way . . . now."

When Josie returns, she has obviously been crying but defiantly starts off toward the door when she sees Jim coming along the road. Phil is furious over the way he has made Josie wait, and the pair think up a new scheme. Josie will continue as if she knows nothing, and Phil will pretend to be so drunk that he does not remember anything of what was said at the inn; this he does, and Josie orders him out of the house as Jim enters, eyes glazed, vague in movement and speech, but otherwise not appearing very drunk. Phil departs singing, "The praties they grow small," in such a "stinko" state that Jim is puzzled because Phil hadn't seemed so bad earlier. Josie then suggests that Jim apologize for keeping her waiting and says that if she had any pride she wouldn't speak to him; to this Jim responds that Josie has too much pride, a remark that Josie finds curious and unsettling.

The two of them sit down on the front steps, Jim one step lower. For a moment or two he is silent, but then he speaks of "the old heebie-jeebies" and tells her, "I've really begun to love you a lot, Josie," recalling that he had had some mad idea to go to bed with her and lay his head on her breast. Josie then suggests that maybe he can do that later, but in the meantime she draws his head down on her breast as he relaxes. Phil's song is heard in the distance as Tyrone reacts with lines from Keats's "Ode to a Nightingale"; "Now more than ever seems it rich to die." Josie bitterly remarks that Tyrone must have a bad conscience, a remark that he treats with suspicion until she suggests that it is for wanting to go to bed with her. He says he wants tonight to be different and insists that Josie lay off her rough talk, as he sits there and she again bitterly talks of his promises. Finally, she suggests that she get him a drink and goes into the house, revealing the living room and a section of her bedroom. Tyrone stares into emptiness and then suddenly says, "You rotten bastard," and attempts to light a cigarette, but his hands are trembling so violently that he cannot.

Act III: The same, except that the living room wall has been replaced. No time has elapsed, and Tyrone is still trying to light his cigarette. When he succeeds, he starts walking back and forth and then swears at himself before singing an old Gay Nineties tearjerker: "And baby's cries can't waken her/In the baggage coach ahead." This causes his sneer to change to "a look of stricken guilt," and it is with relief that he sees Josie coming out with a quart of whiskey, two tumblers, and a pitcher of water. She pours for both of them, somewhat to Tyrone's surprise, but despite her claim to drinking once in a while, she is clearly so inexperienced that he later prevents her from drinking any more. She recalls that it is Jim's "pleasure to have me pretend I'm an innocent virgin tonight" after he tells her to cut out "the raw stuff," but then he looks at her with real desire and kisses her passionately. However, he stops there and turns away, while Josie reacts with a mixture of "fright, passion, happiness, and bitter resentment." Josie keeps the drinks coming, and Jim asks if she is trying to get him drunk, but Josie says she wants him "to forget all sadness" and feel happy. She continually refers to his "Broadway tarts," and Jim says he finds her more beautiful than they. Every time he kisses her, he begins to feel physical desire, but he turns away, claiming he doesn't want to poison their relationship; as he says later, "When I poison them, they stay poisoned."

Slowly, punctuated with drinks and with compliments, and even with some anger directed against Josie's rough talk, Jim reveals that Phil has tricked Josie into this compromising situation. At the inn, Jim had told her father that he had no intention of accepting the Harder offer of ten thousand dollars for the farm and that he and his brother were agreed that Phil could buy it. He and Phil had celebrated the end of probate together. This discovery makes Josie almost hysterical because she realizes that her father is trying to trick her into bed with Jim who knows that indeed she is a virgin: "You pretend too much. And so do the guys. . . . They all lie to each other. No one wants to admit all he got was a slap in the puss when he thinks a lot of other guys made it." What is more, Jim is sure that Phil is aware of the situation, something that upsets Josie even more—that he would wish to hurt her. This brings Josie to confess her virginity to Jim and offer herself to him in love, knowing that he wants her: "As if I gave a damn what happened after! I'll have had tonight and your love to remember for the rest of my days." But then she recalls that he must leave before sunrise (and Phil's return).

Jim then makes a serious drunken pass at her, acting as if she is a whore. Josie is appalled and he stops, turning to her in "bitter accusation" for leading him on when he wanted this night to be different from the other nights he had spent with a woman. With this, Josie runs after him, kisses him with almost maternal solicitude, and gets him to sit down with his head on her bosom: "Sure if there's one thing I owe you tonight, after all my lying and scheming, it's to give you the love you need, and it'll be my pride and my joy." In this situation, with Jim resting on the bosom of this almost freakish earth-mother of a woman, Jim is finally able to tell his tale of hate, love, sorrow, and degradation, his loss of hope, the hurt with which his mother died, and his own contributing fault when he "was too drunk to go to the funeral." He had managed to beat the liquor for the sake of his mother, but shortly before she died of a brain tumor he had gone back to it, and toward the end she had seen him drunk. After that, he brought her body back on the train to New York, en route to Connecticut so that she could be buried with her husband. But on the train, the memory of her laid out in her coffin, looking so young, pretty, and innocent, tormented him. As a result, he drank solidly, making a total nuisance of himself to the other passengers until he found a "blond pig," a prostitute, whom he invited to share his drawing room for fifty dollars a day, trying desperately to forget his mother's body "in the baggage coach ahead."

He also recalls his father's miserliness and his own search for happiness. Acting was no good because he was "a third-rate ham," and following the horses made no profit because he was too concerned with their meaningless beauty and returned again to the bottle as a means of forgetting. He looks on Josie as "simple and kind and pure of heart," words he used to speak of his mother; on her breast he confesses and exorcises his past, finding forgiveness in the moonlight and Josie's insistence that "*she* hears. . . and I know she understands and forgives me too, and her blessing lies on me." Jim, who has at last been able to weep for his faults, then falls asleep as Josie gazes tenderly on him: "Sleep in peace, my darling. Oh, Jim, Jim, maybe my love could still save you, if you could want it enough!" But then common sense takes over; she realizes the impossibility of this dream and looks derisively on the situation: "God forgive me, it's a fine end to all my scheming, to sit here with the dead hugged to my breast."

Act IV: Dawn; Josie is sitting in the same position as at the end of Act III. She does not seem to have moved, and Jim's head is still on her breast. She looks exhausted from her motionless vigil but is afraid to move in case she wakens him. Phil Hogan appears from behind the barn, looking as if he has slept in the haystack. He approaches Josie quietly, but she has heard him. He attempts to keep up the pretense that he returned to the inn and came back blind drunk, but Josie taxes him with "the scheme behind your scheme"; yet witnesses would have been unnecessary, as Phil says, because nothing has happened. But Josie claims that there has been a miracle, "a virgin who bears a dead child in the night, and the dawn finds her still a virgin." Hogan tries to laugh off Josie's virginity, but she tells him to stop lying, saying that nothing has happened; the sadness in her face comes from the sorrow a woman feels "for the man she has loved who has died." But, like Nora Melody* in *A Touch of the Poet*,* she speaks of the "pride" that is also in her heart. She had thought there was hope in James Tyrone, but "I didn't know he'd died already—that it was a damned soul coming to me in the moonlight, to confess and be forgiven and find peace for a night." Then she turns on her father, enraged at his greed and his lies, knowing that Josie loved Jim yet lying about the farm so that she would do the scheming, force Jim to offer marriage to her, and then, after he would leave her and drink himself to death, she would be the legal widow. She says that she now intends to leave the farm, just as her brothers have done, to leave Phil to his dirty schemes. But Phil says that he had taken the chance in the hope of bringing Josie some happiness, despite any consequences.

With this, the sun has risen on a beautiful morning, and Josie sends Phil away while she wakens the sleeping Tyrone "with a maternal tenderness," saying, "I hate to bring you back to life, Jim, darling. If you could have died in your sleep, that's what you would have liked, isn't it?" Then as he stirs she hopes that he will remember "that one thing and forget the rest." Awakening, Jim reacts as if he is with one of his "tarts" but realizes with surprise that he is with Josie, who treats him with her accustomed good-humored friendliness, complaining that she is numb from holding him all night. Jim, not even finding interest in another drink, finds himself strangely peaceful after a night without nightmares. She finds that he remembers very little of what went on, and therefore she speaks of the beauty of the night; and in answer to his question about whether he had tried to go to bed with her, she says they had just "kidded."

He feels "at peace with myself and this lousy life—as if all my sins had been forgiven," and as he looks at the sunrise in the terms of a dramatic curtain rise, he becomes genuinely emotional to Josie : "I'll never forget it—here with you." Josie is pleased, hoping that he would "feel beauty in it—by way of a token," a remark that puzzles him. Troubled, Jim asks if he has tried to "get out of order last night," but Josie assures him otherwise. However, as soon as he takes a drink of Phil's good liquor, memory returns, and he starts to leave. Josie is stricken and begs him not to leave like that because they will never meet again, "and I know that's best for us both." She wants him "to remember my love for you which gave you peace for a while," but Tyrone "defensively" claims he doesn't know what she is talking about. Josie then agrees that she doesn't remember, either; but when she wishes him "good-bye and God bless you," Tyrone comes to her, kisses her twice, saying that he will always remember Josie and her love, bids her the same farewell, and walks away as Josie sobs.

Phil Hogan looks after him with hatred, and when Josie says she will prepare breakfast, he looks at her "pleadingly," telling her that his scheme was not aimed at getting Tyrone's money but rather at bringing the two of them together "to face the truth that you loved each other," hoping that her love would save Tyrone. As for the money, he claims he thought of it only so that Josie would have a better life than a shanty farm. Josie believes and forgives her father, teasing him about playing Cupid, saying she will not leave him. With this, Phil lights up, claiming that he had thought of committing suicide in Harder's ice pond, and in an attempt to restore the old relationship, he calls for his breakfast; but when he vents his rage at Jim, Josie stops him in anguish: "Father, I love him!" Phil apologizes, and the two try to act in their normal adversary manner.

As Phil goes in, Josie looks after Tyrone: "May you have your wish and die in your sleep, soon, Jim, darling. May you rest forever in forgiveness and peace."

Comments: This play has not been a favorite of either critics or playgoers because of its singularly static quality and also because of the difficulty in casting the central role. Josie Hogan is a woman of such unusual physical characteristics that any actress possessing them would probably have been advised against entering the theatrical profession, and as a result, audiences are forced into a mighty suspension of disbelief. In addition, the part of Jim Tyrone is exceedingly difficult to play. In its original production, which O'Neill worked on, he continually complained that the actor playing Jim was too coarse, unlike Jamie O'Neill, his original. Nonetheless, the part contains more grossness than gentility. In addition, the overall structure of the play does not fully mesh with the seriousness of its content. In essence, the situation is farcical, if not trite, with its attempt to trick the "lovers" into bed with each other, and O'Neill spends most of the play leading the audience to expect a sexual consummation but then turns expectations into disappointment with the *dénouement* (hinted at throughout) that Josie really is a virgin, not the wanton woman of the neighborhood, a variation on the idea of the prostitute with a heart of gold.

Once again, O'Neill also shows his curious attitude toward the relationship between man and woman. As in *The Great God Brown,** Josie is the great earthmother, a Cybel,* but here a virgin believed to be a prostitute, which leads one also to a recollection of *Dynamo** and Henry Adams's essay, "The Virgin and the Dynamo." But in *A Moon for the Misbegotten*, Josie also shows some of the qualities of Nora Melody in *A Touch of the Poet*, in the way she celebrates the "pride" of her love and the self-abnegation with which she sees herself as the comforter of the afflicted, whether it be her brothers, her father, or James Tyrone, Jr. The play also has an important autobiographical significance, because Jim's account of his mother's death and his journey from California to New York is a recreation of Jamie O'Neill's own journey back with his mother's body. What O'Neill seems to be doing in this play is to exorcise his own guilt concerning his brother, as he had earlier done with his father in *Long Day's Journey into Night*, though that play was not produced until much later. But he seems never to have forgiven his mother for her dope addiction.

The original production of *A Moon for the Misbegotten* took place in Columbus, moving on to Pittsburgh, Detroit (where it was briefly closed for "obscenity"), and St. Louis, closing out of town, the only other O'Neill play to do so having been *Chris Christophersen.** *A Moon* achieved a modest run in New York in 1957 and reasonable runs in 1968 and 1973. It was published in book form in 1952, largely because the playwright needed the money. Two later revivals indicate that serious theatregoers are beginning to appreciate the essentially psychological action of the late O'Neill plays, with their intensity of emotion and familial feeling. The playwright seems to have gone beyond fashionable Freudian and Jungian interpretations and instead has come to depend on the integrity of his memory and the intensity of his emotions and familial feeling.

Production Data: Written 1941–1943. Produced by the Theatre Guild* at the Hartman Theater, Columbus, Ohio, February 20, 1947. Toured to Detroit, and St. Louis, closing there March 29, 1947 (total of 30? performances).
  Director: Arthur Shields
  Designer: Robert Edmond Jones*
  Cast: Josie Hogan: Mary Welch
        Mike Hogan: J. Joseph Donnelly
        Phil Hogan: J. M. Kerrigan
        James Tyrone: James Dunn
        T. Stedman Harder: Lex Lindsay
Revived at the Bijou Theatre, New York City, May 2, 1957 (68 performances).
  Producers: Carmen Capalbo and Stanley Chase
  Director: Carmen Capalbo
  Designer: William Pitkin
  Cast: Josie Hogan: Wendy Hiller
        Mike Hogan: Glenn Cannon
        Phil Hogan: Cyril Cusack
        James Tyrone: Franchot Tone
        T. Stedman Harder: William Woodson
Revived at the Circle in the Square, New York City, June 12, 1968 (199 performances).
  Director: Theodore Mann
  Designer: Marsha Eck
  Lighting: Jules Fisher
  Costumes: Domingo Rodriguez
  Cast: Josie Hogan: Salome Jens
        Mike Hogan: Jack Kehoe
        Phil Hogan: W. B. Brydon
        James Tyrone: Mitchell Ryan
        T. Stedman Harder: Garry Mitchell
Revived at the Morosco Theatre, New York City, December 29, 1973 (175 performances), with Jason Robards, Jr.,* and Colleen Dewhurst*; José Quintero, director.
A Note on Text: The text used is that published by Yale University Press.

MOON OF THE CARIBBEES, THE, a one-act play, part of the S.S. *Glencairn** group. The action takes place aboard the S.S. *Glencairn* anchored off an island in the West Indies. It is night, the moon is full, and the sound of "a melancholy negro chant" is heard across the water. The crew members are sprawled out on and around the deck awaiting the arrival of a bumboat woman who, with the connivance of the captain, is bringing women aboard for both officers and sailors. She also intends to smuggle rum aboard. The men find that the chant continually intrudes upon their consciousness, and their characters are developed through their reactions to it. Driscoll* calls it keening; Smitty* finds that it awakens old, sad memories; Big Frank* thinks it is a funeral; and Cocky* makes bad cannibal jokes. Attempting to drown out the unknown, the unfamiliar, the sailors have Paul,* the Norwegian, play sea chanteys for them so that they can sing. When the women—Bella,* Susie,* Violet,* and Pearl*—arrive, they are picked out by various sailors. Pearl tries to attach herself to Smitty, the young blond Englishman who obviously has a past. He buys a bottle of booze at her invitation, and after downing some of it he speaks to Old Tom,* the donkeyman, about the incessant chant. Tom compares it to "listenin' to the organ outside the church on Sundays," but Smitty can only recall his sad memories, seeing himself and Old Tom in terms of the Yale Whiffenpoof song: "poor little lambs who have lost our way." The two then discuss their reasons for going to sea. Smitty is trying to escape the hurt of a love affair that foundered on the shoals of his drinking. The donkeyman, with a philosophy born of an acceptance of his fate and a sobriety forced on him for health reasons, merely listens as Smitty relates his tortured memories. Pearl returns from the forecastle to Smitty, telling him that he should drink less and that he is not like the rest of the crew because he is really a gentleman. Soon all the seamen and women pour out the forecastle to dance drunkenly on the deck. Big Frank, the fireman, trips Cocky, the Cockney sailor, and his woman; a fight erupts in which the seamen side against the firemen, and Paddy* receives a flesh wound. The First Mate* then appears and orders the women back ashore, refusing to pay them for their services since they had illegally brought rum aboard. The ship returns to normal, and the chant is heard again: "the mood of the moonlight made audible."

Comments: The play, which has very little action, is basically a mood piece. The technique is poetic, based on reactions to the mysterious chant. But the ship is also a microcosm of the world, a common image for O'Neill. It is no accident that so many different nationalities are included among the crew. The chant, and the women, indicate to some extent the impact of a different and alien race upon this enclosed group. The physical action is somewhat melodramatic, particularly the stabbing and the sudden hustling away of the women. The inner action, however, is more important. The men belong to the sea, though some of them challenge their fate. Only in drunkenness can there be relief. The chant itself, timeless like the sea and mysterious like the moonlight, strikes fear into those who think. The seamen's pleasure is short-lived, and at the end of the play, the universe returns to what it was in the beginning; the brief interlude the audience has just witnessed makes no difference in the scheme of existence. The permanence and unchangeability of nature, particularly the sea which is a symbol of man's harsh and inevitable fate, constitute the real center of the internal action.

Of the four plays in the S.S. *Glencairn* group, O'Neill took most pride in *The Moon of the Caribbees*. In 1924, when he organized the series in its entirety, he placed this play first.

Production Data: Written 1917–1918. First produced by the Provincetown

Players* at the Playwrights' Theatre, New York City, December 20, 1918 (performances, unknown).

Director: Thomas Mitchell
Designer: unknown
Cast: Yank: Harry Winston
       Driscoll: Hutchinson Collins
       Olson: William Forster Batterham
       Davis: W. Clay Hill
       Cocky: O. K. Liveright
       Smitty: Charles Ellis
       Paul: Percy Winner
       Lamps: Phil Lyons
       Chips: Fred Booth
       Old Tom: William Stuart
       Big Frank: Howard Scott
       Max: Jimmy Spike
       Paddy: Charles Garland Kemper
       First Mate: Louis B. Ell
       Bella: Jean Robb
       Susie: Bernice Abbott
       Pearl: Ruth Collins Allen
       Violet: Unknown

Revived as part of a triple bill, April 25, 1921 (21 performances).
Revived frequently as part of the S.S. *Glencairn* group. *See* that entry for performance statistics.
[*See also* Appendix B for operatic version by Adriano Lualdi; also film adaptation of the entire series under the title *The Long Voyage Home*.]

MORAN. In *The Iceman Cometh** a middle-aged plainclothes policeman who comes with his companion, Lieb,* to arrest Theodore Hickman.*

MORAN, Tim. In *The Web*,* a safecracker. "He is short and thick-set, with a bullet head, close-cropped black hair, a bull neck, and small blue eyes close together. Although distinctly a criminal type his face is redeemed in part by its look of manliness. He is dressed in dark ill-fitting clothes." He appears with a loaded revolver to save Rose Thomas* as Steve,* her pimp, has knocked her down. Moran and Rose are two of a kind. Where Rose has been forced into prostitution, Tim has been drawn into crime. He was made to take the blame for a crime committed by an older gang member and was sent to reform school. On his release he attempted to go straight, but whenever his record was discovered, he was dismissed from his job. As a result, he stole again and drew a five-year sentence. After that he joined a gang of "yeggmen" and learned to be a safecracker. He has just pulled a job and is currently in hiding, but despite his vulnerable situation, he rushes in to save Rose when he hears Steve beating her. He admires Rose for her forbearance and love for her child and therefore gives her some of the stolen money so that she can go to the mountains to cure her tuberculosis. He is shot down by the jealous Steve just as the police arrive to arrest him. Steve escapes, and Rose is accused of robbery and murder.

Like the other characters of the play, Moran is not deeply drawn. He is the stereotypical victim of society who nonetheless has a gentle heart, and he admires Rose for herself, perceiving her innate decency. He is caught in *The Web* of circumstances and cannot escape except in death.

MORELLO, Chuck. In *The Iceman Cometh*,* "a tough, thick-necked, barrel-chested Italian-American, with a fat, amiable, swarthy face." He is Cora's* pimp and a roomer at Harry Hope's saloon. His pipedream is that he will lay off the booze "tomorrow," marry Cora, and move to a farm in New Jersey or Long Island, despite the fact that he knows nothing of farming. Under the influence of Theodore Hickman,* the salesman who comes to the bar annually to celebrate Harry's birthday, Morello attempts to translate the dream into reality, but Cora gets drunk and Chuck realizes its impossibility. After Hickey's arrest on the charge of murdering his wife, Chuck, along with other denizens of the bar, seizes on his plea of insanity, a pipe-dream explanation which discredits what he has taught them, and then he is happy to get drunk in order to forget the outside world and regain illusions.

MORE STATELY MANSIONS, a play in three acts and six scenes, the sixth play of the abandoned cycle, "A Tale of Possessors, Self-Dispossessed."* Originally entitled "Oh, Sour-Apple Tree," this play opens four years after *A Touch of the Poet*.* The fortunes of Deborah Harford,* Simon Harford,* and Sara Melody* (Mrs. Simon Harford) are carried farther here (1832–1841).

Act I, Scene i: An abandoned log cabin in the woods near a village in Massachusetts, the site of Simon Harford's earlier experiment in living close to nature in *A Touch of the Poet,* just before 3 P.M. of an October day in 1832. Sara Melody, now twenty-five and married to Simon Harford, enters, six months pregnant and wearing deep mourning. Her typical Irish beauty (blue eyes, dark hair, fair skin, and rosy cheeks) remains undimmed, while her curious mixture of peasant and aristocratic features remains notable. Her finely chiseled nose and high forehead are offset by a heavy jaw and sensual mouth, while her figure has the bad points of big feet and heavy, stubby, peasant hands. She takes a key from her pocket, lets herself in, and locks the door after her. Deborah Harford then enters, a tiny woman of forty-five, under five feet, slender, and tastefully dressed in white. She looks very little different from four years ago in *A Touch of the Poet* except that her wavy hair is now white, surrounding a face so youthful that she almost seems to be wearing a period wig for a costume ball. While she waits for the arrival of her son, Simon, she dreams erotically of being "a noble adventuress of Louis's court" at Versailles but then warns herself against such romantic self-indulgence in case she might not be able to find her way back to the world of reality. She then contemplates Simon, lost to the arms "of that vulgar Irish biddy," and allows her mind to wander again to the court of King Louis where she is a courtesan leading the king "into the little Temple of Love he built for me," as Simon appears for the first time in both plays. He is twenty-six, "tall and loose-jointed with a wiry strength of limb. [He has] a long Yankee face,...straight nose, a wide sensitive mouth, a fine forehead, large ears," and wide-set light brown eyes whose expression super-imposes shrewdness over contemplation.

They commence by playing a mildly flirtatious game because they have not seen each other for some time and try to catch up on the past. Simon is at first surprised to discover that he has lost the key to his cabin of dreams where he had planned to write an idealistic work about a world in which humanity is not acquisitive, a notion which Deborah had inspired in him. They speak of Simon's marriage, his other children and the one which is coming, then of the Harford family—the business acumen of Simon's father and the plodding mentality of Joel Harford,* Simon's brother, who has just become head bookkeeper of the family firm. Deborah then reveals her secret romantic dream, but instead of sympathetic understanding, Simon at first exhibits shock and then derisive laugh-ter, reactions which enrage Deborah so that she turns to a discussion of Simon's own business success. Obviously she is jealous of Sara, whom she considers responsible for the death of Simon's ideals, but is reassured when he says that he plans to retire when they have sufficient money and claims that Sara's hap-piness is sufficient reward for the dullness of the counting house grind. He may have suspended work on his book, but his ideals remain intact. Contritely, Deborah embraces him, saying, "love is worth everything," and Simon departs, having told his mother again of his happiness with Sara. Deborah looks after him knowing that "he will forget in her arms. I have dismissed that Irish biddy's husband from my life forever. I shall never see him again."

Overhearing these last words, Sara lets herself out of the cabin and reveals that she has heard the entire exchange, responding to Deborah's insulting com-ments about her origin with the assertion that she will take from life what she wants "and make it mine." Unlike Deborah, with her dream of being "a greedy, contrivin' whore," Sara is not afraid of life. Nonetheless, she regrets Simon's cruelty in laughing at his mother's folly, a sentiment that momentarily endears her to Deborah. But Sara continues to speak of Simon's business ability, her own desire for economic security and for upward mobility, so understandable in view of her early poverty, and finally tells Deborah, "Stay in your dreams and leave me and mine alone. Simon is mine now." With arrogant disdain Deborah says she will never communicate with Simon again and will certainly not "touch anything of yours." Sara draws the battle line by saying, "You know I wouldn't let you." Deborah looks after her. "Vulgar, common slut!" she calls her, and then momentarily wanders off into her dreamworld. But recalling Simon's mirth, she swears she will never dream again and will instead become resigned to "change and ugliness, and Time and Death." She can do nothing else now that her son has shown her her folly.

Act I, Scene ii: Deborah Harford's garden "on a warm moonlight night in June 1836." In the center is an octagonal summer house, a "Temple of Liberty," built by her Jacobin father-in-law. It has "a narrow arched door, painted a Chinese lacquer red," three steps in front of it, two stone benches before a small oval pool, and two paths, one leading to the house and the other to a green door with a lighted lamp in the high brick wall enclosing this space. There is a line of cypress trees, and the shrubs around the summer house are clipped into a variety of geometrical shapes. The whole atmosphere is artificial, and the psychological implications of door, house, wall, and trees are very clear. Nicholas Gadsby,* now a short, tubby fifty-six and as self-important and pretentious as in *A Touch of the Poet*, speaks as the family lawyer to Joel Harford. He is twenty-nine, pale, and handsome, slightly stooped, prematurely old, "a methodical mediocrity. . . . His whole character has something aridly prim and puritanical about it." They are dressed in mourning and have come to speak with Deborah. To Gadsby's shock, she has retired inside the summer house, "deliberately deranged," Joel suggests, by his father's death, though Gadsby is more charitable.

As they wait, Deborah opens the door of the summer house, backing out of it, and then turning around. She is greatly changed, now looking much older than forty-nine, her face beginning to have a death's head look, though her white-clad figure is still youthful. She seems glad to see Gadsby, saying that she will never go inside the little house again because she is afraid that she might succumb to the temptation to open another door, this time a door in the mind, and escape from living into insanity. She claims that she has accepted the facts of human existence and indeed is "possessed by facts—like a whore in a brothel," a comparison which shocks Gadsby. Joel and Gadsby reveal that the Harford company is in a tottering condition financially because Mr. Harford has been gambling in Western lands, and the only hope of its recovery is for Simon to take it over. Since the firm has been left jointly to Deborah and Joel, her consent is required; in fact, both Joel and Gadsby suggest that she make the proposition and convince Sara to accept. In addition, her husband had also suggested that Simon's family move into the Harford residence with Deborah, a prospect that gives her a momentary satisfaction, but then she refuses utterly to have anything to do with "such a low intrigue." She is now tired of life, "an ugly, resigned old woman whose life is only in the mind."

Gadsby eventually convinces her through his curious gallantry to fall in with the plan. Joel, who is not close to his mother and who has been rather shamelessly exploited by his father, leaves to make travel arrangements, leaving the lawyer and Deborah alone to discuss future plans. Gadsby suggests that the arrival of her grandchildren will give her a renewed interest in life. She announces her pleasure at this thought and suggests that she will beg for "this chance to be reborn!" She will even love Sara and make her love back, and her children will love their grandmother. Perhaps she, too, will relearn the art of loving. She decides to exorcise "my devil, the old Deborah—drag her from her sneering-place in my mind and heart, and push her back where she belongs—in there—in perpetual darkness." With this she shuts and locks the door, leaving her dreaming self inside. Suddenly she stops to listen to the footsteps of life beyond the wall: "Life remembers he has forgotten me and is turning back." Then "she bursts into natural teasing laughter" at Gadsby's face as the curtain falls.

Act I, Scene iii: Sara Harford's sitting room "in a textile-mill town about forty miles from the city. The following night." The room is small and furnished in an unremarkable manner. The noise of small boys arguing is heard from upstairs and then Sara's voice ordering them to be quiet. Simon enters. He is now thirty-one and looks it. He has put on some weight, but the most notable difference is in his face, which looks harried and tense. His preoccupied air lightens as he hears the family noise and then Sara's voice insisting on quiet. He picks up a newspaper, reads it for a moment, his face turning hard and bitter; then he puts it down, staring into space. But as soon as he hears Sara he cheers up as she enters, slightly dishevelled from a pillow fight, looking happy and maternal, her figure buxom but slim-waisted and well proportioned. They discuss the death of Simon's father, the fact that Simon was not invited to the funeral, and that Joel had been the one to notify them. Deborah has not been in touch since their meeting at the cabin four years ago, and Sara recalls the way she used to write about Simon's book, the book which Sara had also been pushing him to complete. Simon, however, now realizes that he cannot write it and suspects that Sara was forcing him to work on it so that he would find the truth out for himself. Sara agrees that she had not believed in Simon's idealistic dream "with men and women what they are." But Simon instantly starts on a new dream—a work which will concern a courageous facing of life for what it is and the founding of a new morality. Sara twits him with his new notion, and Simon speaks of money, business, and acquisition of more companies, but momentarily he falls into what Sara calls "that black loneliness" as there is a knock at the door. Deborah and Joel arrive.

Joel leaves to discuss business with Simon while Deborah discusses her business with Sara. She announces that she has come to beg charity from Sara, a chance to live again, "to live in others' lives for their sake and not my sake," and be a true mother-in-law and grandmother. Sara is touched, yet wary, but Deborah slowly persuades her that they complement each other and can indeed be friends; she needs "the happy, greedy laughter of children" instead of merely waiting for death. In sympathy, Sara agrees, and then Deborah reveals that Joel has come to offer Simon a controlling interest in the financially ailing Harford Company and also that her late husband had suggested that she make over to Sara a half-interest in the Harford house and garden. Deborah's only condition is that she continue to live there with them, but with Sara in charge. Then, as Sara is greedily about to consent, Deborah asks to see the children. Sara departs to be sure they are asleep while Deborah shows her divided self: is she an actress, or is she sincere in her offer? She insists on sincerity as Simon enters with an expression of triumph in contrast to Joel's humiliation. He puts his hand on his mother's shoulder, promising to save her from ruin—but he has insisted that *his* company absorb that of his father. Joel leaves, having been promised his job as head bookkeeper, and Simon insults him to Deborah: "He isn't a man. He's a stuffed moral attitude!"

When Sara returns she is hurt that Simon has made this important decision without consulting her, and similarly, Simon is hurt that she and Deborah have come to an agreement about the house. Deborah notes that Sara has made Simon "your eldest son as well as your husband." He is disturbed with this new turn of events and the sudden friendship between the two women, expressing his doubts that "two such opposites" can live in daily harmony, telling them he wants no domestic dissension. Deborah gives "a solemn oath" that she will never complain to him, and Simon, convinced of their good faith, kisses them both.

Act II, Scene i: Simon Harford's private office, late summer, 1840, a conservatively furnished room with dark panelling and portraits of the Founding Fathers and John C. Calhoun. Simon enters, considerably changed. He looks older than his thirty-five years, has put on weight, and has the suggestion of a paunch. His face is thinner, his hair graying, his expression tense, and his manner "curtly dictatorial." He is well dressed but wears his clothes carelessly. He sits down and reads his mail with extraordinary speed. Joel enters and waits to be recognized, until Simon finally turns to him with exasperation. Obviously this is a frequently replayed scene in which Joel questions Simon's unscrupulous methods in running the company and his questionable expansion tactics—just like those of his father. Joel is about to leave when Simon calls him back so that he may unburden himself to Joel. Simon feels driven to complete these deals, but with each success he feels "empty, yet at the same time restless and aimless." He feels left out of his family life now, since Deborah and Sara have become such friends—his mother's doing, he is sure. In fact, she seems to have "taken possession of Sara in order to make of. . .[her] a second self through which she could live again." The two women seem to have become "a spirit of Woman made flesh and flesh of her made spirit, mother and wife in one." He himself now seems useless, since mother-become-wife has his sons as substitute for him, and his wife, possessing them, no longer needs a husband for begetting. Now he is an unwanted son, a discarded lover, nothing more than "a domestic slave whose greed can be used to bring in money to support Woman!" However, he has decided that they are both about to discover "that whenever I wish, I take back what belongs to me." After Joel's exit, he continues with his meditation. He hates what he has become, "a Napoleon among traders," and feels himself divided. And here one is forced to recall Deborah's cryptic warning to Sara in *A Touch of the Poet* that the Harford men never give up their dreams. Thus the dreamer still exists under the skin of the businessman, and he wishes to regain control of his own destiny.

For this reason he has asked Sara to come to his office, and when she enters it is clear that his concern is justified, for Sara seems to have appropriated some of the manner of Deborah, and her attitude toward her husband is maternal rather than the "passionate tenderness" of old. Simon and Sara start to spar verbally; clearly they have been living almost separate, circumscribed lives, working apart rather than together, a distance demonstrated by their use of the first person singular rather than the old, affectionate plural. Simon has even started sleeping separately, and he capitalizes on that hurt by arousing her sexual jealousy: "You probably think I must be secretly keeping some beautiful mistress who has stolen your place in bed!" He is successful in arousing her possessive instincts and in this way manages to drive a wedge between her and Deborah, suggesting that the two have become one woman to him and further that "Mother has always been extremely greedy for others' lives." Sara seizes on this, is abruptly contrite, and then is convinced when Simon suggests that the time the children spend with Deborah in the garden may make them "dependent on her for life," as had almost happened with Simon himself. The boys are to grow up in a world of "reality so when the time comes they will be capable of serving our company," and now he uses the plural again.

Sara is perturbed because she had promised to trust Deborah, but Simon convinces her that his mother is trying to steal their children, confusing them about the priority of their affections. He himself has become similarly confused at home, but here in his own world of business Sara becomes "yourself, my wife, my partner—my mistress, too, I hope." Sara is convinced, and they decide that the boys must be forbidden to visit their grandmother in her garden; Sara will do that, and "with feigned reluctance" Simon agrees to tell Deborah. What he wants of Sara is that she will again become the source of his success, work with him "in the company as my secretary and secret partner." But she will "have to pay for this opportunity" by playing the role of his mistress. Sara, at first embarrassed, then agrees joyfully: "I'll play any game with you you like, and it will be fun playing I'm a wicked lustful, wanton creature and making you a slave to my beauty." They embrace passionately, but then Simon talks mysteriously of the "game" she must play, the "identical lust" she will perceive. With her "adversary across the table," she will play with marked cards and loaded dice; and in the acceptance of them, the adversary "becomes oneself." Sara is both frightened and mystified by this comment but is placated when Simon tells her to draw plans for the magnificent country estate she has always wanted and speaks, to her concern, of love as business.

Finally she agrees, and after her departure, Simon makes his motivation clear— he has taken Sara back and will put Deborah in her own place. But then he becomes dreamy: "It will be pleasant to find myself in her garden after all these years." The old relationship and the old dreams are not dead. Suddenly Joel, the representative of the world of reality, enters to tell him that the directors of the latest company Simon has acquired are waiting, and Joel is doing these important folk the courtesy of announcing them. Maliciously Simon rejoices in his power and mocks Joel's consideration as the curtain falls.

Act II, Scene ii: Late afternoon in Deborah Harford's garden, as it appeared in Act I, Scene ii. The artificiality of the place "is of nature distorted and humiliated by a deliberately mocking, petulant arrogance." Deborah, dressed in white, sits on the summer house steps, looking like "a surprisingly youthful grandmother." She looks at peace, though her eyes and smile "still retain their old imaginative, ironical aloofness and detachment." She is reading from Byron's poems as she hears Simon's call, which brings "a little smile of gloating scorn" to her lips. She drops her book and opens the door to him. He leads her along, telling her that he has invited Sara to his office to tell her of a "new arrangement," a new private secretary who is "a young and very beautiful woman." Deborah reacts with "vindictive satisfaction and gloating pity," seeing this as "an inevitable step in the corruption of your character . . [into an] unscrupulous greedy trader, whose one dream was material gain."

But Simon turns the tables on her by recalling her own erotic fancies of the past, suggesting that she, in her role of "doting old Granny" is now out of place in her own garden, implying that it reflects her old dreams. He then tells her of his acquisitions, his monetary success, and his lack of self-fulfillment. Deborah seems to understand, recalling the way in which she longed for escape into madness, to push open that door of the summer house and of the mind and exist only in her dream world. She tries to leave, but Simon speaks of her as she was and what both this garden and her dream have meant to him. He wishes to return to this garden, with his mother "the good, kind, beloved, beautiful Queen [of it]. I have become so weary of what they call life beyond the wall, Mother."

He then tells her that Sara and he have decided that she is a bad influence on the children and consoles her for their loss by suggesting that she has fallen under Sara's influence, a comment which makes Deborah claim that *she* has influenced Sara "as part of my scheme!" Then, as with Sara, he speaks of seeing his mother and wife as one woman, a concept that Deborah takes up: "united against" you. But now she realizes that Simon has still remained hers, and she asks her place in this new scheme of things. With barely hidden eagerness, he says he will come every afternoon to see her: "A little rest here each day will restore the soul—the change I so badly need." With this he turns to the book of Byron's poems, looking for the parts he has marked, and the two trade lines back and forth. Ironically, this is the identical poem quoted by Cornelius Melody* in *A Touch of the Poet*: "I have not loved the World, nor the world me."

From the house Sara is heard calling Simon, but he and Deborah remain together, Simon asking his mother about the door to the summer house and her refusal to allow him to enter, recalling also the tale she had told him of the enchantress behind the door who warned the young king that behind that "magic door" lay disaster and not his "lost kingdom." Deborah tries to laugh the tale away, but Simon says that it has always been associated with the summer house and suggests that someday they will open that door and enter together. Deborah greets this proposal "with forced scorn," exacting as a condition of his being allowed to visit her that he never mention the matter again. Sara calls once more, and the two leave, arm in arm, each rejoicing in the return of the other. Simon has succeeded in sowing discord between Sara and Deborah, and now he warns his mother not to interfere in "this reorganization of my home."

Act II, Scene iii: "Parlor of the Harford mansion—a high-ceilinged fine proportioned room" in Massachusetts Federal style. It is 9 P.M. the same evening. Simon, dressed in black, sits at the table; Sara, in a blue semiformal evening gown, is across from him; and Deborah, in white, on the sofa at the rear of the room, attempts to read. Sara pretends to work at needlepoint, and Simon pretends to read. There is a curious air of tension as each of the three speaks inner thoughts in an approach reminiscent of *Strange Interlude*.* Sara is concerned that there is some secret between her husband and his mother. Deborah feels less certain of her son than she had felt in the garden, and Sara thinks possessively of Simon, her home, and her children: "let [Deborah] sit and dream herself into the madhouse." With equal hostility, Deborah looks ahead to Sara's becoming "no more than the empty name of wife, . . . our Irish biddy nurse girl and houseservant." Meanwhile, Simon gloatingly notes that they are not sitting together as has been their custom. He must take care that the game he now controls is played as he wishes.

Each in thought voices various hostilities until suddenly and simultaneously Sara and Deborah speak each other's name and forgive, uniting against Simon because they, with four sons, do not really need him. Simon can feel this hatred and blames Deborah for it, seeing her as "a cannibal witch whose greed will devour." The two women react to this hostility with teasing and maternal humoring, but as they move toward him they start to look like coquettish prostitutes, and, standing behind him, they both embrace him while their other arms remain intertwined. The three-way struggle continues until Simon leaves for his study, telling them to leave him alone while they fight their battles to the death. But then he turns to them as if "begging for pity," explaining that "when you unite to dispossess me . . . you compel me to defend what is mine—all I ask is that each of you keep your proper place in my mind."

He then taunts them with the secrets they have not yet shared. First Sara tells of Simon's plans for her at the office, his unscrupulous greed, and his "acting as if I was a street whore." Deborah speaks of Simon's plan to visit her nightly in her garden; she has agreed because he seemed such a lost little boy again. They strike a bargain: Sara will have him at the office and will have her sons to herself, while Deborah will entertain him in her garden. The two women, now almost one person, hope to bring him back to beg for family peace and reentry into their home. But their hostility lingers as Deborah looks at Sara as "the vulgar grasping harlot you were born to be," whom Simon will eventually drive back into the gutter. Sara looks on Deborah, swearing, "I'll keep what's mine from her if I have to drive her into the asylum itself!" Each looks for exclusive possession of Simon, and they smile confidentially at each other as the curtain falls.

Act III, Scene i: One year later, an early midsummer morning in 1841. The scene is Simon Harford's office, to which has been added a "garishly expensive and luxurious" sofa at center stage, an ornate mirror over Sara's desk, and an architect's drawing of a "nouveau-riche country estate on the shore of a small lake." The house is huge, a mixture of architectural styles, but based on a medieval castle reminiscent perhaps of Melody Castle in *A Touch of the Poet*. Sara is working at her desk. She has changed and "has grown strikingly voluptuous and provocatively female," dressed in seductive clothes. Her face has become dissipated-looking, her mouth "repellently sensual, ruthlessly cruel and greedy," with "cunning and unscrupulous" eyes. Her manner combines the curtness of a businesswoman with "calculating feminine seductiveness." Joel Harford enters, looking exactly the same, but his "insecure, and furtive" manner and his staring at Sara "with a sly desire" indicate a change in his moral stance.

As in Act II, Scene ii, Joel is announcing the head of another business which the Harford firm has absorbed. The two are alone because Simon is paying his morning visit to Deborah in her garden, and Joel makes it clear that he understands what has been happening in the office, that Sara has used her body to get Simon to sign over to her his business interests—but she is the one who has been swindled because Simon's properties are all deeply in debt: "He has abandoned all caution," like his father. Joel is also disgusted with the immorality of the situation but then begs forgiveness as Sara does the same. "It's Simon. I've got to be what he wants. He makes me want to be what he wants." At this, Joel offers to sell his share in the business; Sara "laughs teasingly," and Joel flings out of the room. She looks admiringly in the mirror and congratulates herself with the power and possessions she has won, but then she realizes, "He's made me think that life means selling yourself, and that love is lust." She has even felt momentary desire for Joel, but "was any one of us ever content with one man?" Nonetheless, Simon's lateness irks her, and she sees it as a plan of Deborah to torment her.

On his arrival she flings herself on him with sobs, but Simon is still in the daydream world of his mother until Sara reawakens him with her passion. He "tries to take her to the couch," but Sara insists that he "earn" her—this time with the new bank—and again they bicker over Deborah, Sara wanting undisputed possession of Simon. Her acquisitiveness seems insatiable, and her desire for more additions to the proposed house is similar. "With a mocking irony tinged with a bitter, tragic sadness," Simon quotes from Oliver Wendell Holmes, Sr., "The Chambered Nautilus," the lines which give the title to the play: "Build thee more stately mansions, O my soul." But Sara wishes to build this mansion for the material things of life, not the spiritual. This poem, Simon suggests, should be the motto for their house, their company, and Deborah's summer house, over the magic door.

The banker, Benjamin Tenard,* now appears for his appointment, and Simon insists that Sara interview him. This she does and offers him a position in his old business, planning to use his name and reputation for probity as a cover for her own unscrupulousness. With regret he accepts, because he can do nothing else, but then Sara realizes what Simon has made her; she is angry at the way in which he and Deborah must laugh at her as a "low, common slut," and momentarily wishes to go back to the old farm. A hint of the company's true position would ruin them. Greed has brought her so far. Now she feels she cannot go on, but Simon forces her to do so, with more grandiose dreams of owning the world: "You would have life under your feet then, just as you have me!" They embrace like lovers, and Sara tells him not to be late again, but Simon resentfully notes that neither woman will ever allow him to forget the other in their jealousy and desire to possess him. As he leaves, he offers Sara an ultimate temptation: "Can't you rid our life of that damned greedy evil witch?" She understands "with dread—but with a fascinated eagerness too," realizing that he is giving her *carte blanche* to drive Deborah into insanity.

Act III, Scene ii: Deborah Harford's garden about 9 P.M. that evening. There is a full moon that is frequently obscured by clouds. Deborah is walking in front of the summer house. She is "terribly emaciated," and her face looks like "a mask of death," appallingly wrinkled, with eyes that "smoulder with a bitter, jealous hatred." She seems on the edge of nervous collapse. As usual she is dressed in white and her hair is becomingly dressed, but her make-up is calculating, grotesque, coquettish, and she looks like a creature from the eighteenth century "come back to haunt the scene of long-past assignation." She has been waiting for some hours for Simon, and in her frantic reverie she speaks of her hatred of Sara and her desire to live "happily ever after" with her son. But the garden frightens her at night, and she fears insanity; perhaps Simon will trick her into unlocking the magic door and will push her "inside alone with that mad woman I locked in there." But, perhaps, she might leave him inside instead.

With that she dreams herself away into "the gardens at Malmaison" as Sara enters, looking "worn out and dissipated" and gazes on the old woman "with a cruel mocking leer of satisfaction." Still dreaming, Deborah goes to the little red door and unlocks it, about to enter with her imaginary lover to seek "love and forgetfulness." Sara's initial reaction is to wish her inside so that she and Simon will be together, but just as Deborah is turning the knob, Sara springs on her and pulls her back, finally telling her that Simon will never come to her garden again. That is the price that Sara has exacted from him. As Deborah looks upon Sara as 'a filthy harlot," the younger woman taunts her with what she has been in her erotic "crazy dreams." Deborah's dream is being destroyed, and she would rather enter the door, go insane, than face the truth. Sara claims she has come to seek peace; but again they battle over possession of Simon, Deborah saying she can take him with her, but Sara threatens murder if Deborah attempts to drive him into insanity. Deborah taunts Sara with being "weakly sentimental and pitiful," ordering her out of the garden. But when she hears Sara say that Simon is waiting to hear that his mother has gone beyond the little red door so that he can commit her to an asylum, she rushes after Sara, begging for help and promising anything: "Only—don't leave me here!" Sara believes she has won and they start to go, but then Deborah recalls Simon who has goaded them "into this duel to the death" because they have both loved him, and, as Sara says, "when only one is living, he knows she'll never have strength to claim her body or soul her own again!"

Unseen by them, Simon has entered, "in a state of terrific tension," with eyes that are "calculating and threatening and at the same time baffled and panic-stricken." He listens as Deborah proposes that she and Sara unite as one woman against Simon—"to fight it out with himself," as Sara puts it—for he has made them what they are. At this, Simon speaks his new creed, that belief in man's goodness is evil, for "he is, a hog." The "idealistic fallacy" that man is naturally good "is responsible for all the confusion in our minds, the conflicts within the self, and for all the confusions in our relationships with one another. . . . All one needs to remember is that good is evil, and evil, good." He has now realized that he must choose "in self-defense" one of his conflicting selves, not between one woman and the other, but what each represents in the duel which is ripping apart his mind.

The two women speak possessively of him as "our" son, husband, lover, saying that they have forgiven him. But Simon remains confused, and just as they are about to sit down, he gets rid of Sara by telling her the children are waiting for her. Simon then speaks disparagingly of Sara, telling Deborah he wants to rid himself of her, and Deborah tells once more the hatred she has felt for Simon, who has forgotten her in Sara's arms. But when he proposes doing away with his wife, Deborah is terrified. Simon has a new morality now in his philosophy of the worthlessness of human life and the meaninglessness of existence with death the only release, "Or, obsessed by a fairy tale, we spend our lives searching for a magic door and a lost kingdom of peace." Again, Simon speaks of murder, for "the murderer possesses the true quality of mercy." Deborah is afraid, for she has dreamt a similar dream, and then Simon announces that he has chosen his mother; there will be no murder; they will take another way "away from reality . . . You have only to open that door—" She attempts to put him off, but Simon insists that she restore to him "the faith you stole from me, or I will choose her!"

Simon longs for freedom from one of his conflicting selves and must either choose one or go insane. With that he says he chooses Sara and says farewell to Deborah, who promises to do anything as they speak again of the magic door. Opening it will readmit Simon into the love of his mother: 'The kingdom of peace and happiness in your story is love. You dispossessed yourself when you dispossessed me. Since then we have both been condemned to an insatiable greed for substitutes." But Deborah had wished for freedom from such emotional entanglements: "You were such a stubborn greedy little boy...And how can you admit you hated your mother and wished her dead!" He tempts her closer and closer to opening the door: "Let us leave this vile sty of lust and hatred and the wish to murder! Let us escape back into peace—while there is still time!'' ''With forced eagerness'' Deborah goes up the first step, hurried along by Simon; but Sara returns panic-stricken, raging against Deborah, and calling Simon to turn back. But the door fascinates him, and he orders Sara away as if she is a whore. She fights back, calling on Deborah to have pity, finally flinging herself at her feet, admitting defeat, telling her that she has won and that she herself will go away, ''sign everything over to you. All I'll keep is the old farm, so I'll have a home for my children.... You know no woman could love a man more than when she gives him up to save him.'' She is now ''beyond scheming,'' and in words that are reminiscent of her mother, Nora Melody,* and also Josie Hogan,* she wishes, ''God bless you, Simon, Darling, for all the joy and love you gave me, and give you peace and happiness!'' As she starts to leave, Deborah thanks her, but then decides that she will prove who loves Simon most, and turns to the dark doorway. He presses toward her as she pushes him away, goes in, and shuts the door of her ''Temple of Love.''

Simon falls, hitting his head as Sara goes to him, admiring Deborah for her renunciation and confessing her own part in Simon's ruin, through her own greed and her ''father's crazy dreams.'' Now she plans to devote her life to ''setting you free to be the man you were when I first met you—the man I loved best— the dreamer with a touch of the poet in his soul, and the heart of a boy.'' She will even smash the Harford company to prove her love, and they and the boys can return to a simple life on the old farm where Simon can again write his poetry and his book. But, practical to the last, Sara plans to see that Joel and Deborah are provided for so that she will have 'the comfort and riches and luxury that's due the great Princess on her great estate she'll be in her dream till the day she dies.''

Deborah reenters, dreamy and trancelike, looking many years younger, happy, and at peace with herself. She comes down the steps and orders Sara, ''the Irish kitchen maid,'' out of the ''palace grounds.'' She looks at Simon, asking if he is her lover, and says, ''I understand everything a woman's love could possibly compel her to desire. I know she can even kill herself to prove her love, so proud can she be of it,'' and again there is a curious echo of Nora Melody. Sara is suddenly frightened that Deborah is pretending in order to set Simon free, and Sara asks if she is happy. Deborah affirms her happiness and arrogantly offers Sara her hand to kiss. For a moment Sara is insulted but then kneels to thank her, adding ''And God bless you.'' Deborah looks back as she mounts the steps with ''gracious understanding amusement.'' ''I think that I may say that He has blessed me.'' With that, she closes the door behind her. Sara miserably realizes she will never know the whole truth, as Simon awakens, speaking again of ''peace and happiness'' beyond the door. But Sara raises him, and when he addresses her as ''Mother,'' she replies, ''Yes, I'll be your mother, too, now, and your peace and happiness and all you'll ever need in life!''

Comments: It is singularly difficult to discuss this rather clumsy play because of the manifold difficulties inherent in the text. The manuscript, which accidentally survived O'Neill's attempt to destroy it and is currently in the O'Neill collection at Yale University, is about five times the length of a normal play. It is impossible to know how O'Neill would have altered it for production and what he might have chosen to emphasize. As it stands in the published version, it is basically a psychological drama concerning the divided self of Simon Harford. The division is here represented by the two women of the play, Deborah, the mother, and Sara, the wife. But at the same time, the play contains echoes and themes of earlier plays. The tripartite aspect of woman (Mother, Wife, Mistress), for instance, is the same as that embodied in Nina Leeds* in *Strange Interlude*. And *Mansions* also shares the technique of the interior monologue spoken aloud. But it also contains the old theme of the dreamer whose dreams are destroyed through the machinations of Woman, which can be observed in *Bread and Butter,* *Beyond the Horizon,* *All God's Chillun Got Wings,* and *Before Breakfast,* most notably. In addition, the theme of the unfulfilled artist can be seen through the conflict between acquisitive Babbittry and romantic idealism, the ideals of *Marco Millions,* and through Juan Ponce de Leon* in *The Fountain.* As in *Beyond the Horizon,* the artist makes a destructive choice through his desire for a woman, but in *More Stately Mansions*, there is a suggestion that the woman, Sara, reaches some kind of understanding because of the sacrifice of another woman, Deborah, and is now prepared to serve that ideal in the manner of marital servitude that O'Neill constantly invoked with approval. As Alice Roylston* had said in *Servitude,* "Love is servitude," and Nora Melody in *A Touch of the Poet* embodied the same principle. The important thing is that the woman have no pride in herself but rather take pride in her love, which seems to lead to complete submission.

More Stately Mansions is filled with psychological symbols: the tower, the red door, the green door in the wall, the tortured garden, and even the little pool. The character drawing is symbolic, almost in the manner of case study, but the symptoms and the conflict are not entirely clear. Where in *Days Without End,* John Loving* reaches a final integration of personality through a religious experience, in this play Simon is left to place his faith in Sara, the ultimate woman who will be there to serve rather than devour him. In a sense, their future would seem to be a time of rest, similar to that of Nina Leeds when, with her son grown and all passion spent, she settles for a father figure. Sara seems also to have gone beyond passion and become the ultimate figure of womankind, with the erotic predatory component common to both Deborah and Sara (and presumably all women, in O'Neill's mind) exorcised. At the same time, Sara dreams of acquisitiveness and materialism, the epitome of what O'Neill in the uncompleted *Dynamo* trilogy wished to show as the failure of American society. But *Mansions* concentrates on Simon Harford with his psychic wound, his rejection as son by his mother and then her cultivation of him as lover, which leads him to look continually for Woman who like Cybel* in *The Great God Brown* will minister to him. By the end of the play, Sara has become that woman, and curiously, she has adopted the self-abnegation of her mother, Nora Melody.

Production Data: Written : 1935?–1941? dates uncertain. Unfinished manuscript dated 1938. First produced at the Royal Dramatic Theatre (Kungl. Dramatiska Teatern), Stockholm, Sweden, in a version shortened from the original manuscript by Karl Ragnar Gierow,* September 11, 1962, in a translation by Sven Barthel* (49 performances).

Producer: Dramaten
Director: Stig Torsslow
Set Design: Sven Fahlstedt
Costumes: Agneta Pauli
Cast: Deborah Harford: Inga Tidblad
    Simon Harford: Jarl Kulle
    Sara Melody Harford: Gunnel Broström
    Joel Harford: Henrik Schildt
    Benjamin Tenard: Olof Sandborg
    Nicholas Gadsby: Tord Stål

First American production produced by Elliot Martin at the Ahmanson Theatre, Los Angeles, California, September 12, 1967; transferred to the Broadhurst Theatre, New York City, October 31, 1967 (142 performances).

Director: José Quintero*
Settings: Ben Edwards
Costumes: Jane Greenwood
Lighting: John Harvey
Cast: Jamie Cregan: Barry Macollum
    Mickey Maloy: Vincent Dowling
    Nora Melody: Helen Craig
    Sara Melody Harford : Colleen Dewhurst*
    Simon Harford: Arthur Hill
    Cato: John Marriott
    Deborah Harford: Ingrid Bergman*
    Nicholas Gadsby: Fred Stewart
    Joel Harford: Lawrence Linville
    Benjamin Tenard: Kermit Murdock

A Note on Text: The text used is that published by Yale University Press. This was shortened from the author's manuscript by Karl Ragnar Gierow and edited by Donald Gallup; it contains less than half of O'Neill's typescript. In the Quintero version, the play begins with the wake of Cornelius Melody* to emphasize the connection with *A Touch of the Poet*, hence the larger cast. The play was fairly successful, achieving its modest run largely because of the presence of Ingrid Bergman, though Colleen Dewhurst proved the finer actress.

MOSHER, Ed. In *The Iceman Cometh*,* a former circus worker. He is around sixty and "looks like an enlarged, elderly, bald edition of the village fat boy...congenitally indolent, a practical joker, a born grafter and con merchant. . .essentially harmless,'' dressed in flashy, worn clothes. He is the brother-in-law of Harry Hope,* the saloon proprietor, and the friend of Pat McGloin,* the ex-police lieutenant dismissed from the force for graft. He knows that Bessie, Hope's late wife, was really a shrew, but he goes along with Hope's near-sanctification of her memory, partly because Harry allows him booze on the house. Mosher rents a room from Harry, and his pipe dream is that he will go back to the circus and get his old job again. Under the influence of Theodore Hickman,* the salesman who comes to the bar annually to celebrate Harry's birthday, Mosher attempts to translate the dream into reality, but he cannot go through with it. After Hickey's arrest on the charge of murdering his wife, Mosher and other denizens of the bar seize on his plea of insanity, a pipe-dream explanation which discredits what he has taught them. They then gladly get drunk as a means of forgetting the outside world and of regaining illusions.

MOTHER OF LAZARUS, in *Lazarus Laughed*,* ''a gentle, simple woman, tall and stout, over sixty-five.'' She sides with the Orthodox against Lazarus,* and Martha* and Mary.* She dies as the result of a conflict between the followers of Lazarus and a combination of Nazarene and Orthodox Jews, which escalates into an attack on both by the Roman soldiers. She is thus among the first martyrs to Lazarus's cause.

MOTT, Joe. In *The Iceman Cometh*,* a light-skinned black man about fifty years old. He is one of the roomers at the saloon kept by Harry Hope,* doing odd jobs to get money for liquor. Mott is the former proprietor of a ''colored'' gambling house and is dressed in worn sporty clothes which still ''preserve an atmosphere of nattiness.'' His pipe dream is that someday he will be able to open up a gambling hall again, with the help of his old connections with the chief of police and with Harry's influence with Tammany Hall. Under the influence of Theodore Hickman,* the salesman who comes to the bar annually to celebrate Hope's birthday, Mott attempts to translate the dream into reality but, realizing its impossibility, becomes angry against what he perceives as racial discrimination from among the other bar room inhabitants. After Hickey's arrest on the charge of murdering his wife, Joe and other denizens of the bar seize on his plea of insanity, a pipe-dream explanation which discredits what he has taught them. They then gladly get drunk in order to forget the outside world and to regain illusions.

MOURNING BECOMES ELECTRA, the title of a trilogy of plays (thirteen acts) in which Eugene O'Neill reinterprets the *Oresteia* using a New England setting and placing the action in 1865–1866, just after the American Civil War. The titles of the individual plays, which are performed as a unit, are *Homecoming, The Hunted,* and *The Haunted.* Except for the fourth act of *The Hunted*, the action ''takes place in or immediately outside the Mannon residence, on the outskirts of one of the small New England seaport towns.'' A curtain gives the appearance of the house as seen from the street and also shows something of "the extensive grounds—about thirty acres—which surround the house," with woods, orchards, flower garden, and greenhouse. There are locust and elm trees along the street frontage, with a white picket fence and "a tall hedge" to separate the property from the street. Before the house is a large lawn with a curving driveway leading to it from two entrances. The house itself is on a slight rise. "It is a large building of the Greek temple type.... A white wooden portico with six tall columns contrasts with the wall of the house proper which is of gray cut stone. There are five windows on the upper floor and four on the ground floor, with the main entrance in the middle, ... The window shutters painted a dark green. Before the doorway a flight of four steps leads from the ground to the portico."

HOMECOMING Act I: "Exterior of the Mannon House on a late afternoon in April, 1965.... It is shortly before sunset and the soft light of the declining sun shines directly on the front of the house." The sound of a band playing "John Brown's Body" is heard from the distance, and then closer, the thin, aged voice of Seth Beckwith,* the Mannons' seventy-five-year-old gardener, is heard singing "Shenandoah." These pieces of music introduce two themes of the trilogy, the return from the war, and the sea. Beckwith enters, followed by Amos Ames,* his wife, Louisa Ames,* and her cousin, Minnie,* all dressed in their Sunday best. Ames is a carpenter in his fifties, "the townsfolk type of garrulous gossip-monger" but not evil. Louisa "is taller and stouter than he and about the same age. Of a similar scandal-bearing type, her tongue is sharpened by malice.... Minnie is a plump little woman of forty, of the meek, eager-listener type,... [All] three are types of townsfolk rather than individuals," and they constitute a chorus similar to that in Greek drama which is used here as an expository device to inform the audience of the following facts about the Mannons: Ezra Mannon,* a West Point graduate, fought in the Mexican War but left the army when his father died and took over the family shipping business. He also learned law and became a judge and mayor of the town, but when the War between the States began, he resigned and went to fight. His wife, Christine Mannon,* is "French and Dutch descended,... Furrin lookin' and queer," the impecunious daughter of a New York doctor. Ezra's brother, David Mannon,* married a "French Canuck nurse girl he'd got into trouble" and was disinherited by the family. In his rage, Ezra's father, Abe Mannon, tore down the house in and erected the present dwelling.

As the group watches, they see Christine Mannon,* a woman with a "fine, voluptuous figure," enter through the front door of the house. She is about forty and "moves with a flowing animal grace." She has extraordinary hair, a mixture of copper brown and bronze gold, and her handsome face in repose is like a "mask in which only the deep-set eyes, of a dark and violet blue, are alive." She listens "defensively" to the band music and then walks past the hidden group toward the flower garden. Seth, grumbling about chores he has been asked to do, returns to invite the townspeople to accompany him on a conducted tour of the grounds just as Lavinia Mannon* appears "where her mother had stood."

She is twenty-three but looks older, a tall, thin, angular young woman, flat-chested, square-shouldered, almost military in her bearing. She is the picture of repression, with facial characteristics and hair that almost duplicate her mother's; but where Christine is voluptuous, Lavinia deemphasizes her femininity, pulling her curly hair back into a severe knot and wearing black rather than the green that suits her mother so well. As she looks after her mother, her eyes are bleak with enmity.

Lavinia and Seth speculate about the end of the war, and Lavinia reveals that she has made a recent trip to New York. Seth starts to warn her about ''that Captain Brant,'' but their conversation is cut short by the arrival of Hazel Niles* and Peter Niles.* Hazel is a frank, pretty girl of nineteen and Peter a straight-forward, heavily built young man of twenty-two, a captain in the Union Army who has recently been invalided home with a wound. They discuss the imminent end of the war, and Hazel asks after Orin Mannon,* Lavinia's brother. Peter again asks Lavinia to marry him, and she refuses him, as she had done a year earlier, saying that her father needs her; however, she relieves Peter's anxiety in telling him that Adam Brant* is not courting her. This ship captain is ''a darned romantic-looking cuss'' who reminds Peter of someone. Just then Christine returns, and the mother and daughter exchange looks of bitter hatred. After Peter leaves, Lavinia asks about the health of her grandfather, whom Christine has recently visited in New York, and Christine, after answering her, meditates on the ''whited sepulchre'' look of the Mannon house. She also mentions Captain Brant, saying that she ''happened to run into. . .[him] on the street in New York'' and that he had asked if he could come to see Lavinia. He is coming to dinner this evening. Lavinia asks if that is why her mother has been getting flowers for the house and then discusses the end of the war and her father's return. The two women seem to have an armed truce, but as Christine enters the house, Lavinia announces that she wants to talk with her ''before long.''

When Lavinia is left alone, Seth reenters to return to the discussion of Captain Brant and reveals to her his suspicion that Brant is the son of Ezra Mannon's brother, David, and the ''French Canuck nurse girl,'' Marie Brantôme,* whom he had married after making her pregnant. Seth suggests that Lavinia should try to find out the truth. Almost immediately on Seth's departure, Adam Brant appears. He is almost Byronically romantic in appearance and dress, dark-haired and almost foppish, but his face has the same masklike quality of the Mannons. He greets Lavinia with winning gallantry, and they talk about the conclusion of the war and Ezra Mannon's return, Lavinia saying, ''I love Father better than anyone in the world. There is nothing I wouldn't do–to protect him from hurt!'' The two spar verbally, until Brant finally asks Lavinia what she has against him. He recalls the night he tried to kiss her and then suggests that his talk of the sea and his love for clipper ships may have made her jealous. But he also notes her interest in his tales of the South Seas. Lavinia takes up the topic, recalling his comments on ''the naked native women. You said they had found the secret of happiness because they had never heard that love can be a sin.'' Brant starts to expatiate on what he calls "the Blessed Isles," but as he attempts to take her hand, she turns on him insultingly: "But I suppose it would be foolish to expect anything but cheap romantic lies from the son of a low Canuck nurse girl."

Brant is stunned, but then he asserts that his parents had loved each other and that he feels shame only for his Mannon blood. His father eventually turned to drink, but his mother always loved her husband in spite of his abuse of her. Brant ran away to sea, refusing to use the Mannon name, and forgetting about his mother until two years ago when he found her ill and dying, having been refused help by Ezra Mannon. "I swore on my mother's body I'd revenge her death on him.' Lavinia suggests, "I suppose you boast that now you've done so,...in the vilest, most cowardly way—like the son of a servant you are!" She thus intimates her knowledge of Christine's affair with him. He tries to put her off, but Lavinia orders him to stay outside while she goes in to confront her mother, leaving Brant stammering that Lavinia is his love.

Act II: Ezra Mannon's study, an austere room with pictures of George Washington, Alexander Hamilton, and John Marshall, the Founding Fathers, and a large portrait of Ezra, painted in his judicial robes some ten years earlier when he was in his forties. He is shown as a stern, aloof, handsome, yet cold and emotionless man. His face has the masklike Mannon quality. The setting sun illuminates the room with gold which changes during the action to crimson and finally darkness. Lavinia stands by the table looking at her father's portrait: "Poor Father!" Christine enters, and Lavinia taxes her with an illicit affair in New York with Adam Brant, revealing that she had followed her mother to her assignation in the city, had seen her meet Brant, and had heard her tell him of her love. Shaken, Christine tries to explain what it has been like, married to a man she has hated.

Certainly, she had once loved Ezra: "He was handsome in his lieutenant's uniform! He was silent and mysterious and romantic! But marriage soon turned his romance into—disgust!" Lavinia recalls her feeling that her mother has always hated her, and Christine says she had tried to love her, but "You were always my wedding night to me—and my honeymoon." However, things are different with Orin Mannon, Lavinia's brother, because while Christine was carrying him, Ezra was away in the Mexican War, "and when Orin was born he seemed my child, only mine, and I loved him for that!" But she has turned against him since Lavinia nagged him into going to the war as an act of duty. In her loneliness for Orin, and a longing for love, she met Adam, who told her he loved her. She is surprised that Lavinia has discovered the secret of Adam's parentage but recovers well and asks what she intends to do when her father returns from the war.

Lavinia promises to keep silent if Christine will give up Brant and continue as a dutiful wife to Ezra. Christine suggests that this is Lavinia's mode of vengeance; since she cannot have Adam for herself, she will ensure that Christine will not gain him, and she accuses her daughter in a Freudian context: "You've tried to become the wife of your father and the mother of Orin! You've always schemed to steal my place!'' Lavinia denies this accusation and insists that Christine give her an answer, pointing out the revenge that Ezra Mannon could inflict on Adam Brant if they were to go away together. He could be blacklisted and lose his command, while Ezra Mannon would never divorce Christine. And then Lavinia cruelly points out that her mother is five years older than her lover. At this, Christine almost strikes Lavinia, but agrees to stop seeing Adam. Then she gains some revenge by telling Lavinia, ''I made him flirt with you, so you wouldn't be suspicious.'' Threateningly, Lavinia says that she has already written to her father and Orin, telling them that people have been gossiping about Christine and Brant. This knowledge enrages Christine, who warns Lavinia, ''You'll be responsible if—!'' leaving her sentence unfinished. Finally, Christine seems to realize that she has no choice but to agree to Lavinia's proposal.

After Lavinia has marched out, Christine writes two words on a slip of paper which she hides in her dress sleeve as she calls for Adam. As she waits, she addresses her husband's portrait, ''You can thank Vinnie, Ezra!'' Adam then enters the room, the first time he has entered the Mannon portals. They speak of Lavinia's discovery of Brant's identity and of their own love. Desperately, Brant proposes to kill Ezra or fight a duel with him, but Christine dissuades him. She wishes Ezra dead but does not want to lose Adam because she hopes to go away with him on his ship. She then hands him the paper, asking him to obtain the poison that is listed there; her plan is to administer it to Ezra and let everyone think he has died of heart failure, for she has tricked the family doctor into believing that Ezra's heart is very weak. Brant demurs, but Christine taunts him with cowardice and then arouses his rage by reminding him that Ezra Mannon is coming back to her bed. At this, Adam Brant agrees, and as the cannon booms from the harbor entrance announcing the end of the war, Christine reminds her lover of his dream of his own ship and his forthcoming possession of her. Left alone, she reveals her secret fear: ''You'll never dare leave me now, Adam— for your ships or your sea or your naked Island girls—when I grow old and ugly!'' She turns around, looks at Ezra's portrait (so curiously resembling Adam Brant) with a shudder, and leaves the room.

Act III: The exterior of the Mannon house at about 9 P.M. a week later. The light of a half-moon illuminates the facade, giving the white columns the air of ''an incongruous mask fixed on the somber stone house.'' Lavinia, dressed in black, is sitting stiffly on the top of the portico steps, staring straight ahead. The sound of Seth's voice singing ''Shenandoah'' is heard approaching. He is a trifle intoxicated, and when Lavinia taxes him with being drunk twice this week he says that first he celebrated Lee's defeat, now he has been drowning his sorrow over Lincoln's assassination, and he plans to be drunk a third time, when Ezra Mannon returns. In answer to Lavinia's questioning, Seth recalls the charm and friendliness of Adam's mother, Marie Brantôme, noting that Ezra had hated her worse than anyone else ''when it got found out she was his uncle David's fancy woman,'' a statement Lavinia as a loving daughter refuses to accept. Just then Christine enters and stands behind Lavinia in an attitude that accentuates both their facial resemblance and their physical hostility and dissimilarity. Tauntingly, Christine suggests that Lavinia had better marry Peter Niles to avoid being left an old maid, but the young woman insists that she won't marry: "I've got my duty to Father!" Christine dislikes this word "duty" and seems unhappy to be reminded of it, but her curious quietness leads Lavinia to suspect that she is plotting something, perhaps to see Adam again, though she denies it.

Footsteps are heard in the distance, and Ezra Mannon comes into view, "a tall, spare, big-boned man of fifty, dressed in the uniform of a Brigadier-General." His face has the masklike look of the Mannons, and he moves almost like a wooden soldier. His voice is hollow and unemotional, "his air is brusque and authoritative." Lavinia rushes to him and throws her arms around him, kissing him, and then bursting into tears. Christine and Mannon greet each other stiffly, and Ezra compliments her on her appearance. She suggests that they sit out in the moonlight for a while, but Lavinia tries to compete for his attention by suggesting food. Mannon, a trifle embarrassed by this "coddling," though he likes it, sits down with Christine. Almost immediately Ezra Mannon raises the question of Adam Brant's visit, which Christine laughs off by suggesting that he is Vinnie's "latest beau." Lavinia, caught off balance, says that she had only walked out with him until she discovered that Brant was "the kind who chases after every woman he sees" and suggests that Brant had even thought Christine was flirting with him. Since this might have caused town gossip, she, Lavinia, had written to Ezra. Finally, Mannon tries to put a stop to their bickering by ordering Lavinia indoors, but as she leaves she kisses him: "You're the only man I'll ever love! I'm going to stay with you!"

After Lavinia goes indoors ("Don't let anything worry you, Father. I'll always take care of you"), Mannon and Christine discuss the matter of Adam Brant, he being angry at the possibilities for gossip, and Christine claiming that Brant is believed by everyone to be courting Vinnie. He has been welcomed because he brought news of Christine's ailing father, and then she imposes calculatingly on his sympathy by talking of the strain she has endured.

Mannon, deeply moved, kisses her, but as he attempts to caress her she turns away in repulsion. Again Mannon is about to kiss her but is stopped by the fact that her eyes are shut and there is some great emotional distance between them. He starts to tell her how strange he feels, at home now, after the crowded camps; he has wanted to communicate with Christine, but "your eyes were always so— so full of silence! That is, since we've been married." She tells him not to talk, but he goes on, telling her that his experience of death has made him think of life, and he has been thinking about the wall that has separated them throughout their marriage. He recalls that she seemed almost pleased when he went to the Mexican War, perhaps hoping he would die. On his return he discovered that she had become more attached to Orin than him, so then he "turned to Vinnie, but a daughter's not a wife." After that he worked to make a success of the shipping business, then became judge and mayor, just so that he could leave

Christine "alone in your life and not care." Above all else, he has wanted her love, the love he had once had from her and which she does not deny. He offers himself to her: "I came home to surrender to you—what's inside me. I love you. I loved you then, and all the years between, and I love you now." He suggests that they try to start again, go away together, . . . I've got to make you love me."

Christine springs up wildly, telling him to stop talking, but then quite calculatingly she tells the emotionally wounded man, "There is no wall between us. I love you." Mannon wishes be could believe her and kisses her passionately as Lavinia comes out. She watches after her parents as they go upstairs to their room: "I hate you! You steal even Father's love from me again! You stole all love from me when I was born!" She decided that it is her duty to inform him about "that shameless harlot" and calls out "Father! Father!" But when her father opens the shutters she "stammers lamely," claiming that she had forgotten to say goodnight. As the curtain falls, Lavinia is staring up at the window and "wringing her hands in pitiful desperation."

Act IV: Ezra Mannon's bedroom with a big four-poster bed and a door leading to Christine's room. As the light comes up Christine slips silently from the bed, goes over to a chair, and puts on her dressing gown. Mannon asks her the time: "Must be near daybreak." Neither has slept, but Christine reacts with dread to the suggestion that they light the lamp and talk. She keeps her head turned away as they speak about their relationship and notes that Vinnie was pacing outside the house like a sentry until 2 A.M. "There is one who loves me, at least," says Ezra, but then when he says he feels strange, she asks if it is his bad heart. Suddenly Ezra understands why she gave herself willingly to him. She is wishing for his death to set her free. Christine claims that he has acted as if she is his property, and the two of them castigate each other until finally Christine reveals the truth about her affair with Brant and also about his parentage.

This triggers a heart attack, and instead of medication, Christine administers the poison she had asked Brant to obtain. Mannon, realizing what has happened, calls for Lavinia, and with his dying voice he gasps, "She's guilty—not medicine." Lavinia cannot believe that Christine would be quite so evil as to poison him, thinking at first that the revelation of the affair with Brant was the cause of his death, but Christine who has been concealing the small box of poison behind her back, falls in a faint and drops it. Lavinia, in "strident denunciation," threatens that she will punish her mother and will prevent her marriage to Adam. When she finds the box, she sinks on her knees by her father's bed, embracing him and crying out, "Don't leave me alone! Come back to me! Tell me what to do!"

Comments: By now the equations with the Orestes legend are clear, Lavinia (Electra), Christine (Clytemnestra), Ezra (Agamemnon), Orin (Orestes), and Brant (Aegisthos). The next play is concerned with a second murder, that of Aegisthos (Brant).

THE HUNTED   Act I: The exterior of the Mannon house on a moonlit night two days after Ezra Mannon's murder. The shutters are closed, and two funeral wreaths are visible, one on a column and the other on the front door. Josiah Borden,* Everett Hills,* and their wives, together with Dr. Blake,* are being ushered out. As in *Homecoming*, these five people act as the chorus for the play. Josiah Borden, the manager of the Mannon shipping company, is sixtyish, "shrewd and competent." His wife, about ten years younger, is a horse-faced, assertive woman. Everett Hills, the minister, is "stout and unctuous, snobbish and ingratiating, in his fifties, [with] a sallow, flabby, self-effacing" wife. Dr. Joseph Blake, the family doctor, is "a stout, self-important old man with a stubborn, opinionated expression." The women discuss the reactions of Christine and Lavinia Mannon to Ezra Mannon's sudden death, noting that Christine had insisted that Peter Niles escort Lavinia to the train station to meet Orin, her brother. They join the men who are discussing the arrangements for Ezra's funeral, which is to be a very quiet one, according to his own wish, Christine says. Dr. Blake is quite certain that Ezra has died of angina, judging from the symptoms Mrs. Mannon had described to him, taken from a letter allegedly sent her by Ezra. He also suggests to Borden that Ezra died as the result of lovemaking with Christine; and as the two of them change salacious grins, Christine enters.

She is obviously under a terrible strain, barely in control, looking momentarily as if she wishes to flee, but when Hazel Niles, appearing the same as in *Homecoming*, comes out to stand behind her, she pulls herself together. The two discuss Orin's imminent arrival, Christine asking the young woman whether she loves Orin, and warning her that Lavinia will try to prevent their marriage because of her possessiveness toward her brother. Hazel attributes Lavinia's silence and continual observation of Christine as grief-stricken response to her father's death, a suggestion that makes Christine realize how "good and pure of heart" Hazel is and also causes her to regret her own lost innocence. She suggests that they wait inside; she can't bear to see Orin coming up the drive because he looks so like his father: "Let's go in. I hate moonlight. It makes everything so haunted."

After a moment, Orin Mannon enters, followed by Peter and Lavinia. He is astonishingly like both his father and Adam Brant, "but his body is thin and his swarthy complexion sallow." His chin also has a "weakened" refinement alien to his father. His head is bandaged, and his jerky military bearing seems vaguely unnatural. He is only twenty but looks ten years older. He is dressed as a first lieutenant in the Union Army, but his uniform is baggy and ill-fitting. He looks at the house, perceiving it as "ghostly and dead," and says that he had been told by Ezra "the trouble he had wasn't serious." This comment corroborates Lavinia's recollection, and she manages to send Peter inside while they discuss the Brant scandal. Then Lavinia warns him against allowing Christine to cosset him again. Christine's voice is heard, berating Peter for leaving Orin with Lavinia, and then she rushes out to embrace her son. She sends him in to Hazel as Lavinia gives him another warning.

Left alone with her daughter, Christine tries to explain her affair with Brant
and then asks the whereabouts of "some medicine I take to put me to sleep."
She suggests that Lavinia has been waiting for Orin's return to inform the police
of her suspicions concerning Ezra's death. In fury she tries to get her daughter
to tell her what she plans to do but recovers her composure when she hears
Orin's voice calling her from within the house.

Act II: "The sitting room of the Mannon house." It is larger than the study,
a severe room with a "bleak" atmosphere; nothing is out of place, and grim
ancestral portraits hang on the walls. Even the two feminine portraits have the
masklike appearance seen in the Mannon men. Hazel is sitting on a chair, center-
front, while Peter is on the sofa, right. Orin's voice can be heard calling, as at
the end of Act I. No time has elapsed, and they are discussing the surviving
Mannons, stopping "self-consciously" as Orin and Christine enter. Orin is
enjoying the coddling that his mother is giving him, but at the same time he is
aware that since his father's death a subtle change has come over the house,
though Hazel has remained "sweet and good."

Orin, and to some extent Peter, are recalling the war when Lavinia enters and,
in a voice that sounds like that of her dead father, orders Orin to look at his
body. Embarrassed, Hazel and Peter leave, and Orin taxes his mother with not
having written to him, asking also about Captain Brant. Christine suggests that
the whole matter is "nonsense," an accusation invented by Lavinia who will
stop at nothing. She tries to take Orin back to their old secret world of his
childhood when they stood together against the Mannons, claiming that Ezra
had even hated Orin, his own son. Now the two of them can be happy together,
as long as Orin does not allow Lavinia to fill him with lies. She claims that
Lavinia's hostility toward her arises from her having fallen in love with Brant,
when he was merely trying to use her influence to get a new ship. Skillfully she
tells the truth about Brant's origins, her own assignation with him in New York,
and her part in Ezra's death interpreting this information as evidence of her
daughter's insane suspicions. Orin believes and comforts her but still retains a
nagging suspicion about Brant, saying he would kill the man if the accusation
were true. He sits on the floor at her feet telling her about his dream of the South
Sea islands depicted in Herman Melville's *Typee*, islands of peace like those of
which Christine and Brant have spoken earlier. To Orin, Christine has come to
be the personification of the security and beauty of those islands, and slowly the
two begin to adopt the relationship of lovers rather than mother and son: "We'll
get Vinnie to marry Peter and there will be just you and I."

This moment of abnormal tenderness is interrupted by Lavinia, who again
orders Orin to view the body of his dead father. When he leaves, Christine
defiantly dares Lavinia to do her worst because Orin is convinced of his mother's
innocence. Further, he won't go to the police because he does not want the
Mannon name disgraced. And she herself would claim that Lavinia is "a daughter
who desired her mother's lover and then tried to get her mother hanged out of
hatred and jealousy." But then her recklessness crumbles, and she pleads to

Lavinia to keep Orin out of the matter. He would kill Adam, and she could not live without her lover. Left alone, she is terrified: "I've got to see Adam! I've got to warn him!" She sinks into a chair as the curtain falls.

Act III: Ezra Mannon's study with his body, dressed in uniform, laid out in front of his father's portrait which his dead face almost duplicates. Orin stands at the foot of the bier, looking at his father, and his face almost reproduces that of his ancestors. He wonders about the truth of the accusations he has heard and then meditates on death and Ezra Mannon's embodiment of it. Perhaps they can now be friends since Ezra is dead. Lavinia then enters, having overheard his strangely callous comments, but Orin proceeds to speak of his hatred of war, his own accidental heroism, and his father's treatment of him. Lavinia openly accuses Christine of murdering Ezra, producing the box of poison as evidence. She tries to convince Orin, swearing upon the body of their father; her brother still tries not to believe her, wresting the box of poison from her hand and hiding it. But Lavinia manages to hit Orin on a tender spot when she suggests that he might not care that Christine had poisoned his hated father—but "I hope you're not such a coward that you're willing to let her lover escape!" To Orin's horror she alleges that Christine is plotting to run off and marry Brant.

Enraged, Orin threatens, "I'll kill that bastard!" and agrees to Lavinia's suggestion that they give Christine the chance to flee to Brant as a means of corroborating Lavinia's tale. Suddenly, Christine's voice is heard at the locked door of the study, and Lavinia takes the box of poison from Orin's pocket, placing it prominently on Ezra's body in an attempt to gain proof. Christine enters in a state of semicollapse. She calls on Orin for protection against Lavinia, saying that they must avoid scandal; she addresses the body of her dead husband, but suddenly sees the poison box and gives a stifled scream. Orin, devastated by these events, "laughs with savage irony." He had thought home would give him a respite from death: "You're my lost island, aren't you, Mother?" Left alone with her mother, Lavinia asks whether Brant had procured the poison. Christine denies it, but Lavinia knows the truth. The curtain falls as Christine stares after her daughter and then cries out to her dead husband: "Ezra! Don't let her harm Adam! I am the only guilty one! Don't let Orin—." As she looks on him she seems to see something there that terrifies her and she backs out the door, her eyes fixed on the face of her husband.

Act IV: "The stern section of a clipper ship moored alongside a wharf in East Boston," at night two days after Ezra Mannon's funeral. The moon is rising to the left and the sound of "Shenandoah" is heard floating across the water, sung by a Chanteyman with the crew as chorus. Another Chanteyman, a dissipated-looking man of about sixty-five, criticizes the singing and repeats the song. As he sings and reminisces, Adam Brant enters, concerned about the safety of his ship: "I'm lacking a watchman and I've got to keep my weather eye open." The Chanteyman asks if Brant needs a chanteyman for his next voyage and then mentions Ezra Mannon's death. He could not have died of heart failure because he was such a "skinflint" that he had none; he then wonders who will get his money. "Leave a widder, did he?" Taken aback, Brant changes the subject, and the Chanteyman compliments him on his ship but then launches into a new chant, "Hanging Johnny," when a rattled Brant cuts him short. He has a premonition that he will "never take this ship to sea." He is acting "like a coward hiding behind a woman's skirts! The sea hates a coward!"

At this moment the fearful Christine appears and is greeted by an equally jumpy Brant who has drawn his revolver. She goes on board, and Brant insists that he won't "let them take me alive." Christine reveals that Vinnie knows about the poison, but she is sure that Orin still believes in her innocence. Brant is concerned that Vinnie may have followed her mother, but Christine is confident that she has not. They go into the cabin, and after a pause, Orin and Lavinia enter. "Her manner is cold and grim. Orin is holding in a savage, vengeful rage." They move to the lighted skylight and bend over to listen as the scene fades into darkness.

Several minutes elapse, and when the lights go on, the interior of the cabin is revealed. Brant is seated at the right of a table with a bottle of whiskey on it, and Christine is to the rear. She looks haggard and disheveled as she finishes "her story of the murder and the events following it." Brant berates himself for not having tried to fight Ezra Mannon in a duel, and the two speak of escape. The clipper, *Flying Trades* won't be ready to leave for a month, and so Christine suggests that they take passage on another ship for China and marry there, "out of Vinnie's reach." But Brant will have to give up his ship, something that causes Christine some guilt and Brant much regret. They try to bolster each other's courage by dreaming of the "Blessed Islands," and Brant escorts Christine off the boat; they will leave together in a couple of days.

On the deck above, Orin pulls out his gun but is prevented by Lavinia from shooting Brant as he passes, and they enter the cabin. With great practicality, Lavinia has wanted to avoid the possibility of a shot being overheard, because that way revenge would not be particularly sweet for them. Certainly Christine would be hanged, but their own lives would be ruined and Brant would have gained revenge on the Mannon clan. Brant comes in the door, sadly bidding farewell to his ship: "I wasn't man enough for you!" At this, Orin shoots him at point-blank range. Adam falls, and then Orin starts to smash up the cabin to give the impression that burglary was the motive. Lavinia "prays coldly" over "the soul of our cousin, Adam Mannon," as Orin returns looking with strange fascination at the corpse. It is like his war dream: "I've killed him before— over and over. . . . The faces of the men I killed came back and changed to Father's face and finally became my own? He looks like me, too! Maybe I've committed suicide!" Lavinia tries to pull him away, but he stays, saying that in Adam's place he "would have loved her as he loved her—and killed Father too—for her sake!" Orin's parting words as the curtain falls are "It's a rotten dirty joke on someone!"

Act V: The following night, the exterior of the Mannon house, just after moonrise, with Christine pacing the drive in front of the portico. She is waiting for someone, and Hazel appears, having been summoned by Christine to keep her company in her sadness and nervousness. She sees herself as being in hell and is also concerned that she has not heard from Orin and Lavinia. Hazel offers to stay the night with her but leaves to pick up some clothes, so Christine is alone when Orin and Lavinia walk up the drive. Orin confronts her with the account of their action, their trip to Boston, and their killing of Adam Brant, showing her a newspaper report of her lover's death. She sinks to a sitting position on the lowest step and moans as Lavinia stands, "rigid and erect, her face mask-like," at the left. Orin continues, berating Christine for grieving "for that servant's bastard, . . . that low swine." And then another motivation becomes clear: "I heard you planning to go with him to the island I had told you about— our island—that was you and I! . . . But you'll forget him! I'll make you happy! We'll leave Vinnie here and go away on a long voyage—to the South Seas."

Harshly, Lavinia accuses her brother of becoming his mother's "crybaby" as he begs her forgiveness and then follows his sister's orders, going into the house. Lavinia looks at her mother's masklike face of grief "with bleak, condemning eyes": "He paid the just penalty for his crime. You know it was justice. It was the only way true justice could be done." With these words, Christine seems to awaken; she springs up and looks at her daughter with a gaze "in which a savage hatred fights with horror and fear." Lavinia recoils and calls after Christine as she is about to enter the house: "You can live!" Christine repeats the word "Live!" and bursts into laughter, putting her hands to her face as if to blot Lavinia from her sight and walking inside. Seth, the gardener, is heard singing "shenandoah," and the last lines, "I'm bound away/Across the wide—" are interrupted by the sound of a pistol shot from inside the house. Again Lavinia asserts, "It is justice! It is your justice, Father!" Orin's cry of horror is heard, and he rushes out to join Lavinia to announce that Christine has shot herself. Guilt-ridden, he wishes that he had not boasted about murdering Brant. Had she believed that burglars killed him then "she would have turned to me! . . . How can I ever get her to forgive me now?" Lavinia in reply tells him that she loves him and will help him to forget, and with that he goes inside. She tells Seth to get the doctor and tell him that Christine has shot herself in an insane fit of grief. As he leaves, Lavinia turns back into the house, following Orin.

Comments: This play develops further resonances from its reenactment of the Oedipus myth and its interpretation in Freudian psychology. Orin (Oedipus) is in love with his mother Christine (Jocasta), and therefore wishes to kill his father Ezra (Laius) in order to supplant him. Adam Brant is also another "father" who must be supplanted. Lavinia remains an Electra figure, and her abnormal attachment to her father is her primary motivation. She is the daughter who wishes to supplant the mother, but she is also the figure of puritan, Biblical retributive justice. The earlier equations with members of the House of Atreus continue at the same time.

THE HAUNTED   **Act I, Scene i**: Exterior of the Mannon house...on the evening of a clear day in summer a year later [1866]." The portico is bathed in the afterglow of sunset, but "all the shutters are closed and the front door is boarded up, showing that the house is unoccupied." Five men stand on the drive: Seth Beckwith and Amos Ames, from *Homecoming*, and Abner Small,* Joe Silva,* and Ira Mackel.* "Small is a wiry old man of sixty-five, a clerk in a hardware store...[with] a shrill rasping voice. Silva is a Portuguese fishing captain—a fat boisterous man, with a hoarse bass voice. Mackel, a farmer, "hobbles along with the aid of a cane....He talks in a wheezy cackle." All five are a chorus of town types "representing the town as a human background for the drama of the Mannons." All are drunk, as they sing and comment on the Mannons, especially the ghost of Ezra's wife, Christine, who they believe haunts the house. Small has bet the others ten dollars that he will stay all night in the house, and they are getting him filled with the courage of liquor. As Seth and Abner go inside, the others tell ghoulish ghost stories, and on Seth's return they begin to discuss the curious doings in the Mannon household, Ezra dying his first night home and Christine's suicide—allegedly as a result of grief. As they watch, Peter and Hazel Niles come up the driveway to announce the imminent return of Lavinia and Orin Mannon to New York. Suddenly there is a yell of terror from inside the house, and Abner Small erupts out of it, giving Seth a ten-dollar bill and swearing that he has seen Ezra Mannon's ghost. Seth claims that the place does indeed appear to be haunted, and he himself would not wish to spend the night there: "There's been evil in that house since it was first built in hate—and it's kept growin' there ever since." Hazel and Peter say that the house must be made ready for Vinnie and Orin's arrival, and, they, too, discuss the haunted feeling of the place, as well as Orin's trancelike behavior at his mother's funeral. Hazel doesn't "believe when Vinnie rushed him off on this trip to the East he knew what he was doing or where he was going or anything." She agrees with Seth as they walk in that "you feel something cold grip you the moment you set foot—" but Peter laughs at her. They go in, and noises as of opening windows and setting fires can be heard, "then silence."

Lavinia enters and looks at the house. She has changed, filled out, become more womanly and now bears a remarkable resemblance to her mother, even to being dressed in her color, green. She calls to Orin as to a child, and he comes in, carrying himself like a wooden soldier. He has a beard and a moustache now and as a result looks more like his father than before, even to the masklike expression on his face. He is extremely thin and his clothes seem too large for him. She insists that he look at the house, telling him that there is nothing to be afraid of, for there are no ghosts: "That is all past and finished! The dead have forgotten us! We've forgotten them!" But Orin still remembers the way Christine had stood outside there the last time he saw her alive. Nonetheless, he obeys Lavinia and they go into the house.

Act I, Scene ii: The sitting room of the Mannon house, lighted by two candles on the mantel and a lantern. In this flickering light the room is full of shadows, and the Mannon portraits "stare with grim forbiddingness." Lavinia enters, dressed in green with her hair arranged like her mother's. In fact, at the first glance, she could easily be mistaken for Christine. "The movements of her body now have the feminine grace her mother's had possessed." She advances toward the fireplace, "her eyes...caught by the eyes of the Mannons in the portraits," and then she "addresses them in a harsh resentful voice," asking why they look at her in that way: "I've done my duty by you! That's finished and forgotten!" But then she realizes that she is alone; Orin has not followed her. She calls him and he enters, his face dazed, but "his eyes have a wild, stricken look. He rushes to her as if seeking protection."

He has been looking for his mother, Christine, but can find only ancestral portraits. Christine has "gone forever. She'll never forgive me now!" He alternates between this fear and defiance, asserting his Mannon heritage, but Lavinia continually tries to explain that they must now return to living a normal life and will have the friendship of Hazel and Peter. Orin asks what right they have to love and then notes how pretty Lavinia has become, how like her mother, even to a change in her soul: "I've watched it ever since we sailed for the East. Little by little it grew like Mother's soul—as if you were stealing hers—as if her death had set you free—to become her!" Lavinia tells Orin not to be morbid, but he suggests that "the Mannon dead" will convert her again. He indicates that something curious has occurred in the islands, and Lavinia reminds him that she had gone there for his sake, afraid of what he might tell. They have returned at Orin's own suggestion to face the ghosts in order to rid him of his "silly guilt about the past." She interrogates him to be sure that he has the agreed-upon story correct: Christine murdered Ezra, and Lavinia and Orin had protected her. "She chose to kill herself as a punishment for her crime—of her own free will! It was an act of justice!" When Orin weakly agrees, she holds her weeping brother comfortingly to her breast but then, as a distraction, suggests that they clean up the place, opening the shutters and removing the dust covers. For a moment Orin helps, but then he stares out the window as Peter enters.

Peter Niles is astonished at the change that has come over Lavinia and says that he has never changed in his feelings for her. He thinks she should always wear color rather than black as in the past, and Lavinia replies curiously, "I was dead then." Bossily, Lavinia tells Orin to greet Peter, who shows "pained surprise at Orin's sickly appearance." Peter tries to make conversation, but Orin inquires, "Did you ask her why she stole Mother's colors?" Orin wants to find out the "strange reason" for that, and he continues to tell how Lavinia has "become romantic! Imagine that! Influence of the 'dark and deep blue ocean'— and of the Islands, eh, Vinnie?" They had stopped at the islands of Orin's dreams for a month, "But they turned out to be Vinnie's islands, not mine. They only made me sick—and the naked women disgusted me. I guess I'm too much of a Mannon, after all, to turn into a pagan. But you should have seen Vinnie with all the men—!"

Obviously Lavinia has been sexually awakened while in the islands, partic-

ularly through her relationship with one of the native men. Lavinia claims that
Orin is telling "disgusting fibs" and that he is teasing her. She straightens her
brother's clothing in a curiously maternal way, suggesting that he should look
less military and should shave off his beard, but Orin interrupts: "Not look so
much like Father, eh? More like a romantic clipper ship captain, is that it?" At
this, Lavinia appears frightened of what Orin might reveal, and she hurries him
off to see Hazel.

Left alone with Peter, Lavinia seems "weak and frightened" as Peter inquires
after Orin and then puts his arm protectively around her; she nestles gratefully
against him and asks if he still loves her. Peter tells her that he does but wonders
whether she can still love him. Lavinia says that she can and proceeds to tell
him of the beauty of the islands, concerned that he might believe Orin's comments: "He's become a regular bigoted Mannon.... But remember I'm only
half Mannon." In the islands she says that the natives showed no sense of sin,
and there she found herself free, there where the spirit of love made her forget
death; and as for the native man at whom she "smiled back," he reminded her
of Peter. Above all, she says, "I want to feel love! Love is beautiful! I was a
fool!" She kisses him with a passion that both astonishes and shocks him, a
kiss that he returns, and she speaks of their forthcoming marriage.

But she cannot leave Orin until he is well and free of his guilt for his mother's
death. She asks Peter to warn Hazel that she will have to make allowances for
any "crazy thing he might say." When he agrees she kisses him "lovingly,"
but while they are still embracing, Hazel and Orin enter. Hazel is momentarily
shocked, but then pleased, but Orin looks so enraged that he seems about to
attack them. "So that's it! By God—!" But then he recovers himself and offers
congratulations with a "ghastly" smile. The curtain falls as "Peter takes his
hand awkwardly. Hazel moves towards Lavinia . . . her face full of an uneasy
bewilderment. Lavinia stares at Orin with eyes full of dread."

Act II: An evening one month later. Orin is sitting in Ezra Mannon's study
with a small pile of manuscripts beside him. He has aged during the last month,
and the resemblance between him and the candle-lit portrait of his father has
now become "uncanny." Orin finishes his writing and addresses the portrait in
its judicial robes as if it were Ezra Mannon himself presiding over a court: "The
truth, the whole truth and nothing but the truth!" But "what will the neighbors
say if this whole truth is ever known? A ticklish decision for you, Your Honor!"
There is a knock at the door, and Orin hurriedly puts the script in the desk and
locks it. Lavinia asks him to open the door, and Orin grabs a book to give the
impression he has been reading.

Suspiciously, Lavinia asks what Orin has been doing, locked up in the study
with the shutters closed against the daylight, working always by artificial light.
She tells him he should get out in the fresh air, but Orin maintains that "perpetual
night—darkness of death in life—that's the fitting habitat for guilt." He knows
he cannot escape, and artificial light is best for "my work," which, he maintains,
is "studying the law of crime and punishment." Lavinia expresses anxiety about

his health, but Orin claims he is well. He wonders why Lavinia will never leave him alone with Hazel, even though they are engaged: "You're afraid I'll let something slip." But Orin is really afraid of himself and also of Hazel's pure and unselfish love, a love he feels unworthy of, while her every look of love leads him to want to confess.

This is Lavinia's fear, and Orin tells her that there is no way that either of them can escape retribution: "Confess and atone to the full extent of the law! That's the only way to wash the guilt of our mother's blood from our souls!" She cannot escape through marrying Peter, especially since he, Orin, the last male Mannon, has almost finished the history of the Mannon family, detailing all their crimes, trying to trace the source of "the evil destiny behind our lives," and perhaps foretell their future. He has found Lavinia "the most interesting criminal of us all," and he taxes her with promiscuity when she met a ship's officer who reminded her of Brant, claiming that her hostility against her mother was really motivated by her own desire for Adam Brant. He charges her jealously with discovery of her own sexuality in the islands and accuses her of more than the kiss she admits she exchanged with the handsome native, Avahanni. Momentarily, she taunts Orin, as Christine had defied Ezra just before his murder, but when Orin breaks down, she denies the right to love she had just asserted. Then Orin shocks her: "Can't you see I'm now in Father's place and you're Mother? That's the evil destiny out of the past I haven't dared to predict! I'm the Mannon you're chained to! So isn't it plain—" But Lavinia will not listen to this incestuous suggestion, and Orin threatens her with responsibility in case of his death. Lavinia says she "would give her life to bring you peace," but that is insufficient for Orin. He swears he will put the family history in safe hands to be read if she tries to marry Peter "or if I should die—" Lavinia shakes him frantically, begging him to stop torturing her, and then breaks down; but Orin offers only cold comfort: "Don't cry. The damned don't cry," and orders her out. She leaves sobbing, as Orin pulls out his manuscript and continues to write.

Act III: The Mannon sitting room with two candles on the mantel and lamps turned low. Again the Mannon portraits seem to dominate the room with their staring bitter eyes. No time has passed as Lavinia enters from the study "in a terrific state of tension." She paces up and down, wringing her hands, as her mother had done just before her suicide. She is distraught at Orin's preoccupation with his own death, wishing to save him, yet also wondering why he lacks the courage to kill himself. Seth enters to ask Lavinia to comfort Hannah, the hired girl, who is "throwin' fits again" because she believes she feels ghosts crawling over her.

After Seth and Lavinia leave, Hazel and Peter enter and discuss their respective fiancés. Hazel is convinced that Lavinia has become a bad influence on Orin: "There's something bold about her." She plans to ask Orin to visit them for a time but knows Lavinia will not be receptive to the suggestion. Peter says he will try to persuade Lavinia to agree, and certainly he wishes Orin's recovery, for only then will they be able to marry. Cryptically, Hazel asks, "Do you really want to marry her—Now?" Peter is surprised, and Hazel bursts into tears; Orin then enters, begging to see Hazel alone. Achieving this, he gives her an envelope to be opened only the day before Lavinia's wedding to Peter, and he tells her to stop loving him: "The only love I can know now is the love of guilt for guilt which breeds more guilt." Orin wants to confess to Hazel's purity and be forgiven. She attempts to offer consolation by telling him what Vinnie has said about his feelings of guilt, information which turns Orin to more hostility. He begs Hazel to take him away, but in answer to her offer to have him stay with her, he shows his fear of his sister. He suggests that Hazel make up a story so he can go with her but she scornfully refuses to lie.

Lavinia then enters, sensing that something is up, and tries to interrogate Hazel and Orin. On hearing of the proposed visit, she forbids it, but she has also noticed that Hazel has the envelope with the manuscript. Orin then claims that he will "have the upper hand for a change, from now on!" Enraged by Hazel's insistence that Orin visit, Lavinia insults Hazel, who replies with dignity that their friendship is at an end and attempts to leave. However, Lavinia has now realized what is in the envelope and offers; "Make Hazel give them up and I'll do anything—anything you want me to!" When she insists that she means it, Orin asks for the envelope and tells Hazel that all is over between them: "The Orin you loved was killed in the war. Remember only that dead hero and not his rotting ghost!" After Hazel leaves, he tells Lavinia that she has in effect promised to give up Peter and never see him again, and he also reminds her that she has promised to do anything. Now he makes another proposal: "Vinnie! For the love of God, let's go now and confess and pay the penalty for Mother's murder, and find peace together!" He turns and addresses the assembled portraits, "You'll find Lavinia Mannon harder to break than me! You'll have to haunt and hound her for a lifetime!" With this, Lavinia's control snaps: "You'd kill yourself if you weren't a coward!" Orin reacts first with terror, then with "pitiful pleading," which moves into "harsh mockery" as he asks whether she means to drive him to suicide as a means of exacting justice. But slowly the idea becomes appealing as a means of finding his mother in the Blessed Isles. Lavinia with deep remorse, tries now to dissuade him, but Orin pushes her away: "Mother's waiting!" Just as he gets to the door, Peter arrives looking for Hazel. After telling him that she has gone home, Orin leaves to clean his pistol.

After a stifled cry of "Orin," Lavinia flings herself into Peter's arms: "Nothing matters but love, does it?" Peter is somewhat "alarmed by her hectic excitement" and also by the danger of Orin's working with a pistol in his state of mind, but Lavinia holds him tightly, planning for their future happiness, until suddenly the shot for which she has been waiting is heard. "Orin! Forgive me!" she says as she hides the manuscript in a table drawer after Peter has rushed out. She pulls herself together, preparatory to going into the study, but then turns to the portraits:"Wasn't it the only way to keep your secret, too? But I'm through with you forever now, do you hear? I'm Mother's daughter—not one of you! I'll live in spite of you!'' But as she leaves, ''she squares her shoulders, with a return of the abrupt military movement copied from her father. . .and marches stiffly from the room.'' She is a Mannon after all.

Act IV: Three days later, later afternoon outside the Mannon house, with all the shutters open in the ''soft golden sunlight.'' The reflected light from the glass makes the windows look like ''brooding revengeful eyes.'' Seth walks up the drive, again singing ''Shenandoah'' and meditating on Lavinia's behavior— she is continually gathering his flowers, just like her mother, only worse. He wonders how a soldier like Orin could possibly shoot himself while cleaning his gun. After this, people will keep away from Lavinia: ''A Mannon has come to mean sudden death to 'em.'' But yet he has admiration for Lavinia, believing that she will be a match for anyone: ''Clean Mannon strain.''

Lavinia then enters, dressed once again in black, looking as before, ''flat-chested and thin,'' her face bearing the masklike Mannon expression in its haggard lack of emotion. She is carrying flowers which she asks Seth to see placed in the house because she wants it ''pretty and cheerful.'' She sits on top of the steps, upright, with knees and elbows pressed to her sides. She is waiting for Peter but is curious that Seth has suggested she rest outside rather than inside the house: ''You've been with us Mannons so long! You know there's no rest in this house which Grandfather built as a temple of Hate and Death!'' With this, Seth tells her to marry Peter and leave the place, which Lavinia says she intends to do: ''I'll close it up and leave it in the sun and rain to die. . . . And the Mannons will be forgotten. I'm the last and I won't be one long. I'll be Mrs. Peter Niles.''

Hazel, dressed in deep mourning, comes up the drive with an air of resolution. Lavinia greets her coldly, and then Hazel bursts out to say that Orin had meant to kill himself, and Lavinia had driven him to it. Hazel doesn't know the whole truth but is aware that something was driving him mad. She pleads with Lavinia not to marry Peter and drag him into this same horror: ''You've got to consider his happiness—if you really love him!'' Already the baleful Mannon influence has affected him; he has moved out of the Niles home and broken his mother's heart. If this sort of thing continues, Peter will come to hate her. Hazel appeals to her conscience, and in reply Lavinia threatens to kill herself. Finally, Hazel begs Lavinia to allow Peter to ''read what Orin had in that envelope. Orin asked me to make him read it before he married you. I've told Peter about that, Vinnie.' Almost as if to herself, Lavinia asks, ''Why can't the dead!'' As Peter comes up the drive, Hazel again appeals to Lavinia's conscience and leaves.

Peter sits beside Lavinia, who remains with her eyes closed, and he tells her that they will soon be married. They agree to go away from the house; Peter is becoming superstitious about it, and he bitterly says they can't move far enough away from both house and town. His tone startles her, and she talks about the quarrel he has had with Hazel and his mother. She realizes that Peter is already suffering from his relationship with her and asks if he is concerned about what Orin had written. Peter declares that he is not, and Lavinia asks him never to suspect her of anything, and then, in desperation, asks him to marry her instantly; but Peter demurs, out of respect for Orin, and then "suspicious in spite of himself," inquires whether anything that Orin wrote could stand in their way. With this Lavinia laughs as if beaten and inveighs against the Mannon dead who are "not to be trusted with love! I know them too well! And I couldn't bear to watch your eyes grow bitter and hidden from me and wounded in their trust of life! I love you too much!"

She throws her arms around the bewildered and suspicious Peter, begging him to consummate their love right now without waiting for marriage. She has earned a moment of happiness. "Take me in this house of the dead and love me! Our love will drive the dead away! It will shame them back into death! Want me! Take me, Adam!" But with this she is shocked because of the way the name of her mother's lover has escaped her: "Always the dead between! It's no good trying any more!" Peter believes her to be hysterical, but he is also "repelled by her display of passion." Now she sends him away: "I can't marry you, Peter. You musn't ever see me again." Again Peter is confused, but he returns to "what Orin wrote" and about "what happened to you on the Islands. Was it something there—something to do with that native—?"

Lavinia, "with calculated coarseness," tells Peter she lost her virginity to the native: "I was his fancy woman!" With this, Peter believes his mother and Hazel: "you are bad at heart—no wonder Orin killed himself—God, I—I hope you'll be punished—I—" As she watches him leave she calls, "Peter, it's a lie! I didn't—!" But then she squares her shoulders again as she looks after him. Seth enters, and starts singing "Shenandoah" as a means of attracting her attention. As he reaches the line, "I'm bound away," she picks it up. "I'm bound here—to the Mannon dead!" and with "a dry little cackle of laughter," she moves to go into the house, as Seth tries to dissuade her. She accepts her punishment: "Living alone here with the dead is a worse act of justice than death or prison. . . . I'll live alone with the dead, and keep their secrets, and let them hound me, until the curse is paid out and the last Mannon is let die." As she goes in she orders Seth to "close the shutters and nail them tight. . . . And tell Hannah to throw out all the flowers." Seth goes in, and Lavinia lingers for a while, looking her last upon the sunlight, but "with frozen eyes." As she stands there, "Seth leans out of the window at the right of the door and pulls the shutters closed with a decisive bang. As if this were a word of command, Lavinia pivots sharply on her heel and marches woodenly into the house, closing the door behind her."

Comments: *Mourning Becomes Electra* was an immediate success, for the power of the mythic trilogy transcended all of O'Neill's previous work, and he was compared with Shakespeare and Racine. He was criticized for his hostile attitude toward New England and its inhabitants, but on the whole the critics understood that he was endeavoring to use modern psychology and American mythology along with that of ancient Greece. He objected to the suggestions of Freudian interpretation, claiming that he was more strongly influenced by Jung than Freud, but the fact remains that the play is deepened by its Freudian associations.

O'Neill accomplished an astonishing mythic amalgam in these plays, using the fate of the House of Atreus as a framework for what is also a realistic American historical play combined with undoubted melodramatic qualities. The central emphasis of the basic myth is also changed in that the most important character is Electra rather than Orestes, an approach which follows Euripides rather than Aeschylus. Similarly, the hostile gods are transmuted into psychological forces over which the characters have no control. At times the characters also seem to be clinical studies in abnormal familial relationships, but they are ultimately saved from that fate by their mythic and historical significance. The characters, then, are symbolic, but they act and react within a consciously contrived realistic situation, with careful attention to specific details such as the commission of crimes in such a way as to allay police suspicions.

What remains extraordinary is the skillful melding of disparate elements into a unit. The inevitability of crime and punishment in New England Puritan tradition combines logically with Ancient Greece, while Greek fate and the Mannon crimes translate easily into modern psychology. Similarly, the return from the heroic war at Troy finds its counterpart in Ezra Mannon's return from the Civil War, the last "chivalric" war in which American troops were involved, while Orin Mannon's comments on war still speak to the present. And then there is O'Neill's recurrent mythic world of freedom and escape, the sea, and in particular the South Seas which still provide the locale for the mythic Islands of the Blessed for many people (notably those who have not been there). The sea is also a jealous mistress, as Adam Brant and Christopher Christopherson* discover, while the chantey "Shenandoah" continually provides a counterpoint of foreboding and disaster.

Intellectually, the trilogy is an astonishing achievement and also a superb theatrical one, though some critics did take the playwright to task for its melodramatic qualities. Certainly there is a great load of corpses for one evening, but the same was equally true of much Elizabethan drama, including Shakespeare's *Hamlet*, and this is to some extent unavoidable within the context of the Atreus myth. One wonders whether the melodrama would have been noted if O'Neill had followed through with an early intention of using half-masks for his characters as a means of emphasizing their symbolic significance. He regretted that he had not done so and hoped that someday the play might be performed with masks.

But the greatest weakness of the play lies in the language, because O'Neill was simply not a major poet, even though he could write good dialogue and at least one line, "The damned don't cry," achieved wide currency. But for O'Neill, as for most playwrights, it should be sufficient to be compared with Shakespeare or Racine, and certainly *Mourning Becomes Electra* established him as the best serious playwright of his age.

The setting of the play is most important, with the Mannon house in effect being an emblem of the play: a Greek templelike portico superimposed on the gray New England stone structure. The interiors are equally grim, with the masklike features of ancestral portraits glowering from the walls watching the tragedy of their descendants. The only departure from the house is to the clipper ship *Flying Trades* in the fourth act of *The Hunted*, a scene which reinforces the theme of the sea as a mistress only for the strong and a means of escape to paradisal islands. But escape from the furies of their psychological inferno is impossible for the Mannons, and as the play concludes with a return to the Mannon house, it is perceived now as a mausoleum in which all the Mannons have committed their secret crimes, played out their lives and now must endure their punishment. Lavinia, in her living death, must pay the price for being the last of the family and is working out the curse. In the final analysis, O'Neill must be conceded success in his announced aim to write a modern drama in which the Greek fates are replaced by forces which are more comprehensible to an age without religion and without commitment to gods. Thus in this trilogy he takes the themes of repressed and deviant sexuality and raises the then new science of psychology to the realm of mythic significance.

Production Data: Written 1929–1931. Produced by the Theatre Guild* at the Guild Theatre, New York City, October 26, 1931 (150 performances).

Director: Philip Moeller
Designer: Robert Edmond Jones*
Homecoming   *Cast:* Seth Beckwith: Arthur Hughes
                        Amos Ames: Jack Byrnes
                        Louisa Ames: Bernice Elliott
                        Minnie: Emily Lorraine
                        Christine Mannon: Alla Nazimova*
                        Lavinia Mannon: Alice Brady*
                        Peter Niles: Philip Foster
                        Hazel Niles: Mary Arbenz
                        Adam Brant: Thomas Chalmers
                        Ezra Mannon: Lee Baker
The Hunted   *Cast:* Mrs. Josiah Borden: Augusta Durgeon
                        Mr. Josiah Borden: James Bosnell
                        Mrs. Everett Hills: Janet Young
                        Dr. Joseph Blake: Erskine Sanford
                        Everett Hills: Oliver Putnam
                        Christine Mannon: Alla Nazimova
                        Hazel Niles: Mary Arbenz
                        Peter Niles: Philip Foster
                        Lavinia Mannon: Alice Brady
                        Orin Mannon: Earle Larimore*
                        Chanteyman: John Hendricks
                        Adam Brant: Thomas Chalmers
The Haunted   *Cast:* Abner Small: Erskine Sanford
                        Ira Mackel: Oliver Putnam
                        Joe Silva: Grant Gordon

Amos Ames: Jack Byrnes
Seth Beckwith: Arthur Hughes
Peter Niles: Philip Foster
Hazel Niles: Mary Arbenz
Lavinia Mannon: Alice Brady
Orin Mannon: Earle Larimore

Revived at the Alvin Theatre, New York City, May 9, 1932 (16 performances). *Revived* at the Circle in the Square/Joseph E. Levine Theatre, New York City, November 15, 1972 (53 performances).
[*See also* Appendix B for operatic version by Marvin David Levy; also film adaptation by Dudley Nichols.]

MOVIE MAN, THE, a one-act play. The scene of this comedy is "the main room of a house in the suburb of a large town in northern Mexico," during a revolution. Henry (Hen) Rogers* is the representative of the Earth Motion Picture Company, and Al Devlin* is a photographer for the same company. The two are involved with [Pancho] Gomez,* commander-in-chief of the Constitutionalist Army, and [Luis] Virella,* general of a division. Gomez and Rogers have signed an agreement whereby Rogers will have the right to film all battles of the insurrectionist army, and in turn he will keep the insurgents supplied with suitable arms and ammunition. As the play opens, Rogers and Devlin are complaining about the climate, the fleas, the women, and the generals themselves. Devlin has been trying to pick up a young Mexican woman whom he had found weeping on a park bench, but "Talk about the icy onceover! She looked at me as if I was a wet dog. I turned and beat it like a little man." Gomez and Virella are planning to execute a prisoner, Ernesto Fernandez, the next morning. Both Rogers and Devlin regret this fact because they seem to consider Fernandez a better man than either of the generals. The two discuss the possibility of saving him, but "Virella has a grudge against him and Gomez needs Virella." Anyway, as Rogers points out, "it'll make a great picture. Be sure and get it." While they are conversing, the noise of drunken revelry is heard in the background. The generals are busy drinking up a case of Scotch, a gift from Rogers for signing the film contract.

Anita Fernandez,* a beautiful young woman, enters and reveals herself as the daughter of the prisoner who is to die tomorrow. She has come to plead with the generals for her father's life, prepared to offer anything in return. Rogers advises her against trying to see the drunken generals when Gomez comes in, filled with the courage born of drunkenness, and attempts to make a pass at Anita. When he learns both her identity and her mission, he refuses her request. Gomez then tells Rogers that he has arranged for a night attack on the town, and at that moment Rogers pulls out a copy of the movie contract, which expressly forbids night battles or engagements on any days when the light is too bad for filming. Rogers threatens to withdraw his arms support if Gomez goes through with this idea but then offers to allow a night battle on this one occasion if he will receive in exchange the life of Ernesto Fernandez. Gomez readily agrees, and Anita rushes away to greet her father. Devlin re-enters looking for a drink and says, "I just got another flash at that dame I was telling you about. . . . Some nerve to that greaser chicken giving a white man the foot. . . . She isn't much to look at after all. Back in God's Country we'd use her photo for a before-taking ad." Rogers has the last word: "Cheer up, Al, you're all wrong, my son, you're all wrong."

Comments: This comedy is a very slight piece, but it does show O'Neill trying to deal with language, whether the argot of the filmmakers or the fractured English of the Mexicans. Characterization is minimal, and the stereotypical attitudes of the "gringos" to Mexico and things Mexican are exploited. To some extent this play may have been intended as a satire on both Pancho Villa and American interventionism. Arthur and Barbara Gelb (1973, pp. 262–263) suggest that the central character is modelled on John Silas Reed,* the American journalist who had spent some time in Mexico.

Production Data: Written July, 1914. Produced with *Abortion** and *The Sniper** at the Key Theatre, St. Mark's Place, New York City, October 27, 1959. No further information located.

A Note on Text: The text used is that appearing in *Ten "Lost" Plays of Eugene O'Neill* (New York: Random House, 1964).

MURPHY. In "The Personal Equation,"* he is the first mate of the S.S. *San Francisco*.

MURRAY, Joe. In *Abortion*,* brother of Nellie Murray.* "He is a slight-stoop-shouldered, narrow-chested young fellow of eighteen, with large feverish black eyes, pasty complexion, and the sunken cheeks of a tuberculosis victim. He wears a shabby dark suit." He, along with his sister Nellie, is the sole support of his family of widowed mother and younger brothers and sisters. Joe has just seen his sister die as the result of a bungled abortion procured by Jack Townsend.* In his rage and sorrow he has gone to the doctor responsible and threatened him, receiving payment of his two-hundred-dollar fee to keep quiet. He goes to Jack's room during the parade of commencement week, at the time of Jack's greatest success, to confront the young man with his crime. Joe, a blue-collar worker, speaks with bitterness of the irresponsibility of the upper-class students who play around with "our goils," and Jack expresses regret for his part in the affair, especially when Joe says that Nellie did not speak a word against him. When Jack offers him money to protect the innocent, Joe is infuriated since Jack can marry his Evelyn while Nellie is dead. He draws his revolver and threatens Jack, but Jack wrests it from him. However, Joe had earlier realized that Jack wasn't worth being hung for. He intends to go to the police station and spurns Jack's offer of the revolver to finish the matter. O'Neill uses him as the spokesman for the underdog in this play, the victim of the unthinking behavior of the privileged. Joe's character, however, is rather stereotypical.

MURRAY, Nellie. In *Abortion*,* sister of Joe Murray.* She dies as the result of a bungled operation. She never appears in the play, but she has some importance as a type in O'Neill's drama. She is a working-class girl, a stenographer, and with her brother is the sole support of the family. She is portrayed by her brother as so faithful to Jack Townsend,* the young man responsible, that she wouldn't reveal his name: "She died game. . . . Not a word outa her against you." This kind of submissive endurance is frequently shown as an affirmative trait in O'Neill's treatment of women characters.

MURRAY, Stephen. In *The Straw*,* he is the central male character. He "is thirty years old—a tall, slender, rather unusual-looking fellow with a pale face, sunken under high cheek bones, lined about the eyes and mouth, jaded and tired for one still so young." However, he has "intelligent, large hazel eyes" which, though having "a dispirited expression in repose," can also show "a concealment mechanism of mocking, careless humor whenever his inner privacy is threatened." He seems "dissatisfied with himself," though not yet a bitter young man. He is a patient in the Hill Farm Sanitorium when he meets Eileen Carmody.* He tells her that he has been a reporter for a small-town paper and complains that it was an utterly boring job. He has no family, only two sisters whom he dislikes, even though they are paying his hospital bills, and he cannot stand their "squally brats." Eileen, overwhelmed with having to leave her beloved brothers and sisters, lends Murray a sympathetic ear, and he tells her about his secret ambitions to write stories. She encourages him to write while he is in the sanitorium and offers to type his manuscripts for him. He is almost immediately successful in placing a story.

This gives him motivation and he recovers, while Eileen's health deteriorates. He is astonished when, the night before his discharge, Eileen risks her health to steal out to tell him of her love, because he does not reciprocate, and had not realized the depth of her feelings. With a certain remorse he promises to "do anything in God's world." He leaves the sanitorium in a state of emotional confusion, but he soon forgets his promise to write to Eileen, as his career falters during the next four months. When he returns to see Eileen he finds her appallingly weakened because she has lost the will to live. Believing herself forgotten first by her family and now Stephen she has ceased her cheerful letters to him. Nevertheless, she is still as supportive of his talent as ever, and Stephen assures her "you made it possible." In order to make him feel better, Eileen treats her earlier declaration of love very lightly. At first his pride is hurt, but then Stephen looks as if a great load has been lifted from his conscience. He is still a self-centered young man, though not without integrity.

His basic decency is speedily shown as he develops into a character capable of self-sacrifice. Miss Gilpin,* the nurse in charge of the infirmary, tells him that Eileen's case is hopeless and she is about to be transferred to the state farm. She begs Stephen to become engaged to Eileen, move her to a private sanitarium and work nearby so that he can make her last months happy. Stung with remorse, for he "had never thought much of loving anyone—that way," he rushes to Eileen, brings her to admit her love, and proposes immediate marriage, telling her that he has had a relapse. He dragoons Miss Gilpin into corroborating that statement, and Eileen ecstatically plans for their future: she will help him with his work, and they will both become healthy. Stephen is overwhelmed with a desperate hope and speaks eloquently of the curative power of love. He will take Eileen out West, and they will overcome, despite all the prognostications of doctors. The play concludes ambiguously as Eileen turns to him with plans for the future.

Stephen Murray is clearly a romanticized development of Eugene O'Neill himself as a patient at the Gaylord Farm* Sanitorium, Wallingford, Connecticut in 1912-1913. The concluding act of renunciation is, of course, a dramatic addition. The surname Murray comes from Catherine Murray, a nurse at Gaylord, while the first name, Stephen, may come from James Joyce's Stephen Dedalus in *A Portrait of the Artist as a Young Man* (1916). However, the continuing theme of the writer who is able to work best with the help of a self-sacrificing woman is again presented, but here it has the addition of a new theme that is to be used more than once in the future: the necessity of the saving lie by which a human being can find meaning in life.

"MYTH-PLAYS FOR THE GOD-FORSAKEN," the overall title for an uncompleted trilogy which included *Dynamo,* * *Days Without End,* * and "It Cannot be Mad."* Material from this last play passed through several titles: "On to Betelgeuse," "On to Hercules" and "The Life of Bessie Bowen"* (or Bolan or Bowlan). It was then included in the proposed last play of the abandoned cycle, "A Tale of Possessors, Self-Dispossessed,"* under the title "Hair of the Dog."* It was finally destroyed in February 1943.

N

NANO. In *The Fountain*,* an old Indian chief whose tribe has refused to pay its taxes and who has himself rejected baptism. He is imprisoned and tortured by Juan Ponce de Leon* in an effort to make him tell the location of the sacred fountain which will be revealed only to the chosen. Eventually he lies to Juan and goes with him as pilot to discover ''Cathay.'' As they approach the Florida coast, Nano hatches a plan and gets the Indians there to ambush Juan and his company after Juan finds a fountain. Nano is one of the apparitions whom Juan sees in the fountain, and he is one of the figures who brings Juan to understand the essential unity of the universe. Like most of the characters in this play, Nano is symbolic rather than realistic.

NAZIMOVA, Alla (1879–1945), actress. Born Alla Leventon in Yalta, Crimea, May 22, 1879; died of coronary thrombosis in Los Angeles, California, July 13, 1945. Married Sergei Golovin in 1898; separated 1899. In 1912 married Charles Bryant, an actor, in a union that was declared null in 1925 because she had neglected to divorce Golovin. She studied violin and languages at the conservatory in Odessa, playing in school orchestras under Tschaikovsky and Rimsky-Korsakov and making her professional debut as a violinist at the age of twelve.

Deciding to transfer to acting, Miss Nazimova studied first in the dramatic school of the Philharmonic Society of Moscow (1897–98) and then with Konstantin Stanislavsky at the Moscow Art Theatre. In 1901 she managed a stock company in Kostroma, Russia and in 1902 appeared in *L'Aiglon* in Vilna, Lithuania. In 1903 in St. Petersburg she played Zaza, Magda, Camille, Hedda Gabler, and in Pinero's *The Second Mrs. Tanqueray*. In 1904 she played in *The Chosen People* in Berlin, repeating the role (in Russian) in London and New York the following year. In New York she also performed in *Tsar Theodor, Crime and Punishment, The Brothers Karamazov, Ghosts*, and *The Master Builder*.

Remaining in the United States, she accepted a contract from the Shuberts, fulfilling its major condition that she learn English, a feat she performed in eight months. In 1906 she made her English-language debut in *Hedda Gabler*, following that with *A Doll's House* (later filmed), *Comtesse Coquette*, and *The*

Master Builder (1907), and *The Passion Flower* (1908). She soon established herself as a specialist in Ibsen, Chekhov, and Turgenev, her often-repeated roles of Hedda Gabler, Mrs. Alving (*Ghosts*), Madam Ranevsky (*The Cherry Orchard*), and Natalia Petrovna (*A Month in the Country*) being considered definitive at the time. In addition to these roles, her most famous appearances were in *Little Eyolf, The Wild Duck, Three Sisters, Katerina,* and *The Good Earth.*

Alla Nazimova created the role of Christine Mannon* in *Mourning Becomes Electra,** with Alice Brady* as Lavinia Mannon,* receiving excellent reviews for what is still credited as a definitive performance of the role. O'Neill, however, did not believe that her performance (though admirable) communicated the character he had himself written, a sentiment he also felt about Miss Brady.

From 1916 to 1925, she worked largely in films, occasionally producing them as well: *Camille* (1921), *A Doll's House* (1923), and *Salome* (1923). In 1925 she retired from films to concentrate on the theatre, appearing with Eva Le Gallienne in repertory (with some clashes of temperament), as well as recreating her most famous roles for limited runs both on and off Broadway. She never fully retired from stage or screen, and she even tried television: *This Lonely Heart* and *The Ivory Tower* (1939). She also played in Shaw's *The Simpleton of the Unexpected Isles* (1935) for The Theatre Guild. She frequently accepted character and cameo roles in films, appearing in *Escape* (1940); *Blood and Sand* (1941); *The Bridge of San Luis Rey* and *Since You Went Away* (1941).

She was an arresting actress (very mannered in her later years) with an exotic appearance, a continental air, and an accent which she never quite lost. Though she appeared in plays by contemporary writers, she achieved her greatest successes as a tragedienne in Ibsen roles and plays from the classic Russian repertory, as well as in *Mourning Becomes Electra,* her only O'Neill role. She was one of the earliest Stanislavsky-trained artists in America and was noted for her subjectivity, which in her case also meant that she frequently played the same role quite differently, depending on her mood and the Russian temperament which she exploited. She was held in such regard in her day that she was often billed simply as "Nazimova."

NELSON, Ted. In *Bread and Butter,** one of John Brown's studio-mates in New York. Ted is a struggling author who sells a story and scandalizes Edward Brown, Sr.,* John's father, by arriving drunk with Helene,* a cloak-and-suit model, on his arm. He epitomizes for Mr. Brown everything that is immoral about the artistic world. In appearance Ted "is a small wiry-looking [fellow] with long sandy hair, grey eyes,...a long thin nose, and a large, thick-lipped mouth. He is dressed in a shabby, grey suit of an exaggerated cut,...black patent-leather shoes with grey spats. He carries a grey overcoat over his arm and a grey felt hat."

NICHOLLS, Fred. In *The Straw,** the accepted suitor of Eileen Carmody* and the son of a local manufacturer. He is twenty-three, stocky, good-looking in an undistinguished way, with fair hair and a manner which attempts to cultivate "a suave gentility." He smiles easily and has an attractive, "ready laugh, but there is a petty, calculating expression in his small, observing, blue eyes." His neat, well-fitting clothes indicate "an attitude of man-about-small-town complacency." He has known Eileen since grammar and high school and later when they were both working in his father's company. Their forthcoming marriage has been "sort of understood" between them. He thinks her very different from the rest of her family, particularly her father, Bill Carmody.* When Fred hears about Eileen's illness, the shallowness of his character is shown. Initially, he is afraid of possible infection, and then he accompanies her and her father to the sanitorium as a duty rather than anything else. Clearly, he does not wish to continue the relationship, but he lacks the strength to break it off. Finally Eileen does so by letter, partly as a result of the prodding of Stephen Murray,* who doesn't think Nicholls worthy of Eileen.

NICK. In *The Long Voyage Home*,* a crimp, a man who is paid by captains to complete their crews. They do not care about his methods, which include tricking or shanghai-ing drugged or drunken sailors and delivering them to these vessels. Nick is round-shouldered, pasty-faced, with cruel eyes and a weak mouth. He wears a shabby suit that was formerly "cheaply flashy," a muffler and a cap. He drugs Olson's* drink and grabs him for the *Amindra*, a hell ship on which he had once sailed.

NILES, Hazel. In *Mourning Becomes Electra*,* sister of Peter Niles* and later fiancée of Orin Mannon.* She appears in all plays of the trilogy. She "is a pretty, healthy girl of nineteen, with dark hair and eyes....She has a strong chin and a capable, smiling mouth." From the very first, one can perceive her character as "frank, innocent, amiable and good." And so she remains throughout the play. She is a welcome breath of normalcy and unadulterated goodness in the midst of gloom. She loves Orin and tries to save him when she sees the unhealthy influence that Lavinia Mannon,* his sister, exerts over him, and as a result she breaks off her longstanding friendship with Lavinia. After Orin's death, she begs Lavinia not to marry Peter Niles, her brother. Hazel is aware that there is something extremely peculiar concerning the Mannons because Orin had tried to give her a manuscript to be read by Peter before his planned marriage to Lavinia. However, Orin had taken it back when Lavinia promised she would follow her brother's wishes in everything. Hazel therefore attempts to prevent the marriage by appealing to Lavinia's conscience and love for Peter. She asks Lavinia at least to tell Peter what Orin had written and then leaves her to her own conscience. Hazel remains throughout a young woman of integrity, sympathy, purity, and love, caring unselfishly for the good of others.

NILES, Peter. In *Mourning Becomes Electra*,* brother of Hazel Niles* and later the fiancé of Lavinia Mannon.* He appears in all plays of the trilogy. In

Homecoming, he is the recently wounded captain of artillery in the Union Army who has been sent home to recuperate. He is twenty-two, heavily built, and somewhat awkward in speech and movement, even shy. He is like his sister: "straightforward, guileless and good-natured." He has already proposed to Lavinia, but she has put him off because of her abnormal insistence that her father needs her. Peter also has some suspicion that Lavinia is more attracted to the romantic clipper ship captain, Adam Brant,* thus indicating some jealousy.

Peter Niles plays a very small part in the action of *The Hunted*, chiefly as a minor commentator, but he becomes more important in *The Haunted* when he notes that Lavinia has been sexually awakened. He is overjoyed that she has decided to marry him, yet he is subliminally aware that there is something abnormal about her. He is frightened by her access of passion, though aroused in spite of himself, and he seems determined to marry her, no matter what the cost to his relationship with Hazel and his mother. Nonetheless, he is a trifle suspicious about Lavinia once Hazel informs him of the manuscript that Orin had tried to give his sister, insisting that Peter read it before he marries Lavinia. In this paper Orin had recounted the family history with all its crimes but had retained possession of it when Lavinia promised to conform to his every wish. Peter asks Lavinia what was in the paper and then asks her about what had happened on the South Sea island. Lavinia tells of her affair with a native, doing so in the coarsest manner, aiming to turn Peter away in order to save him from the deleterious consequences of marriage to such a haunted criminal as herself. Her stratagem succeeds, and Peter rushes away from her, his own innate decency violated and appalled by the shamelessness of her passionate sexuality. He never knows the full truth about Lavinia. Throughout the trilogy, he and Hazel are representatives of normalcy and decency in a gloomy and abnormal world.

NOBEL PRIZE   for literature. Awarded to O'Neill in 1936.

NORAH. In *Ah, Wilderness!** the stock clumsy Irish "greenhorn" maid, straight off the boat. She is incapable of doing anything properly, from screwing in a light bulb to serving meals. She finds the intoxicated Sid Davis* completely hilarious in Act II.

"NOTHING IS LOST BUT HONOR,"   the proposed ninth part of the abandoned cycle, "A Tale of Possessors, Self-Dispossessed."* This play, covering the period 1862–1870, was designed to portray the rise and fall of Honey Harford,* the politician, the only one of the four sons of Sara Melody* and Simon Harford* to survive at the end of the cycle. The outline of this play was destroyed in 1943 or 1953.

NOW I ASK YOU, a play in three acts, with a prologue and an epilogue.
   Prologue. A darkened room, "the Library of a house in a fashionable New York suburb." Lucy Ashleigh* Drayton enters, listens, then throws herself

weeping on a chair. She goes to a drawer, pulls out a revolver, looks at it, and puts it on the table "with a convulsive shudder." The sound of an automobile is heard, and Lucy looks as if she is trying to hide. She pulls the curtains, and a brief murmured exchange between chauffeur and maid is heard. Tom Drayton* and Leonora Barnes* can be heard talking as they come downstairs. She is laughing. Tom enters the room and calls for Lucy, but she does not answer. He is in full evening dress. Leonora calls for him, and he leaves. The front door is opened and shut, the car door is slammed, and the noise of the engine is heard. As the curtain starts to fall, "Lucy lifts the revolver to her temple" with her eyes closed. As the curtain touches the floor of the stage, a shot is heard.

Act I: "The living room of the Ashleighs' home in the neighborhood of Gramercy Park, New York City. It is a large, high-ceilinged room furnished in sober, old-fashioned good taste," with an occasional anachronistic modern intrusion. A few ancestral portraits are on the walls, and a number of books are in bookcases, which bespeak "a creditable amount of sound classic culture on the part of the occupants." The time is 1915–1916. Mr. Ashleigh,* a retired banker of sixty, and his wife, Mrs. Mary Ashleigh,* a dignified woman of fifty, are discovered at 8:30 P.M. on a warm June evening. It is the day before the wedding of their daughter, Lucy, and they are discussing what Mr. Ashleigh calls "Lucy's continual attacks of insane faddism." Tom Drayton, Lucy's fiancé, has been putting up with her odd enthusiasms with extraordinary patience. Mrs. Ashleigh details some of Lucy's earlier escapades: buying futurist paintings, writing a tragedy in free verse, trying to play the ukulele, interest in a tramp poet, then in an absinthe-drinking sculptor, psychoanalysis, Yoga. Now, Ashleigh reports, she has dragged Tom to an anarchist lecture on the topic of birth control. He is outraged, but Mrs. Ashleigh expresses agreement with the principle.

At this point the doorbell rings, and Leonora Barnes, a young painter, is announced. She has brought a vivid "synchromist" painting entitled "the Great Blond Beast," after Nietzsche, as a wedding present for Lucy. Mr. Ashleigh has already left to make his peace with Lucy, so Leonora tries to shock Mrs. Ashleigh by rolling her own cigarette and then arguing for free love: "Marriage is for propagation and artists shouldn't propagate. Takes up too much of their time." In spite of herself and her critical comments on the Ashleigh ancestral portraits, "Leo" is rather impressed with Mrs. Ashleigh as a modern-minded woman, though she does suggest that the older woman dye her hair red: "You'd be splendidly decorative." At this point, Tom Drayton enters. Leo first greets him as an acquaintance, then tells him, "You see you attract me physically," and finally, "I mean you have all the outward appearance of my ideal of what the Great Blond Beast should look like." She asks if he has read Nietzsche, "No," Tom replies, "business men don't, do they?. . . Maybe there is something more to you than you realize yourself." With that she grinds out her cigarette in the carpet and departs: "Tell Lucy. . . I think she's a fool to marry."

Tom is stunned, but Mrs. Ashleigh seizes the moment to have a frank talk with her future son-in-law, warning him that he must *pretend* to take Lucy's enthusiasms seriously: "Try to feel something of the spirit of Lucy's rainbow chasing and show her you feel it. It's the old, ever young wild spirit of youth which tramples rudely on the grave-mound of the Past to see more clearly to the future dream." She believes that Lucy will grow out of these phases and will temper her spirit to "a fine, sane, progressive ideal which is of infinite help to the race." Tom agrees to play the role of "promising neophyte" that Lucy has laid out for him, even though he finds Leo's painting rather astonishing, as does the enraged Mr. Ashleigh who arrives with the news that Lucy has been reading him "a lot of nonsense condemning marriage....Then she said she'd decided not to marry Tom after all."

After that bombshell, Lucy enters the room, "dressed in a dark, somber kimono, and Turkish slippers." Her face is powdered to an acceptable pallor, and her expression is tempered into what she imagines must be that of a melancholy heroine of a Russian novel. "In short, Lucy is an intelligent, healthy American girl suffering from an overdose of undigested reading." She speaks accordingly: "Strindberg's daughter of Indra discovered the truth. Life is horrible, is it not?" She drops her pose for a moment to assess Leo's painting, which she pronounces "old-fashioned." Lucy then announces, "there will be no wedding—ever," and continuing her "Russian heroine pose," she consoles Tom with her dream of self-realization: "My highest duty is toward myself, and my ego demands freedom, wide horizons to develop in." To her astonishment, Tom announces his agreement with her. He counters her outrageous statements with an appearance of sincere, even abject agreement. Ashleigh sputters with indignation; his wife and Tom agree, Mrs. Ashleigh even suggesting, "When we have the right to make our own laws we ought to abolish marriage the first thing....I've been in the toils for over twenty years." Lucy is taken aback by this unexpected reception, but she pushes on, suggesting that she and Tom live together "as free spirits, comrades who have no other claims upon each other than what our hearts dictate....Let the marriage only be omitted and I will go with you." After a moment's hesitation, Tom agrees, despite the opprobrium they will have to face. Lucy has not bargained for this and sadly refuses. Mrs. Ashleigh herself comes up with the solution that they should simply go through with the marriage ceremony: "You needn't live up to it in any way. Few people do. You can have your own private understanding—and divorce is easy enough." Finally, after a suitable display of unwillingness, and Mrs. Ashleigh's suggestion that they should make their "marriage a model of all that's best in free love, if you must set an example," Lucy agrees to their signing a prenuptial agreement. As she leaves to bring down the one she has already prepared, Mrs. Ashleigh and Tom laugh. The agreement, which includes a pledge not to have children, allows each the freedom to take lovers and lays down economic independence as a rule. Both sign the document, and Lucy agrees to meet Tom "at the church," but "it's absolutely meaningless, remember."

Act II: Three months later. "The library of the Draytons' home in a fashionable New York suburb. The room is light and airy, furnished unpretentiously but in perfect taste. The only jarring note is supplied by two incredible paintings in the Synchromist manner which are. . . not to be ignored.'' [The similarity in atmosphere to the Ashleigh's living room should be noted.] Lucy and Mrs. Ashleigh are seated there at about noon on a warm September day. Lucy has now found another role. This time she is Hedda Gabler, the Ibsen heroine who thinks herself trapped in a hopelessly bourgeois marriage. Tom has arrived home with tickets for an afternoon concert, but this does nothing to dispel "my blue devils [that] live deep down in my soul.'' Mrs. Ashleigh quickly sees that Lucy has found another heroine and teases her, "You'll be longing next for someone to come 'with vine leaves in his hair,' '' like Ejlert Løvborg. Lucy suggests, "perhaps he will come,'' and Mrs. Ashleigh counters that it will hardly be Gabriel Adams,* a poet who lives with Leonora Barnes "in *free* comradeship,'' according to Lucy. He is more interested in "unfermented grape juice'' and "scientific eating.'' Lucy suggests that "there's much more to Gabriel than you have any idea of,'' and Mrs. Ashleigh recalls that Leonora had said the same thing about Tom when she had told him "she [Leonora] was attracted to him physically.'' Lucy continues with her Hedda Gabler act until she and her mother leave and Gabriel Adams and Leonora enter the empty room.

Gabriel is a young man with "rather long black hair and big soulful eyes'' and a "thin and intelligent'' face. His clothing is "sufficiently unconventional to attract attention'' and "his manner is that of a spoiled child.'' Leonora is dressed "in her usual bizarre fashion.'' The two commence to quarrel over the nature of their art and insult each other until Gabriel finally throws a book to the floor. They then calm down to discuss Lucy and Tom. Gabriel has seen through the Hedda Gabler act, and Leonora is beginning to feel sorry for "the Blond Beast,'' whom Gabriel thinks is "an overgrown clod.'' Another quarrel erupts as each accuses the other of flirting when Lucy enters. After Leonora leaves to find Mrs. Ashleigh, Gabriel and Lucy fall into the roles of Shaw's Candida and Marchbanks. Gabriel draws his chair to hers, speaks of his unhappiness with Leonora, and utters words of adoration to Lucy wishing that he might be the one to "come into your life and take you away, to the mountain tops, to the castles in the air, to the haunt of brave dreams where life is free, and joyous, and noble. . . . Can't you read the secret in my heart?'' As he kneels before her and kisses her hand, Tom enters and manages a greeting with considerable difficulty.

After Gabriel leaves, Tom remonstrates with Lucy, saying that Gabriel makes love to every woman he sees—"I know his kind.'' Lucy, now in her role as Candida, says that Gabriel was indeed making love to her—and she reminds Tom of their prenuptial agreement, claiming she will go with Gabriel in an instant if she finds that she loves him. She leaves and Mrs. Ashleigh enters, taking in the situation quite quickly. When she hears what has happened she suggests that Tom engage in a flirtation with Leonora, just to make Lucy appreciate him. He speedily puts this plan into practice by falling in with Leonora's suggestion that Gabriel escort Lucy to the concert while he goes to an art exhibit with Leonora. Leo promptly announces that she will take a bath since "there's never any hot water where we live." When Lucy returns, Tom announces the change of plans to her. She and Gabriel seem remarkably reluctant but finally agree. Gabriel offers to run up to tell Leo, but Tom forestalls him. However, before he leaves, Leonora enters wearing Tom's oversized dressing gown and demanding some soap as the curtain falls.

Act III: One month later. The same scene as Act II, about 7 P.M. Tom and Leonora are chatting—or rather Leo is talking incessantly, and Tom is pretending interest but with difficulty. Leo says she is glad that Tom is not falling in love with her because "I've given up sex for good. I've been through it all, and there's nothing in it for anyone who wants to accomplish something real." Tom remains abstracted as Leo chatters on, revealing that her real name is Pearl, and so forth, and so on. Lucy, Mr. Ashleigh, and Gabriel then enter. Gabriel appears furious at finding Tom and Leo together, while Lucy is very cold to her. Leo then suggests that they all go in the car to the theatre, but everyone begs off until only Leo and Tom are left. Tom has booked a stage box and Leonora is not dressed for the occasion. Tom then suggests that Leo borrow one of Lucy's dresses and baste it to fit. Lucy is furious, but Gabriel continues his lovelorn-poet approach, much to her annoyance. All is not well with Gabriel either because he fumes about Tom and Leo, especially when Lucy doesn't wish to hear his poems. The two of them start to quarrel until Gabriel inadvertently reveals that he and Leo have been married for two years: "The only reason we concealed it was because we were taking a studio in Greenwich Village together. . . and we were afraid they'd consider us provincial. . . if they knew." Lucy bursts into laughter at this discovery and Gabriel leaves in a huff, but Lucy's laughter soon turns to sobs.

Mrs. Ashleigh then enters and very rationally tells Lucy how foolish she has been and how deeply she may have hurt Tom. Lucy speaks of his flirtation with Leo as a "shameless, disgusting liaison," while Mrs. Ashleigh tries to make her see reason even when Lucy, overacting as always, claims that Leo is Tom's mistress and she will never speak to him again: "I'll go out alone and live my own life as I choose." Mrs. Ashleigh then swears that this whole "liaison" was a plot between her and Tom to bring Lucy to her senses, but the girl is too angry to listen. As Tom enters, she walks right past him. Tom doesn't want to go through with this charade, but Mrs. Ashleigh suggests that he go to the theatre with Leo and have it out with Lucy later. Leo then enters, in Lucy's white dress, clumsily altered, and the scene of the prologue is reenacted. As the curtain touches the stage, "there is the sound of a shot."

Epilogue: Three minutes elapse and the curtain is raised. Lucy is "standing in an attitude of abject terror, the revolver still clutched in her trembling hand." Suddenly it drops from her hand and she falls to the floor. Tom and Leonora enter. He switches on the lights, and they investigate the body of the prostrate Lucy. Leonora tries to revive her. Gabriel enters and stands petrified, while Mrs. Ashleigh rushes over to put a hand on her daughter's heart. Tom is dazed, "She shot herself,'' while Leonora remarks that ''she must have missed'' because there is no visible wound. Tom then opens the revolver and chuckles, ''I forgot—it's never been loaded.'' Lucy is revived, and both couples eventually fall into each other's arms, properly sorted out. However, the shot is not explained until the chauffeur enters, carrying a wheel with a flat tire: ''See, sir! Fix up as good as new.'' There is an outburst of laughter as Leonora points dramatically at the tire and delivers a parody of the last lines of Ibsen's play: ''General Gabler's pistol! Fancy that, Heddy!''

Comments: This play shows O'Neill in an unaccustomed mode, that of satire. He takes the themes of Russian melancholy, self-realization, free love, the Nietzschean superman, the Ibsen New Woman, and Shaw's *Candida* and tries to work them into an articulated whole. To be sure, the mixture is ingenious and the humor broad, but the total effect is one of clever contrivance rather than anything else. The characterization is one-dimensional, and the characters are designed for laughter and passing effect alone. Mrs. Ashleigh, for example, seems intended to be the norm of good sense for the play, yet her behavior does rather beggar belief. Nonetheless, this work is useful as a means of showing that O'Neill did have some ability in parodic comedy, though some of the dialogue does bear a close resemblance to the kind of exchanges that he sometimes expects his audience to take seriously.

The use of the prologue is shrewd because it manages to send the audience off on the wrong track, and as a result the comedy develops deeper overtones that it otherwise would have had. Structurally, the prologue shows a great advance on O'Neill's earlier works. The epilogue, on the other hand, is a monumentally illogical contrivance. First there is the inversion of the old ''I didn't know the gun was loaded'' routine and then the invention of the most efficient chauffeur ever employed by anyone—who can change a flat tire in three minutes. The title derives from the numerous occasions when comment on foolish behavior is introduced by those words.

Production Data: Written 1917. Unproduced.

A Note on Text: The text used is that appearing in *''Children of the Sea'' and Three Other Unpublished Plays by Eugene O'Neill*. Edited by Jennifer McCabe Atkinson (Washington, D.C.: NCR Microcard Editions, 1972, A Bruccoli Clark Book).

O

OBAN, Willie. In *The Iceman Cometh*,* a Harvard Law School alumnus in his late thirties who rents a room above the saloon kept by Harry Hope.* Oban, the son of a former criminal, is a dissipated alcoholic who wears the worst clothes the pawnshop has to offer because he has pawned and repawned everything down to the very lowest value in order to get money for drink. Harry is currently refusing Oban his usual free drink, and as a result Oban is suffering from the d.t.'s: "the Brooklyn Boys" are after him. His pipe dream is that someday he will spruce up, give up drinking, and get a job with the district attorney, a position commensurate with his brilliance as a student. Under the influence of Theodore Hickman,* the salesman who comes to the bar annually to celebrate Harry's birthday, Oban attempts to translate the dream into reality, but of course that is impossible. After Hickey's arrest on the charge of murdering his wife, Oban and other denizens of the bar seize on his plea of insanity, a pipe-dream explanation which discredits what he has taught them. They then gladly get drunk in order to forget the outside world and to regain illusion.

O'DOWD, Paddy. In *A Touch of the Poet*,* one of the low-class Irish. He "is thin, round-shouldered, flat-chested, with a pimply complexion, bulgy eyes and a droopy mouth." He has the insinuating manner "of a born sponger and parasite." He is one of the hangers-on at Cornelius Melody's* tavern and regularly gets drunk there. He and his companions, Dan Roche* and Patch Riley,* are present at Melody's last Talavera Day Dinner, and throughout the play the noise of their merry making often serves as a counterpoint to the serious action. They beat up the Harford family lawyer, Nicholas Gadsby.* Their lack of social class is indicated by their support of Andrew Jackson for president of the United States.

"OH, SOUR-APPLE TREE." Original title of *More Stately Mansions*.*

OLDER MAN, THE. In *A Wife for a Life*,* partner of Jack* who is later revealed to be John Sloan. The Older Man is dressed in rough miner's costume, but his voice and manner suggest a "native refinement" which indicate that he has seen better days. He is the principal character of the play, though he has fewer lines than Jack. The tale that his partner tells of waiting for his beloved Yvette,* who had been married to a drunken mining engineer and remained faithful to her vows despite her love for Jack, turns out to be the tale of his own life and wife. Yvette now believes herself free since the Older Man is presumed dead, and she has telegraphed Jack to offer to marry him.

The action of the play is internal, almost totally concerned with the growing perceptions of the Older Man. First, he realizes that Jack is the enemy that he has sworn to kill—but Jack has saved his life, and he no longer has any hatred for him as an enemy. Next, he discovers that Yvette has been faithful to him, despite his behavior to her, loving him for what he was, not hating him for what he had become. Last, he reaches the conclusion that his only way of repaying his debts to both is to allow the two persons he loves most in the world to work out their own happiness together. Though tempted to withhold the telegram which will lose Jack to him forever, his better self triumphs; he gives the document to his friend and wishes them both well.

The character of the Older Man is developed by his responses to Jack's account of the past: Jack operates on the level of literal narrative and the Older Man in terms of psychological insight. From the beginning, he is perceived as a character with a mysterious past. O'Neill here makes considerable use of the aside, a device he used to very great effect in his later play, *Strange Interlude*.* The conception of both the role and the play indicate O'Neill's indebtedness to the old-fashioned theatre of his father, James O'Neill.* This is the kind of vaudeville-vehicle role in which fading stars used to display their talents for emotion and technical prowess. However, O'Neill here calls for controlled acting rather than unrestrained passion while providing very little motivation. The curtain line, "Greater love hath no man this that he giveth his wife for his friend," is really a rather bad ironic joke which is meant seriously.

"OLDEST MAN, THE." The original title of *The First Man*.*

OLD PETE. In *A Wife for a Life*,* an old miner. He is a down-and-outer who always loses money in saloons. He delivers a telegram for Jack to the Older Man,* who reads it, and this precipitates the exposition which comprises the entire play.

OLD TOM. In *The Moon of the Caribbees*,* donkeyman of the S.S. *Glencairn*, "an old gray-headed man with a kindly, wrinkled face." The philosopher of the boat, he has lived long enough to accept his fate as a seaman. Hence he interprets the mysterious negro chant as reminding him of "listenin' to the organ outside o'th' church." He perceives its religious quality but realizes that he is forever an outsider.

"OLE DAVIL, THE," unpublished and unproduced play in four acts, the second version of *Chris Christophersen*.* The third reworking of this material became *"Anna Christie."**

Act I: The inside of Johnny-the-Priest's* saloon near South Street, New York City. The stage is divided into two sections showing both the main bar and the back room. "It is late afternoon of a day in the fall of 1910." Johnny "the Priest" is reading a newspaper. He is a mild-looking clerical type, but "the man behind the mask [is] cynical, callous, hard as nails." Two longshoremen enter and order drinks. Larry,* the relief bartender, arrives, "a boyish, red-cheeked, rather good-looking young fellow of twenty or so." A Postman brings a letter addressed to Christopher Christophersen* in care of Johnny. The letter is postmarked St. Paul, Minnesota, and Johnny recalls that Chris has a daughter out west. Chris then enters, "a short, squat, broad-shouldered man of about fifty, with a round weatherbeaten face, short-sighted blue eyes, and an expression of "obstinate kindness." He has "stumpy legs. . .large flat feet. . .a clumsy, rolling gait" and is wearing "ill-fitting shore clothes." He is now employed as captain on a coal barge, though he was once a boatswain on a sailing ship. Happily intoxicated, he comes in singing what will be his theme song, "My Yosephine." He orders drinks and then remembers Marthy Owen* in the back room. She has been living with him on the barge. She is a fat woman of about forty or fifty, with a "jowly, mottled face. . .thick red nose. . .thick grey hair piled in a greasy mop," but her eyes still show "a youthful lust for life." She is dressed in a man's cap and jacket, "grimy calico skirt," and oversize men's brogans. As he orders a drink for her, Chris is given the letter which is from his daughter, Anna [*see* Christopherson, Anna]. Chris has not seen his daughter since she was five, and she is now twenty. Since her mother's death, she has lived with cousins in Minnesota, away from "ole davil sea." Chris tells of his two older sons, both lost in a fishing accident. Larry comments that Anna might marry a sailor, a suggestion that Chris angrily resents because a sailor "not for marry gel. . . .Dat damn dirty sea she spoil all tang. She's ole devil." As Chris reads the letter in front of Marthy, he "becomes desperately ill at ease" and goes to the bar to tell Larry that he will have to get rid of Marthy now that Anna's arrival is imminent. Anna has had a job as a nurse-governess for the last two years, and she believes that Chris is a janitor. He plans that she will live with him on the barge. He returns to Marthy, and after she teases him along, she offers to leave without any trouble, certain that she'll find another bargeman. They will part friends, and so they drink—at some length—to Anna's arrival.

As Chris goes out to sober up, Anna Christophersen enters, "a tall, blond, fully developed girl of twenty, handsome after a large Viking-daughter fashion, but now run down in health and plainly. . .belonging to the world's oldest profession. Her youthful face is already cynical beneath its layer of make-up. Her clothes are the tawdry finery of peasant stock turned prostitute." She orders: "Gimme a whiskey—ginger ale on the side. And don't be stingy, baby." She gulps down her drink and sits with Marthy, who realizes her identity as the conversation continues. Anna says she is tired from the long train journey by coach and is out of the hospital just two weeks. She orders drinks for herself and Marthy and begins to smoke. At this, Marthy says, "I got your number," to which Anna replies, "You're me forty years from now," a statement Marthy resents but decides not to argue. Anna then tells Marthy confidentially that she had been given a prison term for prostitution and then had become ill enough to be sent to the hospital. She says she has come to join her father, a janitor, a statement that surprises Marthy, who asks the young woman whether old Chris is her father, telling her, "he's as good an old guy as ever walked on feet." She is attempting to counter Anna's statement that she hates all men and expects Chris to be like the rest. Anna is shocked to hear that Chris is a barge captain and rejects the idea that she should live with him. Angrily she tells Marthy of her miserable life on the farm and Chris's insistence that she stay away from the sea. Her cousins' family had treated her like a slavey poor relation, and "it was one of the sons—the youngest—started me—when I was also treated badly" and sexually harassed. Finally she got a chance to work in a brothel, where again she was exploited by men: "I hate 'em all, every mother's son of 'em." Marthy says that there are some good men, and Chris is one, but Anna remains sceptical even though Marthy tries to convince her of Chris's love for her. Marthy suggests that Anna stick to the nurse story to avoid hurting Chris and also that she make some trips with her father, but Anna is unconvinced.

At this point Chris returns, having eaten, and goes to see Marthy and what Larry calls the "tramp with her." Marthy moves aside to let Anna sit alone, announces her departure from the barge, and leaves. As Chris enters the back room, father and daughter are both awkward, emotional, and embarrassed. Chris takes Anna's tawdry clothes for brilliance and "high-toned" beauty. They kiss and Chris discovers that Anna knows no Swedish. Overwhelmed by her appearance, Chris compliments Anna: "You vas awful pooty gel, Anna? Ay bet all men see you fall in love with you." This remark repels Anna: "You talk same as they all do—all the men."

Anna and Chris exchange confidences, Chris apologizing for his neglect of her, once again blaming "dat ole davil sea." He claims he has had to take the barge job for his health, but "dis ain't real sail yob." Anna tells her father that she had hoped to live with him "till I felt able to get back on the job again." Chris is overjoyed and tries to overcome all her objections. "You don't know how nice it's on barge, Anna," and she agrees to go "for the one trip." Chris then offers her a drink—"yinger ale—sas'prilla, maybe." Anna laughs, and Chris suggests a genteel drink, port wine. As he goes to the bar, he proudly identifies Anna as his daughter, to the profound embarrassment of Larry, who had thought Chris was picking up a "tramp." Chris and Anna drink together, the girl downing hers like a shot of whiskey.

Act II: Ten days later, at 10 P.M. on the stern deck of the "barge *Simeon Winthrop*, at anchor in the outer harbor of Provincetown, Mass.," enveloped in almost impenetrable fog. Anna, wearing black oilskins, is looking "healthy, transformed; the natural color has come back to her face." She looks "out into the fog with an expression of awed wonder." Chris, wearing yellow oilskins, comes out for Anna, concerned about her health and safety, but Anna is overwhelmed by the experience: "I feel as if I was—out of things altogether." Chris, as usual, complains about the "dirty tricks" of "the ole davil sea." This becomes a *leitmotif* of his conversation. Chris sees the fog as an enemy, a danger to them, but Anna has fallen in love with both sea and fog: "It seems to wipe it all out, somehow I feel as if—I'd always been out here—and nothing had ever happened." She tells him to stop complaining about the sea. She "would rather have one drop of ocean than all the farms in the world." Warily, Chris asks if she'd marry a sailor and is overjoyed when he hears her say, "I wouldn't marry the best there is on sea and land." Chris completely misreads the situation, not understanding her motivation, and Anna then asks about her family. Chris tells her that the sea claimed all of them, except his brother, but he, Chris, intends to die in bed. Proudly he announces that he, unlike the rest of his menfolk, was more than an able seaman—he was boatswain. The women of the family had all married sailors, but, he warns Anna, "Any gel marry sailor, the crazy fool." But Anna still speaks glowingly of the sea: "It's like I've come home after a long visit away some place....And I feel clean, somehow, like you feel just after you've took a bath. And I feel happy for once....Happier than I ever been anywhere before." Chris is so disturbed that Anna inquires whether he thinks something might happen, "half-mockingly" suggesting that it would be "Gawd's will," but Chris replies angrily, "Dat ole davil sea, she ain't God!"

At this moment they hear a feeble hail from a dinghy, and four men come on board. Johnson, the barge deckhand, is supporting one man and Chris another. They have been adrift five days since the sinking of their steamer. Mat Burke,* a powerfully built thirty-year-old stoker, then wearily tumbles in and sits down, followed by Johnson, who supports a babbling fourth man. Burke berates his companions for their physical weakness: " 'Tis only in the stokehole you'll find proper men," for he has been doing all the rowing for the past three days. Anna, who has been inside preparing food, is astonished to see Mat as she comes on deck. When she offers him a drink, Mat is sure that he is dreaming, but as he reaches out to touch her, Anna recoils, yet she becomes amusedly interested as he boasts of his prowess. Despite his exhaustion, Burke starts a flirtation, "I'm the proper lad for you," and attempts to embrace her. He is so tired that he is momentarily off balance when she pushes him, and he falls, knocked out for the moment, while Anna, filled with remorse, kneels to help him. When he recovers, Anna explains that she is not "the old squarehead's woman" but his daughter, reproving Mat for his presumption. At first the stoker is apologetic, but he soon returns to blarneying her as "a fine dacent girl."

The two exchange personal information, and Anna allows that she is a governess and has just come from the West. Mat replies with his account of the wreck and his own part in keeping it afloat. The captain had prayed, but the "prayers of a Protestant pup" were naturally ineffectual. Finally, all men but these four on the barge were drowned in the panic-stricken rush for the boats. They survived only "with the help of God." Nonetheless, he thinks the deaths of the others to be "a good end...quick and clane," a remark that strikes a responsive chord in Anna. Despite all the hardships, Mat would do "it all over again for the sake of mating you at the end of it." Mat then talks, almost like Chris, about a sailor's hard life and the prostitutes he meets. Anna is cut by this, but Mat misunderstands: "this is the first time I've had a word with a rale clane woman." But still, Mat will not leave the sea for "digging spuds in the muck from dawn to dark." His dream is to get a berth on a passenger steamer and have a house on land and "a fine dacent girl—the like of yourself, now—would be willing to wed with me." Mat works Anna's uneasy agreement into a real proposal, which Anna rejects "on such short acquaintance." Chris, seeing the two together, is furious and orders Anna inside, but he has chosen the wrong approach and Anna turns on him: "Who d'you think you're talking to—a slave? I'll go in when I get good and ready." Chris calms down, but this time Mat starts to swagger and threaten, though he is too exhausted to do anything and eventually falls. Anna helps him in as Mat insists, "we'll be marrying soon." Chris remains on deck to rage against the sea: "Dat's your dirty trick, damn ole davil, you!" But then he threatens, "But py God, you don't do dat! Not vile I'm living! No, py God you don't."

Act III: "The interior of the cabin of the barge *Simeon Winthrop* (at dock in Boston)....It is afternoon of a sunny day about a week later." Anna is sitting, reading a newspaper, while Chris is pottering about uneasily, singing "My Yosephine." The two start bickering over remaining in Boston and also over the way Anna has been spending so much time with Mat, who has pursued her from Cape Cod. She is angered at Chris's suggestion that "it ain't right kind of fun—not with that damn falla—no," and threatens to "get the hell out" if he thinks evil of her. Chris apologizes but then suggests that Mat as a mere stoker is no proper sailor. He, Chris is not afraid of Mat's strength, "oder vay for fix him," a comment which brings Anna to warn him against taking action—he might get hurt. Once more Chris warns her against marrying a sailor, but the discussion turns into an argument about Mat. Chris is relieved when Anna says that though she would "have jumped at the chance" four or even two years ago, now she "ain't got the heart to fool him." As Anna gets ready to go out, Chris proffers the observation that she and Mat will soon forget each other. Left alone, Chris mutters, "Dirty ole davil you!"

Suddenly Mat appears, dressed in his shore clothes, and Chris reaches for the sheath knife at his belt. Mat asks for Anna and tells Chris he intends to marry her "before this day is out." To this Chris replies that Anna "tal me yust before she go out she never marry fallar like you." Both discuss their wishes for both Anna and themselves: Chris does not want to be alone and wishes Mat would ship out. Mat says that he is anxious to settle down with a decent girl, and since the sea is in Anna's blood the match is really a good one. Certainly Chris will see more of Anna in Boston and New York than he did when she was in

Minnesota. The discussion escalates into insult as Mat celebrates himself as a real man, calling Chris "a liar and a coward," accusing him of fear ("swallowed the anchor"). Chris retorts by speaking of the days of sail, "ships vas ships dem days," while Mat knows only how to shovel coal, which he could do just as well on shore. Insults become ethnic until Chris finally lunges with his knife, and Mat easily disarms him. Anna then returns and asks for an explanation of the argument. On hearing that she was the topic, she asks what they were saying and finally admits, "Sure I love you, Mat!" They kiss, and then Anna, "forcing a broken laugh," says good-bye. The two men continue their bickering until Mat offers Chris his hand. Anna repeats her good-bye: "I can't marry you, Mat." Mat, tortured by her words, suggests that Chris's "blather" against the sea is the explanation, but Anna calls the scrapping men to order: "I got a good reason—and that's all you need to know. I can't marry you." Mat asks if she has already married someone out West, that being the thing he couldn't bear, but Anna replies, "No, I should say not! I hated every one of 'em." Mat then takes her by the arms and starts to bully her into acceptance while Chris orders, "You stay right here, Anna! You hear!"

At this, "the expression of her face freezes into the hardened sneer of her experiences" as she hears them talk *of* her and *to* her as if she were an object. She confronts them with her declaration of independence, "nobody owns me, see?—'cepting myself. I'll do what I please and no man, I don't give a hoot who he is, can tell me what to do!" Then she reveals the horror of her life on the farm, her cousin's rape of her, and finally the way she "give it all up finally—the job—and everything else." She accuses the two men of being "like all the rest!" Chris has never acted like a father, she says, and then she forces them to listen to her recital of horrors: "I was in a house . . . the kind sailors like you and Mat goes to in port . . . and all men, God damn them!—I hate 'em! Hate 'em." Chris collapses, and Anna turns bitterly to Mat, "remember your promise, Mat. No other reason was to count with you so long as I wasn't married already. . . . You're like all the rest. So gimme a kick now when I'm down and beat it for good." Gradually, Anna turns to "pitiful pleading," saying that she has now been totally changed by her life since leaving the West. She felt clean and new and had wanted to marry Mat, but had found herself unable to live a lie. "Will you believe it if I tell you that loving you has made me—clean?" Mat threatens her with a chair, "You slut," but cannot go through with it, but then he berates her as being "the same as others you'd meet in a hooker-shanty in port." As Anna orders Mat out, Chris says, "Ay tank maybe it's better Anna marry you now." Mat refuses Chris and curses Anna as he leaves. Chris also leaves for a drink, but before departing, he comforts Anna: "Ain't your fault, Anna, Ay know dat. It's dat ole davil sea, do dis to me. . . . Dirty ole davil." She sits, staring vacantly, as the curtain falls.

Act IV: "Same as Act III about nine o'clock of a foggy night two days later." Anna enters, carrying a suitcase and dressed as in Act I. She sits down wearily. There is a knock at the door, and the Donkeyman of the barge enters, concerned that Anna might have been leaving and tells her that the crew will always be pleased to help her. He is also concerned that Chris might lose his job if he stays away too long, and therefore he proposes to go to look for him. But then Chris enters, very bleary, very hungover, and carrying a tin pail full of foaming beer. Anna looks at him with contempt and complains at his leaving her alone. He sees her bag, and Anna says that she had decided to go back to New York and prostitution but had thought to wait one more day. She wishes to see Mat because she really is in love with him. Chris asks forgiveness and gives his permission for her to marry Mat. Anna forgives him, too, and he tells her that he has just signed on to go to sea again as boatswain on the steamer *Londonderry*, bound for Cape Town. He is nothing but a "Yonah man" to Anna, thanks to "dat ole davil sea." He has arranged for the steamship office to pay Anna all his money, "So you never gat go back—" He takes off his coat, and as Anna goes to hang it up, she finds a revolver in a pocket, but Chris says he has not bought bullets for it. He had planned to kill Mat, but "killing him don't do no good. It's ole davil, sea, Ay'd like to kill—if Ay could." Sick and exhausted, he goes to bed after they kiss in forgiveness.

Anna, left alone, tries to distract herself, when suddenly she hears Mat. At first she is joyful but then seizes the revolver and hides as Mat bursts in, drunk, violent, battered, and miserable. Anna, he says, has made him such a weakling that he can't kill her. As he sees her suitcase he thinks she is going back to prostitution and runs through emotions, from joy that she has not yet left to rage and potential violence. Anna confronts him, revolver in hand, to ask his business, but Mat advances on her, asking her to shoot him—and then he disarms her. He has tried to forget, but he cannot. He begs her to tell him that all she has told him was a lie, but Anna cannot. She begs him to see how she has changed. She couldn't leave without seeing him once more. Now she will return to New York tomorrow: "What's the use of changing? It's a rotten game and I might as well be as rotten as the rest. . . . Don't you see I'm licked? Why d'you keep on kicking me?" Mat then tells her that he has signed on as a seaman on the *Londonderry*, information that arouses her wild, ironical laughter. She teases him about the women he will find in Cape Town and then asks angrily, "How're you any better than I am?"

Mat then accuses her of having told all her sexual companions "the same lies. . . that you told to me," suggesting that she was in love with them. Stung into fury, Anna answers, "I hated 'em all and I still do and always will! And may God strike me dead this minute. . . if I ain't telling you the honest truth." Mat starts to soften as he wants to believe her: "I'm thinking I'd change you to a new woman entirely." Perhaps, after all, it was not her fault. He then asks her to swear on the crucifix his mother had given him that "I'm the only man in the world ever you felt love for." She willingly does so but then asks Mat to swear, "that you'll forget the whole business once and for all." This he does, but then he asks if she is a Catholic because if not, her swearing would mean nothing. Anna asks, "What's difference? I don't know what I am. I ain't nothing."

Mat then sees himself as an instrument of her salvation—as Anna declares that she will become a Catholic.

They embrace as Chris enters. He looks and then goes back to get the beer so they can drink to this change. Anna then breaks the news that Chris and Mat will be shipmates. She plans to ''get a little house somewhere and—if you both give me ALL your money I'll make a regular place for you to come back to, wait'n see.'' The men drink together as Burke promises an early grandchild. Chris looks into his drink: ''It's funny—you and me shipping on same boat dat vay...it's dat funny vay ole davil, sea do her vorst dirty tricks...yes. It's so.'' Mat brushes away this remark, ''The sea means good to us only,'' but as Chris continues to say ''Dirthy ole davil,'' Burke calls to Anna, ''He's after putting his fists to the sea again.'' And the final word goes to Anna as she laughingly refuses to take Chris seriously: ''Oh, for Gawd's sake.''

Comments: This intermediate version of ''*Anna Christie*'' shows a tremendous advance over the earlier *Chris Christophersen*. The focus of the drama is clearer, the Christophersens' voyage to Buenos Aires is omitted, and the characters of both Anna and Mat Burke are completely redrawn. O'Neill had had difficulty in developing Paul Andersen* as a suitable lover for his misconceived Anna in *Chris Christophersen*. In this second version he hits on a much more plausible characterization than a British typiste hoping to get a college degree. This second Anna is a true daughter of Chris, and she is now given the motivation of earlier mistreatment to explain her past, while Mat, a muscular romantic and lover of the sea, takes the place of the unambitious college dropout ex-farmer turned sailor, Paul Andersen. Curiously, the Anna of ''The Ole Davil'' seems more aggressive, more damaged by her past experiences, and more turned against men than her later counterpart. Chris is given two tags, the words ''ole davil,'' and the song ''My Yosephine,'' both of which tend to become tedious with constant repetition, and his dialect is more consciously Swedish. The conclusion of the second version is certainly more comic than in ''*Anna Christie*,'' and the notion of the sea as ultimate doom is not conveyed. Travis Bogard (1972, p. 162n) may well be right in suggesting the possibility that this ending was used in the original New York production of ''*Anna Christie*'' since reviewers mention the ending as comic.

Production Data: Written 1920. Unproduced. Reworked into ''Anna Christie,'' produced 1921.

A Note on Text: The text used is that of the typescripts at Yale University, and at the Library of Congress. Used by permission.

OLSON, also known as Ollie. In *The Moon of the Caribbees,** *Bound East for Cardiff,** and *The Long Voyage Home,** a seaman on the S.S. *Glencairn*, a ''Swede with a drooping blond mustache,...stocky, middle-aged...with round, childish blue eyes. He is portrayed as a stolid, unintelligent, and at times almost animalistic character. However, even he has a dream, hoping to escape the clutches of the sea and return to Stockholm and buy a farm with his life's savings.

However, in *The Long Voyage Home*, he is drugged and impressed into service on the hell-ship *Amindra*, of which he had formerly been a crew member. His savings are stolen from him, first by the prostitute, Freda,* and taken from her by Fat Joe,* the keeper of a waterfront dive. Olson is O'Neill's symbol for the man who attempts to escape his fate but always is doomed to fail.

O'NEILL, Agnes. *See* Boulton, Agnes.

O'NEILL, Carlotta. *See* Monterey, Carlotta.

O'NEILL, Catherine Givens, wife of Shane Rudraigh O'Neill* and mother of his five children.

O'NEILL, Edmund Burke (1883–1885), second son of James O'Neill* and Ella (Quinlan) O'Neill.* Died in infancy as the result of measles contracted from his brother, James ("Jamie") O'Neill.*

O'NEILL, Ella Quinlan, wife of James O'Neill*; mother of James ("Jamie") O'Neill, Jr.,* Edmund Burke O'Neill (died in infancy), and Eugene [Gladstone] O'Neill. Born in New Haven, Connecticut, August 13, 1857, to Thomas Joseph and Bridget (Lundigan) Quinlan. Died in Los Angeles, California, February 28, 1922. Her given names were Mary Ellen, but at the age of fifteen she began to call herself "Ellen" at boarding school, and her marriage certificate shows this name. At some time after her marriage she adopted the name "Ella," by which she was known henceforth and which appears on her tombstone.

Shortly after Ella's birth, Thomas Quinlan with his wife, son, and daughter moved to Cleveland, where he began his business career as a newsdealer, later expanding into stationery, books, baked goods, candy, and sundries, becoming really a general retail business man. By 1867 he had become prosperous and middle class, and within the next few years he entered the liquor and tobacco business, moving his family into one of the more affluent parts of town. He also interested himself in real estate, making profitable investments. Ella was brought up among books and music, receiving piano lessons at an early age, believing also that she had considerable talent in this regard and might even make her living at it.

In the fall of 1872, Ella Quinlan was enrolled at St. Mary's Academy, Notre Dame, Indiana, a boarding school for young ladies which also accepted members of faiths other than Roman Catholic. There, after an initial period of homesickness, she was extremely happy and even thought of entering the convent but was persuaded to test her vocation by spending at least a year in the world. This excellent advice came from her music teacher, Mother Elizabeth, a remarkably perceptive and cultured woman who correctly assessed the romanticism of Ella's character. At the same time that she thought of the convent, Ellen O'Neill still nourished dreams of becoming a professional musician, winning the gold medal for music at her graduation in 1875, playing the Chopin *Polonaise* No. 22 at the ceremony. In later years she enjoyed returning to St. Mary's to roam around the grounds and recapture the peace, security, and contentment of her life there. Another link to her youth was the grand piano on which she had learned to play and which her father left to her in his will. She took it with her to New London, the only settled home of her marriage. Thomas Quinlan died in May 1874 of tuberculosis brought on by excessive drinking. Apparently he had been a tee-totaler until the age of forty when, as James Tyrone* says of Mary Tyrone's father in *Long Day's Journey Into Night*,* he developed a great taste for champagne, possibly (as Louis Sheaffer suggests, 1973, p. 14) in reaction to his "moralistic wife to whom champagne symbolized sinful living."

After her graduation, Ella returned to Cleveland and found herself somewhat bored. She had met James O'Neill when he had visited her father at home in 1872, but he did not seem to have noticed her, and she left for school, probably with a crush on him. Their paths diverged, and they did not meet again until she went backstage to see him after a New York performance in 1876. Ella had persuaded her mother to come with her to New York, where she had relatives, so that she should continue her musical studies, but whether her real motive was to pursue James O'Neill remains unknown. Certainly he was a good catch, handsome, charming, despite his lack of education, and a successful actor with limitless possibilities. He was thirty years old and was captivated by Ella's tall, dark-golden-haired beauty allied to that indefinable air of deference, innocence, and cultured gentility which used to distinguish the convent-bred.

Despite the opposition of Bridget Quinlan, the two were married at St. Ann's Roman Catholic Church, East Twelfth Street, New York City, then a most fashionable area, before a few relatives, with Bridget acting as matron of honor for Ella. Despite the privacy of the ceremony, Ella had a very elegant and expensive bridal dress of white satin with ruffles of duchesse lace at neck and sleeves as well as at the bustle. She kept this dress, hoping for a daughter to wear it (see *Long Day's Journey into Night**). The wedding ring came from Tiffany's. One reason for the quiet ceremony was James O'Neill's reputation as a bachelor matinee idol. The weather on the wedding day, June 14, 1877, was gloomy and threatening—hardly a good omen (Gelb and Gelb, 1973, pp. 38–39).

Shortly after the wedding James O'Neill went on tour to Chicago, and Ella accompanied him, finding life as a backstage wife rather miserable. She remained in her hotel room most of the time and discovered that her husband liked to drink; but, as he said and *Long Day's Journey* corroborates, he never missed a performance on that account. In September of 1877, a woman named Nettie Walsh brought a paternity suit against James O'Neill, her former lover, alleging marriage to him which had produced a son, and also his adultery. By mid-November the judge ruled that there was insufficient evidence, but Walsh was awarded attorney's fees and fifty dollars a week support until the case for "divorce" was heard. In December 1877 it was dismissed since there was no evidence to support the allegation of marriage. This episode seemed to have affected Ella adversely, and she withdrew farther from her husband's life of superficial glamor, staying in hotel rooms most of the time. One wonders what she could have found to do, before the era of mass entertainment, especially since she was hopelessly undomestic and always had either a maid or nurse.

She continued to follow her husband on tour, and on September 10, 1878, her first child, James, Jr. ("Jamie"), was born in the home of friends in San Francisco while James, Sr., was playing there and also investing in real estate as a hedge against the future. They remained in San Francisco until October 1880 when James O'Neill moved his family back to New York, and once again they went on the road. In the fall of 1883, in a St. Louis hotel, Edmund Burke O'Neill was born, named after the Anglo-Irish member of parliament, not Edmond Dantès in *The Count of Monte Cristo*, the role with which James O'Neill was already closely associated. But with two young children, touring became almost impossible, and Ella and the babies were accustomed to remain in their New York apartment. Then when separation became unbearable, she would leave the children with her mother and go to her husband. This is what happened in early 1885 when she went West to be with him. Her mother and the children were at their apartment in the Richfield Hotel, on West Forty-third Street, when Jamie caught the measles; and ignoring orders to the contrary, he visited the baby, who fell ill on February 27. Ella and James were in Denver; and since he was committed to his run as Monte Cristo, Ella returned East alone, arriving on March 4, 1885 after Edmund's death. She never forgave herself for the death of this baby, and Agnes Boulton* recalled her saying in 1918, "He might not have died if I hadn't left him; we had a good nurse, a very good nurse, and James wanted me to go on tour—he can't seem to manage without me" (Boulton, 1958, p. 233; Sheaffer, 1983, p. 16).

In fall 1885 the O'Neills put Jamie, now seven years old, in a special boarding division of St. Mary's, Notre Dame, so that they could tour more comfortably. The previous year they had bought a summer home-*cum*-permanent residence in New London, Connecticut, 325 Pequot Avenue, and during the next two years they bought adjoining property and added to the cottage, later known as "Monte Cristo Cottage," for James was now completely identified with the role. Despite the presence of her mother in New London, Ella seemed very depressed, not regarding the town as home but attached to it because Edmund was buried there. Her husband, however, enjoyed himself, pottering about the garden and going to his club, while Ella remained retiring. In Summer 1887 they toured Europe, James O'Neill visiting the sites important in *The Count of Monte Cristo* and Oberammergau, though the Passion Play was not being given that year. During their absence, Bridget Quinlan died in New London, another blow to the fragile personality of Ella O'Neill.

She began touring again with her husband, who was by now beginning to sense that he had sold his artistic soul for financial success. On October 16, 1888, Eugene Gladstone O'Neill was born in a room in the Barrett House, a family hotel on Broadway at Forty-third Street, now Times Square. The building was demolished in 1940. Ella had a long and difficult childbirth, and the doctor whom James O'Neill had called to attend her relieved her pain with morphine. This "medicine" was continued to relieve her postpartum depression, and she accidentally and innocently became addicted to the drug. Later, both mother and sons blamed James O'Neill for his miserliness in getting "a cheap hotel doctor" (see *Long Day's Journey*) to attend her instead of a decent doctor, a charge he always denied. As she recovered from her ordeal she took to self-medication, finding that morphine, then readily available in patent medicines, brought not only relief from pain but also from the difficulties and loneliness of daily existence. She seems to have been unaware that she was becoming addicted, while her husband was long in discovering the cause of her dreaminess and unreality. Only when a pharmacist warned him that the patent medicine he was buying for his wife could become habit forming did he have any suspicion. From this time until 1914 Ella was a confirmed addict, attempting cures at various sanitoria with the help of her husband.

The trauma of those dreadful years has been dramatized in *Long Day's Journey into Night*, and the experience had deleterious effects on both Jamie and Eugene. Jamie knew of his mother's drug addiction very early and seems to have blamed himself for his part in his brother's death, while Eugene, who finally learned the truth when he was about fifteen, when she threatened suicide in New London (Sheaffer, 1973, p. 59, and 1983, pp. 17–18), always harbored a residual bitterness toward her. However, the family remained close-mouthed about Ella's weakness, though she was known in New London to be somewhat strange. She seems to have led a shadowy half-life both there and on tour with James O'Neill; however, unlike Mary Tyrone* in *Long Day's Journey*, Ella O'Neill decided, apparently on her own, to make one last attempt to break her habit, choosing her own way—a return to the piety of her convent youth. She went into a Brooklyn convent and there managed to free herself from her twenty-five-year enslavement to drugs. Thus, by the time Agnes Boulton met her, she had again become an elegant, charming, and impressive lady; though still suffering guilt for the loss of her son Edmund, she was now able to deal with it. As before, Ella remained in the background and never really associated with James's friends in the theatre, apparently considering the theatrical life somewhat unacceptable socially. She always seems to have felt, with some justice, that her convent friends ostracized her because of her marriage to an actor, particularly after the Nettie Walsh scandal. Also, the time was not long past when actors were not even welcome in churches for their own funeral services.

An interesting vignette of their life is found in Agnes Boulton's *Part of a Long Story* (1958, pp. 229–235) when she visited them at the Prince George Hotel, Twenty-seventh Street and Fifth Avenue, New York, in late 1918. She noted the elegance of the room, the flowers, the bric-à-brac, and "a picture of a lovely nun, her face bent down, gazing at a crucifix in her hands" (Boulton, 1958, p. 231). She found Ella very beautiful, neat, with "quiet elegance," wearing a "small matched strand of pearls" and lace at the neck and wrists of her black dress. Most particularly, Boulton noted Ella's exquisite shoes and the "faint and elegant flower perfume" she used. Her eyes were dark brown, her skin smooth, soft, and pale, her expression calm and serene. Obviously, her early interest in fine clothes had not evaporated. Sometime around September 1918 Ella O'Neill underwent a mastectomy, and in March 1919 a further nodule was discovered (Sheaffer, 1983, pp. 16–17). Apparently there was no further recurrence.

In retirement, James and Ella O'Neill divided their time between the Prince George Hotel in Manhattan and New London until Monte Cristo Cottage was sold in 1919. They were present at the opening night of *Beyond the Horizon*,* and James O'Neill had earlier offered some advice to members of the Provincetown Players* during rehearsals for his son's productions. They lived comfortably, were frequently seen at the theatre and Ella became a regular communicant.

In 1920, James O'Neill died of cancer, and Ella O'Neill discovered an independence which no one had suspected. She began to look after her investments, apparently assuaging her grief by immersing herself in practicalities. After his father's death, Jamie gave up drinking, and for the rest of Ella's life they were inseparable. At the beginning of 1922, Ella and Jamie went to California, planning to stay for six months for Ella to sell off some of her West Coast properties. She had for some time been suffering from severe headaches, possibly caused by a brain tumor, and while in Los Angeles she suffered two strokes, the second of which, on February 16, left her semiparalysed and scarcely able to talk. She made her will, dividing her estate equally between Jamie and Eugene, but was able only to mark it with an X. She died in Los Angeles on February 28, 1922. During her last days of life, Jamie again began drinking and remained drunk during the railroad journey back to New York with his mother's body, somehow losing or giving away her jewelry on the way. Her funeral service was held in New York at Saint Leo's Church, East Twenty-eighth Street, which she used to attend, and the nuns who had helped her overcome her addiction prayed over her body. Jamie was too drunk to go to the funeral. She was buried in Saint Mary's Cemetery, New London, next to her husband. Jamie O'Neill's account of his mother's last days was later retold by Eugene O'Neill in *A Moon for the Misbegotten*.*

Ella O'Neill's life is a curiously passive one and yet also touchingly romantic. She married a man idolized by many women, and the two of them seem, despite troubles and complaints, to have remained in love with each other. They found it difficult to be separated for long, and despite her dislike of touring and of the backstage life, Ella followed her husband throughout a very rigorous career. She seems always to have been a withdrawn personality, reportedly a bit snobbish, especially toward theatre people, and in New London she remained in the background (perhaps then because of her addiction). Her influence on her sons seems to have been unfortunate because her drug problem caused Jamie to drink and deeply wounded Eugene, who believed his birth was to blame for her plight. Even when she overcame her habit he still could not forgive her totally, perhaps blaming her for not having the strength to break away much earlier. It is interesting to note that in *Long Day's Journey* she is treated tragically, but not with real sympathy in her incarnation as Mary Tyrone. In fact, by the end of the play her condition seems quite as hopeless as Edmund's. To some extent she felt that she had come down in the world by marrying an actor and was concerned about not being socially accepted. She loved beautiful clothes and linens, and was frustrated by not having a beautiful home, Monte Cristo Cottage being exactly what its name implied. Her last years, when Jamie stopped drinking and devoted himself entirely to her, seem to have been happy.

See in "References": Alexander (1962); Boulton (1958); Gelb and Gelb (1973); Sheaffer (1968, 1973, and 1983).

O'NEILL, Eugene [Gladstone] (1888–1953), playwright. Born in a New York City hotel, the Barrett House (Forty-third Street and Broadway), October 16, 1888. Died in Suite 401, the Shelton Hotel, Back Bay, Boston, November 27, 1953, of pneumonia after a long siege of what had been erroneously diagnosed as Parkinson's disease but which an autopsy revealed as a familial tremor, the result of a rare degenerative brain disease. Youngest son of James O'Neill,* Sr., actor, and Ella (Quinlan) O'Neill,* brother of James (Jamie) O'Neill, Jr.,* and Edmund Burke O'Neill. Educated at a Roman Catholic boarding school, the Academy of Mount Saint Vincent, Riverdale, New York; De La Salle Academy, New York City; Betts Academy, Stamford, Connecticut; Princeton University (1906–07 only, being suspended for misbehavior in the spring); Harvard University (1914–15 only), where he took George Pierce Baker's* English 47 Workshop. Married (1) Kathleen Jenkins* (later Pitt-Smith), 1909–12: one son, Eugene O'Neill, Jr.* (2) Agnes Boulton* (later Kaufman), 1918–29: one son, Shane Rudraighe O'Neill*; one daughter, Oona O'Neill Chaplin.* (3) Carlotta Monterey,* 1929–53: no children.

A few days before his death, O'Neill, in words variously reported by his biographers, looked back on a life that had begun and was soon to end in rented rooms. The source of his bitterness and sense of failure may be hard to comprehend in a playwright who had won the Nobel Prize for literature in 1936 and had been awarded three Pulitzer Prizes (and was to receive a fourth one posthumously), as well as having written or drafted over sixty plays. But in 1953 his reputation was in eclipse, and he had been unable to write since 1947–48 because of his nervous disorder. In that same year, two of his plays were not great successes, *The Iceman Cometh** achieving a respectable 136 performances and *A Moon for the Misbegotten** closing out of town. He was, in fact, something of a back number, and his rediscovery as America's premier playwright was some years in the future, beginning with the Jason Robards, Jr.,* and José Quintero* *The Iceman Cometh* (1956). He had sealed away his most autobiographical play, *Long Day's Journey into Night,** leaving it with his publisher,

Random House, with instructions not to open it until twenty-five years after his death. In his declining years he became almost totally isolated from daily living because of his health and the almost suffocatingly assiduous, and sometimes rancorous, care of his third wife.

Throughout his career, O'Neill was an intensely autobiographical playwright, frequently transmuting his personal experiences into drama, but one must always be on guard against taking his autobiographical plays, especially *Long Day's Journey into Night*, as absolutely factual. This is particularly true when one examines the facts of his early life. Certainly he was born in a hotel room, but the Barrett House was a perfectly decent family hostelry. He was, however, haunted by the knowledge that as a result of the pain that followed his long and difficult birth, his mother inadvertently became addicted to morphine, which had originally been prescribed to relieve her pain and depression. Her torture-filled life as an addict lasted until approximately 1914–15, when she managed by sheer will power and the strength of prayer to wean herself from her enslavement, something numerous other sanitoria had been unable to do. Eugene also believed that his mother resented his existence because he was taking the place of her second son, Edmund Burke O'Neill (*see* O'Neill, Ella Quinlan), who had died in infancy. Both O'Neill and his brother Jamie seem to have blamed her problems on the miserliness of their father in getting the services of a "cheap hotel quack" to aid in the birth of Eugene. This attitude seems to have poisoned O'Neill's relations with his father until shortly before the old actor's death in 1920.

But the facts show otherwise: the elder O'Neill was remarkably generous to his wife, frequently sending her to sanitoria that he sometimes afforded only with difficulty. To be sure, James O'Neill lived with a rather legitimately based fear of dying in the poverty in which he had been born, but he seems to have spent money on the education of his sons without a qualm. His apparent desire to economize on Eugene's tuberculosis sanitorium seems in justice to be the result of his firm belief that tuberculosis was incurable. As Eugene and Jamie began to lead what appeared to him to be permanently dissipated and wastrel existences, he still continued to help them, even if reluctantly, finding them jobs in his acting company, financing them, and using his influence to assist them. His anger with them at a time when he could legitimately expect them to be self-supporting is explicable, while his sons' annoyance at the small amounts of money he doled out to them is less so.

After his birth, Eugene O'Neill was looked after by an English nurse, Mrs. Sarah Jane Bucknell Sandy, who remained with the family for seven years, accompanying Ella and Eugene on James's strenuous theatrical tours and summering with them at Monte Cristo Cottage, New London, Connecticut. Jamie, almost ten years older than Eugene, was at this time enrolled in boarding school at Notre Dame, Indiana. O'Neill learned to read at a very early age and became a bookish child. But his nomadic existence exacted a psychic cost, and he always longed for roots and permanency. Monte Cristo Cottage was the one constant in his existence because it was there that the whole family returned every summer to recuperate at 325 Pequot Avenue from the yearly grind of theatrical touring. The house was an unpretentious tree-shaded conglomerate, on a lot that sloped down to the water. Ella O'Neill hated the place, partly because it was rather gloomy, partly because of her drug-induced depression, and partly because she did not feel it did justice to their station. She believed, to some extent correctly, that the O'Neills were not as well received in the community as was Richard Mansfield, another actor, who maintained a luxurious estate in the area. O'Neill and Jamie tended to agree with Ella's evaluation of their residence and also to resent their father's happy reversion to "bog Irish" pottering about the garden. For the first seven years of his life, O'Neill saw Jamie only during these summer vacations, and the difference in age seems at that time to have left O'Neill even more introverted. Also, during these early summers, the other members of the family were preoccupied with their own problems: Ella with her addiction, James with plans for the coming theatrical season, and Jamie with some hell-raising. Thus Eugene seems to have spent his time reading and sketching with Mrs. Sandy, who early regaled him with ghost stories.

At the age of seven he was enrolled at St. Aloysius, the boys' department of the Academy of Mount St. Vincent, run by the Sisters of Charity in Riverdale, New York. This school had moved from its original quarters in what is now Central Park to the former mansion of Edwin Forrest, the Shakespearean actor. Like Monte Cristo Cottage, the campus had a view of the water, this time the Hudson River. O'Neill seems to have remained a loner during this time, immersed in his books, even though his brother Jamie was now a fairly short distance away at Saint John's College (later Fordham University), Rose Hill, the Bronx. Despite occasional visits from his mother and her cousins, O'Neill and Jamie spent almost all of their time at school, except for Christmas, but even then their parents were often away on tour.

In 1900 he transferred to the De La Salle Academy, 58–59 Street, New York City, an institution run by the Christian Brothers. Since his father had an engagement in New York in *The Three Musketeers*, Eugene was a day student, living in his family's West Sixty-fifth Street hotel apartment. Jamie, who had been expelled from Saint John's over a foolish prank, but who was trying to find himself first as a reporter, then as a lumber salesman, also visited frequently. Thus for the first time, O'Neill had a relatively normal home life. However, by 1901 he was a boarding student at De La Salle. This seems to have been the result of his mother's addiction. His father went on tour about this time, and O'Neill seems to have felt the same loneliness he had experienced at St. Aloysius.

In 1902 he persuaded his parents to send him to Betts Academy, Stamford, Connecticut, a nonsectarian preparatory school, where he spent the next four years and lost his faith. In the summer of 1903, Ella O'Neill, having run out of morphine, threatened to throw herself from the dock into the river. As detailed in *Long Day's Journey* and supported by Louis Sheaffer (1968, p. 89, and 1983, pp. 17–18) it was then that O'Neill discovered the truth about his mother. Later, when she did manage to wean herself from the drug, O'Neill still did not fully forgive her, apparently reasoning that she could have made the effort earlier. Despite all these problems, O'Neill again seems to have found relief in reading, particularly the kind of "shocking" reading detailed later in his plays: Baudelaire, Dowson, and Oscar Wilde, among others. By the age of fifteen he was beginning to imitate the drunken dissipation of Jamie, who eventually introduced him to a brothel in what was apparently an embarrassing experience. When he left Betts in the spring of 1906, he had done an extraordinary amount of reading, ranging from the romantic novels of Dumas and the Irish history in his father's library to Kipling and writers like Shaw and Ibsen. He was also "flirting" with anarchism.

In fall 1906, O'Neill became a freshman at Princeton University but he stayed less than a year. He was noted for his appetite for reading, his visits to the red-light districts of Trenton and New York, his boredom with the English classes and sermons of Henry Van Dyke, his impatience with library regulations, and his drinking proclivities. On one occasion in Spring 1907, he tried drinking absinthe, which had been supplied him by Louis Holladay,* an experiment which caused an episode of berserk behavior frightening both to Holladay and O'Neill's classmates, who kept the matter secret from the authorities. Though his grades were marginal, O'Neill was not dismissed from the university, but in April 1907 he was suspended for two weeks as the result of a drunken prank which involved damage to the property of Pennsylvania Railroad. (*See* Hastings and Weeks, 1968, for reminiscences of classmates concerning this and other incidents involving O'Neill at Princeton. *See also* Sheaffer, 1968, pp. 124–125.) By June 1907, O'Neill had cut too many classes to take examinations in some courses, and he did not bother to take the others, with the result that he was then dropped for poor scholastic standing. The discipline of Princeton was not for him; he preferred to indulge his voracious reading habit in an unstructured way.

O'Neill returned to New London and then to New York where James O'Neill was preparing for a Broadway venture, which failed. In the fall of 1907, through the influence of his father, O'Neill gained a secretarial job in the New York-Chicago Supply Company at a salary of twenty-five dollars per week. He took little interest in his work and was more concerned with wandering around Greenwich Village and Hell's Kitchen, the Tenderloin district, in company with Edward Keefe, a New London acquaintance, and George Bellows, later a noted artist. They also sampled the New York theatre, from Ibsen to vaudeville. During the year he spent in business, O'Neill continued his acquaintance with Louis Holladay, meeting other Greenwich Village folk through him and his sister, Polly. Losing his job, O'Neill subsisted on an allowance paid him by his father, with some justifiable reluctance because James O'Neill now saw himself saddled with two ne'er-do-well sons. In January 1909, in company with Keefe and Bellows, O'Neill spent a freezing month on a farm owned by James O'Neill in New Jersey, where he did some writing.

In Spring 1909, Eugene met Kathleen Jenkins,* a pretty, well-bred young woman with whom he seems to have had little in common intellectually. Apparently wishing to end the romance, O'Neill confided in his father, who suggested that he join a mining expedition to Honduras which was being financed by a company in which James O'Neill had invested some money. O'Neill was excited by this prospect but discovered that Kathleen, who was now pregnant, expected marriage. The two were secretly married in Trinity Protestant Episcopal Church, Hoboken, New Jersey, on October 2, 1909. Two weeks later, O'Neill left for Honduras in the company of Frank Stevens, a mining engineer from Columbia University, and his wife, Ann.

O'Neill found Honduras distinctly distasteful because of its poverty, heat, disease, and general hardship. In addition, personal relationships were complicated by his romantic interest in Ann Stevens, which his early play, *A Wife for a Life*,* exploits. His affair with Kathleen Jenkins was also exploited in *Abortion*,* while aspects of *The Emperor Jones** show a clear recollection of his jungle experiences. He remained in Honduras only a few months, coming down with a severe attack of malaria and returning home in the spring of 1910. His return to New York signalled another violent episode, similar to the absinthe drinking experience at Princeton, a pattern that was repeated on several occasions throughout much of his life.

James O'Neill arranged for his son to join the touring company of *The White Sister*, in which he himself was playing, in a minor managerial capacity. On May 6, 1910, Eugene Gladstone O'Neill, Jr.,* was born, while both Kathleen and her mother apparently believed the father still in Honduras. In June 1910, O'Neill journeyed to Buenos Aires as a working passenger aboard the Norwegian windjammer *Charles Racine*, allegedly in the company of a friend, perhaps Louis Holladay (see Sheaffer, 1968, pp. 161–162), a journey which gave him some first-hand experience of seafaring life that would prove valuable as local color in his sea plays. After a rough voyage of fifty-seven days, O'Neill reached Buenos Aires, where he gained brief employment with the Singer Sewing Machine Company. With a new acquaintance and roommate, Frederick Hettman, he visited the varied entertainment possible in that city. He also visited bars, brothels, and tough waterfront dives with an unknown acquaintance. He worked briefly on a German vessel, the *Timandra*, and then took another short-lived job. Apparently he was also writing poetry at the time, if one can trust the recollection of Charles Ashleigh, a young Englishman and future member of the Industrial Workers of the World. In later years O'Neill also claimed that he had voyaged to Durban, South Africa, tending mules on a cattle steamer, a voyage that Louis Sheaffer (1968, pp. 183–184) considers fictitious. He seems to have touched rock bottom in Buenos Aires and also to have suffered a recurrence of malaria. On March 20, 1911, he signed on as a crew member of the *Ikala*, bound for New York, a forecastle experience he was later to use in his S.S. *Glencairn** plays.

O'Neill returned to New York in a restless and unsettled frame of mind, incurring some undesirable publicity from his mother-in-law for his failure to visit his wife and son. O'Neill and Kathleen Jenkins were finally divorced in White Plains, New York, in 1912 on the grounds of adultery, then the only one admitted in New York City. The evidence was gathered on December 29, 1911; the uncontested case was heard on June 10, 1912, an interlocutory decree awarded on July 5, and the final decree was signed on October 11, giving Kathleen custody of the child. She asked for neither alimony nor child support, and later O'Neill was to remark that she, whom he had hurt the worst of his three wives, had troubled him the least. O'Neill moved downtown to "Jimmy-the-Priest's,"* a bar and flophouse at 252 Fulton Street, operated by James T. Condon,* on the site of the present World Trade Center. O'Neill seems to have spent his time there on an almost permanent binge, sleeping in a three-dollar-a-month room. These experiences were later to be celebrated in "*Anna Christie*"* and *The Iceman Cometh*. On July 19, 1911, he sailed to Southampton, England, as an able seaman aboard the S.S. *New York*, returning on her sister ship, the S.S. *Philadelphia*. Though he hated the experience, he was able to make use of it in the scenario "The Personal Equation"* and the play *The Hairy Ape*,* both of which have realistic forecastle scenes. While on the *Philadelphia* he met a sailor named Driscoll,* whom he was later to memorialize in the S.S. *Glencairn* plays. Some years later, Driscoll jumped overboard from his ship.

On August 11, 1911, O'Neill returned to New York and went briefly to New London, returning to Jimmy-the-Priest's in mid-September, subsisting on an allowance that his father, who was away on tour, insisted that he pick up personally from James O'Neill's theatrical agents. He seems to have done some writing but was basically soaking up experiences and meeting those who eventually peopled his plays. At the same time, he seems to have been showing an interest in the New York theatrical scene, particularly in performances given by the Abbey Theatre Company of Dublin who were touring America. However, his state of mind in January 1912 was so bad (partly as a result of his impending divorce) that he attempted suicide by taking an overdose of veronal. Fortunately, James Findlater Byth* discovered him comatose in his room, and Byth and some other lodgers managed to revive him. There are differing accounts of this incident, and Agnes Boulton (1958, pp. 20–24) retails a hilarious one in which O'Neill was taken to Bellevue Hospital and released, while his drunken escorts were admitted to the alcoholics ward. *Exorcism*,* the play he wrote about this incident, achieved a single production, but later O'Neill destroyed it.

Shortly afterward, he joined his father's vaudeville tour with a truncated version of *Monte Cristo* in New Orleans, where Jamie was also part of the cast. The entire family was now together, and O'Neill made his own stage debut in Ogden, Utah, in walk-on roles. The tour was, in general, a disaster: Jamie was drinking too much, Ella was taking morphine, James O'Neill was finding vaudeville most exacting, and all seemed to have been concerned over Eugene. They finished their engagement in St. Paul, Minnesota, and in March returned to New York. O'Neill used to tell amusing stories of drunken merrymaking during this period.

Going back to New London in the summer of 1912, he continued reading, bar-hopping, and visiting the Second Story Club, a mildly Bohemian place in the home of Dr. Joe Ganey. At this time he began to get some of his experiences down on paper, though later O'Neill was to claim 1913 as the beginning of his career as playwright. He seems, however, to have begun by writing poetry which, to judge from a recently printed collection, was not very good, to say the least (*Poems 1912–1944*, ed. Donald Gallup, 1980). His first theatrical work seems to have been *A Wife for a Life*, in the summer of 1913.

During the summer of 1912, O'Neill got a job as a cub reporter for the New London *Telegraph*, again through the influence of his father, who secretly paid his wages. As a reporter, O'Neill seems to have been remarkably deficient, frequently neglecting facts in favor of emotional content and human interest. Nonetheless, he did learn the discipline of deadlines and profited from the criticism of the editor, Judge Frederick P. Latimer, the original of Nat Miller in *Ah, Wilderness*!* He also wrote satirical poems in a column entitled "Laconics." At this time, he had a brief affair with a local girl, Maibelle Scott, the model for Muriel McComber* in *Ah, Wilderness*! In October 1912, they mutually decided to wait until O'Neill was financially secure before thinking of marriage.

That same month, O'Neill became ill with what first seemed to be pleurisy, a situation which sent Ella into greater morphine dependence. In November he was diagnosed as having tuberculosis. At first he was looked after at home with a private nurse, and he continued to write for the *Telegraph*. By December his condition had worsened and hospitalization was necessary, something that seems to have precipitated a lasting conflict between father and son. James O'Neill wanted to send his son to the Fairfield County State Tuberculosis Sanitorium in Shelton, Connecticut, a state-run institution, while Eugene objected since the institution took mainly charity cases. This episode is recounted in *Long Day's Journey into Night*. In actual fact, O'Neill did go to Shelton, an arrangement reported in the *Telegraph* on December 9, 1912 (Sheaffer, 1968, p. 243). He stayed only two days and had himself discharged when he learned that his case was mild and eminently curable. He returned to New York where his father, apparently ashamed of his action, obtained good professional advice. Accordingly, O'Neill applied to, and was accepted by, the Gaylord Farm* Sanitorium, Wallingford, Connecticut, run by Dr. David Lyman. This institution had an excellent record of success and, in addition, was not very expensive since it was endowed by the Anti-Tuberculosis Association of New Haven County. O'Neill arrived in the midst of a blizzard on Christmas Eve, 1912, and was discharged on June 3, 1913. He had responded well to treatment, and his case was considered arrested. While at Gaylord, he engaged in a great deal of reading, particularly the plays of Strindberg, Hauptmann, Synge, Yeats, and Lady Gregory. In addition, he found the local color he needed later when he wrote *The Straw*,* using his friendship with a fellow patient, Kitty MacKay, as a model for the more intensely romantic relationship in the play.

In Summer 1913, he returned to New London and spent the time reading, sailing, and writing his first play, *A Wife for a Life*. When his parents returned to New York for the winter, O'Neill moved into the boarding house of a Mrs.

Rippin, where the family had been accustomed to taking their meals. It is interesting to note that even then his hand tremor embarrassed him so much that he preferred to eat alone. During this time, he wrote *The Web** and attempted to work on film scenarios in the hope of making money. He was happy in New London and continued to toughen his body by sleeping outdoors and even swimming throughout the winter. Through the Rippin family he met Clayton Hamilton, a drama critic who further encouraged him. During this time he wrote *Warnings,** *Recklessness,** *Bread and Butter,** *Abortion, The Movie Man,** and *Children of the Sea** (later revised into *Bound East for Cardiff**). In 1914 Ella O'Neill overcame her morphine addiction. That year, O'Neill took up with Beatrice Ashe, another New London woman, the romance with Maibelle Scott being at an end. His writing at this time included *Servitude,** and in August 1914, *Thirst and Other One Act Plays* was published at the expense of James O'Neill. (In addition, this publication included *Fog,** *Recklessness, The Web*, and *Warnings.**) O'Neill also received more specific and discouraging advice concerning playwriting from Clayton Hamilton, who supported his proposal that he enroll in George Pierce Baker's playwriting course at Harvard. He was accepted on the basis of two of the one-act plays he submitted and enrolled in English 47 at Harvard in September 1914.

Older than most of the students and already a published playwright, O'Neill was something of an oddity and a loner who, because of his lifelong experience with the theatre, had very specific ideas which he was given to expressing definitively. He made the acquaintance of only a few classmates and while at Harvard wrote "Dear Doctor,"* *The Sniper,** "Belshazzar"* (with Colin Ford), and "The Personal Equation"* (originally entitled "The Second Engineer"). The most important thing O'Neill learned from Baker was the method of beginning with a scenario and then putting in the dialogue, an approach he followed for the rest of his life. His affair with Beatrice Ashe had continued by correspondence, and after completing the fall semester he returned to New London when he wrote "A Knock at the Door"* (destroyed) and apparently began his four-act farce, *Now I Ask You.** Though invited by Baker to return for the advanced class, O'Neill declined. In later years he claimed that he had lacked the money, which might indeed have been true since his father's producing company had gone bankrupt.

After the summer of 1915, the entire family returned to New York, the parents to the Prince George Hotel and Jamie and Eugene nearby at the Garden Hotel, near the original Madison Square Garden. O'Neill, who was also frequenting Greenwich Village, now submitted the *Thirst* volume and *Bound East for Cardiff* to the Washington Square Players.* He also went to the Greenwich Village Liberal Club and as a result met a myriad of well-known socialists and liberals who were, or would later become, famous in one way or another. They included John Silas Reed,* Louise Bryant,* Max Eastman, Dorothy Day,* Lawrence Langner,* Ida Rauh, George Cram ("Jig") Cook,* Susan Glaspell,* Edna and Norma Millay, Djuna Barnes, Mary Heaton Vorse, Terry Carlin,* Louis Holladay, and his sister Polly. He became a well-known habitué of such bars as "The Hell Hole" (really "The Golden Swan"), where he became acquainted with the Hudson Dusters, a local gang of stevedores and truckdrivers who doubled as hijackers and thieves. They seem to have had some respect for O'Neill, whose other haunts also included a bar called "The Working Girls' Home." He also took delight in following six-day bicycle races, a pastime to which he later introduced the reluctant Carlotta Monterey, his third wife.

In the spring of 1916, O'Neill and Carlin went to Provincetown where a number of Village denizens summered because it was cheap. That particular year, a group of these friends began to excoriate the current commercial American theatre and decided to perform plays that they themselves had written, notably those by Jig Cook, Susan Glaspell, and Neith Boyce. The Provincetown Players began operations on the verandah of Mary Heaton Vorse's home and later they took over an old wharf owned by her and her husband. Later that summer, the group decided to perform O'Neill's *Bound East for Cardiff*, which on July 28, 1916, became his first performed play. Later that summer, *Thirst* was performed, with Louise Bryant playing the dancer. She and O'Neill had an affair, with the initiative coming from her. It is believed that the triangle of O'Neill, Bryant, and John Reed is the basis for the love triangle in *Strange Interlude*.*

Writing during this summer of 1916 included *Before Breakfast** and the short story, "Tomorrow"* (later published with Reed's help). O'Neill seems also to have worked again on his first comic attempt, *Now I Ask You*. Though O'Neill, like most of the Provincetown group, was very short of money at the time, the summer proved profitable in other ways. Chiefly, of course, there was his contact with a group that appreciated, criticized and performed his plays, but also he made the acquaintance of John A. Francis, who owned some real estate in Provincetown and on more than one occasion arranged food and shelter for the playwright and his companion, Terry Carlin, and later for Jamie, Harold De-Polo, and Agnes Boulton O'Neill. In addition, O'Neill collected more of the characters and relationships he was later to use dramatically. At the end of the summer, the friends returned to New York, flushed with a certain success deriving from the publicity they had received from their essentially amateur productions. On his return, Cook leased a building on Macdougal Street and made it into a rather primitive but adventurous experimental theatre club with a subscription clientele—both a means of avoiding fire department citations and raising money from a "captive" audience. As for O'Neill, he continued his affair with Bryant while her husband, John Reed, was in the hospital. It is also said that she had an abortion at this time. As was always the case in his relations with women, O'Neill was intensely possessive of Bryant, who wished to keep the status quo. That fall and spring, the Provincetown Players presented four O'Neill plays: *Bound East for Cardiff, Before Breakfast, Fog*, and *The Sniper*.* As before, at the Wharf Theater, O'Neill appeared in his own plays, *Cardiff* and *Before Breakfast* (where the appearance of his poet's hand constituted his farewell to acting). James O'Neill saw these plays and professed himself pleased and surprised with his son's promise, though his attempts to advise the actress in *Before Breakfast* were deplored as a return to old-fashioned acting.

Clearly, relations between son and father had improved, but James O'Neill seems to have kept his son chronically short of funds, and despite the critical success of his plays and the sale of the texts, O'Neill led a penurious existence. However, as people from that era have pointed out, he was never a true Village type, apparently using his acquaintances as a sounding board for his tales of past experiences. During this period (1916–17) he wrote *The Rope** and also met Saxe Commins,* whose connection with O'Neill—first as his dentist and later as his editor, generous friend, and emotional support—was to be one of the most important relationships of the playwright's life. However, O'Neill was becoming disenchanted with Village life and its drinking. He escaped back to Provincetown with a friend, Harold DePolo (later to help him with Jamie). During this time he wrote *In the Zone*,* for which *Seven Arts* magazine paid fifty dollars. Produced in October 1917 by the Washington Square Players, this play achieved some success because of its topicality. During this productive Provincetown time, he wrote three more sea plays: *The Moon of the Caribbees** (his favorite), *The Long Voyage Home*,* and *Ile*,* in an undetermined order.

That summer (1917), O'Neill went back to New London. War was imminent and O'Neill allegedly tried to enlist in the navy, but he also claimed exemption from military service because of his arrested tuberculosis. After a month together, O'Neill quarrelled with his father, who arranged for him to return to Province-town, this time in the company of a life-long New London friend, Arthur McGinley (the last person Eugene, Jr., saw before his suicide in 1950). Two works from this summer, "G.A.M.,"* a farce in one act, and a short story entitled "The Hairy Ape,"* were both destroyed, though apparently the latter was read by an editor who suggested a changed ending.

Again back in the Village in the fall of 1917, O'Neill seems to have had an affair with Dorothy Day, though the details remain obscure. Bryant and Reed were in Russia. Theatrically, things were looking up for O'Neill, beginning with the production of *In the Zone* by the Washington Square Players. This topical piece became a hit on the vaudeville circuit during World War I. Later they produced *The Rope*.* The Provincetown Players followed with *The Long Voyage Home*, *Ile*, and *The Rope*. O'Neill was now attracting serious critical attention as a playwright to be watched, and already the word "genius" was being used. At this time O'Neill's pattern of deliberately avoiding opening nights was established, partly because he never felt that actors really conveyed his meaning, and the act of writing a play was more important to him than its performance. Even at this early time, he was keeping track of his ideas in notebooks, some of which have now been published (*see* Floyd, 1981).

Personally, O'Neill seemed to be at a loose end drinking heavily with Dorothy Day and others from the socialist journal, *The Masses*. But this winter he met Agnes Boulton, who was to become his second wife. She had a child from a previous marriage, had tried farming without success, and was now trying to make a living as a writer. Her account of the meeting is told in her book, *Part of a Long Story* (1958). At first he was attracted to her because of a resemblance to Louise Bryant, but he still continued his friendship with Dorothy Day, who had moved in with Agnes. A friend of Dorothy (Gerald Griffin) suggests that she fought quite hard to hold O'Neill, and Boulton's account seems to corroborate this. Later, Day was to suggest that she was in love with O'Neill's work but that Boulton loved the man. The three of them were intimately involved with events concerning the suicide of Louis Holladay where O'Neill's life-long pattern of avoiding situations concerning death became notable. He went to a bar while Day and Boulton returned to the restaurant where Holladay had died to help deal with the police.

By the end of January 1918, O'Neill and Agnes had moved to Provincetown, to an apartment owned by John Francis. On April 12, 1918, they were married in Provincetown at the house of the Reverend William Johnson. Their idyll had been somewhat clouded by Bryant's unsuccessful attempt to renew her relationship with O'Neill. During this time, O'Neill wrote *Beyond the Horizon,** which had long been germinating. However, his return to New York to oversee rehearsals of *The Rope* turned into an alcoholic disaster, and it was only with the greatest difficulty that Agnes managed to get both him and Jamie back to Provincetown where O'Neill tapered off and tried to write. From this time, the following plays emerged: *The Dreamy Kid** (his first sympathetic treatment of blacks) and *Where the Cross Is Made** (later developed into the less-successful full-length play *Gold**). In its first manifestation, *Where the Cross* prefigures the later *The Emperor Jones** in its attempt to involve the audience in a collective hallucinatory experience. That summer he also wrote *Shell Shock,** a minor topical piece, and began scenarios for *Chris Christophersen** and *The Straw*.

In November 1918, O'Neill and Agnes returned to the Village, where O'Neill engaged in many arguments over the staging of *Where the Cross Is Made*, particularly over the appearance of the ghosts. He also began drinking heavily and for the first time showed his violent streak against Agnes. After lukewarm reviews of the play, the couple moved to Agnes's house, Old House, in West Point Pleasant, New Jersey, where O'Neill continued with his two summer projects *Chris* and *The Straw*. He also went to the city to help with rehearsals of *Moon of the Caribbees*. On December 20, 1918, the opening night of *Moon*, O'Neill began drinking again, and Agnes had to rescue him. They then remained living quietly in New Jersey because of their straitened finances. *Beyond the Horizon* was now under option to John D. Williams, who also took *The Straw* (based on O'Neill's Gaylord Sanitarium experience). Later O'Neill took back the latter play, which was finally produced by George Tyler at the Greenwich Village Theatre in November 1921.

In December 1918, James O'Neill purchased for his son the abandoned Coast Guard station, Peaked Hill Bars, near Provincetown, which had been lavishly decorated by Mabel Dodge and her then husband, Sam Lewisohn. Mrs. Dodge was the wealthy patron and lover of John Reed, and later, when she was living with another husband, Tony Luhan, in Taos, New Mexico, she offered hospitality to D. H. Lawrence and his wife. O'Neill, always closely attuned to the sea and swimming, was extremely happy with this gift and spent some memorable summers there, beginning in May 1919. The couple's first child, a son, Shane Rudraighe O'Neill, was born in Provincetown, on October 30, 1919. Shortly after his birth, O'Neill returned to New York to oversee production of his plays. With a household that also included a nurse for Shane, Mrs. Fifine Clark, O'Neill was short of funds. By the end of January 1920, plans were in hand for production of *Chris Christophersen* and *Beyond the Horizon*, but the Theatre Guild* rejected *The Straw*. On February 3, 1920, O'Neill had his first Broadway success with *Beyond the Horizon* and received the first of his four Pulitzer Prize awards, but *Chris Christophersen* (produced as *Chris*) closed in Philadelphia. In that season the Provincetown Players presented *Exorcism** (his suicide play which he later destroyed) and *The Dreamy Kid*.

James O'Neill died of cancer in August 1920, an event which affected O'Neill profoundly because the two men had finally made their peace and James had seen his son's first success. That summer at Peaked Hill he reworked *Chris Christophersen* into "The Ole Davil"* (and later into "*Anna Christie*"*). He also completed *The Emperor Jones* (originally entitled "The Silver Bullet"), which opened at 133 Macdougal Street on November 1, 1920. This play became a hit with Charles Gilpin* in the leading role, and it was later moved uptown to Broadway, an occurrence which ultimately brought about the demise of the Provincetown Players. [*See* Cook, George Cram.] During this time, he also completed *Diff'rent*,* which was produced in December 1920 by the Provincetown Players. His next play, *The First Man*,* represents something of a creative regression. It was finished in 1921, and then he began work on *The Fountain*.* In June 1921, *Gold* opened and closed quickly on Broadway. Back at Peaked Hill for the summer, O'Neill was now in better financial shape as a result of *The Emperor Jones* and *Diff'rent*. In addition, he had also adopted the then unusual policy of publishing his plays almost simultaneously with their production, a practice which was so financially successful that he continued it throughout his writing career.

However, family relationships were becoming tense because Agnes, wishing to continue with her work, seems to have become depressed and harried over all the demands made on her that summer of 1921 when visitors to Peaked Hill included Jamie O'Neill, Robert Edmond Jones,* Kenneth Macgowan* and his wife, and also Terry Carlin (who was a more or less permanent, and drunken, fixture). By the end of August, *The Fountain* was finished and optioned by Arthur Hopkins the next month. At the celebration which followed, O'Neill became very drunk and publicly threatened Agnes. Plays produced during this season were: "*Anna Christie*," which was a success, and *The Straw*, which was not. O'Neill was also somewhat incensed over criticism of the "happy" ending of *Anna*, maintaining that he had been trying to show the continuous cycle of life rather than giving a conventional Broadway conclusion. He received his second Pulitzer Prize for this play.

In December 1921, O'Neill wrote *The Hairy Ape** in just under three weeks. This play, like *The Emperor Jones*, was first presented by the Provincetown Players and then moved uptown with one major cast change: Mary Blair,* as Mildred Douglas,* was replaced by the more exotic and better known actress, Carlotta Monterey (later to become O'Neill's third wife), at the insistence of the uptown producer, Arthur Hopkins. This success caused George Cram Cook and his wife, Susan Glaspell, to leave for Greece and later to dissolve the Provincetown Players [*see* separate entries]. One of the noteworthy devices of *The Hairy Ape* was the use of masks in the Fifth Avenue scene, a first for O'Neill and a step taken at the suggestion of Blanche Hays, the costume designer.

On February 28, 1922, just before the Broadway opening of *The Hairy Ape*, Ella Quinlan O'Neill, Eugene's mother, died in Los Angeles, California, while on a visit with Jamie to look after her real estate investments. Jamie, who had been "dry" since his father's death two years earlier, now went on a monumental binge, one that O'Neill later incorporated into *A Moon for the Misbegotten.** Ella O'Neill's death sent Jamie into a state of perpetual intoxication, which eventually caused his early death. He visited with O'Neill and Agnes at Peaked Hill that summer of 1922, which was an essentially unproductive one for the playwright. Another visitor was Eugene O'Neill, Jr., O'Neill's son by Kathleen Jenkins (now Mrs. George Pitt-Smith). O'Neill was now paying for his older son's education. Over the years the two men became quite close and essentially remained so (despite Carlotta Monterey's opposition) until Eugene, Jr.'s, suicide in 1950.

Having written nothing that summer, O'Neill now wrote *Welded** in 1922–23, a semi-autobiographical Strindbergian play concerning marriage. It shows no real advancement over his earlier play on the same theme, *Servitude*. This was a restless time for O'Neill. Plans for producing *The Fountain* had been shelved, and he had purchased a new home, which he could now afford as a result of profits from "*Anna Christie*," both the play and the silent film (released 1923). His life at Brook Farm, Ridgefield, Connecticut, has been well described by Malcolm Cowley and other visitors. By the end of 1923, O'Neill was achieving an international reputation with successful London and Moscow productions of "*Anna Christie*" and a failed Berlin production of *The Emperor Jones* (for which the translation was partially responsible).

In the fall of 1923, O'Neill, together with Kenneth Macgowan and Robert Edmond Jones, founded the Experimental Theatre, Inc.,* using the old Provincetown place at Macdougal Street. Macgowan was the director, with Jones and O'Neill as associates. O'Neill, however, did not play a very active role, partly because of his preoccupation with his new project, *All God's Chillun Got Wings,** and his later move to Bermuda. The group disbanded in 1927. In November 1923, Jamie O'Neill died in New Jersey of acute alcoholism.

O'Neill then moved on to his next work, *Desire Under the Elms,** at Brook

Farm which, according to Louis Sheaffer (1973, p. 129), he now disliked. During the composition of *Desire* (January-June 1924), *Welded* opened and closed (twenty-four performances). During this season, his experiment with total theatre in his dramatic interpretation of Coleridge's *The Ancient Mariner** was offered, but without success, and consequently he did not continue with a similar idea, "The Revelation of St. John the Divine."* His other play of the season, *All God's Chillun Got Wings*, achieved an extraordinary *succès de scandale* in May 1924 because it presented Paul Robeson* and Mary Blair*as an interracial couple. Despite the then shocking nature of this situation, the reviews were less than enthusiastic, though the play achieved over one hundred performances. O'Neill then moved on to write *Marco Millions*,* his satire on American Babbittry and his celebration of Oriental religious solutions, in many ways a companion piece to *The Fountain*. He finished the first draft at Peaked Hill in October 1924 and returned to New York where the S.S. *Glencairn* plays opened to excellent reviews on November 3, followed by *Desire Under the Elms* on November 11. Reviews of the latter were not very enthusiastic, though later evaluations consider it among his best works. It is today popular in Eastern Europe but perhaps for political and propagandistic reasons.

By now O'Neill was completely tired of Brook Farm and Northeastern winters. He had become convinced that he worked best in a warm climate near the sea and accordingly decided to move his household to Bermuda, sailing there at the end of November 1924. Agnes was by now pregnant with Oona, who was born in Bermuda on May 14, 1925 (*see* Chaplin, Oona O'Neill). In late January 1925, O'Neill began work on *The Great God Brown*,* in which he began to develop his concepts of masked drama. At its 1926 opening the viewers were bothered by this device, and O'Neill later defended his approach in several essays. (*See* "References"). Throughout the winter and spring of 1925, O'Neill read, drank heavily, swam frequently, and entertained numerous houseguests, including Eugene, Jr. His drinking continued after Oona's birth, but in late May he apparently "tapered off" in time to discuss his problems with Dr. Louis Bisch, a New York psychiatrist who visited with his wife (*see* Sheaffer, 1973, pp. 179–180). That July he returned to New York and then he and his family spent the summer at Nantucket, where he continued drinking. Nonetheless he was still writing and began preliminary work on *Lazarus Laughed** the third of his poetic and mystical plays, the others being *The Fountain* and *Marco Millions*. He also began work on *Strange Interlude*.* He was increasingly concerned about money and felt aggrieved that (as he saw it) Macgowan and Jones were paying insufficient attention to his work. That fall (1925) the family returned to Brook Farm and O'Neill continued with *Lazarus*. During that season, with both *The Fountain* and *The Great God Brown* in rehearsal, O'Neill seems to have been profoundly depressed and seldom completely sober.

With 1926, O'Neill apparently tried to stop drinking, and, through the help of Kenneth Macgowan, both O'Neill and Agnes consulted with a psychiatrist, Dr. Gilbert V. Hamilton (*see* Sheaffer, 1973, p. 188ff.). In February, after the opening of *Brown*, the O'Neill household returned to Bermuda to a large rented house, while O'Neill continued to read and work on *Lazarus* and while his money problems continued. To Lawrence Langner,* who visited him, he confided the news of his latest project, *Strange Interlude*. In this same year he bought "Spithead," a dilapidated seafront estate near Hamilton, and promptly committed more money to its renovation. This house was to remain in the O'Neill family for many years. It was part of Agnes's divorce settlement and proved a place of refuge many years later for Shane and his wife. It was finally sold shortly before Agnes's death in 1968.

The summer of 1926 proved to be an important one for O'Neill. He returned to New York in June and was awarded an honorary degree from Yale University, partly through the offices of George Pierce Baker, his Harvard mentor, who was now at Yale. It was largely because of this recognition that O'Neill's papers were consigned to Yale by his widow, Carlotta. The entire family, including Eugene, Jr., and Barbara Burton, Agnes's daughter, took a cabin at Loon Lodge, Belgrade Lakes, Maine. However, the strain of such a large gathering of children of assorted ages forced Agnes to have a small shed built away from the main house so that O'Neill could continue work on *Strange Interlude*. At this time he seems to have become bored with this familial kind of domesticity which seemed to him a trap. Consequently, he was in a susceptible state when he again met the actress Carlotta Monterey, whom he had not particularly admired as Mildred in the uptown production of *The Hairy Ape* in 1922. She was a well-known beauty whose minor acting career was composed mainly of vamps and exotic female roles. She was summering nearby with a friend, and after some initial sparring she and O'Neill became interested in each other's company. Their acquaintanceship continued during the fall of 1926, and when O'Neill followed his family to Bermuda at the end of November, he was seriously considering leaving Agnes. He was impressed with Carlotta's elegance, sense of order, and *savoir-faire*, as well as her possession of an annuity of fourteen thousand dollars a year from an aunt (as she told O'Neill) but in fact from an old lover and protector, the banker James Speyer. Carlotta seemed to offer emancipation from the clutter of a child-ridden household and also total commitment to him and his needs. In addition, he seems to have been flattered by having this acknowledged beauty pursue him and buy clothes for him.

On his return to Bermuda, O'Neill told Agnes of the Carlotta affair, which he continued at a distance. He was also continuing work on *Strange Interlude*. In March 1927, they moved into the newly renovated Spithead property. By now O'Neill had become a teetotaller, and while this increased his commitment to work, it seemed to interfere with his marriage to Agnes, who, according to his biographers, no longer felt in control of the situation (*see particularly* Sheaffer, 1973, p. 246). That summer, Lawrence Langner of the Theatre Guild* visited O'Neill in Bermuda and read *Strange Interlude*, still in progress. He eventually managed to get the Guild to place it and *Marco Millions* under option. O'Neill then made another brief visit to New York and returned to Bermuda, becoming very tired of the place in the "slack" summer season. Accordingly, he returned to New York at the end of August to discuss his productions with the Guild, telling Agnes (and possibly believing) that all was well between them. In New York he had another bout of ill health, possibly the result of loneliness— Carlotta being away in Baden Baden for a "nerve cure." He was also concerned about the fact that Brook Farm remained unsold. Letters between O'Neill and Agnes indicate increasing bitterness, suspicion, and reconciliation. Then, after Carlotta's return to New York, she and O'Neill became lovers. He returned to Bermuda for a month in October–November 1927 and then left for good, though Agnes did not realize it. That December he asked Agnes to send him the manuscripts he had left at Spithead. She did not give up O'Neill without a struggle, even coming to New York in an attempt to dissuade him. A lawyer was consulted, and Agnes returned to Bermuda, from where she expressed reservations about the proposed divorce settlement. O'Neill's third Pulitzer Prize-winning play, *Strange Interlude*, opened on January 29, 1928, to appreciative reviews, and on February 10, Carlotta and O'Neill (the latter under an assumed name) sailed for England.

Carlotta planned to show him Europe and also to "educate" his taste. This was the first evidence of her desire to control and manage her future husband's life. They toured France and then took a villa near Guéthary, keeping their whereabouts secret from all but a few close friends, notably Kenneth Macgowan, who believed Carlotta might be good for O'Neill. They seem to have been blissfully happy, though Agnes had not yet agreed to a settlement. Both Carlotta and O'Neill were bitter about this, but Agnes seems merely to have been prudent and was actually quite conservative in her requests. During this time he and Carlotta remained in Europe, carefully splitting their household expenses fifty-fifty, while he worked on his next play, *Dynamo*,* the first of a proposed trilogy concerning modern life. Later that year (1928) Carlotta walked out on O'Neill as the result of an evening he spent drinking with an old friend, Louis Kalonyme. However, she thought better of it and returned almost immediately. This episode marks the beginning of her keeping old friends from Provincetown days away from O'Neill. This disapproval did not extend to Saxe Commins and his wife, the concert pianist, Dorothy Berliner, who visited them at Guéthary, after their return from a tour of Spain. By this time he had finished *Dynamo*, which Commins typed, as well as doing other business tasks for him. In August 1928, *Dynamo* was sent to the Theatre Guild for consideration.

His divorce still not settled, O'Neill and Carlotta set off for the Orient, sailing for Hong Kong in October 1928. On the trip, relations between the two became severely strained, partly because of O'Neill's drinking and occasional gambling, and partly because of the combined effects of heat and ill health. Their problems culminated in Shanghai where O'Neill began very serious drinking, once even slapping Carlotta while he was intoxicated. Enraged, Carlotta moved out, but she continued to keep an eye on him, particularly after he was hospitalized on the verge of a nervous breakdown. As was to become the pattern of their later years, O'Neill begged her to return, and she, after punishing him for a few more days, agreed. Partially recuperated, O'Neill and Carlotta left secretly for Manila. By Christmas Eve they were in Singapore, with O'Neill drinking heavily and bickering with Carlotta as a result. In Colombo, Sri Lanka (Ceylon), things became so bad that Carlotta walked off the *Coblenz*, leaving O'Neill to continue without her. However, she took the next vessel out, the *President Monroe*, and the two were reunited with considerable publicity and display of temperament in Port Said. They then went to Genoa and on to the Riviera, taking a villa outside Monte Carlo.

In February 1929, *Dynamo* opened in New York and lasted only fifty performances. O'Neill was bitter over its failure but later admitted that he should have spent more time on it. Two bright spots in that month were a visit from the Comminses and Agnes's decision to seek a Reno divorce. However, O'Neill was restive. Carlotta was beginning to define her role as a watchdog, cutting him off from old friends, preventing him from seeing troublesome newspaper clippings, and even withholding personal mail she considered unsuitable and contrary to her policy of insulating him from the outside world and isolating him within the bonds of their relationship. Still hunting for total privacy, they moved into the rented and renovated Chateau du Plessis, at Saint-Antoine-du-Rocher, near Tours. Here, for the first time, Carlotta demonstrated fully the skills of renovation and building that she was later to display at Casa Genotta, Georgia; Tao House, California; and Point o'Rocks Lane, Marblehead, Massachusetts.

Agnes's divorce became final on July 1, 1929, and on July 22, O'Neill and Carlotta were married in Paris in a civil ceremony. They exchanged rings engraved with words "from *Lazarus Laughed*. 'I am your laughter' (in O'Neill's ring to her), 'And you are mine' (in her ring to him)" (Sheaffer, 1973, p. 332). Though he had arranged for a press announcement, O'Neill was hurt that he received no congratulation from the Provincetown group. It seems that Carlotta had deliberately intercepted their letters, hoping to force O'Neill to make a total break with his past. In later life she maintained that he had wanted her to take total charge of the practicalities of daily living, including his personal correspondence and telephone calls. Certainly O'Neill needed a superbly run household, and if the price was the loss of some old friends, he was apparently willing to pay it, even if it meant (as finally happened) that he had to break with his most devoted friend and editor, Saxe Commins. They remained at Chateau du Plessis for just under two years, though their lease was for three years, and while there he wrote the trilogy, *Mourning Becomes Electra*,* finishing it in the rainy and gloomy autumn of 1930.

They lived rather formally at the chateau, entertaining a number of house guests during the summer, including Eugene, Jr. whose classical knowledge made an impression on his father in view of his own current work. They also acquired a dog, a Dalmatian named Silverdene Emblem,* "Blemie," who was to be with them for the next twelve years. He is buried on the grounds of Tao

House, and was, Carlotta said later, "the only one of our children who has not disillusioned us" (Sheaffer, 1973, p. 518). However, as O'Neill became more engrossed in his work, he became less and less social, and Carlotta began to feel completely isolated. After he finished *Electra*, they took a brief tour of Spain and Morocco and returned to the gloom and damp of Le Plessis. At the end of the year both were ill, and Carlotta was hospitalized. O'Neill was beginning to feel homesick for the United States, and Carlotta was becoming disenchanted with the loneliness of her position as chatelaine, especially when she discovered her servants were dishonest.

On May 17, 1931, the O'Neills returned to New York, an arrival marred by the almost simultaneous suicide of Ralph Barton,* Carlotta's third husband, who left a note lamenting his "beautiful lost angel, Carlotta." The O'Neills resented this unfortunate publicity and soon moved to a rented house in Northport, Long Island, which had a private beach. There Shane visited them, and later Eugene, Jr., whose marriage on June 15, 1931 O'Neill did not attend. O'Neill continued with the revision of *Mourning Becomes Electra* in consultation with Saxe Commins, who had now become his editor at Horace Liveright & Co. At O'Neill's stipulation, Commins remained his editor at Random House, a move Commins advised in 1933 on the bankruptcy of Liveright. In later years Donald Klopfer of Random House mused that in some ways Saxe was the finer acquisition of the two (Sheaffer, 1973, p. 417). Toward the end of Summer 1931, the O'Neills leased an apartment at 1095 Park Avenue, a location that made it easy for O'Neill to sit in on rehearsals for *Mourning Becomes Electra*. The trilogy opened to enthusiastic reviews on October 26, 1931, and a touring company was quickly formed. With this success launched, O'Neill renewed acquaintance with Shane and Oona, the latter of whom could barely remember him.

Finding it difficult to work in New York, O'Neill and Carlotta looked for a new place in which to settle so that they could have more privacy. They finally decided upon Sea Island, Georgia, where Carlotta had a twenty-one-room, Spanish-style house built, with a study for O'Neill that looked like the captain's cabin of a Spanish galleon. Thanks to the foresight of Saxe Commins and the success of *Mourning Becomes Electra*, O'Neill was able to afford this project. They moved to Sea Island before Casa Genotta (named for a combination of their first names) was quite finished. At this time, O'Neill was apparently starting to rough out his monumental American cycle "A Tale of Possessors, Self-Dispossessed,"* and was also engaged in writing another drama of marriage. Then entitled "Without Ending of Days," and later produced as *Days Without End*,* the play aimed at conveying the essence of his marriage with Carlotta, as before he had done with his marriage to Agnes in *Welded*. Delighted to be back by the sea, O'Neill reverted to his usual pattern of several hours of writing every day, keeping himself healthy by swimming and fishing. Once he married Carlotta, his days of heavy drinking were over—except for a few well-publicized lapses. Once again, Carlotta ran a thoroughly efficient and elegant establishment, paying meticulous attention to every detail.

He had considerable difficulty in writing *Days Without End*, perhaps because of his emotional closeness to the subject, and therefore temporarily shelved it in favor of *Ah, Wilderness!** which gives a comic view of the material he was later to exploit tragically in *Long Day's Journey into Night*. However, he did not wish to release it until after the 1932–33 season. Money was something of a problem in those depression years, but O'Neill had received something from the films of *Strange Interlude*, *Recklessness** (of which only the title was the work of O'Neill), and *The Emperor Jones*, starring Paul Robeson (*see* Appendix B for film adaptations). *Ah, Wilderness!* was produced by the Theatre Guild on October 2, 1933, and was enthusiastically received. It was immediately bought by Metro-Goldwyn-Mayer for a film. At this time, Carlotta bought O'Neill his only musical instrument, a player piano he called "Rosie." Rosie moved with them from Sea Island to Tao House where the room she shared with Blemie, the dog, was the most cheerful of the entire house.

Finally finishing *Days Without End* after great difficulty and many discussions with Roman Catholic friends, the play opened briefly in Boston and then moved to New York on January 7, 1934, where it received unfavorable reviews, except for those in some Catholic publications. This play fueled the belief that O'Neill had decided to return to the church of his parents, something O'Neill denied. Later in the year, it was well received in a Dublin production by the Abbey Theatre. After this New York failure, O'Neill took his doctor's advice and began an almost complete vacation from writing that lasted most of the year. He visited New York occasionally and summered in the Adirondacks. Returning to Sea Island in October 1934, he started work on "The Life of Bessie Bowen"* (or Bolan or Bowlan), the third play in his projected trilogy of American life, planned to follow *Dynamo* and *Days Without End*. This new title took the place of the earlier one, "It Cannot Be Mad."* He soon gave up this project, tentatively titled "Myth-Plays for the God-Forsaken,"* and in 1935 began his massive American cycle, "A Tale of Possessors, Self-Dispossessed."* "Bessie Bowen" was to be part of this now, and it was to concern modern mechanized industry. This grandiose project staggered O'Neill's friends as its plan grew inexorably to encompass eleven plays.

Although they had many house guests in Georgia, O'Neill began to become so committed to his cycle that he remained in Georgia for the summer and went to New York for only a brief visit in October. As at Le Plessis while he was writing *Mourning Becomes Electra*, he became so engrossed in his work that Carlotta and everything else became secondary. In March 1936, he finished the first draft of *A Touch of the Poet** and proceeded to the second of the series, *More Stately Mansions*.* Again they remained in Georgia for the summer, this time suffering intensely from the heat and humidity of the worst season in memory. O'Neill finished the first draft of "And Give Me Death"* in August, feeling exhausted. In addition, Carlotta found herself fighting a losing battle against such natural environmental hazards as snakes, mold, and mildew.

Out of this came the idea to move to a cooler climate, again by the sea. They thereupon decided to move to Seattle, near Sophus K. Winther, O'Neill's first biographer and a professor at the University of Washington. He and his wife, Eline, had visited at Casa Genotta, and they became friends with Carlotta and Eugene, later being of very great assistance to both the O'Neills during their complicated estrangements. By the end of September 1936, both O'Neill and Carlotta were ill, and in October they went to New York and on to Seattle without waiting to sell Casa Genotta.

In Seattle they rented a house overlooking Puget Sound, and while they were there, news came that O'Neill had been awarded the Nobel Prize for Literature for 1936. Refusing to become a literary lion, he declined to attend the public ceremony of award, sending a prepared address for the occasion and paying tribute to the influence exerted on his own work by the Swedish playwright, August Strindberg. In order to escape publicity, the O'Neills moved to San Francisco in December 1936, where O'Neill was hospitalized for an appendectomy and Carlotta took a room also, probably to counter his roving eye. As a third wife currently married to a fourth husband, Carlotta may be forgiven a little paranoia in this regard. The Nobel medal was finally awarded in a hospital ceremony on February 17, 1937.

With the sale of Casa Genotta (at a considerable loss) and with the cash award from the Nobel prize, the O'Neills were now ready to build another house. O'Neill had tired of hotel life at the Fairmont in San Francisco, and so they rented an estate in Lafayette while Tao House was being constructed on 160 acres in the Las Trampas Hills above Danville, Contra Costa County, California. Again Carlotta threw herself into the multifarious activities of nesting and designing, which she apparently loved. Once she managed to get an establishment running perfectly, she seems to have tired of it and was ready to move on. Another curious pattern also manifested itself: whereas in New York O'Neill had dragged Carlotta to six-day bicycle races, enjoying the anonymity conferred by large crowds, now he became a follower of the University of California, Berkeley, football team.

Much has been written about Tao House, and its opulence has been greatly exaggerated. Certainly the site and view are magnificent, but the house (before later improvements) did not make adequate use of the superlative view, and Carlotta usually kept the shades drawn because of her eye problem. Though almost every room has direct access to the outside, the house, with its walled back garden, seems to turn in upon itself, begging for privacy. A swimming pool was built, eerily seeming suspended between sky and nothingness, so that trees were planted to give a sense of location. The entire compound was surrounded by a tightly winding path to ward off evil spirits, which, according to oriental philosophy, can only travel a straight path. Carlotta indulged her passion for things oriental in the interior decor. When they moved into Tao House at the very end of 1938 their isolation was fairly complete, although San Francisco was about an hour away by car.

O'Neill had now finished his first draft of "Greed of the Meek,"* part of the cycle, and was beginning to be of two minds about the theatre. Rather than have his work performed on Broadway, he thought solely of publication; but then he also talked of forming a repertory company which would dedicate itself entirely to the performance of his cycle. Despite repeated requests from the Theatre Guild, whose current policies he disliked, he refused to release even the two cycle plays which were under contract to them, though he remained grateful for their earlier help. He continued his regimen of daily writing, and by September 1938, *More Stately Mansions* was completed and typed by Carlotta. It was O'Neill's pattern to write his plays in longhand in pencil, using a script which steadily became more minuscule as his tremor increased, and for Carlotta to type the first draft. Another draft would then be prepared by a typist or sometimes (as for *Iceman* and *Long Day's Journey*) by Saxe Commins.

From the Tao House period come some of O'Neill's finest plays: *The Iceman Cometh* (1939–), *Long Day's Journey into Night* (1939–1941), and *A Moon for the Misbegotten* (1941–43, revised 1944), while he also continued working on the cycle. At Tao House, where O'Neill said he had been happiest, he seems to have exorcised his ghosts. In *The Iceman Cometh* he recalled the denizens of Jimmy-the-Priest's bar in Lower Manhattan while at the same time revealing his continuing bitterness (and even hostility) toward the institution of marriage. But it was in the two allied autobiographical plays, *Long Day's Journey into Night* and *A Moon for the Misbegotten*, that O'Neill finally laid his family ghosts to rest. Carlotta recalled that no play took such an emotional toll of him as *Long Day's Journey* where he made his peace with his father, and the words of his dedication of the play to her indicate this: "This play of old sorrow, written in tears and blood." In *A Moon* he offered a final tribute to the memory of his brother, Jamie. But still O'Neill refused to release his plays for performance, despite the fact that he had had no new Broadway productions since 1934.

Now, also, the outside world began to impinge on his self-imposed isolation, particularly after the September 1939 beginning of the European war. He continued to have house guests, among them his three children, including Oona whom he had not seen for some years. Other guests were Russel Crouse; Saxe Commins; Lawrence Langner; and Carlotta's daughter, Cynthia, and her husband. As always, no one visited except by invitation. However, ill health began to plague both O'Neill and Carlotta: O'Neill's tremor increased until in 1943 handwriting became almost impossible, and he also suffered from neuritis and, later, prostate trouble; Carlotta developed arthritis in the spine, and her lifelong eye problems increased to the point that she had to employ her daughter as secretary-typist. In December 1940 their dog Blemie died and was buried near the house where a headstone still marks his grave. As consolation for them both, O'Neill wrote "The Last Will and Testament of Silverdene Emblem O'Neill" and presented it to Carlotta. The next year was one of continued ill health but also produced *Hughie*,* a monologue of the same ilk as *Iceman* and designed as part of a series (never completed) entitled "By Way of Obit."* In February 1942, he was diagnosed (erroneously, as it later turned out) as having Parkinson's

Disease and was accordingly put under medication, which caused unwelcome reactions.

O'Neill's pessimism increased, and finances were also something of a problem, though the 1940 John Ford-Dudley Nichols collaboration on the film of *The Long Voyage Home* [*see* Appendix B], based on the S.S. *Glencairn** plays, provided some relief; it was the only film version of his plays that O'Neill liked. In addition, in 1941–42, Carlotta's annuity from James Speyer was jeopardized with the death of her old protector, but his heirs decided not to contest the matter. Further financial relief came from a 1941 revival of *Ah, Wilderness*! and the selling of *The Hairy Ape* to the films [*see* Appendix B] in 1943. More and more, O'Neill came to resent his alimony payment to Agnes, particularly as he came to disapprove of Oona's debutante lifestyle. With her 1943 marriage to Charles Spencer [Charlie] Chaplin,* O'Neill rejected his daughter totally and forever. He finally made a cash settlement with Agnes in 1947.

As the war continued, gasoline rationing and the servant problem increased Carlotta's burdens. Since she did not drive, they were dependent on the kindness of neighbors for transportation and deliveries. Accordingly, she obtained O'Neill's permission to sell Tao House, which she did in February 1944 for about sixty thousand dollars, again a substantial loss. She sold back her oriental furniture to Gump's, and the O'Neills moved into the Fairmont Hotel. "Rosie," some books, and objets d'art were sent to storage in New York. Overwork had made Carlotta ill, and their stay at the Fairmont proved difficult because of the close quarters; they then moved to the Huntington Hotel. With O'Neill's children almost totally rejected, Carlotta now rejected her own daughter, Cynthia, not even saying good-bye when they left for New York in 1945. Carlotta, now unable to type, employed Jane Caldwell, a young woman, as O'Neill's secretary, but she still stayed on guard, wary of his susceptibility. In the summer of 1944 when the Langners visited, O'Neill showed them four completed plays. This resulted in a plan to release them after the war in the following order: *A Moon, Iceman, A Touch of the Poet, Hughie*, and another play (which was to remain unwritten).

In 1945 they flirted briefly with the idea of returning to Sea Island, even purchasing some property there. However, they remained in San Francisco, until their hostilities came to a peak over O'Neill's alleged relationship with Jane Caldwell; on one occasion their dispute escalated into O'Neill's using physical violence against Carlotta. In mid-October they returned to New York, taking a small suite at the Hotel Barclay, sharing a bedroom for the first time since their marriage. Again turmoil resulted from their close quarters, and Saxe Commins was the embarrassed witness of an incident one evening when O'Neill hunted despairingly for his "lost" manuscripts, while Carlotta (who had hidden them as some kind of punishment) taunted him, saying that his mind was going [*see* Commins, Saxe; and Monterey, Carlotta]. As a result of this incident, O'Neill deposited his manuscripts with Random House for safekeeping. *Long Day's Journey*, however, had the further stipulation that it not be opened until twenty-five years after his death. Another cause of friction was O'Neill's desire for a more social existence, something Carlotta discouraged, partly because of his health but possibly from fear of his roving eye. Once again he began attending sports events and also jazz concerts with male friends. Eugene, Jr., and Shane again intruded on their existence. Carlotta now disapproved of Eugene, Jr.'s new nonacademic lifestyle, and finally father and son were reduced to meeting secretly. She similarly disapproved of Shane's marriage, and when their baby died of Sudden Infant Death Syndrome, she made some rather unprintable allegations about the young couple.

In the spring of 1946 they moved into a six-room penthouse at 35 East Eighty-fourth Street, formerly the residence of Edward Sheldon, the most successful graduate of George Pierce Baker's "47 Workshop," who had recently died after a lifetime of appalling suffering borne with extraordinary gallantry and fortitude. The O'Neill finances improved with the sale of *Mourning Becomes Electra* to RKO, though the film was not a success. *The Iceman Cometh* began rehearsals in September that year, with the Theatre Guild anxious to restore O'Neill's reputation after his long silence. He attended rehearsals, apparently intimidating both director and cast, with the result that the play, though carefully cast and well promoted, was not a major success. James Barton,* in the role of Theodore Hickman,* proved unequal to the role, the direction was pedestrian, and the text was considered too verbose. Only after O'Neill's death did this play achieve its current classic status as a result of the 1956 performance of Jason Robards, Jr., as Hickey and José Quintero as director. Despite this disappointment, O'Neill was in good health and spirits that year and began to socialize with Russel Crouse, Irving Berlin, Burl Ives, and others (*see* Sheaffer, 1973, p. 589). Carlotta was still afraid of younger women, but O'Neill was probably never serious, well aware of his dependence on her.

In January 1947, the Theatre Guild began rehearsals for *A Moon for the Misbegotten*, which opened in Columbus, Ohio, in February, to mixed reviews. In Pittsburgh it was considered "vulgar" and at first prohibited in Detroit because of "obscenity." After a two-week run there, it moved to St. Louis for a week and closed. The Guild wanted to recast the play, but O'Neill refused and also declined to allow production of *A Touch of the Poet*. Later he allowed publication of *A Moon for the Misbegotten*, largely for financial reasons.

By now O'Neill's health was making work impossible, and relations between him and Carlotta were bad, partly because of his frustration and partly because of her continuing suspicion, partially induced by his friendship with Patricia Neal, then a young actress. In late 1947, Carlotta recounted O'Neill's shortcomings to the visiting Sophus Winther and his wife, but the great explosion came in January 1948 when M. Eleanor Fitzgerald, an old Provincetown friend, telephoned to ask for a loan. Saxe Commins was again an embarrassed spectator (*see* Commins, Saxe, and Monterey, Carlotta, for fuller accounts). Carlotta, after an episode of violence during which she destroyed O'Neill's only photograph of his mother, packed her things and walked out. Saxe Commins, knowing that

O'Neill could not be left alone because of his tremor, arranged for himself or someone else always to be present. Despite these precautions, O'Neill fell one night after a few drinks, fractured his left shoulder, and was hospitalized.

After more than a month, progress began on a reconciliation which took place at the end of March. For a time there was a comic opera situation with Carlotta also in Doctors Hospital unbeknown to O'Neill. The major cost of this quarrel was the friendship of Saxe Commins, whom Carlotta believed to have been working against her. The two agreed to move to the Boston area where O'Neill would have access to excellent medical care, and on April 19, 1948, they left New York. Their next house was a seven-room cottage at the end of Marblehead Neck, almost in the ocean. Winterizing and renovating took several months, and on moving in Carlotta was forced to scale down their possessions. Finances were still a problem, and Carlotta had to sell off some investments to pay for the alterations. She continued to keep O'Neill away from prying eyes, allowing only a few selected guests.

By the end of 1949 he finally realized that medication could not cure him and that he would never work again. A combination of frustration, close quarters, loneliness, and ill health on both sides (Carlotta was again having trouble with arthritis) began to cause turmoil. In 1950, Eugene, Jr., committed suicide, and when O'Neill's lawyer telephoned the news, Carlotta is alleged to have said, "How dare you invade our privacy," and then to have slammed down the receiver. Neither she nor O'Neill attended the funeral, though each sent separate floral arrangements.

In the same year Carlotta, not wishing to spend another winter at Marblehead and also tired of another finished house, obtained O'Neill's permission to sell. But in the meantime, with both of them under heavy medication that had reached toxic levels and was impairing their judgment, tensions were extremely high. On February 5, 1951, O'Neill walked out of the house after an argument, insufficiently clad for the cold, slipped, and fractured his right leg. Apparently Carlotta looked at him, jeered, and went inside. It was about an hour before a doctor arrived to find O'Neill lying in the snow; he called an ambulance and took O'Neill to the hospital. Carlotta remained behind and was discovered the next evening by the police wandering alone in the snow. She refused to return to the house on Point o' Rocks Lane and later became so hysterical that she, too, had to be taken to the hospital (*see* Monterey, Carlotta). Eventually O'Neill agreed to follow the advice of a psychiatrist and have her declared incompetent and institutionalize her. Carlotta's lawyer prevented that, and she sued O'Neill for separate support, having by now been released from the hospital and living in a hotel suite in Boston with a trusted friend from San Francisco days.

Meanwhile, friends rallied around O'Neill, whose leg was in a cast, and on March 30, 1951, he reluctantly took their advice and went to New York, where he was eventually admitted to Doctors Hospital. After initiating the guardianship petition against Carlotta, he also changed his will, removing her as executrix. Carlotta interpreted this as an attempt by Lawrence Langner to gain control of

A Moon for the Misbegotten, and since Langner had arranged for her psychiatric examination, her paranoia is understandable. In the hospital, O'Neill contracted pneumonia but recovered well, while in Boston Carlotta was threatening lawsuit and publication of the story of her difficulties with her husband. O'Neill seems to have enjoyed the attention he was getting, but he would also become lonely and depressed. Most of his friends believed that this separation was and ought to be permanent, in order to save O'Neill from Carlotta. Saxe Commins in particular believed this, and he and his wife offered O'Neill a permanent home with them. In mid-April 1951, O'Neill announced his intention of returning to Carlotta, and finally a reconciliation was effected through the intervention of Russel Crouse, whom both parties trusted. O'Neill agreed to live in the Hotel Shelton with Carlotta. On May 17, 1951, after a long run of farewells, he returned to Boston.

On his return, Carlotta repaid a loan from the Theatre Guild, paid his hospital bills, and discontinued relationships with everyone who had assisted O'Neill, with the exception of Russel Crouse. Their reunion appeared to be happy, and O'Neill spent the last two years of his life in Suite 401 overlooking the Charles River, with Carlotta devoting herself entirely to his care. Again, finances were a problem, because the Marblehead cottage had brought only about forty thousand dollars, again a loss. The O'Neills were never fortunate in their real estate. To ease the situation O'Neill allowed publication of *A Moon for the Misbegotten*, and in Fall 1951 he corrected the proofs. Nevertheless, there was still friction between them. As time went on, O'Neill was more and more under sedation, Carlotta claiming that he continuously begged for more drugs, which she would refuse; on the other hand, two doctors thought he was overmedicated (Sheaffer, 1973, p. 661). After his brief hospital stay in November 1951, O'Neill seems to have begun his preparations for death, giving Carlotta an inscribed typescript of *Long Day's Journey* with the poignant conclusion to his dedication: "I have loved you for twenty-three years now, Darling, and now that I am old and can work no more, I love you more than ever." Nevertheless, Sheaffer (1973, p. 665) reports her as saying that his last words to her were "quite bitter." He also revised his will, giving Carlotta complete control of all his works and papers, disinheriting his children. [For comments on this *see* Commins, Saxe.]

In 1952 there were two unsuccessful New York revivals of *"Anna Christie"* and *Desire Under the Elms*, and even the publication of *A Moon for the Misbegotten* failed to increase O'Neill's reputation. Carlotta refused to allow a production of this play unless O'Neill cut some of the vulgarity—which he stubbornly refused to do. In Winter 1952–53, O'Neill went through all his papers, including those he had deposited at Random House after the 1948 incident, but with the exception of *Long Day's Journey into Night*. According to Carlotta, they tore up scripts page by page and fed them to the fire. Later, when reminded that Suite 401 had no fireplace, Carlotta said that the torn manuscripts were sent to the furnace. As his palsy worsened, O'Neill became almost totally dependent on Carlotta, refusing to let her away from him, even when she was totally exhausted. A local Catholic priest tried to get in touch with him, but Carlotta rebuffed him.

In November, Eugene O'Neill contracted pneumonia, and died on November 27, 1953. Among his last recorded words were: "I knew it, I knew it! Born in a hotel room—and God damn it—died in a hotel room" (Sheaffer, 1973, p. 670; Gelb and Gelb, p. 939). After an autopsy it was revealed that O'Neill's illness was a rare one, "a degeneration of the cells of the cerebellum" (Karl Ragnar Gierow,* quoted in Sheaffer, 1973, p. 671), the symptoms of which mimicked Parkinson's disease. He was buried in a very small private ceremony just outside Boston. Carlotta Monterey survived until 1972.

Much has been written and surmised about their tempestuous relationship, but these two strong-willed people seem to have needed each other. Their past marital histories indicate that each was rather impossible to live with because each possessed the kind of personality that would have engulfed and destroyed a lesser one. Their frequent rages with each other may therefore be seen as assertions of independence which each occasionally found necessary. O'Neill needed Carlotta to hold life at a distance, while she felt the need to be part of the life of a great man whose work, intellect, and (in the early days) body she could respect.

In her last years she became a most redoubtable "keeper of the flame." She had long been angry at the American theatre's neglect of O'Neill's work—and said so—noting that her husband's plays were being performed more frequently outside the United States than in it. For this reason she gave his unproduced plays to the Royal Dramatic Theatre of Stockholm, beginning with *Long Day's Journey into Night* (1956), going against O'Neill's wishes to do so [*See* Commins, Saxe; Monterey, Carlotta; and *Long Day's Journey into Night*]. This was followed by *A Touch of the Poet* (1957), *Hughie* (1958), and *More Stately Mansions* (1962). All these plays were translated by Sven Barthel, and the last was constructed and condensed by Karl Ragnar Gierow from a manuscript that O'Neill had overlooked in his mass destruction in 1952–53. All these plays speedily reached Broadway, and *Long Day's Journey into Night* (November 1956) reestablished O'Neill as a major Broadway figure, winning him a fourth Pulitzer Prize.

But the O'Neill revival had actually begun a little earlier with the Circle in the Square revival of *The Iceman Cometh* (1956), which established Jason Robards, Jr., as the definitive Hickey and José Quintero as the quintessential O'Neill director. Since that time, O'Neill's reputation has remained solid; unproduced and lesser-known plays are being performed, and theatrical people like Colleen Dewhurst,* Geraldine Fitzgerald,* Robards, and Quintero have become almost inseparable from the works of O'Neill. Now there even seems to be a specific theatrical *genus* known as an "O'Neill actor" or an "O'Neill director."

See in "References": Alexander (1962); Bogard (1972); Boulton (1958); Bowen (1959); Carpenter (1979); Commins (1978); Floyd (1979, 1981); Gelb and Gelb (1973); Hastings and Weeks (1968); Sheaffer (1968, 1973, 1983). Additional sources will be found at the end of other entries and in the Bibliography.

O'NEILL, Eugene Gladstone, Jr. (1910–1950), son of Eugene [Gladstone] O'Neill* and Kathleen Jenkins* O'Neill (later Pitt-Smith). Born in New York City, May 6, 1910; died in Woodstock, New York, by his own hand, September 25, 1950. Educated at Peekskill Military Academy; Horace Mann School, New York City; and Yale, receiving a Ph.D. in classics (1936).

He was the result of O'Neill's early, and very short-lived, marriage to Kathleen Jenkins which took place October 2, 1909, and was terminated by divorce on October 11, 1912. James O'Neill* had disapproved of this marriage and had arranged for his son to go to Honduras on a mining expedition, and apparently O'Neill never saw his wife again. Custody of the child was awarded to Kathleen, who did not ask for alimony. In 1915 she married George Pitt-Smith, a divorced office manager whose wife had custody of his son, who was a little younger than Eugene, Jr. Young Eugene was given the name of Richard Pitt-Smith and did not know his real father until he was twelve years old. Mrs. Pitt-Smith, having noted the playwright's success with *Beyond the Horizon*,* and being in some financial difficulties, decided to ask her ex-husband's help with his son's education. Coincidentally Eugene, Jr., had been rather difficult, hating the military academy he attended and running away more than once. He met his father for the first time in May 1922, and the two made mutually good impressions on each other. O'Neill agreed to help with his son's education and at the Horace Mann school, New York City, his academic performance improved markedly. O'Neill also invited the boy to stay with him, Agnes Boulton* (his second wife), and young Shane Rudraighe O'Neill* (his son with Agnes) at Peaked Hill Bars, near Provincetown, in the summer. Young Eugene, who seems to have had fairly good relations with his stepfather, was pleased to discover that he also liked his real father, though Mrs. Pitt-Smith thought that perhaps she was losing her own son, particularly since he reverted to his baptismal name of Eugene O'Neill shortly after meeting his father.

A pattern of familial visits soon evolved, with Eugene, Jr., visiting with Agnes, his father, half-brother, and later his half-sister at Peaked Hill Bars; Bermuda; and Loon Lodge, Belgrade Lakes, Maine. Agnes's daughter from her first marriage, Barbara Burton, was sometimes part of this ménage and was very impressed with her relative. With O'Neill's commitment and later marriage to Carlotta Monterey* (1929) the friendly relations between father and son continued, O'Neill informing his son of his plans to go abroad before Agnes obtained a divorce. After this, Eugene, Jr., who entered Yale at seventeen, seems to have revised his former liking for Agnes and adopted his father's hostility toward her. As a result he severed communications with her, and relations between him and his half-brother, Shane, and his half-sister, Oona (*see* Chaplin, Oona O'Neill), were never close. In August 1929, in the course of a summer tour to Germany financed by his father, Eugene, Jr., visited him and Carlotta at Chateau du Plessis, where their friendship was strengthened further, O'Neill taking particular pride in his son's brilliant scholastic record at Yale. To some extent, his son's interest in classics led O'Neill to attempt the integration of classic myth into modern drama which he performed in *Mourning Becomes Electra.**

On June 15, 1931, Eugene, Jr., married Elizabeth Green, the first of three ill-fated marriages. He was still an undergraduate and therefore had to receive the permission of the Yale faculty for the marriage. O'Neill seems to have had no objection to the marriage, but he did not attend the ceremony, perhaps in order to avoid meeting his first wife. Eugene, Jr., was awarded the Winthrop Prize for classics and was listed as one of the top scholars of his senior year. When he graduated A.B. in June 1932, he won the Berkeley Scholarship (a traveling fellowship), was elected to Phi Beta Kappa, and was also Ivy Laureate of his class. His plan to continue his studies at the University of Freiburg, Germany, was later changed as a result of his distaste for Hitler Germany, and he completed his Ph.D. degree at Yale in 1936. After his initial visit to his father at Casa Genotta, relations between him and Carlotta began to sour. She seems to have disapproved of his early marriage without the money to support a household. However, Eugene, Jr., continued to visit at Tao House, near San Francisco, and one indication of the friendship between the two men was O'Neill's earlier gift to his son of Peaked Hill Bars, the converted Coast Guard station which had been James O'Neill's gift to Eugene, Sr. Unfortunately, Eugene, Jr., was able to enjoy it for only a year or so before it washed into the sea on January 10, 1931.

After receiving his Ph.D. from Yale, Eugene, Jr., was appointed to the Yale classics department where he began to establish himself as an excellent classical scholar. However, he was beginning to show signs of instability. In 1942 he applied for a commission in the Intelligence Corps, hoping to make use of his command of six languages, including ancient Greek. However, he was not accepted by the three services, perhaps because of his left-wing politics, demonstrated by a six-month membership in the communist party. He left Yale and trained as a mechanic so that he would not have to be drafted for the infantry. However, he failed to pass an army physical because of the fractured skull he had suffered as the result of a childhood bicycle accident and also a slight hand tremor which he thought might be hereditary, in view of his father's condition. He took a wartime job in a cable factory in New Haven and began to drink heavily. After the war was over he did not return to Yale but co-edited *The Complete Greek Drama* (two volumes) with the influential Whitney J. Oates, chair of classics at Princeton, a commission obtained for him by Saxe Commins.* By now his personal life was in disarray. His first marriage had ended in divorce, and his second (to Jane Hunter Longley) the daughter of a Yale mathematics professor) was about to go the same way, while a potential third wife was waiting in the wings.

According to an old friend, Frank Meyer, he was spreading himself too thin, and growing less committed to teaching at Yale with its rules and regulations. He was becoming interested in mass education, radio and television work, and briefly held a position as a radio announcer in Hartford before moving to Greenwich Village where he lived with Ruth Lander, a divorcée and artist's agent. He supported himself with guest lecturing, thanks to Whitney J. Oates, at Princeton University for two terms until his cavalier attitude toward teaching and his heavy drinking forced his termination. He also began to work as a television commentator where his learning, handsome appearance, and excellent voice were important assets. However, he seems to have had a self-destructive urge and publicly disgraced himself one evening when interviewing Adolphe Menjou, an actor noted for his natty appearance. Eugene, Jr., appeared not only sloppily dressed but also somewhat drunk. Needless to say, relations between him and Carlotta had seriously deteriorated, because she disliked his left-wing politics and his apparent shiftlessness. Eventually, father and son had to continue their friendship almost surreptitiously, as was demonstrated by O'Neill's secretiveness in aiding his son in the purchase of some property in Woodstock, New York, where he went in 1947 with Ruth Lander. Psychologically, Eugene, Jr., had recently been battered by two deaths, those of George Pitt-Smith, his invalid stepfather, and his maternal grandmother, to whom he had been particularly close. He realized also that since the death of his step-brother, George Pitt-Smith, Jr., in a fall from a New York skyscraper window in 1930, there was no one to take care of his mother except himself. Therefore, Eugene, Jr., took out a twenty-five-thousand-dollar life insurance policy with her as the beneficiary; and in what was taken to be a jocular remark to friends, he indicated that he could now commit suicide since she would be provided for.

He remained at Woodstock with Ruth Lander after 1947, in a stormy and sometimes even violent relationship during which she left him several times. He supported himself with part-time teaching, including courses at Fairleigh Dickinson College and at the New School for Social Research. By 1950 he was drinking very heavily, and his behavior was notorious even in an artists' colony. He was also involved with and considered marriage to a New York woman, Flora Rheta Schriber. He was almost totally estranged from his father, a situation that was partially the result of his having taken O'Neill's side in a brief separation from Carlotta, who thenceforward seems to have considered him an enemy. Eugene, Jr., and Ruth Lander finally broke up around September 18, 1950, and during that week he tried to raise money from O'Neill so that he would be able to pay the bank loan which had become due on the Woodstock property. By now Eugene, Jr., was certain that Carlotta was intercepting his letters to O'Neill, and he was probably right. On the night of September 23, 1950, he was depressed and drinking heavily but the next day visited friends for dinner. Early that morning, while staying over, he began to drink again with his friend, Frank Meyer, while the two reminisced. He returned home, and at some point between 5 A.M. and 1 P.M. on September 25 (medical testimony suggests about midday), he got into a bathtub of hot water and slashed his left wrist and ankle, attempting a classical suicide. Then, apparently changing his mind, he tried to go for help but bled to death at the bottom of the stairs; he was unable to telephone because service had been discontinued for nonpayment of bills. He left a note beside an empty bottle of bourbon: "Never let it be said of O'Neill that he failed to empty a bottle. *Ave atque vale.*" (Sheaffer, 1973, p. 631; Gelb and Gelb, 1973, p. 904). The elder O'Neill seems almost to have had a premonition of his son's death, because when Carlotta spoke cryptically on the telephone in an apparent attempt to spare him, he instantly understood the situation.

With Eugene, Jr.'s, death, one major objection to publication of *Long Day's Journey into Night** was removed. O'Neill had said that he wished it published only twenty-five years after his death, but Carlotta claimed that this restriction had been made because of a request by Eugene, Jr., who had read the play in the early forties and thought that it might damage his own academic career. This statement has been disputed by Saxe Commins,* among others.

Altogether, the relationship between Eugene O'Neill, Jr., and his father seems to have been at times satisfying yet also destructive. Louis Sheaffer (1973, p. 99) has suggested that he might have been better off had he never known his real father, yet their friendship seems to have been fruitful for O'Neill and useful to the son. Certainly, in his later years Eugene, Jr., was fond of identifying himself in bars and elsewhere as the playwright's son, to some extent capitalizing on his father's reputation; and undoubtedly his radio and television career was advanced as a result. Certainly Eugene, Jr., possessed a self-destructive streak, from whatever cause, and the significance of his committing suicide just after his fortieth birthday should be noted because he seems to have feared that he would become "sexually unattractive" after that date. Louis Sheaffer (1973, p. 626) suggests that he was perhaps trying to prove himself by replicating the career of his uncle, James ["Jamie"] O'Neill, Jr.,* whom his father now romanticized. Apparently his motive for suicide was not financial because he did have back lecture fees due and was scheduled to teach three courses at the New School for Social Research. One can only regret the destruction of such brilliant promise.

The funeral took place at Frank Campbell's, Madison Avenue, New York City, with his mother the only blood relation present. Both Carlotta and O'Neill sent separate floral pieces, Carlotta a wreath and O'Neill a blanket which reportedly nearly covered the casket. His Yale Skull and Bones Fraternity Brothers made the arrangements. Eugene, Jr., left his Ph.D. diploma to his father, a significant bequest giving tangible evidence of shared intellectual values and an expression of gratitude for educational assistance. Curiously, his obituary makes no mention of Shane Rudraighe O'Neill* as a relative. *See* in "References": Alexander (1962); Bowen (1959); Commins (1978); Gelb and Gelb (1973); Sheaffer (1973).

O'NEILL, Eugene, III (1945–1946), son of Shane Rudraighe O'Neill* and his wife, Catherine Givens O'Neill*; first grandchild of Eugene O'Neill. Born in New York City, November 19, 1945; died February 10, 1946, of what is now called Sudden Infant Death Syndrome. At the time there were some allegations of neglect, and when Carlotta Monterey* O'Neill felt particularly vindictive toward Shane and his wife, she would both repeat and embroider on them.

O'NEILL, James (1846–1920), father of Eugene O'Neill. Born County Kilkenny, Ireland, probably October 14, 1846, to Edward and Mary O'Neill (or O'Neil). Died New London, Connecticut, August 10, 1920. Seventh of nine children, youngest of three sons. His father, an unskilled laborer, was illiterate. His mother, almost twenty years younger than Edward, could read as well as write.

The O'Neills emigrated to America in 1850, when James was four years old. Their long and appallingly difficult trip was so traumatic that he was never to allude to it later. Settling in Buffalo, New York, the family moved from one wooden shack to another in the town's depressed boatyard area. For not quite a dollar a day, Edward, then in his sixties, slaved at dockside jobs from dawn to dusk in order to support his large family.

Five years after settling in Buffalo, Edward abandoned his family. He returned to Ireland, where he soon died. The despair of the stranded family heightened James's lasting hatred of his father.

Mary and two of her daughters found employment as seamstresses and scrubwomen (the older sons had left earlier and were fending for themselves), while the younger girls took care of housekeeping. At the age of eleven James became an apprentice filemaker. For fifty cents a week he worked twelve hours a day, under wretched conditions. The family's combined incomes were too meager to prevent their remaining perpetually hungry and threadbare. They were evicted from their homes at least twice, their furnishings dumped outside while they all stood by, weeping. These memories left an indelible impression on James, shaping his life as well as those of his own wife and sons.

In 1858 one of his older sisters, who had married a saloon owner, brought the family to Cincinnati. There James continued to work as a machinist. When the Civil War started, his brother-in-law opened a military uniform store in Norfolk, Virginia, and took James in. He helped in the business, later claiming that during that time he was also provided with a tutor, who introduced him to the theatre.

When the war ended, James returned to Cincinnati and moved in with his mother. He drifted into his career by chance. Playing billiards in the saloon next door to the National Theatre on a September evening, he agreed to go on stage as an extra. He performed creditably—and the experience exhilarated him. For twenty-five cents a performance, he became a member of the company. Almost immediately, he proudly listed himself in the new city directory as "James O'Neill, Actor."

For some months after that first appearance in 1865, O'Neill performed lowly roles in various then-popular romances, melodramas, and tearjerkers. Assiduously, he learned as much as he could about the theatre, working hard and manifesting his quick mind and his charm—the ingredients that were soon to propel him to fame. Diffident and kind as well as friendly and gregarious in private, he was single-minded and almost ruthless in his profession. Yet, though ambitious and indefatigable, he was also hesitant about taking risks. These conflicting drives and pulls ultimately limited his career and precluded his reaching the very pinnacle of his profession.

In his apprentice years, O'Neill played in the stock companies of St. Louis and Baltimore as well as in Cincinnati, constantly improving his skills. His good looks, his bearing, and his voice, which has been considered among the finest ever heard on the American stage—though he was occasionally criticized for the brogue he was never quite able to overcome—attracted the attention of women in the audience, reviewers, and touring stars. Edwin Booth, Edwin Forrest, Joseph Jefferson, and other notables gave the promising young actor the needed advice and encouragement. He quickly rose through the ranks. Having started as a super (extra), he soon became a utility (bit player), then a "walking gentleman," then the juvenile (romantic) lead. And in 1870, John Ellsler engaged him as leading man in his Academy of Music in Cleveland.

Though this was the stock company's top position, the leading man usually played a subordinate part: it was the visiting stars who were the attraction. Nonetheless O'Neill did get the opportunity to play big roles, also supporting visitors such as the aging and crippled Forrest's Virginius (as Icilius), Jean Davenport Lander's Queen Elizabeth (as Essex), and Jefferson's ever-popular Rip van Winkle (as Hendrick). He devoted most of his time to mastering his profession and learning as many roles as possible. Though he found memorizing to be the most difficult part of his work, he knew some fifty roles, including many Shakespearean ones, by the end of his first season in Cleveland. And his reputation was rising.

During that first year in Cleveland, he became friendly with another self-made Irish American, Thomas J. Quinlan, whom he probably met at his liquor-and-cigar store near the theatre and who invited him to his luxurious home. It would have been surprising if the Quinlan's thirteen-year-old daughter, Mary Ellen ("Ella"), was not infatuated with Cleveland's matinee idol. At the time, however, O'Neill's attentions were focused on someone else, a prematurely-developed fifteen-year-old redhead named Nettie Walsh.

In 1872, O'Neill was offered the position of leading man in McVicker's Theatre in Chicago, the foremost theatre in the west. During his three-year period in Chicago, O'Neill reached his artistic peak. McVicker's featured much Shakespearean and other classical drama and attracted the greatest stars of the age for long engagements. As its stock company's leading man, O'Neill now played important roles. Though in 1874 he moved to Hooley's Opera House, McVicker's principal Chicago competition, it was at McVicker's that O'Neill experienced the climax of his career.

O'Neill was to become obsessed by that event for the rest of his life, and he recounted it frequently. Edwin Booth, during a month's engagement, alternated with O'Neill in the parts of Othello and Iago. The story is dramatized in *Long Day's Journey into Night**: "The first night I played Othello, he said to our manager, 'That young man is playing Othello better than I ever did!' That from Booth, the greatest actor of his day or any other! And it was true! And I was only twenty-seven years old!' " (Like many actors, O'Neill was prone to misstate his age.)

Also eventful at this time in Chicago was his personal life. O'Neill's name was romantically linked with that of Louise Hawthorne, his leading lady; she later died in an accident but was believed to have committed suicide for love of O'Neill. And the redheaded Nettie Walsh, though at this time she also kept company with other men, visited him in Chicago. He had just decided to end their affair once and for all when she informed O'Neill that she was carrying his child. She refused O'Neill's offer to raise it himself if she left him alone thereafter.

In the spring of 1875, Hooley's moved to San Francisco. There, as well as in periodic tours, O'Neill played with actors who, like O'Neill himself, shortly became the new leading American theatrical figures. One of them, Clara Morris, in late 1876 obtained an engagement for O'Neill at Palmer's Union Square Theatre in New York, the city which was already the country's theatrical center. One of his costars there was Charles Thorne. Also popular in romantic, swashbuckling roles, he was O'Neill's most immediate rival.

In the meantime, O'Neill's friend, Thomas Quinlan, had died. For reasons probably not irrelevant to O'Neill's appearance at the Union Square Theatre, Ella in early 1877 prevailed upon her now-widowed mother to resettle in New York. There Ella saw O'Neill frequently. They were married that June. Despite many later problems, their great and lifelong love for each other withstood many personal and familial tribulations. Rumors that commonly accompany actors' lives never touched those of the O'Neills. No scandal ever marred their marriage, and there was never another woman in his life. But his premarital doings haunted their first year. Nettie Walsh, claiming to have been married to O'Neill who had then deserted her and their child, filed for divorce. The artistic success of O'Neill's engagement with the Union Square Company visiting Chicago that fall was overshadowed by the publicity generated by the trial. Ultimately, however, Walsh's suit was dismissed.

The O'Neills' marriage was to experience more lasting trials. The seeming glamor of an actor's life vanished as Ella experienced its reality. Like other nineteenth-century stars, O'Neill had to lead a rough, nomadic life. He was used to it, and being outgoing by nature, enjoyed it. But the naturally retiring and pious Ella resented it—the drinking, the "week after week of one-night stands, in trains without Pullman, in dirty rooms of filthy hotels, eating bad food" (as Mary Tyrone* says in *Long Day's Journey into Night*). Yet their mutual love and need again and again made them share its hardships.

Later that first winter, the "black moustached Adonis," as he was called, was warmly welcomed back to San Francisco with his new wife. His good looks and graceful bearing had heretofore typecast him in romantic leads. Now he was enabled to extend his range and create different character and comic roles, his prestige having grown after his New York performances. And his personal happiness was heightened in September (1878) by the birth of his first son, James ["Jamie"] O'Neill, Jr.*

His fortunes grew—and suddenly were shattered the following March. Reassured by Catholic prelates, O'Neill had agreed to impersonate Christ in Salmi Morse's *The Passion*, a colossal spectacle David Belasco modeled on the Oberammergau pageant. Belasco judged O'Neill's talent as "the greatest performance of the generation," and O'Neill, a devout Catholic who frequently expressed ambitions to become a priest, announced that "if the public will support me, I shall devote the remainder of my life to this great work" (Timberlake, 1954, p. 610). Reverent audiences knelt in devotion, but others rioted against what they considered sacrilege. The authorities thereupon closed the show and arrested the cast, including O'Neill. Subsequent attempts to stage *The Passion* were unsuccessful. Later O'Neill revealed that he was convinced that his acting career had come to an end at that point.

The reverse turned out to be the case. After completing his engagement in San Francisco, O'Neill returned east. While touring there, he was invited to Booth's Theatre in New York, to finish the engagement of Charles Thorne, who had suddenly died. On February 12, 1883, O'Neill opened in the scheduled play, *The Count of Monte Cristo*, Charles Fechter's adaptation of Dumas's romance. Though the reviews were not encouraging, the piece soon became enormously successful. That first season it ran long beyond the originally scheduled run, and when Booth's had to be vacated, O'Neill bought the rights to the play and took it on tour. It became one of the most profitable plays of the nineteenth century.

Monte Cristo galvanized O'Neill's career. Immediately his income soared. (That same fall, too, during the first *Monte Cristo* tour, his second son, Edmund, was born in a hotel in St. Louis.) Audiences never tired of it, though O'Neill came to loathe "that God-damned play" (Sheaffer, 1968, p. 35), as he privately called it (publicly he extolled its dramaturgy and sentiments). Periodically he tried other plays, but such changes were short-lived. Popular demand and O'Neill's congenital terror of the poorhouse enslaved him to the creaky but lucrative melodrama. He was to play Edmond Dantès until he retired a quarter of a century later. Well over six thousand times he climbed on his chair behind simulated waves, stretched out his arms, and shouted the play's famous words, "Mine the treasures of Monte Cristo! The Wor-r-r-ld is mine!"

The O'Neills' lives now remained intertwined with *Monte Cristo*. Despite the growing fame and financial fortune the play brought him, O'Neill was increasingly frustrated by his failure to achieve the artistic heights that had seemed within his grasp. His frustrations inevitably affected his whole family.

Since James and Ella O'Neill found even short separations painful, she accompanied him as often as possible. While they were in Denver in early 1885, Edmund died in New York before she was able to get back. Her guilt feelings probably helped trigger her subsequent drug addiction (*see* O'Neill, Ella Quinlan). James O'Neill, grief-stricken, mechanically went through his lines onstage that night: he had never before permitted anything to prevent his fulfilling professional commitments.

Though perpetually and heavily investing in real estate, he and his family lived in New York apartment hotels. Their only permanent home was the "Monte Cristo Cottage." O'Neill purchased it in 1884, in New London, Connecticut, which appealed to him when they visited Ella's mother there. Unassuming and simple in his tastes, O'Neill enjoyed working his bit of land, fishing and swimming, and socializing with ordinary townspeople. Until he sold the cottage the year before his death, the O'Neills spent most summers there.

They toured Europe in the summer of 1887, visiting Marseilles, Oberammergau, and other places related to his acting. The following year saw the birth of their third son, Eugene. It was a difficult birth, and the doctor, as was customary at the time, administered morphine. Too late did O'Neill realize that Ella, who continued taking the drug which was then available without prescription, had become addicted.

In the following years, though he continued to try his luck in other dramatic vehicles, O'Neill principally toured *Monte Cristo*, the play that became ever more identified with O'Neill—and ever more popular. In 1895 he was among the few stars who dared oppose the powerful Klaw-Erlanger syndicate. His fame reached its highpoint, and despite many unsuccessful real estate ventures, his wealth kept increasing.

But notwithstanding his confident, cheerful public posture, he was becoming increasingly depressed. Repeated attempts to cure Ella in expensive sanatoria failed, and though he loved her deeply, he also felt despair and resentment. Similar were his feelings toward his growing sons. Jamie, enormously gifted but feeling unable to live up to his father's towering image, soon gave up. He blamed his father for his mother's addiction, became a dissipating cynic, and influenced the much younger Eugene to emulate him.

O'Neill kept trying to escape *Monte Cristo*. In 1904 he produced a gala revival of *The Two Orphans*, and the next year, following the example of other stage stars, he made his debut in vaudeville, performing scenes from another old hit, *Virginius*. But soon he was back in *Monte Cristo*, playing to packed houses from coast to coast. Ella continued to accompany him, and Jamie was given a minor acting role, though he often disgraced O'Neill with his drunkenness. (Though O'Neill also drank, he was always completely sober on stage.)

O'Neill now determined to give up his vehicle forever. Beginning in 1906, he announced numerous "farewell" performances. After a trip to Great Britain with Ella that summer, he starred on Broadway in *Virginius*, which he then toured. He also played in *Julius Caesar* and in the dramatization of F. Marion

Crawford's sentimental religious novel, *The White Sister*. But notwithstanding all these efforts, he was again and again forced back into *Monte Cristo*. Its final and ignominious run was as a twice-a-day tabloid version in a vaudeville show— a painful, humiliating national tour that O'Neill cut short in March 1912. Later that year he played Edmond Dantès for the very last time, in the film version of *Monte Cristo*. As that still extant performance illustrates, O'Neill's acting was overly histrionic by our current standards. But he was ahead of his own age: time and again reviewers criticized his underplaying, his "undramatic," "natural" acting.

Nearing seventy but still energetic, O'Neill thought up a number of new projects. None of them ultimately materialized. During the years of World War I, he took subordinate roles in *Joseph and His Brethren* and in *The Wanderer*, two biblical spectacles that ran on Broadway and then went on tour. And then he finally retired. Family life had improved now, for Ella had been cured of her addiction since 1914. While Jamie's alcoholism persisted and continued to cause his parents grief, Eugene had apparently settled down happily with his new wife (Agnes Boulton*) and with his work. Though quite pleased with him, O'Neill was puzzled by his son's "depressing" early plays, so different from those he himself had starred in all his life. "Where did you get those ideas?" he would ask. "People come to the theatre to forget their troubles, not to be reminded of them. What are you trying to do—send them home to commit suicide?" (Basso, quoted by Sheaffer, 1968, p. 477). But his puzzlement did not prevent his being the happiest and expansively proudest of fathers when he attended his son's first Broadway opening, *Beyond the Horizon*.*

Always gregarious, fun-loving, and popular with his colleagues, O'Neill was content in those last years, too, in the Lambs' Club. He participated in its "Gambol," and then was given a leading role in the Friars' parody of that event, the "Giggle." And he was elected to leading positions in the Green Room Club.

In December 1918 he was struck by a car while crossing Fifth Avenue near his hotel apartment. He was not injured seriously, but though he had always been vigorous and robust, his health now began to deteriorate. Early in 1920 he had a stroke. He partially recovered but soon was found to have intestinal cancer. Thereupon he was moved to the New London hospital, where he died in August.

His legacy was enormous. Apart from his financial fortune, he bequeathed to his youngest son—and therefore to America and to the world—the love for and knowledge of the theatre that made him the playwright he was to become. As Doris Alexander noted, "Had James O'Neill not been one of America's last great actors, Eugene O'Neill might never have been its first great playwright."

It is amusing to recall the young and then-rebellious Eugene's exasperated exclamation, to the great merriment of his office companions, at always being pointed out as the famous star's son: "Some day James O'Neill will be remembered, if at all, as the father of Eugene O'Neill" (Sheaffer, 1968, p. 225). While that ironically indeed turned out to be the case, the surviving image of his "tightwad" father, as portrayed in *Long Day's Journey Into Night*, is as unfair as it is false. That resentful prophecy was made in the offices of the *New London Telegraph*, whose publisher was James O'Neill's friend. Eugene O'Neill, that summer of 1912, was a twenty-dollar-a-week cub reporter. What he did not know was that he got that job because of—and that his salary was secretly subsidized by—his father, James O'Neill. *See* in "References": Alexander (1962); Matlaw (1979); Patrick O'Neill (1942); Sheaffer (1968, 1973, 1983); Timberlake (1954). © Myron Matlaw.

O'NEILL, James, Jr. ("Jamie"), (1878–1923), eldest son of James O'Neill,* actor, and Ella Quinlan O'Neill*; brother of Edmund Burke O'Neill and Eugene O'Neill. Born in San Francisco, September 10, 1878; died in Riverlawn Sanitarium, Paterson, New Jersey, November 8, 1923, of complications and general physical collapse arising from chronic alcoholism. Educated at a Roman Catholic school, Notre Dame, Indiana (1885–93); Saint John's Preparatory School (1893–95) and Saint John's College, the Bronx, New York (later known as Fordham Preparatory School and Fordham University, 1895–99). Expelled from Saint John's six months before his scheduled graduation after being detected in an attempt to pass off a prostitute as his sister, the result of a drunken bet. This was the last and greatest of his college drinking escapades. His academic career had been excellent at both Notre Dame and preparatory school, and he had continued to do well at Saint John's College, despite his sexual experimentation among Broadway showgirls and his overindulgence in alcohol.

At the same time, he was beginning his almost life-long rebellion against his father and also his religion. Part of Jamie's rage toward his father seems to have been induced by James O'Neill's alleged stinginess in obtaining cheap medical assistance for Ella when Eugene was born in 1888. As a result of a difficult delivery, she became addicted to morphine and remained so for the next twenty-six years (see *Long Day's Journey into Night*). To some extent his attitude toward Eugene was also affected by this circumstance because he considered him partially responsible for his mother's addiction. Later in life he alleged that he had initiated Eugene into his world of chorus girls, prostitutes, horse racing, booze, and cynical irreligion as a kind of revenge, first for his mother's illness and later out of jealousy for his brother's success. Jamie also felt considerable guilt over the death of his eighteen-month-old younger brother, Edmund Burke O'Neill (1883–85). Left with him and his grandmother in New York while his parents were on tour in the West, Jamie contracted measles; and despite being warned to keep away from the baby, he did not obey. The child contracted measles and died; for many years Ella seems to have blamed Jamie for acting out of deliberate vindictiveness.

After his dismissal from college, Jamie tried newspaper work and then went on the road as traveling salesman for a lumber company. Unsuccessful at either occupation, he drifted into his father's acting company, playing a small supporting role and then graduating to the part of the son to his father's *Monte Cristo*. Though he undoubtedly had talent, he lacked the capacity for hard work that had brought his father to stardom. To judge from contemporary reviews, he showed promise in his smaller roles, but his performances were erratic, at times marred by drunkenness, a condition that offended his father's sense of responsibility. The older man boasted that he had never missed a performance because of drink. Nonetheless, Jamie continued to gain parts through his father's influence. In 1902 he played in *Audrey*, moving on to roles in *The Adventures of Gerard* and *The Two Orphans*. In Spring 1905 he played in the one-act vaudeville version of *Virginius*, also with his father. In the 1907 season, James O'Neill developed the idea of forming a repertory company to produce the classics (including a series of Shakespeare revivals) and train young actors in the old tradition. He began with a grandiose revival of *Virginius*, in which both he and Jamie appeared. While the father was well reviewed, Jamie was not, partly because of his decision to adopt a contemporary hair style rather than a historically correct one (Sheaffer, 1968, p. 128). Two weeks later the show folded, and James O'Neill was forced to turn again to *Monte Cristo*, which he took on the road, also planning to play Shakespeare. Again he was unsuccessful, and Jamie's reviews once more revealed his shortcomings as an actor. As James Tyrone* in *Long Day's Journey* indicates, he might never have been given parts had it not been for his father's influence.

Jamie's career continued in this manner, with the whole family spending almost every summer in New London, Connecticut, as they had done since 1884, and where they seem to have lived in a state of armed truce and sometimes open warfare (see *Long Day's Journey*). Jamie had a bad reputation there among women and prostitutes, though he was popular in bars. In 1905 he lived apart from the family in New London but continued to see his mother. In the fall of 1908 Jamie opened with his father in *Abbé Bonaparte*, which failed. In January 1909 he commenced touring in the second company of *The Travelling Salesman* in the role of the salesman Watts, also obtained through his father's influence. He was to stay with this company for the next two and one-half years playing one-night stands in small towns and doing extensive primary research among their bars and brothels. His acting seems to have displayed a certain facility in farcical comedy, but as usual he did not work hard at his craft and his performances were often marred by drunkenness.

By 1910–11 Eugene was back in New York, and the two brothers seem to have enjoyed much drinking together. In 1911 Jamie again toured, this time with his father's vaudeville company of *Monte Cristo* on the Orpheum circuit, to be joined by Eugene in New Orleans in January 1912, just after his suicide attempt. The two brothers appear to have boozed their way across stages and across the United States with this company, on one occasion forcing cancellation of a performance, while Jamie's drinking steadily increased. After the tour closed early, the O'Neill family returned to New York, and later in 1912 James and Jamie appeared in a film version of *Monte Cristo* that was never commercially released. By late 1912, Eugene was in a tuberculosis sanitarium and Jamie was rehearsing with his father for *Joseph and His Brethren*, a most opulent production. He is said to have fallen in love with Pauline Frederick, one of the stars of the cast. The play went on tour in August 1913, and Jamie was frequently drunk. He alleged (though some of her acquaintances denied it) that he had declared his passion to Miss Frederick, who renounced him with the words "No. Mr. Jimmy. It's liquor or me. Not both—never!" (*see* Boulton, 1958, p. 210). One thing seems certain: Jamie was unable to keep away from liquor for more than a few weeks at a time. It has been suggested that the relationship between Lily Miller* and Sid Davis* in *Ah, Wilderness!** was suggested by this circumstance. Jamie and his father remained with this company into the 1914 season, but during the fall, Jamie's alcoholic misbehavior onstage became even more noticeable, though James refused to sanction his dismissal. Both O'Neill men left the company in April 1914, ostensibly because of Ella O'Neill's "serious illness," which is thought by Louis Sheaffer (1968, pp. 280–281) to have been the time of her final "cure" from morphine addiction. Jamie, James, and Pauline Frederick returned to the company for a tour in the 1914–15 season, which was truncated because of the bankruptcy of the producers. Jamie and James returned to New York, with Jamie's drinking and general misbehavior becoming habitual. Despite the hostility between the two men, and the way in which both Jamie and Eugene ganged up on "the old man" (as detailed in *Long Day's Journey*), James O'Neill did give both his apparently "prodigal" sons a small allowance, which in Jamie's case, particularly, usually went for liquor.

By 1917, Jamie was becoming jealous of Eugene's growing success. His own looks were gone and he was unemployed, but he still affected superiority when he visited with his brother among the denizens of Greenwich Village. When Eugene met Agnes Boulton,* Jamie initially approved of her, and after their marriage in April 1918, he went with them to their flat in Provincetown for the summer. In June 1918, James O'Neill issued what sounds like a press "puff" to the effect that Jamie regretted his rejection by army doctors. Agnes has retailed with some humor her difficulty in getting both O'Neills sober enough to travel (she had to cancel reservations several times). She also tells of the antics of Jamie, together with his two dogs, adopted serially, and of his "pastoral love" for a young girl he met while clam digging at Provincetown. (Boulton, 1958, pp. 125–138, 161–168, 208–213). However, Jamie's self-destructive behavior continued in New York, as did his hostility toward his father, though he continued to see his mother almost daily. A description of the strained relations among the family members is given by Agnes Boulton in an account of her first meeting with Eugene's parents (p. 233). The three men grew farther apart as James O'Neill began to look upon his young actor-protegé and playwright Brandon Tynan as the successful son he wished he had had, though shortly before his death James O'Neill became reconciled to Eugene and proud of his success in *Beyond the Horizon.** But as Eugene and his father were growing closer together, Jamie was feeling not only jealous but excluded, and the two brothers became more distant, Jamie now having come to disapprove of Agnes. At the moment of his father's death in August 1920, Jamie was drunk.

After this, Jamie became devoted to his mother. He stopped drinking to please her, and while he continued to play the horses, he also became her dapper constant companion and escort. Relations between the brothers began to mellow, and he even visited Eugene and his family at Peaked Hill, though his derogatory view of women still extended to Agnes. He continued his career of sobriety, helping his mother with her new-found business interests in winding up his father's tangled affairs. In early 1922 he accompanied his mother to Los Angeles, California, to look after her real estate holdings there. She had been suffering from headaches, later believed to be the result of a brain tumor, and while there she had a stroke, finally dying in February 1922. Just before her death, and unable to cope with the situation, Jamie resumed his compulsive drinking and took up with a woman to whom he apparently promised some of Ella's effects. It seems that his mother was aware of his drinking at the last, if one can trust the recollection of those who were with her at the time. The story of his drunken railroad journey from Los Angeles to New York seeking solace from a fifty-dollar-a-day prostitute in his drawing room, while Ella O'Neill's coffin was "in the baggage car ahead" has been told by O'Neill in A Moon for the Misbegotten.* But the reality seems to have been even more appalling. Somehow Ella O'Neill's jewelry had disappeared; Jamie remembered nothing and arrived too drunk to collect the coffin. He was also unable to attend the funeral, being in a drunken stupor.

From now on, the final disaster was just a matter of time. He continued to drink away his portion of Ella O'Neill's estate, and, as he had earlier put it, "the boys from Brooklyn are coming over the bridge." He was suffering from delirium tremens. For a time he moved in with Harold DePolo, a mutual friend of the O'Neill brothers, in Darien, Connecticut. He continued his drinking there and in New London, and in February 1923 he made an outrageous public spectacle of himself during a performance by a touring company of "Anna Christie"* in Stamford, Connecticut. In June of that same year he was taken (allegedly in a strait jacket) to a sanitarium in Norwich, Connecticut, and then to Riverlawn Sanitarium, Paterson, New Jersey, where he continued to obtain liquor. By this time he was a physical and mental wreck, almost blind; after some days of lunacy he died of arteriosclerosis and cerebral apoplexy, obviously induced by chronic alcoholism, on November 8, 1923. Even at the last, ill fortune dogged him. Agnes Boulton, who represented Eugene O'Neill at the funeral, discovered to her horror that Jamie was to be buried in a cheap "undertaker's" half-suit in a plain pine coffin. She delayed the funeral an hour to arrange for a better one (Sheaffer, 1973, p. 117).

Jamie O'Neill seems to have led a totally wasted and self-destructive life, for whatever cause. Doris Alexander (1962) looks for a psychological interpretation: guilt over his brother's death, rage at his father for the addiction of his beloved mother, and jealousy of both father and brother. Eugene O'Neill also attributes some vengeful motivation to his brother in initiating him into the Broadway world. But whatever the reason, the pattern of his life began early. Agnes Boulton records that he believed he would be impotent by the age of forty and hence undesirable to the whores he frequented (1958, pp. 211–212). He had a low opinion of women and never married, so that with the death of his mother, his last anchor to reality was gone and he found himself committed to his own speedy death. In his younger days he had been handsome, charming, witty, and popular, with undoubted talent, but without a sense of responsibility. In later years O'Neill's attitude toward Jamie softened considerably as indicated by Josie Hogan's* pity for Jamie's equivalent in *A Moon for the Misbegotten*. O'Neill even used to recount some of Jamie's undeniably funny drunken escapades with some amusement. Crosswell Bowen (1959) believes that O'Neill's son, Shane Rudraighe O'Neill,* was affected by this nostalgic tolerance and patterned his own tragic life after that of his uncle. *See* in "References": Alexander (1962); Boulton (1958); Bowen (1959); Gelb and Gelb (1973); Sheaffer (1968, 1973, 1983).

O'NEILL, Kathleen. *See* Jenkins, Kathleen.

O'NEILL, Oona. *See* Chaplin, Oona O'Neill.

O'NEILL, Shane Rudraighe (1919–1977). Son of Eugene O'Neill and his second wife, Agnes Boulton*; brother of Oona O'Neill Chaplin.* Born in Provincetown, Massachusetts, October 30, 1919; died in Brooklyn, New York, June 23, 1977, as the result of a suicide attempt. The name is said to have been suggested to O'Neill by James Stephens, the Irish author, but O'Neill may well have chosen it himself because of his interest in his own distinguished family history. The original Shane O'Neill, nicknamed "Shane the Proud," led diplomatic and military opposition in Ireland (1558–1567) against the government of Queen Elizabeth I. He was one of the last of the great Gaelic chieftains and uncle of Hugh O'Neill, Earl of Tyrone, who also led a rebellion against Queen Elizabeth (1598–1603). (See also *Long Day's Journey into Night*.) Educated at a series of schools, including Catholic schools in Bermuda and Point Pleasant, New Jersey; boarding school in Lenox, Massachusetts; the Lawrenceville School, New Jersey; Florida Military Academy; Ralston Creek School, Golden, Colorado; the Art Students League, New York. Married Catherine Givens, July 1944, by whom he had five children: Eugene O'Neill III* (died as an infant), Maura, Sheila, Ted, and Kathleen.

Shane O'Neill seems, even more than his half-brother, Eugene Gladstone O'Neill, Jr.,* to have been a highly sensitive person and as a result was more deeply affected, even destroyed, by his relationship to his famous father, whom he worshipped. All accounts of Shane's early life speak of him as a lonely yet singularly beautiful child brought up from his babyhood by his nurse, Mrs. Fifine Clark, his beloved "Gaga." Apparently there was some conflict between her and Agnes Boulton, who felt that the nurse had come between mother and child. At their varied residences in Provincetown, Peaked Hill Bars, Brook Farm (Ridgefield, Connecticut), Bermuda, Nantucket, and Belgrade Lakes (Maine),

Shane is spoken of as loving the solitary sport of fishing and enjoying swimming and boating. One of the few people who took an interest in the boy at Peaked Hill was the old anarchist Terry Carlin,* who played games with him and generally entertained him. O'Neill, however, was too occupied with his work to pay much attention, and since he needed complete quiet in order to write, he found children an annoyance. This was particularly marked during the summer of 1926 which was spent at Loon Lodge, Belgrade Lakes, Maine, when Oona was one year old and Eugene, Jr., and Barbara Burton, Agnes's daughter by her first marriage, were present. O'Neill grew so nervous at the presence of so many progeny that Agnes finally arranged for the construction of a separate shack so he could work in peace. All in all, O'Neill seems to have been distant from Shane, while the child desperately sought approval and emotional commitment from his father.

When O'Neill separated from Agnes in 1927, Shane seems to have been particularly disturbed, additionally so because Mrs. Clark had had to return to Provincetown because of illness, and he was now doubly bereft. O'Neill wrote fairly frequently to Shane, assuring the boy of his love yet at the same time using a letter to the child to convey misinformation. He said he was going to Pasadena to help with rehearsals of *Lazarus Laughed** while in fact he and Carlotta Monterey* were planning a trip to Europe. Then, after his illness in Shanghai, O'Neill used a letter to convey to Shane the message that he no longer felt any bitterness toward anyone. By this time Agnes was living with Oona and Shane in Old House, West Point Pleasant, New Jersey, and Mrs. Clark was once more with them. However, just before Agnes went to Reno to secure her divorce, Shane was sent in 1928 to boarding school in Lenox, Massachusetts, where he was so desperately unhappy that he was brought home. Shortly afterward, Mrs. Clark died while Agnes was still in Reno, and the child felt more lost. He was then at parochial school in Point Pleasant. He also took odd jobs connected with boats around Point Pleasant, making a little pocket money. He continued to write to his father, but correspondence began to languish as O'Neill worked on *Mourning Becomes Electra*,* though he did not forget his children's birthdays.

In the fall of 1931 Shane entered the Lawrenceville School at the early age of twelve. He had needed some tutoring to prepare him for the rigorous curriculum of the school, which Agnes had chosen both for its reputation and its geographical location reasonably close to Point Pleasant. He might not have been accepted had he been other than the playwright's son. At Lawrenceville, Shane's natural shyness seemed to lead to great insecurity, and his academic performance suffered accordingly. O'Neill was by now married to Carlotta, who began to assume responsibility for correspondence other than that related to her husband's work. She refused Shane's request for tickets to *Mourning Becomes Electra* and similarly refused to pass on a letter from a concerned Lawrenceville master asking O'Neill to counsel his son. Shane's academic performance at Lawrenceville was not good, and Agnes sent him to Florida Military Academy in 1934 where his marks improved, he edited the school newspaper, learned how to drink, and ceased going to church.

Shane had seen his father only briefly since the divorce, twice during the summer of 1931, once with Oona, a meeting that was rather unsuccessful. Apparently they did not spend significant time together until the summer of 1936 when Shane visited with O'Neill and Carlotta at Casa Genotta, Sea Island, Georgia. Apparently he enjoyed himself but did not get close to his father, while Carlotta spoke of her displeasure at having to write letters of courtesy to him and Oona because their father was too busy. Shortly after this visit, O'Neill and Carlotta moved to the West Coast.

In his senior year, Shane was sent by his mother to the Ralston Creek School, Golden, Colorado, so that he could improve his grades and perhaps obtain admission to Yale. He did well in the fall but suffered a great falling away by Christmas. In February of 1938, Shane began to consider giving up the idea of university to adopt ranch life, something Agnes did not wish O'Neill to encourage. In April 1938, Shane visited O'Neill and Carlotta at Tao House, their first meeting in over a year. Once again relations between father and son were somewhat distant, Shane wanting advice and not receiving it. He spoke of becoming a writer, but his father discouraged him, while Carlotta emphasized the importance of going to university and studying hard in order to achieve economic independence. The following September, Shane left Ralston and reentered Lawrenceville but was dropped for poor academic performance at the end of the winter term. He had done well only in art, where he drew pictures of horses. The following spring he took courses at the Art Students' League in New York City, dividing his time between New York and Point Pleasant. He visited Tao House again that summer and showed his drawings to his father, who agreed that he did have some talent. He also proposed enrolling in a veterinary course preparatory to starting his own horse ranch, something that his father discouraged. On the whole, the trip was not a success, except for visits to the San Francisco exposition in the company of the O'Neill chauffeur.

Back in New York, Shane began frequenting Greenwich Village bars and took up with a young painter named Margaret Stark, visiting Tao House briefly again in the summer of 1940. Again O'Neill kept insisting that Shane ought to become independent, suggesting that he might use his talent for drawing in ship design. Now twenty-one, Shane decided he should try to make some money and took a series of odd jobs as a carpenter's helper, and in 1940 he worked as a painter of stage flats for Cleon Throckmorton, while trying to write. In December 1940 he toured with Marc Brandel to Mexico, a trip which degenerated into a great deal of drinking and Shane's initial experiment with marijuana. Running out of money, he was helped out first by O'Neill and then by Agnes, his mother. On his return he moved into the apartment rented by Marc Brandel in Greenwich Village, and the two divided their time between New York and Point Pleasant where Brandel helped Agnes with her novel and Shane worked the charter boats. He and Brandel then took jobs as civilian employees for the U.S. Navy and took out seaman's papers just after Pearl Harbor. Shane was by this time experimenting more regularly with marijuana and continuing to see Margaret Stark. In March 1942, Shane began the first of a series of voyages, sometimes in dangerous waters, and began to drink heavily. He is also said to have become addicted to morphine at that time through raiding emergency medical supplies. He made his last voyage in the fall of 1943, returning in a highly nervous state, suffering from shock, drinking too heavily, and attempting suicide on two occasions by leaving the gas jets on. He began to see a psychiatrist but soon ceased. He continued to use marijuana and broke up with Ms. Stark in 1944. His half-brother, Eugene O'Neill, Jr., was by this time also living in Greenwich Village, and the two renewed their sketchy acquaintance, which placed Eugene, Jr., in the role of advice giver and Shane as listener.

On July 31, 1944, Shane married in a civil ceremony in Norwalk, Connecticut. His bride, Catherine Givens, a young woman from Connecticut, was living in Greenwich Village and working as a saleswoman, while Shane was working for a window display company. Two impractical people married each other in this case, and for a time they drifted from one temporary place to another. In early 1945 they visited Agnes and Oona in Hollywood, returning to Greenwich Village in the spring, where they took back their apartment from Eugene, Jr., who took another in the same building. Shane saw his father for the first time in five years just before the birth of Eugene O'Neill III on November 19, 1945. Carlotta visited Cathy in the hospital and in their cold-water flat in the Village, and later the younger couple visited with the O'Neills. During that winter Shane saw his father frequently, but when the baby died at the age of just under three months, probably of Sudden Infant Death Syndrome, Eugene O'Neill did not attend the funeral of his first grandson. Allegations of child neglect were made, particularly by Carlotta.

After this they went to Bermuda for a vacation at Agnes's expense (deducted from her alimony by O'Neill), and stayed in a cottage on the grounds of Spithead for four months. When they returned they were not immediately able to get work, and when, after a great deal of difficulty, Cathy found the O'Neill telephone number, Carlotta indicated that O'Neill did not wish to see them. However, O'Neill did arrange to have a doctor examine Shane when he was ill, but unfortunately, the doctor mistook a friend for Shane, much to O'Neill's annoyance at what he saw as a deliberate hoax. He did not again communicate with his son (Sheaffer, 1973, p. 567).

During the winter of 1945, Shane's health began to deteriorate noticeably; he was depressed, drinking, and taking marijuana, if not something stronger. In 1947 Agnes settled her accounts with O'Neill and arranged for the sale of a part of the Spithead property, the proceeds of which were divided equally between Shane and Oona, about nine thousand dollars apiece. Oona gave her share to Agnes, who had recently married "Mack" Kaufman and moved to Hollywood with her ailing mother. After her departure, Shane became almost pathologically depressed, and he and Cathy moved to Florida, where his second child was born.

They returned to New York in early Spring 1948, and during that season and early summer he developed a large and costly addiction to heroin in the amount of about thirty dollars per day. For him, the prosecution of this habit had become a purpose for existence. On August 10, 1948, while trying to make a purchase, he was arrested for possession of three capsules of heroin and sent to jail. Despite requests made by Cathy and a friend, O'Neill refused to make bail, and Eugene, Jr., said he did not have sufficient funds. Accordingly, Shane was indicted while undergoing the trauma of being removed from drugs "cold turkey." The case was heard on August 20, 1948, and he was given a two-year suspended sentence on condition that he go to the federal hospital, Lexington, Kentucky, for no less than four months or until cured. Needless to say, Shane was bitter that no one had made bail, but he went to Kentucky, in accordance with the court ruling, and was discharged as cured after six months.

On his return, he and his wife and child went to Bermuda, staying two years, first with Agnes and "Mack" Kaufman at Spithead and then in a small cottage where Shane's third child was born. Back at Spithead, Shane was in a bad way, drinking heavily and smoking marijuana. In June 1951 he returned to New York, possibly to avoid a proposed Bermuda newspaper article on the Spithead "pot" parties. However, he did not send any funds back to Cathy, who was forced to sell the contents of Spithead, which included some of the effects of Ella Quinlan O'Neill,* Shane's grandmother, to a second-hand dealer. Spithead was finally sold in 1961, and Agnes and Shane divided the proceeds. Meanwhile, Cathy had joined her mother in Florida where in early 1952 a fourth child was born. They returned to New York where they stayed through the rest of the year, moving into Old House, West Point Pleasant, in late winter because they were again penniless. Shane was registered there as a convicted narcotics addict, though he declared that he no longer used drugs. He began to spend his time shuttling between New York and Point Pleasant, even being picked up by police and sent to Bellevue because of his confused condition and aimless wandering in Manhattan.

When O'Neill died in 1953, Shane, like Oona, was purposely excluded from his father's will, a situation which was no surprise to him. He continued to live in Point Pleasant, occasionally getting odd jobs but unable to hold them because of his eccentric behavior. On one occasion he was arrested for disorderly conduct, possibly the result of too much benzedrine. His fifth child was born in February 1955, and by then the family was living in an apartment in Point Pleasant, Agnes having returned to Old House. At this low ebb in their fortunes, Cathy received a windfall trust fund of sixty thousand dollars which was left to her as the result of her mother's murder by her fourth husband.

In 1956, Shane was sentenced to twenty days in the Ocean County jail as a disorderly person. Since he seemed in very poor physical condition and was now addicted to benzedrine, he was committed to Ancora State Hospital. There he was given medical treatment. His health improved, and, having been informed that he must keep away from drugs, he was released on September 12, 1956.

He went to the house in Point Pleasant which Cathy had bought with her inheritance. In 1959 he was again arrested and jailed in Perth Amboy as a disorderly person, and in 1961 he was briefly jailed on charges, later dismissed, of "neglecting to provide proper support for his children." In 1962 he was arrested in Greenwich Village for possession of narcotics and in 1967 jumped from the second floor of a police station where he had been taken on a similar charge.

After the death of Carlotta O'Neill in 1970, Shane and Oona had shared royalties from *A Moon for the Misbegotten*,* which provided Shane with financial security because Oona gave him her share. The two also shared royalties with Yale University from sundry other O'Neill plays, as the result of a quirk in the copyright laws. Again Oona is said to have given her share to her brother.

Perhaps this newfound independence explains why Shane O'Neill drops from sight insofar as published reports of drug or alcohol offenses are concerned. At some point he separated from his wife and died in circumstances that appear to have been drug or alcohol related. On June 22, 1977, he jumped from the fourth-floor apartment of a woman friend with whom he had been having an argument shortly before midnight. He died in Coney Island Hospital the next day. At the time he was said to be living in New York City. So completely was his existence forgotten by journalists that no obituary appeared in the *New York Times* until December 7, 1977, and even then it was a sketchy one. *See* in "References": Alexander (1962); Boulton (1958); Bowen (1959); Gelb and Gelb (1973); Sheaffer (1973).

"ON TO BETELGEUSE," preliminary title of "It Cannot be Mad."* This was planned as the third part of the uncompleted trilogy "Myth-Plays for the God-Forsaken."* The two completed plays were *Dynamo** and *Days Without End.** The material proposed for the third part passed through several titles: "On to Hercules," "The Life of Bessie Bowen" (or Bolan, or Bowlan). It was then planned for inclusion in "Twilight of Possessors, Self-Dispossessed" later titled "Hair of the Dog,"* the last play of the abandoned cycle "A Tale of Possessors, Self-Dispossessed."* In February 1943, O'Neill finally became convinced of the intractability of this material and destroyed the longhand draft. It concerned the automobile industry.

"ON TO HERCULES," a second preliminary title for "It Cannot Be Mad."* *See also*: "On to Betelgeuse,"* "The Life of Bessie Bowen,"* "Hair of the Dog,"* and "A Tale of Possessors, Self-Dispossessed."*

O'ROURKE. In "The Personal Equation,"* a big red-headed stoker. In an offstage fight he knocks out Schmidt,* a German fellow stoker on the S.S. *San Francisco*. He takes part in the attempt to sabotage the engines of the vessel. As in the later *The Hairy Ape*,* O'Neill includes a number of different ethnic groups in his portrait of the stokehole.

OVIEDO, Alonzo de. In *The Fountain*,* a swashbuckling young man. As the play progresses, he remains exactly the same in his ambitious aims. He is the type of bold adventurer who went forth to conquer the new world for Spain and line his own pockets as well. His only advance is in cruelty.

OWEN, Marthy. In *"Anna Christie,"** the live-in companion of Chris Christopherson* on his coal barge. She is about forty or fifty with a "jowly, mottled face, with its thick, gray hair piled anyhow in a greasy mop on top of her round head." She is flabby and fat, speaking "in a loud, mannish voice, punctuated by explosions of hoarse laughter." She has some teeth missing and breathes wheezily, but somehow her eyes indicate that she has retained a lusty, gusty attitude toward life. She is dressed in a man's cap and jacket, "grimy calico skirt," and oversize men's brogans. She is a variation on the character of the prostitute with a heart of gold, but she insists that Anna Christopherson* is wrong in her assessment: "You're me, forty years later." She quite willingly leaves the barge when Anna appears and takes a great deal of trouble to inform Anna that her father Chris is "as good an old guy as ever walked on two feet." She obviously has affection for Chris, but she has been buffeted about by life long enough to realize that nothing is permanent.

She also appears in the two earlier versions of *"Anna Christie,"* and her physical description remains constant throughout. In *Chris Christophersen*,* she is first discovered on board the coal barge, and she seems to have anticipated Chris's wish to be rid of her; and, as in the later drafts, they part friends. One interesting little touch which appears only in *Chris Christophersen*, however, is that as Marthy passes Anna on her way off the barge, she pretends to be a saleswoman of seafaring goods in order to save Chris from embarrassment.

In *"The Ole Davil"** her role is increased to almost the same extent as in *"Anna Christie."* She is now the expository figure who is used to explain to Anna what kind of person Chris actually is. This situation indicates the change between the two versions. The bar room banter exposition has been greatly reduced, and Marthy is used for this purpose, informing both the audience and Anna of Chris's past and his good qualities. With the change in Anna's social class and profession, O'Neill can now bring the two women together in conversation, and Anna can also use the occasion for an account of her own past. Marthy is obviously a "Tugboat Annie" type of character, as Frances Marion clearly realized when she wrote the movie version (*see* Appendix B) and insisted on Marie Dressler for the role.

P

PADDY [Meehan]. In "Tomorrow,"* O'Neill's only published short story, the deepwater sailor. He, Lyons,* and Art* (the Eugene O'Neill character) frequently get drunk together. They are roomers in the saloon of "Tommy-the-Priest," which is really the saloon of James J. Condon,* "Jimmy-the-Priest,"* at 252 Fulton Street near the old Washington Market. This story contains elements of the later play, *The Iceman Cometh.**

PADDY. In *The Moon of the Caribbees*,* a seaman on the S.S. *Glencairn*, "a squat, ugly Liverpool Irishman," who is wounded in the melee. See also *The Hairy Ape*,* and Driscoll.*

PADDY. In *The Hairy Ape*,* a wizened Irishman given to dreaming of the past and continually recalling the lost days of sail when man and the sea were one. See also Driscoll,* Paddy* of the S.S. *Glencairn** plays, and *Children of the Sea.**

PARRITT, Don. In *The Iceman Cometh*,* eighteen-year-old son of Rosa Parritt, the former lover of Larry Slade.* He is a good-looking, gangly, blonde young man with an unpleasant personality: "There is a shifting defiance and ingratiation in his light-blue eyes and an irritating aggressiveness in his manner." He is a recent addition to the roomers above the saloon operated by Harry Hope.* Parritt has just come from the West Coast where his mother has been arrested for complicity in a bombing incident on information given by someone inside "the Movement." He has come to seek out Larry Slade, his mother's former lover, whom he remembers as the only person in the movement who treated him well. In fact, Don once suggests that Larry might be his father, an assertion the older man, now disenchanted with anarchism, vehemently denies, but the truth remains ambiguous.

Don is an abrasive personality who does not seem to belong among the hopeless misfits in the saloon, partly because of his new clothes and his possession of a considerable amount of money, which he is not ready to spend treating others to a drink. He sneers constantly at Larry, maintaining that despite his protestations of being through with the Movement, he still cares greatly for it. Larry, in turn, wonders how Parritt has managed to elude the police he claims are looking for him. When Theodore Hickman,* the salesman who comes to the bar annually to celebrate Harry Hope's birthday, meets Parritt, he detects some subliminal similarity between them. This later becomes clear when Hickey reveals that he has killed his wife. Parritt, who has been excessively concerned with the fate of his mother in prison—"she's always been so free"—finally confesses that he is the informer who is responsible for her arrest, and his reason is the same as Hickey's: "I don't give a damn about the money. It was because I hated her." This statement is echoed by Hickey's confession just before he is arrested.

Left in the bar room with the rest of Harry Hope's companions, Larry has a wish for Hickey, "May the Chair bring him peace at last, the poor tortured bastard," a comment which brings Parritt to a full confession of his guilt in his mother's imprisonment. "It was the tart the detective agency got after me who put it in my mind," but, like Hickey, he realizes that he, too, has been full of hate. His mother has made all the decisions: "She doesn't like anyone to be free but herself." And now he is utterly guilty of her betrayal, and "You're the only one who can understand how guilty I am.... Because she is dead and yet she has to live. But she can't last long in jail," and he will live in guilt knowing that she will never have any peace knowing what he has done to her. Then, in total despair, he blurts out the hatred that led to his betrayal: "You know what you can do with your freedom pipe dream now, you damned old bitch!" This statement brings Larry to take a judgmental stance, "Go! Get the hell out of life,...Before I choke it out of you! Go up—!" and his unfinished sentence recalls Parritt's sneer that Larry was too yellow to commit suicide, to "take that hop off the fire escape" he had always talked of. Larry's words seem to transform Parritt: "Thanks Larry. I just wanted to be sure. I can see now it's the only possible way I can ever get free of her." But even then he leaves with a jeer: "You know her, Larry! Always a ham!" As he walks out with a certain "dramatic bravado," he promises to buy Hugo a drink "Tomorrow! Beneath the willow trees." As the merriment in the bar increases, Larry sits alone listening for the inevitable, the sound of a falling body which passes almost unnoticed in the noise of revelry from those trying to forget and to regain illusions.

The character of Don Parritt may be based on that of Don Vose, who informed on the anarchists in the McNamara Case of 1910 which concerned the bombing of the *Los Angeles Times*. Rosa Parritt is based on the character of Emma Goldman.

PASATIERI, Thomas (1945–   ), composer. Born in New York, October 20, 1945. Educated on Long Island and at the Juilliard School of Music, to which he was awarded a scholarship at the age of sixteen, gaining the first doctorate for composition offered by the institution. His composition teachers there were Vittorio Giannini and Vincent Persichetti; he also worked with Darius Milhaud at Aspen, Colorado.

Pasatieri has proved a very prolific composer of orchestral and vocal works but has devoted himself particularly to opera, frequently acting as his own librettist and adapting literary works to this genre. His operas include: *The Women* (1965), *La Divina* (1966), *Padrevia* (1967, after Boccaccio), *Calvary* (1971, libretto from W. B. Yeats), *The Trial of Mary Lincoln* (1972, television opera with libretto by A. H. Bailey), *Black Widow* (1972, after Miguel de Unamuno), *The Seagull* (1974, libretto by K. Elmslie after Anton Chekhov), *Signor Deluso* (1974, after Molière's Sganarelle), *The Penitentes* (1974, libretto by A. H. Bailey), *Inez de Castro* (1976, libretto by B. Stambler), *Washington Square* (1976, libretto by K. Elmslie after Henry James), *Before Breakfast* (1981, after Eugene O'Neill [*see* Appendix B]).

This last opera was presented at the New York State Theatre by the New York City Opera and was not well received. The libretto has little relationship to O'Neill's play, the woman being portrayed as a former marathon dancer, and performing a jazz sequence. It seems to have been designed in conscious comparison to François Poulenc's *La Voix Humaine*. Pasatieri is considered to be a traditional "neo-romantic" composer whose work is often likened to that of Gian Carlo Menotti.

PAUL, a seaman on the S.S. *Glencairn*, a Norwegian who plays the accordion; appears in all the shipboard plays of the S.S. *Glencairn** group.

PAYNE, Captain Enoch. In the scenario of *The Calms of Capricorn*,* husband of Nancy Drummond Payne* and captain of the clipper ship *Dream of the West*. He is in his sixties, a man of average height, "solid and imposing," with white hair, giving an impression of conservatism; he is greatly in love with his wife who has traveled on the ship with him for the past five years since their child died. He is a seaman of the old school, cautious, and careful of both his ship and his passengers. For this reason he is dubious about temporarily promoting Ethan Harford* to the position of first mate because he is aware of Ethan's desire to break a record no matter what the cost. The current first mate, Thomas Hull,* has been advised to remain ashore for this voyage in order to recuperate from a heart attack, so the position is vacant. Payne is relieved when Hull returns to make the voyage, and so he demotes Ethan; but when Hull dies as the result of a fall (and a blow by Ethan), he is forced to promote him. Nonetheless, he is concerned, noting that both of Ethan's promotions have come as the result of "accidents." Slowly he begins to realize that Ethan and Nancy are in love, and wonders whether they would like to see him dead. One day he falls down the companionway, and for a moment both Ethan and Nancy consider murder, but then they think better of it. Nancy penitently nurses him, and Ethan, an honorable man to a certain extent, does not go to bed with her. Payne finally asks Ethan directly whether he has slept with Nancy and is relieved to get a negative answer. However, as the ship remains becalmed, nerves fray; the crew and the gold-seekers on board demand that Payne, the "Jonah," resign his command to Ethan, who refuses to accept it. Finally the strain is too much for Ethan, who picks up a pillow to smother the sleeping captain, but Nancy enters and commits the murder herself. Reverend Samuel Dickey,* a minister and passenger, officiates at the funeral service and almost immediately after at the wedding of Ethan and Nancy, almost like a double ceremony.

PAYNE, Nancy Drummond. In the scenario of *The Calms of Capricorn,* wife of Captain Enoch Payne* of the clipper ship *Dream of the West*. She is thirty-eight, pretty, with "brown hair,...[and] big brown eyes...shy, bashful, reserved, gentle." At the beginning of the scenario, she shows great respect for her sixty-year-old husband. She has been going to sea with him since the death of her son some five years ago and says that the clipper is now home to her. She has fallen in love with Ethan Harford,* son of Sara Melody* Harford and Simon Harford,* the second mate of the ship, but realizes that the twenty-eight-year-old man has no chance of advancement. She suggests to Sara that Ethan be encouraged to find another ship, but he does not. When the entire Harford family embarks on the *Dream of the West*, Ethan has been temporarily promoted to first mate because his predecessor, Thomas Hull,* is expected to remain ashore to recuperate from a heart attack. However, Hull does not, and in a fit of anger Ethan accidentally kills him. By keeping quiet and cooperating with Leda Cade,* Nancy becomes an accessory after the fact. Now she wishes that her "old fool" of a husband would die, and almost in answer to her wish, he falls and is hurt. Momentarily both Ethan and Nancy consider helping him to die, but they then think better of it. Nancy nurses him with despairing devotion until she finally decides she can wait no longer to go to bed with Ethan. She returns to her husband's cabin to find Ethan about to smother him with a pillow. She grabs it from him and commits the murder herself. The two are married instantly, but their love becomes poisoned by their sense of guilt. Their crime seems to have prevented Ethan's chance of making a speed record into San Francisco because the elements have become hostile. Finally they realize that they must expiate their sins, and Nancy believes that hell in the company of Ethan will be all the heaven she would ever want. Accordingly, they both jump into the sea near Golden Gate.

Since this is only a scenario, motivations are sketchy, but Nancy is brought to gratify her desires with Ethan through murder as a result of her relationship with the prostitute Leda Cade, a passenger on the vessel and the embodiment of feminine emotion and intuition.

PEARL. In *The Moon of the Caribbees,* a West Indian negress. "The youngest and prettiest" of the women, she is first seen with Yank's* arm about her waist, but she chooses Smitty,* the "gentleman," and tries unsuccessfully to attach herself to him.

PEARL. In *The Iceman Cometh*,* a dollar streetwalker, just over twenty years old. She and Margie* are whores who are run by Rocky Pioggi* and are roomers at Harry Hope's* saloon. They both have the remains of youthful freshness. Pearl is stereotypically Italian in appearance and is "sentimental, feather-brained, giggly, lazy, good-natured and reasonably contented with life." Her pipe dream is that she is a "tart," not a whore, and her attitude toward Rocky, who insists he is a bartender, not a pimp, is that of a sister "toward a bullying brother." Under the influence of Theodore Hickman,* the salesman who comes to the bar annually to celebrate Harry's birthday, the girls finally admit they are whores, treat Rocky like a pimp, then go on strike and take the day off to visit Coney Island. After Hickey's arrest on the charge of murdering his wife, they, along with other denizens of the bar, seize on his plea of insanity, a pipe-dream explanation which discredits what he has taught them, and then gladly get drunk in order to forget the outside world and to regain illusions.

PEDRO. In *The Fountain*,* servant to Juan Ponce de Leon.*

PERKINS, Thomas. In "The Personal Equation"* father of Tom Perkins.* He is a short, awkward, bespectacled man in late middle age, has a timid voice, and is partially bald with straggly gray hair. He is the second engineer of the S.S. *San Francisco*, a rank he has held for thirty years. He totally lacks self-assertiveness and since the death of his wife has devoted himself entirely to the care of his engines, which he loves. When Perkins discovers that the stokers are about to sabotage the engines of the vessel, he threatens them with a revolver and shoots the first man who touches them. The man he injures is his own son, Tom, who has shipped as a stoker on the ship but is really an activist for the International Workers of the Earth. He thought he had aimed over Tom's head, but in fact he has inflicted such massive brain injuries that the young man will probably remain a vegetable. The company which owns the ship sees Perkins as a hero and gives him a gold watch and offers him a promotion. The company also denies the relationship between Perkins and his son and assures Perkins that Tom is sure to recover. In remorse, Perkins pays for Tom's private hospital room. When he returns to Liverpool after his next transatlantic crossing, Perkins is shocked to discover that his company has lied to him. He has also decided to forego the promotion and now intends to look after Tom himself, with the help of Mrs. Allen,* his long-time housekeeper. Olga Tarnoff,* a young revolutionary and Tom's mistress, also wishes to take care of Tom, feeling remorse that she led him into this situation. Perkins and Olga argue but are reconciled when Olga reveals her pregnancy and threatens to kill her unborn child if she cannot take care of Tom. Perkins will take her and the child to live with him as well. He is a scarcely drawn character, but his devotion to his engines prefigures the extraordinary attachment felt by Reuben Light* to the dynamo in O'Neill's later play of that name, *Dynamo*.*

PERKINS, Tom. In "The Personal Equation,* a healthy-looking young man in his twenties, over six feet tall and "handsome in a rough, manly, strong-featured way." He is the lover of Olga Tarnoff,* who follows her commitment to the cause of the International Workers of the Earth. His father, Thomas Perkins,* is the second engineer of the S.S. *San Francisco*, a man in love with his engines who has refused a promotion in order to stay on his ship. Tom despises his father as a spineless worker for the capitalists. Tom is a most active unionist and is fired from his job in the Ocean Steamship Company, for which his father works, for his activities. He is happy to take on the task of damaging the engines of one of the company's vessels, even when he discovers that it is his father's ship. Tom had one year of college, but was radicalized by doing one round trip as a stoker, and so he is suitably qualified for the task laid on him by Hartmann,* the union activist. Tom, under the false papers of Fred [later Tom in the text] Donovan, becomes a stoker on the S.S. *San Francisco* and attempts to destroy the boat's engines so that it cannot leave Liverpool Harbor. Tom tries to safeguard his father from harm; but when Perkins sees Tom attempting to sabotage his beloved engines, he shoots him in the head. Perkins is devastated because he thought he had aimed high. As a result of the wound, Tom becomes almost a vegetable and can do nothing except mimic the words of Olga. She and Perkins argue over who will take care of Tom, but when Olga reveals her pregnancy, Perkins agrees to take her into his house as well. They will both care for Tom, hoping that there is a glimmer of possibility that Tom will recover. The play ends on a note of tremendous irony as Olga delivers a passionate endorsement of the revolutionary cause, and Tom imbecilically echoes her: "Long Live the Revolution!"

"PERSONAL EQUATION, THE," unproduced and unpublished play in four acts and five scenes.

Act I: Hoboken, New Jersey, the main room of the offices of the International Workers of the Earth on a dark evening. Two gas lights provide harsh illumination. The furniture consists of a small table with a typewriter on the right, and a long table center with newspapers and magazines. The walls are covered with cartoons and a picture of naked Liberty at the rear between two windows. Olga Tarnoff,* a young woman with dark hair and eyes, a strong face, and slender figure, is reading a newspaper at the table. She and Enwright,* a "thin, round-shouldered, middle aged, clean-shaven [man who] wears glasses," discuss the comments in the socialist newspaper while they wait for Tom and Hartmann.* Enwright is dubious about Tom's commitment to the cause, wondering whether it is the result of love for Olga, curiosity, or what, because he seems too much of an intellectual.

After Enwright has left, Tom Perkins* enters, a healthy-looking young man of over six feet, in his early twenties, "handsome in a rough, manly, strong-featured way" with a manner that combines naiveté and enthusiasm. He kisses Olga, and the three of them wait for Hartmann, wondering why he has summoned them. Olga thinks he wishes to talk about the forthcoming dock and firemen's strike which is being planned secretly. She reads an unflattering account of the speeches both of them gave in Union Square, New York, the previous Saturday. She is being billed as an anarchist in the socialist press when she is really a pacifist, while Tom is excoriated as a college boy. Actually he has spent only a year in college. His attitude toward Olga is most chivalric, and Olga scoffs at that. Clearly they are in love and are living together, though unmarried, and they discuss the implications of this choice. Olga is opposed to marriage, seeing it as a mode of enslaving women; she wishes to assert her freedom. But Tom is concerned about the possibility of their having children. Olga says she would "die first." Again they embrace. Enwright returns, but Hartmann has still not come.

Tom tells Olga and Enwright that he has lost his job as assistant cashier of the Ocean Steamship Company because he was caught distributing leaflets on board the S.S. *San Francisco*, on which his own father is second engineer. He plans to inform his father this evening when they meet for dinner. Tom despises his father as spineless, always afraid of losing his job, and lacking in ambition: "Thirty years in the same little rut—and contented!" He is so lacking in assertiveness that no one thinks of promoting him, and he will never ask; his chief virtue is that he really loves his ship and its engines.

Hartmann enters, a short man in his early forties with long black hair brushed back in artist style. He is dressed in black with a white shirt and a "flowing black Windsor tie." His head seems too big for his short body, and he wears thick-rimmed glasses to counter his myopia. He has a black mustache and imperial. He apologizes for his tardiness and says that he has been discussing the forthcoming European war with the union executive. Olga suggests that a general strike be declared against war, a suggestion that Hartmann ridicules, saying that the workers will march off as they always do. Enwright suggests that war might kill off "the unenlightened" and therefore war should be encouraged. Olga asks what will happen to women in the event of war, and Hartmann says they will revert to their earlier state of inequality. She protests but looks forward to a possible surplus of women after the cessation of hostilities.

Hartmann's real topic is the forthcoming dock and firemen's strike. Since the Ocean Steamship Company has been selected as the first target, Hartmann is glad that Tom has been dismissed and that he is prepared to do "anything" for the cause. Tom once did a round-trip voyage as a stoker, and that experience has radicalized him. Hartmann's plan is for Tom to ship as a stoker and strike a blow against the shipping cartel through its leader, the Ocean Steamship Company. Tom is to call himself Fred Donovan, and papers are already available for him under that name. On his arrival in Liverpool he is to get in touch with Whitely,* the only honest member of the Liverpool group—the others are really working with the shipping companies. Whitely will procure some dynamite for Tom, who will use it to destroy the ship's engines. The idea is to give confidence to the men so that they will strike when the company retaliates; this is to be the

first of such assaults against the shipping cartel. Tom asks the name of the vessel
that has been chosen and to his shock learns that it is the S.S. *San Francisco*,
his father's ship. However, he says he will go through with the job and make
sure he does it when his father is ashore. Hartmann is momentarily afraid that
Tom will tell his father but is reassured when Tom expresses his determination.

Act II: Jersey City, the living room of Thomas Perkins's home. He is a short,
awkward, bespectacled man in late middle age with a timid voice and is partially
bald with straggly gray hair. He is wearing cheap, ill-fitting clothes and carpet
slippers. He is playing cards with Henderson,* the ship's engineer, a tall, thin
Scot. The living room is crammed with cheap, mass-produced furniture. Perkins
and Henderson are arguing about their bets; Perkins is unable to concentrate
because his son Tom is late and has kept Mrs. Allen's* dinner waiting. Mrs.
Allen, Perkins's long-time housekeeper, castigates Perkins and Henderson for
drinking and then goes on to complain about Tom's attitude toward his father—
the result of too much education. She speaks of Tom's failure to drop by ever
since he got a job and a girl. Perkins asks the name of Tom's girlfriend and says
he likes the name Olga, clearly not understanding the situation and looking
forward to their marriage. Mrs. Allen is about to tell all, but Henderson manages
to shut her up. Left alone, the two men discuss their ship over scotch and water.
Henderson plans to leave after this coming trip and gain employment in the
marine works in Liverpool. Perkins is sad because the two have worked together
for over twenty years, and he discusses his own lack of assertiveness and his
love of his engines. Now that Henderson is leaving, Perkins may stay on board
his ship permanently with the engines that he has come to love like friends ever
since the death of his wife. As a result, he hardly knows Tom but he will be
happy to give him this house when he marries because it is now free and clear.
Suddenly he remembers that the head of the shipping company had said something
to him about Tom and his involvement with the International Workers of the
Earth.

At this moment, Tom enters "with careless indifference" to apologize for his
tardiness. Left alone with his father after the departure of Mrs. Allen and Henderson, Perkins tells him about his friend's plan to leave the sea. With heavy
irony Tom mocks his father's love for his engines *and* the shipping company.
The two spar verbally, Perkins eagerly suggesting that his son and Olga move
into this house. Tom is surprised at his father's broadmindedness, but Perkins
is shocked when he hears that Tom and Olga are not yet married. Innocently,
Perkins thinks that this unconventional arrangement was what the shipping company official had meant regarding Tom's "involvement" with the International
Workers, but Tom reveals that he is a member of the union and is so committed
that he would obey an order to dynamite the engines of the S.S. *San Francisco*.
Perkins is horrified and says he would not allow that. Tom pretends that he has
been joking, but he tries to force his father to see what a rotten company he
works for, attacking him for his "servile fidelity" to a bunch of "crooked
capitalists" who run the shipping cartel. Perkins is also shocked at Tom's dis-

missal and is afraid that his own may follow. He offers to talk to the company if that would help his son, thinking that Tom would be rehired if he broke his ties with Olga and the union. He looks upon himself as a total failure and says he has looked to Tom to achieve success. Tom is furious at this and leaves.

Act III, Scene i: The firemen's forecastle on board the S.S. *San Francisco* in Liverpool, two weeks later at night. Three tiers of bunks with benches and portholes are visible. It is four bells, and stokers are sitting around or lying in their bunks, stripped to the waist or in their undershirts to gain relief from the heat. Tom is discovered at the center, smoking and staring in front of him. Other stokers in this scene represent a selection of different types and ethnic backgrounds: O'Rourke* is a big redhead; Cocky* is squat, broad-shouldered, and pasty-faced; Harris* is a wiry gray-haired man; Schmidt* is a giant German. All of them are talking about what will happen tonight. If the Union Officers back down while the officers are ashore at a company dinner, then Tom and the other stokers will take action. Only the mate and the second engineer are aboard, and they will be hopelessly outnumbered. Tom, after some difficulty, manages to get them to agree not to hurt the second engineer (his father, though his fellow stokers do not know it, given his alias of Fred Donovan). As Tom is trying to make his companions remember what Olga Tarnoff had said to them, Hogan* enters, very drunk, and insults Schmidt, who knocks him down. O'Rourke, Schmidt, and the others then go out to continue the fight while Hogan falls asleep.

Tom tramps up and down restlessly, and then Olga enters, dressed in dirty dungarees. Whitely has sent her to warn Tom that the strike is off because it would not be a patriotic action. Both Tom and Olga deride this sentiment, and Olga declares that she'll bring up their child "with a soul freed from all adorations of Gods and governments." Tom picks up this remark, but Olga says she is talking theoretically. Tom kisses her, and she goes on to tell him that Whitely will send the dynamite for Tom's use. Tom is concerned about getting his father out of the way, while Olga is worried about the danger of a premature explosion, suggesting that he should let Whitely do it. Tom disagrees and also notes that Olga seems changed. She says she thinks "everything is different now" and is unsure whether the action will have the effect Hartmann expects. Tom tells her that he is perfectly safe as long as no one squeals and that Whitely already has a safe place for him. Nonetheless, Olga remains unconvinced and breaks down, begging Tom to leave the job to Whitely, but she can't tell him the reason for her fear.

At this moment Whitely enters, "a swarthy, dark-eyed, bull-necked, powerfully built man" of about thirty-five. He announces that there will be no dynamiting because the man who had hidden the explosives has been arrested. Nonetheless, he wishes that there were some way to stop the S.S. *San Francisco* from sailing. Tom has a plan, but it means mutiny. The idea is to consolidate all the men under the International Workers as an umbrella organization rather than as a series of small unions. Whitely will stimulate a strike by telling the stokers that they have been betrayed by their union. Therefore, when the stokers return, O'Rourke having beaten Schmidt, who remains outside unconscious, Whitely tells them that the strike is off because their union leaders were bribed and that he, Whitely, has resigned as a result. (Suddenly O'Neill changes the name of "Fred Donovan.") He tells them to follow Tom Donovan. Some way must be found to prevent the vessel from sailing. Tom and the men decide to go to the stokehole, join with the other men there, and smash the engines. Olga tries to stay, but Tom refuses. He kisses her as the curtain falls.

Act III, Scene ii: The engine room of the S.S. *San Francisco*. Perkins, covered in grease, is looking over his beloved engines, continually cleaning them. He and Murphy* the mate, discuss them, comparing them favorably with those of another vessel. Perkins asks about the strike, wondering whether the men are content. Murphy says he is not a union member, and Perkins expresses his concern that some of the men might have been listening to inflammatory speeches in Liverpool. Obviously he is still concerned about his son. Jack, a youthful, fresh-faced apprentice, rushes in to announce that he has overheard Tom Donovan and a woman talking about dynamite, unions, and strikes, and reveals the plan to smash the engines. Perkins swears he'll never permit that to happen; he will stay with the engines. The chief engineer has left him a revolver for use in such an emergency. He sends Jack away to find the chief.

The stokers enter to find "old Molly Perkins" in the engine room. They threaten him, and he tries to stop them, begging them not to hurt the engines. Tom has sent O'Rourke to make sure that Perkins is not hurt, but the engineer brandishes his revolver. Tom enters with an iron bar, and Perkins seems to wither away. The mayhem begins, and Perkins points his revolver at the man who began the destruction, but Tom tries to protect his father. The men dislike this display of weakness, and in response to an ironic "Who is he—your old man?" Tom reveals the truth, begging his father to go on deck. Perkins refuses and points the revolver at the men, threatening to shoot the first man who damages the engines. Tom gets to work with his iron bar, and Perkins shoots him. Panic-stricken, the stokers leave. Olga enters to find an appalled Perkins saying, "I pointed it—over his head."

Act IV: A room in a private hospital in Liverpool, three weeks later. Tom is in a rocking chair in the white-painted room while his bed is being made. The nurse finishes her task and helps him back into bed. A doctor enters and discusses Tom's case with the nurse. He is permanently brain-damaged and has not spoken since the incident. No one even knows who he is. The tale that he was the son of Perkins has been discredited by both the shipping company and the second engineer, and they dismiss Tom's relationship with Olga Tarnoff as an example of "free love."

Olga and Whitely enter. She looks very ill and distraught. She calls Tom's name and then her own, telling him that she loves him. Tom merely mimics her: "Olga! Olga!" The doctor tells her that there is almost no hope of Tom's recovery. Olga has told the doctor she was engaged to Tom, but she had earlier told Whitely they were "just comrades." Now, left alone with Tom, she and Whitely are appalled to see him almost a vegetable. Olga announces her intention to take care of Tom, and they discuss Perkins's actions. He has received a promotion and a gold watch from the company for his bravery, and he has also paid for Tom's private room. There is no longer any mention of their relationship. War has now broken out, the "rotten fizzle" of violence of the S.S. *San Francisco* is now forgotten, and the attempted strike was a "fiasco." However, even Whitely is beginning to feel the stirrings of patriotism. Perkins is due in port this day; the company has hustled him away, telling him that Tom was certain to get well. Olga is filled with remorse because she had talked Tom into working for the International Workers, and "he followed blindly where I had led him." She says that Tom had stayed in the union only because he feared that she would have contempt for him. Whitely says that she would indeed have felt that, but Olga swears that she loves Tom.

Perkins arrives, sobbing, from his ship, appalled to discover that Tom's condition is permanent. Olga taxes him with denying his son, and Perkins says that he believed he had acted for the best and that Tom is the only thing he has ever loved. Olga deliberately adds to his anguish by saying, "You have your engines," but Perkins now says he hates them. Left alone with Tom, the father and Olga engage in a battle over who shall look after him. Perkins has refused his offered promotion and will live on shore in his house with Mrs. Allen as housekeeper. After all, as the young man's father he is sure to be awarded custody. Olga begs him to understand, and obviously each feels the need to make some reparation to Tom. Finally Olga reveals her pregnancy, threatening to kill the unborn child if she can't have Tom. In a scene of reconciliation, Perkins agrees to take Olga in as well. She agrees, and together they will try to help Tom, pinning their hopes on the unlikely possibility of recovery the doctor has mentioned. When Tom is well, then he and Olga can marry. Tom takes both their hands and appears to recognize them.

Whitely rushes in, complaining of the latest German atrocity and saying that he intends to enlist. To justify his decision he quotes anti-German sentiments uttered by other revolutionaries. Olga is shocked, and Whitely suggests that she ought now to hate the movement after what it has done to her life, but Olga delivers a passionate speech supporting the revolution, concluding with "Long Live the Revolution!" Tom mimics these words imbecilically as Whitely turns away and Olga bursts into tears, covering her face with her hands.

Comments: This is one of the plays written during O'Neill's time in George Pierce Baker's* English 47 workshop. It is very contrived and derivative but has some importance for themes and situations that O'Neill later used to much better advantage. The conclusion is similar to that of Ibsen's *Ghosts*, while Olga's expression of freedom from patriotism derives from Nietzsche's *Also Sprach (Thus Spake) Zarathustra*. The stokehole scenes with the use of dialect look ahead to *The Hairy Ape*,* while Perkins's love for his engines prefigures Reuben Light's* love of the machinery in *Dynamo*.* The characters are really stock figures who speak in stereotypical dialogue, while there is rather too much contrivance and coincidence.

A Note on Text: Written in 1915 or earlier, the play exists in a typescript in the Harvard Theatre Collection. It was submitted during O'Neill's participation in the English 47 workshop course of George Pierce Baker. Originally it was entitled "The Second Engineer." Used by permission.

PIOGGI, Rocky. In *The Iceman Cometh*,* night bartender and pimp. "He is a Neapolitan-American in his late twenties, squat and muscular, with a flat, swarthy face and beady eyes." He rooms above the saloon operated by Harry Hope* and runs two prostitutes, Margie* and Pearl.* He treats them like performing animals, and his pipe dream is that he is really a bartender and not a pimp. Under the influence of Theodore Hickman,* the salesman who comes to the bar annually to celebrate Hope's birthday, the girls admit they are really whores, not "tarts," and taunt Rocky with being "a Ginny pimp." This enrages Rocky, who does not want to face this truth. He reacts with violence, drawing his gun on Chuck Morello,* another pimp, and later threatens to punch him. At the end of the play, after Hickey's arrest for murdering his wife, Rocky and other denizens of the bar seize on his plea of insanity, a pipe-dream explanation which discredits what he has taught them. They then gladly get drunk in order to forget the outside world and to regain illusion.

POET, The. In *Fog*,* he is the "humanist," the spokesman for the downtrodden, and full of melancholy over the human condition. He is clearly a portrait of O'Neill himself with a face "oval with big dark eyes and a black mustache and black hair pushed back from his high forehead." This unnamed character wishes for death rather than to deal with a life which has, for some unexplained reason, become unbearable for him. He engages in a dialogue with the Man of Business* about the nature of life.

POLISH PEASANT WOMAN. In *Fog*,* a mute character. Her child had died before the play opens, and she dies during the course of the dialogue. The supernatural cry of her dead child guides the rescuers to the lifeboat containing the Man of Business* and the Poet.*

POLO, Maffeo. In *Marco Millions*,* brother of Nicolo Polo* and uncle of Marco Polo.* Maffeo is middle-aged, "tall and stout with a round, jovial face and small, cunning eyes." He has traveled once to the court of Kublai Kaan* with his brother, and this time he is taking his nephew Marco to learn the business. The brothers continually read their travel notes from their earlier journey which reveal them to be crassly insensitive to the culture and religion of the lands through which they pass. He is the more enterprising brother of the two and advises Marco to ask the Kaan for the civil service position which will garner the best perquisites. He, like the rest of the family, embodies the materialism of the profit-obsessed businessman.

POLO, Marco. In *Marco Millions*,* son of Nicolo Polo* and nephew of Maffeo Polo*; later betrothed to Donata.* He is first seen as an eighteen-year-old youth, handsome, dark, well-formed, serenading Donata through a barred window and exchanging vows of love with her. She gives him a locket with her picture. But for Marco business must always take first place, and he leaves to accompany his father and uncle on a journey to the court of Kublai Kaan* to prepare for his part in the family business.

As they retrace old routes, the older men consult their journals which indicate a total blindness to the culture and religion of the lands through which they pass. But if they are crassly materialistic, Marco is even more so. He sees everything in terms of profit and loss. Even in his attempt to write a love poem to Donata he is materialistic—"You are as lovely as gold in the sun"—and he describes her in terms of precious metal and precious stones. Like his elders he is insensitive to the culture and religion of others. No intellectual, he hates being idle and dislikes the opportunity to think. Action is all important to him, particularly when it leads to making money, increasing efficiency, and gaining a high position. He is a quintessential salesman, confident, brash, adaptable, filled with primary certitude concerning such abstract notions as the existence of the immortal soul. He merely parrots forth the words of the catechism and says "it doesn't need proof." The papal legate, Tedaldo,* later Pope Gregory X, ironically tells Marco that he "will be worth a million wise men" to the Great Kaan "in the cause of wisdom." The Kaan has asked for a hundred wise men to dispute the superiority of Christianity to his Eastern religions. Marco does not see that Tedaldo is seeing in him the perversion of Christianity into profit and loss and materialism, and he takes the pope's remark literally, informing the Kaan accordingly. The Great Kaan has a glimmer of understanding, as does his philosopher-adviser Chu-Yin,* and so Marco is offered a position in the civil service.

Advised by his uncle, Marco chooses the post of second-class government commission-agent. At first he wants nothing less than first class but relents when he is informed that there are more perquisites in this position. He is appointed mayor of Yang-Chau and proves himself as insensitive there as he had shown himself on the journey to the court of the Kaan. As before, he has no interest in individuals, only what can be squeezed out of them. Consequently he taxes everyone, making sure that he "sweats" money out of beggars and poor people as well as the rich because it is more "democratic." He orders everyone to be happy and imprisons those who are not as malcontents. He "supports" local culture by passing a law saying "that anyone caught interfering with culture would be subject to a fine"; he suppresses the right of free speech, and in short acts like a dictator of the Fascist (or later, Nazi) model. He also invents paper money and the cannon, which, in a parody of the pitch of an international arms salesman, he sells to the Kaan so that others will not have it. Obviously, he values the concept of "preemptive strike capability." He has also invented a garishly costumed order, the Mystic Order of Confucius, which parodies such organizations as the Knights of Columbus and the Knights of Pythias.

However, he has captured the heart of the Princess Kukachin,* who sees him as an exotic, a prince, a knight, someone who brings her unexpected gifts, like a chow puppy—pedigreed, of course. The Kaan, who has been using Marco as a kind of humorous experiment, is appalled by this discovery, especially since the lady is affianced to the king of Persia. When Marco returns unannounced to the court and tells of his "triumphs," the Kaan finds himself no longer amused by Marco's "spiritual hump" and wonders whether he really does have an immortal soul. Kukachin defends him and asks that he be allowed to captain her fleet en route to Hormuz, from whence Marco and his relatives will return to Venice. The Kaan reluctantly agrees, and Chu-Yin, as an additional experiment and perhaps as an assistance to Kukachin, says that the Kaan wishes Marco to look deeply into Kukachin's eyes every day and report what he sees. With his usual pragmatism, Marco thinks that the request is made for medical reasons. The royal junk leaves after six slaves have died as a result of the speed-up of the assembly line loading system—an acceptable figure, and after Marco has arranged for a brass band. He does not realize that the crowd which farewells them would have come unbidden to see the princess.

Two years later the royal junk arrives at Hormuz after an eventful voyage in which the princess has nearly died on three occasions: (1) by falling overboard; (2) during a pirate attack; (3) by fever. In each case Marco saved her, though she wished for death, despairing in the knowledge that Marco does not love her. On their last night on the vessel, Marco seeks an interview with her, recapitulates the problems of the voyage, and asks her to request a bonus for him on account of these extra services so well performed. She is almost hysterical with despair and asks him to look into her eyes and report what he sees there, as Chu-Yin had requested. Thinking that she may have fever, Marco touches her feet and pulse and then looks deeply into her eyes. There is a moment in which passion momentarily moves him, they almost kiss—but Maffeo calls out the money count, "one million." This recalls Marco to materialistic reality, and he explains the Princess's eyes as "delirious." He tells her to get some sleep, but she draws a dagger. Marco is now sure of her illness.

Blind to her despair, he then tells her about his engagement to Donata, "the best little girl in the world." When she realizes that it is an economic marriage, Kukachin knows herself defeated; and like the Great Kaan, one wonders whether Marco does indeed have an immortal soul. Even when she grinds Donata's portrait under her heel, Marco is blind. What he wants is a well-run household with a bourgeois wife who is not very bright. Money is his sole object. When Ghazan,* who is to marry Kukachin, comes, Marco again asks for a bonus and suggests that the princess's spleen is out of order as a result of the passage. She, in a fit of despairing hysteria, takes from Ghazan the Order of the Lion, worn only by heroes, and gives it to Marco, mocking its appearance "on the breast of a sheep." But Marco is impervious to the insult.

In the final scene, Marco and Donata speak of his travels; he allows that there have been some women, but he would not have married "the prettiest girl in Cathay" in preference to his fat, bovine fiancée. He shows her his locket, claiming falsely that it was damaged in an encounter with pirates. Then a great feast is held, with tables vulgarly overladen with gold plate and food. Marco and his partners exhibit the carelessness of conspicuous consumption as they give away their outer garments to servants and musicians. Then, dressed once more in their traveling clothes, they slit the seams of their sleeves and pour forth precious stones to the general astonishment of the multitude. Donata almost swoons at the sight, and her engagement is announced to thunderous applause. All sit down to eat, but first Marco is called upon to make a speech. He begins with the usual insincere display of emotions one sees on such occasions and then starts into a long "Chamber of Commerce" memorized speech on silkworms which is almost drowned out by the noise of feasting.

For O'Neill, Marco Polo represents the ultimate development of the materialistic American businessman, notably of the kind immortalized by Sinclair Lewis in *Babbitt*. He has no heart, no soul, no emotions—or if they exist, they are kept rigidly under control. His god is money, and his heaven ultimate riches. Philosophy for him is a waste of time because thinking does not make money— action does. The Epilogue of the play sums up not only Marco, but also the audience. As the lights go up full, a man dressed as Marco Polo gets up from a front aisle seat, yawns, stretches, and walks out with the rest of the audience a trifle puzzled and perhaps bored by what he has seen, if not disturbed. Unaware of the stir he causes, he mingles with others in the lobby, then strides out to wait impatiently for his "luxurious limousine" and be chauffeured away to resume his life. In other words, Marco Polo lives even today, and the audience may well also be a collection of Babbitts.

POLO, Nicolo. In *Marco Millions*,* father of Marco Polo* and brother of Maffeo Polo.* Nicolo "is a small thin middle-aged man, with a dry, shrewd face." He has traveled once to the court of Kublai Kaan* with his brother, and this time he takes his eighteen-year-old son, Marco, in order to teach him the business. He is a less enterprising businessman than his brother, operating in his shadow. However, like all the Polos, he is concerned solely with the acquisition of money and material goods. The notes taken by the two brothers during the course of their earlier journey reveal a total lack of interest in the religion or culture of the lands through which they pass. They embody the crass materialism of a capitalist-oriented society.

POMPEIA. In *Lazarus Laughed*,* the favorite mistress of Tiberius Caesar.* She appears as a young woman wearing an olive-colored half-mask "with the red of blood smouldering through," but under it her mouth indicates "agonized self-loathing." At first she is both intimidated and puzzled by the luminescent confidence of Lazarus,* and on a wager with Caligula* she tests Lazarus by offering his aged wife Miriam* a poisoned fruit, with the consent of Tiberius. She knows from Caligula that Lazarus really loves his wife, and she wishes to see how he will accept her death. When Miriam dies and Lazarus does not really mourn but instead looks toward his own death, she realizes that she loves Lazarus and therefore she cannot give her body to Caligula. Nonetheless, she is still hostile to Lazarus and influences Tiberius to burn Lazarus. But as Lazarus cries out, "O men, fear not life! You die—but there is no death for Man," the crowd falls silent, and almost hypnotized, Pompeia walks, laughing with Lazarus, into the funeral flame. She has learned not to fear death, and in that moment she, too, has welcomed it as a means to further life.

PONCE DE LEON, Juan. In *The Fountain*,* he is the central character. O'Neill takes considerable liberties with historical fact in this romantic re-creation of the search for the fountain of youth. Juan is thirty-one years old when the play opens in 1492, and the play ends with his death circa 1514. He is a hard, brave, reckless young man, dedicated to finding new lands for Spain. He has never really loved, though he has had a "rare friendship" with Maria de Cordova,* who loves him deeply. For Juan, the defeat of the Moors at Granada ushers in an era of effete peace, and he is ready to go forth with Christopher Columbus* for the greater glory of Spain. Nonetheless, Juan is also something of a dreamer and is not impervious to the spell of the Moorish minstrel's song sung before a fountain in a captured Moorish palace in Granada. The minstrel sings of a fountain where old men come to bathe, and where their years fall away from them, they are ever afterward at peace with themselves and the world, and they are revered as holy men. Juan is challenged to a duel by Vicente de Cordova,* husband of Maria who believes his honor has been impugned, and Juan has to leave court because of the ensuing scandal when he wounds Vicente slightly.

On the way to the "East" Juan discovers himself at odds with Columbus, who wishes to gain money not for himself but in order to finance "the Last Crusade." Juan ridicules this motive and says instead that he will not look back to the old "fanaticism" of religion. He wants new land for the glory of Spain, not the conversion of Indians. When land is sighted and Columbus orders the cross to be raised, Juan raises the hilt of his sword.

Twenty years pass and Juan is governor of Porto Rico, but he has never ceased to think of a voyage to Cathay and also of the mysterious fountain. He has imprisoned an Indian, Nano,* whose tribe has refused to pay taxes and who has himself rejected baptism. Juan has even resorted to torture in order to gain information about the location of the fountain. In the meantime, Maria de Cordova has sent her daughter, Beatriz de Cordova,* to Juan as his ward, and Juan falls in love with her but sadly realizes that he is too old. He has been given his patent to search for Cathay, but he will not leave without knowing the location of the fountain. Finally, he is forced to sail as the result of a plot fomented against him by Diego Menendez,* a churchman. He takes Nano with him. Nano tricks him into believing that he has found the fountain in "Florida," of which Juan takes possession for Spain. However, after drinking of the fountain, he is wounded by the arrows of Nano's Indian allies.

In his delirium he discovers the spirit of the fountain and undergoes something like a theophany as a result of which he perceives the oneness of man with nature, the oneness of all religions, and that youth and age are both the same. The spirit of youth, which is personified in Beatriz, leads him to the discovery that each soul is but part of the great eternal soul. The "tenderness" that Maria had hoped he would learn has now become his, and in that knowledge he has found spiritual enlightenment, but not in the conventional sense of religion, in a more romantic manner. He has in fact discovered the fountain of life, the source of life's mystery.

Juan survives his wound and this experience only to discover that Beatriz is now in love with his nephew, who is the duplicate of Juan himself in his youth; and having learned the glory of renunciation, Juan gives his blessing to the lovers and dies.

The character of Juan is not deeply drawn, but he demonstrates the conflict of action and romantic spirituality with which much of the play is concerned. He despises the forced conversions of the churchmen but is quite capable of cruelty in order to subjugate lands to Spanish hegemony. Only with love and beauty does he discover his spiritual source, and Beatriz, the personification of both these things, is his unwitting guide.

PROVINCETOWN PLAYERS, THE. It was with the Players in Provincetown in the summer of 1916 that the twenty-eight-year-old O'Neill had the first productions of his plays in the rough theatre the group had fashioned in a large fish shed on an old wharf. When the Players moved to their theatre in Greenwich Village that fall, O'Neill's work began to get exposure in New York, and there he had a place for growth and experimentation. In turn, O'Neill's work helped sustain the life of the Players. He was their chief legacy, but many other talents and notable spirits were nurtured in this group. Had its legacy been less, it would deserve notice nevertheless for the spirit of experiment it embodied for the era and for its supportive communion of artists and rebels of the era.

The group was formed by writers and artists from the Village who were summering in Provincetown, by then the summer retreat of many in the developing counterculture, including artists returning from Europe after the outbreak of World War I. In their beginnings on Cape Cod in the summers of 1915 and 1916, they performed first in a private home and then in their Wharf Theatre, provided by Mary Heaton Vorse at 621 Commercial Street in Provincetown. In September 1916, the group organized—to the dismay of a few who thought it should be informal and spontaneous—and brought the experiment back to the Village with them. There they performed for six seasons, occupying successively two theatres on Macdougal Street between West Third and Fourth streets. From

1916 to 1918, the group performed in what was called—at O'Neill's suggestion—the Playwrights' Theatre, a converted brownstone at 139 Macdougal. From 1918 to 1922, they occupied what was called the Provincetown Playhouse at 133 Macdougal, a converted stable and bottling works. (The basic theatre still stands at that address today.) The original Wharf Theatre in Provincetown was destroyed by fire and ice in 1922. (There are plans for the rebuilding of its distant cousin-by-tradition, the Provincetown Playhouse on the Wharf.) As the group evolved in those Provincetown summers, it became the only group in America's little-theatre movement devoted solely to nurturing new American playwrights. Through the years of the original Players, the inspirational leader was George Cram Cook.*

The Provincetown Players is part of an intellectual and artistic awakening in America in the second decade of this century, of a growing rebellion against the cultural traditions of mainstream America. There was more spirit than system to it, but the revolt was characterized by the individual rejection of conventional moral values and traditional religious doctrines. One sees among the prewar rebels an intense awareness of self and mortality; the rejection of the materialistic life, urgent quests for new kinds of personal fulfillment, and expectations that new overarching meanings and designs for living were just on the horizon. There was a hungry exploration of modern art and ideas from Europe, an increasing sensitivity to instances of social oppression, increasing criticism of the capitalistic system, and special sympathy with the labor movement. The revolt, like bohemia itself, was sometimes a dramatic construct. The Provincetowners saw themselves as the artistic and spiritual antithesis of the commercial, complacent theatre of Broadway, which O'Neill characterized as "the showshop." The Provincetown caught the winds of the new poetry and the new stagecraft in its robes and almost every other wind of artistic, social, and personal protest that blew. The Players' theatre south of Washington Square became something of the ceremonial center of Village unorthodoxy.

The list of those who contributed to the work of the original Players is a litany of America's early moderns for cultural historians. Among those who wrote plays for them (besides O'Neill) were John Silas Reed,* Louise Bryant,* Susan Glaspell,* George Cram Cook, Alfred Kreymborg, James Oppenheim, Maxwell Bodenheim, Floyd Dell, Hutchins Hapgood and Neith Boyce, Edna St. Vincent Millay, Djuna Barnes, Wilbur Daniel Steele, Saxe Commins,* Mike Gold, Kenneth Macgowan,* and Wallace Stevens. Among those who created settings for them were Robert Edmond Jones,* Cleon Throckmorton, William and Marguerite Zorach, B.J.O. Nordfeldt, and Frank Lloyd Wright. Among those who acted and directed were (in addition to many of the above) E. J. Ballantine, Max Eastman, Ida Rauh, Charles Ellis, Charles Demuth, James Light, Nina Moise, Norma and Kathleen Millay, Jasper Deeter, Charles Gilpin,* Michio Itow, Mary Blair,* Ann Harding, and Louis Wolheim.*

In the charter the Provincetowners drew up in September of 1916, they declared their primary objectives: "To encourage the writing of American plays of real artistic, literary, and dramatic—as opposed to Broadway—merit. That such plays be considered without reference to their commercial value, since this theatre is not to be run for pecuniary profit.'' From their beginnings on the Cape, they operated on a subscription membership basis, and in the flush of their early communal enthusiasm, their theatre was a resolutely amateur one; the intent was to remain unencumbered by professional production costs in order to be free to experiment. The intention—inspired by ''the new stagecraft''—was to stage plays simply, without elaborate, pictorial scenery, the better to stimulate audience imaginations. ''Jig'' Cook offered, in his inspired moments, altruistic visions of a creative community, and the group's supportive fellowship did help sustain new artists. But it must be noted, too, that the group was a collection of independent personalities with strong egos, that conflicting ambitions for art, self, and the integrity of the group often existed within the same breasts, and that, ultimately, amateurism was not enough either to sustain them or to satisfy them— including George Cram Cook.

In its eight seasons, the group produced ninety-three new plays by forty-seven American authors (sixteen of them women). Most were one-act plays. About eighty are extant in print or in manuscripts. Those O'Neill contributed are of special interest, of course; few others have wide, abiding interest. But taken together, the plays are valuable for the life of the theatre they sustained and for what they tell us about these early American moderns. Most of them are realistic in nature. A number explore the problems of the manners and *mores* of liberated Village moderns. Neith Boyce's *Constancy* is a moderately amusing portrait of the love affair of Jack Reed and Mabel Dodge (Luhan). Cook and Glaspell's *Suppressed Desires* is a lightweight comedy on the new Freudian fad on Washington Square. Glaspell's *The People* deals earnestly with the struggles of a newspaper modeled on *The Masses*. Rita Wellman's *Funiculi-Funicula* depicts a self-centered, artistic young couple whose very sick child is a burden on their dreams and bohemian ways. In Floyd Dell's *King Arthur's Socks*, Guenevere [*sic*] and Lancelot discover their desires for one another are not strong enough to overcome their allegiance to conventional love and marriage. A few of the plays are American gothic horror stories of repressive Puritan or provincial worlds, and there are several vignettes of urban ghetto life. Pendleton King's *Cocaine* is a sympathetic, naturalistic depiction of two young addicts in love and poverty. In Alice Rostetter's comedy, *The Widow's Veil*, the lives of two Irish families in a tenement are glimpsed as the characters appear at the openings of the building's dumbwaiter shaft. Mike Gold's *Money* is a pathetic tale of theft among poor Jewish immigrants saving money to bring over relatives. Such realism was radical enough at the time, but there were also several dramas that were responses to current social or political issues. Wilbur Daniel Steele's *Contemporaries* is an allegory on a 1914 clash in New York City between a group of unemployed men and a church that closed its doors to them. Plays of a pacifistic spirit included O'Neill's *The Sniper,** Jack Reed's *The Peace That Passeth Understanding*, which satirizes President Wilson and the Paris peace talks of 1918, and Edna St. Vincent Millay's *Aria Da Capo*, which uses *com-*

media dell'arte and pastoral characters in a precious allegory on the cycle of human greed and war.

The Players experimented with some poetic dramas that wanted stylized, overtly theatrical scenic décor. Louise Bryant's *The Game* is a quasi-morality play on love, death, and life for which the Zorachs provided stylized staging, with actors positioned in the manner of figures in Egyptian painting in front of a handsome, modernistically painted curtain by Marguerite Zorach. Millay's *Aria Da Capo* was staged in front of a series of wittily painted black and white screens. James Oppenheim's *Night* offered earnest meditations on the human condition by a priest, a scientist, and poet, none of whom can console the woman who comes to their hilltop carrying her dead, newborn child. The setting was created by silhouetting the figures on a mound against a violet-lighted cyclorama. Alfred Kreymborg's *Lima Beans* and Maxwell Bodenheim's *Knotholes* deal more light-handedly with human frailty and mortality. The Players had difficulties with the less realistic works, but the scenic challenges such works posed did help prepare the way for the effective solutions to the problems posed by *The Emperor Jones** and *The Hairy Ape.**

The first O'Neill play the Players produced was *Bound East for Cardiff** in the Wharf Theatre on July 28, 1916. They also used it to open their theatre in the Village that fall. Contrary to Susan Glaspell's account in her biography of Cook, the group probably rejected some of the plays O'Neill first proffered (*The Movie Man* and those in his privately printed volume of 1914, *Thirst and Other One Act Plays*), ultimately staging *Cardiff* on the second bill of the summer. This seminal play was a rewrite of his *Children of the Sea* (1914), revised in large part during O'Neill's Harvard year with Baker* (1914-1915). The value to O'Neill of his work with the Players was considerable, as he himself acknowledged in later years. The group was there when he needed counsel and the opportunity for the first trial of his work in a working theatre (he directed *Cardiff*, a duty required of the playwrights); with the Players he had an audience sympathetic to experiment and new visions but not uncritical. With them he continued to have a place to test unconventional theatrical forms, as he did in *The Moon of the Caribbees,* The Emperor Jones*, and others. In his plays for the Provincetown, he can be seen seeking theatrically effective ways of handling the individual's quest for some spiritual meaning, the tragic illusions, and the ironic life-forces—matters that occupy him throughout his career. In these works, too, are the biographical strains characteristic of O'Neill.

It was not in O'Neill to be an acolyte in Cook's communal temple, but he was responsive to Cook's continual pleas for new plays from the group's best writer to help sustain the theatre. The Players produced fifteen of his plays altogether. In chronological order they were *Bound East for Cardiff, Thirst, Before Breakfast,* Fog,* The Sniper, The Long Voyage Home,* Ile,* The Rope,* Where the Cross Is Made,* The Moon of the Caribbees, The Dreamy Kid,* Exorcism,* The Emperor Jones, Diff'rent,** and *The Hairy Ape*. While O'Neill's exposure to New York begins with the Players and their subscription audiences, it should be noted that the Washington Square Players'* productions of *In the Zone** and *The Rope* in their 1917–18 season (together with the publication of some of his plays) advanced him faster because of the attention critics gave to that semi-professional, open-to-the-general-public theatre.

In O'Neill's ability to create characters of complex human dimension, with strong passions, and in the developing modern tragic vision implicit in these early works, he had no equal among the other Provincetown writers. His nearest rival in talent, seriousness of theme, and sustained output in these years was Susan Glaspell. But her vision remained romantic, for all the realistic surfaces of her plays. Today her work has some feminist interest (not much explored), but her serious, full-length works for the group, the best of which is *Bernice* and her later Pulitzer Prize-winning *Alison's House* (1930), while interesting as evidence of the spiritual hungers of her era, have little appeal now because of their constrained worlds, their sentimentality, and their undramatic, obscure transcendental preoccupations.

It was with *The Emperor Jones* (1920) and *The Hairy Ape* (1922) that the Players achieved wide public recognition. These first American experiments with expressionism were imaginatively staged and acted, and these works by the author whose *Beyond the Horizon** had just won acclaim on Broadway were moved uptown to Broadway houses. The casting of the professional black actor, Charles Gilpin*, in the leading role of Brutus Jones* was done without hesitation by the group, but it represented a dramatic crossing of the American theatre's racial lines.

The O'Neill successes brought into sharp focus problems present in the group from the beginning. There had been a gradual shift toward more effective, professional production and away from the experimental, independent atmosphere of the nurturing workshop. Also, George Cram Cook's second full-length play, *The Spring* (1920), failed to win him recognition; the acclaim and even the attentions of his own group were now going to O'Neill's works. With this identity crisis for the group and the personal crisis for Cook, with the factor of fatigue from the search for new plays and sustaining the inspiration upon which the amateur operation depended, season after season, the Players decided early in 1922 to declare a year's interim. Jig Cook now departed America before the last plays of the season (which included one of his wife's), saying in essence that in a commercial-minded, success-driven country, he and his followers had failed their ideals, failed to build his spiritual community. He left, deeply disappointed, to seek in his beloved Greece those gods that had eluded him on Macdougal Street. He died near Delphi in 1924, with Glaspell at his side, after a final try, like a character O'Neill might have created, to answer to his tragic illusions and find a place for his immortal soul near the ancient monuments.

The original Players' organization did not resume where it had left off. In its stead a new organization, the Experimental Theatre, Inc.,* took up production at the Provincetown Playhouse at 133 Macdougal Street in the fall of 1923.

Distinctions have not always been made between the offspring and the original Players, but the policies and practices of the new organization were much different.

For further reading, *The Provincetown, A Story of the Theatre* (1931) by Helen Deutsch and Stella Hanau briefly surveys all phases from 1915 to 1929, with emphasis on the later phases in which the authors joined the theatre. Full-length studies of the original Players to 1922, with different emphases, are Robert K. Sarlós's *Jig Cook and the Provincetown Players: Theatre in Ferment* (1982). On the Experimental Theatre, Inc., see *"The Theatre We Worked For," The Letters of Eugene O'Neill to Kenneth Macgowan*, edited by Jackson R. Bryer and Ruth M. Alvarez, with introductory essay by Travis Bogard (1982). © Gary Jay Williams.

PULITZER PRIZE , awarded annually for the best American play. Won an unprecedented four times by Eugene O'Neill for: *Beyond the Horizon** (1920); *"Anna Christie"** (1922); *Strange Interlude** (1928); and posthumously for *Long Day's Journey into Night** (1957).

PUTNAM, Abbie. *See* Cabot, Abbie Putnam.

Q

QUESADA, Friar, a Franciscan friar, exemplar of the qualities of the church militant in *The Fountain*.* He is a worldly priest who is usually shown in dress which symbolizes his dual function. He wears his robe tucked up to show his riding boots and spurs, or he has a belt with a pistol in it over his brown habit. He is a priest who will put down uprisings with violence and enforce conversion. He is killed in Florida after a plot hatched by Nano,* an Indian, succeeds. He misunderstands the motivations of the Indians who want to give the impression they worship the Spaniards' "totem pole." When he sees they have raised the cross in an inverted position, symbol of the Black Mass, he is enraged and fatally wounds the Medicine Man* who in turn kills him.

QUINTERO, José (1924–   ), director, producer, author; full name José Benjamin Quintero. Born in Panama to Carlos Rivira and Consuelo (Palmorala) Quintero. His father was a cattleman and politician. Educated at La Salle High School, Panama; Los Angeles City College, California; B.S., University of Southern California, 1948; Goodman Theatre, Chicago, 1948–49.

More than any other professional theatre person, Quintero has been responsible for the revival of interest in O'Neill's work. His production of *The Iceman Cometh** at the Circle in the Square, New York City, in 1956 was considered superior to the original production, largely as the result of the superb performance of Jason Robards, Jr.* From this time on he became a confidant of the ailing Carlotta Monterey* O'Neill, who took a great interest in him and seemed at times to consider him almost a reincarnation of O'Neill. Quintero also took an interest in Carlotta while she was a patient in Saint Luke's Hospital, New York City, and attempted to alleviate some of her distress.

Quintero hopes eventually to direct the entire corpus of O'Neill's work, and in furtherance of this ambition he revived *Welded** at Columbia University in 1981. Other notable O'Neill productions by Quintero are: *Long Day's Journey into Night** (New York, 1956; toured to Cleveland, 1957; Los Angeles, 1958); *The Iceman Cometh* (Amsterdam, Holland, 1957); *A Moon for the Misbegotten** (Spoleto, 1958; Buffalo, New York, 1965; Circle in the Square, New York City, 1968; Morosco Theatre, New York City, 1973; and ABC-TV, 1975); *Desire

*Under the Elms,** (Circle in the Square, New York City, 1963); *Strange Interlude** (for the Actors Studio at the Hudson Theatre, New York City, 1963); *Marco Millions** (for the Repertory Co. of Lincoln Center, ANTA Washington Square Theatre, 1964); *Hughie** (Royale Theatre, New York City, 1964); *More Stately Mansions** (Ahmanson Theatre, Los Angeles; Broadhurst Theatre, New York City, 1967); *Mourning Becomes Electra** (Circle in the Square/Joseph E. Levine Theatre, 1972). Quintero seems to have a singularly close empathy to the work of O'Neill, and his productions of individual plays are eagerly awaited. He received the Vernon Rice Award for *The Iceman Cometh* (1956); the *Variety* and Antoinette Perry awards for *Long Day's Journey into Night* (1956); and the Antoinette Perry and Drama Desk awards for *A Moon for the Misbegotten* (1973–74).

Quintero's work is not confined to the Eugene O'Neill canon, and he has directed the plays of many other writers, as well as opera at the Metropolitan Opera, New York City, and elsewhere; a film, *The Roman Spring of Mrs. Stone* (1961); and television productions. He also wrote an autobiographical work, *If You Don't Dance They Beat You* (1974), which contains much fascinating information concerning his connection with the O'Neill canon and his sometimes stormy relationship with Carlotta Monterey.

R

RECKLESSNESS, a one-act play. The action takes place in "the library of Arthur Baldwin's* summer home in the Catskills"; all the furnishings indicate "the typical sitting room of a moderately wealthy man who has but little taste and is but little worried by its absence." Mildred Baldwin,* his wife, is waiting for her husband's return, but finally decides that he is not coming home. Thinking that she is quite safe, she calls for Fred Burgess,* the chauffeur, and the pair exchange words of love in a close embrace which is observed by Gene,* Mrs. Baldwin's maid, who "glares at them" vindictively, for Fred had once loved her. Mildred speaks of the horror of her existence with a husband whom she hates, but Fred says they can't go away together because they have no money. Mildred offers to sell her jewels, but Fred refuses, saying that he will soon pass his engineering examinations, and then "we'll go away together. I won't be anybody's servant then." Mildred tearfully begs him to take her away at once, romantically asking, "What difference does the money make as long as I have you?"

Fred very sensibly points out that she has never been poor, as he has, and therefore does not understand what it is like. After having been used to everything, she would eventually come to blame Fred for her poverty and her love would die. Further, Baldwin might not even give her a divorce, out of sheer spite. Mildred disagrees, saying that Baldwin has been good to her, "a very considerate 'owner'," though she hates him. The marriage was arranged by her parents, solely for his money, despite the fact that he was much older than she. Fred then reveals that he has been investigating Mr. Baldwin's past and has found it "none too spotless," so that he will probably allow a very quiet divorce if Fred goes to him. Suddenly the noise of an automobile is heard—Baldwin has come home. Fred rushes out to greet him.

Arthur Baldwin enters and embraces Mildred, who flinches at the kiss of this undersized, dissipated-looking man as he discusses the performance of his new car, noting that he was delayed because something had gone wrong with the steering gear and he had had to drive very carefully. Mildred answers him abstractedly, and Arthur treats her with a cruel cynicism. She leaves to change her clothes, and soon after Gene, the maid, enters, saying that Mildred has a headache. Baldwin treats Gene with a cynical salaciousness as she tells him that Fred no longer loves her. Under his mocking comments she hints at the identity of Fred's new lover until finally Baldwin comprehends; enraged, he threatens to throttle her and demands proof. She produces a letter and asks him to confront the guilty pair after she has left the next morning: "I'd like them to know it was me who spoiled their fun." Baldwin reads the letter and hears about a number of assignations. Suddenly he thinks of a mode of vengeance and telephones Fred at the garage, ordering him to rush to the village to get a doctor for Mildred, claiming that she "has been taken very ill. Hemorrhage, I think—blood's running from her mouth. She's unconscious—it's a matter of life and death. Drive like hell, do you hear?" The noise of a car is heard, and as it dies away, Baldwin waits impatiently until the telephone rings to announce that there has been a fatal accident.

He asks that the body be brought straight to the house and calls for Mildred to come downstairs. She has heard the car depart, and he tells her that Fred has apparently tried to find the source of the steering gear trouble by himself this very night, instead of waiting until morning: "Fred is very careless—very, very careless in some things. I shall have to teach him a lesson. He is absolutely reckless, especially with other people's property." As Mildred tries to keep her self-control, Baldwin continues cruelly: "Chauffeurs—even overzealous ones— are to be had for the asking, but cars like mine are out of the ordinary." Baldwin, playing a cat and mouse game, then asks if Mildred is "perfectly happy up here," and when she answers affirmatively, he claims that he has been conscience-stricken leaving her alone. Perhaps if he were to let Fred go, and with him the second car, she could enjoy the advantages of a more fashionable and livelier resort. The sparring continues as Mildred asserts her love of "motoring," because Fred is "very careful,...the best chauffeur we have ever had." The conflict slowly concentrates as Mildred says that Gene alone of all the help is unsatisfactory. She will discharge her as soon as she can find a suitable replacement. Baldwin replies, "in the same soft, half-mocking voice he has used during the whole conversation," that she has already announced to him her intention of leaving and in reply to Mildred's outburst alleges that Gene is or was the lover of Fred, claiming that he has visual evidence.

He continues torturing Mildred with hints about Fred's ambition and the possibility of his leaving now that Gene has gone until finally he hands her her own letter and she admits her love for the chauffeur. Mildred pleads for her freedom, and Baldwin announces his intention to "let" her get a divorce. In her gratitude she kisses his hand, and the two discuss the monetary reasons for their marriage, Mildred being quite honest, while Baldwin, with his superior knowledge of events, cynically leads her on. She suggests that she has been simply a "plaything" for her husband, who says he "was only accepting the valuation your parents set upon you when they sold you." Then, when Baldwin says that Mildred may have Fred, she kisses him: "Oh, I do love you now— you are so good to me." Baldwin looks sneeringly at her as the sound of a car is heard, and completely aware of the accident, he says that it is Fred: "We will have him in and relieve his mind."

Almost immediately after these words, Fred's body is brought in. Mildred faints and is carried out. Within a few minutes Baldwin returns, and the sound of a shot is heard. He is momentarily startled but quickly realizes that "Mrs. Baldwin has just shot herself."

Comments: This melodrama is a slight piece, but it does show O'Neill's ability to exploit suspense. It bears a superficial resemblance to Strindberg's *Miss Julie*, and it discusses topics which evoke memories of Ibsen's *A Doll's House*. Mildred discusses the horror of a loveless marriage, and both she and Baldwin speak of the matrimonial relationship in terms of property rights. The dialogue, however, is rather clumsy, chiefly because the play at times has the light tone of a matrimonial farce, but it is meant to be taken seriously. The characters of Fred and Mildred are not developed sufficiently to allow the audience to identify with them, while Baldwin is a singularly repellent personality. As a result, their problems and their quest for "freedom and dignity" in love seems rather more trivial than tragic. The conclusion with a shot is therefore almost an obligatory conclusion rather than one which arises from depths of feeling within the character. The sense of inevitability which O'Neill was presumably trying to evoke is not achieved. The play is a curious mixture of problem play, matrimonial farce, and melodrama. The title comes from Baldwin's comment that Fred is notably "reckless, especially with other people's property."

Production Data: Written 1913. Unproduced. The script supplied the title for the 1933 film, *The Constant Woman* (see Appendix B), which bears no resemblance to the O'Neill text.

A Note on Text: The text used is that appearing in *Ten "Lost" Plays of Eugene O'Neill* (New York: Random House, 1964).

"RECKONING, THE," a scenario.

Act I, Scene i: Hillvale, Ohio; interior of a blacksmith's shop in the late afternoon of a spring holiday, 1890. Bessie Small* is waiting for Jack Gardner, her stepfather's helper in the blacksmith shop. Jack has been drinking. On his arrival they argue about his playing around with another girl, named Alice, and in the course of conversation it is revealed that Stephen Donohue,* Bessie's stepfather, disapproves of the relationship between Bessie and Jack. The young man swaggers in a macho way, saying that he is not afraid of Donohue, but he is somewhat deflated when Bessie tells him she is pregnant. Jack turns from her, saying that he can't be sure it is his, though Bessie insists that it is. He has a right to his fun and has no intention of marrying her. Nonetheless, he will take her to the dance tonight. He leaves.

"Big Steve" Donohue, the town blacksmith, enters to berate Bessie for playing around with Jack because she is shaming the family by her behavior. He finally gets Bessie to admit that Jack is her lover but only after he threatens to have the young man run out of town unless he hears the truth. Bessie, very calculatingly, reveals that she is pregnant by Jack, and Donohue swears that he will force Jack to marry her. Jack returns, having had a few more drinks, and Donohue confronts him with Bessie's information and says that he had better marry her. Jack, made courageous by alcohol, defiantly laughs and refuses. At this he and Donohue fight; the blacksmith picks up a hammer and tries to hit Jack with it, but Jack wrenches it from him and hits the older man on the head. Donohue falls, and both young people think he is dead. Bessie instantly takes command, telling Jack to flee, to hop a fast freight train to Chicago where she will write to him (in care of general delivery) under the name of Jack Cockran* and will join him as soon as possible. She will spread the story that her stepfather fell on his anvil while drunk and died as a result. Jack kisses her and leaves. After his departure Donohue stirs and is revived by Bessie. The angry man rushes after Jack, but he is too late.

Act I, Scene ii: Chicago, about one month later, a small bedroom in a cheap rooming house. Jack, looking crushed by circumstances, enters, followed by Bessie. He asks after Donohue, and Bessie lies by saying that he died without regaining consciousness. Now suffering from guilt, Jack says he will give himself up, but Bessie dissuades him by insisting that no one suspects him because everyone believes her story of the drunken fall. She then blackmails him by promising to keep silent if he will give up drinking and marry her. Jack agrees, saying that he has already become an abstainer but insists that he had never loved Bessie, his affections being committed to Alice. The marriage then will be one based on fear of betrayal, completely without love, because Jack has no desire to renew his connection with Bessie, whom he perceives as guilty.

Act II: Jack Cockran's living room, ten years later, in a large northeast manufacturing town. Present are Mathew Lathrop, Jack's business partner; Isiah King, a brigadier-general in the Grand Army of the Republic; and Jim O'Brien, Democratic Party boss of the district. They are trying to convince Cockran to run for Congress. In ten years he has made the mill a model of productivity and sustained tranquil relations between management and labor with the result that he has earned the combined support of both the millowners and the unions. His reputation is good, and his wife is noted for her good works, while everyone admires his rise from mill hand to partner in such a short time. Cockran is not enthusiastic about the idea and makes excuses; eventually the others leave O'Brien behind to convince him. After O'Brien's departure, still unsuccessful, Mrs. Elizabeth Cockran (the former "Bessie" Small), who has overheard everything, enters. Cockran is furious because she is attempting to interfere in his business, but she continues to advise him to take this chance, for the sake of little Jack Cockran, Jr.*

The nine-year-old child then enters, and when the two are alone it is clear that his mother's life is centered entirely on the child, an affection he reciprocates. The maid brings a card from an old man who is waiting outside. It is Stephen Donohue. At first Mrs. Cockran refuses to see him, then changes her mind and sends the child away to confront Donohue alone. She is very shaken when she sees him because he has aged greatly; his hands shake, and he seems vague and "half-witted." He addresses her as "Bess," but she insists that he is mistaken. Donohue then tells the story of his deterioration during the last ten years through the loss of his stepdaughter, his permanent weakness as the result of Jack's hammer blow, the loss of his shop, and his enforced nomadic life. He swears he will kill the man who maimed him. Mrs. Cockran asks the old man what he wants, and when he says that his wish is to return to Ireland, she offers to buy his passage and leave the ticket for him. She gives him money and offers more, but there is no love in her generosity: she wishes to be rid of him. Donohue is at first grateful, but then he recognizes her. At first he threatens her in his rage, but then he subsides and leaves.

She breaks down, but when the child enters again, she asks whether he would like to see his father become president of the United States. Young Jack's enthusiasm for the proposal makes her light up. Cockran re-enters, and Bessie continues to persuade him to take the congressional nomination, but Cockran is bitter. He would like to take the job but fears the revelation of his past. Bessie says that that was a long time ago, but in a momentary lapse she almost reveals the truth. However, she is afraid of losing him and attempts to exorcise her guilt feelings by forcing him to accept this opportunity, threatening to take young Jack away and tell him about his father's past. Once again she is blackmailing him, and the result is the same as at the end of Act I. Jack agrees but only out of hatred for her. He strikes a hard bargain: she must give up all claims on his life, and the child must be sent to a boarding school. Bessie agrees with dull resignation because she has gained her wish.

Act III: The library of Senator Cockran's Washington, D.C., house in early April 1917. Albert Simms, Cockran's secretary, is working on papers when King enters, and they start to discuss World War I. Brigadier-General Isiah King is in favor of entering the war and excoriates all antiwar senators. He has faith that Cockran's speech favoring war will change minds because Cockran is both popular and respected. He leaves with Simms to talk to the senator.

Jack, Jr., enters with Harriet Lathrop,* the daughter of Cockran's business partner, obviously in love with her. She and her mother are house guests of the Cockrans. A love scene ensues, and the two express their patriotism as well. Jack, Jr., who is now twenty-six years old, plans to enlist, and Harriet enthusiastically offers to go with him to the recruiting office, without even waiting to hear the senator speak. In answer to her inquiry, Jack says that he thinks his father will be proud of his decision, but he is uncertain about his mother's reaction since he barely knows her, having been so long away from her. Harriet, however, senses his mother's affection for her son and suspects that Bessie fears that Harriet will take him away and that therefore she hates the young woman. Mrs. Lathrop, Harriet's mother, enters, and small talk ensues until the entry of Bessie Cockran, greatly aged and terribly timid. After the young people leave, Mrs. Lathrop talks about war and the draft, topics that terrify Mrs. Cockran. She says that Jack, Jr., would surely be exempt as the son of a senator, but Mrs.

Lathrop, noting that he is a perfect physical specimen, assures Mrs. Cockran that Jack would volunteer. Mrs. Cockran is appalled and awakens from her "dull resignation" to say that she is certain that her husband will not allow a declaration of war. Mrs. Lathrop disabuses her, informing her that her husband is a hawk on the subject and is about to speak in favor of it. Distraught, Mrs. Cockran leaves to speak to her husband. Mrs. Lathrop remains until Cockran, Simms, and King enter, and then she leaves. Cockran sends Simms on an errand, and then King leaves. When his wife enters, Cockran tries to ignore her and then finally tells her to say her piece as briefly as possible. The two debate his stance on war, Mrs. Cockran speaking of Jack and her husband extolling patriotism. She remains unconvinced, and finally he explodes into anger and starts to leave. Mrs. Cockran repeats her pattern of blackmail; she will reveal the elder Cockran's past if he does not speak against war. She will smash him totally.

As before, she has made her point, and her husband is abject. She insists that she is thinking only of young Jack, whom she loves despite her husband's keeping them apart; but when the senator remonstrates with her, saying that he has little real influence, she threatens him again. If the senator does not work against war she will reveal his past—and will begin by telling his son. With this threat Cockran crumbles, agreeing to speak against war. He will ruin himself politically to avoid revelation of his crime. He is alone when Jack and Harriet enter conspiratorially. He begs them not to come to the Senate to hear his speech, and they tell him they have already planned something else.

Act IV: The library, as in Act III. It is night. Mrs. Cockran is alone, almost hysterical about the coming war, when Jack, Jr., enters with the news that he has already enlisted in the aviation service and that Harriet had been with him at the time. Mrs. Cockran now realizes what she has done; she has destroyed her husband's political career for nothing. Frantically, she tries to persuade Jack to run away because she is certain he will be killed. Jack refuses and delivers a patriotic speech about duty, honor, and country which awakens Mrs. Cockran's conscience.

She now tells her son about the fight between Donohue and Cockran, and her own deception, promising to make a clean breast of it to her husband. However, she omits one crucial fact—her premarital pregnancy. Shocked at her duplicity, Jack turns against her. She then tells him of the way she blackmailed his father into trying a political career. Jack reproaches her, but she is beyond caring. She attempts to tell him that she had used the same tactics earlier in the day, but Jack continues his reproaches. They are interrupted by Senator Cockran, who tells them he has just spoken in favor of the war, and he is surprised at his wife's approval. She tries to leave, but Jack forces her to remain while he retells her story.

Cockran is furious at her violation of their bargain and threatens to strike her, but Jack intervenes. Cockran asks his son if he knows the real reason for their marriage, while Mrs. Cockran tries to prevent his continuing. The senator has realized that she was trying to preserve his son's respect for him and blames himself for their long years of unhappiness. He tells Jack the truth. His mother had wanted marriage to give her child a name, and Cockran now sees that he has "stifled" her life and punished her by making her miserable and trying to separate her from young Jack. He has made her suffer for his sin. But then it occurs to him that her threats, allied to his own guilty conscience and desire to make reparation, have made him successful. This time, Jack is crushed as his father tells him that he alone must be the judge of his parents—and he begs him to be charitable. Jack replies that he loves them as he loves his country, "right or wrong, my country." Now they must each forgive the other. Mrs. Cockran dissolves into tears, and her husband is deeply moved. Harriet calls out to Jack, who replies and turns to leave. Mr. Cockran extends his hand to his wife, who takes it as he assures her that Jack will return safely: "The good God owes us that." The curtain falls on this scene of reconciliation.

Comments: It is unfair to attempt a full analysis of this scenario, since it is merely a draft. Motivations are not fully established, and the facts are at times contradictory—this is particularly true of the chronology, which as it stands would make young Jack twenty-six years old, instead of the youth he appears to be at the end of the play. What one does note is that even at this early stage, O'Neill shows a woman who is prepared to give up almost everything to make her husband a success. The final reconciliation scene, comingled with a rather jingoistic patriotism, is also very contrived.

Agnes Boulton* O'Neill, with some help from her husband, developed from this scenario a play entitled "The Guilty One."* According to Louis Sheaffer (1968, pp. 147–148, 166) it was placed under option by William Brady, who asked for revisions. It remained unproduced, and in 1925 it was withdrawn, on O'Neill's insistence, largely because of Brady's attitude toward play censorship and morality, particularly in reference to *Desire Under the Elms.* *See also* Floyd (1981), pp. xxxiii, 84–91.

A Note on Text: Written in 1917 or 1918. The scenario exists in a typescript in the Harvard Theatre Collection. Used by permission.

REED, John Silas (1887–1920), American revolutionary and journalist. Born Portland, Oregon, October 22, 1887. Died in Moscow, USSR., of typhus, October 17, 1920. Son of Charles Jerome and Margaret (Green) Reed. His father was a businessman and his mother was a member of the Portland aristocracy. Educated at the Portland Academy, Morristown School, New Jersey, and Harvard University, B.A., 1910. Married Louise Bryant* (1916–1920).

Somewhat delicate as a child because of a kidney ailment, John Reed read voraciously. Despite some family financial reverses, Reed was educated in private schools, first at the Portland Academy, then at the Morristown School, New Jersey, and finally at Harvard where he became editor of the *Lampoon* and a member of the Hasty Pudding Club. He was not a distinguished student and on one occasion was rusticated to Concord for a term after overstaying his vacation because of an impulsive trip to Bermuda. As a student of the renowned Charles Townsend Copeland he developed a love of literature, and poetry in particular, though his own attempts were less impressive than he believed. His years at Harvard were, however, profitable in teaching him journalism and giving him an insight into politics. But above all else, John Reed made himself noticed at college through his incessant activity, joining clubs, writing for student-run papers, and attempting creative writing. He graduated from Harvard in 1910, and finding himself short of money, he shipped on a freighter with a classmate, Waldo Peirce, who swam back to shore after the first meal on board. As a result, Reed had to face murder charges on his arrival in Manchester, being saved by the opportune appearance of Peirce, who had come by liner. He spent the rest of the year wandering through France and Spain, becoming engaged to a young French woman, Madeleine Filon, in early 1911.

Returning to the United States with the intention of making money and then getting married, he found his father in a most precarious financial situation in Portland. Lincoln Steffens, an old family friend, helped Reed get a half-time position in New York on the *American* where he assessed manuscripts and learned the magazine business, while also writing poetry and articles. He began to move in artistic and literary circles, and in June 1911 he broke his engagement. During the summer of 1911 he moved into Greenwich Village, at 42 Washington Square South, with three other Harvard men. Lincoln Steffens later moved into the same building. Supporting himself with his poetry and journalism, Reed continued to look closely at the inexhaustible life of New York City, but after his father's death in July 1912, he was forced to spend several months in Portland, disentangling the family finances. By October of 1912 he was back in New York and had become a member of the Industrial Workers of the World (IWW). At this time, Greenwich Village was full of intellectuals, artists, and radicals, and Reed took in Robert Edmond Jones,* a Harvard classmate, as a roommate and helped him to make theatrical contacts. Later, Jones teamed with Kenneth Macgowan* and Eugene O'Neill in producing O'Neill's plays. In December 1912, Reed met Max Eastman, editor of *Masses*, a radical magazine, and became an editor of it. When his poem, "The Day in Bohemia," was published in February 1913, he became the epitome of the Village life.

In 1913 he met William D. Haywood, head of the IWW, and heard "Big Bill" speak of the causes of the silkworkers' strike in Paterson, New Jersey, and the violence with which the authorities were treating the workers who were striking for an eight-hour day. Haywood believed that national publicity was needed, and accordingly John Reed went to Paterson to look at the situation. There he was arrested and sent to jail where he met Carlo Tresca, another IWW leader. After four days of not very arduous incarceration he was released, and he returned to New York where he began to write about the strike, gaining support for the workers. Somehow the idea arose to perform what came to be known as the Paterson Pageant, a performance at Madison Square Garden in which the strike was reenacted, with the workers themselves playing their real-life roles on the stage. The originator of this scheme is unclear (Mabel Dodge, John Reed, or an unnamed person), but Reed certainly wrote the scenario and staged the production, with Robert Edmond Jones designing it and John Sloan painting scenery. The performance on June 7, 1913, was extraordinarily successful, but it showed a deficit of around two thousand dollars. Exhausted by the work of the pageant, Reed left for Florence with Mabel Dodge to recuperate. After what was diagnosed as a diphtheria attack, Reed and Dodge returned to New York in September 1913, and he moved into her apartment at 23 Fifth Avenue. But by November 21 the romance was temporarily over, and by the end of the month Reed was off to Mexico to cover the rebellion of Pancho Villa for the *Metropolitan* magazine.

This commission made Reed's reputation as a reporter, and his account of a battle in which he participated with "La Tropa," a group of one hundred, stimulated tremendous interest. His book, *Insurgent Mexico* (1914), a collection of his impressions and an account of the rebellion, remains eminently readable, though it is less trustworthy as history. The book was completed at the end of Summer 1914, and the romance with Mabel Dodge was on again. With the outbreak of World War I in 1914, Reed became a supporter of nonintervention and set off for Europe to cover the action, joining Mabel Dodge in Naples. They went north to Paris as the German forces approached while Reed tried to get a story; he was appalled at the selfishness and gaiety of London and fashionable watering places in Europe, as yet untouched by war; and when Mabel Dodge went back to the United States, freeing Reed from her, he went to Berlin and then to the western front. While there he fired a couple of shots in the direction of the French trenches, an action which caused him to be barred from that country as a war correspondent. He returned to the United States still convinced that America should stay out of the war and in 1915 went to Italy and thence into Serbia, the eastern front, and Petrograd.

In December 1915 he was in Portland, Oregon, where he met Louise Bryant.* Their attraction was both instant and mutual, and within a few weeks she followed him to New York. They were married on November 9, 1916, after her divorce from Paul Trullinger, a Portland dentist. In the summer of 1916, Reed and Louise Bryant summered at Provincetown, where she had an affair with Eugene O'Neill of which Reed apparently knew nothing, given that he was helpful to O'Neill in his career. Reed was part of the group that founded the Provincetown Players, and he wrote a play for them, *The Eternal Quadrangle*, a satire on "triangle" plays. He is said to have been present, along with Louise Bryant, at the often reported evening at which *Bound East for Cardiff** was first read at the home of George Cram Cook* and Susan Glaspell,* and played a role in the original production. He also played the role of Death in Bryant's one-act morality drama, *The Game*. In November 1916 he was hospitalized for the removal of a bad kidney.

Throughout 1917 he worked to keep the United States out of the war, incurring the opprobrium of influential politicians and others, particularly after writing a headline over a reprinted article from the *Tribune* on mental illness in the military: "Knit a Straight-Jacket for Your Soldier Boy." Louise Bryant spent several months in France during this year, attempting unsuccessfully to cover the war.

In August 1917, Reed and Bryant went to Russia to observe the political situation, sending back articles on the Bolshevik revolution. Reed remained in Petrograd until March 1918, Louise having left the previous January. The book that grew out of these experiences and articles, *Ten Days That Shook the World* (1919), has become a classic account of the Bolshevik Revolution. It has all the virtues of observation and recreation of the moment that made *Insurgent Mexico* so vivid, and also some of the romantic reorganization of facts that weaken both works. Reed had some difficulty returning to the United States because of his unfortunate acceptance of the position of "consul of the Russian Republic in New York," an action for which he later found himself unable to gain a passport. After his return, Reed, along with Max Eastman and other members of the *Masses* staff, were tried on charges of disloyalty but were acquitted. For the next year, 1918–19, Reed devoted himself to furthering the aims of the American Socialist Party, testifying with Louise Bryant before a Senate committee about what they had observed during the revolution. Louise went on a speaking tour while Reed finished his book on the Bolshevik revolution. Wishing to ensure the recognition of the Communist Labor Party of the United States by the Communist International in Russia, Reed left clandestinely for Moscow in September 1919, arriving there in November. Unsuccessful in his attempt, he tried to return to the United States but seems to have been betrayed by his Bolshevik friends who wished to keep him in Russia; as a result, he was imprisoned for some five months in Finland. Returning to Moscow, he was joined by Louise on September 15, 1920, after his return from the great Bolshevik convention in Baku. But in the course of that trip he had contracted typhus and died on October 17, 1920. On October 24, he was buried in the Kremlin. There is some doubt over whether or not Reed was disenchanted with communism at the time of his death, but he was revered as an American hero of the Bolshevik Revolution.

His connection with O'Neill arises from their mutual acquaintanceship with the radical Bohemians in Greenwich Village, some of whom, like Hippolyte Havel,* served as models for characters in O'Neill plays. The triangular relationship among O'Neill, Bryant, and Reed seems to have served as a model for *Strange Interlude** and also *Beyond the Horizon*,* while the character of Don Parritt's* mother in *The Iceman Cometh** is based on Emma Goldman, a friend of Reed and the aunt of O'Neill's editor, Saxe Commins.*

See in "References": Rosenstone (1975) and Hicks (1936), the latter of which should be treated with caution. Also useful are the sources listed under the entry Louise Bryant, as well as biographies of O'Neill which make brief mention of Reed. The movie *Reds* (1981) is somewhat inaccurate in its portrayal of the relationship between Bryant and O'Neill and tends to romanticize Reed, but it does capture some of the euphoria of *Ten Days That Shook the World*.

"REVELATION OF ST. JOHN THE DIVINE, THE," an unstaged lyric interpretation of the Book of Revelations, written 1924. The speaker is Saint John, who is ordered to write after an appearance by the Son of Man. The vision is staged, and there are choruses of elders, angels, kings, merchants, and sailors. The stage directions are taken directly from the Bible. In this attempt at staging a poetic experience, there is interesting use of dance and lighting: the Four Horsemen appear bathed in red light for instance, while moonlight is used continually. The scenes that are staged are: the fall of Babylon, the New Heaven, the New Earth, and the description of the New Jerusalem. The work ends with a heavenly voice as John lies prostrate on the stage. He rises, exalted, and with his last words he blesses the audience. The conclusion is the only dramatic moment in the work, the rest being better described as lyric, choric reading of the biblical text. It is really a reverential oratorio without music.

A Note on Text: The above information is from the typescript in the Harvard Theatre Collection. Used by permission.

RILEY, Patch. In *A Touch of the Poet*,* an old piper. He "is an old man with a thatch of white hair." His eyes are "washed-out blue," and his expression is half-witted. He is dressed in tattered clothing and carries an Irish bagpipe. He seems sensitive to insult, unlike the other low-class Irish spongers of Cornelius Melody's* tavern, and Sara Melody* feels obliged to compliment him on his music after she has been curt to the others. He and his companions, Dan Roche* and Paddy O'Dowd,* are present at Melody's last Talavera Day Dinner, and throughout the play the noise of their merrymaking often serves as a counterpoint to the serious action. They beat up the Harford family lawyer, Nicholas Gadsby.* Their lack of social class is indicated by their support of Andrew Jackson for president of the United States.

"RIME OF THE ANCIENT MARINER, THE." See *The Ancient Mariner*.

RIO GRANDE. In the unpublished scenario "S.O.S."* this is the name of the steamer on which John Lathrop* is wireless operator. It is sunk by a German raider because John, as a result of his deafness, fails to monitor a warning signal.

ROBARDS, Jason, Jr. (1922–   ), actor. Born in Chicago to Jason and Hope Maxine (Glanville) Robards. Educated at Hollywood High School, California (graduated 1940); the American Academy of Dramatic Art (1946); studied acting with Uta Hagen. Married to Eleanor Pitman (1948–58), Rachel Taylor (1959–61), Lauren Bacall (1961–69), Lois O'Connor (1970–   ).

Since his debut in 1946, this singularly versatile actor has appeared in comedy, tragedy, classical theatre and popular theatre, film and television (including even the D'Oyly Carte Opera Company). He has worked in all aspects of theatre from summer stock to Broadway and as stage manager and director. Since his remarkable performance as Theodore Hickman* in *The Iceman Cometh** (Circle in the Square, 1956) initiated a Eugene O'Neill revival, he has become increasingly associated with performance of O'Neill roles, though not, of course, confined to them. Though physically he does not fit the part, his interpretation of the role of Hickman is almost definitive, something that was illustrated in his free outdoor public "reading" (really a performance) in 1982 of the monologue in an Actors Equity attempt to save the Morosco and Helen Hayes theatres (New York City) from destruction to provide a site for a Times Square Portman Hotel. He received the *Village Voice* Off-Broadway award in 1956 for this portrayal, repeating it for television on "Play of the Week" (November 14 and 21, 1960). Other acclaimed performances in O'Neill roles (frequently in productions directed by José Quintero*) were: James Tyrone, Jr.,* in *Long Day's Journey into Night* (Helen Hayes Theatre, New York City, 1956); "Erie" Smith* in *Hughie* (Royale Theatre, New York City, 1964; Huntington Hartford Theatre, Los Angeles, 1965; and on tour); James Tyrone, Jr., in *A Moon for the Misbegotten* opposite Colleen Dewhurst* as Josie Hogan* (Academy Theatre, Lake Forest, Illinois; Eisenhower Theatre, Washington, D.C.; and the Morosco Theatre, New York City, all in 1973; Ahmanson Theatre, Los Angeles, 1974; and on ABC-TV, May 27, 1975); James Tyrone,* Sr., in *Long Day's Journey into Night*, which he also directed (Mendelssohn Theatre, Ann Arbor, Michigan; Eisenhower Theatre, Washington, D.C.; Brooklyn Academy of Music, 1975–76). He received the New York Drama Critics' Award as Most Promising Actor in 1956–57 for his performance as James Tyrone, Jr., in *Long Day's Journey into Night*. Mr. Robards has also appeared in numerous film and television productions. Like José Quintero, who directed him in the 1956 performance of *The Iceman Cometh*, he has a remarkable empathy with O'Neill characters, managing to make their weaknesses credible and their agony heartrending. For an account of the first American production of *Long Day's Journey into Night*, see the memoir by José Quintero, *If You Don't Dance They Beat You* (1974), which also includes material concerning the director's work with Robards.

ROBESON, Paul (1898–1976), actor and singer. Born in Princeton, New Jersey, April 9, 1898, to the Reverend William Drew Robeson, a former slave, and Maria Louisa (Bustill) Robeson. Died in Philadelphia, January 23, 1976. Married Erlanda Cardozo Goode in 1921, who died in 1965. Educated in the public schools of Princeton and Somerville, New Jersey; Rutgers University (B.A., 1919); and Columbia University (LLB, 1923); honorary LLD, Rutgers (1932).

At Rutgers, Robeson was a Renaissance man, being the first black All-American football player, college basketball player, valedictorian of his class, and a member of Phi Beta Kappa. However, as a black he was neither allowed to live in a dormitory nor to join the Rutgers Glee Club. He had a brief professional football career and made his stage debut in 1920 in a New York YMCA production of *Simon the Cyrenian*. In 1922 he played in *Taboo* on Broadway, a role he repeated in London opposite the legendary Mrs. Patrick Campbell, when the play was called *Voodoo*.

He created the role of Jim Harris* in *All God's Chillun Got Wings** (1924, co-starring with Mary Blair*) for which he found himself the target of much vilification and exploitation because the play was repellent to critics as a result of its alleged approval of interracial marriage. In 1925 in London Robeson replayed the role of Brutus Jones* in *The Emperor Jones**, a role he had essayed earlier in 1924, in the New York City revival arranged just before the opening of *All God's Chillun Got Wings*. O'Neill was ecstatic about Robeson and at first preferred his performance to that of Charles Gilpin,* the creator of the role, an opinion not shared by the critics, who considered Gilpin's more elemental approach superior to the intellectuality of Robeson. Later, O'Neill's opinion favored Gilpin. Some glimmering of the quality of Robeson's performance may be found in the otherwise unsatisfactory film adaptation (*See* Appendix B) of the play. He repeated the stage role on numerous occasions in Europe and also appeared in a concert performance of the opera (*See* Appendix B) by Louis Gruenberg.* Robeson's other roles included Porgy in *Porgy and Bess*, *Showboat*, *Othello* (1930, 1943–44), *Plant in the Sun*, *Toussaint L'Ouverture*, *Stevedore*, *Black Boy*, and *John Henry*.

Always sensitive to the racial hostility directed against him, Robeson moved to England (1927–39) where he felt there was a climate of greater tolerance, giving concerts, playing theatrical roles, and also making films, sometimes in Hollywood, but always with the aim of providing an affirmative black image. Apart from *The Emperor Jones* (1933), his films include: *Body and Soul*, *Sanders of the River* (1935), *Show Boat* (1936), *King Solomon's Mines*, *Big Fella*, *Jericho*, and *Dark Sands* (1937), *Proud Valley* (1940), and *Tales of Manhattan* (1942). In 1942, Robeson severed his connections with Hollywood and in 1946 had political difficulties with the California State Legislative Committee under Martin Dies. In 1948 he was a founder of the Progressive Party, and in 1949 he and Pete Seeger were the victims of a raid by goons in Peekskill, New York, when a concert they were giving for the benefit of the Human Civil Rights Congress was broken up. In 1950 his United States passport was revoked because of his refusal to sign the required anticommunist affidavit. In 1952 he was awarded the Stalin Peace Prize and was blacklisted as a performer in the United States. In 1958 he returned to England, occasionally giving concerts, and returned to the United States in 1963. After the death of his wife in 1965, he lived with a sister until his death.

Paul Robeson was one of the greatest black performers of his era, a tireless fighter for civil rights and a frequent victim of racial discrimination. Because of his high visibility and his refusal to remain silent, he was frequently attacked, and his career was irreparably damaged as a result. In 1958 he published his autobiography, *Here I Stand*. It is to O'Neill's credit that he pioneered the use of racially integrated casts on Broadway. Prior to the work of Gilpin and Robeson, the usual approach was to have black roles played by whites in blackface.

ROBINSON. *See* Second Mate.*

ROCHE, Dan. In *A Touch of the Poet*,* one of the low-class Irish. He "is middle-aged, squat, bowlegged, with a potbelly and short arms lumpy with muscle." His face is porcine and his clothes dirty and patched. He is one of the spongers at Cornelius Melody's* tavern and regularly gets drunk there. He and his companions, Paddy O'Dowd* and Patch Riley* are present at Melody's last Talavera Day Dinner, and throughout the play the noise of their merrymaking often serves as a counterpoint to the serious action. They beat up the Harford family lawyer, Nicholas Gadsby.* Their lack of social class is indicated by their support of Andrew Jackson for president of the United States.

ROGERS, Alf. In *Diff'rent*,* a "husky young fisherman of twenty-four" who marries Harriet Williams,* sister of Caleb Williams.* He appears only in the first scene, where he has the reputation of fooling around with women. He is the father of Benny Rogers,* a total ne'er-do-well who gulls Emma Crosby.* Alf Rogers is drowned in the company of Jack Crosby.* Apparently he mistreated his wife during their marriage and never settled down. He is almost as bad as his son.

ROGERS, Benny. In *Diff'rent*,* son of Alf Rogers* and Harriet Williams*, nephew of Caleb Williams.* He is a completely rotten young man who has stolen money from his mother, a widow, and joined the army. He boasts of his valor but was merely a loader of supplies. He returns to his hometown to drink and consort with the town prostitute and also to inveigle Emma Crosby* out of her money. He calculatingly makes her believe that he is in love with her, even promising to marry her. But when he thinks that his Uncle Caleb, whom he hates because he has been a disciplinarian, will buy him off; he throws Emma away with singular cruelty. He is a coarse-featured, cruel young braggart.

ROGERS, Harriet. In *Diff'rent*,* sister of Caleb Williams*; later wife of Alf Rogers* and mother of Benny Rogers.* She first appears as a plain yet vital young woman of twenty-four who scoffs at Emma Crosby's* idealism in expecting premarital and even postmarital chastity from Caleb. She knows that Alf Rogers plays around and expects that all men subscribe to this double standard. When Alf is drowned in company of Jack Crosby,* she moves next door to Caleb Williams, who acts as disciplinarian to her no-good son, Benny, who takes after his father. In the second act she is a fretful, irritable, disappointed woman beaten down by life. She loves her brother and hopes that eventually Emma will come to her senses and marry him. She tries to talk Benny out of his calculating treatment of Emma.

ROGERS, Henry (Hen). In *The Movie Man*,* representative in Mexico of the Earth Motion Picture Company. He is "tall, blond, clean-shaven, in his early thirties." He is dressed in the stock "uniform" of colonialists: Stetson hat, khaki shirt, riding breeches, puttees. He has made an agreement with the leader of the insurrection in Mexico to supply arms for the fighting in return for film rights to all the battles. He discovers that a prisoner, Ernesto Fernandez, is to be shot the next day, and when Anita Fernandez,* the unfortunate man's beautiful daughter, appears, he manages an agreement with the general, Gomez.* Rogers will allow him to make a night attack, in violation of his film contract, in exchange for the life of Fernandez. He is very much the stock figure of an American in Mexico, one who cares nothing at all for the people or the culture. However, he has a certain quality of romance in coming to the aid of a maiden in distress. His character is very lightly drawn.

ROPE, THE, a one-act play. Abraham Bentley,* an old man of about sixty-five who appears to be senile, is living on his poverty-stricken farm with his daughter, Annie Sweeney,* her husband, Pat Sweeney,* and their daughter, Mary Sweeney,* a stupid ten-year-old. Old Bentley is eaten up with hatred and religious mania, given to biblical quotations and insane rages against his family. He loathes Annie because, in marrying Pat Sweeney, she has become a Roman Catholic. He hates his own granddaughter, Mary, because she is "a Papist brat." He hates Pat, also, as a drunken Irishman, despite the fact that it is Pat's hard work that keeps the farm even minimally productive. Most of all, he seems to hate his son by his second wife. Luke Bentley* ran away from home at the age of sixteen, some five years before the opening of the play, after stealing one hundred dollars from his miserly father.

Old Bentley's hatred is returned by his family. Annie hates him for the way in which he drove her mother to her grave and speedily married Luke's mother, whom she considers a harlot. She casts doubts on Luke's parentage and taunts old Bentley with the way Luke's mother left him. Pat, Annie, and old Bentley are also eaten up with greed. The younger people feel that their work is unappreciated, and Pat in particular wants to know where the old miser keeps his money because Bentley had borrowed one thousand dollars in twenty-dollar gold pieces and Pat is still working to pay off the interest, but the money is nowhere to be found. Pat finds out from the lawyer that the old man has made no mention of money in his will and that apparently there will be none left for him.

Suddenly Luke reappears after having spent some time bumming around and at sea. He gives Mary a silver dollar and then takes her out to throw rocks into the sea, but Mary insists on throwing the silver piece instead. Luke allows this act of bravado, of deliberate waste, to intimidate his half-sister and her husband.

Old Bentley is told of his son's return, and after numerous quotations from the biblical prodigal son tale, he shows his son the rope he had prepared for him when he ran away five years earlier, telling him to hang himself on it. Bentley has checked on this rope almost daily. Thinking the old man is joking, Luke gets on a chair and puts his head through the noose. To his horror he realizes that old Bentley really does want to see him hang, and in a rage he beats his father. Annie takes Abraham away, and Luke and Pat plot over a bottle of whiskey to find the old man's hoard, even if they have to torture him for information. They leave the barn empty with the rope noose dangling, as it has been for the last five years. Mary enters and decides to swing from the rope, which breaks loose, allowing a bag containing the gold pieces to fall to the ground. It has been used as a counterweight. Obviously this is why old Bentley has kept such a careful watch on the rope, wishing for Luke to discover the hidden hoard. He has loved his son after all. Mary looks at the money, scoops up a handful of gold pieces, and runs to the nearby headland to throw them one by one into the sea to see them skip. She runs back for a second handful as the curtain falls on her words, "Skip! Skip!"

Comments: The play is really a moral treatise on greed, as demonstrated in this study of hatred given and returned. All the characters in the play seem to lack redeeming social qualities, though old Bentley does have affection for Luke. The only person lacking in hatred, Mary, is a thoroughly stupid child. Everyone else is eaten up with avarice and self-interest. The play lacks consistency given that at one point Luke is said to have been absent five years and to have left home at sixteen, but the stage directions suggest he is about twenty-five. Similarly, it seems rather too fortuitous that Mary has taken five years to swing on the rope which has been there all that time. Perhaps, too, the moral lesson of *radix malorum est cupiditas* is a trifle too pat, as also is the final irony of Mary's throwing the money away.

Production Data: Written 1918. First produced by the Provincetown Players at the Playwrights' Theatre, New York City, April 26, 1918 (performances, unknown).

Director: Nina Moise
Designer: Unknown
Cast: Abraham Bentley: O. K. Liveright
Annie: Dorothy Upjohn
Pat Sweeney: H. B. Tisdale
Mary: Edna Smith
Luke Bentley: Charles Ellis
Produced May 13, 1918, by the Washington Square Players, at the Comedy Theatre, New York City (performances unknown).

ROUGON. In *The Sniper*,* a sixty-five-year-old Belgian peasant who has lost his son. He enters bearing the body of his son, Charles, whom he has seen killed in battle. He is consoled by a Village Priest* who speaks of God's "infinite will.'' Rougon, however, refuses pity because he is overwhelmed with grief. He has lost almost everything—his horses, his cow, his house, his harvest, and now his only son on the day which was to have been his wedding day. He takes a little comfort in the knowledge that Louise, Charles's fiancée, and Margot, Rougon's wife, have escaped to Brussels. Then Jean,* a peasant boy who had been sent away with the women, arrives to tell Rougon that they, too, have been killed.

Rougon now disregards the earlier warnings given by both his son and a German captain against committing violence against the Germans. As the German troops come by, Rougon takes out his old long-barrelled rifle and shoots twice, once for Louise and once for Margot. He refuses to pray to a God who has treated him unjustly, and he stands proudly before the four German privates who shoot him down in reprisal. He spits on the ground as an insult to ''your God who allows such things to happen.'' The German captain says, ''It is the law,'' and as the priest gazes on the two dead bodies he says, ''Alas, the laws of men.''

Rougon speaks in a language which sounds like a literal translation from the French and is sometimes a trifle awkward. His is the principal part in the play, and to him belongs most of the exposition. This ''great hulking old man,'' broken by grief, is a very moving character in this antiwar play. His death is well motivated, as also is his desire for vengeance, in ironic contrast to the priest's plea for resignation.

ROWLAND, Alfred. *See* Rowland, Mrs., and *Before Breakfast.*

ROWLAND, Mrs. In *Before Breakfast,** a slovenly-looking woman in her early twenties who looks much older. ''She is of medium height and inclined to a shapeless stoutness.'' Everything about her, from drab hair to nondescript blue eyes, is dull. Her expression is pinched, and her mouth is ''weak, spiteful.'' She is the only speaking character, and her monologue consists of a continual recital of grievances against her husband, Alfred Rowland, starting with her resentment at having to work. She had married the son of the town millionaire, who had gotten her, the grocer's daughter, ''into trouble.'' He had persuaded her to marry him, despite his father's offer to buy her off, but now the ''town millionaire'' is dead, owing everyone money, and Alfred, ''the Harvard graduate, the poet, the catch of the town,'' has turned into a failed poet, a frequenter of Washington Square bars.

She tells Alfred that the rent is due, that he must get a job, that she has read his letter from ''Helen,'' and that she is aware of his ''goings-on'' and certainly will not grant him a divorce so that he can marry another woman. The large glass of gin she has gulped down to begin her morning has clearly started her off on a tirade. Luckily their child was stillborn, but her health has been ruined, and Alfred is always too drunk or too hungover to get a job. Indeed, that allegation seems correct, because when Alfred puts out his long slender artistic hand to take his bowl of shaving water, it is shaking rather badly. When Mrs. Rowland reaches her crowning insult, calling Helen "no better than a common street-walker," there is a groan of pain from the bedroom, then the sound of water dripping, and suddenly something crashes heavily to the floor. Mrs. Rowland rushes to the bedroom door, stands transfixed with horror for a moment, and then rushes out the other door "shrieking madly."

This character is one of O'Neill's Strindbergian women who cannot understand the artistic capacity of their men and drives them to suicide or unhappiness. It is really little more than a vaudeville sketch but useful as a development of themes the playwright had already used in *Warnings** and *Bread and Butter** and was later to use in *Beyond the Horizon** and *The Great God Brown.** The theme of the girl in "trouble" is also used in *Servitude,** a play which indicates O'Neill's ideal of a successful matrimonial relationship.

ROYLSTON, Alice. In *Servitude,** wife to David Roylston* and mother of Davie and Ruth. Alice "is a pretty woman of thirty or so, with a mass of light curly brown hair, big thoughtful eyes, rosy complexion, tiny hands and feet, and a slight girlish figure." Her children are "healthy, noisy, delightful." She was the stenographer to David's father when she had an affair with David, who felt himself obliged to marry her. Her father-in-law is said to have died of grief over this marriage, and Alice has never ceased to feel herself unworthy of her husband. She claims that despite her eleven years of marriage, she has always believed that she would leave David as soon as he no longer needed her. She has always felt that the day would come when he would find her nothing more than a weight because now that he is successful, she is unworthy of him. All she has had to offer him is her love, and therefore she has devoted herself to making his life as comfortable as possible; she is the perfect housekeeper who keeps the problems of life at a distance for David so that he can devote himself entirely to his art. When they were poor she had done all his typing for him, and now she makes his home run as if on wheels.

As a reward, David consistently underestimates her, thinking that she has no feelings. He has never bothered to analyze his "domestic bliss," but he enjoys both his home comforts and the adoration of the assorted young women who write to him. Alice is hurt by the way in which he reads their letters aloud to her, but when he ceases she is suspicious, and she reads them without permission. With the arrival of Ethel Frazer,* Alice takes her for the latest, most importunate admirer, and on learning that the lady has stayed the night in her own absence, she jumps to the logical conclusion that she and David have been intimate. She instantly takes the stand that she must therefore withdraw from the marriage because its continuance would not be in David's best interests. She sees Mrs. Frazer as the embodiment of all that she dreaded and thinks that she must now pay for her earlier sin by freeing David to marry his "love." For her, "love means servitude; and *my* love is *my* happiness," and if that is insufficient, then she must go. Finally, when Mrs. Frazer brings Roylston to an appreciation of his egotism he is reconciled to his wife; and as he tells her, "Don't you understand that you have stifled your own longings, given up your own happiness that I might feel self-satisfied—'' she replies, "That was my happiness."

Alice Roylston seems almost too good to be true, and certainly she is the total opposite to the "new woman," the "liberated female." She seems also to be a portrait of the O'Neill feminine ideal. Indeed, his attitude toward his second wife, Agnes Boulton,* when he wished for a divorce in order to marry Carlotta Monterey,* would seem to indicate that he wished her to act in the same manner as Alice Roylston, while Carlotta herself seems to have endeavored to live up to that same ideal of "servitude," according to her account.

ROYLSTON, David. In *Servitude*,* a successful playwright and novelist and husband of Alice Roylston.* He is the egotistical author who preaches self-realization for all, including women, and a defiance of conventions. "He is a tall, slender, dark-haired man of thirty-five with large, handsome features, a strong ironical mouth half-hidden by a black mustache, and keenly-intelligent dark eyes." His dress is "white shirt with soft collar and black bow tie, grey trousers, and low tan shoes with rubber soles." Clearly, in his physical appearance he resembles O'Neill himself. He is exceedingly attractive to young women who find themselves liberated by his works, and some of them attempt to put his unconventional principles into action in their daily lives. They write him letters asking for advice, and some even come to see him, but he is always careful to distance himself from any emotional entanglement. He was "caught" only once, by his wife Alice, his father's stenographer, with whom he had been intimate before his marriage to her. He has never tried to analyze his familial relationships, satisfied only that everything runs smoothly, and has no conception of the hurt he offers to his wife when he reads aloud to her some of the adoring letters he receives.

Only the arrival of Ethel Frazer,* who misses the last train home and must therefore stay overnight in his wife's absence, finally brings about his awakening. For the first time he is himself trapped, and therefore he shows himself no disciple of his own teaching by moving out to the local hotel. Mrs. Frazer finally brings him to an understanding of his own selfishness and his wife's totally unquestioning love for him. At the end of the play they are reconciled, and Roylston sets himself the task of paying back to some extent the debt of love he owes to his wife, Alice, who would even give him up if that would assure his complete happiness. One does, however, doubt the longevity of his resolution because it sounds like a new enthusiasm. He rephrases the central statement of the play, "Happiness is servitude," as "Logos in Pan, Pan in Logos!" There is also a curious echo, which probably did not occur to O'Neill, of Piccarda's statement in the *Paradiso* section of Dante's *Divine Comedy*: "la sua volontate è nostra pace,"—His will is our peace.

ROYLSTON, Herbert. In *Shell Shock*,* lieutenant of infantry, U.S.A., a blond, clean-shaven young man of about twenty-seven, who has just returned from the front after being severely wounded. He was brought in from No Man's Land after three days and nights by Jack Arnold,* a college hero who later has a nervous breakdown as a result of questioning his own motivations for this heroic act.

S

SANDS, Evelyn. In *Abortion*,* fiancée of Jack Townsend.* She "is a tall, dark-haired, beautiful girl about twenty years old. Her eyes are large and brown; her figure lithe and graceful. She is dressed simply but stylishly in white." She is adoringly in love with Jack, her hero, and she tells of her secret joy in her ownership of him as everyone cheers his achievements. She sees Jack as an ideal character, playing "the game of life—fairly, squarely, strengthening those around you, refusing to weaken at critical moments, advancing others by sacrifices, fighting the good fight for the cause, the team, and always, always, whether vanquished or victor, reserving a hearty, honest cheer for the other side." She is used as the spokesperson for the external nature of Jack, who knows very well that he is an idol with feet of clay. She also represents a common O'Neill feminine type character: the woman who adores her man and accepts him unquestioningly as the guiding star of her life. She discovers Jack's dead body and faints on it as the curtain falls.

SARAH ALLEN, the name of the schooner in *Gold*,* prepared for the purpose of seeking the buried treasure.

SCHMIDT. In "The Personal Equation,"* a huge blond German stoker. He is beaten in a fight by another stoker named O'Rourke* on the S.S. *San Francisco*. He does not take part in the sabotaging of the engines because he has been knocked out. As in the later *The Hairy Ape*,* O'Neill includes a number of different ethnic groups in his portrait of the stokehole.

SCOTT, Dick. In *Beyond the Horizon*,* captain of the *Sunda*, a sailing vessel. He is the brother of Kate Mayo* and uncle of her two boys, Robert Mayo* and Andrew Mayo.* He "is short and stocky, with a weatherbeaten, jovial face and a white mustache." He is fifty-eight. At the beginning of the play, he is waiting to take Robert with him on a three-year voyage to the Far East on the *Sunda*. Robert, a delicate, romantic person, decides to remain at home to marry Ruth Atkins.* Andrew, also in love with Ruth, thereupon decides to undertake the voyage. Captain Scott is a "typical old salt," given to the occasional tall story and also concerned with what his crew thinks of him. He is very concerned that they will think he was jilted by a woman when Robert decides not to occupy the refurbished cabin on the *Sunda*. He is relieved when Andrew takes his brother's place. Indeed, Scott had all along considered that the physically stronger Andrew would make a better seaman than his brother.

SCOTTY. In *Bound East for Cardiff*,* a seaman on the S.S. *Glencairn*, ''a dark young fellow.''

"SEA-MOTHER'S SON, THE." An idea for an autobiographical play which O'Neill mentioned first in the late 1920s but never wrote. Virginia Floyd (1981, pp. 180–182) recounts its history and gives an entry from O'Neill's *Work Diary* noting that it was discussed there from 1927 to 1931. It bears some relationship to *Dynamo*.*

"SECOND ENGINEER, THE." The original title of ''The Personal Equation.''*

SECOND MATE (Robinson), of the S.S. *Glencairn*. In *Bound East for Cardiff*,* he is ''clean-shaven and middle-aged,'' wearing a simple blue uniform.

SELBY, Wint. In *Ah, Wilderness!*,* friend of Arthur Miller.* Selby is a Yale college-sport type on vacation. He wants his friend, Arthur, to visit the Pleasant Beach Inn with him and two ''tarts'' from New Haven, but finding that Arthur is unavailable, he asks Richard Miller* to come instead. Selby is strictly a piece of stage machinery.

SERVITUDE, a three-act play. The action takes place in the study of David Roylston,* a successful playwright and novelist, in his home at Tarryville-on-Hudson, New York. The time is 1913–1914.

   Act I: It is 10 P.M. ''on a sultry night in early May'' when David Roylston is discovered in his study, seated and writing at a table. The study is a book-lined room with doors in the back wall and to the right of the fireplace, which is on the left wall. The right wall contains a leather sofa and armchairs with an open window looking onto the garden. ''A few framed prints of Old Masters are hung on the walls.''

   Benton,* a manservant in livery, enters to ask whether Roylston wishes to have the windows shut, noting that the impractical writer has forgotten to perform this task the night before. He also tells Roylston that his wife and two children have arrived safely in New York for their theatre visit. Roylston asks whether any telephone calls have been received, and on hearing that there have not been any, he inquires, ''Not even the young lady who has '*(ironically)*' asked my advice so frequently of late?'' On receiving a negative answer, he continues, ''Well, whenever the young lady in question calls up again you are to tell her

I am writing and cannot be disturbed.'' Benton leaves and then returns with a card from a Mrs. George Frazer who wishes to see the writer; he says she is "young and pretty'' and apparently has come alone. Roylston seems surprised and sarcastically notes, "A lady, you say?'' as Benton notes that she is "dressed shabby, almost as if she'd seen better days.'' Cynically, Roylston suggests he should perhaps get out his checkbook; but Benton says that she doesn't look the type who would beg, so Roylston opts for "another aspiring playwright who wants me to write her last act for her.'' Benton then shows in Ethel Frazer,* a strikingly beautiful woman of about twenty-eight, "her manner is troubled, nervous, uncertain. She has on a plain black dress as is worn by the poorer class of working women.'' Left alone with Roylston, Mrs. Frazer apologizes profusely for her intrusion upon his privacy and for "such a breach of all the conventions.'' Roylston dryly claims to see "nothing strange'' in her coming in this manner: "You are the very first to accuse me of conventionality.'' Reassured, Mrs. Frazer says that they had met, very briefly, at a ball given at an artist's studio about a year ago. Roylston, trying to put her at her ease, suggests that she remove her hat: "To see you sitting there with your hat on gives me the uncomfortable impression that this is a lawyer's office and you are consulting your attorney— and I warn you I am far from being a *legal* advisor.''

Mrs. Frazer then explains that she has indeed come to Roylston for advice concerning her current situation, and she tells the story of her life. She had been brought up in a privileged environment: "governess, private tutors, and finally a finishing school.'' She then married her husband, "a broker on the New York Stock Exchange.'' Fascinated by his work and financial connections, she married him, had "the usual honeymoon trip to Europe,'' and was very happy until, after seven years, she fell in love "with an ideal—the ideal of self-realization.'' She had read one of Roylston's novels, about Wall Street, and disillusion set in. Her husband had treated this attitude with some tolerance, but she read all of Roylston's novels, went to see all his plays, and "It dawned upon me gradually that the life he and I were living together was the merest sham; that we were contented because he was too busy and I was too lazy to analyze our position, to stop and think.'' Finally, after seeing Roylston's play, *Sacrifice*, she followed the example of the principal character and left her husband. Since then she has modeled her life on that character, becoming a wage-earner. But now the loneliness and misery of her life has caught up with her. Instead of finding liberation, self-realization, and freedom, she has discovered that "the men were all such beasts and the women I had to come in contact with were so unintelligent and ordinary.'' And all this time, George Frazer* has been pleading with her to return to him, "trying to force money'' on her. Now she has come to Roylston to have him tell her that she has made the right choice.

Roylston is "*plainly embarrassed*'' and offers her "help...in—er—a pecuniary way,'' an offer Mrs. Frazer indignantly refuses. All she wants is "the assurance that I am on the right path''; she wonders whether she has a right to make her husband so unhappy, and in her wavering faith she has come to

Roylston: "I demand that you restore my peace of mind by justifying me to myself." Roylston, "*deeply moved*," urges her "not to give up the battle, for in the end you will achieve a victory well worth the winning," and asks her to call on him whenever she may "need help in the future." He also suggests that he might find some work for her in the city, but "In the meantime I have lots of work which should be typewritten," an offer which Mrs. Frazer accepts with joy: "Your encouragement has made me feel so hopeful, so full of energy, I am ready for anything. A new life of wonderful possibilities seems opening up before me."

With these words she gets ready to return to her "little hall room" in her dingy boarding house, only to discover that she has missed the last train to New York City. Roylston offers her a bed in the house, but Mrs. Frazer is shocked by this breach of convention, especially when she discovers that Mrs. Roylston and the family are not home. Finally, after Roylston explains that the local hotel is not a place of good repute, she agrees to stay overnight. He says that Benton is "a model of discretion," and as for his wife, "she would not think anything. If it would ease your conscience, I will tell her the whole thing. I'm sure she'd forget all about it ten minutes later (*contemptuously*) when the butcher came for his order." Then in answer to Mrs. Frazer's question concerning his love for his wife, he admits that he has not really bothered to analyze his "home relations": "My work comes first. As long as my home life gives free scope for my creative faculty I will demand nothing further of it....I accept my domestic bliss at its surface and save my analytical eye for the creations." Mrs. Frazer agrees to stay, but as she leaves the room she confesses that she has never actually met Roylston and that she had deliberately missed her last train "to see if you were a real man with the courage of your convictions or just a theorist." Roylston starts to move toward her, but she claims that she knows she is safe with such a man who would "protect the helpless." Roylston watches her departure, sits down, tries unsuccessfully to work, and with an exclamation of "Damnation!" leaves the room.

Act II: It is about 9 A.M. the next morning when Benton enters to discover Ethel Frazer's hat lying on the sofa. With "a low whistle of amazement" he sees Weson,* the old gardener, who reports "a feller hangin' round the house s'picious like." Benton loses his reserve for a moment and engages Weson in discussion concerning Mrs. Frazer and notes, "I don't blame him, though; she's a beauty." However, he does offer a warning: "Once caught, twice shy, they say; and he was caught once, good and proper. (*With a short laugh*) It'll do the Missus good to get a dose of her own medicine. It broke the old man's heart when the young fellow married her." Then the old retainer remembers himself and ends the conversation as Mrs. Frazer comes downstairs. He greets her affably and tells her that Roylston doesn't usually rise this early; then in a moment of confidence, he tells her that his master isn't in the habit of having young women stay overnight, even though "the others" are "all crazy about him" and he likes it: "It tickles him...to have them adoring him, asking for his advice."

Suddenly Alice Roylston* and the children return unexpectedly because the little girl, Ruth, has taken ill (probably too much candy). She and her older brother, Davie, exchange a few words. Ethel Frazer, "too overcome with fear and shame to think," slips out the rear door before they enter. After Benton arranges for the doctor to call, Mrs. Frazer enters to confront Mrs. Roylston: "I lost my head completely for a moment, and ran away, I was so afraid of what you might think. In there I regained my senses. I had done no wrong. Why should I be afraid of you? So I came back." Mrs. Roylston greets her appearance with "I knew it! I knew it!" and gradually discovers that Mrs. Frazer has spent the night in the house. Instantly Alice thinks the worst: "I have prayed this would never happen, but I have seen it drawing nearer every day in spite of my prayers; and I am prepared for it." Sadly she refuses to accept Mrs. Frazer's assurance of her innocence, "Haven't I read your letters to him?" but Mrs. Frazer denies ever having written. Alice refuses to accept the explanation that Mrs. Frazer does not love Roylston and had never seen him before last night.

Alice Roylston then tells the tale of her own married life, how they had had to get married, and how as a result she had foreseen the day when Roylston would tire of her. He has read letters from many women to her, not knowing how hurt she was, and then "all at once he stopped showing them to me—and they kept coming, all in the same handwriting." At that point she read the letters. Hopelessly, Alice recounts that she had been stenographer to Roylston's father and that she had loved the son "too well." She takes the entire blame for everything upon herself, for allowing her husband "to make too great a sacrifice." She thinks her father-in-law even died of grief over their marriage, but when she married Roylston she resolved to leave him as soon as he could take care of himself: "I knew he would come to regret his sacrifice and I would become a dead weight holding him back." But then the children came, so she stayed. She looks back on their early days of poverty—when she would do her husband's typing—as the happiest of her life; but now he is successful, and "lately he has grown more and more indifferent to me and to the children; so that now I'm afraid he only looks on me as a sort of housekeeper. . . . He'll have to acknowledge I'm a good one. I've protected him from all the small worries he detests so much. I don't believe he realizes; he thinks things just run along by themselves."

Mrs. Frazer notes that indeed Roylston "has never analyzed his home relations" and asks Alice whether she has ever attempted to assert herself, to tell her husband how she has felt. Alice says that she has simply "loved him with all my heart and soul; . . . If that has no power to hold him,—then I have lost him." Her only happiness has been in serving him, but now that her husband's "future happiness" no longer depends on her, she will leave: "I can only thank God for granting the beauty and joy of the past eleven years to a woman who sinned and was too cowardly to pay." She will make her supreme sacrifice of love by letting him go, and in face of that, Ethel Frazer agrees: "Compared to you I am a weakling." The two women seem almost to develop a confidence in each other as Alice Roylston says that she has daily laid her soul bare to her husband, "but he never saw it," and the pair make the central statements of the play: *Mrs. Frazer*: "How much you have taught me! Happiness, then, means servitude?" *Mrs. Roylston*: "Love means servitude; and *my* love is *my* happiness." But Alice still believes that Ethel Frazer is her rival and looks upon her, quite legitimately, as an enemy. Suddenly she hears Roylston enter, presumably from a morning walk, and she turns on Mrs. Frazer, accusing her of lying.

On her husband's entrance, Alice explains the circumstances of her unannounced return, and in a bantering tone he tries to explain away the events of the previous night: "My dear Alice, you are really the perfect wife. I told you, Mrs. Frazer, that Caesar's wife is above harboring suspicion. I welcome you to the model household, where truth reigns, where conventions are as naught, where we believe each other implicitly because we have found each other so worthy of belief. And I salute you, My Angel of Trustfulness." With this, Alice pushes him away. Roylston sees that all is not mutual trust, so he tells her that "Mrs. Frazer is going to do some work for me," but she refuses to believe him.

Revelations abound as Alice confesses to reading her husband's letters from an admirer—who is not Ethel Frazer. In response, Roylston rages that Alice has dared to read his mail and insists that she is in the wrong. At this moment the doorbell rings to announce the doctor, and Mrs. Roylston starts to leave, but Roylston stops her by adopting a holier-than-thou attitude: "I will have Benton pack up my things at once. I do not care to live with a wife who is also an evil-minded spy." Alice cringes and says that it is she who no longer belongs in the household, and therefore she will give him his freedom: "I want you to be happy, and—I know I am only in the way—now. Please forgive me." As he turns away from her, Ethel says indignantly, "For shame, Mr. Roylston," but Alice refuses the intercession, "Don't you know how I hate you," as she rushes out.

Act III: No time has elapsed, and Roylston and Ethel Frazer remain standing looking at the door. Roylston breaks the silence: "I have lived with that woman eleven years, and I have never known her until ten minutes ago." The tension is broken by Benton, who mentions Weson's tale of a prowler but suggests that Roylston should "look out for the badger game, sir," a clear suggestion that Mrs. Frazer might be planning blackmail. Self-righteously, Roylston continues to inveigh against Alice for reading his letters. Now "the muddy depths" of his family relationships have been stirred up, and he sees that he has "trusted in a sham." He turns to Mrs. Frazer, noting that they are both in the same boat, the "prop is worm-eaten." Mrs. Frazer sarcastically agrees, noting that they share "bruises on the soul." Roylston sees he will have to find a new illusion and recalls Mrs. Frazer's words of the last evening when she feared "the crowning disillusionment," something she has clearly discovered. Finally she turns on him to denounce him as "insighted": "you see nothing beyond yourself. . . . You are only a cruel egotist. . . the only individual in the world." In her rage she refutes his argument that he has spoken of "the duty of the individual to triumph over environment. . . . Last night I thought—you were on such a high pedestal—

I thought of the superman, of the creator, the maker of new values. This morning I saw merely an egotist whose hands are bloody with the human sacrifices he has made—to himself."

After this outburst the two calm down a trifle, and Ethel Frazer admits she is trying to overcome her "attack of hero-worship," but she then goes on to praise Alice as "the most wonderful woman I have ever known." Roylston cannot agree, and she warns him not to judge by appearances, telling him that he had no right to receive adoring letters from another woman. Gradually she draws the facts out of him: he has persuaded a pretty twenty-one-year-old girl to break her engagement and leave her home—all for self-improvement, and love of him. Ethel suggests that Roylston write to her and reveal himself for the egotist he is, but Roylston tells her that his method, a cynical piece of affected pathos, is better. Mrs. Frazer, now in control, tries to speak seriously and notes that Roylston always avoids compromising himself—according to Benton. Roylston then says he will get Benton to pack his clothes so that he may move out, but Mrs. Frazer stops him, telling him how blind he has been, and recounts her interview with his wife; she speaks of the way Alice has gloried in her servitude to him, how the days of their poverty were happier than those of prosperity, and how in her everlasting generosity she is prepared to give him up in order to serve his future happiness.

Gradually, Roylston sees the truth of her comments, and he starts to understand that he knows neither Alice nor their children; he will now try to make up for the time he has lost, to "pay off a part of this enormous debt of love which has accumulated against me!" Ethel Frazer repeats her remark in Act II, "Happiness is servitude," a remark which Roylston takes up and rephrases, "Of course it is! Servitude in love, love in servitude! Logos in Pan, Pan in Logos! That is the great secret." Then he discovers that it is Alice who should be credited with the solution to that great enigma. Now he will love: "My love will be a superlove worthy of the superman." Mrs. Frazer laughs at his "determination to be exceptional though the heavens fall."

Ethel Frazer then says she will leave, having accomplished her mission. She will return to her husband, and if Alice will allow it, she will be her friend. At that moment, George Frazer enters, and seeing the two standing together, he draws a revolver. Mrs. Frazer flings herself between the two men, and George throws the revolver to the floor and collapses into sobs while Benton creeps off with the gun. Now Frazer confronts Roylston and says he has not spared him for himself. He then tells his wife that he has had a nervous breakdown, the result of overwork. He has had her followed ever since she left him because he was afraid of the kind of game "these gentlemen play." Above all, he expresses his love for her. Swearing her innocence, Ethel Frazer asks if he wants her back. George replies in the affirmative, and his wife promises an explanation as Alice Roylston enters. Ethel introduces her to George, saying that "Mrs. Roylston is the most wonderful woman in the world," and the newly reconciled couple depart.

David Roylston and his wife are then themselves reconciled with his confession that he had spent the night at the local hotel and not alone with Mrs. Frazer in the house. Alice then reveals that she had been prepared to ensure his future happiness, and they fall into each other's arms as Roylston tells her, "it was your duty to claim your right as an individual, to shake off the shackles my insufferable egotism had forced upon you.... you have... given up your own happiness that I might feel self-satisfied." Alice interrupts him tenderly with the curtain line, "That was my happiness."

Comments: This early well-made play is also an attempt at a problem play in the manner of Ibsen and it tries to answer the question of what happened to Nora Helmer in *A Doll's House* after she slammed the door. Ethel Frazer is almost as helpless a character as Nora, and she learns what Alice Roylston had always known, that "happiness is servitude." At the same time, the dialogue has a Shavian quality to it, and the play is concerned with the theme of the superman, not so much in the Nietzschean sense but rather that of Bernard Shaw. What constitutes a happy marriage is the real theme, but the situations with continual insinuations of adultery seem almost like French farce. The first act is an unalloyed exposition, while the second is a revelation scene in which the two women discover themselves. The third act is a combination of revelation for Roylston and Frazer, and a double reconciliation of both couples which is serious rather than comic. The final revelation is that of Roylston's basic conventionalism.

One of the most important things in *Servitude* is its presentation of what apparently remained O'Neill's attitude toward the marriage relationship both in his works and in real life. Throughout his plays, the women characters he most admires are those who, like Nora Melody in *A Touch of the Poet*,* give up their whole lives to their husbands, thinking that in self-abnegation lies happiness. Women who attempt to assert themselves, like Lavinia Mannon* in *Mourning Becomes Electra*,* are doomed to perpetual misery. In real life, also, O'Neill in his marriage to Agnes Boulton,* and even more so in his third marriage, to Carlotta Monterey,* showed that what he most particularly wanted was a relationship which would relieve him from all the tasks of daily living and leave him free to pursue his art. O'Neill, both in his real and his artistic life, seems to have considered matrimony as a trap to catch the unwary male, especially if he was an artist. In that case, his desires for self-expression would probably be thwarted by the practical economics of the wife: see *Bread and Butter*,* and *Beyond the Horizon*,* for instance.

Servitude has a curiously mixed tone, because its dialogue is a combination of attempted wit and attempted philosophy, neither of which is fully realized, while the relentless procession of confrontations and revelations leads to a certain monotony. The characters are cardboard figures, and it is hard to believe today in such total unselfishness as that shown by Alice Roylston, or such idealism as that of Ethel Frazer. Perhaps only the intense self-absorption of Roylston remains viable, though the play has, of course, dated badly with the "new morality" and women's liberation.

In this play O'Neill does not quite seem to have made up his mind whether he is satirizing the Shavian "New Woman" and the desire for self-realization expressed by the Ibsen woman, or writing a work which upholds his own serious view of marriage as a relationship in which the woman must serve her man unstintingly and unquestioningly. The exaggerated idealism of Mrs. Frazer as the "new woman" is indeed laughable, particularly when one considers the qualities of Roylston, the egotistical superman. But then the exaggerated unselfishness of Alice Roylston ought to be equally laughable, but O'Neill seems to take that seriously.

Production Data: Written 1913–1914. Produced by Tom Del Vecchio at the Skylark Theatre, New York International Airport, April 22, 1960. No further information located.

A Note on Text: The text used is that appearing in *Ten "Lost" Plays of Eugene O'Neill* (New York: Random House, 1964).

SHAW, Gordon. In *Strange Interlude** engaged to Nina Leeds* and killed before the action of the play begins. Nonetheless, he is the ghost who haunts the entire play because both Nina and her husband, Sam Evans,* keep his memory alive. Nina never forgets the lover who is killed shortly before the Armistice (1918) and attempts to mold her son after his pattern. The character of Gordon Shaw is probably based on that of Hobart Amory Hare Baker (1892–1918), whose career is very similar to that of Shaw. He remains to this day the legendary Princeton athletic hero by whom all later prowess is judged. He joined the American Expeditionary Force and served as pilot and squadron commander. He was killed shortly after the Armistice while testing a repaired plane and under orders to return home. He epitomized the F. Scott Fitzgerald ideal of university youth, and displayed "the spirit of manly vigor, of honor, of fair play, and the clean game." (President Hibben of Princeton, quoted in Leitch, 1978, p. 38). Interestingly, O'Neill insists snobbishly on the fact that Gordon's people were really rather ordinary and also that great college athletic heroes do not normally succeed later in life; after that brief time of adulation, everything is downhill.

Gordon Shaw is remembered in the play as a latter-day knight in shining armor, but his ethic is not very viable: one of athletic prowess, commitment to self-denial, honor, masculine strength, and very little introspection. Nina and Sam Evans always continue a belief in that ideal, while both Charles Marsden* and Edmund Darrell* rebel against it, each seeing this commitment as poisoning their relations with Nina. As a result, both Charlie and Edmund (though opposed, almost inimical characters) hope that Nina's son, Gordon Evans (the re-creation of the Gordon Shaw ideal), will lose in his last regatta crew race. This ideal is really rather adolescent and to some extent dated, and it does make some of the other characters of the play seem a trifle shallow.

SHEFFIELD, Esther (Jayson). In *The First Man*,* wife of Mark Sheffield* and sister of Curtis Jayson.* She is "a stout, middle-aged woman with the round, unmarked, sentimentally contented face of one who lives unthinkingly from day to day, sheltered in an assured position in her little world." She dislikes Martha Jayson* because of her aggressive personality and also because she has little in common with her. Like the rest of the Jayson family, she quickly believes that Martha's child is Edward Bigelow's* rather than Curtis Jayson's. However, she is not totally devoid of sympathy during Martha's agonizing childbirth and even weeps "for Curt" at Martha's funeral.

SHEFFIELD, Mark. In *The First Man*,* husband of Esther (Jayson) Sheffield.* He is a tall, slightly stooped lawyer of about forty-five. His face is "alert, shrewd, cautious, full of the superficial craftiness of the lawyer mind." He is most concerned with the family honor, and in the fourth act it is he who tries to impress upon Curtis Jayson* the importance of his recognizing Martha Jayson's* child "for appearance's sake." He readily believes the family gossip that the child is really that of Edward Bigelow.*

SHELL SHOCK, a one-act play. The scene is "a corner in the grill of the New York club of a large Eastern University." It is mid-afternoon on a hot day in September 1918. A bored middle-aged waiter surveys the room whose only other occupant is a uniformed medical corps officer about thirty years old. As the curtain rises, Herbert Roylston* enters in the uniform of an infantry first lieutenant. He is about twenty-seven, but his face seems to indicate "recent convalescence from a serious illness." He greets the medical officer, Robert Wayne* (who used to room with Jack Arnold* at college).

As they chat together, Roylston reveals that he had been saved by the bravery of Jack Arnold who had crawled out into No Mans Land and carried him back to the American trenches. Wayne is surprised because he had heard that Arnold had brought back the body of a dead officer. Roylston laughingly remarks that everyone probably thought he was "a gone goose" at the time. The two then discuss Jack's extraordinary exploit of holding out with his company for three days without relief, and Roylston tells how he had lain out between the trenches for three days and nights, badly wounded. He suddenly tried to stand up, was hit again, and then he saw Jack Arnold coming for him. Wayne is surprised when Roylston says that Arnold had picked him up on the *third* night, after the company had been relieved, but thinks little of this odd discrepancy, remarking that Arnold has been invalided home, the victim of either a nervous breakdown or shell shock. A friend has sent a note to Wayne saying, "Watch Arnold— cigarettes," which he thinks strange since "Jack never smokes." Roylston quickly tells him that in France, Arnold had become a compulsive smoker. They continue their reminiscences about Jack Arnold and his football exploits, and Roylston leaves.

Arnold enters. He is a tall, athletic-looking young man of about thirty whose suntan has faded to a sickly yellow with illness. His face is tense and he continually raises his hands to his lips as if smoking an imaginary cigarette. Wayne and Arnold talk about generalities and then move on to a discussion of the war. This triggers a curious reaction in Arnold. He continually cadges cigarettes from Wayne, even though he has full boxes in his pockets; he seems afraid that he may run out, and to his annoyance he finds himself " 'sniping butts'. . . whenever the silence comes over me." Asked to explain his frequent reference to "the silence," Arnold speaks of the everlasting racket of the trenches, the screams of the dying, the stench of corpses, until Wayne remarks that Roylston has been in the club that day, "the man you dragged out of No Mans Land after Chateau Thierry which won you your load of medals." Arnold refuses to believe this: "Herb was dead, I tell you."

Through Arnold's flood of reminiscences the story comes out. When relief came, the troops did not bring any cigarettes with them; at that point, as Jack recalls it, he remembered that Roylston was out there—dead, as he believed— and he had some cigarettes on him. "After that—I forget. It's all a blank. I must have gone over the top and brought him back." Wayne looks at him in disbelief: "You saved Roylston—for a cigarette—God!" That is the basis of Arnold's fear—a distrust of his own motivations. Wayne then asks if he had gone out to Roylston because he had seen him stand up in the shell hole—no— but then when Wayne asks if he had heard Roylston screaming, Arnold remembers that there were screams—"like this"—which came into a moment of silence. Suddenly Arnold's burden of guilt is lifted, and he realizes that it must have been Roylston's screaming that drove him out, not merely the cigarettes: "all the time I've been going mad—slowly inside—thinking I was a damned cur." Wayne is now quite convinced that Arnold is cured, and at that moment Roylston enters and the two bear-hug each other. But when he offers Arnold a cigarette, Jack says, "Not on your life! Never another! A pipe for me for the rest of my life."

Comments: This slight sketch has very little importance except for its timeliness, and it is a fairly typical antiwar piece, far more contrived than even *The Sniper*.* There is, however, one character who appears for the first time, that of the college athlete who enlists in the army as soon as possible in order to fight the Germans.

Production Data: Written 1918. Unproduced.

A Note on Text: The text used is that appearing in *"Children of the Sea" and Three Other Unpublished Plays by Eugene O'Neill*, edited by Jennifer McCabe Atkinson, with Foreword by Frank Durham (Washington, D.C.: NCR Microcard Editions, A Bruccoli-Clark Book, 1972).

SHORTY. In *All God's Chillun Got Wings*.* He starts the play as a young punk and ends as a pimp and dope peddler.

SILVA, Joe. In *The Haunted*, the last play in the trilogy, *Mourning Becomes Electra*,* "a Portuguese fishing captain—a fat boisterous man, with a hoarse bass voice." He is sixty years old. He forms part of the Chorus of Townsfolk who comment on the Mannon family and the events with which they have been involved. He is one of those who successfully bets Abner Small* that the latter cannot stay overnight in the haunted Mannon mansion.

"SILVER BULLET, THE." The original title of *The Emperor Jones.**

SILVERDENE EMBLEM ("Blemie") (1927–1940), Dalmatian dog, pet of Eugene and Carlotta Monterey* O'Neill. Died of old age and was buried at Tao House. O'Neill composed for Carlotta's consolation *The Last Will and Testament of Silverdene Emblem O'Neill*, which was later privately printed, "For Carlotta," by Yale University Press (1956). She once commented that "Blemie" was "the only one of our children who has not disillusioned us (Sheaffer, 1973, p. 518). His headstone, which still stands, reads: "Blemie/(Silverdene Emblem)/Born September 27, 1927, England/Died December 16, 1940, Tao House/Sleep in Peace, Faithful Friend."

SIMEON WINTHROP. The name of Chris Christopherson's* coal barge in *"Anna Christie"** and its two earlier drafts *Chris Christophersen,** and "The Ole Davil."**

SIMMS, Doctor. In *The Straw,** the assistant to Mr. Sloan.* He "is a tall angular young man with a long sallow face, and a sheepish, self-conscious grin."

SLADE, Larry. In *The Iceman Cometh,** a sixty-year-old disenchanted anarchist. He is "tall, raw-boned, with coarse straight white hair, worn long. . . . He has a gaunt Irish face" and is unshaven and dirty. He has "an expression of tired tolerance giving his face the quality of a pitying but weary old priest's." He is one of the roomers above Harry Hope's* saloon. Theodore Hickman,* a salesman who comes to the bar annually to celebrate Hope's birthday, has characterized him as "the old foolosopher" in recognition of the total detachment from life that Larry has tried to cultivate. He acts as chorus for the entire play and assesses Hope's establishment as "the No-Chance Saloon. It's Bedrock Bar, The End of the Line Cafe, The Bottom of the Sea Rathskeller!" He also understands that "The lie of a pipe dream is what gives life to the whole misbegotten mad lot of us, drunk or sober." He was once active in "the Movement" and was the lover of Rosa Parritt, a leader recently imprisoned on the West Coast for complicity in a bombing incident as the result of information furnished by an insider. Larry, along with the other denizens of Hope's saloon, is waiting for Hickman's annual visit and blowout.

However, the long-time camaraderie of the saloon population has been disrupted this year by the arrival of Don Parritt,* the eighteen-year-old son of Larry's former lover, Rosa Parritt. He latches on to Larry as the only friend he has in the world, even suggesting that Larry was his father, a statement the older man denies, but the truth is left ambiguous. Parritt sneers at Larry's philosophical detachment and world-weariness, maintaining that he still has a commitment to the movement and that the only reason he doesn't take that suicidal hop from the fire escape is that he is basically afraid. Hickey also suggests that Larry is more committed to living than he would care to admit. This similarity of understanding is underscored when Hickey meets Parritt and recognizes that "you're having trouble with yourself." Larry is suspicious of Don Parritt from the first, and their relationship throughout the play is one in which Parritt is continually trying to confess his complicity in the capture of Rosa, his mother, and asks Larry's advice on how to deal with his guilt. But Larry wants to keep his uncommitted stance—his belief in his philosophical detachment is his pipe dream, the only way he can deal with life. His awareness of his situation is shown by the way he locks his door against Hickey when he comes selling his new line of facing the truth, destroying pipe dreams, and thereby achieving peace.

As commentator on the characters and action of the play, Larry is quick to realize that Hickey has killed his wife, just as he is fairly sure quite early that Parritt has betrayed his mother and "the Movement." However, he does not want to get involved and tries to prevent bar room speculation about Hickey. Similarly, he refuses to be drawn into Parritt's life when the young man insists on confessing to him. In their confessions, both Hickey and Parritt lie to themselves, Hickey claiming at first that he killed Evelyn, his wife, to bring her peace, and Parritt that he informed in order to get the money for a prostitute. Finally each admits that his true motivation was hatred. In the case of Hickey, Slade hopes that he will find peace in his death in the electric chair, and for Don he sees suicide as the only possible way of overcoming his guilt. He has been forced into a judgmental position and into abandonment of his philosophical detachment. When he turns on Parritt, "his quivering voice has a condemning command in it," as he orders him, "Go! Get the hell out of life,. . .before I choke it out of you." With this, Parritt is transformed, "suddenly at peace with himself," and departs to jump off the fire escape. Larry sits waiting until he hears the sound of a falling body almost masked by the merriment in the bar made by the other denizens who are drinking to forget.

Larry alone of the group concludes the play without illusions and without looking for any. Hickey has adopted the pipe dream that Evelyn's murder was an act of insanity; Parritt believed that in suicide he would be rid of his mother, yet his last words indicated an interest in what her reaction will be. Larry, however, realizes that "there's no hope!. . .I'll be a weak fool looking with pity at the two sides of everything till the day I die! May that day come soon." And with that comment he realizes that he is "the only real convert to death Hickey made here." He now seems to believe the couplet from Heine's poem to morphine which he had earlier quoted sardonically to Parritt:

Lo, sleep is good; better is death; in sooth
The best of all were never to be born.

SLOAN, John. *See* Jack in *A Wife for a Life*.

SLOAN, Mr. In *The Straw*,* he is a short, stout, fiftyish businessman, one of the benefactors of the Hill Farm Sanitorium. He is on a tour of the place and is used solely as an expository figure.

SLOCUM. In *Ile*,* the second mate of the whaling ship *Atlantic Queen*, a man of thirty-two, "a rangy six-footer with a lean weatherbeaten face." He warns Captain David Keeney* that the crew is mutinous because it has been kept ice-bound looking for apparently nonexistent whales for two years. Now that the term of their contract has expired, the men will try to force Keeney to return to Homeport. Keeney suggests that Slocum might side with the men, an accusation that Slocum denies. His assistance to Keeney in foiling the threatened mutiny shows his professionalism. At the end of the play he, along with the men, is eager to go hunting after the school of whales that has just appeared.

SMALL, Abner. In *The Haunted*, the last play in the trilogy, *Mourning Becomes Electra*,* "a wiry old man of sixty-five, a clerk in a hardware store. He accepts a bet of ten dollars that he can stay overnight in the Mannon mansion, popularly believed to be haunted. His companions get him drunk to give him courage, but he rushes out of the house in quick order, refusing to stay and paying off his bet in fear. He, along with his companions, forms part of the Chorus of Townsfolk who comment on the Mannon family and the events in which they have been involved. He has "a shrill rasping voice."

SMALL, Bessie, later Mrs. Jack Cockran. In "The Reckoning,"* stepdaughter of Stephen Donohue,* the blacksmith. When she is made pregnant by Jack Gardner, the blacksmith's helper, he refuses initially to marry her because he really loves Alice (who never appears). Bessie, however, calculatedly reveals her pregnancy to her stepfather, who tries to force Jack to marry her. In the course of a fight between the two men, Jack Gardner hits Donohue over the head with a hammer, and he falls senseless. Both believe him to be dead, and Bessie instantly plans to save Jack by advising him to flee to Chicago and live there under the name of Jack Cockran* while she will spread the tale that Donohue died as the result of a drunken fall. She will join Cockran in Chicago. This she does, a month later, and Cockran finds himself forced to marry her because otherwise Bessie will reveal everything. He cruelly explains to her that he has no affection for her and that their relationship is really one of guilt. In truth, Bessie has deceived Jack, because Donohue is actually alive, but she is determined to marry Cockran. Later her motivation is shown to be a desire to legitimize the child.

Ten years later Bessie blackmails Cockran with the same threat of revealing the crime when she persuades him to run for senator, now that he is a successful businessman. This time Cockran demands as his price complete control over the upbringing of their son, Jack Cockran, Jr.* This Bessie agrees to, with "dull resignation." In 1917, with the United States about to enter the war, Bessie blackmails him once more with the same threat, this time trying to force Cockran into speaking against the war in order to prevent Jack, Jr., from being drafted. Unbeknownst to Bessie, Jack has already enlisted, in the full flush of super-patriotism, and she later discovers that she may well have destroyed her husband's political career for nothing. Bessie then reveals the truth about her deception to young Jack, who is appalled and turns on her. However, she omits the crucial fact of her premarital pregnancy (apparently to preserve Jack's admiration of his father). Cockran follows his conscience and speaks in favor of the war, convinced that Bessie intends to ruin him. He is appalled that Bessie has informed Jack of his crime because keeping it from him had been part of the bargain he had earlier struck with her. However, he realizes that Bessie, in not revealing her pregnancy, has assumed all the blame. With this he becomes reconciled to his wife and asks Jack's forgiveness for them both. Jack forgives them both in a jingoistic speech equating family with country, and the play ends with Cockran offering Bessie his hand, which she takes in forgiveness. He has come to realize that through her "blackmail" he has become a success, and he has treated her very badly. She has always remained faithful to him and has devoted herself to his well-being and that of their son.

The character of Bessie is not very well developed, and in justice one must recall that the source of this material is merely a draft scenario. Bessie seems throughout to be both calculating and deceptive, but at the same time she is also the victim of Cockran's vindictiveness. She is basically the kind of woman who will do anything for love, but her deceptive tactics are not appealing. She seems to regard her stepfather as rather a nuisance, especially when he tracks her down later and she buys him off by sending him back to Ireland. Her total commitment is to her love for her husband (which is not well portrayed) and devotion to her son (which seems a trifle smothering). Her dislike of Harriet Lathrop,* Jack's girlfriend, is reminiscent of the attitude of the later Nina Leeds* of *Strange Interlude.**

SMITH, "Erie." In *Hughie*,* an unsuccessful Broadway gambler and horse-race handicapper. He is a man in his early forties, of medium height but appearing shorter because of his figure, which is stout with fat legs a trifle too short for his body. His pasty face is round, his neck so short that it disappears into beefy shoulders, his sandy hair is thinning, his nose is round and snub, and his pale blue eyes have a shifty expression. He is dressed in a tight-fitting Broadway-type suit of light gray with a loud blue shirt, red and blue silk tie, tan and white shoes, white silk socks, and a braided leather belt with a brass buckle. He mops his perspiring face with a blue and red silk handkerchief and carries a Panama hat.

This lonely and sentimental wise guy has just returned to his seedy westside

New York hotel after a long drunk induced by the death and funeral of Hughie, the former night clerk. He meets Hughie's replacement, Charlie Hughes,* and tells him about his predecessor and also about himself. He had to leave his birthplace, Erie, Pennsylvania, to avoid a shotgun wedding and decided to follow the horses. He is a failure, but Hughie, who had played the role of confidant and straight man to him, had managed to assist Erie in keeping his confidence alive. Erie has even gone into debt to send a floral piece to the funeral and is now afraid that his creditors will beat him up because he is unable to pay. With Hughie's death, Erie has lost his luck and now is "forlornly" trying to communicate with the new night clerk who is so busy with his own dreams of excitement that he pays little attention to Smith.

Finally the two manage to communicate, and Erie begins the same kind of pipe-dream boasting he had done with Hughie, and Charlie Hughes starts to respond. The play concludes with Erie and Charlie shooting dice with Erie's loaded "bones." Erie has regained his confidence in himself, as he looks on Charlie as a "sucker," while Charlie, the good listener, is participating vicariously in the excitement of Broadway. Each character is in effect helping the other.

SMITHERS, Henry. In *The Emperor Jones*,* the Cockney trader, "a tall, stoop-shouldered man of about forty," bald, with a long neck and a large Adam's apple. His dress is that commonly associated with colonial oppressors. His pasty-yellow face and rum-reddened nose are set off by his dirty white drill riding suit, puttees, spurs, and pith helmet. He wears a cartridge belt and an automatic revolver around his waist. He carries a riding whip. His eyes are pale blue, red-rimmed and ferretty. He is unscrupulous, mean, "cowardly and dangerous." He took in Brutus Jones* when the latter landed on the island, hiring him despite his gaol record, or perhaps because of it since Jones accuses Smithers of having once been in prison, an accusation he vehemently denies. Basically he is an expository device in the play, serving to introduce information and at the end delivers the epitaph on Jones, for whom he has some curious respect. Smithers sees Jones as a more advanced person than the natives of the island, represented by Lem.*

SMITH, Robert, the real name of Yank* in *The Hairy Ape*.*

SMITTY. A seaman on the S.S. *Glencairn*, "a young Englishman with a blond mustache" who appears in all shipboard plays of the S.S. *Glencairn* plays.* The "gentleman" of the ship, he obviously has an unhappy past. In *The Moon of the Caribbees*,* the sound of the negro chant torments him with memories of a lost love, and drink is hinted as being the cause. Smitty cannot accept his fate and sees himself and Old Tom* as "poor little lambs who have lost our way," a quotation from the Yale Whiffenpoof song. Throughout the series there are continual statements that Smitty is out of his educational and social class on the S.S. *Glencairn*. He speaks in too literate a manner, for instance. The revelation of his past comes in *In the Zone** when Smitty's carefully hidden black iron box leads his fellow crew members to suspect him of being a German spy. The box is forcibly opened and found to contain love letters. When Driscoll* reads the letters aloud, it is discovered that Smitty's real name is Sidney Davidson and that his girl, Edith, an aspiring singer studying in Berlin, has thrown him over because of his drinking. She berates him for his cowardice in going to sea. Smitty weeps silently, well aware of his weaknesses and unable to change himself. The sea is symbolic of his failure and the "dark shadow" of his drunkenness.

SNIPER, THE, a one-act play. The action takes place in "the main room of a ruined cottage on the outskirts of a small Belgian village." The stage directions are exceedingly detailed and include a description of two breaches in the rear wall made by artillery; on the left wall there is a crucifix over the door. "The time is about sundown on a September day," as Rougon,* "a great hulking old man of sixty-five,...dressed in the usual peasant fashion," enters, bent under the heavy burden of the body of a young Belgian infantryman, his only son, Charles. In anguish the old man weeps over the body as an old white-haired Village Priest* enters. He attempts to comfort Rougon, speaking sincerely of the will of God, but the distraught peasant cannot accept comments on the goodness of a God who would kill a young man on his wedding day. Luckily, Louise, the young man's fiancée, and Rougon's wife have been sent away to Brussels earlier this same day, but even this knowledge does not comfort Rougon who feels "like a coward, me, to stand by and do nothing." However, he has been warned by his son not to take arms against the Germans for fear of reprisals.

Rougon then tells of his son's killing, which he has watched from the farmhouse. He has seen his barn destroyed, together with the cow he was giving to his son as a wedding present. Now he has lost almost everything, but the Priest continues to remind him that at least his "wife is safe in Brussels," and Rougon says, "Were it not for the thought of my poor Margot I had let these butchers kill me before this." The two arrange for the funeral to take place the next night, and they pray for the repose of the young man's soul. "The priest commences to intone a prayer in which the words 'Almighty God,' 'Merciful,' 'Infinite justice,' 'Infinite love,' 'Infinite pity,' 'Thy son Jesus,' 'We, thy children,' 'Praise thy infinite goodness,' stand out from the general mumble of sing-song sentences." Rougon finally breaks down: "Charles, Charles, my little one! Oh, why did not God take me."

After another moment of shared sorrow, a young German Captain walks into the room, seeking the Priest. He stops, embarrassed at his intrusion in this private moment: "I honor the brave dead on whichever side they fall." The Captain asks the Priest to "warn the inhabitants against committing any violence against our soldiers. Civilians caught with arms will be immediately shot." The Priest agrees, not because he respects the orders of the German commander, "or admits his right to give them to a man of peace," but solely "because I have the welfare of my people at heart." When the Captain leaves, Rougon rages, "Dog of a Prussian." As the Priest bids him to be silent, Jean,* a peasant boy of about fifteen, appears, mudstained and trembling with a cut on his forehead. Gradually, the frightened boy reveals that both Margot and Louise have been killed on the road to Brussels. As the Priest intones, "Merciful God, have pity!" Rougon says, "Everything is gone." After a long silence a bugle call is heard, and the terrified Jean rushes in to say that the Germans are coming.

Rougon leaves the room and re-enters "carrying a long-barrelled rifle." He goes to the back wall and kneels at one of the breaches, "takes careful aim and fires." "That for Margot! That for Louise!" As he reloads, "the Captain and four German privates rush in." They disarm Rougon who "stands proudly, calmly awaiting his fate." Rougon tells the Germans that the Priest had endeavored to dissuade him from violence, and then as the Captain offers him time to say a prayer, Rougon refuses: "I want no prayers....To hell with your prayers!" In reply to the Priest's "Make your peace with God, my son," Rougon spits on the floor and says, "That for your God who allows such things to happen! I am ready, pig!" Rougon is then shot down, and the Captain turns to the Priest: "It is the law." The Priest is left looking compassionately at the bodies of father and son: "Alas, the laws of men."

Comments: This play is notable for being one of the two surviving plays that O'Neill wrote for George Pierce Baker's* English 47 Workshop playwriting course at Harvard. The other surviving play is "The Personal Equation"* in four acts. *The Sniper* is a carefully wrought piece in which revelation proceeds slowly and builds to a very strong curtain. The dialogue is, however, still somewhat on the fractured French model, reminiscent of the fractured Spanish of *The Movie Man.** Nonetheless, there is some skillful use of irony in the prayer of the Priest, and the curtain is a strong one. Characterization is minimal and arises entirely from the developing situation, with dramatic exposition by the father, Rougon, aimed at intensifying the pathos of the play. O'Neill here took advantage of public opinion concerning the unprovoked attack of the Germans on "little Belgium" in 1914. Later, because of its contemporaneity, the play achieved a professional production. There is a sense of inevitability about this short work which emphasizes the powerlessness of individual human beings caught up in circumstances beyond their control. Unlike some of O'Neill's earlier plays, the violent death of the principal character is well motivated.

Production Data: Written 1914–1915 at Harvard as part of the "English 47 Workshop" of George Pierce Baker, where it achieved a student performance. First professional production by the Provincetown Players* at the Playwrights' Theatre, New York City, February 16, 1917 (performances, unknown).

Director: Nina Moise
Designer: Unknown

Cast: Rougon: George Cram Cook*
        Village Priest: Donald Corley
        German Captain of Infantry: Theron M. Bamberger
        Private of the Regiment: Morton Stafford
        Another Private: Robert Montcarr
        Jean, a Peasant Boy: Ida Rauh

Revived with *Abortion** and *The Movie Man* at the Key Theatre, St. Mark's Place, New York City, October 27, 1959. No further information located.

A Note on Text: The text used is that appearing in *Ten "Lost" Plays of Eugene O'Neill* (New York: Random House, 1964).

"S.O.S." unpublished scenario of disputed date. The typescript notes West Point Pleasant, New Jersey, as the place of writing, which would place it in 1918–1919. O'Neill himself said it was written in Provincetown, 1917 (*see* Floyd, 1981, p. 389). This work is usually referred to as a novelette, but the typescript specifically calls it a scenario. It is an adaptation of *Warnings.** John Lathrop,* in his early sixties, is the resident telegraphist of the small town of Acropolis. He is also noted for his weekly drinking sprees. He lives in the local boarding house of Mrs. Perkins, until, much to the surprise of the town, he marries Susannah Darrow,* a woman of forty who has nursed her father, a retired whaling captain until his death. Lathrop instantly stops drinking and moves into Susannah's house where the two enjoy six months of total "blessedness." Unfortunately for John Lathrop, his newfound happiness and responsibilities lead him to take much greater care in his work, with the curious result that he makes more mistakes than before, thus attracting the attention of his superiors who note that he has reached retirement age and discharge him. Though Susannah has enough money for them to live on, John feels that he must work, so they rent her house and move just across the Hudson River from New York City where John looks for a job. As he is repeatedly refused because of his age, he becomes increasingly dispirited, and they begin to drift apart.

Finally, he manages to talk his way into a position as radio operator on a steamer, the *Rio Grande*, bound for Buenos Aires. But when he breaks the news to Susannah that this will entail a four-month separation, she decides that she will travel as a passenger on the same ship. She discovers that she enjoys the arrangement and so they continue it for the next two years, living in Brooklyn between voyages. Lathrop then discovers that he is going deaf. At first he blames inefficient wireless apparatus, but finally he sees a specialist who warns him that he may become totally deaf at any time and says that there is no cure for his disorder. Susannah, at almost the same time, discovers that the fish-packing house, from which most of her money comes, has gone bankrupt, and therefore she must return to Acropolis to straighten things out. John, who has not told Susannah of his condition, now realizes that he must make at least one more voyage because they need the money.

   Alone on the *Rio Grande* for the first time, Lathrop finds his hearing getting worse and worse, a serious matter since there are rumors of a German raider in the vicinity. The raider chases them, and at that point Lathrop does send an S.O.S. He is now completely deaf, and when the other members of the crew think he is a coward, he finally breaks down and confesses his inability to hear. Stevens,* a radio operator traveling as a passenger, informs the captain that Lathrop is to blame for missing a signal the previous night, and as a result they are in the path of the raider. The *Rio Grande* is captured, the raider transfers the crew, and the sea-cocks of the steamer are opened. Lathrop, suddenly realizing that he has left Susannah's photograph on board, tries to go back but is restrained. On board the raider, Stevens tells the survivors that Lathrop is to blame, with the result that everyone treats him with hostility, but Lathrop cannot hear what is being said about him.

   Still, he is racked with guilt. The raider's commander, a man with a curious sense of humor, decides to "reward" Lathrop for his contribution to the capture of the *Rio Grande* by giving him the run of the ship. Grateful for the opportunity to hide from the accusing gaze of his fellows, Lathrop spends most of his time forward on deck. An American vessel comes in sight, and the raider prepares to fire. The crew, also with a warped sense of humor, decide not to warn Lathrop but to watch him jump when he feels the concussion of the raider's guns. However, the shock restores Lathrop's hearing, with the result that he can now hear what is being said about him, and he becomes both angry and almost insane. He then resolves to take some expiatory action. He kills the German wireless operator and sends out a signal giving the position of the raider. Fortunately he contacts a cruiser which steams in their direction. As the American cruiser *New Orleans* comes into sight, the raider's commander has John Lathrop executed by firing squad and buried at sea. On the way home his story becomes that of a hero, and by tacit consent his responsibility in the loss of the *Rio Grande* is forgotten. He is given a medal posthumously, and Susannah is also lionized. However, she has now sold her house and Brooklyn is no home for her since her husband's death. Finally, she moves back to Acropolis to take up residence in Lathrop's old home, Mrs. Perkins's boarding house.

   Comments: This scenario, written in 1917–1919, is similar to *In the Zone** in its exploitation of the wartime scene. It is basically a revision of the early one-act play *Warnings.** As it stands, "S.O.S." has some possibilities, but O'Neill clearly had not fully decided on the true focus of the work.

A Note on Text: The text used is that in the Harvard Theatre Collection. Used by permission.

S.S. *GLENCAIRN* Plays, a group of four one-act plays concerning the crew of a British tramp steamer. Those plays are: *The Moon of the Caribbees,** *Bound East for Cardiff,** *The Long Voyage Home,** and *In the Zone.** Individually produced between 1916 and 1918, with *Cardiff* first and *Caribbees* last, they were rearranged by O'Neill in the above order when they were first produced together in November 1924.

The basic theme of the series is that mankind, represented by the complement of the S.S. *Glencairn*, is the plaything of an unalterable destiny. While there are isolated acts of free will or attempted rebellion against fate, the seamen (the voyagers) are unsuccessful, for the sea always wins and takes its own. A secondary theme of camaraderie among those forced into a difficult situation is also found in *In the Zone*, and the bonds of friendship are celebrated in *Bound East for Cardiff*. The quality of the plays is somewhat uneven, and at times O'Neill resorts to rather obvious structural devices. *The Moon of the Caribbees*, however, is relatively free from these defects; when placed first in the series, it casts its poetic shadow over the more literal-minded plays. It helps convey the inevitability of fate and the immutability of the universe.

Production Data: Performed as a group by the Barnstormers at Barnstormers' Barn, Provincetown, Massachusetts, August 14, 1924. Produced at the Provincetown Playhouse, New York City, November 3, 1924; moved to the Punch and Judy Theatre, New York City, December 16, 1924; moved to the Princess Theatre, January 12, 1925 (total performances 99).

New York Production
  Director: James Light
  Designer: Cleon Throckmorton
  Music in the First Episode arranged and directed by Norma Millay
  Cast: Yank: Sidney Machet
       Driscoll: Lawrence Cecil
       Olson: Walter Abel
       Davis: Harold McGee
       Cocky: Walter Kingsford
       Smitty: E.J. Ballantine
       Ivan: James Meighan
       Swanson: Samuel Selden
       Scotty: Archie Sinclair
       Paul: Abraham Krainis
       Lamps: Clement O'Loghlen
       Old Tom: Stanley Howlett
       Big Frank: William Stahl
       Paddy: H. L. Remsten
       Captain: Edgar Stehli
       First Mate: Lewis Barrington
       Bella: Mary Johns
       Susie: Louise Bradley
       Violet: Rilla Romaine
       Pearl: Jeannie Begg
       Joe: Stanley Howlett

Nick: Edgar Stehli
Mag: Barbara Benedict
Kate: Dorothee Nolan
Freda: Helen Freeman
First Rough: Clement O'Loghlen
Second Rough: H. L. Remsten

Singers: Misses Cozine, Derr, Du Mont, Marlowe, Millay, Myrshkin, Pendleton, Shreve, Wenclawska; Messrs. Brush, Thayer (*See* Deutsch and Hanau, 1931, pp. 268–269).

Revived September 1, 1929 at the Provincetown Playhouse, New York City (90 performances).

Revived October 29, 1937, at the Lafayette Theatre, New York City (68 performances).

Revived May 20, 1948 at the New York City Center (14 performances), directed by José Quintero.

[*See also* Appendix B for the film adaptation entitled *The Long Voyage Home*,* the only film version of his plays that O'Neill liked.]

S.S. *SAN FRANCISCO*. In the unproduced and unpublished play, "The Personal Equation,"* the name of the vessel owned by the Ocean Steamship Company. The revolutionary movement, International Workers of the Earth, plans to sabotage the engines in order to frighten the international shipping cartel and drive the firemen and dockworkers to strike.

STANTON, Doctor. In *The Straw*,* the physician in charge of the Hill Farm Sanitorium. He is about forty-five, handsome, with a grave, lined face enlivened "by a kindly humorous smile." His gray eyes are "saddened by the suffering they have witnessed," yet he projects both sympathy and "real understanding." Somehow he seems to have retained a sense of hope. "He speaks with a slight Southern accent, soft and slurring." He seems to have been drawn from the real-life personality of Dr. David Russell Lyman, of the Gaylord Farm,* Wallingford, Connecticut. Lyman had been educated in Virginia, though born in Buffalo. He himself had had tuberculosis and had made Gaylord a showplace for new methods of treatment. When O'Neill knew him, he was about thirty-six years old.

STEELE, Maud. In *Bread and Butter** fiancée, later wife, of John Brown.* She is a remarkably pretty girl of twenty with great blue eyes, golden brown hair, and small delicate features. Of medium height, her figure is lithe and graceful." She has a kittenish manner and a pouting red mouth. "Her voice is petulant, soft, all-too-sweet," and she is clearly spoiled. She loves John Brown and tries to understand his commitment to art, but she cannot comprehend how much his painting means to him. She thinks solely in terms of commercial art. At first she agrees to a long engagement, but later she becomes impatient and goes to New York with Edward Brown, Jr.,* and Mrs. Brown* to coerce John to return. After marriage to Maud, John gives up his painting and drawing and takes a position in her father's business. She is the type of totally philistine woman who destroys the artist in a number of O'Neill plays. Maud becomes fretful, then quarrelsome and antagonistic, driving her husband to drink and women. She is also vindictive when she finds herself unhappy with her bargain and refuses to give him a divorce. She would have been better suited as the wife of Edward Brown, Jr.,* John's older brother, the alderman, later Mayor of Bridgetown and congressional candidate who loves her and twice proposes to her. She is totally materialistic and as destructive as any Strindberg wife. Finally, when she attacks the virtue of John's sister, Bessie Brown,* John nearly throttles her and then shoots himself, much to her horror. Maud Steele is the first full-length study of the destructive woman in O'Neill, a character type that reappears in *Beyond the Horizon** and *All God's Chillun Got Wings.**

STEELE, Mr. In *Bread and Butter,** father of Maud Steele.* He "is a tall, stout, vigorous-looking man of about fifty-five. . . . He has grey hair and a short-cropped grey mustache; a full florid face with undistinguished features, and small grey eyes. He is carefully dressed in a well-fitting light suit and looks the part of the prosperous small-town merchant." He is a resident of Bridgetown, Connecticut, and takes himself seriously. He is a widower who spoils his daughter outrageously. He suggests that John Brown* be allowed to have a year in New York at art school rather than become a lawyer. He agrees that John has talent and believes that he will make money as an illustrator. He, like the other in-habitants of Bridgetown, is a philistine and does not understand the art world. He gives John a job in his business and provides a home for him and Maud after they marry. He is disappointed in John's inability to succeed in business.

STEVE. In *The Web,** a "cadet," or a pimp. He is flashily dressed, rat-eyed, weak of mouth, undersized, and showing on his face the effects of drink and drugs." He is the cowardly "protector" of Rose Thomas,* a tubercular pros-titute, whom he exploits. He takes all her earnings and refuses to allow her medical expenses. He will not allow Rose to keep her baby daughter and gives her one week to put the child in an orphanage. When Rose threatens to act like her friend Bessie and keep some of her earnings, Steve threatens her with the police and knocks her down. At this point Tim Moran,* a safecracker, frightens Steve off with a loaded gun. Enraged, Steve climbs the fire escape and finds the two embracing. As Tim turns to leave, Steve shoots him at point-blank range and escapes, while Rose is left to take the blame.

Steve is not a fully drawn character, being a collection of stereotypical external details rather than a well-motivated character. He, like Rose and Tim, appears to be victim of his social circumstances, but apart from the mention of his having been an orphan, this influence is not fully established. Nonetheless, this rudi-mentary motivation seems to underline the recurrent O'Neill theme that human beings are victims of circumstances beyond their control, but Steve, unlike Rose and Tim, lacks any redeeming qualities.

STEVENS. In the unpublished scenario "S.O.S."* he is the young, efficient wireless operator traveling as a passenger on the *Rio Grande*. It is he who realizes that something is very wrong with the ship's wireless operator, John Lathrop.* He thinks Lathrop a coward when in fact Lathrop is totally deaf. Stevens also arouses the animosity of the survivors of the vessel against Lathrop by revealing that it was Lathrop's failure to pick up a warning signal that caused their capture by a German raider.

STEWARD of the whaling ship *Atlantic Queen*. In *Ile*,* "an old grizzled man" with a "sullen and angry manner." He opens the play; and through his discussion with Ben,* the cabin boy, as well as through his own frightened clumsiness, he acts as an expository figure. He explains the parlous situation of the icebound whaler, and by serving as the focus of Captain David Keeney's* rage, he demonstrates the fanaticism of his superior officer.

STILLWELL, Dr. Herbert.* In *Days Without End*,* a sharp-faced, gray-haired doctor in his early fifties who attends Elsa Loving.* He makes the pertinent observation that her pneumonia is "more a means than a cause." He realizes that her problem is psychological rather than physical and that she has lost the will to live.

STRANGE INTERLUDE, a play in two parts and nine acts, covering twenty-five years, 1919–1944, though chronological dates are irrelevant to this play, the personal passage of internal time being much more important. The play, which gained O'Neill his third Pulitzer Prize, is famous for its dramatic use of the interior monologue, really a development of the soliloquy, to convey the thoughts of the individual characters.
FIRST PART
   Act I: "The library of Professor Leeds'* home in a small university town in New England." The room is lined with books, mainly editions of Latin, Greek, and other "classics in French and German and Italian" as well as early English writers and a few more recent ones, "the most modern probably being Thackeray." The room gives the impression of being a retreat from reality. The other furnishings include a sizable table with an armchair beside it, at left, a rocking chair at center, and bench with cushions. This arrangement of furniture is repeated throughout the play. It is late afternoon in August 1919.
   Voices are heard, and the maid shows in Charles Marsden,* a tall, thin, meticulously tailored man of thirty-five, delicately built, slightly effeminate, poised, somewhat dreamy, but "always willing to listen, eager to sympathize, to like and be liked." His expression is both ironical and sad around the mouth. He looks around the room and starts to meditate aloud beginning with the unchanging character of the room, the loss of his own father, his memories, his inability to write in war-destroyed Europe, and then his own charming novels of manners. He thinks of the widowed professor and his daughter, Nina Leeds,*

who bosses the professor and Charles himself. She has "become quite queer lately" as the result of the death of her fiancé, Gordon Shaw,* shot down in flames two days before the armistice. Marsden's mother has seemed jealous of her son's concern for Nina, and obviously he is tied to her apron strings. He wonders why he has never fallen in love physically with Nina—but then sex is "all dreams with me . . . my sex life among the phantoms!" This leads him into a meditation concerning his disgust with sex-obsessed society, and he recalls his disastrous visit to a brothel at the age of sixteen when he felt that he had defiled both his mother and himself "forever!"

The entry of Professor Leeds breaks in upon his thoughts. He is an intelligent, small, slender, gray-haired man of fifty-five, slightly timid, but relaxed with Marsden, a former student, whom he has known since childhood. He greets Marsden cordially and thinks with relief that Marsden has always been a "calming influence on Nina." In reply to Marsden's inquiry, he says that Nina is much changed; she seems to be haunted by Gordon's ghost and even to hate her father. This the professor can understand because he suggested that Gordon ought not marry Nina before going to war, that it would not be the honorable thing to do, to tie her down, possibly with a child: "In justice to Nina, they must wait until he had come back and begun to establish his position in the world. That was the square thing." Gordon, the soul of honor, was vulnerable to this argument, and so he told Nina that they must wait. The girl now suspects that her father had "deliberately destroyed her happiness," even hoping for Gordon's death and being secretly pleased when the news came—and she is right. None of this has been said directly to her father, but she has hinted at it. The two men wait for Nina with conflicting emotions: Charles's heart is pounding, but he knows Nina sees him only as "dear old Charlie," while the professor hopes that she won't make a scene and worries about the state of her mind.

At this moment Nina enters. She is twenty, tall, athletic-looking, with blond bobbed hair and extraordinary eyes of "deep greenish blue." She looks the picture of health, but her manner conveys "a terrible tension of will alone maintaining self-possession." She announces, "I have made up my mind, Father," and at that Charlie comes forward to greet her. She greets him coolly and turns to talk to her father, who reminds her of her manners. In her thoughts she dismisses Charlie, the timid man who has never done anything "and never will." He will watch the "swimmers drown at last," but he will never jump in. And with that in her thoughts, her kiss is cold. The two engage in social inanities, but Nina shows her bitterness by saying that coming back safe from Europe is nothing, now that the war is over. Charlie takes this as a taunt, for he had worked in the press office while others like Gordon had died, but he covers up with cheery banter.

Nina now announces her decision to leave home and go to nurse the war-crippled in a soldier's hospital. She has arranged this through a friend of Gordon. Her father is appalled that she should think of such a step in her condition, but Nina can only think of "Gordon, my dear one! . . . gone forever from me."

She plans to leave that very evening and asks Charlie to help her pack. "I must pay for my cowardly treachery to Gordon," she says, believing that she must give her health for the survivors. Only when she can give herself "for a man's happiness without scruple, without fear, without joy except in his joy," only then will she be able to live her own life once more, having expiated her holding herself away from Gordon. Both the professor and Marsden are appalled by her shameless physical longing as she speaks of that unconsummated relationship and the emptiness she now feels: "I didn't make him take me! I lost him forever! And now I am lonely and not pregnant with anything at all, but—but loathing."

Professor Leeds now explains his intervention in the affair, confessing that he had been actively opposed to the marriage but that he had acted out of fatherly concern for her. Nina, however, will not be placated and tries to leave. She teases Charlie about using this in a book, and when he jestingly suggests that he will have to propose to her, she suggests he help her pack. After their exit the professor begins to think all is for the best and believes that the ghost of Gordon will now be gone. As the curtain falls, he pulls out a Latin text at random and starts to read from it, "like a child whistling to keep up his courage in the dark."

Act II: The study, about 9 P.M. "in early fall, over a year later." Nothing in the room has changed except that the window shades are drawn. Charles Marsden is sitting center, dressed in a dark blue suit with "a gloomy brooding expression" as if in mourning. He looks weary, and his eyes stare unseeingly ahead. He meditates on the death of Professor Leeds, recalling his loneliness, and then his thoughts turn to Nina, whom he has visited twice at the hospital, wondering what she has "been doing in that house full of men . . . particularly that self-important young ass of a doctor! . . . Gordon's friend," through whom she was accepted there. As he broods, the doorbell rings and Nina enters, dressed in her nurse's uniform. She has changed, coarsened a trifle, but is still "strikingly handsome" and gives the impression of hidden experience. She looks about the room, recalls herself as "Daddy's girl," and then realizes that her father has been dead to her for a long time; she has written letters but has not seen him since going to work at the hospital. She has brought Dr. Edmund Darrell* with her from the hospital in case something could be done for her father, but now, of course, his presence is not needed. Charlie upbraids her for her neglect of her father, but Nina replies that "I didn't want him to see what he would have thought was me," a callous-sounding remark that brings tears to Charlie's eyes.

His reverie is interrupted by the entrance of Sam Evans,* a very blond, coltishly collegiate-looking young man of twenty-five who looks younger than his years. He is, as Marsden notes, no genius but a likable fellow nonetheless. In the course of conversation, Evans reveals that he has only recently come to know Nina, though he had met her some years ago at a prom when she was with Gordon Shaw, a classmate of Evans. Clearly Evans still worships Gordon and all that he stood for. He himself was no good at athletics, but he always kept trying; and when Marsden attempts to console him with the remark that sports heroes usually fade after college, he enthusiastically disagrees, pointing out that Gordon had become an air ace, "And he always fought just as cleanly as he'd played football! Even the Huns respected him!" Evans explains his presence by saying that Darrell had been his college dorm mate, a senior when Evans was a freshman. The two men then engage in conflicting thoughts, Marsden hoping that he might have been the one to comfort Nina, and Evans hoping that Nina will marry him, while Marsden, in turn, wonders about Nina's relations with Darrell. Suddenly Sam Evans starts to speak of his hopes of marrying Nina, treating Marsden as if he is Nina's guardian. In panic, Charlie sees himself relegated to the role of Nina's father but then reconsiders, thinking that there might be a chance for him, "what a vile thought," if Nina "were married to this simpleton." Pulling himself together, Marsden wishes Evans luck and suggests that they drop the matter as Darrell enters and sends Sam out for a sedative for Nina.

Darrell is twenty-seven, "short, dark, wiry, his movements rapid and sure, his manner cool and observant," rigidly controlled, the pure scientist who considers himself "immune to love through his scientific understanding of its real sexual nature." Darrell and Marsden spar in their interior monologues, the doctor sizing up the author as all "surface" like his novels and Marsden resenting the scientific evaluation he realizes he is being given. Darrell comes into the open and tells Marsden that between them they must straighten Nina out; she has been promiscuous at the hospital (but he softens the words for the super-sensitive Marsden), and he suggests that the best thing for her would be to marry Sam Evans because "his unselfish love, combined with her real liking for him, will gradually give her back a sense of security and a feeling of being worth something to life again, and once she's got that, she'll be saved!" Darrell says he is prescribing for Sam, as well as Nina, because Sam needs self-confidence, but Marsden suggests that Darrell might himself be in love with Nina, something the doctor denies: "In my mind she always belongs to Gordon. . . . And I couldn't share a woman—even with a ghost!" And in saying that he mentally recalls all the other men who have had her. Marsden has a curious feeling that Darrell is hiding something, but then Nina enters and starts to speak about her father's death and her own, turning to Charlie as "Dear old Charlie," torturing him with this approach, speaking lies, and finally asking him to say "lie" and then "life": "You see! Life is just a long drawn out lie with a sniffling sigh at the end!" Marsden in agony thinks how hard Nina has become, and then she speaks sarcastically about him to Darrell: "He believes if you pick a lie to pieces, the pieces are the truth! I like him because he is so inhuman. But once he kissed me—in a moment of carnal weakness! . . . And he looked so disgusted with himself! I had to laugh!" She treats him "with a pitying scorn," and Darrell remembers her indifferent treatment of *him*.

Then, her mind seeming to wander, she speaks of God, "the modern science God," "any God at any price" and her desire to believe. With this she turns to Charlie and asks why he has always been so afraid—drawing from him the answer, "I'm afraid of—of life, Nina." In reply Nina suggests, "The mistake began when God was created in a male image." Had God been perceived as a mother, then "we should have imagined life as created in the birth-pain of God the Mother" and thus have been able to understand pain and perceive death as a "reunion with Her, a passing back into Her substance, blood of her blood again, peace of her peace!" Excitedly, Marsden agrees that such an image is superior to that of a male God, and Nina, crying out a desire to believe in something, flings herself sobbing on her knees and hides her face in her hands on his knees. At this instant, Marsden perceives the kind of lover he must be for Nina, "a father, a pure lover." She then turns to him as if to a confessor, telling him of what she has done and how she wishes to be punished for it. Her promiscuity was an attempt to atone for keeping herself from Gordon, but now she sees herself as a fool. Charlie is horrified and feels himself almost contaminated by "this little whore," but then he accepts the role of father, picking her up to take her to bed. Just then Sam Evans enters and Marsden tells him that they have spoken of him and that Sam should "have every reason to hope." Respectfully, Sam refers to him as Mr. Marsden, and when Charlie suggests that he use his first name, Evans calls after him "Good old Charlie," a comment that is underlined by Marsden's bitter laugh—almost as if he had heard what Evans had said.

Act III: "Seven months or so later—the dining room of the Evans' homestead in northern New York State," about 9 A.M., late spring 1921. The room is large and depressingly ugly with brown water-stained wallpaper, a large table in the center, and high-backed chairs against the wall. Nina now married to Sam, is writing a letter to Edmund "Ned" Darrell. She is puzzled about the atmosphere of the old place, hideous despite its being surrounded by apple trees in full bloom. She has found it hard to sleep there, feeling that even the ghosts of the past have abandoned the place. She then looks up from her letter wondering whether she should tell Ned about her pregnancy and deciding against it since she has not yet told Sam. She wishes to keep her secret to herself a little longer. Sam and Nina are visiting with Charles Marsden in his car since Charlie is too fussy to allow either of them to drive. Mrs. Amos Evans,* Sam's mother, also puzzles Nina because she is totally unlike Sam, who hardly seems to think of her and indeed didn't even mention her until she began importuning them to visit. Charles Marsden enters, and she teases him, as usual, about his timidity, "you slacker bachelor." As Nina leaves him alone he starts to wonder about her happiness and is sure she is pregnant. Then he becomes exasperated about having invited Nina and Sam to tour with him—all he wanted was a new setting for a novel. He considers Sam's mother, noting the sadness and grimness of her eyes, as he leaves.

Mrs. Evans and Sam then enter. She is a tiny woman of forty-five who "looks at least sixty." Once upon a time she must have been a delicate, almost romantic beauty, but now all softness seems to have vanished. "She is very pale. Her big dark eyes are grim with the prisoner-pain of a walled-in soul," but she still retains a vestigial sweetness. Sam looks eminently collegiate and happy as he prattles to his mother about the success he will be now that he is married. She will never have to concern herself about the apple crop again. Mrs. Evans seems rather abstracted, and then quite suddenly she asks whether Nina is going to have a baby. Sam says he doesn't think so, and his mother is relieved; Sam, however, expresses inward concern that she is not yet pregnant and says he will go upstairs to visit his aunt. But Mrs. Evans forestalls him, saying that Aunt Bessie wouldn't know him, suggesting instead that he join Charlie in a drive to town. Sam runs out, and Mrs. Evans looks after him, glad to see his happiness and hoping again that Nina is not pregnant.

When Nina returns, Mrs. Evans asks her whether she has noticed anything strange about the house and then asks whether she loves Sam, finally coming to the point and asking Nina whether she is going to have a baby. When Nina replies in the affirmative, Mrs. Evans asks whether it isn't too soon, but Nina, wondering at this, says that she wants a baby "beyond everything! We both do!" To Nina's terror and bewilderment, Mrs. Evans tells her, "But you can't! You've got to make up your mind you can't!" She then explains the hereditary insanity that exists in Sam's family, despite his apparent normalcy. She had married Sam's father in total ignorance of this horror, finding out only later when her husband begged her forgiveness, saying "he loved me so much he'd have gone mad without me, and I was his only hope of salvation." She believes that she might indeed have been able to save him, had they not accidentally had Sammy. For years she lived in fear of Sam's insanity, and then her husband "gave up and went off into it" when Sam was about eight years old. At that she sent Sammy to boarding school and later told him his father was dead, never letting the boy come home until now, years after his father's death. She has nursed Sam's father and also poor idiot Aunt Bessie, and she begs Nina to have an abortion so that the curse of the Evanses will die out and Sammy will live a normal life.

Bitterly, Nina says she has only married Sammy for *his* need and her own desire to have children. She sees the necessity of the abortion but is appalled to realize that she cannot leave Sam lest she be guilty of causing his insanity. Mrs. Evans begs her to stay with her son and then diffidently says that at times she used to wish, when she was carrying him, that she had deliberately "picked a man, a healthy male to breed by, same's we do with stock, to give the man I loved a healthy child," even though it would be adultery. She hints that this might be an answer for Nina, since Sam so loves children and it would make him happy: "Being happy, that's the nearest we can ever come to knowing what's good! It's your rightful duty!" With this she tells Nina that they must never see each other again and gathers her into her arms as "the daughter of my sorrow!"

Act IV: About seven months later on a winter evening, Sam is sitting in Professor Leeds's old chair, and the disarrangement of the room betrays the presence of a confused mind rather than the meticulous intellect of the former inhabitant. Sam is smoking and sitting at the typewriter, looking thinner and drawn, desperately trying to write advertising copy. He seems deeply troubled both by his lack of success in his job and Nina's refusal to sleep with him for the past five months. He is puzzled about what happened between Nina and his mother, and then Nina "crashed . . . strain of waiting and hoping she'd get pregnant . . . and nothing happening." He wishes distractedly that they would have a child so that he would have something to work for and be able to succeed. Then he remembers that he has asked Ned Darrell to come out to check Nina: "Ned's the only one I can trust." With that he starts back to his typing as Nina enters, looking on him with contempt and dislike for his weakness; but then remorse sets in, and she pities him for his love and for trying so hard. She must sleep with him again soon, but then she recalls the "poor dead baby I dared not bear." Sam apologizes for his typing and confides that he has been told to shape up—or else—and Nina looks ahead to an endless vista of similar situations as she endeavors to comfort him by telling him of her love—and indeed she almost does love him as she says, "I want you to be happy, Sam," suggesting that they sleep together again soon. Then she says that Charlie is coming over to discuss her outline for Gordon Shaw's biography, an announcement that shatters Sam's happiness, but to Nina's surprise he says that Ned Darrell is also coming that very evening.

When Charlie arrives, he speaks of his mother's ill health and then discusses his corrections to Nina's biography of Gordon Shaw. As Sam looks them over, Charlie thinks about the abortion he is sure that Nina has had performed and snobbishly looks again at Sam as if he is a simpleton. Both Sam and Nina adored Gordon, "when actually he came from the commonest people." He repeats this thought aloud to Sam, who is busy checking the manuscript, when the doorbell rings and Sam says that it is Darrell. Charlie reacts "with anger mixed with alarmed suspicion and surprise" and thinks of leaving, but he is too late. Darrell has become more authoritative than before and looks on Marsden as an old woman, acting quite brutally when Charlie asks his advice about his mother's illness, suggesting that it might be the cancer she fears.

Marsden leaves, taking Sam with him, and Darrell speculates first about Charlie, then about Sam's lack of success and Nina's failure to have a child, as she enters, looking younger and prettier than before. She likes the touch of Ned's strong capable hands, unlike Sam's, as Darrell looks diagnostically at her. They momentarily discuss the book on Gordon Shaw, and then Nina turns to Darrell, asking whether he is getting married. On hearing his denial, she speaks in a "bitterly sarcastic" way, recommending that he have a baby, "a fine, healthy baby!" Then, "in a dull, monotonous tone recalling that of Sam's mother," she tells the story of Sam's family and of her abortion, suggesting that Darrell should not have tried to play God the Father in abetting their marriage. Darrell is horrified and suggests that she get Sam to give her a divorce, but Nina says that she could not bear the guilt of that.

Then she makes her proposition, making use of curiously formal language and taking pains to be objective and unemotional, as does Darrell, when they speak: "What is it precisely that Sam's wife has thought so much of doing?" Nina, after much timidity: "Sam's wife is afraid," and she asks, "you, Doctor, to suggest the father." Nina has changed now that she has married Sam: "She can't bear the thought of giving herself to any man she could neither desire nor respect." Finally she suggests that Ned, who used to attract her and has a superior mind, should be the man, and finally he agrees: "I must confess the Ned you are speaking of is I, and I am Ned." "And I am Nina, who wants her baby." In a spirit of gratitude on Nina's part and humility on Ned's, they agree: Ned thinks he will be happy for a while, and Nina says, "I shall make my husband happy."

Act V: "A bright morning in the following April" in the sitting room of a rented house in a seashore suburb of New York. The house is of the dull mass-produced type, but the arrangement of the furniture is similar to that of Act I: table and Morris chair at left, chair at center, and sofa at right. Nina is sitting in the center chair, trying to read. She is pregnant, "but this time there is a triumphant strength about her expression, a ruthless self-confidence in her eyes." She has just felt her baby move for the first time, and she thinks back to the begetting of the child, remembering the way that she and Darrell discovered desire for each other. Now she glories in her impending motherhood: "I am a mother . . . God is a Mother." She leans back happily as Sam enters, looking shabby, harried, and unshaven, trying to screw up his courage to speak to Nina and feeling that he has failed her by not giving her a child. He is beginning to feel suicidal, and he thinks he should offer her a divorce. His voice trembles as he calls her name; she opens her eyes, looking calmly and evaluatively at him while thinking about divorcing him because he has proved himself unable to give her anything—not even a home. He has lost his job and is depending on Ned to get another—but then Nina feels contrite because she had decided to sell her house to be near Ned.

Sam attempts to be cheerful, saying that he hopes to be back on the job soon. He also wonders about Charlie, whose mother has just died. Whenever Sam speaks, Nina treats him with incivility, but fortunately the doorbell rings, and Darrell enters. He looks older. "There is an expression of defensive bitterness and self-resentment about his mouth and eyes. This vanishes into one of desire and joy as he sees Nina." He moves toward her and stops on seeing Evans, who greets him. Darrell has indeed brought him a letter of recommendation, and Sam offers thanks, only to have Nina brusquely tell him to go and shave.

Left alone, the two lovers speak of their mutual happiness, though Darrell sometimes confesses to hatred for her. He believes now that she loves *him* rather than Gordon, but he cannot compromise either Sam or his career by taking any action, even though he does admit his love for her, after she has done the same. But almost instantly he must deny this avowal as Nina rejoices in it.

At this moment, Charles Marsden enters, haggard and in deep mourning but as immaculately dressed as ever. He is completely devastated by the death of his mother. Nina offers a sympathy she really does not feel because Mrs. Marsden had always disapproved of her. Darrell welcomes Marsden's arrival because it cools the passions between himself and Nina—but Charlie picks up their sensual vibrations and hates both of them, yet he realizes that he cannot hate his "little Nina" and tries to cover up his thoughts by discussing his mother's last days and her death from cancer. But suddenly he turns on Darrell: "I think you doctors are a pack of God-damned ignorant liars and hypocrites!" Then he apologizes and talks wildly about the "repulsive" nature of the room, a comment Nina takes literally. He asks after Sam, noting that he cannot understand his loss since Sam seems to care very little for his mother. Inwardly, Nina recalls the wish of Sam's mother for her son, "Make my boy, Sammy, happy!" and feels both remorseful and trapped. But when Charlie leaves, Nina and Ned resume their tormented conversation, Darrell regretting his loss of scientific objectivity and Nina claiming that "only your love can make me happy now! Sam must give me a divorce so I can marry you." Darrell, inwardly thinking of his career, uses Sam as a reason to deny her request, but Nina maintains that she has given Sam enough of her life and that she is now entitled to happiness. She holds his hands and forces him to look at her, and Sam finds them in this position, innocently misconstruing it as part of a medical examination, but then he wonders why she shrinks away from him when he touches her.

Nina then suggests that Darrell stay for lunch, and as she leaves she remarks, "after lunch we'll tell Sam," leaving her husband wondering what she means. Darrell cannot look Sam in the face, and conflicting emotions sweep over him; thoughts of his career, of the effect that news of their love would have upon Sam, of Nina's continuing love for Gordon, of his own desire to get away from her tentacles; then he resolves to tell Sam about the baby.

Returning to reality, he says he is going to Europe in a few days and therefore must rush off instantly. Then he reveals that Nina is pregnant: "You're going to be a father, old scout." With that he leaves "honorably! . . . I'm free!" Sam stands in a "state of happy stupefaction," and as Nina enters, he takes her in his arms, kissing her happily, saying that Ned had told him the good news. Wildly, Nina asks after Ned, and Sam is surprised that he has not told Nina that he plans to be in Europe for at least a year studying and will be out of town visiting until the ship sails. Nina frantically thinks that Ned has left her, not like Gordon but "like a sneak, a coward! . . . a liar!" Enraged, she decides that she'll make Sam hate Ned. But then pity overcomes her and she cannot tell him the truth. Almost pathetically, Sam asks Nina if she will be happy now, and Nina replies, "I'll try to make you happy, Sammy." But in her thoughts she speaks of the child moving within her: "my life moving in my child . . . God is a Mother." She perceives this child as wholly hers but then with anguish remembers the "afternoons with you, my lover . . . you are lost . . . gone from me forever!"

SECOND PART

Act VI: The same room a little over a year later. It now seems to reflect "a comfortable homey atmosphere, . . . [with] a proud air of modest prosperity." Sam looks "healthy and satisfied," stolid, determined, and even confident. Nina "looks noticeably older, the traces of former sorrow can be seen on her face," but she seems contented and calm." Marsden has aged greatly." His grief is turning to resignation. As usual, he is immaculately dressed, this time in dark tweed. Sam is reading the newspaper, Nina is knitting a baby sweater, and Marsden is pretending to read a book. The thoughts of the three are spoken: Nina is maternally concerned about her baby son, Gordon, and wonders why Darrell has not written to her. However, she forgives him because of the wonderful baby, and Sam has made a superb father. Marsden wonders what had been going on between Nina and Ned, recalling that the doctor had really been "going the pace" when he had seen him in Munich. For Darrell as for him, running away to Europe was no cure for sadness. He must write novels again, and he wants to remember his mother without pain. Evans thinks exceedingly practical thoughts. He has been doing well in his business and wonders if Charlie might invest some of his money in it: "he'd be an easy partner to handle." Marsden looks evaluatively at the pair, thinking that he preferred the old, more vulnerable Sam, and then announces that he is going to bring his widowed sister, Jane, to live with him, to assuage his loneliness and also to circumvent his mother's will because she had disapproved of Jane's marriage.

As usual, Nina teases Charlie about being a timid bachelor, threatening to pick out a wife for him. Somewhat nettled, Charles mentions having seen Ned Darrell in Munich and rather maliciously says that "he was with a startling looking female— . . . I gathered they were living together." Marsden gets the jealous reaction from Nina that he had wanted and proceeds to twist the knife by suggesting that Darrell had nothing at home to be faithful to. Nina recovers and treats the matter airily but then tortures herself with being jilted. Again she teases Marsden with possibly being the father of "little Marsdens," but when Charlie replies, "It's a wise father who knows his own child," Nina is afraid, a feeling that evaporates when she hears that Ned has asked after her. However, she exerts herself to win Charlie over again but thinks contemptuously of him when she does, while he hates himself for wanting to hurt her. Charlie realizes that he has almost admitted his love for Nina, while she is concerned to keep him as a "dependable friend." However, he rejoices inwardly, "Nina likes me!" But then he bitterly realizes that he is only her comfortable "old doggie." Sam recalls him to reality as he returns to speak glowingly about his baby and his wish that the child be everything that Sam himself wanted to be at college and couldn't: "I want him to justify the name of Gordon and be a bigger star than Gordon ever was, if that's possible." Marsden is inwardly contemptuous of this adolescent dream. Then Sam starts to talk of his business plans and hints to Charlie about needing one hundred thousand dollars—but Charlie is impervious and Sam realizes this, suggesting that Charlie might have some ideas to contribute instead. He is becoming progressively more shrewd, and Charlie evaluates this new situation and also his own aimless life.

The doorbell rings, Marsden answers it, and finds Darrell, "pale, thin, nervous, unhealthy looking. There are lines of desperation on his face, puffy shadows of dissipation and sleeplessness under his restless, harried eyes." His dress is careless, almost shabby. In answer to Marsden's rather nasty inquiry, he says that he has come back to wind up the estate of his father, who died three weeks ago. Now he realizes that he still loves Nina and has returned in the hope of claiming some happiness for himself; otherwise he is finished. Marsden realizes Darrell and Nina love each other and is therefore singularly waspish to Darrell, deciding to protect Nina from herself and also to look after Sam, the "simpleton" who may well decide to ask Darrell to back him. He praises Sam's energy and success ever since the baby was born as well as his paternal instincts. Both Ned and Nina wish desperately to be alone; but when Ned hears that Nina has called the baby Gordon, he sees himself left out of a closed corporation: "Gordon, Sam, and Nina! . . . and my son!" In an internal rage he promises to tell Sam the truth. Meanwhile, Nina has come to the realization that she needs Sam for a husband and Ned for a lover, while Marsden has suddenly stumbled on the possibility that Gordon is Ned's child. Rejecting this thought, he promises to fight for Sam and his baby against the two of them, and then he leaves them alone.

The lovers fall into a passionate embrace, and Ned tells Nina she must come away with him; but Nina reminds him, "You're forgetting Sam—and Sam's baby!" Ned says they will take *their* baby with them and Sam will have to give Nina a divorce, but Nina refuses. The happiness of her child comes first, and Ned had given him to Sam for Sam's salvation. Now that Nina feels she has made Sam happy, she loves his joy and "the devoted father in him." In other words, she cannot leave him, even though she still loves Ned. Darrell says he will go away forever, but Nina wishes him to remain as her lover, wanting to keep both men. This angers Darrell, who looks upon Nina as "inhuman and calculating" and threatens to tell Sam. Just then, Sam enters with such evident joy in seeing his old friend and such pride in the child that Darrell is disarmed. Nina calls for Charlie, who enters with the words, "Here, Nina. Always here!"

She looks around her at her three men as they sit, Evans at the table, Marsden in the center, and Darrell on the sofa on the right, all absorbed in their own thoughts. Darrell, with a curious objectivity, notes the success of his "experiment" with Sam and Nina but sees his own deterioration as he gloats over Sam, the putative father of his child. Sam is concerned about the health of both Ned and Nina, and Marsden tries to assess the situation of Nina and her three men: "I feel, with regard to Nina, my life queerly identified with Sam's and Darrell's. . . her child is the child of our three loves for her. . . . I would like to be her husband in a sense. . . and the father of a child, after my fashion. . . I could forgive her anything. . . permit everything." He perceives that Nina is using Darrell's love only for her own happiness and thus Nina will always be his.

Nina looks on the three men with triumph: "I feel their desires converge in me!...to form one complete beautiful male desire which I absorb....I am pregnant with the three!...husband!...lover!...father!...and the fourth man...little man!...little Gordon!...he is mine too!...that makes it perfect." She then says she is tired, and Evans orders her to bed. As she leaves, "the eyes of the three men follow her."

Act VII: Eleven years have passed [1934], and the Evans family is now ensconced on Park Avenue, New York City. The sitting room of the apartment retains the same general arrangement of the furniture, but there are more pieces, obviously expensive. Nina is now thirty-five, slimmer than before and healthy; but her face shows great internal strain in its many lines, and "her eyes are tragically sad in repose and her expression is set and masklike." Gordon is a healthy, athletic-looking child who looks older than his eleven years, with "quick-tempered" sensitive eyes. He is different from any of the people we have seen. Darrell has aged greatly; his hair is gray-streaked and he has grown heavy, while his face has an unambitious look and his eyes are embittered. His manner is one "of cynical indifference."

It is an early fall afternoon, Gordon's birthday, and the youngster is resentful that Darrell is there to be in the way. Obviously he dislikes Ned and wants to be rid of him; he would smash any birthday presents from him. Nina looks tenderly upon her child and wishes now "to rot away in peace! . . . I'm sick of the fight for happiness!" She looks over at Darrell, wondering what has kept them together all these years and wonders about her part in turning him aside from his promising career and corrupting him. But then she refuses to take the blame, saying that she had "shamed him into taking up biology and starting that station in Antigua." Otherwise he would have simply stayed around, idle. However, she now wants to see the last of him for a while because she gets the feeling that he is really waiting for Sam to die. Darrell looks with "apathetic bitterness" on Nina and wonders what she is thinking. He can't understand the hold she has over him—he has always come running back after breaking with her. Once upon a time, he used to hope that Sam would succumb to the family madness, but he has become healthy. "Sam is the only normal one!...we lunatics!...Nina and I!...have made a sane life for him out of our madness." He looks at the child and again expresses his dislike of the name Gordon, blaming Nina for the mess he has made of his own life.

Nina breaks the silence to ask when he plans to return to the West Indies, wondering how he can leave his work for "such long periods," to which Darrell replies that his best experiment was concluded twelve years ago and he no longer wants to meddle with human lives. Cynically, he notes that Sam's business acumen has made both himself and Marsden so wealthy that they can afford to take up hobbies, to be dilettantes. However, he really is interested in the work of the station, particularly in his young assistant, Preston, who will one day do great things if he "never carries his experiments as far as human lives!" Nina rebukes him for his bitterness on Gordon's birthday as Darrell bitterly says that the child gets more and more like Sam. Nina says he reminds her of Gordon Shaw, but Darrell disagrees, sniping at her vision of the "rah-rah hero!" Gordon, overhearing all this, sees Darrell forever belittling his father as the doctor mocks Sam as a material success in terms of money, the right club, and so on. Finally, Gordon leaps to Sam's defense and tells Darrell to shut up, at which Nina insists that he apologize to "Uncle Ned," a title which angers Gordon—"He's not my anything!"—and he is ordered out of the room.

Left alone, Nina and Ned indulge in pointless recriminations and also in some psychological analysis, Darrell suggesting that Gordon "realizes subconsciously that I am his father, his rival in your love; but I'm not his father ostensibly, . . . so he can come right out and hate me to his heart's content!" He reproaches Nina for no longer loving him, and she begs him not to start that again, though she knows that she will again become lonely and call him back once more. She begs Ned to remember that Gordon is the child of their love, but Darrell gives another analysis of the situation: "He feels cheated of your love—by me. So he's concentrating on Sam whose love he knows is secure, and withdrawing from you." Nina thinks this comment is foolish, suggesting that Darrell has never tried to seek Gordon's love; he has not even bothered to bring him a birthday present. At this, Ned says that he has indeed done so, but he has left it outside so that he will not have to see the child destroy it, as he has destroyed all the other gifts he has brought in the past. The two of them then look tenderly at each other, Nina regretting the ruin she has been to him and Darrell saying that she has brought him his only happiness.

After these frank avowals, Nina begs him to go away for two years—without bitterness, this time—and to work really hard and then return. They kiss to seal the bargain, and as they kiss again, Gordon enters and watches them with a combination of "jealousy and rage and grief." He decides not to reveal himself, but Nina has the curious feeling that someone has observed them. Gordon's voice is heard announcing "Uncle Charlie," and the lovers wonder what the child might have seen; but then Darrell snipes at Marsden, "The damned old woman," jealously wondering what Gordon can see in "that old sissy." His rage goes deeper than that: he is still angry that Marsden wanted to put up half the money that Sam needed to set himself up in business, even though Ned had offered the whole amount. He does not wish to share anything with Charlie.

As Marsden enters, Darrell is quite nasty, suggesting that it must be "a great comfort" to have his sister to take the place of his mother. Nina is embarrassed because Charlie has "become such a comfort." The two men then make derogatory remarks about their respective professions, biology and writing novels of manners. Marsden realizes that Darrell knows that he, Charlie, has really lost Nina to him: "we have built up a secret life of subtle sympathies and confidences." He does not "lust" physically for Nina; his love is finer than anything Nina has ever known. Nina, watching him, sees Marsden as a perfect lover for old age "when one was past passion." Suddenly her thoughts turn against all her three men; "the wife and mistress in me has been killed by them," and she makes an excuse to leave with Charlie. Left alone, Darrell does not wish to stay for lunch as a "ghost" at his son's feast. At this, Gordon enters with an exquisitely made model yacht. He loves it, wants it badly, but regretfully must smash it because Darrell is the giver. Then it comes out: "I saw you kissing Mother!" and he accuses Ned of cheating on Sam. But Ned appeals to the child's sense of honor, and Gordon agrees to keep silent as Sam enters.

Sam has grown prosperous and stout with an air of command. He greets Gordon fondly, and Darrell cringes at the sight, deciding he has had enough and must leave. As before, he announces that he must leave immediately because he is sailing in a few days. To his own surprise, Gordon calls him "Uncle Ned" as he leaves, but Darrell thinks that is because he is glad to see the last of him. Left alone with his father, Gordon discusses his birthday presents, finessing the question of Ned's gift by asking to hear again about Gordon Shaw and the reason for his being named after him. When he hears that "Mother loved him a lot," the child intuitively realizes that Darrell dislikes the name Gordon because it means that Nina loved Shaw more than him. Therefore young Gordon resolves to "be just like Gordon and Mother'll love me better'n him!" He asks Sam if he resembles Gordon Shaw, and Sam tells him that if he can be like his namesake, "I'll give you anything you ask for!"

Contentedly, Gordon asks Sam to retell the story of a boat race in which Shaw managed to "talk" a weaker crewmate to the finish and then collapsed himself. Gordon talks to his father about athletic prowess, whether his father used to fight, and whether he could "lick Darrell." This disturbs Sam, and Gordon probes on, coming to the conclusion that Nina must have loved Gordon Shaw better than Sam. Nina, at first jealous of the rapport between Sam and young Gordon, then breaks into the conversation and hears that Ned has left. She lies to Gordon, with the conscious motivation of getting back her son's devotion, saying that she is beginning to find Ned a bore, and then she explains her kissing him as a sentimental good-bye. Gordon is overjoyed, while Sam thinks she might be too hard on their oldest friend, saying that it is a pity that Ned has never married. Gordon kisses Nina—to take away Ned's kiss—and she hugs him. But then she feels remorse for being too cavalier about Ned, and Gordon senses the direction of her thoughts and moves away from her. Sam tells her to stop babying the child, warning him that that was probably what made Marsden the way he is. Nina treats this remark with submissive scorn, but Sam asserts his authority, insisting that he is right. The curtain falls as Nina, "with intense hatred," thinks, "O Mother God, grant that I may some day tell this fool the truth!"

Act VIII: "Late afternoon in late June, ten years later [1944], aboard the Evans' motor cruiser anchored in the lane of yachts near the finish line at Poughkeepsie.... Two wicker chairs are at left," a table with a chair at center, and a chaise longue at right. In other words, the original arrangement of furniture is almost repeated here. "Nina is sitting by the table at center, Darrell in the chair farthest left, Marsden in the chaise longue at right. Evans is leaning over the rail directly back of Nina, looking up the river through a pair of binoculars.

Madeline Arnold* is standing by his side." Nina, now forty-five, has aged notably; her hair is completely white, and her make-up succeeds only in emphasizing her age. Her face is thin, her smile forced, but she has retained her excellent figure. "She is dressed in a white yachting costume....Her eyes...now seem larger and more deeply mysterious than ever." She resembles the neurotic, passionately embittered, and torn Nina of the first act. Darrell, by contrast, seems the cool, scientific doctor of Act II, slender, suntanned, with iron-gray hair. He looks his age, fifty-one, but no more. "Marsden has aged greatly," his stoop is more noticeable, and he is once more in mourning as in Act V, this time for the death of his sister, Jane, two months earlier. However, he seems more resigned than despairing. Sam Evans has remained much the same, except that he has become stouter and more opinionated, as befits a successful businessman. Madeline Arnold is nineteen with dark hair and eyes, athletic, suntanned, reminiscent of a young Nina: "She gives the impression of a person who always knows exactly what she is after and generally gets it, but is also generous and a good loser. . . . She is dressed in a bright-colored sport costume.

Evans and Madeline are desperately trying to see the race upriver, and Evans fusses because his radio has gone dead at this crucial moment. Both of them are concerned about Gordon; and Nina, realizing that she is losing her son, is bitter and antagonistic to this younger woman. Her remarks to Madeline are distinctly acid, and Sam thinks she is "the prize bum sport." Without his efforts the engagement would never have happened, and he is determined to see that "their marriage goes through on schedule, no matter how much Nina kicks up!" Darrell notes Nina's dislike and realizes that she would like to break this engagement as she once did his. He is no longer her slave, yet he has come to this boat race—"duty to Gordon." As Evans becomes excited, Nina pleads a headache, and Sam wishes she were not such a "killjoy." He would like to have had Gordon's friends on the cruiser, but instead he is saddled with her, Darrell, and Charlie. Darrell looks at her, noting her reversion to the Nina of Act I, and then with remorse thinks that her men are deserting her now. Marsden is on the verge of tears. Everyone is tense, and Evans upbraids Nina when she insists that "Gordon *is* you," though as good an athlete as Gordon Shaw, "but there the resemblance ceases." Evans looks so apoplectic that Nina notes his high blood pressure, a remark that Darrell correctly takes for a momentary death wish, and he rejoices that he no longer is really concerned or in love with her. Evans then takes Madeline and Charlie below, leaving Darrell and Nina alone, at her request.

Both Marsden and Madeline leave with some hostility toward Nina. The two former lovers look on each other, Darrell "with melancholy interest" and Nina with sadness, recalling the past: "the only living life is in the past and future...the present is an interlude...strange interlude in which we call on past and future to bear witness we are living." Nina tells Ned she has asked him to come so they can be friends and compliments him on his youthful appearance. Proudly, Darrell speaks of the success of his biology station and the work of his assistant, Preston, who is becoming world-famous: "He's what I might have been . . . if I'd had more guts and less vanity." With some bitterness Nina realizes that he must regard their affair as a mistake, and she thinks that he has forgotten Gordon in his affection for Preston, whom he does agree might be an unconscious "compensating substitute." Obviously, Darrell is not really impressed with the fact that his son is recreating the feats of the famous Gordon Shaw, but he is surprised to discover that Nina has really lost her son to Sam, who has made all the decisions concerning him. At this moment she doesn't care if Gordon comes in last, a sentiment with which Darrell silently agrees: "it's time these Gordons took a good licking from life!"

Madeline appears, saying that the race has begun and that Gordon is third. Darrell notes that Madeline cares about his winning, and Nina indicates her disapproval of their marriage. Ned sees Nina as a possessive mother in action and interprets her wish to enslave Madeline as she had him, and therefore he defends Gordon. Without listening to him, Nina speaks of her fear of losing Gordon, their son, suggesting that Darrell give him "a good talking to." With deep internal struggle, Darrell says he is not going to interfere. "I won't touch a life that has more than one cell!" he tells Nina, "You've got to give up owning people, meddling in their lives as if you were God and had created them!" The two admit a residual affection for each other, but Darrell still refuses to interfere, even when Nina starts to discuss Sam's high blood pressure. But with a slip of the tongue, Darrell indicates his own secret wish for Sam's death.

Sam then comes out, looking upriver for the approaching shells saying that Charlie has been drinking far too much. As he goes in, Darrell secretly hopes that Gordon will lose, while Nina thinks of a way to tell Sam about Gordon's parentage, but she will need Ned to corroborate her statements. She suggests that Sam's mother was lying about the hereditary insanity, but Darrell has already checked that story and found it true. Desperately she tries to rekindle the old passion and get Ned to tell Sam, but the doctor refuses, even though he believes that "if it hadn't been for Sam I would have been happy! . . . I would have been the world's greatest neurologist!" But finally he refuses to tell Sam, explaining that he himself was only a body to Nina, "a substitute for your dead lover," Gordon Shaw. From then on he wishes Gordon to lose. As Nina desperately thinks of a way to get young Gordon back, Charlie comes out and also starts to root against Gordon: "I don't like him since he's grown up!" He believes that "these Gordons are too infernally lucky—" And then in a curious outburst, he suggests that he and Nina will eventually be married.

Madeline and Evans come out excitedly to watch the race, but Marsden seems oblivious, thinking of plans for his married life with Nina and for the book he will write, "the book of us!" the last chapter of which is currently in the making. Nina seems also removed from the race and plots a way to tell Madeline of the hereditary insanity in Sam's family as a way of explaining her objection to the engagement. As the shells draw closer, Nina insists on talking to the exasperated Madeline, telling her that she must break their engagement; but Darrell intervenes, claiming that Nina is not herself, having just passed the menopause and being "morbidly jealous of you and subject to queer delusions!" Nina is in despair as Darrell maintains he wants Gordon's best interests yet hopes that he will be beaten in this race. Marsden realizes that something important was almost revealed in that moment, and he moves by taking Nina's hand. With that, she reveals the whole story of Sam, his hereditary insanity, Darrell, and Gordon's parentage, finally looking at Marsden: "Only you are alive now, Father—and Gordon!" And with that they exchange forgiveness as the shells come close to the finish, Darrell encouraging Gordon's opponent, Navy; but when Sam expostulates, Darrell bitterly goes on: "Meant Gordon, of course! Gordon is always meant—meant to win!" Nina calls silently on "Mother God" to protect Gordon: "Madeline will bring you down in flames!"

As expected, Gordon wins, and Sam takes Nina in his arms: "Our Gordon! The greatest ever!" Nina despairingly tries one last protest, "Gordon is Gordon's!" as Sam humors her. Suddenly he staggers and falls down with a bad stroke. "With a cry of grief" Nina asks, "Oh, Ned, did all our old secret hopes do this at last?" But Ned professionally pooh-poohs this idea, telling Nina that Sam will need "perfect care" and "absolute quiet and peace of mind." At first Nina is crushed, but she vows: "I will never leave his side! I will never tell him anything that might disturb his peace!" Inwardly Marsden thinks, "I will not have long to wait now." But then, ashamed, he speaks something like a priestly valediction over Sam as Darrell says, "I will give my life to save you," and Nina says, "Save—again?" But then she remembers all that Sam has done: "Dear husband, you have tried to make me happy, I will give you my happiness again! I will give you Gordon to give to Madeline." Madeline, looking after Gordon's shell, dreams ahead to the consummation of their marriage: "your head will lie on my breast...soon!"

Act IX: "Several months later. A terrace on the Evans estate on Long Island" overlooking a harbor and the sea. "There is a stone bench at center, a recliner at right, a wicker table and a chair at left," the same furniture arrangement to the last. Gordon, the handsome, sun-bronzed all-American athlete, is sitting on the bench while Madeline has her arm around his shoulders. Gordon, materialistically raised though he has been, still has enough sensitivity to grieve. Madeline seems more maternal toward him than before as she attempts to console him for his father's death.

Gordon blames first himself and then Nina for not having had Sam take better care of himself, but they both praise his mother's total devotion to Sam during his last months. Gordon then says that he has had the curious feeling that it was really the result of a feeling of duty and that her grief is more for the loss of a friend than a husband. He still believes that perhaps she loved Darrell more than Sam but that she had sent him away; he considers Darrell's continual visits the result of the doctor's weakness. Now he expects that they will marry, "and I'll have to wish them good luck!" Madeline does not believe Gordon, thinking that Nina and Darrell would have acted upon their love against all obstacles, as she and Gordon have done.

As they kiss, Marsden enters and is quite shocked by what he sees. But then, with "self-mockery" he realizes that Sam was not Gordon's father and that he himself will soon be able to marry Nina: "dear old Charlie . . . yes, poor dear old Charlie!—passed beyond desire, has all the luck at last!" At this he interrupts the "biological preparations" of the lovers, giving Madeline a rose: "Hail, love, we who have died, salute you!" Madeline finds this statement uncanny but writes it off as coming from "poor old Charlie!"

Gordon then says he wants to see both Nina and Darrell alone, and Madeline moves away. He wants to be fair, but he is in a state of mixed emotions—in love with Madeline, loving his father more than his mother, still confused by the way she had kissed Darrell on his own eleventh birthday. He recalls Nina's last months of devotion, but when he sees Darrell, the old desire to hit him comes back. Nina is dressed in mourning and looks much, much older, having given up any attempt to defeat time. Darrell has lost his suntan and also seems older. Both Nina and Darrell wonder why Gordon has asked to see them. Nina suspects that he is critical because she cannot weep any more, and Darrell expects a "final accounting." Nina looks forward to being left "free at last to rot away in peace." She will return to her father's house, which Sam bought back for her, and Charlie will come to visit, and they will talk of the days before she even knew Gordon Shaw. Darrell compares Gordon unfavorably with Preston, his own protégé and surrogate son, as "a well-muscled, handsome fool!"

To Darrell's surprise, Gordon mentions a curious provision in Sam's will in which a half-million dollars is left "to the Station to be used in biological research work." It is not left to Darrell but specifically to the station, "but I suppose if you won't carry on, whoever is in real charge down there will be glad to accept it." Darrell sees this as Sam's attempt to steal Preston, and Nina thinks that "even in death Sam makes people suffer," though she urges Darrell to accept "for science." Insultingly, Gordon suggests the same. When Nina tells him to be silent, he says that he wishes to speak further, and Darrell authoritatively tells him to go ahead. With this, Gordon threatens to spank Darrell, while Nina thinks "the son spanks the father." As she laughs at Gordon, Darrell goes to her, and Gordon slaps Darrell across the face: "I realize you've acted like a cur!" Hysterically, Nina cries out, "what would your father say? You don't know what you're doing! You're hitting your father!" Darrell says that it is all right, "you didn't know—" and the two are reconciled, even though Darrell reveals his hope that Gordon would lose his last race.

This great revelation of his parentage passes over Gordon's head, and he addresses Darrell by his last name, as an equal. Now Gordon reveals his knowledge that the two were always in love and his own hatred of the idea. But since they both are free, he hopes they will marry and "be as happy as you deserve." It is Darrell's turn to try to tell Gordon the truth, but Nina intervenes, asking Gordon if he had ever suspected her of infidelity with Darrell. When Gordon denies it with horror, she releases him to Madeline, while Darrell, even when given the chance to speak decides to keep forever silent.

Left alone, Darrell asks Nina to marry him, prefacing the proposal with the wish that she refuse—as a favor to him. However, he must ask since Gordon expects it. Nina, without that prodding, refuses: "Our ghosts would torture us to death. But I wish I did love you, Ned. Those were wonderful afternoons long ago! The Nina of those afternoons will always live in me, will always love her lover, Ned, the father of her baby!" Darrell kisses her hand in farewell: "And that Ned will always adore his beautiful Nina! Forget me! I'm going back to work!" He advises her to marry Charlie as a reward for his lifelong devotion and also if she wishes to find peace. With this Marsden appears, and Nina tells him she has refused Ned and asks Charlie if he wants to marry her. As Charlie stands there in secret ecstasy, Darrell says, "Bless you, my children" and then Charlie speaks of his plans for their marriage in late afternoon and then living in Nina's old house. Life is coming full circle.

Suddenly the noise of a plane taking off is heard. It is Gordon with Madeline, and as they circle overhead, Nina waves farewell to "my dear son!" At this Darrell shouts up, "You're my son, Gordon! . . . [and then] Good-bye, Gordon's son!" Nina calls up to her son, "You've got to be happy!" as Darrell comments on that wish, which he himself had once shared. Now he will return to "sensible unicellular life that floats in the sea and has never learned the cry for happiness!"

But Nina no longer seems to hear him, and so he goes into the house as she seems to return to the year 1918, when she received the cable telling of Gordon Shaw's death. Now her son, Gordon, has flown to a new life, and she and Charlie are alone as before. She realizes that her "having a son was a failure, wasn't it? He couldn't bring me happiness. Sons are always their fathers. They pass through the mother to become their father again. The Sons of the Father have all been failures!" In paternal comfort, Charlie suggests that they should forget that whole time since her meeting with Gordon Shaw, "regard it as an interlude of trial and preparation, say, in which our souls have been scraped clean of impure flesh and made worthy to bleach in peace." Nina's reply reveals identical sentiments: "Strange interlude! Yes, our lives are merely strange dark interludes in the electrical display of God the Father!" With this she leans on his shoulder, wishing to return home, with Charlie, to live in peace and "to be in love with peace together—to love each other's peace—to sleep with peace together—! — to die in peace! I'm so contentedly weary with life! Charlie . . . who passed beyond desire, has all the luck at last!" Act IX thus repeats Act I, and Nina is again safe with a father figure. She is where she belongs.

Comments: Though a performance of *Strange Interlude* ran from 5:30 P.M. to after 11 P.M. (including a one-hour dinner intermission at 8 P.M.), this play became O'Neill's greatest hit to date, giving 426 Broadway performances in its first production and gaining his third Pulitzer Prize. The subject matter of the play created a furor, and predictably, the work was banned in Boston because it dealt with abortion, adultery, and homosexuality. In addition, it developed the Freudian and Jungian themes that O'Neill had earlier used in *Desire Under the Elms.** In *Strange Interlude* the subconscious is really the focus of the action.

The external plot action of the play is eminently simple and can be condensed into very few lines, but the complex interweaving of thought and action, sometimes in opposition, is what gives the play both its extraordinary length and its strength. To be sure, some of the Freudian comments and explanations of *Strange Interlude* (though denied by O'Neill) may seem simplistic today, but in 1928 they were daring, shocking, and offered new material for the serious commercial theatre.

Also, in trying to combine a novelistic theme with drama, O'Neill made use of a new theatrical device, the interior monologue, in which he may have been influenced by the novels of James Joyce. In effect he set himself the task of developing a play which would be viable on two distinct levels, the interior and the exterior, and to do this he developed the old Elizabethan device of the soliloquy to its logical (and some suggest its undramatic) conclusion. Some of the interior monologues of individual characters run almost one page of the printed text, while, at times, for several printed pages the reader/audience is presented with a series of interacting monologues, each delivered for the information of the audience rather than the characters, who can only guess at the thoughts of others in the room. This technique exploits what Bertrand Evans (1960, p. 8) has called the gap of "discrepant awareness," for here the audience knows a great deal more than any or all of the characters and is therefore in a judgmental situation, particularly since it knows the complete truth. The conventions of the Elizabethan soliloquy are carefully observed: each of the characters tells the truth about himself or herself insofar as motivations, emotions, and general understanding of situations are concerned. To be sure, some characters have limitations of comprehension, Sam and Gordon Evans, for instance, and there are critics who would disagree with Darrell when he blames Nina for his own failure in medicine. Overall, the characters are devastatingly honest, something that often leads to the most intense dramatic irony—and also to clumsiness when a remark is made in a monologue and then repeated openly to one of the other characters.

The staging of these interior monologues presented a notable challenge. Whereas the Elizabethan soliloquy was delivered with a character alone on the stage, here the audience is asked to distinguish between conversation and thought, almost the way one is expected to do in a novel where the structural conventions are notably different. The original director, Philip Moeller, hit upon what might be called in film parlance the "freeze-frame": when one character is engaged in an interior monologue, all other characters "freeze" in place. This was very effective on stage, and even in an exchange of interior monologues it was apparent to the audience that what it was hearing was spoken thoughts rather than dramatic conversation. Of course this device gave rise to parody, most notably that of Groucho Marx in *Animal Crackers* where he and S. J. Perelman (the scriptwriter) adopted the somewhat inflated language that O'Neill on occasion used for these musings. But the fact remained that *Strange Interlude* succeeded in communicating on various levels and also in making a tremendous emotional impact on its original audiences.

One aspect of the material of the play is most noteworthy: it is O'Neill's only full treatment of the American Ivy-League, business-oriented, Long Island, Park Avenue set, and it also seems to represent his major memory connection with his freshman term at Princeton. The unseen hero, Gordon Shaw, with the athletic prowess and honor code by which he lived and died, is clearly based on that quintessential Princeton hero, Hobart Amory Hare Baker (1892–1918) who excelled in every sport offered at Princeton, joined the American Expeditionary Force and was killed in a flying accident shortly after the World War I armistice. His life seemed to epitomize the romance of American college life, and his fate partook of the same aura that surrounded the death of such as Rupert Brooke (who actually died of sunstroke and was buried at Lemnos) and the central figures of both A. E. Houseman's "To an Athlete Dying Young" and Laurence Binyon's "Recessional" poems. Onto this archetypal figure O'Neill grafted the tale of a girl whose fiancé had died in circumstances similar to those of Baker. She had a nervous breakdown and later married, not for love but in order to have a child and wring some happiness from life. The knowledge of this young woman seems to come from about 1923, long before O'Neill began this play. However, and possibly because he was in effect an outsider in this Scott Fitzgerald-like world, O'Neill reveals himself as frequently uncomfortable with the "Gordon-Shaw-ethic" in its glorification of the athlete, the surface quality of such a mind, its materialism and its lack of real sensitivity. Almost as self-justification, the playwright continually has characters remark that college athletes have their greatest success in their youth; after that, almost everything is downhill, and they rarely achieve success. In some respects this ethic represents a deep flaw in the play itself: the central ideal is so adolescent, so empty, that it tends to tarnish the other characters of the play. Darrell sees through the Gordon-myth, yet he is partially destroyed by it. Charles Marsden also perceives its futility, but since he is drawn as a hypersensitive, mother-ridden non-sexual being, his comments are biased. Neither Nina nor Sam ever rises above dedication to this ideal, and in that fact their weakness as human characters lies.

The most important person in the play is Nina Leeds, and the entire action, both internal and external, revolves around her relationship with six men: her father, the professor; her unseen lover-ideal, Gordon Shaw; her husband, Sam Evans; her actual lover, Ned Darrell; her son, Gordon, who re-creates the ideal of Gordon Shaw; and Charles Marsden, the gentle, mother-obsessed, latent homosexual who finally takes on the role of father for Nina. In effect, for six different men, O'Neill has drawn four different relationships, father, lover, husband and son; and through Nina's reactions to each he has drawn what is, in his view, the progress of woman. But the woman he portrays is ultimately a destructive personality, to some extent a Strindbergian character, yet, as Doris Alexander has also suggested (1953, pp. 213–228), she also partakes of Schopenhauer's idea of the will to live.

Nina, violently deprived of her fiancé, has a mission in life: the fulfillment of her procreative function and also the perpetuation of her ideal lover, Gordon Shaw. Even the nine-act structure suggests the nine months of pregnancy. Thus she marries Sam, who shares her admiration for Gordon, but then she makes use of Ned Darrell, Gordon's friend, to beget the healthy son (both mentally and physically) that Sam is unable to provide. However, throughout the play Nina is also seen as the victim of some kind of hostile will in the universe over which she has no control, and so she is forced as the feminine embodiment of this force, this life-force (though not in the Shavian sense), to make use of all the men in her life to achieve her end as woman. Thus, she ruins Darrell's life by turning him aside from his career as neurologist and forcing him into the furtherance of her life-mission (though some critics and Darrell himself in the play seem to think that his weakness is also responsible). She also contributes to the early death of her father through her devotion to Gordon Shaw and her abandonment of him, her father, to pursue what she sees, neurotically, as her salvation through a promiscuity which horrifies Darrell.

To some extent, one must allow that as a wife Nina succeeds because she does indeed save Sam from the insanity that has destroyed other members of his family. Yet at the same time she is a contributor to Sam's stroke at the end of the play. In the role of wife, Nina is closer to the ideal that O'Neill had already depicted in *Servitude*,* but her self-sacrifice is far from a voluntary one, being imposed upon her by forces over which she has no control. But Sam is a character who can be manipulated, and through apparent submission, Nina remains some-what in control. However, she fails to control in the case of her son. She has wanted him so that she can mold him and possess him utterly, but she is defeated by the Gordon Shaw ethic which she thinks she espouses. In that view of masculine superiority, athletic achievement, and material success, Sam, the nonparticipant, is a truer role-model than Nina realizes. In dedicating her son to this view, Nina loses him, as she of course must, to another woman, and O'Neill here imposes a curious contrast between Gordon Evans and Charles Marsden, the timid, mother-controlled bachelor who waits quietly until Nina is ready for the asexual, protective, paternal relationship that he is able to offer her. At the end of the play, Golden Boy Gordon Evans flies off into the clouds, recalling the Gordon Shaw who fell out of the sky in flames; but the young Gordon is moving toward some kind of achievement, while Nina, finding herself now superfluous, turns back to Charlie Marsden, as if to a father. At the sur-prisingly early age of forty-five she has aged markedly and wishes now merely to "rot in peace." For her, as Hamlet put it, "the heyday of the blood is cold"; and all passion spent, she is content merely to rest.

The ending of the play, then, is curiously romantic, indeed inconclusive, as Nina in effect goes off into a golden sunset and reverts almost to a state of childhood, defining the struggles of life as a "strange interlude" of pain imposed by God the Father. It is in her anguished complaints against God the Father that Nina attempts to find belief in God the Mother who understands the nature of pain, while God the Father becomes the hostile Schopenhauerian will who merely imposes it. But Nina does to some extent endure (in the Faulknerian sense), and so she and Charlie manage to ride out the storms of this strange interlude with some peace.

The victims of this play are Darrell, who has allowed his intellect to be turned aside by his emotions, and Professor Leeds, who appears so briefly that the audience has little time to gain sympathy for him. Sam, though initially a victim, is eventually saved in a material sense in that he achieves happiness on earth, which throughout the play is denied to all the other participants until the final act. But this is gained at the expense of sensitivity and results in the slightly vulgar display of recently acquired wealth. Sam is a decent Babbitt, with good instincts, but wedded to pursuit of an essentially materialistic and adolescent ideal. Actually, the true central character of the play is really Gordon Shaw, the ghost at Sam's marriage and in Darrell and Nina's bed on those glorious afternoons they remember.

All the men of the play define themselves in relationship to Nina, the woman-force who controls them all and who brings such disparate characters together under one roof. Each man attempts to rid himself of this relationship, but each finds himself trapped; even Sam thinks he has not satisfied Nina's expectations and considers offering her a divorce, though Nina never knows this. She is sensual, restless, questing, looking not for sexual freedom or equality but rather for control, only to find that what she really wants is protection.

Basically, then, the true action of *Strange Interlude* is psychological and philosophical. O'Neill was particularly daring in his attempt to display the innermost thoughts of his characters on the stage, not, he insisted, in a Freudian manner, though there does seem to be some influence of Freud. On the whole he is successful, and the varied reactions of the four men who represent the basic relationships between the sexes are admirably differentiated with good use of dramatic irony. The antennae of these characters are all sensitively attuned to the subconscious (even those of Sam and young Gordon), and through the sometimes open opposition of what is thought and what is said, the play derives a density of meaning which might otherwise be impossible of achievement in drama.

Two curious aspects of this play which often pass unnoticed are the use of milieu and time. When one realizes the extraordinary social upheavals that took place during the years covered by this play, 1919–1944, it is astonishing that no notice is taken of any of them. But then one must realize that O'Neill in 1928, when this play was first produced, was projecting his action some sixteen years into the future; he was no visionary, and his play world remains static. Hence the characters in the play are isolated from external events. They seem to live in a world removed from reality, a time warp in which everything material remains static and only the characters grow old. This notion of the unchanging nature of the world and the development of human characters is signified by the repetitive furniture arrangement throughout the entire play. No matter where the characters are, and no matter how they change economically or emotionally, the world around them is the same and has little impact on them. In effect, both chronological time and milieu are irrelevant. What matters is the internal conflict of each character, doomed to come to some kind of rapprochement with existence inside an isolated, circumscribed group. Thus the specifics of Sam's business and his success in it are unstated, as is the actual college which Gordon attended. Even the jazz age does not matter, and there is no thought of the impending stock market crash: the hermetically sealed world alone has importance here.

Production Data: Written 1926–1927. Produced by the Theatre Guild* at the John Golden Theatre, New York City, January 30, 1928 (426 performances).

   Director: Philip Moeller
   Designer: Jo Mielziner
   Cast: Charles Marsden: Tom Powers
             Professor Leeds: Philip Leigh
             Nina Leeds: Lynn Fontanne* (Pauline Lord* played Nina on tour)
             Sam Evans: Earle Larimore*
             Edmund Darrell: Glenn Anders
             Mrs. Evans: Helen Westley
             Gordon Evans (as a child): Charles Walters
             Madeline Arnold: Ethel Westley
             Gordon Evans (as a man): John J. Burns

Revived at the Hudson Theatre, New York City, March 11, 1963 (104 performances).

[*See also* Appendix B for film adaptation].

STRAW, THE, a play in three acts and five scenes.

   Act I, Scene i: "The kitchen of the Carmody home on the outskirts of a manufacturing town in Connecticut. . . . It is about eight o'clock in the evening of a bitter cold day in late February." As the curtain rises, Bill Carmody* is reading the newspaper and smoking. He is about fifty, "heavy set and round-shouldered." His face is bony yet fleshy, and "the expression of his small, blue eyes is one of selfish cunning." He is dressed like a working man in baggy pants and muddy shoes. "His voice is loud and hoarse." Sitting with him is his eight-year-old-daughter, Mary Carmody,* a quiet, dark-haired child who is reading. Carmody is complaining that Mary, like her sick sister, Eileen Carmody,* reads too much. They are both awaiting the return of Doctor Gaynor* who is with her. Two other children, Tom Carmody,* age ten, and Nora Carmody,* age eleven, enter. They are robust and merry. Finally, Billy Carmody,* a fourteen-year-old replica of his father," joins them. In the course of family talk we learn that Mrs. Carmody, apparently a quiet delicate woman, died a year ago and Eileen has been looking after the family.

   Obviously, Carmody is incapable of controlling his rambunctious family as Doctor Gaynor enters and in a dictatorial manner orders that two prescriptions be filled. Carmody, in a whining tone, complains about the cost of the medicines, and Gaynor informs him that Eileen is suffering from pulmonary tuberculosis and will have to be sent to a sanitorium immediately. Carmody complains and the doctor threatens him with reporting to the Society for the Prevention of Tuberculosis. Clearly he blames Carmody for having allowed Eileen to work herself to exhaustion, while Carmody complains about expense and inconvenience.

There is a knock at the door, and Fred Nicholls,* who is unofficially engaged to Eileen, enters. He is a fairly handsome, though commonplace young man, the son of a local manufacturer. Dr. Gaynor tells him about Eileen's illness, and Fred is clearly very disconcerted, indeed frightened by the news, especially when the doctor says that he will have to take the responsibility of her health when she returns from the hospital. Carmody continues to complain about his hard lot as Nicholls becomes progressively closer to panic when Eileen Carmody enters. "She is just over eighteen" with dark hair, blue eyes, full lips, and high color. She is thin and dressed in black. The doctor's announcement has clearly shocked her, but she tries to act cheerfully. Carmody runs off to get a drink while Eileen and Fred are left alone. She speaks sadly of having to leave the children, while Fred is so petrified of infection that he can barely bring himself to touch her, let alone kiss her. Eileen recognizes his fear, and finally he kisses her on the forehead.

Act I, Scene ii: "The reception room of the Infirmary, a large, high-ceilinged room painted white, with oiled, hardwood floor." In general, the room is as cheerful as a hospital can be, with a wood fire, easy chairs, magazines, and a Victrola. "It is nearing eight o'clock of a cold morning about a week later." Stephen Murray* is sitting in an armchair as the curtain rises. He is about thirty years old, pale, lined, and worn. He has hazel eyes and a somewhat dispirited expression, an impression compounded by his failure to get up to turn off the Victrola. Miss Gilpin,* a middle-aged, dark-haired nurse who combines efficiency with sympathy, and Miss Howard,* a pretty blond nurse in training, enter, and the younger woman jokes with Murray about the Victrola.

Murray complains about the depressing atmosphere of the hospital, and Miss Howard says that perhaps the new patient may be good company for him. At this moment Eileen, followed by her father and Fred Nicholls, enters. Miss Gilpin is considerate, Carmody is drunk, and Nicholls is eager to get away. Murray observes the two men as they quarrel about Carmody's drinking and Nicholls's evident desire to leave, something that Carmody taxes him with. Carmody introduces himself to Murray, and then Eileen returns and is introduced to Murray. Desperately, Eileen tries to give final instructions to her father, who turns them aside, while Nicholls suggests that Eileen is already setting her cap at Murray. They leave in a flurry of misunderstanding, with Eileen totally exhausted.

Murray and Eileen exchange details about themselves, and Murray is found to be a former newspaper reporter on a small-town newspaper. He tries to cheer her up and in so doing reveals how despondent he is and how he has hated his job, wishing that he had had the time to write stories. Eileen suggests that he should try out this talent while he is in the sanitarium and offers to type his manuscripts for him. They agree, and the act ends with Murray and Miss Howard joking together with a macabre tubercular-hospital parody of Omar Khayyám.

Act II, Scene i: "The assembly room of the main building of the sanitorium— early in the morning of a fine day in June, four months later." The large airy room, painted white, has armchairs and a pianola. Windows look out over the woods and hills. Doctor Stanton,* the sanitorium head, his assistant, Doctor Simms,* and Mr. Sloan,* a successful businessman and contributor to the Hill Farm Sanitorium, are discussing the patients and their treatment. Dr. Stanton points out that tuberculosis is not considered cured, only arrested, and notes the high success rate of the sanitorium. However, in reply to a direct question concerning the number of deaths, he speaks of "a very hard, almost cruel imperative" which mandates that those whose cases are absolutely incurable are sent away from Hill Farm, perhaps "to one of the State Farms if they lack the means," in order to make room for others for whom a cure might be possible. Again, in answer to Mr. Sloan, Dr. Stanton says that love affairs between patients are actively discouraged. He then says that he must start with the weekly weighing of each patient as a means of determining individual progress.

As the patients enter, Murray tells Eileen that he has sold a story and has been asked for others. Exuberantly he kisses her, but she tells him to avoid such public affection, reminding him that they have been warned against being so much together. Murray is highly optimistic, saying that he has been promised release if he has gained weight again. Eileen, on the other hand, is certain that she has lost weight and that she is again running a temperature—a situation that will lead to her being returned to bed for a complete rest. The other patients discuss their own hopes, and one of them plays a rag on the pianola in an attempt to relieve tension. One by one the patients are weighed; all have gained weight except one young woman, Miss Bailey, and Eileen, who is devastated to learn that she has lost three pounds. Murray, however, has gained three pounds and is merrily preparing to pack and leave. Eileen, who has managed to get a reprieve from bed rest for one more day (much to Miss Bailey's annoyance) generously says to Stephen, "Oh—I'm so glad—you gained—the ones I lost, Stephen—so glad!" before breaking into sobs. Murray desperately tries to soothe her.

Act II, Scene ii: "Midnight of the same day. A crossroads near the sanito- rium." Eileen is standing in the middle of the road as the curtain opens. Hearing a noise, she hides, and Stephen Murray appears. He calls to her and she appears. She has stolen out of her room to say good-bye to Stephen. They speak of Murray's imminent return to the outside world and his two sisters (whom he cares little about, even though they have paid his hospital bills). Eileen then reveals that she has finally written a letter to Fred Nicholls breaking off their relationship, "the letter you've been advising me to write." Murray is somewhat disturbed at this and wonders whether he has been completely fair to Fred. Eileen, however, seems quite certain that Fred will be happy to break off the "engagement" because " he couldn't love anyone but himself." Stephen hopes that she'll "get one of the right sort—next time," but Eileen interrupts him with a cry of pain and they say good-bye. Suddenly she calls him back and tells of her love for him, asking his forgiveness for telling him, and speaking of the loneliness she will feel without him. Her family seems to have forgotten her, and they no longer need her. She begs him to write often, and Murray promises to "find something." With a final "I love you—love you—remember!" Eileen runs back, and Stephen starts to follow. He calls "Eileen!" but then with a furious stamping of feet he clenches his fists "in impotent rage at himself and at Fate." "Christ!" he says as the curtain falls.

Act III: "Four months later. An isolation room at the Infirmary. . . . Late afternoon of a Sunday toward the end of October." Eileen is in bed on a sleeping porch. Whereas in Act II she had seemed a bit more robust, now she is thinner, her eyes lack fire, and "she gazes straight before her into the wood with the unseeing stare of apathetic indifference." Bill Carmody, Mrs. Brennan,* and Mary Carmody enter. He is in his stiff and unfamiliar Sunday-best; Mary is tall, skinny, and wears an outgrown dress. She looks sullen and furtively rebellious as she looks at Mrs. Brennan, her new stepmother. This lady is a florid, coarse-faced, permanently irritable-looking woman of about fifty, also dressed "in her ridiculous Sunday-best." They discuss Eileen's condition, saying Eileen must not be told that she is to be sent to the state farm in a few days because the news would upset her. Mrs. Brennan attacks Eileen for not writing to them and draws Carmody's annoyance. She tells him to be sure and tell the girl of their recent marriage. Clearly she sees Eileen as unwelcome competition.

They go out to look at Eileen, who doesn't notice them at first. Mrs. Brennan attempts to take her hand, but Eileen pulls away. Carmody treats her "with rough tenderness," leaning forward to kiss her but then withdrawing in fear. Eileen greets Mary with joy, but the girl approaches her gingerly, and when Eileen tries to hug her she whines, "Let me go." With that rebuff, Eileen "in a dead voice" says, "You, too! I never thought you—Go away, please." Carmody attempts to give her news of home, of Billy and Nora, "the smartest girl in the school." Mrs. Brennan keeps fidgeting to be gone, and finally the news of the marriage is broken. Eileen greets the announcement with notable lack of enthusiasm, and the senior Carmodys quarrel. Mrs. Brennan walks out as Eileen rejects her, and Carmody "in a whining tone of fear" asks, "Is your last word a cruel one to me this day, Eileen?" She remains silent as he walks out angrily, followed by the frightened Mary. Eileen covers her face and shudders with relief.

Miss Howard enters and with unconscious irony asks if Eileen has had "a nice visit with your folks." Then, in an attempt to cheer her up, Miss Howard announces that "Mr. Murray" has arrived. He is no longer the healthy-looking young man who left the sanitorium. He is thinner and his eyes are puffy, showing signs of sleeplessness and dissipation. But he is well and expensively dressed. He is shocked to see how much Eileen's condition has deteriorated. She looks at him "with wild yearning," but what she hopes he was going to say is not forthcoming. She says that she finally got tired of writing without receiving an answer, and gradually she reveals that her cheerful letters were only a pose.

Murray has not been happy with life on the outside. He doesn't need money, but he has lost the real urge to write: "I'm sore at everything because I'm dissatisfied with my own cussedness and laziness—and I want to pass the buck." Eileen speaks encouragingly to him, and Murray begins to wonder aloud whether she again is helping him to work, and he speaks of the way in which she had made his career possible. Her letters had continually given him courage. He asks if she remembers that last night on the road near the hospital, and Eileen tries to laugh that off, claiming she hardly remembers what happened because she was so sick and "crazy." At first Stephen seems a trifle hurt but then is somewhat relieved as he departs, promising to be back in time to say good-bye.

As he leaves Eileen on her sleeping porch, he meets Miss Gilpin who tells him that Eileen is being sent to the state farm in a day or two: "Her father is unwilling to pay for her elsewhere now he knows there's a cheaper place." Stephen is shocked, and Miss Gilpin tells him that whatever he thinks, Eileen has continued to love him. She herself understands because something similar happened to her, and she also loves Eileen. Murray, in answer to her direct question, says that "I've never thought much about loving anyone—that way." Miss Gilpin sadly wishes they had spoken earlier so that Eileen might not have had to face that truth, and now with her imminent departure for the state farm she will despair utterly, and will die there—alone. She begs Murray to tell Eileen he loves her just as means of making her happy in the time left her. He must become engaged to her and then take her away to a small, private sanitorium where he can work nearby. Murray agrees, but "I won't do this thing by halves. . . . I'm going to marry her." Miss Gilpin suggests that this shock might be fatal, but Murray goes out to propose marriage. As Miss Gilpin had predicted, Eileen wants to wait until she is well, but she does want Stephen to move nearby so she can help him. He announces, as if it had been planned, the move to another sanitorium. Eileen is ecstatic, but suddenly Stephen seems to realize the fact of her imminent death, and Eileen realizes it, too, "with a childish whimper of terror." Murray then begs her to marry him immediately, as Eileen breaks down. Miss Gilpin enters to remonstrate with Murray, who concocts the lie that he has had a relapse and asks the nurse to confirm his statement. Somehow Miss Gilpin feels impelled to go along with the deception. Murray exultantly announces the curative power of love against all the knowledge of doctors. He will take Eileen to the West, or anywhere, and she will recover. Miss Gilpin leaves with "God bless you both!" knowing the truth. As the curtain falls, Murray kisses Eileen as she strokes his hair and speaks fondly of the way they will undergo a curative regimen together.

Comments: *The Straw*, written in 1918–1919, is a highly autobiographical play, based on O'Neill's sojourn at the Gaylord Farm,* Connecticut, in 1912–1913. Stephen Murray, the young reporter, is a recreation of O'Neill himself. The name Murray seems to have been taken from one of the nurses at the sanitorium, while the first name of Stephen is thought to have been inspired by James Joyce's Stephen Dedalus, who in *A Portrait of the Artist as a Young Man* (1916) goes forth to create as a writer (Sheaffer, 1968, p. 447). Other characters of the play have certain equivalents: Dr. Stanton is Dr. Lyman, head of Gaylord; Miss Gilpin is Miss Mary A. Clark, to whom O'Neill later sent a volume of his plays containing *The Straw*; while Eileen Carmody is Kitty Mackay, a fellow patient of O'Neill. It seems certain that they had a flirtation, she encouraging him to write and he giving her books to read. Any commitment would appear to have been more on her side than O'Neill's, and after his release from the sanitorium, they never saw each other again. She died in 1915 of tuberculosis. Miss Howard is a composite of two other nurses at Gaylord Farm, Wilhelmina Stamberger and Catherine Murray (*see* Gelb and Gelb, 1973, pp. 230–231).

The significance of the title concerns the proverbial straw to which a drowning man clings. In other words, it is meant to underline the mixed conclusion of the play rather than the "last straw" which finally reduces a human being to despair. Certainly the hope which this title indicates is frail, even nonexistent, but it does show the indefatigability of human beings in the face of disaster, as well as the power of the saving lie.

The interest of this play lies more in its autobiographical elements than in its content or character drawing. Some of the changes between its original version and the final text, however, show some interesting second thoughts. Travis Bogard (1972, p. 110) notes that in the manuscript, Stephen Murray is given more family background which makes his character closer to that of the young James Tyrone, Jr.,* in *Long Day's Journey into Night.** In particular, James O'Neill,* who originally sent Eugene to the "state farm," the Fairfield County State Tuberculosis Sanitarium, is the basis of the character of Bill Carmody, the father of Eileen. However, the major change between the first draft and the acting text is that the emphasis is now on the fate of Eileen rather than that of Stephen. The romantic conclusion is, of course, completely divorced from the realities of O'Neill's experience and bears a curious resemblance to the novella, "Sanitorium," by Somerset Maugham.

Nonetheless, *The Straw* does show skill in the handling of exposition and construction, particularly in the ambiguously optimistic conclusion. It also demonstrates the first use of a theme which O'Neill uses on more than one later occasion—the saving lie which makes life (or what remains of it) bearable and the almost imperative necessity of protective illusion. The authenticity of the hospital setting is impeccable, even to the grimly macabre humor of those who are doomed to a lifetime of fragility rather than cure. O'Neill manages with this first-hand knowledge to construct dramatic tension out of mundane aspects of hospital routine such as the weekly weighing. He also treats the character of Eileen Carmody with skillful understanding and delicate sympathy. As is usual, the O'Neill persona, Stephen Murray, becomes an edited version of O'Neill himself, but there seems no reason to infer that he should have had any feelings of guilt toward Kitty Mackay. Once again, O'Neill draws his central feminine character as one who is prepared to sacrifice herself totally to the talent of the man she loves.

Production Data: Written 1918–1919. First produced by George C. Tyler at the Greenwich Village Theatre, New York City, November 10, 1921 (20 performances).

Director: Unknown
Designer: Unknown
Cast: Partial list
   Bill Carmody: Harry Harwood
   Nora: Viola Cecil Ormonde
   Tom: Richard Ross
   Billy: Norris Millington
   Dr. Gaynor: George Woodward
   Fred Nicholls: Robert Strange
   Eileen Carmody: Margalo Gillmore
   Mary Carmody: Unknown
   Stephen Murray: Otto Kruger
   Miss Gilpin: Katherine Grey
   Mr. Sloan: Unknown
   Miss Howard: Dothea Fisher
   Dr. Simms: Unknown
   Mrs. Abner: Nora O'Brien
   Mrs. Turner: Grace Henderson
   Miss Bailey: Alice Haynes
   Dr. Stanton: George Farren
   Mrs. Brennan: Jennie Lamont

SUNDA. In *Beyond the Horizon,** a sailing vessel captained by Dick Scott.*

SUSIE. In *The Moon of the Caribbees,** a West Indian negress.

SWANSON. In *In the Zone,** a seaman on the S.S. *Glencairn,* "a squat, surly-faced Swede."

SWEENEY, Annie. In *The Rope,** daughter of Abraham Bentley,* half-sister of Luke Bentley,* wife of Pat Sweeney,* and mother of Mary Sweeney.* Annie is "a thin, slovenly, worn-out looking woman of about forty," she is perpetually whining in voice, and her expression is pinched and bitter. She is living with her husband and child on her father's farm, trying to make ends meet. She has never forgiven Abraham Bentley for marrying so soon after her own mother's death, and moreover, she believes that his miserliness was the cause of it. She taunts him with the remembrance that the "harlot" had been unfaithful to him and casts doubts on the paternity of her half-brother, Luke. She had been jealous of Luke as her father's favorite, and therefore she takes perverse satisfaction in reminding the old man of the way Luke ran off with one hundred dollars of her father's money five years ago. When Luke returns, there is no reconciliation between them. Annie seems to be totally self-absorbed, caring for nothing but getting her father's money. She resents the old man's continual anti-Catholic slurs and his everlasting biblical references. She does seem to have some companionship in Pat Sweeney, but it is based on mutual self-interest rather than love. Her daughter Mary seems to be a thoroughly stupid child of ten.

SWEENEY, Mary. In *The Rope*,* daughter of Annie Sweeney* and Pat Sweeney,* granddaughter of Abraham Bentley,* and niece of Luke Bentley.* She is "an overgrown girl of ten" with carrot-colored hair, a stupid expression, and a whining voice. She is thoroughly unlikable. When her prodigal uncle, Luke, appears, he gives her a silver dollar, much to her mother's rage. Mary then suggests to Luke that he throw the coin over the water instead of rocks to see it skip. Luke, eager to enrage his half-sister, Annie, does so, saying that he is teaching Mary to be "a sport." The little girl later discovers where old Bentley has hidden his hoard of fifty twenty-dollar gold pieces by swinging on the noose which the old man had left in readiness for Luke to hang himself. The rope breaks, and the bag of money, which had been used as a counterweight, falls to the ground. Mary, with the nearest approach to glee shown by anyone in the play, takes a handful of gold pieces and throws them one by one into the water to see them skip. The play ends with heavy irony as she returns for a second handful, saying, "Skip! Skip!"

SWEENEY, Pat. In *The Rope*,* husband of Annie Sweeney,* father of Mary Sweeney,* and son-in-law of Abraham Bentley.* "He is a stocky, muscular, sandy-haired Irishman, "with bullet head and pugnacious jaw. His expression is one "of mean cunning and cupidity." In *The Rope*,* he is trying to eke out a living on Abraham Bentley's farm, but more than anything else he wants to get hold of the old man's money. He is certain that there is some because Bentley had borrowed one thousand dollars on which Sweeney is still paying interest, but he doesn't know where it is hidden. He has discovered by getting Bentley's lawyer drunk that no money is left to him in the will, and he is more than eager to get Luke Bentley also drunk so that the pair of them can torture old Bentley into revealing the hiding place of the hoard. To be sure, Pat has reason for resentment against Abraham Bentley, but at the same time, greed has shriveled any redeeming qualities he may at one time have possessed.

T

"TALE OF POSSESSORS, SELF-DISPOSSESSED, A," the overall title of the massive cycle devoted to the Harford family, which eventually grew to a projected eleven plays, only two of which have survived, the completed *A Touch of the Poet*,* and the unfinished manuscript from which *More Stately Mansions** was adapted. In addition, the scenario of *The Calms of Capricorn** has been printed and developed into a play by Donald Gallup (1982). Other plays, outlines, and drafts were destroyed by O'Neill in 1943 and the winter of 1952–1953. The overall plan, which occupied O'Neill more or less continuously from 1931 to the end of his active writing career, was to show the history of the United States and the development of its society from 1775–1932. He planned to use the saga of one family to illustrate the central theme of the corrupting influence of possessions upon their owners. At the height of his enthusiasm in 1936 O'Neill spoke with Theresa Helburn* of the Theatre Guild* hoping that a repertory company could be set up to produce all these plays, but Ingrid Bergman,* like other performers O'Neill hoped to use, could hardly commit themselves for the four years O'Neill expected. Insofar as one can piece the cycle together, the planned plays with titles and periods covered, were probably as follows: (*See also* separate entries for each play.)

Play Title	When Written
1. "Greed of the Meek" (1755?–1775)	June 1936-February 1943. Destroyed, February 1943.
2. Proposed portion of the above (1776?–1793?)	
3. "And Give Me Death" (1793–1805?)	September 1935-February 1943. Destroyed, February 1943.
4. Proposed portion of the above.	
5. *A Touch of the Poet* (1828)	January 1935- Revised 1942. Completed.
6. *More Stately Mansions* (1832–1841)	February 1935—January 1941. Surviving manuscript dated 1938, not revised by O'Neill.

7. *The Calms of Capricorn* (1857–1858)	December 1932—June 1939. Scenario survives. Later printed and adapted by Donald Gallup into play form.
8. "The Earth Is the Limit" (1860s)	June 1935. Outline destroyed, 1943 or 1953.
9. "Nothing Is Lost But Honor (1862–1870)	July 1935. Outline destroyed, 1943 or 1953.
10. "The Man on Iron Horseback" (1876–1893)	August 1935. Outline destroyed, 1943 or 1953.
11. "Hair of the Dog" (1900–1932)	1927-1943. Longhand draft destroyed February 1943.

The final play, "Hair of the Dog," began as "It Cannot Be Mad,"* part of the uncompleted trilogy, "Myth-Plays for the God-Forsaken,"* the other plays of which were *Dynamo** and *Days Without End.** There the heroine was Bessie Wilks. The play was reworked as "On to Betelgeuse" and "On to Hercules," and again as "The Life of Bessie Bowen" (or Bolan, or Bowlan). O'Neill then tried to integrate this material about the automobile industry into the last play of his cycle. He seems to have been very reluctant to get rid of this play and destroyed it in 1943 only when he was totally convinced of its intractability in its new setting.

"In [the] original conception of the Cycle each of the four sons of Simon Harford* and Sara [Melody*] Harford was to be the principal character of a particular play; Ethan [Harford*], the sailor, would be protagonist of *The Calms of Capricorn*, . . . 'The Earth Is the Limit' was to be built around Wolfe [Harford*] the gambler; . . . 'Nothing Is Lost But Honor' would trace the rise and fall of the politician, Honey [Harford*]; and . . . 'The Man on Iron Horseback' would follow the career of Jonathan Harford* as a railroad and shipping magnate." Honey, aged ninety-three, was to be the sole survivor of the family. (*See* O'Neill, ed. Gallup, 1982, pp. vi–vii; Floyd, 1981, *passim.*)

Gradually, O'Neill found himself obliged to go backward and forward in time until the final cycle was extended to a total of eleven constituent plays. Fearful of leaving uncompleted work that he considered unworthy, he and his wife Carlotta Monterey,* in winter 1952–1953 destroyed most of the manuscripts that had survived an earlier destruction in February 1943.

The history of the Cycle's expansion and change is told in the following section:

A. "The Calms of Capricorn." Four Plays, 1935.
   1. *The Calms of Capricorn*
   2. "The Earth Is the Limit"
   3. "Nothing Is Lost But Honor"
   4. "The Man on Iron Horseback"
B. "A Touch of the Poet." Five Plays, 1935.
   A Touch of the Poet (Original title "Hair of the Dog"; retitled April 1936), dramatizing the lives of Sara Melody* Harford, her parents, Cornelius Melody* and Nora Melody*

together with Sara's courtship and marriage to Simon Harford becomes the first of the series.

C. "Threnody for Possessors, Self-Dispossessed." Six Plays, 1935.

A Touch of the Poet remains the first play, but "Oh, Sour-Apple Tree," first title of *More Stately Mansions*, the story of Deborah Harford* (originally Abigail) and her life with Sara and Simon is inserted to become the second play.

D. "Twilight of Possessors, Self-Dispossessed." Seven Plays, 1935.

This also becomes the title of a proposed new seventh play which later is given the title "Hair of the Dog," the former title of *A Touch of the Poet*. It includes the Bessie Bowen material which dates back to "It Cannot Be Mad"* (1927).

E. "A Legend of Possessors, Self-Dispossessed." Eight Plays, 1935.

A new play concerning Deborah (Abigail) Harford and her marriage, entitled "Greed of the Meek" is placed first.

F. "Lament for Possessors, Self-Dispossessed." Nine plays, 1937.

First draft is done of a new first play entitled "Give Me Death." Its action precedes what has gone before, apparently beginning about the year 1755. This play was written in June 1936. In August, 1937, the titles of the two "first" plays in proposals E and F are reversed: "Give Me Death" is now entitled "Greed of the Meek," and remains the first play, while the second play becomes "Give Me Death."

G. "A Tale of Possessors, Self-Dispossessed." Eleven Plays, 1940.

O'Neill became absorbed in these first two plays tracing the history of the Harford family from farm to French Revolution. He finally realized that he would have to expand each of them into two separate plays. He retitles the second play "And Give Me Death." The drafts of both plays were destroyed in February 1943.

TARNOFF, Olga. In "The Personal Equation,"* a dark-haired, dark-eyed, slender young woman. She is a young revolutionary who persuades her lover, Tom Perkins,* to join her commitment to the International Workers of the Earth. Later, when Tom is assigned to destroy the engines of a ship on which his father, Thomas Perkins,* is second engineer, she tries to talk him out of performing the task. She is afraid for his personal safety, and also she has just discovered that she is pregnant by Tom. All her previous talk of free love and freedom from commitment is now subordinate to this new discovery. When Tom is reduced to the state of permanent vegetable as the result of being shot by his father in an attempt to damage the engines, Olga wants to take care of Tom in reparation. She disputes this issue with Tom's father, but when he hears of her pregnancy and her threat to kill the unborn child, he agrees to take her in as well. Despite what the revolution has done to her life, Olga remains committed to the cause, and the play ends with her delivering an impassioned speech in support of it, concluding with "Long Live the Revolution," words which are echoed in an imbecilic manner by the brain-damaged Tom.

TEDALDO. In *Marco Millions*,* the papal legate, later Pope Gregory X. He is about sixty years of age, a man with a sense of humor and intelligence. He is amused by the Polos' total preoccupation with business. He evaluates Marco Polo* skillfully when he hears his poem to Donata,* noting that the lady is "too mineral'' and that Marco's conception of heaven is "too monetary." Jestingly, he tells Marco to announce to Kublai Kaan* that he, Polo, will be worth more than a million wise men "in the cause of wisdom." Perhaps Tedaldo realizes the way in which the church he is to head has been perverted by materialism.

TENARD, Benjamin. In *More Stately Mansions*,* a failed banker. He is a fine-looking man in his sixties, well and conservatively dressed with a face like a Roman coin. Simon Harford's* firm has taken over his bank, and Sara Melody* Harford interviews him, offering him his old position as bank manager, and planning to make use of his known probity as a means of covering her own ruthlessness and sharp practice. Tenard is at first insulted, but she points out to him that that is the only way he will be able to support his family. This incident is meant to show how low Sara has fallen in her dedication to greed.

THARSING, Hazel, the original name of Carlotta Monterey* O'Neill.

THEATRE GUILD, THE. This producing group was first organized in early 1919 with a managerial board that included Helen Freeman, Lawrence Langner,* Philip Moeller, Rollo Peters, Justus Sheffield, Lee Simonson, and Helen Westley. An outgrowth of the Washington Square Players,* it also included some of the earlier Provincetown Players,* such as Edna St. Vincent Millay, and Mary Blair.* For many years the Theatre Guild was noted for its performances of the plays of George Bernard Shaw, so much so that its theatre (later the ANTA Theatre, New York City) was nicknamed "the house that Shaw built." The Guild's policy in the 1920s was to produce the work of young American playwrights as well as that of important European dramatists. At this time it had a large subscription audience and prospered under the management of Theresa Helburn,* Lawrence Langner, Philip Moeller, Lee Simonson, Maurice Wertheim, and Helen Westley. Notable Guild actors of this period included Earle Larimore,* Florence Eldridge* and Fredric March,* Alfred Lunt* and Lynn Fontanne,* Dudley Digges,* and Henry Travers. During the 1930s the Guild fell upon lean depression times and also suffered a series of box-office failures, but the successful run of *Oklahoma* (1943) revived its finances. Today the Theatre Guild continues as a producing organization with a film department.

The Theatre Guild staged the original productions of the following O'Neill plays: *Marco Millions* (Guild Theatre, New York City, January 9, 1928; revived, Liberty Theatre, New York City, March 3, 1930); *Strange Interlude* (John Golden Theatre, New York City, January 30, 1928); *Dynamo* (Martin Beck Theatre, New York City, February 11, 1929); *Mourning Becomes Electra* (Guild Theatre, New York City, October 26, 1931); *Ah, Wilderness!* (Nixon Theatre, Pittsburgh, September 25, 1933); Guild Theatre, (October 2, 1933; revived October 2, 1941); *Days Without End* (Plymouth Theatre, Boston, December 27, 1933); (Henry Miller's Theatre, New York City, January 8, 1934); *The Iceman Cometh* (Martin Beck Theatre, New York City, October 9, 1946);

and *A Moon for the Misbegotten* (Hartman Theater, Columbus, Ohio, February 20, 1947, toured to Pittsburgh and Detroit and closed in St. Louis, March 29, 1947). It turned down *The Straw,** *Gold,** *The Fountain,** *Welded,** *The First Man,** and *"Anna Christie,"** this last being a decision that caused much later regret. [Accounts of the group's history may be found in the memoirs of two of the founders: Langner (1951), and Helburn (1960).]

THIRST, a one-act play. Three persons, a Gentleman,* a Dancer,* and a West Indian Mulatto Sailor,* have been floating for some time on a single raft without food and water under a blazing tropical sun, somewhere off the normal shipping lanes. Sharks swim lazily around them, waiting for the inevitable victim. The three characters seem to have been chosen to represent a microcosm of the world. The middle-aged Gentleman, clearly a first-class passenger, is dressed in the remains of his evening dress. The Dancer, even more grotesquely, is in black velvet and spangles, as if interrupted in the midst of a performance; she wears a valuable diamond necklace. The West Indian Sailor is dressed in his sailor's uniform. All are slowly being driven mad by their thirst. The Dancer and the Gentleman speak of their hardships, and the Gentleman maintains that the Sailor has stolen the last of the water. They decide to coax him into letting them drink from the private store they are convinced he has secreted somewhere on his person. Throughout a large part of the play, the Sailor sings a strange song which he says is a charm to prevent the sharks from eating them.

As the three go slowly mad, the Gentleman tells of the way he was going home: "After twenty years of incessant grind, day after weary day, I started my first vacation." Similarly, the Dancer "was coming home, after years of struggling, home to success and fame and money." Under the Gentleman's questioning, she realizes that she was saved by the second officer, who had loved her and sent her out on this raft after kissing her good-bye. The Gentleman, on the other hand, had swum to the boat, in deathly fear of the waiting sharks. He recounts how the captain had shot himself as the vessel sank, and both the Gentleman and the Dancer recall that he had deliberately chosen a risky route to make time. He has paid for his folly.

Gradually their insistence intensifies that the Sailor share his alleged store of water with them. The Dancer offers him her diamond necklace, the gift of an English duke and worth five thousand dollars; then she straightens her clothing, and in a grotesque scene of seduction she offers him her body. Again the Sailor says he has no water. The Dancer stands up, performs her last insane dance of death, and falls lifeless. The Sailor then suggests that he and the Gentleman eat her body in order to survive. As he sharpens his knife, the Gentleman throws the Dancer's body overboard. The Sailor lunges at the Gentleman, killing him, but in death the Gentleman holds on to the Sailor as they both fall into the sea to join the Dancer as victims of the waiting sharks. Only the necklace remains on the raft.

Comments: This play is basically a melodrama, but O'Neill even at this early stage demonstrates his frequent theme that human beings are victims of a hostile universe and a hostile God; the final stage direction includes the words, "The sun glares down like a great angry eye of God." Mankind struggles in situations that are not of his own making. Beauty, money, success, civilization—all these things are stripped away. In this play, the only reality is survival, something that the Sailor understands but the civilized Gentleman does not. The price of survival is cannibalism, something that the Gentleman, who had earlier said he would sell his soul for a drop of water, cannot bring himself to pay. Throughout the play the irony of human existence is commented upon: the Dancer wears a valuable necklace, the Gentleman discovers that he has seized an old menu from a dinner in his honor instead of his wallet, and both have been shipwrecked in their moment of success. The Sailor, whom both consider an inferior, is in this situation their equal. The plot is highly ironic and melodramatic, ending with the conventional violence, and the dialogue is stilted. The sense of place and atmosphere which O'Neill had earlier demonstrated in *A Wife for a Life** is well developed here, while the mysterious, magic chant of the Mulatto Sailor (a portrayal created by O'Neill himself) looks ahead to the use of the tom-tom in *The Emperor Jones.**

Production Data: Written 1913. First produced by the Provincetown Players* at the Wharf Theatre, Provincetown, Massachusetts, August 1916 (Performances unknown).

    Director: George Cram Cook*
    Designer: William Zorach
    Cast: Gentleman: George Cram Cook
          Dancer: Louise Bryant*
          West Indian Mulatto Sailor: Eugene O'Neill

A Note on Text: The text used is that appearing in *Ten "Lost" Plays of Eugene O'Neill* (New York: Random House, 1964).

"THIRTEENTH APOSTLE, THE." Original title of "The Last Conquest."*

THOMAS, Rose, a tubercular prostitute of twenty-two who looks thirty. In *The Web,** she is the mother of a baby girl. She is "dressed in the tawdry extreme of fashion" with gaudy hat and an excessive amount of cheap costume jewelry. Her pale face, feverish eyes, and hacking cough indicate the seriousness of her illness. She is full of maternal love for her baby and wishes to keep it, despite the threats of her pimp, Steve,* because it is the only thing in her life that means anything to her. Steve tries to force her out onto the street and knocks her down. Tim Moran,* a safecracker, intervenes, threatening Steve with a revolver.

Rose and Tim exchange life stories. Rose has tried many times to give up streetwalking and even managed to hold a situation as a housekeeper. But someone who knew of her past informed her mistress, and Rose was dismissed. This happened more than once, and now, with a baby, she is even less likely to gain a good position, let alone regain her shattered health. She sees herself as the victim of a hostile society which will not allow her to go straight but will malevolently push her down the moment she tries to change. Tim has had a similar experience, and he gives her money so that she can go away.

The vengeful Steve manages to shoot Tim just as the police enter to arrest the safecracker. When they find Rose with the money, she is accused of murder and robbery. Her earlier fears are borne out: no one will believe her, and she suddenly "realizes the futility of all protest, the maddening hopelessness of it all." Tim has told her that she is basically decent, but no one else, especially in the virtuous area of society, will believe her. This sudden enlightenment comes to Rose just as she is to be taken off to prison, and she stands in a trance "aware of something in the room none of the others can see—perhaps the personification of the ironic life force that has crushed her."

As a character, Rose is drawn from a selection of external details rather than intense psychological insight. Her life story follows the typical pattern of social injustice and protest, and the actual nature of her revelation is not fully treated. She is a variation on the stock character of the prostitute with the heart of gold. Nonetheless, her character and her plight are capable of evoking sympathy.

"THRENODY FOR POSSESSORS, SELF-DISPOSSESSED," the title of the six-play version of the abandoned cycle "A Tale of Possessors, Self-Dispossessed."*

TIBERIUS CAESAR, a seventy-six-year-old man, corpulent yet still muscular. In *Lazarus Laughed*,* he is shown as a man weakened by debauchery, who has called for Lazarus* to come to his villa at Capri. There he has crucified a male lion as a warning to this new prophet who confronts him shining with an incandescent light and fearless of his power. Tiberius lives in fear of death by assassination and keeps around Caligula,* his heir and chief threat, mainly because he will be a fit instrument for his own vengeance. In his pride he decides to kill Lazarus, who shows no fear of death, even though Miriam,* his aged wife, has been poisoned by Pompeia* with the open connivance of Tiberius. However, Lazarus manages to touch the soul of Tiberius by revealing to him his loneliness and the love that Lazarus himself bears toward this wicked man. Tiberius speaks of the crimes committed by his family and himself, and finally he orders the death of Lazarus by fire, at the suggestion of Pompeia. He has not been able to accept Lazarus's assurance that after death "there is peace" and wishes to see how this strange prophet will face death. When Lazarus cries out, "O men, fear not life! You die—but there is no death for man!" Pompeia walks into the pyre with Lazarus, and Tiberius is strangled by Caligula as the entire assemblage joins in the laughter of Lazarus. In that moment, Tiberius has wished for death and has accepted it.

"TILL WE MEET," a play written in 1918. Destroyed. Contents unknown.

TOMMY-THE-PRIEST. In "Tomorrow,"* a saloon keeper.

"TOMORROW," O'Neill's only published short story (written 1916–1917: *Seven Arts*, 2, June 1917): 147–170. Reprinted in *Eugene O'Neill Newsletter* 7, iii (Winter 1983): 3–13.

The first person narrative is told by Art,* an ex-sailor who has just been paid off after a voyage from Buenos Aires as an able-bodied seaman on a British tramp steamer. He and an old friend, another "gentleman ranker," Jimmy Anderson,* share a room over an all-night dive near South Street known as Tommy-the-Priest's. Art is subsisting on a small allowance from his family but is currently out of money, dying for a drink, but since no one is treating he goes upstairs. In his room Jimmy's typewriter is broken, but he is always planning to do something tomorrow. He seems starved for affection because he lavishes attention on a geranium that never blooms. Another idiosyncracy is his forever buying unreadable books which fill the small room the two men share. Next door is "a broken-down telegrapher—'The Lunger,' " who later dies of tuberculosis. Art tries to read, but the lamp goes out because Jimmy has not yet returned with the necessary oil—more evidence of his fecklessness.

Eventually Jimmy does return, dressed in his best suit, shoes shined, and sober. He tells Art of the horrors of drunkenness. Art listens mechanically, wondering "what Jimmy would do if he ever saw his face in the clear cruel mirror of truth. Struggle on in the same way and cease to have faith in mirrors." In other words, he would cling to his illusions. As Jimmy continues to tell his story, Art loses interest but then notices that it does not differ from the tale he tells when he is drunk: Anderson estate in Scotland, now heavily mortgaged, but there is still one old aunt who will certainly leave him money, and the whole gang will have a "rare blowout." He tells of spending time at Edinburgh University, graduating with honors, becoming a journalist, covering the Boer War (1899–1902) as a journalist, then crashing and taking to drink. But contrary to Art's expectations, Jimmy has gotten a job. He has also heard from his Aunt Mary—but has lost the letter. He says that his aunt is unaware of his straitened circumstances because he never writes to her, and Art suggests that he should because the bar room gang expects the blowout "tomorrow." This word upsets Jimmy, but Art consoles him with the remark that he will start work "tomorrow."

Lyons,* the stoker, and Paddy* Meehan the old deepwater sailor, tramp in to invite Art and Jimmy for a drink. Art goes with them, but Jimmy will not. The next day Art goes on a binge with Lyons and Paddy, seeing Jimmy only briefly on the fourth day and notes that he looks drawn and tired. On the fifth day Jimmy looks very sick; and though he is still sober, the gang believes he needs a drink, and they send Art up to offer one. He twits Jimmy with working too hard, and Jimmy replies with anger. The next morning Art realizes that Jimmy's bed has not been slept in and is so concerned that he waters Jimmy's geranium plant, which has been dying from neglect. That evening, after Art, Lyons, and Paddy have bummed around all day, they return to the dive, expecting a celebration for Jimmy's payday. The gang is drinking courtesy of Old McDonald when Jimmy enters just before midnight, looking haggard, to announce that he has lost his job, and even if he had not been fired, he would have had to quit: "I couldn't do the work," he admits. He now realizes that he is a failure, "But it's hell, Art, to realize all at once—you're dead!"

Jimmy then gets drunk, and when he and Art are alone he confides the story of what started him drinking. He discovered his wife, Alice, in bed with a staff officer in Cape Town. He loved this English girl, and she had never divorced him—hoping for some of his Aunt Mary's money. Eventually he goes to sleep, and Art goes downstairs to the bar. There he dozes off, but is awakened from his snooze by the sound of a crash—a bottle has fallen from the fire escape, he thinks—but suddenly Jimmy bursts in. He has knocked over his beloved geranium in his drunken haze, and it has been smashed. He "cries heartbrokenly like a sick child whose only remaining toy has been smashed," goes upstairs, and jumps out the window.

Comments: This slight piece is based on O'Neill's own experience in the saloon operated by James J. Condon* at 252 Fulton Street, a man who was known as Jimmy-the-Priest.* It is, however, interesting as containing the germ of the later play, *The Iceman Cometh.* The tale of Jimmy is remarkably similar to those of James Cameron,* "Jimmy Tomorrow," and Captain Cecil Lewis* of the later work. The concept of "tomorrow" appears here for the first time as the "pipedream" which Jimmy attempts to translate into reality. When he realizes the truth about himself he, like the later Don Parritt,* finds life impossible and follows in death the geranium which seems to be the only thing he has loved in recent years—and that flower, symbolically, has failed in its purpose in life; it has never bloomed. Art, of course, represents Eugene O'Neill himself. Jimmy Anderson, like his later development as James Cameron, may well be James Findlater Byth.* And Lyons, the stoker, is Driscoll,* who appears under his own name in the S.S. *Glencairn* series.* Byth later attempted suicide by jumping out a window and died without gaining consciousness. Driscoll apparently also committed suicide by jumping overboard while his ship was at sea.

TOUCH OF THE POET, A, a play in four acts, part of the abandoned cycle, "A Tale of Possessors, Self-Dispossessed."* When the cycle consisted of five plays, this was the title of the entire corpus, and the play was called "Hair of the Dog."* It was retitled in April 1936. The entire action takes place in the dining room of Cornelius Melody's* tavern from morning to night of July 27, 1828, the nineteenth anniversary of the Duke of Wellington's victory over Napoleon's army during the Peninsular War (1808–1814). Melody's tavern is situated in a village a few miles from Boston, a breakfast stop on what used to be the main stagecoach line. With its discontinuance the tavern has gone downhill;

the large dining room is now divided into two rooms with a flimsy partition painted in a clumsy attempt to match the fine old wood panelling on the walls. "At left front, two steps lead up to a closed door opening on a flight of stairs to the floor above. Farther back is the door to the bar" with a mirror between the two doors and a small wall cabinet beyond the bar entrance. On the rear wall are four windows separated in the middle by the street door. "At right front is another door, open, giving on a hallway and the main stairway to the second floor, and leading to the kitchen. Farther front at right there is a high schoolmaster's desk with a stool." Four tables are set with white cloths, and two in the foreground are not.

Act I: It is around 9 A.M. on July 27, 1828. Mickey Maloy,* a sturdy, twenty-six-year-old with "an amiable, cunning face," is reading a newspaper as "Jamie Cregan* peers around the half-open door of the bar." Obviously Irish, Cregan has a gaunt face, with a saber scar over one cheekbone. He is middle-aged and neatly dressed "in old, worn clothes. His eyes are bloodshot, his manner sickly." He greets Maloy with a wan grin; obviously he is suffering from a hangover, and Maloy takes a decanter and glass from the cabinet to revive him. It is part of Cornelius Melody's private store, and Cregan speaks of the absent host, whom he has not seen since serving under him in Spain as a corporal in the Seventh Dragoons. Cregan was very drunk the night before and made a number of allegations unfamiliar to Maloy, the barkeep; and now in the unkind day of sobriety, he questions the visitor about the major.

Melody's father had come from Galway where he was "a thievin' shebeen keeper who got rich by moneylendin' and squeezin' tenants." When he had made his pile he married, settled on an estate as a gentleman with a pack of hounds, but shortly after "his wife died givin' birth to Con." The surrounding gentry had refused to accept the elder Melody as one of them, and as revenge he determined to raise his son as a great gentleman, sending him to Dublin to school with enough money to support his gentility. However, Con discovered that money did not bring acceptance, and as a result of his touchiness, he fought his first successful duel. "It gave his pride the taste for revenge and after that he was always lookin' for an excuse to challenge someone." This proclivity led to his resignation from the British Army. He had reached the rank of major when he killed a Spanish nobleman who had caught him seducing his wife. "If it wasn't for his fine record for bravery in battle, they'd have court-martialed him." Con Melody was an extraordinarily handsome man in those days, welcome in the homes of Portuguese and Spanish gentry, where the women were very different from the prostitutes he had known. Apparently Con still tries his old seductive approach, but without success, on the women of the Yankee gentry who pass by. He despises all the local Irish, and when he is drunk he taunts Nora Melody* because he had to marry her. Maloy believes Con's tale that "the priests tricked him into marrying her," but Cregan, who was raised on the Melody estate, says that he had loved her yet was ashamed of her because her people were poor peasants. He married her, went off to Spain, and left her alone to have his child. On his return he raised what money he could, took her and the child, Sara Melody,* and emigrated to America. Cregan accepts another drink, but the sound of a girl's voice is heard, and both men seem afraid. Maloy returns the whiskey to the cabinet and picks up his paper, while Cregan leaves to avoid a tonguelashing from Sara for getting her father drunk the preceding night.

"Sara is twenty, an exceedingly pretty girl with a mass of black hair, fair skin with rosy cheeks, and beautiful, deep-blue eyes." She is a curious blend of the aristocrat and the peasant. Her face, with its high forehead and thin straight nose, enhanced by small ears and slender neck, is well bred, but her mouth is a trifle coarse and sensual above a heavy jaw. She has a full, graceful figure with a small waist but also has the large feet and hands of a peasant. She speaks softly and musically but self-consciously, because of her attempt to hide her brogue. She is cheaply but neatly dressed. She has come to look over the bar account book. As she does, Maloy speaks of the way she has been setting her cap for "the young Yankee upstairs" whom she has been nursing, and then, when Sara resents his teasing about Simon Harford,* tells her that a grand carriage with a black coachman came with a Yankee lady as passenger to ask the way to the lake. She wanted a cup of tea, and when Maloy, impatient of "Yankee airs," told her the waitress was out and the tavern still closed, she left. The two speculate on the identity of this thirtyish woman, "a pale, delicate wisp of a thing with big eyes," and Sara says that was Simon's mother, suggesting that Maloy should have told her that her son is at the tavern. She returns to check figures.

Her mother, Nora Melody,* enters. She is forty, but hardship and worry have made her look older. When young she must have been pretty, like Sara, who has her fine eyes, "But she has become too worn out to take care of her appearance." She is dumpy, her dark hair straggly, her hands red and rheumatic; she is dressed in what looks as bad as a sack tied in the middle with old, down-at-heel working shoes on her bare feet. "Yet in spite of her slovenly appearance there is a spirit which shines through and makes her lovable, . . . and somehow, dauntless. She speaks softly "with a rich brogue."

Sara, with "her habitual manner toward her . . . of mingled love and pity and exasperation," tells her to see a doctor about her rheumatism, but Nora demurs both because of the expense and her own distrust. She has some fresh eggs ready for Con when he comes for breakfast, she says, but Sara is bitter because he was drunk the previous night as on every other night. Nora excuses him because "he hasn't seen James since—" Nora, however, is worried about money: the grocery bill is long overdue, but at least she has the mortgage money saved. Sara wants to take charge of the money, but Nora says that would cause farther dissension between father and daughter. In answer to Nora's question, Sara says that she failed to pay the grocery bill last week because she had had to pay the feed bill for Melody's thoroughbred mare, which is "his greatest pride. He'd be heartbroken if he had to sell her," his last reminder of past gentility.

Sara, however, refuses to accept this explanation uncritically. She is angry that he seems to love the horse better than his own family, but Nora reminds Sara that he had sent her to a good school to learn to talk like the local gentry, even if she had insisted on leaving. Sara again complains about her father's airs, his refusal to tend bar, his mistreatment of her mother, and particularly his "blaming his ruin on having to marry you." She turns on her mother for accepting all his insults, but Nora stubbornly defends him, saying that she could never leave him because of her pride in her love for him. "With a strange superior scorn" she says that Sara doesn't understand the nature of love and never will: "It's when, if all the fires of hell was between you, you'd walk in them gladly to be with him, and sing with joy at your own burnin' if only his kiss was on your mouth!" This outburst gains Sara's reluctant respect, but she defiantly says, "I'll love where it'll gain me freedom and not put me in slavery for life." Nora at first replies, "There's no slavery in it when you love," but then breaks down, begging her daughter not to "take the pride of my love from me," for without it she is nothing but an old sick woman.

As Sara continues to check the figures, Nora speaks with concern of Con, who has adopted the politics of the Yankee gentry "against Jackson and the Democrats and . . . with the Yankees for John Quincy Adams," another aspect of his contempt for the local "shanty Irish." This rouses Sara's anger at her father's pretensions and also his folly, because he had the chance in his new country "to make himself all his lies pretended to be." He was better educated than most Americans and had sufficient money to make a start, but instead he allowed himself to be fleeced into buying this tavern in the belief that a new coach line was going to stop there. "Oh, if I was a man with the chance he had, there wouldn't be a dream I'd not make come true." Nora, however, seems not to have heard and returns to the subject of Father Flynn, whom she had met yesterday when he discussed Con's politics. He is very concerned that the Melody family is no longer going to church. Sara now finishes her accounts and offers to speak to the grocer for more credit.

Discussion then turns to Simon Harford, the son of wealthy parents, Harvard graduate, embryonic poet, who has spent the last year "living like a tramp or a tinker," as Nora puts it, by the lake "to prove his independence,... support himself simply, and feel one with Nature, and think great thoughts about what life means and write a book" against greed. Of course, Simon has only notes for such a book, and in the last few months he has written nothing but love poems. Nora has not been asleep during these months, and she has noted Sara's frequent long walks by the lake and suggests that "young Master Harford has a touch of the poet in him—the same as your father," an addition that annoys Sara: "just because he shows off reciting Lord Byron." Sara triumphantly says that Simon has fallen in love with her, and she intends to marry him in spite of all obstacles; but Nora warns that "maybe it's not marriage he's after." If Simon marries Sara he will probably be disinherited. But Sara has confidence that his father will come around, though she is less certain of his mother, who "never goes out at all but stays home in their mansion, reading books, or in her garden." She sings Simon's praises, his gentleness, his reverence for her purity, and then speaks of the way that they will conquer the world together once they are married, whatever his father may do. At this Cornelius Melody enters.

He "is forty-five, tall, broad-shouldered, deep-chested and powerful, with long muscular arms, big feet, and large hairy hands." His bearing is still that of a soldier, and his body shows few signs of the dissipation that disfigures his once handsome face which is now reminiscent of a Byronic hero. He has a fine nose, sensual mouth, hollow cheeks, gray hair and bloodshot eyes which look coldly on the world in anticipation of insult. His manners are extremely polished, almost as if he is playing a role, and he is dressed in the foppish style of the "English aristocracy in Peninsular War days." He greets Nora formally and with condescension as she scrambles to prepare his breakfast, which he refuses to consider, wishing instead to have some peace to read the paper. His nerves are obviously shaky, and when Nora suggests a drink to steady them, he agrees but then turns on her, "I hate the damned meek of this earth," despising her for her resignation, but quickly he feels ashamed of himself.

Suddenly he realizes the date: July 27, the anniversary of Talavera, the day on which the Iron Duke of Wellington himself commended Major Melody for bravery. At first he prefers to forget the day, but Nora insists that there should be a special dinner; this year Con will invite Jamie Cregan, "A brave soldier, if he isn't a gentleman," Patch Riley,* Paddy O'Dowd,* and Dan Roche,* the local Irish rabble. As usual, the major will wear his uniform to dinner: "It makes me feel at least the ghost of the man I was then." Nora loyally says he is still handsome and does not tell him about their perilous finances. Melody tries to discuss the news with Nora but then insults her ignorance and again apologizes, this time for his drunkenness the previous evening. His attitude toward his wife swings between affection and revulsion: he kisses her and then complains that her hair smells of cooking, for instance. When she leaves, he drinks again and quotes from Byron's *Childe Harold*, particularly two lines which recur throughout the play: "I have not loved the World, nor the World me" and "I stood among them, but not of them."

As he is reciting histrionically to himself in the mirror, Sara enters. He bows to her, but she speaks of having to beg for credit so that his mare's feed bill can be paid. Melody ignores this and complains about his room, which Sara reminds him is the best in the house. Then, as her father compliments her on her appearance, for she is dressed in her Sunday clothes, she drops a "mocking, awkward, servant's curtsy" and speaks to him in broad brogue to enrage him. At first she succeeds, but then Melody remembers, "Your mother warned me you only did it to provoke me." As Con takes another drink, he asks after the progress of Sara's romance with Simon Harford, saying in a curiously aristocratic manner that they have his consent, that Simon has "a romantic touch of the poet'' to compensate for his ''Yankee phlegm,'' and that ''I find his people will pass muster,'' despite the fact that they are ''in trade,'' but at least his mother ''springs from generations of well-bred gentlefolk.'' Throughout this exchange, Sara, stung to anger, berates him for keeping the mare ''to prove you're still a gentleman'' and allowing her mother to slave so that he may keep the horse. But Melody continues, asking for an interview with Simon so that the young man can declare his intentions and also discuss the financial arrangements which must be made—the amount of Sara's settlement, for instance (although Melody has nothing for a dowry but a mortgage). Sara is angry with the way Melody insists on the reality of his dreams of gentility and tells him to keep out of her affairs: ''Is it stark mad you've gone, so you can't tell any more what's the living truth?''

He looks at her ''as if something vital had been stabbed in him—with a cry of tortured appeal'' and half-threatens her as his rage increases, but then he sinks into his chair as Dan Roche, Paddy O'Dowd, and Patch Riley crowd in, all hung over and three different types of Shanty Irish: Roche, a middle-aged, squat, muscular, porcine type; O'Dowd, a born sponger; and Riley, an old, gaunt, skinny piper. All are either seedy or ragged. Melody treats them like dirt, but Sara shows some kindness when she sees that she has hurt the feelings of Patch, the piper. They all go into the bar, and Sara derisively tells her father that his retainers ''respect the master.'' She switches from brogue, ''Don't let me keep you from joining the gentlemen!'' and leaves as he calls pleadingly after her. Nora appears with Con's breakfast tray, which he refuses condescendingly and goes into the bar, leaving Nora weeping quietly as the curtain falls.

Act II: a half-hour later. Melody enters after having had two more drinks and no breakfast. He gives orders to those in the bar to be quiet so he can be with his memories; he turns aside with a Byronic gesture but then collapses into ''hopelessness and defeat'' so that he does not hear Sara's return. She is momentarily afraid that he really is ill. But then when she is told that it is the anniversary of Talavera, she bitterly says that she will wait on table for him and his friends just this one more time and then only to please her mother, informing him that she has just had to beg more credit which the storekeeper has given out of pity for Nora: ''But what do you care about that, as long as you and your fine thoroughbred mare can live in style!''

For a moment Con is shaken, and then as Nora brings in a glass of milk for Sara to take to Simon, he speaks vindictively of the way ''you two scheming peasants'' are trying to trap the young man, suggesting ''there's always one last trick to get him through his honor.'' Sara is furious. After she leaves, Nora speaks of her ''sin'' yet recalls Con as ''that handsome, no woman could resist you. And you are still.'' He speaks scornfully of her ''lying, pious shame'' because when they went to bed together ''It was love and joy and glory in you and you were proud,'' a sentiment that Nora says she will hold to her dying day. The conversation then turns to Simon, and Nora says he is extremely shy, a lack of ''romantic fire'' that rouses Con's scorn. He looks ahead to allowing the marriage, if the financial arrangements are satisfactory. Sara will have great economic and social advantages. She has "the looks, the brains—ambition, youth—." But Nora speaks of love. As Sara comes downstairs, Melody returns to the bar rather than face what he terms her insults. She comes in, "her eyes full of dreamy happiness." Simon has just kissed her but only because she made it almost impossible for him not to. He might have asked her to marry him, but she was so shy herself that she left. With this, Nora embraces her, but Sara berates herself for letting her heart rule her head, yet still looks ahead to becoming Mrs. Simon Harford. The two then go to the attic to unpack Melody's old uniform for the dinner that evening.

Con Melody, waiting for the arrival of Jamie Cregan, walks to the mirror where he repeats both the poem and the mirror-gazing of Act I as Deborah Harford* enters. She is forty-one but looks thirty, a tiny, fragile creature just over five feet tall with a face beautiful in its bone structure, "thick, wavy, red-brown hair," and enormous brown eyes. She "is dressed in white with calculated simplicity." Her whole personality shows an aloofness, a detachment, yet at the same time a curious assertiveness which brings her "to the point of whimsical eccentricity." Mrs. Harford attracts Melody's attention, and he instantly adopts his air of the gallant gentleman, which impresses her in spite of herself. He completely misunderstands the situation, not realizing who she is. When asked if he is "the innkeeper, Melody," he replies that he is "*Major* Cornelius Melody, one time of His Majesty's Seventh Dragoons." Gradually Deborah plays up to him, and Melody takes up his old role of successful seducer, almost managing to kiss her until she pulls back from him, having smelt the whiskey on his breath, and scornfully puts him in his place as Sara enters, recognizes Mrs. Harford, and realizes what has happened. Deborah announces that she has come to see Simon and thanks Sara for her careful nursing of her son. She "is repelled by Nora's slovenly appearance, but feels her simple gentleness," as Sara introduces her. Melody, enraged by Nora's peasant curtsey, adopts his fine gentleman air once more, suggesting that Mrs. Harford might like to visit her son. When she and Sara have left, Melody upbraids himself but then speaks with hatred of the "cursed Yankee upstart."

As a means of calming him down, Nora says that she and Sara have brushed his uniform and laid it out for him. At first he says he wants nothing to do with it but then decides that he will put it on to impress Deborah, who has obviously disbelieved his tale of Talavera. After he leaves, Sara enters, furious with her father but then also wondering whether Deborah might have liked "his drunken love-making," a suggestion she dismisses as "craziness." However, she is no longer sure of Simon now that his mother has come before the young man has committed himself, because she perceives that Deborah hates her. She has been listening at the door and has learned that Simon's father has gone to see his lawyer about preventing the affair, and she feels sure that Deborah's influence will also be strong. The two women obviously are enemies, and Sara looks on the situation as a war. She herself has the brains for the combat, but she feels

Deborah's strangeness "behind her lady's airs, and it'll be hard to tell what she's really up to."

At this, Sara hears her antagonist coming and sends Nora away so the two may be alone. Once again Deborah thanks Sara formally for her kindness to Simon and starts to speak at some length of her son, his inveterate dreaminess and his attempt to find peace with nature. She also speaks of the "rigidly unforgiving" qualities of Simon's father when his material dreams have been interfered with, as Simon has done, for "the Harfords have been great dreamers, too, in their way." In reply Sara says "I know there's a true poet in Simon." This leads Deborah to give a rapid account of the acquisitive dreams and financial successes of the Harford family; but they did not succeed in owning Deborah, who slipped through their fingers. She believes that the greedy Harfords would approve of Sara: "They would see that you are strong and ambitious and determined to take what you want." But then she tells of her own private dream that she was the Empress Josephine; she recalls that the Harford sister-in-law, Simon's father, and she went together on the honeymoon trip to Paris to see their admired Napoleon crowned emperor. She comes to herself to warn Sara "that the Harfords never part with their dreams even when they deny them," a cryptic comment which she clarifies by suggesting that Simon will never finish his proposed book denouncing greed and ambition and that Sara knows this to be true. With this she turns to leave, and Sara starts impulsively to say something, only to realize that this moment of communication has passed. They engage in civilities, and Mrs. Harford leaves, wearing her metaphorical mask of formal manners.

Nora returns, distressed that the lady has left before Melody has seen her again, while Sara tries to assess what has happened, coming to the conclusion that she has asked her son to wait before making a decision. Nora, afraid of Melody's rage, runs out just before her husband makes a grand Byronic entrance dressed in his major's uniform, looking undeniably impressive. Anticlimactically, he attempts to explain his choice of costume. As Sara turns with contempt to look at him, she is forced into impulsive and reluctant admiration for him, but then she asks sadly, "why can't you ever be the thing you seem to be? The man you were." Melody attempts to explain away his unfortunate *faux pas* with Mrs. Harford, suggesting that she had rather enjoyed his pass at her. Sara agrees but then announces that the lady has left and he won't have the chance to dazzle her with his uniform. Once again, Melody recovers himself, suggesting that he now doesn't need to humble himself. Sara's anger is cut off by the entrance of Jamie Cregan, who is surprised at Melody's appearance, and the two drink to the memory of Talavera, Melody carefully insisting on Cregan's rank of corporal and Cregan responding to the major with a kind of admiration as the two raise their glasses.

Act III: The same, around 8 P.M. The bar door is closed, and candles are lighted on the center table, presided over by Melody in full uniform with Cregan at his right. At another table sit Riley, O'Dowd, and Roche, the troops distinct from the rankers. All are drunk: the rabble boisterous, Melody "holding his liquor like a gentleman," and Cregan the least removed from sobriety. Sara, in working dress and apron, is clearing the table as Melody is refighting the battle of Talavera with the silverware and china. Melody's strategic studies are punctuated by the rowdy behavior of the rabble and by Sara's attempts to clear the table, to which her father reacts with deliberate cruelty. He plays the role of squire well, responding to a toast from his underlings with another stanza from Byron's *Childe Harold*; and when that meets with blank stares, he suggests an old hunting song in which all can join. But that sends him into recollections of his youth at Melody Castle, as Sara watches with a sneer.

Deflated, he follows her suggestion to order everyone else into the bar, and he remains to talk to her. She reproaches him for his inability to face the truth about himself, while Melody tells her about his talk with Simon after his accustomed afternoon gallop. The young man "finally blurted out that he wanted to marry her," but his mother has suggested a wait of a year, basically as a means of avoiding gossip. Melody says he approves of such a delay, speaking loftily of financial arrangements and the settlement that Henry Harford will make on a son who plans to be a poet-philosopher, remaining quite oblivious to the possibility that the Harford family might consider such a match less than an honor. Momentarily Sara accepts his dream, but then Melody comments that "all I can see in you is a common, greedy, scheming, cunning peasant girl whose only thought is money."

He plans to decline this offer of marriage. Such a match would be "a tragic misalliance for him . . . and ruin to all his dreams." He would wish to save the young man from the consequences of such infatuation (in other words, his own fate in marriage to Nora) and insultingly suggests that a more suitable match would be with Mickey Maloy, the bartender. Sara reminds him of his own lowly origins, and in reply Melody furiously makes a proposition: "if you trick Harford into getting you with child, I would not refuse my consent." But then he recalls his own marital situation. Enraged, Sara almost strikes him but scathingly promises to remember what he has said. This sobers Melody somewhat, and he takes a conciliatory approach, which Sara does not wait to hear. Momentarily crumbling, Melody shores up his courage by again quoting from Byron.

He is so self-absorbed that he does not at first hear the knocking that precedes the entrance of Nicholas Gadsby,* the Harford family solicitor, a stout, florid, "best-family attorney" with all the pomposity that implies. There is momentary confusion on both sides, Melody surprised that the visitor is a gentleman and Gadsby "impressed by Melody's handsome distinction." The tavernkeeper attempts to atone for his rudeness with old-fashioned courtesy, and then Gadsby announces his wish to speak with "the proprietor of this tavern, by name, Melody." In response to Gadsby's question, Melody denies his status, instead announcing himself by his military rank. The two treat each other with a combination of insolence and sarcasm, particularly when Gadsby recognizes Sara in her position as waitress and Melody denies the relationship. Gadsby curtly announces Mr. Harford's desire to make a settlement with Melody, who completely misunderstands the proposition so that the two proceed at cross purposes until Gadsby finally states Henry Harford's unalterable opposition ''to any further relationship between his son and your daughter, whatever the nature of that relationship in the past.'' Melody is stung by the insinuation but Gadsby continues, offering three thousand dollars as payment for an agreement to drop all claims on Simon and move away from the area. Melody's fury grows, and despite Sara's remonstrations, he threatens Gadsby; then with the arrival of the ''rabble from the bar,'' they push the lawyer out as Melody speaks of a duel of honor with Henry Harford. Nora wails in fear, while Sara attempts to make him see common sense, but Melody has gone too far in rage and drink, threatening to horsewhip the Yankee.

Sara tries to dissuade him, saying she still wishes to marry Simon, even though Melody sees his honor as being compromised. Again he insults Sara as a ''filthy peasant slut! You whore!'' moving threateningly on her until Cregan suggests they should proceed to the Harford residence before the lawyer returns. Sara makes ''a last, frantic threat'' that she will be forced ''to go to Simon—and do what you said'' as the ''rabble'' return, speaking of the mayhem they have wrought on Gadsby. But it goes unheeded, and Sara is left alone as her mother enters, speaking with a curious pride mingled with fear that Con is again duelling. Sara decides to ''play at the game of gentleman's honor, too!'' telling her mother she is going to bed. Nora doesn't fully realize her daughter's plan, but she gives inadvertent support to it as she speaks of love: ''If there's true love between you, you'll not let a duel or anything in the world kape you from each other, whatever the cost! Don't I know!'' With this, Sara kisses her mother, leaving her alone as the curtain falls.

Act IV: The same, around midnight. The sound of Riley's bagpipes and dancing comes from the bar. Nora is sitting in her old shawl at the foot of the center table, almost in a state of collapse with worry because Melody and Cregan have not returned. Mickey Maloy comes in to offer a little whiskey, which she finally accepts. The boys are drinking to the rout of the Harfords, and Nora curiously shares their belligerence. She will not hear a word against Sara, and Mickey is roused to admiration for her love.

She is alone again as Sara enters in nightgown, old wrapper, bare feet, her hair down, and an expression of calm, of dreamy exaltation on her face. The two women await Melody's return, and in her fear Nora accidentally reveals the fact that she, too, sees through her husband's dream: ''His pride indade! What is it but a lie? what's in his veins, God pity him, but the blood of thievin' auld Ned Melody who kept a dirty shebeen?'' But then in horrified loyalty she recovers: ''It would break his heart if he heard me! I'm the only one in the world he knows nivir [*sic*] sneers at his dreams!'' In her fear she wants to go to confession for her old sin with Con but feels she cannot ''betray'' him in this way. With that, Sara tells her mother that she has been to bed with Simon and has consummated their relationship, speaking of his tenderness, his handsome appearance, and his talent as a poet. Above all, she speaks of the exaltation of their love and her pride in it.

Dreams of riches seem "crazy" to her now, though Simon has, with practicality, thought of earning a living; all Sara now believes in is whatever would bring happiness to her beloved. Nora understands, and she also understands the guilt arising from it, but Sara refuses any thought of guilt for herself, though Simon has felt it. In sudden kinship with her mother Sara announces, "It's love's slaves we are, Mother, not men's—and wouldn't it shame their boasting and vanity if we ever let them know our secret." She can now even understand her mother's love for her father, but then she turns to bitterness, wishing Con to face the truth about himself, though she expects him to speak of his victory over the Harford clan.

At that moment Cregan enters and then goes out to support Con Melody into the room, pallid, battered, and tattered, with eyes that are "empty and lifeless." Obviously he has been fighting and has gotten the worst of it, but he will not take a drop of liquor to comfort or rouse him. As Melody remains silent, Cregan reports with a certain glee the way the two of them laid siege to the Harford mansion, Nora appearing to enjoy the account. But then Melody speaks "in a jeering mumble to himself," seeing his behavior not as Wellington's victory but instead as the behavior suitable to "a drunken, foul-mouthed son of a thieving shebeen keeper who sprang from the filth of a peasant hovel, with pigs on the floor," and he recalls that Deborah, "that pale Yankee bitch," watched it all from her window. Con Melody now sees the truth about himself, and Sara understands this as he leaves the room followed by Nora.

For a moment Sara is afraid he might do harm to Simon but then rejects this thought as Cregan continues with his account, telling how Con has been blathering on about Mrs. Harford and the beauty of his thoroughbred mare "and beggin' her forgiveness and talkin' of dishonor and death—." Nora returns terrified, because Con has gone to the barn with his duelling pistols. And over the noise of the bar room revelling, the sound of a pistol shot is heard, which frightens Sara even more than her mother because for a moment Sara had taken some joy in thinking, "Then he's not beaten."

Cregan returns, supporting Melody, who "appears completely possessed by a paralyzing stupor." He has shot the mare, the last symbol of his gentility, and has planned to kill himself as well, but he realized that that would "be a mad thing to waste a good bullet on a corpse." As he had cradled the dying animal's head, he realized that she understood that he, too, was dying along with her and forgave him; Major Melody is dead, and without his dream Con can be nothing more than a low-class tavernkeeper. Significantly, Melody is now talking in the brogue he despises. Nora attempts to comfort him, and Sara begs him to stop his "game," but Melody insists that "it was the Major played a game all his life, the crazy auld loon, and cheated only himself."

He suggests that Sara seduce Simon, and when she says she has done so, he momentarily returns to his old arrogant role as major, then congratulates her with the deepest sarcasm and raises his duelling pistol against her. Nora grabs his arm, and Con again congratulates Sara, "Lave it to her to get what she wants by hook or by crook," but he also observes that she will "have some trouble, rootin' out his dreams." He is confident that she will have some further trick to manage that. He puts down his pistols then, for they belong to the major; he embraces Nora and, to her ecstasy, tells her he loves her and will begin to run the tavern himself. But his military bearing has gone, and "he looks like a loutish, grinning clown." As he kisses Sara good-night, again congratulating her on her day's work, she begs him, "Won't you be yourself again?" With this remark, Con Melody consigns Talavera and his dreams to perdition and once more repeats his Byronic quotation, this time with a guffaw of contempt. She begs him not to shame himself so utterly, but Melody is impermeable, even declaring himself a supporter of the hated Andrew Jackson, "the friend av the common men like me."

Sara regrets the loss of the dream, discovering now that she has taken pride in it. She will even refuse to marry Simon for the insult offered to her father's honor. Melody is in agony because Sara has stripped him psychologically naked. But when her mother interposes, asking for peace, he adopts his new role of "leering peasant," turns on Sara, and "cuffs her on the side of the head," telling her not to interfere. "That'll teach you, me proud Sara! I know you won't try raisin' the dead any more." He will make certain that the marriage takes place now that Sara has seduced Simon, and with that he goes to join his "friends in the bar," no longer taking his liquor from the cabinet in the dining room. Nora tries to make peace, while Sara realizes that Melody is "beaten at last and he wants to stay beaten," but she cannot understand why she wants to prolong his illusion—perhaps it's her inherited pride—but her loss of it will make her a better wife for Simon.

As mother and daughter sit there, Nora rejoices to hear Melody's voice in praise of Jackson, while Sara says: "it wasn't anyone I ever knew or want to know." All Nora can think of is Con's love for her and his unexpected kiss. She will "play any game he likes and give him love in it. Haven't I always?" Sara speaks with admiration of her mother's nobility and also of Simon; but then the sound of Patch Riley's bagpipe is heard, and Sara understands that it is really a requiem: "May the hero of Talavera rest in peace!" But the last words come from Nora: "Shame on you to cry when you have love. What would the young lad think of you?"

Comments: This play constitutes the introduction of the two families of Melody and Harford whose fortunes were designed to parallel and illustrate the period of American history, 1755–1932, through a series of eleven plays. This is the sole completed play of the cycle, "A Tale of Possessors, Self-Dispossessed."* *More Stately Mansions,* another play in this cycle, was posthumously edited from O'Neill's manuscript, as was the scenario of *The Calms of Capricorn.* *A Touch of the Poet* not only introduces some of the themes of the cycle but also develops others which O'Neill had treated earlier. The most obvious echo of a theme used before is that of the saving lie, which forms the basis of *The Iceman Cometh*.* Con Melody holds to his past gallantry at the battle of Talavera and also to his brief period of gentility. The first is conveyed visually by the wearing of his carefully preserved old uniform and the second by his thoroughbred. When he, like the derelicts in Harry Hope's* bar in *Iceman*, perceives that his dream is but a chimera, he is lost and kills his horse as a means of exorcising the influence of the past. But in so doing he kills himself—not literally, but psychologically—and almost instantly adopts a new role, that of a leering peasant lout, a "thievin' shebeen keeper" like his father before him. Byronic posturing gives way to the illusion of happiness in self-abnegation.

But there is also another theme which is endemic in O'Neill's treatment of man-woman relations: that of the man who is ruined by an imprudent marriage. Melody sees himself as the victim of this situation, though the facts do not fully support it since he was a willing participant in his own ruin in Spain. This is the reason for his ambivalence toward both his wife and his daughter. However, a further repetitive element in O'Neill's treatment of matrimonial relations is the position of wife vis-à-vis her husband. Here the playwright seems to have remained fixated at the stage of development of his early play, *Servitude*,* and repeated in *Welded*,* *The First Man*,* and *Days Without End*.* Like Alice Roylston* in *Servitude*, Nora Melody feels she must pay for her past sin, and also like her, "Love means servitude; and *my* love is *my* happiness."

A final theme in *A Touch of the Poet* is the acquisitiveness which O'Neill treated at greater length in *Marco Millions*.* Sara Melody in this play shows the beginnings of this trait, which will be developed farther in *More Stately Mansions*,* but in her case it is complicated by her initial physical infatuation. She will become closer to the character of Nina Leeds* in *Strange Interlude** because of her combination of feminine roles as her saga progresses. And like earlier women in *Bread and Butter** and *Beyond the Horizon*,* Sara will destroy her husband's dreams.

Production Data: Written 1935–1942, but O'Neill decided not to release it for Broadway after the failure of *A Moon for the Misbegotten** during its tryout. Robert Edmond Jones* had actually made preliminary set drawings, and Spencer Tracy or Laurence Olivier had been suggested for the role of Cornelius Melody, with O'Neill favoring Patricia Neal for the part of Sara (much to Carlotta Monterey* O'Neill's annoyance).

Produced at the Royal Dramatic Theatre (Kungl. Dramatiska Teatern), Stockholm, Sweden, March 29, 1957, in a translation by Sven Barthel (34 performances).

Producer: Dramaten
Director: Olof Molander
Designer: Sven Fahlstedt
Cast: Mickey Maloy: Björn Güstafson
      Jamie Cregan: Bengt Eklund

Sara Melody: Eva Dahlbeck
Nora Melody: Sif Ruud
Cornelius Melody: Lars Hanson
Deborah Harford: Inga Tidblad
Dan Roche: Arthur Cederborgh
Paddy O'Dowd: Olle Hilding
Patch Riley: John Norrman
Nicholas Gadsby: Rune Carlsten

First New York production by Robert Whitehead Productions, October 2, 1958; at the Helen Hayes Theatre, New York City (284 performances).

Director: Harold Clurman

Designer: Ben Edwards

Cast: Mickey Maloy: Tom Clancy
Jamie Cregan: Curt Conway
Sara Melody: Kim Stanley
Nora Melody: Helen Hayes
Cornelius Melody: Eric Portman
Deborah Harford: Betty Field
Dan Roche: John Call
Paddy O'Dowd: Art Smith
Patch Riley: Farrell Pelly
Nicholas Gadsby: Luis Van Rooten

Revived May 2, 1967, at the ANTA Theatre, New York City (5 performances).

A Note on Text: The manuscript was sent to Yale in 1951 and published in 1957. The printed text is used here.

TOWNSEND, Jack. The principal character in *Abortion*,* engaged to Evelyn Sands.* He is handsome, blond, and blue-eyed, with the easy confidence that accompanies collegiate fame and athletic prowess. He is the epitome of the college athlete, somewhat over-protected, and perhaps the type for whom the rest of his life will be a disappointment after the glory of his undergraduate days. "He wears a dark coat, white soft shirt with a bright colored tie, flannel trousers, and white tennis shoes."

Before the play opens, Jack has gotten Nellie Murray,* a "Townie" stenographer, pregnant and has sent her to an abortionist after getting a "loan" of two hundred dollars from his understanding father. Jack quite clearly wishes to be through with his obligations to Nellie and has neither answered her letter nor telephoned her since the operation. He writes off the incident as a passing act of "the male beast," and to some extent he also blames the moral values of society for his fault. He is irresponsible rather than heartless, however, and does have the decency to feel and express guilt when his father remonstrates with him. Nonetheless, his penitential statement seems a trifle self-justificatory, as does the convoluted logic by which he claims that this occurrence will make him a man more worthy of Evelyn.

His confidence that the incident is closed disappears with the arrival of Joe

Murray,* the brother of Nellie who is, together with her, the sole support of their family. Joe informs Jack that Nellie has died as the result of the operation and calls Jack a "dirty murderer." Jack expresses his sorrow and begs Joe not to harm "the innocent," even offering him money and anything else he wants if he will keep silent. Joe, enraged at the suggestion, draws his revolver. Jack wrests it from him but offers it back, suggesting that he go ahead and shoot: "Let the thing end with me and leave the innocent alone." Joe departs for the police station, leaving the revolver behind, and Jack shoots himself in the temple as the triumphal parade cheers him for his contributions to the athletic success of the college. Jack dies as the crowd sings, "For he's a jolly good fellow."

TOWNSEND, Lucy. In *Abortion*,* sister of Jack Townsend.* "She is a small vivacious blond nineteen years old, gushing with immense enthusiasm over everything and everybody." She teases Jack's roommate, Donald ["Bull"] Herron,* unmercifully, calling him "Pluto" and "Jumbo." She looks forward to being "just the most stunning bridesmaid" at Jack's forthcoming wedding to Evelyn Sands. She seems a pleasant empty-headed little person, enthusiastically basking in her brother's glory.

TOWNSEND, Mr. In *Abortion*,* father of Jack Townsend* and Lucy Townsend.* He is a tall, kindly old man of sixty or so with a quantity of white hair. He is erect, well-preserved, energetic, dressed immaculately but soberly." He is a loyal, successful alumnus of the same college at which his son has become the sports hero, and he delights in the rituals of parade and commencement week in general. He was apparently "no St. Anthony" during his college years, and he shows himself tolerant towards Jack's peccadillo. However, he is still a decent enough human being to criticize Jack's failure to communicate with his pregnant girlfriend, Nellie Murray,* after her abortion. Mr. Townsend has a conservative moral outlook, but at the same time he has a trusting, if sometimes awkward, relationship with his son. He tends to gloss over the incident as a part of maturing and has willingly lent Jack the two hundred dollars to finance the operation. Like Mrs. Townsend,* he seems to be somewhat overprotective and indulgent toward Jack, rejoicing in his son's athletic prowess but refusing to allow him to go out for football.

TOWNSEND, Mrs. In *Abortion*,* mother of Jack Townsend* and Lucy Townsend.* She is "a sweet-faced, soft-spoken, gray-haired lady in her early fifties ... dressed in dark gray." She has little to say, but she epitomizes the upper-class suburban matron who dotes on her perfect family, Jack, the college hero, and Lucy, the pert teenager. Her statement that when "John first entered college his father and I made him promise not to go in for ... [football] on any account" indicates an overprotectiveness which may have prevented Jack's maturing.

TRITON. The name of Captain Isaiah Bartlett's* wrecked whaling vessel in *Gold*.*

"TRUMPET, THE,"   a play written in 1919. Destroyed.

TURNER, Mrs.   In *The Straw*,* she is "stout, motherly, capable-looking with gray hair." She is the matron of the Hill Farm Sanitorium and is probably drawn from the character of Mrs. Florence R. Burgess, a widow and senior nurse at the Gaylord Farm,* Wallingford, Connecticut, while O'Neill was a patient there (Gelb and Gelb, 1973, p. 230).

"TWILIGHT OF POSSESSORS, SELF-DISPOSSESSED,"   the title of the seven-play version of the abandoned cycle, "A Tale of Possessors, Self-Dispossessed."* It was also briefly the title of the seventh play, which finally received the title "Hair of the Dog."*

TYRONE, Edmund. In *Long Day's Journey into Night*,* younger son of James Tyrone* and Mary Cavan Tyrone;* brother of James ["Jamie"] Tyrone, Jr.* Edmund is twenty-three with large dark eyes in a long Irish face, sunken cheeks, and is very underweight. He discovers in the course of the play that he has consumption and must be sent to a sanitorium. True to form, James Tyrone tries to send him to the cheapest sanitorium possible, the state farm, but when his son protests, he suggests another place at seven dollars a week but where one gets ten times the value. The character of Edmund Tyrone is really that of Eugene O'Neill himself, with his wandering the world as a sailor, his drunkenness, and living in low dives—even his attempted suicide at "Jimmy-the-Priest's."* Like Edmund, O'Neill contracted consumption in 1912 (the year of this play) and after a brief stay at the state farm was sent to the Gaylord farm* where he was cured. Also like Edmund, O'Neill worked on a local newspaper for awhile. In his portrait of himself, however, O'Neill is a trifle editorial in that he omits the tale of his first marriage to Kathleen Jenkins* and the birth of his son, Eugene Gladstone O'Neill, Jr.*

In the play, Edmund is a sensitive, artistic young man, given to the reading of romantic poetry and philosophy. He and his brother, Jamie, seem to be good, though occasionally bickering, companions with real affection between them. The major change in familial relationships in the play comes in Act IV when Edmund, after hearing his father's account of his life and honest regret for the artistic chance not taken, comes to an understanding of the real tragedy of his life. He settled for money rather than art, and part of the reason for his thwarted ambition is the morphine addiction of his wife, Mary Tyrone.

Edmund's attitude toward her is complex, since she blames him for her addiction. It was to relieve the pain she experienced after his birth that "a cheap hotel quack" gave her the medicine to which she later became addicted. As a result, she seems to waver between love and hatred of him, and Edmund cannot forgive her for this rejection. Throughout the play he tries to break through to her emotionally; in a desperate cry for help he tells her that he has consumption, but she is so far gone that she believes him to be talking about *her* father and forbids him to mention the disease. There is no scene of mutual communication between Edmund and his mother that compares with the one between Edmund and his father. Edmund feels some sympathy toward his mother, but he cannot forgive her for her weakness. At one point in his characterization of Edmund, O'Neill allows his alter ego a moment of real insight into the author's mind. When James Tyrone suggests that his son has the "makings" of a poet, Edmund says that he can only stammer because he does not have the language to communicate the intensity of his feelings: "Well, it will be faithful realism, at least. Stammering is the native eloquence of us fog people." At this moment father and son reach true understanding, and O'Neill gives a major critical assessment of his own talent and achievement.

TYRONE, James. In *Long Day's Journey into Night*,* husband of Mary Cavan Tyrone*; father of James ["Jamie"] Tyrone, Jr.,* and Edmund Tyrone.* James looks at first ten years younger than his sixty-five years. A former romantic actor, he is still very handsome with a good profile and light-brown eyes, though his gray hair is thin with a bald spot at the center, and his face is beginning to go. He has retained a good carriage and graceful movement, together with a fine resonant voice, and his manner is slightly stagey, as befits his former profession. At bottom he is "a simple, unpretentious man" from Irish peasant stock who has risen from abject poverty, the memory of which has made him frugal.

His father had deserted the family when James was ten years old, and he had to go to work in a machine shop. As he tells his son, Edmund, in the play, he worked on his education by reading Shakespeare and trained his voice out of its natural brogue. But then after a promising career as a leading man, he bought a play which had in it a matinée-idol starring role, a part he repeated for the rest of his acting life. His regret is that he was so afraid of being poor that he settled for an easy financial success instead of artistic fulfillment. He does not get along with Jamie, whom he sees as a ne'er-do-well, a drunk, and a whoremonger. He has more sympathy with Edmund, his more literary-minded son. His wife has become a morphine addict, and while James still loves her, he is tortured by what she has become and by her incessant accusations of his responsibility for her situation. The particulars of James Tyrone's life closely parallel those of James O'Neill,* the father of Eugene O'Neill, who appears in this play as Edmund.

On the whole, the character of James Tyrone is portrayed in a sympathetic light, particularly in Act IV when James tells his son of his regret about choosing economic security over art. And again O'Neill seems to imply that a wife caused the loss of artistic fulfillment, a frequent theme throughout the canon, from *Bread and Butter** through *Beyond the Horizon*,* *All God's Chillun Got Wings*,* and beyond. James also understands to some extent the yearnings of his son and has enough flexibility to respect and appreciate Edmund's talent, even if he disapproves of his tastes in literature. In this portrait O'Neill seems to come to terms with the memory of his own father, treating him with tolerance and understanding.

TYRONE, James, Jr. (Jamie or Jim). In *Long Day's Journey into Night*,*
son of James Tyrone,* and Mary Cavan Tyrone*; brother of Edmund Tyrone.*
He is thirty-three, good looking with brown hair and eyes, about five feet seven,
but lacking the graceful carriage and the vitality of his actor father. He already
shows the signs of dissipation, and his face is beginning to go, but he retains a
certain "humorous irresponsible Irish charm," despite the fact that his aquiline
nose and "habitual expressions of cynicism" give "his countenance a Mephistophelian cast."

Jamie is deeply wounded because he has very early discovered his mother's
addiction to morphine, and he blames her current state on his father's miserliness
in obtaining a cheap hotel doctor to attend her at his brother's birth. He has tried
acting with his father but was unable to succeed, partly because he lacked talent
and partly because he was too often drunk. Throughout the play the two snipe
at each other, but they do have something of a common understanding in their
hope that Mary Tyrone will recover.

The relationship between Jamie and his brother, Edmund, is important here.
Jamie has initiated his brother into the world of bars and prostitutes, partly, he
admits, out of a desire to ruin him as he himself is ruined, because he resents
the fact that Edmund's birth began Mary Tyrone's problems. Nonetheless he
loves his twenty-three-year-old brother, fighting for his rights when James Tyrone, Sr., clearly thinks Edmund is doomed to an early death from consumption.
Jamie tells both his father and Edmund not to accept a cheap sanitorium, and
then late in the evening of that *Long Day's Journey into Night*, Jamie reveals
his affection for Edmund, as well as his bitter disappointment in his mother, an
emotion he masks in the cruelly cynical epithets and comments he uses. He
considers Mary Tyrone completely lost, while Edmund still believes that she
can be saved from herself.

*A Moon for the Misbegotten** takes up his story about ten years later, with
Jim Tyrone now "in his early forties." The marks of steady drinking are clearly
upon him, and his good physique is beginning to become flabby; his incipient
bald spot is now very noticeable, and his "Mephistophelian quality . . . is
accentuated by his habitually cynical expression." However, he still retains
remnants of that old Irish charm which still makes him popular among women
and men (especially drinking companions) alike. James and Mary Tyrone are
now dead, with Mary's estate just about to come out of probate. It appears that
Jim is about to become a reasonably affluent man, and he teases Phil Hogan,*
his tenant farmer, about thinking of selling his farm to the highest bidder, the
Standard Oil heir, T. Stedman Harder.* However, it is made clear early in the
play that this is unlikely because of his glee in overhearing Harder outsmarted
by Phil and his freakishly large daughter, Josie Hogan,* who loves Jim but
recognizes his faults. Jim intends to take his inheritance and leave.

To prevent this, Phil tries to trick Josie into bed with Jim, as she has often
wanted, by pretending that Jim has decided to sell the farm. This galvanizes
Josie into suggesting a moonlight rendezvous at the farm, but when Jim arrives,

she realizes the truth about him, that he has already died inwardly, and also that her father has tricked her. Jim, with the acuteness of the deeply wounded, also understands the depth of Josie's sadness, for she is so freakish that no man would want her; as a result she has pretended promiscuity to cover the fact of her virginity. She gets Jim extremely drunk, and while he makes one sensualist's pass at her, he tells her that he wants this night to be different from other ones and has hoped to lay his head on her breast.

Josie realizes that what he most needs is maternal affection, and they spend a long night together, in a pietà-like position, with Josie holding the "dead" man. But before he sleeps, Jim confesses his past faults to Josie, telling of the way he had accompanied his mother's body from the West Coast, too drunk to care, and taking a prostitute to his drawing room throughout the trip. Finally he was too drunk even to attend the funeral. He was not merely grief-stricken for his mother's death but also because of the hurt he had inflicted on her by returning to drinking before she died. It is not directly stated, but understood, that she had cured her morphine addiction.

Josie, in her roles of earth-mother (like Cybel* in *The Great God Brown**), the virgin mediatrix, and Jim's own mother, absolves Jim and forgives him his faults, with the result that for the first time in years he is able to rest. On his awakening he feels an unfamiliar sense of blessed peace, complicated only by his recollection of the way he had tried to seduce Josie. Again she forgives him and lets him go, feeling a pride that her love through its chaste maternal quality has brought him peace. Marriage between them would be impossible, and Josie's last wish for Jim is that he will die soon, as he undoubtedly wishes to do.

The character of James Tyrone, Jr., is directly based on O'Neill's own brother, James ["Jamie"] O'Neill, Jr.,* and the facts of his confessions are biographically accurate, from his attempt to pass off a prostitute as his sister (a prank that had Jamie expelled from college) to his conduct on the train from the West Coast. In these plays O'Neill exorcises his own ghosts in what is meant to be a basically understanding and sympathetic portrait of his brother, who eventually drank himself to death.

TYRONE, Mary Cavan. In *Long Day's Journey into Night*,* wife of James Tyrone*; mother of James ("Jamie") Tyrone, Jr.,* and Edmund Tyrone.* She is fifty-four, "a trifle plump" but with a thin face dominated by large, beautiful, long-lashed dark brown eyes. At the beginning of the play, she has been home at the Tyrone summer house for the past two months after having undergone a "cure" for her morphine addiction. The action of the play chronicles her regression, her return to addiction, and her reliving of the past. She was a convent-girl student when she first met James Tyrone backstage after a performance and fell instantly in love with him, marrying him and travelling with him during his lucrative road tours playing his starring role which made him money but did not give him artistic fulfillment. During the years, Mary came to feel very lonely, partly because her convent friends no longer found her acceptable after her marriage with an actor and also because James Tyrone seemed to prefer the company of the bar room to that of his family.

She tells of living in "second-rate hotels" and regrets that she has never had a proper home, except the cheap little cottage they occupy during the summer. She continually berates James for his meanness and blames him for her addiction, claiming that he had obtained a cheap doctor to look after her when Edmund was born. In order to relieve her pain, the doctor had prescribed morphine, and inadvertently Mary became addicted. Throughout the play Mary recalls the happy times of her life—as a promising piano student at the convent and as a young woman who believed that she had a religious vocation but gave it all up when she married James Tyrone. The portrait of Mary is based on that of O'Neill's own mother, Ella Quinlan O'Neill,* who did, however, manage to cure herself of her addiction largely as the result of a strong religious faith and the use of prayer. In *Long Day's Journey*, Mary Tyrone continually regrets the loss of her religious faith, and the conclusion of the play offers no hope for the recovery.

Mary Tyrone speaks bitterly against both her sons. Jamie is an object of her antagonism because he had visited his younger brother when he himself had measles and the baby died as a result. Then she berates Edmund for having been the cause of her addiction, believing that she should have never had him. To be sure, she does not fully believe these allegations, but she is so far gone with morphine that she says more than she means. Geraldine Fitzgerald* suggests that she is trying to "un-bear" Edmund.

O'Neill does not draw her character with as much sympathy as that of her husband, James Tyrone, perhaps because O'Neill was not prepared to forgive his own mother for the trouble she had caused him. There is no scene of mutual communication and understanding to parallel the one between Edmund and his father. Mary Tyrone seems to be a totally lost cause, a character living in a fog which shuts out reality, one who finds existence only in the past. Nonetheless, she does remember James and their early life together as a relationship of love. Throughout the play she is portrayed as a tortured creature unable to muster sufficient willpower to break herself of her drug habit. O'Neill manages to convey the terror and total denial of the addict superbly, but while the portrait shows some understanding, and even sympathy, it remains at bottom somewhat hostile. Mary is not weak but shrewdly manipulative, managing to set her three men against each other in order to avoid confronting herself with what she has become. Again, too, the failure of a wife to serve her husband's artistic ambitions has meant that the husband, in this case, James Tyrone, has been forced to forgo his dream.

V

VILLAGE PRIEST, A, an elderly, white-haired man "with a kindly, spiritual face." In *The Sniper*,* he vainly preaches resignation and the love of God to Rougon,* the old peasant who has lost his son at the beginning of the play and who at the end has discovered that his wife and his son's fiancée have also been killed. Even then he exhorts Rougon against violence, remembering that the German captain has promised reprisals for such action. He is a patriot but still believes that Rougon should not take up arms against the enemy. When Rougon does so and is about to be shot, the Priest begs him to pray, but Rougon refuses to pray to a God who has treated him unjustly. He spits on the ground and dies with an insult on his lips. The Priest is given the final words of the play as he gazes on the dead bodies: "Alas, the laws of men!" The priest is the source of dramatic irony in the play, preaching resignation in a world of violence and the wisdom and love of God to a man who can see only the injustice of a hostile deity. His prayer in which words of Christian love and acceptance suddenly surface out of singsong formulas acts as counterpoint to the rage and grief of Rougon.

VIOLET, a West Indian negress in *The Moon of the Caribbees*.*

VIRELLA, Luis. In *The Movie Man*,* general of a division of insurgents. He "is an undersized man with shifty, beady black eyes and a black mustache." He has a grudge against the prisoner, Ernesto Fernandez, who has been condemned to death. He has very little to say in the play and is, like Gomez,* a caricature of a Mexican general.

"THE VISIT OF MALATESTA," notes for a proposed gangster comedy originally entitled "Malatesta Seeks Surcease." It concerns "the legendary Italian insurrectionist," Enrico Malatesta (Floyd, 1981, p. 298). O'Neill worked on it from January 4, 1940, to March 2, 1941. The scene is New London, Connecticut, and the characters include anarchist figures who also appear in *The Iceman Cometh*.* The notes also show O'Neill's preoccupation with political and social themes, including the plight of the Italian immigrants in the United States. Floyd (1981), who gives an extensive analysis of these notes (pp. 298–316), maintains that this would have been America's "richest comedy" (p. 301). The manuscript materials are at Yale University.

W

WARNINGS, a realistic one-act play in two scenes concerning the wireless operator of the S.S. *Empress*, James Knapp,* who discovers that he is going deaf.

Scene i: A cramped Bronx apartment where Knapp lives between voyages with his wife, Mary Knapp,* a wornout woman of forty, and their five children. In this long expository scene, the tensions within the family are shown to be almost unbearable as the children bicker constantly and Mary Knapp complains bitterly about their poverty: she even has to take in washing so that they can make ends meet. The two adolescent elder children, Charles and Daisy (*see* Knapp Children), are rebellious and on the verge of getting into trouble, but their pettiness seems motivated by a poverty that does not even allow them decent clothes.

Mary and Charles discuss James Knapp's odd conduct since his return from his last voyage, Charles saying that he has had to speak loudly because his father doesn't seem to hear. When James returns from a visit to the doctor he seems profoundly depressed, something he attributes to the fact that he is to set off on a three-month voyage the next morning. Charles asks him for a new suit, and his father sorrowfully refuses, promising that he will have one after the completion of this forthcoming assignment.

James tells Mary that the doctor has told him that he is going deaf. He will "probably be able to hear for a long time yet but I got to be prepared for a sudden shock which'll leave me stone-deaf." Knapp says that if anyone on the ship were to know, he would lose his job instantly. However, he intends to tell his superiors, citing the responsibility of his job. Mrs. Knapp first points out that the doctor had said her husband's hearing "would hold out for a long time yet," and then she fastens on the word "responsibility," pointing out that he himself had told her that there was little wireless traffic. She glosses over the verdict as a means of getting Knapp to return to see the doctor. Then when Knapp suggests he should resign and look for another job, she berates him with their poverty-stricken existence and with bitter scorn asks, "Oh, why did I ever marry such a man? It's been nothin' but worryin' and sufferin' ever since." Tortured by this tonguelashing, Knapp cries out, "I'll go! But this is going to be my last trip. I got to do the right thing."

Scene ii: "A section of the boat deck of the S.S. *Empress*," which is obviously sinking. Knapp is in the wireless room sending out calls and listening intently for replies. Captain Hardwick* continually asks if he has contacted anyone, and Knapp says, "Not a single answer, sir. I can't account for it." This circumstance concerns the captain and Mason,* the first officer, because they know that some vessels are in the vicinity. Time is running out, and the bulkhead may collapse at any moment when finally the captain, enraged at Knapp's apparent incompetence or cowardice, asks, "Are you deaf?" At this, Knapp collapses and reveals that he has indeed lost his hearing, saying that he had made this last trip only to support his family. The captain finds another wireless operator, Dick Whitney,* a passenger. Captain Hardwick's initial sympathy for the distraught Knapp is turned to fury when he discovers that one nearby vessel, the *Verdari*, has been trying to communicate with the *Empress*. In fact, the day before she had broadcast a report of a derelict and warned ships in the area. Obviously, the *Empress* has struck it. Captain Hardwick berates Knapp as a "miserable, cowardly shrimp" and has Mason write out the circumstances of the *Verdari*'s warning. The boats are then lowered as Knapp reads the paper and realizes that he has caused the loss of the ship. He stumbles to the wireless room, pulls out a revolver, and shoots himself in the temple.

Comments: This play bears a narrative resemblance to Joseph Conrad's *The End of the Tether*, in which Captain Whalley goes almost totally blind but continues with his last command in order to send money to his favorite daughter. The character of the operator may also be based on a tubercular wireless operator who was a fellow resident with O'Neill at Jimmy-the-Priest's* (Gelb and Gelb, 1973, p. 162).

The heroic quality of the Conrad narrative, however, is not present in *Warnings*, chiefly because the realistic setting and the relentless misery of the Knapp household reduce the circumstances to the realm of nagging rather than tragedy. The children are unlikable, even Charles, who is the best of them, while Mary Knapp, the mother, is drawn as a mean-spirited, pathetic creature, too preoccupied with her own situation to understand that of her husband. Even James Knapp is pathetic rather than tragic, and his death seems perhaps a fitting punishment for his moral weakness rather than a major sacrifice. O'Neill seems here to have been developing a theme which he had raised, but not treated, in *Thirst*,* when the captain shoots himself for losing his ship—he has made an error of judgment and he must pay. In the earlier work, however, there is more emphasis on humanity as being controlled by outside cosmic forces instead of the economic determinism of this play. The suicide of Knapp does seem rather melodramatic, and it is interesting to note the number of O'Neill's early plays that end with violence.

Note: O'Neill later revised this play into a scenario entitled "S.O.S."* in 1917-1919.

Production Data: Written 1913. Unproduced.

A Note on Text: The text used is that appearing in *Ten "Lost" Plays of Eugene O'Neill* (New York: Random House, 1964).

WARREN, Elizabeth. In the scenario of *The Calms of Capricorn*,* daughter of Theodore Warren* and later wife of Jonathan Harford.* She is eighteen, "tall, dark, slender, with a boyish figure, . . . [and] a coldly beautiful, calm, disciplined exterior" which hides "intense nervous energy." She has no love for her father and operates in an aloof manner until she meets Leda Cade,* a prostitute and passenger on the clipper *Dream of the West* bound for San Francisco. Leda awakens Elizabeth to a sense of her own body, teaching her about "life" and bringing her to make use of physical attraction to seduce Jonathan Harford and then marry him. Elizabeth has to learn about the use of femininity in order to gain what she wants; in this situation she will marry Jonathan Harford, not for love but in a businesslike partnership, working to make money and achieve success together. However, in him she meets her match because this is precisely the kind of relationship he wants. They seem to deserve each other. Presumably she would have appeared in "The Man on Iron Horseback," the play in the proposed cycle, "A Tale of Possessors, Self-Dispossessed,"* which would have chronicled Jonathan's career as a railroad and shipping baron.

WARREN, Theodore. In the scenario of *The Calms of Capricorn*,* father of Elizabeth Warren* and owner of the clipper *Dream of the West*. He is forty-eight, tall, successful-looking, and dressed with expensive conservatism. He represents the typical sharp-practicing businessman. He cheats at cards, and his daughter points out that that is the way he has succeeded in business; he is quite ruthless, as is shown in his attitude toward Captain Enoch Payne* and Ethan Harford,* who succeeds the captain. At first he agrees with Payne's conservative approach to sailing, but when the vessel remains becalmed he begins to change his mind; after Payne's death he becomes intoxicated with the notion of breaking the record of the *Flying Cloud*, even though it means that the ship has been overstrained and is leaking. He plans to patch her up and sell her in England at a handsome profit.

However, when Ethan Harford fails to break the record, Warren begins to be concerned that the truth about the voyage may come out, and he dismisses Ethan just before the ship reaches San Francisco harbor. He has no love for his daughter, whom he rightly perceives as cold and calculating; Jonathan Harford* is not really the husband he would have picked out for her, but he perceives that they deserve each other. Like all the characters in the action, he, too, is affected by his meeting with Leda Cade,* a prostitute and passenger on the *Dream of the West*,* and goes to bed with her.

WASHINGTON SQUARE PLAYERS, THE. This group lasted from 1915 to 1918 and operated out of the rented Bandbox Theatre, East Fifty-seventh Street. It produced sixty-two one-act plays and pantomimes as well as six full-length plays. The Theatre Guild* was a development of this organization, which included some of the earlier Provincetown Players* group. It mounted the first production of O'Neill's *In the Zone** and revived *The Rope.**

WAYNE, Robert, Medical Corps, U.S.A. In *Shell Shock,** he is a young man of about thirty, a doctor who is an expert on shell shock. When Jack Arnold* returns from the front after suffering a nervous breakdown, Wayne interrogates him concerning his heroic action in saving Herbert Roylston* from No Mans Land. Wayne brings Arnold to a recognition that he did not merely go out there for the purpose of getting his "dead" friend's cigarettes but rather because he had heard Roylston's screaming. To be sure, there is some doubt about this more acceptable explanation, but it satisfies Arnold, who is now pronounced cured.

WEB, THE, a one-act play. The action takes place in "a squalid bedroom on the top floor of a rooming house on the Lower East Side, New York." Rose Thomas,* a consumptive prostitute of twenty-two (but who looks thirty), is forced by her pimp, Steve,* to work on the street this particularly wet night. Rose begs him to allow her to stay home and go to a doctor, but Steve refuses. In answer to her request for some of the money she has given him, he says he has spent it all. Rose realizes that, as before, it has gone on drink and drugs, and she threatens to act like her friend, Bessie, holding back on some of her takings. At the sound of loud voices, Rose's baby wakes up and cries, a circumstance that arouses Steve to rage. He refuses to allow the child to sleep in the bed with him and tells Rose to give it to an orphan asylum where it will be taken care of. He himself had been brought up in an orphanage. Finally, Steve gives Rose two weeks to get rid of the child because it interferes with her earnings; if she doesn't comply, Steve threatens to inform the police of her activities and have her imprisoned. Rose struggles with Steve.

Suddenly, Tim Moran* enters, pointing his automatic revolver at Steve. Tim orders Steve to get out, and as Rose consoles her baby, Tim comforts Rose. They tell each other their life stories. Rose has tried to break away from prostitution and once even held a housekeeping position in a decent house, but someone recognized her and she was dismissed. Society has made it impossible for her to do anything except remain a prostitute, and she has never been trained for any kind of work. Tim's case is similar. He was sent to reform school as the "fall guy" for an older gang. There he was really made into a crook. Upon his release he tried to go straight but always met discrimination because of his past. Once again he stole and received a five-year sentence; on his release he learned the trade of safecracking and has just pulled off a job. Like Rose, he sees that it is impossible for him to go straight.

Tim has been hiding next door for a week and has developed sympathy for the young woman and her child. That is why he has intervened, and he even gives Rose some money so that she can go to the mountains with her child in an attempt to cure her tuberculosis. But Tim is afraid that he has been recognized, and as they hear noises in the hallway, Steve's face appears on the fire escape outside the window. He sees the two of them embrace and holds his fire, but as Tim prepares to leave by the fire escape, Steve fires point blank at Tim's chest. While Rose is still leaning over the dead Tim, the police break in, and finding some of the loot from the safecracking job in Rose's possession, they jump to the conclusion that she has robbed Tim and then shot him. No one believes her as she attempts to tell the truth, and she is taken off to jail. As she leaves crying, "Gawd! Gawd! Why d'yuh hate me so?" a plain-clothes man attempts to comfort the child: "Mama's gone. I'm your mama now."

Comments: This bleak little play is written in the German naturalistic manner, and its title, *The Web*, refers to the web of external circumstances in which the two major characters are caught. They are the little people whom society forces into criminality, even against their will. The play was originally entitled "The Cough," but its present title implies greater universality. Perhaps, too, it is meant to recall *Die Weber* (*The Weavers*) of the German naturalistic playwright Gerhard Hauptmann, whose work seems to have influenced O'Neill here.

Though the title expresses universality, the impact of the play is more local and limited, perhaps because of the playwright's attempt at a too literal recreation of reality. Consequently, the most important statement concerning Rose appears in the stage directions where only the reader can see it: "She seems to be aware of something in the room—perhaps the personification of the ironic life force that has crushed her." Clearly , this is different from the "life force" of Bernard Shaw, but this is not the center of the situation. O'Neill does not communicate this "ironic life force" to his audience, and it is difficult to see how an actress could possibly convey it. The problem may well be that at this early stage he was not capable of dealing dramatically with such internal conflicts and discoveries, perhaps because he is too preoccupied with the external details and conflicts of the characters—something that often troubles a naturalistic writer. The dialogue adopts the argot of criminals and the streets, and though used a trifle self-consciously, it has more life than that of his play *Thirst*,* written in the same year. Once again, there is some melodramatic action, and perhaps coincidence is overworked when Steve appears quite so opportunely to kill Tim just as the police break in. The theme of a malevolent God, in this case a malevolent Society, is continued, and human beings are portrayed as the victims of circumstances from which they cannot escape. Justice is not done, and Steve escapes. O'Neill's sympathy for the underdog, the underprivileged, and the victim, a recurrent theme, is well shown here.

Production Data: Written 1913. Unproduced.

A Note on Text: The text used is that appearing in *Ten "Lost" Plays of Eugene O'Neill* (New York: Random House, 1964).

WELDED, a play in three acts and four scenes. The play opens in a studio apartment at night. In the rear is a balcony with a stairway leading down to the main floor. Initially the room is in darkness, and then a circle of light reveals Eleanor Cape* lying on a chaise longue. She is a tall woman of thirty with "high, prominent cheekbones . . . passionate, blue-gray eyes . . . high forehead . . . dark brown hair combed straight back. The first impression of her whole personality is one of charm, partly innate, partly imposed by years of self-discipline." She picks up a letter from the table, kisses it with an expression of love on her face, lets it drop, and falls into a reverie. The door beneath the balcony opens noiselessly, and Michael Cape* enters. He, too, is surrounded by a circle of light. "These two circles of light, like auras of egotism, emphasize and intensify Eleanor and Michael throughout the play. There is no other lighting." Michael is thirty-five, tall, dark, with a face that "is a harrowed battleground of supersensitiveness, . . . the forehead of a thinker, the eyes of a dreamer, the nose and mouth of a sensualist." He projects an aura of "powerful imagination tinged with somber sadness." He seems both "sympathetic and cruel at the same time." Yet he also seems tortured between a "defiance of life and his own weakness, a deep need for love as a faith in which to relax."

Eleanor suddenly perceives Michael, and they embrace passionately, Eleanor remarking that "it's positively immoral for an old married couple to act this way," while Michael notes with happiness that after five years of marriage she is still reading his love letters. He inquires concerning her reverie, but she caressingly refuses to gratify his egotism by telling him. She asks about his progress on the play he has been writing for the past few weeks in the country. Michael says that since he has now finished the fourth act, he has returned. She asks whether he had hurried his work because he was lonely, but Michael sternly denies it.

Enthusiastically, he tells Eleanor that this play "is going to be the finest thing we've ever done." Eleanor seizes on the use of "we" and notes deprecatingly that she is only the interpreter of a part Michael has created. Michael sweeps this remark aside with "You're an artist," claiming that she has taught him how to write parts for women. She attempts to get him to read her the last act, but Michael refuses "because I've been hoping for this night as our own." They speak of the way that they have remained lovers, even though married, and recall their first meeting and first impressions, each having heard rumors of the love affairs of the other. This conversation injects a little awkwardness into the situation as they speak of the "grand ideal" for their marriage, "a new faith." "We swore to have a true sacrament—or nothing! . . . a consummation demanding and combining the best in each of us! Hard, difficult, guarded from the commonplace, kept sacred as the outward form of our inner harmony." Together they muse over the difficulty, success, and exaltation of this undertaking.

As they fall into a passionate embrace and walk toward the stairway, there is a noise outside and then a knock at the door. Michael doesn't want her to answer, but Eleanor says she must in case it is "something important." She opens the door, relieved and surprised to find that it is John.* "He is a man of about fifty, tall, loose-limbed, a bit stoop-shouldered, with iron-grey hair, and a gaunt, shrewd face." John speedily sees that he has interrupted something and asks about Michael's play. Michael, clearly angry at John's presence, replies icily; and when Eleanor tries to patch things up by offering the visitor a cigarette, she is greeted with "a hot glance of scorn." John then notes that Michael looks tired and on hearing that he has just finished the play, asks to see it. Michael is acting in a very prickly way, and Eleanor tries to calm things by suggesting that he read them the last act. Michael fiercely says that he hates the whole play, but John, finding a graceful way to leave, says he is sure it will be a major triumph for them both.

On John's departure, Michael explodes, asking Eleanor why she had answered the door given that anyone outside would have gone away. He maintains that she should have been thinking only of him, "oblivious to everything," but now she has destroyed "a rare moment of beauty." Eleanor does feel guilty and tries to smooth things over, but they fall into spoken thoughts, each talking past the other, "neither appearing to hear what the other has said." Eleanor speaks of being "crushed" in the relationship, "Even my work must exist only as an echo of yours," while Michael speaks of "some knock at the door, some reminder of the life outside that calls you away from me." He thinks that he should be sufficient for her in all ways.

Michael then begins to discuss John and the curious manner of his visit, asking whether he has been in the habit of calling in Michael's absence. Eleanor defends herself, saying that John is her oldest friend and one to whom she owes her success because of "his advice and direction." Michael reacts with possessive jealousy, recalling that John had once asked Eleanor to marry him, even suggesting that there might have been more than mere friendship. They momentarily make up, and then Eleanor speaks of Michael's intense absorption in his work, a comment that Michael instantly perceives as jealousy. As they argue about the value of his work and her success, John's contribution is mentioned by Eleanor, causing Michael to explode into recriminations about her past until Eleanor insists that she and John were not lovers. Michael does not respond, and Eleanor says, "How could I ever love you?" Then, after he kisses her passionately, she coldly announces that John was her lover while Michael was away. At that, Michael breaks into anguished tears and accuses her of "dragging our ideal in the gutter— with delight." Enraged, he says he will drag it even lower; as he created that ideal, he will destroy it "and be free." With these words, he rushes out of the door and Eleanor, after an initial cry of despair, announces her own freedom, rushes upstairs, returns with a hat and coat, and goes out the door, leaving it open behind her.

Act II, Scene i: A library with a large couch and a picture of Eleanor on the wall. John is sitting wearily bent over on the extreme edge of the center of the couch as a car is heard arriving and departing and the doorbell rings. Eleanor enters as John greets her amazedly, "Nelly!" Eleanor reminds him of his earlier promise that she might always come and asks if she may now stay. In answer to his question about Michael she says, "I've forgotten—as if he's never lived. Do you still love me?" John admits his continuing love, and when she asks, he kisses her passionately on the lips, only to discover that she is merely submitting to his embrace. She says she is tired, but she will not discuss in detail what has gone on between her and Michael. She throws herself at John, who suggests that she go to bed. As she starts up the stairs she seems to see Michael standing at the top—as he had been when John had knocked at the door earlier in the evening. She offers herself to John but discovers, as John has sadly realized, that she does not really love him. Eleanor repeats her hatred of Michael, and John again says he will "nurse along that crumb of hope you gave," while Eleanor reveals the hurtful lie she had told Michael about having been John's mistress while her husband was away. John is amazed, but Eleanor says she made him believe, and her aim is to be revenged on Michael. Finally John tells her that while he does love her, she has twice treated his love with "humiliating contempt," once as a means of furthering her career and now as a means of revenge, suggesting that she had better go home. Eleanor agrees, and John says that the three of them will have a fine theatrical success. John then offers to drive her home, and Eleanor assents, saying that "I'll always believe Fate should have let me love you, instead." John wonders aloud whether he could have made it happen, but Eleanor says that there was always something within her heart that would have prevented that. And so they compromise on continuing as friends.

Act II, Scene ii: a sleazy bedroom in darkness except for the light from a street lamp. A Woman,* obviously a foreigner and dressed like a prostitute, enters followed by Michael. He is dishevelled, feverish, and wild-looking. The Woman, who moves like "a tired scrubwoman," takes off her hat and speaks of her weariness, recalling the way Michael had flung himself at her, kissing her until she thought they might be arrested. Michael sits with his head in his hands until the Woman asks if he wants to stay all night. Michael asks, "where else would I go?" and when the Woman suggests "home," he takes the remark as a bad joke: "from now on Hell is my home! I suspect we're fellow-citizens." This blasphemous remark shocks the Woman, but Michael looks upon her as his salvation: "You have the power—and the right—to murder love! You can satisfy hate!"

As she undresses, Michael continues to talk in what she sees as riddles: "You're all the tortures man inflicts on woman—and you're the revenge of woman!" Finally he bursts into tears, and she comforts him. He kisses her frenziedly, but he can do nothing more, and the woman comments, "Well, I'm glad one of youse guys got paid back like you oughter!" Michael then says that "love must live on in me" and starts to leave as the Woman suggests that he kiss and make up with his wife.

Suddenly she turns on him, angrily refusing to become his instrument of revenge. She won't even take money from him. She won't have anything to do with him "if you was to get down on your knees!" She refuses to forgive him for treating her like an object, and Michael perceives that her life has not totally broken her spirit. He asks for a kiss because love has brought them together as two lonely human beings.

Finally she allows Michael to kiss her on the forehead and address her as "Sister." She even accepts Michael's money because she will have to give it to the man who keeps her and will beat her. She admits that she loves this man: "I'm lonesome." After all, as she says, the whole game of life is funny: "You've got to laugh, ain't you? You got to loin to like it!" Michael picks up this speech: "To learn to love life—to accept it and be exalted—that's the one faith left to us." He leaves, closing the door after him.

Act III: The studio apartment, as in Act I. Eleanor stands by the table, trembling and frightened, watching the door as Michael is entering. They move toward each other, hands groping "in a strange conflicting gesture of a protective warding off and at the same time seeking possession." They clasp hands, look at each other, then speak, but to no real purpose except to discover a draught, so Michael shuts the door.

Michael again seems to think that a fleeting moment of wordless understanding has passed, but he must attempt to explain things. Perhaps they now know that they love and, as Eleanor says, "Now—we know peace." But Michael replies, "Peace isn't our meaning." Slowly they reveal the incidents of their parallel search for love, but the battle is not yet over. Michael talks of choosing an end, as Eleanor talks of renunciation. He suggests that she should "act nobility" and go. As she puts her hand on the doorknob and stops, he "jumps toward the door with a pleading cry." She knocks on the door and says in a kind of exorcism, "No. Never again, come out." Then she opens the door: "It opens inward, Michael." She turns to face him, and since it is nearly dawn, she says she will say "good-night instead of good-by."

Everything now becomes both clear and simple for them. They belong together even though "we'll torture and tear, and clutch for each other's souls!—fight— fail and hate again—but fail *with pride*—with joy." They exchange love and forgiveness and decide that they have their old dreams back again, "deeper and more beautiful." "We love," says Eleanor. As she reaches the top of the stairs, she turns and stretches out her arms to form a cross. Michael, two steps below her, looks wonderingly; then his hands reach out for hers, and between them they form a cross. Finally, they embrace and kiss as the curtain falls.

Comments: This play is highly autobiographical and concerns O'Neill's marriage with Agnes Boulton.* In attitude and approach, it is also heavily influenced by the work of August Strindberg, whose battle of the sexes it echoes. Written in 1922–1923, it achieved twenty-two performances and was not well received. Critics saw it as second-rate Strindberg and also as a continuing love-hate battle without much insight or motivation. The attitude toward marital relationships, however, does show O'Neill's preference for a kind of servitude as demonstrated in his early play of the same name, *Servitude.** In *Welded*, however, the characters are overly theatrical and the dialogue is at times highly pretentious, especially when Michael tries to deliver philosophical statements. The feeling of imprisonment in marriage is something that Agnes O'Neill seems to have felt, but O'Neill here makes the debate between his characters as one on the relative quality of their work, one between creator and interpreter, and the ultimate insult Michael delivers to Eleanor is "You actress."

The last tableau, the couple's embrace making a cross, is clearly meant to symbolize the sacrificial, painful, yet perhaps ennobling aspects of marriage, and it is overdrawn. The stage directions are very important here, since O'Neill seems to require very complex gestures. His lighting directions are also very specific, with the characters illuminated only by two spotlights to signify their "auras of egotism." However, this might make the rest of the stage invisible and further prevent any suitable illumination of the two other characters. Altogether, this is not a very successful play, but it is important in showing O'Neill's attitudes toward matrimony and his concern with the topic throughout his theatrical career.

Production Data: Written 1922–1923. First produced by Kenneth Macgowan,* Robert Edmond Jones,* and Eugene O'Neill in association with Edgar Selwyn at the Thirty-ninth Street Theatre, New York City, March 17, 1924 (24 performances).

Director: Stark Young
Designer: Robert Edmond Jones
Cast: Eleanor Cape: Doris Keane
        Michael Cape: Jacob Ben-Ami
        John: Curtis Cooksey
        Woman: Catherine Collins

Revived at Columbia University, June 10–July 5, 1981, at the Horace Mann Theatre, Teachers College, Columbia University, New York City, under the auspices of the Columbia University Summer Session and the Center for Theater Studies.

Producer: Andrew B. Harris
Director: José Quintero*
Designer: Quentin Thomas
Lighting: Michael Valentino
Cast: Eleanor Cape: Ellen Tobie
        Michael Cape: Philip Anglim
        John: Court Miller
        Woman: Laura Gardner

WESON. In *Servitude*,* the elderly gardener. He is withered and myopic "with a drooping gray mustache stained yellow by tobacco juice." He is an expository character who warns of a prowler in the garden and serves as a sounding board for Benton.*

WEST INDIAN MULATTO SAILOR, A. In *Thirst*,* dressed in a sailor's uniform and wearing sailor shoes. He constantly intones a magical chant of his people which is reputed to drive away the sharks which surround the life raft on which he and two companions, a Dancer* and a Gentleman,* are drifting, half-crazed by thirst and hunger. He is suspected of having a secret store of water, and the other two try to coerce him out of it. He repeatedly says there is no more water and continues with his chant. On the death of the Dancer he proposes to the Gentleman that the pair consume the body to ensure their survival. When the Gentleman reacts with horror, flinging the body overboard, the Sailor stabs the Gentleman but is carried in his victim's death grasp to meet his destruction by the sharks. As a character the Sailor indicates the equality of all human beings before a hostile God and a hostile universe. The sailor alone does not complain about injustice. He seems to concentrate solely on survival. His constant intoning of the mysterious chant points ahead to O'Neill's use of the tom-tom in *The Emperor Jones*.* Though the other characters consider him beneath him, they will humble themselves to get what they want from him. He seems more capable of survival than they, and consequently one may take him as a comment on the inability of civilization and its denizens to cope in such a situation. But the hostility of the universe destroys all alike. O'Neill himself created this role in the original production.

WETJOEN, Piet. In *The Iceman Cometh*,* a Boer ex-general in his fifties. He is the Dutch-farmer type, now run to fat and drink but with "a suggestion of old authority lurking in him like a memory of the drowned." His name is a conflation of those of two famous Boer guerrilla generals, De Wet and Viljoen. He is the friend of Captain Cecil Lewis,* a former British army officer who fought on the opposite side in the Boer War (1899–1902). The two met at the St. Louis World's Fair. Wetjoen is running from a reputation for cowardice, which he sees as caution, and rents a room over the saloon operated by Harry Hope.* His pipe dream is that someday he will be able to return to South Africa and be welcomed there. Under the influence of Theodore Hickman,* the salesman who comes to the bar annually to celebrate Hope's birthday, Wetjoen tries to translate this dream into reality, and as a result he temporarily breaks off his friendship with Lewis and insults the black man Joe Mott,* calling him a Kaffir. However, he realizes the impossibility of his dream and returns to the bar to get drunk in order to forget the outside world and to try to regain old illusions. Like his companions, he wants "to pass out in peace" but willingly accepts Hickey's insanity plea—a new pipe dream which discredits Hickey's message.

WHERE THE CROSS IS MADE, a one-act play, the first version of Act IV of *Gold*.* Isaiah Bartlett,* a whaling captain, has been living for the past three years in his "cabin" at the top of his house awaiting the return of his wrecked ship, the *Mary Allen*. He is looked after by his daughter, Sue Bartlett,* who loves him, and his crippled son, Nat Bartlett,* who hates him, blaming him for forcing him to go to sea and the consequent loss of his right arm. Nat, a frustrated writer, has made plans to have his father committed to a mental institution so he can sell up his father's property and finish his book.

Nat tells his father's story to Dr. Higgins* of the mental hospital. Seven years earlier, Captain Bartlett's whaling vessel was wrecked in the Indian Ocean. Six men and the captain reached a desert island, but only four survived, and there were suspicions of cannibalism. Nat then retails what he calls the "dream." They discovered two chests of gold and precious stones, which they buried on the island, intending to return. He claims that his father has made him heir to the treasure and in the presence of the survivors, Silas Horne,* Cates,* and Jimmy Kanaka,* had given him a map showing that the treasure is buried "where the cross is made." Nat insists that the map is real, but as the tale progresses the audience perceives that Nat's own sanity is suspect. Captain Bartlett has mortgaged his property and has sent his three companions in search of the treasure, but their ship, the *Mary Allen* (named for the captain's late wife), is lost with all hands in a hurricane off the Celebes. Captain Bartlett refuses to believe it and waits obsessively for their return with the treasure. Arrangements are made for Dr. Higgins and two attendants to take the captain away that night. When Sue finds out about this, she berates Nat for his lack of love, saying that she would not wish to accept her share of the property sale, calling it "blood money." Nat, however, sees this as a chance to free himself from his hated father and also from his own obsession with the buried treasure, so he burns the map.

At that moment, the ghosts of the three companions of the captain appear, and in an hallucination shared by father and son, the three, bathed in a greenish light and clearly the victims of drowning, present the old man with two heavy, inlaid chests. At that moment, the captain dies and the hallucination disappears. His companions, rather than the attendants of the mental institution, have fetched Captain Bartlett away. The obsession, however, has passed to Nat, who picks up his father's copy of the map and swears he will seek the treasure himself. The play ends with the horrified Sue trying to pull her brother away.

Comments: The play is a curious mixture of melodramatic cliché and psychology. The O'Neill theme of frustrated son trying to break from the power of a father is well shown, but the treasure is treated in an almost jocular manner, while the appearance of the three sailors is well handled in an attempt to involve the audience actively. There is very little action in the drama, most of it being exposition. Later, O'Neill reworked this play into his longer melodrama, *Gold*, a play which he later came to dislike and which is less powerful than the shorter version, though certainly easier to stage since the ghosts do not appear.

Production Data: Written 1918. Based on "The Captain's Walk," a short story idea by Agnes Boulton.* First produced by the Provincetown Players* at the Playwrights' Theatre, New York City, November 22, 1918 (Performances unknown).

Director: Ida Rauh
Designer: Unknown

Cast: Nat Bartlett: James Light
Dr. Higgins: O. K. Liveright
Sue Bartlett: Ida Rauh
Captain Isaiah Bartlett: Hutchinson Collins
Silas Horne: Louis B. Ell
Cates: Foster Damon
Jimmy Kanaka: F. Ward Roege

WHITE, Walter. *See* "Blind Alley Guy."

WHITELY. In "The Personal Equation,"* "a swarthy, dark-eyed, bull-backed, powerfully built man of about thirty-five." He is a member of the union executive in Liverpool which represents the firemen and dockworkers. He is the only honest revolutionary among them and resigns when the executive is bribed by management. He attempts to get dynamite so that Tom Perkins* can blow up the engines of the S. S. *San Francisco*, a vessel owned by the Ocean Steamship Company, leader of the shipping cartel. When this falls through, Whitely aids Tom in his plan of sabotaging the engines.

After Tom is shot in the head by his father, Thomas Perkins,* the second engineer of the ship, Whitely and Tom's mistress, Olga Tarnoff,* visit him in his hospital room. Tom is so brain-damaged that he will remain a vegetable. Whitely, now that World War I has broken out, is beginning to feel twinges of patriotism and by the end of the final scene is about to enlist, justifying his action by citing patriotic statements made by other revolutionaries. He tells Olga he is surprised that she can still support the cause of revolution after what has happened to Tom. Whitely is the epitome of those "committed" workers and revolutionaries who will march away to war in support of their country, blind to the fact that they are acting contrary to their announced revolutionary principles.

WHITHORNE, Emerson, composer of incidental music to *Marco Millions*,* published as a piano score entitled *At the Court of Kublai Kaan* (New York: Carl Fischer, c1948), eight pages.

WHITNEY, Dick, the wireless operator/passenger in *The Web.**

WIFE FOR A LIFE, A, a one-act play. The action takes place on the edge of the Arizona desert in a mining camp. An elderly man of about fifty who seems to have seen better days and who has a "native refinement" is sitting before a smouldering fire outside a tent waiting for someone. Old Pete,* dressed in "rough miner's costume," brings a telegram for Jack* (John Sloan), and the men discuss their claims, Pete remarking that he won't get rich because cities always clean him out, but the other claimholders will do well. After he leaves, the Older Man* opens the telegram, thinking it might concern the mine, and finds the message, "I am waiting. Come."

This disturbs him because he hopes to keep Jack with him now that they have struck it rich. With the arrival of Jack, a young man in his early thirties, the two partners discuss their mine and discover that it is indeed a fine one. Jack suggests that he go East to help form a company to work it, and the Older Man jokingly suggests that his increasing eagerness to return to "the effete East" is caused by a woman. "An angel, rather," replies Jack, to which the Older Man cynically indicates that such women do not exist in his experience. The two then toast the success of their mine, which Jack names "the Yvette mine," a name which gives a start to the Older Man. When questioned about this choice of name Jack tells the tale of his lady.

When he first met Yvette,* she was married to a drunken mining engineer many years her senior, who had abused her. Jack had offered her sympathy in her marriage to the "drunken brute" and finally told her of his love. She, too, loved him but felt herself bound irrevocably to her marriage vows and said they must never see each other again. Jack then went off to the Transvaal where he saved the life of the Older Man, and they have been partners ever since. The lady, however, did write to Jack, telling him that her husband had disappeared shortly after Jack's departure, and it was rumored that he was seeking to kill Jack. She also told him that if her husband did not return after another year, then she would be legally free to marry.

The Older Man becomes progressively more agitated, and it is clear that he is the lady's husband. He is tempted to burn the telegram; but his finer instincts prevail, and he gives it to Jack, who rejoices in his happiness. The Older Man debates whether to reveal himself to Jack but decides against such an action. All his hatred of John Sloan has now vanished, and he feels some joy that Yvette had stayed faithful to him for what he had been and had not left him because of what he has become. Now he must see himself excluded from the mutual happiness of the only two people in the world that he has ever loved. He wishes Jack every happiness, and as the curtain falls he says, "Greater love hath no man than this that he giveth his wife for his friend."

Comments: This piece, begun while O'Neill was a patient at the Gaylord Farm* sanitorium (1913), is really an exercise in extended exposition. From an early point in the play, the audience is well aware of the situation, and the entire action of the play consists in the psychological reactions and asides of the Older Man. It is noteworthy that at this premature stage of his career, O'Neill was experimenting with the aside, a device he was to use most notably in *Strange Interlude*.* O'Neill himself identified this early effort as a vaudeville skit rather than a play, considering *Thirst** his first real play. Certainly *A Wife* employs the techniques of the two-man vehicle with star and straight man, a genre with which he had become familiar while accompanying James O'Neill,* his father, on a 1912 vaudeville tour. It was quite common for stars to perform in such skits while "resting" between major productions. The character of the Older Man looks ahead to Smitty* of the S.S. *Glencairn** plays, but the setting of a mining camp is based on O'Neill's recollections of his own mining experiences in Honduras. It has been suggested that the characters of the Older Man and his wife may have had real-life counterparts in a Mr. and Mrs. Stevens whom O'Neill met on his expedition [Gelb and Gelb, 1973, p. 134].

The play is clumsy, with stereotyped characterization and motivation, while the final line (meant to be taken seriously) is merely risible. However, there is also an early version of the ideal, long-suffering wife who endures uncomplainingly all manner of abuses from her husband. This play along with others was reprinted in 1950, without O'Neill's permission, when its copyright expired, in *Lost Plays of Eugene O'Neill*. Despite its old-fashioned and simplistic theatrical qualities, recalling the starring vehicles of his father's theatre, this work has importance as O'Neill's first known play. It exhibits techniques of focus, narrative, psychological insight, use of atmospheric setting, and theme, all of which return and are refined later in his career.

Production Data: Written 1913. Unproduced, though James O'Neill did offer to appear in it as a vaudeville skit.

A Note on Text: The text used is that appearing in *Ten "Lost" Plays of Eugene O'Neill* (New York: Random House, 1964).

WILLIAMS, Caleb. In *Diff'rent*,* fiancé of Emma Crosby,* brother of Harriet Williams,* and uncle of Benny Rogers.* Caleb is at first a "tall and powerfully built" whaling master of about thirty, bronzed and healthy-looking, and dressed in his dark Sunday-best suit. At the end of the play he is sixty years old, white-haired, and weatherbeaten but in many ways remarkably similar to his appearance in Act I.

He was the victim of a joke played on him by drunken crewmen in the South Seas. They persuaded a native girl that Williams wanted to go to bed with her, and as a result she swam out to the ship where Williams had remained to avoid temptation. He lost his virginity to her and was later extremely repentant. However, as the vessel left the South Sea island the girl swam out after it calling for Caleb—much to the amusement of the crew and the humiliation of Caleb. The crew finally had to shoot around her in the water before she would return to her home. Everyone treats this as a good joke on Caleb, but Emma is appalled when she hears of it, and she refuses to marry him. Caleb tries to explain things, and even before Emma finds out about the incident, he begs her not to make him out to be a "plaster saint." When Caleb realizes that Emma is serious in her refusal, he says that she may change her mind after his next two-year voyage; but when she says that she will not marry him even then, he promises to wait for twenty, thirty years, if necessary. On his return after thirty years, he finds that his ne'er-do-well nephew, now twenty-five, whom he has helped to bring up, has calculatingly insinuated himself into Emma's heart, even going so far as to propose marriage in order to get his hands on the small amount of money Emma has inherited. When she tells Caleb that she loves Benny better than she has ever loved him, Caleb is enraged and is so despairing that he goes to the barn and hangs himself.

The character of Caleb is curiously one-dimensional, and his reason for continuing to hope for Emma to change her mind is not motivated at all. In fact, his action seems rather foolish in its obstinacy. There seems to be no connection between his name and the novel by William Godwin, *Caleb Williams*.

WILLIAMS, Harriet. *See* Rogers, Harriet.

"WITHOUT ENDING OF DAYS," a preliminary title for *Days Without End*,* which also temporarily bore the title of "Without Endings." This constitutes the second play of a projected trilogy (later abandoned) of which *Dynamo**
is the first. The entire trilogy was to be called "Myth-Plays for the God-Forsaken."*

WOLHEIM, Louis (1881–1931), actor. Born to German-Polish parents, March 28, 1881, on the Lower East Side of New York; died of stomach cancer, Los Angeles, California, February 18, 1931. His father, Elias, was a painter of walls, murals, and portraits, the last of which shocked his Orthodox Jewish circle. Educated in the public schools of New York City, the City College of New York (B.E., 1904), and Cornell University (M.E., 1906).

Wolheim played fullback as "Wallie" Wolheim on the Cornell football teams of 1904–5, when his nose was broken three times. His role on these teams seems to have been one of intimidation rather than the starring one later attributed to him both by himself and his publicity. After graduation, he went to New York to work for a Manhattan engineering firm. He returned to Cornell, ostensibly to work for a Ph.D., but in fact taught mathematics at the Cornell University Preparatory School, engaged in free-lance mathematics tutoring, and clerked behind the cigar counter of the Ithaca Hotel. During 1910–12 he seems to have been in Mexico, first as an engineer with an American firm, losing his job when a revolution broke out after a few months. He later claimed that he was a messenger for Madero, operating between El Paso and Chihuahua, but like many of Wolheim's fanciful personal anecdotes, this one is suspect. He returned to Cornell in 1912, tutoring, clerking, and nurturing his reputation for boozing and tall tales, while also working as an extra in the various films that were being shot in the neighborhood, making his debut as an Indian in 1914.

Lionel Barrymore, who saw him at the Ithaca Hotel, encouraged him to try acting, suggesting that his broken-nosed ugliness could make his fortune. Taking this advice, Wolheim returned to New York City in 1915, playing bit parts (mainly villains) in films (1916–17) and taking odd jobs. He played in the film *The Eternal Mother* (1917), with Ethel Barrymore, and also in serials. The Barrymore family seems to have continued to help Wolheim, and in 1919 he achieved his first notable stage role in *The Jest*. At his original audition for this play, he was awarded a large part but was removed because of his stage fright and given a smaller role. However, when the production re-opened after the summer recess, he was returned to the larger part, having now conquered his nervousness. He also tried his hand at playwriting in *The Idle Inn* (1921) with

Isaac Goldberg, a show which included Jacob Ben-Ami of the Yiddish Theatre and a City College graduate, Edward G. Robinson. In the same year he helped adapt Henri Bernstein's play, *The Claw*, with Edward Delaney, though the nature and extent of his contribution are both disputed and unclear.

In 1922 he gained Broadway fame as Yank* in O'Neill's *The Hairy Ape** when the play moved uptown from Macdougal Street. Mary Blair,* the original Mildred,* said that the ferocity of his performance frequently frightened her. She was replaced in the uptown production by Carlotta Monterey* (later O'Neill's third wife), who was thought to be a better box-office attraction. Wolheim received enthusiastic reviews for this role but was even more successful as the original Captain Flagg in *What Price Glory* (1924), by Laurence Stallings and Maxwell Anderson. He left the cast after 299 performances to continue his screen career. Altogether, Wolheim made over forty-five films as extra, featured player, and principal. He also tried to direct with *Sin Ship* (1931), an unsuccessful film in which he also starred. His most famous film roles were in *Dr. Jekyll and Mr. Hyde* (1920) opposite John Barrymore, and as Sergeant "Kat" Katczinsky in the brilliant production of *All Quiet on the Western Front*, with Lew Ayres, a film whose subsequent remake underscores the superiority of the original. He married Ethel Dale, a sculptor and actress, in Los Angeles, May 5, 1923; she survived him. As Lionel Barrymore had predicted, Wolheim's ugliness made him a successful actor, though it also caused him some anguish because it typecast him. His publicity frequently contained notice of his intent to have a "nose job."

WOMAN. In *Welded*,* she is the prostitute whom Michael Cape* visits in an act of vengeance on his wife. She is about twenty-six, heavily painted, "bovine," and has an Eastern European accent. She cannot understand Michael's semi-philosophical and literary maunderings, but she understands what he is trying to do. She tells him to go home but then she berates him for treating her like an object. In this way she echoes the attitude of Eleanor Cape,* who sees Michael's possessiveness as a prison. She shows that the difficulty of her life has not destroyed her spirit, and in her comforting of the weeping Michael she demonstrates the nurturing qualities that he seeks.

Y

YANK, a seaman on the S.S. *Glencairn*, "a rather good-looking rough" American; appears in *The Moon of the Caribbees** and *Bound East for Cardiff.** He dies after a fall into the hold in the latter play. The action of *Bound East for Cardiff* consists almost entirely of a dialogue between Yank and his friend, Driscoll,* who has been his shipmate for five years. They exchange reminiscences as Yank is dying and discover that each has independently yearned to buy a farm and take the other away from the sea. Yank has wanted to be buried on land, fearing the clutches of the sea, but his wish is unfulfilled—there is an unspoken implication that the sea will punish those who rebel against it. Yank's wish for a farm is thus an act of rebellion for which he must pay. As the fog of death covers his eyes, he remembers Fanny the barmaid who once offered to lend him money, and asks Driscoll to buy her the biggest box of candy he can find. Yank dies, therefore, after an act of charity and in the company of a friend. In *The Moon of the Caribbees*, Yank is a slighter character who attempts to appropriate Pearl,* "the youngest and prettiest" of the West Indian girls who come aboard. She, however, prefers Smitty.* See also *Children of the Sea.**

YANK, a fireman, the central character in *The Hairy Ape** (real name Robert Smith). Yank, at the beginning of the play is an ugly, squat, truculent, almost simian figure, the leader of all the firemen on board an unnamed steamship. He glories in his strength and identifies himself with the machinery he serves. He perceives himself as the prime mover of all machinery, the maker of steel, "the bottom," but someone on whom the entire movement of the industrial world depends. He "belongs," a favorite word with him. He has found a place for himself, one which satisfied him, in the inferno of the stokehole. This dream is shattered when Mildred Douglas,* a jaded young society woman, visits the stokehole in search of a new experience and sees Yank. She is appalled, frightened, and cries out, "The filthy beast." Yank is destroyed psychologically by this experience because he is forced to reevaluate his existence. From this time on, whenever he wants to think, he falls into the pose of Rodin's "The Thinker," and one ought to recall that this piece of sculpture was intended for the central position on top of the monumental work, "The Gates of Hell."

Yank is taken by his friend, Long,* a radical activist, to visit Fifth Avenue on a Sunday morning. There he sees firsthand the conspicuous consumption of the capitalist class. In an expressionistic scene, he bumps into assorted members of this group as they come out of church, but they merely say, "I beg your pardon" or fail completely to notice him. Finally, one man calls the police when Yank becomes violent, and he is imprisoned for thirty days. Yank does not belong on Fifth Avenue.

In prison he learns about the Industrial Workers of the World (IWW). He joins this organization in an attempt to get even with Mildred by blowing up the steel company her father owns. Steel has betrayed him. He has thought himself to be the personification of steel, but as a result of his experience he now sees steel as something that imprisons him in some kind of cage, whether it be the cage of the stoker's forecastle, the cage of prison, or the cage of social injustice. However, his incendiary ideas are too violent even for the IWW, and Yank is thrown onto the street.

In the final scene, Yank visits the gorilla in the zoo. He looked at the beauty of a sunrise and realized that he does not belong with that, and now he has come to see how it is with a real hairy ape in the zoo. Everyone has been calling him that, so he might as well be one. As he confides his sense of displacement to the gorilla, there almost seems to be communication between them, and Yank realizes the ugliness that Mildred has seen in him. He claims that the gorilla is more fortunate than he because the animal can at least have some memory of a more pleasant past in the jungle. He, however, has never had a place in which he belongs. He goes between heaven and hell, trying to find a place; but the gorilla, by definition, does not belong among men, and therefore he is put in a cage. He suggests that he and the gorilla take a stroll down Fifth Avenue—anything is better than merely dying passively in a cage. He opens the door and attempts to shake hands with the animal, who responds by crushing his ribs and then shuffling off. Yank realizes that he is dying and crawls into the gorilla's cage, holding himself upright by the bars, and then dies. O'Neill's final stage direction suggests that "perhaps the Hairy Ape at last belongs," a rather pessimistic thought.

Yank is a symbolic rather than a polemical figure. He reacts against society because he can find no place in it, and he is destroyed by his discovery that society has no use for such a man as he. But he is not to be read as a disappointed revolutionary. Rather, he is a symbol of modern man searching for certainties in a world which has lost its ancient truths. The days when men and the sea were one (as Paddy* suggests) are finished, and at first Yank believes that steel and machinery have taken their place. He is, therefore, the exemplar of a man who has accepted the dreams and promises of industrial society, only to find them wanting, like Willy Loman in Arthur Miller's *Death of a Salesman* (1949), or destructive, as Reuben Light* in *Dynamo** discovers when he wishes to become one with the machine. For some people, and this includes Brutus Jones* in *The Emperor Jones*,* society has no place, and therefore they must look elsewhere. Jones is forced to relive his lost past; but Yank, having no such resources, takes on the identity of the animal he resembles. But even the animal refuses this identification, and Yank is destroyed. Originally O'Neill had planned to make this character an Irishman but later had second thoughts. The play gains immediacy by the change.

YUSEF. In *The Fountain*,* the Moorish Minstrel of Scene i. He sings the song of the mysterious fountain which brings youth and enlightenment to some few chosen old men who are ever afterward revered as holy. He appears as one of the apparitions in the fountain to Juan Ponce de Leon,* who believes he has found what he seeks—the mystery of life and its essential unity. The minstrel appears first in his own person and later as a priest of Islam to indicate the real unity of all the major religions, Buddhism, Islam, paganism (represented by the Medicine Man*) and Christianity, represented by Luis de Alvarado.*

YVETTE. In *A Wife for a Life*,* the faithful wife of the Older Man,* the drunken mining engineer. She does not actually appear in the play, but she is described as the epitome of the long-suffering wife. At the time of the play she is only twenty-five, but she had been forced into marriage with the Older Man, some twenty years her senior. She put up with his drunkenness and brutality, and although she returned Jack's* love, she sent him away because she believed in fidelity to her marriage vows. After her husband disappears while seeking vengeance on Jack, she waits until she is legally free to marry before telegraphing Jack to say that she will marry him. The Older Man discovers the situation and rejoices that she has continued to love him for what he was, not hating him for what he has become. Deciding not to stand in the way of their happiness, the Older Man does not reveal himself, and Jack goes East to marry his "angel."

Chronology of Completed Plays of Eugene O'Neill by Date of Completion

It is not possible to establish a definitive chronology for O'Neill's plays, even after a study of notebooks, work diary, the Copyright Division of the Library of Congress, and the playwright's own statements on the subject. Frequently O'Neill was working on several plays simultaneously, while others existed as ideas in notebooks years before they were worked up. *The Hairy Ape,** for instance, was a short story rejected for publication and destroyed before the material was reworked into the play we know today.

The following chronology lists those plays known to have been completed, whether or not they have been produced. However, it is not really possible to determine whether a given play still remains unproduced, since documentation for productions worldwide is not definitive. Plays known to have been completed but later destroyed are included, but I have deliberately excluded consideration of destroyed plays in the abandoned cycle, "A Tale of Possessors, Self-Dispossessed,"* since the chronology of those materials is treated at length under that entry.

For further reference, the following tables of composition, all of which have some differences of approach and opinion, should be consulted: Törnqvist, 1969, pp. 256-65; Jordan Y. Miller, 1973, pp. 15-43; Floyd, 1981, pp. 388-393.

For more detailed accounts of composition the user is referred to individual entries.

The abbreviation NC stands for Not Copyrighted.

Completed Plays of Eugene O'Neill by Date of Completion

TITLE	DATE OF COMPLETION	DATE OF FIRST PRODUCTION
A Wife for a Life (1 act)	1913	—
The Web (1 act)	1913	—
Thirst (1 act)	1913	August ??, 1916
Recklessness (1 act)	1913	—
Warnings (1 act)	1913	—
Fog (1 act)	1914	January 5, 1917
Bread and Butter (4 acts)	1914	—
Children of the Sea (1 act), revised and produced as *Bound East for Cardiff* (1 act)	1914	— July 28, 1916

Abortion (1 act)	1914	October 27, 1959
The Movie Man (1 act)	1914	October 27, 1959
Servitude (3 acts)	1914	April 22, 1960
[The?] Dear Doctor (1 act)	1915 or earlier	Destroyed. NC.
"The Personal Equation" (4 acts), original title "The Second Engineer."	1915 or earlier	—
The Sniper (1 act)	1915	February 16, 1917
"A Knock at the Door" (1 act)	1915	Destroyed. NC.
"Belshazzar" (6 scenes), written with Colin Ford	1915	Destroyed. NC.
Before Breakfast (1 act)	1916	December 1, 1916
"Atrocity" (1 act)	1916	Destroyed. NC.
"The G.A.M." (1 act)	1916	Destroyed. NC.
Now I Ask You (3 acts)	1917	—
Ile (1 act)	1917	November 30, 1917
In the Zone (1 act)	1917	October 31, 1917
The Long Voyage Home (1 act)	1917	November 2, 1917
"The Reckoning" (4 acts)	1917 or 1918	—NC.
The Rope (1 act)	1918	April 26, 1918
Beyond the Horizon (3 acts)	1918	February 2, 1920
The Moon of the Caribbees (1 act)	1918	December 20, 1918
"Till We Meet"	1918	Destroyed. NC.
Shell Shock (1 act)	1918	—
The Dreamy Kid (1 act)	1918	October 31, 1919
Where The Cross Is Made (1 act)	1918	November 22, 1918
The Straw (3 acts)	1919	November 10, 1921
Chris Christophersen (3 acts)	1919	Produced as *Chris*, March 8, 1920
"Honor among the Bradleys" (1 act)	1919	Destroyed. NC.
"The Trumpet" (1 act)	1919	Destroyed. NC.
"Exorcism" (1 act)		March 26, 1920 Destroyed, N.C.
Gold (4 acts)	1920	June 1, 1921
"The Ole Davil" (4 acts) revised into "Anna Christie" (4 acts)	1920 1920	— November 2, 1921
The Emperor Jones (8 scenes)	1920	November 1, 1920
Diff'rent (2 acts)	1920	December 27, 1920
The First Man (4 acts), original title "The Oldest Man"	1921	March 4, 1922
The Hairy Ape (8 scenes)	1921	March 9, 1922
The Fountain (11 scenes)	1922	December 10, 1925
Welded (3 acts)	1923	March 17, 1924
All God's Chillun Got Wings (2 acts)	1923	May 15, 1924
The Ancient Mariner (1 act)	1923	April 6, 1924. NC.
"The Revelation of Saint John the Divine" (1 act)	1924	—NC.
Desire Under the Elms (3 acts)	1924	November 11, 1924

Marco Millions (3 acts)	1925	January 9, 1928
The Great God Brown (4 acts)	1925	January 23, 1926
Lazarus Laughed (4 acts)	1926	April 9, 1928
Strange Interlude (9 acts)	1927	January 30, 1928
Dynamo (3 acts)	1928	February 11, 1929
Mourning Becomes Electra (3 plays of 4, 5, and 4 acts)	1931	October 26, 1931
Ah, Wilderness! (4 acts)	1933	September 25, 1933
Days Without End (4 acts)	1933	December 27, 1933
The Calms of Capricorn (4 acts?)	1935?	—Not completed by O'Neill.
More Stately Mansions (3 acts)	1938?	September 11, 1967, not completed by O'Neill.
The Iceman Cometh (4 acts)	1939	October 9, 1946
Long Day's Journey into Night (4 acts)	1941	February 2, 1956
Hughie (1 act)	1941	September 18, 1958
A Touch of the Poet (4 acts)	1942	March 29, 1957
A Moon for the Misbegotten (4 acts)	1943	February 20, 1947

Film, Musical, Operatic and Balletic Adaptations of Works by Eugene O'Neill

FILM ADAPTATIONS

AH, WILDERNESS!, film version
Metro-Goldwyn-Mayer, 1935. Black and White
Producer: Hunt Stromberg
Director: Clarence Brown
Screenplay: Albert Hackett and Frances Goodrich
Music: Herbert Stothart
Camera: William Daniels, Clyde de Vinna
Cast: Sid: Wallace Beery
 Nat Miller: Lionel Barrymore
 Lily: Aline MacMahon
 Richard: Eric Linden
 Muriel: Cecilia Parker
 Tommy: Mickey Rooney
 Essie Miller: Spring Byington
 Mr. McComber: Charley Grapewin
 Arthur: Frank Albertson
 Wint Selby: Edward Nugent
 Mildred: Bonita Granville
 Belle: Helen Flint
 Miss Hawley: Helen Freeman

This film has some nice moments but suffers from too much respect for Wallace Beery. His role is expanded to the overall detriment of the play. The lighting in the love scene is rather dim. Mickey Rooney does a good job as Tommy. His success in the role led to the creation of the Andy Hardy series. A very free adaptation.

"ANNA CHRISTIE," film version
First National, 1923. Black and White. Silent
Producer: Thomas H. Ince

Director: John Griffith Wray
Titles: Unknown
Adaptation: Bradley King
Camera: Harry Sharp
Cast: Anna: Blanche Sweet
    Chris: George F. Marion
    Mat Burke: William Russell
    Marthy: Eugenie Basserer
    Brutal Cousin: Ralph Yearsley
    Tommy: Chester Conklin
    Anna's Uncle: George Siegman
    With Victor Potel and Fred Kohler

"ANNA CHRISTIE," film version
Metro-Goldwyn-Mayer, 1930. Black and White. Sound
Producer: Clarence Brown
Director: Clarence Brown. Additional director for German and Swedish versions, Jacques Feyder
Screenplay: Frances Marion
Art Director: Cedric Gibbons
Gowns: Adrian
Photography: William Daniels
Editor: Hugh Wynn
Sound: Douglas Shearer
Cast: Anna Gustafson: Greta Garbo*
    Mat Burke: Charles Bickford
    Chris Gustafson: George F. Marion
    Marthy Owen: Marie Dressler
    Johnny-the-Harp: James T. Mack
    Larry: Lee Phelps

This film opens up the action and changes the scene frequently, including Chris's barge in a storm, Anna and Mat at an amusement park, and also at a restaurant. The part of Marthy Owen is increased by including her in the last scene mentioned and also using her in dialogue with Chris to open the action of the entire film, cutting back on the bar room scenes. Liberties are taken with O'Neill's dialogue, even with Garbo's first words: "Gimme a whiskey—and fill it up." Garbo was considered excellent in this, her first talking role, and the return of Marie Dressler was celebrated as Marthy. In fact, she topped Garbo. This was a successful film and a good Garbo vehicle, though some critics objected to the Coney Island scene. George Marion recreated his stage role successfully, though at times his acting is too broad for the screen.

"ANNA CHRISTIE," film version
Metro-Goldwyn-Mayer, 1930. Black and White. Silent Version of the Preceding
Additional Credits:
Film Editor: Everett Douglas
Titles: Madeleine Ruthven

"ANNA CHRISTIE," film version
Metro-Goldwyn-Mayer, 1930. Black and White. German Version of the Preceding
Director: Jacques Feyder
Cast: Anna Gustafson: Greta Garbo*
      Mat Burke: Hans Junkermann
      Marthy Owen : Salka Viertel
      Chris Gustafson: Theo Shall

CONSTANT WOMAN, THE, film adaptation of *Recklessness**
The original title was to have been "Auction in Souls." World-Wide Films, distributed
by Fox, 1933. Black and white
Producer: E. W. Hammons
Continuity and Dialogue: Warren B. Duff and F. Hugh Herbert based on a play by Eugene
O'Neill
Director: Victor Schertizinger
Cast: Walt: Conrad Nagle
      Lou: Leila Hyams
      Jimmy: Tommy Conklin
      Marlene: Claire Windsor
      Beef: Stanley Fields
      Bouncer: Fred Kohler
      Leading Man: Robert Ellis
      Character Man: Lionel Belmore
      Radio Magnate: Alexander Carr

This film bears no resemblance to the play of *Recklessness*, from which it was allegedly
adapted. The major locales are those of a traveling tent show, a New York hotel, a
Galveston speakeasy, and a circus. Some of the publicity attached to the film will indicate
the general approach: "Human hearts on the block." "One woman wanted fame—another
was happy with love—and a boy was the pawn in the game they played." "Missing
mother love—a boy—caught in a maelstrom of confusions about his own parenthood."
The climax of the play, which leads to the ultimate reconciliation of Jimmy and his future
stepmother, involves an elephant stampede, a circus fire, and a fight with a tiger, from
which Jimmy is rescued by "the constant woman," Lou, who shields Jimmy from the
knowledge of his illegitimate birth. O'Neill received five thousand dollars for the rights
to the script, and his picture appeared prominently on the film's publicity posters.

DESIRE UNDER THE ELMS, film version
Paramount, 1958. Black and White
Producer: Don Hartman
Director: Delbert Mann
Screenplay: Irwin Shaw
Music: Elmer Bernstein
Camera: Daniel L. Frapp

Cast: Anna Cabot: Sophia Loren
      Eben Cabot: Anthony Perkins
      Ephraim Cabot: Burl Ives
      Simeon Cabot: Frank Overton
      Peter Cabot: Pernell Roberts
      Lucinda: Rebecca Welles
      Florence: Jean Willes
      Eben's Mother: Anne Seymour
      Fiddler: Ray Faut

This was a faithful, but overlong adaptation of the original, with certain adaptations necessitated by Miss Loren's accented English. Her performance was good, but Burl Ives was simply miscast as Ephraim. Anthony Perkins was good as Eben, but his concern for his dead mother was omitted, with concomitant weakening of his motivation. There was too much music, and one wonders whether it was necessary for the brothers to return to the farm with "fancy women." Altogether, the film lacked a consistent style of acting.

EMPEROR JONES, THE, film version
United Artists, 1933. Black and White
Producers: John Krimsky and Gifford Cochran
Director: Dudley Murphy
Screenplay: DuBose Heywood
Sound Recorder: J. Kame
Camera: Ernest Haller
Scenic Designer: Herman Reese
Cast: Brutus Jones: Paul Robeson*
      Smithers: Dudley Digges*
      Jeff: Frank Wilson
      Undine: Fredi Washington
      Dolly: Ruby Elzy
      Lem: George Haymid Stamper
      Marcella: Jackie Mayble
      Carrington: Brandon Evans
      Stick-Man: Taylor Gordon

There are two main problems with this film: (1) it attempts to "open up" the action by using a long expository section which reenacts the whole course of Brutus Jones's career before he becomes emperor of the island; (2) the special effects are clumsy and stagey. The literal reenactment tends to draw tension away from the climactic last quarter of the film which uses most of the O'Neill text, with, however, the excision of the third scene, that of the slave auction. The influence of the Hays Office can also be seen in minor changes in dialogue. The special effects, however, are very poorly handled, even for a film of that time. The crocodile looks too much like the papier-maché model it probably was, and the apparitions are too transparent to seem really frightening. The Witch Doctor, for instance, is too vaguely seen to arouse fear. The change of tools in the rockbreaking scene (Scene iv) to hammers rather than shovels gives Robeson a chance to sing "If I Had a Hammer," and this occurs again in the last quarter of the film. Scenes v-vi, dealing with the slave era of black American history, are excised, and Jones staggers into the clearing to die rather than being carried there. The film is best when it deals with the specific O'Neill material, and is reasonably faithful to the lines, except for the omitted scenes and some minor dialogue changes. Added scenes are laboriously contrived, in particular the throne-room scene presenting the Duke and Duchess of Manhattan, the Duke and Duchess of Newark, Lord and Lady Baltimore, and so forth. This is both clumsy and condescending. Dudley Digges is suitably nasty as Smithers, but the added characters are merely fillers. The best single thing about this film is, of course, the performance of Paul Robeson, which preserves for posterity some glimmering of that remarkable musical and theatrical performer in one of his most famous roles. Curiously, it also increases the stature of Charles Gilpin's* interpretation if, as contemporary critics allege, it was greater than that of Robeson. Among the additions to the play are Robeson's renditions of the songs "Water Boy," "Now Let Me Fly," and "I'm Travelin'."

HAIRY APE, THE, film version
United Artists, 1944. Black and White
Producer: Jules Levey
Director: Alfred Santell
Screenplay: Robert D. Andrews and Decla Dunning
Music: Michel Michelet and Edward Paul
Camera: Lucien Andriot
Cast: Yank: William Bendix
    Mildred: Susan Hayward
    Lazar: John Loder
    Helen: Dorothy Comingore
    Paddy: Roman Bohnen
    Long: Tom Fadden
    MacDougald: Alan Napier
    Gantry: Charles Cane
    Aldo: Raphael Storm
    Portuguese Proprietor: Charles La Torre
    Concertina Player: Don Zelaya
    Waitress: Mary Zavian
    Musician: Egon Becher
    Refugee Wife: Geseia Werbsek

William Bendix did a fairly good job and was at his best in the prison scene. Susan Hayward was rather artificial, and an attempt was made to boost her part by giving her a romance with a character not in the original play, Lazar. The film includes a great deal of mist and fog, reminiscent of the film of *The Long Voyage Home.**

ICEMAN COMETH, THE, film version
American Film Theater, 1973. Black and White
Producer: Ely Landau
Director: John Frankenheimer

Cast: Hickey: Lee Marvin
   Harry Hope: Fredric March*
   Larry Slade: Robert Ryan
   Don Parritt: Jeff Bridges
   Willie Oban: Bradford Dillman*
   Hugo Kalmar: Sorrell Booke
   Margie: Hildy Brooks
   Pearl: Nancy Juno Dawson
   Cora: Evans Evans
   Captain Cecil Lewis: Martyn Green
   Joe Mott: John McLiam
   Chuck Morello: Stephen Pearlman
   Rocky Pioggi: Tom Pedi
   General Piet Wetjoen: George Voskovec
   Moran: Bart Barnes
   Lieb: Don McGovern

Like the others in the American Film Theater series, this film was designed as a faithful rendition of the play. No attempt was made to open up the action, and the result was really that of a filmed play rather than an adaptation. Lee Marvin gave a good performance as Hickey, but he was disadvantageously compared with Jason Robards, Jr.,* whose stage performance of the role has reached legendary, definitive status.

LONG DAY'S JOURNEY INTO NIGHT, film version
Twentieth-Century Fox, 1962. Black and White
Producers: Ely Landau, Jack Dreyfus, Jr., Joseph E. Levine
Director: Sidney Lumet
Music: André Previn
Costume Design: Motley
Camera: Boris Kaufman
Production Design: Richard Sylbert
Cast: Mary Tyrone: Katharine Hepburn
   James Tyrone, Sr.: Ralph Richardson
   James Tyrone, Jr.: Jason Robards, Jr.*
   Edmund Tyrone: Dean Stockwell
   Cathleen: Jeanne Barr

This film follows the play very closely, without attempts to open up the action. Ralph Richardson gives an excellent interpretation of "the golden voice" of James Tyrone, Sr.; Katharine Hepburn gives her standard fey performance; while Jason Robards, Jr., is at times mesmerizing. Dean Stockwell is simply outclassed. A reverent translation from stage to screen.

LONG VOYAGE HOME, THE, film adaptation of the S.S. *Glencairn* plays
United Artists, 1940. Black and White
Producer: Walter Wanger
Director: John Ford
Screenplay: Dudley Nichols

Music: Richard Hageman
Music Director: Edward Paul
Art Director: James Basevi
Camera: Gregg Toland
Editor: Sherman Todd
Special Effects: R. T. Layton and R. O. Binger
Interior Decorations: Julia Heron
Cast: Ole Olson: John Wayne
      Driscoll: Thomas Mitchell
      Smitty: Ian Hunter
      Cocky: Barry Fitzgerald
      Captain: Wilfred Lawson
      Freda: Mildred Natwick (debut)
      Axel Swanson: John Qualen
      Yank: Ward Bond
      Donkeyman: Arthur Shields
      Davis: Joseph Sawyer
      Crimp: (Nick): J. M. Kerrigan
      Tropical Woman: Rafaela Ottiano
      Bumboat Girls: Carmen Morales, Carmen D'Antonio, Tina Menard, Judith Linden,
         Elena Martinez, Lita Cortez, Soledad Gonzales
      Scotty: David Hughes
      Joe, Proprietor: Billy Bevan
      First Mate: Cyril McLaglan
      Second Mate: Douglas Walton
      Frank: Constantine Romanoff
      Cook: Edgar "Blue" Washington
      Mr. Clifton: Lionel Pope
      Kate: Jane Crawley
      Mag: Maureen Roden-Ryan
      Paddy: Bob Perry
      Norway: Constant Franke
      Max: Harry Tenbrook
      Tim: Dan Borzage
      Captain of the *Amindra*: Arthur Miles
      First Mate of the *Amindra*: Henry Woods
      Dock Policemen: James Flavin, Lee Shumway
      British Naval Officer: Wyndham Standing
      Bald Man: Lowell Drew
      Seaman: Sammy Stein
      Bergman: Jack Rennick

This is a faithful adaptation of the spirit of the original, but there is an overabundance of fog. Of all the film adaptations of O'Neill plays, this is the only one which met with the approval of the playwright. He deeply respected the work of John Ford, and Dudley Nichols treated the text with great consideration and careful alteration. O'Neill received twenty thousand dollars for the rights.

MOURNING BECOMES ELECTRA, film version
RKO, 1947. Black and White
Producer, Director, Adapter: Dudley Nichols
Music: Richard Hageman
Camera: George Barnes
Art Director: Albert D'Agostino
Cast: Lavinia Mannon: Rosalind Russell
　　　Orin Mannon: Michael Redgrave
　　　Ezra Mannon: Raymond Massey
　　　Christine Mannon: Katina Paxinou
　　　Adam Brant: Leo Genn
　　　Peter Niles: Kirk Douglas
　　　Hazel Niles: Nancy Coleman
　　　Seth Beckwith: Henry Hull
　　　Landlady: Sara Allgood
　　　Dr. Blake: Thurston Hall
　　　Amos Ames: Walter Baldwin
　　　Mrs. Hills: Elizabeth Risdon
　　　Josiah Borden: Erskine Sanford
　　　Abner Small: Jimmy Conlin
　　　Reverend Hills: Lee Baker
　　　Joe Silva: Tito Vuolo
　　　Mrs. Borden: Emma Dunn
　　　Louisa Ames: Nora Cecil
　　　Minnie Ames: Marie Blake
　　　Ira Mackel: Clem Bevans
　　　Eben Nobel: Jean Clardenden

In general the film follows the original, though compressing the action from six hours to three. Scenically the film is good, though the continually shifting camera angles tend to weaken the focus of the action. Michael Redgrave gives a good performance, but the women are less effective, Rosalind Russell lacking sufficient malevolence and Katina Paxinou sufficient sexuality. Overall, it is tedious rather than moving.

STRANGE INTERLUDE, film version
Metro-Goldwyn-Mayer, 1932. Black and White
Producer: Irving Thalberg
Director: Robert Z. Leonard
Screenplay: Bess Meredyth and C. Gardiner Sullivan
Camera: Lee Garmes
Editor: Margaret Booth
Art Director: Cedric Gibbons
Cast: Nina Leeds: Norma Shearer
　　　Ned Darrell: Clark Gable
　　　Sam Evans: Alexander Kirkland
　　　Charles Marsden: Ralph Morgan
　　　Gordon (as a child): Tad Alexander
　　　Gordon (as a man): Robert Young
　　　Mrs. Evans: May Robson

Madeline: Maureen O'Sullivan
Professor Leeds: Henry B. Walthall
Maid: Mary Alden

The adapters managed a skillful compression of this extremely long play, cutting long speeches and monologues to bare essentials and eliminating repetition. For instance, Nina's recounting to Darrell of Mrs. Evans's advice is begun, then a log falls off the fire to take over the screen; and when that image dissolves, Nina has reached the end of her tale. The film is also given circularity of structure by the insertion of opening sequences in which a whirling globe and stock war shots are seen, with Nina crying, "Gordon, come back to me," as his plane falls in flames. In the concluding scene, Gordon's "hydroplane" flies away as the camera pans from plane to the ground. The action is continually opened up, and Nina is given two scenes in which she looks at Gordon's portrait and then at Sam's, to indicate the comparison. Dr. Leeds also dies on screen, and there is a rather coarse foreshadowing of and emphasis on the lunacy in the Evans family when Aunt Bessie is shown looking out of an upper window, laughing insanely. Her laughter also appears on the soundtrack during Mrs. Evans's narrative, a scene which concludes with Nina being taken upstairs to see the old lady. There are film tours of all the Evans and Leeds dwellings, and there is a rather sentimental exploitation of Nina's maternal feelings in sequences showing her, for example, bathing her child. The film-makers also show their technical skill in the boat race and final scenes. However, this continual shifting of focus tends to blur the inner lives of the characters so that the external action becomes a trifle melodramatic. On the whole the film was unusually frank and advanced for its time; it was well photographed, and the sensational aspects were understated. Unfortunately, it was designed as a star vehicle in which Norma Shearer and Clark Gable were miscast. The filmmakers handled the interior monologues most effectively, doing them as voice-overs, with the result that the action was speeded up. This film was a respectable attempt to transfer a noteworthy play to the screen. Much publicity was given to the voice-over device: "You hear their secret thoughts."

SUMMER HOLIDAY, film adaptation, musical of *Ah, Wilderness!*
Metro-Goldwyn-Mayer, 1948. Color
Producer: Arthur Freed
Director: Rouben Mamoulian
Screenplay: Adapted by Irving Buechner and Jean Holloway from the screenplay of *Ah, Wilderness!* by Albert Hackett and Frances Goodrich
Music: Henry Warren
Music Director: Lenny Hayton
Camera: Charles Schoenbaum
Cast: Richard Miller: Mickey Rooney
Muriel: Gloria de Haven
Mr. Nat Miller: Walter Huston
Uncle Sid: Frank Morgan
Tommy: Butch Jenkins
Belle: Marilyn Maxwell
Cousin Lily: Agnes Moorehead
Mrs. Miller: Selena Royle
Arthur Miller: Michael Kirby

Mildred: Shirley Jones
Wint: Hal Hackett
Elsie Rand: Ann Francis
Mr. McComber: John Alexander
Miss Hawley: Virginia Brissac
Mr. Peabody: Howard Freeman
Mrs. McComber: Alice MacKenzie
Crystal: Ruth Brady

A travesty of the original in which Mickey Rooney plays his Andy Hardy role. There are some good scenes, but the film lacks a coherent style.

OPERAS AND MUSICAL ADAPTATIONS

ALL GOD'S CHILLUN GOT WINGS, opera in three acts.
Composer: John Frans Ruivenkamp
Libretto: John Frans Ruivenkamp
Copyright 1982.
No further information located.

"ALWAYS, ALWAYS, FOREVER AGAIN," song, words from *The Great God Brown.*
Composer: William Moyer
No further information located.

"AT THE COURT OF KUBLAI KAAN." Incidental Music to *Marco Millions*, composed by Emerson Whithorne.* Published as a piano score (New York: Carl Fischer, c1948), eight pages.

BEFORE BREAKFAST, an opera, loosely based on the O'Neill play. In the libretto by Frank Corsaro, the unnamed Woman, who sings the forty-minute monologue, is a former marathon dancer for whom everything afterwards has been a decline. She is hostile and cruel to her husband, but she is hereby given both motivation and also a three-minute jazz sequence. The music is composed in the mode of Gian Carlo Menotti, and the work is really a forty-minute mad scene.
Production Data: First performed by the New York City Opera at the New York State Theatre, Lincoln Center, New York City, October 9, 1980
Composer: Thomas Pasatieri*
Libretto: Frank Corsaro*
Staging: Frank Corsaro
Dance Sequence: Zoya Leporska
Conductor: Imre Pallo
Cast: Woman: Marilyn Zschau

While Zschau's performance was praised, the opera was not well received. "Do we really need two Menottis?" asked the *New York Times*. The piece was considered "weak."

DESIRE UNDER THE ELMS, operatic adaptation. Workshop performances under the auspices of the Eugene O'Neill Theatre Center, Connecticut, held at Connecticut College,

New London, August 10, 12, 1978, assisted by a grant from the National Endowment for the Humanities.
Composer: Edward Thomas
Libretto: Joe Masteroff
Director: Joseph J. Krakora
Music Director: Paulette Haupt-Nolen
Cast: Eben Cabot: Tenor, Michael Best
        Abbie Cabot: Soprano, Carol Todd
        Ephraim Cabot: Bass-Baritone, William Fleck
        Peter Cabot: Baritone, Sean Barker
        Simeon Cabot: Baritone, Ken Bridges

This performance was given without orchestra, the musical accompaniment being provided by two pianos. At the time, the composer had been working for eight years on the work.

EMPEROR, JONES, THE, operatic adaptation. World premiere, Metropolitan Opera House, New York City, matinee, January 7, 1933 (on a double bill with Leoncavallo's *I Pagliacci*). (11 performances).
Composer: Louis Gruenberg*
Libretto: Louis Gruenberg; printed libretto compiled, *but not written*, by Kathleen de Jaffa
Conductor: Tullio Serafin
Chorus Master: Giulio Setti
Stage Manager: Alexander Sanine
Set Design: Jo Mielziner
Cast: Brutus Jones: Baritone, Lawrence Tibbett
        Henry Smithers: Tenor, Marek Windheim
        Old Native Woman: Soprano, Pearl Besuner
        Congo Witch Doctor: Dancer Hemsley Winfield
        Soldiers, "Formless Fears," Jeff, Convicts, A Prison Guard, A Planter, An Auctioneer, Slaves, and others

Act I: In the palace of the Emperor Jones on a West Indian island in the 1920s. Act II: In the forest, nightfall, night, and dawn. There is a prologue and an interlude. The second act is divided into five scenes.
    The action of the opera follows the play quite closely, except for the omission of the final scene and also one very important change: Brutus Jones *commits suicide* with his last remaining silver bullet. This change has often been criticized as diluting the character of Jones and lacking motivation, but it is important to note that O'Neill read and approved Gruenberg's libretto. The Congo Witch Doctor, followed by a pack of blacks, becomes the pursuer; and after Jones's death before the crocodile god under a voodoo moon, the natives pick up Jones's body, carrying it out in triumph to the sound of orgiastic stamping and fierce cries, a conclusion that Paul Rosenfeld (*New Republic*, February 22, 1933) thought too theatrical. Olin Downes (*New York Times*, January 8, 1933) hailed the opera as a triumph and liked the performance of Lawrence Tibbett whom Rosenfeld thought overacted somewhat. Downes also noted that Jones had curiously little singing to do, while Rosenfeld remarked that the outstanding vocal number, the spiritual, "Standing in the Need of a Prayer," was an interpolation. Downes considered the music "superbly

potent," particularly as a dramatic emphasis to the plot. However, in his more critical comments, Rosenfeld maintained that Gruenberg really did little more than accentuate what was already in the O'Neill play, finding the music rather derivative, though showing "considerable technical facility," and also lacking in progression, "a sort of superior bogey music which plays entirely on the nerves." Also, as a result of the orchestration, the sound of the tom-tom was less effective in the opera than the drama. The composer makes use of "song-speech, discordant sounds, complex rhythmical patterns, loud out-cries, leading to orgiastic intensity with little relief for the audience."

Despite achieving a front-page column in the *New York Times* on January 8, 1933 (along with the funeral of former President Calvin Coolidge), the opera soon dropped from the repertory, although it was given seven times in 1933 and four more in 1933–1934. It also received a noteworthy performance at the Mecca Temple (now New York City Center) with an all-black cast headed by Jules Bledsoe. In 1946 it was performed in Chicago and later in Rome and Palermo. In 1950 the National Broadcasting Company planned a television performance of the work, and William Warfield (famous for his interpretation of Porgy in Gershwin's *Porgy and Bess* in the all-black touring cast of the work) was signed for the role of Jones. However, the project was shelved, despite sporadic attempts to revive it, on the grounds that the work was demeaning to blacks, a shift in opinion which may militate against its return.

Gruenberg himself was hurt by this implication of racism, particularly in view of his pioneering attempts at integrating jazz and classical music. In his last years he was perceived (and quite unfairly) as more a writer of Hollywood film scores than the serious composer he really was. He took care to separate these two parts of his career, but critics tended to assess them in comparison, with the ironic result that his operatic and orchestral work was considered too commercial and his Hollywood work too serious. (Prepared with the help of Dr. Irma Gruenberg.)

ILE, opera in one act.
Composer: Beatrice Laufer
Libretto: Beatrice Laufer
Copyright 1957. Reregistered 1981 with new changes in music.
No further information located.

LA LUNA DEI CARAIBI, opera based on *The Moon of the Caribbees.*
Composer: Adriano Lualdi*
Libretto: Adriano Lualdi
Premiere: 1953, printed score 1952, written 1944
Cast: Pearl, a West Indian black: Soprano, lyric or spinto
      Bella, a West Indian black: Alto
      Gianni, ship's boy: Mezzo or singing boy
      Smitty, a sailor: Lyric tenor
      Cocky, a sailor: Comic tenor
      Loris, a sailor: Comic baritone
      Yank, a sailor: Dramatic baritone or comic bass
      Driscoll, a sailor: Comic bass
      Old Tom, donkeyman: Bass
      Captain: Bass
      Susie, Violet, Black Women, other blacks: mixed chorus.

Other sailors, stokers, engineers: chorus of tenors and basses, no more than twenty-four.

The opera follows the play closely. It is composed in music noted for its coloristic qualities. The opera has not been performed in the United States.

MOON OF THE CARIBBEES, THE, operatic adaptation by Adriano Lualdi.* See *La Luna dei Caraibi.*

MOURNING BECOMES ELECTRA, operatic adaptation in three acts and seven scenes. Commissioned and given its world premiere by the Metropolitan Opera Association, New York City, March 17, 1967.
Composer: Marvin David Levy*
Libretto: Henry Willis Butler
Conductor: Zubin Mehta
Stage Director: Michael Cacoyannis
Costume and Set Designer: Boris Aronson
Cast: Christine Mannon: Soprano, Marie Collier
        Lavinia Mannon: Soprano (spinto or dramatic), Evelyn Lear
        Jed: Bass, Raymond Michalski
        Adam Brant: Dramatic Baritone, Sherrill Milnes
        Peter Niles: Lyric Baritone, Ron Bottcher
        Helen Niles: Lyric Soprano, Lillian Sukis
        Gen. Ezra Mannon: Bass Baritone, John Macurdy
        Orin Mannon: High Baritone or Tenor, John Reardon
        Chorus: Servants (Sopranos); Townswomen (Altos); Townsmen (Tenors); Field-Workers (Basses); Soldiers, Sailors, Dockworkers.

The action of the opera follows that of the trilogy quite closely, each play here being compressed into one act. The name of Hazel Niles has been changed to Helen, obviously for purposes of euphony. Permission for unrestricted adaptation of the O'Neill text was given by Carlotta Monterey* O'Neill after the intercession of her old friend, Carl Van Vechten, and minimal advance royalties were requested. After a preliminary hearing of the work, Rudolf Bing, then director of the Metropolitan Opera, offered Marvin David Levy a commission for it, and the work was performed during the opening season in the Met's new house at Lincoln Center. In general, the critics were not particularly kind to the music, thinking that the play itself overpowered it. Also, the necessary compression of the action tended to give a version that was considered too truncated (though this was probably unavoidable), even though the work ran over three and one-half hours. It was later trimmed, by the omission of an orchestral interlude.

Harold Schonberg (*New York Times,* March 18, 1967) commented on the lack of melody in the score and the dependence on "heightened recitative," noting that the music was not particularly original and drawing attention to the Benjamin Britten-esque quality of the Orin-Lavinia encounter. When the production was again performed, the *Times* reviewer thought the score "weak and pretentious" and said that the success of the opera was one of production rather than musical merit, criticizing the obvious nature of some of the devices employed: string glissandos in the incest scene, for instance. Overall, the score was considered glorified "background music" with a curiously "neutral" and "old fashioned" approach, projecting an eerie and ghostlike quality, yet leaving the hearers

curiously unsatisfied. The two sopranos, Marie Collier and Evelyn Lear, were praised, though some considered their acting a trifle exaggerated. Along with Samuel Barber's *Antony and Cleopatra*, the other American work commissioned for the opening season of the new Metropolitan Opera House, this work soon dropped from the repertory, though a later revival was planned in Wisconsin.
European Premiere: Dortmund Opera, West German, November 1969.

NEW GIRL IN TOWN, musical in two acts based on *"Anna Christie."*
Produced by Frederick Brisson, Robert E. Griffiths, and Harold S. Prince at the Forty-sixth Street Theatre, New York City, May 14, 1957 (431 performances).
Book: George Abbott
Music and Lyrics: Bob Merrill
Dances and Musical Numbers: Bob Fosse
Sets and Costumes: Rouben Ter-Arutunian
Musical Direction: Hal Hastings
Orchestrations: Robert Russell Bennett and Philip J. Lang
Dance Music Devised by Roger Adams
Hair Styles: Ronald DeMann
Production Stage Manager: Fred Hebert
Cast: Lily: Lulu Bates
       Alderman: Michael Quinn
       Chris: Cameron Prud'homme
       Seaman: H. F. Green
       Marthy: Thelma Ritter
       Oscar: Del Anderson
       Pete: Eddie Philips
       Mrs. Smith: Dorothy Stinnette
       Bartender: Mark Dawson
       Anna: Gwen Verdon
       Pearl: Mara Landi
       Mat: George Wallace
       Mrs. Hammacher: Jean Handzlick
       Masher: John Aristides
       Politician: H. F. Green
       Krimp: John Ford
       Henry: Edgar Daniels

The show was considered to have a dated, lightweight book, but it was a well-produced extravaganza with outstanding performances by Gwen Verdon and Thelma Ritter, though Miss Verdon was a better dancer than a singer. There were two good numbers: "Look at 'Er" and "Flings," particularly the latter (sung by Miss Ritter).

TAKE ME ALONG, musical in two acts based on *Ah, Wilderness!*
Produced by David Merrick, with Edward Fuller, assistant, at the Sam Shubert Theatre, New York City, October 22, 1959 (448 performances).
Book: adapted by Joseph Stein and Robert Russell
Music and Lyrics: Bob Merrill
Choreography: Onna White

Staged by: Peter Glenville
Scene Designer: Oliver Smith
Lighting: Jean Rosenthal
Costumes: Miles White
Musical Direction and Vocal Arrangements: Lehman Engel
Ballet and Incidental Music: Laurence Rosenthal
Orchestrations: Philip J. Lang
Production Supervisor: Neil Hartley
General Stage Manager: Lucia Victor
Cast: Nat Miller: Walter Pidgeon
      Mildred Miller: Zeme North
      Art Miller: James Cresson
      Tommy Miller: Luke Halpin
      Essie Miller: Una Merkel
      Lily: Eileen Herlie
      Richard Miller: Robert Morse
      Muriel Macomber [sic]: Susan Luckey
      Dave Macomber [sic]: Fred Miller
      Sid: Jackie Gleason
      Wint: Peter Conlow
      Bartender: Jack Collins
      Belle: Arlene Golonka
      The Drunk: Gene Varrone
      Salesman: Bill McDonald
      The Beardsley Dwarf: Charles Bolender
      Salome: Rae McLean

The *New York Times* reviewer was enthusiastic about the second act in which all elements of the show came together, including a bizarre Aubrey Beardsley ballet. Robert Morse was universally praised for his performance, as were all the women. Jackie Gleason, as Sid, was thought to have given a slightly cheap vaudeville-drunk characterization in Act I but to have improved in Act II. While the first act suffered from excessive exuberance and blaring noise, the second act managed to convey the mood of gently comic nostalgia of the play.

BALLETS

EMPEROR JONES, THE, ballet based on the play by Eugene O'Neill.
Performed by the José Limón Dance Company at the Empire State Music Festival, Ellenville, New York, July 12, 1956.
Choreography: José Limón
Music: Heitor Villa-Lobos
Conductor: Heitor Villa-Lobos
Orchestra: The Symphony of the Air
Costumes: Pauline Lawrence
Design: Kim Edgar Swados

Cast: Jones: José Limón
Smithers: Lucas Hoving
Natives, Witch Doctor, and others: Richard Fitzgerald, Michael Hollander, Harland
MacCallum, Martin Morginsky, Chester Wolenski.

The performance was well reviewed, both Limón and Hoving being singled out for
favorable comment. Pauline Lawrence's costume for Limón was particularly admired.
The music was considered to be suitable, managing to rise to atmospheric heights, though
the incessant drumbeats which O'Neill wanted throughout the play appeared to have been
overlooked.

"GREAT GOD BROWN, THE," story outline for choreography.
Writer: Beatrice Laufer. Copyright 1982.
No further information located.

O'Neill's Theory and Practice of the Theatre: An Assessment

(*Note:* Dates of plays are completion dates.)

EXPERIMENTS IN REALISM

Throughout his career, O'Neill was an experimenter, reacting against the theatre of his own day and continually asserting the seriousness of his dramatic art. He began with a conscious reaction against the melodramatic, commercial theatre epitomized both by the career of his own father, James O'Neill,* as the perennial Count of Monte Cristo, and ironically, by the short, minimally successful career of his third wife, Carlotta Monterey.*

Nevertheless, some of his earliest experiments showed the influence of melodrama, particularly *Thirst** (1913) and *Fog** (1914), while *Bread and Butter** (1914) and *Abortion** (1914) end with suicides. *The Moon of the Caribbees** (1917), however, represents something of an advance in its attempt to integrate both music and drama to create a mood. O'Neill was to try the same kind of thing in *Where the Cross Is Made** (1918) in attempting to involve the entire audience in a collective hallucinatory experience with the appearance of the ghosts of drowned sailors.

However, his first successful plays, particularly *Beyond the Horizon** (1918) and "*Anna Christie*"* (1920), are exercises in dramatic realism, and they, and others, betray the influence of continental dramatists, including Henrik Ibsen, August Strindberg, Gerhard Hauptmann, and Frank Wedekind. Like Ibsen, O'Neill displayed some interest in social problems, but that was short-lived, and the basic Ibsen influence appears only in his early technique. From Strindberg, however, the influence was lasting, particularly in O'Neill's approach to relationships between men and women. Even in the early *Bread and Butter*, one finds the deleterious influence of woman as wife, which he was to use again in *Before Breakfast** (1916) and *Beyond the Horizon*. In this third play, his first Broadway success, the blame for the failure of both Andrew Mayo* and Robert Mayo* rests with the woman, Ruth Atkins* Mayo. Another Strindberg influence should be noted in his use of another theme: that of the weak character who manages to control the apparently stronger one. Clearly seen in this early play, it is repeated time and again; as late as *More Stately Mansions** (begun 1935 and unfinished), Deborah Harford* battles Sara Melody* for control of the life of her son, Simon Harford.*

At this earlier time, O'Neill also chose unexpected themes and locales. In *The Straw** (1919) he wrote of romance in a tuberculosis sanitorium, and in the four plays that later became known as the S.S. *Glencairn* group* (1914–1918), he wrote of the forecastle life of semi-articulate sailors. *The Dreamy Kid** (1918) represents his first major use of black characters in a drama which seems almost a companion piece to his very early *The Web** (1913) in its portrayal of the seamy world of prostitutes and criminals. Nonetheless, he had not quite liberated himself from the theatrical tyranny of the happy ending. Even in *Beyond the Horizon*, some people have taken the bleak conclusion as an ambiguous one, believing that Andrew and Ruth may find happiness of some kind. Similarly, in "*Anna Christie*" (1920), what O'Neill meant as an incipiently tragic ambiguity was misinterpreted as a conventionally happy matrimonial conclusion. He is also making use of stock theatrical devices and characters, even here, the culminating work of his "realistic" period, particularly in the situation of Anna Christopherson,* the reluctant prostitute, who is reformed by a combination of nature (the sea) and love (Mat Burke*). However, there is a glint of something original in Anna's outburst against men and society for having made her what she is (Act III).

EXPRESSIONISM AND BEYOND

That O'Neill was already moving beyond the conventional is evidenced in *The Emperor Jones** (1920). Here he tries to involve his audience in a collective experience that goes beyond his experimental *Moon of the Caribbees* and *Where the Cross Is Made* and now makes use of C. J. Jung's theory of the racial memory. As Brutus Jones* replays the entire history of American blacks in reverse, the audience is meant to experience an almost total physical and emotional involvement through the hypnotic beat of the tom-tom as it increases in speed and intensity, while Jones achieves a symbolic status. This play also shows O'Neill's developing habit of pressing against the boundaries of stage illusionism, and moving into expressionism.

Diff'rent* (1920) represents a return to realism, but it does have some importance as introducing the theme of the Blessed Isles that O'Neill was later to use in *Mourning Becomes Electra** (1931). *The First Man** (1921), however, shows O'Neill in a milieu in which he never really succeeded—upper-middle-class suburbia—and is eminently forgettable.

His next foray into expressionism is *The Hairy Ape** (1921), and he uses the formal elements of this approach even more self-consciously than before. The forecastle is barred to look like a prison, while the stokehole is representative of hell, and the stokers are a carefully chosen collection of men representing the major races of the world. The Fifth Avenue scene has both expressionistic set and behavior, while some of the characters are masked. And throughout the play the motif of the cage is visually evoked. There is also some social commentary in that Yank,* the symbolically named protagonist, is a victim of industrialism, though at first he is unaware of it. When he does discover his situation and learns that he does not "belong," he, like Brutus Jones before him, regresses until he is finally reduced to seeking companionship from the animal world, which destroys him.

After these plays, O'Neill's experiments became more daring, pressing the resources of stage mechanics even further and finally reaching the almost completely unstageable in *Lazarus Laughed** (1926). He also began to develop and practice his theories of the drama, insisting upon high seriousness in the theatre as a means of teaching his audience a philosophy of life. In *The Fountain** (1922), he finds the solution in Juan Ponce de Leon's* search not just for the fountain of youth, but for the mystery of human existence. He finds it in love, reconciliation, and unselfishness. The high point of the play comes when representatives of the major world religions appear in the fountain, along with the young Beatriz de Cordova who is Love.

A quasi-expressionist return to the subject of marriage comes with *Welded** (1923), in which the inability of husband and wife to communicate is shown by the device of having each inhabit a separate circle of stage lighting, and only after they climb the stairs to reconciliation (in a kind of calvary scene) do their pools of light merge. This play is clearly based on the playwright's own marriage to Agnes Boulton* O'Neill. Marriage is also the theme of *All God's Chillun Got Wings** (1923), compounded with the added theme of interracial coexistence in the face of inherited racial stereotypes. A Strindbergian theme recurs here in the apparently weak woman-wife, Ella Downey,* who destroys her husband, the stronger Jim Harris.* Significantly, an African tribal mask is an important element in this play, prefiguring a greater interest in masking yet to come. Also, like the later Nina Leeds* in *Strange Interlude** (1927), Ella Downey regresses to a childish state.

With *Marco Millions** (1925), O'Neill attempts a synthesis of themes within a mixed play which includes expressionistic approaches. Marco Polo* is, of course, a recognizable American Babbitt, an exploitive businessman in pursuit of the almighty dollar, a go-getting technocrat. For him, money transcends love, and in the death of the Princess Kukachin,* the audience is to know that Marco has made the wrong choice. However, the play fails to hold together because the satire overwhelms the message, which seems to be that death is but a rite of passage to something greater (but unspecified) and that love is the center of existence. The play does show O'Neill's interest in oriental philosophy, but it offers a rather woolly-minded solution.

At this time O'Neill was also becoming interested in the development of "total theatre," or "plastic theatre." In *The Ancient Mariner** (1923), he attempted what was essentially a dramatic staging of the Coleridge poem, with masked actors, suitable sound effects, and evocative lighting. When this failed he did not bother to stage its experimental counterpart, "The Revelation of St. John the Divine" (1924).

EXPERIMENTS IN MYTH

The year 1924 is important in O'Neill's development because he began to work seriously with mythic elements in *Desire Under the Elms*.* This play and the later *Dynamo** (1928) indicate the two differing approaches to myth that O'Neill was to exploit for the remainder of his career. In *Desire*, O'Neill should be perceived as a *myth-user*, while in *Dynamo* he attempts to be a *myth-maker*, seeking a creed that will suit the modern temper, which rejects the claims and beliefs of orthodox religion. Significantly, O'Neill is more successful as myth-user than myth-maker, as *Desire* and the later trilogy, *Mourning Becomes Electra** (1931), indicate. Perhaps the strength of O'Neill's mind lay in eclecticism rather than original thought, and whenever he attempted to propound a new philosophy or creed he stumbled badly, retreating into romanticism, as in *The Fountain* and *Marco Millions*, or incoherence, as in *Dynamo*.

In *Desire Under the Elms*, however, O'Neill takes the Phaedra, Medea, and Oedipus myths and embeds them in puritanism, in the granitehard religious world of New England, itself part of the American mythic past. "God's not easy," as Ephraim Cabot* points out, understanding that he must pay for his Dionysian experiments and inclinations. Yet another mythic element lies behind this play in the theme of stubborn fertility, while another O'Neill theme intrudes once more—that of the weaker subduing the stronger. Eben Cabot's* mother reaches from beyond the grave to achieve vengeance upon the husband who had killed her with hard work. The stage set with its simultaneous staging seemed revolutionary in its day (but it was really a return to earlier conventions), and there is a visual evocation of the symbiotic relationship between the maternity of the trees and the action of the play. The somewhat melodramatic ending is curiously unprepared for, and the sudden transformation of lust into sacrificial love in both Abbie Putnam Cabot* and Eben Cabot is unconvincing. Nevertheless, the play has power and remains one of O'Neill's great achievements, while it also introduces the Dionysus-Apollo opposition which O'Neill was later to use in *The Great God Brown** (1925).

O'Neill's most creative use and amalgamation of diverse myths comes with *Mourning Becomes Electra*. Here, in the form of a classical trilogy, O'Neill evokes the *Oresteia* in form and action while exploiting archetypal American historical time and place: Brigadier-General Ezra Mannon's* return from the War Between the States (a war that still has the mythic resonances of ancient chivalry) is superimposed on the Puritan tradition, New England, and the mercantilism of modern America, all of which have mythic significance. O'Neill also includes the sea and the world of sail, as well as the Civil War, in the chantey, "Shenandoah," and makes use of the mythic response evoked by South Sea islands—"The Blessed Isles"—with their supposed freedom from cant and restrictions, the epitome of escape from an oppressive past. The equation of characters with their classical counterparts is deliberately inexact, with changes made for dramatic impact, to make this play a brilliant intellectual feat of mythic integration and synthesis. The conclusion in which Lavinia Mannon* follows her destiny by entering the Mannon house and closing the door is not only a superlative dramatic conclusion but an equally fine recension of classic archetypal myth in terms of American mythic and religious history.

Having tried some myth-making in *The Fountain* and *Marco Millions*, O'Neill attempted to forge an entirely new belief for modern man in a proposed trilogy, "Myth-Plays for the God-Forsaken."* In the first of these plays, *Dynamo*, he sought a center of belief in a curious mixture of material. He takes off from Henry Adams in "The Virgin and the Dynamo," exalting the power of the machine and having his hero (symbolically named Reuben Light*) sacrifice himself on the dynamo, after killing his girlfriend, Ada Fife,* because her kind of sexual love has turned him aside from his worship of the totemic machine and dedication to that totem in human form, the bovine May Fife,* the earth-mother. The play was so difficult to write that O'Neill frequently turned aside, finishing it in 1928.

The second play of the trilogy, *Days Without End** (1933), is based on his marriage to Carlotta, who is the original of Elsa Loving.* But again he had problems in forging his mythology and his credo for love and marriage. The conclusion he finally chose, with John Loving* prostrate before the crucifix in a Roman Catholic church, has a vague recollection of *Welded* and a very specific affinity with the conclusion of *Dynamo*. But while Reuben dies as the result of a sacrificial act, John Loving is supposed to be moving into a new life. So roundly was this solution attacked that O'Neill abandoned the trilogy entirely, stung by the suggestion that he was returning to Catholicism. The material of the proposed third play, "It Cannot be Mad"* (also once entitled "On to Betelgeuse,"* and "On to Hercules,"* was later transferred to "The Life of Bessie Bowen" (or Bolan, or Bowlan)* and planned as the last play of the abandoned cycle "A Tale of Possessors,

Self-Dispossessed.* There it ran through the title "Twilight of Possessors, Self-Dispossessed,* before finally becoming "Hair of the Dog."* It was destroyed in 1943.

EXPERIMENTS IN MASK

With *The Great God Brown* (1925), O'Neill offered his first attempt at fully masked drama. Certainly he had used masks earlier in *The Hairy Ape*, but they were an afterthought, suggested by the costumer of the play, Blanche Hays. He had also tried masks in *The Ancient Mariner*, his unsuccessful attempt at "total theatre," and had given symbolic importance to an African tribal mask in *All God's Chillun Got Wings*. Now, in *The Great God Brown*, he consciously explored the possibilities of masking, allying it also to a combination of mythic meanings. From Friedrich Nietzsche he develops the Dionysus-Apollo opposition, combining it with the Christian asceticism of Saint Anthony and the mystical *Imitation of Christ* of Thomas à Kempis. The spiritual development (or regression) of the central characters, particularly Dion Anthony* and William A. (Billy) Brown,* is shown by the masks they wear (and exchange). In this way, O'Neill seeks to achieve a philosophical and psychological expression of ideas and spiritual states in a manner that transcends realism. What he was attempting is best stated in his own words: "One's outer life passes in a solitude haunted by the masks of others; one's inner life passes in a solitude hounded by the masks of oneself" from *Memoranda on Masks* (1932, reprinted in Cargill, 1961).

The use of masks, then, helps to develop "a drama of souls" by giving another dramatic means of arriving at "insight into the inner forces motivating the actions and reactions of men and women." Masks are "a proven weapon of attack," and by their very formalism they enforce a specific intellectual reaction, insisting also that one reject a mere emotional response, listening instead to what is being said. The mask thus intrudes itself between actor and audience, insisting that one observe the primacy of content. Later, O'Neill realized that the use of masks required a greater gift of language than he possessed.

Certain themes and characters from earlier plays are developed in *The Great God Brown*. Margaret Anthony,* the Faustian beloved, turns into the destructive wife, and for the first time, the full-blown character of the earth-mother appears in Cybel,* who is also a development of the prostitute of *"Anna Christie."* In her role of mother-confessor to both Dion Anthony and Billy Brown, Cybel also prefigures Josie Hogan* in *A Moon for the Misbegotten** (1943). Though there were some complaints about the masks, *Brown* achieved a respectable eight-month run.

Emboldened by this success, O'Neill went further in *Lazarus Laughed* (1926), endeavoring to create a complete ritual theatre aimed at the promulgation of ideas. He believed he was returning in spirit to:

the one true theatre,...that...legitimate descendant of the first theatre that sprang,...out of the worship of Dionysus. I mean a theatre returned to its highest and sole significant function as a Temple where the religion of a practical interpretation and symbolical celebration of life is communicated to human beings, starved in spirit by their soul-stifling daily struggle to exist as masks among the masks of the living. [*A Dramatist's Notebook* (1933, reprinted in Cargill, 1961)]

In the play all the characters are masked, except for Lazarus, who no longer fears death, having already experienced it and is now above and beyond the sufferings of the world and able to embody the words of Nietzsche in *Thus Spake Zarathustra*:

How many things are still possible! So *learn* to laugh beyond yourselves! Lift up your hearts, ye good dancers, high! higher! and do not forget the good laughter!

   This crown of laughter, this rose-garland crown; to you, my brethren, do I cast this crown! Laughing have I consecrated; ye higher men *Learn*, I pray you,—to laugh. *See* in "References": Nietzsche (1927), p. 337.

However, though the design is great, and O'Neill believed that the play contained some of his best thinking and writing, the execution is repetitive and rather static. Lazarus brings his message to representatives of each of the world's great civilizations, leading them to an affirmation of life that transcends the fact of death. The message is received in varying ways by a masked chorus representing the seven ages of man and seven different character types within each civilization, with the result that there are over 420 roles in the play. The size of the production (and its problems) overwhelms the message which always turns out to be that "men forget," until finally Lazarus dies at the hands of enemies. In this play O'Neill wrote a work that is barely stageworthy, as its production history makes clear. This cavalier attitude toward the limits of the stage indicates O'Neill's ambivalence toward the performance of his plays, particularly in the 1930s. He felt that actors always diminished his work and, indeed, once said that no actor ever recreated precisely the character he had written.

   As he was to do on more than one later occasion, he tested the endurance of his audience with the nine-act *Strange Interlude* (1927). Here, though he disclaimed the influence of Freud, he nonetheless makes use of some popular knowledge (even misconceptions) of Freudianism, that most pervasive behavioral myth. Technically, O'Neill's major experiment here lies in his use of interior monologues, conveying the innermost thoughts of the characters by means of extended soliloquies. In this manner he conveys the idea that the characters are wearing figurative rather than literal masks because outward behavior does not mirror inward thought. In later years he said that he wished he had chosen to use masks for this play. Difficult as these soliloquies were to stage, they also increased the length of the play to dimensions that extended it beyond dramatic logic, with the result that it is rarely revived. To some extent this play lends itself better to film technique because close-ups can take the place of characters who must remain frozen in place, and voice-overs can be done as the character continues apparently normal activities. Yet the film version (*see* Appendix B) was merely adequate.

   Themes from earlier plays reappear, notably in the character of Nina Leeds, who is the mother-wife-mistress (and later nurse) that O'Neill was in real life to find in his third wife Carlotta Monterey. Each aspect of Nina's existence is fulfilled by the men in her life: son, husband, lover. But then like Ella Downey in *All God's Chillun Got Wings*, she eventually finds peace in regression to childhood. "All passion spent," she crawls into the arms of "good old" Charles Marsden,* who takes her back to end her life in the home of her father where it began. All the turmoils of her existence were thus a "strange interlude in the electrical display of God the father." It is interesting to note here that O'Neill uses the same kind of electrical image that he was also to employ in *Dynamo*.

   Shocking in its time because of the theme of Nina's seeking a surrogate father for her child, the play seems tame today. Even the experimental use of time by which the action of the play (1919-1943) extends some seventeen years past the date of original performance seems less astonishing now. Certainly O'Neill did not predict or consider the Second World War, but the outside world is almost totally irrelevant to *Strange Interlude*, whose characters expend almost all their energy on their inner psychic conflicts.

A DETOUR INTO COMEDY

In 1932 O'Neill took a single detour into comedy in the nostalgically romantic *Ah, Wilderness!** perhaps as a relief from his struggles with *Dynamo* and *Days Without End* and as a reaction against the tragic gloom of *Mourning Becomes Electra*. In *Ah, Wilderness!* O'Neill makes use of the myth of the typical American family and the young man's ritual experience of growing up. Arthur Miller* is Eugene O'Neill's alter ego, and the Miller family is the O'Neill family in New London, the way he idealized and fantasized them into comic myth.

THE LAST PLAYS

Obsessed with continuing work on his cycle, "A Tale of Possessors, Self-Dispossessed,"* which eventually grew to a projected eleven plays, O'Neill aimed at creating a great American saga of mercantilism and economic success—another kind of American myth. In 1936 he moved to the West Coast where he spent the rest of his actual working life as a playwright, for after 1943 his hand tremor made writing impossible. During these years at Tao House he wrote the autobiographical plays which have now reestablished the primacy of his reputation. Though he still tested his actors and audience with his logorrhea, he had pretty much abandoned real theatrical experimentation. He is now more sensible in his demands on stage carpenters and designers, but the addiction to repetition and monologue, particularly in *The Iceman Cometh** (1939) and *A Moon for the Misbegotten** (1943), is still very evident while the short piece *Hughie** (1941) is really a self-contained monologue. He also returned to his old mode of realism, touching naturalism, too, in *Iceman**, which takes its form from Maxim Gorky's *The Lower Depths* and its theme of the saving lie from Ibsen. Both here and in *Hughie*, O'Neill managed to transform his pitiable failures into characters who possess symbolic meaning. This statement is also true of Cornelius Melody* in *A Touch of the Poet,** the only completed play of the cycle; he, too, takes shelter from existence in "the saving lie." In effect, all these last plays continue the theme of the mask which hides the psychic identity of the individual, while the action of each play shows characters being stripped of pretense. *See* in "References": Eugene Waith, *Eugene O'Neill: An Exercise in Unmasking*, reprinted in Gassner, 1964.

With *Long Day's Journey into Night** (1941) and *A Moon for the Misbegotten* (1943), O'Neill made his peace with most of his family ghosts in plays of "old sorrow." Here he is unashamedly autobiographical, even if he does edit his own character of Edmund Tyrone.* There is no indication that Edmund's original was already a divorced man with a child at the time depicted in *Long Day's Journey*. In this play O'Neill is also reconciled with James O'Neill (James Tyrone*) and in their Act IV dialogue he confesses his own inefficiency as a poet. Edmund Tyrone says he can only stammer, and in some ways this comment exemplifies O'Neill's great weakness. He had the mind of a poet but lacked the verbal gift to express it (as an examination of his attempts at poetry, 1912–1944, clearly indicates). Father and son come to an understanding and so do the two brothers, James Tyrone, Jr.,* and Edmund. However, there is no forgiveness for drug-addicted Mary Cavan Tyrone,* no hint that in later years her real life counterpart, Ella Quinlan O'Neill,* did recover through an extraordinary combination of willpower and prayer.

Final peace with Jamie comes later with the extremely moving *A Moon for the Misbegotten*. Certainly the play is flawed and based on the outmoded structure of a farcical bed-trick which does not succeed. The figure of Cybel,* earth-mother of *The Great God Brown*, reappears as Josie Hogan, the so-called whore, who in fact is the virgin-mother-confessor to the tortured Jamie, as Cybel was to Dion Anthony and Billy Brown. Josie, like O'Neill himself, absolves Jamie, and the remaining Tyrones/O'Neills can now rest in peace.

Of the projected cycle, "A Tale of Possessors, Self-Dispossessed," only one completed play remains, *A Touch of the Poet* (1942). It is a competent piece of work but of lesser stature than the autobiographical plays of O'Neill's last phase. In the winter of 1952–1953, realizing that he would never finish this extraordinary project, O'Neill (with the help of Carlotta) destroyed his uncompleted manuscripts, so that no one could finish what he had been unable to do. In this plan, however, he was unsuccessful, because the manuscript of *More Stately Mansions** somehow escaped destruction and was later cut down to manageable length by Karl Ragnar Gierow* and produced in Stockholm. The American production (1967) by José Quintero* uses a slightly different text. This play, even when shrunk, remains too long-winded, and it is really unfair to discuss it since the author himself did not consider it ready for performance. In 1982, the scenario of *The Calms of Capricorn*,* another surviving part of the cycle, was published and also turned into a play by Donald Gallup. This has not been produced, though a reading has been given. The manuscript of *Hughie*, part of a projected series entitled "By Way of Obit,*'' also survived and has been published and produced.

O'NEILL'S REPUTATION

The reputation of Eugene O'Neill now seems secure, as theatrical revivals and the proliferating scholarship listed in the accompanying bibliography indicate. Despite the uneven quality of the canon, he is now recognized as America's premier classic playwright, one who almost singlehandedly restored seriousness to American drama. His fame now rests more solidly on his final, less-experimental plays, particularly those with autobiographical significance. Curiously, he finally found the secret of symbolism and the final mastery of the dramatic form he had sought all his life by means of a paradoxical solution. By digging deeply into his psyche through the history of his friends and that of his own tormented family, he succeeded in creating a paradigm of familial relations. As the noted O'Neill actress, Geraldine Fitzgerald,* once pointed out in an interview, almost everyone can identify with the human relationships he depicts, even though few (if any) of us have a miserly father, a dope-fiend mother, and an alcoholic brother. O'Neill's autobiographical plays have the stamp of truth on them, and the psychological and literal experiences he depicts are twentieth-century reality writ large.

O'NEILL: CRITICAL LETTERS AND ESSAYS, PUBLISHED IN NEWSPAPERS AND PERIODICALS.
(Interviews and incidental references are excluded.) In chronological order.

"A Letter from O'Neill." *New York Times* (April 11, 1920), Sec. VI, p. 2. [Concerning *Beyond the Horizon*.]

"Eugene O'Neill's Credo and His Reasons for His Faith." *New York Tribune* (February 13, 1921), pp. 1, 6. [Article in defense of *Diff'rent*.] Reprinted in Cargill, 1961.

"Letter." To the drama editor, *New York Times* (December 18, 1921), Sec. V, p. 1. ["*Anna Christie*," especially the conclusion.]

"Strindberg and Our Theatre."*Provincetown Playbill*, no. 1 (1923–24), pp. 1, 3. Reprinted in *New York Times* (January 6, 1924), Sec. VII, p. 1. Also reprinted in Cargill, 1961. [Used on playbill for *The Spook Sonata*.]

"*All God's Chillun*." *New York Times* (March 19, 1924), p. 19. [Article in its defense.]

"Playwright and Critic: The Record of a Stimulating Correspondence." *Boston Transcript* (October 31, 1925), Sec. III, p. 8. [Correspondence with George Jean Nathan. Reprinted in Cargill, 1961.]

"Are the Actors to Blame?" *Provincetown Playbill*, no. 1 (1925–26). Reprinted in *New York Times* (November 8, 1925), Sec. VIII, p. 2. Also reprinted in Cargill, 1961. [Used on playbill for *Adam Solitaire*.]

"*The Fountain*." *Greenwich Playbill*, no. 3 (1925–26), p. 1.

"The Playwright Explains." *New York Times* (February 14, 1926), Sec. VIII, p. 2. [Essay on *The Great God Brown*.]

"Letter." To the drama editor, *New York Times* (March 7, 1926), Sec. VIII, p. 2. [In defense of *Goat Song*, by Franz Werfel.]

"Letter to George Jean Nathan." *The American Mercury* (January 16, 1929), p. 119. [On *Mourning Becomes Electra*.]

"O'Neill's Own Story of Electra in the Making." *New York Herald Tribune* (November 8, 1931), Sec. VII, p. 2. [Notebook excerpts concerning *Mourning Becomes Electra*.]

"O'Neill Says Soviet Stage Has Realized His Dreams." *New York Herald Tribune* (June 19, 1932), Sec. VII, p. 2. [Letter from O'Neill to the Kamerny Theatre (June 2, 1930), concerning their production of *Desire Under the Elms* and *All God's Chillun Got Wings*, is quoted.] Reprinted in Cargill.

"Memoranda on Masks." *American Spectator* (November 1932), p. 3. [Important essay on masked drama arising from the reception of *The Great God Brown*.] Reprinted in Cargill, 1961.

"Second Thoughts." *American Spectator* (January 1933), p. 2. [Addenda to "Memoranda on Masks."] Reprinted in Cargill, 1961.

"A Dramatist's Notebook." *American Spectator* (January 1933), p. 2. [Concerning masks, especially in *Lazarus Laughed*.] Reprinted in Cargill, 1961.

"Professor George Pierce Baker."*New York Times* (January 13, 1935), Sec. IX, p. 1. [Tribute to his former teacher.]

"Gustav Presents Nobel Prize to 3." *New York Times* (December 11, 1936), p. 34. [News story includes text of O'Neill's acceptance speech which was not personally delivered by him.]

Searched in card catalog
By Reference Dept. 6/86

References Cited

The following alphabetical listing gives full references to items cited in short form within the text. For journal abbreviations see listing in Bibliography, pp. 771-772.

Adams, Henry. *The Education of Henry Adams*. Introduction by James Truslow Adams (The Modern Library). New York: Random House, © 1931. See Chapter XXV.

Alexander, Doris. "*Strange Interlude* and Schopenhauer." *AL* 25 (1953): 213–28.

———. *The Tempering of Eugene O'Neill*. New York: Harcourt, Brace, 1962.

Atkinson, Jennifer McCabe. *Eugene O'Neill: A Descriptive Bibliography*. Pittsburgh: University of Pittsburgh, 1974.

Avrich, Paul. *The Modern School Movement*. Princeton: Princeton University Press, 1980.

Baker, George Pierce. *Dramatic Technique*. Boston: Houghton Mifflin, 1919.

Barnes, Djuna. *Nightwood*. New York: Harcourt, Brace, 1937.

Basso, Hamilton. "The Tragic Sense." *New Yorker*, February 28, March 6, and March 13, 1948. (Profile of Eugene O'Neill.)

Bogard, Travis. *Contour in Time: The Plays of Eugene O'Neill*. New York: Oxford University Press, 1972.

Boulton, Agnes. *Part of a Long Story*. Garden City, N.Y.: Doubleday, 1958.

———. *The Road Is Before Us*. Philadelphia: Lippincott, 1944.

Bowen, Crosswell, with the assistance of Shane O'Neill. *The Curse of the Misbegotten: A Tale of the House of O'Neill*. New York: McGraw-Hill, 1959.

Bryant, Louise. *Mirrors of Moscow*. New York: T. Seltzer, 1923.

———. *Six Red Months in Russia*. New York: George Doran, 1918.

Bryer, Jackson, and Ruth M. Alvarez, editors. *"The Theatre We Worked For": The Letters of Eugene O'Neill to Kenneth Macgowan*. Introductory Essay by Travis Bogard. New Haven: Yale University Press, 1982.

Cargill, Oscar, N. Bryllion Fagin, and William J. Fisher, editors. *O'Neill and His Plays: Four Decades of Criticism*. New York: New York University Press, 1961.

Carpenter, Frederic I. *Eugene O'Neill*. Rev. ed. (Twayne United States Authors Series No. 66). Boston: Twayne, 1979. (Original edition published 1964.)

Clark, Barrett H. *Eugene O'Neill: The Man and His Plays*. New York: Dover, 1967. (A revision and expansion of the 1926 and 1947 editions.)

Commins, Dorothy [Berliner]. *What Is an Editor? Saxe Commins at Work*. Chicago: University of Chicago Press, 1978.

Commins, Saxe, and Lloyd Coleman. *Psychology: A Simplification*. New York: Liveright, 1927.

Cook, George Cram. *Greek Coins*. Edited by Susan Glaspell. Introductions by Floyd Dell, Edna Kenton, and Susan Glaspell. New York: George H. Doran Co., 1925.

Day, Cyrus. "The Iceman and the Bridegroom: Some Observations on the Death of O'Neill's Salesman." *MD* 1 (1958): 3–9.

Deutsch, Helen, and Stella Hanau. *The Provincetown: A Story of the Theatre*. New York: Farrar and Rinehart, 1931.

Evans, Bertrand. *Shakespeare's Comedies*. Oxford: Clarendon Press, 1960.

Falk, Doris V. *Eugene O'Neill and the Tragic Tension*. New Brunswick, N.J.: Rutgers University Press, 1958.

Floyd, Virginia, editor. *Eugene O'Neill at Work: Newly Released Ideas for Plays*. New York: Frederick Ungar, 1981.

———, editor. *Eugene O'Neill: A World View*. New York: Frederick Ungar, 1979.

Gassner, John, editor. *O'Neill: A Collection of Critical Essays*. With Introduction. Englewood Cliffs, N.J.: Prentice-Hall, 1964.

Gelb, Arthur, and Barbara. *O'Neill*. Revised edition. New York, 1973. (Original publication 1962.)

Gelb, Barbara. *So Short a Time: A Biography of John Reed and Louise Bryant*. New York: Norton, 1973.

Glaspell, Susan. *The Road to the Temple*. New York: Frederick Stokes, 1927, reprinted 1941.

Hamilton, Gilbert V., and Kenneth Macgowan. *What Is Wrong with Marriage*. New York: A. & C. Boni, 1929.

Hapgood, Hutchins. *A Victorian in the Modern World*. New York: Harcourt, Brace, 1939.

Hastings, Warren H., and Richard F. Weeks. "Episodes of Eugene O'Neill's Undergraduate Days at Princeton." *PULC*, 29 (1968): 208–15.

Helburn, Theresa. *A Wayward Quest: The Autobiography of Theresa Helburn*. Boston: Little, Brown & Co., 1960.

Hicks, Granville. *John Reed: The Making of a Revolutionary*. New York: Macmillan, 1936.

Jones, Robert Edmond. *The Dramatic Imagination*. New York: Duell, Sloan and Pearce, 1941.

———. *Drawings for the Theatre*. New York: Theatre Arts Books, 1970. (Original publication 1925.)

Joyce, James. *A Portrait of the Artist as a Young Man*. New York: B. W. Huebsch, 1916.

Jung, Carl G. *Psychological Types*. Translated by H. Godwin Baynes. London: K. Paul, Trench, Trübner, 1946. (Original translation appeared in 1923.)

Langner, Lawrence. *G.B.S. and the Lunatic*. New York: Atheneum, 1963.

———. *The Magic Curtain*. New York: Dutton, 1951.

Larson, Orville. "Robert Edmond Jones and His Art." *Theatre Design and Technology*, No. 16 (May 1969): 14–24.

Leitch, Alexander. *A Princeton Companion*. Princeton, N.J.: Princeton University Press, 1978.

Macgowan, Kenneth. *Footlights across America*. New York: Harcourt, Brace, 1929.

——. *The Theatre of Tomorrow*. New York: Boni & Liveright, 1921.

——, and Robert Edmond Jones. *Continental Stagecraft*. New York: Harcourt, Brace, 1922.

——, and Herman Rosse. *Masks and Demons*. New York: Harcourt, Brace, 1923.

Mannes, Marya. "The Power Behind the Throne." *New Yorker*, December 6, 1930. (Profile of Theresa Helburn.)

Matlaw, Myron. "English and American Dramatizations of *Le Comte de Monte Cristo*." *Nineteenth-Century Theatre Research* 7 (1979): 39–73.

Miller, Jordan Y. *Eugene O'Neill and the American Critic: A Bibliographical Checklist*. Second edition, revised. Hamden, Connecticut: Archon, 1973.

Miller, William. *Dorothy Day: A Biography*. San Francisco: Harper & Row, 1982.

Nietzsche, Friedrich. *The Philosophy of Nietzsche*. New York: Modern Library, 1927.

O'Neill, Carlotta Monterey. Letters to Frances McComas. Huntington Library Manuscripts, Nos. 85, 87, 88, 90, 91, 92, 93.

——. Theatrical Scrapbook. Chamberlain and Lyman Brown Agency. Billy Rose Theatre Collection, New York Public Library at Lincoln Center, New York City. (Covers 1922–1924.)

O'Neill, Eugene. "The Ancient Mariner." Edited with an Introduction by Donald Gallup. *YULG* 35 (1960): 61–86.

——. *The Calms of Capricorn*. A Play Developed from O'Neill's Scenario by Donald Gallup. New Haven: Ticknor & Fields, 1982. (Contains a transcription of the scenario.)

——. *"Children of the Sea" and Three Other Unpublished Plays by Eugene O'Neill*. Edited by Jennifer McCabe Atkinson. With Introductory Foreword by Frank Durham. A Bruccoli-Clark Book. Washington, D.C. NCR/Microcard Editions, 1972. (Includes *Bread and Butter, Children of the Sea, Now I Ask You*, and *Shell Shock*.)

——. *Chris Christophersen*. Foreword by Leslie Eric Comens. New York: Random House, 1982.

——. "A Dramatist's Notebook." *American Spectator*, January 1933. Reprinted in Cargill, 1961. (On Masks.)

——. *Inscriptions: Eugene O'Neill to Carlotta Monterey O'Neill*. Privately Printed. New Haven: Yale University Press, 1960.

——. *The Last Will and Testament of Silverdene Emblem O'Neill*. Privately printed "For Carlotta." New Haven: Yale University Press, 1956.

——. "Letter." To the Drama Editor, *New York Times*, December 18, 1921, Sect. V, p. 1. ("*Anna Christie*," especially the conclusion.)

——. *"Lost" Plays of Eugene O'Neill*. New York: New Fathoms Press, 1950.

——. "Memoranda on Masks." *American Spectator*, November 1932. Reprinted in Cargill, 1961.

——. Poems, 1912–1944. Edited by Donald Gallup. New Haven: Ticknor & Fields, 1980.

——. "Second Thoughts [On Masks]." *American Spectator*, December 1932. Reprinted in Cargill, 1961.

——. *Ten "Lost" Plays of Eugene O'Neill*. Preface by Bennett Cerf. New York: Random House, 1964. (Includes all the plays reprinted in the 1950 New Fathoms Press volume (see above). These were *Abortion, The Movie Man, The Sniper*,

Servitude, and *A Wife for a Life*. In addition, the following plays appear: *Thirst, The Web, Warnings, Fog*, and *Recklessness*.)

———. *"Thirst" and Other One Act Plays*. Boston: Gorham Press, 1914. (Includes *Fog, Recklessness, Thirst, The Web*, and *Warnings*.)

———. *Work Diary, 1924–1943*. Transcribed by Donald C. Gallup. Preliminary Edition. New Haven: Yale University Press, 1981. 2 vols.

O'Neill, Peter. *History of the San Francisco Theatre*. Vol. XX: *James O'Neill* (San Francisco: Works Progress Administration for Northern California, 1942). Typescript.

Peck, Seymour. "Talk with Mrs. O'Neill." *New York Times*, November 4, 1956, Sect. 2, pp. 1, 3. Reprinted in Cargill, 1961.

Pendleton, Ralph. *The Theatre of Robert Edmond Jones*. Middletown, Conn.: Wesleyan University Press, 1958.

Quintero, José. *If You Don't Dance, They Beat You*. Boston: Little, Brown & Co., 1974.

Raleigh, John Henry. *The Plays of Eugene O'Neill*. Carbondale: Illinois University Press, 1965.

Reaver, J. Russell. *An O'Neill Concordance*. Detroit, Mich.: Gale Research Press, 1939. 3 Vols.

Reed, John. *Insurgent Mexico*. New York: D. Appleton, 1914.

———. *Ten Days That Shook the World*. New York: Boni & Liveright, 1919.

Robeson, Paul. *Here I Stand*. New York: Beacon Press, 1958.

Robinson, James A. *Eugene O'Neill and Oriental Thought: A Divided Vision*. Carbondale & Edwardsville: Southern Illinois University Press, 1982.

Rosenstone, Robert A. *Romantic Revolutionary: A Biography of John Reed*. New York: A. A. Knopf, 1975.

Sarlós, Robert Karoly. *Jig Cook and the Provincetown Players: Theatre in Ferment*. Amherst: University of Massachusetts Press, 1982.

Sheaffer, Louis. "Correcting Some Errors in Annals of O'Neill (Part I)." *EON* 7, No. 3 (Winter 1983): 3–25.

———. *O'Neill: Son and Artist*. Boston: Little, Brown & Co., 1973.

———. *O'Neill: Son and Playwright*. Boston: Little, Brown & Co., 1968.

Simonson, Lee. *The Stage Is Set*. New York: Harcourt, Brace, 1932. (Contains material on Robert Edmond Jones, and peripherally on O'Neill.)

Timberlake, Craig. *The Life & [sic] Work of David Belasco, the Bishop of Broadway*. New York: Library Publishers, 1954.

Törnqvist, Egil. *A Drama of Souls*. New Haven: Yale University Press, 1969. (Also published Stockholm, 1968.)

Vorse, Mary Heaton. *Time and the Town*. New York: Dial Press, 1942.

Waterman, Arthur E. *Susan Glaspell* (Twayne United States Authors Series, No. 101). New York: Twayne, 1966.

Winther, Sophus Keith. *Eugene O'Neill: A Critical Study*. Second revised edition. New York: Russell & Russell, 1961. (Original publication, 1934).

Bibliography

BIBLIOGRAPHIC ESSAY

Introduction

Scholarship on Eugene O'Neill has not yet reached the proportions of Shakespearean scholarship, but since the revival of interest in his work, which began with the 1956 production of *The Iceman Cometh*, publication has accelerated. During the 1960s and 1970s dissertations proliferated, the fruits of which are only now being seen in print. Additional scholarly work was generated with the founding of the Eugene O'Neill Society at the end of 1978, twenty-five years after the death of the playwright. Also, the Eugene O'Neill Theater Center, Waterford, Connecticut, was founded to aid the work of contemporary and often highly experimental playwrights. This group is also restoring Monte Cristo Cottage, New London, Connecticut, which is open to the public as a museum. Tao House, above Danville, California, was declared a National Historical Monument in 1976, but owing to access problems it is not yet open to the public.

The following bibliographical essay attempts to assess briefly the major achievements and trends of O'Neill scholarship. It contains brief citations within the text to material listed fully in classified and alphabetical order in the selected bibliography.

Bibliographical Studies

Bibliographical studies of Eugene O'Neill indicate both competence and completeness. In 1931 (reissued with additions, 1965), Ralph Sanborn and Barrett H. Clark produced the first bibliography of the published works of O'Neill, also reprinting some of the poems he published in the *New London Telegraph*. This material was ably reworked, extended, and redeveloped by Jennifer McCabe Atkinson into an indispensable reference work: *Eugene O'Neill: A Descriptive Bibliography* (1974). It includes blurbs, material quoted in catalogues, anthologized plays, and an appendix of film, radio, and musical adaptations. There is no section on television. In 1962, Jordan Y. Miller offered his extremely comprehensive *Eugene O'Neill and the American Critic* (revised edition, 1973), which also pays attention to the production and chronological composition of the plays. A chronology of O'Neill's life is also given, together with a critical prologue. In 1979–1980, Charles Carpenter published addenda to Miller by listing "Elusive Articles, Books, and Parts of Books about O'Neill." Miller's 1965 anthology, *Playwright's Progress: O'Neill and the Critics*, though designed for student use, has a good selection of fugitive material and a select bibliography.

Jackson R. Bryer in 1961 gave an account of "Forty Years of O'Neill Criticism," following it in 1971 with a *Checklist of Eugene O'Neill*. In 1976, Ernest G. Griffin, in *Eugene O'Neill: A Collection of Criticism*, included a select bibliography. An extremely useful aid to scholarship appeared in 1969; J. Russell Reaver, compiler, *An O'Neill Concordance* (3 volumes), though such later releases of O'Neill works as the 1982 *Chris Christophersen*, and *The Calms of Capricorn* are, of course, excluded. Two useful dissertations have not yet appeared in print: Kathy Lynn Bernard, "The Research Library of Eugene O'Neill," and Clarence Sturm, "Scholarly Criticism of Eugene O'Neill in Periodicals, 1960–75, with a Bibliographic Overview of American and German Studies." In addition, Horst Frenz developed "A List of Foreign Editions and Translations of Eugene O'Neill's Drama" (1943), supplementing it over the years with installments on specific countries. In general, this material is more easily found in the *Index Translationum*, an annual publication of UNESCO (1932–), which lacks a cumulative index. In short, it is fair to say that the basic bibliographical work has been done, and the scholar now has the tools to continue.

Manuscripts

The basic documents for consultation here are *American Literary Manuscripts* (second edition) and the *National Union Catalogue of Manuscripts* (1959–), now an annual publication of the Library of Congress. By far the largest O'Neill manuscript collection is at the Beinecke Library, Yale University, since Carlotta Monterey* O'Neill deposited all her husband's remaining papers there. Yale also has the papers of Harry Weinberger, O'Neill's lawyer for many years, and the papers of George Pierce Baker,* O'Neill's Harvard teacher of playwriting. Substantial holdings also exist in the Harvard Theatre Collection, Harvard College Library, which has material deposited by Agnes Boulton* O'Neill, including a considerable body of correspondence. Cornell University has the George Jean Nathan papers, which contain O'Neill material. Princeton University has the papers of George C. Tyler, the theatrical producer, and those of Saxe Commins,* O'Neill's editor and friend. There are also some autograph manuscripts. The New York Public Library has, among other papers, typescripts of several plays, three drafts of *Days Without End*, and the papers of Dudley Digges,* the actor, long associated with O'Neill roles. In 1969 the library also acquired the papers of Mrs. Beatrice Ashe Maher, which included letters, photographs, and poems relating to her romance with O'Neill in New London, Connecticut. This library also has an extensive collection of promptbooks, reviews, theatrical scrapbooks, and production documents. Columbia University has the papers of Manuel Komroff, O'Neill's original editor at Boni & Liveright, as well as files from Random House. At the University of Texas, Austin, the Humanities Research and the Hoblitzelle Library have numerous letters to and from Carlotta Monterey O'Neill, together with manuscripts, promptbooks, production documents, and pictures. Some of this material is not yet catalogued. The Library of Congress has typescripts of O'Neill plays. The Museum of the City of New York also has a sizable O'Neill collection, in particular, papers and memorabilia relating to James O'Neill,* the playwright's father, as well as longhand drafts of some early O'Neill plays. Smaller collections and single items exist elsewhere (at C. W. Post College of Long Island University, and the Henry E. Huntington Library, for example), and these may be located by using the basic documents listed above. The researcher wishing to use manuscript materials should be warned that restrictions on their use frequently remain in force, even though O'Neill has been dead over twenty-five years, while some documents cannot be published until all the persons concerned are dead.

Text

For plays published during O'Neill's lifetime, the standard texts are those issued by Random House, which took over the earlier publications from Boni & Liveright. O'Neill's first published collection, *Thirst and Other Plays* (Boston: Gorham, 1914), was underwritten by James O'Neill, and it, too, was later taken over by Random House. O'Neill involved himself intimately in the publication of his plays and corrected the published texts himself, though some prefaces appearing over his name were in fact written by Saxe Commins, his editor. An exception to the above comments is *Lost Plays of Eugene O'Neill* (New York: New Fathoms Press, 1950), subsequently taken over by Random House. This collection was printed because O'Neill had inadvertently allowed copyright on this juvenilia to lapse, and its appearance was unauthorized. Other plays have been posthumously published by a variety of publishers: *Hughie, Long Day's Journey into Night, More Stately Mansions*, and *A Touch of the Poet*, (New Haven: Yale University Press); *The Calms of Capricorn*, a scenario (New Haven: Ticknor & Fields, 1982); *Children of the Sea and Three Other Unpublished Plays* [*Now I Ask You, Bread and Butter, Shell Shock*] (Washington, D.C.: Microcard Eds., 1972) A Bruccoli Clark Book; *Chris Christophersen* (New York: Random House, 1982). *Poems, 1912–1944*, has been printed by Ticknor and Fields (1980). For these and other material posthumously published see the bibliography to this text. Also, for an admirable bibliographical survey of published works by O'Neill (including acting texts of individual plays), the reader should consult Jennifer McCabe Atkinson, *Eugene O'Neill: A Descriptive Bibliography* (University of Pittsburgh, 1974).

Biography

The finest biography of O'Neill is the two-volume one by Louis Sheaffer, *O'Neill: Son and Playwright* (1968), and *O'Neill: Son and Artist* (1973), which is arguably the best biography to date of any American literary figure. It is well researched and trustworthy, with few errors and sympathetic objectivity. It also reads very well, with biographical and critical details skillfully integrated. Next is the equally monumental work of Arthur and Barbara Gelb (1962, revised edition 1973). Like Sheaffer, they seem to have spoken to everyone with recollections of O'Neill. As journalists, they emphasize the human and psychological interest of the author, as well as O'Neill's intensely autobiographical approach. Preceding Sheaffer by some years, they have some information that he was later to disprove, and therefore this volume should be used in conjunction with the later work. Doris M. Alexander, *The Tempering of Eugene O'Neill* (1962) gives a psychologically oriented account of the years to 1920, including some comments that Sheaffer supersedes. Agnes Boulton's* *Part of a Long Story* (1958) is the first volume of a contemplated and unfinished two-volume account of her marriage to O'Neill. It ends with the birth of Shane Rudraighe O'Neill* in 1919. The book is a curious mixture of lyricism, vagueness, and at times what seems to be total recall. Sometimes her account may even be unique. Crosswell Bowen in *The Curse of the Misbegotten* (1959), written with the assistance of Shane O'Neill, regards the history of O'Neill and his family as demonstrating the existence of some kind of ancestral curse. His comments should be checked against Sheaffer.

Barrett H. Clark was the first to attempt an O'Neill biography in 1926 (revised in 1967). He interviewed the playwright who (as Clark himself noted) sometimes gave the edited spirit of an anecdote refined by art, rather than the unvarnished truth. The same difficulty exists in the famous *New Yorker* profile by Hamilton Basso, "The Tragic Sense" (February-March 1948). O'Neill's account of the escapade that led to his rustication from Princeton, for instance, does not square with the recollection of classmates (*see* Hastings and Weeks) or with university records. Brief biographies and chronologies can be found in many places, including the work of Jordan Y. Miller, as well as in prefaces to individual plays. Travis Bogard, *Contour in Time* (1972) (*see* Critical Studies: General Section) gives a few biographical facts at the beginning of each chapter that is devoted to the plays of that period.

In addition, details concerning O'Neill's life and work may be found in the biographies and autobiographies of persons associated with the playwright. These are listed under "Ancillary Biographies" in the sections that follow. O'Neill's correspondence with various friends and acquaintances is also being published and should be consulted. *See*, particularly, *The Theatre We Worked For*, edited by Jackson R. Bryer and Ruth M. Alvarez (1982), which consists of the letters of O'Neill to Kenneth Macgowan.*

Criticism

Until the publication of Barrett H. Clark, *Eugene O'Neill: The Man and His Plays* (1926, revised in 1967), most commentary on O'Neill was to be found in newspapers and periodicals, consisting mainly of play reviews and articles aimed at a general audience, but also including some thoughtful evaluation in literary reviews. In fairness, of course, one should point out that the academic discipline of American literature is of rather recent vintage; for instance, the publication of *American Literature* began in 1929. Similarly, theatre history, as opposed to a study of the literary content of plays, is also a latecomer, *Theatre Survey* beginning publication in 1959 and *Modern Drama* in 1958. It is highly significant that the December 1960 issue of the latter was devoted to Eugene O'Neill, an event which was to prove of lasting significance.

The next major landmark in O'Neill scholarship is that of Sophus Keith Winther, *Eugene O'Neill* (1934, revised edition 1961). He was the first to attempt a full-length thematic study of O'Neill's work, and his comments gain added weight because of his friendship with the playwright. Also, though critics did not know it at the time, the bulk of O'Neill's work had already been completed, though some of his greatest triumphs were still to come: *The Iceman Cometh* (in its 1956 revival), *A Moon for the Misbegotten* (in its 1968 and 1973 revivals), *Long Day's Journey into Night* (1956), *A Touch of the Poet* (1958), and *Hughie* (1964). With the 1936 award of the Nobel Prize for Literature to O'Neill, differences of evaluative opinion became exacerbated. Lionel Trilling in the *New Republic* (1936, reprinted in Cargill, 1961), though not a complete devotee, hailed "The Genius of O'Neill," while Bernard de Voto in the *Saturday Review* (1936, reprinted in Cargill, 1961) gave a "Minority Report," wondering why O'Neill had deserved such recognition. For some time the lines remained drawn in this manner, Eric Bentley in particular "Trying to Like O'Neill" (1952, reprinted in Cargill, 1961) but without success. A truce has more or less been reached with the arrival of the final and posthumously produced plays. Recent critics such as Travis Bogard and Walter J. Meserve (see *Revels History*) readily admit the extraordinary inconsistency of O'Neill's output but draw attention to its serious purpose and frequent brilliance.

An excellent anthology of O'Neill criticism to 1958 is found in Oscar Cargill and others, editors, *O'Neill and His Plays: Four Decades of Criticism* (1961). This indispensable volume contains critical comments by O'Neill, theatrical reviews, international critical assessments, and some excellent special studies, notably that of Cargill himself on "Fusion-Point of Jung and Nietzsche" (pp. 408–414). This book gives a representative study of fashions in and concerns of O'Neill criticism. Jordan Y. Miller's *Playwright's Progress: O'Neill and the Critics* (1965), though aimed at a college audience, does the same thing with excerpts from theatre reviews. Other useful anthologies of reprinted criticism are: John Gassner, editor, *O'Neill: A Collection of Critical Essays* (1964); John Henry Raleigh, editor, *Twentieth Century Interpretations of "The Iceman Cometh"* (1968); and Ernest G. Griffin, *Eugene O'Neill: A Collection of Criticism* (1976).

Book-length critical studies of O'Neill, some showing scholarship of a very high order, have been appearing regularly. Travis Bogard, *Contour in Time: The Plays of Eugene O'Neill* (1972), is a distinguished contribution, easy for a neophyte to use because of its chronological approach and invaluable cast lists. John Henry Raleigh, *The Plays of Eugene O'Neill* (1965), on the other hand, offers a thematic, psychological approach. Two earlier studies remain valuable: Edwin A. Engel, *The Haunted Heroes of Eugene O'Neill* (1953), and Doris V. Falk, *Eugene O'Neill and the Tragic Tension* (1958), Engel looking at themes of the entire canon (to 1947) and Falk studying "the lifelong torment of a mind in conflict." Similarly, the work of Joseph Wood Krutch bears examination as that of one of O'Neill's early champions (*see* particularly Chapter III of *The American Drama Since 1918* [1939]). Another important early study is Richard Dana Skinner, *Eugene O'Neill: A Poet's Quest* (1935). He sees O'Neill as a thoroughly serious artist aiming at poetic fulfillment and also comprehends the almost religious significance the playwright attached to his work. An elegant short introductory study is that of Clifford Leech, *Eugene O'Neill* (1963), while Frederic I. Carpenter, *Eugene O'Neill* (1964, revised edition 1979), has some good insights and a useful section of O'Neill's greatness and limitations. The most recent short study is that of Normand Berlin, *Eugene O'Neill* (1982).

European writers early noticed O'Neill, Hugo von Hofmannsthal writing on him as early as 1923 (reprinted in Cargill, 1961), and some extremely good work has been done by Karl Ragnar Gierow,* mainly in producing the plays in Stockholm. Egil Törnqvist, in *A Drama of Souls* (1969) has added a book-length study to a distinguished body of shorter critical essays, as has Timo Tiusanen, *O'Neill's Scenic Images* (1969). Sections on O'Neill's foreign reputation (including in Eastern Europe) appear in Virginia Floyd, editor, *Eugene O'Neill: A World View* (1979), a collection which also includes some useful critical studies and comments by theatrical figures who have played O'Neill roles with distinction.

Influence and source studies are many, with the emphasis falling heavily on Greek tragedy, Jung, Strindberg, Nietzsche, Ibsen, the German expressionists and naturalists, Bergson, and, to a lesser extent, Schopenhauer. The articles of Törnqvist, Valgemae, and Winther, among many others, are important here. Dissertations in these areas have been many, and one now awaits with considerable interest book-length treatments arising from them. Allied to influence studies are those of psychology, and here the thoughtful pieces of Arthur H. Nethercot are useful. Other studies are concerned with O'Neill's tragic theories and his aesthetics, particularly in his relationship to Nietzsche.

Treatment of specific themes, such as despair, suffering, and death, throughout the entire canon, has become a popular dissertation approach, as has the influence of philosophy and religion. One new approach is that of James A. Robinson, *Eugene O'Neill and Oriental Thought* (1982). Of course O'Neill's relationship to the Roman Catholic faith of his Irish ancestors has been frequently studied, notably by John Henry Raleigh and also Harry Cronin, *Eugene O'Neill: Irish and American* (1977). Puritanism has also been extensively studied, particularly in relation to *Desire Under the Elms* and *Mourning Becomes Electra*, while O'Neill's attempt to forge a new creed through an amalgam of myth, religion, mysticism, and philosophy is also being well researched. In addition, with the development of scholarly feminist criticism, O'Neill's dramatic treatment of women is now being examined. Although O'Neill is alleged to have had a poor ear for language and to have been a poet *manqué*, studies of his use of language are now being undertaken; one should note here Jean Chothia, *Forging a Language* (1969). The number of dissertations on O'Neill's dramatic techniques and theories of drama also indicates future directions for scholarship.

Concerning individual O'Neill plays, the weight of learning falls heaviest on the last plays, *The Iceman Cometh* and *Long Day's Journey into Night*, in particular, followed by the earlier *Mourning Becomes Electra* and *Desire Under the Elms*. The "mystical" plays of the twenties seem to have fallen out of favor, and there is a curious lack of interest in *Strange Interlude*. O'Neill's experiments, which in their day seemed revolutionary, are now either commonplace or outmoded, and his fame seems now to rest on the final naturalistic plays which possess a universality and a symbolic value which seems likely to make them lasting dramatic documents. With the passage of time and the removal of restrictions from manuscripts, letters and papers are being sifted and more original material is being published, not always to the enhancement of O'Neill's reputation, as in the case of *Poems 1912–1944* (1980). Though it is good to have the text of *Chris Christophersen* (1982), one might also wish for "The Ole Davil," the intermediate text between *Chris* and "*Anna Christie*". Virginia Floyd's edition of O'Neill's notebooks, *O'Neill at Work* (1981), sheds new light on the author's work habits and plans, and while one wonders about the propriety of Donald Gallup's (1982) devising a play from O'Neill's scenario of *The Calms of Capricorn* the reprinted text of that scenario enhances our understanding of the destroyed cycle, "A Tale of Possessors, Self-Dispossessed." O'-Neill's *Work Diary, 1924–1943* has been transcribed by Donald Gallup, and exists in a two-volume preliminary edition (1981); one looks forward to its general distribution as an aid in dating the plays.

The Future of O'Neill Scholarship

Much of the groundwork has now been done, but there is room for more—basic scholarship in particular. Definitive texts need to be established in some cases. Studies of promptbooks will yield interesting variations from the published text and will indicate patterns of revision. The work of Judith Barlow (1979) on *Long Day's Journey* is exemplary in this regard. Original performances need to be researched and documented. For instance, exactly which ending was used in the first production of "*Anna Christie*"? Correspondence between O'Neill and others, including publishers, may yield new information. Andrew B. Myers (1979) in an article on *Days Without End* indicates the intelligent use that can be made of such material. And above all, some demythologizing is needed, as Gary Jay Williams has discovered from his Provincetown Players* research. We also need to know more about that fascinating actor-father, James O'Neill,* a project happily being undertaken by Myron Matlaw. A detailed study of O'Neill films already exists in the dissertation of Janet Klotman Cutler (1977), and one looks forward to more. Certainly O'Neill studies are alive, and now is the time for scholarship to consolidate the material, avoid hagiography, admit the warts and all of O'Neill, and in that way fully establish his reputation, not only as America's most prolific and serious playwright but probably her very best and the one with the highest international standing.

ABBREVIATIONS OF PERIODICAL
TITLES

The abbreviations listed below are the standard ones used by the Modern Language Association of America in its annual publication, the *MLA International Bibliography*.

AL	American Literature
ALitASH	Acta Litteraria Academiae Scientiarum Hungaricae
AQ	American Quarterly
AR	Antioch Review
ArQ	Arizona Quarterly
ASch	American Scholar
BB	Bulletin of Bibliography
BSUF	Ball State University Forum
Caliban	(Toulouse, France)
CE	College English
CEA	CEA Critic (College English Association)
CL	Comparative Literature (Eugene, Oregon)
CLAJ	College Language Association Journal
Clio	CLIO: A Journal of Literature, History, and the Philosophy of History
CompD	Comparative Drama
ComQ	Commonwealth Quarterly
Criticism	A Quarterly for Literature and the Arts (Detroit, Michigan)
CritQ	Critical Quarterly
DA	Dissertation Abstracts. *See also* DAI
DAI	Dissertation Abstracts International
DQR	Dutch Quarterly Review of Anglo-American Letters
DR	Dalhousie Review
EA	Études Anglaises
EJ	English Journal
ELWIU	Essays in Literature (Macomb, Illinois)
EngR	English Review of Salem State College
EON	The Eugene O'Neill Newsletter
ES	English Studies
ESC	English Studies in Canada
ETJ	Educational Theatre Journal (now Theatre Journal)
ForumH	Forum (Houston, Texas)
GyS	Gypsy Scholar: A Graduate Forum for Literary Criticism
JEGP	Journal of English and Germanic Philology
JPC	Journal of Popular Culture
KanQ	Kansas Quarterly
KR	Kenyon Review
L&P	Literature and Psychology
LCrit	The Literary Criterion (Mysore, India)
MD	Modern Drama

MLN	Modern Language Notes
MLQ	Modern Language Quarterly
Mosaic	A Journal for the Interdisciplinary Study of Literature
MR	Massachusetts Review
MSE	Massachusetts Studies in English
MuK	Maske und Kothurn: Internationale Beiträge zur Theaterwissenschaft
NEQ	New England Quarterly
NMAL	Notes on Modern American Literature
NR	The Nassau Review (Nassau Community College, N.Y.)
NS	Die Neueren Sprachen
NYTM	New York Times Magazine
OL	Orbis Litterarum: International Review of Literary Studies
PMLA	Publications of the Modern Language Association of America
PR	Partisan Review
PULC	Princeton University Library Chronicle
QJS	Quarterly Journal of Speech
RLC	Revue de Littérature Comparee
SAB	South Atlantic Bulletin
SAQ	South Atlantic Quarterly
SB	Studies in Bibliography (University of Virginia)
ScanR	Scandinavian Review
SDR	South Dakota Review
SHR	Southern Humanities Review
SLitI	Studies in the Literary Imagination (Atlanta, Georgia)
SMLit	Studies in Mystical Literature (Taiwan)
SN	Studia Neophilologica
SR	Sewanee Review
SS	Scandinavian Studies
TCL	Twentieth Century Literature
TDR	The Drama Review (formerly Tulane Drama Review)
TJ	Theatre Journal (formerly Educational Theatre Journal)
TQ	The Texas Quarterly (Austin, Texas)
TSLL	Texas Studies in Literature and Language
Univ	Universitas: Zeitschrift für Wissenschaft, Kunst und Literatur (Stuttgart, West Germany)
WVUPP	West Virginia University, Philological Papers
YULG	Yale University Library Gazette

SELECT BIBLIOGRAPHY OF EUGENE O'NEILL SCHOLARSHIP—TO 1983

BIBLIOGRAPHICAL STUDIES

Atkinson, Jennifer McCabe. *Eugene O'Neill: A Descriptive Bibliography*. Pittsburgh Series in Bibliography. Pittsburgh, Pa.: University of Pittsburgh, 1974. [Indispensable; contains reproductions of original title pages.]

Bernard, Kathy Lynn. "The Research Library of Eugene O'Neill." *DAI* 38 (1977): 259A–260A.

Bryer, Jackson R. "Forty Years of O'Neill Criticism." *MD* 4 (1961): 196–216.

———. *Checklist of Eugene O'Neill*. Merrill Checklists. Columbus, Ohio: Charles F. Merrill, 1971.

Carpenter, Charles A. "Further Addenda to Miller: Elusive Articles, Books, and Parts of Books about O'Neill." *EON* 4, no. 3 (1980): 16–17.

———. "Parts of Books on O'Neill, 1966–78: Addenda to Miller." *EON* 2, no. 3 (1979): 29–31.

Frenz, Horst. "A List of Foreign Editions and Translations of Eugene O'Neill's Dramas. *BB* 18 (1943): 33–34.

Index Translationum. International Bibliography of Translations. Paris: UNESCO, 1932–. [Annual volume with names of translators. No cumulative index.]

Miller, Jordan Y. *Eugene O'Neill and the American Critic: A Bibliographical Checklist*. 2d ed. rev. Hamden, Conn.: Archon, 1973. [Original edition 1962. Indispensable. Contains cast lists for first productions and major revivals.]

———. *Playwright's Progress: O'Neill and the Critics*. Chicago: Scott, Foresman, 1965.

Reaver, J. Russell. *An O'Neill Concordance*. 3 vols. Detroit: Gale Research Press, 1969.

Sanborn, Ralph, and Barrett H. Clark. *A Bibliography of the Works of Eugene O'Neill*. New York: Random House, 1931. Reissued with additions, 1965.

Sturm, Clarence. "Scholarly Criticism of Eugene O'Neill in Periodicals, 1960–75, with a Bibliographical Overview of the American and German Studies." *DAI* 38 (1978): 5469A.

GUIDES TO MANUSCRIPT COLLECTIONS

American Literary Manuscripts: A Checklist of Holdings in Academic, Historical, and Public Libraries, Museums, and Authors' Homes in the United States. Compiled by J. Albert Robbins and others. 2d ed. Athens: University of Georgia Press, 1977.

National Union Catalogue of Manuscript Collections. Washington, D.C.: Library of Congress, 1959–. Annual, with index.

BIOGRAPHIES

Alexander, Doris M. *The Tempering of Eugene O'Neill*. New York: Harcourt, Brace, 1962. (Biography to 1920.)

Basso, Hamilton. "The Tragic Sense." *New Yorker*, February 28, March 6, March 13, 1948. (Profile of Eugene O'Neill.)

Boulton, Agnes. *Part of a Long Story*. Garden City, N.Y.: Doubleday, 1958.

Bowen, Crosswell, with the assistance of Shane O'Neill. *The Curse of the Misbegotten: A Tale of the House of O'Neill*. New York: McGraw-Hill, 1959.

Clark, Barrett H. *Eugene O'Neill: The Man and His Plays*. New York: Dover, 1967. (Based on earlier editions of 1926, 1947, but heavily revised.)

———. "O'Neill and the Guild." *Drama* 18 (1928): 169–71.

Frenz, Horst. *Eugene O'Neill*. Berlin: Colloquium Verlag, 1965. English translation, New York: Frederick Ungar, 1971.

Gassner, John. *Eugene O'Neill*. University of Minnesota Pamphlets on American Authors, no. 45. Minneapolis: University of Minnesota Press, 1965.

Gelb, Arthur and Barbara. *O'Neill*. Rev. ed. New York: Harper, 1973.

Hastings, Warren H., and Richard F. Weeks. "Episodes of Eugene O'Neill's Under-
    graduate Days at Princeton." *PULC* 29 (1968): 208–15.
Highsmith, James M. "A Description of the Cornell Collection of Eugene O'Neill's
    Letters to George Jean Nathan." *MD* 14 (1971): 420–25.
Jensen, George Henry. "The Eugene O'Neill-Theatre Guild Correspondence." *DAI* 40
    (1979): 853A.
Raleigh, John Henry. "Eugene O'Neill and the Escape from the Chateau d'If." In *Ideas
    in the Drama: Selected papers from the English Institute*, edited by John Gassner.
    English Institute Essays, 1963. New York: Columbia University Press, 1964.
    Reprinted in John Gassner, *O'Neill: A Collection of Critical Essays*. Englewood
    Cliffs, N.J.: Prentice-Hall, 1964.
Sheaffer, Louis. "Correcting Some Errors in Annals of O'Neill (Part I)." *EON* 7, iii
    (Winter 1983): 3–25.
———. *O'Neill: Son and Artist*. Boston: Little, Brown, 1973.
———. *O'Neill: Son and Playwright*. Boston: Little, Brown, 1968.
Voelker, Paul Duane. "Eugene O'Neill and George Pierce Baker: A Reconsideration."
    AL 49 (1977): 43–58.

ANCILLARY BIOGRAPHIES: BIOGRAPHIES AND AUTOBIOGRAPHIES OF PERSONS
CLOSELY ASSOCIATED WITH O'NEILL

Commins, Dorothy [Berliner]. *What is an Editor? Saxe Commins at Work*. Chicago:
    University of Chicago Press, 1978.
Cook, George Cram. *Greek Coins*. Edited by Susan Glaspell [Poems]. Introductions by
    Floyd Dell, Edna Kenton, and Susan Glaspell. New York: George H. Doran,
    1925. (The introductory material is important here.)
Deutsch, Helen, and Stella Hanau. *The Provincetown: A Story of the Theatre*. New York:
    Farrar & Rinehart, 1931.
Gardiner, Virginia. *'Friend and Lover': The Life of Louise Bryant*. New York: Horizon
    Press, 1982.
Gelb, Barbara. *So Short a Time: A Biography of John Reed and Louise Bryant*. New
    York: Norton, 1973.
Glaspell, Susan. *The Road to the Temple*. New York: Frederick A. Stokes, 1927, and
    reprinted 1941.
Goldberg, Isaac. *The Theatre of George Jean Nathan*. New York: Simon and Schuster,
    1926.
Hapgood, Hutchins. *A Victorian in the Modern World*. New York: Harcourt, Brace,
    1939.
Helburn, Theresa. *A Wayward Quest: The Autobiography of Theresa Helburn*. Boston:
    Little, Brown, 1960.
Hicks, Granville. *John Reed: The Making of a Revolutionary*. New York: Macmillan,
    1936.
Langner, Lawrence. *The Magic Curtain*. New York: Dutton, 1951.
Miller, William. *Dorothy Day: A Biography*. San Francisco: Harper and Row, 1982.
Pendleton, Ralph, ed. *The Theatre of Robert Edmond Jones*. Middletown, Conn.: Wes-
    leyan University Press, 1958.
Quintero, José. *If You Don't Dance, They Beat You*. Boston: Little, Brown, 1974.

Rosenstone, Robert A. *Romantic Revolutionary: A Biography of John Reed.* New York: A. A. Knopf, 1975.

Sarlós, Robert Karoly. *Jig Cook and the Provincetown Players: Theatre in Ferment.* Amherst: University of Massachusetts Press, 1982.

Simonson, Lee. *The Stage Is Set.* New York: Harcourt, Brace, 1932. [Contains material on Robert Edmond Jones and peripherally on O'Neill.] *PN 2037 S5 1713*

Vorse, Mary Heaton. *Time and the Town.* New York: Dial Press, 1942. [First years of the Provincetown Players.]

Waterman, Arthur E. *Susan Glaspell.* Twayne United States Authors Series, no. 101. New York: Twayne, 1966. *PS 3513 L35 Z93*

O'NEILL: MATERIAL DRAWN FROM MANUSCRIPT SOURCES AND PUBLISHED: 1960–

Bryer, Jackson R., and Ruth M. Alvarez, eds. *"The Theatre We Worked For": The Letters of Eugene O'Neill to Kenneth Macgowan.* With introductory essay by Travis Bogard. New Haven, Conn.: Yale University Press, 1982.

Davenport, William H. "The Published and Unpublished Poems of Eugene O'Neill." *YULG* 38, no. 2 (1963): 51–66.

Floyd, Virginia, ed. *Eugene O'Neill at Work: Newly Released Ideas for Plays.* New York: Frederick Ungar, 1981. [Materials drawn from O'Neill's notebooks.]

O'Neill, Eugene. *The Calms of Capricorn: A Play Developed from O'Neill's Scenario by Donald Gallup.* New Haven, Conn.: Ticknor & Fields, 1982. [With a transcription of the scenario.]

———. *"Children of the Sea" and Three Other Unpublished Plays by Eugene O'Neill.* *PS 3529* Edited by Jennifer McCabe Atkinson, with introductory foreword by Frank Durham. Washington, D.C.: NCR/Microcard Eds., 1972. (A Bruccoli-Clark Book.) *N5 A6 1972*

———. *Chris Christophersen.* Foreword by Leslie Eric Comens. New York: Random House, 1982.

———. *Inscriptions: Eugene O'Neill to Carlotta Monterey O'Neill.* Privately printed. New Haven, Conn.: Yale University Press, 1960.

———. *The Last Will and Testament of Silverdene Emblem O'Neill.* Privately printed "For Carlotta." New Haven, Conn.: Yale University Press, 1956.

———. *Poems, 1912–1944.* Edited by Donald Gallup. New Haven, Conn.: Ticknor & Fields, 1980.

———. *Ten "Lost" Plays of Eugene O'Neill.* Preface by Bennett Cerf. New York: Random House, 1964. *PS 3529 N5 A6 1964*

———. *Work Diary, 1924–1943.* Transcribed by Donald Gallup. Preliminary edition. 2 vols. New Haven, Conn.: Yale University Press, 1981.

CRITICAL STUDIES: GENERAL

Bentley, Eric. "Trying to Like O'Neill." *KR* 14 (1952): 476–92. (A hostile view.)

Berlin, Normand. *Eugene O'Neill.* New York: Grove, Evergreen, 1982.

Bogard, Travis. *Contour in Time: The Plays of Eugene O'Neill.* New York: Oxford University Press, 1972.

Bowling, Charis C. "The Touch of Poetry: A Study of the Role of Poetry in Three O'Neill Plays." *CLAJ* 12 (1968): 43–55.

Cargill, Oscar, N. Bryllion Fagin, and William J. Fischer, eds. *O'Neill and His Plays: Four Decades of Criticism.* New York: New York University Press, 1961. (Indispensable.)

Carpenter, Frederic I. *Eugene O'Neill.* Rev. ed. Twayne United States Authors Series, no. 66. Boston: Twayne, 1979. (Originally published 1964.)

Chabrowe, Leonard. *Ritual and Pathos: The Theater of O'Neill.* Lewisburg, Pa.: Bucknell University Press, 1976.

Chaitin, Norman C. "O'Neill: The Power of Daring." *MD* 3 (1960): 231–41.

Chiaromonte, Nicola. "Eugene O'Neill (1958)." *SR* 68 (1960): 494–501.

Chothia, Jean. *Forging a Language: A Study of the Plays of Eugene O'Neill.* Cambridge: Cambridge University Press, 1969.

Cronin, Harry. *Eugene O'Neill: Irish and American.* New York: Arno, 1977.

Doyle, Louis F., S.J. "The Myth of Eugene O'Neill." *Renascence* 17 (1964): 59–62, 81.

Engel, Edwin. *The Haunted Heroes of Eugene O'Neill.* Cambridge Mass.: Harvard University Press, 1953.

————. "O'Neill, 1960." *MD* 3 (1960): 219–23.

Fagin, N. Bryllion. "Eugene O'Neill." *Antioch Review* 14 (March 1954): 14–26.

Falk, Doris V. *Eugene O'Neill and the Tragic Tension.* New Brunswick, N.J.: Rutgers University Press, 1958.

————. "That Paradox, Eugene O'Neill." *MD* 6 (1963): 221–38.

Falk, Signi. "Dialogue in the Plays of Eugene O'Neill." *MD* 3 (1960): 314–25.

Fergusson, Francis. "Eugene O'Neill." *Hound & Horn* 3 (1930): 145–60.

Fleisher, Frederic, and Horst Frenz. "Eugene O'Neill and the Royal Dramatic Theatre of Stockholm: The Later Phase." *MD* 10 (1967): 300–11.

Floyd, Virginia, ed. *Eugene O'Neill: A World View.* New York: Frederick Ungar, 1979.

Gassner, John, ed. *O'Neill: A Collection of Critical Essays.* Englewood Cliffs, N.J.: Prentice-Hall, 1964.

Geddes, Virgil. *The Melodramadness of Eugene O'Neill.* Brookfield, Conn.: Brookfield Players, 1934.

Goldman, Arnold. "The Vanity of Personality: The Development of Eugene O'Neill." In *American Theatre Today*, edited by John R. Brown and Bernard Harris. Stratford-upon-Avon Studies 10. London: E. Arnold, 1967, pp. 28–51.

Griffin, Ernest G. *Eugene O'Neill: A Collection of Criticism.* New York: McGraw Hill, 1976. (With selected bibliography.)

Halio, Jay L. "Eugene O'Neill: The Long Quest." In *Modern American Drama: Essays in Criticism*, edited by William E. Taylor. Deland, Fla.: Everett Edwards, 1968, pp. 13–27.

Hofmannsthal, Hugo von. "Eugene O'Neill." Translated by Barrett H. Clark. *Freeman* 7 (March 21, 1923): 39–41.

Josephs, Lois S. "The Women of Eugene O'Neill: Sex Role Stereotypes." *BSUF* 14, no. 3 (1973): 3–8.

Kemelman, H. G. "Eugene O'Neill and the Highbrow Melodrama." *Bookman* 75 (1932): 482–91.

Klavsons, Janis. "O'Neill's Dreamer: Success and Failure." *MD* 3 (1960): 268–72.

Krutch, Joseph Wood. *The American Drama since 1918.* New York: Random House, 1939. [Chapter 3, "Tragedy: Eugene O'Neill."]

Lee, Robert C. "The Lonely Dream." *MD* 9 (1966): 127–35.

Leech, Clifford. *Eugene O'Neill*. Edinburgh: Oliver & Boyd, 1963; New York: Grove Press, 1963.
———. "Eugene O'Neill and His Plays." *CritQ* 3 (1961): 242–56, 339–53.

Lindell, Richard L., II. "Eugene O'Neill from Play into Film." *Filmograph*. 4, no. 3 (1975): 2–15.

Miller, Jordan Y., comp. *Playwright's Progress: O'Neill and the Critics*. Chicago: Scott, Foresman, 1965.

Moleski, Joseph J. "Eugene O'Neill and the Cruelty of Theater." *CompD* 15 (Winter 1981–82): 327–42.

Mullaly, Edward. "O'Neill and the Perfect Pattern." *DR* 52 (1972–73): 603–10.

Nathan, George Jean. "O'Neill: A Critical Summation." *American Mercury* 63 (1946): 713–19.

Pallette, Drew B. "O'Neill and the Comic Spirit." *MD* 3 (1960): 273–79.

Parks, Edd Winfield. "Eugene O'Neill's Quest." *TDR* 4, no. 3 (1960): 99–107.

Raghavacharyulu, Dhupaty V. K. *Eugene O'Neill: A Study*. Bombay, India: Popular Prakashan, 1965.

Raleigh, John Henry. *The Plays of Eugene O'Neill*. Carbondale: Southern Illinois University Press, 1965.

The Revels History of Drama in English. Vol. 8, *American Drama*. Edited by T. W. Craik. London: Methuen, 1977. (Contains two chapters on O'Neill: Travis Bogard, "O'Neill versus Shaw," pp. 66–76; Walter J. Meserve, "Arrival of a Master Playwright, Eugene O'Neill," pp. 219–26.)

Rollyson, Carl Jr. "O'Neill's Mysticism from His Historical Trilogy to *Long Day's Journey into Night*." *SMLit* 1 (Spring 1981): 218–36.

Ryan, Pat M. "Stockholm Revives O'Neill." *ScanR* 65, no. 1 (1977): 18–23.

Skinner, Richard Dana. *Eugene O'Neill: A Poet's Quest*. New York: Longmans, Green, 1935.

Tiusanen, Timo. *O'Neill's Scenic Images*. Princeton, N.J.: Princeton University Press, 1969.

Törnqvist, Egil. *A Drama of Souls*. New Haven, Conn.: Yale University Press, 1969.
———. "O'Neill's Work Method." *SN* 49 (1977): 43–58.
———. "Strindberg and O'Neill." In *Structures of Influence: A Comparative Approach to August Strindberg*, edited by Marilyn Johns. Chapel Hill: University of North Carolina Press, 1981, pp. 227–91.

Whitman, Robert F. "O'Neill's Search for a Language of the Theatre." *QJS* 46 (1960): 153–70.

Winther, Sophus Keith. *Eugene O'Neill: A Critical Study*. 2d ed. New York: Russell & Russell, 1961. [Originally published 1934.]
———. "Eugene O'Neill: The Dreamer Confronts His Dreams." *ArQ* 21 (1965): 221–33.

Young, Stark. "Eugene O'Neill: Notes from a Critic's Diary." *Harper's Magazine* 204 (June 1957): 66–74.

CRITICAL STUDIES: INDIVIDUAL PLAYS

A representative selection of criticism, mainly American, written primarily during the 1960–1981 period. Short notes are included. Divided into three sections, according to O'Neill's major writing periods: I, –1922; II, 1923–1934; III, 1935–.

Section I: –1922

Alexander, Doris M. "Eugene O'Neill: *The Hound of Heaven* and The Hell Hole." *MLQ* 20 (1959): 307–14. [Regarding *Servitude, Welded, Days Without End.*]

Bogard, Travis. " *'Anna Christie'*: Her Fall and Rise." In *O'Neill: A Collection of Critical Essays*, edited by John Gassner. Englewood Cliffs, N.J.: Prentice-Hall, 1964.   *PS/3529/ A5/ Z 648*

Clark, Marden J. "Tragic Effect in *The Hairy Ape.*" *MD* 10 (1967): 372–82.

Cooley, John R. "*The Emperor Jones* and the Harlem Renaissance." *SLitI* 7, no. 2 (1974): 73–83.

Dave, R. A. "Have We Lost the Tragic Sense? Eugene O'Neill's *Beyond the Horizon*: A Study." *LCrit* 6, no. 4 (1965): 26–35.

Fish, Charles. "Beginnings: O'Neill's *The Web.*" *PULC* 27 (1965): 3–20.

Flory, Claude R. "Notes on the Antecedents of *Anna Christie.*" *PMLA* 86 (1971): 77–83.

Floyd, Virginia. "The Search for Self in *The Hairy Ape*: An Exercise in Futility?" *EON* 1, no. 3 (1978): 4–7.

Frazer, Winifred. "Chris and Poseidon: Man versus God in *Anna Christie.*" *MD* 12 (1970): 279–85.

Goldhurst, William. "A Literary Source for O'Neill's *In the Zone.*" *AL* 35 (1964): 530–34.

Highsmith, James Milton. " 'The Personal Equation': Eugene O'Neill's Abandoned Play." *SHR* 8 (1974): 195–212.

Hinden, Michael. "*The Emperor Jones*: O'Neill, Nietzsche, and the American Past." *EON* 3, no. 3 (1980): 2–4.

———. "Ironic Use of Myth in *The Hairy Ape.*" *EON* 1, no. 3 (1978): 2–4.

Kagan, Norman. "The Return of *The Emperor Jones.*" *Negro History Bulletin* 34 (1971): 160–62.

McAleer,, John J. "Christ Symbolism in *Anna Christie.*" *MD* 4 (1961): 389–96.

Nolan, Patrick J. "*The Emperor Jones*: A Jungian View of the Origin of Fear in the Black Face."*EON* 4, nos. 1–2 (1980): 6–9.

Roy, Emil. "Eugene O'Neill's *The Emperor Jones* and *The Hairy Ape* as Mirror Plays." *CompD* 2 (1968): 21–31.

———. "Tragic Tension in *Beyond the Horizon.*" *BSUF* 8, no. 1 (1967): 74–79.

Rust, R. Dilworth. "The Unity of O'Neill's *S.S. Glencairn.*" *AL* 37 (1965): 280–90.

Scarbrough, Alex. "O'Neill's Use of the Displaced Archetype in *The Moon of the Caribees.*" *WVUPP* 19 (1972): 41–44.

Scheick, William J. "The Ending of O'Neill's *Beyond the Horizon.*" *MD* 20 (1977): 293–98.

Törnqvist, Egil. "Platonic Love in O'Neill's *Welded.*" In *Eugene O'Neill: A World View*, edited by Virginia Floyd. New York: Frederick Ungar, 1979.

Voelker, Paul D. "The Uncertain Origins of Eugene O'Neill's *Bound East for Cardiff.*" *SB* 32 (1979): 273–81.

Section II: 1923–1934

Adler, Jacob H. "The Worth of *Ah, Wilderness!*" *MD* 3 (1960): 280–88.

Alexander, Doris M. "Captain Brant and Captain Brassbound: The Origin of an O'Neill Character." *Modern Language Notes* 74 (1959): 306–10.

———. "*Lazarus Laughed* and Buddha." *MLQ* 17 (1957): 357–65.

———. "Psychological Fate in *Mourning Becomes Electra*." *PMLA* 68 (1953): 923–34.

———. "*Strange Interlude* and Schopenhauer." *AL* 25 (1953): 213–28.

Asselineau, Roger. "*Mourning Becomes Electra* as a Tragedy." *MD* 1 (1958): 143–50.

Berkelman, Robert. "O'Neill's Everyman." *SAQ* 58 (1959): 609–16 [Regarding *The Great God Brown*.]

Blesch, Edwin J. "Lots of Desire, No Elms: A Reconsideration of Eugene O'Neill's *Desire Under the Elms* on Film." *NR* 4, no. 2 (1982): 14–22.

Bowles, Patrick. "Another Biblical Parallel in *Desire Under the Elms*." *EON* 2, no. 3 (1979): 10–12.

Cunningham, Frank R. "*The Ancient Mariner* and the Genesis of O'Neill's Romanticism." *EON* 3, no. 1 (1979): 6–7.

———. "*The Great God Brown* and O'Neill's Romantic Vision." *BSUF* 14, no. 3 (1973): 69–78.

Curran, Ronald T. "Insular Typees: Puritanism and Primitivism in *Mourning Becomes Electra*." *Revue des Langues Vivantes* (Brussels), 41 (1975): 371–77.

Dahlström, Carl E.W.L. "*Dynamo* and *Lazarus Laughed*: Some Limitations." *MD* 3 (1960): 224–30.

Day, Cyrus. "*Amor Fati*: O'Neill's Lazarus as Superman and Savior." *MD* 3 (1960): 297–305.

Feldman, Robert. "The Longing for Death in O'Neill's *Strange Interlude* and *Mourning Becomes Electra*." *L&P* 13 (1981): 39–48.

Frenz, Horst, and Martin Mueller. "More Shakespeare and Less Aeschylus in Eugene O'Neill's *Mourning Becomes Electra*." *AL* 38 (1966): 85–100.

Gallup, Donald. "Eugene O'Neill's *The Ancient Mariner*." *YULG* 35 (1960): 61–86. [Includes text of the play, pp. 63–86.]

Gey, Guy. "*Dynamo* de Eugene O'Neill: 'La maladie contemporaine' et l'exploitation d'un mythe moderne." *Caliban* 7 (1970): 35–41.

———. "Unité et dualité du mythe de Dionysos dans *Lazarus Laughed* de Eugene O'Neill." *Caliban* 6 (1969): 69–72.

Hannzeli, Victor E. "The Progeny of Atreus." *MD* 3 (1960): 75–81. [*Mourning Becomes Electra* and Sartre's *The Flies*.]

Hartman, Murray. "*Desire Under the Elms* in the Light of Strindberg's Influence." *AL* 33 (1961): 360–69.

Herron, Ima H. "O'Neill's Comedy of Recollection: A Dramatization of 'The Real America'," *CEA* 30, no. 4 (1968): 16–18.

Hinden, Michael. "*The Birth of Tragedy* and *The Great God Brown*." *MD* 16 (1973): 129–40.

———. "Desire and Forgiveness: O'Neill's Diptych." *CompD* 14 (1980): 240–50. [*Desire Under the Elms* and *A Moon for the Misbegotten*.]

———. "*Desire Under the Elms*: O'Neill and the American Romance." *ForumH* 15, no. 1 (1977): 44–51.

———. "The Transitional Nature of *All God's Chillun Got Wings*." *EON* 4, no. 2 (1980): 3–5.

Lemanis, Mara. "*Desire Under the Elms* and Tragic Form: A Study of Misalliance." *SDR* 16, no. 3 (1978): 46–55.

Lucow, Ben. "O'Neill's Use of Realism in *Ah, Wilderness!*" *NMAL* 1 (1977): item 10.

McDonnell, Thomas P. "O'Neill's Drama of the Psyche." *Catholic World* 197 (1963): 120–25.

McDonough, Carole, and Brian McDonough. "*Mourning Becomes Electra*: A Study between Puritanism and Paganism." *EngR* 3 (1975): 6–19.

Macgowan, Kenneth. "O'Neill and a Mature Hollywood Outlook." *Theatre Arts* 42 (April 1958): 79–81. [*Desire Under the Elms*.]

Meyers, Jay R. "O'Neill's Use of the Phèdre Legend in *Desire Under the Elms*." *RLC* 41 (1967): 120–25.

Myers, Andrew B. " 'Hysteria Night in the Sophomore Dormitory': Eugene O'Neill's *Days Without End*." *Columbia Library Columns* 28, no. 2 (1979): 3–13.

Nagarajan, S. "Eugene O'Neill's *Mourning Becomes Electra*: The Classical Aspect." *LCrit* 5, no. 3 (1962): 148–54.

Nolan, Patrick J. "*Desire Under the Elms*: Characters by Jung." *EON* 5, no. 2 (1981): 5–10.

Racey, Edgar F. "Myth as Tragic Structure in *Desire Under the Elms*." *MD* 5 (1962): 42–46.

Robinson, James A. "Christianity and *All God's Chillun Got Wings*." *EON* 2, no. 1 (1978): 1–3.

Roy, Emil. "O'Neill's *Desire Under the Elms* and Shakespeare's *King Lear*." *NS* 15 (1966): 1–6.

Sogliuzzo, A. Richard. "The Uses of the Mask in *The Great God Brown* and *Six Characters in Search of an Author*." *ETJ* 18 (1966): 224–29.

Stafford, John. "*Mourning Becomes Electra*." *TSLL* 3 (1962): 549–56.

Stroupe, John H. "O'Neill's *Marco Millions*: A Road to Xanadu." *MD* 12 (1970): 377–82.

Törnqvist, Egil. "O'Neill's Lazarus and Christ." *AL* 41 (1970): 543–54.

Tuck, Susan. " 'Electricity Is God, Now': D. H. Lawrence and O'Neill." *EON* 5, no. 2 (1981): 10–15.

Valgemae, Mardi. "Eugene O'Neill's Preface to *The Great Good Brown*." *YULG* 43 (1968): 43–49. [Includes photostat and transcript.]

Van Laan, Thomas F. "Singing in the Wilderness: The Dark Vision of Eugene O'Neill's Only Mature Comedy." *MD* 22 (1979): 9–18.

Weissman, Philip. "*Mourning Becomes Electra* and *The Prodigal*: Electra and Orestes." *MD* 3 (1960): 257–59.

Winther, Sophus Keith. "*Desire Under the Elms*: A Modern Tragedy." *MD* 3 (1960): 326–32.

Section III: 1935–

Alexander, Doris M. "Hugo of *The Iceman Cometh*: Realism and O'Neill." *AQ* 5 (1963): 357–66.

———. "The Missing Half of *Hughie*." *TDR* 11, no. 4 (1967): 125–26.

Andreach, Robert J. "O'Neill's Women in *The Iceman Cometh*." *Renascence* 18 (1966): 89–98.

Arested, Sverre. "*The Iceman Cometh* and *The Wild Duck*." *SS* 38 (1966): 331–50.

Barlow, Judith E. "*Long Day's Journey into Night: From Early Notes to Finished Play*." *MD* 22 (1979): 19–28.

Berlin, Normand. "Ghosts of the Past: O'Neill and *Hamlet*." *MR* 20 (1979): 213–23.

Bilman, Carl. "Language as These in Eugene O'Neill's *Hughie*." *NMAL* 3 (1979): item 25.

Brashear, William R. "The Wisdom of Silenus in O'Neill's *Iceman*." *AL* 36 (1964): 180–88.

Butler, Robert. "Artifice and Art: Words in *The Iceman Cometh* and *Hughie*." *EON* 5, no. 1 (1981): 3–6.

Carpenter, Frederic I. "Focus on Eugene O'Neill's *The Iceman Cometh*: The Iceman Hath Come." In *American Dreams, American Nightmares*, edited by David Madden. Crosscurrents/Modern Techniques. Preface by Harry T. Moore. Carbondale and Edwardsville: Southern Illinois University Press, 1970, pp. 158–64.

———. "*Hughie*: By Way of Obit." *EON* 1, no. 1 (1977): 1–3.

———. "The Romantic Tragedy of Eugene O'Neill." *CE* 6 (1945): 250–58.

Chabrowe, Leonard. "Dionysus in *The Iceman Cometh*." *MD* 4 (1961): 377–78.

Day, Cyrus. "The Iceman and the Bridegroom: Some Observations on the Death of O'Neill's Salesman."*MD* 1 (1958): 3–9.

Driver, Tom F. "On the Late Plays of Eugene O'Neill." *TDR* 3 (December 1958): 8–20.

Egri, Peter. "*The Iceman Cometh*: European Origins and American Originality." *EON* 5, no. 3 (1981): 5–10.

———. "The Reinterpretation of the Chekhovian Mosaic Design in O'Neill's *Long Day's Journey into Night*." *ALitASH* 22 (1980): 29–71.

Fiet, Lowell A. "O'Neill's Modification of Traditional Themes in *A Touch of the Poet*." *ETJ* 27 (1975): 508–15.

Finkelstein, Sidney. "O'Neill's *Long Day's Journey*." *Mainstream* 16, no. 6 (1963): 47–51.

Fitzgerald, John J. "The Bitter Harvest of O'Neill's Projected Cycle." *NEQ* 50 (1967): 364–74.

———. "Guilt and Redemption in O'Neill's Last Play: A Study of *A Moon for the Misbegotten*." *TQ* 1 (1966): 146–58.

Frazer, Winifred. *E.G. and E.G.O.: Emma Goldman and "The Iceman Cometh."* University of Florida Monographs/Humanities Series, no. 43. Gainesville: University of Florida, 1974.

———. *Love as Death in "The Iceman Cometh": A Modern Treatment of an Ancient Theme*. University of Florida Monographs/Humanities Series, no. 27. Gainesville: University of Florida, 1967.

———. "King Lear and Hickey: Bridegroom and Iceman." *MD* 15 (1973): 69–78.

———. "O'Neill's *Iceman*—Not Ice Man." *AL* 44 (1973): 677–78.

———. " 'Revolution' in *The Iceman Cometh*." *MD* 22 (1979): 1–8.

Gierow, Karl Ragnar. "Eugene O'Neill's Posthumous Plays." *World Theatre* 7 (1958): 46–52. [Includes identification of O'Neill's nervous tremor.]

Hartman, Murray. "The Skeletons in O'Neill's *Mansions*." *Drama Survey* 5 (1967): 256–79.

Hayes, Richard. "Eugene O'Neill: The Tragic in Exile." *Theatre Arts* October 1963. Reprinted in *O'Neill: A Collection of Critical Essays*, edited by John Gassner. Englewood Cliffs, N.J.: Prentice-Hall, 1964.

Josephson, Lennart. *A Role: O'Neill's Cornelius Melody*. Stockholm Studies in the History of Literature, no. 19. Stockholm: Almqvist & Wiksell, 1977.

Kennedy, Joyce Deveau. "O'Neill's Lavinia Mannon and the Dickinson Legend." *AL* 49 (1977): 108–13.

Lee, Robert C. "Eugene O'Neill's Remembrance: The Past Is the Present." *ArQ* 23 (1967): 293–305.

———. "Evangelism and Anarchy in *The Iceman Cometh*." *MD* 12 (1969): 173–86.

McDonald, David. "The Phenomenology of the Glance in *Long Day's Journey into Night*." *TJ* 31 (1979): 343–56.

Mayberry, Robert. "Sterile Wedding: The Comic Structure of O'Neill's *Hughie*." *MSE* 7, no. 3 (1980): 10–19.

Miller, Jordan Y. "Murky Moon." *KanQ* 7, no. 4 (1975): 103–05. [*A Moon for the Misbegotten*.]

Muchnic, Helen. "Circe's Swine: Plays by Gorky and O'Neill." *CL* 3 (1951): 119–28. Reprinted in *O'Neill: A Collection of Critical Essays*, edited by John Gassner. [Regarding *The Iceman Cometh*.]

Nagarajan, S. "A Note on O'Neill's *Long Day's Journey into Night*." *LCrit* 7, no. 3 (1966): 52–54.

Nethercot, Arthur H. "O'Neill's *More Stately Mansions*." *ETJ* 27 (1975): 161–69.

Pallette, Drew B. "O'Neill's *A Touch of the Poet* and His Other Last Plays." *ArQ* 13 (1957): 308–19.

Petite, Joseph. "The Paradox of Power in *More Stately Mansions*." *EON* 5, no. 3 (1981): 2–5.

Presley, Delma E. "O'Neill's *Iceman*: Another Meaning." *AL* 42 (1970): 387–88.

Quinn, James P. "*The Iceman Cometh*: O'Neill's Long Journey into Adolescence." *JPC* 6 (1972): 171–77.

Raleigh, John Henry. "The Irish Atavism of *A Moon for the Misbegotten*." In *Eugene O'Neill: A World View*, edited by Virginia Floyd. New York: Frederick Ungar, 1979, pp. 229–36.

———. "O'Neill's *Long Day's Journey into Night* and New England Irish Catholicism." *PR* 26 (1959): 573–92. Reprinted in *O'Neill: A Collection of Critical Essays*, edited by John Gassner.

———, ed. *Twentieth-Century Interpretations of "The Iceman Cometh."* Englewood Cliffs, N.J.: Prentice-Hall, 1968.

Real, Jere. "The Brothel in O'Neill's *Mansions*." *MD* 12 (1970): 383–89.

Redford, Grant H. "Dramatic Arts vs. Autobiography: A Look at *Long Day's Journey into Night*." *CE* 25 (1954): 527–35.

Reilly, Kevin P. "Pitching the Mansion and Pumping the Morphine: O'Neill's *Long Day's Journey into Night*." *GyS* 5 (1978): 22–33.

Reinhardt, Nancy. "Formal Patterns in *The Iceman Cometh*." *MD* 16 (1973): 119–28.

Rich, J. Dennis. "Exile Without Remedy: The Late Plays of Eugene O'Neill." In *Eugene O'Neill: A World View*, edited by Virginia Floyd, pp. 257–76.

Rothenberg, Albert, and Eugene D. Shapiro. "The Defense of Psychoanalysis in Literature: *Long Day's Journey into Night* and *A View from the Bridge*." *CompD* 7 (1973): 51–67.

Scheibler, Rolf. "*Hughie*: A One-Act Play for the Imaginary Theatre." *ES* 54 (1973): 231–48.

———. *The Late Plays of Eugene O'Neill*. Bern: Francke Verlag, 1970.

Schvey, Henry I. "The Past Is the Present, Isn't It? Eugene O'Neill's *Long Day's Journey into Night*." *DQR* 10 (1980): 84–99.

Shaughnessy, Edward I. "The Iceman Melteth: O'Neill's Return to Cultural Origins." *EON* 3, no. 2 (1979): 3–6.

Shawcross, John T. "The Road to Ruin: The Beginning of O'Neill's *Long Day's Journey into Night*." *MD* 3 (1960): 289–96.

Thurman, William R. "Journey into Night: Elements of Tragedy in Eugene O'Neill." *QJS* 53 (1966): 139–45.

Tuck, Susan. "House of Compson, House of Tyrone: Faulkner's Influence on O'Neill." *EON* 5, no. 3 (1981): 10–16.

Watson, James G. "The Theater in *The Iceman Cometh*: Some Modernist Implications." *ArQ* 34 (1978): 230–38.

Weales, Gerald. "Eugene O'Neill: *The Iceman Cometh*." In *Landmarks of American Writing*, edited by Hennig Cohen. New York: Basic Books, 1969, pp. 353–67.

Welch, Dennis M. "Hickey as Satanic Force in *The Iceman Cometh*." *ArQ* 34 (1978): 219–29.

Wiles, Timothy J. "Tammanyite, Progressive, and Anarchist: Political Communities in *The Iceman Cometh*." *Clio* 9 (1980): 179–96.

Winther, Sophus Keith. "*The Iceman Cometh*: A Study in Technique." *ArQ* 3 (1947): 293–300.

———. "O'Neill's Tragic Themes: *Long Day's Journey into Night*." *ArQ* 13 (1957): 295–307.

Wright, Robert C. "O'Neill's Universalizing Technique in *The Iceman Cometh*." *MD* 8 (1965): 1–11.

CRITICAL STUDIES: INFLUENCES AND THEMES

Alexander, Doris M. "Eugene O'Neill and Light on the Path." *MD* 3 (1960): 260–67. [Theosophical publication.]

———. "Eugene O'Neill as Social Critic." *AQ* 6 (1954): 349–63.

Andreach, Robert J. "O'Neill's Use of Dante in *The Fountain* and *The Hairy Ape*." *MD* 10 (1967): 48–56.

Blackburn, Clara. "Continental Influences on Eugene O'Neill's Expressionistic Dramas." *AL* 13 (1941): 109–33.

Brashear, William R. "O'Neill and Shaw: The Play as Will and Idea." *Criticism* 8 (1966): 155–69.

———. "O'Neill's Schopenhauer Interlude." *Criticism* 6 (1964): 256–65.

———. " 'Tomorrow' and 'Tomorrow': Conrad and O'Neill." *Renascence* 20 (1967): 18–21, 55.

Carpenter, Frederic I. "Eugene O'Neill, the Orient, and American Transcendentalism." In *Transcendentalism and Its Legacy*, edited by Myron Simon and Thornton H. Parsons. Ann Arbor: University of Michigan Press, 1966, pp. 204–14.

Cerf, Walter. "Psychoanalysis and the Realistic Drama." *Journal of Aesthetics & Art Criticism* 16 (1958): 328–36.

Chioles, John. "Aeschylus and O'Neill: A Phenomenological View." *CompD* 14 (1980): 159–87.

Clark, Barrett H. "Aeschylus and O'Neill." *EJ* 21 (1932): 699–710.

Egri, Péter. "The Use of the Short Story in O'Neill's and Chekhov's One-Act Plays." In *Eugene O'Neill: A World View*, edited by Virginia Floyd. New York: Frederick Ungar, 1979, pp. 115–44. In *Ideas in the Drama: Selected Papers from the English*

Institute, edited by John Gassner. English Institute Essays, 1963. New York: Columbia University Press, 1964, pp. 101–24. *PN* / *16 2] / G 28*

Fagin, N. Bryllion. "Freud on the American Stage." *ETJ* 2 (1950): 296–305.

Fleischer, Frederic. "Strindberg and O'Neill." *Symposium* 10 (1956): 84–93.

———. "Swedes in the Published Plays of Eugene O'Neill." *OL* 12 (1957): 99–103.

Fluckiger, Stephen L. "The Idea of Puritanism in the Plays of Eugene O'Neill." *Renascence* 30 (1978): 152–62.

Frenz, Horst. "Eugene O'Neill and Georg Kaiser." In *Eugene O'Neill: A World View*, edited by Virginia Floyd, pp. 172–85. *PS* / *3 5 2] / N 5 / Z 6 3 7*

———. "Eugene O'Neill's *Desire Under the Elms* and Henrik Ibsen's *Rosmersholm*." *Jahrbuch für Amerikastudien* 9 (1964): 160–65.

Fuchs, Elinor. "O'Neill's *Poet*: Touched by Ibsen." *ETJ* 30 (1978): 513–16.

Gatta, John, Jr. "The American Subject: Moral History as Tragedy in the Plays of Eugene O'Neill." *ELWIU* 6 (1979): 227–39.

Gillett, Peter J. "O'Neill and the Racial Myths." *TCL* 18 (1972): 111–20.

Griffin, Ernest G. "Pity, Alienation, and Reconciliation in Eugene O'Neill." *Mosaic* 2, no. 1 (1968): 66–76.

Hartman, Murray. "Strindberg and O'Neill." *ETJ* 18 (1966): 216–23.

Hays, Peter L. "Biblical Perversions in *Desire Under the Elms*." *MD* 11 (1969): 423–28.

Hayward, Ira N. "Strindberg's Influence on Eugene O'Neill." *Poet Lore* 39 (1928): 596–604.

Innes, Christopher. "The Salesman on the Stage: A Study in the Social Influence of Drama." *ESC* 3 (1977): 336–50.

Jackson, Esther M. "O'Neill the Humanist." In *Eugene O'Neill: A World View*, edited by Virginia Floyd, pp. 252–56. *PS* / *3 5 2 9 / N 5 / Z 6 3 7*

Josephs, Lois S. "The Women of Eugene O'Neill: Sex Role Stereotypes." *BSUF* 14, no. 3 (1973): 3–8.

LaBelle, Maurice M. "Dionysus and Despair: The Influence of Nietzsche upon O'Neill's Drama." *ETJ* 25 (1973): 436–42.

Lawrence, Kenneth. "Dionysus and O'Neill." *University Review* 33 (1966): 67–70.

Marcus, Mordecai. "Eugene O'Neill's Debt to Thoreau in *A Touch of the Poet*." *JEGP* 62 (1963): 270–79.

Nethercot, Arthur H. "Madness in the Plays of Eugene O'Neill." *MD* 18 (1975): 259–78.

———. "The Psychoanalyzing of Eugene O'Neill." *MD* 3 (1960): 242–56, 357–72.

———. "The Psychoanalyzing of Eugene O'Neill: Postscript." *MD* 8 (1965): 150–55.

———. "The Psychoanalyzing of Eugene O'Neill: P.P.S." *MD* 16 (1973): 35–48.

Pettegrove, James P. "Eugene O'Neill as Thinker." *MuK* 10 (1964): 617–24.

Pommer, Henry F. "The Mysticism of Eugene O'Neill." *MD* 9 (1966): 26–39.

Raleigh, John Henry. "The Last Confession: O'Neill and the Catholic Confessional." In *Eugene O'Neill: A World View*, edited by Virginia Floyd, pp. 212–28. *PS* / *3 3*

Robinson, James A. *Eugene O'Neill and Oriental Thought: A Divided Vision*. Carbondale and Edwardsville: Southern Illinois University Press, 1982.

———. "O'Neill's Grotesque Dancers." *MD* 19 (1976): 341–49.

———. "O'Neill's Symbolic Sounds." *Modern Language Studies* 9, no. 2 (1979): 36–45.

———. "Taoism and O'Neill's *Marco Millions*." *CompD* 14 (1980): 152–62.

Salem, James M. "Eugene O'Neill and the Sacrament of Marriage." *Serif* 3, no. 2 (1966): 23–35.

Scrimgeour, James R. "From Loving to the Misbegotten: Despair in the Drama of Eugene O'Neill." *MD* 20 (1977): 37–53.

Sproxton, Birk. "Eugene O'Neill: Masks and Demons." *Sphinx* 3 (1975): 57–62.

Stamm, Rudolph. "The Dramatic Experiments of Eugene O'Neill." *ES* 28 (1947): 1–15.

———. " 'Faithful Realism': Eugene O'Neill and the Problem of Style." *ES* 40 (1959): 242–50.

———. "The Orestes Theme in Three Plays by Eugene O'Neill, T. S. Eliot, and J. P. Sartre." *ES* 30 (1949): 244–55.

Steinhauer, H. "Eros and Psyche: A Nietzschean Motif in Anglo-American Literature." *MLN* 64 (1949): 217–28.

Strauman, Henrich. "The Philosophical Background of the Modern American Drama." *ES* 26 (1944): 65–78.

Stroupe, John H. "The Abandonment of Ritual: Jean Anouilh and Eugene O'Neill." *Renascence* 28 (1976): 147–54.

Törnqvist, Egil. "Ibsen and O'Neill: A Study in Influence." *SS* 37 (1965): 211–35.

———. "Jesus and Judas: On Biblical Allusions in O'Neill's Plays." *EA* 24 (1971): 41–49.

———. "*Miss Julie* and O'Neill." *MD* 19 (1976): 351–64.

———. "Nietzsche and O'Neill: A Study in Affinity." *OL* 23 (1968): 97–126.

———. "Personal Nomenclature in the Plays of Eugene O'Neill." *MD* 8 (1966): 362–73.

Valgemae, Mardi. "O'Neill and German Expressionism." *MD* 10 (1967): 111–23.

Winther, Sophus Keith. "Strindberg and O'Neill: A Study of Influence." *SS* 31 (1959): 103–20.

CRITICAL STUDIES: REPUTATION

Dobree, Bonamy. "The Plays of Eugene O'Neill." *SR* 2 (1937): 435–46.

Fagin, N. Bryllion. "Eugene O'Neill." *AR* 14 (1954): 14–26.

Falb, Lewis W. "The Critical Reception of Eugene O'Neill on the French Stage." *ETJ* 22 (1970): 397–405.

Freedman, Morris. "O'Neill and Contemporary American Drama." *CE* 23 (1962): 570–74.

Frenz, Horst. "Notes on Eugene O'Neill in Japan." *MD* 3 (1960): 306–13.

Herbert, Edward T. "Eugene O'Neill: An Evaluation by Fellow Playwrights." *MD* 6 (1963): 239–40.

Jaräb, Josef. "The Lasting Challenge of Eugene O'Neill." In *Eugene O'Neill: A World View*, edited by Virginia Floyd. New York: Frederick Ungar, 1979, pp. 84–100.

Kpreneva, Maya. "One Hundred Per Cent American Tragedy: A Soviet View." In *Eugene O'Neill: A World View*, edited by Virginia Floyd, pp. 145–71.

Krutch, Joseph Wood. "Die Wiederentdeckung Eugene O'Neills." *Deutsche Universitätszeitung* 14 (1959): 286–89.

———. "Why the O'Neill Star is Rising." *NYTM* March 19, 1961), pp. 36–37, 108, 111.

Leech, Clifford. "O'Neill in England: From *Anna Christie* to *Long Day's Journey into*

Night: 1923–1958.'' In *Eugene O'Neill: A World View*, edited by Virginia Floyd, pp. 68–72.

Loving, Pierre. ''Eugene O'Neill.'' *Bookman* 53 (1921): 511–20.

Lüdeke, Henry. ''O'Neill—der grosse Dramatiker der heutigen Weltliteratur.'' *Univ* 19 (1964): 587–94.

Olsson, Tom. ''O'Neill and the Royal Dramatic.'' In *Eugene O'Neill: A World View*, edited by Virginia Floyd, pp. 34–60.

Reardon, William R. ''O'Neill since World War II: Critical Reception in New York.'' *MD* 10 (1976): 289–99.

Sienicka, Marta. ''O'Neill in Poland.'' In *Eugene O'Neill: A World View*, edited by Virginia Floyd, pp. 101–14.

Tiusanen, Timo. ''O'Neill's Significance: A Scandinavian and European View.'' In *Eugene O'Neill: A World View*, edited by Virginia Floyd, pp. 61–67.

CRITICAL STUDIES: O'NEILL'S THEORIES OF DRAMA

Adler, Thomas P. ''Through a Glass Darkly: O'Neill's Esthetic Theory as Seen through His Writer Characters.'' *ArQ* 32 (1976): 171–83.

Gelb, Arthur and Barbara. ''As O'Neill Saw the Theatre.'' *NYTM* November 12, 1961), pp. 32, 34, 37, 39.

Halfmann, Ulrich. *Unreal Realism: O'Neills dramatisches Werke im Spiegel seiner szenischen Kunst*. Munich: Franke, 1969.

Highsmith, James M. ''O'Neill's Idea of Theater.'' *SAB* 23, no. 4 (1968): 18–21.

Krutch, Joseph Wood. ''O'Neill's Tragic Sense.'' *ASch* 16 (1947): 283–90.

Long, Chester C. *The Role of Nemesis in the Structure of Selected Plays by Eugene O'Neill*. Studies in American Literature, no. 8. The Hague: Mouton, 1968.

O'Neill, Joseph P., S.J. ''The Tragic Theory of Eugene O'Neill.'' *TSLL* 4 (1963): 481–98.

Parks, Edd Winfield. ''Eugene O'Neill's Symbolism.'' *SR* 43 (1935): 436–50. [O'Neill's symbols and philosophy.]

Prasad, Hari Mohan. ''Nuances of Soliloquy in the Theatre of Eugene O'Neill.'' *ComQ* 5, no. 17 (1980): 48–59.

Roy, Emil. ''The Archetypal Unity of Eugene O'Neill's Drama.'' *CompD* 3 (1969–70): 263–74.

Stroupe, John H. ''Eugene O'Neill and the Problem of Masking.'' *Lock Haven Review* 12 (1971): 71–78.

Törnqvist, Egil. ''Personal Addresses in the Plays of O'Neill.'' *QJS* 55 (1970): 126–30.

Voelker, Paul Duane. ''Eugene O'Neill's Aesthetic of the Drama.'' *MD* 21 (1978): 87–99.

Waith, Eugene M. ''Eugene O'Neill: An Exercise in Unmasking.'' *ETJ* 13 (1961): 182–91. Reprinted in *O'Neill: A Collection of Critical Essays*, edited by John Gassner. Englewood Cliffs, N.J.: Prentice-Hall, 1964.

DISSERTATIONS, POST–1960: A SELECTED LIST

Drawn from listings in *Dissertation Abstracts* and its successor, *Dissertation Abstracts International*.

Adrian, Mary Tinsley. "Two Biographicial Plays by Eugene O'Neill: The Drafts and the Final Versions." *DAI* 31 (1970): 1297.

Barlow, Judith. "Three Late Works of Eugene O'Neill: The Plays and the Process of Composition." *DAI* 36 (1976): 6095A.

Bell, Wayne E. "Forms of Religious Awareness in the Late Plays of Eugene O'Neill." *DA* 28 (1967): 2220A.

Bernstein, Samuel. "Eugene O'Neill, Theatre Artist: A Description of and Commentary upon the Craftsmanship of Four Plays by Eugene O'Neill." *DA* 25 (1964): 4683.

Blackburn, Ruth M. "Representation of New England Rustic Dialects in the Plays of Eugene O'Neill." *DA* 28 (1968): 4616A.

Brennan, Joseph J. "The Comic in the Plays of Eugene O'Neill: The Use of Character-ization, Situation, and Language in Relation to Bergson's Theory of Comedy." *DAI* 35 (1974): 1088A.

Brown, Susan Rand. " 'Mothers' and 'Sons': The Development of Autobiographical Themes in the Plays of Eugene O'Neill." *DAI* 36 (1976): 4481A–4482A.

Cook, Thomas Edwin. "Eugene O'Neill's Use of Dramatic Imagery, 1920–30: A Study of Six Plays." *DA* 22 (1962): 4353–54.

Corrigan, Ralph L., Jr. "The Function of the Green World in Selected Plays of Eugene O'Neill." *DAI* 35 (1974): 51621–63A.

Cunningham, Frank R. "Eugene O'Neill's Romantic Phase." *DAI* 31 (1971): 5394A.

Cutler, Janet Klotman. "Eugene O'Neill on the Screen: Love, Hate, and the Movies." *DAI* 38 (1977): 3109A.

Dalven, Rae. "The Concepts of Greek Tragedy in the Major Plays of Eugene O'Neill." *DA* 22 (1962): 4343–44.

Diamond, George Saul. "The Ironic Use of Melodramatic Conventions and the Con-ventions of *The Count of Monte Cristo* in the Plays of Eugene O'Neill." *DAI* 38 (1977): 2123A–2124A.

Elrod, James Frederick. "The Structure of O'Neill's Serious Drama." *DA* 20 (1959): 1898–99.

Fiskin, Abram Maurice I. "Eugene O'Neill: The Study of a Developing Creed through the Medium of Drama." *DA* 25 (1965): 4697–98.

Fleckenstein, Joan P. "Eugene O'Neill's Theatre of Dionysus: The Nietzschean Influence Upon Selected Plays." *DAI* 34 (1973): 2805A.

Fleming, William P., Jr. "Tragedy in American Drama: The Tragic Views of Eugene O'Neill, Tennessee Williams, Arthur Miller, and Edward Albee." *DAI* 33 (1972): 1168A–1170A.

Floyd, Virginia I. "Eugene O'Neill's 'New England' Cycle: The Yankee Puritan and New England Irish Catholic Elements in Five Autobiographical Plays by Eugene O'Neill." *DAI* 32 (1971): 963A.

Friedman, Lois, O.S.F. "The 'Dark of the Soul' in Selected Dramas by Three Modern Catholic Authors." *DAI* 39 (1978): 872A.

Hambright, Jeanne K. "The Journey Out: Contributions of German Dramatic Expres-sionism in the Social Protest Plays of Eugene O'Neill." *DAI* 34 (1973): 5178A–5179A.

Hanson, Eugene Kenneth. "The Earth Mother/Mother of God: The Theme of Forgiveness in the Works of Eugene O'Ncill." *DAI* 39 (1978): 1567A–1568A.

Hartman, Murray. "Strindberg and O'Neill: A Study in Influence." *DAI* 33 (1972): 1169A–1170A.

Highsmith, James M. "Eugene O'Neill: Apprenticeship with Dramatic Presentational-ism." *DA* 28 (1968): 3671A.

Hinden, Michael G. " 'Tragedy,' the Communal Vision: A Critique and Extension of Nietzsche's Theory of Tragedy with Attention Devoted to the Early Plays of Eugene O'Neill." *DAI* 32 (1972): 5186A.

Horner, Harry N. IV. "Love, Agony, Ambivalence: Background and Selected Studies in the Artistic Failures of Eugene O'Neill." *DAI* 33 (1972): 756A.

Hsia, An Min. "The Tao and O'Neill." *DAI* 40 (1980): 4037A.

Hunt, Doris Ann. "Dialects of the Black Characters in the Plays of Eugene O'Neill." *DAI* 37 (1977): 4327A–4328A.

Hurley, Daniel F. "The Failed Comedies of Eugene O'Neill." *DAI* 34 (1973): 3401A–3402A.

Jiji, Vera M. "Audience Response in the Theater: A Study of Dramatic Theory Tested Against Reviewers' Responses to the Plays of Eugene O'Neill." *DAI* 33 (1972): 1171A–1172A.

Jordan, John Wingate. "An Examination of Eugene O'Neill's Plays in the Light of C. G. Jung's *Collected Works* and Recorded Conversations." *DAI* 40 (1980): 5056A.

Karadaghi, Mohamed R. "The Theme of Alienation in Eugene O'Neill's Plays." *DAI* 32 (1972): 5232A.

Kilker, Dorothy K. "Eugene O'Neill's Methods of Characterizing the Secret Self." *DAI* 32 (1972): 3311A.

Koplik, Irwin J. "Jung's Psychology in the Plays of O'Neill." *DA* 27 (1967): 3872A.

Lee, Robert C. "Eugene O'Neill: A Grapple with the Ghost." *DA* 26 (1965): 2754–55.

Lichtman, Myla Ruth. "Mythic Plot and Character in Euripides' *Hippolytus* and Eugene O'Neill's *Desire Under the Elms*: A Jungian Analysis." *DAI* 40 (1979): 1750A.

McNicholas, Sister Mary V., O.P. "*The Quintessence of Ibsenism*: Its Impact on the Drama of Eugene Gladstone O'Neill."*DAI* 32 (1972): 5328A.

Mandel, Josef Lorenz. "Gerhart Hauptman and Eugene O'Neill: A Parallel Study of Their Dramatic Technique in Selected Naturalistic Plays." *DAI* 37 (1976): 1045A–1046A.

Mihelich, Christine, I.H.M. "The Rite of Confession in Five Plays by Eugene O'Neill." *DAI* 38 (1977): 265A.

Miller, Robert R. "Tragedy in Modern American Drama: The Psychological, Social, and Absurdist Conditions in Historical Perspective." *DAI* 36 (1975): 3717A.

Olson, Esther Judith. "An Analysis of the Nietzschean Elements in the Plays of Eugene O'Neil." *DA* 17 (1957): 695.

Orlandello, John Richard. "Stage to Screen: Film Adaptations of the Plays of Eugene O'Neill." *DAI* 37 (1976): 1271A.

Pampel, Brigitte, C. G. "The Relationship of the Sexes in the Works of Strindberg, Wedekind, and O'Neill." *DAI* 33 (1972): 2946A–2947A.

Phillips, Julien Lind. "The Mask: Theory and Practical Use in the Plays of Eugene O'Neill." *DAI* 38 (1978): 5802A.

Pickering, Christine P. "The Works of Eugene O'Neill: A Greek Idea of the Theatre Derived from the Philosophy of Friedrich Nietzsche." *DAI* 33 (1972): 732A.

Poulard, Regina. "O'Neill and Nietzsche: The Making of a Playwright and Thinker." *DAI* 35 (1974): 2291A.

Ratliff, Gerald Lee. "An Examination of the Parabolic Nature of 'Suffering' in Selected Plays of Eugene O'Neill, 1913–23." DAI 36 (1975): 1900A.

Ray, Helen Houser. "The Relation between Man and Man in the Plays of Eugene O'Neill." *DA* 26 (1966): 7324.

Rich, J. Dennis. "Eugene O'Neill: Visions of the Absurd." *DAI* 37 (1977): 5446A.

Robinson, James Arthur. O'Neill's Expressionistic Grotesque: A Study of Nine Experimental Plays by Eugene O'Neill." *DAI* 36 (1976): 6689A–6690A.

Roland, Laurin Kay. "Biography and Culture in the Later Plays of Eugene O'Neill." *DAI* 39 (1979): 6134A.

Ross, Gwendolyn DeCamp. "Comic Elements in the Late Plays of Eugene O'Neill." *DAI* 36 (1975): 1511A.

Ryba, Mary Miceli. "Melodrama as a Figure of Mysticism in Eugene O'Neill's Plays." *DAI* 38 (1977): 2794A.

Scarbrough, John A. "Eugene O'Neill's Sense of Place: A Study of his Locative Archetypes." *DAI* 31 (1970): 2938A.

Swanson, Margaret Millen. "Irony in Selected Neo-Hellenic Plays." *DAI* 40 (1979): 2995A.

Swanson, Mary Stewart. "The Themes of Time and Mortality in the Dramas of Eugene O'Neill." *DAI* 38 (1977): 3491A–3492A.

Tinsley, Mary A. "Two Biographical Plays by Eugene O'Neill: The Drafts and the Final Versions." *DAI* 31 (1970): 1297A.

Turner, Clarence Steven. "Man's Spiritual Quest in the Plays of Eugene O'Neill." *DA* 23 (1962): 1709–10.

Voelker, Paul Duane. "The Early Plays of Eugene O'Neill, 1913–1915." *DAI* 35 (1975): 5433A.

Vunovich, Nancy W. "The Women in the Plays of Eugene O'Neill." *DA* 28 (1967): 1089A–1090A.

Walker, Herbert Kenneth, III. "Symbolism in the Later Plays of Eugene O'Neill." *DAI* 39 (1979): 6768A–6769A.

Watkinson, Sharon Anne Onevelo. "An Analysis of Characters in Selected Plays of Eugene O'Neill According to Erik Erikson's Identity Theory." *DAI* 41 (1980): 464A.

White, Jackson E. "Existential Themes in Selected Plays of Eugene O'Neill." *DA* 27 (1967): 4270A–4271A.

Williams, Julia Willa Bacon. "Eugene O'Neill: The Philos-Aphilos of a Mother's Eternal Son." *DAI* 39 (1978): 3235A–3236A.

Index

571, 601; source of, 83, 614; writing of, 543

Bible, The: New Testament, 162, 322; Old Testament, 90, 91, 92, 93, 168; scripture quoted, 52, 93, 162, 168, 169, 255, 256, 257, 258, 259, 260, 261. *See also* Religion

Bigelow, Edward (*The First Man*), 62-63, 217-22

Big Frank (*The Moon of the Caribbees*), 63, 467, 469, 645

Bijou Theatre (New York City), 467

Birth of Tragedy, The (Nietzsche), 266, 365

Bisch, Louis (psychiatrist), 546

Blair, Eugenie (actress), 33

Blair, Mary (actress), 63-64; *All God's Chillun Got Wings*, 18, 21, 546, 617; *Before Breakfast*, 51; *Desire Under the Elms*, 177; *Diff'rent*, 184; *The Hairy Ape*, 187, 282, 440, 545, 725; *Marco Millions*, 421; and Provincetown Players, 598; and Theatre Guild, 682

Blake, Doctor (*Mourning Becomes Electra—The Hunted*), 64, 491, 504

Bledsoe, Jules (singer), 271

"Blemie" (Silverdene Emblem), 64, 446, 549, 550, 551, 553, 636

"Blind Alley Guy," 64

Bodenheim, Max, 153, 154, 598, 600

Bogard, Travis (critic), 32, 183, 267-68, 322, 367, 527, 676

Boije, Alexander (actor), 282

Boleslavski, Richard, 213

Book of Common Prayer, 162, 392

Booth, Edwin (actor), 383, 564-65

Booth, Fred (actor), 469

Borden, Emma (*Mourning Becomes Electra—The Hunted*), 64, 491, 504

Borden, Josiah (*Mourning Becomes Electra—The Hunted*), 64-65, 491, 504

Bosnell, James (actor), 504

Boulton, Agnes, 65-68, 83, 111, 152-54, 301, 623, 632, 717; as author, 65, 83, 248, 530-32, 538, 543, 571, 611, 720; as O'Neill's second wife, 112, 117, 133, 162-63, 222, 272, 333, 391, 397, 440-41, 533, 542-43, 544, 545, 546-

47, 548, 549, 559, 568, 571, 573, 574, 576, 718; with Oona and Shane O'Neill, 117-19

Bound East for Cardiff, 69-70, 119-20, 136, 187, 247-48; character analyses, 112, 132, 151, 191, 527-28, 583, 626, 727; evaluation of, 69; first reading, 83, 247, 613; production of, 69-70, 541, 600, 613, 644

Bowen, Crosswell (critic), 573

Bowler, Richard (actor), 324

Boyce, Neith (playwright), 541, 598, 599

Bradley, Louise (actress), 645

Brady, Alice (actress), 70, 352, 504, 505, 510

Brady, Matthew (producer), 272

Brady, William (producer), 66, 70, 611

Brandel, Marc (acquaintance), 575

Brant, Adam (*Mourning Becomes Electra—Homecoming; The Hunted*), 70-71, 486-94, 504

Brantôme, Marie (*Mourning Becomes Electra*), 71, 486-88

Bread and Butter, 71-78; character analyses, 78-81, 115, 252, 290, 295, 510, 646-47; evaluation of, 77-78; writing of, 540

Brecher, Egon (actor), 238

Brennan, Mrs. (*The Straw*), 78, 674, 677

Brewster, John (actor), 24, 208, 209

Broadhurst Theatre (New York City), 178, 483, 604

Broad Street Theatre (Philadelphia), 126, 227

Brook Farm (Ridgefield, Conn.), 66, 397, 545, 546, 548, 573

Brooklyn Academy of Music, 616

Brooks, Patricia (actress), 324

Broström, Gunnel (actor), 483

Brown, Arvin (director), 387

Brown, Bessie (*Bread and Butter*), 72-77, 78-79

Brown, Charles D. (actor), 251

Brown, Edward, Jr. (*Bread and Butter*), 71-76, 79

Brown, Edward, Sr. (*Bread and Butter*), 71-74, 79-80, 82, 268

About the Author

MARGARET LOFTUS RANALD is Professor of English at Queens College of the City University of New York and Associate Editor of *Renaissance Quarterly*. She has written numerous critical essays and articles and has recently completed a book on the social context in Shakespeare's works. She was Executive Secretary of the American Society for Theatre Research 1977–1983, and is currently the American representative on the University Commission of the International Federation for Theatre Research. She is editorial consultant for the American Society for Theatre Research International Bibliography of Theatre Research.

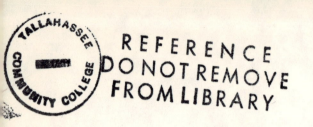
REFERENCE
DO NOT REMOVE
FROM LIBRARY

TALLAHASSEE
COMMUNITY COLLEGE